MW00570180

PSYCHOLOGY

Principles and Applications

David G. Martin
University of Manitoba
Contributing authors: Gary Hawryluk and Michael Stambrook

Prentice-Hall Canada Inc., Scarborough, Ontario

Canadian Cataloguing in Publication Data

Martin, David G., 1939–
Psychology : principles and applications

Includes index.

ISBN 0-13-734773-1

1. Psychology. I. Title.
BF121.M37 1991 150 C91-093035-X

Prentice-Hall, Inc., Englewood Cliffs, New Jersey
Prentice-Hall International, Inc., London
Prentice-Hall of Australia, Pty., Ltd., Sydney
Prentice-Hall of India Pvt., Ltd., New Delhi
Prentice-Hall of Japan, Inc., Tokyo
Prentice-Hall of Southeast Asia (Pte.) Ltd., Singapore
Editora Prentice-Hall do Brasil Ltda., Rio de Janeiro
Prentice-Hall Hispanoamericana, S.A., Mexico

Credits are listed throughout the book and at the back of the book. Every reasonable effort has been made to find copyright holders. The publishers would be pleased to have any errors or omissions brought to their attention.

ISBN 0-13-734773-1

Production Editor: Maryrose O'Neill
Project Editor: Maurice Esses
Cover and Interior Design: Bruce Farquhar
Contributing Illustrators: Bruce Farquhar, Irma Ikonnen, Jim Loates, Marjorie Pearson, and Jane Whitney
Cover Image: Eric Curry/First Light
Production Coordinator: Florence Rousseau
Typesetting: Compeer Typographic Services Limited
Printed and bound in the United States by Arcata Graphic Company

1 2 3 4 5 AGC 95 94 93 92 91

To my mother
Sylva Martin
You were always there

OVERVIEW

CONTENTS

CHAPTER 4 *Perception* 124

CHAPTER 5 *Principles of Learning* 160

PART V *DISORDER AND THERAPY* 493

PSYCHOLOGY IS EXCITING. My main goal in this book is to arouse the student's excitement for psychology *first as a science and then as a body of knowledge that can significantly improve human existence.* I have set out to explain the basic principles and to show the methods which we use to test those principles. I hope that this book will contribute toward the development of real scientists who are rigorous, demanding, and searching, at the same time as they are open to all possibilities, humble about the extent of our knowledge, and full of wonder. In the many places where psychology touches everyday life, students will find themselves challenged by applications of psychology to personally relevant issues. While this is not a self-help book (I often caution the reader about the limits and potential dangers of a "little knowledge" in psychology), psychology does have much to offer the student, both as an applied science and as a pure science.

Guiding principles

To achieve my goals for this book, I have followed several general guidelines:

Integrating principles, research, and applications. It is common to present psychology in a fragmented way, separating discussions of principles and data from discussions of the significance or application of such basic knowledge. Sometimes this is necessary, but whenever possible, I have presented the principles and data in the context of their meaning. Sometimes this context gives rise to provocative questions that challenge the student's worldview. Sometimes the implications of research bear directly on how humans live, and sometimes the new understanding simply has its own "gee whiz" quality.

Encouraging critical inquiry. Whenever possible, I have tried to show that science develops step-by-step, with each researcher building on and expanding the limits of previous work. I have also tried to include the most up-to-date research possible. At times, early research led to a conclusion that was later contradicted by more refined work. Since the reader learns about methodology in the first chapter, he or she can see what was lacking in the earlier research and how improvements in research design may have clarified a particular issue.

In this book, we discuss many controversial issues; in each case, I try to describe different positions in the controversy and to encourage the student to think critically. Psychology is a diverse field. The student must learn not to accept whatever appears in print.

Conveying the excitement of psychology. Behaviour, especially human behaviour, is fascinating, and the acquisition of knowledge about behaviour is exciting. I want my readers to capture that excitement because it is so motivating. I have designed this book to motivate the student and thereby to reinforce learning.

Continuity of ideas. Many threads weave through the book, linking the various principles and applications that we discuss. As just one example, the issue of the relationship between cognition and emotion is important in the basic chapters on motivation, emotion, learning, thinking, and language. But this relationship also has enormous implications for consciousness, abnormal behaviour, psychotherapy, and health. Whenever there is a link between some current topic and a previous or future discussion, we alert the student to that connection. This encourages the reader to view psychology as a more unified whole, and it motivates the reader to learn the current material, since it will be necessary for understanding later material.

Clear language. Advice that is often given to public speakers is "talk as though you were explaining this to your cousin." In other words, use plain, clear language. I hope I have done that. Pedantic language inhibits learning. Another principle my high school debating coach liked was "tell them what you're going to tell them; tell them; then tell them what you told them." Whenever a new concept appears in the book, it is defined in a concise sentence to give an overview of the discussion to follow. Then the concept is described, illustrated, and expanded. Finally, concepts are integrated and summarized.

Reinforcing learning. Everything about this book is aimed at giving the reader clear new knowledge. It is not enough simply to convey information. The information must be received and processed. The use of clear language is one way to encourage learning. More importantly, that learning must be reinforced. I always try to write with this question in mind: "If I were a student, why would I want to know this particular information?" When possible, I use examples and observations that touch the student's life or that challenge, fascinate, amuse, or startle the reader.

Facilitating teaching. I have tried to make the instructor's job as rewarding as possible. Of course, the instructor's manual is the primary vehicle for this, but I hope that the text also paves the teacher's way. Making the book up-to-date, easy to read, and interesting should help to create a personal and positive mood within a class. Provocative questions and balanced presentation of controversial issues should stimulate student response. Finally, the organization and integration of materials in this book will, I hope, facilitate the planning and conducting of classes.

Canadian emphasis. Many areas of psychology are not related to national issues, so it may seem unusual to think of a text as a "Canadian psychology text." While I have consistently tried to present the best research available (without regard to the location in which it was done), whenever appropriate I have emphasized the work of Canadian researchers. I want the student to appreciate the

quality and quantity of research and writing that characterize psychology in Canada. One of the most important reasons for doing this is to motivate students to pursue psychology as a discipline — to make them aware of the opportunities available for them in Canada. It also makes clear the many implications of psychology for Canadian society. In some areas, such as social psychology and bilingualism, there is important research with national implications for Canada. Such research seldom appears in introductory psychology texts.

Chapter features

Each chapter includes several features designed to facilitate students' learning. My goal is not just to present the material; it is to "get it in," to have it understood and retained.

Chapter Outline. The *Study Guide* leads the student through the SQ4R method of study. Since the "S" stands for "Survey" we start each chapter with an outline that gives the reader an overview of the chapter.

Special Topics. Special Topics give a more in-depth discussion of a specific topic related to the chapter.

Close-ups. The Close-up boxes present interest builders related to the main content of the chapter. Although close-ups appear to be "lighter" than text material and Special Topics boxes, each one is making a point or illustrating a concept in real-life terms.

Chapter Summaries. The Chapter Summary does more than simply repeat what was in the chapter. Through numbered points, it integrates each section of the chapter in a concise way. It will not substitute for reading the chapter, but a reader who has done the reading will find that it draws everything together. Main concepts are not defined in the Chapter Summary. That is the job of the Key Terms section.

Key Terms. A thorough glossary follows every chapter. This facilitates learning more effectively than having one glossary at the back of the book. This method also makes the key terms more accessible as the student reads the chapter and permits a more meaningful review of individual chapters. If the reader wants to look up a term without knowing the chapter number, each key term is indexed in the Key Term index. Since some terms are important in more than one chapter, there is some duplication of terms in different chapters. This makes each chapter an independent unit.

Suggested Readings. Many students will want to pursue particular topics or perhaps to write papers on them. The Suggested Readings at the end of each chapter provide annotated references to more advanced textbooks, popular treatments of important topics, and—in some cases—to annotated research bibliographies.

Organization of the book

Like many texts, this one starts with an overview of psychology as a discipline and of the methods by which psychology investigates phenomena. Starting with Chapter 2, there is a general "bottom up" organization. Foundations for later chapters are laid with a discussion of the biology of behaviour and basic processes such as sensation, perception, learning, thinking, and language. A chapter on consciousness then builds on these foundations by discussing controversial subjects and discussing consciousness in terms of brain functioning. Developmental, clinical, and social psychology occupy the middle portion of the text. The final three chapters extend the student's basic understanding to the applied areas of gender roles, health, and organizational psychology.

Alternative approaches to using the text. Instructors differ in the emphasis they place on different areas of psychology, especially when time is limited for a course. It would be possible to present a "basics only" course by omitting Chapters 9, 11, 13, 18, 19, and 20. Conversely, an instructor who wished to emphasize the applied aspects of psychology could focus on the later chapters. In this case, however, it would be important to include at the very least Chapters 1, 2, 5, 7, and 8. All of the preliminary chapters lay groundwork for later chapters. In most cases, when a discussion requires knowledge from earlier chapters, I have included a brief statement of the necessary knowledge to refresh the reader's memory.

Supplements

Test Item File. The Test Item File was written by Allan Moore. He also prepared the sample test items in the students' *Study Guide*, giving continuity and consistency of level and style. Over 1500 questions are included in this file. Most are multiple-choice questions, but fill-in-the-blank and short-answer questions are also provided for each chapter. The questions are keyed to specific pages in the text.

Computerized Test Item File. In addition to the printed test item file, a computerized test item file is available. This is much more than the simple listing of test items on a computer disk. It is a self-contained software program which will be tailor-made to work with any major North American computer hardware. A few examples of its many features are total and immediate control over item selection, comprehensive options for arranging items, and many printing options. It is even possible to generate tests that require no separate student answer sheets.

Instructor's Manual. The Instructor's Manual uses many aids to make a lecturer's life easier and teaching more effective. Chapter outlines and summaries written for the instructor give an overview and perspective from which to lecture. Advice about lecturing on each of the topics is accompanied by suggestions for articles and other resources. I have included potential lecture topics, suggestions for films, possible student projects, and practice essay questions.

Transparencies. A set of colour transparencies is available to instructors for overhead projection. Some of the illustrations also appear in the text, but many do not. The instructor can use these to supplement text material.

Study Guide. The Study Guide that accompanies this text has two themes. First, it guides the student toward a better understanding of each chapter's content. By giving the "big picture" of each chapter, along with sample questions, the study guide both prepares the student for examinations and enhances comprehension. Second, it talks to the student as a "friend who has been there." Allan Moore has included "all the things I wish someone had told me when I was a student" in an introductory chapter on study skills. The Study Guide is based on the SQ4R study strategy, as discussed in Chapter 7 of the text.

Acknowledgements

Many people have contributed to producing this book. Prentice-Hall Canada has supported and encouraged me at every step of the way. Patrick Ferrier's enthusiasm and belief in the project inspired me and kept me going through occasional periods of discouragement. I am especially grateful to Prentice-Hall Canada for providing me with wonderful editors—Maurice Esses and Maryrose O'Neill. They gave constant support and guidance that improved the manuscript enormously. They edited for writing style, of course, but they also read the manuscript through the eyes of the student, focusing on how a reader would understand each concept. They both gave parts of themselves that are now part of this book. Kathy Burchill saved me many hours in the library and prepared the name index, and Kristen Martin gave important help with the bibliography. Allan Moore prepared the test item file and the study guide.

Colleagues at several colleges and universities made many helpful suggestions and offered insights that improved the book. I want to thank the following individuals for their reviews of the manuscript:

Emir Andrews, Memorial University
Michael L. Atkinson, University of Western Ontario
Margaret Caron, Marianopolis College
Nicola Matteo Ciavarella, Vancouver Community College
Annabel Evans Coldeway, Concordia College
Katherine Covell, University of Toronto
Richard B. Day, McMaster University
James Enns, University of British Columbia
Jim Kelly, Algonquin College
John Mitterer, Brock University
James L. Mosley, University of Calgary
James L. Mottin, University of Guelph
Ed Pomerory, Brock University
John D. Roth, Ryerson Polytechnical Institute
Dolf Ryks, Grant MacEwan College
Leo Spindel, Centennial College
Jan Szumski, John Abbott College
K. H. Vandonselaar, University of Saskatchewan.

Finally, I want to thank Melissa, Kristen, Mark, Kathy, Charles, Laura, Troy, Nancy, and Joel for being who they are and Yvonne for being both steadfast and sensitive.

David Martin
1991

PART I

INTRODUCTION

CHAPTER 1

What is Psychology?

MOST PEOPLE have some idea of what "psychology" is, but each person probably has a different reaction to the term, different ideas about what it covers, and different notions about what psychologists do. Take, for example, the common uses of the word "psychology." "Use a little psychology on him"; "She must have some deep psychological reasons for needing so much attention"; "The market advance today was based upon investor psychology"; or, "Mr. Jones doesn't have any pain—it's all psychological." All these statements suggest that psychology is something deep, mysterious, and complex. We hope that by the end of this book you will find it less mysterious, despite its complexity, and that you will have acquired some knowledge that will help you to understand yourself and others.

DEFINING PSYCHOLOGY

Psychology is the scientific study and understanding of behaviour. This may seem an obvious statement, but each word has been chosen carefully. *Scientific study* means a systematic collecting and testing of observations and data, not the random gathering of information. *Understanding* follows logically after studying. It often involves making inferences based upon study and investigation and then coming up with the most reasonable explanation for why something has occurred. **Behaviour** is defined broadly to include overt (i.e., external and observable) actions and covert (i.e., internal and hidden from view) actions such as brain firings, stomach contractions, and the secretion of hormones. This broad definition of "behaviour" means that scientists observe some behaviours directly and others indirectly. Indirect observation requires that we make inferences. For example, we often infer what a person is thinking (covert behaviour) from what he or she says (overt behaviour). Inferred behaviour is, of course, more difficult to study because there is seldom a simple, direct correspondence between covert and overt behaviour. Thus, in our example, we might draw a different inference about what the person was thinking if when saying the same words, the person started to show beads of sweat around the upper lip (another overt behaviour).

In psychology, we study human behaviour without making moral judgments. As psychologists, we do not classify behaviours as good or evil, right or wrong, natural or unnatural. We do examine deviant behaviour, but we define such terms as "abnormal" and "mental health" very carefully (see Chapter 13, Abnormal Psychology).

The goals of psychology

Psychology is concerned with (i) the description of behaviour in ways that can be agreed upon by several observers, (ii) the explanation and understanding of behaviour, (iii) the prediction of behaviour under specific conditions, and (iv) the control or influence of behaviour.

Description

The first step in understanding is to describe reality in an objective and precise manner. We can describe something without necessarily understanding what we are describing or its underlying causes. It is useful, for example, to know that there is a higher incidence of severe psychological problems the closer one is to the core of a large city, even if current research can't explain this finding. We need to know how things are. Determining *why* they are that way is the next step in psychological research.

Explanation and understanding

Our knowledge is more powerful if we know the principles and causes that govern behaviour — if we know explanations. Why is there more severe psychological disturbance near the city core? Does inner-city life cause human problems? Do troubled people drift toward the city centre? Perhaps the city core and emotional problems have nothing to do with each other causally. Does some third factor, such as patterns of family living, account for the psychological disturbance found near the city centre? Good research would be designed to test each of these questions and eliminate all but one as a possible explanation.

Prediction

One purpose of describing and explaining behaviour is to be able to predict what people and animals will do under different circumstances. If we can determine the relevant principles and if we are given enough descriptive information, we should be able to predict who would benefit most from a particular training program or what people will do during times of unemployment. Such predictions would have direct practical value.

Control

The word "control" may arouse thoughts of manipulating people in the manner described by Aldous Huxley in his *Brave New World* (1932). It would probably be less provocative to call this aim "influence" or "modification." The fact is, though, that psychology as a science does strive to change human behaviour. Description, explanation, prediction, and control are the goals of all sciences, but they sound more benign when a chemist says them than when a psychologist says them. We do not want our own behaviour to be manipulated by others. Nevertheless, we should emphasize that the field of psychology is dedicated to using its knowledge for the improvement of human life through changes such as reducing fear, improving child rearing, and helping students learn to study more effectively.

Levels of analysis

Analysis and understanding of behaviour can take place on many levels: social, behavioural, physiological, anatomical, and biochemical. Thus, we can try to affect behaviour by intervening at any or all of these levels. The picture is further complicated by the interplay between levels. An example will help clarify these ideas.

Stress or conflict produces emotional arousal. In our culture, a great deal of importance is given to being financially successful and well-educated (social level). Financial worries or anxiety about passing one's final exams (behavioural level) may lead to muscle tension, increased respiration, perspiration, and heart rate (physiological level). If this tension lasts long enough, physical changes such as duodenal ulcers (anatomical level) may occur. We can intervene to try to make changes at any of these levels. We might attempt to modify the value systems within the culture (social). We might recommend a higher pay scale or provide guidance to improve study skills (behavioural). We might try physiological interventions such as giving the person tranquilizers (biochemical) or surgically removing the ulcer (anatomical).

Moreover, as we mentioned above, we should take into account the interplay between the various levels. Thus, in our example, we should consider that a high level of physiological arousal will impair problem-solving, which may further interfere with an individual's ability to cope with financial challenges or exams. Similarly, the stomach pains associated with ulceration may be an additional stressor leading to further physiological arousal, thereby compounding the problem.

In trying to understand and change human behaviour, we must be aware of all of the levels of analysis that contribute to "humanness." To neglect some or to be excessively reliant on one level leads to incomplete understanding and less effective intervention and treatment.

HISTORY AND PERSPECTIVES

Psychology is a social science which, like other sciences such as biology, physics, and chemistry, relies upon the scientific method. In the development of psychology, however, this was not always the case. Psychology, like many other fields, had its origins in philosophy. Its roots can probably be traced back to the ancient Greeks who, in fact, coined the term "psychology" (*psyche* means soul and *logos* means discourse or discussion). Philosophy relied heavily upon developing rules and systems of logic for understanding nature and the universe. Logical reasoning was the benchmark of this approach, and we can imagine a group of philosophers discussing and speculating about the nature of the shapes of objects in the universe. Philosophical arguments about forms and shapes are important. However, when Archimedes discovered that the volume of irregular shapes can be calculated by measuring the amount of water they displace, his approach reflected a shift in the way we pursue knowledge. He was supplementing the rules of logic with a cornerstone of scientific understanding—namely, observation.

Observation is the key to understanding in psychology, although psychologists have long debated what qualifies as the best form of observation. Early psychology was characterized by various schools of thought, whose founders and disciples strongly advocated the superiority of their particular mode of observation. Even today, psychologists disagree about some basic issues, and the true scientist must approach the field with a combination of openness and humility. Let's look at some of the different theories from the past and present in psychology.

Wilhelm Wundt (1832–1920).
SOURCE: The Bettmann Archive.

Structuralists and functionalists

Wilhelm Wundt (1832–1920) is often credited with being the founder of scientific psychology. He argued that controlled observations were necessary for studying the discipline, and he established a laboratory for that purpose in 1879. To understand mental processes, Wundt focused his research on brain mechanisms. His ideas led to what later became known as the structuralist school or **structuralism**. According to structuralism, the human mind can best be understood by studying its components or parts — that is, its structures. These structures combine to form what we call the mind. The main method used by structuralists to study the mind was called **introspection**. It consisted of having trained observers examine their own mental processes and report their private mental experiences in detail.

Prior to Wundt's research, there were other structuralist theories which were rather unscientific, and which we now look upon with amusement. For example, in about 1800, Franz Joseph Gall developed a theory later known as **phrenology**, which stated that specific mental characteristics result in specific bumps and indentations in the skull. Gall held that our psychological makeup is comprised of "faculties," each located in a particular area of the brain. Well-developed faculties were associated with a greater amount of tissue in certain brain areas, which in turn were supposed to be indicated by bumps or prominences in the overlying skull. A bump in one place might indicate musical skill, and a dent in another a lack of social skills (see Figure 1-1.). By feeling a person's skull (literally "hands-on" personality testing), one was supposed to be able to determine an individual's personality. Phrenology was very popular during the 19th century. However, later scientific research discredited the theory completely.

FIGURE 1-1 A map of the human skull according to the old theory of phrenology
SOURCE: The Bettmann Archive

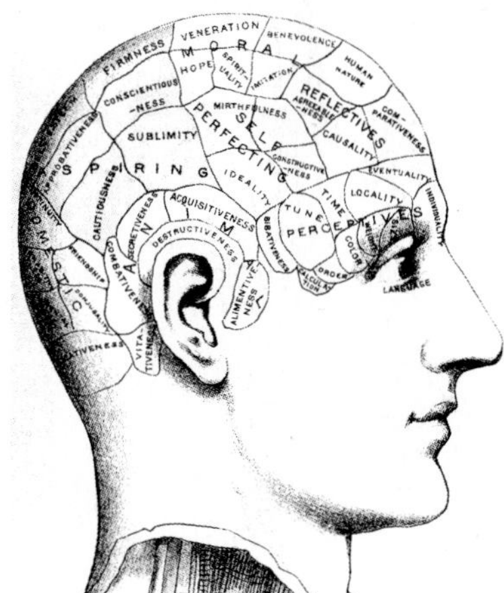

The structuralist school of thought that developed from Wundt's ideas was soon opposed by the so-called functionalist school or **functionalism**. According to functionalism, the human mind can best be understood by studying its ongoing processes, rather than its component parts. One of the leading exponents of functionalism was William James (1842–1910). He was greatly influenced by Charles Darwin's theories of evolution and natural selection. James held that for humans, the mind is the most important organ for survival of the

William James (1842–1910).
SOURCE: Archives of the History of American Psychology.

species. He argued that thoughts are continually flowing through the human mind, which is responsible for individuals learning and adapting to the environment. In general, the functionalists were more interested in the process of thinking and adaptation than in the faculties (structures) studied by the structuralists. For the functionalists, the mind can be better understood by studying process rather than structure.

The origins of modern psychology

Dissatisfaction with both the structuralist and functionalist approaches led to the formulation of other theories which are more common in modern psychological thought. Readers are often surprised to discover that there are several different schools of thought in psychology and that they differ from each other in fundamental ways. There is no one answer to the question "What do psychologists think about basic human nature?" One of our goals is to present each viewpoint for you to consider and integrate with your own view of human nature. In this chapter, we will give a brief overview of the different perspectives. In Chapter 10, we will elaborate on them.

Gestalt psychology

Gestalt psychology stands in direct contrast to the structuralist school. One of its founders was Wolfgang Köhler (1887–1967). According to **Gestalt psychology**, the mind and perception can be understood only as an integrated whole, rather than as component parts. Gestalt psychologists maintain that "the whole is greater than the sum of the parts," and that overall impressions are crucial for understanding the mind. They disagree with the idea that the individual elements of the mind are important, as the structuralists said. Gestalt psychologists argue that the mind can be understood only as an overall, unified pattern. Therefore, they have focused their research on how individuals view the world around them, rather than simply on how individuals behave. Thus, Gestalt psychologists have adopted a phenomenological approach. **Phenomenology** is the study of the individual's subjective perception and inner experiences. According to Gestalt psychologists, an individual's perceptions determine his or her behaviour.

Wolfgang Köhler (1887–1967).
SOURCE: UPI/Bettmann Newsphotos.

Psychoanalysis

Sigmund Freud (1856–1939) provided another response to structuralism and functionalism. He developed a set of theories, and by extension a method of treatment, known as **psychoanalysis**. Freud claimed that human behaviour is fundamentally biological and instinctual, driven by sexual and aggressive energy. According to Freud's theory of psychoanalysis, the unconscious exerts a powerful influence on an individual's behaviour. Freud also maintained that early childhood experiences play a leading role in shaping an individual's personality. Freud was fond of saying, "There are no accidents." Freud believed in **determinism**, the view that human behaviour is completely determined by prior events. Determinism implies that our behaviour is caused by forces beyond our control. It denies the existence of free will.

Rather than relying on laboratory observations, Freud developed his theories out of observations he made in his own psychiatric practice, working with patients. Freud's work continues to influence modern psychological thinking, particularly in theories about normal and abnormal behaviour. Two of Freud's most important ideas were major departures from the thought of his day. But both are now commonly accepted: (1) early childhood development strongly affects adult personality, and (2) unconscious influences strongly affect behaviour.

Sigmund Freud (1856–1939).
SOURCE: The Bettmann Archive.

Behaviourism

Another major school which developed at the turn of the century took a different approach by focusing on observable behaviour. One of its founders was John B. Watson (1878–1958). Watson was dissatisfied with other theories that made direct observation and verification difficult, if not impossible. Consequently, he formulated a theory called **behaviourism** (also known as **learning theory**). According to behaviourism, virtually all behaviour is the result of prior learning. In other words, even though an organism is born with some genetic characteristics, almost everything a person or animal does is the result of that individual's learning history. Learning, in turn, is the result of various types of conditioning. The legitimate area of study for psychology should be behaviour, rather than unobservable factors. Like psychoanalysis, behaviourism is clearly deterministic. It states that although behaviour may be very complex, behaviour is just as much the result of antecedent events as is the movement of billiard balls.

John B. Watson (1878–1958).
SOURCE: Archives of the History of American Psychology.

Watson rejected introspection as a valid method for understanding human behaviour. Watson argued that the only legitimate approach in the science of psychology is the direct observation of events and behaviours, not the description of unobservable concepts such as motives, desires, thoughts, and the mind. He reasoned that because the mind cannot be seen, touched, or observed, the mind does not exist in a scientific sense. Therefore Watson concluded that the mind is not a reasonable object for study. According to behaviourism, all that is necessary and sufficient for the understanding of behaviour is to introduce or observe stimuli and to note the resultant responses. This behaviourist view is known as **stimulus-response (S-R) psychology**.

When behaviourism was first formulated, it appeared to be much more objective and scientific than the other schools. Even today, learning theory is one of the most powerful influences—some would say the most powerful influence—in the psychology departments of North American universities. Moreover, behaviour therapy has proved to be a successful treatment for solving some behavioural problems. One of the best known and most influential psychologists is the American behaviourist, B. F. Skinner (1904–1990), whose work we will discuss in Chapter 5. Behaviourism continues to be a very

B.F. Skinner (1904–1990).
SOURCE: Susan Hogue/Courtesy of the late B.F. Skinner.

Abraham Maslow (1908–1970).
SOURCE: Archives of the History of American Psychology.

important method of approach in psychology. However, in recent years, many theorists have been modifying their focus to include thoughts, emotions, and images as legitimate behaviours to be studied.

Humanism

Humanism is the theory that each individual strives for self-actualization based on the way he or she perceives the world. Humanism is sometimes called the "third force," to emphasize its differences from psychoanalysis and behaviourism. Psychoanalysis claims that human behaviour is driven by powerful internal forces that need to be brought under control. Behaviourism asserts that we are programmed by conditioning. Humanism presents a more optimistic view by rejecting the determinism of psychoanalysis and behaviourism. According to humanism, the basic human drive is toward self-actualization. Individuals are driven to achieve healthy growth or self-fulfilment unless they are thwarted somehow. Furthermore, humanism takes a phenomenological approach. According to phenomenology (which we briefly discussed under Gestalt psychology), what each person perceives as reality *is* that person's reality in terms of guiding his or her behaviour. Humanism maintains that people's subjective perceptions determine their behaviour. Each individual will make the best choices possible, as he or she perceives those choices. Faulty behaviour results from faulty perceptions. Humanists are fond of saying that psychoanalysts and behaviourists claim that behaviour is determined by the past, but actually behaviour is determined by the future—by one's perceptions and expectations.

Abraham Maslow (1908–1970) focused attention on the need to achieve maximum potential or self-actualization. The most influential humanist has been Carl Rogers (1902–1987). He developed both a theory of personality and an approach to psychotherapy called the "person-centred approach." Humanism's influence is strongest among counsellors and psychotherapists, rather than at universities.

Carl Rogers (1902–1987).
SOURCE: Courtesy of the Carl Rogers Memorial Library.

Cognitive psychology

We said earlier that learning theory may be the most powerful influence in the psychology departments of North American universities. However, some people would argue that cognitive psychology is replacing behaviourism as the most important perspective in psychology today. The so-called "cognitive revolution" has been going on for about 20 or 30 years (Mandler, 1985). **Cognitive psychology** is the theory that cognitions (thinking, learning, remembering, and other mental processes) are the most important causes of behaviours. The strict behaviourism of Watson tried to eliminate the study of internal processes such as consciousness, desires, and thoughts; and for many years, psychological research did just that. Later, however, many psychologists argued that it was a mistake to ignore cognitions just because they are difficult to study. They claimed that in order to understand behaviour, it is both possible and necessary to study cognitions scientifically. Thus, cognitive psychology represents a shift in focus from strictly observable behaviour to internal processes.

To complicate the picture a bit, there are two general groups of cognitive theorists. One group is known as **cognitive behaviourists**. They believe that cognitions (primarily thinking) control behaviour, but that cognitions themselves are simply behaviours that happen to occur inside the skin. A thought cannot be seen, but that doesn't make it any different — or operate by different rules — than any observable behaviour, such as scratching one's head. Feelings, desires, wishes, and memories are also simply behaviours that occur inside the skin. The other group of cognitive theorists, who take a different view, are not known by any special name. These theorists also believe that cognitions are of primary importance in understanding behaviour. However, they argue that cognitions themselves are something more than observable behaviours, such as scratching one's head. They contend that cognitive processes don't always follow the same laws as observable behaviours.

Where are we now?

Our brief overview shows that there are different opinions and theoretical perspectives in psychology, none of which hold the whole "truth." Many psychologists identify strongly with one theoretical perspective. Often, bad feeling exists between different "camps," almost as though they were rival religious factions. Nevertheless, a large number of researchers and practitioners are **eclectic** in their approach. In other words, they select from the various theoretical perspectives whatever seems to work best to solve a particular problem. In some settings eclecticism is more common than any one theoretical approach. For example, according to one survey of Canadian hospitals (Arnett, Martin, Streiner, and Goodman, 1987), 43% of psychologists described themselves as eclectic in orientation. Psychologists with single theoretical orientations were less numerous.

THE FIELD OF PSYCHOLOGY

Traditionally, the psychologist earned a Ph.D. degree, which is primarily a research degree. Recently, however, some programs have been developed which tend to emphasize applications rather than research. They focus on training in the practice of psychology, using knowledge developed from its scientific and research base. Many of these more applied programs award a Psy.D. (doctor of psychology) degree.

Generally, individuals in psychology have an orientation that is predominantly either experimental or applied. An **experimental orientation** focuses on theory and extending existing knowledge through research, whereas an **applied orientation** focuses on practice and using existing knowledge to deal with practical problems. However, many psychologists would not identify themselves as belonging solely to one orientation. Perhaps it would be more accurate to say that most psychologists choose to emphasize one perspective over the other. In Canada, the line between experimental and applied orientation has become even more blurred because university teaching positions have become more scarce. In the past, most people who were trained in psychological research found academic (experimental) jobs rather than applied jobs. In discussing Canadian psychology, John Adair (1981, p. 166) points out that is no longer the case:

> Also partly responsible for more applied psychologists was the spill-over from experimental graduates trained for no longer available academic positions. Many quickly and effectively transformed their laboratory research training into careers as research psychologists, program evaluators, and practitioners in penitentiaries, social service agencies, government departments or in private industry. Such positions in turn became legitimate career options, rather than merely 'parachutes' for those unable to be placed in academia.

Recent developments have demonstrated that people with sound training in the principles of psychology have the flexibility to apply their skills in a variety of settings.

Areas of specialization

The field of psychology is large and complex. It contains many subspecialties, each with its own way of looking at behaviour. In this section, we will describe the main areas of specialization. Perhaps one or more will strike you as being particularly interesting and useful.

Clinical psychology

A **clinical psychologist** is one who diagnoses and treats emotional and behavioural disorders. When most people hear that a person is a psychologist, they often say, "Don't psychoanalyze me!" However, not all psychologists are clinical psychologists, and only a minority of clinical psychologists use psychoanalysis. Nevertheless, clinical psychology is the largest area of specialization within psychology. According to surveys conducted by the American Psychological Association (Stapp, Fulcher & Wicherski, 1984; and Stapp, Tucker & VandenBos, 1985), and the Canadian Psychological Association (Martin, Ritchie, & Sabourin, 1988), most psychologists work in the clinical or counselling areas.

Counselling psychology

A **counselling psychologist** is one who treats relatively mild emotional and social problems. Some counselling psychologists offer help in dealing with marriage difficulties. Others provide guidance for academic and vocational problems. Your university or college probably has a counselling service where students can obtain guidance about study skills, career decisions, and personal problems. It is sometimes difficult to tell where counselling psychology ends and clinical psychology begins. In general, however, the counselling psychologist treats less severe problems than the clinical psychologist does.

School psychology and educational psychology

After clinical and counselling psychology, the next largest areas of specialization are school psychology and educational psychology (Stapp, Fulcher, Wicherski, 1984; Stapp, Tucker, & VandenBos, 1985; and Martin, Ritchie, & Sabourin, 1988). A **school psychologist** applies psychological principles to assess and counsel students in elementary and high school. School psychologists may evaluate test results, deal with behavioural problems, and help to identify learning disabilities. Unlike clinical psychologists, almost all of whom have doctoral degrees, most school psychologists have teaching certificates and master's degrees, usually in educational psychology. Educational psychology is the theoretical counterpart of school psychology. An **educational psychologist** is one who researches all aspects of formal education and who helps to train teachers and school psychologists at the university.

Personality psychology

A **personality psychologist** is one who studies individual differences in human behaviour. Personality psychologists try to understand how and why people differ from each other. They conduct research on abilities and traits, and they work to develop theories about the basic nature of human beings. Most personality psychologists are employed in universities, where they combine research and teaching. In Chapter 10, we will discuss several different theories of personality.

Social psychology

A **social psychologist** is one who studies the behaviour of individuals in relationship to others as well as the behaviour of groups. Why do people conform to the demands of others, even when it is not in their own best interests? Who is most likely to fall in love with whom? Under what circumstances are people likely to help others or hurt others? Why does prejudice persist in some areas? The questions asked in social psychology concern issues that often affect us directly, as you will see in our discussion in Part VI (Chapters 16–18).

Applied social psychology

As its name suggests, applied social psychology is the applied counterpart of social psychology. Most social psychologists spend their time doing research and teaching. An **applied social psychologist** uses the findings of social psychology to deal with social problems. How do advertisers influence people? How can community access to child-rearing information be made more efficient? Is there a way to increase the use of seat-belts or to encourage conservation? Applied social psychologists often have to carve out their own job in an organization, but many such opportunities do exist. Although this specialty is often listed under social psychology, applied social psychology is growing as an independent area. For example, the University of Saskatchewan now has a Ph.D. programme in applied social psychology.

Experimental psychology

An **experimental psychologist** is one who uses experimental methods to study the basic psychological processes and cognitive processes in humans or animals. In Part II, we will explore the basic psychological processes of sensation, perception, learning, motivation, and emotion. In Part III, we will investigate the cognitive processes of memory, thinking, and language. Experimental psychologists devote much of their time to research. Because most of them work in universities, they also engage in teaching. It is a little misleading to call this area of specialization "experimental," because researchers in most of the other areas also do experiments. Nevertheless, the term is used to refer to those psychologists who research basic psychological processes and cognitive processes.

Physiological psychology

If you are interested in both biology and psychology, you might be attracted to physiological psychology. A **physiological psychologist** is one who studies the role of biology and physiology in behaviour. In Chapter 2, we will discuss the biological basis of behaviour. Some physiological psychologists study the impact of kidney malfunction on high blood pressure. Others are interested in how hormones change mood. Still others explore the relationship between brain function and behaviour. Sometimes it is hard to tell where the study of physiology ends and physiological psychology begins. Nevertheless, we can say that the physiological psychologist focuses on behaviour.

Developmental psychology

Developmental psychology is commonly called "child psychology," but that term is misleading. A **developmental psychologist** is one who studies human growth and change throughout the lifespan. How do children form bonds with their parents? How does intelligence change with old age? These are the types of questions we will consider in Chapter 12. Most developmental psychologists teach and do research at universities. Often, they also serve as consultants for child development agencies, educational programmes, and certain government departments.

Health psychology

Health psychology is one of the newest specialties in psychology. It has become important enough to warrant its own chapter in this book. A **health psychologist** is one who applies psychological knowledge to the prevention and alleviation of physical disease. It is becoming clear that emotions and behaviour have an important influence on nearly all diseases. Coping with stress is a major concern in today's society. Being a patient in a hospital requires survival skills that few of us learn in everyday life. The threat of AIDS calls for significant changes in behaviour and presents special challenges to help victims. These are some of the issues that we will discuss in Chapter 19.

Organizational psychology

Often called "industrial psychology," organizational psychology is another important area of specialization. An **organizational psychologist** is one who applies psychological knowledge to the world of work and business. Organizational psychologists may even help design jobs in order to make them more meaningful and productive. What makes one person an effective leader and another a failure? How does the structure of an organization affect the productivity of its workers? How can workers be motivated to be more productive? What are the needs of workers? We will address these sorts of questions in Chapter 20.

The legal regulation of psychology

Who is a "psychologist"? In Canada, the profession of psychology is regulated by the Province (or Territory). Some inter-provincial differences do exist. Generally, however, in order to call oneself a psychologist or to practice psychology, one must be registered or certified by the appropriate provincial regulatory body. To obtain registration, one normally must first have a doctoral degree (Ph.D. or Psy.D.) in psychology and one or two years of post-doctoral supervised experience. Then, one must pass special written and oral examinations (and you might have thought exams ended with university). In most provinces, it is against the law for anyone to sell services using the title "psychologist" without being registered. Thus, a physiological psychologist who wanted to sell services as a "consultant psychologist" would have to be registered. By contrast, anyone can use the title "research consultant" or "behavioural advisor" or even "family counsellor" without legal penalty.

RESEARCH METHODS

The scientific method

When we say that psychology is a science, we mean nothing more than that we use the scientific method to build up our store of knowledge. The **scientific method** consists of (i) gathering information through systematic observation, (ii) formulating an explanation (theory), (iii) deriving a prediction (hypothesis) from the theory, and (iv) testing the prediction in a controlled and reproducible manner. For example, a person might say, "My experience is that people are basically friendly if I'm friendly first." This might be true, but it is not a scientific observation because it is based on anecdotal and unsystematic observations. It could be biased by a tendency to ignore unfriendly behaviour in others. Scientific observation would require that we make our observations of friendly behaviour in a controlled way that eliminates such biases.

The scientific method entails the public sharing of information so that others can confirm or disprove (disconfirm) one's findings. In practice, people use many ways to acquire information and knowledge. Much of what we know and do is *not* based on scientific methods. If you relate to a lover solely on the basis of what has been discovered scientifically, you are going to be a very lonely person. There are limits to scientific observation. Nevertheless, in many areas (some of which may not be obvious), the scientific method is the most dependable source of knowledge.

It is both exciting and discomforting to realize that some of the information in this book contradicts what passed for knowledge in introductory psychology 30 years ago. Although recent research has confirmed some earlier findings, it has shown others to be false. Some years from now, new research will inevitably contradict parts of this book. This is the way knowledge grows. Science is not something magic or sacred. It is simply a relatively objective and reliable way to observe and understand reality.

According to the scientific method, in order to know, we must observe. The methods we use to observe will differ depending on the problem that we are trying to investigate and the means we have available for investigating it. The observations made by an investigator interact with his or her hypotheses. A **hypothesis** is a prediction to be tested through research. Hypotheses can come from the researcher's "hunches," based upon similar research done in the past. But most commonly, hypotheses are derived from theories. A **theory** is a logical set of ideas designed to explain some set of facts in a way that best approximates truth. A good theory organizes current knowledge in a way that points toward new knowledge. Confidence in a particular theory is increased if a hypothesis derived from that theory is confirmed. Confidence is decreased if the hypothesis is disconfirmed. A theory may be modified or eventually even discarded if further hypotheses derived from it are also disconfirmed. Theories are scientifically useful to the extent that they lead to testable hypotheses which may be examined in actual research. (See Figure 1-2.)

FIGURE 1-2 The relationship between theory and research Predictions or hypotheses are derived from a theory in accordance with basic principles of logic. Hypotheses are then tested in actual research. If they are confirmed, confidence in the theory is increased. If they are disconfirmed, the theory may be modified, and new predictions tested. If these, too, are disconfirmed, confidence in the theory's accuracy is reduced and ultimately the theory may be rejected.

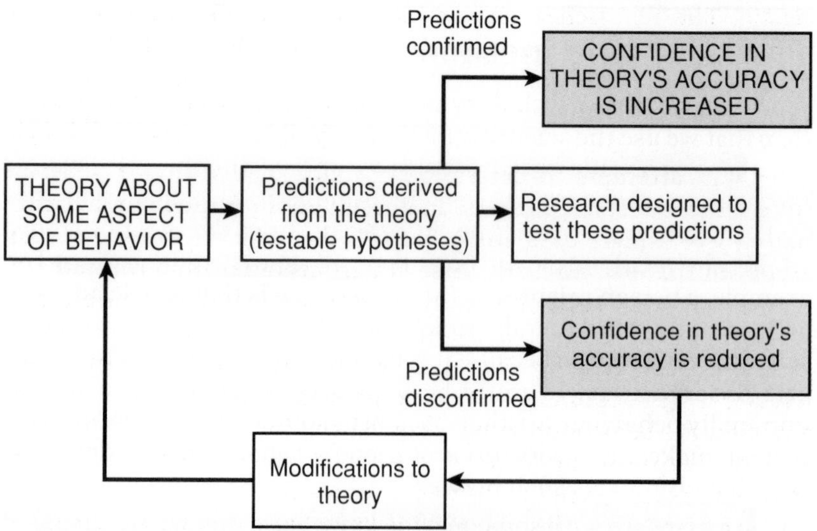

SOURCE: Reprinted with permission from Allyn and Bacon, 1989.

Perhaps the simplest form of observation is to study events in a natural setting. We use the term **naturalistic observation** to refer to a non-intrusive gathering and recording of observations of events as they naturally occur in the environment without interference or distraction from the researcher. This is a valuable method of observation because in many instances artificial control or manipulation will alter the events or behaviours as they would otherwise occur naturally. For example, suppose we are interested in what people do in reception areas while waiting for an employment interview. Do they read, talk, solve crossword puzzles, or bite their nails? To collect this data in a systematic manner, we could record the number of people engaging in these activities at 15-minute intervals or we could count the number of occurrences of each event. By the way, we must be careful to **operationalize** the behaviour under investigation. In other words, we must describe our measure of it in a clearly observable and quantifiable way. We must carefully specify our observations so that any other people observing the situation will come up with the same set of data. For example, does leafing through a magazine back to front constitute reading? Does tugging on a hangnail count as nail biting? We must provide clear definitions.

We said that the effects of the observer should be minimized. We will get a different set of observations if we observe from behind a small one-way mirror than if we sit in the waiting room, pencil and clipboard in hand, glancing about and writing furiously.

March 5, 1984: After several months, I now feel that these strange little rodents have finally accepted me as one of their own.

SOURCE: *The Far Side* by Gary Larson. Reprinted by permission of Chronicle Features, San Francisco, CA.

Studies

There are many ways in which to collect observations in a *non-naturalistic* way. Non-naturalistic observation methods involve varying amounts of intervention by the observer or the experimenter. These methods are more appropriately classified as studies.

Single case studies

The simplest type of study is the **single case study** (or simply **case study**). The researcher gathers extensive data on one individual through interviews, testing, observation, and other methods. When a physician compiles information by taking a patient's history and then examining the patient, the physician is conducting a single case study. Another example of a single case study occurs when a driving instructor attempts to determine an individual's driving abilities from written tests, road tests, and observation. A much more informal type of single case study occurs when we try to evaluate an escort on the first date. All these situations differ from the naturalistic observation method because in the case study, the observer is usually present. Thus, we have to consider the possibility that our presence is influencing what is happening. We might be employing a **reactive measurement**, that is, a method of measurement that is affecting the behaviour being observed and investigated. If the presence of the driving instructor frightens the person about to take the road test, then driving performance may well suffer. When we are out on a first date with someone, the knowledge that we are carefully observing and evaluating each other tends to affect the behaviour of both parties.

Survey studies

In the **survey study**, groups of subjects are asked for information through interviews or questionnaires. If the total number of potential subjects is too great to be questioned individually, then a random sample of this population is used instead. (We will discuss sampling techniques later in this chapter.) Suppose we are interested in improving the quality of our introductory psychology course. Let's assume that we want the changes to be improvements from the individual student's point of view. We could devise a survey of the students which might include such questions as "What do you find most difficult about this course?", "What do you find most helpful?", or "How could this course be made better for you?" Alternatively, we could design a somewhat different survey. Instead of asking open-ended questions, we could quantify our data by having the students respond to questions on a numbered five-point scale (from very poor to excellent). We could ask such questions as "How would you rate the effectiveness of the lectures?" and "How would you rate the usefulness of your textbook?" Whichever type of questions we ask, we should formulate them so that they will address specific strengths and weaknesses that we suspect exist. The answers we obtain will then serve as tests for our hypotheses.

The survey method is relatively easy to use and can be applied to problems that cannot be studied in other ways. However, there are serious limitations to the survey method. First, what people *say* they do or think is often different from what they *actually* do or think. Second, the researcher's questions are not always as clear or unbiased as he or she may think they are. Third, if those being questioned are a sample from a larger group, then it may be difficult to ensure that the sample truly represents the entire population.

Longitudinal versus cross-sectional studies

In a **longitudinal study** the same subjects are examined repeatedly over time, usually over the course of years. Longitudinal studies are used primarily to assess changes in individuals or groups over time. If, for instance, we want to study how people's television-viewing habits change as they grow older, we could examine the viewing habits of a carefully selected sample group at five-year intervals. This approach permits the researcher to measure the subject's current score against his or her earlier scores. This means that the individual is used as his or her own referent or *control* (more about controls and control groups later). By comparing individuals at one time in their lives with themselves at other points in time, the researcher is able to eliminate some of the extraneous variables that creep in when different groups are compared with each other.

However, there are some disadvantages to longitudinal research. For one thing, it is both expensive and time consuming and thus not practical for many research applications. Our longitudinal study of changing television-viewing habits from childhood through old age is certainly going to be a protracted and costly investigation, and one that would also, no doubt, involve more than one investigator. Another problem with longitudinal studies is that historical changes make it difficult to interpret findings. It would be simplistic to attribute all changes in television-viewing habits solely to age, because so many other factors might also change during these same years: social habits, forms of recreation, television programming, and the marketing of new gadgets that compete with television.

Another research method, quite different from the longitudinal study, is the **cross-sectional study**, in which data is collected on individuals or groups of different ages at one point in time. In our example about television viewing, we might explore age-related changes in viewing habits by collecting data on groups of individuals of different ages. We could compare viewing habits of five-year-olds and fifty-year-olds, without waiting for the toddlers to age. This approach has both advantages and shortcomings. On the positive side, it is less expensive and more practical to conduct a study that will take months, rather than years or even decades. Because many research questions are concerned with describing current conditions, comparisons of different age groups at one time are appropriate. On the negative side, our groups of subjects have had different prior experiences, and this will distort our interpretations of the data. Fifty-year-olds have had life experiences, have grown up in social circumstances, and likely have had child-rearing practices imposed upon them that are all quite different from today's five-year-olds. Thus, we are comparing groups that are different in more respects than just age. A general comparison of cross-sectional and longitudinal studies is shown in Figure 1-3.

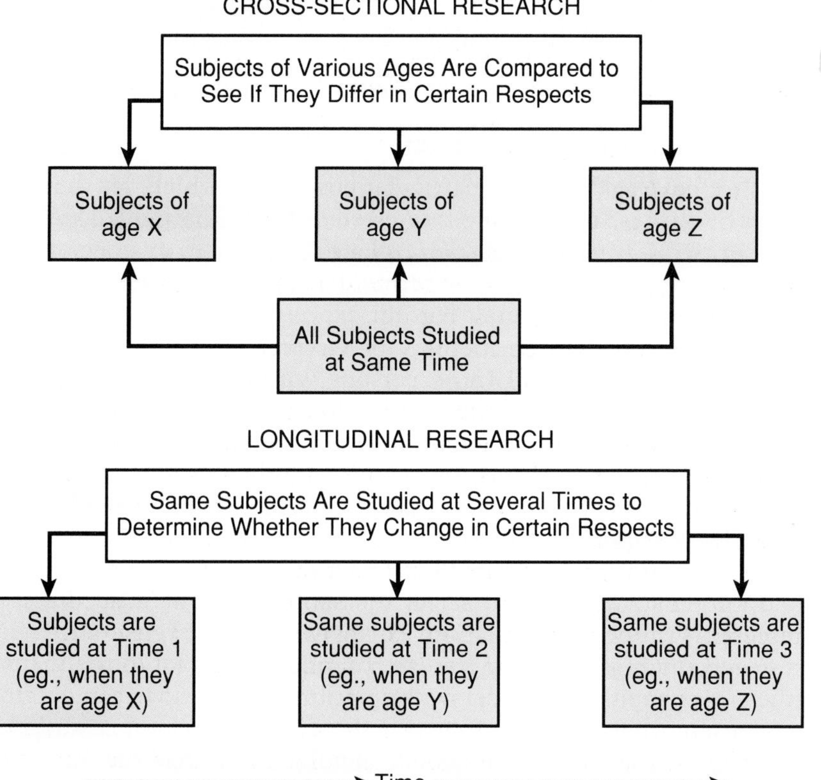

SOURCE: Adapted with permission from Allyn and Bacon, 1989.

FIGURE 1-3 Comparison between cross-sectional and longitudinal research
There are two major research methods used in psychological research comparing subjects of different ages. In cross-sectional research (upper panel) subjects of different ages are compared in order to determine if they differ in certain respects. In longitudinal research (lower panel) a single group of individuals is studied at different points in time to determine whether they change in various respects with the passage of time.

Experiments

Perhaps the most important tool in the acquisition of scientific knowledge is the experiment. Experiments lead to more reliable conclusions about causality than do other methods. An **experiment** is a research method in which the researcher manipulates one or more variables (independent variables) and measures the impact of that manipulation on some outcome measure (dependent variable). In a good experiment, the researcher can isolate each of the variables and observe any resulting changes precisely. This abstract definition will become clearer as we describe an experiment and define a few terms.

Suppose we want to see whether a particular drug can help to improve a person's memory after a head injury. Our hypothesis is that it will. The obvious thing to do would be to give the drug to a group of people who have suffered head injuries and see if their memories improve. However, in order to test our hypothesis, we have to design our experiment carefully. The goal of our experiment is to be able to conclude that the drug caused improvement in memory. If we simply give our drug to this group, a critic of our experiment could cite many plausible alternative explanations for any memory improvement. For example, it is possible that memory generally improves after a head injury because of bed rest or spontaneous nerve regeneration or some other such cause. We could also be accused of making inaccurate observations because we expected memory to improve when our drug was administered. We want to eliminate such plausible alternative explanations for our findings.

Throughout the remainder of this chapter, we will be introducing statistical terms and concepts. They are discussed in more detail in the Statistics appendix at the end of this book.

Sampling from a population

First we have to define the particular population which, for the purposes of our research, we are interested in. A **population** consists of the entire group about whom knowledge is sought. For some experiments, the population might be middle-class males. For others, it might be people in general. For our experiment to investigate the effects of a drug on the memory of victims of head injuries, the population would be all those persons who have suffered a head injury which results in memory impairment. This is a large population, and it would not be economical or feasible to test all of these individuals. Having defined our population, however, we can then take a sample of the population. A **sample** is a representative subset of an entire population.

There are many factors to consider in choosing a sample. First and foremost, we want to select the sample so that it accurately represents the entire population. This will allow us to generalize our research findings from the few (the particular sample) to the many (the entire population under consideration). Usually, we can obtain a representative sample by selecting the subjects randomly. **Random selection** is a process of selecting a sample so that every member of a population has an equal chance of being chosen. Random selection should eliminate all bias from the sample. In other words, the resulting sample should not differ in any systematic way from the population. How could we arrange for a random selection in our hypothetical experiment about the effects of a drug on memory recovery? One way would be to choose as subjects every third individual admitted to hospital who has been diagnosed as suffering a head injury with memory impairment. We would not expect that every third individual would differ in some systematic way from the others admitted with the same diagnosis. Another way of arranging for a random selection would be to number all the patients and then choose the subjects for our experiment by means of a random number table. (See the Statistics appendix for information about random number tables.)

It is easy to make our first research mistake at this point. For example, if we wish to make some statements about the effects of our memory-recovery drug on the adult population, we should not use only males in our sample. If we did use males only, then our results might not be applicable to females who had experienced a head injury. (Actual research suggests that there are sex differences in recoverability from head injuries.) By the same token, if we wish to make inferences about possible memory recovery in adults, we should not include children in our sample.

There are other, more subtle, ways that sampling bias can creep into our data. **Sampling bias** is a systematic disproportionate selection of some subgroup of the population so that the resulting sample is not representative of the entire population. Suppose that we were available only on Mondays to collect data for our memory experiment. Is it possible that our patients might differ in some systematic way from the larger population of head-injured adults? Perhaps we would be seeing a greater proportion of individuals injured after consuming alcohol at weekend parties. Without intending to do so, we might disproportionately be sampling heavy drinkers. Thus, when we came to interpret our experimental findings, we would not be able to separate out the effects of alcohol on head injuries and memory recovery. Representative sampling is one prerequisite for good research that is often neglected.

Dependent and independent variables

Since, in our hypothetical experiment, we are investigating memory loss and recovery, we have to have some way of defining and measuring memory. Clinical psychologists often use standardized tests of memory for this purpose. We will go into more detail about psychological tests in Chapter 11, but for now let us assume that we have selected a test which will accurately measure a person's memory. This test will give us a numerical score indicating a person's level of memory functioning. Let's assume that 100 is an average score, which can be defined statistically as "normal" memory. The score a person obtains on this test of memory in our study would be called the dependent variable. In general, a **dependent variable** is the factor that changes as a result of whatever manipulation the researcher has carried out. In other words, it is our outcome measure.

Now that we have our sample and our dependent variable, we could simply give our group of head-injured patients the drug, and then score them on the memory test. The drug, in this case, would be considered the independent variable. In general, an **independent variable** is the factor that the researcher deliberately manipulates in order to study its effects. For our hypothetical experiment, suppose we now have a random sample, a dependent variable (a memory test that can be scored), and an independent variable (the drug). Do we now have everything we need? Not yet. Imagine that we gave our sample individuals the drug, tested their memory, and found the average score for the group was 100. What could we conclude from this? Nothing. All we would have is a score which indicates that, after administration of our drug, these people are functioning at a normal level of memory. The score does not answer our question about whether the drug has had a positive, negative, or neutral effect on the return of memory. This is where we need a control.

Controls: eliminating alternative explanations

In the design of scientific experiments, a crucial objective is to control the conditions. **Controls** are techniques used in experiments to ensure that the results are attributable solely to the chosen independent variables, and not to anything else. As researchers, we want to know that there is only one plausible explanation for our findings. In other words, we want to design our experiments so that all confounding variables are eliminated.

A **confounding variable** is a factor that allows a plausible alternative explanation for results of research, thereby making it impossible to attribute the findings only to the independent variable.

Let us reconsider our memory-drug experiment. Perhaps one useful way of incorporating controls would be first to test the memories of our subjects, then give them the drug, and lastly retest their memories. In this way, each member of the group would serve as his or her own comparison or control (as in a longitudinal study). We could then make statements about memory functioning both before and after administration of the drug. This arrangement is known as a **pre-post design**, a design in which dependent measures are taken of each subject both before and after the experimental manipulation of an independent variable.

Suppose our group average on the memory test was 80 prior to the administration of the drug and 100 afterward. Can we now safely say that the drug has a positive effect on the return of memory function? Not yet. Suppose that the time elapsed between the first testing of memory and the second was a month. The passage of time could have influenced the recovery of memory and perhaps the drug had little or even no effect. We would not have eliminated the effects of time as an alternative explanation in our study. In other words, time would be a confounding variable here.

To overcome this problem, we can select another sample or group in the same way that we selected our experimental group to whom we administered the drug. (An **experimental group** is that group of subjects who are exposed to the researcher's manipulation of the independent variable.) The new sample will serve as our control group. (See Figure 1-4.) In general, a **control group** is that group of subjects who are not exposed to the researcher's manipulation of the independent variable, but who are exposed to all the other conditions of the experiment. In the new design of our memory-drug experiment we now have two groups of subjects. The experimental group will receive the drug and the control group will not. In order for us to be able to make valid statements about the drug's effects on memory, it is essential that the control group be selected in the same random way as the experimental group. Furthermore, we also need to ensure that the two groups are treated similarly in all ways. Thus, we should realize the control group might not feel that they are getting the special attention that goes along with receiving a pill. As a result our control subjects might become somewhat depressed and less likely to do well on a test of memory. By the same token, the experimental subjects might have an expectation that their memory will improve because they are receiving a "memory enhancing" drug. Hence, they might well be more motivated in the memory testing. To avoid such confounding variables, we could design the experiment as a blind study. In general, a **blind study** is one in which the subjects do not know whether they belong to the experimental group or to the control group. In other words, the subjects do not know whether they are being exposed to the independent variable. How can we arrange our experiment so that it will be a blind study? We could try to find a way of making all the subjects think that they are receiving the drug. The most common technique for achieving this is to give the control group a **placebo**, a substance or treatment which resembles that given to the experimental group but which actually lacks the critical element under study. For our purposes, we could use a pill identical in appearance to the pill that the experimental group receives, except that there would be no active drug in the capsule. Usually, some inert substance serves as a substitute. By utilizing

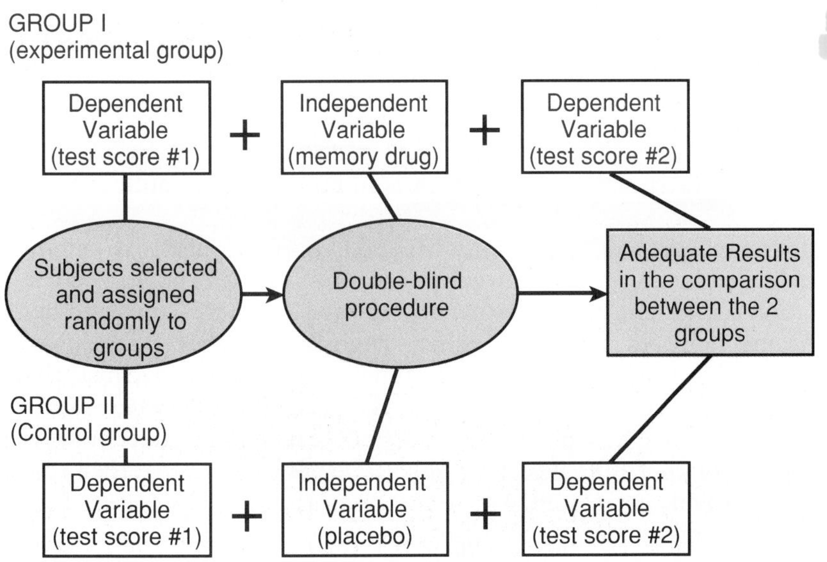

FIGURE 1-4 An adequate experimental design

placebos, researchers are following the principle that the experimental group and the control group should be treated identically in all ways except for the all-important independent variable.

Suppose each of our two groups receives an average score of 80 prior to the administration of the drug or the placebo. If both the experimental group and the control group were selected in the same way, we would expect them to have identical pre-drug scores because both samples are representative of the same population. After the administration of the drug or the placebo, suppose that the experimental group obtains a score of 100 and the control group a score of 80. Can we then conclude that our drug has improved memory functioning? We're closer, but not quite there.

An important control issue in all studies is that of *experimenter bias*. Research has shown that experimenters can unintentionally affect the results of their experiments (Rosenthal & Rubin, 1978). A researcher can inadvertently, and quite subtly, communicate his or her expectations to the subjects of both groups. To prevent this from happening, an experiment is designed where possible as a **double-blind study**, in which both the experimenters and the subjects are kept unaware of which subjects are in the experimental group and which subjects are in the control group. How could we arrange our memory-drug experiment as a double-blind study? One way would be to use a secret code to distinguish the real pills from the placebos. The code would not be revealed to any of the experimenters who come into contact with the subjects. This would include those who administer the substance (drug or placebo) and those who give and mark the memory tests.

Suppose that as a double-blind study, our experiment yields the results described above (pre-drug score of both sample groups = 80; post-drug score of experimental group = 100; and post-placebo score of control group = 80). Because we have taken the proper precautions in the design of our experiment, we are on reasonably safe ground in saying that our new drug has improved memory functions in our sample of people who had suffered memory loss from head injuries. Furthermore, we can reasonably apply our results to the entire population of such victims.

Correlational studies

Another statistical concept which is important in research is correlation. A **correlation coefficient** is a statistical measure of the direction and degree of relationship between two variables. It is usually indicated by a number between −1.00 and +1.00. A positive correlation coefficient indicates that two variables tend to occur together. As one increases, so does the other. Height and weight tend to covary positively. That is, taller people tend to be heavier. Because this relationship does not always hold, the correlation between height and weight will be a positive number but less than a perfect positive correlation of +1.00. If two variables tend not to occur together, they are negatively correlated. As one increases, the other decreases. Temperature and incidence of frostbite are certainly correlated with each other, but the higher one is, the lower the other tends to be. They covary negatively. If two variables are completely unrelated to each other, their correlation coefficient will be zero. For instance, shoe size and visual acuity are not related to each other. We would expect to find a correlational coefficient between these two variables of about 0.00.

In an experimental design (such as our memory-drug experiment), we introduce one variable, the independent variable (the drug) to see what effect it will have on another variable, the dependent variable (memory test scores). In correlational research, we would try to examine relationships that already exist and are not the product of any experimental intervention.

Suppose that in looking over the memory data in our hypothetical experiment, we found what appeared to be an interesting pattern in the scores. Perhaps on the initial memory test (before the administration of the drug or placebo), older people obtained better scores than younger people. If we found this to be true in every single case in our sample group, then the correlation between memory and age would be +1.00. By contrast, if we found that the older the patient, the lower the memory test score, then the correlation between memory and age would be a negative one (indicating an inverse relationship). If this occurred in every instance, we would have a perfect correlation, a negative correlation of −1.00. Finally, if there was no relationship between age and memory score, then the correlation coefficient would be somewhere around zero (0.00). See Figure 1-5.

Correlation is not causation

A word of caution is appropriate here: *Correlation is not causality.* We cannot emphasize this too strongly. A correlation shows a relationship between variables, but the relationship is not necessarily causal. Age does not necessarily cause higher (or lower) memory scores, even though our data suggest that some relationship does exist.

In Europe many years ago people observed a strong correlation between the number of storks nesting on a house and the number of babies born in that house. In spite of folkloric tradition, it would be wrong to conclude from these observations the causal relationship that storks bring babies. Actually, a number of other variables affected both measures at the same time. For instance, most storks nested in rural areas, and rural families tended to have large families to help with the farming. In another correlation that does not necessarily show causation, some studies have shown that married people tend to be happier than those who are unmarried. Can we conclude from this that marriage causes happiness? Maybe happiness causes marriage, or maybe other variables independently cause both. Perhaps, having opportunities, education, money, intelligence, and good looks increases the probability both of getting married and of being happy. We simply can't tell what causes what from a correlation.

Let's reconsider our memory-drug experiment. Suppose the time (on the 24-hour clock) when patients suffered their head injuries correlates with their memory score, such that lower scores are obtained at greater clock values. We can be relatively confident that

FIGURE 1-5 Scatterplots of different correlations
The first two graphs (A and B) represent perfect correlations. In practice perfect correlations are extremely rare. The second two graphs (C and D) represent more realistic correlations.

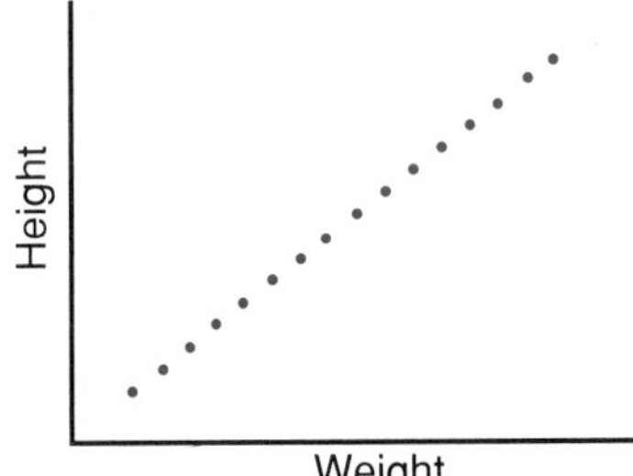

A. A perfect positive correlation of +1.00

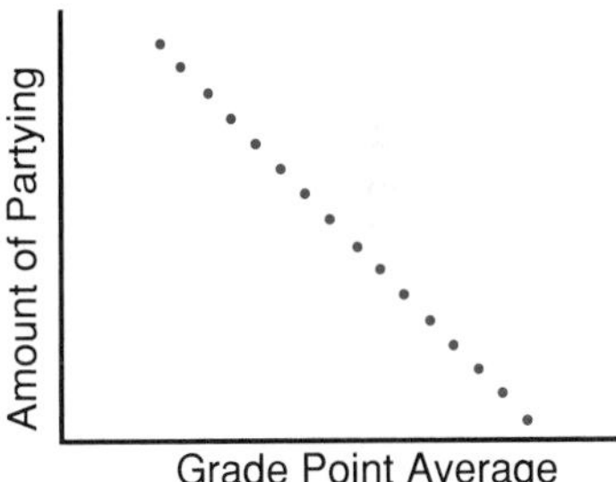

B. A perfect negative correlation of −1.00

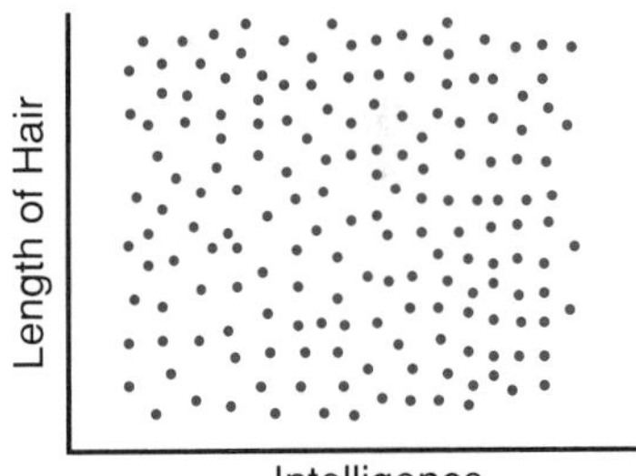

C. Uncorrelated variables-correlation = 0.0

D. Moderately positive correlation of approximately +0.5

time of day does not cause a particular memory score, but a relationship does exist. Perhaps an intervening variable is responsible for the correlation. An **intervening variable** is a hypothetical variable which is not observed directly in a study but which may account for the observed relationship between the independent variable and the dependent variable. In our experiment, any intervening variable would have to relate to both the time of day and the severity of memory impairment. One possibility would be the severity of the accident. It might be that the most severe accidents occur before midnight and the least severe in the early morning hours.

Many advertisers try to capitalize on the *misconception* that "correlation equals causality." Perhaps there is a relationship between the number of brushings with a certain toothpaste and the number of friends an individual has, but the relationship is not necessarily causal. (See the "Close-up: Television Commercials and Research," near the end of this chapter.)

Using statistics to interpret our results

Once the observations, test scores, or data are collected, how can we be sure that the differences in scores are really meaningful? In our memory-drug experiment, the sample groups would consist of individuals who are not, of course, identical in all respects. This, in itself, would account for at least some differences in their test scores. Moreover, it could happen that even with random selection, we might end up with a disproportionate number of heavy drinkers for the control group. Other chance factors could also affect our findings. How sure can we be that the results obtained are not attributable to chance alone? To answer this question, we have to analyse our results statistically. We can make use of statistics to find out the likelihood or probability that the findings from our sample groups apply to the total population under consideration.

For some reason, many students in psychology experience mild nausea in contemplating statistics. Perhaps they are confronted with too much detailed information at once. To avoid this problem, we will briefly consider here only a few more statistical concepts. We encourage you to read at your leisure the more thorough discussion of statistics given in the Appendix.

Let us imagine, once again, that in our hypothetical experiment, the pre-drug score of both sample groups was 80, the post-drug score of the experimental group was 100, and the post-placebo score of the control group was 80. Let us assume that our groups each have three individuals in them (although this is usually too small a number from which to draw conclusions in an experiment). Suppose the patients in our experimental group obtained post-drug scores of 80, 100, and 120, giving an average of 100. And suppose the patients in our control group had post-placebo scores of 60, 80, and 100, giving an average of 80. Only one patient in the drug group scored above the highest in the control group. This might have been caused by a factor not controlled in our study. Compare these scores with another hypothetical outcome. Suppose the subjects in the experimental group obtained post-drug scores of 99, 100, and 101, giving an average of 100. And suppose the subjects in the control group obtained post-placebo scores of 79, 80, and 81, giving an average of 80. Here there is absolutely no overlap in scores between the two groups. How can we assess the meaningfulness of the results in each example?

In comparing groups statistically, we can first consider the **mean**, the arithmetic average of a group of scores (i.e., the sum of the scores divided by the number of scores). But we should also consider the **variability** of the scores, or the degree to which a group's scores deviate from the mean. In our two examples above, the means of the scores by corresponding groups are the same (100 for the experimental group and 80 for the control group). However, in the first example, the variability of the scores is relatively high, and there is even considerable overlap between the two groups. By contrast, in the second example, the variability of the scores is relatively low (they are clustered tightly around the means), and there is no overlap between the two groups. (See Figure 1-6.) Consequently, with the second example we are on stronger ground in concluding that we have a meaningful result.

Figure 1-6 The effect of variability on statistical significance

Distribution of scores in two hypothetical experiments. Even though both experiments yielded identical differences in average scores, the difference in Experiment 2 is more likely to be statistically significant. There is less variability and thus less overlap between the groups.

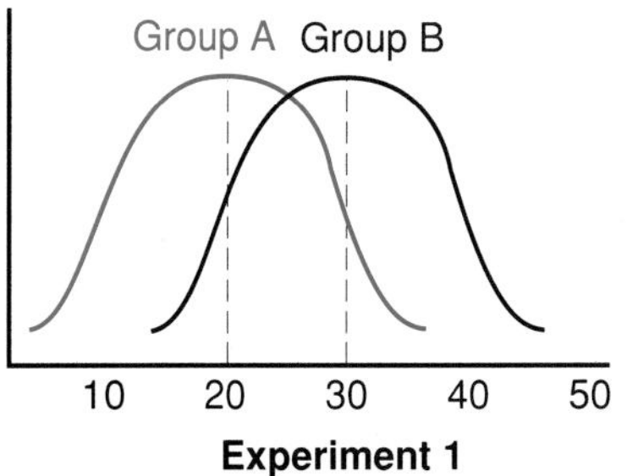

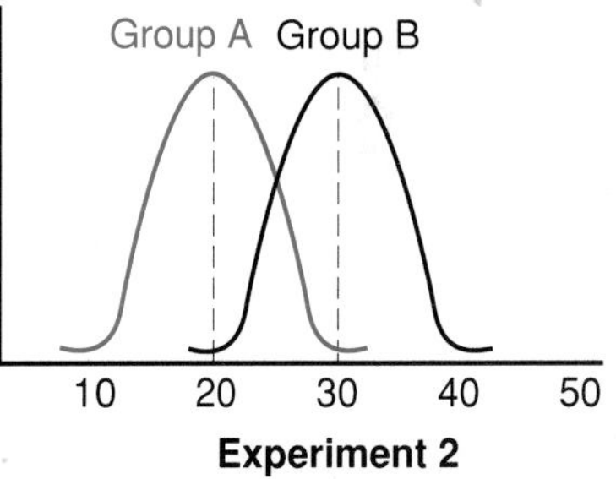

Statistics enable us to measure and compare the strength of experimental results with precision. By applying certain statistical tests to such properties as the mean and variability, we can calculate the likelihood that our findings are attributable to the independent variable rather than to chance factors. By convention, we use the term **statistically significant** to designate research findings whose likelihood (probability) of being "real" (that is, not due to chance) has been calculated to be at least 95%. Research articles usually refer to their findings with such phrases as "statistically significant at $p < .05$" (this reads: "*p* less than point zero five"). The "*p*" stands for probability. The statement means that the probability that the results obtained are attributable to chance factors is less than 5%, or 1 in 20. Thus, a research finding that is "statistically significant at the $p < .001$ level" is a more powerful finding than one that is "statistically significant at the $p < .05$ level." In other words, with $p < .001$, we can generalize our findings to the population with more confidence, since the probability is less than 1 in 1000 that the results were caused by chance factors.

Ethical standards

Is psychology manipulative and dangerous? Earlier, we pointed out that one goal of the science of psychology is to influence behaviour. To the extent that we can discover the principles of behaviour, our knowledge could be used for good or evil. Thus, there is no easy answer to our question. On the positive side, nearly all of psychology's applications of knowledge are aimed at the improvement of human life. The primary goal of clinical and counselling psychology is the relief of human suffering. Social psychologists have discovered principles about eyewitness testimony that have improved the system of legal justice. Physiological psychologists have discovered relationships between brain chemistry and schizophrenia. The list of such contributions is long, and we will read about many of them in the coming chapters. The profession of psychology is governed by a strict set of ethical guidelines. These guidelines serve to promote the socially constructive applications of psychological principles.

The ethical standards of the Canadian Psychological Association (1986) are based on four principles: (i) respect for the dignity of persons, (ii) responsible caring, (iii) integrity in relationships, and (iv) responsibility to society. These principles are summarized in Figure 1-7.

The ethical standards of psychology are enforced in many ways. Practitioners can be reviewed by provincial licensing or registration organizations. Researchers must submit their research plans to ethical review boards of various kinds. For example, a researcher in a university would submit a plan for each study to one or more committees within a university. If the researcher applied for a grant to support the research, then the granting agency would also evaluate the research according to the ethical code of the Canadian Psychological Association.

In applying these standards, a psychologist can sometimes face difficult dilemmas. For example, a psychotherapist must protect the privacy of the therapy relationship. However, if a client reports current child abuse, many provinces require this information to be shared with authorities. Or, in another scenario, if a client were to threaten to kill someone or to commit suicide, there would be a clear conflict between the privacy of therapy and the safety of the individual. In such instances, the psychologist must weigh the relative importance of opposing principles before coming to a decision.

FIGURE 1-7 A summary of the Canadian code of ethics for psychologists (1986)

PRINCIPLE I: **Respect for the Dignity of Persons.**

"Each person should be treated as a person or an end in him/herself, not as an object or a means to an end" (p. 1).

This principle includes a general recognition of respect and individual rights. It also includes non-discrimination, seeking informed consent from clients and research subjects, freedom of consent, and confidentiality.

PRINCIPLE II: **Responsible Caring.**

"Ethical conduct by psychologists is characterized by an active concern for the welfare of any individual, family or group with whom they come into relationship in their roles as psychologists" (p. 4).

This principle includes both a general caring and an obligation to act only in areas in which the psychologist has a high level of competence. Each activity requires a risk/benefit analysis in which the psychologist acts to maximize benefit and minimize harm.

PRINCIPLE III: **Integrity in relationshps.**

"The relationships formed by psychologists . . . embody . . . fairness; impartiality; straight-forwardness; avoidance of misrepresentation; avoidance of conflicts of interest; and, the provision of accurate information" (p. 12).

PRINCIPLE IV: **Responsibility to society.**

"Two of the legitimate expectations of psychology as a discipline are that it will increase knowledge and that it will conduct its affairs in such ways that it will promote the welfare of all human beings" (p. 16).

SOURCE: Adapted with permission from Canadian Psychological Association (1986).

The ethical standards also direct researchers to minimize the impact of research on participants' physical and mental integrity. The goal of the Canadian Psychological Association is to maximize benefit and to minimize harm. In many cases, research has created knowledge that has relieved human suffering. Each potential benefit must be carefully weighed against the cost to research subjects. To this end, the standards spell out the limits on the use of animals as research subjects. They also present guidelines for the use of deception when doing research with human subjects.

CLOSE-UP

Television Commercials and "Research"

Have you ever wondered about those authoritative-sounding television commercials proclaiming the effectiveness of a particular product based on "scientific research"? In fairness to the advertisers, perhaps the "research" was appropriately conducted, with due attention given to sampling, control, adequacy of dependent measures, and statistical analyses, none of which are provided during the 30-second presentation. It is certainly possible that the beauty on the beach might be able to purr into her lover's ear with 95% certainty ($p < 0.05$), that her soft, clear complexion is attributable to her newly discovered skin cream. It is also possible, however, than certain features of the "research" design may have had an inappropriate influence on the outcome of the study.

"Ninety-five percent of physicians surveyed said that they prescribe Throbofree for headache relief." This sounds like a very impressive testament to this medication, but does it result in headache relief? Remembering the importance of sample size in research, one might consider this a more powerful statement if 2000 physicians were surveyed, instead of 20. What was the sample size? What is the population of physicians which the sample represents? Is it headache specialists, general practitioners, or the consulting staff to the pharmaceutical company? Assuming that prescribing this medication does have some reasonable correlation with headache relief, how is this measured? Was a placebo used? Was the research conducted as a double-blind study?

"The friction-proofing of Slidem motor oil is unsurpassed!" Presumably the originators of this product have conducted research into the friction-reducing properties of this oil and compared it with other motor oils. Particularly with a small sample size (which the manufacturer may favour in this type of research), the variability in the scores of friction-reduction may be great. Greater variability and a small sample size are likely to result in differences that are not statistically significant. If no differences are found, the advertiser is free to say "there is nothing better" and the product is "unsurpassed." These phrases certainly have more advertising appeal than "not statistically different from" or "the same as" in reference to the competition. In fact, these phrases are legally correct even if in the research study other oils achieved higher friction-reducing scores — as long as the difference was not statistically significant!

Somehow numbers and percentages seem to convey a more definite and rigorous impression of product evaluation. "Zappo kills 71% of household germs." Although you will never see an advertisement claiming that a product kills, cures, alters, changes, or enhances less than 50% of anything, 71% does sound impressive. Certainly, because it is a number not ending in zero or five, we tend to think that it must be a reflection of careful scientific study. We might wonder, however, what the "kill-rate" is for other, less exotic products, such as plain soap and water. We might also wonder who was responsible for counting these microscopic casualties, and by what methods? Moreover, what are "household germs"? Do they differ from "garden germs," and are we in any danger from the surviving 29%?

SPECIAL TOPIC Isn't Psychology Just Common Sense?

Sometimes the lay reader responds to psychological studies by saying (or thinking), "That was a waste of time! My own common sense could have told me as much!" However, although common sense may sometimes be correct, psychological research often reveals that some of our widely held beliefs are wrong. After all, prejudice is common sense to the bigot. It is also true that the dictates of common sense are often contradictory. We all know that absence makes the heart grow fonder *and* that out of sight is out of mind. Which is true? If birds of a feather flock together, then why do opposites attract?

Spear, Penrod, and Baker (1988) describe a study in which Eva Vaughan, a university psychology teacher, gave a test of common sense psychology to her first-year students. Each of the following statements from her test has been contradicted by psychological research, but most people believe them. After each discredited statement is the percentage of university students who agreed with it. Test yourself and think about the importance of research as a check on the accuracy of common sense.

1. To change people's behaviour toward members of ethnic minority groups, we must first change their attitudes. (92% said this was true; but the evidence suggests that, under certain conditions, it may be more important to first change behaviour—see Chapter 16.)

2. The basis of a baby's love for its mother is the fact that the mother fills its physiological need for food. (84% agreed; but research indicates that touch may be more important—see Chapter 12.)

3. The more highly motivated you are, the better you will do at solving a complex problem. (80% agreed; but very high motivation interferes with the completion of complex tasks, even though it facilitates simple tasks—see Chapter 13.)

4. A schizophrenic is someone with a split personality. (77% were wrong on this one. Schizophrenia does not involve split personality; rather, it includes grossly illogical thinking and loss of contact with reality—see Chapter 14.)

5. The best way to ensure that a desired behaviour will persist after training is completed is to reward the behaviour every single time it occurs throughout the training period. (77% would apply the wrong principle here. Intermittent rewards result in much longer-lasting behaviour—see Chapter 5.)

How did you do? We all need to check our common-sense beliefs against the evidence and be willing to change those beliefs when we discover that they are invalid.

SPECIAL TOPIC How Can Experiments on Animals Tell Us about People?

This question reflects a partial misunderstanding of psychology. Psychology is the science of behaviour, not just of human behaviour. The study of animal behaviour is interesting and useful in its own right. But there is another reason to do experiments with animals. We can often control variables more thoroughly in animal experiments and thus discover basic principles of behaviour. Of course, it would be a mistake to extend the findings of animal experiments directly to humans. However, experiments on animals can help us isolate variables that will then guide us in doing research with humans. For example, many of the basic principles of learning theory (which we will discuss in Chapter 5) were discovered and refined in work with animals. Humans are, after all, animals, and we share many similarities in physiology and nervous-system functioning with other species. Subsequent research with humans has confirmed most of the principles of learning theory, and these research findings have many applications to the relief of human suffering.

As interesting as animal behaviour can be, our ultimate interest is in human behaviour. It is that focus which has guided the writing of this book. In the following chapters, you will encounter many brief descriptions of animal research that established particular principles and of human research that clarified the applications of those principles to human beings.

Special Topic: How Does Psychology Contribute to Canadian Society?

In 1984, Brendan Rule and John Adair (writing in the journal *Canadian Psychology*) outlined the ways that psychology as a social science has contributed to Canadian society. They excluded from their review the many contributions made by psychologists acting as biological scientists or as health professionals. They focused solely on psychology as a social science. Nevertheless, the list of contributors is impressive. For example, during World War II, Canadian psychological research helped to improve both pilot training and pilot morale.

Some studies have addressed uniquely Canadian problems. For instance, psychological research has strongly influenced the development of second-language learning programmes, especially French immersion training. "The research demonstrated the greater effectiveness in second-language learning of total immersion in early years, with a concomitant absence of detrimental effects on the native language" (Rule and Adair 1984, p.53). The adaptation of Native peoples to cultural change has been another important area of study in recent Canadian psychological research.

Some psychological research is directly linked to government policy. For instance, the Canadian legal system has relied on psychological findings to help it formulate its own definition of the insanity verdict. Moreover, there are many indirect ways in which psychology influences both public perceptions and public policy. Consider just a few examples: (i) research done on eyewitness testimony both in Canada and the United States led to some limiting of eyewitness accounts in criminal trials; (ii) Canadian research showing that children are especially vulnerable to TV advertising resulted in legal regulation of such advertisements in Quebec and a self-regulatory code in the broadcasting industry in the rest of Canada; and (iii) studies done in Canada have shown that police officers are less likely to arouse hostility if they keep their guns concealed when making routine checks.

Often, people may wonder about the usefulness of some of the Canadian psychological experiments they read about. But many principles derived from the laboratory have important applications. Much of what we know about adapting to life in the arctic, for example, was influenced by research on sensory isolation. On another front, Canadian research on pain has had enormous implications for the delivery of health care. For example, it has been discovered that severe pain can be reduced by increasing certain kinds of stimulation. Society clearly is affected and improved by basic psychological research.

Chapter Summary

1. Psychology is the scientific study and understanding of behaviour. The goals of psychology are description, understanding, prediction, and control of behaviour.
2. Psychology had its roots in philosophy. It also incorporated the scientific perspective by adding observation and data collection to rational analysis and logic as sources of knowledge.
3. The earliest theorists in psychology were the structuralists and functionalists. Structuralists studied the mind and its mechanisms through introspection. Their goal was to understand the mind by understanding its structures. By contrast, functionalists were more interested in the flow of thoughts through the human mind. They focused their research on the process of mental operations.
4. Behaviour can be analysed from many different perspectives. In order to try to change behaviour, we might intervene at one or more of the following levels: social, behavioural, physiological, anatomical, and biochemical.

5. In modern psychology, there are several different schools of thought, some of which contradict each other. The main theories are Gestalt psychology, psychoanalysis, behaviourism, humanism, and cognitive psychology.

6. Gestalt psychology claims that the whole is greater than the sum of the parts. Gestalt psychology rejects the idea that one can understand human behaviour completely by studying the individual components of mental processing. Instead, one should view mental processing as an organized whole. Gestalt psychology is also phenomenological in that it places great importance on the individual's subjective perceptions.

7. Freud's psychoanalysis maintains that human functioning is primarily biological and instinctual. The driving forces are sexual and aggressive energy. Freud developed his deterministic theories from clinical observations rather than from laboratory experiments. He argued that childhood experiences shape the adult personality. He also claimed that the unconscious powerfully influences behaviour.

8. Behaviourism focuses on observable behaviour. In its early days, behaviourism rejected the idea that internal processes could be studied scientifically. According to behaviourism, virtually all behaviour is the result of prior learning, which in turn is the result of conditioning. This behaviourist view is known as stimulus-response psychology.

9. Humanism provides a more optimistic view by rejecting the determinism of psychoanalysis and behaviourism. Humanism claims that the basic human drive is a healthy one toward self-actualization. Humanism is also a phenomenological theory in that it assumes that a person's subjective perceptions are critical in influencing behaviour.

10. Cognitive psychology stresses the importance of thinking and other cognitions in determining behaviour. Cognitive psychology claims that it is both possible and necessary to study internal processes. One group of cognitive theorists, known as cognitive behaviourists, believes that cognitions operate by the same rules as observable behaviours.

11. Today, many psychologists are eclectic. Rather than confining themselves to one school of thought, they draw upon the various theories to deal with particular problems.

12. We can distinguish two general orientations in psychology: experimental and applied. In Canada today, a growing number of psychologists are employed outside the university in applied positions.

13. The field of psychology contains many areas of specialization. The largest areas in terms of number of practitioners are clinical

psychology and counselling psychology. Next in size come school psychology and educational psychology. Other relatively traditional areas of specialization include personality psychology, social psychology, experimental psychology, physiological psychology, and developmental psychology. Three newer applied specialties are applied social psychology, health psychology, and organizational psychology.

14. In Canada, the profession of psychology is regulated by the provincial governments. In general, one must be registered or certified by a provincial body to market services using the title "psychologist."

15. Psychologists use the scientific method, by which they test their hypotheses against observation. Scientific theories are refined, corrected, or replaced in light of new research.

16. Systematic observation can be conducted in a number of ways. The simplest method is naturalistic observation. Other methods commonly used by psychologists include the single case study, the longitudinal study, and the cross-sectional study.

17. The experiment is one of the most powerful tools that scientists use to test the validity of their hypotheses. Researchers must design their experiments with care in order to be able to draw accurate conclusions about the independent variables that they are manipulating. Scientists should strive to eliminate all bias and confounding variables from their experiments. First, to avoid sampling bias, researchers often select their samples randomly so that they truly represent the entire population under consideration. Second, researchers normally select a control group as well as an experimental group. Third, to eliminate any bias on the part of the subjects or the experimenters, researchers generally design their experiments as double-blind studies.

18. Correlation coefficients indicate the strength and direction of relationships between pairs of variables. But correlation is not equivalent to causation. In some instances, researchers make use of intervening variables to account for observed relationships between an independent variable and a dependent variable.

19. Psychologists make use of statistics to help assess the meaningfulness of their research findings. They focus on specific statistical properties such as the mean and variability. By convention, findings are considered statistically significant if the probability that they are attributable to chance is less than 5% ($p < .05$).

20. The profession of psychology is governed by a strict set of ethical guidelines. The guidelines of the Canadian Psychological Association are based on four principles: (i) respect for the dignity of persons, (ii) responsible caring, (iii) integrity in relationships, and (iv) responsibility to society.

KEY TERMS

Applied orientation A focus on using existing knowledge to deal with practical problems.

Applied social psychologist A psychologist who uses the research findings of social psychology to deal with social problems.

Behaviour All actions an organism performs, including overt (i.e., external and observable) actions and covert (i.e., internal and hidden from view) actions.

Behaviourism The theory that virtually all behaviour is the result of prior learning.

Blind study A study in which the subjects do not know whether they belong to the experimental group or to the control group.

Case study See *single case study*.

Clinical psychologist A psychologist who diagnoses and treats emotional and behavioural disorders.

Cognitive behaviourists Cognitive psychologists who believe that cognitions (primarily thinking) control behaviour, but that cognitions themselves are simply behaviours that happen to occur inside the skin.

Cognitive psychology The theory that cognitions (thinking, learning, remembering, and other mental processes) are the most important causes of behaviour.

Confounding variable A factor that allows a plausible alternative explanation for results of research, thereby making it impossible to attribute findings to the independent variable.

Control group In an experiment, a group of subjects who are *not* exposed to the researcher's manipulation of the independent variable, but who are exposed to all the other conditions of the experiment.

Controls Techniques used in experiments to ensure that the results are attributable solely to the chosen independent variables, and not to anything else.

Correlation coefficient Statistical measure of the direction and degree of relationship between two variables.

Counselling psychologist A psychologist who treats relatively mild emotional and social problems.

Cross-sectional study Research method in which data are collected on individuals or groups of different ages at one point in time.

Dependent variable In an experiment, the factor that changes as a result of whatever manipulation the researcher has carried out.

Determinism The view that all human behaviour is completely determined by prior events. Determinism denies the existence of free will.

Developmental psychologist A psychologist who studies human growth and change through the lifespan.

Double-blind study A study in which both the experimenters and the subjects are kept unaware of which subjects are in the control group and which are in the experimental group.

Eclectic Selecting from the various theoretical perspectives whatever seems to work best to solve a particular problem.

Educational psychologist A psychologist who researches all aspects of formal education and who helps train teachers and school psychologists at the university.

Experiment Research method in which the researcher manipulates one or more variables (independent variables) and measures the impact of that manipulation on some outcome measure (dependent variable).

Experimental group In an experiment, that group of subjects who are exposed to the researcher's manipulation of the independent variable.

Experimental orientation A focus on theory and extending existing knowledge through research.

Experimental psychologist A psychologist who uses experimental methods to study the basic psychological processes and cognitive processes in humans or animals.

Functionalism The early theory that the mind can best be understood by studying its ongoing processes, rather than its component parts.

Gestalt psychology The theory that mind and perception can be understood only as an integrated whole, rather than as component parts. "The whole is greater than the sum of the parts."

Health psychologist A psychologist who applies psychological knowledge to the prevention and alleviation of physical disease.

Humanism The theory that each individual strives for self-actualization based on the way he or she perceives the world.

Hypothesis A prediction, usually derived from a theory, to be tested through research.

Independent variable In an experiment, the factor that the researcher deliberately manipulates in order to study its effects.

Intervening variable A hypothetical variable which is not observed directly in a study but which may account for the observed relationship between the independent variable and the dependent variable.

Introspection A research method used by structuralists in which trained observers examine their own mental processes and report their private mental experiences in detail.

Learning theory Another term for *behaviourism.*

Longitudinal study Research method in which individual subjects are examined repeatedly over time.

Mean Statistical term for the arithmetic average of a group of scores (i.e., the sum of the scores divided by the number of scores).

Naturalistic observation A non-intrusive gathering and recording of observations of events as they naturally occur in the environment without interference or distraction from the researcher.

Operationalize To describe a measure of something in a clearly observable and quantifiable way.

Organizational psychologist A psychologist who applies psychological knowledge to the world of work and business.

Personality psychologist A psychologist who studies individual differences in human functioning.

Phenomenology The study of the individual's subjective perceptions and inner experiences.

Phrenology The theory that specific mental characteristics result in specific bumps and indentations in the skull.

Physiological psychologist A psychologist who studies the role of biology and physiology in behaviour.

Placebo A substance or treatment which resembles that given to the experimental group but which actually lacks the critical element under study.

Population In research, the entire group about whom knowledge is sought.

Pre-post design A research design in which dependent measures are taken of each subject both before and after the experimental manipulation of the independent variable.

Psychoanalysis A set of theories, and by extension a method of treatment, developed by Sigmund Freud. According to Freud, human behaviour is fundamentally biological and instinctual, driven by sexual and aggressive energy.

Psychology The scientific study and understanding of behaviour.

Random selection A process of selecting a sample so that every member of a population has an equal chance of being selected.

Reactive measurement A method of observation that affects the behaviour being observed and investigated.

Sample In research, a representative subset of an entire population.

Sampling bias A systematic, disproportionate selection of some subgroup of the population so that the resulting sample is not representative of the entire population.

School psychologist A psychologist who applies psychological principles to assess and counsel students in elementary and high school.

Scientific method A method of inquiry which consists of (i) gathering information through systematic observation, (ii) formulating an explanation (theory), (iii) deriving a prediction (hypothesis) from the theory, and (iv) testing the prediction in a controlled and reproducible manner.

Single case study Research method in which extensive data is gathered on one subject, through interviews, testing, observation, and other methods.

Social psychologist A psychologist who studies the behaviour of individuals in relation to others as well as the behaviour of groups.

Statistically significant Research findings whose likelihood (probability) of being "real" (that is, not due to chance) has been calculated to be at least 95%. This probability is usually stated as "$p < .05$."

Stimulus-response (S-R) psychology The behaviouristic view that all that is necessary and sufficient for the understanding of behaviour is to introduce or observe stimuli and to note the resultant responses.

Structuralism The early theory that the human mind can best be understood by studying its components or parts, largely through introspection.

Survey study Research method in which groups of subjects are asked for information through questionnaires, or interviews.

Theory A logical set of ideas designed to explain some set of facts in a way that best approximates truth.

Variability Degree to which a group's scores deviate from the mean.

Suggested Readings

American Psychological Association. (1986). *A career in psychology.* This free booklet can help you consider potential careers in psychology. It can be obtained by writing the American Psychological Association, 1200 17th Street, N. W., Washington, DC 20036.

Agnew, N. M. & Pike, S. W. (1987). *The science game: An introduction to research in the social sciences.* 4th ed. Englewood Cliffs, NJ: Prentice-Hall. A very readable description and explanation of various research methods.

Canadian Psychological Association. (1985). "Psychologist: Guidance Centre occupational information." A Canadian listing of potential careers in psychology. It can be obtained from the Guidance Centre, Faculty of Education, University of Toronto, Toronto, Ontario, M4V 2Z8.

_____ (1989). *Graduate guide: A directory of graduate training programs in psychology in Canada.* This booklet has been prepared for students who wish to enrol in graduate schools in psychology. It can be obtained from the Canadian Psychological Association, Vincent Road, Old Chelsea, Quebec, J0X 2N0.

_____ (1986). "A Canadian code of ethics for psychologists." The strict code of ethical guidelines that govern the profession of psychology in Canada and promote the socially constructive applications of psychological principles. Reprints can be obtained from the Canadian Psychological Association.

Evans, R. I. (1976). *The making of psychology: Discussions with creative contributors.* New York: Knopf. A collection of interviews with eight very influential psychologists.

Stark-Adamac, C. & Kimball, M. (1984). "Science free of sexism: A psychologist's guide to the conduct of nonsexist research." This document was approved and endorsed by the Canadian Psychological Association's Board of Directors in June 1983. Reprints can be obtained from the Canadian Psychological Association.

PART II

BASIC PROCESSES

CHAPTER 2

SOURCE: Sorel Etrog, Detail from Untitled lithograph (n.d.).

The Biology of Behaviour

AS WE SAW in Chapter 1, psychologists can investigate behaviour from many different perspectives: developmental, behavioural, social, educational, clinical, or biological. In this and the next two chapters, we will focus on the biological basis of human behaviour, a study that includes molecular, biochemical, physiological, and anatomical elements.

Perhaps you are surprised to see the importance given to biological functions in an introductory psychology book. Moreover, if you don't have a strong background in biology, you may find Chapters 2, 3, and 4 to be among the most challenging chapters in this book. But, although biological topics may seem quite removed from the interests that motivated you to study psychology, they are basic to the understanding of behaviour.

Indeed, almost everything we will discuss in this book can be traced back to brain functioning and its relationship to our other organ systems. The very act of reading this page requires you to use a complex network of muscle, organ, brain, and nerve functions. A short time ago you used hand, arm, and shoulder muscles to pick up and open this book. At this very moment you are using your eyes to see these words. Your brain is now working to understand and remember the meaning of the words and to relate the ideas they represent to other topics that you have stored in your memory. And this whole elaborate set of activities is being coordinated and directed by your entire nervous system. Whatever else we can say about ourselves, we are biological.

The study of the biology of behaviour raises important philosophical issues about human nature. Many topics in this book will make you think through your view of what a person is. While we're on it, what *is* a person or a personality? Do you have a personality? That seems a silly question; of course you have one. But if this personality is something you can possess, it must be a thing. Where is yours? Similarly, what is a mind? If you have one, where is it? Is it something different from your personality? Our very language implies that personality, mind, and thoughts are *things*. For example, we have all probably said something like "I have several thoughts in my mind right now, but the one I was going to tell you is gone. It was there a minute ago." Such statements imply that the mind is a place in which things called thoughts may or may not exist. But is this true? We should realize that our language can influence our thinking in subtle ways. One question that seems deceptively simple will arise in many chapters: what is a thought? And we can also ask, where is a thought when it is not being thought? We can pursue this line of questioning even further. Close your eyes and picture a green horse. Where is that picture? If it isn't anywhere, why can you "see" it? Beginning in this chapter, we will try to lay a foundation for tackling these and hundreds of similar questions.

THE NERVOUS SYSTEM: AN OVERVIEW

The nervous system is a complex network made up of about 100 billion **neurons** or nerve cells that conduct stimulation from one location in the body to another (Hubel, 1979). Each of us has about as many neurons as there are stars in our galaxy. Neurons are the basic building blocks of the nervous system. Some neurons send **afferent** (or **sensory**) **neural signals** to the spinal cord and brain, bringing information *into* the nervous system through the sense receptors. Other neurons send **efferent** (or **motor**) **neural signals** *outward* from the spinal cord and brain to the muscles and glands of the body.

The nervous system contains two types of cells: neurons and glial cells. **Glial cells** serve to nourish, hold, protect, insulate, and provide a supporting environment for the delicate network of neurons. All the space in the nervous system not taken up by neurons is occupied by glial cells.

As shown in Figure 2-1, the human nervous system is composed of two major subsystems: the central nervous system and the peripheral nervous system. The **central nervous system** (**CNS**) consists of the neurons within the brain and the spinal cord. The CNS is of great interest to us because of its importance in thinking, memory, and other higher brain processes. The **peripheral nervous system** consists of all the neurons that lie outside the brain and spinal cord. It includes special cranial nerves and spinal nerves that can carry stimuli to the brain and spinal cord respectively.

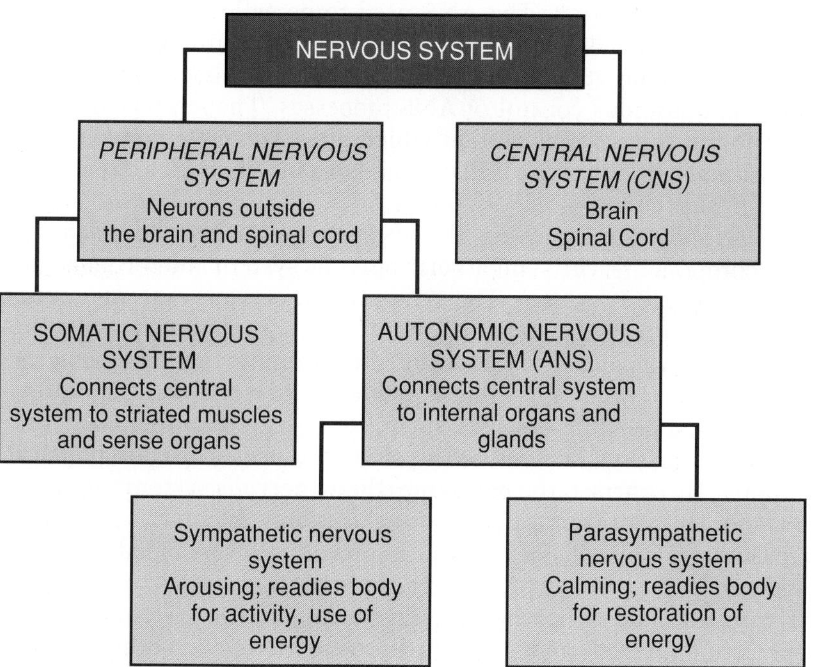

FIGURE 2-1 **Major subdivisions of the human nervous system**

SOURCE: Adapted with permission from Allyn and Bacon, 1989.

The peripheral nervous system itself can be subdivided into two branches: the somatic nervous system and the autonomic nervous system. The **somatic nervous system** controls the muscles connected to the skeleton and transmits information from the sense organs to the CNS. Thus, it consists of both motor neurons and sensory neurons. The skeletal muscles controlled by these motor neurons are those that move the bones. For example, it is the somatic nervous system that goes into action as you turn the pages of this book. In general, the skeletal muscles are called **striated muscles** because they appear striped (i.e., striated) under a microscope. The somatic nervous system is commonly thought to be under voluntary control. Therefore, in everyday language, the somatic nervous system plus the central nervous system are often referred to as the *voluntary nervous system*. However, we will soon see that this term is somewhat inaccurate. The **autonomic nervous system (ANS)**, the other main branch of the peripheral nervous system, connects the internal organs and glands to the CNS. It helps regulate such processes as heart rate and digestion. It also connects to some smooth non-skeletal muscles, such as the sphincters which control bladder and bowel retention. This branch of the peripheral nervous system is called *autonomic* (from the word "autonomous") because its functions *may* be carried out without any conscious effort on the person's part. During sleep, for example, our heart rate is continuously adjusted by the ANS. After eating, stomach movements increase, hydrochloric acid is secreted into the stomach, and blood vessels around the area dilate to make more blood available to the stomach. This elaborate procedure is controlled by the ANS and occurs without our awareness or our effort. This is a good thing for otherwise we would have little time for anything but heart-rate adjustment and sphincter contraction. The ANS used to be called the *involuntary nervous system*. But the term is not strictly accurate, because we now know that it is possible, through biofeedback training, to develop conscious control of ANS processes. The ANS is also that division of the nervous system which plays the most active role in emotional behaviour. We will discuss both biofeedback and emotion later in this chapter.

As shown in Figure 2-1, the ANS in turn can be subdivided into two components: the sympathetic nervous system and the parasympathetic nervous system. The **sympathetic nervous system** arouses the body for activity and the use of energy. It comes into play for vigorous physical activity, emotional excitement, and emergencies. When it is activated, this system increases heart rate and respiration, raises blood pressure, releases sugar (for energy) into the blood, and increases the flow of blood to the striated muscles (used in physical actions). By contrast, the **parasympathetic nervous system** calms the body for the conserving and restoring of energy. When it is activated, this system lowers heart rate and respiration, lowers blood pressure, and diverts the flow of blood from the striated muscles to the digestive organs. The sympathetic and parasympathetic systems work in opposite directions and are often antagonistic to each other. In general, the activation of one system tends to suppress the other.

NEURONS AND SYNAPSES

Before going further with our discussion of the systems that operate within the nervous system, let us take a closer look at the neurons, the so-called building blocks of the human nervous system.

There are different kinds of neurons that perform different functions within the body. Neurons occur in various forms and sizes. Some neurons, such as some in the spinal cord, are longer than one metre. Other neurons, such as some in the brain, are shorter than a few thousandths of a centimetre. Despite this variety, every neuron consists of dendrites, a cell body, and an axon (usually covered by a myelin sheath and ending in terminal buttons), as illustrated in Figure 2-2.

A **dendrite** is a branched part of a neuron that receives stimulation and conveys it toward the cell body. The **cell body** is the central part of a neuron which contains the cell nucleus. It is this cell body that controls the mechanisms that maintain the cell. An **axon** is a projecting part of a neuron that conveys impulses away from the cell body. At the branching end of the axon there are small swellings called terminal buttons which contain **synaptic vesicles** filled with neurotransmitters. In a sense, neurons are one-way channels of communication. Information usually moves from the dendrites, through the cell body, and then outwards along the axon.

In many neurons, the axon is covered by a **myelin sheath** composed of a particular type of glial cell. This covering insulates the neuron from nearby neurons and speeds up the transmission of impulses. In Figure 2-2, the myelin sheath can be seen covering the axon in segments. One reason that the nervous system of a newborn baby cannot perform some functions well (such as bladder control) is that the infant's neurons are not yet completely *myelinated* (i.e.,

FIGURE 2-2 **The basic structure of neurons**

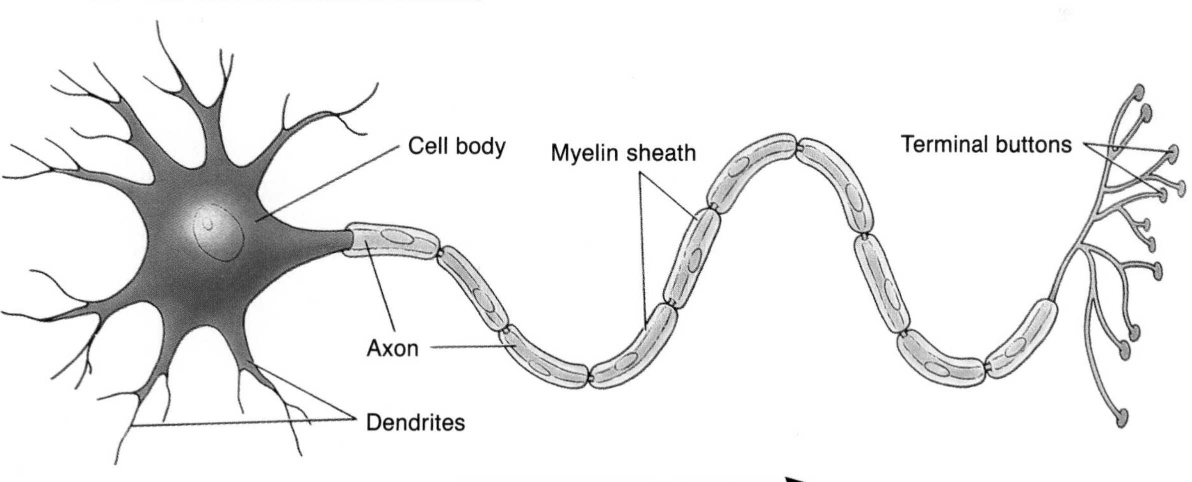

SOURCE: Adapted with permission from Allyn and Bacon, 1989.

FIGURE 2-3 The action potential: How neurons "fire"

SOURCE: Reprinted with permission from Allyn and Bacon, 1989.

A

When the neuron is at rest, the inside is negatively charged relative to the outside.

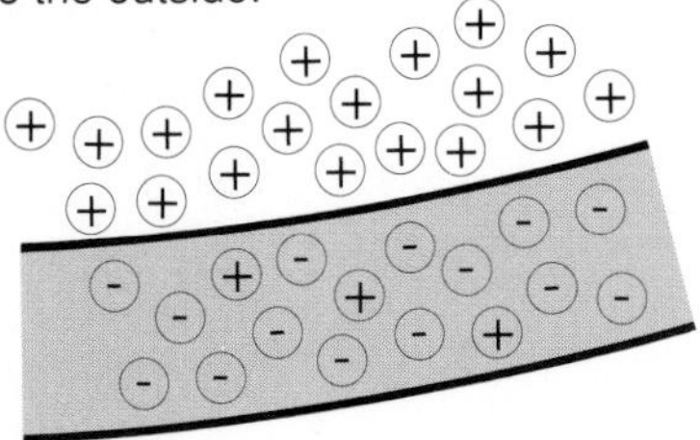

B

When the neuron is stimulated, positively charged particles enter.

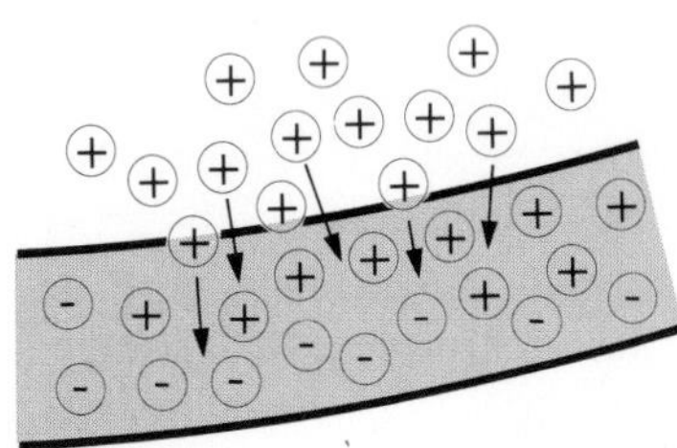

C

After a brief period, these particles are actively pushed outside.

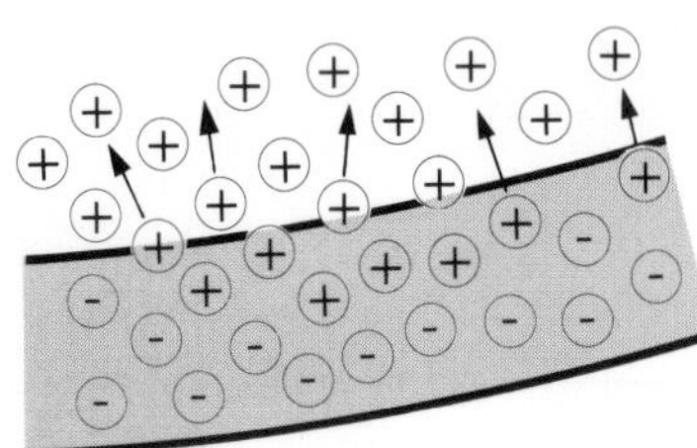

D

Soon, the neuron is returned to its initial resting state.

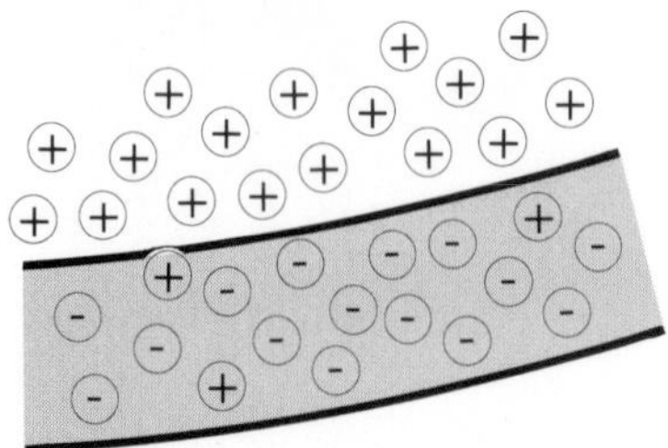

covered with myelin sheaths). As time passes and *myelinization* progresses (i.e., the axon becomes coated with myelin sheaths), the baby becomes able to perform new behaviours.

How neurons fire

The firing of a neuron begins with the impingement of a stimulus on the dendrite. If the stimulus is strong enough, an electrochemical impulse is transmitted through the cell body and then along the axon. According to the so-called **all-or-none law**, a neuron can fire at only one particular strength, when and only when its stimulation threshold has been exceeded. In other words, a neuron cannot partially fire in response to a weak stimulus; nor can it fire more strongly or quickly in response to a very powerful stimulus. A neuron either fires fully (all) or not at all (none).

We have said above that an electrochemical impulse is transmitted when a neuron fires. By this we mean that a chemical causes an electrical charge to travel along the neuron. (We will discuss this chemical change further when we look at neurotransmitters and synapses). When a neuron is at rest, there are more positively charged particles (sodium ions) outside the cell membrane, and more negatively charged particles inside. Thus, a small negative electrical charge exists across the cell membrane. The state of a neuron when it is at rest and ready to fire in response to stimulation is known as its **resting potential**. (See Figure 2-3.) In a sense, each neuron is like a battery that has potential energy because of the electrical imbalance between the charges of ions inside and outside the neuron's membrane. When the dendrites of the neuron are stimulated, positively charged particles enter the neuron rapidly, causing the cell's polarity to change at the point where it was stimulated. For a brief instant the inside of the cell is more positively charged than it was before. This sudden change is called the **action potential**, the actual firing of the neuron. Within a few milliseconds (thousandths of a second) positive ions are actively pumped back outside the neuron to restore the resting potential. Inside the neuron the sudden, momentary change in polarity travels down the length of the axon. When this impulse reaches the axon terminals, chemicals called neurotransmitters are released in order to stimulate or inhibit other neurons. Thus, the "firing" of the neuron is a moving electrical change that results from a chemical change and causes another chemical change. While the neuron is firing, it is in the **absolute refractory period**. It is unable to fire again until it has returned to its resting potential. For a few thousandths of a second after it has fired, the neuron is in a **relative refractory period**. During this time, it will not fire unless it receives extremely strong stimulation.

Neurons stimulate and interrelate with one another in an enormously complex network. No neuron can, by itself, form a complete arc or circuit. They connect with one another; the dendrites of one neuron connect with the *axon terminals* of many other neurons. Look at Neuron A in Figure 2-4. Each of the dendrites of Neuron A is connected with axon terminals from other neurons. One or a combination of these other neurons could serve to stimulate Neuron A.

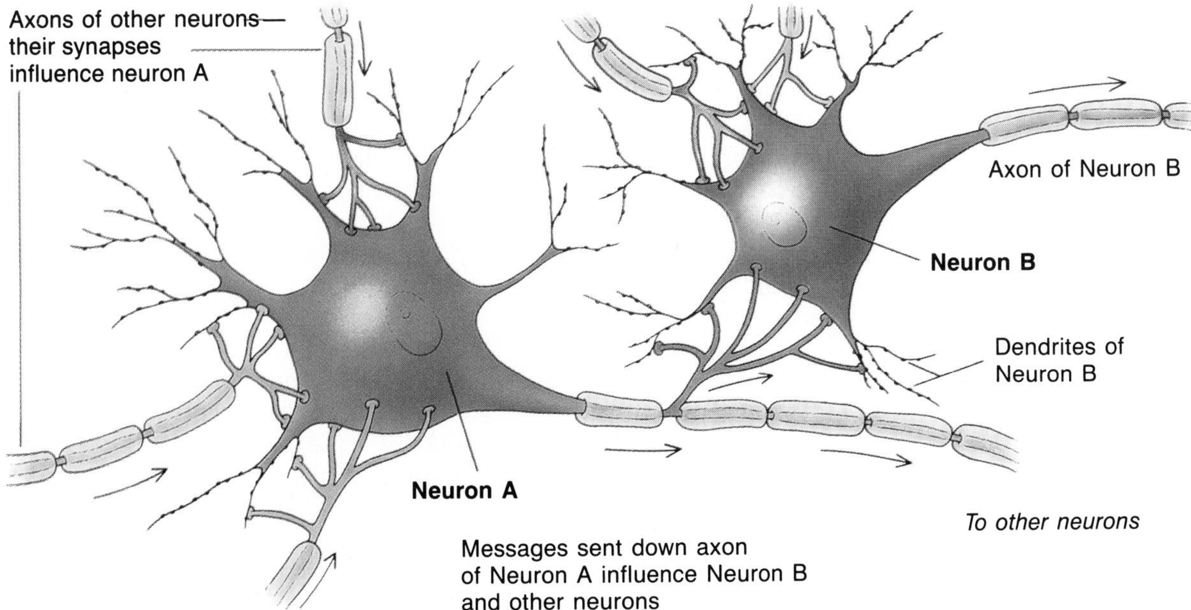

SOURCE: Adapted with permission from Allyn and Bacon, 1989.

FIGURE 2-4 **Synapses between neurons**
Neurons communicate across synapses. Conjunctions of terminal buttons of one neuron influence the cell body or dendritic membrane of another neuron. Many terminal buttons form synapses with a single neuron, and this neuron in turn forms synapses with many others. This drawing is considerably simplified. An individual neuron can have tens of thousands of synapses on it.

In turn, it could stimulate any or all of the dendrites of a whole new set of neurons, represented by Neuron B. Kolb & Whishaw (1985) say that one neuron can have as many as 15 000 connections with other neurons. If we remember that there are over 100 billion neurons in the nervous system and that one neuron can be stimulated by thousands of other neurons and can in turn stimulate thousands of new ones, the enormous complexity of the interrelationships in the nervous system begins to become clear. It has been estimated that the circuitry in one human brain has connections comparable to 17 000 Canadian telephone systems.

Synapses and their functions

At the point at which two neurons connect, axon of one neuron to dendrite of the next, there is a **synapse** or small gap (about .00002 centimetres wide) across which the impulse must somehow jump. It is crucial to understand the functions of this gap that is also the point of connection between neurons. The synapse serves to inhibit as well as to facilitate the sending of impulses from neuron to neuron. Without something to stop the impulse, once one stimulus impinged on one neuron, a chain reaction would be set up in which all the neurons in the body would soon be firing. This would make it, at the very least, difficult to relax.

How the synapse is "jumped"—neurotransmitters

Scientists believe that an impulse jumps the synaptic gap chemically. When the electrical impulse reaches the axon terminal, a chemical called a **neurotransmitter** or **transmitter substance** is released from the terminal buttons of the axon. The function of the neurotransmitter is to enable the neural electrical impulse to jump the synapse by chemically stimulating the dendrite or cell body of the next neuron. Some transmitter substances excite and some inhibit the dendrites of the next neuron (see Figure 2.5). These neurotransmitters are stored in small spaces called synaptic vesicles. Once this transmitter substance has reached special receptors in the membrane of the next neuron and has stimulated the second neuron, the substance is quickly destroyed by enzymes present in the synapse. The impulse doesn't always jump all possible synapses, of course, since if the transmitter substance always stimulated the next dendrites, it would be as though there were no synapses at all. All the neurons would be firing at once. There are two main reasons that impulses don't always successfully jump the synapses. First, the transmitter substance from one nerve impulse is seldom strong enough to surpass the firing threshold or the all-or-none response of the next neuron. The **firing threshold** is the level of stimulation necessary to make a particular neuron fire. The neuron only fires once this threshold is reached. It is usually necessary for several axons to stimulate a dendritic area

FIGURE 2-5 Excitatory and inhibitory neurotransmitters
There are two types of neurotransmitters: excitatory and inhibitory. When the terminal buttons of a neuron release excitatory neurotransmitters, they excite the neurons with which they form synapses. The effect of this excitation is to make it more likely that the synapsed-upon, or postsynaptic, neurons will fire. Inhibitory neurotransmitters do just the opposite. When they are activated, they lower the probability that the axon of the postsynaptic neuron will fire. Thus the rate at which a particular axon fires is determined by the activity of the synaptic inputs to the dendrites and cell body.

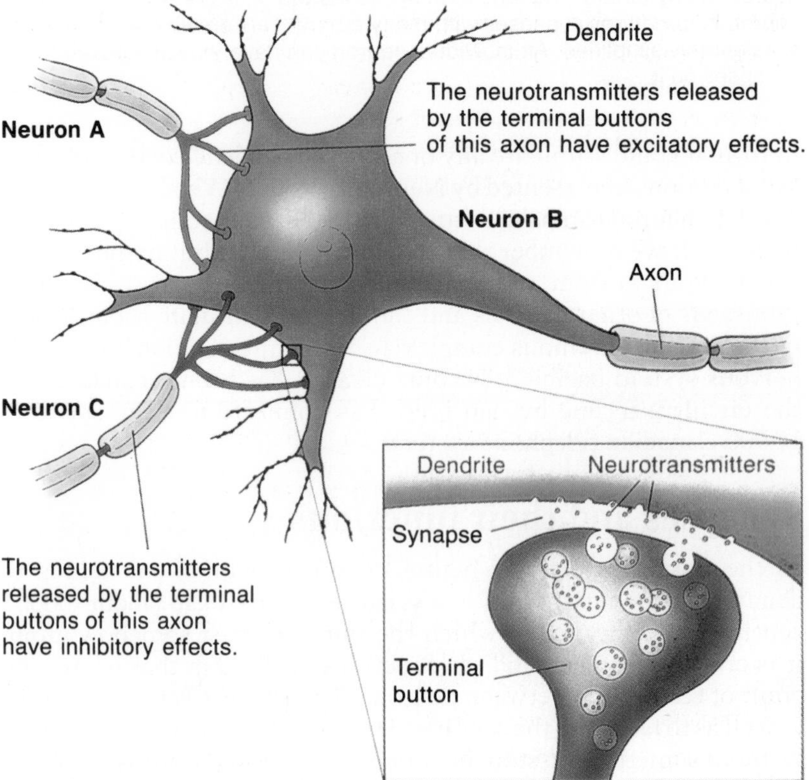

SOURCE: Adapted with permission from Allyn and Bacon, 1989.

to the point of firing. Second, some transmitter substances act to inhibit the action of other transmitter substances and prevent them from stimulating the dendrite strongly enough to cause the neuron to fire.

More than 50 different transmitter substances have been identified, and new ones are constantly being discovered (McGinty and Szymusiak, 1988; Panksepp, 1986). All of these substances affect the **postsynaptic neuron** which is the neuron whose membranes are stimulated or inhibited by the release of a neurotransmitter from another neuron. **Acetylcholine**, the most common neurotransmitter, is usually excitatory. It is discharged at synapses in the brain, spinal cord, and autonomic nervous system. **Epinephrine** is an adrenal hormone discharged in response to emotion, particularly fear. It can act as an excitatory neurotransmitter in the sympathetic nervous system. **Norepinephrine** is another adrenal hormone discharged in response to emotion, particularly anger. It can act as an excitatory or an inhibitory neurotransmitter in the brain and the sympathetic nervous system. **Gamma-amino butyric acid** or GABA is an amino acid that also acts as an inhibitory neurotransmitter especially in the brain and spinal cord. Two other common neurotransmitters are serotonin and dopamine. See Figure 2-6 for a summary of six of the most common transmitter substances and the locations of their effects.

The beauty of all this complexity is that the functioning of the neurotransmitters at synapses provides a mechanism for establishing different complicated pathways through the nervous system. As we will see later in this chapter, these pathways are formed and changed by experience. They allow us to store our learning experiences.

A word of caution: we do not mean to imply that the nervous system is just a passive reactor, a network that responds only to external stimulation. The nervous system is electrically active all the time. Some nerve cells sometimes fire "spontaneously," without any apparent external stimulus. Some neurons are likely to fire when

Transmitter Substance	Where Found	Effects
Acetylcholine	Brain, spinal cord, autonomic nervous system, target organs of the parasympathetic system	Excitation in brain and autonomic nervous system; excitation or inhibition of target organs
Epinephrine	Brain, spinal cord, target organs of sympathetic system	Inhibition in brain, excitation or inhibition in target organs
Norepinephrine	Brain, spinal cord, target organs of sympathetic system	Inhibition in brain; excitation or inhibition of target organs
Dopamine	Brain	Inhibition
Serotonin	Brain, spinal cord	Inhibition
GABA	Brain, spinal cord	Inhibition

SOURCE: Adapted with permission from Allyn and Bacon, 1989.

FIGURE 2-6 Neurotransmitters: Locations and effects

Neurotransmitters are key ingredients in the transmission of impulses from one neuron to another. They can be excitatory or inhibitory in nature.

they have not been stimulated externally for a time and to reduce their rate of firing in response to increased stimulation.

Further, our nervous system is constructed in such a way that its own structure influences what stimuli have what kinds of effects on it. Some neural functioning, for example, reduces the sensitivity of other parts of the system to incoming stimuli. This often happens when inhibitory neurotransmitters prevent the firing of specific neurons. The nervous system is much more than a passive reactor.

THE PERIPHERAL NERVOUS SYSTEM

The word "peripheral" means "toward the outer edges." The peripheral nervous system consists of the nerves outside the brain and spinal cord. **Nerves** are bundles of neurons that are physically adjacent to each other, somewhat like a "cable" of neurons. These are the nerves that connect us with the world; they help us operate our muscles and internal organs, and they help us experience sensation. As we have already described in brief, the peripheral nervous system has two major divisions, the somatic system and the autonomic system.

The somatic nervous system

The word soma is from the Greek word for body. The somatic nervous system controls the operation of the striated muscles, information from the senses (touch, taste, sight, hearing, and smell), and the bodily reflexes. Internal organs like the heart are made of **smooth muscle** and are under the control of the autonomic nervous system.

We are able to move because our striated muscles are attached to bones, to other muscles, and to skin. Complex neural messages are sent from the brain to the muscles, telling one set to contract and the opposing set to relax. So we are able to kick or bend or flex our arms. Some movements may require sets of muscles to contract together; other movements may require the same muscles to move in opposite directions. An action as common as threading a needle requires an enormously complicated series of tiny contractions and releases of muscles. Such complex patterns are constantly being coordinated by the somatic nervous system.

Motor neurons are neurons in the somatic nervous system that convey messages from the brain to muscle fibre. They control the contraction and relaxation of muscles. They connect to muscle fibres across synapses. When a muscle is to contract, the axon terminals of the motor neurons release the neurotransmitter acetylcholine. This bridges the synapse and causes the muscle fibre to contract. The strength of the contraction depends on both the number of motor neurons firing and the frequency with which they fire.

We will wait for Chapter 3 to discuss the senses in detail, but we will note in passing that the sense organs contain **receptor neurons**. These neurons receive stimulation from the environment and transmit that information to the brain for processing.

The autonomic nervous system

The feelings that we identify as emotion usually involve the arousal of our autonomic system. This system connects the glands and the internal organs (e.g., the heart, the liver, and the lungs), the gastrointestinal tract, and the sex organs to the central nervous system. It controls motor functions other than those performed by the skeletal muscles: sweating, crying, salivation, secretion of digestive juices, changes in the size of blood vessels (which cause changes in blood pressure), and secretion of hormones. The ANS can be divided into two parts with somewhat different functions, the sympathetic nervous system and the parasympathetic nervous system. Figures 2-7 and 2-8 list the effects of the sympathetic and parasympathetic branches and illustrate the organs affected by the autonomic nervous system.

In general, the sympathetic nervous system arouses the body in times of strong emotion, such as fear, excitement, joy, and surprise. Most of its functions serve to use the body's energy to respond to arousing situations. For example, to facilitate action the heart speeds up and pumps more blood to the exterior muscles. In addition, to provide support for intense muscular activity, blood vessels in the

FIGURE 2-7 The major functions of the autonomic nervous system

	EFFECT OF ACTIVITY OF AUTONOMIC NERVE FIBERS	
Bodily Systems	**Sympathetic**	**Parasympathetic**
Adrenal medulla	Secretion of epinephrine and norepinephrine	
Bladder	Inhibition of contraction	Contraction
Blood vessels		
Abdomen	Constriction	
Muscles	Dilation	Constriction
Skin	Constriction or dilation	Dilation
Heart	Faster rate of contraction	Slower rate of contraction
Intestines	Decreased activity	Increased activity
Lacrimal glands	Secretion of tears	
Liver	Release of glucose	
Lungs	Dilation of bronchi	Constriction of bronchi
Pupil of eye	Dilation	Constriction
Salivary glands	Secretion of thick, viscous saliva	Secretion of thin, enzyme-rich saliva
Sweat glands	Secretion of sweat	
Sexual systems male (penis)	Ejaculation	Erection
female (clitoris, vagina)	Orgasm	Erection, and secretion of lubricating fluid

SOURCE: Adapted with permission from Allyn and Bacon, 1989.

interior of the body contract and those in the peripheral muscles expand. Breathing increases; the mouth dries up as salivation is inhibited; stomach motility decreases; and the pupils of the eyes become larger. In addition to directly stimulating certain organs, the sympathetic nervous system stimulates the adrenal glands to secrete epinephrine (**adrenaline**) and norepinephrine (**noradrenaline**). Since these hormones also arouse strong activity, this causes even greater arousal. The sweat glands also become more active in these circumstances. This gives rise to increased electrical activity in the skin that we can measure as the **galvanic skin response** (**GSR**). (The GSR is often used in research as a measure of emotional arousal and in the treatment of stress.) The sympathetic system tends to become aroused as a unit, so that there is a general pattern of arousal throughout the body rather than a separate arousal of specific emergency functions.

In general, the parasympathetic nervous system calms the body for the conserving and restoring of energy. Its effects are the opposite of the sympathetic system's. Further, unlike the sympathetic system, the parasympathetic system often affects one or a few organs separately. As you will see in Figure 2-8 most of the organs are connected to both systems. The major exception is the adrenal glands, which are specifically active during emotional arousal. As regards most of the body organs, the parasympathetic system functions to maintain the organism: to slow the heart and breathing, to speed up digestion in the stomach, to constrict the pupils, and to cause the flow of saliva.

Patterns of autonomic arousal

There are some exceptions to the generalization that the sympathetic and parasympathetic systems act in opposition and tend to inhibit each other. There is some parasympathetic arousal in excitement, for example. And often a complex physical action such as sexual intercourse requires the systems to act in sequence. The early stages of sexual arousal are under parasympathetic control, and orgasm in the male and female is under sympathetic control. This means that the systems must act in sequence. If for some reason there is strong sympathetic arousal during the early stages of sexual arousal, the male will be unable to maintain an erection. This observation helps to explain why erectile dysfunction is often the result of some form of fear.

With a few minor exceptions, patterns of autonomic arousal are not distinguishable in different emotions. Autonomically, fear looks

FIGURE 2-8 The organs and glands affected by the parasympathetic and sympathetic nervous systems

Neurons of the sympathetic nervous system, which lead from the central nervous system to the internal organs and glands, carry commands that rouse the body for action. The impulses it carries stimulate the heart, cause sugar to be released into the bloodstream, and slow digestion and other bodily processes that might interfere with the ability to meet danger either by fighting or fleeing. The parasympathetic system is primarily concerned with recuperative and life-sustaining functions, such as digestion and the slow, steady beating of the heart.

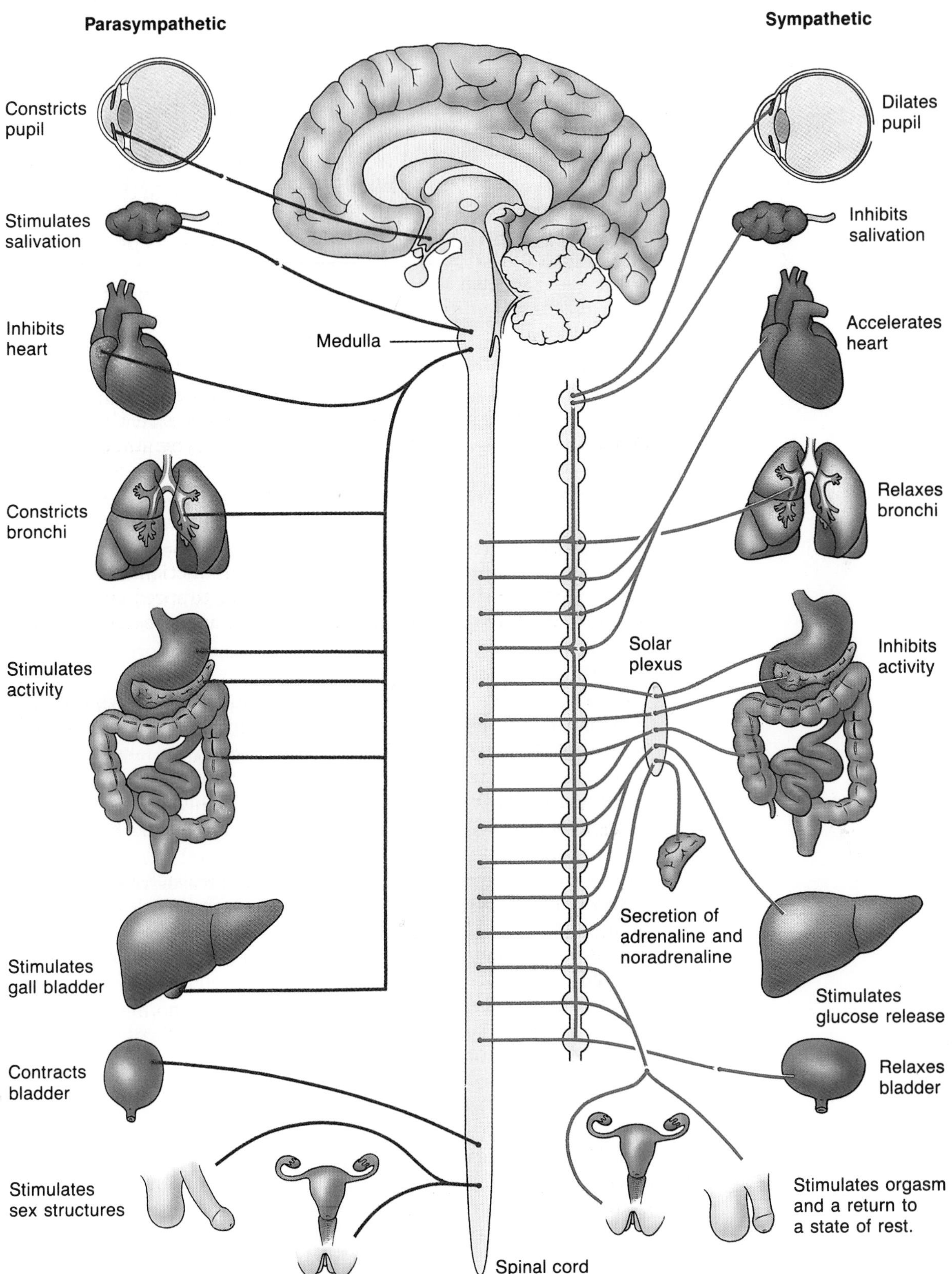

SOURCE: Adapted with permission from Allyn and Bacon, 1989.

pretty much like joy. We tend to label our emotions more on the basis of the situation we are in when we experience them and on what we have learned about such situations in the past. Autonomic arousal in the presence of a loved one talking softly would be labelled differently from the same arousal in the presence of that loved one screaming. However, a physiologist might not be able to tell the difference simply from the pattern of autonomic arousal. One exception to this "arousal is arousal" principle is that a task which requires a person only to take in information and not to act overtly sometimes results in **directional fractionation** (Lacey, 1967). This is a pattern of autonomic arousal in which one response (such as GSR) increases while another (such as heart rate) decreases. Normally, sympathetic arousal acts in a unitary way, but apparently not in such situations.

Biofeedback and voluntary control of the ANS

You would think it silly if we were to tell you to slow your stomach contractions, blush in your left ear, and make your heart beat at the rate of exactly one beat per second. These seem unlikely tasks because we usually think that such actions can't be controlled consciously. In recent years, however, each of these tasks has been partially brought under intentional control through biofeedback. **Biofeedback** is a treatment procedure in which a person who is provided with ongoing information about his or her autonomic functions can learn to modify those functions. We all learned to touch our nose successfully because we could tell when we were hitting and missing and so we could learn to adjust our performance. Some of us learned to wiggle our ears by looking in a mirror for feedback. If people are provided with feedback about functions for which there is no naturally occurring feedback, they seem to be able to gain some control of such actions as stomach contractions (Deckner, Hill, & Bourne, 1972), heart rate (Lang, 1970), and blushing in one ear (Miller, 1969). Actually, it was a rat that learned to blush in one ear on command, but you could probably handle it and make a big hit with your friends.

Some subjects have learned to use biofeedback to alter their heart rate by monitoring that rate with an instrument that provided them with visual information. A moving dot on a screen in front of each subject remained stable between two lines as long as the heart rate did not deviate from the one-beat-per-second rate by more than a few milliseconds. Whenever the dot drifted to the right or left side of the screen, the subject knew that the rate was too fast or too slow. Subjects gained some conscious control over heart rate. A similar procedure was used to give subjects control over the movements of their stomachs (Deckner et al., 1972). Part of the digestive process includes rhythmic contractions of the stomach, although we can't feel these movements. To provide their subjects with biofeedback, Deckner and his colleagues used an electronic measure of stomach motility that moved a pen on a moving strip of paper. The subjects could see a record of their stomach movements. The researchers also provided auditory feedback (through earphones); a tone changed pitch according to the speed of stomach movements. In 4 training sessions of 24 minutes each, the subjects acquired an increasing amount of control over their stomachs, and the results suggested that further training would have resulted in even more control.

It is interesting that subjects in biofeedback experiments often find it difficult to describe what they are doing to achieve their acts of control. They "just do it." But that's not too surprising. Many acts we perform every day are nearly impossible to put into words. How does a rider stay upright on a bicycle? Few people know that they are constantly making minute turns in the direction the bike is beginning to fall. Similarly, how would you describe the process by which you retain and release urine at will? Urination is one autonomic function over which most of us learn conscious control. It is one of the few autonomic functions on which we naturally get feedback.

The early expectations for the applications of biofeedback to human problems were very high. As with certain other areas of psychological research, biofeedback caught the attention of the popular press and was oversold (Miller, 1985). The sweeping claims that it can cure human ailments have diminished, but biofeedback still holds out some hope for useful applications. For example, about two-thirds of a group of patients with high blood pressure were successfully weaned off medication. Their program provided them with biofeedback as their medication dosage was lowered gradually (Fahrion, Noris, Green & Green, 1986). In another instance, when combined with other treatment methods, biofeedback has been found to help reduce the effects of stress by promoting relaxation (Miller, 1983).

The usefulness of the polygraph (lie detector) is based on the premise that most people find it upsetting to lie, especially when they might be found out. The polygraph measures the response of certain elements of the subject's sympathetic nervous system. These measurements are then interpreted as evidence of the truthfulness or untruthfulness of the subject's responses. However, the polygraph is not a very reliable device, as we will see in the Special Topic section of Chapter 6. The unreliability of this instrument arises partly from the fact that it doesn't work with people who aren't upset by lying. It even seems possible that really devoted liars could, through biofeedback procedures, gain control of their autonomic functioning to beat the machine. In any case, it is clearly no longer accurate to speak of the ANS as the "involuntary nervous system."

The Central Nervous System

The brain and spinal cord comprise the central nervous system (CNS), which resembles a long-stemmed mushroom with a very wrinkled grey top. As we move up from the bottom (the spinal cord) to the top (the cerebrum), the complexity of both structure and function increases. The lower structures are very similar in humans and other animals; it is the higher structures that define our humanness.

The brain and spinal cord are the most protected parts of the body. The brain is encased in the **skull**, which consists of a very tough set of bones. The spinal cord runs through the middle of a

FIGURE 2-9 The central nervous system

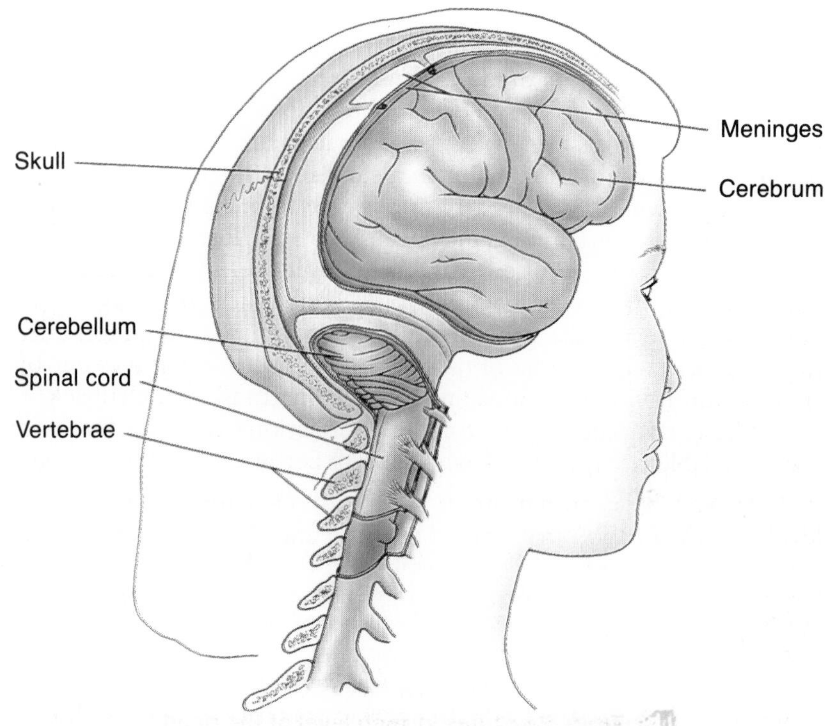

SOURCE: Adapted with permission from Allyn and Bacon, 1989.

column of hollow bones known as the **vertebrae**. Both the brain and spinal cord are surrounded by the **meninges** (singular: "**menix**"). These are three different sets of membranes which encase the brain; the outer one is a thick, tough, unstretchable wrapping—rather like soft parchment. The inner one is thin and delicate and adheres to the brain, while the middle layer is spongy and filled with fluid. See Figure 2-9.

The spinal cord

The "lowest" segment of the central nervous system is the **spinal cord**, which consists of a strand of nerve fibres running down the middle of the spine. It connects most of the nerve fibres in the body to the brain and controls some stimulus-response reflexes.

Our interest in the central nervous system will be primarily in the brain. This is where nearly all learning takes place. However, the neurons in the spinal cord do have some influence on behaviour. For example, some reflexes operate through the spinal cord. When we inadvertently place a hand on a hot surface, the stimulus travels from the hand, through neurons in the spinal cord, and directly back to the muscles of the hand and arm. This causes us to remove the hand before we feel the pain or can make any kind of a conscious (brain) decision. Simple reflexes also help control our posture. For example, if we are standing and start to fall forward, our calf muscles stretch from the pulling. This stimulus alerts sensory neurons connected to these muscles; the message is carried to the spinal cord where it passes through a reflex arc and connects with motor neurons. These motor neurons carry a message to other muscles in our feet to push our toes down so we won't fall. This all happens in less than one-twentieth of a second and our conscious brain knows nothing of what happened, although it may get the information after the event (Greer, 1984).

In addition, some simple conditioning or learning can take place exclusively in the spinal cord. A cat with its spinal cord cut can be conditioned to lift its foot when its tail is brushed if tail-brushing has been paired with shock to the foot (Patterson, 1976). This conditioned reaction cannot involve the brain, since the connectors to the brain have been severed. Beyond this simple kind of learning, though, the neurons below the brain are not very plastic. In other words, experience does not change them much.

The spinal cord ends at the base of the brain, which we will look at next. The human brain can be divided into three general levels: (1) the *hindbrain*, (2) the *midbrain*, and (3) the *forebrain*. (See Figure 2-10.) In general, the functions of these three sections of the brain are arranged in an ascending order of complexity. However, no one layer operates independently of the others, and they are interconnected by complex pathways of neurons.

FIGURE 2-10 The major structures in each level of the brain
The human brain can be divided into three general levels: the hindbrain, the midbrain, and the forebrain.

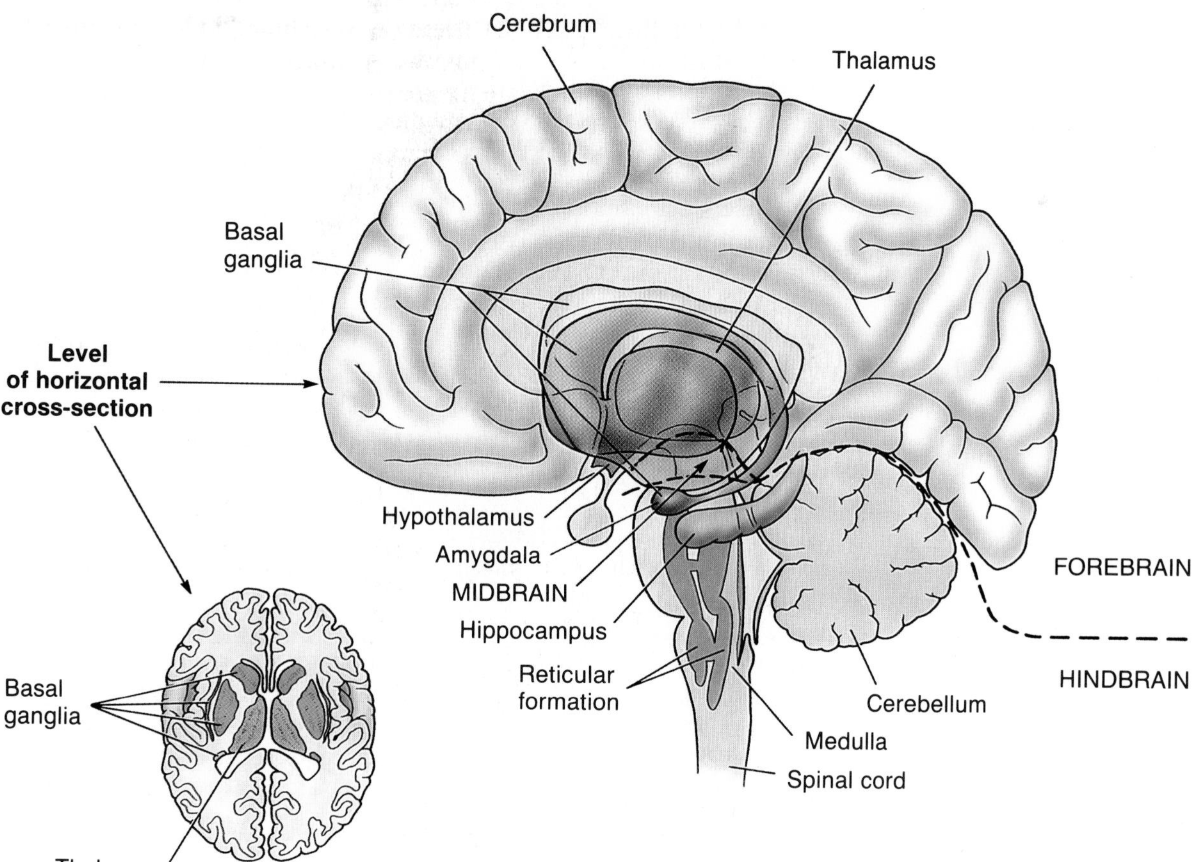

The brain

The hindbrain

The **hindbrain** is the lowest and most primitive part of the brain and its most important structures are the medulla and cerebellum. It strongly resembles the brains of many lower animals and serves several primitive functions, without which we could not live. The **medulla** helps control breathing and circulation, and helps the body maintain particular postures. The **cerebellum** is important in coordinating smooth motor movement and in maintaining balance. A person with a damaged cerebellum can sit quietly enough, but as soon as he or she starts to move, jerky tremors appear. The cerebellum is also probably involved in the conditioning and memory of motor movements (McCormick & Thompson, 1984).

The midbrain

The **midbrain** lies between the hindbrain and the forebrain and is especially important in coordinating and relaying auditory and visual information to the brain. It contains the reticular formation and is an essential connector and relay station between the higher and lower portions of the brain.

The **reticular formation** is a structure of the midbrain that is made up of neurons and nerves and that serves to alert the organism to prepare for incoming stimulation. It controls sleep and wakefulness. In general it arouses the other parts of the brain and determines their readiness to act (Kelly, 1985). Wooldridge (1968) has called the reticular formation a "consciousness switch," because without it an individual would go into a state of coma even if the rest of the brain was intact. When a certain frequency of electrical impulse is used to stimulate an animal's reticular formation, that impulse will reliably produce sleep; a different frequency will awaken it. If the reticular formation is made inactive by a drug that does not affect the rest of the brain, an interesting phenomenon occurs. A stimulus such as a pinprick will arouse the expected electrical activity in the brain, but the person will be unaware of the pain because the cortex has not been aroused by the reticular formation. The cortex must be alerted before there will be a conscious experience.

The forebrain

The **forebrain** contains the structures that make complex human functioning possible: the cerebral hemispheres, the hypothalamus, the thalamus, the basal ganglia, the limbic system, and the hippocampus. We make plans for the weekend while talking with a friend as we drive downtown. Our talk stimulates several memories from last weekend and a vague sense of worry over work we have left until the last minute. We decide to ignore a sense of mild hunger and are distracted by a momentary glimpse of a face in a crowd. It turns out to be our cousin. All of these activities require the structures of the forebrain.

The **hypothalamus** is located above the brain stem and below the thalamus. It is a brain structure that controls much of the activity of the autonomic nervous system. It also helps to regulate the homeostasis (stability or equilibrium) of bodily functions and of some aspects of the emotions. This control is apparently achieved by **homeostats**, structures within the hypothalamus that respond when levels of functioning are too high or too low. Homeostats operate something like thermostats do in controlling the temperature in a house. A thermostat turns the furnace on when the temperature drops below the preset level and turns it off again once the temperature has risen to that level. For example, the hypothalamus has considerable influence over our experience of hunger and subsequent eating behaviour. It signals the body when satiation is reached. Lesions in the hypothalamus of experimental animals, or of humans who have suffered brain damage, have led to uncontrolled eating and resultant obesity. The mechanism for signalling satiation to the body apparently doesn't work, and the homeostat fails to "turn off" after an appropriate amount of eating.

The **thalamus** rests at the top of the brain stem deep in the centre of the brain. It acts primarily as a relay station for signals from the sensory systems and from other brain centres (particularly the reticular formation) to the cerebrum.

The **basal ganglia** are a set of structures just below the cortex and in front of the thalamus. They are necessary for the coordination and control of motor movements. Damage to the basal ganglia can lead to the kind of spontaneous and uncoordinated movements (either the sudden jerking of body parts or the slowing of movements) that are made by the victims of Parkinson's disease.

The **limbic system**, often referred to as the old brain, resides underneath the cerebrum, around the central core of the brain. It is not a specific structure but rather a system of structures in the forebrain. It is influential in the inhibiting and arousal of strong emotion (e.g., rage), in carrying out behaviours that require a specific sequence of steps, and in storing memories. These actions that require performance of a sequence of behaviours could include any habitual behaviour, such as feeding oneself or finding and sharpening a pencil, that consists of several successive steps. A person with damage to the limbic system may set out to complete some such simple sequence but may be unable to do so. What would normally be considered relatively minor distractions interrupt the process (Milner, 1966). The limbic system is also involved in strong emotion. The **amygdala**, which is part of the limbic system, seems to arouse rage in both animals and humans. Other parts of the system produce timidity. So, the different parts serve to inhibit each other.

The **hippocampus**, another part of the limbic system, is involved in the storage of memories. Damage to the hippocampus can result in the inability to form new permanent memories, even though a person may be able to function in the present quite well. For such people each experience is entirely new and each meeting with another person seems to be a new introduction.

The cortex: The crown of the forebrain

Because it evolved later than the lower structures of the human brain, the area we are about to discuss is called the new brain. In this area occur many of the functions that we think of as constituting our humanness. The **cerebrum** is the entire, outer, convoluted portion of the brain; this is the area that is responsible for higher mental functions. The outermost layer of cells (and it is an understatement to call this a *layer* of cells) make up the **cerebral cortex** which contains 80–90% of all the neurons in the brain. This is the most important structure in the brain for dealing with higher mental functions such as language, thinking, memory, and creativity. The cortex is where actions are initiated, memories are stored, thoughts occur, and feelings are registered. It is highly organized; indeed it is the most complexly functioning single object that we know of (Kass, 1987).

The cerebral cortex, which is divided down the middle, consists of two halves, the left and the right **cerebral hemispheres**. The brain and body are organized contralaterally. **Contralateral organization** is the "cross-over" system of the brain whereby the left hemisphere generally controls the right side of the body, and the right hemisphere generally controls the left side of the body. Thus, an object placed in the left hand will be perceived first by the right hemisphere of the brain. Within a few thousandths of a second, however, the left hemisphere will also know about the object. The message will travel via the **corpus callosum**, a thick bundle of neurons connecting and carrying messages between the two hemispheres.

Each hemisphere is divided into the four lobes illustrated in Figure 2-11. Although there are some differences between the activities of the four lobes, it is important to remember that their functions overlap a good deal. The main reason we label the lobes and distinguish them one from another is for convenience in discussing the anatomy of the brain. The **occipital lobe**, at the rear of the cortex, is primarily responsible for visual functions. The **temporal lobe**, along the lower side portion, is most involved in hearing. At the front of the cortex, the **frontal lobe** seems to affect both the control of voluntary movement and the higher mental processes that make up intelligent functioning. The frontal lobe is separated from the temporal lobe by the **lateral fissure** and from the parietal lobe by the **central fissure**. It is the **parietal lobe** (the upper, side portion of the cortex) that plays an important role in bodily sensation. In general, the area of the cortex behind the central fissure is important for sensation and perception, concept formation, and storage of most memories. The area in front of the central fissure is largely responsible for movement-related activities, such as planning and initiation of behaviour.

Throughout the lobes of both hemispheres there are a great many **association areas**. These are large and diffuse and seem to be responsible for most of what we call the "higher functions" of the brain: thinking, logic, artistry, and memory (Kupferman, 1985). However, these areas can only be vaguely defined at our present level of knowledge of brain structure.

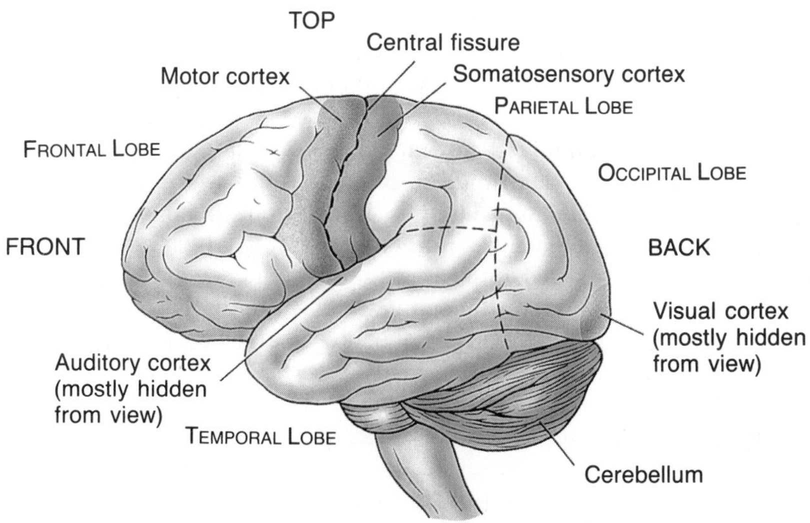

FIGURE 2-11 The four lobes of the cerebral cortex
The cerebral cortex is divided into four areas, or lobes, named for the bones of the skull that cover them. The central fissure is a deep fold that divides the frontal area of the brain and the posterior regions. The lateral fissure divides the frontal lobe and the temporal lobe.

THE BIOLOGY OF THE WORKING BRAIN

It is clear that experiences are somehow registered in the brain and that memories are stored there for later retrieval, but the processes by which these phenomena occur have been difficult to establish. In later chapters we will discuss sensation (Chapter 3), perception (Chapter 4), learning (Chapter 5), memory (Chapter 7), thinking (Chapter 8), and even consciousness (Chapter 9) in more detail. In this chapter, we want to establish the biological foundations of these topics. First, our interest is in the biology of learning and memory—how the brain changes as the result of learning.

Recent work has told us a lot, but the exact processes are more complex than what we can look at here. Keep in mind, as we talk about the basic processes, that we are talking about changes as though they were occurring in one or a few neurons. Actually, however, thousands of changes can occur among the billions of neurons within part of a second and changes in one area effect changes in many others.

Neural storage and memory

You will recall (from our discussion on neurons earlier in this chapter) that when any stimulus impinges on the nervous system, that stimulus sets off a series of neural firings that follow pathways through the nervous system. The electrical impulse in a neuron travels the length of its axon to its terminal buttons. Then the impulse either stops at the synapses between it and other neurons or jumps one or more synapses by releasing enough neurotransmitter substance to stimulate the next neuron or neurons to the threshold of firing. Each of the neurons in the chain then returns to its previous state of rest.

But what of memory in all this? If each of these chains of neuron-firings was discrete and left no trace of its occurrence, there would be no memory and no learning. What appears to happen is that once a pathway through the nervous system has been travelled by a stimulus, that pathway will subsequently be easier for the next stimulus to follow. In other words, once a particular sequence of neurons has fired in a particular order, that sequence is more likely to fire in the future. Synapses that have already been crossed by an impulse from a particular stimulus are more easily crossed by the next similar stimulus.

There seem to be two major ways that memories are stored. **Short-term memory** (**STM**) describes briefly active memories, the retention of which is apparently caused by temporary *electrical* changes in the neurons. **Long-term memory** (**LTM**) is the apparently permanent retention of memories. It seems to be caused by *chemical* changes (probably at the synapses between neurons) and occurs as a result of learning experiences (see Chapter 7).

The effects of electrical stimulation of the human cortex

Some years ago the famous Canadian brain surgeon, Wilder Penfield (1969, 1975), made a discovery that has greatly increased our understanding of the brain's functioning. He was performing operations to relieve epileptic seizures by cutting an opening in the skull and removing the brain tissue associated with the seizures. Occasionally, if too much brain tissue was removed, the patient also lost some other function, such as sight in one eye. To minimize such losses it was necessary to locate as precisely as possible the seizure-related tissue. For this reason, before removing any brain tissue Penfield would "map" the brain by touching the exposed cortex with a mildly charged electrode and then observing the function aroused. Touching certain areas of the exposed cortex would cause the patient to say that he or she saw fuzzy lights or perhaps primitive visual images. Patients were able to report orally on the effect of the electrical stimulation because the surgery was carried out under local anaesthesia and they remained conscious throughout the operation. As soon as Penfield stimulated areas that led the patient to report that he or she felt a seizure coming on, he could map just the area that had to be removed. However, a number of other interesting phenomena also occurred. For example, when Penfield touched areas associated with speech, he caused a temporary aphasia. **Aphasia** is a blocking of speech functions caused by brain injury or other brain malfunction in the speech areas of the cortex. Patients would be unable to speak, although they might know what they wanted to say. Showing one of these patients a pencil might elicit many hand movements indicating an understanding of what the object was, but the person would be unable to say the word "pencil." As soon as the electrode was removed, the word was easy to say.

Wilder Penfield (1891–1976).
SOURCE: Davidson, National Archives of Canada/PA1287000, Montreal Star.

One day Penfield applied the electrode to the right hemisphere of a woman's cerebral cortex and she reported that she seemed to be re-experiencing the birth of her baby girl. Penfield noted but initially didn't pursue the incident. Eventually, another patient, a girl, reported (after Penfield applied an electrode to her cerebral cortex) that she felt as though she were running through a meadow in a specific incident from her past. Another patient exclaimed, "Oh gosh! There they are, my brother is there. He is aiming an air rifle at me." (Penfield and Perot, 1963, p. 617). Subsequently, Penfield collected many such incidents in which patients knew that they were in the operating room talking with the surgeon. Nonetheless, they reported that, under the electrical stimulation of the cerebral cortex, specific memories became very vivid to them, as though they were re-experiencing the events and even feeling the accompanying emotions. This flow of experiencing stopped either immediately or a few seconds after the electrode was removed. For example, one patient said, "Oh, everybody is shouting at me again, make them stop!" The stimulus from the electrode lasted 2 seconds, but the voices lasted 11 seconds. She explained, "They are yelling at me for doing something wrong, everybody is yelling" (p. 630).

These findings raise fascinating questions about the permanence of memories. Although the matter is far from settled, it is possible that if a memory has been stored in long-term memory, it may be permanently encoded in the brain. Some evidence suggests that many memories do not go from short-term to long-term storage, but it is likely that the chemically stored memories do not decay. In other words the neurons probably do not completely change back to the condition they were in before the onset of the chemical change. Forgetting is probably better understood as the result of processes other than simple decay, as we will see in Chapter 7.

Early experience and the structuring of the cortex

Parts of the brain are genetically structured. That is, the functions of such structures as the reticular formation and the hypothalamus are essentially predetermined, regardless of the organism's experiences. Parts of the cortex are also biologically committed to certain functions. If, for example, a particular place on the cortex is stimulated the thumb will rotate inward. But by far the major portion of the cortex is what Penfield has called the "uncommitted cortex" (1969). *Experience structures the cortex.* This has many implications. It suggests, for one thing, that we aren't born with anything resembling ideas and that stimulation early in life has a significant effect on the very neural structure of the cortex.

This hypothesis is supported by evidence from experiments in which rats were raised in an "enriched environment." They had problems to solve, objects to manipulate, and new places to explore. Compared with the control rats that were raised in an unstimulating environment, these animals had thicker and heavier cortexes. Some evidence even suggests that the cortical neurons of the enriched rats had more branches on their dendrites, which would mean that they could connect with more neurons (Rosenzweig, 1984; Rosenzweig, Bennett, & Diamond, 1972).

Presumably, the nature of early experience could significantly affect an individual's eventual level of intelligence. Penfield has argued that the parts of the uncommitted cortex that are associated with speech are affected by early experience in the acquisition of language. He calls the child a "genius of language imitation," since the uncommitted cortex of a child can be conditioned to foreign tongues so easily (Penfield, 1969, p. 139).

The localization of cortical functions

In Chapter 1, we mentioned the system of phrenology (Gall & Spurzhiem, 1810). While the phrenologists' argument that the brain is the organ of the "mind" was correct, their claim that specific mental traits are localized in specific parts of the human brain was foolishly overstated and unsupported. They also claimed that well-developed parts of the mind would correspond to well-developed parts of the brain and that these could be felt as bumps on the skull. Poorly developed parts of the mind (and brain), that is, less important characteristics of the individual, could be felt as depressions in the skull. Thus, a phrenologist could presumably read people's characters by feeling their heads. Although phrenology met with well-deserved ridicule, there is still controversy about how much localization of function there is within the cortex. There is no quick and easy answer to the controversy. Although there does seem to be some localization of function, it is only in general areas of the cortex, rather than in specific locations. Damage to a particular area of the cortex can in some cases result in a permanent loss of a particular function, while in other cases the loss of function may be only temporary. Other parts of the cortex often take over the functions formerly controlled by the damaged area or serve as the location of new learning.

Sensory and motor functioning can be localized within specific parts of the cortex. So too can the **speech area**, since damage to this region causes aphasia. For the large majority of humans a speech area appears only in the left hemisphere, which primarily serves the right side of the body. However, among the relatively few people whose speech areas are in the right hemisphere, a large proportion are left-handed.

As we noted in our discussion of the cerebral cortex, the association areas are large diffuse regions in which most of what we call thinking occurs. Memories are stored, information is integrated, and most learning takes place in these areas. Although we can identify some general functions of the association areas, current evidence seems to suggest that there is little localization of function within them. Penfield's report of stimulating a patient's cortex and eliciting a specific vivid memory might seem to suggest that one particular memory is stored at one particular place, but other evidence suggests that this is an oversimplification.

Although memories do seem to be stored in specific neuron changes, these changes occur diffusely in complex networks throughout the association areas. This would help to explain why even though considerable brain damage to one part of the cortex may dim specific memories, it does not necessarily destroy them. We do know that something learned by one half of the brain is also recorded in the other half, so it would be retained by the second, recording hemisphere even if the initial memory area was destroyed in the first hemisphere.

If this view of memory storage is correct, it suggests the following possibility. If we could locate and destroy all the millions of neural connections involved in a specific memory—such as running through a meadow—then there would be no such memory, even if the running occurred yesterday. We could show the person a movie of herself running through the meadow, and she would say, "I see the movie, but I still don't remember doing it."

SOURCE: *Cathy* by Cathy Guisewite. Copyright 1984 Universal Press Syndicate. Reprinted with permission. All rights reserved.

Lateralization of brain functioning and the split-brain

Lateralization of brain functioning refers to the observation that, in general, the left hemisphere is superior to the right at processing speech and language; at logical thinking; and at sequential, step-by-step tasks. The right hemisphere seems to be superior at visualizing objects in space, and recognizing faces. The right hemisphere seems to be the area of the brain where our experience of music and emotion is centred and where we attend to other "all at once" tasks. (See Figure 2-12.) Notice that we say that one hemisphere is superior to the other, not that one hemisphere does logic and the other does music (Gazzaniga & Ledoux, 1978; Sperry, 1982). Some of the evidence for the lateralization of brain functioning comes from research monitoring brain-wave activity in normal subjects while they are exposed to different kinds of stimuli.

Our popular culture has exaggerated recent research on the different functioning of the two brain hemispheres. In fact, there is considerable overlap between the hemispheres and they nearly always work together in an integrated way. It is misleading to say, "He's so right brained you just can't talk to him" or "My right brain took over." Even the term "my right brain" is misleading because it implies that we have two separate brains, whereas in fact we have one brain with two halves that work together (Levy, 1985).

Keeping this caution in mind, we will look at some research on the functioning of the cortical hemispheres and at some fascinating findings obtained by research on patients who have had their hemispheres separated surgically. This severing, in effect, creates two brains that cannot communicate with each other. As a result of this split-brain phenomenon, subjects are unable to use the speech and language capabilities of the left cerebral hemisphere to describe activities carried out by the right hemisphere.

As you know, the two hemispheres of the brain are connected by a complex network of neurons called the corpus callosum. Material that is registered in one half of the brain is also registered nearly instantly in the other half. If we learn a task with the right hand, we can later perform that task to some extent with the left hand even though the learning occurred in the right hemisphere (because of the contralateral organization of body and brain).

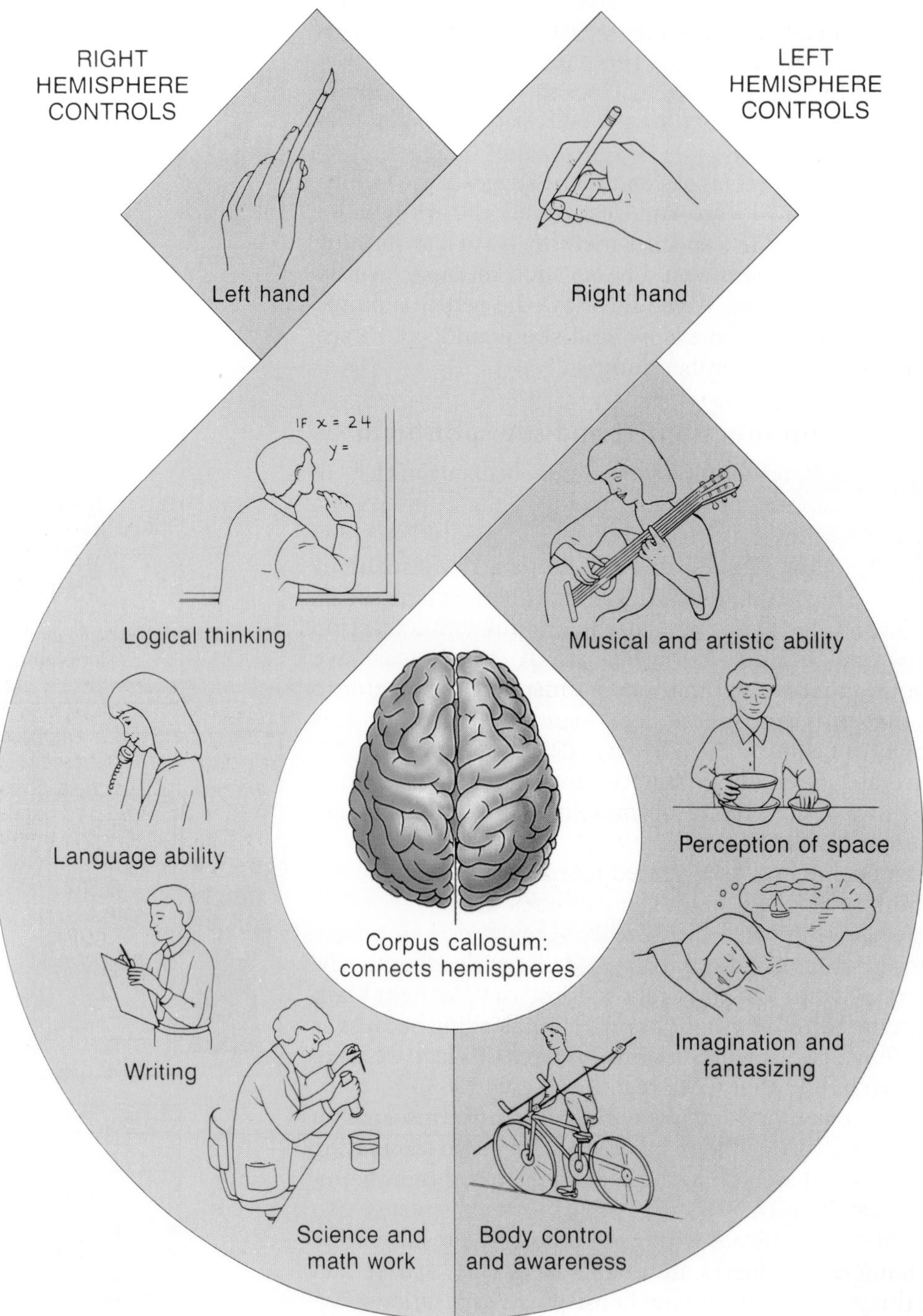

Source: Adapted with permission from Allyn and Bacon, 1989.

Figure 2-12 Lateralization of brain functions
Scientists have shown that in most humans one cerebral hemisphere, usually the left, is specialized for processing speech and language, and for sequential analysis. The other hemisphere, usually the right, appears to specialize in spatial tasks, in musical and artistic talent, in the recognition of faces, and in other mental processes that require "all at once" analysis.

Note that in the intact brain some visual stimulation from each eye goes to each hemisphere. (See Figure 2-13.) Normally, visual information in the left visual field (the area to the left of centre) strikes the right side of both retinas (the areas at the back of the eye where vision is first registered). This image then goes to the right hemisphere of the brain. Objects in the right visual field cast their image on the left side of both retinas and go to the left hemisphere.

From research studies done with both animals and humans, we now know that it is possible to cut the corpus callosum. After this surgical procedure the subject's brain seems, under certain circumstances, to operate as two separate brains. For example, an animal that has had a split-brain operation can be taught to solve a problem with one eye but will be unable to perform the task if that eye is covered and the other eye is uncovered. In order to do these experiments, the split-brain operation would have to include the severing

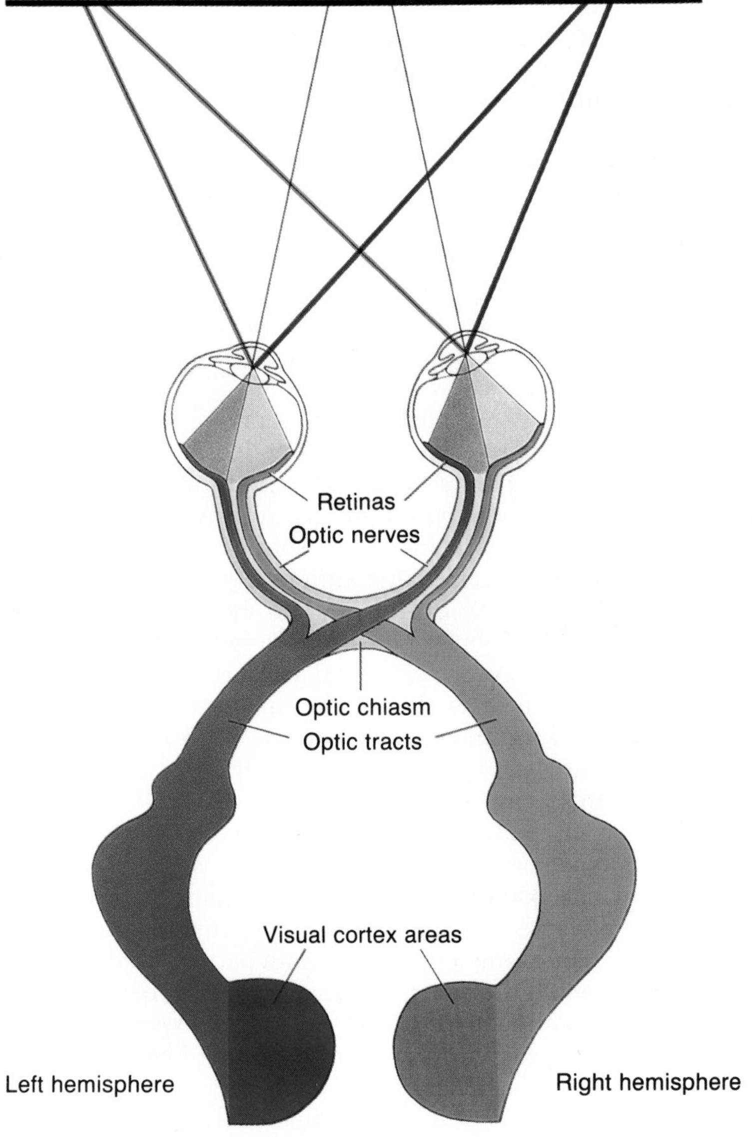

FIGURE 2-13 The visual fields of the left and right eyes
Each eye is connected to both sides of the brain. Some impulses go to one side of the brain, and others cross over to the opposite side. This cross-over of impulses at the optic chiasm allows the brain to process two sets of signals about an image and helps us perceive form and depth. Notice that images from the left visual field go to the right hemisphere and images from the right visual field go to the left hemisphere.

of the corpus callosum *and* the severing of part of the optic chiasm. The **optic chiasm** is the point at which the optic nerves from the eyes cross over from one side of the brain to the other. Under these circumstances images reaching the right eye would go only to the left hemisphere and images reaching the left eye would go only to the right hemisphere.

For such an animal, the image presented to one eye would register in only one half of the brain (Sperry, 1964; Gazzaniga, 1967, 1986). In fact, if the animal is presented with two panels, one bearing a circle and the other a cross, it can be taught to push the circle when it is looking with one eye and to push the cross when it is looking with the other eye. The animal learns different correct responses with the different brain halves, and as long as one eye is covered there is no confusion. If both eyes are uncovered, there is some initial conflict, but the animal eventually seems to choose one response and then stick with it. One fascinating finding in this research is that in certain kinds of problems a split-brain monkey can handle more visual information than a normal monkey. If the experiment is set up as in Figure 2-14, there is a fairly complicated problem to be solved. The animal pulls a knob, and 8 of the 16 panels light up for a very brief period (0.6 seconds). The animal then must push only the panels that lit up. A normal monkey can get up to only the third row of panels before forgetting which panels were lighted. However, we can fit a split-brain monkey with polarizing filters that let each eye see only half the board. This monkey can solve the entire problem with only 0.2 seconds of light exposure. The left half of its brain and the right half of its body solved part of the problem and the right half of its brain and the left half of its body solved the other part. (See Figure 2-14.)

FIGURE 2-14 A split-brain monkey handling a visual-information problem

SOURCE: Adapted from Gazzaniga (1967).

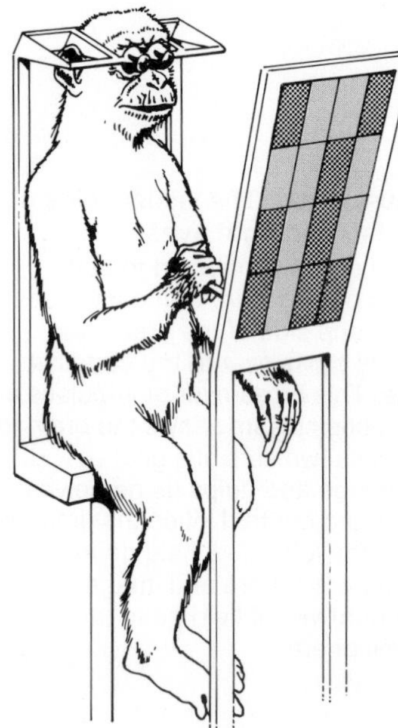

When it was discovered that a split-brain operation on humans could be used to prevent the spread of epileptic seizures from one hemisphere to the other, several such operations were performed. These operations also provided an opportunity to study the split-brain in humans. In both instances, split-brain subjects (whether monkeys or humans) seem to function nearly normally in everyday situations in which they can move their eyes freely. However, in special situations, split-brain humans have specific performance deficits. These deficits reveal a great deal about the brain hemispheres.

In most people it is the left hemisphere that is primarily involved in verbal and analytical behaviour. The right hemisphere is usually more involved with nonverbal thinking—in such tasks as spatial problem-solving (Kimura, 1973; Ornstein, 1977). In a person whose brain is intact, the two hemispheres work together; however, in a split-brain person the two hemispheres are more independent of each other. Consequently, there are circumstances under which a person with a severed callosum cannot perform what appears to be a simple task. For example, if a split-brain patient holds a pencil in his right hand and if the pencil is behind a screen where he can't see it, he can still describe it verbally. If he is asked to perform the same task under the same circumstances with his left hand, though, he is unable to describe the pencil verbally. His right hemisphere knows he is holding a pencil, but his left, which controls speech and most verbal thought, does not. However, the right hemisphere can recognize some simple words. If the word "pencil" is flashed on a screen in the left visual field (the signal would then go to the right hemisphere), the person can, with his left hand, pick out the pencil from among a number of objects behind a screen. He knows what the object is but he is unable to describe it verbally. Split-brain subjects differ in their ability to complete certain other performance tasks. For instance, the left hand (which is controlled by the right hemisphere) can copy a square, a spatial task, but the right hand (which is controlled by the left hemisphere) can't do as well. Conversely, the right hand can easily copy a word, while the left hand will have great difficulty doing so.

We will return to this split-brain phenomenon when we discuss human consciousness in Chapter 9.

The brain and emotion

Emotion is another topic we will cover in more detail later (Chapter 6), but it is important to have some understanding of the connection between emotion and biology. Strong emotional reactions have widespread effects throughout the body. They include ANS arousal, increases in the secretion of the hormones epinephrine (adrenaline) and norepinephrine (noradrenaline), and changes under the control of striate muscles — frowning, grimacing, whining, snarling, and screaming. The brain is involved in both the coordination of all these activities and in the arousal and inhibition of emotional reactions. Although a great many areas of the brain are involved in emotional behaviour, there are two systems that play especially important roles —the hypothalamus and the limbic system.

Emotion and the hypothalamus and limbic system

Research evidence suggests that within the hypothalamus and the limbic system, there are *excitatory and inhibitory centres* that operate in conjunction with each other (Albert & Walsh, 1984; Carlson, 1986). Experiments have been performed on cats and monkeys to study the behavioural effects caused by the removal of progressively greater parts of the brain. Some analogous behavioural effects have been observed in human subjects who have suffered brain damage to the hypothalamus and limbic system. When a normal cat has its tail pulled, it exhibits signs of rage and turns on its attacker with a well-coordinated counterattack. If the cat's cortex is removed, leaving the limbic system and all lower systems intact, the animal becomes very placid and tame, showing little or no reaction to considerable provocation. The cortex controls the intentional attack behaviours that would be the normal reaction to such provocation. If the limbic system is then removed, the animal will become enraged at very slight stimulation, such as gentle stroking of its tail. This response has been called "sham rage" because it is not directed at the target in an organized way. The animal spits and snarls but not *at* anything in particular, apparently because the neocortex is necessary for coordinating behaviour in relation to external stimuli. This rage seems to be caused by a centre in the hypothalamus that under normal circumstances is inhibited by other centres in both the cortex and the limbic system. (We've greatly oversimplified the functioning of these centres, since there are several, all acting in conjunction with one another to stimulate and coordinate emotional behaviour.)

Further evidence of the role of the hypothalamus in emotion comes from studies in which specific parts of this structure were stimulated electrically. An electrode implanted in specific areas of the hypothalamus will elicit a different reaction from one implanted in other areas. In many parts of the hypothalamus, stimulation will arouse rage and fighting responses, while in other parts stimulation will arouse two different patterns of fear reactions — the patterns associated with flight and with alarm.

In 1954, Olds and Milner discovered a related phenomenon involving the hypothalamus and the brain tissue surrounding it. In placing an electrode in a rat's brain they inadvertently missed the reticular formation, the area they intended to study. Instead, the electrode connected up with the hypothalamus. This particular animal kept returning to the place where the electrical stimulation was delivered, and Olds and Milner realized that this stimulation somehow served to reinforce the rat's behaviour. Further experimentation revealed that rats would learn to run mazes just to get the brain reward. It was even possible to locate areas in which the stimulation was so reinforcing that the animals would continue to perform a reinforced response, such as bar pressing, until they dropped from exhaustion. (See Figure 2-15.) They would even ignore food nearby. Because the animals would do all kinds of things to get the stimulation and because they reacted so wildly, even ecstatically, a number of people have concluded that there may be some kind of "pleasure centre" in the brain. This is a bit misleading, however. Further studies indicate that there are a number of areas (including areas outside the hypothalamus) where stimulation is reinforcing. Hence it is unlikely that one or only a few "centres" are involved (Kornetsky, 1986).

Research has also shown that there are some intriguing differences between brain stimulation as a reinforcer and other kinds of natural reinforcers, such as food (Gallistel, 1973). First, a response reinforced with brain stimulation seems to become extinguished very quickly. When the reinforcement is withdrawn, the behaviour

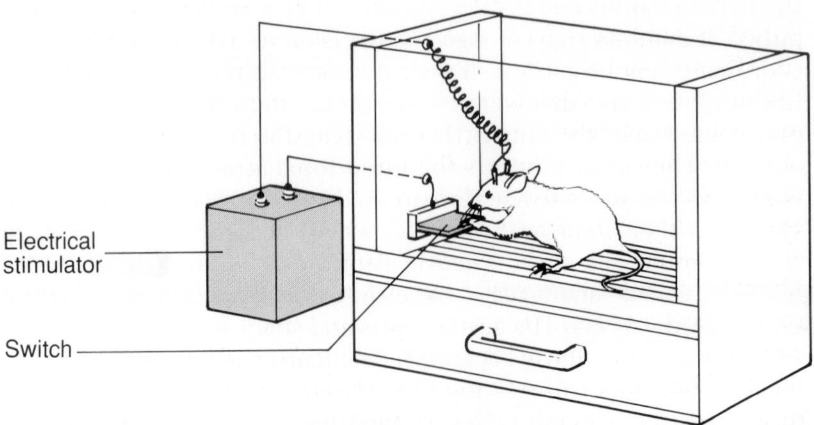

FIGURE 2-15 Pleasure centres in the brain

Research has shown that rats found stimulation of certain areas of the brain to be so reinforcing that they would continue to perform a reinforced response, even to the point of exhaustion.

stops very quickly compared to the extinction rate for responses reinforced by something like food. Gallistel has reported results that indicate that this decay in response rate is not really extinction but seems to be the result of rapid decay of the memory of the electrical reinforcement. He rewarded animals with brain stimulation at the end of a runway. Then, if he let them run again immediately, they would do so quickly. On the other hand, if he delayed the next test by five minutes, most of the animals wouldn't run at all. With natural reinforcers, extinction is a function of the number of unreinforced responses, not of the length of time between trials (see Chapter 5). However, with brain stimulation, elapsed time results in reduced performance. Other research suggests that behaviour developed with brain stimulation as a reinforcer may be very powerful behaviour but will not reappear after a day's rest. So this research too suggests a rapid memory loss of learned behaviours that were reinforced by artificial brain stimulation. It is interesting to note that if, on the second day, an animal is given a "free jolt" as a reminder, it will again perform as though it had not had the day's rest. A second difference between brain stimulation and more natural rewards is that animals will work for the brain stimulation in the absence of any apparent state of deprivation. An animal must first be made hungry or thirsty before food or water can act as a reinforcer, but no analogous situation has been found for brain stimulation.

It is still not clear how brain stimulation works. The last few years of research have raised more questions than they have answered, especially about the function of brain stimulation in humans. As with many new discoveries in psychology, brain-stimulation work received a lot of publicity in the popular press and was sensationalized with stories of the "electronic-ecstasy" variety. However, no research has shown that human subjects whose brains are electronically stimulated experience the frantic excitement that rats show. Generally, human subjects have been more casual and passive when given brain stimulation. Brain stimulation has been tried in a few cases: to reduce pain in terminally ill patients, and to treat severe brain disorders that do not respond to conventional methods. These cases include one woman who had severe seizures that resulted in episodes of uncontrollable rage in which she often would attack others with a knife or with scissors. Electrodes were implanted in her limbic system at several places, and a transceiver permitted both the measurement of electrical activity as she went about her life in the hospital and the stimulation of particular areas by her doctors. During periods of rage, there was abnormal electrical activity in her amygdala and hippocampus, two parts of the limbic system. It was also discovered that stimulating one centre in the amygdala would cause a brief rage reaction, and this knowledge was instrumental in her later treatment (Delgado, 1969). In another patient, stimulation of a particular area caused a sensation of fearful apprehension that strongly resembled anxiety. After the stimulation stopped, she could remember having felt the fear, but there seemed to be no lasting emotional effect. One man with narcolepsy (excessive falling asleep) received implanted electrodes over which he had control, permitting him to stimulate several areas of his own brain. He showed a clear preference for one particular area that somewhat relieved his narcolepsy and also gave him a good feeling. He felt as though he were building up to sexual climax, although he never did achieve orgasm.

We do need to note that Valenstein (1977) made a number of observations that should make us cautious about over-interpreting studies of electrical stimulation of the brain. Even among animals, the effects of this procedure are not very consistent. Changes in the environment, for example, can cause changes in the way an animal responds to a particular stimulus. Humans' responses are even less consistent, so the practical applications of electrical stimulation of the human brain are very limited. The point we wanted to emphasize in this section is that the brain, particularly its "lower" parts, is deeply involved in emotional behaviour.

CHEMICAL INFLUENCES: THE ENDOCRINE SYSTEM

The brain is a chemical as well as an electrical structure. Brain functions and behaviour are greatly influenced by hormones. **Hormones**, which are chemicals secreted by the endocrine system, activate and integrate a wide variety of bodily changes, including growth and emotion.

The **endocrine system** is a series of ductless glands that produce and secrete hormones directly into the bloodstream and affect the workings of the whole body. There are a number of endocrine glands and pairs of glands in the body. These include: the thyroid, the pancreas, the adrenal glands (adrenal medulla and adrenal cortex), the sex glands, and the pituitary gland. The hypothalamus and kidneys also qualify as endocrine glands because they secrete hormones.

The hypothalamus receives information from the sensory receptors and is thus informed about changes in the organism's physiological status. It also controls the **pituitary gland** which is located on the end of a stalk attached directly to the base of the hypothalamus and which is called the "master gland" because it controls the activity of the rest of the endocrine system.

The **thyroid gland** is responsible for producing thyroxin, a chemical that affects metabolism. The **pancreas**, which secretes insulin, helps the system metabolize sugar and determines energy level. The **kidneys** are glandular organs that secrete renin, a hormone that helps maintain the body's homeostasis (especially the balance of water in the organism). There are two **adrenal glands**: the cortex and the medulla. The **adrenal cortex** (the outer) controls metabolism and the body's response to stress and some sex hormones in women. Through the secretion of epinephrine and norepinephrine, the **adrenal medulla** (the inner) also controls metabolism and response to stress. (We will have more to say about the adrenal medulla in the next section). In the female, the sex glands are the **ovaries** which secrete the hormones estrogen and progesterone. In the male, the sex glands are the **testes** which secrete the hormone testosterone. The functions of these glands are summarized in Figure 2-16 and their location is shown in Figure 2-17.

Gland	Hormone	Function
Adrenal gland		
Cortex	Aldosterone	Excretion of sodium and potassium
	Androgens	Growth of pubic and underarm hair; sex drive (women)
	Cortisol	Metabolism, response to stress
Medulla	Epiephrine, norepinephrine	Metabolism, response to stress
Hypothalamus[a]	Releasing hormones	Control of anterior pituitary hormone secretion
Kidneys	Renin	Control of aldosterone secretion; blood pressure
Ovaries	Estrogen	Maturation of female reproductive system; secondary sex characteristics
	Progesterone	Maintenancy of lining of uterus; promotion of pregnancy
Pancreas	Insulin, glucagon	Regulation of metabolism
Pituitary		
Anterior	Adrenocorticotrophic hormone	Control of adrenal cortex
	Gonadotrophic hormones	Control of testes and ovaries
	Growth hormone	Growth; control of metabolism
	Prolactin	Milk production
	Thyroid-stimulating hormone	Control of thyroid gland
Posterior	Antidiuretic hormone[b]	Excretion of water
	Oxytocin[b]	Release of milk
Testes	Testosterone	Maturation of male reproductive system; sperm production; secondary sex characteristics; sex drive (men)
Thyroid	Thyroxin	Energy metbolism; growth and development

[a]The hypothalamus, although it is part of the brain, secretes hormones; thus it can be considered to be an endocrine gland.
[b]These hormones are produced by the hypothalamus but are transported to and released from the posterior pituitary gland.
SOURCE: Adapted with permission from Allyn and Bacon, 1989.

FIGURE 2-16 The major endocrine glands, the hormones they secrete, and their principal features
Endocrine glands are ductless glands that secrete hormones directly into the bloodstream and that can influence a person's behaviour dramatically.

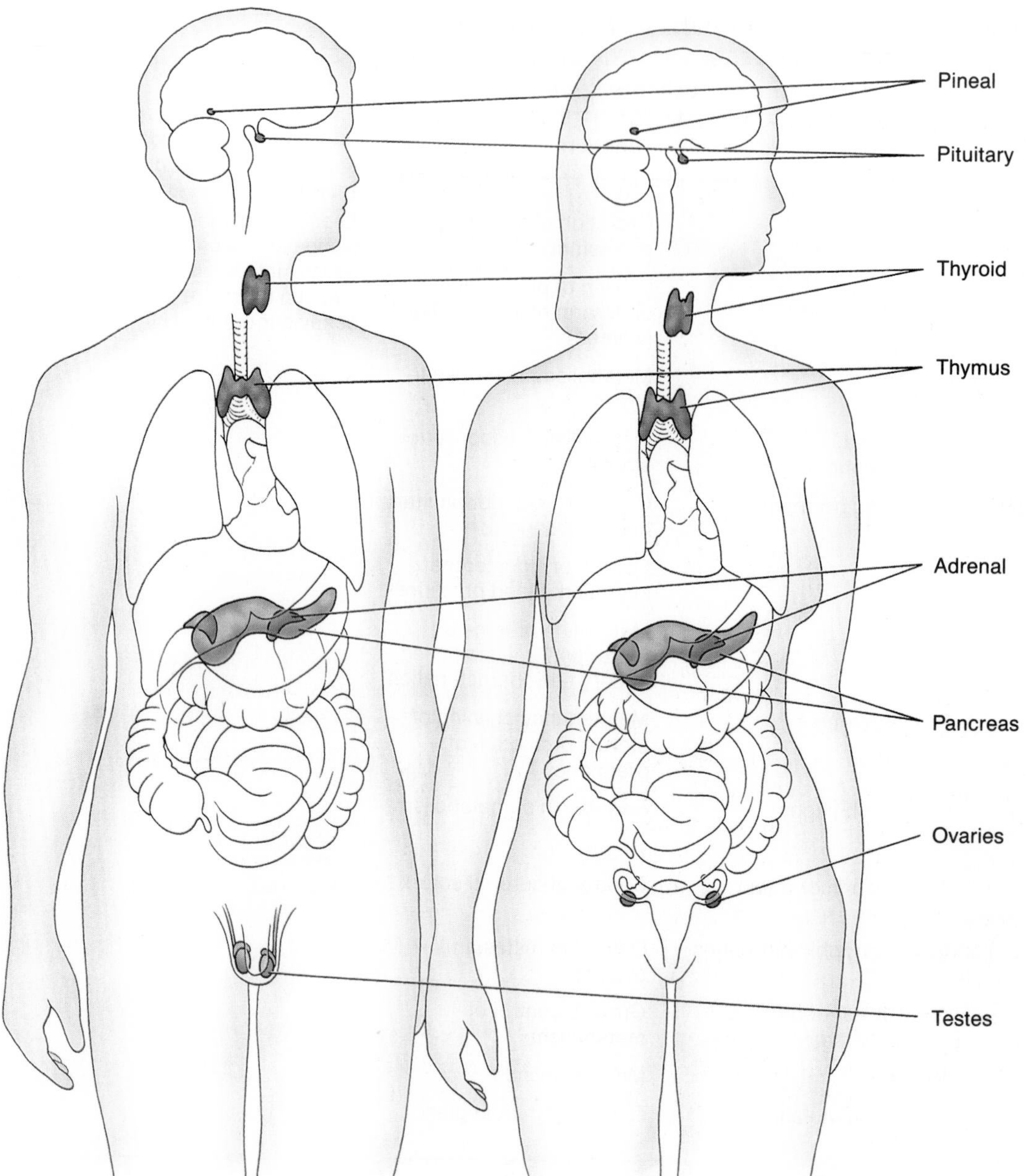

Source: Adapted with permission from Allyn and Bacon, 1989.

Figure 2-17 The localization of the endocrine glands

Hormones and emotion: The adrenal medulla

Each of the endocrine glands can influence emotional behaviour. (The thyroid, for example, can overproduce thyroxin and cause feelings of agitation that resemble anxiety or it can underproduce thyroxin and cause lethargy.) In this section we will focus on one endocrine gland, the *adrenal medulla*.

As we have seen, the adrenal medulla secretes two of the hormones that we know to be connected with the arousal of strong emotion, epinephrine and the more recently discovered norepinephrine (also known as adrenaline and noradrenaline). These hormones facilitate the arousal of the sympathetic nervous system and exert some direct effects of their own. Norepinephrine acts as a transmitter substance to enable nerve impulses to cross synapses; it also increases blood pressure by causing a general constriction of blood vessels. While epinephrine has many similar effects to norepinephrine, it also has certain characteristics of its own. For example, it produces blood-vessel constriction in some parts of the body but dilation in other parts, such as the striated muscles—a reaction that is adaptive in emergency situations that call for quick action. Both of these hormones also interact with the sympathetic nervous system in these emergency situations. The sympathetic system may be aroused by some stimulus; one effect of this arousal will be the stimulation of the adrenal medulla. The adrenal medulla will in turn secrete epinephrine and norepinephrine, which will further stimulate the sympathetic system and keep the emergency reaction going longer than it would have if the organism were dependent on only neural arousal.

Although the evidence is still somewhat inconclusive, it seems likely that these hormones also have a number of effects on brain functioning. Norepinephrine, especially, seems to act as a neurotransmitter in many places in the nervous system, especially the autonomic system (Rogawski, 1985). Drugs such as the amphetamines increase the amount of norepinephrine in the brain and result in states of excitement and "speeding." On the other hand, drugs that suppress norepinephrine in the brain lead to depression and/or have sedative effects. The point of greatest interest to us in all this is that chemicals can cause mood alterations by facilitating and/or inhibiting brain functioning. Change the chemical structure of the blood reaching the brain and you can change the mood.

We have mentioned a few subtle differences in the effects of epinephrine and norepinephrine. These differences raise some interesting questions about whether the two hormones are somehow differentially effective in emotional reactions. Such questions must be answered in a fairly complex and careful way. There is some evidence to suggest that epinephrine is related to fear behaviour and norepinephrine is related to aggressive behaviour. However, we can't conclude that particular hormones cause particular emotions because other evidence shows that environmental cues can lead people to label their emotions completely differently, even though the arousal involved is due to the same hormone (Schachter & Singer, 1962; see Chapter 6, Motivation and Emotion).

In Chapter 2, we will look at the evidence that suggests that epinephrine and norepinephrine are related to fear and anger, respectively. Years ago, Von Euler (1933) suggested that those animals that typically flee in the face of danger have high levels of epinephrine in their blood, while aggressive animals have high levels of norepinephrine. Some years later, Ax (1953) caused subjects to feel either fear or anger while their physiological functions were being measured. He reported that the physiological reactions to fear were those typically caused by epinephrine, such as dilation of blood vessels in the muscles but constriction of blood vessels elsewhere in the body. The arousal of anger resulted in patterns similar to norepinephrine arousal. Unfortunately, Ax did not report any direct measurement of increases in the secretions of particular hormones. In 1960 Hoagland reported some fascinating findings when he measured the epinephrine and norepinephrine levels of hockey players and boxers. Hockey players showed a marked increase in the secretion of norepinephrine during a game (the two players who did not get to play showed an increase in epinephrine secretion). Before a boxing match, the epinephrine levels of the boxers were elevated in general, but among those fighters who aggressively shadowboxed, norepinephrine levels were elevated. Schachter and Latane (1964) followed up this general lead with studies of the effects of epinephrine on avoidance learning in both rats and humans. They injected rats with either epinephrine or a placebo substance and found that the first group of rats learned more quickly in an avoidance-learning situation, presumably because elevated levels of fear motivated quicker learning. In their study of humans, they identified two groups of criminals according to whether they had been labelled as being "sociopathic." Briefly, "sociopathic" is an older term for individuals who have few feelings of conscience and who tend to act for immediate gratification. It has been strongly suggested that this deficit in the behaviour of the sociopath results from a lack of normal levels of fear and anxiety development. Research has found that such persons are, in fact, slower than normal subjects at learning an avoidance task, as well as being slower to condition generally (Eysenck, 1964). Schachter and Latane designed an experiment in which a subtle avoidance-learning task would permit the avoidance of electric shocks and found that the sociopathic group was slower to learn than the nonsociopathic group. However, when they administered injections of epinephrine to the sociopathic group, there was a marked reversal in the findings so that this group performed faster than the nonsociopathic group. Although these results can't be considered conclusive, they strongly suggest that epinephrine is related to fear behaviour and that norepinephrine may be more related to aggressive feelings and behaviour.

CLOSE-UP

Determining Your Speech Laterality

You might want to enlist the services of a friend to determine a little about how your brain is organized. Have your friend measure, over several trials, the length of time that you can balance a pencil on your index finger. First use your right hand, then your left. For right handers, balancing is generally easier with the right hand. Now repeat these time trials when you are speaking. If you are left-hemisphere-dominant for speech, you will be using this hemisphere for both talking and control of your right hand. You should find that your balancing time will decrease for your right hand, but increase for your left. If the opposite change occurs, you may have your speech centre in the right hemisphere.

SPECIAL TOPIC How the Nervous System Is Studied

Since the nervous system is the foundation of our efforts at understanding behaviour, we need powerful tools to study it. However, studying the nervous system presents special problems because it is inside the skin, and largely inside the skull. It is hard to reach without being invasive and destructive. Although our tools are still relatively crude and our subject is so complex that the brain and nervous system will continue to be a research frontier for many years, we have, in recent years, made some advances in the development of these tools.

Surgical lesions: Destroying parts of the brain

One of the oldest and crudest tools is still in use, especially with animals. Specific areas of the nervous system are lesioned (cut) and destroyed or removed. The impact of these lesions on behaviour is studied and inferences are made about which brain structures are responsible for which behaviours. In Chapter 6, for example, we will read about animals that became obese as a result of a specific brain lesion. Among humans, we can study victims of head injuries. The location and extent of nervous-system damage can be mapped fairly accurately, and behavioural changes give clues about human brain function. We can also study patients who have had **psychosurgery** to relieve specific disorders but who have also exhibited other changes in their behaviour. We have had an example of this in this chapter: those patients with intractable epilepsy who had their corpus callosums lesioned to control the spread of seizures. This also, as you will recall, provided the opportunity to learn important information about how the brain hemispheres interact.

Electrical and chemical stimulation

In this chapter we also have seen examples of electrical stimulation of the human brain. Parts of the brain can be exposed surgically, under local anaesthetic. The patient remains conscious and can talk about his or her experiences when different areas of the brain are stimulated by tiny electrical probes. There are no pain receptors in the brain, so patients feel no pain unless specific pain pathways are stimulated.

When studying animals it is also possible to deliver chemicals to precisely defined areas of the brain through an extremely thin metal tube called a cannula. The impact of the chemical on the animals' behaviour can then be studied. Among humans, chemicals (such as drugs) clearly have an enormous impact on brain functioning. However, we have to study these chemicals more indirectly, since we don't have ways to deliver the chemicals to precise locations.

Experimental methods with the normal, intact brain

It is unusual and expensive to have opportunities to study the human brain directly, so researchers have devised techniques to study normal, intact brains. You may have been a subject in brain research without even knowing it. Two of the most popular and powerful research techniques are dichotic listening and tachistoscopic viewing.

Dichotic listening. Dichotic listening is a research procedure in which a subject is given two different auditory messages simultaneously, one in each ear. This is usually accomplished through the use of stereo earphones. The nerves from the ears are arranged *contralaterally*, so that most of what goes into the left ear travels first to the right brain hemisphere and most of what goes into the right ear travels first to the left hemisphere. However, there is a weaker **ipsilateral** (near side) **connection**, so that under normal life circumstances both ears are feeding both hemispheres, although the contralateral effect is stronger. During dichotic listening, however, it appears that the ipsilateral connection is inhibited, so there is nearly complete crossover of information. This knowledge permits us to study such topics as hemispheric differences in word recognition. If we present words to one ear and distracting sounds to the other, we will find that the right ear (and left hemisphere) is superior at word recognition. This data supports the idea that language is primarily a left-hemisphere function.

Tachistoscopic viewing. Another non-invasive tool is tachistoscopic viewing, in which visual images are exposed for a very brief period on a screen. Review Figure 2-11 (on the optic chiasm); images in the left visual field (everything to the left of centre) go first to the right hemisphere, and the reverse is true for the right visual field. (There is some overlap in the very centre of the visual field). An experimenter can, for example, have a subject focus on a centre dot and then flash an image in the left visual field so quickly that the eyes cannot move to centre on the image. It takes a person at least one-eighth of a second to react and move the eyes. We would then know that the image reached the right hemisphere first; we might discover that words flashed in the left visual field took longer to say because the word stimulus goes to the right hemisphere and information must cross the corpus callosum before the left hemisphere can speak the word (Martin, Verman, and Miles, 1984).

Non-invasive technologies

Technology has provided several non-invasive methods for studying both brain structure and brain functioning. Most of these techniques were developed for medical diagnosis, but they are also powerful research tools.

Electroencephalography (EEG). Electroencephalography measures the electrical activity of the brain through small electrodes placed directly on the scalp. The waves of small electrical signals pass from the brain through the skull and then are amplified thousands of times. These signals are recorded on paper or on a computer to give an electroencephalogram (EEG). In Chapter 9, we will see that particular patterns of waves of electrical activity are typical of different stages of sleep. Other patterns can help diagnose specific diseases or nervous system malfunctions. Some patterns are indicative of rest and others of activity, so we can study brain activity under different circumstances. For example, we might find the right hemisphere "idling" during a verbal task but active during a visualization task. Such idling would be indicated by brain activity characterized by a regular "alpha rhythm" of about ten cycles per second (see Chapter 9).

Computerized axial tomography scan (CAT scan). A computerized axial tomography scan (CAT scan) provides a very detailed x-ray picture of a "slice" of the brain. X-ray images are taken from many different points around the brain and then a computer integrates these many pictures into one image of brain anatomy.

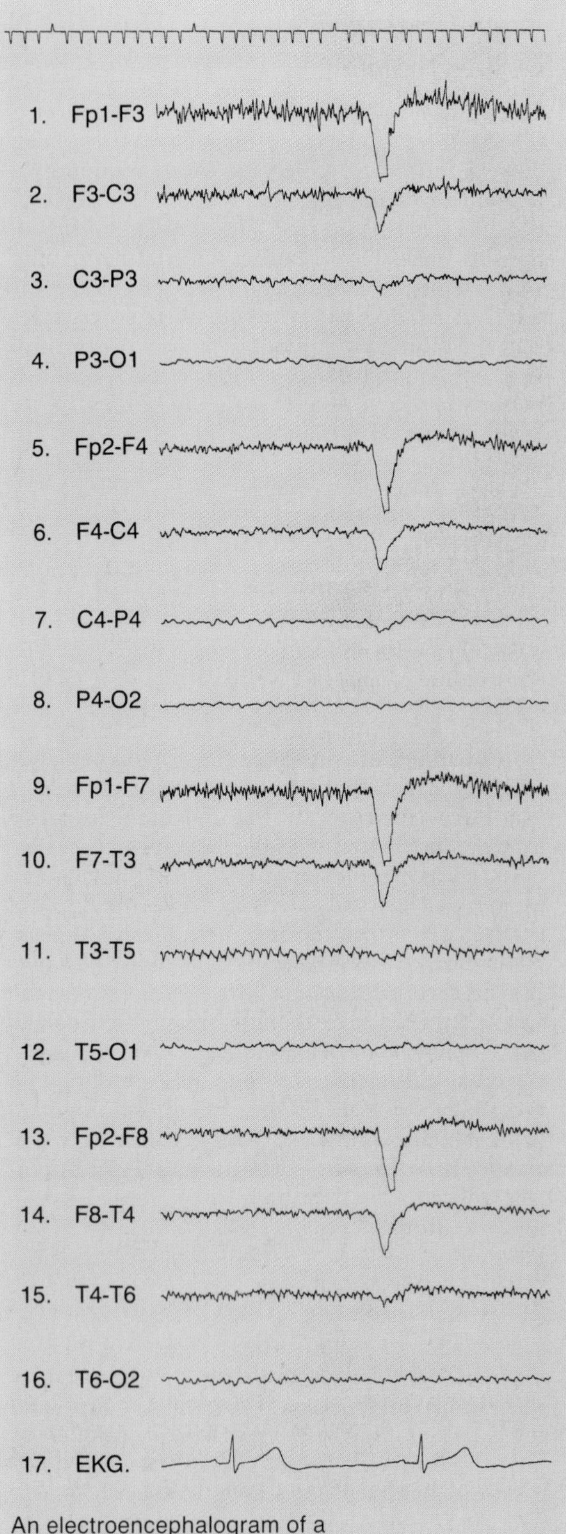

An electroencephalogram of a normal human brain.
SOURCE: Toronto Western Hospital.

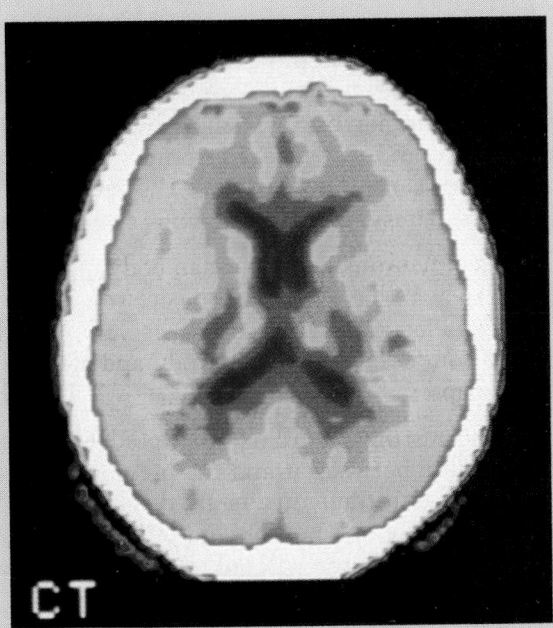

A CAT scan of a normal human brain.
SOURCE: UBC/Triumpf PET program.

Magnetic resonance imaging (MRI). An even more detailed three-dimensional image of brain structures or other soft tissue organs is possible with magnetic resonance imaging (MRI). MRI scanners use magnetic fields, radio-frequency waves, and computers to construct the images. It was originally called nuclear magnetic resonance.

Positron emission tomography scan (PET scan). Both CAT and MRI provide good images, but they are static. The EEG gives a measure of ongoing activity in the brain, but it is not as precise as we would like because the skull distorts and diffuses the electrical signals. A powerful new technology called a positron emission tomography scan (PET scan) is like a moving version of a CAT scan. Neural firing uses energy, so active neurons are constantly absorbing sugar from the blood. A half hour before receiving a PET scan, a patient is injected with radioactive sugar. The PET scan sensitively measures radioactivity in the brain, so the more active parts of the brain will show more radioactivity as they absorb the radioactively "labelled" sugar more quickly than other parts of the brain. Even more precise work can be done by radioactively "labelling" drugs that bind to specific neurotransmitters.

Magnetoencephalography (MEG). Instead of measuring electrical activity, as with the EEG, magnetoencephalography (MEG) measures magnetic fields that are created by the brain's electrical activity. The advantage is that these magnetic fields are not affected by passing through the bone of the skull. The MEG measures both the source and the strength of the magnetic field.

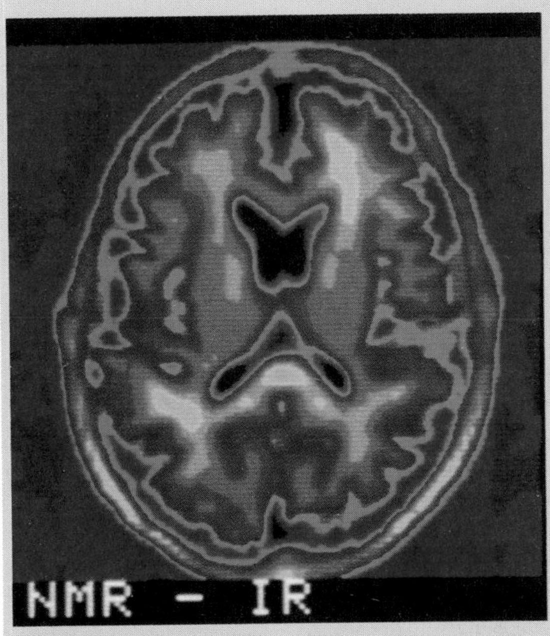

An MRI scan of a normal human brain.
SOURCE: UBC/Triumpf PET program.

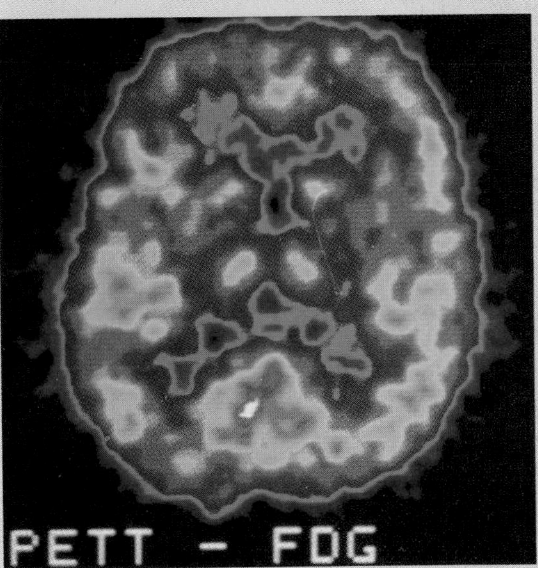

A PET scan of a normal human brain.
SOURCE: UBC/Triumpf PET program.

Chapter Summary

1. The human nervous system is composed of nerve cells (neurons) and glial cells. It is a complex system which is divided into the central nervous system (CNS) and the peripheral nervous system. In turn, the peripheral nervous system is divided into the somatic nervous system and the autonomic nervous system (ANS). Finally, the ANS can be divided into the sympathetic nervous system and the parasympathetic nervous system.
2. Although the billions of neurons in the human body may differ in length and shape, they all have the same basic structure and mode of operation. An electrical impulse travels very quickly through the neuron (from dendrites to cell body and along the axon) and into the synapses.
3. A postsynaptic neuron's resting potential is disrupted by a chemical change in the synapse between it and the previous neuron in the chain. Chemical neurotransmitters are discharged from the axon terminal buttons of one neuron and either inhibit or stimulate the next neuron. A neuron will only fire when its firing threshold has been crossed.
4. The somatic nervous system conducts messages from the receptor neurons in the sense organs and muscles to the central nervous system, and carries messages from the central nervous system through motor neurons to the muscles of the body.
5. While the two divisions of the autonomic nervous system work together to maintain the system's viability (neurons of one system lead to many of the same organs as the neurons of the other), they do have somewhat opposing effects. The sympathetic system responds to situations of danger and excitement; the parasympathetic system controls body-conserving functions.
6. Biofeedback has modified our understanding of the autonomic nervous system. Subjects have been able to learn to exert some control over bodily functions that were formerly thought to be automatic (involuntary).
7. The central nervous system is made up of the spinal cord and the brain. Through a complex network of neurons throughout the body, the spinal cord carries messages to and from the brain. It is also responsible for certain reflex reactions and for some simple learning.
8. Of the three sections of the brain, the hindbrain is the most primitive. The midbrain relays impulses to and from the higher faculties of the forebrain and controls sleep and wakefulness. The forebrain, the most advanced section in terms of evolution, controls most of our higher mental functions.
9. The forebrain, the area above the core of the brain, contains centres that control higher mental functioning; learning and memory; the emotions of fear, rage, and pleasure; motor functioning; and the reception and processing of sensory data. While different areas tend to control different functions, the healthy

forebrain also integrates all of these activities into a smooth-running whole.

10. Some memories are retained in neurons only for a short time. Other memories are retained for much longer periods, perhaps even permanently. Through the work of Wilder Penfield, we now know that many of these long-term memories are stored in association areas throughout the cortex.

11. The left hemisphere of the brain seems to be superior at performing certain skills and the right at performing other skills. However, the two hemispheres do work together and, when the corpus callosum is no longer intact, the subject (whether animal or human) usually suffers some performance deficits.

12. Research indicates that the hypothalamus and the limbic system work together to control emotion. Different areas of the hypothalamus are control centres for bodily reactions to both painful and pleasurable emotions. Electrical stimulation of the pleasure centre in the hypothalamus of rats seems to be a strong (if short-lived) reinforcer.

13. Closely connected with (but operating more slowly than) the nervous system, the endocrine system produces various chemical substances that affect behaviour. One indication of the close relationship between the two systems is that certain of these hormones also act as neurotransmitters.

14. Among the most important of the hormones/neurotransmitters that affect human emotion are the two that are secreted by the adrenal medulla. Research indicates that epinephrine is related to the experience of fear and that norepinephrine is related to the experience of aggression and, further, that both hormones have effects on subsequent behaviour.

Key Terms

Absolute refractory period The time during which a neuron is firing and cannot fire again. It is unable to fire again until it has returned to the resting potential.

Acetylcholine The most common neurotransmitter, usually excitatory. It is discharged at synapses in the brain, spinal cord, and autonomic nervous system.

Action potential The actual firing of the neuron. A sudden, momentary reversal of the polarity of the resting potential, with the inside of the cell membrane more positively charged than it was before.

Adrenal cortex The outer portion of the adrenal gland which controls metabolism and the body's response to stress and some sex hormones in women.

Adrenal gland See *adrenal cortex* and *adrenal medulla.*

Adrenal medulla The inner portion of the adrenal gland which secretes epinephrine and norepinephrine. It controls metabolism and the body's reaction to stress.

Adrenaline See *epinephrine.*

Afferent (or sensory) neural signals Neural signals that travel the spinal cord and brain, bringing information into the nervous system through the sense receptors.

All-or-none law The principle that a neuron can fire at only one particular strength, when and only when its stimulation threshold has been passed. It either fires fully or not at all.

Amygdala Structure of the limbic system that seems to arouse rage.

Aphasia Blocking of speech functions caused by brain injury or other brain malfunction in the speech areas of the cortex.

Association areas Large and diffuse parts of the cerebral cortex which seem to be responsible for thinking and memory.

Autonomic nervous system (ANS) The branch of the peripheral nervous system that connects the internal organs and glands to the central nervous system.

Axon A projecting part of the neuron that conveys impulses away from the cell body.

Basal ganglia A set of structures just below the cortex and in front of the thalamus in the forebrain. They are necessary for the coordination and control of motor movements.

Biofeedback Treatment procedure in which a person who is provided with ongoing information about his or her autonomic functions can learn to modify those functions.

Cell body The central part of a neuron which contains the cell nucleus.

Central fissure Deep fold that separates the frontal lobe and the parietal lobe in each hemisphere of the brain.

Central nervous system (CNS) One of two major divisions of the nervous system. It consists of the neurons in the spinal cord and the brain.

Cerebellum Structure of the hindbrain that is important in coordinating smooth motor movement and in maintaining balance.

Cerebral cortex Outer layer of cells of the cerebrum. The most important structure for dealing with higher mental functions such as language, thinking, memory, and creativity. Contains 80–90% of all the neurons in the brain.

Cerebral hemispheres Left and right halves of the cerebral cortex, which is divided down the middle.

Cerebrum The entire, outer, convoluted part of the brain. Responsible for higher mental functions.

Computerized axial tomography scan (CAT scan) A very detailed x-ray of a "slice" of the brain. Many images are integrated by a computer into one picture.

Contralateral organization The "cross-over" system of the brain whereby the left hemisphere generally controls the right side of the body, and the right hemisphere generally controls the left side of the body.

Corpus callosum Thick bundle of neurons that connects up and carries messages between the right and left cerebral hemispheres.

Dendrite A branching part of a neuron that receives stimulation and conveys it toward the cell body.

Dichotic listening Research procedure in which a subject is given two different auditory messages simultaneously, one in each ear.

Directional fractionation A pattern of autonomic arousal in which one response (such as GSR) increases while another (such as heart rate) decreases.

Efferent (or motor) neural signals Neural signals that travel outward from the spinal cord and brain to the muscles and glands of the body.

Electroencephalography (EEG) Research and clinical method of measuring the electrical activity of the brain through small electrodes placed directly on the scalp.

Endocrine system A series of ductless glands that secrete hormones directly into the bloodstream and affect the workings of the whole body.

Epinephrine An adrenal hormone discharged in response to emotion, particularly fear. Can act as an excitatory or inhibitory neurotransmitter.

Firing threshold The level of stimulation required for a particular neuron to fire.

Forebrain The highest and largest portion of the brain, including the cerebral hemispheres, the hypothalamus, limbic system, thalamus, and the basal ganglia. Responsible for complex emotional and intellectual functioning.

Frontal lobe Front portion of the cortex, seems to affect both the control of voluntary movement and the higher mental processes that make up intelligent functioning.

Galvanic skin response (**GSR**) Increased electrical activity in the skin that is caused by sympathetic nervous system arousal. Often used as a measure of emotional arousal.

Gamma-aminobutyric acid or **GABA** An amino acid that also acts as an inhibitory neurotransmitter especially in the brain and spinal cord.

Glial cells A type of cell found in the nervous system. Glial cells serve to nourish, hold, protect, insulate, and provide a supporting environment for the delicate network of neurons.

Hindbrain The lowest and most primitive part of the brain. Most important structures are the medulla and cerebellum.

Hippocampus Structure of the limbic system that seems especially involved in the storage of memories.

Homeostats Structures within the hypothalamus that control various bodily functions by responding when levels of functioning are too high or too low.

Hormones Chemicals secreted by the endocrine glands. Activate and integrate a wide variety of bodily changes, including growth and emotion.

Hypothalamus A structure of the forebrain that controls much of the activity of the autonomic nervous system. Located above the brain stem and below the thalamus. Regulates the homeostasis of both bodily functions and some aspects of the emotions.

Ipsilateral connection A connection between two objects on the same side.

Kidneys Glandular organs that secrete renin, a hormone that helps maintain the body's homeostasis (especially the balance of water in the organism).

Lateral fissure Deep fold that separates the frontal lobe and the temporal lobe in each hemisphere of the brain.

Lateralization of brain function The observation that, in general, the left hemisphere is superior to the right at processing speech and language; at logical thinking; and at sequential, step-by-step tasks. The right hemisphere seems to be superior at visualizing objects in space; and at musical, perhaps emotional, and other "all at once" tasks.

Limbic system Set of structures underneath the cerebrum, around the central core of the forebrain. Influential in the inhibiting and arousal of strong emotion, in carrying out behaviours that require a specific sequence of steps, and in storing memories.

Long-term memory (**LTM**) The apparently permanent retention of memories. Seems to be caused by *chemical* changes, probably at the synapses between neurons. Occurs as a result of learning experiences.

Magnetic resonance imaging (**MRI**) A very detailed three-dimensional image of brain structures or of other soft tissue organs. MRI scanners use magnetic fields, radio-frequency waves, and computers to construct the images.

Magnetoencephalography (**MEG**) A measurement of the magnetic fields that are created by electrical activity in the brain.

Medulla Structure of the hindbrain that helps control breathing and circulation and helps the body maintain particular postures.

Meninges (**singular: menix**) Three sets of membranes that encase and protect the brain.

Midbrain Part of the brain that lies between the hindbrain and the forebrain. Especially important in coordinating and relaying auditory and visual information to the brain. Contains the reticular formation.

Motor neurons Neurons in the somatic nervous system that convey messages from the brain to muscle fibre. They control the contraction and relaxation of muscles.

Myelin sheath A coating made up of one kind of glial cell. The axons of some neurons are covered to facilitate firing and to insulate the neuron from nearby neurons.

Nerve A bundle of neurons that are physically adjacent to each other, somewhat like a "cable" of neurons.

Neuron A nerve cell that conducts stimulation from one location in the body to another.

Neurotransmitter A chemical substance that is released at the terminal buttons of the axon. Its function is to jump the synaptic gap by chemically stimulating the dendrite of the next neuron. Some transmitter substances excite and some inhibit the dendrite of the next neuron.

Noradrenaline See *norepinephrine.*

Norepinephrine An adrenal hormone discharged in response to emotion, particularly anger. It can act as an excitatory or inhibitory neurotransmitter.

Occipital lobe The rear portion of the cortex, which is primarily responsible for visual functions.

Optic chiasm The point at which the optic nerves from the eyes cross over from one side of the brain to the other.

Ovaries Female sex glands that secrete estrogen and progesterone.

Pancreas Endocrine gland responsible for secreting insulin, a hormone that metabolizes sugar and determines energy level.

Parasympathetic nervous system The branch of the autonomic nervous system that calms the body for the conserving and restoring of energy.

Parietal lobe Upper side portion of the cortex, plays an important role in bodily sensation.

Peripheral nervous system One of two major divisions of the nervous system. It consists of all of the neurons outside the spinal cord and brain.

Phrenology Outmoded theory that specific mental abilities and traits are reflected by bumps on the skull.

Pituitary gland The "master gland" of the endocrine system. Attached directly to the base of the hypothalamus (which controls it) and is called the "master gland" because it controls the activity of the rest of the endocrine system.

Positron emission tomography scan (PET scan) A detailed moving picture of the functioning brain. It sensitively measures the activities of the brain.

Postsynaptic neuron Neuron whose membranes are stimulated or inhibited by the release of a transmitter substance from another neuron.

Psychosurgery Surgical procedures designed to correct emotional and behavioural disorders.

Receptor neurons Neurons in the sense organs. They receive stimulation from the environment.

Relative refractory period The few thousandths of a second after a neuron has fired, during which time it is capable of firing again only if it receives greater than normal stimulation.

Resting potential The state of a neuron when it is at rest and ready to fire in response to stimulation.

Reticular formation A structure of the midbrain that serves to alert the organism to prepare for incoming stimulation. Controls sleep and wakefulness.

Short-term memory (STM) Briefly active memories, the retention of which is apparently caused by temporary *electrical* changes in the neurons.

Skull Strong set of bones that encase and protect the brain.

Smooth muscle The muscles of internal organs such as the heart. Generally affected by the autonomic nervous system.

Somatic nervous system The branch of the peripheral nervous system that controls the muscles connected to the skeleton (i.e., the striated muscles) and transmits information from the sense organs to the central nervous system.

Speech area Specific area of the cortex (usually in the left hemisphere) responsible for the production of speech.

Spinal cord The "lowest" segment of the central nervous system. It is a strand of nerve fibres running down the middle of the spine. It connects most of the nerve fibres in the body to the brain and controls some stimulus-response reflexes.

Striated muscles Muscles connected to the skeleton. They move the bones.

Sympathetic nervous system The branch of the autonomic nervous system that arouses the body for activity and the use of energy.

Synapse Tiny gap between the dendrites of one neuron and the axon terminals of another. Point of connection between two neurons.

Synaptic vesicle Small area within the terminal buttons at the end of the axon for storage of neurotransmitters.

Tachistoscopic viewing Research procedure in which visual images are exposed on a screen for a very brief period.

Temporal lobe Lower side portion of the cortex, primarily responsible for hearing.

Testes Male sex glands which secrete testosterone.

Thalamus Structure of the forebrain that acts primarily as a relay station for signals from the sensory systems and from other brain centres (particularly the reticular formation) to the cerebrum.

Thyroid gland Endocrine gland responsible for secreting thyroxin, a hormone that affects metabolism.

Transmitter substance Another term for neurotransmitter.

Vertebrae Hollow bones that make up the spine and protect the spinal cord.

Suggested Readings

Bloom, F.E., Lazerson, A., & Hofstadter, L. (1985). *Brain, mind, and behavior*. New York: Freeman. A colourful, well-illustrated popular summary of recent brain research.

Hunt, M. (1982). *The universe within: A new science explores the human mind*. New York: Simon & Schuster. This is a wide-ranging book written for the lay reader. It explores what we know about mental function as an expression of brain functioning. Hunt covers topics that will come up in later chapters of this book too, such as the nature of thinking, artificial intelligence, and the evolution of the brain.

Ornstein, R., & Thompson, R. G. (1984). *The amazing brain*. Boston: Houghton Mifflin. Well-written summary of brain research that covers a wide range of topics. Both authors are active brain researchers and Ornstein has published a lot of material for the educated layperson.

Sacks, O. (1985). *The man who mistook his wife for a hat and other clinical tales*. New York: Summit. This collection of clinical case histories often has a marked impact on readers. The patient described in the title had a kind of brain damage that impaired his ability to recognize faces and even to distinguish faces from other objects. Such a specific disability is nearly always the result of right hemisphere malfunction. It can be startling to read about real people and the bizarre world they must adapt to because of brain damage.

CHAPTER 3

SOURCE: William von Moll Berczy, Detail from *Study of a Right Hand* (n.d.).

Sensation

Knowing the World
- What are sensation and perception?
- What is reality?

Sensory Psychology
- Psychophysics and sensory thresholds
- Adaptation and context

Vision
- Properties of light
- Structure of the eye
- Adaptation
- Neural pathways
- Colour vision

Hearing
- What is sound?
- Structure of the ear

Taste and Smell (Chemical Senses)
- Gustation
- Olfaction

Somatosenses (Body Senses)
- Kinesthetic (bodily position) sense
- Vestibular (balance) sense
- Skin senses

Special Topic Subliminal Perception

KNOWING THE WORLD

At this moment, you are being bombarded with an enormous number of stimuli. Light is bouncing off the page and entering your eyes; the sound of your own breathing is reaching your ears; the seat of your chair is pressing against you; and various odours are in the air around you. As you concentrate on this book, most of these sources of stimulation have little effect on you; but if a whispering couple mentions your name, you probably will notice. Let's investigate how all this stimulation enters our nervous system and how we then process it to give ourselves a meaningful view of the world.

What are sensation and perception?

A **stimulus** is any form of energy that arouses some response from an organism. It may be light, sound, touch, pressure — any energy that elicits a response. **Sensation** is the impact that stimuli have on sensory organs and the nervous system. Sensation is the reception of "raw data" from the environment. In this chapter, we will consider how stimuli from the environment get into our systems and we will investigate how these stimuli create sensations. In the next chapter, we will study **perception**, which is the process by which the brain interprets and organizes stimuli to make them meaningful. Thus, in Chapter 4 we will explore how the brain gives meaning to the millions of sensations that strike us.

As we saw in Chapter 2, the nervous system is wonderfully complex, powerful, and adaptive, but it is cut off from the external world. The only way the brain can establish contact with the environment is through a network of neural connections that start at the sense organs—namely, the eyes, ears, skin, nose, and mouth. Internal sense receptors also exist that tell the brain such things as the position of the body's muscles.

It is useful to think of sensation as the "raw data" we receive from the environment and perception as the "processed data." However, it is often difficult to draw a clear line between sensation and perception. In fact, many psychologists today no longer try to do so. We are presenting sensation and perception as separate chapters, primarily to help you organize the large amount of material that both concepts embrace. As you read through these two chapters, you should note areas of overlap.

What is reality?

Most of us trust our senses almost completely. "Seeing is believing," we say. And often we insist that an event was just as we perceived it because, "I was there; I *saw* it." One of the strange lessons of this chapter and the next is that none of us perceives reality as it is. Our perception is a construction of reality that is filtered through our limited senses and distorted by our processes of interpreting what those senses permit us to receive.

For example, we don't perceive the motions of our breathing until they are pointed out; but they are part of reality. By the same token, we are surrounded right now by many sounds that our pets can hear but we can't; such sounds are part of reality too. Later we will present evidence to show that all of us distort our perceptions to some extent because of what we expect to perceive. Two witnesses to the same event actually perceive different things. Obviously, we misperceive reality when we look at visual illusions such as the one in Figure 3-1.

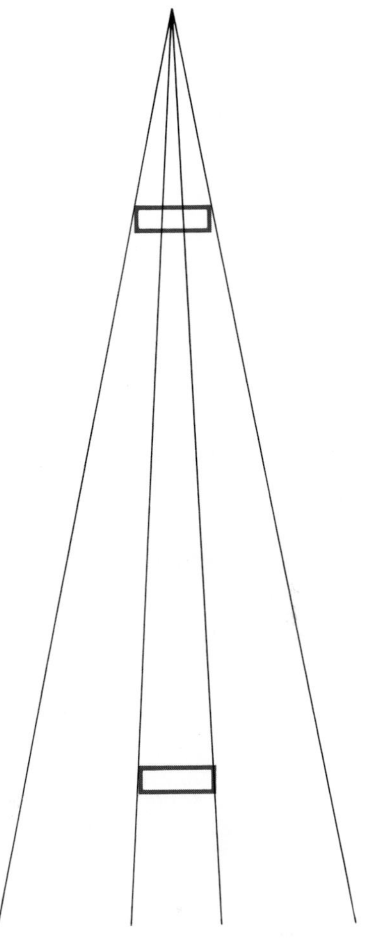

FIGURE 3-1 The Ponzo illusion The two rectangles in this drawing are the same length.

Use a ruler to prove to yourself that the two rectangles have the same length. You're a reasonable person, so you should be able to use your reason to make your brain see the two rectangles as the same size. But you will find that reason does not work here. Logic won't change the way your brain perceives the illusion. (Later, we will see that new experiences might.) This illustration demonstrates that our perceptions are our construction of reality, not literal representations of reality.

Fortunately, for most of us, our construction of reality is accurate enough to permit us to function well in the environment. We can also protect ourselves against our distortions by comparing our perceptions with those of others and by using instruments such as rulers. It is humbling, however, to learn that seeing is not necessarily believing.

SENSORY PSYCHOLOGY

To understand sensation, we need to know how the physical energy from an environmental stimulus is transduced (i.e., changed or transformed) into the firing of neurons. How does a physical stimulus, such as a sound wave or a light wave, get changed into the experience of hearing or seeing? We know a considerable amount about the early stages of this process — how the sense organs receive stimuli and how that leads to the firing of neurons. We will focus on these early stages in this chapter. We still know relatively little about how neural firings become the mental events that each of us experiences.

Psychophysics and sensory thresholds

The volume dial on our stereo is graded from 0 to 10. As we turn the dial up from 2 to 4, does our experience of loudness double? When the dial is set at 10, is it five times louder than when set at 2? These are the kinds of questions asked in psychophysics. **Psychophysics** is the study of the relationship between physical stimuli and how we sense those stimuli. Let's look at some of the things that psychophysics has uncovered.

In everyday language, we often use the word "threshold" to refer to the entrance or doorway of a building. On one side of it we are outdoors, and on the other side of it we are indoors. In psychophysics, we use the term *threshold* to denote a limit or line. There are two broad categories of sensory thresholds: *absolute thresholds* and *difference thresholds*.

FIGURE 3-2 **Absolute thresholds for several human senses in selected terms**

VISION A candle flame seen at 45 kilometres on a dark, clear night.

HEARING The tick of a watch at 6 metres under quiet conditions.

Absolute thresholds

An **absolute threshold** is the minimal intensity of a stimulus needed before our sensory receptors can detect the presence of that particular stimulus. It represents the line between no sensation and experienced sensation; it is the lowest intensity of a stimulus that can produce a response. Suppose someone presses a soft feather against your arm with steadily increasing pressure. At first, you may "feel nothing," even though there clearly is physical contact. As the pressure increases, you will eventually become aware of the contact. At that point, you will have crossed your *touch threshold*. Suppose someone grabs your arm and starts squeezing it more and more tightly. At some point, you will say that the sensation changes from pressure to pain. When you cross that line, you will have reached your *pain threshold*.

Figure 3-2 shows the absolute thresholds for several human senses in selected terms. For instance, hearing is described here in terms of loudness. But we can also consider the absolute threshold of human hearing in terms of pitch (i.e., the "highness" and "lowness" of a sound). As we shall discuss later in this chapter, pitch is determined by frequency, which is usually measured in cycles per second. One cycle per second is called one **hertz** (**Hz**). Human hearing has both a minimum and maximum limit of sensitivity to pitch. Our hearing is limited to sound waves that are between 20 and 20 000 Hz. We experience "sounds" below 20 Hz (subsonic) as vibration rather than as sound, and we have no conscious experience of "sounds" that are above 20 000 Hz (ultrasonic). It might seem odd to describe such stimuli as "sounds," inasmuch as we can't hear them. However, refusing to call them "sounds" would only reflect our human-centred illusion that reality is what humans perceive. Some of the thresholds in Figure 3-2 seem quite remarkable—one drop of perfume in a three-room house, for example. But again, they only seem remarkable in

TASTE One teaspoon of sugar dissolved in 7.6 litres of water.

SMELL One drop of perfume diffused into the entire volume of a three room house.

TOUCH The wing of a fly falling on your cheek from a distance of 1 centimetre.

terms of the limits of human sensation. Many animal species have vastly more sensitive senses of smell than humans have.

There are two other important points we should emphasize about the thresholds shown in Figure 3-2. First, thresholds vary somewhat from individual to individual. One person may be able to hear sounds or see light that another person cannot sense. Second, each individual experiences some fluctuations in his or her own thresholds. Our thresholds would change, for example, if we were tired, hungry, bored, or surrounded by observers intently staring at us. The physical capabilities of the human senses and the strength of the signals (stimuli) are very important in our sensing of stimuli. But according to the **signal-detection theory**, our ability to detect signals (stimuli) is influenced by various factors, including our motivations and expectations (Gesheider, 1985). The lonely and desperate can often hear the telephone ring when others can't. We will discuss this further in the next chapter.

Given this sort of variability, how should we measure absolute thresholds? The answer is somewhat arbitrary. By convention, psychologists define the absolute threshold for a particular person as the intensity of the stimulus at which that person detects the stimulus 50% of the time. A common procedure for determining this measure runs as follows. An experimenter exposes the subject to various intensities of a stimulus in no set order. Each intensity level is presented numerous times. For each intensity level, the experimenter records the percentage of times the subject detects the stimulus. The relationship between the intensity level of the stimulus and the percentage of accurate detections is an example of a psychometric function. In general, a **psychometric function** is a pattern of human functioning that has been measured. Figure 3-3 is a graph of a typical psychometric function. We see that the results do not include a straight line marking the threshold. In other words, in practice there is not an abrupt change at the threshold. On the contrary, a person's accuracy in detecting a stimulus usually increases gradually, as indicated by the S-shaped curve in Figure 3-3.

Figure 3-3 A psychometric function
This curve represents a psychometric function showing a zone of transition from no detection of the stimulus to 100% accuracy in detecting the stimulus. The 50% accuracy point is arbitrarily designated as the threshold.

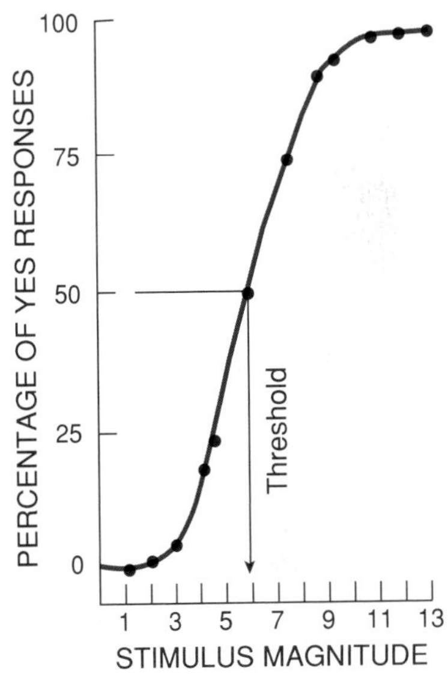

Difference threshold

Suppose someone puts two feathers on your hand. Would you be able to tell which is heavier? How different would their weights have to be before you could discriminate between them—before you could tell them apart? This difference would be your difference threshold.

The minimal difference in intensity between two stimuli needed to tell them apart is called the **difference threshold**. This minimal difference is also known as the **just noticeable difference (JND)**.

Like the absolute threshold, the difference threshold varies from person to person and from time to time. For example, if a person is fatigued or aroused, the JND will be affected. Background stimulation can also increase the JND. It is harder to discriminate between two specific sounds in a noisy room. Again, by convention, psychologists have agreed to define the difference threshold for a particular person as the minimal difference that person can detect 50% of the time.

FIGURE 3-4 **Difference thresholds (JND) ratios for several sense modalities**

SOURCE: Adapted from Schiffman (1976).

Sense modality	JND ratio
Weight	1:50
Loudness	1:10
Brightness	1:60
Pressure on skin	1:7
Pain (heat) on skin	1:30
Salty taste	1:3

The JND also varies in proportion to the intensity of the initial stimulus. Thus, the JND increases (or decreases) when the intensity of the original stimulus increases (or decreases). You can probably easily tell the difference between a 10-gram weight and a 20-gram weight. But we would be wrong to conclude that 10 grams exceeds your difference threshold for weight. We have to take into account the intensity or magnitude of the initial weight. For instance, you probably would not be able to discriminate between a 4000-gram weight and a 4010-gram weight. The work of the German psychologist Ernst Weber (pronounced VAY-bear) during the early 1800s led to the discovery that there is a constant ratio between stimulus intensity and the difference threshold. Thus, if you can just detect the difference between 1000 grams and 1020 grams (a 20-gram JND), we would have to add 40 grams to a 2000 gram weight before you could tell the difference. The ratio between stimulus intensity and JND remains the same (constant). This is called **Weber's Law**. However, it is a little exaggerated to call this a "law." The ratio does hold for a wide range of values, but not for extremely intense and extremely weak stimuli (Carlson, Drury, & Webber, 1977).

The ratio of Weber's Law is different for different types of stimuli. For weight, the ratio (or JND) is about 1:50. That means the difference between 50 grams and 51 grams is just detectable. For sound intensity, however, the ratio is 1:10. In other words, the intensity of a sound must increase by 1/10 for the change to be detectable. Other senses have different ratios. Figure 3-4 illustrates different threshold ratios for different sense modalities.

Adaptation and context

An important feature of our nervous system is **sensory adaptation**, the process by which sensory systems reduce their responses to prolonged, unchanging stimuli. If a person climbs into a hot bath, the water is almost painfully hot at first. After a few minutes of soaking, the person no longer experiences the water as hot, even though its actual temperature has changed little. The person's neurons (in this case the temperature receptors) decrease their firing to steady-state (unchanging) stimuli. In other words, they adapt to such stimuli. Our other sensory systems also adapt. If we enter a room which has a strong odour, our nose quickly adapts even to an unpleasant smell, which then seems to disappear. A new person might enter the room and surprise us by expressing disgust at the odour. Again, the nervous system has adapted to the steady-state stimulus with reduced firing. Sensory adaptation has evolutionary survival value, because we normally need to be less vigilant for unchanging stimuli than for new stimuli.

One consequence of sensory adaptation is that our experience of a stimulus depends in part on what we were experiencing before it was introduced. According to the so-called **context effect**, the sensation of a new stimulus is affected by the stimuli immediately preceding it. Sometimes the effect is quite dramatic. For example, many of us have probably experienced the sensation of heat after running cold water over extremely cold fingers. The pre-existing condition of temperature receptors provides the context for the later processing of new stimulation. Another way to demonstrate this is to have three pails of water: one ice-cold, one lukewarm, and one hot. Leave your right hand in the cold and the left in the hot for several minutes. Then plunge both hands into the lukewarm water. You will have the strange sensation that the same water feels hot with your right hand and cold with your left. There are many ways in which our sensations can be misinterpreted because of the context in which they occur. We will discuss other examples in Chapter 4, Perception.

The area of study in which we investigate the biology of how we make contact with the world is known as *sensory physiology*. Here we try to understand the neural mechanisms responsible for converting physical energy into the electrochemical energy of our nervous system. Let's now explore this conversion process by examining our sensory systems individually.

VISION

As humans evolved, vision was the most important sense for survival. So it is no surprise that more of the brain should be devoted to seeing than to any other sensory system. Nor is it surprising that for many of us, vision is our most powerful sense.

Properties of light

Electromagnetic energy is energy that radiates from a source as tiny packets or units called *electrons*. Electrons are negatively charged particles that circle atoms. When these electrons bounce out of their orbits, electromagnetic waves travel off through space. Electromagnetic energy varies in terms of *wavelength* (i.e., the distance from the trough of one wave to the trough of the next wave). Some wavelengths, such as radio waves, range from hundreds of metres to many kilometres in length. At the other end of the scale are cosmic rays such as gamma rays that are only trillionths of a centimetre long. The entire range of energy waves created by the release of electrons from atoms is called the **electromagnetic spectrum**.

Figure 3-5 illustrates that what we call visible light forms only a small part of the electromagnetic spectrum. Moreover, the length of visible wavelengths is so short that scientists measure it in terms of a special unit known as a nanometre. One **nanometre (nm)** equals one billionth (10^{-9}) of a metre. Visible light is the same kind of energy as radar, x-rays, and radio waves. Light differs from them only in the length of the waves formed by the energy. We define some electromagnetic energy as light simply because it is what human eyes can sense. Our visual systems evolved to sense this narrow band of the electromagnetic spectrum because it promoted survival of the species. Exactly how we sense this energy is a function of the three properties of light: hue, intensity, and purity.

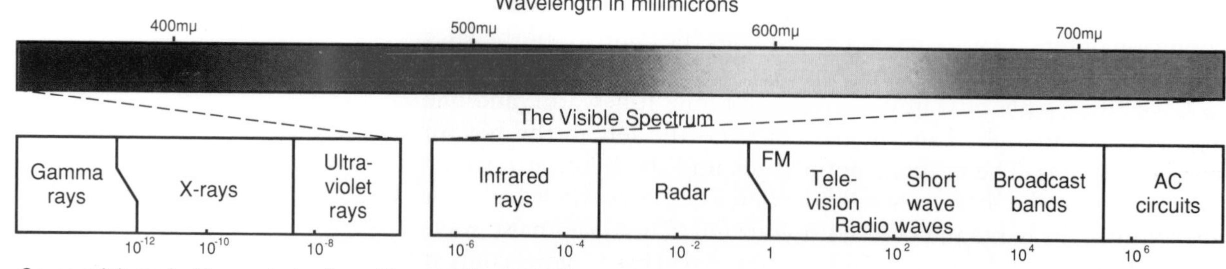

SOURCE: Adapted with permission from Allyn and Bacon, 1989.

FIGURE 3-5 The electromagnetic spectrum
The entire range of electromagnetic wavelengths is known as the electromagnetic spectrum. At one extreme are radio waves, whose length from crest to crest can exceed thousands of metres. At the other extreme are tiny gamma rays, whose length is unimaginably small: ten-trillionths of a metre. The human eye is sensitive to only a small part of the spectrum, from 350 nanometres to 750 nanometres.

Hue

We sense light of a given wavelength as a specific colour or **hue**. The wavelength at 500 nanometres will be seen as green, while energy with the longer wave pattern of 700 nanometres will be seen as red.

Intensity

Another property of light is its **intensity**, which is perceived as brightness. Intensity is determined by the amount of energy in the electromagnetic waves. The more electrons that reach the eye's receptors per second, the more intense the light.

Purity

The **purity** of a light wave refers to its composition of wavelengths or the purity of its hue. Some light may consist predominantly of one wavelength or hue. Other light may be a mixture of several different wavelengths. If the eye receives only one wavelength, the colour will be sharp and "pure." If other wavelengths are mixed in, the colour will be duller. A very pure colour is called *highly saturated*.

Structure of the eye

The main structures of the eye are shown in cross-section in Figure 3-6. The eyeball, approximately 2.5 cm in diameter, sits within a protective bony socket called the **orbit**. The eyeball is sheltered from damaging external stimuli by an eyelid that closes reflexively when the eye is threatened. The *extraocular* ("outside the eye") *muscles* are connected to the eyeball in three different bundles. They move the eye around by contracting and relaxing in various combinations. The outer white layer of the eyeball, called the **sclera**, is extremely tough. It contains receptors for pressure, pain, and temperature. The sclera forms the "whites of the eyes."

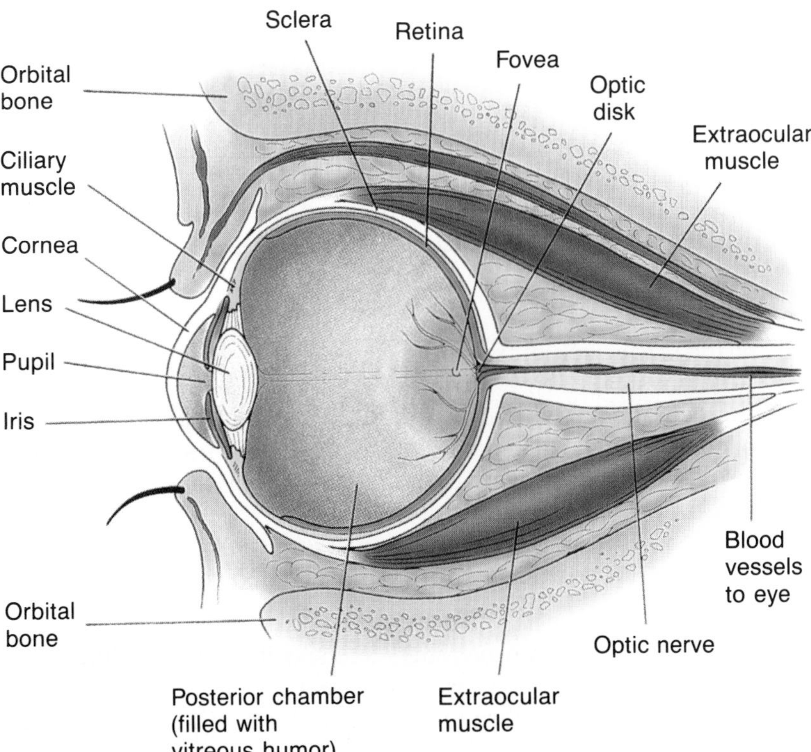

SOURCE: Adapted with permission from Allyn and Bacon, 1989.

FIGURE 3-6 A cross section of the human eye

The eye is a remarkable structure. It allows light waves to enter in controlled amounts. Then it focuses the light on the appropriate receptors, thereby beginning the process of sensation and perception. Let us follow this course of events step by step.

Light first enters the **cornea**, which is a slightly protruding, transparent coating on the front of the eye. The cornea is responsible for the initial bending of the light so that it can be focused clearly on the inner portions of the eye. From the cornea, light passes through a small, circular aperture called the **pupil**, which is an opening in the coloured portion of the eye, the **iris**. The size of the pupil, which is controlled by muscles in the iris, determines the amount of light that enters the eye. In bright light, the pupil is relatively small or constricted. In dim light, the pupil is relatively large or dilated. This mechanism guards the sensitive inner eye structures from being flooded with light or not receiving enough light.

After the light passes through the pupil, it crosses the lens. The **lens** is a flexible, transparent, inner structure that focuses light on the retina at the back of the eye. The shape of the lens can be adjusted by *ciliary muscles*. These muscles stretch and squeeze the lens to the right shape for focusing the light. These fine adjustments to the shape of the lens are called **accommodation**. The lens reverses and inverts the visual image so that the retina receives a picture of the world that is upside-down and backward. Those who are nearsighted or farsighted have difficulty changing the lens to precisely the right shape to focus light on the retina. Wearing glasses or contact lenses can compensate for difficulties with accommodation. (Artificial lenses provide the extra bending of the light necessary to yield a clear image on the retina.) After the light goes through the eye's lens, it is focused, inverted, and reversed. Then, the light passes through a large, inner cavity (known as the *posterior chamber*) that is filled with a transparent, jelly-like substance called the *vitreous humour* ("glassy fluid"). Finally, the light reaches the retina at the back of the eye, where actual sensation will begin.

The retina

The **retina** is the back inner surface of the eye where light is sensed. Here, the physical energy carried in the light waves is transformed into the neural code which the brain can process. This transformation occurs through specialized nerve cells (neurons), called **photoreceptors**, which are specifically designed to receive light wave energy. Through chemical reactions, they transduce (transform) the physical energy into the electrochemical energy of the nervous system. The retina contains approximately 120 million of these photoreceptors.

There are two kinds of photoreceptors, rods and cones. Their names come from the shape of the cells. **Rods** are a long and narrow type of photoreceptor. They are sensitive to light of low intensity, and therefore they are used for seeing in relatively dark environments (e.g., for night vision). Rods can distinguish between black, white, and various shades of grey. But they cannot distinguish between different hues (colours). By contrast, **cones** are a cone-shaped type of photoreceptor. Unlike rods, the cones are sensitive to different hues. Thus, they enable us to see colour. Furthermore, cones are less sensitive than rods to light intensity. Therefore, they work well in bright light and are responsible for providing fine detail to visual images. Rods and cones also differ from one another in number. Of the 120 million photoreceptors in each retina, only about 6 million are cones.

The rods and cones are not distributed evenly across the retina (see Figure 3-7). Moreover, most of the 6 million cones are located in the centre of vision, directly behind the lens in an area of the retina called the **fovea**. When we need to focus on a task that requires fine discriminations, such as looking through a microscope, we use central vision. We should try to perform such tasks in bright light so that the cones of the fovea will be activated. A telescope is difficult to use in dim light because our centrally located cones do not work well in the dark.

Unlike the cones, the rods are more densely distributed toward the outer edges of the retina. There are no rods at all in the fovea. You may have had the experience of seeing an object clearly with peripheral vision under dark conditions. However, when you looked directly at the object, it became much less distinct. In dim light, the greater sensitivity of the rods in peripheral vision provide a clearer image than do the cones in the central portion of vision.

Figure 3-8 illustrates that there are three levels of neurons in the retina. The backmost layer consists of photoreceptors, which respond to light. Therefore, the light must pass through layers of two

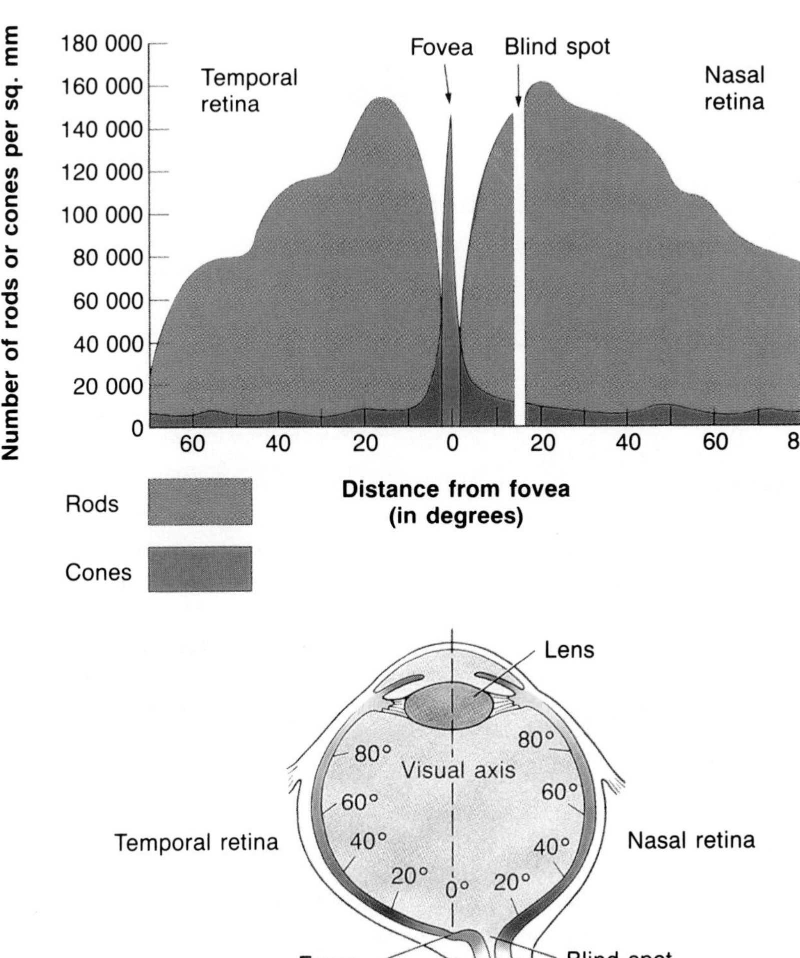

FIGURE 3-7 The densities of rods and cones across the retina

SOURCE: Adapted with permission from Allyn and Bacon, 1989.

other kinds of cells and a maze of blood vessels that lace the retina before it reaches the rods and cones where it can be sensed. The middle layer of the retina consists of **bipolar cells**, which relay signals from the photoreceptors to the top level of the retina. Each bipolar cell forms synapses with more than one photoreceptor. The top layer of the retina consists of **ganglion cells**. Each ganglion cell forms synapses with several bipolar cells. Thus a ganglion cell can receive information from many different photoreceptors. There are only about one million ganglion cells in all. The axons of the ganglion cells form the fibres of the **optic nerve**, which carries the visual information to the brain.

As indicated in Figure 3-8, light must pass through the layer of ganglion cells and then through the layer of bipolar cells before it reaches the photoreceptors. And yet the response to this stimulus (which occurs in the photoreceptor cells first) must then pass back through the bipolar cells and on to the ganglion cells before a message can be sent along the optic nerve to the brain.

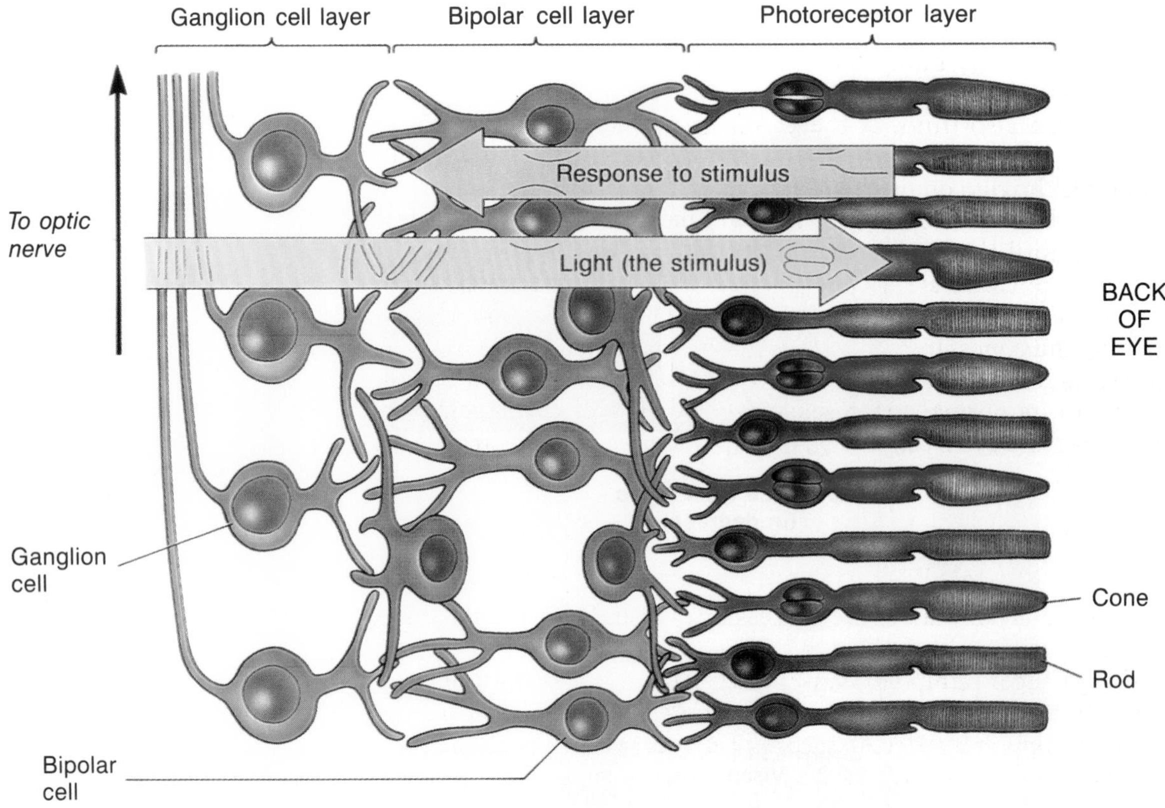

SOURCE: Adapted with permission from Allyn and Bacon, 1989.

FIGURE 3-8 The cells of the retina
The retina, which performs the sensory functions of the eye, consists of three principal layers. Light passes successively through the outermost ganglion cell layer, the middle bipolar cell layer, and the innermost photoreceptor layer. Photoreceptors respond to light and pass the information to the bipolar cells by means of a transmitter substance. Bipolar cells transmit this information to the ganglion cells, neurons whose axons travel across the retina and through the optic nerves to the brain.

Adaptation

How does sensory adaptation work when applied to brightness (i.e., light intensity)? When we enter a dark theatre on a sunny day, it is usually necessary to stop for a moment before finding an empty seat; we need to wait until our eyes "adjust." If we have to sit in the dark for some time before the movie begins, we become able to see more and more clearly. The process by which the eyes become more sensitive to light under dim or dark conditions is called **dark adaptation**. It occurs because rods and cones have different sensitivity to the intensity of light. Rods are much more sensitive than cones to light. In bright light, the photochemicals in the rods break down or bleach out to such an extent that we are relying almost totally on cones for vision. When we enter the theatre, both the rods and cones begin to restore the photochemicals that were bleached out in the brighter light. This process is faster for the cones, which function well in the bright light. However, because cones are not very sensitive to low light, we are without the use of the cones while the rods have not yet recovered from the bright light. Thus, for a very brief period, we are temporarily blind. As the rods restore their photochemicals, vision in the dark improves.

We can also think of these changes working in the opposite direction. The process by which the eyes become less sensitive to light under bright conditions is known as **light adaptation**. When we leave the dark theatre, the sunlight will be almost painful for a few minutes, until the visual pigment in the rods rapidly bleaches out and only the cones are active. There is a delicate balance between the processes of bleaching out and restoring the visual pigments in the rods and cones. Imagine driving at night when an oncoming car flashes its highbeams at you. It takes some time before your vision returns to its normal night sensitivity because of the momentary flooding of the eye by light and the rapid, but short-lived, bleaching of the rods.

Neural pathways

A considerable amount of the processing of visual information takes place in the retina itself. The 120 million photoreceptors feed into a smaller number of bipolar cells, which feed into a smaller number of ganglion cells, until about one million ganglion axons leave the eye in the optic nerve. This means that even though each photoreceptor cell responds only to the light that reaches it, any one ganglion cell can fire in response to information received from many photoreceptors. The area of the retina that relays signals to a particular ganglion cell is called that cell's **receptive field**.

After leaving the retina, axons from the ganglion cells join to form the fibres of the optic nerve. The area at the back of the eye through which the optic nerve exits is called the **optic disk**. (See Figure 3-9.) It is also known as the **blind spot** because it does not contain any rods or cones and hence is completely insensitive to light. How is it that we have a blind spot in each eye but no blank spaces in the reality we perceive? Remember that our perceived reality is a construction. Our perceptual processes fill in the blind spot and create the illusion of a continuous picture. To convince yourself of this, you can do the exercises in Figure 3-10. In the top picture, you can find your blind spot and make the X invisible. In the bottom picture, you can line up the break in the line so that it falls on your blind spot. Even though you know the line is broken, your brain will "fill in" the black spot and you will perceive an unbroken line.

As the optic nerve extends toward the back of the brain, it enters the *optic chiasm*. As you will recall from Chapter 2, the **optic chiasm** is the point at which the axons in the optic nerve from the inside portion of each retina cross over to the opposite side of the brain. (You may find it helpful to review Figure 2-13.) Thus, each retina sends information to both hemispheres of the brain. Visual information is relayed to the *occipital lobe* at the back of the brain for processing. While perceptual organization of visual information occurs at many levels in the brain, with vision, as with all the other senses, the information becomes conscious fairly late in the process, when the signals reach the cortex.

FIGURE 3-9 Neural connections in the visual region

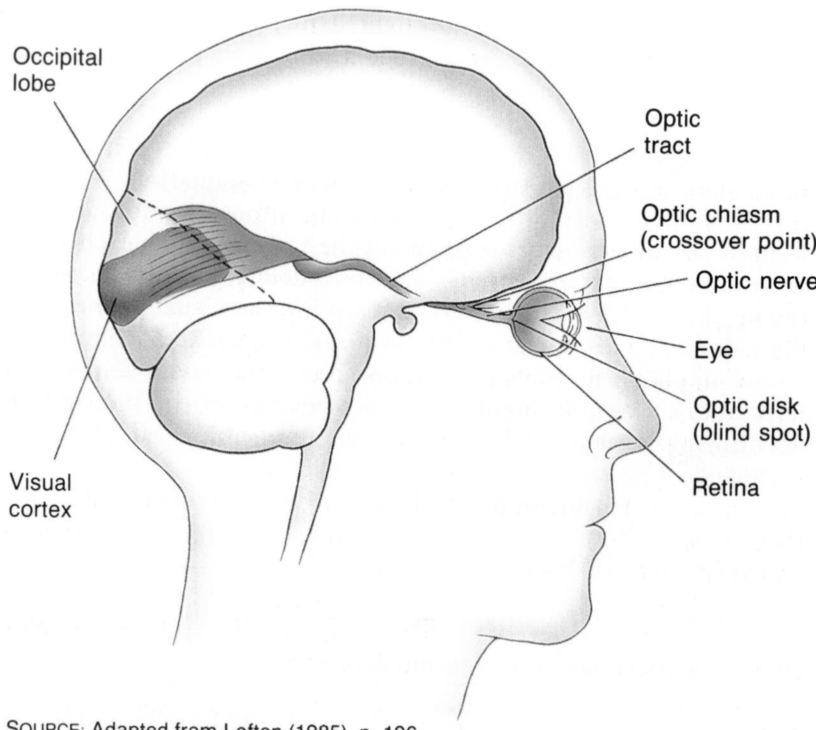

SOURCE: Adapted from Lefton (1985), p. 196.

The visual cortex

As we move deeper into the visual system, neurons become more and more specialized. The **visual cortex** is that area in the occipital lobe of the brain where visual information is processed. It appears to contain three kinds of specialized neurons: *simple cells, complex cells*, and *hypercomplex cells*. Each kind of cell has a different role in the visual perception of patterns. The discovery of these cells was so important to our understanding of vision that David Hubel and Torsten Wiesel (1979) won the Nobel prize for medicine in 1981 for their research on them.

Simple cells are neurons of the visual cortex that are specialized to detect stationary lines or edges at specific orientations in the visual field. They are sometimes called **edge detectors**, because most of the lines we see in the environment are in fact the edges that mark the

FIGURE 3-10 Finding your blind spot

Close your right eye and stare at the cross in Diagram A. Hold the book about 30 cm from your eye and slowly move it towards you and then away from you. At some point the X on the left will disappear because its image is projected on the blind spot in your left eye. Then do the same exercise with Diagram B. Stare at the cross and move the book until the blank spot in the line disappears. You will see the line as unbroken because your brain will "fill in" the blind spot.

boundaries of objects. Some simple cells are specialized to respond to horizontal lines, some to vertical lines, and others to lines at specific angles. If you look at a pencil in front of you and slowly rotate it to different angles, you will be switching rapidly among the simple cells you are using in your occipital lobe. If an animal is reared in an environment with no edges to detect, these cells seem to die off, with the result that the animal cannot discriminate lines from each other. Simple cells are so specialized that this effect seems to be specific to the angles one sees during development. If a kitten is raised in a way that it never sees diagonal lines, as a cat it will be blind to diagonal lines (Mitchell, 1981).

Complex cells are neurons of the visual cortex that are specialized to detect moving lines at specific orientations in the visual field. For example, some complex cells respond most to vertical lines moving sideways, whereas others respond most to diagonal lines moving up and down. **Hypercomplex cells** are neurons of the visual cortex that are specialized to detect moving lines at specific orientations and at specific angles in the visual field. They can be so specialized that a given cell might respond only to lines at an 80-degree angle moving in a diagonal direction. The complex cells and hypercomplex cells are sometimes called **motion detectors.**

In our description, we have deliberately oversimplified the activity of the visual cortex. With millions of neural cells firing together in patterns, the visual cortex is able to construct something like an "outline drawing" of the patterns seen by the eye. No one cell can sense an entire visual image. Thousands of these cells must work together in any one instant. This intricate play of neural firings forms the foundation on which the brain constructs the perceived image. But we do not yet fully understand how the brain synthesizes all this information.

Aftereffects

Knowing that there are motion detectors in the visual cortex helps us understand the phenomenon of aftereffects of visual movement. An **aftereffect** is the illusory perception of motion in a stationary object that occurs after one has been staring at another object moving continuously in the opposite direction. You can demonstrate this phenomenon to yourself quite easily. Stare at a record rotating clockwise on a turntable for several minutes. Then, look at the floor. You will have a strong sensation that a round area in the floor is rotating counterclockwise. The same phenomenon will happen if you watch a waterfall and then look away at the riverbank. The riverbank will seem to be moving up.

Aftereffects occur because specific motion detectors become fatigued. Normally our clockwise-moving motion detectors and our counterclockwise-moving motion detectors balance each other's effects, and the world holds still for us. When we fatigue one set, the opposing set takes over temporarily and we "see" motion that is not occurring. We know that this effect is taking place in the brain and not in the eye. If we stare at the record with one eye, we can get the aftereffect by later looking at the floor with the other eye.

Colour vision

We are capable of distinguishing approximately 150 different pure hues. However, if we take into consideration variations in purity and intensity, we can differentiate among more than 7 million colour shades. Nevertheless, by definition, there are only three **primary colours**: pure red, pure green, and pure blue. The hundreds of thousands of shades of colours that humans can discriminate can be produced by combinations of the three primary colours. A colour television monitor, for example, has three electronic "guns" that shoot colour on the screen. Each produces only red, green, or blue light, but we see virtually all the possible shades of colours on the screen as the three primary colours combine. White light results when all wavelengths combine. Actually, white light can be produced by the combination of particular pairs of colours. Two colours are called **complementary colours** if they produce white or grey when combined. As suggested by the *colour wheel* in Figure 3-11, each hue has a complement.

There are two major theories of how we see colour: the trichromatic theory and the opponent-process theory. Although they offer different explanations for colour vision, we will see that they are compatible with each other. Trichromatic theory focuses on the rods and cones, whereas opponent-process theory focuses on the ganglion cells.

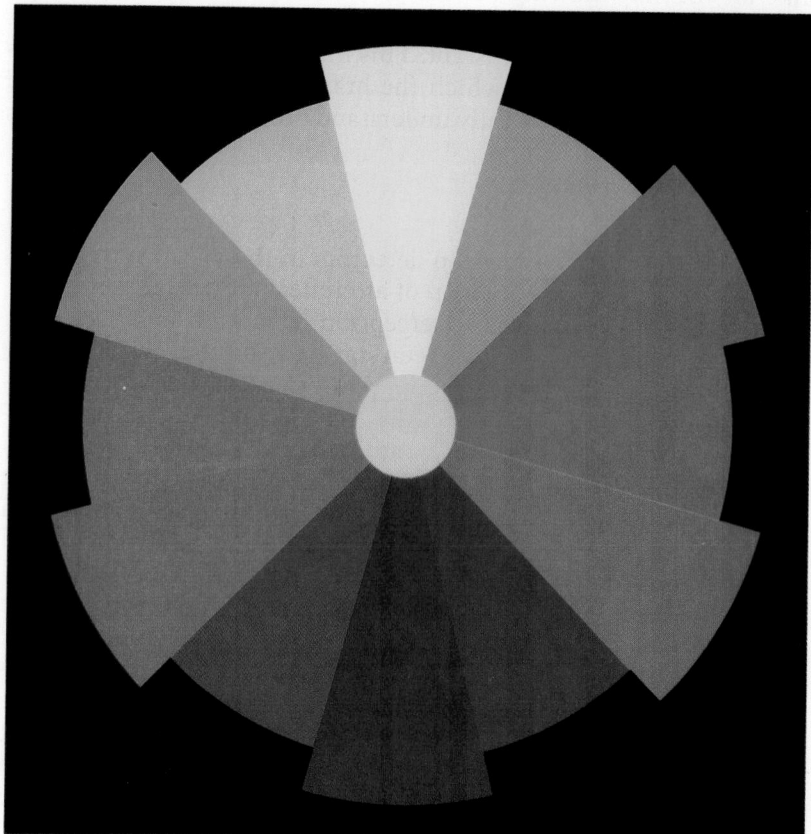

FIGURE 3-11 A standard colour wheel

The colours opposite each other are complementary colours. This means that when they are combined, they produce white or grey light.

SOURCE: Color wheel from *The PANTONE® Book of Color* by Eiseman and Herbert © 1990. Published by Abrams.

The trichromatic theory of colour vision

As early as the 1800s, some researchers theorized that there are three kinds of cones, each sensitive to one of the primary hues, red, green, and blue. This theory of colour vision is known as the **trichromatic theory**. It wasn't until the 1960s, however, that evidence was found to support this theory (Marks, Dobelle, & MacNichol, 1964). Three types of cones were identified by means of different molecular structures in their visual pigments. These molecules absorb different wavelengths of light and each type is most efficient at absorbing red, green, or blue. The neural signals from these three kinds of cones combine to produce the sensation of all the colours we can see.

The opponent-process theory of colour vision

The trichromatic theory explains colour mixing, but it does not explain some visual phenomena that we will discuss shortly, such as negative afterimages. Therefore, in the 1880s, Ewald Hering (1920) proposed another explanation known as the opponent-process theory, and subsequently others have expanded it (Hurvich & Jameson, 1957; DeValois & DeValois, 1975). According to the **opponent-process theory**, there are three systems in colour vision: a red/green system and a yellow/blue system for hue and purity, and a black/white system for intensity. Within each system, the two members work in opposition to each other. Thus, they are literally "opponent" processes. Each system is represented by a type of ganglion cell. Thus, we have red/green ganglion cells, yellow/blue ganglion cells, and black/white ganglion cells. This theory builds on trichromatic theory because it describes what happens to the ganglion cells after the photoreceptors (the rods and cones) are stimulated.

Figure 3-12 demonstrates how the stimulation of each kind of cone affects each kind of ganglion cell. The red/green ganglion cells produce the sensation of red when they are *excited* (fire quickly) and green when they are *inhibited* (fire slowly). This is why we cannot see a reddish-green colour. The red/green ganglion cells cannot fire both quickly and slowly at the same time. Similarly, we cannot see yellowish-blue. However, we can see a reddish-blue colour. Figure 3-12 shows how stimulation from cones sensitive to red excite the red/green ganglion cells and inhibit the yellow/blue ganglion cells to produce the sensation of reddish-blue. Green-sensitive cones, on the other hand, inhibit both kinds of ganglion cells. Blue-sensitive cones only act to excite the yellow/blue ganglion cells. All three kinds of cone excite the black/white ganglion cells. Combinations of the millions of firings of these ganglion cells produce all the colours we can see.

Afterimages

The opponent-process theory helps explain the phenomenon of afterimages. An **afterimage** is the sensation of light after the light source has terminated. For example, when a flashbulb goes off in front of us, for several seconds afterward we experience "seeing" spots of white and black. The white spots are **positive afterimages** (same

FIGURE 3-12 Hypothetical connections between the three types of cones and the three types of ganglion cells according to the opponent-process theory
This figure indicates the effects from stimulation of each type of cone on the firing of each type of ganglion cell. The arrows do not imply direct neural connections, only effects, and show why we never see a reddish green or yellowish blue.

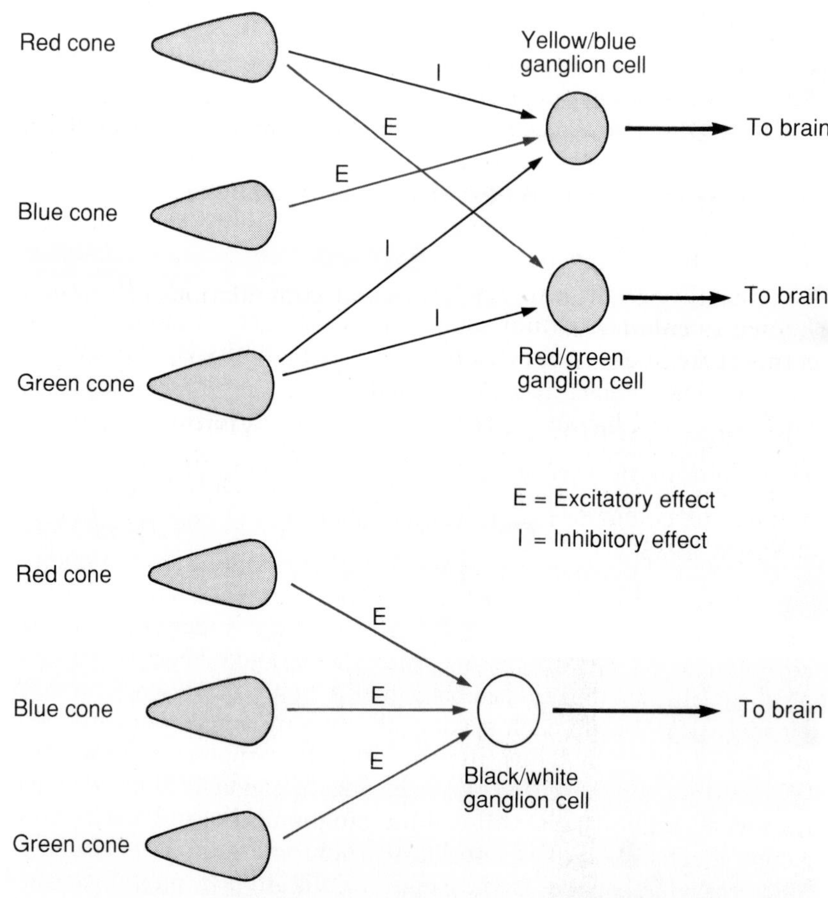

SOURCE: Adapted with permission from Allyn and Bacon, 1989.

colour as the light source), and the black spots are **negative afterimages** ("opponent" colour of the light source). The positive afterimages occur because our receptors have been so strongly stimulated that they continue to fire. The explanation of the negative afterimages is a little more elaborate.

A negative afterimage is the sensation of colour which is the opponent of the colour at which one has been staring. (Note that opponent colours are complementary.) You can demonstrate this for yourself by doing the exercise in Figure 3-13. Stare at the dot in the middle of the black and green flag for 45 seconds. Then quickly look away to the dot in the white part of the page. You should "see" the familiar white and red of the maple leaf. Staring at green fatigued the green system of your red/green ganglion cells. Thus, red was no longer counterbalanced and you "saw" red. Similarly, with the black and white pair, we can surmise that the black system became fatigued. By the same token, the afterimage of the flagpole is yellow, since blue system cells were fatigued by looking at the blue flagpole.

The mechanism responsible for afterimages occurs in a different location than the mechanism responsible for aftereffects of motion which we discussed earlier. Motion aftereffects occur because motion detectors are fatigued in the *brain*. Colour afterimages occur because ganglion cells are fatigued in the *eye*. Thus, an aftereffect created by looking at a moving object with one eye can be seen by looking at a stationary object with the other eye. Afterimages, on the other hand, will only occur in the eye that stares at the target object. You can prove this to yourself by staring at the flag in Figure 3-13 with one eye. You will get the afterimage only in that eye.

Colour blindness

The inability to discriminate particular combinations of colour is known as **colour blindness** or **colour deficiency**. It occurs in many forms and degrees. The inability to see colour normally is inherited as a sex-linked characteristic. We will discuss sex-linked characteristics more in Chapter 12. But for our purposes here, it is sufficient to note that females can carry genes for colour deficiency but are very unlikely to have impaired colour vision. Only half of 1% of females are colour deficient, whereas about 8% of men are (Pokorny & Smith, 1986).

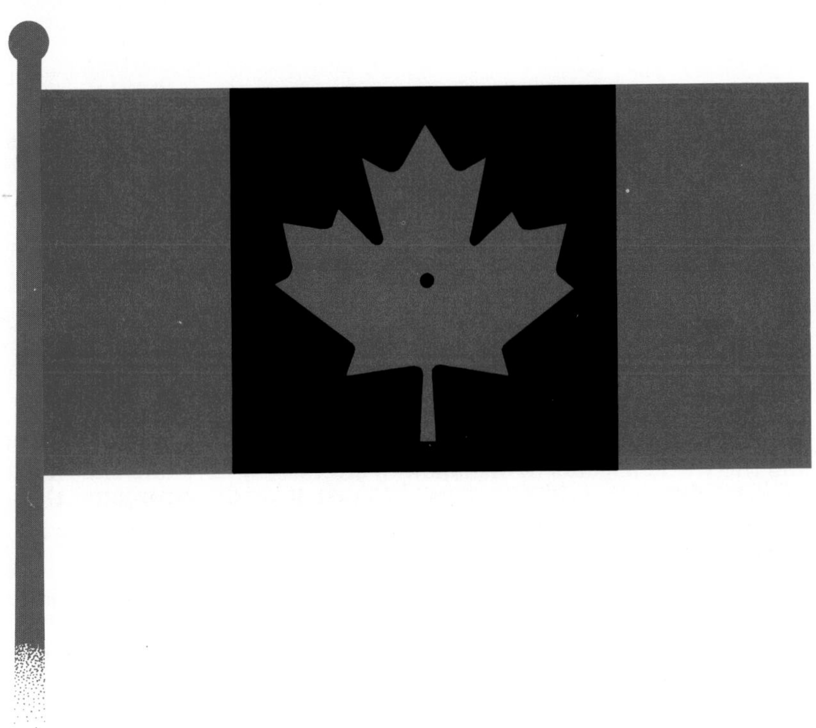

FIGURE 3-13 Afterimages
To see how afterimages work, stare at the dot in the middle of the flag for about 45 seconds. Then stare at the dot in the white space below. You should see an afterimage of a normal Canadian flag. The afterimage of green will be red and the afterimage of black will be white. The flagpole should appear yellow in the afterimage.

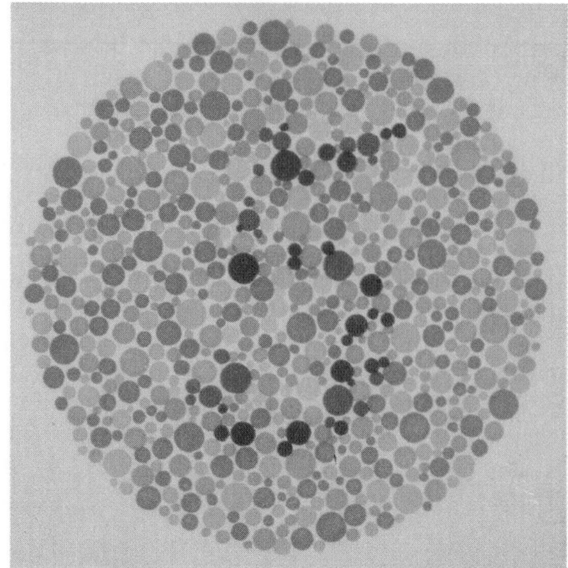

FIGURE 3-14 Testing for colour deficiency (colour blindness)
A person with red-green colour deficiency will not be able to perceive the number 5 in this figure.
SOURCE: The Stock Shop/Grace Moore

The patterns found for colour deficiency are consistent with the trichromatic theory. As this theory predicts, there are three general types of colour deficiency. Each type is associated with the malfunction of one kind of cone. In red-green colour blindness or deficiency, the person cannot distinguish red from green, suggesting the loss of red cones. See the colour deficiency test in Figure 3-14. Red and green both appear yellow, as we know from those rare individuals who are red-green colour deficient only in one eye (Graham & Hsia, 1958). Blue-cone colour deficiency is very rare but does occur. There are also rare cases in which only one type of cone functions, and the world appears in black and white. Even more rare and much more serious are cases in which no cones function. Not only is the world black and white, but the person is nearly blind during the day because rods don't function well in bright light. In addition, the person has poor visual acuity, since fine discriminations are normally made by the cones at the fovea.

HEARING

Hearing, or *audition* (the process of hearing), is, for most of us, one of our primary means of relating to other humans. Much of human interaction depends on speaking to others and hearing what they say to us. If this was true before the telephone was invented, it is even more true now. Hearing may be less important than vision in negotiating the environment, but without hearing we are vulnerable to dangers from behind and out of sight. We need to understand hearing and the new dangers threatening it in today's noisy environment.

What is sound?

Sound consists of vibrations in a medium. Most sound results from vibrations of air molecules that reach our ears in waves. As a wave of sound moves outward from its source, molecules of air are compressed together and then expand to press against other molecules of air. For example, when a guitar string is set vibrating, it causes waves or pulses of air to travel away from it. If the string vibrates 8000 times a second, then 8000 waves of dense air followed by thin air will hit our eardrum, and we will hear a fairly high note. If 200 waves hit our ear per second, we will hear a very low note.

Sound can also travel through other media. A doctor may have tested your hearing by striking a tuning fork on the desk and then pressing it against a bone in your head. Although you may have been barely able to hear the sound at first, the tone likely became quite clear when the tuning fork touched your head. The vibrations in the air were weak, but the vibrations set up in your bones stimulated your auditory system. We can put an ear against a railroad track to hear if a train is coming because vibrations travel through the metal to make sound. These examples illustrate that sound must have a medium to travel through. The largest bell in the world would make no sound if it was ringing inside a vacuum jar. If a tree falls in the forest with no one there to hear it, there is sound because sound is defined as vibrations in the air. But if a tree were to fall on the moon there would be no sound, no matter how many people were there, because there is no air.

Sound travels at 340 metres per second, far more slowly than light, which travels at almost 300 000 kilometres per second. We can watch a carpenter pounding nails across the street and see that the hammer hits the nail an instant before we hear the sound of it. If we could time the interval between the sight and sound of the hammer blow, we could calculate the distance between us and the carpenter. As a child, you may have counted off the time between a lightning flash and the thunder that followed. Each three seconds means that the storm is about a kilometre away.

We define sound as having three basic characteristics: frequency (pitch), amplitude (loudness), and complexity (timbre). Figure 3-15 illustrates frequency and amplitude.

FIGURE 3-15 Characteristics of a sound wave: Frequency and amplitude

SOURCE: Adapted with permission from Allyn and Bacon, 1989.

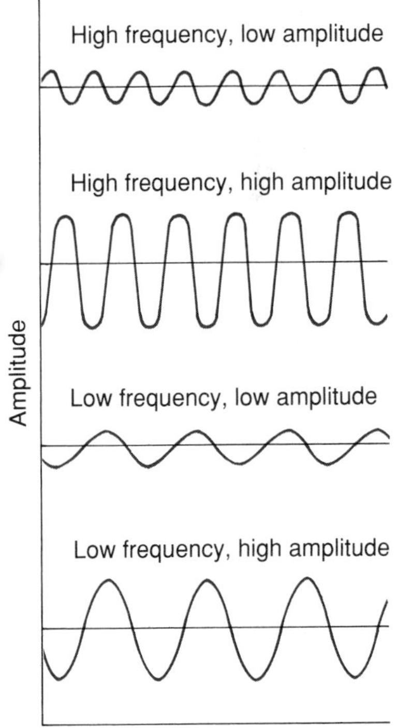

Frequency

The **frequency** of a sound is the speed at which air pressure waves reach the ear. It corresponds to the pitch ("highness" or "lowness") that we hear. When the waves are tightly packed together, the resultant high-frequency sound is shrill. Low-frequency sounds are low. As we noted earlier in this chapter, frequency is usually measured in *hertz* (*Hz*), which simply means "cycles per second." Normal human speech varies between about 100 and 3500 Hz (a high-pitched scream is about 3000–4000 Hz). The limits of human hearing range from about 20 Hz to 20 000 Hz. However, a dog can hear up to about 80 000 Hz.

FIGURE 3-16 A comparison of two sound waves of different complexity
a) The sound wave of a flute played softly at 488 hz.
b) The sound wave of a saxophone played moderately at 209 hz.
SOURCE: Jeans, (1937), plates VIII and IX.

a.

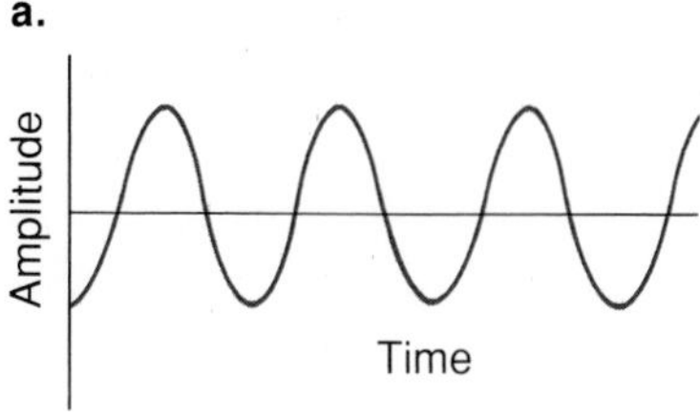

b.

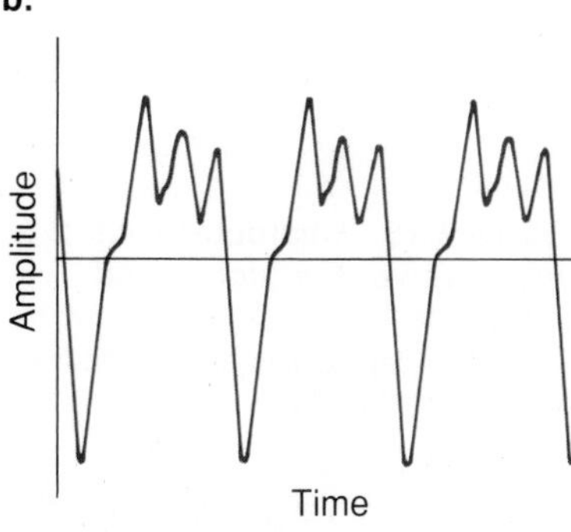

Amplitude

The **amplitude** of a sound is determined by the amount of pressure or intensity with which sound waves reach the ear. Amplitude corresponds to the loudness of a sound. If a sound is of high amplitude (loud), more air molecules hit the ear with each wave than if the sound is of low amplitude (soft). Loudness is measured in **decibels (dB)**. A gentle whisper is about 20 dB; conversation is about 60 dB; and standing next to a rock band is about 110 dB. The decibel scale is logarithmic, which means that for every increase of 20 decibels, the intensity of the sound increases by a factor of ten.

Complexity

Complexity is the purity or timbre of a sound. It is determined by the proportion of various frequencies which combine to form a particular sound. Very few sounds are "pure" in the sense that only one frequency occurs. (A tuning fork does produce a pure sound.) Usually there are other, less intense, frequencies (known as *overtones* or *harmonics*) that make the sound wave more complex. For example, a note played on a flute sounds different than the same note played on a saxophone. The flute's note consists primarily of one frequency, and its sound wave is smooth. By contrast, the saxophone's note incorporates several frequencies, and its sound wave contains prominent indentations. See Figure 3-16.

Structure of the ear

Our ear is the structure designed to capture sound waves and transduce them into the neural signals that we perceive as sounds. Figure 3-17 shows the major parts of the external and inner ear. The external ear is like a funnel that collects sound waves and channels them into and down the auditory canal. The **auditory canal** is the passageway that carries sound from the external ear into the inner ear. At the end of the auditory canal, the sound waves strike a thin membrane that is called the eardrum or **tympanic membrane**. Like the skin on a drum when the drum is hit, the tympanic membrane begins to vibrate. This mechanical energy is transmitted to the **ossicles**, three small bones called the **malleus**, **incus**, and **stapes** that are linked together in the middle ear. These Latin names describe the shape of these three bones: *malleus* means hammer, *incus* means anvil, and *stapes* means stirrup. The bones of the ossicles begin to vibrate and pass this vibration on to the cochlea.

The **cochlea** is a coiled, fluid-filled structure which is the primary hearing organ of the inner ear. The stapes is attached to a part of the cochlea called the **oval window** which vibrates in response to the ossicles and sets into motion the fluid contained in the cochlea. Running down the centre of the cochlea is a special band of tissue called the **basilar membrane**. It contains rows of cells with tiny hairs (*cilia*) protruding from them. Figure 3-17 illustrates the cochlea in its normal coiled position. Figure 3-18 shows how the cochlea would look if it were partially uncoiled and cut away to display the basilar membrane. The cochlear fluid vibrates in waves that bend the specialized cilia in the basilar membrane. It is this act of bending the

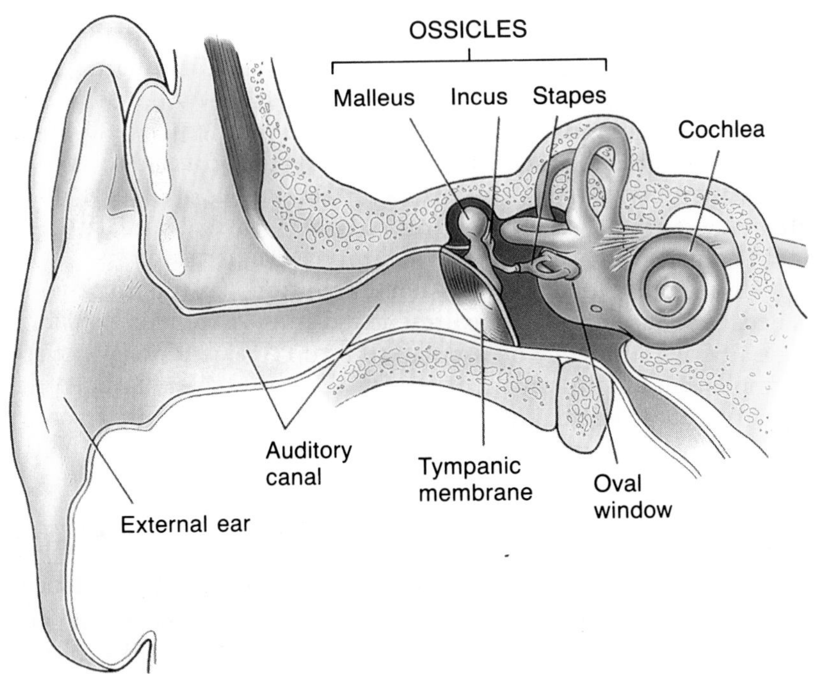

FIGURE 3-17 Anatomy of the auditory system
The tympanic membrane responds to sound waves and passes the vibrations on to the ossicles. The vibrations are then transmitted to the oval window and on into the cochlea.

cilia that stimulates neural firings of receptor cells in the basilar membrane. The impulses are then transmitted along the auditory nerve to the auditory cortex of the temporal lobe.

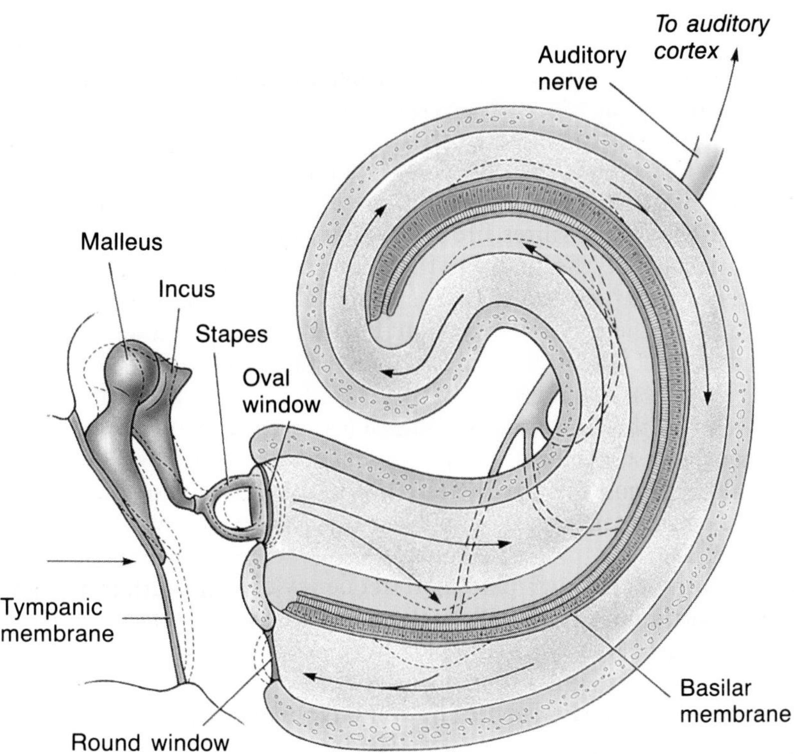

FIGURE 3-18 Structure of the middle and inner ear
In this diagram, the cochlea is shown as if it is partially uncoiled.

Hearing loudness

Loudness, as we have seen, is a function of the pressure with which sound waves strike the ear. We know that loudness cannot be caused by individual neurons firing more or less strongly (remember the all-or-none principle discussed in Chapter 2). In fact, loudness is coded in the auditory system by increases in the number of hairs that are deformed on the basilar membrane. Louder sounds deform more of these hairs and thus cause more auditory nerve fibres to fire.

Excessively loud noise or "noise pollution," as it is commonly called, can cause hearing impairment and stress. Extended exposure, over a period of eight hours or so, to 80 dB (inside a noisy car, for example) can cause permanent hearing damage. At very loud levels, impairment can occur after only a few minutes. There is also research showing that constant loud noise in the workplace can produce harmful psychological effects (Glass & Singer, 1972).

Hearing different pitches: Place versus frequency theory

As we listen to speech and music, we can hear very subtle differences in pitch. There are two major theories of how we register this difference. **Place theory**, the first of these theories, proposes that sound waves of different frequencies stimulate different places on the basilar membrane of the cochlea. For example, high-frequency waves tend to stimulate areas in the basilar membrane close to the oval window. Low-frequency sounds stimulate areas at the far end of the basilar membrane. Place theory helps explain how a person can be deaf to only certain tones or frequencies. In these cases, place theory would say that the basilar membrane or its cilia are damaged at one location. However, this explanation is not entirely satisfactory. Research has shown that some tones, particularly low-frequency ones, are registered at multiple sites along the basilar membrane. This finding is inconsistent with place theory.

Frequency theory is the second explanation of the coding of pitch. According to **frequency theory**, there is a direct correspondence between the frequency of the sound wave and the frequency of neural firing. With low sounds, the cilia are bent more slowly, and hence the auditory nerve fibres fire more slowly. As the frequency of the sound increases, the neurons fire more rapidly. The problem with frequency theory is that there is a limit to how fast auditory neurons can fire. The theory cannot account for our perception of high-pitched sounds. One attempt to extend frequency theory is the **volley principle** which says that groups or "squads" of neurons fire in sequence in response to high-pitched sounds. Even though one nerve fibre cannot fire faster than 1000 times a second, it might have "partners" that also fire quickly and in sequence with it. Even this volley principle, however, cannot explain hearing sounds above about 4000 Hz (Matlin, 1988).

We must use both place and frequency theories to explain how we hear different pitches. Place theory seems to explain how we hear high sounds above 3000–4000 Hz, whereas frequency theory seems to explain how we hear very low-pitched sounds (i.e., from 50–3000 Hz) such as the deep hum of a large machine. Both principles seem to operate in the range between 500 and 4000 Hz. It is probably no accident that this is also the range of the human voice. Our hearing is most acute for the sounds we most need in order to communicate with other humans.

Locating sounds

It is easiest to locate sounds that originate from either side of us. Castillo & Butterworth (1981) have demonstrated that even very young infants will turn toward a sound coming from one side. However, with our eyes closed, it is very difficult to tell whether a sound is coming from directly in front of us, directly over our head, or directly behind us. As soon as the sound is moved slightly to one side or the other, though, we can locate it quite accurately. We locate sounds in space in two ways. Consider a sound off to the left side. First, it reaches the left ear an instant before it reaches the right ear. This instant is enough for the brain to interpret that the sound is coming from the left side, especially if it is a low-frequency sound. Second, the head forms a "sound shadow" so that the sound will be slightly louder in the left ear than in the right ear. This difference in amplitude is especially important in locating high-pitched sounds.

Hearing loss

Understanding the physical dimensions of sound waves and how they are transduced into auditory nerve firings helps us understand several causes of hearing impairment. For instance, blockage of the auditory canal will prevent sound waves from reaching the tympanic membrane. Deformation of the tympanic membrane itself will result in a distortion of the mechanical vibrations needed for the middle ear bones to transmit the mechanical energy to the cochlea. Infection in the middle ear may cause the ossicles to fuse which would also distort the sound wave vibrations. Damage to a portion of the basilar membrane or to the hairs imbedded in it could lead to impaired hearing. Finally, damage to the auditory nerve resulting from a tumour, infection, or injury can also lead to hearing impairment.

TASTE AND SMELL (CHEMICAL SENSES)

Our senses of taste and smell are called chemical senses because their receptors are stimulated by physical contact with molecules of chemicals. It may seem obvious that taste entails solid or liquid molecules entering the mouth. It is perhaps less obvious that smell entails vaporized molecules entering the nose.

The significance of taste and smell differs among species, as do the sensitivities of the corresponding sensory systems. For humans, neither of these senses is required for survival. For some species, however, a highly developed sense of smell is essential for detecting predators in an environment where vision is limited by distance, darkness, or dense woods. Thus, for example, we use dogs to sniff

SOURCE: *The Far Side* by Gary Larson. Reprinted by permission of Chronicle Features, San Francisco, CA.

out drugs or explosives packed in luggage, which is obviously something no human could do.

Taste and smell are important to human life, however, and for much more than just the enjoyment of food and drink. Most substances that are dangerous to us taste bad and have a repulsive smell. Smell even influences human relationships in subtle ways (and some not so subtle ways). People can smell the difference between their own clothes and those of other people. They can also discriminate the smells of their own family members from those of other people (Filsinger & Fabes, 1985). Babies turn more toward breast pads worn by their mothers than to pads worn by other nursing mothers. Babies are more peaceful when smelling cloth worn by their own mothers. An experiment conducted by Balogh & Porter (1986) even found a gender difference in infants' discrimination of smells. They exposed newborns to one of two odours (ginger or cherry) for one full day. Subsequently, both smells were presented to the infants in two different locations in their bassinets. The amount of time each infant spent orienting toward each smell was observed. Figure 3-19 shows that female infants spent more time than male infants orienting toward the odour they had previously become familiar with. Male infants did not show this preference. This study certainly shows that female infants are capable of discriminating smells at a very young age and of expressing a preference for the familiar stimulus. We do not know if male newborns are unable to discriminate the smells or

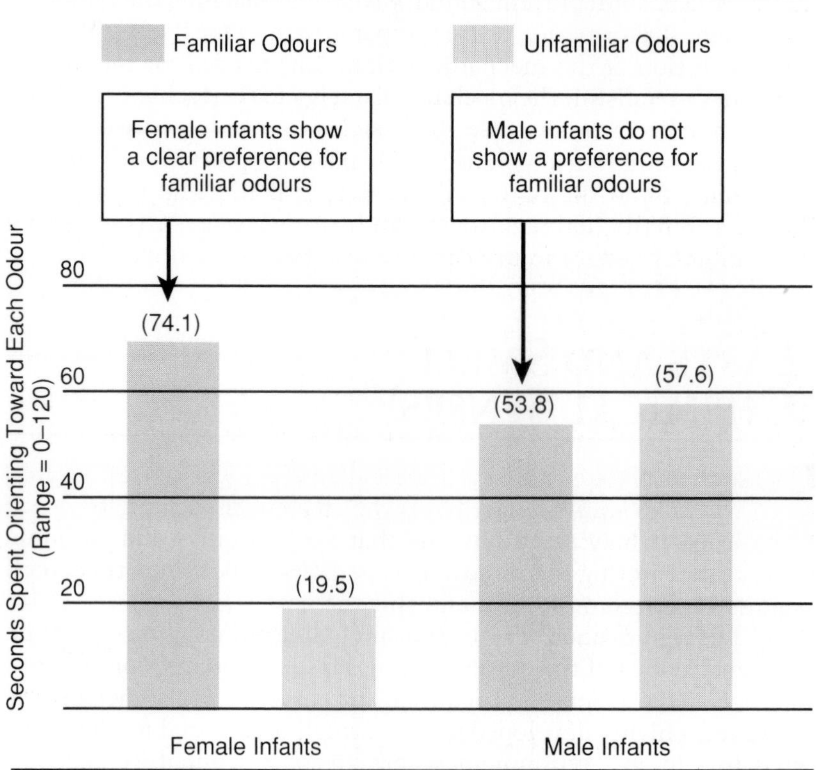

FIGURE 3-19 Odour recognition in human infants: Gender difference
This figure shows the results of an experiment performed by Balogh and Porter (1986) designed to study the ability of infants to differentiate between odours.

SOURCE: Adapted with permission from Allyn and Bacon, 1989.

if they simply have less tendency to orient toward familiar stimuli. Why such a gender difference should exist so soon after birth is not clear.

Gustation

Gustation is the technical name for the sense of **taste**. The sensory receptors responsible for gustation are located on the top and sides of the tongue and to a lesser extent in other places in the mouth. **Taste buds** are groups of sensory receptors in the mouth that are specialized to respond primarily to one of four major dimensions of taste: sweet, salt, sour, and bitter. These four fundamental types of taste combine to create the wide diversity of tastes that we can sense. We have approximately 10 000 taste buds in our mouths, and each taste bud contains several receptor cells and each is shaped like a segment of an orange. The bumps on the upper surface of the tongue are **papillae**, each of which contains many taste buds, in some cases as many as 200. Figure 3-20 shows that the papillae form trenches that reach down into the tongue. The receptor cells in each taste bud have small hair-like projections called **microvilli** that protrude into the wet environment of the trench. The microvilli are stimulated by whatever is in the saliva that coats the tongue and fills the trenches of the papillae. Molecules of food bathed in saliva begin to degrade in the mouth, and the chemicals in the food then interact with the taste buds by stimulating the receptor cells. These receptor cells, in turn, form synapses with dendrites of neurons that send axons to the brain through several cranial nerves.

FIGURE 3-20 Papillae on the surface of the tongue: A taste bud

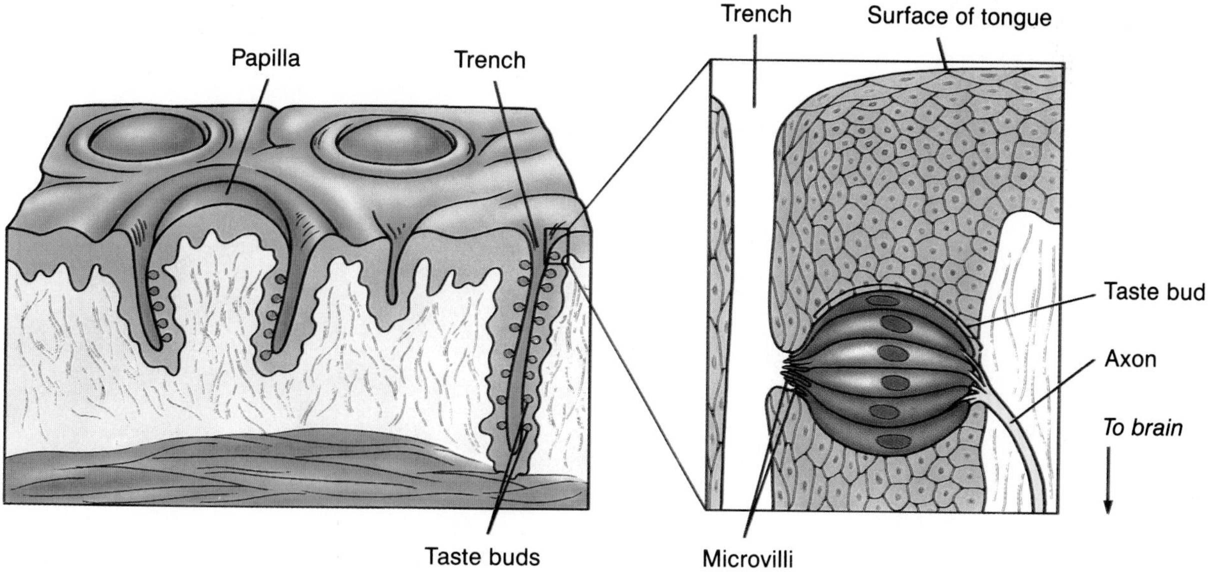

SOURCE: Adapted with permission from Allyn and Bacon, 1989.

The taste that we experience is coded by the relative firing of neurons in taste buds in the region stimulated. Different areas of the tongue are more sensitive to different tastes. The sides are most sensitive to sour tastes, and the tip to sweet, salty, and bitter (McBurney & Collings, 1984). Actually, all taste buds can respond to all four basic tastes, but each is most sensitive to one taste.

The cells responsible for taste live for approximately seven days and are then replaced with new cells. For much of our lifetime this relatively rapid turnover continues. However, the process seems to slow down with age, which may account for our loss of acuity in the sense of taste (and smell) as we get older.

Olfaction

Olfaction is the technical name for the sense of **smell**. The sensory receptors responsible for olfaction are embedded in the **olfactory mucosa**, a mucous membrane that lines the upper nasal passages. More precisely, this membrane is located on the roof of the nasal sinuses, just under the base of the brain. The smell receptor cells are packed in between supporting cells, as shown in Figure 3-21. Each smell receptor has hair-like projections (called cilia) that stick out into the nasal cavity and are stimulated by chemicals that enter the nose in air molecules. When stimulated, the cilia make the olfactory receptor (or neuron) fire. The signal is sent along the axons of the

FIGURE 3-21 The anatomy of the olfactory system

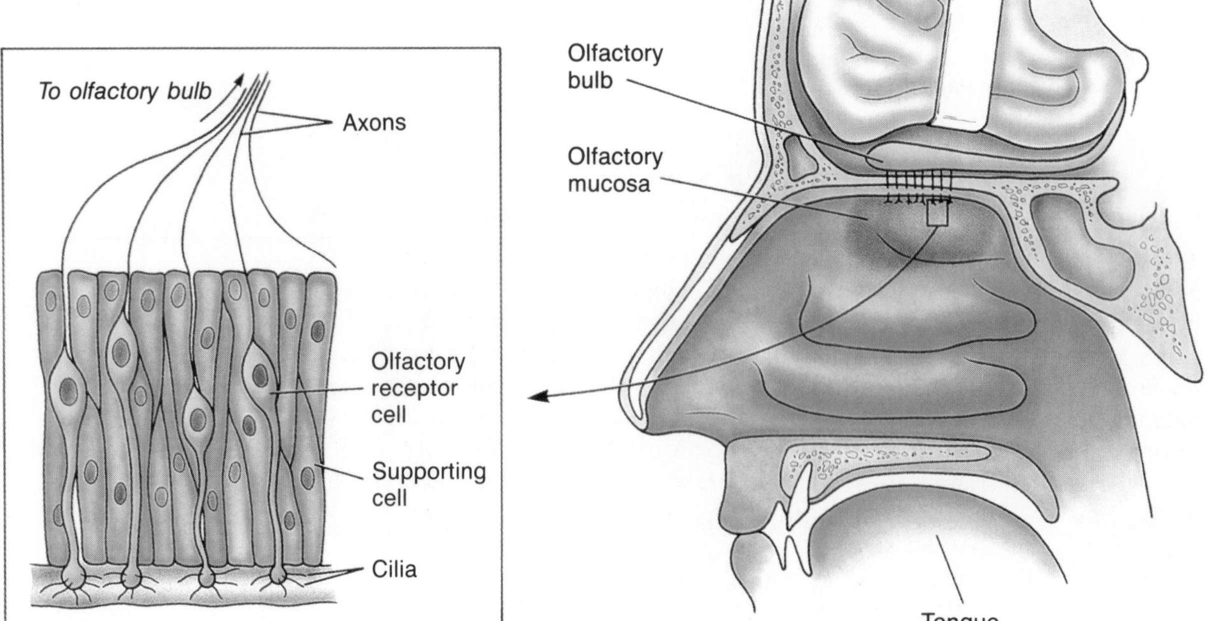

SOURCE: Adapted with permission from Allyn and Bacon, 1989.

receptor through the bony plate at the top of the nasal cavity to the **olfactory bulbs**, which are swellings at the ends of the olfactory nerves. From here, the stimulation is relayed to the brain.

There is some controversy about the number of basic odours that humans are sensitive to. Research on the sense of smell is not as conclusive as that on vision or hearing because it is difficult to study smell precisely. First, in practice it is extremely difficult to deliver an odour to specific receptors because most of the molecules are absorbed by the lining of the nose. Second, we don't have clear classifications or definitions for different odours.

Nevertheless, we do know from research that it is possible to develop an **anosmia**, which is the inability to smell one or more specific odours. This suggests that there are specific receptors for specific odours. It is unlikely, though, that there are olfactory receptors as specific as the different kinds of cones in the eye. It is more likely that each receptor is stimulated by many molecules or groups of molecules (Gesteland, 1986). It is interesting to note that molecules with similar odours are also similar in molecular structure. It is as though each molecular structure fits best in specific receptors. In fact, the **lock and key theory** of smell postulates that chemicals with particular smells have specific molecular structures that fit into specific olfactory receptor cells.

Flavour

The experience of flavour involves much more than taste or odour separately. Through sensory integration, we experience **flavour** as a combination of taste, odour, texture, cognitive expectations, and sometimes pain (with very spicy foods). Food usually does not taste as good if the nose is stuffed up, for example. This is because flavour depends in part on the molecules that drift into the nose as we eat.

Somatosenses (Body Senses)

The **somatosenses** are our bodily senses. They help us respond to pain, touch, temperature, bodily position, vibration, and speed and direction of bodily movement. The somatosenses can be grouped into three major categories. The **kinesthetic senses** provide information on bodily position. The **vestibular senses** provide information on balance and position relative to gravity. The **skin senses** provide information for pressure, pain, cold, and warmth. We often take the bodily senses for granted until we are deprived of them. For instance, perhaps on one occasion your dentist has given you a local anaesthetic that also anaesthetized parts of your tongue. You would then feel no pressure or pain in your tongue. Without this sensory information, it would be quite easy to bite your tongue inadvertently. The only way you would become aware that you had bitten it would be by the taste of blood in your mouth.

Kinesthetic (bodily position) sense

The kinesthetic or body senses function within a special system that allows us to know where our body parts are in relation to each other and to the environment. When we move, hundreds of muscles carry out complicated sequences of contracting and relaxing. Movement requires constant and instantaneous feedback on where each muscle is. Otherwise we would move like robots, in a jerky, uncoordinated manner. The receptors that sense muscle and body position and give this constant feedback are located in the joints, muscles, and tendons of the body. For example, Figure 3-22 shows **muscle spindles**, a kind of "stretch detector" which we have in our muscles. When a muscle is stretched by an increase in load, the muscle spindles fire and send a signal to the spinal cord. This signal rapidly stimulates motor

FIGURE 3-22 Muscle spindles
Muscle spindles, one kind of stretch detectors, are distributed throughout the muscle system. If we hold our forearm parallel to the ground and a weight is suddenly placed in our hand, stimulation from the muscle spindle causes an automatic increase in the strength of the muscular contraction, thereby compensating for the additional weight.

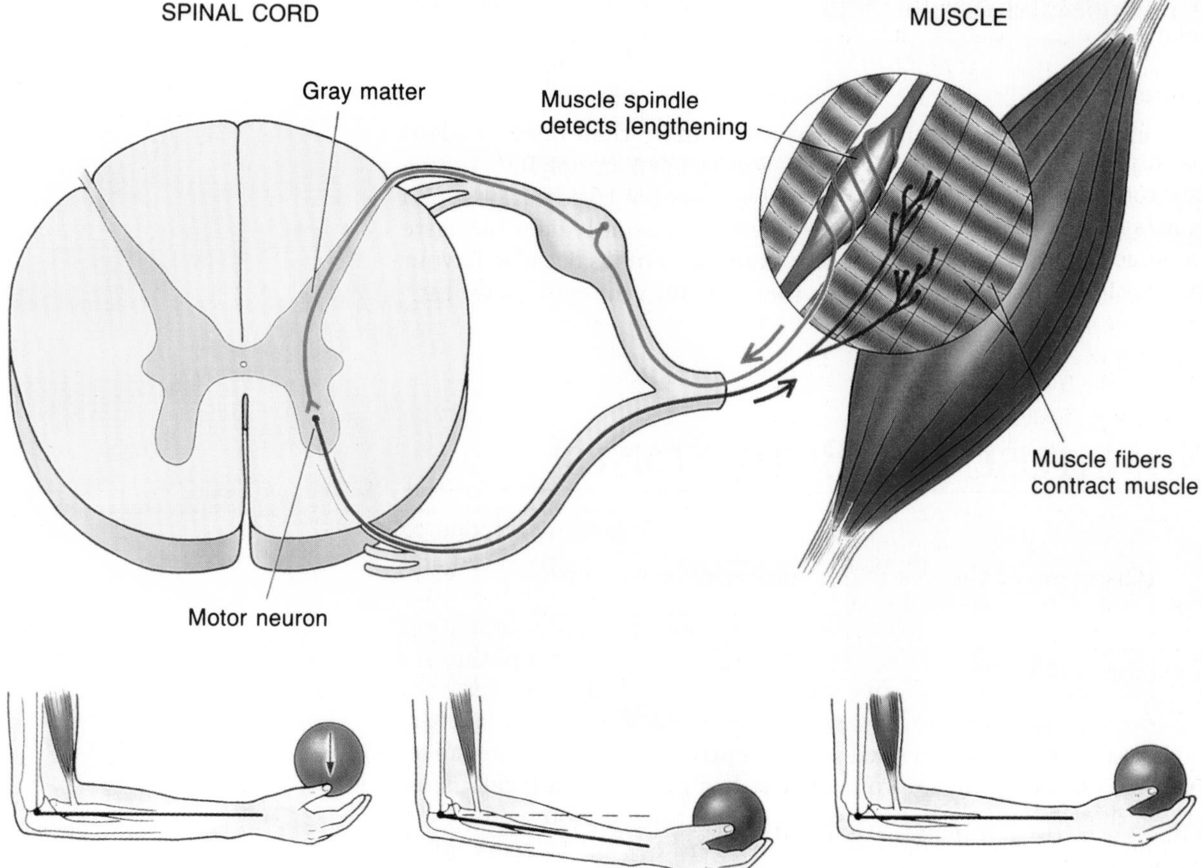

SOURCE: Adapted with permission from Allyn and Bacon, 1989.

neurons leading to the muscle; these motor neurons cause the muscle to contract and thereby compensate for the increased load. This whole chain of action and reaction happens rapidly and without the person's awareness. We cannot "feel" the information from the muscle spindles, but the brain uses the information from these receptors and from joint receptors to keep track of the location of parts of the body, and to control muscular contractions.

Our vestibular apparatus enables us to perform acts of balance.

Vestibular (balance) sense

The vestibular sense helps us know the position of our head and body relative to the pull of gravity. If we turn slowly as we float underwater in near weightlessness, our muscles won't provide us with reliable information about whether we are upright or sideways. However, we can still sense our position because of the *vestibular apparatus*. This is a structure of the inner ear that is sensitive to the force of gravity. This apparatus includes the **semi-circular canals**, a set of three circular tubes which are at right angles to each other in different planes. These canals give us information about our position relative to gravity. They contain liquid that moves around as we move and tiny hairs line the inside of the tubes and bend as the liquid moves. This bending fires receptor cells that give us information about our position relative to gravity. If we are upright, the liquid is at the bottom of the semi-circular canals. When we lie down on our back the fluid flows to the back.

It is easy to fool the vestibular apparatus. When we spin in place rapidly, the world seems to keep spinning when we stop. We have vigorously stimulated the semi-circular canals so that the fluid continues to move when we stop. You may have taken the carnival ride in which riders are held against the wall of a spinning drum by centrifugal force. People who have experienced such rides have reported a powerful sensation that they are lying on their backs looking up. This is because centrifugal force is throwing the fluid against the back of the semi-circular canals, just as though the person were lying down. I once tipped over while running rapids in a canoe. I lost all sense of which way was up as the water tumbled me (and the fluid in my semi-circular canals) around. If a life jacket hadn't pulled me to the surface I might have joined the many drowning victims who swam down in error.

Disorders of the vestibular sense can cause **vertigo**, a loss of sense of balance. Victims of vertigo often fall over in the same way that we do when we spin around repeatedly. Inner ear infections, some kinds of medication, and tumours can all confuse the vestibular sense.

Skin senses

The skin senses respond to *pressure*, *cold*, *warmth*, and possibly *pain*. The receptors are located just under the skin. That we have specialized receptors sensitive to temperature and pressure is a widely held belief, but there is controversy over whether there are specific receptors for pain. It is possible that the sense of pain comes

FIGURE 3-23 Heat illusion apparatus
When cold water flows through one of the intertwined pipes and warm water through the other, the subject senses heat. This illustrates that the sense of heat results from simultaneous stimulation of warm and cold receptors.

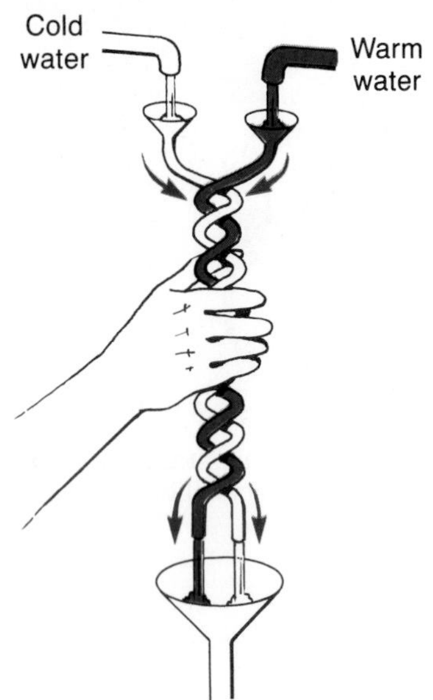

from the overstimulation of any of the other skin senses. (We will wait for Chapter 4 to discuss the Special Topic of "Pain Perception and Control.")

Our sense of touch is based on pressure receptors just under the skin. These receptors are not distributed evenly around the body. This is demonstrated by the **two-point threshold determination**. This is a procedure for mapping the sensitivity of the skin to touch. The threshold is the minimum distance between two points (of stimulation) at which the two points can be discriminated as separate and distinct. Touching a fingertip with two points only 2 or 3 millimetres apart will result in the sensation of two points. The same stimulation to the upper arm will be sensed as one point. In fact, these two points will be sensed as one even if they are 30 millimetres apart. The fingertips are more sensitive to pressure because they are more densely populated with pressure receptors.

It may surprise you that we have receptors for cold and warm temperatures but no specific receptors for hot temperatures. Sensations of heat result from the simultaneous stimulation of both cold and warm receptors. This is illustrated by the heat illusion apparatus pictured in Figure 3-23. The intertwined tubes carry cold water in one and warm in the other. The person who grasps the apparatus feels a sensation of heat.

SPECIAL TOPIC Subliminal Perception

The issue of sensory thresholds becomes more complex when the notion of **subliminal perception** is introduced. This is a controversial topic that involves the effect of stimuli presented below detectable threshold. The controversy probably originated with sensational claims made by some people in the field of advertising. One early report said that if the words "eat popcorn" and "drink cola" were flashed on a movie screen so quickly that patrons did not know they had been presented, there were increases in sales of popcorn and cola. A number of controlled experiments, however, failed to document the dramatic effects that had been claimed in the popular press (e.g., George and Jennings, 1975). The earlier findings were based on poorly controlled "studies" that had not taken into account factors such as the weather, the type of films that were being shown, snack bar displays, and the kind of audience that was present. Subliminal stimulation is also supposed to be present in other places. Exaggerated claims have been made for the effect of subliminal messages in popular songs. Large amounts of money are apparently still being made by those who sell cassette tapes with subliminal messages. Presumably, these hidden messages can help you lose weight, stop smoking, love yourself, become smarter than your professor, and be incredibly attractive to others. Such are the claims, but what does the evidence tell us?

For many years, psychologists entirely rejected the notion of subliminal perception as not supported by research. Recently, however, there has been research done on learning without awareness and other interesting phenomena, and some of this research has had positive results (Dixon, 1971; Stambrook & Martin, 1983). On the basis of current research, it seems most reasonable to conclude that subliminal effects have been demonstrated in research, but that these effects are very subtle. Martin, Hawryluk, and Guse (1974), for example, presented short bursts of ultrasound (sound that is too high-pitched for humans to hear) to a group of subjects and indeed the subjects were unable to detect the ultrasound. However, EEG measures showed that the stimulus was being received and processed by the brain. We will discuss these matters further in Chapter 9.

Subliminal perception does seem to work. We make this statement cautiously because the valid findings are a far cry from the exaggerated claims of those who would have us "eat popcorn" or purchase tapes that would ensure for us "subliminal brain-booster breakthroughs." Nearly all the support provided for commercial subliminal tapes is based on testimonials from users. Some users may actually benefit from the tapes, but there is no way to know if this is because the subliminal suggestions work or because of the placebo effect. There seems to be no controlled research on the effectiveness of these tapes. Backward subliminal messages hidden in rock songs and other forms of subliminal advertising have also fared badly in research. No effects have been demonstrated to result from either the messages or the advertisements (Vokey & Read, 1985).

Chapter Summary

1. Our sensory organs transduce stimulation from the environment into neural firings. Our brain then interprets and organizes these signals to form our perception of reality. However, our construction of reality is not entirely accurate. Our sensory organs are limited in what they can receive, and our interpretative processes can distort information.
2. In the field of psychophysics, much attention has been devoted to sensory thresholds. Research indicates that the experience of sensation varies somewhat from person to person. Each individual also experiences fluctuations, as explained by the signal-detection theory. Psychologists have developed procedures for determining the absolute thresholds and the difference thresholds for a given person. Psychometric functions reveal that these thresholds mark gradual changes, not abrupt ones. For difference thresholds, the ratio of Weber's Law depends upon the intensity of stimulus being measured.
3. Because of sensory adaptation, our nervous systems respond most strongly to changes in stimuli. Our experience of a new stimulus is affected by the stimulus immediately preceding it.
4. Visible light, which is the stimulus for human vision, forms only a small part of the electromagnetic spectrum. The three main properties of light are hue, intensity, and purity.
5. Light is focused on the retina at the back of the eye by passing through the cornea, pupil, lens, and posterior chamber. The retina is divided into three layers. The backmost layer consists of two types of photoreceptors, which begin the process of converting light into the sensation of seeing. The rods are distributed mostly around the periphery of the retina. They are sensitive to light intensity and they can distinguish between black, white, and various shades of grey. The cones, which are fewer in number, are concentrated at the fovea. They are sensitive to hues and

they work best in bright light. Electrochemical impulses from the photoreceptors are transmitted via the bipolar cells to the ganglion cells and then along the optic nerve to the brain.

6. Dark adaptation and light adaptation occur because rods are more sensitive than cones to light intensity. With the onset of dim light, the rods take some time to replenish their photochemicals. With the onset of bright light, the rods are rapidly bleached out before the cones become active.

7. Each retina sends information to both hemispheres of the brain. Because perception is a construction of a reality, we are normally unaware of the blind spot we possess in each eye at the optic disk.

8. The visual cortex contains simple cells, complex cells, and hypercomplex cells. These specialized neurons respond to particular features of stationary or moving stimuli. Together they enable us to form an outline drawing of the sensed image. When specific motion detectors become fatigued, we may experience aftereffects of visual movement.

9. There are two theories of colour vision. The trichromatic theory emphasizes the role of the photoreceptors, whereas the opponent-process theory emphasizes the role of the ganglion cells. These theories are not incompatible with each other. According to the trichromatic theory, the retina contains three types of cones, each of which is most sensitive to one of the primary colours. Malfunction of one or more of these types of cones causes colour blindness. According to the opponent-process theory, the three types of cones interact with three types of ganglion cells to form three systems: red/green, yellow/blue, and black/white. The phenomenon of afterimages (positive or negative) lends support to the opponent-process theory.

10. The human auditory system senses vibrations within the range of 20 Hz to 20 000 Hz as sound. The three basic properties of sound are frequency, amplitude, and complexity.

11. Sound waves are funnelled into the ear along the auditory canal. Vibrations are then passed from the tympanic membrane to the ossicles and then through the oval window to the cochlea. The vibration of fluid in the cochlea bends the cilia, thereby stimulating neural firings in the basilar membrane.

12. There are two theories of how we register different pitches. The place theory seems to explain high pitches. The frequency theory seems to explain low pitches. Both theories are satisfactory for the frequency range of the human voice. The volley principle is a hypothesis that would extend the frequency theory up to 4000 Hz.

13. We are able to locate sounds in space because signals reach each ear at slightly different times and with slightly different volumes.

14. Gustation and olfaction comprise our chemical senses. The receptors for both are stimulated by physical contact with chemical molecules. Each taste bud responds most strongly to sweet, salt, sour, or bitter. Each olfactory receptor may respond to smells with specific molecular structures. Flavour is an experience that combines input from taste, odour, texture, cognitive expectations, and sometimes pain.

15. Our somatosenses are also necessary for survival. The kinesthetic senses help us maintain our bodily position and muscle movements, the vestibular senses help us keep our balance in the face of gravity, and our skin senses help us respond to touch through specialized receptors under the skin.

Key Terms

Absolute threshold The minimal intensity of a stimulus needed before our sensory receptors can detect that stimulus.

Accommodation Fine adjustments to the shape of the lens for focusing light on the retina.

Aftereffect The illusory perception of motion in a stationary object after one has been staring at another object moving continuously in the opposite direction.

Afterimage The sensation of light after the light source has terminated. Positive afterimages are the same colour as the light source. Negative afterimages are the "opponent" colour of the light source.

Amplitude The amount of pressure or intensity with which sound reaches the ears. Corresponds to the loudness of a sound.

Anosmia The inability to smell one or more specific odours.

Auditory canal Passageway that carries sound from the external ear into the inner ear.

Basilar membrane Band of tissue running down the centre of the cochlea. Contains rows of cilia which produce neural stimulation when bent by the fluid in the cochlea.

Bipolar cell Neuron in the middle layer of the retina that relays stimuli from the photoreceptors to the ganglion cells.

Blind spot See *optic disk.*

Cilia Hair-like projections that stick out from receptor cells to receive stimulation.

Cochlea Coiled, fluid-filled structure which is the primary hearing organ of the inner ear.

Colour blindness The inability to discriminate particular combinations of colours. It is also known as colour deficiency.

Colour deficiency See *colour blindness.*

Complementary colours Two colours which produce white or grey when combined.

Complex cells Neurons of the visual cortex that are specialized to detect moving lines at specific orientations in the visual field.

Complexity The purity or timbre of a sound. It is determined by the proportion of various frequencies which combine to form a particular sound.

Cones A cone-shaped type of photoreceptor. Cones are sensitive to colour and respond well to bright light.

Context effect The sensation of a new stimulus is affected by the stimuli immediately preceding it.

Cornea Protruding, transparent coating on the front of the eye.

Dark adaptation The process by which the eyes become more sensitive to light under dim or dark conditions.

Decibel (dB) Measure of the loudness of a sound.

Difference threshold The minimal difference in intensity between two stimuli needed to tell them apart.

Edge detectors See *simple cells*.

Electromagnetic spectrum The entire range of energy waves created by the release of electrons from atoms.

Flavour The experience that results from integrating input from taste, odour, texture, cognitive expectations, and sometimes pain.

Fovea Central spot on the retina, directly behind the lens, that is densely packed with cones. It is especially sensitive to colour and fine discriminations.

Frequency The speed at which air pressure waves reach the ear. It corresponds to the pitch of the sound that we hear.

Frequency theory According to this theory of pitch perception, there is a direct correspondence between the frequency of the sound wave and the frequency of neural firing.

Ganglion cell Neuron in the top level of the retina that receives visual information from the photoreceptors, via the bipolar cells, and passes it along to the brain.

Gustation The sense of taste.

Hertz (Hz) (plural: *hertz*). One cycle per second. A unit of measurement of the frequency or pitch of a sound.

Hue The colour of a particular wavelength of light.

Hypercomplex cells Neurons of the visual cortex that are specialized to detect moving lines at specific orientations and at specific angles in the visual field.

Incus Second of three bones (known as ossicles) that transfer vibrations from the tympanic membrane to the cochlea. It is shaped like an anvil.

Intensity The brightness of light that results from the amount of energy in the electromagnetic waves.

Iris Coloured portion of the eye.

Just noticeable difference (JND) Another name for the *difference threshold*.

Kinesthetic senses The type of somatosenses that provide information on bodily position.

Lens Flexible, transparent, inner structure of the eye that focuses light on the retina.

Light adaptation The process by which the eyes become less sensitive to light under bright conditions.

Lock and key theory The theory that chemicals with particular smells have specific molecular structures that fit into specific olfactory receptor cells.

Malleus First of three bones (known as ossicles) that transfer vibrations from the tympanic membrane to the cochlea. It is shaped like a hammer.

Microvilli Small hair-like projections that protrude into a trench of the mouth from receptor cells in the taste buds.

Motion detectors Another name for the complex cells and hypercomplex cells of the visual cortex, specialized to sense moving lines.

Muscle spindles A kinesthetic receptor that detects stretch in muscles.

Nanometre (nm) A unit of measurement equal to one-billionth (10^{-9}) of a metre. It is used to describe the wavelengths of visible light.

Negative afterimage See *afterimage*.

Olfaction The sense of smell.

Olfactory bulbs Swellings at the ends of the olfactory nerves. Relay smell stimulation to the brain.

Olfactory mucosa Mucous membrane that lines the upper nasal passages and contains the smell receptors.

Opponent-process theory The theory that colour vision results from three systems of ganglion cells: a red/green system, a yellow/blue system, and a black/white system.

Optic chiasm The point at which the axons in the optic nerve from the inside portion of each retina cross over to the opposite side of the brain.

Optic disk (or **blind spot**) The area at the back of the eye through which the optic nerve exits.

Optic nerve Bundle of axons of the ganglion cells which relays signals from the retina of the eye to the brain.

Orbit Bony socket that houses the eyeball.

Ossicles A set of three bones (malleus, incus, and stapes) linked together in the inner ear which transfer vibrations from the tympanic membrane to the cochlea.

Oval window The place where the stapes connects to the cochlea. It vibrates in response to the ossicles and sets into motion the fluid contained in the cochlea.

Papillae The bumps on the upper surface of the tongue, each of which contains many taste buds.

Perception The process by which the brain interprets and organizes stimuli to make them meaningful.

Photoreceptors Specialized neurons in the backmost layer of the retina that transduce light energy into the electrochemical energy of the nervous system.

Place theory According to this theory of pitch perception, different locations on the basilar membrane of the cochlea are sensitive to different pitches of sound.

Positive afterimage See *afterimage*.

Primary colours Pure red, pure green, and pure blue.

Psychometric function A pattern of human functioning that has been measured.

Psychophysics The study of the relationship between physical stimuli and how we sense those stimuli.

Pupil Circular aperture in the iris. Its size determines the amount of light entering the eye.

Purity The composition of wavelengths in a light or the purity of its hue.

Receptive field The area of the retina that relays signals to a given ganglion cell.

Retina The back inner surface of the eye where light is sensed.

Rods A long and narrow type of photoreceptor. Rods are sensitive to light of low intensity but not to different hues.

Sclera The outer white layer of the eyeball.

Semi-circular canals A set of three circular tubes in the inner ear. All at right angles to each other, they give information about position relative to gravity.

Sensation The impact that stimuli have on sensory organs and the nervous system.

Sensory adaptation The process by which sensory systems reduce their responses to prolonged, unchanging stimuli.

Signal-detection theory The theory that our ability to detect signals (stimuli) is influenced by various factors, including our motivations and expectations.

Simple cells Neurons of the visual cortex that are specialized to detect stationary lines or edges at specific orientations in the visual field. They are also known as edge detectors.

Skin senses The type of somatosenses that provides information about pressure, pain, cold, and warmth.

Smell See *olfaction*.

Somatosenses Bodily senses of pain, touch, temperature, bodily position, vibration, and speed and direction of bodily movement.

Sound Vibrations in a medium, usually air.

Stapes Third of three bones (known as ossicles) that transfer vibrations from the tympanic membrane to the cochlea. It is shaped like a stirrup.

Stimulus Any form of energy that arouses some response from an organism.

Subliminal perception The influence of stimuli too weak to be detected consciously.

Taste See *gustation*.

Taste buds Group of sensory receptors in the mouth that are specialized to respond primarily to one of the four major dimensions of taste: sweet, sour, salt, and bitter.

Trichromatic theory The theory that colour vision results from the combined stimulation from three types of cones, each sensitive to red, green, or blue.

Two-point threshold determination Procedure for mapping the sensitivity of skin to touch. The minimum distance between two points (of stimulation) at which the two points can be discriminated as separate and distinct.

Tympanic membrane The eardrum, a thin membrane at the end of the auditory canal which vibrates in response to sound waves.

Vertigo Disorder of the vestibular senses that results in loss of sense of balance.

Vestibular senses The type of somatosenses that provide information on balance and position relative to gravity.

Visual cortex The area in the occipital lobe of the brain where visual information is processed.

Volley principle An elaboration of frequency theory that says that groups or "squads" of neurons fire in sequence in response to high-pitched sounds.

Weber's law The observation that there is a constant ratio between stimulus intensity and the difference threshold.

SUGGESTED READINGS

Matlin, M.M. (1988). *Sensation and perception*, 2nd ed. Boston: Allyn & Bacon. This is a comprehensive text on sensation and perception. It would probably be the best source to use if you wish to pursue these topics further.

Dixon, N.F. (1971). *Subliminal perception: The nature of a controversy*. London: McGraw-Hill; and by the same author (1981), *Preconscious processing*. New York: Wiley. These two books by Dixon give a positive summary of the evidence on subliminal perception. The more recent book goes beyond perception to discuss unconscious mental processes, a topic that we will discuss in Chapter 9.

Gregory, R.L. (1978). *Eye and brain: The physiology of seeing*, 3rd ed. New York: McGraw-Hill. A well-illustrated and well-written description of visual perception.

CHAPTER 4

SOURCE: Photo by Kathy Bellesiles.

Perception

AN EXPERIMENTAL PSYCHOLOGIST once discovered that some of his white rats had escaped from their cages. The rats were dead and some had been partially eaten. Although the psychologist wasn't sure how they had escaped their cages, he felt quite sure that he knew how the rats had died. In his opinion, they had been killed by wild rats that had gotten into his animal-storage room. Later, in order to fill a container with water, he had to leave the room. When he returned after a few minutes, he saw a grey rat standing in front of the empty cages. By making a sudden motion as if to throw the water container at the wild rat, he tried to scare it away. However, the grey rat didn't move. When the psychologist gingerly moved closer to the "rat," he discovered that it was nothing more than a crumpled piece of grey paper (Haney, 1979). Had the psychologist actually seen a rat? He certainly thought so. Whatever the actual *sensory* data he received, the psychologist, because of his state of mind after his gruesome discovery, *perceived* a wild grey rat.

Perception is the process by which we organize and make meaningful the mass of sensations we receive. Our past experience and our current state of mind influence the intricate series of steps between sensation and perception. The experimental psychologist who had found the mutilated bodies of his laboratory rats was convinced that the grey mass in front of the cages was the perpetrator of the destruction. As we pointed out in the previous chapter, we perceive a construction of reality, not reality itself.

DATA-DRIVEN PROCESSING VERSUS CONCEPTUALLY DRIVEN PROCESSING

We can look at the process of perception from two different perspectives. If we focus on the external stimuli of the environment and their impact on the nervous system as a biological entity, we are emphasizing **data-driven processing**. If we focus on the higher, internal processes of the perceiver (such as expectations, past experiences, knowledge, and mood) and their impact on perception, we are emphasizing **conceptually driven processing**. The difference between these two processes is an example of the "nature-nurture" controversy that occurs in many areas of psychology. There are differences of opinion over how much human functioning is innate and genetically determined (nature) and how much is learned (nurture). Do we learn to perceive or are our perceptual processes "built in"? Both perspectives are needed for a complete understanding of perception. In order to recognize the face of your best friend in a crowd, you must have specific stimuli (the data) impinging on your senses. The friend's nose, eyes, cheeks, jaw, and chin have specific shapes and colours that must be sensed in order that we may perceive this particular face. However, the process of perception must also involve integration of all the separate components of your friend's face. It is unlikely that you could describe the parts of your friend's face so that another person could pick it out of a crowd as you can, with only a momentary glimpse. If asked how you knew which face was your friend's, you would probably say something such as "I just knew." You would think of the pattern made up of all the elements. You would probably not think of a slightly pointed chin, medium cheeks, blue-grey eyes, and so on. This process of integration is based on our internal processes—that is, it is determined by our conceptual understanding. As we will see in this chapter, we learn to interpret and organize the mass of stimuli that reach our senses. In short, *we learn to perceive.*

Gestalt Principles of Perceptual Organization

In Chapter 1, we quoted the famous dictum of the Gestalt school of psychology: "The whole is more than the sum of its parts." This principle is most applicable in the field of perception. It is common in psychology to use the word **gestalt** as a noun meaning the perception of an entity as an integrated whole rather than as a collection of separate elements. When you spot your friend in the crowd, you do not see her face as a collection of parts but as one integrated and meaningful image. You perceive it as a gestalt.

We perceive the picture in Figure 4-1 as a barnyard with animals. In fact, we *see* only fragments of some of the animals because they are partially obscured by other objects, but we *perceive* whole animals. It would be absurd if we had to consciously build up our perception out of all the separate elements of the picture: a leg, several

FIGURE 4-1 Gestalt perception
Most of the objects that we see in this picture are actually only fragments because they are partially obscured by other objects. However, we perceive them as complete because we construct our perceptions on our past experience with similar perceptions.

FIGURE 4-2 Gestalt principles of perceptual grouping

SOURCE: Reprinted with permission from Allyn and Bacon, 1989.

A

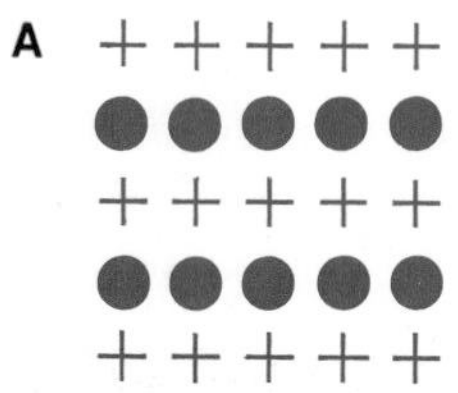

The law of *similarity*: the crosses will tend to be seen as grouped together in horizontal rows, not alternated with dots in vertical columns.

B

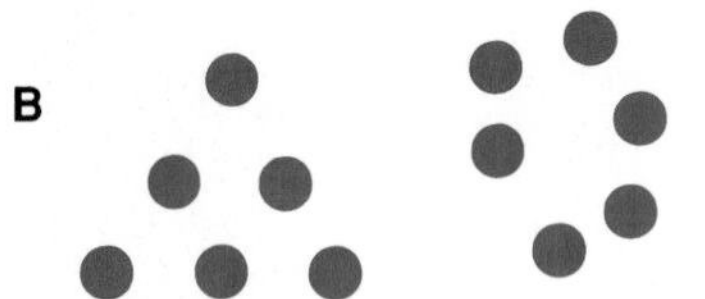

The law of *proximity*: because they are closer together, the dots on the left will be seen as a group, and the dots on the right will be seen as another group.

C

The law of *closure*: the line will be seen as enclosing a circle, despite the gap.

D

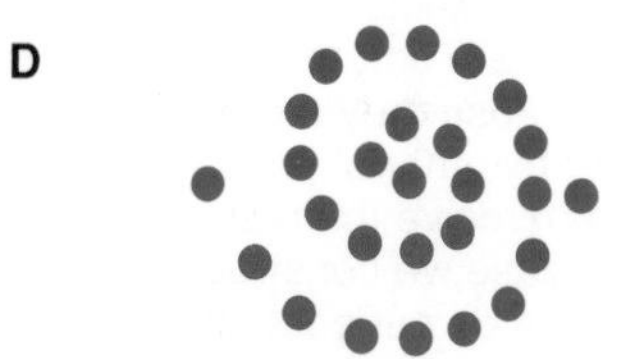

The law of *good continuation*: the dots will be seen as a spiral because they seem to flow in that direction.

horizontal lines, some ovals, horns, and so on. We organize our perception of such pictures without consciously thinking about it. Gestalt psychologists have developed a number of principles that help us understand how we organize the stimuli of our sensations into perceptions.

Grouping

We have a strong, automatic tendency to organize our perceptions by **grouping** certain kinds of objects together. The principles of grouping (and of figure and ground which we will discuss shortly) were first studied by Gestalt psychologists in Germany in the early 1900s. Figure 4-2 illustrates the four principles of grouping: similarity, proximity, closure, and good continuation.

According to the law of **similarity**, we tend to perceive similar objects as a group. In Example A in Figure 4-2, people tend to perceive five rows rather than five columns. Logically, the picture could just as well be five columns of alternating crosses and circles, but we automatically group the similar objects as a unit.

According to the law of **proximity**, we tend to perceive objects that are near each other as a group. In Example B of Figure 4-2, it seems quite obvious that there are two groups of six circles. However, they could just as well make up one group of twelve circles or even four groups of three circles if we chose to organize the circles on some basis other than nearness to each other.

According to the law of **closure**, we tend to fill in gaps in order to perceive objects in familiar form. We perceive as complete what we expect to experience as complete. This tendency is also sometimes called the principle of *continuity*. Example C of Figure 4-2 is not a complete circle, but most people would insist that it is a circle. The principle of closure does more than help us group objects. It also helps us make sense out of a world in which we usually see incomplete objects. This is the principle that allows us to *see* complete animals in Figure 4-1.

According to the law of **good continuation**, we tend to perceive objects according to the apparent flow of direction of surrounding objects. This tendency would seem to arise from our experience with motion. The dots in Example D of Figure 4-2 seem to be flowing in a spiral, even though one dot doesn't fit the pattern. For most of us, the general line of motion will be perceived as a spiral.

Figure and ground

Another way in which we organize visual stimuli into perceptions is to distinguish between objects and the spaces around the objects. The **figure** is that part of a set of stimuli which we perceive as objects. The **ground** is that part of a set of stimuli which we perceive as the space around the objects.

To a large extent, our perception of what is figure and what is ground depends on what part of the stimuli we are focusing on at a given moment. This is demonstrated most dramatically by our perception of specially designed drawings where the figure and the ground are reversible. Consider, for example, Figure 4-3. Sometimes it looks like a vase and sometimes it looks like the profiles of Queen Elizabeth II and Prince Philip, depending on what we attend to. When we focus on the vase, we can perceive it as the figure. The profiles then fade away to form the ground. Similarly, when we focus on the profiles, we can perceive them as the figure. Then it is nearly impossible to perceive a vase even though we know it is represented there. With such an ambiguous figure-ground relationship, most people will perceive this drawing as a shifting back and forth between the vase and the profiles.

The Dutch artist C. M. Escher (1898–1972) exploited the ambiguities between figure and ground in some of his works. In his drawing *Symmetry Work 105*, reproduced as Figure 4-4, Escher has divided the plane into interlocking outlines of a prancing horse. If we attend to the white stimuli, we perceive oblique rows of white horses. If we attend to the dark stimuli, we perceive oblique rows of black horses. Again, we will find it almost impossible to perceive the white and black stimuli simultaneously as the figure. Nevertheless, because the outlines interlock and fill the plane, we will experience a very rapid oscillation between perceiving white horses and black horses.

Drawings with reversible figures and grounds illustrate the importance of attention in the construction of perception. Let's now consider the concept of attention more closely.

FIGURE 4-3 Figure versus ground
This vase was created for the Silver Jubilee of Queen Elizabeth II and shows the profiles of the Queen and Prince Philip. It is almost impossible to perceive a vase and the profiles at the same time. When one is the figure, the other becomes the ground.
SOURCE: Courtesy Kaiser Porcelain.

ATTENTION

We are limited in the number of stimuli that we can attend to at any given moment. We seem to be able to "pay attention" to only one set of stimuli at a time, but that doesn't mean we are not processing other information. At a party we can carry on a conversation at the same time as we pour a drink, but, if we get engrossed in our conversation, we might reach out and pick up someone else's drink instead of our own. The typical apology for such a mistake ("I'm sorry. I just wasn't paying attention") is quite accurate. At that moment we were more focused on the conversation than on the drink.

By its very nature, **attention** is "selective." Therefore, we use the technical term **selective attention** to refer to the state of focused processing of one set of stimuli among many competing stimuli. We know from experience that it is quite possible (and often necessary) for us to "tune out" some of the competing stimuli that assault our senses. At a party, there are usually many conversations going on all around us, but they fade into a jumbled hum as we make sense out of our own conversation. If asked, we could not describe what was being said next to us. However, if someone mentions (or worse, whispers) our name within earshot, we immediately notice. How can this be? Evidently, we are receiving and processing much more sensory data than we are consciously aware of. Most of this data is blocked from reaching our awareness. But stimuli that have special meaning for us will somehow be processed so that we become aware of them. We will discuss the issue of unconscious processing of unattended information further in Chapter 9.

FIGURE 4-4 *Symmetry Work 105* by M.C. Escher
In this drawing we can perceive the figure as either white horses or black horses.
SOURCE: M.C. Escher (1989), p. 30.

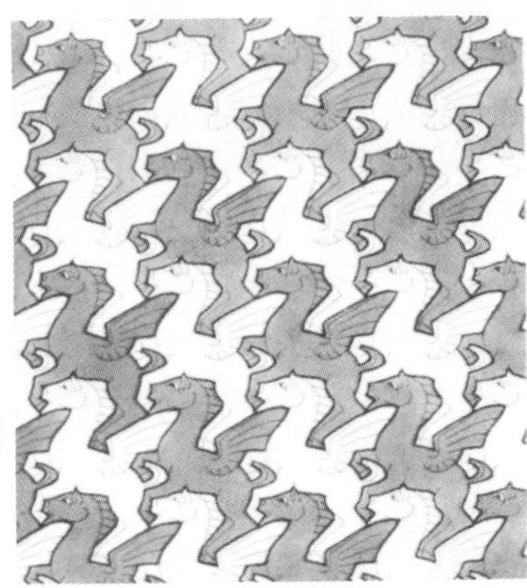

PERCEPTUAL CONSTANCY

If the world existed exactly as we sense it, cars would shrink as they drove away, a rose garden would disappear in the dark of the night, and all objects would change shape as they moved. We have many ways, however, whereby we maintain perceptual constancy. **Perceptual constancy** is the tendency to maintain stable perceptions even when sense data change. Sometimes our perceiving faculty can be fooled by illusions, as we will soon see, but normally our brains make unconscious inferences that keep the world stable. **Unconscious inferences** are automatic conclusions the brain draws about the actual qualities of sensed objects in order to maintain perceptual constancy. The perceiving faculties of the brain are constantly making informed "guesses" based on principles such as "larger objects are generally closer." Sometimes we modify such an inference by factoring in other information such as "adults are usually larger than children" (Rock, 1983). As a moving car "shrinks" in size relative to the stationary lamp posts, we make inferences about distance and we deduce that the car is going away from us.

Most research on constancies has been done on how we maintain visual constancies and we will focus on visual constancies here. But there are also perceptual constancies in our other senses. For example, we would speak of loudness constancy. If one of your intimates was whispering in your ear while another one was screaming obscenities at you from across the room, the two auditory messages might reach the ear at exactly the same amplitude. The sounds would be *sensed* as being of the same loudness even though you *perceived* them to be different. Your brain would maintain the constancy that screaming is loud and whispering is soft.

FIGURE 4-5 The Ames room
The illusion of the Ames room makes the child seem taller than the adult. This room in the Manitoba Museum of Man and Nature is constructed as the drawing shows, with non-parallel walls. The false perspective tricks the brain into making inaccurate comparisons of the size of objects.
SOURCE: David Martin.

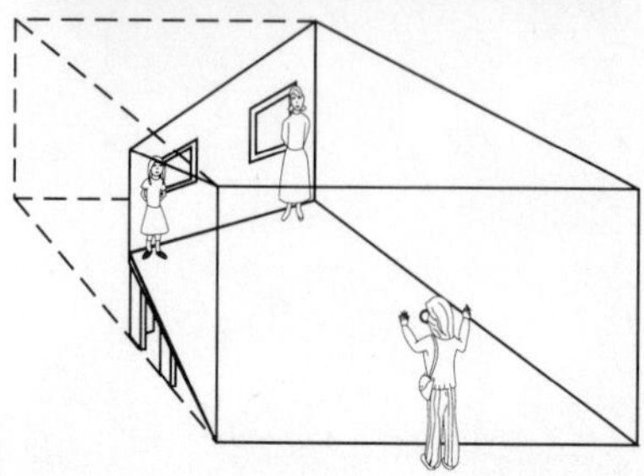

Size constancy

We maintain a sense of the size of objects in spite of our distance from them. **Size constancy** is the tendency to perceive familiar objects as being a fixed size, even though the size of the retinal image of the object changes when our distance from the object changes. The further an object is from us, the smaller is the image it projects on the retina. Size constancy depends in part on perspective. **Perspective** is the principle that guides us to perceive foreshortened (smaller) objects as being farther away from us and larger objects as being closer. Perspective also helps us perceive a three-dimensional world even though our retinal images are only two-dimensional. According to the geometrical laws of **linear perspective**, parallel lines seem to converge as they recede into a "vanishing point" in the distance.

However, using converging parallel lines as a distance cue can be used against us in illusions such as the Ames room in Figure 4-5. The "hidden lines" drawing shows how the room has been specially constructed so that the perspective lines trick the brain into perceiving both side walls as the same length. We consciously know that the adult is taller and farther away than the child, but we perceive them as the same distance away.

Shape constancy

As objects move, the retinal image they cast constantly changes shape. **Shape constancy** is the tendency to perceive an object as being a constant shape, even though the retinal image of that object changes shape depending on our angle of vision. In Figure 4-6, our retinal image of the closed door is a rectangle, but our retinal image of the same door partially open is not. However, we still perceive the door as a rectangle. Try to imagine how confusing it would be if we did not have this space-constancy faculty among our tools of perception. The door and all the other familiar objects in our world would change their shapes whenever we or the objects moved.

FIGURE 4-6 Shape constancy
The door changes shape as it opens, but we maintain the constant perception of it as a rectangle.

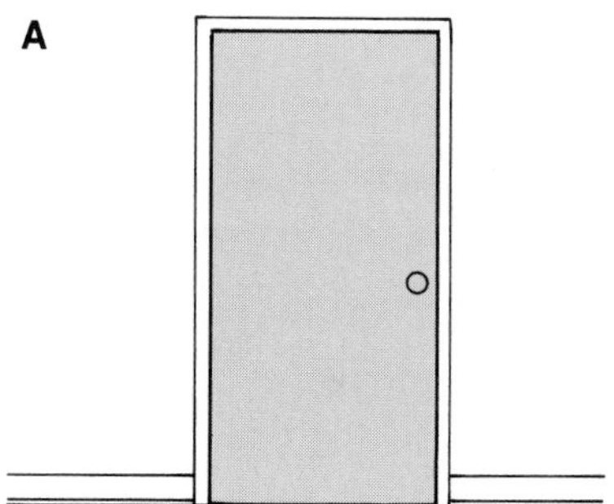

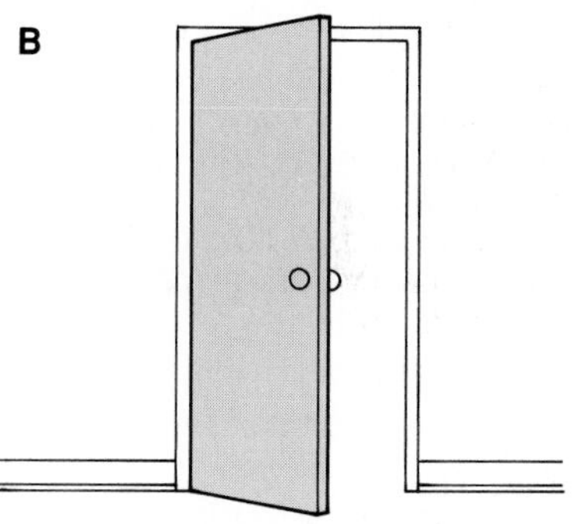

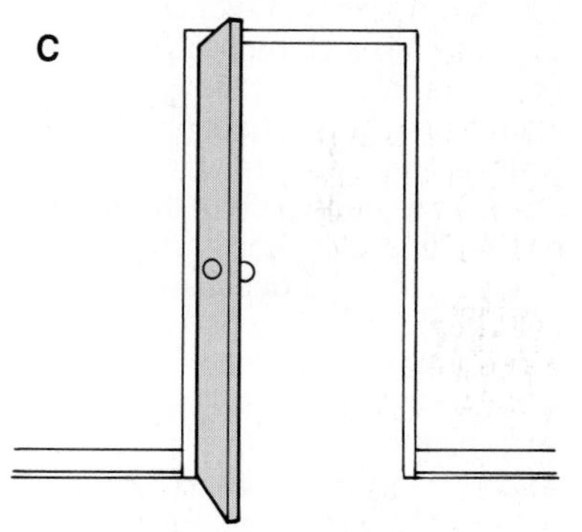

Brightness constancy

The sensation of brightness and contrast changes with every change in the intensity of light. **Brightness constancy** is the tendency to see a known object as being more or less of a constant brightness even when the prevailing light intensity changes. Reading this page in bright light will produce a strong contrast between the white page, which reflects the light, and the black print, which absorbs the light. In dim light, this contrast will be less pronounced. The black print will still absorb light and will be of the same intensity as it was in the bright light, but the white paper will have less light to reflect. Nevertheless, even in dim light, we would still perceive the contrasting black and white as constant.

Colour constancy

As the brightness and wavelength of light changes, the colours of the objects around us change. We perceive the colour of the object remaining the same, except when the wavelength of the light changes dramatically. **Colour constancy** is the tendency to perceive an object as being more or less of a constant colour even when the brightness and wavelength of light change. As we move around under different lights at a party, friends do not *perceive* our skin as changing colour. Even when a green light shines directly on our face (a dramatic change in wavelength) and we are seen as green, people still assume that our natural colour has not changed.

How We See Depth

The image on our retina has only two dimensions, height and width. However, we are able to perceive three dimensions and to judge depth accurately. **Depth perception** is the ability to judge the relative distance of objects and to perceive objects in three dimensions. Some of the ways we do this seem to be learned. However, it is possible either that depth perception is partly innate or else that we have a propensity for learning depth perception at a very early age. Let's explore some of the evidence for each of these possibilities.

Is depth perception innate?

One way to study depth perception in the very young is by using the **visual cliff** apparatus designed by Gibson and Walk (1960). It consists of a flat glass-covered table with a checkerboard design directly underneath half of the table and a checkerboard dropoff ("cliff") under the other half. See Figure 4-7. The visual cliff provides dramatic depth *cues* for an infant or animal on the surface. Cues are stimuli that provide useful information. Examples of depth cues provided by the visual cliff are perspective (the converging lines going down into the dropoff) and relative size (the squares on the bottom of the dropoff appear smaller). Gibson and Walk reported that very few infants would crawl across the glass, even when their mothers were coaxing them to do so. The infants seemed to be aware of the apparent dropoff underneath the glass surface. Because these infants were 6-14 months old, they had already had some experience with depth cues. Thus, we cannot be sure whether their perception of the dropoff was innate or learned. It is likely, for example, that learning to crawl involves a lot of falling, with floor-rushing-at-the-face learning. However, Banks & Salapatek (1984) reported that two-month old infants showed a slowing of heart rate when placed on the visual cliff, suggesting that they perceived the dropoff. Slowing of heart rate is usually a sign of increased attention; yet these infants did not show genuine fear responses such as crying and retreating from the "edge." We can conclude from this that young babies notice the sudden change in visual cues at the edge of the visual cliff. However, we don't know if they perceive these cues as depth or simply as a change.

FIGURE 4-7 The visual cliff
Gibson and Walk (1960) used the visual cliff to test the depth perception of infants. The child was placed on a large sheet of glass. A checkerboard pattern was pressed against the underside of the glass on the "shallow" side of the cliff. At the "cliff," the checkerboard pattern abruptly dropped about a metre. Infants will seldom crawl across the cliff, even when beckoned by their mothers.

SOURCE: Gibson and Walk (1960), p. 65. Photo courtesy of William Vandivert and the *Scientific American*.

Gibson and Walk also reported that young kittens, freshly hatched chicks, and a one-day old goat recoiled from the visual cliff. However, even this evidence does not prove conclusively that the capacity for depth perception is innate. Most young animals recoil from any sudden changes in their environment and this recoil response to a changed environment does seem to be innate. So, it could be that the young goat that recoiled from Gibson and Walk's visual cliff could have been reacting not because of its capacity to perceive depth but because of its capacity to notice and react to any change in its environment.

One other line of evidence suggests that human infants do indeed develop depth perception fairly early, usually by the age of approximately four months. In these experiments infants were fitted with special goggles that made some views stand out as three-dimensional while other stimuli remained two-dimensional. The infants started orienting toward the "3-D" pictures at about age four months, indicating that they could discriminate them from the flat views. This suggests that the capacity to perceive depth may, in part, emerge quite naturally as the brain develops rather than be learned through specific individual experience (Aslin & Smith, 1988). In other words, although the depth perception faculty may not be itself present from birth, the developmental clock that brings the infant to the depth perception stage does seem to be built in.

Next, we need to ask what are the cues (whether innate or learned) that help us transform our two-dimensional retinal image into the perception of depth. Some of these cues are binocular ("two eyes") and some are monocular ("one eye").

Binocular cues

Binocular cues are cues that depend on the use of both eyes at the same time. Our eyes are approximately six centimetres apart. Consequently, each eye receives visual input from a slightly different angle. One retinal image is slightly different from the other and both images are two-dimensional. Having two eyes helps us perceive objects in depth and in three dimensions. If we didn't have the use of both eyes, binocular disparity and convergence would not make sense to us experientially.

Binocular disparity

Binocular disparity is the difference between the retinal images of the left and right eyes. It serves us as a depth-perception cue. Each eye sees a slightly different picture, as is shown in Figure 4-8. The brain interprets the differences between these pictures to create the perception of depth. We are not usually aware of any difference between our two retinal images because the images are perceived as one three-dimensional picture. If we intentionally cross our eyes or press on the outside of one eyeball we will see two pictures because the brain can no longer fuse the two very different images.

FIGURE 4-8 Binocular disparity Binocular disparity causes each eye to see a slightly different picture. These two views of the same scene correspond to the view of each eye.

SOURCE: Photos courtesy of the National Museum of Science and Technology.

Binocular disparity leads to **stereopsis**, the process of seeing in stereo. We see a slightly different image with each eye. This is the basis of 3-D movies and viewers. Looking through a 3-D viewer gives the dramatic illusion of depth, as objects in the two pictures seem to be in different planes, one behind the other. Closing one eye immediately eliminates the perception of depth. This loss of depth perception will also happen if we close one eye in the natural environment, but it is usually less obvious than when we look through a 3-D viewer. If you lift your eyes from this page and look at the scene around you, first with one eye closed and then open, you will find that the sense of depth will lessen when you use just one eye. Stereopsis also helps us calculate the movement of objects away from us and toward us. As an object moves toward us, the difference between the two retinal images changes for that object but not for the surrounding objects that have remained stationary.

Convergence

The second way that binocular vision helps us perceive depth is through **convergence**, which is the degree to which the eyes move toward the centre of the face. Convergence is most helpful in judging the distance of objects that are moving closer to us. This is because the change in the angle of the eyes is greater the closer the object is. Hold a finger at arm's length and then look at that finger as you move it back and forth toward and away from your nose. As your eyes strive to keep your finger in focus, you can feel changes in the muscles that control your eyes. The visual cortex of the brain reads these changes for depth perception cues.

Monocular cues

Monocular cues depend on the use of one eye only. When you closed one eye to eliminate the three-dimensional effect, you saw the world the way it appears to a person who is blind in one eye. Such a person will never see the depth in a 3-D viewer or in the world. However, he or she can learn to navigate the environment perfectly well because there are also many monocular cues to depth.

Accommodation

We said in Chapter 3 that **accommodation** is the process whereby fine adjustments are made to the shape of the eye lens. This lens is stretched and contracted by the eye muscles in order to focus an image on the retina. But accommodation also gives the brain information about depth. The eye muscles send different sensations to the brain as they change the shape of the lens. Because this process occurs with each eye, accommodation is a depth perception cue that is especially helpful to those with monocular vision.

Motion parallax

As we move through the environment, closer objects appear to change position faster relative to more distant objects. **Motion parallax** is the movement of images (their direction and their speed) across the retina as either the objects in the environment move or as we move through the environment. This apparent motion is an especially important depth perception cue for judging objects at some distance, because many of the other cues we have mentioned are more useful for nearby objects. Parallax is especially obvious when we are driving in a car. The telephone poles that border the highway seem to whiz by, while the cows in the more distant fields seem to pass more slowly. But you don't need to be in a moving car to observe motion parallax. Hold your finger in front of you and look beyond your finger at an object a hundred metres away. As you move your head from side to side, the distant object seems to move in the same direction as your head, while your finger "travels" in the other direction. As a child riding in a car, many of us have asked, "Why does the moon follow us everywhere?" The moon's apparent lack of motion relative to the immediate environment is a parallax cue for great distance.

Size

Another primary cue for distance is relative size. **Size** can be a depth cue by which more distant objects appear smaller than similar objects closer to us. In our discussion of size constancy, we mentioned that the size of the retinal image of an object changes when our distance from the object changes. As an object moves closer to us, it projects a larger image on the retina. Our brains quickly calculate that the car in front of us is not really getting bigger but is getting closer. The changes in relative size of our retinal images permit us to make the rapid adjustments necessary for us to avoid the other car.

Perspective

Perspective (which we discussed under "Size Constancy") also serves us as a depth perception cue. You will recall that perspective is the principle whereby objects appear to be farther away from us as they decrease in size, and that linear perspective is the principle whereby parallel lines seem to converge to a vanishing point. It is because of linear perspective that railroad tracks seem to come closer to each other as they recede into the distance.

FIGURE 4-9 **The Ponzo illusion**

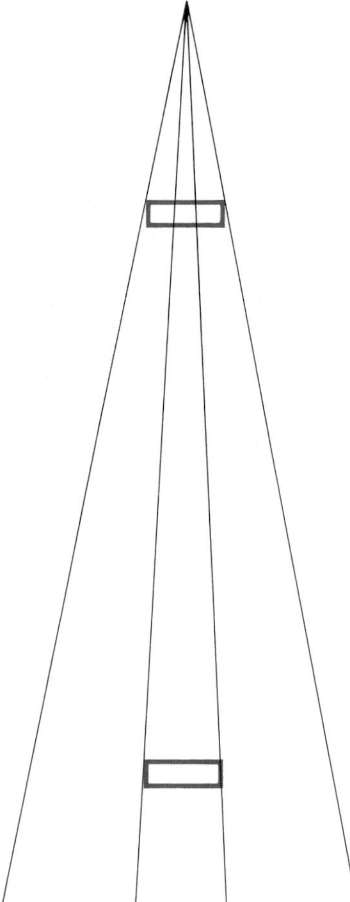

In the Ponzo illusion (see Figure 4-9, previously presented as Figure 3-1), we expect the two rectangles to be of unequal size because of the converging lines. We are accustomed to associating these converging lines with distance. Our perspective cues tell us that the top rectangle is farther away from us than the bottom rectangle, and so we *perceive* the top rectangle as longer than the bottom rectangle even though we *see* that they are the same size.

Perspective is the primary cue that tricked us in the picture of the illusion room in Figure 4-5. The drawing in Figure 4-10 uses linear perspective and foreshortening to give a strong illusion of depth on flat surfaces.

FIGURE 4-10 **The Illusion of depth**
The lines we perceive as going off into the distance greatly enhance the illusion of depth.
SOURCE: Set design by Ferdinando Tacca for the opera *Hipermestra* by Francesco Cavalli, staged in Florence in 1658.

Texture gradient

Texture gradient is a depth perception cue in which the perception of an object's texture is related to the distance between viewer and object. In Figure 4-11, we perceive the tray of marbles on the left as being vertical because its texture (and depth of shadows) is the same over its whole surface. The entire picture is on the one plane. We perceive the tray of marbles on the right as being partially horizontal because the texture is coarser near the bottom or foreground of the

FIGURE 4-11 **Texture gradient**
The texture of the picture on the left is uniform because the marbles are all on one ground. In the picture on the right, the size of the marbles and the clarity of their outlines diminish as the marbles recede.

picture, and gradually becomes finer as we look higher into the background of the picture. This change in texture is another instance of how we use size as a cue for distance. The marbles appear smaller and less differentiated as they recede into the distance.

Shading

Shading is a depth perception cue in which patterns of light and darkness indicate the relative position and shape of an object. Artists use shading to create the appearance of depth in paintings such as Figure 4-12. The artist's manipulation of light and shadow mimics the physical world: shadows fall near an object and shading appears on the object itself. In general, round objects appear to become gradually darker on the side that is away from the source of light, and it is also on this side that the object casts a shadow.

FIGURE 4-12 Shading
Shading can almost make objects leap out of a picture.
SOURCE: Gerald Brockhurst, *Ballynakill Woman*, 1926; etching, 13.7 × 10.5 cm (imp). Art Gallery of Ontario, Toronto. Gift of Mr. and Mrs. Ralph Presgrave, 1977. Reproduced with permission.

Interposition

Interposition is a depth cue in which close objects partially block the view of distant objects. But is this always true? Although interposition is quite dependable in the normal world, it can be used to fool the perceiver as in Figure 4-13.

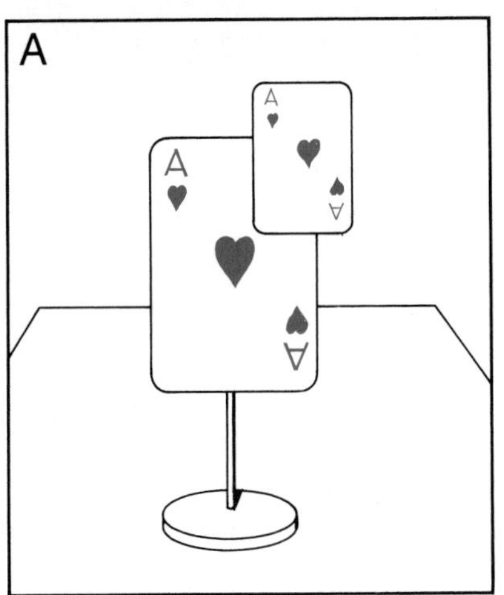

FIGURE 4-13 Interposition
Interposition usually tells us which objects are farther away. We perceive the smaller card as closer in picture A, even after seeing the trick in picture B.

VISUAL ILLUSIONS

Perceptual constancies allow us to perceive the world accurately in most circumstances, but they can also lead us astray. Because we come to depend on these "constants," we are vulnerable to false perceptions. **Visual** (or **optical**) **illusions** are false perceptions or interpretations caused by discrepancies between our visual cues and physical fact. For example, the white checkers in the upper portion of Figure 4-14 are parallel to the four solid white sections in the lower portion. Because of the placing of the checkers, we perceive them to be on an angle. But, if you take your ruler and measure the dark "lines," you will find them to be parallel.

FIGURE 4-14 An optical illusion
Although the white checkers in the upper portion of this figure appear to be on an angle, they are actually parallel to the four solid white bars in the lower portion.

As we saw in the Ponzo illusion in Figure 4-9, some arrangements of objects do not fit what we have learned from experience, in this case from our experience of linear perspective. We are so used to converging lines indicating distance that our perceiving faculties automatically adjust the perceived size of the two rectangles. The rectangles are the same size, so they cast the same size image on the retina of the eye, but the brain perceives the top rectangle as larger because the perspective lines suggest that it is farther away. We can reason that the two rectangles are the same size, but we still can't rid ourselves of the illusion that they are of different lengths. However, it may be that extensive practice could improve our capacity to detect illusions since such practice would give the brain new experiences with which to interpret the cues.

A person who grew up in dense bush or on a small island would not understand what we are talking about because he or she would not experience the Ponzo illusion. Leibowitz (1971) compared university students from Guam with students from the United States. The American students were more vulnerable to the Ponzo illusion, especially as more perspective cues were added. Only a person with a lifetime of experience of lines converging as they recede into the distance is fooled by the Ponzo illusion.

In the Müller-Lyer illusion in Figure 4-15, we perceive Line A as longer than Line B, even though they are of equal length. As in the Ponzo illusion, the apparently more distant lines in A and C are perceived as longer, even though they are the same length as the vertical lines in B and D. Researchers have found that this illusion is strongest for those who live in "carpentered" environments, that is, environments with square-cornered buildings. Apparently, the brain interprets the outward-pointing lines at the ends of Line A as perspective lines "going away" toward a distant corner. On the other hand, the lines at either end of Line B seem to be receding perspective lines that indicate Line B is itself in the foreground. In one study, American Navajos who had spent at least their first six years in traditional round houses were less vulnerable to the Müller-Lyer illusion than Navajos who had grown up in square-cornered houses (Pederson & Wheeler, 1983).

Ironically, the more perceptual experience an individual has, the more that person will be affected by illusions (Matlin, 1988).

FIGURE 4-15 The Müller-Lyer illusion
The apparently more distant lines in A and C are perceived as longer, even though they are the same length as the vertical lines in B and D.

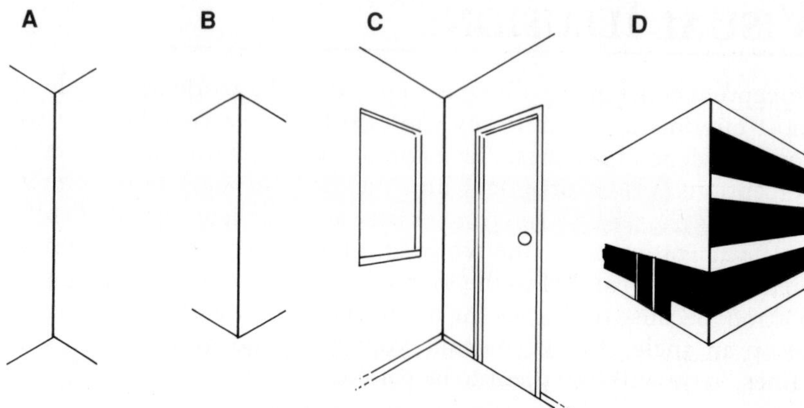

Illusions of movement

Have you ever sat in a bus when all you could see out the window was another bus? If the other bus started to move backward, you probably had the strong perception that you were moving forward. A friend of ours was sitting in his car at a railway crossing waiting for a train to pass. There were cars on either side of him headed in the same direction. As he sat daydreaming, both cars beside him coincidentally started to back up. The illusion that he was rolling into the train was so powerful that he leaped up in the seat and with his heart pounding in his ears slammed the brake pedal as hard as he could. In both of these cases, the relative position of moving objects caused a false perception about movement.

Our perceiving faculties tell us that if an image on the retina moves to another location on the retina, either the object moved or the eye moved. The brain makes its decision about which of these

FIGURE 4-16 A schematic explanation of why passive movement of the eye results in perception of movement of the visual scene

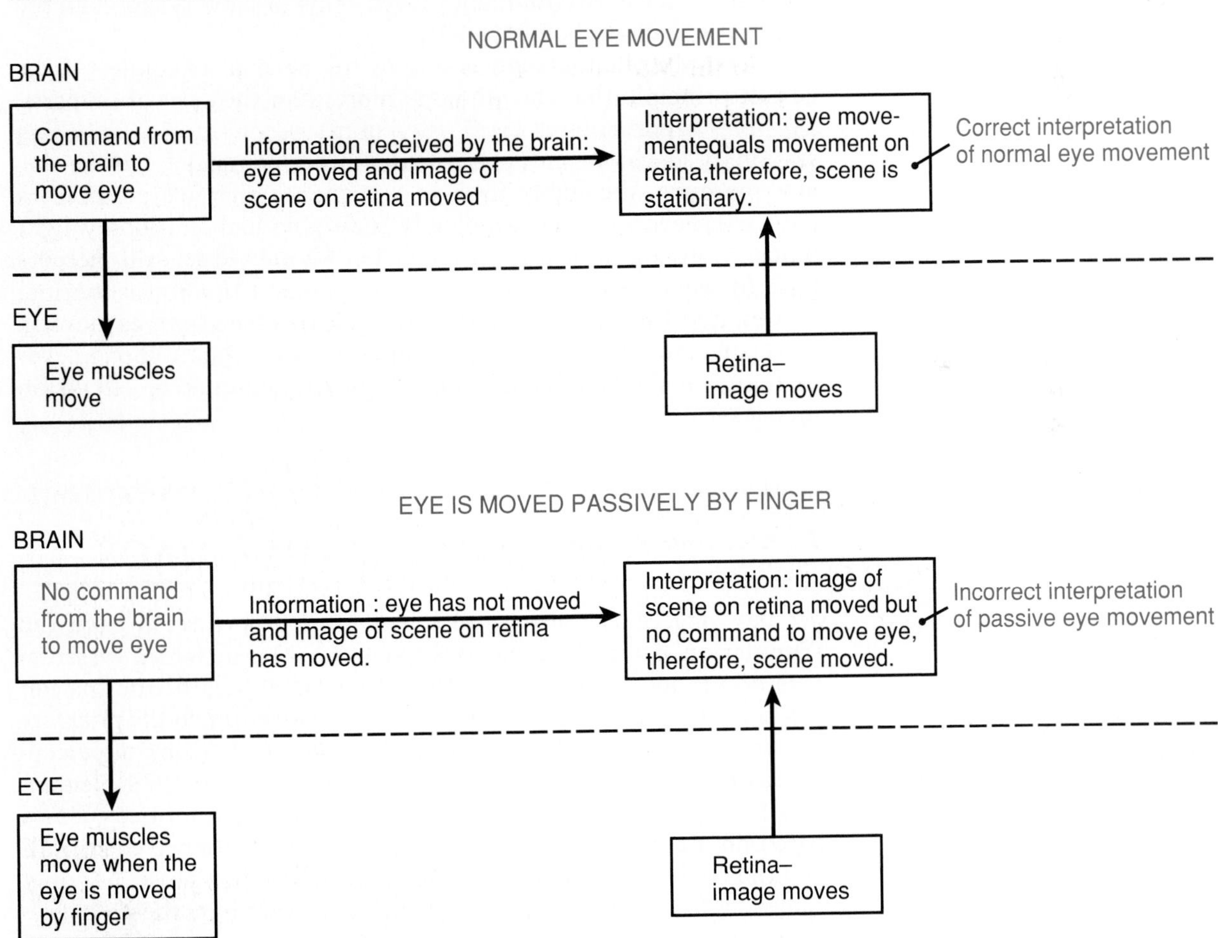

SOURCE: Adapted with permission from Allyn and Bacon, 1989.

has happened based on information it receives from the eye muscles. If there is an intentional movement of the eye muscles, the object being watched is perceived as not moving. If the brain does not get this message of movement from the eye muscles, the brain calculates that the eye hasn't moved, so the object must have. However, even this kind of feedback is subject to illusion. If we sit in a dark room staring at a small light, we will perceive nonexistent movement. Since we would have no cues from other objects in the environment about the relative position of the light, we would have to depend on the position of the retinal image. Our eyes would eventually tire and make small involuntary movements of which we would not be aware. Thus, the retinal image would move, tricking the brain, which wouldn't know about the small eye movements. We would perceive the stationary light as moving. You can get a similar effect by closing one eye and looking slightly downward with the other. Gently pushing the open eye sideways will make objects in the environment seem to move, even though we know they are stationary. Because the retinal image moves and the brain does not receive information about any eye muscle movements, the perception is that the stationary objects in the environment moved. This illusion is shown in the schematic diagram of Figure 4-16.

The phi phenomenon is one of the clearest examples of the gestalt principle that the whole is more than the sum of its parts. The **phi phenomenon** is the illusion of movement created by seeing stationary visual stimuli presented in rapid succession. On the theatre marquee, the lights flash in a sequence that we perceive as animation even though we clearly see individual, stationary light bulbs. More dramatically, on television 60 individual still pictures flash in sequence every second, and we perceive this too as motion. Indeed, it is impossible not to perceive television pictures as moving. This perceived motion emerges from the whole gestalt. It can never be found in the individual "frames" of the marquee or television broadcast.

GETTING MEANING FROM CHAOS

We have traced the process of sensation and perception from the stimulation of our sense organs through the ways by which we structure, group, and organize perceptions. In the next stage of information processing we interpret, classify, and assign meaning to the products of our sensory experience. Cognitive psychologists think of perception as an active hypothesis-testing process (Hockberg, 1978; Neisser, 1967). We are constantly and automatically making informed guesses based on a combination of both our sensory experience of stimuli and the context in which we sense that stimuli. In a sense, our only knowledge of the world is our speculations. Our hypotheses or perceptions are usually correct enough to help us navigate life, but our expectations, motivations, and personality can bias our perceptions.

Factors that prepare us to perceive

Let's look at some of the factors that bias perceptions. Remember that perception is a process of constructing a view of the world. These biasing factors are not simply a nuisance. They actually change our perceptions of our environment.

Context

Sometimes we encounter friends in unfamiliar surroundings and fail to recognize them. We would recognize them instantly in their usual surroundings, that is, in the context in which we are accustomed to perceiving them. **Context** is the situation in which a sensory stimulus is embedded. We often take the meaning of a stimulus from its context. In Figure 4-17, we readily read the words "THE CAT," even though the middle letter in each word is the same shape. Is it an "H" or an "A"? The ambiguous shape casts the same image on the retina whether we look at it in the first or the second word, but context makes it one letter or the other. Context also creates the illusion in Figure 4-18. The two centre circles are exactly the same size, but the one above is in a context of small circles. Therefore it is perceived as larger than the one below in its context of large circles.

FIGURE 4-17 An illusion based on context
Context determines the perception of the middle letter in each word.

Schemas

We have a tendency to perceive what we expect to perceive, even if, in order to do so, we must distort the evidence of our senses. Of course, we don't always and only perceive what we expect to perceive. The reality of the stimuli determines much of our perception. But we do form schemas that influence the process of perception. **Schemas** are organized and complex expectations we hold about the nature of reality — a "blueprint" of what we can expect from the situations and experiences of our individual world. Throughout this book we will see instances where schemas influence memories, emotional reactions, and even social relationships. In this chapter, we want to emphasize the fact that schemas also influence perceptions.

One schema that is common to most of us is the expectation that playing cards are made up of black spades and clubs and red hearts and diamonds. Jerome Bruner and Leo Postman (1949) set up an experiment in which subjects looked at playing cards which were flashed rapidly in a tachistoscope (an instrument that is used to show words or pictures for very brief spaces of time). Subjects were to name the card that was flashed. Most of the cards were coloured normally, but occasionaly an anomalous one was flashed, such as a black three of diamonds or a red ace of clubs. Many subjects *corrected* the data from their senses and gave responses such as identifying the black three of diamonds as the three of spades. What did they actually see? It seems that they *sensed* a black three of diamonds which was the reality, and *perceived* a three of spades, which fit their schema for playing cards. The three of spades was what they really perceived. Remember, our perceptions are a construction. When the experimenters modified the subjects' expectations by suggesting that

FIGURE 4-18 An illusion based on context
The two centre circles are the same size.

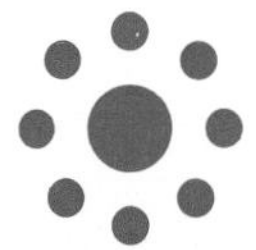

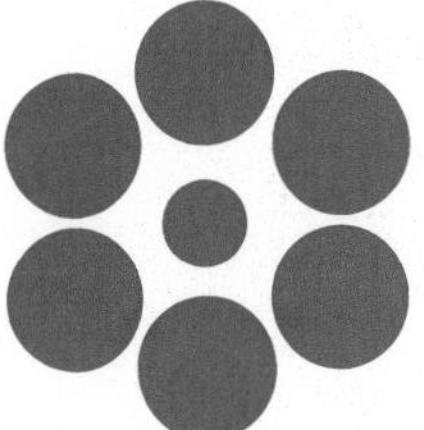

hearts are not necessarily always red, many individuals quickly became able to perceive the anomalous cards accurately. Their schemas had been broadened.

Set

Like a schema, a set is a complex expectation. A **set** is a well-learned predisposition about how to perform a specific task or perceive a particular situation. If our way of perceiving and performing is rigid, we will miss new solutions to problems and even misperceive the world around us. Try this experiment with some friends. Tell them you are going to spell a common word which they are to pronounce without writing the word down. Spell "b-a (pause) s-e-b (pause) a-l-l." Even with it printed here in front of you, you may have had trouble seeing the word "baseball." Many of us would struggle to make sense out of the letters if they are clustered in this way. We have a strong set to perceive words in syllables. The word is easy to see and hear when it is spelled "b-a-s-e (pause) b-a-l-l." The same tendency to form sets applies also to visual stimuli. Figure 4-19 is an ambiguous figure. It first appears to be a mass of variegated spots. However, once it is explained to us that this is actually a dalmatian dog sniffing the ground in a dappled sunlit scene, we create a set, a fixed expectation for this picture. We can now readily perceive the dog and we find it difficult to perceive what we formerly thought to be a mass of spots.

FIGURE 4-19 An ambiguous figure that will become clear as soon as the correct set is created by reading the text.
SOURCE: R. James

Motivation and need

We're more apt to see restaurant signs among a mass of other signs if we are hungry. Our motivational state sensitizes us to food-related stimuli. In an experiment done by Wispe and Drambarean (1953), hungry subjects could identify food-related words more quickly than other subjects, even though the groups did not differ in their ability to identify non-food-related words. Motivation has such a powerful influence on perception that each of us really does perceive a different world. We all have different personalities, and we have different, fluctuating needs and motives. For instance, someone who is starved for affection will perceive a facial expression very differently from someone who is driven to dominate others. The same wide-eyed look could be perceived as affectionate longing or vulnerable weakness.

In a classic study, Bruner & Goodman (1947) found that emotional factors related to socioeconomic status influenced children's perceptions of the size of coins. When the children were asked to estimate the size of various coins, those who were from a lower socioeconomic class overestimated the size of the coins, and those who were from a higher socioeconomic class underestimated their size. To the poorer children, the coins were more important or "larger" psychologically. This greater importance influenced their perceptions of the coins' size.

Perceptual adaptation

In Chapter 3 we discussed sensory adaptation, in which a sensory system stops responding to a stimulus that does not change. Perceptual adaptation is similar but more complex. **Perceptual adaptation** is the tendency not to perceive a repetitive set of stimuli, even when those stimuli are being received by the sense organs. We form a complex set of perceptual expectations and, as long as the environment fits those expectations, we no longer notice.

Karl Pribram (1969) described what he called the "Bowery El" effect. At one time loud elevated trains ran along Third Avenue in New York City. One train ran late each night. The people who lived in the area seldom woke up when the train passed. They were used to it. Interestingly, when the train was torn down, residents frequently phoned police to report that something was wrong at about the time the old train had gone through their neighbourhood. They tended to hear strange noises. What they "heard" of course was the *unexpected* silence. Presumably, as time passed, the residents changed their expectations. That is, they formed revised schemas.

Data-driven versus conceptually driven again: The interactionist view of perception

Earlier in this chapter we contrasted the data-driven perspective on perception with the conceptually driven perspective. **Nativists** are those who favour a data-driven view of perception and who believe that important aspects of the ability to perceive are innate. They emphasize the importance of the nature of the stimulus and say that perceptual processes are inborn, "native," and direct (Gibson, 1979). **Constructivists** or **empiricists** are those who favour a conceptually driven view of perception and who believe that learned abilities enable us to perceive. They think that little of our capacity to perceive is innate, and that we construct our perceptions from what we have learned.

The interactionist view

The evidence we have studied in this chapter and in Chapter 3 (Sensation) leads us to conclude that both the nativist and the constructivist viewpoints are partially correct but that neither is completely true. Nativists can point to sensory structures that result in similar perceptions for virtually all humans. They can mention evidence such as the visual cliff experiments which suggest that depth perception is either innate or very easy for a young infant to learn. On the other hand, empiricists point out that even the neural structure of the visual cortex depends on experience. Kittens who never see horizontal lines are blind to horizontal lines (Mitchell, 1981). Constructivists also emphasize the many cultural and personal factors that influence perception, some of which we have described in this chapter.

Interactionists believe that perception emerges from both inherited biological factors and learning experiences. The evidence on the development of depth perception provides strong support for this position. We have said that depth perception in infants seems to be present at about four months of age. This seems to support a nativist view. However, the development of the visual cortex is influenced by experience, as we saw with the kittens blind to certain lines. Researchers have found that experience plays a large part in the development of binocular neurons. **Binocular neurons** are detector cells in the visual cortex that receive stimulation from both eyes and are used in depth perception (Singer, 1986). In one experiment, kittens were raised with one eye covered one day and the other covered the next for several months (Blake & Hirsch, 1975). Later, the animals could not perceive depth correctly. They had not developed the binocular ability in the neurons that are normally connected to both eyes. Such experimental data tells us that in order to understand perception we must consider both the innate potential of the brain and the experience needed to bring out that potential.

A less dramatic but similar finding has been reported in research done on adult humans (Ball & Sekuler, 1982). Training seemed to modify the experimental subjects' motion detectors. Each subject sat in front of a screen on which dots were scattered. Sometimes the dots moved a tiny distance and the subjects practised detecting this movement. Performance at detecting movement increased with practice. For each subject, however, the dots always moved in one direction only. Later testing showed that the subjects had improved at detecting tiny movements *only* in the direction they had been trained to detect. They did not experience a general improvement in motion detection. When the subjects were retested ten weeks later this effect was still present. It seems likely that the subjects' visual systems were modified by experience in a very specific way. It is possible that specific motion-detector cells in the visual cortex developed because of the training. This is further evidence that the structure of the brain interacts with experience.

Coordination of perceptual and motor systems

We seldom consider what an amazingly complex act it is to catch a ball. We plot its trajectory through the air, constantly projecting how many metres farther along it will be seconds from now. We judge its depth in the environment, calculating changes instantly, all the while factoring in information from our own bodily senses about where we are relative to the ball and where we need to be two seconds from now. It is not enough to have good depth perception and good kinesthetic sense. In order to catch that ball, the two processes must be well integrated.

In a well-known study with kittens, Held and Hein (1963) demonstrated the need for coordination between these two processes. One kitten in a pair was permitted to walk around a circular enclosure in a harness. The other was restrained in a holding device illustrated in Figure 4-20. Every movement by the first kitten caused the second one to *be moved* around the same environment. Thus, their perceptual experiences were identical. However, the first kitten was learning to integrate motor movements with external perceptions. Immediately following the experiments, only those kittens who had been allowed to move could navigate the environment effectively. The kittens who had been exposed to visual stimuli passively failed a number of tests of visual recognition. However, after a few hours experience with normal movements, the second group (the passive kittens) quickly acquired the same perceptual abilities as the first group.

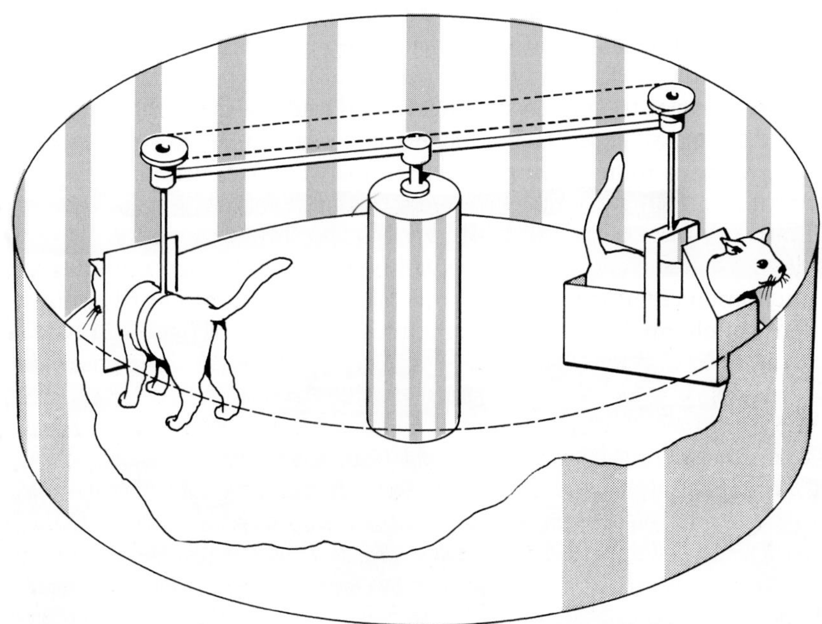

FIGURE 4-20 Perception and movement

Although both kittens saw the same environment, only the active kitten learned to integrate bodily movements with external perceptions.

SOURCE: Adapted from Held and Hein (1963).

A reconstructive process

We can think of the whole sensory-perceptual process as a process of reconstruction. We form hypotheses which we hope will enable us to reconstruct the reality of our world. We have seen that the early stages of the process are influenced primarily by relatively mechanical factors. The later stages, however, are partly the product of our past experiences and of our personality, motivation, and various higher mental processes. We really do reconstruct reality, but it is according to our own image. This process occurs so effortlessly and automatically, however, that we believe that our perceptions and interpretations are really the way the world is. The study of perception is a little humbling. Perhaps it will make all of us more tolerant of others' perceptions.

PERCEPTION WITHOUT SENSATION (ESP)?

SOURCE: *Bizarro* by Dan Piraro. Reprinted by permission of Chronicle Features, San Francisco, CA.

Interest in psychic phenomena is very high in our culture. Many people report having had psychic experiences or know someone who has. Of all the disciplines of knowledge, psychology is the one that comes closest to including extrasensory perception (ESP) as an area of interest. Feelings run very high among psychologists, however, over whether research should even be done on such topics. Wagner and Monnet (1979) found that about one-third of psychology professors considered ESP to be either an "established fact" or a "likely possibility." However, another one-third of the professors said that ESP is "an impossibility." Since it is rare for a scientist to say that anything is impossible, it is clear that parapsychology arouses passionate feelings among psychologists. In other academic fields, teachers were somewhat more likely to be positive about ESP. However, the most interesting finding was that among professors in the natural sciences, only 3% said ESP was impossible. In the other social sciences, none of 166 professors questioned said it was an impossibility.

Before we examine evidence and controversies in parapsychology, we need to define some basic terms, starting with parapsychology itself. "Para" means "beyond," and the term **parapsychology** was coined to describe the study of phenomena beyond the normal realm of traditional psychology. This subfield of psychology includes all phenomena related to mental perception that doesn't use the known sensory channels or known principles of physics. The general term used for paranormal abilities is **psi**. **Telepathy** is the transfer of information from one person (or animal, some would say) to another without the use of known sensory channels — mind reading. **Clairvoyance** is the perception of distant or hidden events or objects without using known sensory channels. It differs from telepathy because clairvoyance does not involve another person's thoughts. **Precognition** is the perception of future events. This can involve specific predictions and prophetic dreams about future events. **Psychokinesis** is a mental operation whereby thought affects material objects without the aid of known physical channels. Usually referred to as "mind over matter," psychokinesis can include such acts as controlling the roll of a die or bending a spoon or a key. Although psychokinesis is not a form of perception, it is usually included in discussions of ESP.

Evidence on ESP

There are many kinds of evidence that influence what a person believes. We saw in Chapter 1 that several beliefs that seem obvious from a common-sense viewpoint are not supported by controlled research studies. Common sense and everyday experience often mislead us. On the other hand, formal research methods are not suitable to study some aspects of human life, and they can mislead us if they are used inappropriately. The conflict between evidence from personal experiences and evidence from formal research is probably most obvious in the area of ESP.

FIGURE 4-21 The five symbols used on Zener cards in ESP experiments

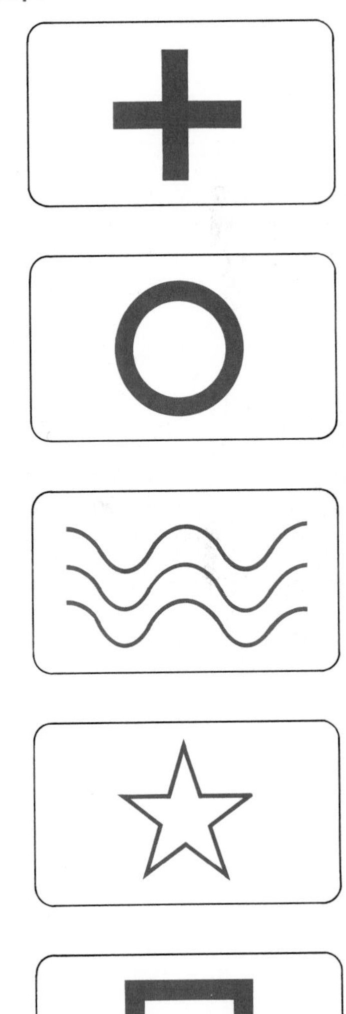

Individual experiences of ESP

Personal experience is the basis of most people's belief in ESP. For instance, someone notices that he or she often thinks of a particular person just before that person phones. Or, to take a more dramatic example, someone experiences an inexplicable sense of dread at the moment a loved one has died some miles away. Such stories are difficult to study systematically because they are unpredictable, and they may happen only once or twice in a lifetime. Further, the details of such occurrences are subject to the vagaries of selective memory. They can neither be confirmed nor be disconfirmed by formal research. Such occurrences are often referred to as **anecdotal evidence**. This evidence is composed of specific incidents, stories, or anecdotes that are cited to support a particular belief and that are gathered without the control typical of formal research. For many people, this kind of evidence is sufficient to support belief, but some researchers have tried to gain an acceptance for parapsychology within the discipline of traditional psychology by designing experiments to explore ESP.

Formal research

The most famous pioneer of ESP research was J. B. Rhine, who established a parapsychology lab at Duke University. He tried to formalize research on ESP by developing a deck of cards (Zener cards) to use in experiments (see Figure 4-21). The cards had five different symbols on them and were used for various experiments. For research into telepathy, one subject would look at a card while another tried to identify it. For research into clairvoyance, a subject would try to identify a card that no one could see. For research into precognition, a subject would try to predict the order that the cards would take after they were shuffled. Performance runs that were greater than the probability of chance were taken as evidence of ESP.

Although the early results of these experiments seemed to indicate strong support for the existence of ESP, these results were later discredited because many factors were not well controlled. For example, early batches of Zener cards were poorly printed and, under certain lighting conditions, the symbol could be seen through the back of the card. Also, experimenters did not usually "blind" themselves and sometimes unconsciously gave subjects cues.

Some subjects had remarkable runs of success but later reverted to chance levels of performance. Sceptics said that the successful runs had also been the result of chance and that, when all runs were calculated together, the results indicated a chance-level performance. Believers in ESP countered that psi ability is probably stronger at some times than others and that subjects probably fatigue over time (Rhine, 1977).

Questioning the evidence

The role of chance and coincidence

If we threw two dice long enough, we would eventually have a run of ten throws in a row when both dice would come up with the same number. Such an occurrence would not seem remarkable if we had been throwing for ten hours, but if it happened on the first ten throws, we would all be amazed. Obviously, it *could* happen on our first ten throws if it can happen after ten hours. If a thousand other people were also throwing dice, it is likely that somebody would have the amazing run. Should we consider that person "psychokinetic"? Sceptics, of course, would say no. All subjects' runs would have to be considered before we could eliminate the role of chance in our results.

Alcock (1981) has argued that the laws of chance make it inevitable that many coincidences will occur in everyday life. They should be expected and not interpreted as evidence of ESP. Like other sceptics, Alcock says that believers notice coincidental happenings and selectively remember them while forgetting hundreds of similar incidents when the coincidence did not happen—for example, when we felt sure that a particular person was phoning but it turned out to be someone else. Believers argue just the opposite about sceptics —that they are so closed-minded they selectively ignore and forget remarkable instances of what Carl Jung called synchronicity. **Synchronicity** is the belief that the components of the universe are interconnected in ways that cause seemingly separate events to influence each other.

The problems of replication and fraud

As we said in Chapter 1, the *scientific method* consists of (i) gathering information through systematic observation, (ii) formulating a theory, (iii) deriving a hypothesis, and (iv) testing the hypothesis in a controlled and reproducible manner. Science is built on public procedures that permit others to replicate research findings. This tradition helps protect against both deliberate fraud and self-deception by researchers who may want the data to support a particular conclusion. As far as we know, there is no ESP phenomenon that has been reliably replicated by independent researchers. Supporters of ESP argue that this could be because the phenomena are fleeting or the research methods are insufficient. However, most scientists still want *some* finding that can be replicated before they will accept psi as a reality.

Although numerous ESP experiments have resulted in positive findings, these studies tend to be published in journals devoted to parapsychology. In general, when researchers hostile to ESP try to replicate these apparently successful experiments, they are not successful. Their interpretation is that positive findings by believers are thus demonstrated to be unreliable. The believers, on the other hand, respond that the very hostility of the researchers could be masking or preventing the subtle mental processes being studied.

In addition to the problem of unintentional bias, two kinds of fraud have plagued parapsychology. The first is scientific fraud of the sort that can occur in any science. Sometimes researchers fake their data. Normally this is discovered when other scientists cannot replicate the original findings or when colleagues become suspicious and point out flaws in the method or interpretation of the experiments. As in other areas of psychology, some parapsychology researchers have been caught cheating. The impact on the field has been more damaging than it would be in another field, however, because of the replication problem we just discussed. We can't count on replication to unmask the cheaters.

The second kind of fraud is the use of conscious trickery to fool researchers. There are hundreds of ways to fake psychic phenomena very convincingly and many reasons why people try this trickery. One such attempt was designed to demonstrate that parapsychology researchers are vulnerable to deception (Randi, 1983a, 1983b). Two teenage magicians, Steve Shaw and Michael Edwards, presented themselves to the parapsychology laboratory of Washington University as potentially psychic subjects. For three years they fooled researchers into thinking they were actually psychic by using trickery to perform such illusions as bending spoons, appearing to see hidden objects "clairvoyantly," and moving objects across a table "psychokinetically." (They used an almost invisible type of thread for this last trick.) They then revealed their scam at a news conference with James Randi, the professional magician who had taught them the magic tricks.

Stage psychics

Nearly all psychologists agree that successful stage psychics must use magic tricks and illusion to get such consistently good results. Most scientists are naive lambs in the hands of a clever magician, perhaps in part because science is based on being able to trust the work of others. James Randi (1980) has devoted much of his career to calling into question performing psychics (such as Uri Geller) and the validity of the evidence for psychic phenomena. Randi performs public key bending, spoon bending, and amazing acts of apparent telepathy. He then explains to his astonished audience that it was all trickery. Some of his audience members have been known to angrily accuse Randi of having true psychic powers which he exploits by pretending they are magic tricks! If you want to know how he does his tricks, you can buy his books.

Magicians never tell their secrets for free, but we're not magicians, so we will tell you one way to do public key bending. First of all you should know that at least 90% of successful magic is the skillful misdirection of the audience's attention. The secret manoeuvre of misdirection in key bending is quite simple. Gather three or four keys, preferably from different audience members. In the confusion you purposefully create—having the audience check the keys for "secret markings," for example—you slip the tip of one key into the slot of another. This will give you plenty of leverage to bend the key with two fingers while your audience is otherwise occupied. Then have a volunteer offer to hold the keys in an upstretched hand. You apply appropriate "psychic powers," and, by golly, one of the keys comes down bent, even though you never touched them during the apparent bending process.

Marks and Kamman (1979) are two psychologists who have criticized many psychic phenomena, especially those performed by Uri Geller. They report instances of having caught Geller cheating when he was presenting his work as authentic psychic phenomena. If you're interested in how conjuring has been used to fake psychic powers, their book would be a good place to start.

Distortions on both sides

Most adverse criticism and accusations of inaccurate reporting have been aimed at supporters of ESP. However, in 1985 Irving Child of Yale University wrote an article in *The American Psychologist* in which he argued that psychologists opposed to ESP have tended to distort the evidence too. They have done this through selective reporting of evidence and through outright inaccuracies in describing evidence (Child used the word "falsification" rather than "inaccuracies").

Child focused on a series of studies in which an attempt was made to influence the content of dreams through ESP. This research was carried out at the Maimonides Medical Center in Brooklyn, New York. The general procedure was to have a subject sleep in an isolated room while being monitored on an EEG machine in another room. (As we will see in Chapter 9, it is possible to tell when a person is dreaming by the nature of the EEG reading and by eye movements.) As soon as the subject was dreaming, the experimenter pressed a button to signal a second subject in a remote room of the building. The second subject concentrated on one target picture that had been chosen randomly from a pool of pictures. The content of this picture was known to no one but the second subject, who had not opened the packet containing the picture until after being isolated for the night. Near the end of the dreaming period, the experimenter woke the first subject by talking through an intercom. The subject related his dream as the experimenter probed and questioned him. Neither the subject nor the experimenter knew the content of the target picture during this phase.

Later, independent raters judged the similarity between the reported dream and each of the potential target pictures. They, of course, had no information about which pictures had been used in a particular experimental session. In summarizing the results of many such sessions, Child concluded, "The outcome is clear. [There is] significant evidence that dreams (and associations to them) tended to resemble the picture chosen randomly as target more than they resembled other pictures in the pool" (Child, 1985, p. 1223). Writing in *The American Psychologist*, Oliver Hill called these studies "well designed, with results that are extremely compelling" (Hill, 1986, p. 1170). Further, there have been a number of successful replications of the Maimonides findings. However, most of these other studies have not controlled all variables as well as did the original research. Child also reports two programs that attempted careful replications by having greater control of these variables. One of these obtained chance findings and the other got results that were not statistically significant but were "encouraging."

While this research is interesting and merits attention, it doesn't settle any questions about ESP. However, the main point Child wanted to make came in the second part of his article. He described the way in which five books by psychologists presented the Maimonides dream research. Each book was a critique of ESP. One book made no mention of the research, and the other four presented blatantly inaccurate descriptions of the procedure. For example, Zusne and Jones incorrectly reported that the experimenters had provided many relevant clues to the dreamer prior to the dream session. They accused the experimenters of "preparing the receiver through experiences that were related to the content of the picture to be telepathically transmitted during the night" (Zusne and Jones, 1982, p. 260). This simply was not true. Had this been true the research would, of course, have been invalid and the experimenters incompetent. Child provides many such examples of misrepresentation and concludes, "Readers who doubt that the falsification is as extreme as I have pictured it need only consult the sources I have referred to" (1985, p. 1228).

This is the emphasis we want to leave with the reader on this question of the existence of ESP. In a controversy where feelings run so high, writers on both sides tend to distort facts. It is important to stay open-minded and to read the original arguments from both supporters and detractors.

Conclusion

It is fair to say that 130 years of research on paranormal phenomena have not produced a finding that has been reliably replicated in scientific experiments. Many psychologists consider this lack of replicable findings sufficient reason to abandon the notion of ESP. Clemmer says, "Since the time of William James, the scientific case for parapsychology has not been convincing. Why should researchers devote any more time to such research?" (Clemmer, 1986, p. 1174). The National Research Council in the U.S. conducted an extensive review of the evidence for and against the existence of ESP and concluded that there is no scientific justification for belief in parapsychological effects (Druckman & Swets, 1988). Critics of this position counter with several arguments. First, the tools of psychological research are crude and probably not well suited to finding these phenomena. Or second, there have been positive results, but they are fragile and psychologists distort them. Or third, there are so many experiences of psychic connection under extremely emotional conditions, such as at the time of a loved one's death, that it is foolish to abandon the search yet.

The comment, "We'll never know anything for sure, probably," seems to apply to this question of ESP. Oliver Hill has argued for the "serious consideration of apparent anomalies (as) an essential part of the procedure of science." But he also knows how difficult it is to keep up with the information explosion in the study of psychology. "Often, however, scientific psychologists have difficulty keeping on top of the literature within even a narrow domain of interest and never venture beyond the boundaries of their immediate research" (1985, p. 1170). Nonetheless, in spite of this overload psychologists must remain open to developments not only in their own discipline but also in other fields of knowledge. Hill went on to describe "recent anomalous findings in the area of quantum physics that have great implications for all of the natural sciences, including psychology." Quantum physics does have some truly mysterious findings (such as massless particles, probabity waves, and event horizons) that seem to be paradoxical. None of this, of course, really tells us whether psychic phenomena are valid or invalid. What Hill's comments mean is that because there is so much we don't know, it is essential to be open-minded. On the other hand, it is also important not to be gullible, especially in areas with a history of deception and self-deception. Is it possible to retain a sense of wonder and be a sceptic at the same time? We hope so.

SPECIAL TOPIC Pain Perception and Control

We all experience pain, and many of us have experienced excruciating pain. Wallis (1984) estimates that approximately one-third of our population experiences chronic pain. Pain is associated with the knocks and bruises of everyday life, as well as with almost all forms of illness.

Pain is a complex phenomenon that has evolved for the purpose of signaling the organism that something is amiss. As much as we dislike pain we would not survive without it. Those rare individuals born with no ability to feel pain seldom live long. They are at risk because they do not notice injuries, of course, but there are other, less obvious dangers. For example, most people change position fairly regularly during sleep because lying in one position becomes uncomfortable. The person who feels no pain often has severe — even fatal — bedsores because there is no discomfort to motivate the small movements needed to prevent bedsores.

Two systems for pain

As we mentioned in Chapter 3, there is some controversy over the nature of the pain system. Some people believe that there are specialized pain receptors in the skin and within the body. Others contend that the sensation of pain results from over-stimulation of any receptor in the body.

Whichever side is correct in this controversy, we do know that there are two major pain systems in the peripheral nervous system. One system is responsible for the sharp jabbing or pricking sensation of pain that can be localized to specific body parts. It has been called the body's warning system (Melzack & Dennis,

1978). This **warning system** delivers sharp, temporary pain while the organism is in immediate danger and it uses fast, large, myelinated nerve fibres to transmit the messages quickly. (Remember from Chapter 2 that myelinated neurons fire more efficiently than nonmyelinated neurons.) The second system, the **reminding system**, leads to a slower, aching, long-lasting pain that is more diffused throughout an area of the body. This system uses smaller, unmyelinated nerve fibres. A toothache or the pain of a bruise or of a tumour give a constant reminder of longer-term danger. We are forced to protect the bruised place or to take action against the illness. Sometimes the reminding system continues to function even when it no longer serves its purpose, such as in the case of terminal illnesses or of injuries that have already healed.

Gate control theory

Melzack (1973, 1980) and Wall (1979) have developed the gate control theory to explain pain control or pain modulation. They suggest that the sensory system has a limited capacity and so there are only a limited number of neural pathways for pain to follow. According to **gate control theory**, spinal mechanisms or "gateways" in the spinal cord control the perception of pain by permitting one source of stimulation to block another. In this way the system is kept from overloading and some information is blocked from reaching higher centres and conscious awareness. If you have ever severely banged your arm or leg and then rubbed the area vigorously, you were using this gate control mechanism. You were using the principle of **counter irritation**, a procedure for blocking intense pain by causing a competing stimulation. Rubbing your arm caused stimulation that competed with the pain for the use of sensory neural pathways.

Endorphins: The brain's painkillers

Endorphins (or **endogenous morphines**) are a class of neurochemicals (found in the brain) that diminish pain. They are similar to morphine in chemical structure (Snyder and Childers, 1979) and function as an analgesic to reduce the perception of pain. Evidence suggests that both pain and stress initiate a release of endorphins from various brain sites (Kruger & Liebskind, 1984). People who suffer from chronic pain may have reduced amounts of endorphins in their systems (Akil, 1978).

The action of endorphins may account for the "runner's high" experienced by some long-distance runners. These runners report an intense feeling of pleasure or elation ("the runner's high") that allows them to tolerate extreme levels of pain. After running so far that the body has to initiate pain-control measures, the person may actually get "high" on natural painkillers.

Pain relief

Gate control theory and the action of endorphins help us understand some very old and some new ways to cope with pain.

Transcutaneous electrical stimulation (TENS) is a pain-reducing procedure that uses low-intensity current to block pain stimuli at the spinal pain gates. The subject experiences as a mild tingling the current that is applied through surface electrodes on the skin. TENS can sometimes decrease the perception of chronic pain because the electrical stimulation competes for pathways in the limited capacity pain system. Because TENS stimulates the large, fast nerve fibres of the warning system, it blocks the slower but more agonizing pain coming from the reminder system. It thus "closes the gate" on the chronic pain.

Acupuncture is a procedure in Chinese medicine used to diminish pain and treat various ailments. The acupuncturist uses needles inserted in the skin and then stimulated by being twirled, heated, or electrified. The procedure is used widely in China for the relief of pain during dental work and sometimes as an anaesthetic for surgery. Chinese doctors also use acupuncture to treat a wide range of other disorders, but this is not commonly known in the West. Chinese medicine explains the effect of acupuncture on the basis of life energy flowing along "meridians" in the body (see Figure 4-22). However, this explanation is not widely accepted in Western science, so researchers have tried to tie acupuncture into what we already know about the nervous system.

Melzack and Wall (1983) believe that acupuncture needles stimulate the small, slower nerve fibres of the reminding system. They go through the pain gate in the spine and up to a "central biasing system" in the brain. This system is like a control centre that redirects neural signals to different functions. Then some of these stimuli return to the spinal cord and close the pain control gates against chronic and intense pain.

FIGURE 4-22 The meridians of energy-flow as understood by Chinese medicine
Chinese medicine teaches that acupuncture affects the flow of life energy along these pathways in the body.
SOURCE: Photo courtesy of the Consulate General of the People's Republic of China.

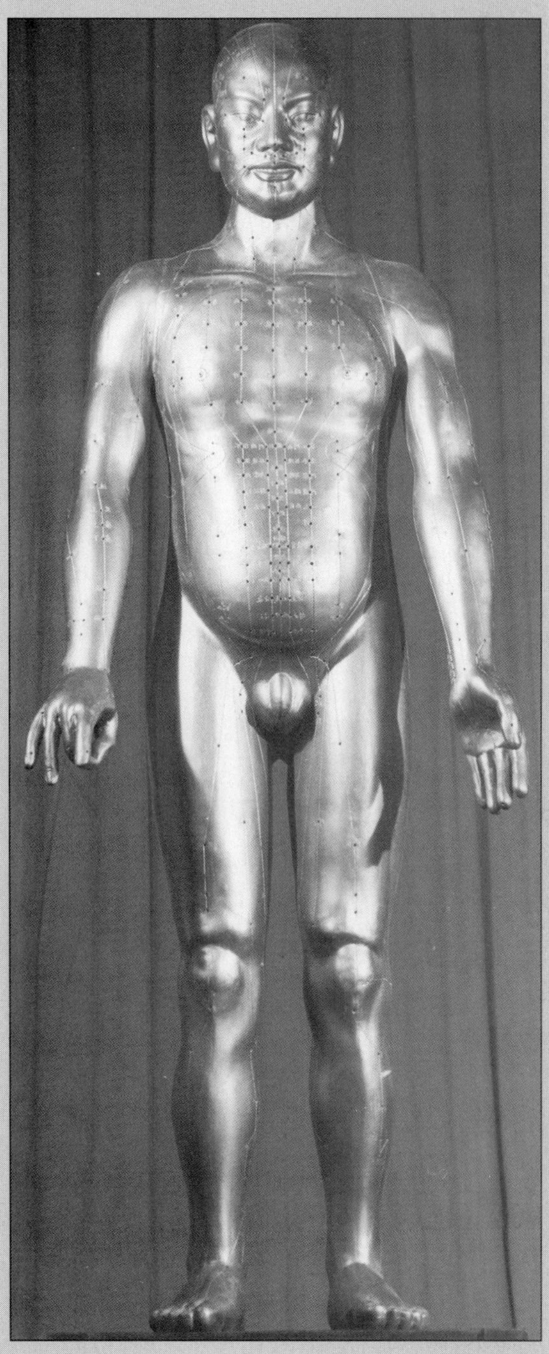

Acupuncture seems also to reduce pain by releasing endorphins. Patients sometimes experience euphoria, deep relaxation, and feelings of light-headedness during treatment, suggesting that something is happening in addition to the closing of pain gates. Pomeranz (1984) demonstrated that acupuncture reduced sensitivity to pain in mice. A second group of animals was injected with a drug (naloxin) that blocks the effect of endorphins and then given acupuncture. They remained sensitive to pain, suggesting that the pain-reducing effect of the acupuncture in the first group resulted from endorphin release.

Higher mental functions can also act on spinal cord mechanisms to effectively close the gate to pain. Active involvement in strenuous mental activity may result in a very high threshold to pain. Athletes sometimes finish an important game with broken bones, never feeling pain until the game is over and there is no more excitement to compete with the pain. We can be hit quite hard in the middle of an intense sporting activity and "not feel it," while the same injury at another time would be extremely painful.

This may explain how hypnosis can be effective in pain management. As we will discuss in Chapter 9 (Consciousness), hypnosis combines a high degree of focused attention with a powerful state of suggestibility.

Social influences on pain

Pain is intensely emotional and usually occurs in a social context. Children often get hurt and somehow bravely hold back tears until a parent arrives. Even later in life our pain behaviour is strongly influenced by our social environment and by the reaction we get from others. There are gender-role stereotypes and ethnic differences in response to pain (Zborowski, 1969).

Research has also shown that our complaints of pain generally increase when they gain us the sympathy and attention of others, and they decrease when these rewards are not given (Block, 1980). This means that caring for a victim of pain, especially chronic pain, requires a sensitive balance between giving needed support and avoiding unnecessary reinforcement of the pain. Pain can become the central focus of a lifestyle, especially if the pain and pain-related behaviour become valued. The person might avoid work, receive compensation benefits, not have to do housework, and be dependent on others. These reinforcements can actually extend the duration of the pain; the person would not be faking the extension of pain. Sometimes pain restricts a person's quality of life well beyond the time when the patient should be medically fit to return to an active lifestyle. For such people, an integrated treatment program that attends to their medication, lifestyle, reactions of important others to their pain, work, and psychological problems needs to be implemented (Fordyce, 1973).

1. Perception is the process by which we organize and make meaningful the mass of sensations we receive. Perception is influenced both by the stimuli that impinge on our senses and by our internal mental processes.
2. The data-driven perspective on perception focuses on external stimuli and the innate structure of the nervous system. The conceptually driven perspective focuses on the influence the perceiver's internal processes have on perceptions. Both perspectives help us to understand perception.
3. Gestalt principles of perception help us understand how we perceive integrated wholes, rather than a collection of separate elements.
4. We tend to group perceptions along lines of similarity, proximity, closure, and continuation, and we tend to organize perceptions into figure and ground.
5. We usually, at any given moment, focus our attention on one set of stimuli from the mass of competing stimuli in our environment, though we do seem to process these other stimuli at another level. Under the right circumstances a different set of unattended stimuli can interfere with this focus and draw our attention to itself.
6. Even though our visual sensations are always changing, we learn to perceive size, shape, brightness, and colour constancy in the world we see.
7. Through a number of binocular and monocular cues we are able to experience depth perception in spite of the fact that our retinal images are flat and two-dimensional. We seem to possess either innate depth perception or the capacity to learn it at a very early age.
8. Binocular depth perception cues include binocular disparity and convergence. Monocular cues for both stationary and moving objects include accommodation, motion parallax, relative size, perspective, texture, shading, and interposition.
9. Visual illusions occur because the monocular and binocular cues that usually help us perceive our world accurately can sometimes be deceived. Our susceptibility to some visual illusions seems to be influenced by cultural learning.

10. Illusions of movement can occur when we are deprived of the visual cues that usually tell us which objects are moving and which objects are stationary or when our normal eye muscle movements are interfered with. The phi phenomenon occurs when stationary stimuli are presented rapidly and in sequence, as in a motion picture.

11. Perception can be seen as an ongoing, largely conceptual process of making and testing hypotheses about the nature of the environment. Our perceptions are embedded in the context in which they occur. They are also influenced by our sometimes distorted expectations about the nature of the world, and the schema and sets we have developed to help us understand and deal with the data from our senses.

12. Personal motives and needs also influence perceptions by sensitizing us to particular stimuli. We tend to adapt to repetitive perceptions, so that they are less likely to be perceived.

13. The interactionist view is that biologically determined and learned processes interact with each other in the development of our perceiving faculties. Certain cerebral cortex neurons seem to be essential for perception and seem to develop only with certain developmental experiences. These neurons can be affected, even changed, by a controlled perceptual environment.

    Perception is best understood as a reconstructive process, in which we interpret reality through the filters of our past experience.

14. Parapsychology is a controversial area in psychology. About one-third of psychology professors believe that ESP is impossible and another one-third believe that it is either an established fact or at least highly likely to exist. The scientific evidence for telepathy, clairvoyance, precognition, and psychokinesis is very weak, primarily because none of these phenomena have been replicated in research. While some believers have falsified evidence in favour of parapsychology, some nonbelievers have distorted and ignored other, potentially valid evidence. Supporters of parapsychology claim that traditional methods of psychological research are not appropriate for studying these phenomena.

KEY TERMS

Accommodation Fine adjustments to the shape of the lens of the eye. A depth perception cue that is especially helpful to those with monocular vision.

Acupuncture Procedure in Chinese medicine used to diminish pain and treat various ailments. Uses needles inserted in the skin and stimulated by being twirled, heated, or electrified.

Anecdotal evidence Specific incidents, stories, or anecdotes that are cited to support a particular belief. They are gathered without the control typical of formal research.

Attention See *selective attention*.

Binocular cues Cues that depend on the use of both eyes at the same time.

Binocular disparity The difference between the retinal images of the left and right eyes. A depth perception cue.

Binocular neurons Feature detectors in the visual cortex that are connected to both eyes and used in depth perception.

Brightness constancy The tendency to see a known object as being more or less of a constant brightness even when the prevailing light intensity changes.

Clairvoyance The perception of objects or events without using known sensory channels.

Closure A gestalt principle of perceptual grouping, by which we tend to fill in gaps in order to perceive objects in familiar form.

Colour constancy The tendency to perceive an object as being more or less of a constant colour even when the brightness and wavelength of light change.

Conceptually driven processing The perspective on perception that focuses on the higher, internal processes of the perceiver (such as expectations, past experiences, knowledge, and mood) and their impact on perception.

Constructivists (or **empiricists**) Those who favour a conceptually driven view of perception and who believe that learned abilities enable us to perceive.

Context The situation in which a sensory stimulus is imbedded.

Continuation See *good continuation*.

Convergence The degree to which the eyes move toward the centre of the face. A depth perception cue.

Counter irritation Procedure for blocking intense pain by causing a competing stimulation.

Data-driven processing The perspective on perception that focuses on the external stimuli of the environment and their impact on the nervous system as a biological entity.

Depth perception The ability to judge the relative distance of objects and to perceive objects in three dimensions.

Empiricists See *constructivists*.

Endorphins (or **endogenous morphines**) Neurochemicals that diminish pain. Similar to morphine in chemical structure.

Figure That part of a set of stimuli which we perceive as objects.

Gate control theory The view that spinal mechanisms control the perception of pain by permitting one source of stimulation to block another.

Gestalt The perception of an entity as an integrated whole, rather than as a collection of separate elements.

Good continuation A gestalt principle of perceptual grouping, by which we tend to perceive objects according to the apparent flow of direction of the surrounding objects.

Ground That part of a set of stimuli which we perceive as the space around the objects.

Grouping A gestalt principle of perception by which we tend to organize our perceptions by grouping objects together.

Interactionists Those who believe that perception emerges from both inherited biological factors and learning experiences.

Interposition A depth cue in which close objects partially block the view of distant objects.

Linear perspective A geometrical law which dictates that parallel lines seem to converge as they recede into a "vanishing point" in the distance.

Monocular cues Cues that depend on the use of one eye only.

Motion illusions False perceptions in which surrounding cues distort the person's perception of motion.

Motion parallax Movement of images (their direction and their speed) across the retina as either the objects in the environment move or as we move through the environment. A depth perception cue that is especially helpful to those with monocular vision.

Nativists Those who favour a data-driven view of perception and who believe that important aspects of the ability to perceive are innate.

Optical illusions See *visual illusions*.

Parapsychology The study of phenomena beyond the normal realm of traditional psychology.

Perception The process of organizing and making meaningful the mass of sensations we receive.

Perceptual adaptation The tendency not to perceive a repetitive set of stimuli, even when those stimuli are being received by the sense organs.

Perceptual constancy The tendency to maintain stable perceptions even when sense data change.

Perspective The principle whereby foreshortened objects are perceived as being farther away and larger objects are perceived as being closer. Perspective also helps us perceive a three-dimensional world even though our retinal images are only two-dimensional. A monocular depth perception cue.

Phi phenomenon An illusion of movement created by seeing stationary visual stimuli presented in rapid succession.

Precognition The perception of future events.

Proximity A Gestalt principle of perceptual grouping, by which we tend to perceive objects near each other as a group.

Psi The general term for paranormal ability.

Psychokinesis A mental operation whereby thought affects material objects without the aid of known physical channels.

Reminding system (*for pain*) The system that delivers slower, diffuse, aching, long-lasting pain that is more diffused throughout an area of the body. Uses smaller, unmyelinated nerve fibres.

Schema An organized, complex expectation we hold about the nature of reality.

Selective attention A state of focused processing of one set of stimuli among many competing stimuli.

Set Well-learned predisposition about how to perform a specific task or how to perceive a particular situation.

Shading A depth perception cue in which patterns of light and darkness indicate the relative position and shape of an object.

Shape constancy The tendency to perceive an object as being a constant shape, even though the retinal image of that object changes shape depending on our angle of vision.

Similarity A gestalt principle of perceptual grouping, by which we tend to perceive similar objects as a group.

Size A depth cue by which more distant objects appear smaller than similar objects that are closer to us. Especially helpful to those with monocular vision.

Size constancy The tendency to perceive familiar objects as being a fixed size, even though the size of the retinal image of the object changes when our distance from the object changes.

Stereopsis The process of seeing in stereo, that is, seeing a separate image with each eye.

Synchronicity The belief that the components of the universe are interconnected in ways that cause seemingly separate events to influence each other.

Telepathy The transfer of information from person to person without using known sensory channels.

Texture gradient A depth perception cue in which the perception of an object's texture is related to the distance between viewer and object.

Transcutaneous electrical stimulation (TENS) Pain-reducing procedure that uses low-intensity current to block pain stimuli at the spinal pain gates.

Unconscious inferences Automatic conclusions the brain draws about the actual qualities of sensed objects in order to maintain perceptual constancy.

Visual cliff Apparatus for studying depth perception in infants. It consists of a flat glass-covered table with a checkerboard design directly underneath half of the table and a checkerboard dropoff ("cliff") under the other half.

Visual illusions (or **optical illusions**) False perceptions or interpretations caused by discrepancies between our visual cues and physical fact.

Warning system (*for pain*) The system that delivers sharp, temporary pain while the organism is in immediate danger. Uses fast, large, myelinated nerve fibres to transmit the messages quickly.

Suggested Readings

Several of the textbooks suggested at the end of Chapter 3 also would be a good source for further reading in perception, especially Matlin (1988).

Marks, D. & Kammann, R. (1979). *The psychology of the psychic*. Buffalo, N.Y.: Prometheus Books. This sceptical view of psychic phenomena explains most of the best known psychic phenomena as the result of illusions, fraud, or coincidences to be expected by chance. The authors report interesting first-hand contacts with famous investigators and self-proclaimed psychics.

Held, R. & Richards, W. (eds.). (1972). *Perception: Mechanisms and models*. San Francisco: W. H. Freeman. Includes a detailed discussion of illusions.

Sekuler, R. & Blake, R. (1985). *Perception*. New York: Knopf. A useful, general text on perception.

Sternbach, R. A. (ed.). (1986). *The psychology of pain*, 2nd ed. New York: Raven Press. Psychological methods for the control of pain are an important part of this general book on pain.

CHAPTER 5

SOURCE: Walter Trier, Detail from "Der Bücherbote," *Illustrierte* Zeitschrift für Bücherfreunde (n.d.).

Principles of Learning

CLASSICAL CONDITIONING
- The basic process
- Higher-order conditioning
- Generalization and discrimination
- Extinction and counterconditioning
- Temporal contiguity and conditioning
- Classical conditioning and human experience

OPERANT CONDITIONING
- Positive reinforcement
- Negative reinforcement
- Shaping and fading
- Extinction
- Primary and secondary reinforcement
- Schedules of reinforcement
- Superstitious learning
- Timing of reinforcements

PSYCHOLOGY OF FEAR
- Emotional conditioning
- Escape and avoidance learning
- Principles of fear reduction
- Why fears are persistent

BIOLOGICAL CONSTRAINTS
- Classical conditioning
- Operant learning
- A common misunderstanding of behaviour theory

PUNISHMENT AND BEHAVIOUR CONTROL
- The basic process of punishment
- Disadvantages of punishment
- Long-term influence on behaviour

COGNITIVE LEARNING
- Inside the black box
- Cognitions as behaviours
- Observational (vicarious) learning

CLOSE-UP The Only Way to Make Money in Las Vegas

SPECIAL TOPIC The Truth about Little Albert

WE SPEND a lot of our life trying to influence others. We want people to like us and to behave the way we think they should behave. We want our friends to do certain things, our children to have certain values, and our parents to share our opinions. It sounds better to call this process "influence" rather than "manipulation," but whatever we call it, the fact is that we all engage in the process. Our investigation into the principles of learning is designed to help explain why people do what they do and how their behaviour can be changed. In other words, an understanding of the principles of learning can help us understand ourselves and show us how we might change our own behaviour.

Behaviour can change as a result of experience. We refer to such changes as *learned* changes in order to distinguish them from changes that result from fatigue or some physical injury or aging or direct physical intervention (as with drugs). For our purposes, let us define **learning** as behaviour change that occurs as a result of experience. By far, most of what we do and feel—such as reading, writing, the feelings we get upon seeing our worst enemy or our best friend, and the subtle way our speaking voice sounds like that of our parents—is the result of learning. Kimble (1961, p. 6) defines learning as "a relatively permanent change in behavior potentiality which occurs as a result of reinforced practice." Through the years, psychologists have discovered a great deal about the basic principles of learning.

Most of the research on learning principles has been done by psychologists who are called *learning theorists*. **Learning theorists** (also called **behaviourists** or **behaviour theorists**) are psychologists who believe that virtually all behaviour is the result of prior learning. In its most strongly stated version, learning theory says that although humans (and animals) are born with certain genetic "equipment" that influences how they develop, it is largely one's experience that determines behaviour, thinking, and personality. This position was stated very strongly by Watson in 1930, when behaviourism was first becoming influential:

> Give me a dozen healthy infants, well-formed, and my own specified world to bring them up in and I'll guarantee to take any one at random and train him to become any type of specialist I might select—doctor, lawyer, artist, merchant chief, and yes, even beggar-man thief, regardless of his talents, penchant, tendencies, abilities, vocations, and races of his ancestors (Watson, 1930, p. 104).

Most learning theorists today would not take such a strong position. It is even possible that Watson was taking an extreme position purposefully in order to arouse people's interest and invite controversy, which he certainly got. However, learning theory does say that everything we think and do is influenced by our learning history, and what we call "personality" simply consists of our *learned* thoughts, feelings, and overt behaviours.

There are two general categories or types of learning: *classical conditioning* and *operant conditioning.*

CLASSICAL CONDITIONING

In **classical conditioning** (sometimes called **respondent conditioning**), a neutral stimulus is paired with some stimulus that already elicits a specific response. If this is done repeatedly, eventually the neutral stimulus will come to arouse the specific response when presented alone. For example, a puff of air in the eye will cause an eye blink; if a bell rings regularly just before the puff of air hits the eye, eventually the subject will automatically blink in response to just the bell. Most people have heard of Pavlov and his dogs; classical conditioning was first associated with salivation in dogs (Pavlov, 1927). Pavlov discovered classical conditioning by observing and following up an incidental occurrence in his work as a physiologist studying salivation. Earlier, he had won the Nobel Prize for his study of the digestive process. Not until he was 50 did he start doing research on conditioning — the work for which he is best remembered. Pavlov studied salivation by putting meat powder on dogs' tongues to elicit saliva. Some experiments were thrown off, however, because the dogs started to salivate too early — at the sight of the food and probably even at the sight of Pavlov, who brought the food. By noticing that a previously neutral stimulus could acquire the power to arouse responses, Pavlov discovered classical conditioning. Other physiologists had noticed the association between the experimenter's presence and unexpected salivation and had mentioned it in their writing, but none of them thought to follow it up with systematic study as Pavlov did. There is an important lesson about the process of science in all this. Many important discoveries result from being open to the unexpected.

Ivan Pavlov with his students.
SOURCE: The Bettmann Archives.

FIGURE 5-1 The basic process of classical conditioning
During conditioning, Pavlov paired a light (a formerly neutral stimulus) with food powder. The food powder was a US that caused the UR of salivation. Eventually the light became a CS that caused the salivation which had become a CR.
SOURCE: Adapted from Sanford and Wrightsman (1970).

BEFORE CONDITIONING

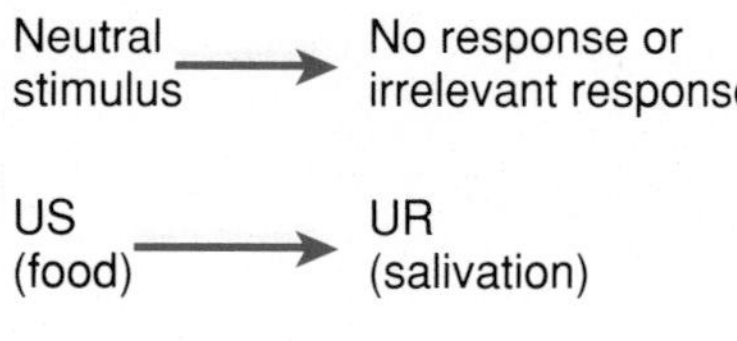

DURING CONDITIONING

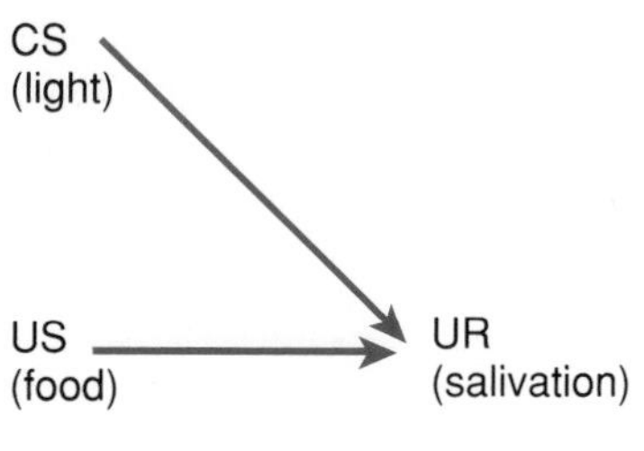

AFTER CONDITIONING

The basic process

The process of classical conditioning is illustrated in Figure 5-1. At the most basic level, we start with an unconditioned stimulus. An **unconditioned stimulus** (**US**) is any stimulus that arouses a particular response in an organism in the absence of prior learning. Every time we apply this stimulus, the person or animal responds in the same way. The **unconditioned response** (**UR**) is the particular response that is aroused by an unconditioned stimulus. A bright light in your eye is a US that always leads to the UR of pupil constriction. A puff of air in your eye is a US that always leads to the UR of an eye blink. Pavlov's meat powder was a US which led to the UR of salivation.

Figure 5-2 illustrates Pavlov's equipment which delivered meat powder (the US) through a tube into the dog's mouth and measured the amount the dog salivated (the UR). The delivery of the meat powder could be precisely timed to follow the onset of a light, buzzer, bell, or other conditioned stimulus.

If we present a US along with some other neutral stimulus, we will of course still get the UR, because of the US. We could play middle C on the piano just before we blow a puff of air in a cat's eye. The cat will blink because of the puff of air. If we do this repeatedly, the musical note will become a *conditioned stimulus*, and the cat will blink when it hears middle C even before the puff of air. In Pavlov's initial experiments, he himself had become a conditioned stimulus to the dog after being associated with the presentation of meat powder many times. A **conditioned stimulus** (**CS**) is a previously neutral stimulus that has acquired the power to arouse a particular response because it has been associated with an unconditioned stimulus. A classically **conditioned response** (**CR**) is that response that is aroused by a conditioned stimulus.

It is tempting to think that the cat blinks to middle C because it *expects* the puff of air, but a classically conditioned response is not entirely under conscious control. Think of your own eye blink

FIGURE 5-2 Classical conditioning apparatus

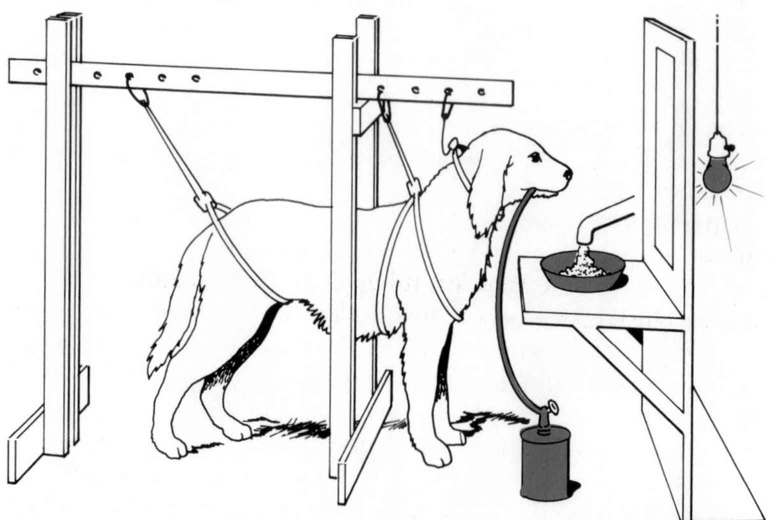

response. When something is coming toward your face quickly, you blink well before you feel any contact, even before you feel any air movement—*and* before you have time to think. You don't decide to blink. Even if we were to warn you that we were going to throw a ball at your face and show you that the ball is on a tether so it cannot reach your face, you still would either blink or prevent the blink only with a great deal of effort.

It is remarkable that virtually anything can come to serve as a CS. Controversy does exist about whether some stimuli are easier than others to establish as CS's. We will discuss this later. The importance of classical conditioning is reflected in some of our own CR's and how "natural" they seem. The word "natural" means "from nature," something we're born with. But we usually use the word in a much broader sense. Most of us would say it is quite natural for a hungry person to drool at the sight of *good* food. However, we might think it unnatural for a hungry person to drool at the sight of insects. Some people *do*, however, drool at the sight of insects; chocolate-covered grasshoppers are a delicacy in parts of the Orient. This is a result of culturally determined classical conditioning.

If your parents had wanted to explore classical conditioning, they could have built a special table that hid your food from sight as it entered your mouth. Usually, the sight of the food immediately precedes the taste of the food on your tongue, so the sight of the food becomes a CS. In your hypothetical case, just before the food hit your tongue, your parents could have shown you something else — say, buttons—every time. You would then drool at the sight of buttons, a response that could create a number of awkward situations for you. Actually, your drooling at buttons would probably have died out by now, but we'll deal with that below under "Extinction."

Higher-order conditioning

So far, we have discussed *first-order* classical conditioning. First-order conditioning always starts with a US, a stimulus with biologically built-in effects. Obviously, however, we have many conditioned reactions that are difficult to trace back directly to some unconditioned stimulus. You may fear snakes, even though you have never been hurt by a snake or ever been in the presence of snakes. Likely, you learned it by seeing another person's fear of snakes. Therefore, first you learned to fear the causes of other people's fears. In general, a great deal of what we learn comes through imitating what other people do.

Higher-order conditioning is the establishment of a conditioned stimulus by pairing a new neutral stimulus with an existing conditioned stimulus. The new stimulus alone then acquires the power to arouse the original conditioned response. To demonstrate higher-order conditioning, we could use a CS that has already been established (we could call this CS1). We could then repeatedly pair this CS1 with some other neutral stimulus and thereby establish the second stimulus as a new conditioned stimulus (CS2). For example, in some experiments Pavlov rang a bell just before putting the meat powder in the dog's mouth. Eventually, the bell alone made the dog

FIGURE 5-3 First-order and higher-order conditioning

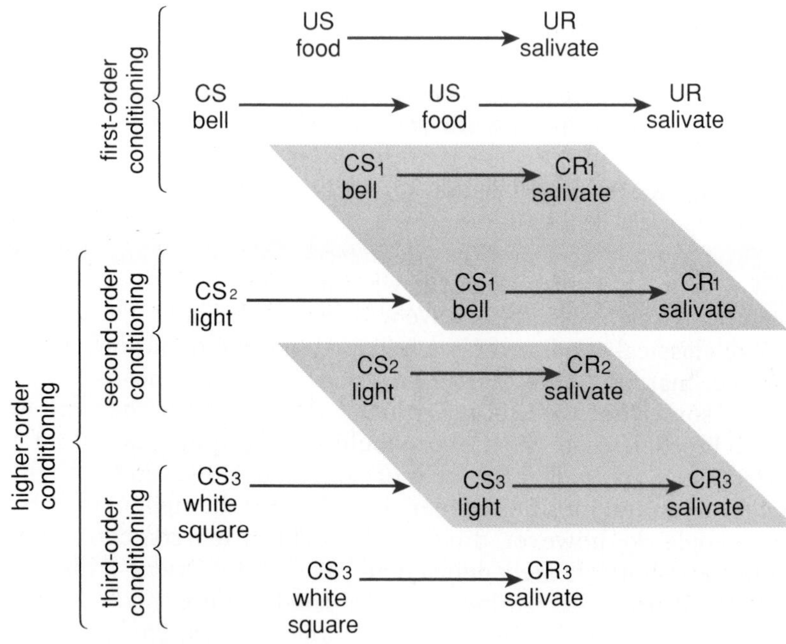

SOURCE: Reprinted with permission from Sanford and Wrightsman (1970).

salivate. Then, without using meat powder anymore, Pavlov turned on a light and rang the bell. Eventually, the dog salivated to the light, even though it was never directly associated with meat powder. The bell was CS1 and the light was CS2. This is an example of *second-order* conditioning.

We can go on to third-order and fourth-order conditioning by using CS2 to establish CS3 and then CS4. (See Figure 5-3.) However, with CS3 and CS4 we seem to be approaching the limit of higher-order conditioning because the effect of CS1 weakens every time it is presented without the US (Schwartz, 1984). This is the extinction effect we will discuss below.

Generalization and discrimination

In learning theory, **generalization** is the process by which stimuli similar to a CS will also elicit the CR, but the strength of the CR will be diminished. If your parents had always used red buttons in their food experiment, you would also salivate to other colours of buttons but not as much. Pink buttons would give you a lot of trouble but not as much as red ones. Zippers might even get to you a little because of the similarity of function. If an animal is conditioned to fear the playing of middle C on the piano, then other notes will also arouse the fear response, and the effect will diminish as we play notes farther up or down the scale from middle C (Schwartz, 1984).

These examples illustrate the **gradient of generalization**, which is the tendency for the strength of generalization to diminish as stimuli become less similar to the original conditioned stimulus. In the experiment illustrated in Figure 5-4, a CR was established to the CS of a vertical line. The subject's strongest CR is to a line at 90 degrees of tilt. Other lines also elicit the CR but less strongly. The more similar a stimulus is to the original CS, the more strongly it will elicit the CR. Thus, lines at 60 and 120 degrees of tilt arouse the CR more strongly than lines at 30 or 150 degrees of tilt. This gradient has an important adaptive value, since we need to apply lessons we learn from one situation to many others. For example, we learn certain emotional reactions to the characteristics of people who have hurt us, and we generalize our feelings to other similar people. It would be very painful to have to learn the lesson with each new person of this kind. In a more positive vein, getting pleasure from one book gives us good feelings about books in general and helps guide our behaviour toward reading.

Generalization can also lead to conflict. If you were strongly conditioned to jump up when a red light came on (let's say you could avoid a shock that way), you would also jump at the sight of an orange light because of generalization. If you were also strongly rewarded for crouching quickly at the sight of yellow light, that response would also generalize to orange, because orange is a combination of yellow and red. But when the orange light was unexpectedly flashed, what would you do? It may sound strange, but your body would be inclined to both crouch and jump at the same time. Likely you would just freeze in place, quivering in conflict.

In a sense, *discrimination* is the opposite of generalization. Conditioned responses do have a tendency to generalize, but a person can be taught **discrimination**, which is the process of learning to respond to a particular stimulus but not to similar stimuli. In this type of conditioning, the specific stimulus that the person is taught to respond to is called the **discriminative stimulus**. You can be conditioned to respond to yellow buttons and not to orange buttons. A sweet roll with spots of green mould still looks a lot like a sweet roll, but it probably won't make you salivate. Discrimination also has survival value for us.

FIGURE 5-4 A gradient of generalization

If a vertical line is used as a conditioned stimulus, lines in other orientations will also arouse the conditioned response because of generalization. However, the farther the line is from vertical, the weaker will be the response.

SOURCE: Adapted with permission from Allyn and Bacon, 1987.

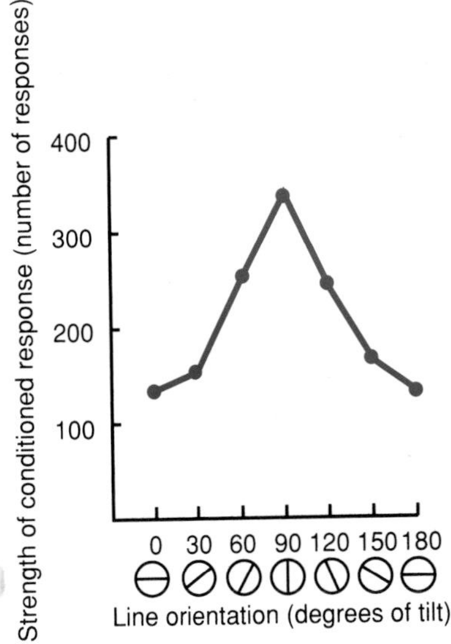

Extinction and counterconditioning

Since some classically conditioned responses (such as fear) are often undesirable, it is important to know ways to weaken or get rid of them. The two primary methods used by psychologists are *extinction* and *counterconditioning*. These two processes underlie much of what we will discuss in Chapter 15 under the heading "Behaviour Therapy."

Extinction

The term *extinction* refers to the weakening of conditioned behaviour. **Extinction in classical conditioning** will occur (i.e., a CR will weaken) *if (1) the CS is presented, (2) the CR occurs, and (3) there is no presentation of the US.* Every word in this sentence is important. Take fear as an example. Fears do not weaken with the passage of time; extinction is required. You must face the CS, the thing you fear, usually in small steps; you must feel at least some of the fear; and finally you must have nothing bad happen. We know people who are afraid of flying on commercial aircraft even though they have

FIGURE 5-5 Extinction of your response to buttons over trials of exposure to the CS

SOURCE: Adapted with permission from Allyn and Bacon, 1987.

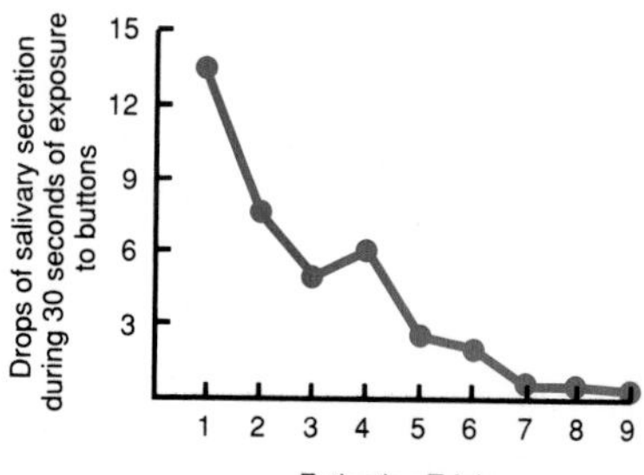

been flying for years. In every case but one, they either drank or took tranquillizers when they flew. This means that they left out one of the three components of extinction. They faced the CS (flying), and there was no US (crash or other pain), but the CR did not occur—they felt no fear. There was one person who was still afraid of planes even though he had flown hundreds of thousands of miles without drinking or taking tranquillizers. He was a student we once had when we taught a course in a penitentiary. We couldn't figure out why the principles didn't seem to apply in his case until he mentioned that he had been running drugs each time he had been flying. Thus, his fear of flying was repeatedly reconditioned because he was in a constant state of fear of being caught. He was a victim of higher-order conditioning. His CR1 was the fear of being caught. Flying became his CR2 because whenever he flew he felt so much aversive emotion from CR1.

It may *seem* as though conditioned responses lose intensity with time. But if they actually do weaken, it is probably because during that time we have real-life experience with the CS's without the US's, and this causes extinction to happen "naturally." You may not have seen a snake for years but may be just as fearful of them as ever. The passage of time will not weaken your fear. Only extinction will actually weaken it. As the subject of our hypothetical food and button conditioning, you may argue that the fact that you don't drool at the sight of buttons anymore illustrates a CR weakening with the passage of time. At one time, the very thought of buttons might have made you drool. However, since childhood you have had years of seeing buttons all around you without being presented with food. This happened in the absence of the US, since we assume your parents no longer follow you around giving you ice cream and showing you buttons. Through the years the CS (buttons) has been presented many times under many circumstances, and though in the early days the CR (drooling) occurred, there has been no US (food) paired with the CS. See Figure 5-5. In other words, you have had years of extinction experience.

Spontaneous recovery and reconditioning

Though a CR may be extinguished enough times that it no longer appears when the CS is presented, two phenomena demonstrate that extinction is almost never complete. The first of these phenomena is **spontaneous recovery**, which is the reappearance, after a period of time, of an apparently extinguished CR when the CS is presented again. Each time spontaneous recovery occurs, however, it will be weaker than the previous time. If you fall off a motorcycle, you will probably feel some fear when you resume riding, and people will advise you to ride frequently to get rid of the fear. Eventually, extinction will let you ride with little or no fear. But if you take a break from riding, some of the fear will probably return the next time you ride.

If you go through the spontaneous recovery enough times, even it should stop occurring. Nevertheless there is a second phenomenon that indicates that extinction is rarely complete. You will find that the effects of your original conditioning persist to some degree, inasmuch as a new conditioning experience will establish the conditioned response more rapidly than before. In general, there is a residual effect of the original learning that leads to easier reconditioning (Schwartz, 1984). **Reconditioning** is the relatively rapid re-establishment of an apparently extinguished CR by means of new conditioning trials. We could recondition you to salivate to buttons more rapidly than we could a person who was never conditioned to salivate to buttons.

Counterconditioning

Counterconditioning is also designed to get rid of a CR, but it seems to work through a different process. **Counterconditioning** is the process by which a newly learned response is paired with and replaces an older learned response. We present the CS along with some new stimulus whose effects work counter to the original CR. We might present you with a button and put something terribly bitter in your mouth, establishing buttons as a CS for inhibition of salivation. We are establishing a new CR to *compete* with the old one. Counterconditioning does not actually weaken the original CR; it merely suppresses the original CR by means of the competing response.

Temporal contiguity and conditioning

The term **temporal contiguity** refers to the closeness in time of the presentation of two stimuli, such as a CS and a US. As a general principle, the closer the link in time between a US and a potential CS, the stronger will be the conditioning. In the Pavlovian experiment, if a buzzer sounds a few seconds before the meat powder hits the tongue, conditioning will be stronger than if there is a two-minute gap between the two stimuli. The most effective time intervals are somewhat different for different types of responses. For example, for a motor response such as an eye blink, the most effective time gap is about one-half second between CS and US; but for internal bodily responses such as heart rate and salivation, between five and fifteen seconds is best.

We can distinguish four different temporal relationships between the CS and US. They are illustrated in Figure 5-6.

In **delayed conditioning**, the CS is presented prior to the US. The CS either overlaps with the US or terminates exactly when the US begins. A buzzer might start, and then a puff of air begins and they both stop together. This is the most effective pattern. It is called "delayed" conditioning because the US does not start until after the CS does. But note that there is *no* time gap between the two. In **trace conditioning**, the CS is presented prior to the US with a time interval between the offset of the CS and the onset of the US. For instance, the buzzer starts and stops, and a brief time later the puff of air starts and stops. This is called "trace" conditioning because it depends on a memory trace of the CS to form a link between the CS and US. It is fairly effective but less so than delayed conditioning. Both delayed conditioning and trace conditioning are types of forward conditioning, which is generally effective because the CS acts as a signal or

FIGURE 5-6 Four patterns of CS–US timing, in the order of their effectiveness

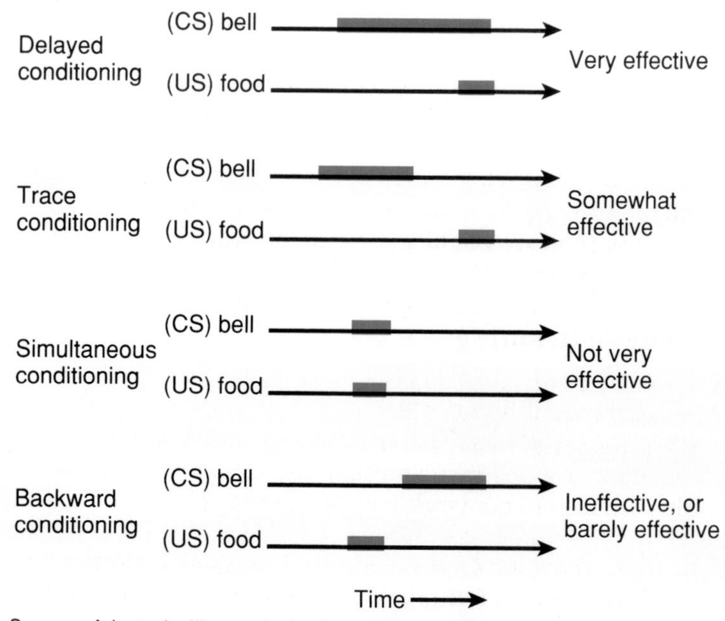

SOURCE: Adapted with permission from Allyn and Bacon, 1987.

warning that the US is coming. In **simultaneous conditioning**, the US and CS occur together and terminate together. For instance, the buzzer starts the instant the puff of air does, and both end at the same instant. This pattern can work but not very well. The fourth pattern is more difficult to execute. In **backward conditioning**, the US is presented first, and the CS follows after the US is terminated. For instance, the puff of air comes first, and after it ends the buzzer is sounded. Because the CS does not function as a signal that the US is coming, this timing is not as effective as forward conditioning. It is sometimes said that backward conditioning is nearly impossible to perform. Nevertheless, Keith-Lucas and Guttman (1975) gave rats one experience of a substantial electric shock to the feet and then presented a toy hedgehog. Subsequently, the rats avoided the hedgehog as an aversive stimulus. This was backward conditioning, because the CS followed the US. It is no surprise that rats should have evolved the ability to acquire a conditioned connection between the sight of a potential predator and a prior pain experience. Although Keith-Lucas and Guttman's rats had no previous experience with predators, it is possible that they had a *biological preparedness* to learn this CR very readily. We will discuss biological preparedness and conditioning later in this chapter. Spetch, Wilkie, and Pinel (1981) reviewed this and many other studies and concluded that backward conditioning is difficult but not impossible to achieve.

Because the CS usually acts as a signal, it is not surprising that conditioning is most effective when the CS is *intense* and when it is *novel* (Kalat, 1974; Lubow, Rifkin, & Alex, 1976). An intense CS works well because it grabs the attention of the subject. A stimulus is novel when it is unusual itself or when it appears in an unusual context. A novel CS is an effective signal because it does not carry other learned associations from previous experience. We could condition you to blink at the sight of pizza, but it would be more effective to use a CS that you had never seen before. For most people, pizza is already a CS for other responses. Therefore, it would not be very effective as a signal for the puff of air in your eye (the US).

The important principle to learn from this section on temporal contiguity is that immediate reinforcement is more powerful than delayed reinforcement. In other words, the shorter the time between the CS and US, the stronger will be the conditioning. This principle will have many applications for understanding some complex behaviours—like self-defeating emotions, for example—that we will discuss later in our study of human behaviour.

Classical conditioning and human experience

Conditioned responses play very important roles in our lives. Fears for which we can find no "reasonable" cause, feelings of peace and satisfaction, and many other subtle emotional reactions probably involve at least some classical conditioning from our pasts. We are not saying that one's emotional life is nothing but classically conditioned reactions. The picture is obviously more complicated than that. Nevertheless, from a study of classical conditioning we can learn much about ourselves and gain a great deal of understanding of how to help people with their problems.

Turkkan (1989), who has drawn together much recent research on this question, has pointed out that classical conditioning affects a wide range of phenomena in human functioning. The following sample of these areas will give you an appreciation of how pervasive and important classical conditioning is. We will often return to classical conditioning later in the book to show how psychologists use it to help people with problems.

Classical conditioning and the placebo effect

The **placebo effect** occurs when a physiologically inactive substance has a measurable effect on physiological functioning. Demonstrations of the placebo effect can be dramatic. Injections of salt water (which has no physiological effect) resulted in fewer ulcers a year later when the original injection had been given by a doctor rather than a nurse. Significant placebo effects have been demonstrated for angina, blood-pressure problems, common cold, cough, fever, stomach secretions and movements, headache, insomnia, generalized pain, rheumatoid arthritis, the effects of vaccines, and warts (Evans, 1985). Classical conditioning probably plays a part in such healing. The "sugar pill" acts as a CS for many healing experiences because similar pills have been followed by relief in the past. Thus, in its role as a CS, a placebo can arouse the internal reactions that bring relief (see also Wickram, 1989).

Classical conditioning and immune-system responses

In Chapter 19 (Psychology and Health), we will see that psychological factors have a significant impact on the immune system, our internal defence against disease. It has been established that the immune system can be classically conditioned. If animals are fed saccharine as a CS, followed by a drug that suppresses the immune system, the taste of saccharine alone can later suppress the immune system. This finding has enormous implications for the control of illness. It may also help explain the power of placebo effects. Perhaps some placeboes are CS's for improved functioning of the immune system.

Classical conditioning and substance abuse

Drug users often develop strong CR's to the surroundings in which they use drugs. Consequently, using the drug among friends in a familiar setting will have a more powerful effect than the same dose in a different setting. People who are falsely led to believe that they have ingested alcohol sometimes become quite "drunk." These studies suggest that the treatment of alcoholism and other substance-abuse disorders is far more complicated than simply treating the chemical effects. The passage of time will not eliminate the CR's that chemical abusers develop to the surroundings in which they use drugs. The CR's must be explicitly extinguished.

Classical conditioning and eating behaviour

Virtually any of our internal processes can be classically conditioned. Thus, it is no surprise that the mechanisms that control hunger are often affected by previous learning experiences. The production of insulin by the pancreas, for example, can be a CR. In a person's conditioning history, the sight of food is regularly followed by eating, which raises the level of blood sugar. This rise in blood sugar acts as a US to stimulate the pancreas to produce insulin, which metabolizes the blood sugar. Eventually, the mere sight of food can become a CS that stimulates the production of insulin and drives down blood sugar. Seeing good food can thus create a real and compelling hunger. If one frequently eats sugar at night, it is even possible that evening time can become a CS that stimulates the pancreas, causing powerful cravings when the insulin lowers blood sugar levels. Over time, it should be possible to extinguish such a response by never eating sugar in the evening.

Seeing good food can create a real and compelling hunger.

SOURCE: *Betty Crocker's Best Recipes of the Year*, © 1989 by General Mills, Inc. Used by permission of the publisher, Prentice Hall, New York.

Classical conditioning and language

There are many ways that classical conditioning can affect language. In certain situations particular words can act as powerful conditioned stimuli. Thus, words that make you feel disgust or desire are functioning as CS's. In other situations intense experiences can result in the explosive uttering of certain words. Uttering those words represents a CR to whatever stimulated the person.

Classical conditioning and sexual behaviour

In the next chapter, we will discuss sexuality and assert that the only unconditioned stimulus for sexual behaviour in humans is touch. This means that the sight of breasts or buttocks or genitalia or ear-lobes is arousing because it is a conditioned stimulus. Domjan and Nash (1989, p. 138) maintain that, "considerable evidence is available indicating that sexual physiology and behavior are subject to modification by conditioning procedures." Throughout the animal kingdom, sexual behaviour is influenced by classical conditioning. For instance, "arbitrary" stimuli (such as a dog being aroused by a pillow) can be established as being sexually arousing. Animals can be taught to behave sexually toward inanimate objects and to ignore opportunities with another animal. For that matter, humans can be aroused by shoes and scared by people.

Operant Conditioning

The second major category of learning concerns behaviour that is *instrumental*, behaviour that achieves a purpose in the environment. The person or animal learns *operations* to perform in order to accomplish goals. We define **operant conditioning** (sometimes called **instrumental conditioning**) as the process of learning in which the organism emits a response, and the consequences either strengthen or weaken that response. The central difference between classical conditioning and operant conditioning lies in the nature of the origin of the response to be strengthened. In classical conditioning, the original response is *elicited* by some external stimulus, the US. In operant conditioning, the person or animal *emits* (that is, performs) a response, and then reinforcement may or may not follow. When reinforcement does occur, the response that most immediately preceded the reinforcement is strengthened (i.e., is more likely to occur again). One way to remember the difference between classical and operant conditioning is that the organism is performing *operations* on the environment in operant conditioning. A **reinforcer** follows a behaviour and increases the likelihood of that behaviour occurring again. In other words, a reinforcer is anything that leads to a strengthening of a response. Most people think of reinforcers as roughly the same as *rewards*; but this is not quite accurate, as we will see in a moment.

Edward L. Thorndike (1874–1949).
SOURCE: Archives of the History of American Psychology.

Historically, operant conditioning is most closely associated with the work of Edward L. Thorndike and B. F. Skinner. In 1898, as part of his doctoral thesis, Thorndike performed an experiment in which cats learned tasks for the reward of escaping from a cage. Thorndike found that the cats' performance improved *gradually* with repeated successes. Because there was no sudden improvement in the cats' performance, he argued that the cats were not learning by "insight." To account for the results of his experiment, Thorndike proposed *the law of effect*. This law essentially states that if a response in the presence of some stimulus is followed by satisfying effects, the association between the stimulus and the response will be strengthened. At first, the cats performed many responses, but only one particular response was followed by the reward of escaping from the cage. The particular response was somewhat strengthened by the effect of the reward, and other responses were weakened by the lack of reward.

The young B.F. Skinner.
SOURCE: Courtesy of the late B.F. Skinner.

B. F. Skinner's work is so extensive and has had such a powerful influence that psychologists who strongly subscribe to the importance of operant conditioning often refer to themselves as "Skinnerians," and experimental chambers in which an animal presses a lever or pecks a key for reinforcement are often called "Skinner boxes" (see Figure 5-7).

Skinner has published research, written a behaviouristic novel (*Walden Two*), published many books on psychological theory and social issues, and is probably the most famous American psychologist in the world. In the sections that follow we will detail his position that behaviour is controlled by its consequences, that is, a behaviour becomes stronger or weaker depending upon what happens after it.

Positive reinforcement

Learning theorists call pleasure-giving reinforcers **positive reinforcers**. It is positive reinforcers that most people are thinking of when they think of rewards. Psychologists define reinforcement *empirically* (that is, according to its observable effects). This means that whether a particular thing is a reinforcer depends on whether it serves to strengthen behaviour. There is virtually no one thing that *always* works as a reinforcer. Sometimes ice cream is a reinforcer, but to a person nauseous with overeating, it could well serve as a punishment.

A useful extension of this idea is the **Premack Principle**, which states that an activity that is preferred can be used to reinforce one that is less preferred at a particular time (Premack, 1965). On the one hand, a hungry rat will run in an exercise wheel to get the reinforcer of food. On the other hand, an exercise-deprived rat will eat more than usual if that eating is reinforced by the chance to run in an exercise wheel. In the first case, the eating was the reinforcer of the running behaviour because it was the preferred activity. (Note that this does not mean that eating is always the reinforcer in a situation.) In the second case, the wheel-running was the reinforcer because it

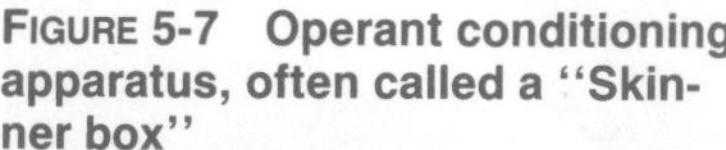

FIGURE 5-7 Operant conditioning apparatus, often called a "Skinner box"

An animal placed in the box would perform some response, such as lever pushing, in order to receive reinforcement.

SOURCE: Photo courtesy of Gerbrands Corporation.

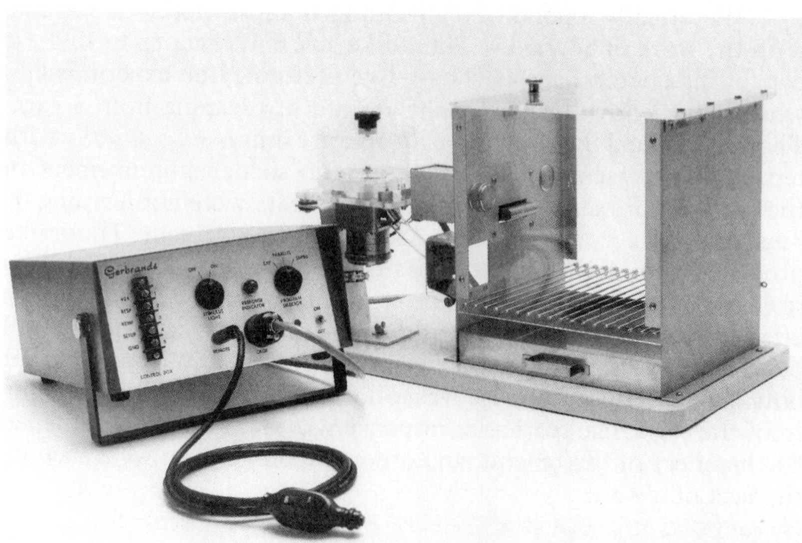

was the preferred activity. In fact, the animal was reinforced for eating more than it normally would have because of the presence of the preferred activity of wheel-running. If there is something you have trouble getting yourself to do, such as study enough, you could set a contingency for yourself so that for every two hours of studying, you take a break and do something you enjoy. This can make the studying more enjoyable because it is being reinforced by a preferred activity. To do it the other way around would be less effective. If you do the preferred activity first, the studying will be harder to get to and may almost seem a punishment for the preferred activity.

It is very important to understand just how much emphasis learning theorists place on positive reinforcement. A learning theorist might argue that the most powerful principle of his or her theory is that *people do what they are reinforced for doing*. At first glance, this seems so obvious it's not worth saying. But it has many applications we seldom think of. Many parents try to get their children to get along with each other by threatening them. The learning theorist would say this won't work in the long run. If you want to change behaviour, you have to change the reinforcers. The children will get along only if it is somehow reinforcing to do so. We will see many examples illustrating this principle throughout this book.

You should also think about the strongly stated version of these statements. Some learning theorists would say that, with a few minor exceptions, people do *only* what they are reinforced for doing. Is this true of you? Do you *ever* do anything for which you are not somehow reinforced? Then why do you do it? These are provocative questions that merit reflection.

Negative reinforcement

A second kind of reinforcement is negative reinforcement. **Negative reinforcers** strengthen a behaviour by following it with a reduction in discomfort. A common misunderstanding in psychology is that of confusing *negative reinforcement* with *punishment*. Negative reinforcement is *not* the same thing as punishment. **Punishment** is an attempt to deal with undesirable behaviour through the offset of an appetitive stimulus or the onset of an aversive stimulus. In fact, the purpose of punishment is the opposite of the purpose of negative reinforcement. The purpose of punishment is to weaken a behaviour; the purpose of all reinforcement is to strengthen a behaviour. "Reinforce" means "strengthen." We stress this confusion because it appears so often, even in textbooks and professional journals (Hines, 1988).

If a behaviour is immediately followed by escape from discomfort, that behaviour is more likely to happen again. In a sense, the escape from discomfort is a reward for doing the behaviour. If you are anxious and you find that talking with a friend gives you an insight that relieves your anxiety, then the anxiety-reduction will reinforce your talking behaviour. Your pleasure has not been increased; your discomfort has been decreased. Either an increase of pleasure or a decrease of discomfort would function as a reinforcer. We call the first *positive reinforcement* and the second *negative reinforcement*.

FIGURE 5-8 Reinforcement and punishment produced by the onset or removal of an appetitive or aversive stimulus

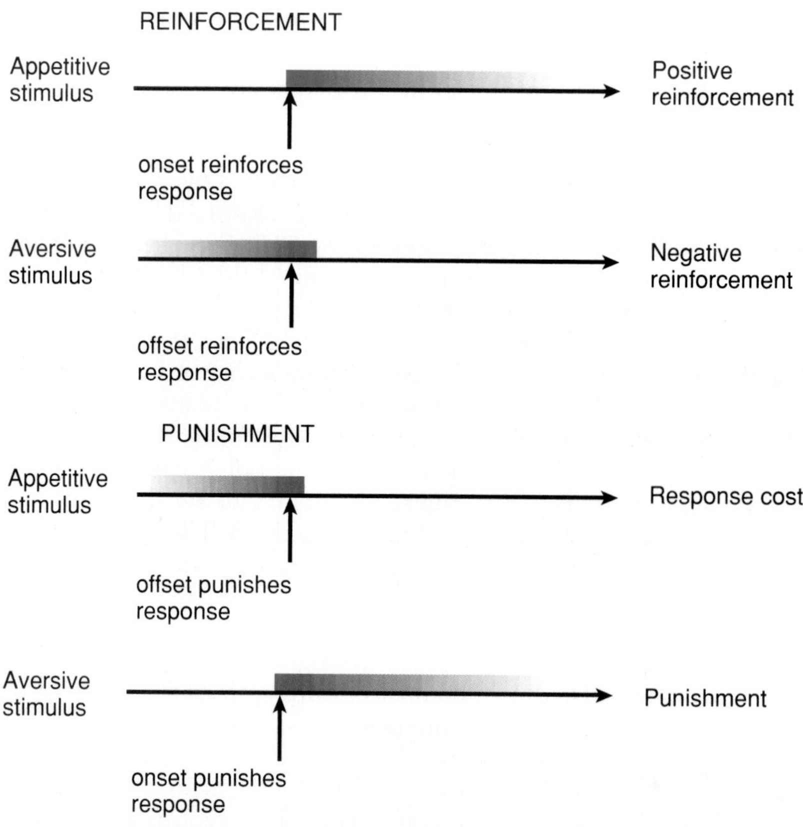

SOURCE: Adapted with permission from Allyn and Bacon, 1987.

Figure 5-8 outlines the differences between reinforcement and punishment. *Reinforcement* occurs either with the onset of a pleasant stimulus (positive reinforcement) or the offset (removal) of an unpleasant one (negative reinforcement). *Punishment* occurs either with the offset of a pleasant stimulus (a loss called *response cost*) or the onset of an unpleasant one (what is usually thought of as punishment).

Shaping and fading

If you want to increase a behaviour, you should arrange reinforcement contingencies to reward that behaviour. However, this is easier said than done. If you want to train your dog to get your slippers in the evening, you can't wait around for her to do this and then shower her with rewards. A complex behaviour like this must be built up by small steps. This building up of a behaviour is called shaping. **Shaping** occurs through reinforcing successive approximations of the final desired behaviour. After supper, you wait until the dog walks toward the bedroom and then say "slippers . . . good dog" and give some special treat. It should be easy to establish the behaviour of going toward the bedroom. Then you say "slippers" and wait until the dog has explored the bedroom and come near your slippers before reinforcing her. Then reinforcement comes only when she picks up the slippers, and so forth. Each step is a successive approximation that you will want to establish securely before you move on to the next step.

One kind of shaping is called fading. In **fading**, an already established behaviour is gradually modified to more closely resemble the desired behaviour. A child might mispronounce the dog's name as "pot." The parent uses the existing behaviour and modifies it by teaching an "ssss" sound separately from "pot" and having the child say them in sequence faster and faster until he or she says "Spot."

Many people might react to this section by saying shaping and fading needlessly complicate things. Most children "just learn" to say "spot," and dogs "just learn" to get slippers. In fact, however, the things we "just learn" are nearly all taught to us in small steps—through shaping and fading that our parents and other teachers do intuitively (and probably less efficiently than they might). In teaching, it is more efficient to know you are looking for small steps that are successive approximations of the final desired behaviour.

Shaping can result in some amazing animal behaviours.
SOURCE: Courtesy of Marineland, Niagara Falls, Canada.

Extinction

As you recall, the only way to weaken a classically conditioned response is through extinction: the CS is presented, the CR occurs, and no US follows. In a similar vein, **extinction in operant conditioning** is also a weakening of conditioned behaviour, but in this case the response weakens when the reinforcement is absent. If your dog scratches up the door to get out and you scold, "Stop scratching!" and also open the door, then the scratching will be reinforced. For scratching to disappear, you must never open the door after a scratch. Of course, you will have to open the door when the dog does what you want, perhaps when it whines. This way, you will establish a desired behaviour and extinguish an undesired one. Understanding the importance of extinction has many implications for how we bring about behaviour change. In too many cases, when we want to get rid of an operant behaviour, we punish the one who is performing the behaviour. However, later in this chapter, we will see that punishment does not actually weaken the behaviour. It merely suppresses the behaviour. Sometimes punishment is necessary, but only extinction actually weakens a behaviour.

In some studies, experimenters observed adults' interactions with disruptive children. They determined that the adults paid attention to these children primarily when they were being disruptive, much like our example of the dog scratching at the door. Teachers often have encounters such as the following:

CHILD: Can you help me draw a house?

TEACHER: That would be nice. (essentially ignoring the request, which serves to extinguish reasonable question-asking)

CHILD: I can't do this!

TEACHER: Uh huh.

CHILD: (pokes child at next desk and yells) I hate drawing houses!

TEACHER: John, sit down! I mean it! (quickly draws the house)

Such a teacher directly reinforces disruptive behaviour by fulfilling the request for the drawing right after such behaviour. Even though the teacher might intend the loud reprimand as punishment, it is probably also a reinforcer because it is the only attention the child receives. When adults ignore this disruptive behaviour, it markedly decreases. In studies by Baer, Harris, and Wolf (1963) and Patterson, Ray, and Shaw (1968), such behaviour was extinguished in children when it was no longer reinforced. It is important to note that the adults were giving the children the same amount of attention but at other times.

Extinction begins when an expected reinforcer is not delivered. At first, this leads to frustration and a brief *increase* in the behaviour. But eventually the behaviour weakens. Of course, there are circumstances where a behaviour cannot be ignored. However, where ignoring a learned operant behaviour is possible, it is the most effective way to reduce it.

Primary and secondary reinforcement

Reinforcers such as food and sex are called **primary reinforcers** because they are based on physiological needs. Much of what motivates us on a daily basis, however, also includes things like praise, money, affection, and even abstract notions such as patriotism or devotion to duty. The learning theorist argues that these motivators are **secondary reinforcers**—acquired reinforcers that have taken on motivating power because of our past learning experiences. For example, how do we define praise empirically? Praise is simply certain patterns of sound in the air or patterns of print on paper. However, praise has meaning for us because we have had experiences in which it was associated with direct rewards of various kinds. In other words, it has acquired reinforcement value for us. A simple example of secondary reinforcement would be making a clicking sound every time we gave a special treat to an animal. Eventually, the animal would perform and learn simply for the reinforcement of hearing the clicking sound. The click is now a secondary reinforcer analogous to praise for a human.

Schedules of reinforcement

A **continuous reinforcement** (**CRF**) **schedule** is one on which reinforcement is given for every performance of the desired response. This pattern of reinforcement leads to quick initial learning. However, when such reinforcement is later withheld, the behaviour will extinguish quickly. A **partial reinforcement schedule** is one on which reinforcement is *not* delivered after every desired response. Initial learning is slower, but the behaviour is more resistant to extinction. Partial reinforcement is very important because nearly everything we learn is learned on a partial reinforcement schedule of some kind. It has often been said that no child in history has ever been raised correctly because parents are inconsistent. We will see that different kinds of partial reinforcement have very different effects.

There are formal names for the different partial reinforcement schedules. If a reinforcer for a desired response is delivered once at the end of some fixed time period, regardless of the number of additional correct responses in the interim, then the schedule is called a

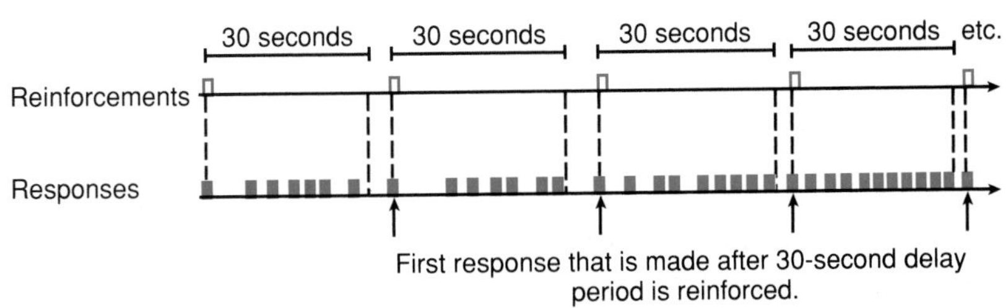

FIGURE 5-9 An example of a fixed-interval 30-second schedule of reinforcement

SOURCE: Reprinted with permission from Allyn and Bacon, 1987.

fixed-interval (FI) schedule. For example, Figure 5-9 shows the results of a test in which an animal was given a food pellet the first time it pushed a lever (the desired response) *after* a time interval of 30 seconds. Note that the other correct responses that are given during that time period are ignored. Nevertheless, this schedule tends to result in increased responding near the end of the designated time period. At our university, the mail is distributed about 11:00 a.m. every day. Starting about 10:30, there is often a group of mail-hungry faculty members hovering around the mail boxes, fruitlessly checking for mail.

On a **fixed-ratio (FR) schedule** of reinforcement, a reinforcer is delivered after some set number of correct responses has been performed, say after every sixth push of a lever. This schedule tends to produce fairly steady and high rates of responding. Both fixed-interval and fixed-ratio schedules are predictable. The person or animal can learn what the contingencies are. There are two schedules, however, that are unpredictable. They use intermittent reinforcement.

On a **variable-ratio (VR) schedule** of reinforcement, the reinforcer is delivered after an unpredictable or variable number of correct responses. For a while, you might be reinforced every third response, then two in a row, then nothing for six responses, and so forth. In a particular experiment, you might be reinforced every five responses on the average. However, the *range* might be from two to

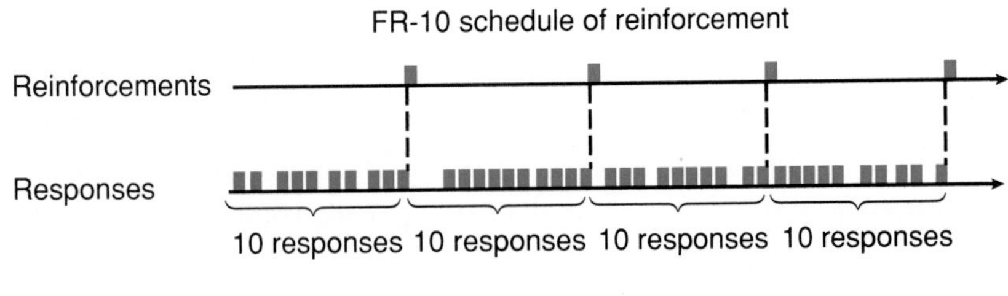

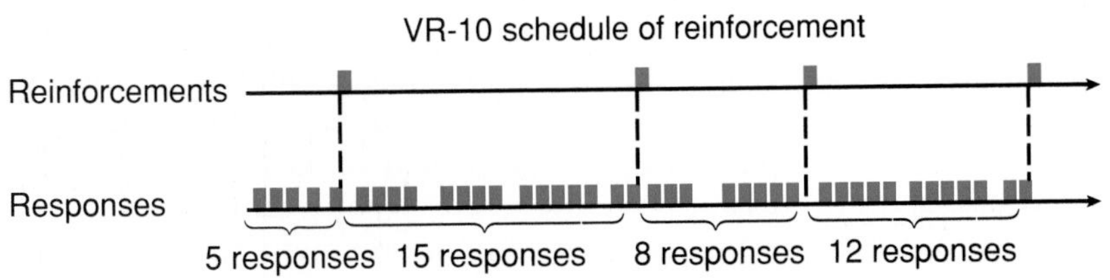

The average number of responses is 10.

FIGURE 5-10 Fixed-ratio 10 and variable-ratio 10 schedules of reinforcement compared

SOURCE: Reprinted with permission from Allyn and Bacon, 1989.

eight. In other words, sometimes you would be reinforced after two responses, but at other times you would not be reinforced until after eight responses. Figure 5-10 compares a fixed-ratio 10 schedule, where every tenth response is reinforced, and a variable-ratio 10 schedule, where *on average* the tenth response is reinforced but the exact number is unpredictable.

Another pattern of intermittent reinforcement is the **variable-interval (VI) schedule** on which the reinforcer for a correct response is delivered after a time interval that varies in length unpredictably. Any other correct responses that are made during that time period are ignored.

These unpredictable schedules result in slower initial learning, but in remarkably persistent learning. This is why they are so important in understanding behaviour, especially behaviour that seems irrational. It is extremely difficult to get rid of behaviour that has been established on intermittent schedules. It has also been shown that being reinforced on such unpredictable schedules on one task makes the subject more persistent on other tasks. In other words, intermittent reinforcement seems to produce a tendency to persist at a wide range of behaviours after having had experience with partial reinforcement for other behaviours. This tendency is called the **generalized partial reinforcement effect** (Pittenger & Pavlik, 1989).

Parents with young children who throw serious tantrums are invariably told by their pediatrician or psychologist to ignore (in order to extinguish) the tantrum behaviour. The child will not die even if it holds its breath and turns blue. Usually the parents had been reinforcing the tantrums by holding and comforting the child when it screamed, banged its heels on the floor, and thrashed back and forth — a very scary thing to see. Now, however, they try to follow the advice and ignore three tantrums in a row. The fourth time, though, the neighbours are visiting, so the parents quiet the child with cuddling. They are headed for trouble to the extent that they continue this pattern of intermittent reinforcement.

The power of intermittent reinforcement is also illustrated by the grip that gambling can have on people. In the long run, the compulsive gambler always loses to the "house" but finds it almost impossible to stop. Gambling is designed so that you might win big on the very next play, but you're only risking a small amount. You lose many of these small amounts and are really hurting, especially when you add up how much you have lost. But you *could* win it back on the very next try. Occasionally you do win, on an unpredictable (variable-ratio) schedule. And when you do, there is an enormous sense of relief of the emotional pain that has been building up. You are receiving powerful negative reinforcement (reduction of emotional pain) on a variable-ratio schedule. Therefore, your gambling behaviour will be very resistant to extinction. Each time you lose is an extinction trial, and your behaviour can be easily shown to be irrational and not in your best interest. But you will have great difficulty stopping. The effects of partial reinforcement operate in similar ways in many aspects of our lives. They are just very obvious in the gambling situation.

Superstitious learning

A fascinating phenomenon was demonstrated by Skinner (1969) using unpredictable reinforcement. A pigeon was in a special box where it received a pellet of food after arbitrary periods of time. The food was in no way contingent on what the bird was doing. However, the bird was doing *something* when the food came. Therefore, whatever it was doing was reinforced and consequently somewhat more likely to be occurring when the next food pellet dropped in. Thus, sometimes when the pigeon performed this particular behaviour it was reinforced, obviously on a variable-ratio schedule. This has been called a "response-independent partial reinforcement schedule." The bird started doing very odd things for long periods of time—turning constantly to the right, vigorously nodding its head, and the like. The behaviour was only reinforced "by accident" but became so irrationally persistent that Skinner called it **superstitious behaviour**. This term refers to behaviour that is inadvertently established through randomly delivered reinforcement. He was obviously taking a shot at human superstitions which also develop through accidental, variable-ratio reinforcements (which are also probably more powerful because they are selectively remembered). These principles will help you understand how a friend of ours consistently made money at Las Vegas (see Close-up).

Timing of reinforcements

As with classical conditioning, the shorter the time between a behaviour and its reinforcer, the stronger will be the effect of the reinforcer. This principle has many implications. We all do things, for example, that are not in our own long-term best interests — self-defeating things. If people do what they are reinforced for doing, why do people hurt themselves? The general principle, says the learning theorist, is that usually there is immediate reinforcement of the self-defeating behaviour. We could be helpless in the face of a chocolate chip cookie in spite of a persistent weight problem and family history of diabetes because the cookie looks so good and tastes so good *right now*. In other cases, some very odd behaviours can lead to immediate anxiety-reduction, and this is a very powerful reinforcer. A person might feel terribly guilty and unworthy for having desires that are unacceptable to him or her. The guilt might be reduced temporarily when the person has been hurt because he or she feels the punishment was deserved. It is possible for that person to find the guilt-reduction so reinforcing that self-mutilation becomes frequent. We will expand on this principle in Chapter 14 when we discuss abnormal behaviour.

The newborn infant responds almost exclusively to immediate reinforcement—the immediate reduction of hunger, pain, and thirst. To survive, however, we must do many things for delayed reinforcement. **Delayed reinforcement** is reinforcement that is delivered after some time period following performance of the desired behaviour. We often work for hours or days without apparent reward. Working for a university or college degree requires sacrificing immediate pleasures and financial resources for a delayed reward. One of our most important lessons as we grow up, then, involves the experience of gradually lengthening the time between behaviours and their reinforcers. This is obvious in training animals. With children, however, parents seem not so aware that they are teaching delay of reinforcement when they say, "Not right now . . . after you clean up your room . . . dessert after spinach." If, after this delay-of-reinforcement lesson the reinforcement is not delivered, the child will learn a different lesson: it doesn't pay to wait for reinforcers.

PSYCHOLOGY OF FEAR

One of the most important applications of learning principles lies in our attempts at understanding fear. The learning theorist argues that the baby is born fearing *nothing* that is not physically discomforting. The learning theorist would say that even though the baby may experience physical discomfort, it doesn't *fear*, say, a loud noise. It cries because of pain, not fear. Fear is our response to something that has become a CS (through conditioning) with pain. Among humans, fears are also learned through such complex ways as imitation and imagination, but even these routes to fear are based on previously learned connections that involve pain somewhere in the individual's learning history.

Emotional conditioning

Emotional conditioning is essentially the classical conditioning of the autonomic nervous system (ANS) to previously neutral cues. A **conditioned emotional response (CER)** is a classically conditioned response in which autonomic arousal is the CR. Autonomic responses can include blushing, increased heart rate, and the like, and they can combine with associated cognitions, as we will see in more detail in the next chapter. It is important to see that an *emotion* involves both cognitive and classically conditioned components. The conditioned components are basically the feeling (ANS arousal), and the cognitive components are our conscious appraisal of the meaning of the emotion. The cognitive component is at least partially separate from the conditioned component. For example, most of us have some fears that are literally irrational, in the sense that they are not under the control of reason. Most people feel some fear when they are in a very tall building and look down off a balcony. There is virtually no chance of falling, but logical thought does not get rid of the feeling. Reason can change the cognitive part of the fear, but the classically conditioned part of the fear can be changed only through extinction.

The CER of fear can be very powerful, and fear-reduction can thus be a very powerful reinforcer. Remember that this kind of reinforcement is called *negative reinforcement* because the *reward* is escape from some kind of discomfort.

Escape and avoidance learning

One kind of behaviour that is strongly established by the reinforcement of fear reduction is **escape behaviour**, which are actions designed to avoid or flee from aversive stimuli. When a person or animal is in discomfort of some kind (and fear is a form of discomfort), whatever leads to escape from that discomfort will be strongly reinforced. This escape behaviour is difficult to change. Obviously, in most cases, there is survival value in learning to escape things that hurt or frighten us. Sometimes, however, escape behaviour is so strongly learned that we continue to escape things that are no longer dangerous.

In a classic study, Solomon and Wynne (1953) put dogs in a "shuttle box," as illustrated in Figure 5-11. A dog was placed in one side of the box. When an electric charge was passed through the floor, the dog first would crouch and whine, but it quickly learned to jump the barrier to the other side of the box and escape the shock. In some cases, a light would come on just before the shock was given. The dog learned to jump as soon as the light came on. In a sense, the dog was learning to fear the light and to escape it. The light served as a fear cue that helped the dog avoid the pain. This is the principle of **active-avoidance learning**, which may be defined as learning to avoid aversive stimuli by taking direct action.

However, when the experimenters stopped delivering shocks, the dogs continued to jump the barrier as soon as the light came on. Some dogs persisted in jumping hundreds of times, even though that cost energy and was eventually very tiring. Obviously, their escape behaviour was so strongly learned that they didn't stay in the first box long enough to learn that there was no longer any real threat. An analogy can be drawn between these dogs and humans that persist in behaviours that at one time helped to escape pain or fear but are no longer necessary. For example, a person who spent years actively avoiding an abusive father might, years after the father died, still avoid contact with middle-aged men, perhaps without even being aware of doing so.

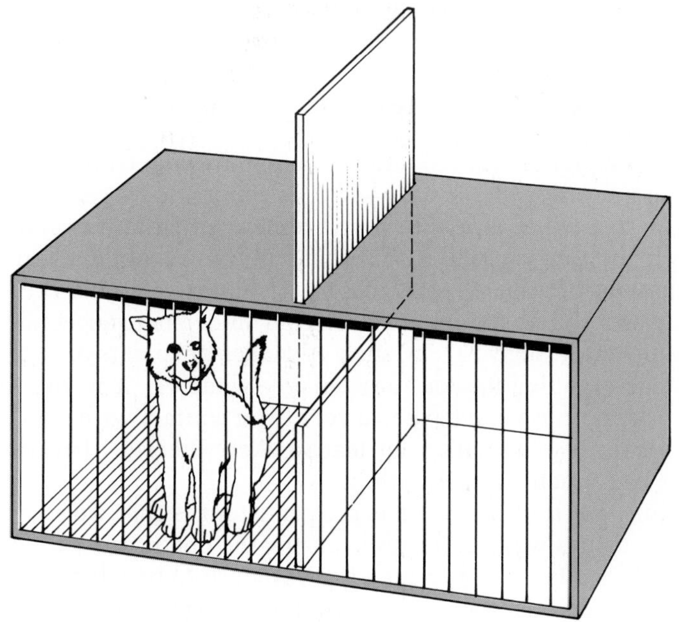

SOURCE: Adapted from Solomon and Wynne (1953).

FIGURE 5-11 Escape conditioning in a shuttle box

Another kind of avoidance behaviour is **passive-avoidance learning**, which may be defined as learning to avoid aversive stimuli by *not* taking particular actions. If we placed the dog in the box that was not electrified, it probably would eventually jump the barrier out of boredom or curiosity. It would land on the electrified floor on the other side of the barrier and would quickly learn *not* to jump, no matter how bored it got. In the future, it would avoid the aversive stimulus, not by actively getting away but rather by passively staying out of the threatening situation. If you fear spiders intensely, you probably avoid going into basements. You are passively avoiding spiders, rather than running from them.

Principles of fear reduction

As you recall, we have two general methods for reducing fears — extinction and counterconditioning. We will see in Chapter 15 (Approaches to Therapy) that these methods are often applied to the treatment of fears. The most common approaches to fear reduction involve (1) exposure to the CS (which could be something as clearcut as a snake or spider or could be something as subtle as one's own thoughts about love and intimacy), and (2a) providing a safe atmosphere where no US occurs (extinction) or (2b) providing a pleasant stimulus to associate with the CS (counterconditioning). The extinction process in which the subject is exposed to the CS in small steps, either by approaching the CS more closely or by being exposed to stimuli that are increasingly more similar to the CS, is called **graduated extinction** or **graduated counterconditioning**.

This process could take the form of being exposed to an object, such as a snake, or to imagined scenes that arouse anxiety, or even to one's own desires, memories, and thoughts just through the process of talking and thinking about them. This is probably why it helps so much to talk to an understanding and accepting friend. You extinguish some of your fears of your own thoughts and feelings by being exposed to them.

Why fears are persistent

These principles of fear-reduction can help us understand why fears often last a long time. It may seem as though fears generally fade with the passage of time. But if you remember what we said earlier about extinction, you will realize that reduction is not just the result of the passing of time. As time goes by, we often experience the things we fear and thus experience extinction under natural conditions. Think of something you fear, such as snakes or spiders or cute little white rats crawling up your arm. Likely whatever it is you fear so much is something you have had very little contact with over a long period of time. Why isn't your fear weaker? Precisely because you haven't had much contact with it.

Thus, the first reason fears are persistent is that we so quickly avoid the things we fear, thus preventing the opportunity for extinction. It takes a few seconds for a fear response to be felt because the autonomic nervous system takes that long to respond. If you avoid the CS quickly, you don't feel the fear; and feeling the fear is a requirement for extinction to take place. A second reason is that our avoidance behaviour becomes extremely strong because every time we avoid a feared situation or object, we feel better. The avoidance behaviour is powerfully reinforced by negative reinforcement and becomes very hard to change. Third, the experiences that cause fear are often unpredictable, so fears and avoidance behaviours are learned on a partial reinforcement schedule, making them that much more resistant to extinction. Finally, fears extinguish more slowly than other conditioned responses (Schwartz, 1984), perhaps for inherited biological reasons. This may seem unfortunate, but it has obvious survival value. The lessons we learn from pain are almost certainly important lessons to remember.

BIOLOGICAL CONSTRAINTS

Recent evidence strongly suggests that there are certain built-in limitations on (1) what can be learned in general and (2) what can be learned more easily by one species than another. A controversy has developed over this evidence, and we will discuss how this controversy has grown out of a widespread misunderstanding of behaviour theory. First, however, let's look at the evidence that there are *biological constraints on learning.*

Classical conditioning

Most of the research suggesting biological constraints has centred on learned taste aversion. A **learned taste aversion** is a previously neutral taste that has become aversive (i.e., to be avoided) because of classical conditioning in which the taste was paired with a painful US. Rats are known for being very "clever" at avoiding poisons, which is one of the abilities that enables them to survive under hostile circumstances. They quickly develop strong aversions for any taste associated with becoming ill. Therefore, a small taste of poisoned food along with the subsequent illness strongly establishes that taste as an aversive CS. In one of a series of experiments by Garcia and Koelling (1966), rats were exposed to clicking sounds and bright lights. Afterwards, some of them (Group A) were given a shock, while others (Group B) were made ill through exposure to radiation. Here only those rats that had been exposed to shock (Group A) developed a strong fear of the lights and clicks. In other words, the lights and clicks had become CS's associated with shock exposure. In a second experiment by Garcia and Koelling (1966), rats were given water sweetened with saccharine, which they drank with apparent relish. After they drank, some of them (Group C) were exposed to shock (a US) and some (Group D) were made ill through exposure to radiation (another US). In this experiment, *only* those rats that had been made ill (Group D) developed a strong fear of the sweetened water. (See Figure 5-12.) In other words, the sweet taste had become a powerful, aversive CS associated with feeling sick. This taste aversion was learned even when there was considerable time—as much as 20 minutes—between the CS (taste) and the US (illness).

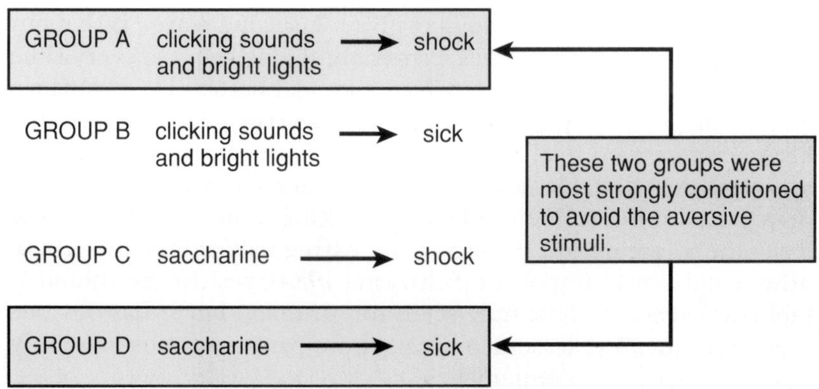

FIGURE 5-12 Selectivity of association
The results of Garcia and Koelling's (1966) experiments. The association between a noisy-bright CS and shock as a US was easier for a rat to learn than the association between taste and shock. The taste-nausea link was easier to learn than a noisy-bright CS paired with sickness as the US. Some associations condition more readily than others.

SOURCE: Adapted with permission from Allyn and Bacon, 1987.

To account for the results of the experiments, Garcia and Koelling proposed that rats are *biologically prepared* to learn an association between taste and illness on the one hand (Group D) and between mechanical stimuli and external pain on the other hand (Group A). This selectivity of association makes good sense from the point of view of evolving survival mechanisms. Rats seem to rely partly on taste in choosing their food. Those that can learn a conditioned aversion for tastes that make them sick—even some time later—will be more likely to survive and pass on their genetic tendencies to offspring. Furthermore, we can argue that in the rats' natural habitat the threat of something external (such as shock) is far more likely to be accompanied by mechanical "warnings" (such as noise and light).

Rats select their food largely on the basis of smell and taste. Some birds, however, use visual cues. In one study, quail were given water that was coloured blue and flavoured sour (Wilcoxin, Dragoin, & Kral, 1971). They were then made sick with a mild poison. Later, the quail strongly avoided unflavoured blue water but drank just about as much clear sour water as before. Depending on the species, there are different patterns of *belongingness* or association of stimuli that the animal has a biological preparedness to learn (Seligman, 1970). **Biological preparedness** is a genetic predisposition to learn some associations between stimuli more readily than others.

Operant learning

As with classical conditioning, there are some built-in connections between certain operant or instrumental behaviours and the reinforcers by which they are learned (Shettleworth, 1972). For example, it is easy to train a pigeon to peck a key to earn food, but it is very difficult to teach a pigeon to peck a key to escape shock. Pecking is food-related behaviour but it is not part of a pigeon's normal escape behaviour (Hineline & Rachlin, 1969).

Breland & Breland (1961) coined the term **instinctual drift** to describe the tendency of many animals, even when strongly taught some new but unusual behaviour, to return gradually to the behaviours that are more common to their species. Breland & Breland arrived at this concept after trying unsuccessfully to train a racoon to drop coins into a piggy-bank. Racoons are smart animals that condition easily, but the Brelands discovered that they could not change the animal's natural disposition. The racoon easily learned to pick up a coin for reinforcement. Then the Brelands used shaping and started reinforcing the animal for dropping the coin into the bank. However, the racoon had a lot of trouble letting go of the coin, even though he got no reinforcement until he did. He would rub the coin against the bank, put it in and pull it back out, and firmly cling to it. Only after much time did he finally release the coin and get the reinforcement. The last step in shaping was to require the racoon to put two coins in the bank. The Brelands eventually gave up. The racoon spent minutes rubbing the coins together, dipping them in the container and pulling them back out, and generally fondling the coins. The racoon's natural food-washing behaviour clashed too strongly with the behaviour of releasing objects into a container. Similar kinds of "drift" back to "natural" behaviour have been reported for several species, in spite of attempts to reinforce the opposite behaviour.

Some behaviours are so "natural" for an animal that it is very likely to perform them even when there seems no need to do so; this phenomenon is called **autoshaping**. Brown and Jenkins (1968) presented pigeons with a small disk which lit up just before a drawer opened to provide food to the birds. The drawer opened *noncontingently*. In other words, the birds did not have to do anything to obtain the food. The birds soon began pecking at the disk anyway. They "shaped" themselves to do the pecking for the food, apparently because they naturally associated food and pecking. The effect of autoshaping can be very powerful. Noncontingent rewards can come to reinforce a very likely behaviour, much as with superstitious learning. Once pecking was established by autoshaping, the pigeons continued to peck the disk, even when this behaviour was mildly punished by a delay in the opening of the drawer (Williams & Williams, 1969). Critics of autoshaping experiments have suggested that classical conditioning actually occurs because the lighted button becomes an attractive CS for the food drawer opening (Turkkan, 1989). Nevertheless, the experiments probably still demonstrate a behaviour that may be *biologically prepared* to be learned easily.

In light of these phenomena, we should point out that we may have oversimplified the earlier case about how you could have just as easily been trained to salivate to buttons as to the sight of ice cream. It does seem true that anything can act as a CS, but some CS-US connections are easier to learn than others, and some behaviour-reinforcer connections are easier to learn and more persistent than others. At least this principle seems true for lower animals. Human learning is so flexible that psychologists are not sure what, if any, biological constraints apply to human classical conditioning.

A common misunderstanding of behaviour theory

Biological constraints on learning, instinctual drift, and autoshaping are often presented as evidence of the limitations of learning theory. This is because many people assume that learning theory includes

SOURCE: *Bizarro* by Dan Piraro. Reprinted by permission of Chronicle Features, San Francisco, CA.

the principle of equipotentiality. **Equipotentiality** is the assumption that any CS-US pairing or any response-reinforcer pairing is just as likely to work as any other. Gleitman, for example, says that one of "learning theory's basic tenets" is that "animals are capable of connecting just about any conditioned stimulus to any unconditioned stimulus (in classical conditioning) or of associating any instrumental response with any reinforcer (in instrumental conditioning)" (Gleitman, 1986, p. 122). According to the principle of equipotentiality, almost any stimulus can be arbitrarily connected with any response with equal success. Gleitman goes on to state that "both Pavlov and Skinner regarded as basic" this principle of the arbitrary equality of stimuli (Gleitman 1986, p. 125). Others have also attributed this position to Pavlov and Skinner and to Thorndike as well (Seligman, 1970; Seligman and Hager, 1972; Shettleworth, 1972). Since Pavlov, Skinner, and Thorndike are three of the most significant names in behavioural theory, it has been widely believed that the theory required equipotentiality.

However, an investigation of the writings of all three reveals that they each anticipated biological constraints on learning. In fact, there is nothing in learning theory that contradicts the concept of biological constraints. Thorndike wrote, "The chick's brain is evidently prepared in a general way to react more or less appropriately to certain stimuli . . . " (Thorndike, 1911, p. 167). Thorndike also maintained that "to any situation an animal will apart from learning respond by virtue of the inherited nature of its reception, connection, and action system" (Thorndike, 1911, p. 243). Pavlov asserted that "if the extraneous stimuli are strong or unusual, the formation of a conditioned response will be difficult, and in extreme cases impossible" (Pavlov, 1927, p. 29). Finally, Skinner explicitly states, "No reputable student of animal behavior has ever taken the position that the animal comes to the laboratory as a virtual tabula rasa [i.e., clean slate], that species differences are insignificant, and that all responses are equally conditionable to all stimuli" (Skinner, 1969, p. 173).

Thus, three of the most prominent behavioural theorists recognized the likelihood of behavioural constraints on learning. Therefore, it seems more accurate to view evidence of biological constraints on learning as elaborations of learning theory, rather than contradictions of it.

PUNISHMENT AND BEHAVIOUR CONTROL

Whether we like to admit it or not, we are all interested in controlling the behaviour of others. "Controlling" seems such a harsh word. We might prefer to say we want to *influence* others. However, the point is that you will want your life partner to love you and act certain ways toward you; you will want your subordinates at work to want to be productive; and you will want your children to grow up with certain values. In our culture, a popular, if not the most popular, method of influencing others is to use punishment. Learning theorists generally argue that punishment does have valid uses but that it also has a number of important disadvantages that people seldom take into account. Punishment seems effective because it often gives the punisher immediate reinforcement when the punished person complies quickly. However, this quick compliance is often misleading because the delayed effects of the punishment are often undesirable. (Recall our earlier discussion of punishment as something quite different from negative reinforcement.)

The basic process of punishment

One of the everyday illusions we have about the nature of punishment is that it seems to get rid of the behaviours we are punishing. There is evidence, however, that punishment works by suppressing or inhibiting the punished behaviour, not by eliminating it. In other words, the punished behaviour is not actually weakened at all. Instead, the punished person learns a *new* behaviour—that of stopping the punished behaviour. The act of inhibiting the punished behaviour is reinforced by negative reinforcement because compliance serves to reduce the discomfort of being punished. Much of this learning goes on without conscious plan or awareness. If we punish a child for kicking, and the kicking stops, it looks as though we have eliminated the behaviour. In fact, however, we have simply reinforced the competing behaviour of "stopping kicking." If somehow we could remove the effects of the punishment, kicking would return in full force. The behaviour has only been suppressed. Campbell and Church summarize this principle well when they say, "Punishment puts down a response by force and tends to conceal it from public view" (Campbell and Church, 1969, p. 111).

The evidence suggests that with mild punishment, the effects of the punishment often "wear off," and the punished behaviour returns. The issue is more complicated with severe punishment. A behaviour can be punished so hard that it never occurs again. It is possible, for example, to punish sexual behaviour so severely that the person never again engages in sexual behaviour and feels strongly that he or she simply has no interest in sexuality. Has sexuality been eliminated from such a person? In this case it is difficult to know if the behaviour has actually been eliminated from the person's behaviour repertoire or if it has been severely inhibited. The difference is that in theory, severely inhibited behaviour can be restored whereas eliminated behaviour cannot. In our example it seems more likely that, as with milder punishment, the behaviour has simply been inhibited. In essence, punishment is a case of avoidance learning, and we have already seen that some avoidance learning can persist for very long periods.

For example, if we were to train an animal to push a lever very actively and then punish it very severely for pushing the lever, the animal might never again perform this act even though lever pushing was a well-learned behaviour. Presumably, the animal would be terrified of levers and never go near them, which means the fear would never extinguish. It would look as though we had eliminated the behaviour of lever pushing. However, if we could give the animal "lever therapy" of some kind, simply to eliminate the effects of the punishment, lever pushing would return in full force. The animal would again be a very active lever pusher. This would mean that the previously learned behaviour had only been suppressed, not weakened.

Disadvantages of punishment

The previous section outlined a major disadvantage of punishment: it doesn't actually weaken the undesirable behaviour; it only suppresses it. There are a number of other disadvantages of punishment that people seldom consider.

1. *Punishment only teaches what NOT to do.* Thus, it is an inefficient tool for influencing behaviour. We will see that for punishment to be effective, it must be combined with plenty of positive reinforcement of the desired behaviour.

2. *Punishment teaches punitiveness by example.* The boss who uses punitive methods sets the tone for what is acceptable practice in the workplace. It is no surprise that the vast majority of violent children have been treated violently. It would be amusing if it weren't so sad to hear a parent say, "If you hit your brother one more time, I'm going to belt you."

3. *Punishment leads to unintended aversive classical conditioning.* The lover who uses insulting language because "I wanted to teach him a lesson" seldom thinks about all the lessons that are learned. She is also becoming an aversive CS. By the same token, arguments in the bedroom can establish that room as aversive in ways that will have an impact on later lovemaking. When the child is punished for talking loudly in school, the teacher seldom thinks that the child is also being punished for being in school, for talking at all, and for being near the teacher. When pain is delivered, everything present can become an aversive CS. The parent who uses punishment is to some degree inevitably becoming an aversive cue. Sometimes it may be worth it (because the immediate consequences of the undesired behaviour are so dangerous, for example), but the punisher should be aware of the price being paid. Skinner (1971) has rhetorically asked why children break school windows when other buildings are more accessible.

Punishment merely suppresses behaviours. It does not weaken them. Punishment also carries a number of serious disadvantages. Nevertheless, *mild* punishment combined with positive reinforcement of desired behaviours can lead to positive results in the long term.
SOURCE: Dick Hemingway.

4. *Punishment leads to quick compliance and long-term resistance.* This principle is related to the previous point. If resentment is established, there often is a motive to retaliate. The authoritarian boss, for example, might frequently see evidence of his or her punitive methods seeming to work. However, punitive bosses have higher turnover rates and have to deal with subtle sabotage and resistance. We will discuss this workplace issue in more detail in Chapter 20.

5. *Punitive methods require continuous enforcement.* The goal is usually long-term influence. The ideal result is that the other person will want to do what you want them to do. If your influence

is based on fear of noncompliance, then when the cat's away, the mice will play.

6. *Punishment arouses emotion that interferes with learning.* The goal is to change behaviour, and this often requires new learning. The arousal of negative emotion that results from punishment often confuses and disrupts the person. As a result, new learning of the desired behaviour is prevented or slowed.

Long-term influence on behaviour

You might think by now that psychologists are entirely opposed to punishment, but that is not the case. There are some obvious situations where punishment is necessary because it has immediate effects. If a child is in immediate danger because of insisting on running into the street repeatedly or touching the stove, or if a crisis demands quick action, or if there are no positive means available for influencing behaviour—in such situations, punishment is useful.

There is another use of punishment, however, that has many real applications. We want to have long-term influence, not just short-term compliance. The learning theorist would say that in the long term, *the most effective way to have an influence is to give lots of positive reinforcement of the desired behaviours combined with mild punishment of undesired behaviours.* However, in practice, one problem seems to be that it is easier to punish than to think of ways to make desired behaviours more rewarding. The effort required to take positive approaches is greater in the short term, but far more effective in the long term. If you want a child to be a reader, you could withdraw TV privileges unless he or she reads a book a week; or you could pay the child $5.00 for each book read; or you could make reading fun by choosing interesting books and reading with the child. The first method uses punishment and will probably get the child reading, but it will also create resentment toward reading. The second approach uses extrinsic reinforcement and will probably only work temporarily. Only the third method is likely to make the child a reader—the child will want to read.

Another example, one that may incorporate some mild punishment, involves sibling rivalry. Parents want their children to get along with each other, but many parents use almost exclusively punitive approaches to make this happen. Some sibling rivalry is probably inevitable, as children compete for parents' limited time and attention. This is an uphill battle for the parents. The battle will be lost if parents frequently say, "Get away from that baby! . . . Why can't you be as good as your sister? . . . If you don't give him back his toy, I'll take all your toys." Each of these statements makes the sibling a source of pain. Rather, it is important that somehow the sibling be made a source of positive things. Again, this is not easy to do. It is easier to use punishment. But punitive approaches yield deep bitterness in the future. The effort of thinking in terms of positive reinforcement is worth it. You might, for example, provide children with toys that are fun only when played with cooperatively. The parent might play with the children when they are being cooperative, but when fighting starts say, "It's no fun for me when you fight, so I'm not going to play." This withdrawal of parental attention illustrates a mild form of punishment. It will be effective, but only when it is combined with much positive reinforcement that comes from parental attention.

One of the most important areas of application of these learning principles is in the treatment of behaviour disorders. We will discuss examples in the section on behaviour modification in Chapter 15.

COGNITIVE LEARNING

So far we have been discussing learning principles in terms of external influences and overt behaviours. One of the most important trends in behaviour theory, however, has been an increasing focus on cognition or thinking.

Inside the black box

Learning theories are sometimes referred to as *S-R* theories, for *stimulus-response*. Behaviourists argued that we could only observe the stimulus that impinged on the organism and then the organism's response. What happened in between, inside the organism, we could not access directly. Thus, there was no way to study it scientifically. All of that internal processing was referred to as going on inside the "black box." The term arose as an analogy to the field of electrical engineering, in which students are sometimes given a black box filled with electronic circuitry. The student's task is to determine what that circuitry is without opening the box; that is, by applying inputs (stimuli) and measuring outputs (responses) and correctly interpreting the results.

S-R theorists have been accused of saying that only overt behaviour exists. But that is a distortion of their position. The strict S-R theorists said, "Of course, there is much going on inside the organism, but we do not have access to it. Therefore, our business is simply to study overt behaviour." The *cognitive trend* in more recent behaviour theory, however, is focusing more and more on the covert behaviour "inside the black box."

Cognitions as behaviours

Cognitive behaviourists say not only that cognition (thinking) is extremely important in the control of behaviour, but that thinking and feeling *are themselves* behaviours as well. They are behaviours that occur "inside the skin," but they are behaviours all the same. They follow the same laws of learning that overt behaviours do. For example, a person will think particular thoughts more if that thinking is operantly reinforced. In addition, it is possible to establish the act of thinking a particular thought as a CS, and then the conditioned response will generalize to related thoughts. The cognitive learning theorist would refer to all the processes we will study in Chapter 8

(Thinking and Language) as *covert behaviour*, behaviour that is not directly observable.

The methods of studying cognition have to be indirect, since we cannot observe thoughts. In later chapters, we will explore many aspects of cognition and see examples of how cognition is studied by making inferences from overt behaviour.

Observational learning is the process of learning by watching and imitating the behaviours of others.
SOURCE: Dick Hemingway.

Observational (vicarious) learning

We have already hinted that much learning takes place without any obvious reinforcement or exposure to unconditioned stimuli. It is likely that much of what we call "personality" as well as many of our subtle behaviours, such as the inflections and accent with which we talk, are not learned through direct reinforcement but rather through imitation. In other words, they are learned through **observational (vicarious) learning**, which is the process of learning by watching others' behaviours. **Modelling** is the act of imitating or matching one's behaviour to that of another person who is acting as a model. It has been argued that anything that can be learned can be learned by imitation. But first the child must learn to imitate. Some psychologists have argued that observational learning must take place through some mechanism other than reinforcement because the child often imitates even when neither the child nor the "model" receives reinforcement (Bandura, 1965), and some babies even tend to imitate others' facial expressions in the first two weeks of life (Field, Woodson, Greenberg, & Cohen, 1982; Meltzoff & Moore, 1977). However, other psychologists have argued that the child is strongly taught a broad class of imitative behaviours that can be called **generalized imitation** (Gewirtz, 1971). These behaviours are established at least in part through frequent and unpredictable reinforcement for imitating others. Nearly from birth, adults are hovering over the child saying things such as "Say daddy. Say daddy." Eventually, the child's random babbling gets around to "du-du," and daddy goes nuts, reinforcing the child for this particular sound but also reinforcing "matching to sample"—that is, matching behaviour to behaviour that just occurred. This training will be given often and on a variable-ratio schedule. Thus, it will become a very powerful behaviour. Imitation probably results from both powerful learning experiences and some kind of "pre-wired" tendency to imitate or at least a strong "preparedness" to learn it. Observational or vicarious learning can result in both conditioned responses and operant behaviours. Bandura (1977) uses the term **social learning theory** for a version of learning theory that emphasizes the importance of learning through interactions with others. One of the central ideas of social learning theory is the strong power of observational learning.

Vicarious classical conditioning

One way we acquire fears and other emotional responses is by observing others. This process might be called **vicarious classical conditioning**. We can define it as the establishment of a CR when a subject simply watches another subject being exposed to a CS followed by the US. In a typical vicarious conditioning experiment, subjects watched another person appear to react with pain after a buzzer sounded (Bandura & Rosenthal, 1966). These subjects later had bodily reactions to the buzzer more than did other subjects, who either thought the person was not getting shocks or who didn't see the other person make gestures and movements indicating pain. In other words, the buzzer was established as a CR for some subjects simply through watching others apparently being conditioned to it.

In real life, this process can be very subtle. If a parent was in serious financial trouble and feared the ringing of the phone, it is entirely possible that his or her children could acquire a fear of the phone ringing, without the parent or the child knowing the source of the fear.

Vicarious extinction

Similarly, **vicarious extinction** has been demonstrated in studies in which subjects' fears were diminished by watching others being exposed to the feared CS's without the US (Geer & Turtletaub, 1967; Bandura, 1969). One common treatment for fears of animals is to have the subject observe other people who are similar to the subject interacting with animals.

Vicarious operant learning

Finally, it is obvious that many examples of vicarious operant conditioning can be found. **Vicarious operant conditioning** is the process of learning operant behaviours simply by watching others perform them. Each person has so much to learn about life that it would be impossible to learn it all firsthand. Vicarious learning is essential for lessons like delay of gratification, perseverance, and calm affection in the face of anger. It is important to note, though, that many types of behaviours can be learned by imitation—not just adaptive behaviours. Children, for example, can learn maladaptive behaviours, as well as a tendency to blame themselves for things, just by watching adult models behave in maladaptive ways (Thelan, 1969; Herbert, Gelfand, & Hartman, 1969).

CLOSE-UP

The Only Way to Make Money in Las Vegas

A psychologist we know likes to tell of his younger days when he would go to Las Vegas and make a profit. He never gambled. First, he went to casinos that provided free drink refills as a way to keep people gambling. Our friend would buy a handful of chips and stand around looking intense and a little worried, shaking his chips every now and then, so that the casino would keep his glass full. When he spotted a high roller at a high-action game such as craps or roulette, he worked his way around so as to be standing next to the wealthy gambler. If the gambler won frequently, he would often pay our friend to continue to stand next to him, since he believed our friend was good luck. Of course, if the gambler lost or won only occasionally, nothing happened. When our friend eventually lost his "power" to bring good luck, the gambler might tell him to leave. However, our friend has a thick skin and he would go off to find some other player to bless with his presence. An understanding of superstitious learning can pay off!

SPECIAL TOPIC The Truth about Little Albert

One of the most famous and repeated stories in psychology is Watson and Rayner's classical conditioning of a baby named Albert (1920). Many introductory psychology textbooks use Albert's story to illustrate classical conditioning. However, we have decided to give you the background of the story as a lesson about being a cautious and critical evaluator of what you read.

At age nine months, Albert was in the hospital and was tested and found not to fear several live animals, such as a rat, a rabbit, and a dog. He did show strong reactions when a steel bar was struck with a hammer unexpectedly behind him. Two months later, Watson and Rayner presented a white rat to Albert and hit the steel bar with the hammer whenever Albert touched the rat. After seven such experiences, Albert cried and tried to move away when the rat was presented. As a demonstration of generalization, Albert was said to show fear toward the rat, a rabbit, a dog, and a sealskin coat, but not to a set of familiar blocks. A month later, Watson and Rayner reported that Albert still showed some of his fears, and then Albert's mother removed him from the hospital. Watson and Rayner clearly said they knew a month in advance when Albert would be taken from the hospital. They wrote that they continued their experimenting up to the time he left.

This story appears in nearly all introductory psychology textbooks and many other books and journals as well. But the accounts often contain incorrect and misleading statements. Benjamin Harris (1979) wrote an article called "Whatever happened to Little Albert?" in which he describes a long series of errors in reporting Albert's story. Textbook writers incorrectly described Albert as being conditioned to other animals, as fearing a wide range of things he was never tested for, and as having been "reconditioned" at the end of the experiment to remove his fear. This last detail seems to have been designed to "brush up" Watson's image. It was clearly unethical for Watson to experiment with Albert and then send him on his way. Therefore many writers added a happy ending to the story. As far as we can tell, no one seems to know what did happen to Albert after his mother took him home from the hospital.

Some writers have erroneously cited the example of Little Albert to show that "it is quite possible for one experience to induce a phobia" (Wolpe & Rachman, 1960, p. 146). Other writers

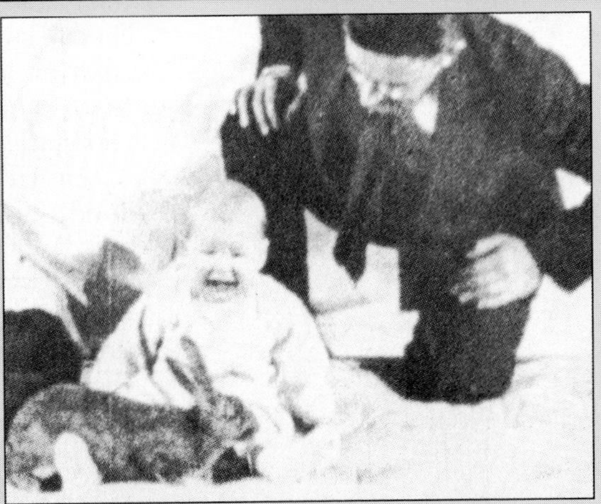

Little Albert reacting to stimuli.
SOURCE: Courtesy of Professor Benjamin Harris.

claimed that "Albert developed a phobia for white rats and indeed for all furry animals" (Eysenck, 1960, p. 5). A phobia is a very severe fear. In fact, however, Albert's behaviour was fairly mild. In one typical instance his reaction to the rat was that he "fell over to the left side, got up on all fours and started to crawl away. On this occasion there was no crying, but strange to say, as he started away he began to gurgle and coo, even while leaning far over to the left side to avoid the rat" (Watson & Rayner, 1920, p.7).

There are many other examples of authors who have incorrectly presented Little Albert's case to make a point. For example, as Harris (1979) points out, Seligman (1971) uses an inaccurate version of the Albert story to support the notion of "biological preparedness" — interestingly, in opposition to the views of Wolpe and Rachmann (1960) and Eysenck (1960), who had also cited Albert's case. Samelson (1980) even criticizes Watson himself for inconsistencies and for omitting "details" in his five published accounts of the Albert story (Watson and Raynor often had to remove Albert's thumb from his mouth before the "conditioned response" emerged, for example, but they rarely mentioned this.)

Some of these mistakes might be amusing if they didn't carry a worrisome message. One should evaluate the written word critically and cautiously. This textbook itself should not elude your scrutiny. We have cited references in order to enable you to pursue points you find interesting or controversial.

CHAPTER SUMMARY

1. Learning can be defined as behaviour change that occurs as a result of experience. In its most strongly stated form, learning theory suggests that it is largely environmental factors rather than biological influences that structure behaviour. Learning theory goes on to suggest that personality consists of our learned thoughts, feelings, and overt behaviours. There are two major categories of learning: classical conditioning and operant conditioning.

2. Classical conditioning begins with a stimulus that has an effect on the organism in the absence of prior learning, called the unconditioned stimulus (US). The response this arouses is called the unconditioned response (UR). When a US is repeatedly paired with some other neutral stimulus, this second stimulus eventually can act alone to arouse a response similar to the UR. The previously neutral stimulus has become a conditioned stimulus (CS) that arouses a conditioned response (CR). In higher-order conditioning, the new CS can be paired with a new neutral stimulus, which can also acquire power as a CS. With third-order and fourth-order CS's, however, we seem to be approaching the limits of higher-order conditioning.

3. A stimulus similar to a CS can also arouse the CR, but in diminished strength. This process is called generalization. The gradient of generalization refers to the fact that the less similar a stimulus is to the original CS, the less effective it is in arousing the original CR. The opposite of generalization is discrimination. In discrimination learning, the subject learns to respond to a specific CS but not to similar stimuli.

4. Classical conditioning affects a wide range of phenomena in human functioning. For instance, classical conditioning is a strong component of emotions. Extinction is the only way to weaken a conditioned response. Extinction consists of exposure to the CS, the performance of the CR, and the absence of the US. To get over a fear, for example, you must be exposed to the thing you fear, feel the fear, and have no painful consequences follow.

5. The establishment of a new CR that competes with an old CR is called counterconditioning. This does not weaken the old CR, but suppresses it with the new, stronger CR.

6. In general, the closer in time the US and CS are presented, the stronger the conditioning. When the US and CS are presented together, this is called simultaneous conditioning. When the CS begins first and overlaps with US presentation or ends just when the US begins, this pattern is called delayed conditioning. When the CS is presented first and ends before the US starts, this is called trace conditioning. Backward conditioning occurs when the CS follows the presentation of the US. It is the most difficult temporal relationship for learning.

7. Classical conditioning affects many areas of human behaviour. Studies have shown that placeboes, acting as CS's, can be effective in alleviating a surprising number of health problems. Substance abuse, eating, sexual behaviour, the responses of the immune system, and the use of language are often classically conditioned to a large extent.

8. Operant conditioning concerns behaviour which operates on or is instrumental in the environment. The major difference between operant and classical conditioning concerns the nature of the origin of the response to be strengthened. In classical conditioning, the response is elicited by a stimulus, whereas in operant conditioning, the person or animal emits a response which is reinforced.

9. A reinforcer is anything that strengthens behaviour for a particular organism. According to the Premack Principle, an activity that is preferred can serve to reinforce an activity that is less preferred. Reinforcers are divided into two types: positive reinforcers, which can be seen as generally giving pleasure, and negative reinforcers, which can be thought of as reducing discomfort.

10. Learning theorists stress the importance of positive reinforcement. Shaping is the technique of rewarding successive approximations of a final target behaviour by reinforcing each step of the complex behaviour.

11. As with classical conditioning, the only way to get rid of an operantly learned behaviour is to extinguish it by having the organism perform the response in the absence of reinforcement. At first this leads to an increase in the behaviour to be extinguished, but in the long run extinction is superior to punishment as a means of eliminating unwanted behaviours.

12. Primary reinforcers are based on physiological needs. Other reinforcers which satisfy psychological needs or have been associated with a reinforcer that satisfies a physiological need are called secondary reinforcers.

13. Reinforcers have different effects, depending on the schedule on which they are provided to the organism. Continuous reinforcement occurs when an organism receives a reinforcer every time it emits the correct response. Continuous reinforcement promotes rapid learning and allows for rapid extinction. Partial reinforcement occurs when reinforcers are not given after every desired response. We can distinguish four different types of schedules of partial reinforcement: the fixed-interval schedule, the fixed-ratio schedule, the variable-ratio schedule, and the variable-interval schedule. In general, the less predictable the schedule, the slower the initial learning but the more resistant the new behaviour is to extinction. Unpredictable reinforcement can produce superstitious learning.

14. As with classical conditioning, reinforcers that are presented immediately after a behaviour has occurred have the strongest effect. An important lesson for survival is to learn to work for delayed reinforcers.

15. Fear is learned through classical conditioning, ultimately based on associating stimuli with some form of pain. Complex fears can be learned through imitation of others and can be made worse by the operant reinforcement of fear. Reason can help combat the thought component of fear, but only extinction can weaken the autonomic nervous system component. Reduction of fear is a very powerful negative reinforcer. Behaviours that are established through fear reduction are called escape behaviours. Fears are persistent because we so effectively avoid feeling fear. We prevent extinction by escaping the feared cue so rapidly that autonomic arousal is prevented. Also, fear reduction is such a powerful reinforcer that our escape behaviour is strongly reinforced and tends to persist. Fears also extinguish more slowly than other responses for biological reasons.

16. It appears that different species of animals have biological constraints on learning. Research on learned taste aversion suggests that different species have a biological preparedness to associate certain types of stimuli more easily than other types. Instinctual drift and autoshaping are further indications of biological predispositions in learning. It is commonly but incorrectly believed that learning theory argues for the principle of equipotentiality —that any conditioned response is as easy to learn as any other.

17. Punishment is probably the most popular way to try to control the behaviour of others. However, the available evidence suggests that punishment does not eliminate the behaviour we wish to control but only inhibits that behaviour. Moreover, punishment has a number of serious disadvantages which people seldom consider. The most effective use of punishment is to apply it in a mild form and combine it with plenty of positive reinforcement.

18. Recently, learning theorists have become more interested in cognition or thinking. Thinking and feeling are considered as behaviours that occur inside the skin but that operate exactly the same way as other behaviours. Imitation itself is a complex behaviour that is acquired through learning. Imitation is generalized to become the foundation of much future learning.

KEY TERMS

Active-avoidance learning Learning to avoid aversive stimuli by taking direct action.

Autoshaping The performance of a "natural" behaviour, even when there seems to be no need for it. Noncontingent rewards can come to reinforce a very likely behaviour, much as with superstitious learning.

Backward conditioning In classical conditioning, the presentation and termination of the US prior to the presentation of the CS.

Behaviour theorists Another term for *learning theorists.*

Behaviourists Another term for *learning theorists.*

Biological preparedness A genetic predisposition to learn some associations between stimuli more readily than others.

Classical conditioning The process of learning in which a neutral stimulus is paired with some stimulus that already elicits a specific response. If this is done repeatedly, eventually the neutral stimulus will come to arouse the specific response when presented alone.

Conditioned emotional response (CER) A classically conditioned response in which autonomic arousal is the CR.

Conditioned response (CR) The response that is aroused by a conditioned stimulus.

Conditioned stimulus (CS) A previously neutral stimulus that has acquired the power to arouse a particular response by being associated with an unconditioned stimulus.

Continuous reinforcement (CRF) schedule A reinforcement schedule on which reinforcement is given for every performance of the desired response.

Counterconditioning The process by which a newly learned response is paired with and replaces an older learned response.

Delayed conditioning In classical conditioning, the presentation of the CS prior to the US. The CS either overlaps with the US or terminates exactly when the US begins.

Delayed reinforcement Reinforcement that is delivered after some time period following performance of the desired behaviour.

Discrimination In learning theory, the process of learning to respond to a particular stimulus but not to similar stimuli.

Discriminative stimulus In discrimination conditioning, the specific stimulus that the subject is taught to respond to.

Equipotentiality The assumption that any CS-US pairing or any response-reinforcer pairing is just as likely to work as any other.

Escape behaviour Actions designed to avoid or flee from aversive stimuli.

Extinction in classical conditioning The weakening of conditioned behaviour. In classical conditioning a CR will weaken if (1) the CS is presented, (2) the CR occurs, and (3) there is no presentation of the US.

Extinction in operant conditioning The weakening of conditioned behaviour. In operant conditioning, the response weakens with performance of the response and the absence of reinforcement.

Fading A type of shaping in which an already established behaviour is gradually modified to more closely resemble the desired behaviour.

Fixed-interval (FI) schedule A partial reinforcement schedule on which reinforcement for a correct response is given after some regular time interval. Any other correct responses that are given during that time period are ignored.

Fixed-ratio (FR) schedule A partial reinforcement schedule on which reinforcement is delivered after some set number of correct responses has been performed.

Generalization In learning theory, the process by which stimuli similar to a CS will also elicit the CR, but the strength of the CR will be diminished.

Generalized imitation A broad class of imitative behaviours that is established at least in part through frequent and unpredictable reinforcement for imitating others.

Generalized partial reinforcement effect A tendency to persist at a wide range of behaviours after having had experience with partial reinforcement for other behaviours.

Gradient of generalization The tendency for the strength of generalization to diminish as stimuli become less similar to the original conditioned stimulus.

Graduated counterconditioning Counterconditioning process in which a new conditioned response replaces an old conditioned response in small steps.

Graduated extinction Extinction process in which the subject is exposed to the CS in small steps, either by approaching the CS more closely or by being exposed to stimuli that are increasingly more similar to the CS.

Higher-order conditioning The establishment of a conditioned stimulus by pairing a new neutral stimulus with an existing conditioned stimulus. The new stimulus alone then acquires the power to arouse the original conditioned response.

Instinctual drift The tendency of many animals, even when strongly taught some new but unusual behaviour, to return gradually to the behaviours that are more common to their species.

Instrumental conditioning Another term for *operant conditioning.*

Learned taste aversion A previously neutral taste becomes aversive (i.e., to be avoided) because of classical conditioning in which the taste was paired with a painful US.

Learning The process through which experience leads to changes in behaviour.

Learning theorists Psychologists who believe that virtually all behaviour is the result of prior learning.

Modelling The act of imitating or matching one's behaviour to that of another person who acts as a model.

Negative reinforcers Reinforcers that strengthen a behaviour by following it with a reduction in discomfort.

Observational (vicarious) learning The process of learning by watching others' behaviours. It underlies a great deal of human learning.

Operant conditioning (also called *instrumental conditioning*) The process of learning in which the organism emits a response, and the consequences either strengthen or weaken that response.

Partial reinforcement schedule A reinforcement schedule on which reinforcement is *not* given after every desired response.

Passive-avoidance learning Learning to avoid aversive stimuli by not taking particular actions.

Placebo effect A measurable effect on physiological functioning which occurs under the influence of a physiologically inactive substance.

Positive reinforcers Reinforcers that increase pleasure. They are usually called "rewards."

Premack Principle The principle that an activity that is preferred can be used to reinforce one that is less preferred at a particular time.

Primary reinforcers Reinforcers that are based on physiological needs.

Punishment An attempt to deal with undesirable behaviour through the offset of an appetitive stimulus or the onset of an aversive stimulus.

Reconditioning The relatively rapid re-establishment of an apparently extinguished CR by means of new conditioning trials.

Reinforcer Anything that follows a behaviour and increases the likelihood of that behaviour occurring again.

Respondent conditioning Another term for *classical conditioning.*

Secondary reinforcers Acquired reinforcers that have taken on motivating power because of past learning experiences.

Shaping In operant conditioning, the teaching of complex behaviours by reinforcing, in small steps, successive approximations of the desired behaviour.

Simultaneous conditioning In classical conditioning, the presentation of the CS and the US together and their termination together.

Social learning theory A version of learning theory that emphasizes the importance of learning through interactions with others. Observational learning is a central concept of this theory.

Spontaneous recovery The reappearance, after a period of time, of an apparently extinguished CR when the CS is presented again.

Superstitious behaviour Behaviour that is inadvertently established through randomly delivered reinforcement.

Temporal contiguity The closeness in time of the presentation of two stimuli, such as a CS and a US.

Trace conditioning In classical conditioning, the presentation of the CS prior to the US and then a time interval between the offset of the CS the onset of the US.

Unconditioned response (UR) The particular response that is aroused by an unconditioned stimulus.

Unconditioned stimulus (US) Any stimulus that arouses a particular response in an organism in the absence of prior learning.

Variable-interval (VI) schedule A partial reinforcement schedule on which the reinforcer for a correct response is delivered after a time interval which varies in length unpredictably. Any other correct responses that are given during that time period are ignored.

Variable-ratio (VR) schedule A partial reinforcement schedule on which a reinforcer is delivered after an unpredictable or variable number of correct responses.

Vicarious classical conditioning The establishment of a CR when a subject simply watches another subject being conditioned.

Vicarious extinction The weakening of a CR when a subject simply watches another subject being exposed to a CS without the US.

Vicarious operant conditioning The process of learning operant behaviours simply by watching others perform them.

Suggested Readings

Axelrod, S., & Apsche, J. (Eds.). (1983). *The effects of punishment on human behavior.* New York: Academic Press. This book deals with both the uses and problems associated with using punishment to influence behaviour. There are suggestions for reducing the negative effects of punishment that we have discussed in this chapter and for grappling with the social issues raised by the use of punishment.

Bandura, A. (1977). *Social-learning theory.* Englewood Cliffs, NJ: Prentice-Hall. The first of two of Bandura's books that we recommend. This is an overview of social learning theory by one of its most famous proponents.

Bandura, A. (1986). *Social foundations of thought and action.* Englewood Cliffs, NJ: Prentice-Hall. Bandura's more recent book focuses on a cognitive view of learning. He has much to say about vicarious learning and stresses how the person interacts with the environment. We are not only influenced by the environment; we also influence the environment.

Schwartz, B. (1984). *Psychology of learning and behavior.* 2nd ed. New York: Norton. This is a comprehensive and well-balanced textbook on learning. It includes material on cognitive learning, basic principles, and animal learning.

Skinner, B. F. (1960). *Walden Two.* New York: Macmillan. This is an interesting and provocative novel written by the famous behaviourist. It is a Utopian novel in which Skinner tries to show how the humane application of behavioural principles could lead to a happier human existence in a commune. This novel is a classic.

Skinner, B. F. (1971). *Beyond freedom and dignity.* New York: Knopf. This is one of Skinner's most influential books written for the educated layperson. He applies his ideas to social issues and grapples with several philosophical questions. He redefines "freedom" and "dignity" within a behaviouristic theory that considers free-will to be an illusion.

CHAPTER 6

SOURCE: Robert J. Flaherty, Detail from *Summer (August) Eskimo in Northeastern Hudson Bay* (ca. 1925).

Motivation and Emotion

WHY DO WE do what we do and why do we feel certain emotions? On an everyday level, we are amateur psychologists each time we speculate about the causes of others' behaviours or try to interpret their emotions. Why *did* you talk to somebody in that way, or go out with that particular person, or eat that strawberry cheesecake in spite of feeling stuffed? How do feelings develop and how are our feelings tied in with our motivations and other mental processes? These are some of the issues that we will explore in this chapter as we survey the way psychologists have tried to grapple with the concept of motivation—the "whys" of behaviour. We will investigate how motivation in humans and in lower species can be studied in the laboratory. After we discuss some different theories, we will take a closer look at three particular motivations: hunger, sex, and the drive for achievement.

One important part of motivation is emotion, which is the feeling part of ourselves that colours life, makes it meaningful, and gives our existence enjoyment. Imagine, for a moment, a life without motivation and without emotion. Tragically, people who suffer from major neurological damage in the frontal lobes of their brains may experience such a life. They are behaviourally inert, lethargic, lacking drive, flat in their emotion, and relatively nonreactive to what goes on around them (Lezak, 1983). They usually do not do anything unless prompted, preferring to watch television, lie in bed, or sit idly. What psychological processes and mechanisms do we all have that allow us to be motivated and involved, and that give our lives the colouring of our emotions? In this chapter we will discuss three leading theories of emotion.

MOTIVATION: GENERAL CONSIDERATIONS

Motivation is a hypothetical construct (i.e., a theoretical concept) that psychologists and others use to account for what determines our behaviours, actions, and thought processes. The term "motivation" comes from the Latin word meaning "to move." The concept focuses on the forces that initiate, sustain, and direct behaviour. The study of motivation seeks to answer the "whys" about human behaviour. It looks at what is inside us that pushes us to act, and what is outside us that functions to elicit certain behaviours. At any one time we are subject to the pushes and pulls of many different kinds and levels of motivation. They range from basic biological drives that maintain a physical equilibrium in our bodies, to drives that are more socially based, which we learn through our upbringing, school experiences, and our culture at large.

Basic concepts

We invariably search for meaning and causes for what happens around us. This search is so solidly rooted in our intellectual life that we are prepared to speculate about causes in situations where the causes are not readily apparent. We frequently ask, "Why did you do that?", when a friend acts irrationally. Or we might speculate, "She married him only for his money." What we are trying to do is make sense out of our world, account for the tremendous range in behaviour around us, and make these behaviours more understandable. This search takes on vital importance in our legal system, for example, where an important feature of trials deals with presumed motives for certain actions. You probably recall courtroom dramas on television where much deliberation goes into the fact that there is circumstantial evidence implicating the accused, but no apparent motive. Consider the legal difference between the following two scenarios:

(1) A woman is walking down the street when she is suddenly assaulted by a strange man. The assailant lashes out at the woman with a racquet and breaks her arm.

(2) A woman is playing racquetball with a friend. Her playing partner lunges for the ball and swings wildly. The racquet misses the ball but strikes the woman and breaks her arm.

The result is the same in each case. The woman's arm has been broken by a blow from a racquet. The difference between the two scenarios lies primarily with presumed motivation. In the first case, there was probably a deliberate intent to injure, whereas in the second case, there seems to have been a pure accident. But how do we know for sure? To help answer such a question, let us look more closely at the concept of motivation.

An intervening variable

We can never see a motive directly. How do you know if somebody is hungry, sexually aroused, competitive, curious, or the like? The use of "motivations" to explain behaviour requires us to infer or hypothesize that some motive is operating. All we actually see are the environmental stimuli and the resulting behaviours. Motivation is an intervening variable. An **intervening variable** is thus a hypothetical construct that represents inferred processes which occur between observed stimulus input and observed response output. When you look at somebody else's actions and speculate about the cause of his or her behaviour, you're going beyond just describing what they are doing; you are explaining, by using motivational concepts as hypothetical causes. We never really do see a motivation. We only see behaviour. In real-life settings, one of the goals of psychological assessment is to understand the reasons behind certain behaviours or the factors that motivate a person. The clinician who is doing the assessment does not really *see* pieces of jealousy, revenge,

We do not *see* jealousy, rage, revenge, despair, or love. We only see the behaviours motivated by such emotions.

SOURCE: *King Lear* (1985), with Douglas Campbell as King Lear and Seana McKenna as Cordelia. Courtesy Stratford Festival.

love, need for power, or achievement. Instead, the clinician makes speculations and inferences about these types of motivations from observations, interviews, and test data. A certain amount of humility is appropriate for those who make such diagnoses because inferences are a step away from actual data. In essence, we are attempting to see what is inside the "black box" by looking at what goes into it and what comes out of it.

Measuring motivation

Because they are intangible, inferred concepts, motivations have to be dealt with in special ways before they become something that researchers can examine. This may sound a long way from our interest in a psychotherapy patient's unconscious fear of success as a determinant of self-defeating behaviour, but it is an important step in beginning to analyze motivation. In scientific terms, if we are interested in researching some form of motivation, we have to operationalize the concept. To **operationalize** is to devise a way to measure something in a clearly observable and quantifiable way. The steps taken to measure the concept must be defined very carefully so that others can repeat our observations and verify them. If we are focusing on a basic internal drive, such as thirst, we cannot directly see the thirst. But one way we can measure it is by the number of hours our subjects have gone without fluid intake. In our experiment, we may deprive subjects of fluid for differing durations and, all other things being equal, be able to say that our subjects differ in their thirst. We have to tie the inferred motivational concept to actual observable behaviours.

The preceding example of thirst illustrates a deprivation procedure that can be used to establish differential motivation among subjects. It is possible to measure motivation in other ways as well. In order to measure a socially based motivation that he called "need for achievement," McClelland (1971) examined and scored stories that subjects made up about pictures they were shown. Although this particular study made use of pre-existing differences among subjects in the need for achievement, the method of approach is the same. A specific operational procedure is used to index or gauge the strength of the motivation. To this end, we can use psychological tests or interviews. In designed experimental settings we often use levels of activity as a measure of the effects of a particular motivation. In general, the researcher should strive to devise procedures for carefully measuring both the strength as well as the effects of a motivation.

Primary and secondary drives

There are many different types of animal and human motivations. A useful way of categorizing them is to consider some of the motives as biologically determined in contrast to others that are more socially or culturally determined.

Primary drives are drives or motives based on innate, biological, and survival-oriented needs. Examples include hunger, thirst, the need for sleep, the need for air, and the need to avoid pain. Some researchers consider the sex drive to be one of the primary drives, and we will classify it as such. Nevertheless, there is some controversy about this because sex is not necessary for an individual organism's survival.

Secondary drives are drives or motives based on learned needs, whether these needs have been acquired through the learning processes of classical conditioning or operant conditioning. In Chapter 5, we showed that previously neutral stimuli may, over time, gain the stimulus value of either the unconditioned stimulus in classical conditioning, or the reinforcer in operant conditioning. In other words, it is possible that the association between a neutral stimulus and the sought-after reinforcement develops so strongly that in time the previously neutral stimulus now has an incentive value equal to the reinforcer. This is how approval, money, or power become something that we search out and work hard to achieve. Money is of no value to an infant, who would gladly chew on your $100 bill. It is only through the learning process that this piece of paper becomes a very powerful motivator of behaviour. We use the term **generalized conditioned reinforcer** to describe an object that acquires broad reinforcing power through association with primary reinforcers. Money, for example, has generalized reinforcing power, as does praise, for most people.

Lower species also develop secondary drives, as has been demonstrated in an experiment conducted by Miller (1948). He applied an electrical current to the floor of a cage in which rats were housed. There were two compartments to this cage, with only one compartment where the shock was consistently applied. The rats learned very quickly to escape from the electric shock by running to the other compartment. Interestingly, later on in the experiment when no shock was being applied, the animals continued to go to considerable effort to leave the previously shocked compartment. They

FIGURE 6-1 The development of secondary drives
In experiments by Miller (1948), rats learned new techniques for escaping from a formerly shocked compartment. Their learned fear had become the motivator or secondary drive for the learning of new responses.

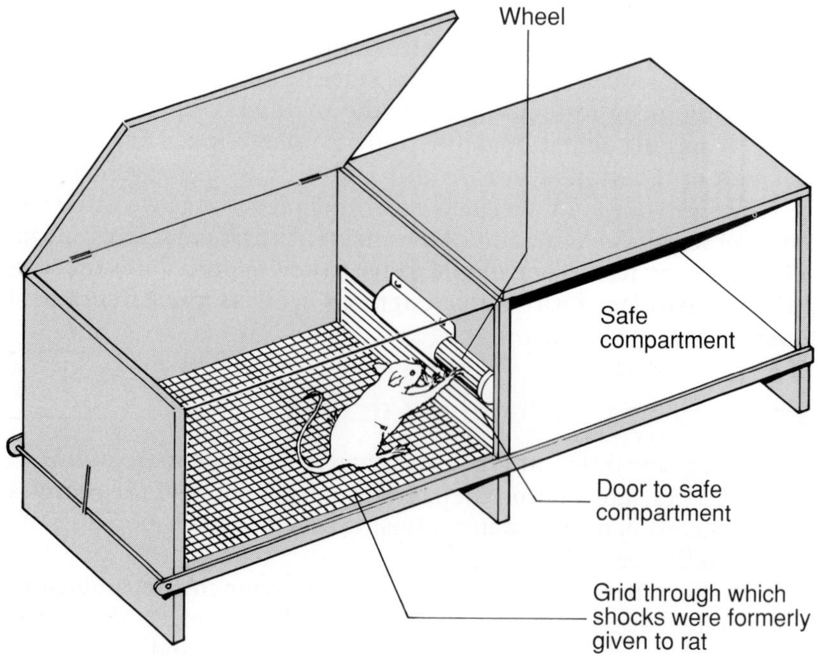

SOURCE: Adapted from Miller (1948), p. 90.

even learned new techniques to escape, including pressing levers or turning a wheel to get out of the previously shocked compartment. It was thought that the rats in this experiment had acquired a learned fear of the shocked compartment through classical conditioning and that this learned fear was a motivator (a secondary drive) for the learning of new responses. See Figure 6-1. Even though the compartment itself was not a source of physical pain, it had become aversive. Thus escaping the compartment was reinforcing, and this reinforcement helped establish avoidance behaviour. The learned fear was difficult to extinguish because the rats did not stay in the formerly shocked side of the cage long enough to find out that the shock no longer occurred. This is also true with human phobias, which persist for long durations unless some specific treatments are instituted.

THEORIES OF MOTIVATION

Throughout history, people have been concerned about what causes behaviour. Early philosophers such as Plato and Aristotle had a strong belief in rationality, and they thought that through reason, choices are made and actions determined. This notion was held by Christian theologians as well, and was thought to be one of the major factors separating humans from the lower species, which are ruled by instincts.

During the last century and a half, scientists have perceived a stronger link between humans and other animals. Many theorists have applied instincts to humans as an explanation of motivation. Other theorists have reduced the importance of instinct explanations in some ways and elaborated on them in others. As you read this chapter, try to see how one theory builds upon another to give a more complete explanation of human motivation. This is the nature of all scientific development: each new theory is a successive refinement of previous ones.

Instinct theories

Instinct theories state that innate, complex, biologically built-in drives are the foundation of motivation. In previous centuries, most philosophers argued for instincts among animals but not humans. They claimed that humans are qualitatively different from animals. The major challenge to this view came with the publication of Charles Darwin's *On The Origin of Species* in 1859. Based upon extensive observations of the changes in species in response to differing environments, Darwin proposed the *theory of evolution* which assumes a continuity among species. Darwin argued that humans, as the highest species, have evolved from lower species through a process which he called *survival of the fittest through natural selection.* According to this theory, different species have had to adjust and adapt to their environments. Those within the species that were able to adjust lived and reproduced. Thus only the fittest survived to produce new generations. For example, see Figure 6-2.

FIGURE 6-2 Survival of the fittest through natural selection

Recent changes in the peppered moth (biston betularius) provide a dramatic example of evolutionary change through selection of the fittest. The normally white moths are well camouflaged against natural predators on birch and other white trees in the wild. However, in places where air pollution has blackened the trees, darker moths are more fit for survival because they are less likely to be seen and eaten by birds. The peppered moth is evolving into a dark species.

A

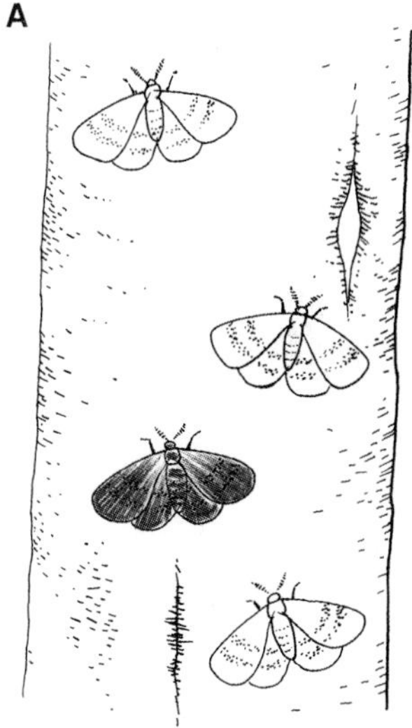

B

This revolutionary idea gave rise to one of the earliest perspectives on motivation—that humans and animals are on a continuum of development. This notion was the foundation of Darwin's book *The Descent of Man* (1871). If there is a continuity among species and if animal behaviour is regulated by instincts, then it is likely that human behaviour is also based on instincts. In other words, we act because of the force of our instincts. As well, we can learn about human behaviour in all of its colour and complexity by studying lower species. The branch of science called **ethology** studies organisms in their natural environments as well as their instinctual patterns of behaviour. **Instincts** are unlearned, biologically built-in, fixed patterns of behaviour. They are relatively constant over a species (i.e., they are characteristic of a whole species) and they often serve a biological purpose. The potential for the instinct may be present at birth, but its actual expression may be delayed until a certain point in the organism's maturation. Ethologists use the more technical term fixed action pattern for an instinct. In other words, **fixed action pattern** refers to the specific behaviours that the organism is preprogrammed to perform under specific conditions. Ethologists call the particular stimuli in the environment that give rise to the fixed action pattern **releasers**. These stimuli "release" the instinctual behaviour. Ethologists say that birds to not have to learn the particular courting ritual that occurs as a prelude to mating. This is a fixed action pattern that occurs at the appropriate time in the bird's maturation, usually in response to some releaser stimulus in the environment. For a male bird, a female who signals her receptivity by certain behaviours would become the trigger stimulus. Do similar factors operate in human courting?

William McDougall (1908) was an early proponent of instinct theory for humans. He argued that all behaviours were the result of a set of inherent dispositions or instincts (such as curiosity, acquisitiveness, and gregariousness) and that he could explain all human thought and behaviour by combining the basic set of instincts.

An alternate conception of instinct theory was developed by Sigmund Freud (1935). He believed that there are two fundamental human instincts and that all human behaviour is caused by them. The first instinct he proposed was what he termed eros. He believed **eros** is the life instinct that supposedly leads to positive actions and sexuality. Later, Freud proposed the instinct he called **thanatos**, which is a death instinct and one that leads to aggression and destructive behaviour. According to Freud, the expression of these instincts is not direct. Freud believed that these instincts are kept in our unconscious so that we are not aware of them, but that they nevertheless exert great effect in our everyday life. Although unconscious, the tension or energy from the instincts pushes for expression, and much of our psychological development has to do with allowing this energy or tension to be relieved in socially acceptable ways. **Libido** is the energy derived from eros that motivates behaviour according to Freud's theory. It is sometimes (somewhat inaccurately) used synonymously with eros. Much motivation stems from attempting to reduce the tension derived from eros and to reconcile it with the demands of everyday life, given the fact that we cannot, for example, go around having sex indiscriminately. We will discuss Freud's theories at greater length in Chapter 10.

While Freudian notions of instincts and of unconscious influences are still used today in many areas (particularly in clinical psychology), ideas about instincts have dropped from the forefront of our understanding about motivation. For one thing, to explain the range and diversity of human behaviour we would have to either speculate about an incredibly large number of instincts or reduce them all to a manageable handful. Some researchers have attempted to catalogue the number of instincts with lists which number over 10 000 (e.g., Bernard, 1924). However, some theorists question whether instincts really explain anything at all. Perhaps instincts are

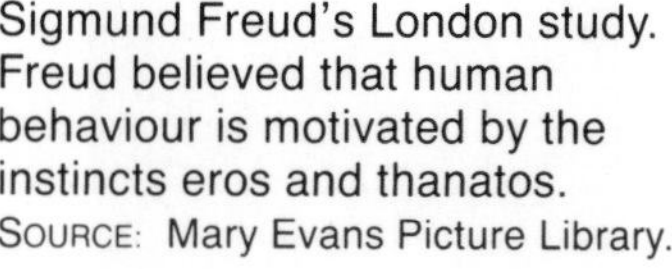

Sigmund Freud's London study. Freud believed that human behaviour is motivated by the instincts eros and thanatos. SOURCE: Mary Evans Picture Library.

simply new labels for particular behaviours. Moreover, some prominent anthropologists studying behaviour in different cultures have failed to see what would have been predicted as the universal expression of instincts regardless of culture (e.g., Mead, 1939). There are large differences between cultures in many behaviours, an observation not easily accounted for by an instinct theory. Perhaps one of the major reasons instinct theories have decreased in their popularity has been the rise of behavioural psychology. We will turn to this next as we discuss drive-reduction and learning-based theories of motivation.

It is important to remember that later theories do not deny the importance of biological influences on motivation. Instead, they put limits on instinct theory as a complete explanation of behaviour.

Drive-reduction theory

Instinct theories have been supplemented by the drive-reduction understanding of motivation, which is based firmly on the physiological concept of homeostasis. **Homeostasis** is that state where systems maintain a balanced, stable environment. You'll remember from Chapter 2 that with regard to physiology, homeostatic mechanisms are the body mechanisms that operate to maintain an equilibrium of functions within the organism. Physiological homeostasis involves complex feedback systems which monitor changes in a body system, decide whether some deviation has exceeded acceptable limits, and then act to re-assert a balance. As we will see when we discuss hunger, the hypothalamus in the midbrain is intimately involved in the neural control of our internal environment and works very much in coordination with the pituitary gland (the master gland of the endocrine system). The homeostatic mechanisms connected with the hypothalamus and pituitary gland influence our temperature regulation, our thirst, and our hunger, for example.

The **drive-reduction theory** of motivation, built on the concept of homeostasis, was most comprehensively stated by Clark Hull (1943). He asserted that changes in body systems have the potential for disrupting the homeostatic balance, thereby producing biological discomfort. This discomfort creates a state of drive that energizes or motivates the organism to action. The energized organism is then mobilized to respond in a certain way in an effort to reduce the drive state and re-establish the body-system equilibrium. The actual actions or responses of the organism are strongly reinforced (strengthened) by the tension reduction, or in Hull's terms, the **drive-reduction**, that occurs with the restoring of homeostasis.

For example, consider thirst as a drive. Our bodies have specialized receptors that are able to determine both intra- and extracellular fluid levels. When reductions in these levels exceed a certain point, homeostasis is disrupted and a biological discomfort is produced. This discomfort leads to a drive state (thirst) that energizes us to search for fluid to intake (drink). See Figure 6-3. The particular actions we take are strongly reinforced if they lead to a decrease in our thirst. We are motivated to restore homeostatic balance, and the act of restoring it is strongly reinforced by the drive-reduction.

FIGURE 6-3 The thirst drive

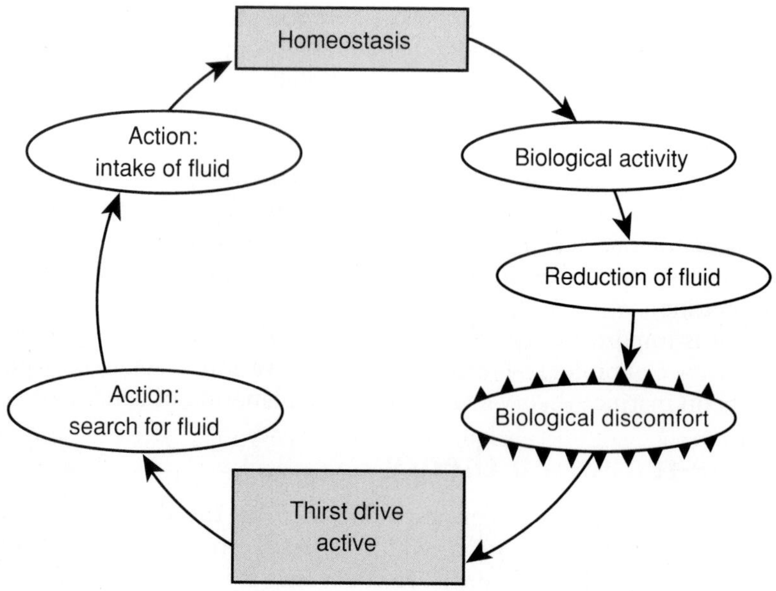

We can use this basic model of drive theory to understand both internally and externally produced motivations. In fact, this drive-reduction theory can be used to tie learning and motivational concepts together, since it shows how motivation can lead to operant learning. A newborn baby motivated by hunger has not yet learned to seek food, for example. The hunger motivates many behaviours such as crying, twitching, moving around, head turning, and toe wiggling. Whichever of these behaviours is most consistently followed by drive-reduction will be most reinforced. With many such experiences, the baby learns goal-directed, food-seeking behaviour. The learning of associations between instrumental (operant) behaviour and consequences is reinforced by the drive-reducing qualities of the reinforcer.

This drive theory also accounts for **acquired drives**, which are secondary or learned sources of motivation acquired through classical or instrumental conditioning. Hull believed that most of human behaviour was motivated by the acquired drives, drives such as the need for achievement or the need for praise. However, if we are to take this drive-reduction motivational theory seriously, we have to believe that all human behaviour has as its real motive the decreasing of arousal or tension. Unfortunately for this theory, but most likely fortunately for us, quite a bit of our everyday life is involved with increasing or seeking out stimulation—in other words, with increasing our arousal level.

We explore, we manipulate, and, at times, we seek out high levels of stimulation and sensation. Butler and Harlow (1954) have shown this to be the case with monkeys who learn to open windows and to perform other tasks when the only reinforcement is their ability to look out at a more interesting visual stimulus (see Figure 6-4). It is difficult to see how tension-reduction or drive-reduction would work here. Similarly, we do a lot of things to give ourselves a thrill or out of intellectual curiosity or out of boredom. Here we do seek to increase stimulation. Indeed, a lot of our leisure time goes into this pursuit. Some theorists have suggested that we all have a certain optimal level of arousal that we seek to maintain which cannot easily be accounted for by drive-reduction theory (Butler & Rice, 1963). An **optimal level of arousal** is the level of stimulation the organism seeks to maintain, sometimes by decreasing stimulation and sometimes by increasing it.

In some experiments, subjects were put into environments in which nearly all external stimulation was eliminated. These experiments with sensory deprivation clearly demonstrate the adverse effects of too little stimulation (Suedfeld, 1980). In extreme situations, sensory deprivation can even lead to marked psychological disturbance, including hallucinations. Our need for a certain level of stimulation seems so strong that when we are denied or restricted from stimulation for long durations, such as in sensory isolation chambers, we produce our own stimulation. We all differ in our tolerance for amount, variety, and complexity of stimulation. This helps to account for the great differences in our leisure activities. Some of us like having the wits scared out of us and enjoy feeling the rush of adrenaline as we watch scary movies or ride on mind-bending and bone-rattling rollercoasters. A few of us might even think that sky-diving is fun and exciting despite the fact that it is something that sends shudders through many people.

FIGURE 6-4 Curiosity

Butler and Harlow (1954) demonstrated that monkeys will explore and manipulate puzzles out of curiosity even when there is no apparent drive reduction.

SOURCE: Butler and Harlow (1954).

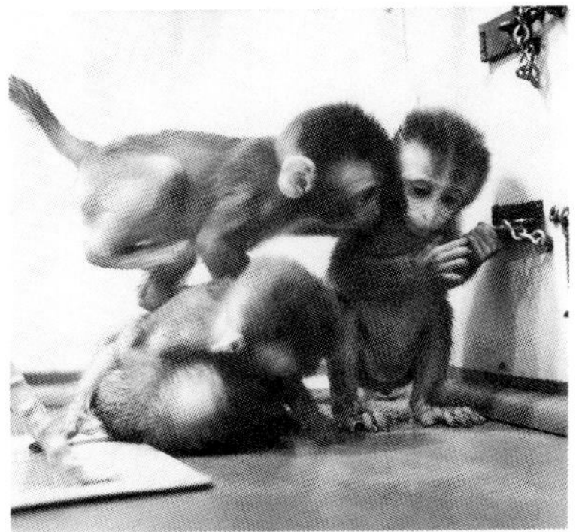

Unfortunately, over time a particular thrill becomes less intense, and we need to find more exciting stimuli to get the same "jolt" as we did previously. This leads to the phenomenon of **sensation seeking**, which is the intentional increase in stimulation, often to levels that are ordinarily uncomfortable. Some research (Zuckerman, 1979) has found that people who score high on measures of sensation seeking more frequently choose risky leisure activities. An unfortunate consequence of this is that sensation seeking may be implicated in the high-speed accidents that kill and otherwise permanently disable people of younger ages.

Drive-reduction theory also has some difficulty dealing with the fact that in the absence of an internal drive, behaviour may be motivated by external stimuli. Drive theory deals mostly with internal drives that seem to "push" from the inside and lead to behavioural expression. It is also possible that our environment "pulls" for certain behaviours. These pulls are usually called **incentives**, which are thought to be external stimuli that have the capacity to energize behaviour even though they don't lead to drive reduction. A classic example is that the sweetener saccharin, which has no nutritional value and does not reduce the hunger drive, is very effective in motivating behaviour. It has been demonstrated that many species will work to attain it (Sheffield, 1966).

There are sophisticated learning-based theories regarding motivation today that are based on internal pushes and external pulls. Many of them show an increased appreciation of the importance of cognitive processes and observational learning in determining actions. In Chapter 5, for example, we saw how the basic processes of learning can be extended by social learning and cognitive processes. We can speculate that motivations and differences among motivations may be due to the differential reinforcement of certain behaviours. We can be influenced by expectations (such as anticipated pay-offs), and we do learn much from watching others. These facts greatly extend the realm of the learning-based psychological study of motivation.

Humanistic theory

A quite different view of motivation has been outlined by Abraham Maslow (1970). Some consider his humanistic view of motivation to be an improvement over the mechanistic and deterministic approach of instinct and drive theories. **Humanistic theory** is based on humans' innate drive toward self-actualization. Maslow proposed that humans have an inborn **hierarchy of needs** (see Figure 6-5) in which basic physiological needs must be met before higher, psychological needs can act as motivators. From lowest to highest the needs are physiological needs, safety needs, social needs, status needs, and self-actualizing needs. The most basic needs are lowest in this hierarchy and are related to restoring physical equilibrium and ensuring physical survival. If we are preoccupied with needs at this level, we usually are not too concerned about self-esteem or aesthetic needs; but these come to the forefront when lower needs have been met. Maslow has not dismissed biological drives. He has simply relegated them to the lowest level in his hierarchy. Maslow's theory is an optimistic and positive view of human nature, because the focus is on human growth and achieving maximal potential. Maslow coined the term **self-actualization** to refer to a striving toward psychological growth and enhancement. According to Maslow, this is the human motive that ranks highest in the hierarchy of needs. Maslow asserted that we each have an innate need to self-actualize; but unfortunately, few of us reach this stage in the hierarchy because we have difficulties satisfying safety needs, relationship needs, or needs related to self-esteem. A self-actualized person is someone who is able to deal fully and completely with the world in non-possessive, non-demanding, and creative ways. Whom do you know in your own circle of acquaintances who is truly self-actualized?

FIGURE 6-5 Maslow's hierarchy of needs
SOURCE: Reprinted with permission from Allyn and Bacon, 1987

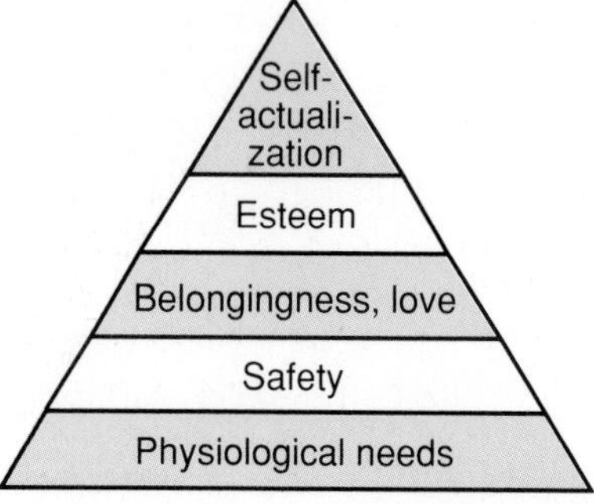

Most of us become entangled in dealing with needs having to do with our self-esteem, our safety, and our relationships with others. The humanistic theorists believe that it is the environment that somehow distorts the self-actualizing process and blocks the striving for growth. Although this theory is a flattering one in terms of its conception of human nature, there has been a lack of research demonstrating that a hierarchy indeed exists or that our needs and motivations actually follow a hierarchical course.

Let's now turn from our overview of different theories of motivation to a discussion of what we know about motivations that are part of our everyday lives. First, we will deal with hunger, a primary drive. Next, we will discuss sex, a drive that can be thought of as a primary drive or as a secondary drive. Lastly, we will consider the need for achievement, a socially based motivation.

HUNGER AND OVEREATING

All of us know what hunger is. At this moment, some of you may even be experiencing the sensations that are going to lead you to say, "I've done enough studying now. I'm hungry, so I'll go and get dinner." What goes on at a physiological level to bring about our food searching and then eating? What are the mechanisms that stop our eating when we've met our nutritional requirements or are full of food? These are important questions that psychologists have examined because eating and concerns about hunger are such major preoccupations in Western society today. The consequences of being overweight are staggering in terms of psychological costs as well as in terms of the greatly increased risk to our physical health. If obesity is defined as being approximately 15% to 20% above ideal body weight for a particular height, it is estimated that one-third of all North Americans are significantly overweight.

Do you worry about your weight? If you do, you share this concern with many others. Discussions regarding weight, diets, and how weight problems can be camouflaged by carefully chosen clothes are major topics of interest amongst friends. These topics are discussed in stories, articles, and ads in many major popular magazines.

Physiological mechanisms

The body requires a certain basic amount of nutrients to fuel its many systems. There is a complex homeostatic mechanism that operates to maintain the organism, with many different body systems playing important roles. Some components of this system are designed to detect the need for food, others to determine the action that then needs to be taken, still others that allow for food searching and eating, and finally, some that terminate the eating because adequate food has been taken in.

The role of the stomach and of hunger pangs was the focus of early research in this area. A physiological psychologist, Walter Cannon, investigated the correlation between reports of hunger and stomach contractions using an ingenious procedure (Cannon and Washburn, 1912). A trained subject swallowed a long rubber tube which had a balloon on the end of it. When this reached the stomach, the balloon was inflated so that stomach contractions would exert pressure onto the balloon. This pressure could then be recorded by equipment attached to the end of the tubing. Although this procedure was not very comfortable for the subject, it clearly did show that there was a strong relationship between the person's subjective experience of hunger (i.e., hunger pangs) and stomach contractions.

We have a correlation here, but not evidence that will allow us to say that stomach contractions *cause* hunger. (Remember our discussion of correlations in Chapter 1.) Both stomach contractions and hunger may occur together, but it would be incorrect to say that one is the cause of the other. In fact, while the stomach does play some role in regulating food intake, there are many other mechanisms involved in our experience of hunger. For example, clinical observations have shown that people who have had their entire stomachs removed because of cancer or other medical conditions nevertheless still experience hunger. So, if hunger can be felt acutely even in the absence of a stomach, there must be more to our hunger than stomach contractions alone. This finding led researchers to look for additional mechanisms that could account for the control of eating. Attention turned to the role of various brain structures—particularly the role of the hypothalamus, a part of the brain that is intimately involved in our body's homeostatic regulation.

Hypothalamic regulation

The brain structures involved in motivation and emotion are so important that we will briefly review some material from Chapter 2. The **hypothalamus** is a small but vital area deep in the centre of the brain. Its major role is the regulation of the body's homeostasis. It plays a role in eating, drinking, and temperature regulation. It also works in concert with the pituitary gland to affect hormonal activity and is involved in emotion. The hypothalamus is rich in connections with other parts of the brain — specifically the limbic system, the reticular activating system, and the frontal lobes. The **limbic system** is a system of neural structures that is involved in motivation (related to hunger and sex) and in emotion (related to fear and aggression). The **reticular activating system** (**RAS**) is a neural structure in the brain stem that helps control arousal, attention, and sleep. Each of the **frontal lobes** is located in a cerebral hemisphere and is concerned with voluntary movements.

There is no single on-off switch for hunger or any other function. Instead there is a complex set of connections and communication channels (bands of axons) that normally work in harmony.

Disruption at any level in this neural network may result in eating disorders. This can be seen in some clinical settings where an eating disorder may be a function of some psychological conflict. There may not be any one part of this neural network that is malfunctioning. Rather, through parts of the brain involved in planning, goal-setting, judgment, and behavioural control or inhibition, there may be widespread effects that result in disturbed eating behaviours. At the other end of the spectrum, in very rare situations, there may be malfunctioning of a specific brain area that can lead to either dramatic overeating or starvation.

Research conducted with animals, using either electrical brain stimulation or destruction of certain brain parts, has shown that two different areas in the hypothalamus play an important role in the motivation cycle of the hunger drive and the regulation of food intake. See Figure 6-6. The outside part of the hypothalamus, called the **lateral hypothalamus** (**LH**), is involved in initiating eating. When this area is electrically stimulated, animals begin to eat even if they are already full. Destruction of the lateral hypothalamus has the opposite effect of leading to the suppression of eating behaviour, a symptom called **aphagia**. The lower-middle part of the hypothalamus, called the **ventromedial hypothalamus (VMH)**, has been shown to play a leading role in the cessation of eating. Hence it is thought to be a **satiety centre**. Stimulation of this part of the brain leads to

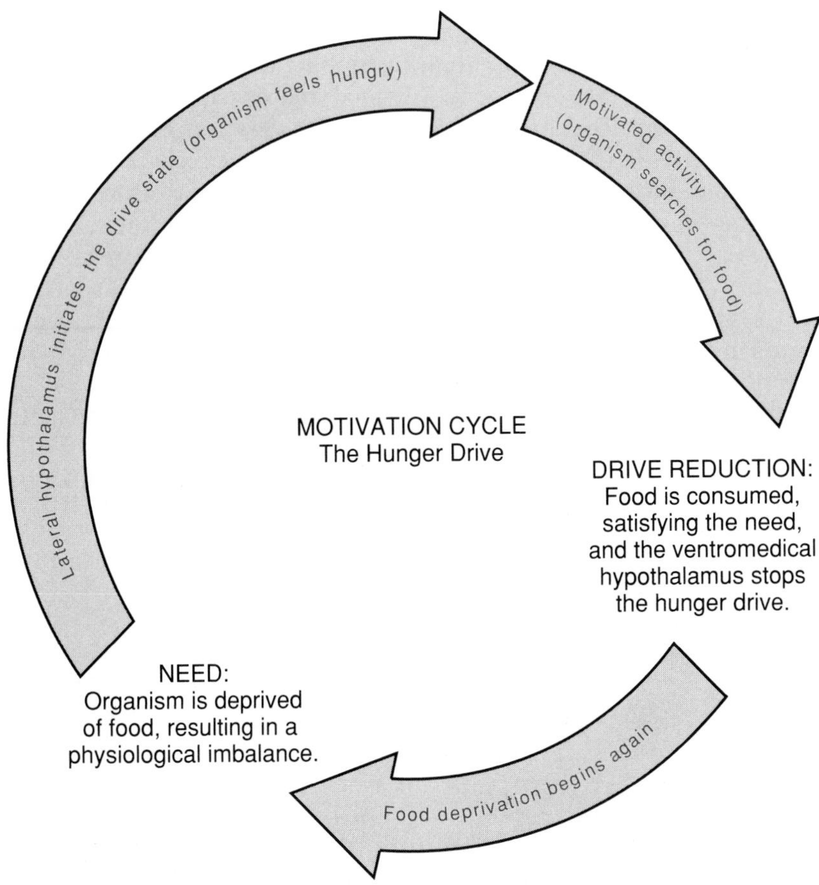

FIGURE 6-6 Motivation cycle: The hunger drive
Hunger is used here to illustrate how the motivation cycle proceeds.

SOURCE: Adapted with permission from Allyn and Bacon, 1987.

the inhibition or cessation of eating, whereas destruction of this area leads to quite dramatic overeating. This symptom of overeating is called **hyperphagia**. It occurs because the mechanism to turn feeding off is no longer present. A rat which had received a lesion in the ventromedial hypothalamus is shown in Figure 6-7. Recent evidence suggests that the control of eating behaviour is more complicated than we thought. The control also seems to involve some brain structures near the hypothalamus (Petri, 1986). Nevertheless, the hypothalamus is the major organ involved.

If you are overweight or underweight, it doesn't mean that you have lesions in your hypothalamus. These findings simply show that the hypothalamus is an important component in a large and complex system governing eating behaviour. Disruptions of this one part do affect eating behaviour. Let's look in more detail at the operation of the hypothalamus in the regulation of food intake.

Some cells in the hypothalamus are sensitive to certain molecules that travel in our bloodstream. These specific molecules vary with our need for nutrition. Some of the cells are particularly sensitive to the level of glucose in the bloodstream and the rate that it is used by our bodies. These cells, known as **glucostats**, are receptors in both the LH and VMH that respond differently to the level of sugar (glucose) in the blood travelling throughout the body. If you haven't

FIGURE 6-7 Obesity and damage to the ventromedial hypothalamus
Lesions in the ventromedial hypothalamus (VMH) caused this rat to eat without restraint until it reached a new plateau weight.
SOURCE: Photo courtesy of Neal E. Miller, Rockefeller University.

eaten for some time, your blood sugar falls. This is detected by glucostats in your LH, causing them to increase their activity. This activation of the LH leads to your mobilization to replenish your nutritional reserves — to seek out food and to eat. This obviously involves many other brain systems and is a very complex process.

But why and how do we stop eating? As our blood sugar rises, glucostats in the VMH become stimulated, leading to the decrease and then cessation of eating. It does take some time for the food you have eaten to be absorbed by your stomach. Sensations of fullness from your stomach also stimulate the VMH to inhibit eating (Deutsch, Young, and Kalogeris, 1978). The operation of the glucostats in the LH and the VMH provide a means for the body to regulate its nutritional status moment by moment.

One of the most important functions of this regulation is to provide to the brain a constant supply of energy in the form of glucose. Figure 6-8 illustrates how eating behaviour supplies this glucose. It comes directly from the digestive system. At the same time,

FIGURE 6-8 Metabolic pathways used when the digestive system contains food and when it is empty

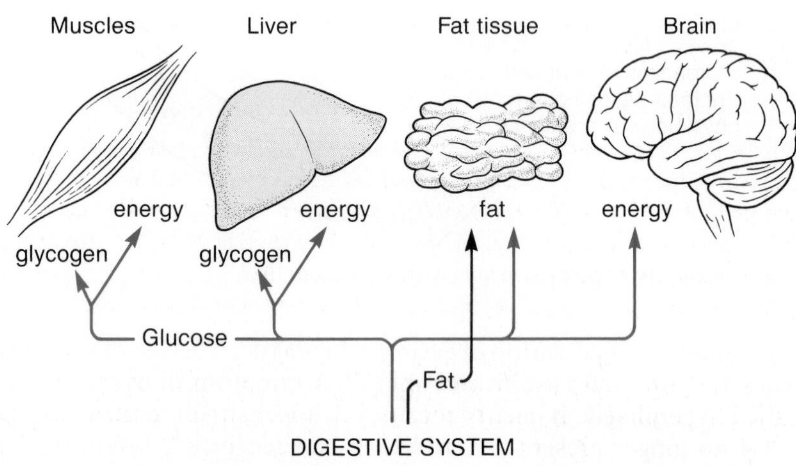

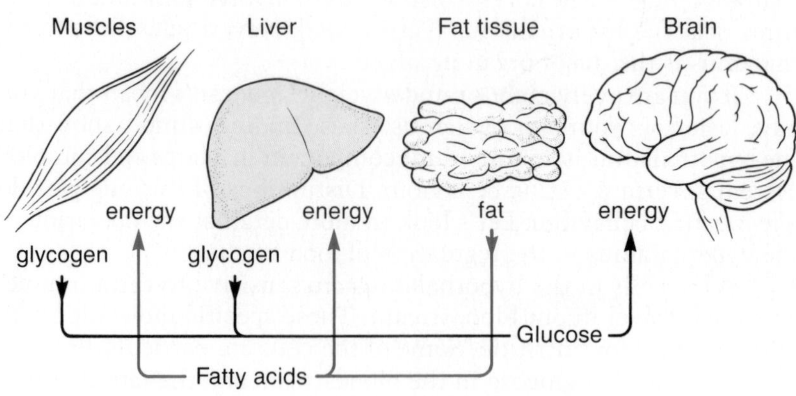

SOURCE: Adapted with permission from Allyn and Bacon, 1989.

the digestive system is providing glucose to the muscles and liver. Some of this glucose is used immediately for energy and some is stored as glycogen. Both glucose and fat are also stored in the fat tissue. When the digestive system is empty, the body draws on its stored energy to maintain functioning. The liver and muscles use fatty acids from the fat tissue for energy and they release their stored glycogen to make glucose for the brain.

There is another way the hypothalamus is involved in food regulation. For better or for worse, our bodies seem to be able to maintain a relatively constant weight over the course of our adult years. Some of us are just plain thin, and others of us seem to be burdened with carrying too much weight around. There are mechanisms in the LH and VMH that monitor the amount of fat stored in our bodies. These mechanisms work to regulate this amount by activating the feeding centre or satiety centre.

One current theory of weight control known as the set-point hypothesis suggests that from an early age we have a stable number of fat cells in our bodies throughout our life (Nisbett, 1972). The **set-point hypothesis** says that the LH and the VMH monitor the amount of fat in fat cells to maintain a specific level. These hypothalamic regions stimulate eating if the fat level is too low and suppress eating if the level is too high. What may change over time is the proportion of fat within these cells, although the LH and VMH work to try to maintain the proportion at a constant level. Although the theory is controversial, some research does show that people who are obese have approximately three times as many fat cells as people of normal weight (Hirsch and Knittle, 1970). The number of fat cells seems to be determined by both heredity and early experiences with nutrition and eating. By the age of approximately two years, the number of fat cells in our body becomes fixed and is stable over the course of our

The number of fat cells in the human body seems to be determined by heredity and early experiences with nutrition and eating.
SOURCE: Dick Hemingway.

lifetime. Hypothalamic mechanisms then monitor the proportion of fat in these cells. When the proportion of fat drops below some critical level, the LH is activated which leads to the initiation of eating. When the proportion of fat in the fat cells rises above the critical level, the VMH is activated which leads to the cessation of eating.

The set-point theory has been used to explain why rats with lesions in their VMH do not continue eating forever, but somehow stabilize their weight at a set-point two or three times their normal body weight. On the other hand, a rat with destruction of the LH will choose not to eat. If it is kept alive by force-feeding, it will eventually begin to eat and it will stabilize its body weight at a much lower weight than normal. For both the LH and VMH rats, destruction of parts of their hypothalamus resulted in the establishment of a new set-point (Mitchel and Keesey, 1974; Hoebel and Teitelbaum, 1966). Interestingly, if both the LH and VMH are lesioned, the animals do not change weight. This would indicate a balance between the effects of disruption to the hypothalamic eating and cessation centres. One of the important implications of set-point theory for human weight-control is that if a person is programmed very early in life to have a fairly large number of fat cells, then that person will have a fairly large number of fat cells throughout his or her life span. Nothing short of major surgery can change this number. All that can change is the proportion of fat within the fat cells. The person who diets and ends up with a lower proportion of fat in fat cells may feel chronically hungry because the proportion of fat is below the critical set-point. This may be one reason why it is difficult for people to keep weight off unless a tremendous amount of effort is expended on changes in lifestyle and modifications in eating behaviour.

There are behavioural similarities between rats who have VMH destruction leading to overeating and humans who have significant weight problems. The hyperphagic animals have a much lower sensitivity to the internal cues for eating and weight control, such as sensations from distention of the stomach and the monitoring of blood sugar. In short, the hyperphagic rat eats despite the absence of internal hunger signals and despite the body not needing the food. These animals, however, become exquisitely sensitive to external food cues and will eat vast amounts of food per meal if the food looks good, tastes good, and is accessible with a minimal amount of work. In comparison with rats of normal weight, the hyperphagic rats are typically less active, faster eaters, and much less willing to work hard for their food (Schachter, 1971; Teitelbaum, 1955).

There is much we can learn about human obesity from the behaviour of animals with artificial and imposed destruction of their ventromedial hypothalamus. Again, we must stress strongly, however, that having a problem with weight does not by any means indicate problems with hypothalamic eating control centres. Research with human subjects does suggest that obese people are very susceptible to external eating cues, such as the palatability of food, taste of food, sight of food, smell of food, the presence of others eating, the time of day, and stressful situations. Research does indicate that a possible difference between normal-weight and overweight individuals is that whereas the normal-weight person is responsive and tuned to internal cues related to hunger, the overweight individual is more sensitized to external cues, independent of internal body state. For example, Schachter, Goldman, and Gordon (1968) devised an experiment in which normal-weight individuals and overweight individuals were first fed a normal meal. When they were then given free access to additional food, the normal-weight subjects ate substantially less additional food than the overweight subjects. The researchers proposed that normal-weight subjects inhibited their later eating because of their evaluation of their internal body state, whereas the overweight subjects were vulnerable to the effect of easy access to attractive food (in this case ice cream) and thus overlooked the fact that their internal state indicated that they were satiated. If just after eating a large meal you have ever been tempted by a double chocolate cake with rich, thick icing, you know well the effects of external cues in determining your eating. This is probably why going to buffet dinners is unwise for those who are dieting. The mere presence of so much good-looking food in one place and the freedom to have unlimited helpings may be too much for those of us who are sensitive to external food cues.

A buffet dinner may be too great a temptation for those who are on diets.
SOURCE: Metropolitan Toronto Convention & Visitors Association.

This brings up an additional issue. Those of us who have dieted know how difficult it is to stay on a diet and control our eating. In fact, control is a very important factor in all diets. Research by Hermann and Polivy (1980) shows that dieters are always attempting to curb their appetite and hence their food intake; but when they seem to lose control by giving in to the external food cues or social pressures to eat, their motivation to control intake decreases substantially and they begin to overeat. These people are referred to as **restrained eaters** because they seem to need constant restraint to limit their eating, and once that restraint is broken they lose control of their eating behaviour. Dieters are familiar with the experience of going over the calorie limit they set for themselves and then giving up and bingeing, often thinking, "I'll start over tomorrow. Today's shot anyway." By contrast, the **unrestrained eaters** simply eat when they are truly hungry. They seem to be less vulnerable to the influence of external cues.

The story for those who are overweight is not as gloomy and pessimistic as it might seem now. We will later touch on some of the ways that can be used to overcome problems with eating. (See the Special Topic, "Obesity and Weight Control" near the end of this chapter.)

Our society is extremely weight conscious.
SOURCE: Courtesy Weight Watchers International, Inc.

Psychological and social pressures

Internal psychological states do have some effect on eating behaviours. Research indicates that some people are particularly vulnerable to overeating when they become anxious, depressed, and stressed, whereas others seem to eat less in these situations. One of the symptoms of severe depression is a disturbance in eating. This disturbance can take the form of substantial weight gain or weight loss. Many other things also affect our eating behaviour. Consider how learning principles apply to eating behaviours. It may not be too much of a

SOURCE: *Cathy* by Cathy Guisewite.

jump to see that through higher-order conditioning, classical conditioning, and stimulus control in operant conditioning, many nonfood stimuli can become associated with food and eating and can become reliable predictors of the presence of food. Most of us are hungry at certain times in the day. For example, we all have had the experience of suddenly becoming hungry when dinner time is approaching. Moreover, the aroma of food is a conditioned stimulus that can be used to predict that food is on its way. Thus, we have all experienced the sensations of increased hunger when we step into a kitchen and actually smell the food. Aroma can also function as a positive discriminative stimulus for eating behaviour. In someone who is vulnerable to external cues, as is the case with overweight individuals, it is quite possible that much in the environment has become a food-related cue, leading to pervasive feelings of hunger.

Having discussed physiological and learning (internal psychological) factors, let us now consider the effects of societal and cultural influences on our eating behaviours. Our society is extremely weight-conscious. We are preoccupied with what we eat, our waistlines, and fat. Many of us are not comfortable with the way our bodies look. This is unfortunate because for the most part we have little control over things that are set by our genetic inheritance and early influences on our development. Nevertheless, we are led to believe that there is an ideal shape for a man or woman by television programs, ads we see, movie stars who are our idols, and sport heroes we admire. A sad consequence of this preoccupation with an unrealistic ideal body image is seen in those suffering from eating disorders such as anorexia nervosa and bulimia. We will discuss these disorders in a Special Topic near the end of the chapter.

SEX

We are sexual creatures. By this we mean not just that we engage in or strongly desire sexual intercourse, but also that sexuality has strong effects on many aspects of our existence. Our morning showers, our shaving and grooming, our perfumes and deodorants, the clothes we wear, the flirting we do, the magazines we look at, the books we read, the movies we watch, and much of our desire and need for touching and stimulation—all these are part of our sexuality. Sexuality is normal and everywhere. However, for many people it is cloaked in anxiety, guilt, and conflicting feelings. This is unfortunate because sexual expression can be one of the most meaningful and satisfying expressions of love when it is embedded in a close, intense, and trusting relationship.

A unique drive

Despite the fact that the sex drive is a very important motivator of many behaviours, it differs quite dramatically from a drive such as hunger. Although hunger may be thought of as a homeostatic drive, sex should not be. Despite what you may think, sex is not necessary for *individual* survival, although it is needed for survival of the species. Sexual arousal is something that is actively sought out, in contrast to our actions relating to other primary drives. As well, sexual arousal can be initiated by almost any stimulus. The only unconditioned stimulus for sexual arousal is touch. But through a conditioning process, almost any stimulus imaginable can become a conditioned stimulus for arousal or a discriminative stimulus for sexual behaviour. Whiffs of cologne or perfume, certain musical recordings, candlelight meals, and many other things are often associated with romance and sexual arousal. Unfortunately, because almost anything can become a conditioned stimulus for sexual arousal, less appealing stimuli may also become a conditioned stimuli for sexual arousal. For example, if sexual arousal through masturbation is consistently associated with stimuli from pornography that displays violent, aggressive, or degrading sexual practices, then such displays may in themselves, through a conditioning process, come to elicit arousal at a later time.

From the beginning to the end of our life, we are all sexual creatures.
SOURCE: Dick Hemingway.

Let's examine sexuality in more detail. We will begin with an examination of sexual arousal, both in terms of what we can learn from lower animals and what we have discovered about humans.

Arousal

The primary determinant of sexual arousal and sexual behaviour differs greatly from species to species. Nevertheless, on a physiological level, there are some marked similarities among mammals. The hormonal activity of the pituitary gland and its interaction with the posterior portions of the hypothalamus are important in sexual behaviour. Again, we find that the hypothalamus and pituitary gland act in combination. With regard to sexuality, the pituitary gland controls the body's hormonal output and is responsible for the fact that all female mammals go through quite large cyclic variations in their hormonal state. In higher mammals (primates and humans), the cycle is called the menstrual cycle. In lower species, it is called the estrous cycle. The **menstrual cycle** is the cycle of hormonal fluctuations in human and other primate females that controls the sequence of fertility and menstrual flow. The **estrous cycle** is the cycle of hormonal fluctuations in non-primate female mammals that controls fertility and often affects patterns of sexual behaviour. Throughout the course of the female cycle, the level of the most important female sex hormone, **estrogen**, varies in the bloodstream. The cycle varies in length depending on the species. It is approximately 28 days long in the human female. In lower species, the level of estrogen determines readiness for sexual activity in the female. At certain times in the cycle the female is in heat, or more technically *in estrous*. However, the link between level of hormones and sexual receptiveness weakens with increases in the evolutionary complexity of the organism. In humans, research has indicated no correlation between female sexual activity and place in the menstrual cycle. In other words, human female sexual activity can occur at any time. This finding suggests that the primary determinants of female human sexuality are learned and are influenced by cognitive, social, and cultural factors.

Through conditioning, almost any stimulus can initiate sexual arousal.
SOURCE: Dick Hemingway.

Infant monkeys raised in isolation have tremendous social deficits that interfere with their development of normal sexual behaviours.
SOURCE: Harlow Primate Laboratory.

The hormonal mechanisms in males are quite different. In all male mammals, the pituitary hormones called, as a group, **androgens**, are the most important sex hormones. They are at a sufficient level following sexual maturity to allow for sexual activity at any time. In lower species, hormones produce a set of inborn, instinctual behaviours that lead from the mating ritual to copulation. The effect of hormones and fixed-action patterns in determining sexual activity decreases with higher mammals as the role of experience, environment, and social factors becomes more important. The decrease is seen even at the level of monkeys, where research has shown that infant monkeys raised in isolation have tremendous social deficits that interfere with their development of normal sexual behaviour (Harlow, 1971). This research shows that although male monkeys raised in isolation are able to masturbate to ejaculation, they are not able to engage in the proper sequence of behaviours to allow for mounting a receptive female. Harlow argued that his research showed that the ability to establish social contact and social bonds is important in sexual arousal and sexual activity, even at the level of subhuman primates. It is no surprise that social contact and bonding play such a prominent role in human sexuality.

Human sexuality

Human sexuality entails a complex interplay of psychological, social, and cultural factors. The last 30 years have seen a tremendous change in values regarding sexuality. Permissiveness is much greater today than it was in the past. For instance, much of what we see on television today was totally unacceptable ten years ago. Whether this is good or bad can be debated at length.

A group of researchers led by Alfred Kinsey (Kinsey, Pomeroy, and Martin, 1948 and 1953) played a major role in demystifying and revealing many normal sexual practices. This group of researchers interviewed approximately 11 000 Americans to get a description of the kinds of sexual activity that people engaged in. The results were surprising at the time, but they were also reassuring to most people, who discovered that their own sexual behaviour was not as unusual as they had believed. Kinsey found, for example, that premarital sex was fairly common. In his study, approximately 66% of the men and about 50% of the women had engaged in premarital sex. Sexual dreams ending in orgasm were reported by 95% of the men and about 35% of the women. Ninety-five percent of the men and 65% of the women reported masturbating. Furthermore, masturbation was found to continue into marriage and apparently did not lead to marital discord or sexual problems. The Kinsey group shattered a lot of social taboos, particularly with regard to masturbation. They helped to legitimize this form of sexual expression as a normal and healthy aspect of sexuality.

Alfred Charles Kinsey (1894-1956).
SOURCE: Photograph by DELLENBACK.

Research by another group (Masters & Johnson, 1966 and 1970) was perhaps even more important because it focused on the actual physiological mechanics of the human sexual response. In controlled laboratory observations, Masters and Johnson measured the phases of sexual arousal during masturbation and intercourse. Their subjects for this experimentation were volunteers willing to participate in research that measured their physical responses at the various stages of the sexual response cycle from arousal to orgasm.

According to the studies by Masters and Johnson, there are four major stages for men and women in the **human sexual response cycle**. The first stage, the **excitement phase**, is characterized by rapid increases in heart rate and in blood flow to the genitals. In the male, the penis becomes erect. In the female, the clitoris swells and elevates somewhat, the vagina becomes moist with lubrication, and the nipples become erect. During the second stage of arousal, the **plateau phase**, there is a sustained, fairly high level of arousal, rather than the rapid increase of the excitement phase. There may be some softening of the male's erection and the woman's clitoris may retract somewhat. Muscular tension and swelling in the vagina gradually increase in preparation for orgasm. Heart rate and involuntary body movements also increase. If intercourse is interrupted during the plateau phase, there will be a long, slow return to the unaroused state. As the person enters the third phase, **orgasm**, there is a heightening of excitement until the person passes a "point of no return" when the orgasm is inevitable. The orgasm is a climax with a reflexive release of tension. The male ejaculates seminal fluid, with the penis rhythmically contracting as the semen is expelled. The female has a similar series of muscular contractions of the vagina, uterus, and abdominal musculature, releasing accumulated tension. The last stage in the human sexual response is known as **resolution**. In both the male and female, this is a relatively rapid physiological return to the pre-excitement state of heart rate, respiration, and muscle tension. The male also enters a **refractory period**, during which he is not able to have another erection. Some women may have one or more orgasms fairly rapidly before they enter resolution.

William Howell Masters and Virginia Johnson
SOURCE: UPI/Bettmann Newsphotos.

Figure 6-9 shows Masters and Johnson's graphs of female and male sexual response cycles. They claim there is more variety among females' sexual experiences than among males'. They distinguish three possible patterns for females. Pattern A consists of arousal,

FIGURE 6-9 Masters and Johnson's graphs of female and male sexual response cycles

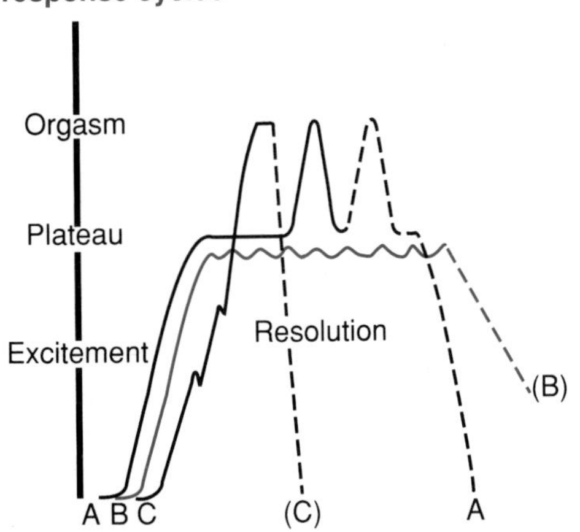

Typical female sexual response cycle.

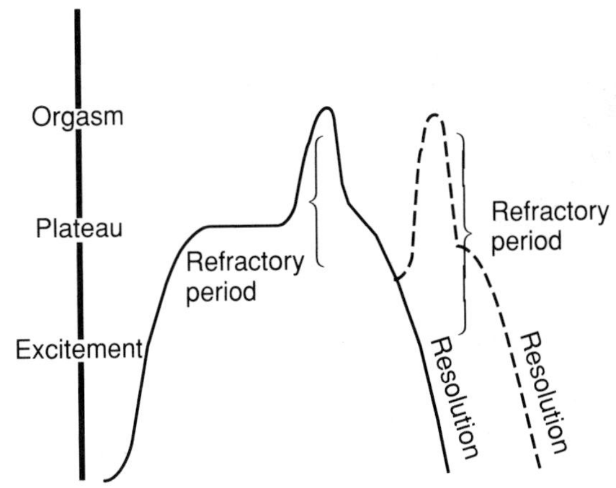

Typical male sexual response cycle

SOURCE: Reprinted with permission from Masters and Johnson (1966).

plateau, intense orgasm, and rapid resolution. Although it resembles the typical male pattern, this female pattern might then continue with further orgasms before going through resolution. Pattern B represents a series of less intense orgasms that can be mistaken for lack of orgasm. Pattern C shows quick arousal, intense orgasm and rapid resolution. In the male pattern, a refractory period nearly always occurs between orgasms.

The research of Masters and Johnson helped to dispel more myths about human sexuality. For instance, they showed that penis size is not an important factor in determining a woman's satisfaction because the vagina is able to adjust to accommodate various penis sizes. Furthermore, simultaneous orgasm was found to be an artificial performance standard for sexual intercourse. In fact, making sexual relations into a *performance* is one of the quickest ways to spoil them. Masters and Johnson found many similarities between men's and women's experience of sex. Their research indicated that the response cycle was the same for intercourse, masturbation, and homosexual contact.

One helpful conclusion they drew was that, on average, women take longer than men to become sexually aroused. It is important to say "on average" here, because there is enormous variability in the sexual responses of different individuals. Therefore we should say that what is "normal" is almost always what feels good for the particular individual. But in the context of a sexual relationship, knowing about normal differences between men and women can provide the basis for developing a caring, giving, and mutually satisfying sexual relationship. Masters and Johnson would advise us that the best bet is to ask our partner what he or she likes. They would say that we can make use of their general findings but that it is much more important to communicate with our partner.

Unfortunately, many people do suffer from sexual problems. Masters and Johnson estimated that *half* the marriages in North America are sexually dysfunctional. Although physical problems (such as hormonal disruptions, diabetes, and certain medications) can cause sexual dysfunctions, most are caused by psychological factors. Personal problems, anxieties, fatigue, drug and alcohol use, and stress may adversely affect sexual enjoyment and fulfilment. Masters and Johnson and others have written about a wide variety of sexual problems and their treatment.

We will discuss two common problems for men. The first, **erectile dysfunction**, is a failure to achieve or maintain an erection. It is sometimes caused by fear and sometimes by physical problems. The second, **premature ejaculation**, occurs when male orgasm comes earlier than desired, often prior to entering the female. The female counterpart of erectile dysfunction is characterized by a lack of excitement and of the vaginal lubrication that usually accompany sexual stimulation. This problem is called **inhibited sexual excitement**. It is very revealing to look at the older terms for some of these problems because they reflect some of society's unhealthy attitudes about sex. "Inhibited sexual excitement" used to be called "frigidity." The older term was used to condemn the woman for her failure to be warm. "Erectile dysfunction" was called "impotence"—and still is by most nonprofessionals. The term "impotence" literally means "lacking power." Its use in this context implies that sex for the male should be an act of power and by extension that sex for the female should be an act of submission. The newer terms are more appropriate. They are descriptive rather than judgmental of the person.

Women may also suffer from what has been termed **orgasmic dysfunction** or **inhibited female orgasm**. Here, although there may be normal sexual excitement, sexual response does not reach orgasm but ends in an earlier phase. When medical causes are ruled out for these problems, sexual therapy has been found to be effective. The focus is on decreasing the anxiety and stress related to sexual activity, teaching individuals how to enjoy and get pleasure from physical stimulation, helping individuals not to worry about their own adequacy of performance, and increasing the communication between sexual partners (Kaplan, 1974). Four of the basic principles underlying therapy for sexual problems are as follows. First, sexual arousal and activity are normal and can be participated in fully without guilt and anxiety. Second, open and clear communication between partners is important. Third, the social stereotypes of sex roles may interfere with the full expression of one's sexuality. Fourth, sex is most rewarding as mutual pleasure rather than as a goal-oriented performance.

Zilbergeld (1978) argues that for all the good they did dispelling old myths, Masters and Johnson have contributed to establishing some new ones. He says that human sexual experience is vastly more varied than the four-stage cycle of response suggests. Moreover, Zilbergeld points out that the graphs of the cycles seem to set up a new but unrealistic standard to live up to, especially for men. As an alternative, he humourously offers the graphs of male sexual response cycles shown in Figure 6-10. Although these graphs are not based on actual scientific data, Zilbergeld presents them to emphasize his view that human sexual experience is extremely varied. Individuals should not worry about fitting some rigid model.

FIGURE 6-10 Male sexual response cycles according to Zilbergeld
Zilbergeld is making the point that tremendous variety in sexual experiences is entirely normal.
SOURCE: Zibergeld (1978), p. 122.

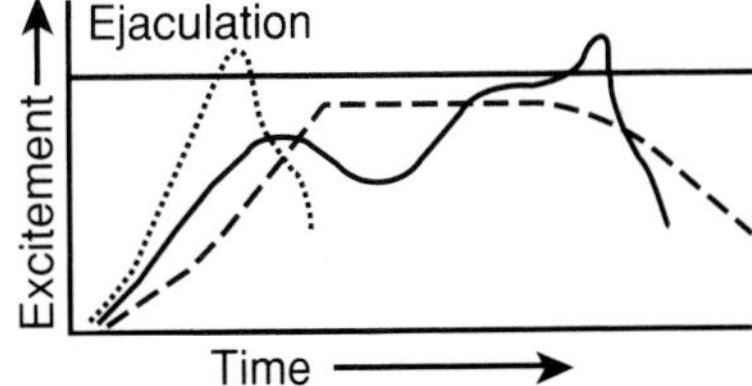

Other male sexual response cycles

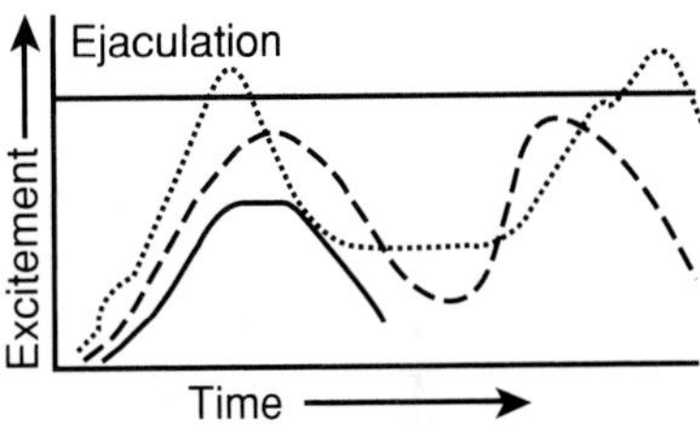

More male sexual response cycles

Sexuality and society

Human sexuality has its physiological basis in the interaction between hormones and brain functioning. Nevertheless, it is strongly influenced by our learning experiences—by the values and standards we have acquired. It has been said that in humans the most important sex organ is the brain. Sexual attitudes and standards are very much culturally determined. There are great differences between the attitudes white middle-class North Americans hold toward human sexuality and the views of sexuality that are held in other cultures. For example, some tribes in Africa vary dramatically in what they feel is appropriate in prepubertal sex. While in certain tribes prepubertal sexuality is encouraged, in others such behaviour may be punished by death.

We do not need to go so far afield to demonstrate variability in sexual standards. A review of our recent past indicates substantially more tolerant and permissive attitudes toward sex and sexually related themes today than were present 30 years ago. As we will see in Chapter 18, our society is a powerful determinant of certain roles and behaviours that limit what men and women are able to be. Stereotypes related to sex even determine how we play the dating game and go through the courting and mating ritual. According to the traditional stereotypes, the male is the person who asks for the dates, acts as the aggressor, and pursues the female, who plays a more passive and submissive role. These roles seem to be slowly changing in our present society, although the older stereotypes still exert a strong influence. Throughout the later parts of this book, we will see how powerfully social influences determine our values. They also very often define and limit our options.

NEED FOR ACHIEVEMENT

We will use the need for achievement as an example of a socially acquired motivation. It illustrates how complex secondary motives can be. What makes us strive for achievement, want to be a part of certain groups, crave power, enjoy the feeling of satisfaction upon completing a major project, or strive to compete? A discussion of these questions is a discussion of our social motivations. They are based on secondary drives that are learned through conditioning and socialization processes (Winterbottom, 1958). They are very much culturally determined. The need for achievement—the drive to produce and succeed—is a major motivation for many people in our fast-paced, 20th-century, North American society. But it is almost totally unheard of in African villages that revolve around traditional native values and standards. Not everyone values achievement as a motive or as a goal. However, it is something that our society places a premium on. We work and sometimes we work very hard, not necessarily for the monetary pay-off but sometimes just for our own feeling of competence, self-esteem, accomplishment, and achievement.

What makes an Olympic athlete strive to excel?
SOURCE: Canadian synchronized swimmer Carolyn Waldo displays gold medal won at the Oympics in Seoul in 1988. Canapress Photo Service (F. Chartrand).

One of the major researchers in this field is David McClelland (1971; McClelland, Atkinson, Clark, and Lowell, 1953). He has defined **need for achievement** as an emotional commitment to meeting personal standards of achievement. He views this need as a drive different from the need for power, which has to do with controlling others. One of the ways that researchers measure the need for achievement is to show subjects ambiguous pictures and ask them to make up a story about each one. The story should indicate what the subject thinks is happening in the picture, what happened before, and what is likely to happen later (Figure 6-11). The rationale for this method is that the stories reveal a particular person's need for achievement, values, and motivations.

For example, consider a picture showing a boy sitting at a table with homework in front of him. A person with a high need for achievement might well see a boy dreaming of medical school, a successful medical and research career, and saving lives. By contrast, someone with a low need for achievement might look at the same picture and come up with a story of a boy who is forced to do homework, hates school, and wishes he could go out and play with his friends. The difference between the invented stories about the same picture is thought to reflect real differences in the need for achievement between the two storytellers.

McClelland (1965) found that the level of the need for achievement in students was related to their later careers. Those students who had scored higher in need for achievement earlier in life had careers with more risk and responsibility than students who had tested lower in their need for achievement. High need for achievement has been found to relate to a need to take risks and to expose oneself to challenge. Presumably the real pay-off for such a person is a sense of satisfaction upon completing a particular task (McClelland, 1971). High-achieving individuals usually attribute success to their own abilities and as a result are very motivated to do well. By contrast, individuals with a low need for achievement seem to prefer a task of low risk or one that is impossible to complete. One reason is that such individuals have a strong fear of failure. If they choose a very simple task, they are confident they will succeed. If they choose an impossible task, they can attribute their failure to the nature of the task, not to a lack of their ability. This was illustrated in an experiment in which subjects chose how far to stand from the target in a ringtoss game (Atkinson & Litwin, 1960). Subjects with high achievement motivation chose an intermediate distance that made the game challenging but not impossible. Those with low achievement motivation tended to choose a close distance (so success was certain) or a very far distance (so success was impossible and therefore excusable).

FIGURE 6-11 A picture similar to those used by McClelland in his need for achievement test
McClelland showed his subjects ambiguous pictures like this and asked them to make up a story about each one. He then tried to interpret the story as a reflection of the subject's attitudes about achievement.
SOURCE: Michael Gibson.

The need for achievement is thought to develop throughout childhood, and the most powerful influence on it seems to come from the parents. Research has revealed that parents of children who score high in need for achievement differ substantially in their behaviour from parents of children who score low. Parents of boys with high need for achievement expected the boys to do more at younger ages, be more independent, be more resourceful, and be more active (Winterbottom, 1958). Parental encouragement, rewards for successes and for persistence, and high but realistic expectations were found to lead to a higher need for achievement in the children (Rosen and D'Andrade, 1959). This research was conducted by observing how parents reacted to their children completing a frustrating and difficult block-building task. The parents were to watch and encourage their children. The results showed that high-achieving children had parents who were supportive, reinforcing, and encouraging. They allowed their children to be independent problem solvers. In short, the parents who valued and communicated to their children trust and faith in the child's own resourcefulness provided the psychological context for the development of a high need for achievement. These parents also acted as models of achievement behaviour, set high standards, and rewarded achievement (Huston-Stein & Higgens-Trenk, 1978).

It is worth noting that achievement motivation is not one single drive that applies consistently to all aspects of an individual's life (Mischel, 1986). A person might be highly motivated musically or athletically but not academically.

It is also worth noting that most of the early research on achievement as a learned motive was done with male subjects. This reflected a general bias that was active in psychological research. Our purpose in this chapter has simply been to use achievement motivation as an example of a secondary motive. In Chapter 18, Gender Roles and the Effective Person, we will look at more recent work on interesting similarities and differences between males and females in achievement motivation.

EMOTION: GENERAL CONSIDERATIONS

Emotion versus motivation

One of the most important sources of motivation is our emotions. Our emotions are feelings that include neurological arousal, hormonal changes, and cognitions about the meaning of those changes. These subjective reactions often motivate behaviour. For example, many of our examples of learned motivation have included emotions like fear. Fear can motivate behaviour intensely. By the same token, we are motivated to act differently toward objects and persons we like and trust. Other types of motives are affected by emotion. We probably will react differently to hunger when we're sad than when we're angry or happy.

Emotion and motivation don't overlap completely, however. Motivation usually directs us toward a goal in the environment, whereas emotion can be entirely internal. In addition, we are sometimes motivated to act without experiencing emotion. Thus, emotion and motivation are closely linked but are not identical.

Defining emotion

One of the most important sources of human motivation is our emotions.
SOURCE: A Soviet militiaman breaks up a discussion that has escalated into a heated argument between a communist supporter and an anti-communist. Canapress Photo Service (Alexander Zemliachenko).

We all have a basic, intuitive understanding of what emotions and feelings are. At times, our emotions are mild preferences and "likings" for one thing over another. At other times they are so strong that we can feel them as powerful bodily reactions. Then, when we say we are hurt, we may mean this not just in a psychological sense, but also in a physical sense. In stressful situations, as in dealing with the death of someone close to us, the emotions may be overwhelming and so strong that we can *feel* the pain and anguish as strongly as we would a physical blow. If you have ever had a near miss when driving your car, you have experienced both the powerful psychological and physical aspects of emotion. Not only would you gasp and feel anxious that you had almost collided with another car, but you would feel a physical jolt, as your blood pressure jumps, your heart rate speeds up, and your muscles begin to shake. When people tell you that they feel happy, sad, depressed, surprised, disgusted, or any one of many different kinds of emotions, you have some understanding of what they are talking about.

Thus, we do have an intuitive understanding of emotion. We deal with it in our everyday lives, and we try to aid those who are suffering emotional distress. Nevertheless, psychologists and other researchers are still struggling to understand emotion and to develop ways to examine and explore it in the laboratory. As with motivation, emotion can be explored only as an intervening variable—a theoretical concept that we use to explain certain behaviours. We cannot see emotions; we see people behave in particular ways from which we infer the occurrence of emotions. Thus to study emotions in research, we have to operationalize them carefully. In other words, we have to devise ways to measure them that are quantifiable and verifiable. For example, we might design an experiment in which the strength of fear of snakes was defined as the closest distance the subject could approach a snake (behavioural), the intensity of galvanic skin response (physiological), adjectives subjects used to describe their reactions (cognitive), or a combination of these measures.

Emotion is a hypothetical construct (i.e., a theoretical concept) used as an intervening variable to explain behaviours marked by a complex pattern of physiological arousal (especially of the autonomic nervous system), internal subjective feelings and thoughts, body language (such as facial expression), and possibly verbalizations. To understand emotion, we need to consider psychological, social, and physical dimensions. Because of this complexity, the study of emotion is difficult despite our intuitive understandings (or misunderstandings).

What colours life?

Emotions tell us how much events, circumstances, and interactions mean to us. How can you explain to somebody why you love them, or why you hate that piece of clothing they gave you for your birthday? We are usually able to articulate some reason that seems to make sense, but it usually comes down to some kind of gut feeling, or emotion. Emotions allow us to measure the impact of what catches our attention. Sometimes, our ability to verbalize why we did a certain thing provides an answer that sounds logical, but it may not be the true reason we carried out some activity. Most people have had the experience of being anxious and frightened and not knowing precisely why. Here we are acutely aware of our emotion, but not of the reasons for it. In this chapter and later in the book, we will see that emotion and reason are probably separate systems in humans. They affect each other, but one does not control the other. Each exerts its own influence.

When we study emotion in the experimental laboratory, we deal with emotion in a much more sterile, cold, and analytic way. It is difficult to study something as intangible and subtle as emotion. One unavoidable barrier is the fact that we are dealing with humans. It would be unethical and inhumane to investigate strong emotions in a laboratory setting where an experiment would have to provoke intense fear, rage, or sadness. Nonetheless, psychologists have been ingenious in their ways of investigating emotion, as we will see.

FIGURE 6-12 Are emotions instinctual?
Facial displays of anger are similar in all cultures. Darwin argued that such expressions show remnants of the growling and aggression of lower species.
SOURCE: Paul Ekman/Consulting Psychologists Press

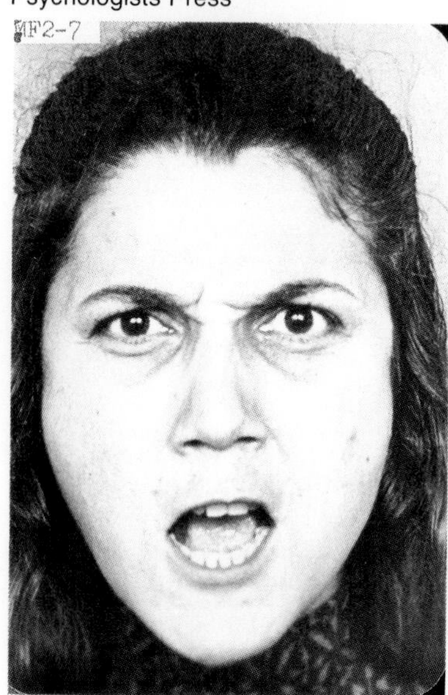

Innate or learned?

A basic question that we have seen in other areas in our study of psychology is whether a particular psychological construct, in this case emotion, is inborn or a product of learning. When we examined motivation, we saw a development of theories that moved from biological explanations to successive refinements that included more psychological factors. We will see the same trend in our study of emotion.

Are we born with a certain set of emotions? Or do our emotions develop over time through interaction with other people, through modelling, and other forms of learning? One early philosophical view was that emotions are instinctual and have to be curbed and restrained by human rationality. This view was elaborated by Charles Darwin in his 1872 classic, *The Expression of Emotions in Man and Animals*. In line with his evolutionary theory, Darwin believed that human emotional expressions are an evolutionary carry-over from the instinctual responses of lower species to their environments. He argued that our own emotional behaviour shows traces of an animal's instinctual behaviour that had survival value. For example, Darwin said that our facial displays of anger — a scowling face and some baring of teeth—is a remnant of growling and the aggressive display of teeth used by lower species to warn of an impending bite (Figure 6-12). Likewise, we sometimes demonstrate our disgust by pretending to spit or by really spitting. This may be a leftover from an animal's need to expel some offending food that may be rancid or poisonous.

A recent elaboration of this Darwinian concept was proposed by Plutchik (1980). He argued that there are eight primary or basic innate emotions, organized into four sets of opposites: joy-sadness, fear-anger, surprise-anticipation, and acceptance-disgust. According to Plutchik, the range of human emotions can be derived from the mixing of these eight primary emotions. For example, contempt results from the combination of anger and disgust, and optimism results from the combination of anticipation and joy.

Some evidence used to support the proposition that we are born with a complement of emotions comes from the observation that infants are born with the capacity to react to their world in particular ways. Children who are blind and deaf express emotions similar to normal children, despite their obvious inability to learn in usual ways about emotional expression. This fact suggests the existence of some inborn set of emotional readiness and capability. It also implies that there are many avenues by which one can learn emotional responding. Furthermore, researchers who have examined emotional expressions cross-culturally maintain that there are at least six emotions that are universal: happiness, sadness, anger, fear, surprise, and disgust (Ekman, Soranson, and Friesen, 1969). See Figure 6-13. The researchers asked individuals in different cultures to identify the emotion being expressed in prepared photographs showing differing facial expressions. Even when researchers travelled into the depths of New Guinea to evaluate a particular tribe that had virtually no contact with Western cultures prior to the study, they

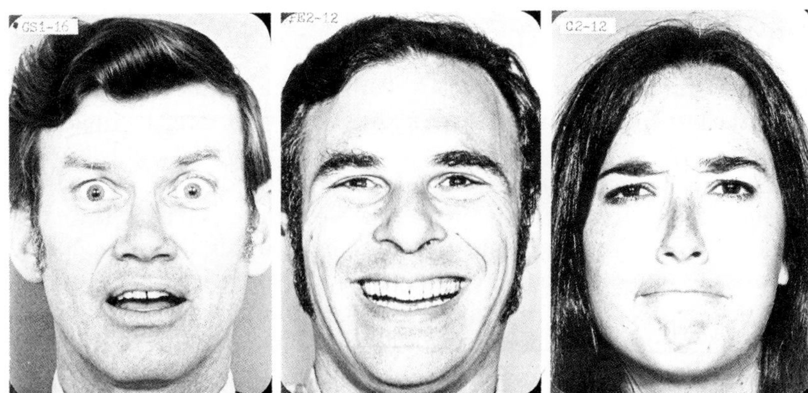

FIGURE 6-13 Some of Ekman's photographs of different emotions from his study of the universality of human emotions
SOURCE: Paul Ekman/Consulting Psychologists Press.

obtained the same set of results. This cross-cultural agreement suggests a certain universality of emotions (Ekman, 1980).

We should qualify this notion of the universality of human emotions. Even though there may be cross-cultural similarities in emotion (suggesting an innate influence), great differences do exist between cultures in the display of particular emotions and in the situations that usually elicit them. The old stereotype of the North American male, as personified by John Wayne, was stoic, determined, and nonemotional. He certainly didn't cry. But this does not necessarily hold true for other cultures. In many countries in Southern Europe, intense emotion (including crying) is acceptable for men. Each society has certain rules that define what is normal for emotional expression. This also applies to the use of gestures, as you will soon find out if you attempt to use the thumbs-up gesture in some areas of Greece where this means the same thing as our use of the extended third finger.

It seems likely that emotions involve both an unlearned (that is, innate) component and a learned component that is dependent upon interactions with others. Izard (1982) argues that two emotions exist at birth: a generalized positive state and a generalized negative state. Over the course of the first few months, joy develops from the positive state, and anger develops from the negative one. Later in the first year, other emotions begin to emerge, such as shame and fear.

There may well be an innate, genetically programmed development of emotions, dependent upon adequate experience and stimulation from the social environment. Early in life, particularly within the first year, our emotions may develop as our nervous system develops (especially as our nerve pathways become myelinated, a process we discussed in Chapter 2). This may explain why infants exhibit "making strange" (fear of strangers) between six and nine months. It is during these months that the neural paths are developing between the limbic system (where emotions are processed), the temporal lobes (where memory is processed), and the cortex (where higher mental functioning is processed). The more complex types of emotions, such as empathy, emerge later. They depend not only upon brain development and maturation but also upon social, interactional, and observational kinds of learning.

Physiology of emotion

Emotion has a physiological basis. Perhaps the simplest way to realize this is to consider our own experience of strong feelings. For example, when we are experiencing fear, we know that our heart rate speeds up, we probably perspire, our mouth feels dry, and sometimes we have difficulty catching our breath. Next time you have the experience of strong emotion, sit back for a moment and try to focus on the changes in your body. You may be quite surprised.

As we discussed in Chapter 2, the **autonomic nervous system** is that branch of the peripheral nervous system that controls the muscles of internal organs and the glands. It is responsible for helping to maintain body homeostasis. One division of the autonomic nervous system, called the **sympathetic nervous system**, plays a prominent role in strong emotional responses. The sympathetic nervous system is responsible for the fight or flight reaction — accelerated heart rate, rising blood pressure, dilating pupils, slowed digestion, speeded respiration, and many other physical changes that are associated with strong emotions. This reaction begins with a stimulus, either internal or external, that increases the neural firing of the reticular activating system (RAS). Through a series of complex connections and pathways, the RAS stimulates the cerebral cortex and other brain structures responsible for higher mental processing. This leads to the mental component of emotion. It consists of intellectual assessment and is called **cognitive appraisal** (Lazarus, 1984). When we experience a particular arousal, we may interpret it in different ways depending on the context. We will investigate this further in our discussion of the Schachter-Singer theory below.

The firing of the RAS also stimulates the hypothalamus and pituitary gland (together with the surrounding structures of the limbic system). The hypothalamus in turn influences the autonomic sympathetic nervous system. We have already discussed the role of the hypothalamus in the hunger drive. The hypothalamus also influences the **pituitary gland**, the master gland of the endocrine system. The pituitary gland is responsible for our hormonal response in emotion.

Thus, emotion leads to many physical changes. These occur through the workings of both the sympathetic nervous system and the endocrine system (which secretes hormones). For example, when we get very excited, we sometimes describe the excitation as "getting a shot of adrenaline" or "getting pumped up." In fact, we really do get **adrenaline** (also known as **epinephrine**) pumped into our system by the adrenal glands (especially during a fear response), and this chemical speeds up our heart rate and increases our blood pressure.

In humans, certain brain diseases can result in dramatic changes in emotional behaviour. Damage to parts of the limbic system may lead to aggressive, rage-like reactions. By contrast, damage to other brain areas, especially the frontal lobes and some of the connections to the limbic system, can result in a lack of all emotion. Here the individual just does not feel any emotion, and life becomes bland. Certain rare forms of epilepsy lead to changes in the experience of emotion. This indicates that certain areas in the limbic system and areas of the hypothalamus are all important in emotional regulation.

However, it is the higher mental functions associated with the cerebral cortex that provide most control over our emotional state. It is this part of the brain that we use to evaluate, inhibit, and determine whether something has significance to us. Let us now turn to some of the theories of emotion that have tried to explain how the physiological and subjective, psychological facets of emotional responding interact.

THEORIES OF EMOTION

James-Lange theory

The James-Lange theory of emotion was the first psychological theory to attempt to account for the generation of emotions. William James and Carl Lange developed similar theories that bodily changes occur first and these changes trigger emotion (Lange, 1922). This theory differs from the common-sense view of emotional responding which would say that we have the subjective experience and this results in physical changes in our body (i.e., we cry *because* we are sad). According to the **James-Lange theory**, the subjective experience of an emotion follows from the perception of the physiological changes that occur. We react in innate and instinctual ways to particular environmental situations. Our body first becomes physically activated or aroused (we cry). We then perceive and become conscious of this through sensory and motor feedback. As a result, we experience an emotion (we are sad). Thus, according to the James-Lange theory, we are sad *because* we cry. It is our perception of the physical changes when we cry that causes us to experience the emotion of sadness (see Figure 6-14).

Although the James-Lange theory may seem backwards to what common sense tells us, some evidence does exist to support it. Suppose our perception of physiological change is indeed important in our experience of emotion. It would then follow that if there were some disruption to our physiological systems, our perception of emotion and our experience of it would be affected. This is what Hohman (1962) found in his research project investigating the emotional experience of patients with spinal-cord injuries. The location of the injury in the spine varied among his subjects. Some patients had damage low in the spinal cord (at the sacral or lumbar level) which eliminates only some functioning of the sympathetic nerves. Other patients had damage relatively high in the spinal cord (at the cervical level), which eliminates all functioning of the sympathetic nerves. According to the James-Lange theory, one would expect that patients with spinal-cord injuries in the cervical region would experience substantially less intense emotions because they lack the normal feedback that usually accompanies physiological activation in emotional situations. The results showed that patients with cervical spinal cord injuries actually did have a decrease in their subjective experience of their emotions compared with those patients who had lower, sacral injuries.

FIGURE 6-14 The James-Lange theory of emotion
According to this theory, we first react physiologically and then interpret these physiological changes as specific emotions.
SOURCE: Adapted with permission from Allyn and Bacon, 1987.

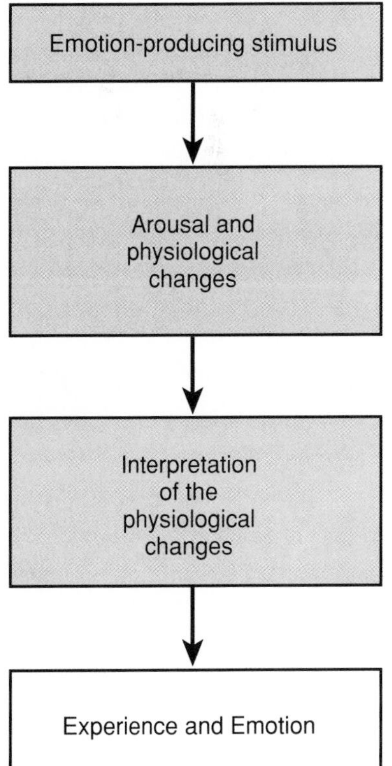

The James-Lange theory, that sensory and motor feedback of body arousal lead to our emotional experience, suggests that facial expression plays a central role in determining emotion. We know that there are neurological connections between our facial muscles, the sensory and motor control areas in our cerebral cortex, and our limbic system. According to the so-called **facial feedback hypothesis**, when we react to stimuli in our environments, these neural connections cause our facial expression to change, and the feedback from our facial muscles *causes* our emotional experience (Izard, 1971; Ekman, 1984).

We know that certain emotions are accompanied by specific changes in facial expression. In fact, we often use people's facial expressions to gauge the way they are feeling. But what evidence is there for the theory that facial expressions can cause emotion? In one study, Ekman (1984) had professional actors move their facial muscles in particular ways to mimic the expressions that are usually correlated with certain emotions. The actors were *not* told to act out certain emotions but just to move their facial muscles. Sensitive recording of the actors' physiological reactions showed that there were differing patterns of body responses, depending on the pattern of facial muscles that were tensed or relaxed. When the actors' faces were positioned in ways usually associated with anger or fear, their heart rates increased. When they adjusted their facial muscles to a happy-looking expression, their heart rates decreased. In a similar way, Lanzetta, Cartwright-Smith, and Kleck (1976) found that subjects who were given a mild electric shock experienced less pain when they consciously minimized their outward emotional expression than when they exaggerated it. Maybe there is something to the old saying, "Smile and you will feel better."

Cannon-Bard theory

Walter Cannon disagreed with the James-Lange theory of emotion. He argued that the physiological changes related to various emotions did not differ sufficiently from each other to allow a person to distinguish certain emotions from others. For example, fear, love, and excitement all involve similar arousal of the sympathetic nervous system. Cannon also maintained that some of the physiological changes correlated with emotion occur much too slowly to account for the speed with which our emotions can change. Cannon developed a theory of emotion (Cannon, 1927) which was later extended by Philip Bard (1934). It is now known as the **Cannon-Bard theory**. According to this theory, the psychological (subjective) experience of an emotion occurs simultaneously with the physical changes that occur. Originally the thalamus was thought to play a central role in determining emotions. (As you will recall from Chapter 2, the thalamus is a structure of the forebrain that acts primarily as a relay station for signals from the sensory system and other brain centres, particularly the reticular formation.) A certain event occurs in the environment and activates the thalamus, which in turn sends nerve impulses simultaneously to both the cerebral cortex and the rest of the body via the sympathetic nervous sytem. Bodily changes include

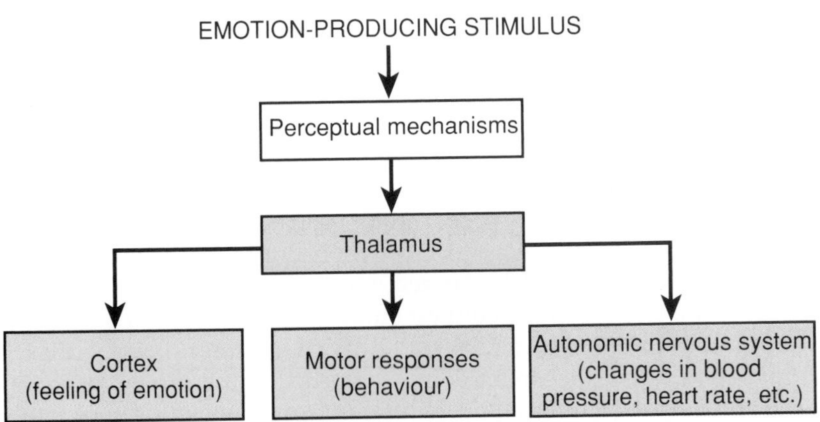

SOURCE: Adapted with permission from Allyn and Bacon, 1987.

FIGURE 6-15 The Cannon-Bard theory of emotion
According to this theory, we react simultaneously at cognitive, physiological, and motor levels.

autonomic responses such as increased heart rate. Thus, emotion is experienced independently of the physical changes, contrary to the James-Lange position (see Figure 6-15). Later research has shown that it is not the thalamus that is involved in emotional regulation and processing but rather the hypothalamus and other parts of the limbic system. This correction, however, does not undermine the basic idea of the Cannon-Bard theory—the idea that the experience of emotion occurs simultaneously with the physical changes.

Schachter-Singer theory

We have seen that emotional responding includes physiological changes as well as subjective experiences. Another important component of emotions seems to be the cognitive processing of the context of our experience. Schachter (1964) proposed the cognitive labelling theory as a two-component view of emotion. According to the **Schachter-Singer theory**, emotion is the product of both physiological arousal and the meaning or label that we attach to the experience through cognitive appraisal of the context (see Figure 6-16). This appraisal is a process that allows a person to determine the meaning of the physiological changes of an arousal in terms of the social context, past experiences, goals, and cognitions.

The classic experiments used to support this theory were conducted by Schachter and Singer (1962). They injected one group of subjects with an inert substance which caused no changes in body functioning and another group of subjects with epinephrine (adrenaline), which quickly led to body arousal by increasing the activity of the sympathetic nervous system (producing trembling and an increase in blood pressure and heart rate). In the group injected with epinephrine, some subjects were then correctly informed about the effects of the injection whereas other subjects were misinformed. (The group injected with an inert substance—a placebo—was a control group.) All subjects were then asked to sit in a waiting room with another person. Unbeknownst to the subject, the other person was a confederate in the experiment. Some "pseudosubjects" acted in a euphoric manner, and others acted in an angry manner. An

FIGURE 6-16 The Schachter-Singer theory of emotion
According to this theory, we first react physiologically. Then, depending on the surrounding context, we interpret this reaction to be a specific emotion.
SOURCE: Adapted with permission from Allyn and Bacon, 1987.

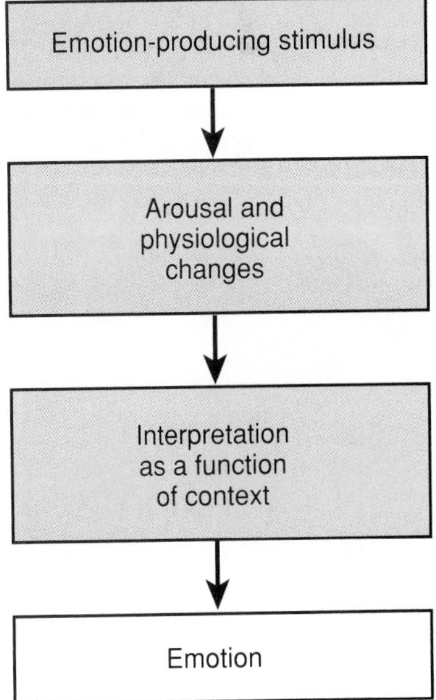

important result of this complex experiment was that subjects who were given epinephrine and were not told about the real effects of this drug tended to label their physiological state in accordance with the kinds of information they perceived in their social setting. Those who were placed in the waiting room with the euphoric confederate tended to feel euphoric; those who were placed with the angry confederate were more likely to feel angry. Apparently, the misinformed subjects had no other way to label their emotional experience. In contrast, the subjects who were accurately informed about the effects of their injections attributed their emotions to the drug, and they did not look to their environment for a way to interpret their feelings.

Thus, this experiment demonstrated that the same physiological arousal can be interpreted in different ways depending upon one's cognitive appraisal. The same physiological state caused by the epinephrine was interpreted in different ways because the subjects were given different cues and information from the social setting.

Further evidence supports the idea that the meaning of a given physical arousal can depend on social cues available in the environment. Two psychologists at the University of British Columbia manipulated physiological arousal in an experiment they conducted in the beautiful Capilano Canyon (Dutton & Aron, 1974). For one group of male subjects, an interview with an attractive woman took place on a low footbridge (low-arousal condition). For the other group of male subjects, the interview with the same woman took place on a swinging suspension bridge approximately 230 feet above the canyon floor (high-arousal condition) (see Figure 6-17).

FIGURE 6-17 The swinging suspension bridge over the Capilano River in British Columbia

This bridge was used for the high-arousal condition in Dutton and Aron's study. When interviewed in the high-arousal condition, men rated the female interviewer as more attractive than did men interviewed on a low footbridge. Apparently they misattributed the source of their arousal.

SOURCE: Dutton and Aron (1974).

Because of the more precarious surroundings, the men on the high suspension bridge experienced more physiological arousal than the men on the low footbridge. The researchers tried to determine how the subjects interpreted their physical arousal. They offered all the subjects an opportunity to call the interviewer later to find out the results of the assessment. More subjects from the high-arousal group phoned than from the low-arousal group. Evidently the female interviewer was considered more attractive by the men on the high suspension bridge. They tended to interpret their physiological arousal as interpersonal attraction, in accordance with the social and environmental cues that were made available.

Although other psychologists have had some difficulty replicating Schachter and Singer's results, research generally supports the conclusion that cognitive appraisal and labelling do influence emotional experience. It would be premature, however, to believe that one existing theory can account for all the data in the study of emotion (Leventhal & Tomarken, 1986; Reisenzein, 1983). On the one hand, there are some physiological differences in the way various people respond to emotionally charged situations. On the other hand, some researchers have argued that we possess unlearned patterns of reacting that are built into the specific types of wiring of our nervous system, and that these patterns have evolutionary value. Thus, without cognitive appraisal or prior learning, when our nervous system is mature enough, we do react in certain universal ways to particular situations that we confront (Tompkins, 1981). Even infants do not need learning to respond to loud sounds. This wide range of data suggests that we need a comprehensive theory of emotion—one that takes into account neurological and physiological components, cognitive and social factors, and unlearned patterns of responding.

SPECIAL TOPIC Lie Detection?

Many businesses, police departments, and government agencies are using lie detection techniques to screen prospective staff and to investigate various kinds of wrongdoing. The use of lie detection raises many issues of human rights and civil liberties, particularly regarding invasion of privacy and the validity of the test results. Psychological evidence has been gathered that questions the accuracy and reliability of this technique. Lie detection or **polygraph testing** is the measurement of physiological functions under autonomic system control in order to determine the truth of responses to a series of questions, some of which relate to the areas of specific interest for the examination. The basic theoretical premise behind polygraph testing is that lying is associated with stress and anxiety —and hence with the arousal of the autonomic nervous system. Proponents of polygraph testing claim that by measuring indicators of this arousal, such as heart rate, respiration rate, blood pressure, and sweating, it is possible to determine whether the person being examined is telling the truth or lying.

Although proponents of polygraph testing assert that the procedure is 90% to 95% accurate, the results of scientific analysis indicate much more modest results. We should be concerned about the failure rate of the procedure, given the tremendous human cost that can result from errors. In an extensive review of research on polygraph testing, Saxe and his colleagues found only ten studies that examined the accuracy of particular lie detection tests in terms of the actual legal outcomes in trials or confessions of crimes (Saxe, Dougherty, and Cross, 1985). They found that the percentage of times a polygraph finding of guilt agreed with the legal outcome ranged from 71% to 99%. By contrast, the percentage of times a polygraph finding of innocent agreed with the legal outcome ranged from 13% to 94%. Of particular concern was the fact that, in some studies, 75% of those examined who were actually found innocent had been declared untruthful (i.e., guilty) by polygraph examination.

Subject being examined by a polygraph expert.
SOURCE: Lafayette Instrument.

If polygraph evidence is given credence in police investigations, in judicial outcomes, or in evaluating fitness for employment in sensitive positions, grave errors are almost certain to occur. Lykken (1981) believes that a polygraph assessment is far more likely to be in error when the subject is truthful. He has documented a number of cases where innocent people have been convicted and have spent from one to five years in prison because of erroneous polygraph data. Polygraph findings are not admissible as evidence in Canadian courts.

Reviews of the polygraph literature do indicate that when polygraphy is used expertly (i.e., with appropriate questioning and after the proper psychological and social testing climate has been provided), the technique can "detect deception at rates significantly better than chance, although the data also suggests that substantial rates of false-positives [subjects incorrectly judged to be lying], false-negatives [subjects incorrectly judged to be telling the truth] and inconclusives are possible" (Saxe et al, 1985, p. 364). Edward Katkin chaired a special committee that examined polygraph testing for the United States government. He concluded that according to the scientific evidence, the utility of polygraph testing exists but it is limited (Katkin, 1985). Consequently, we should not use polygraph results to make decisions that have an important impact on human lives. Furedy (1989, p. 459) says that in most Western European countries, "the polygraph is regarded as akin to tea-leaf reading and astrology, rather than a scientifically based 'test.'" He goes on to criticize the polygraph as an unstandardized procedure whose proponents use deceptive terminology and make unfounded claims for "this peculiarly American flight of technological fancy" (Furedy, 1989, p. 460).

SPECIAL TOPIC Obesity and Weight Control

Not only does being overweight lead to an increased risk for hypertension, diabetes, and cardiovascular disorders, but it also leads to decreased self-esteem, feelings of unattractiveness, and social prejudice. There are probably more diets available than are really needed. The true mark of a successful diet is not just to lose weight while on it but to maintain the weight loss for a long duration afterwards. This is one of the most difficult things for dieters to do, and often over time they regain any weight lost. Nevertheless, programs based on behavioural techniques have been developed that do help people maintain weight loss over long durations (Lebow, 1981 and 1988). Such programs focus on one's eating habits, the cues that control one's eating, and the amount of physical exercise one does.

The first step in a systematic program is to evaluate carefully actual eating behaviour and the stimulus conditions that give rise to eating. What do we eat, when do we eat it, and what do we do after we eat? We need to identify the stimulus cues that help initiate eating behaviour, as well as those that control eating. We have seen that people who are overweight are sensitive to external food cues. This is a good starting place to develop a weight-loss program.

How do we decrease the impact of these external cues? A good place to begin might be with our shopping for food. We should never shop on an empty stomach because when we do, we are tempted to buy more food and to buy food that is less nutritious. We should plan menus out ahead of time, and buy just enough food to make the meals on our menus. This will ensure that our cupboards will not be filled with the kind of junk food that is tempting, tasty-looking, and that contributes to our weight problem. When we cook, we should prepare only the amounts needed to satisfy our menu. Given our sensitivity to external cues, we should not make too much, because we may well eat it all even though we may not need it or be hungry for it. After cooking, we should put the servings of food on the plates before bringing them to the table, and we should give ourselves small, but adequate, servings. If the food is on the table, and we help ourselves, it often happens that "our eyes are bigger than our stomachs."

The next step in our program should be to modify our actual eating behaviour. Here, it would make sense to slow our eating, take smaller mouthfuls, chew for longer durations, and engage in conversation throughout the course of meals. The increased time taken to consume a meal will give the body a chance to "notice" that it is full and send the signal to stop eating. By contrast, if we read or watch television during the time we eat, then we end up eating more and enjoying it less. It is also useful to take short breaks in the course of eating, by putting our knives and forks down and taking the time to finish chewing and swallowing before taking another mouthful. What we are attempting to do here is to control the stimulus conditions associated with eating, as well as to modify actual eating behaviour.

Another important component of an effective behavioural program is to develop ways of preventing eating at times other than meals. Behavioural psychologists talk about the need for using incompatible responses. **Incompatible responses** are more desirable activities that compete with behaviour we want to diminish. These could include any behaviours that make eating less likely because they compete with eating and take its place. Going for a walk, going for a run, playing a game, or doing some work is an effective replacement for eating if you are attempting to curb your appetite.

A successful weight-loss program also needs to be built upon a healthy and active lifestyle, particularly if we want to break the cycle of dieting and then regaining weight. Exercise has some added benefits as well. It may lead to cardiovascular conditioning, as well as a change in the body's basic metabolic rate. Thus it may result in more efficient body functioning (Thompson, Jarvie, Lakey, and Cureton, 1982).

SPECIAL TOPIC Anorexia and Bulimia

Anorexia nervosa is a severe eating disorder in which the individual refuses to eat for emotional reasons, sometimes to the point of starving to death. Persons suffering from anorexia nervosa are usually intensely preoccupied with their body image. Because they have such a fear of becoming fat, they suffer a large decrease in food intake and lose at least 25% of their body weight. A healthy and robust individual of 120 pounds may lose up to 50 pounds through self-starvation. Such staggering weight loss leads to a host of physical problems associated with starvation syndromes. The person suffering from anorexia nervosa does not eat enough to maintain even basic body processes such as body temperature and menstruation. Death can result from heartbeat irregularities caused by imbalances of electrolytes (body fluids).

Anorexia is typically a disorder of adolescence. Although both males and females are susceptible to this disorder, it is most frequently found among girls from families of a high socioeconomic standing where there is a considerable drive for success. The girls are usually high achievers, perfectionists, and well behaved. At times, the onset of anorexia is associated with the failure of a first-love experience. At other times, the onset coincides with the outbreak of family conflict that the adolescent finds difficult to deal with. Some researchers have suggested that the onset of anorexia around puberty represents some psychological conflict over sexuality (Garfinkel and Garner, 1982) and a preoccupation with the ideal body type. A unique part of this disorder is that even though others become appalled at the tremendous loss of body weight, the individuals who are suffering from anorexia do not see this themselves. In fact, they maintain their desire to continue to lose weight, denying that they are even hungry and continuing to refuse food. Moreover, they often engage in intense physical activity.

Another eating disorder that can have serious consequences is called **bulimia**. This is an eating disorder characterized by uncontrolled binge eating followed by purging and laxative abuse to control weight. The person who suffers from bulimia eats in binges, sometimes up to 10 000 calories of junk food in one sitting, and then purges this food either through self-induced vomiting or the use of laxatives. This disorder can be found with anorexia, or it can occur alone. Its physical consequences can be similar to those of anorexia: the high frequency of vomiting and the abuse of laxatives can lead to a dangerous loss of electrolytes.

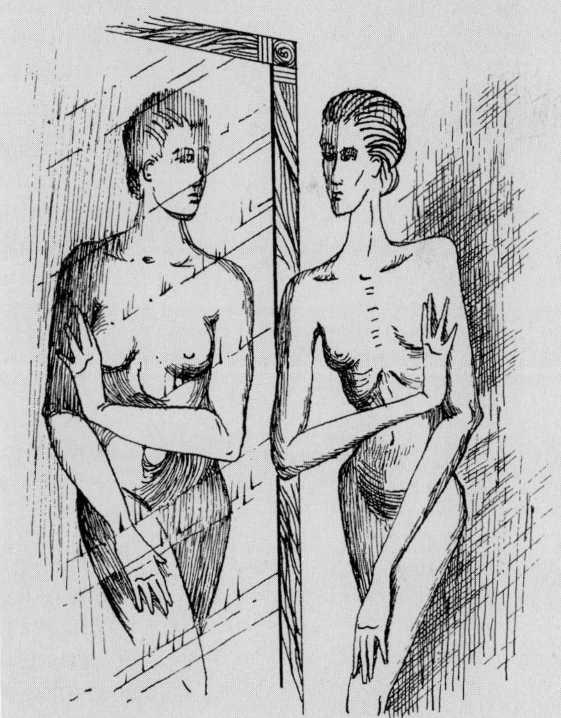

Anorexia nervosa is a life-threatening emotional disorder in which the victim refuses to eat.

To deal with either of these eating disorders, they must first be identified. One of the tragedies of anorexia is that the initial weight loss is reinforced by praise and encouragement, just as any normal successful diet would be. Unfortunately for the anorexic, the weight loss does not stop here. It accelerates until major physical problems develop. The difficulty is that often too much weight loss occurs before people become concerned. Given that research indicates anorexia is increasing in frequency, school teachers, guidance counsellors, and youth-group leaders and others who work with high-risk groups should be attentive and should be prepared to express concern when weight loss begins to look excessive. The anorexic needs treatment. The first goal is to have the patient gain weight. Sometimes hospitalization is necessary to reverse many of the biological consequences of self-imposed starvation. This may require intravenous feedings. After addressing the biological problems, an effective treatment may well include individual counselling, behavioural management, and family therapy. Similarly, a promising approach to dealing with bulimia is to use cognitive behavioural treatment in which one works with the patient's self-image and self-control (Agras, Schneider, Arnow, Raeburn, & Telch, 1989). We will discuss cognitive behaviour modification in more detail in Chapter 15. For now, it is important to note that the causes of anorexia and bulimia may differ from patient to patient. Therefore, the treatment should be geared to the individual.

CHAPTER SUMMARY

1. Motivation is a hypothetical construct that psychologists and others use to account for what determines our behaviours and thoughts. Motivation is an intervening variable that operates between a stimulus and a response. Therefore, to research a motivation effectively, it is important to operationalize it carefully. Our primary motives are innate, biological, and survival-oriented. Our secondary motives are acquired through learning.
2. In the second half of the 19th century Charles Darwin challenged the widely held view that humans are qualitatively different from animals. His revolutionary ideas imply that instinct plays a major role in human behaviour. Three main types of theories of human motivation have since been developed: instinct theories, drive-reduction theory, and humanistic theory.
3. Instinct theories focus on behaviour that is biologically built into the organism. The implication of Darwin's evolutionary theory is that humans and animals are on a continuum—in other words, that we differ from animals only in degree of complexity. Ethologists study animal behaviour and extend their findings on fixed action patterns (i.e., instincts) to humans. Sigmund Freud proposed a complex instinctual theory for human nature. He based it on two fundamental drives: eros and thanatos.
4. Drive-reduction theory proposes that states of drive are caused by changes in the body system that threaten to upset homeostasis. According to Clark Hull, an imbalance in homeostasis creates a biological need to restore the balance. This motivates the organism toward drive-reduction. Given that drive-reduction is reinforcing, this theory can account for the motivation to learn (either by operant conditioning or classical conditioning).

5. The humanistic theory of motivation differs dramatically from the biological theories. Abraham Maslow argued that humans have an inborn hierarchy of needs. The lowest levels consist of physiological needs and ensuring physical safety. The highest level is the need for self-actualization. According to this theory, lower needs must be met before higher ones. In practice, people have difficulty reaching self-actualization because the environment somehow distorts the process and blocks the innate striving for growth.

6. Hunger and eating behaviour illustrate many aspects of motivation. Stomach contractions are associated with hunger, but it is possible to feel hunger without a stomach. The hypothalamus, a brain structure that helps to control homeostasis, plays a leading role in eating. The hypothalamus is rich in connections with the limbic system, the reticular activating system, and the frontal lobes. Consequently, disorders at a variety of levels in the brain can result in changes in eating behaviour. Lesions to different parts of the hypothalamus can lead to significant overeating or to the cessation of eating. The lateral hypothalamus (LH) is involved in initiating eating; the ventromedial hypothalamus (VMH) is involved in stopping eating. Glucostats, special cells in the hypothalamus, apparently detect levels of blood sugar and thereby stimulate or suppress hunger.

7. A theory of weight control called the set-point hypothesis suggests that we have a stable number of fat cells in our bodies. When the amount of fat in these cells falls below (rises above) a critical level, the LH (VMH) acts to initiate (suppress) eating behaviour.

8. People with weight problems and rats with lesions in their VMH exhibit several behavioural similarities in eating. Both show lower than normal sensitivity to internal cues and higher than normal sensitivity to external cues.

9. Considerable research has been done on dieting and the problems of restrained eaters. Evidence indicates that non-food stimuli, internal psychological states, and cultural factors can all influence eating behaviour.

10. Sex is a unique drive. It is not homeostatic because it is not needed for survival of the individual organism. Unlike other primary drives, sexual arousal is actively sought. Touch is the only unconditioned stimulus for sexual arousal. Nevertheless, through conditioning, sexual arousal can be initiated by almost any stimulus.

11. The pituitary gland is physiologically responsible for the hormonal cyclic variations of all female mammals. In animals the cycle is called the estrous cycle. In humans it is called the menstrual cycle. Among animals, the level of the hormone estrogen determines the female's sexual receptiveness. But among

humans, no relation has been found between hormone levels and female sexual activity. In male mammals, the pituitary hormones called androgens are at a sufficient level following sexual maturity to allow for sexual activity at any time.

12. As we move from lower animals to humans, the importance of experience, environment, and social factors increase in determining sexual activity. The primary elements of human sexuality are probably learned.
13. Kinsey's research on human sexuality demystified many sexual practices that were actually more widespread than people thought. Premarital sex and masturbation were found to be common. Masturbation that continued into marriage had no relationship with marital discord or sexual problems. Masters and Johnson studied human sexual response and reported a cycle of four stages: excitement, plateau phase, orgasm, and resolution. They also dispelled some myths about sex. They found no relationship between a woman's sexual satisfaction and the penis size of her partner. They argued that men's and women's sexual responses are quite similar, and that the sexual response cycle is the same for intercourse, masturbation, and homosexual contact. They concluded that simultaneous orgasm is an artificial performance standard. They strongly emphasized the importance of communication between partners for mutually satisfying sexual relations.
14. The incidence of sexual dysfunction in North America has been estimated at about half of all married couples. Common problems for men include erectile dysfunction and premature ejaculation. Common problems for women include inhibited sexual excitement and orgasmic dysfunction.
15. Some recent theorists claim that human sexual experience is more varied than the four-stage cycle of response suggests. They also emphasize that learning experiences and cultural standards exert a strong influence on human sexuality.
16. Achievement motivation is an example of a social motivation. Social motivators are learned through conditioning and socialization. They are greatly determined by cultural values and parental behaviour. Subjects with a high need for achievement have been found to prefer tasks involving risks and responsibility. Considerable research has been done on achievement needs, but much of it neglected women.
17. Emotion is an important source of motivation. Emotion is an intervening variable that is used to explain certain complex patterns of behaviour and that should be carefully operationalized for effective research. Experiments must be carefully designed to meet ethical standards for working with human subjects.
18. Emotion seems to be partly innate and partly learned. It may also depend on brain development and maturation. Darwin argued that our emotional behaviour is instinctual and that it shows traces of an animal's behaviour that had survival value.

Cross-cultural studies and other research suggest that specific emotions are universal, but what elicits emotion is determined by the particular culture.

19. Emotion has a physical component and a mental component. The sympathetic division of the autonomic nervous system is very active in emotional responding. The firing of the reticular activating system stimulates the cerebral cortex and other brain structures. Our cognitive appraisal of the meaning of an arousal plays an important role in emotion. Damage to specific brain structures can arouse certain emotions, such as rage and timidity. Three main theories of emotion have been developed: the James-Lange theory, the Cannon-Bard theory, and the Schachter-Singer theory.
20. The James-Lange theory states that we experience a certain emotion only after we perceive certain physiological changes in our bodies. We are sad because we cry. The emotional responses of patients with various spinal-cord injuries tend to support this theory. One extension of the theory, called the facial feedback hypothesis, states that feedback from our facial muscles causes our emotional experience.
21. The Cannon-Bard theory states that the psychological experience of emotion occurs simultaneously with the physical experience. It was formulated because the James-Lange theory does not adequately explain how we distinguish between certain emotions and how we can change our emotions so quickly.
22. The Schachter-Singer theory, otherwise known as the cognitive labelling theory, emphasizes the importance of thoughts in emotion. It views emotion as having two parts: physiological arousal and the meaning or label that comes from cognitive appraisal. Two different emotions might be quite similar physiologically, but we might appraise one as love and the other as fear.

Key Terms

Acquired drive A secondary or learned source of motivation which is acquired through classical or instrumental conditioning.

Adrenaline One of the hormones secreted by the adrenal glands during strong emotional responses, particularly fear. It is also known as epinephrine.

Androgen The most important male sex hormone.

Anorexia nervosa A severe eating disorder in which the individual refuses to eat for emotional reasons, sometimes to the point of starving to death.

Aphagia The suppression of eating that results from damage to the lateral hypothalamus.

Autonomic nervous system The branch of the peripheral nervous system that controls the muscles of internal organs and the glands.

Bulimia An eating disorder characterized by uncontrolled binge eating followed by purging and laxative abuse to control weight.

Cannon-Bard theory According to this theory of emotion, the psychological (subjective) experience of an emotion occurs simultaneously with the physical changes that occur.

Cognitive appraisal The mental component of emotion consisting of intellectual assessment.

Drive-reduction The basic cause of reinforcement in drive-reduction theory. Discomfort is caused by an imbalance in homeostasis, and restoring this balance reduces the discomfort and is reinforcing.

Drive-reduction theory The theory that behaviour is motivated by the tension of imbalances threatening homeostasis. The imbalances arouse a drive state which motivates the organism toward drive-reduction.

Emotion A hypothetical construct used as an intervening variable to explain behaviours marked by a complex pattern of physiological arousal (especially of the autonomic nervous system), internal subjective feelings and thoughts, body language (such as facial expression), and possibly verbalizations.

Epinephrine Another name for *adrenaline*.

Erectile dysfunction The male's inability to get or maintain an erection, sometimes caused by fear and sometimes by physical problems.

Eros Freud's basic motive, the life instinct, that supposedly leads to positive actions and sexuality.

Estrogen The most important female sex hormone.

Estrous cycle The cycle of hormonal fluctuations in nonprimate female mammals that controls fertility and often affects patterns of sexual behaviour.

Ethology A branch of science which studies organisms in their natural environments as well as their instinctual patterns of behaviour.

Excitement phase The first stage of sexual arousal. It is characterized by rapid increases in heart rate and in blood flow to the genitals.

Facial feedback hypothesis The hypothesis that facial expressions can cause particular emotions. It is an extension of the James-Lange theory.

Fixed action pattern In ethological theory, the specific behaviours that the organism is pre-programmed to perform under specific conditions.

Frontal lobe A lobe in each cerebral hemisphere that is concerned with voluntary movements.

Generalized conditioned reinforcer An object that acquires broad reinforcing power through association with primary reinforcers.

Glucostats Receptors in the LH and VMH that respond differently to the levels of sugar in the blood travelling throughout the body. They help control eating.

Hierarchy of needs An arrangement of needs devised by Maslow. Basic physiological needs must be met before higher, psychological needs can act as motivators.

Homeostasis A state where systems maintain a balanced, stable environment.

Human sexual response cycle Masters and Johnson's portrayal of the four stages involved in human sexual arousal — excitement phase, plateau phase, orgasm, and resolution.

Humanistic theory A theory of motivation based on humans' innate drive toward self-actualization.

Hyperphagia The extreme overeating that results from damage to the ventromedial hypothalamus. It occurs because the mechanism to turn off feeding is no longer present.

Hypothalamus Brain structure that helps to regulate the body's homeostasis. It plays a role in eating, drinking, and temperature regulation. It also works in concert with the pituitary gland to affect hormonal activity, and it is involved in emotion.

Incentives External stimuli that have the capacity to energize behaviour, even though they don't lead to drive reduction.

Incompatible responses More desirable activities that compete with behaviour we want to diminish.

Inhibited female orgasm Another term for *orgasmic dysfunction*.

Inhibited sexual excitement A sexual dysfunction in the female. It is characterized by a lack of excitement and of the vaginal lubrication that usually accompanies sexual stimulation.

Instincts Unlearned, biologically built-in, fixed patterns of behaviour.

Instinct theories of motivation Theories that view innate, complex, biologically built-in drives as the foundation of motivation.

Intervening variable A hypothetical construct that represents inferred processes which occur between the observed stimulus input and the observed response output.

James-Lange theory According to this theory of emotion, the psychological (subjective) experience of an emotion follows from the perception of the physiological changes that occur.

Lateral hypothalamus (LH) Outside portion of the hypothalamus. It is involved in initiating eating.

Libido Sometimes used synonymously with eros. More accurately, the energy derived from eros that motivates behaviour according to Freud's theory.

Limbic system A system of neural structures that is involved in motivation (related to hunger and sex) and in emotion (related to fear and aggression).

Menstrual cycle The cycle of hormonal fluctuations in human and other primate females that controls the sequence of fertility and menstrual flow.

Motivation A hypothetical construct that psychologists and others use to account for what determines our behaviours, actions, and thought processes. It focuses on the forces that initiate, sustain, and direct behaviour.

Need for achievement A socially acquired motive to produce and succeed. It is an emotional commitment to meeting personal standards of achievement.

Operationalize To devise a way to measure something in a clearly observable and quantifiable way.

Optimal level of arousal The level of stimulation the organism seeks to maintain, sometimes by decreasing stimulation and sometimes by increasing it.

Orgasm The third stage of sexual arousal. It is marked by a heightening of excitement until the person passes a "point of no return" when the orgasm is inevitable.

Orgasmic dysfunction A sexual dysfunction, more common among females. Although there may be normal sexual excitement, sexual response does not reach orgasm but ends in an earlier phase.

Pituitary gland The master gland of the endocrine system. It is strongly influenced by the hypothalamus.

Plateau phase The second stage of sexual arousal. There is a sustained, high, and fairly steady level of arousal.

Polygraph testing The measurement of physiological functions under autonomic system control in order to determine the truth of responses to questions. It rests on the assumption that lying will be stressful to the subject and hence arouse the autonomic nervous system. The process is commonly known as "lie detection."

Premature ejaculation A sexual dysfunction in which the male comes to orgasm earlier than desired, often prior to entering the female.

Primary drives Drives or motives based on innate, biological, and survival-oriented needs.

Refractory period Part of the male resolution stage following orgasm. During this period the male is unable to have another erection.

Releasers In ethological theory, the particular stimuli in the environment that give rise to specific fixed action patterns.

Resolution The fourth stage of sexual arousal. It is characterized by a relatively rapid physiological return to the pre-excitement levels of heart rate, respiration, and muscle tension.

Restrained eater Persons, often overweight, who need constant restraint to limit their eating. Once the restraint is broken, they often respond to external cues and lose control of their eating behaviour.

Reticular activating system (RAS) A neural structure in the brain stem that helps control arousal, attention, and sleep.

Satiety centre Term used to describe the ventromedial hypothalamus because of its leading role in the inhibition or cessation of eating.

Schachter-Singer theory According to this cognitive labelling theory, emotion is the product of both physiological arousal and the meaning or label that we attach to the experience through cognitive appraisal of the context.

Secondary drives Drives or motives based on learned needs, whether these needs have been acquired through the learning processes of classical conditioning or operant conditioning.

Self-actualization A striving toward psychological growth and enhancement, proposed by humanistic theory as the human motive that ranks highest in the hierarchy of needs.

Sensation seeking The intentional increase in stimulation, often to levels that are ordinarily uncomfortable.

Set-point hypothesis The theory that the LH and the VMH monitor the amount of fat in fat cells to maintain a specific level. These hypothalamic areas stimulate eating if the fat level is too low and suppress eating if the level is too high.

Sympathetic nervous system The division of the autonomic nervous system that plays a prominent role in strong emotional responses.

Thanatos Freud's later notion of a death instinct that supposedly motivates aggression and destructive behaviour.

Unrestrained eater Persons who are not very vulnerable to the influence of external cues and who tend to eat only when they are actually hungry.

Ventromedial hypothalamus (VMH) Lower-middle portion of the hypothalamus involved in stopping eating.

Suggested Readings

Hyde, J. S. (1986). *Understanding human sexuality*. 3rd ed. New York: McGraw-Hill. A very complete treatment of recent advances in nearly all aspects of human sexual behaviour.

Petri, H. L. (1985). *Motivation: Theory and research*. 2nd ed. Belmont, CA: Wadsworth. A textbook overview of the field of motivation. This is a scholarly, well-written work that is within the grasp of the undergraduate reader.

Spence, J. T. (Ed.). (1983). *Achievement and achievement motives*. New York: Freeman. A good summary and synthesis of recent theory and research on achievement motivation.

Strongman, K. T. (1987). *The psychology of emotion*. 3rd ed. New York: John Wiley & Sons. A textbook overview of the field of emotion. It is comprehensive, scholarly, and up-to-date.

Stuart, R. B. (1978). *Act thin, stay thin*. New York: Norton. A widely used book that outlines a behavioural approach to weight control.

Zilbergeld, B. (1978). *Male sexuality*. Boston: Little, Brown. One of the most useful books available for men exploring their sexuality. It dispels many myths and offers much sound advice. Many women find that a lot of this material applies to their own sexuality as well.

PART III

COGNITIVE PROCESSES

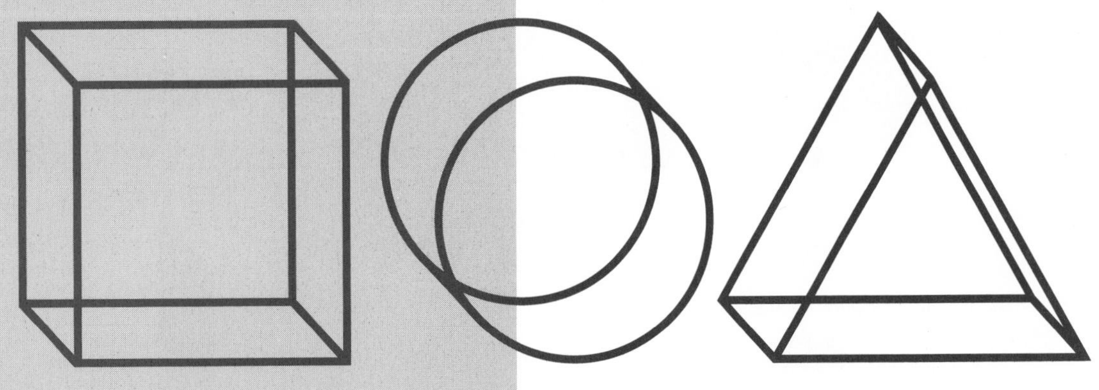

CHAPTER 7

SOURCE: G.A. Reid, Detail from *Sketch for "Adagio"* (n.d.).

Memory

MEMORY UNDERLIES everything we do. In order to be able to repeat any act intentionally, we have to be able to remember something we have learned.

Memory is a fascinating and somewhat mysterious process. How can past experiences be stored in the brain, often for life? When the father of one of us was dying from a brain tumour, he sometimes seemed to be vividly reliving very old experiences. He would say things like, "Grandpa says to get the horses into the barn right now." That 60-year-old memory was somehow still part of him. It had probably been activated by the pressure of the tumour on his brain. Are *all* our memories stored for as long as we live? Nobody knows for sure.

Other instances also raise challenging questions about memory. The father of another researcher, Michael Gazzaniga, had suffered a small stroke. When Michael showed him a carnation, his father, an avid gardener, could say many things about it: it was a flower, it was pink, it goes in one's lapel. But he couldn't retrieve the word "carnation." Even when told the word, he simply said, "Okay, if you say so" (Gazzaniga, 1985, p. 102). How can we account for this type of memory problem? More tragic was the memory loss suffered by the patient, H.M., described by Scoville and Milner (1957; also Milner, 1966). In order to alleviate H.M.'s epilepsy, surgeons removed part of a small structure in his brain called the hippocampus. However, the effect on H.M.'s memory was so devastating that surgeons quickly abandoned this type of operation as a treatment. H.M. could remember his life before the surgery, but he could never again remember anything new for more than about ten minutes. Does this mean that different types of memory are stored in different parts of the brain?

Common incidents in our daily life suggest other important questions about memory. For example, you have probably had the experience of talking with someone who absolutely insists that what happened last night was very different than what you are sure you remember happening. How can two people have such different memories of the same event? Or consider the common but frustrating experience of knowing something but being unable to call it to mind at a particular moment. How do we locate a piece of information in our memory?

In this chapter, we will consider such questions in our investigation of memory. We'll discuss the different components of the memory process as well as the different types of memory that have been identified. We'll also consider the other side of the coin, forgetting. To conclude the chapter, we will use the findings of research and prevailing theory to suggest ways in which we can each improve our own memory.

What is Memory?

We can define **memory** concisely as the persistence of experience and learning over time. We can think of the concept in two ways. On the one hand, we can consider memory as a *place* where past knowledge and information have been stored, ready to be accessed to assist us in our day-to-day activities. On the other hand, we can consider memory as a *process* by which information is first acquired, then stored, and later retrieved. These three stages — acquisition (more technically "encoding"), storage, and retrieval — are sometimes called "remembering behaviour." Either as a place or a process, the concept of memory implies the ability to acquire, store, and retrieve information, events, or skills. Researchers have found it useful to distinguish between these stages of memory. Let us now discuss how researchers go about measuring memory.

Memory is a process by which information or manual skills are first acquired, then stored, and later retrieved.

SOURCE: Courtesy Japan Information Centre, Consulate General of Japan.

Measuring memory

To research memory, we might simply ask an individual what he or she remembers. We could use this technique to investigate remote memories, such as those recollections we have of our early childhood. However, we probably would not be able to verify the accuracy of an individual's responses.

Most research in memory is much more sophisticated than that described above. Information should be presented carefully, recollections should be verified, and memory performance should be measured objectively. To obtain measures of memory, researchers commonly make use of the following tasks: recall, recognition, and relearning.

Recall

Recall is a task used to measure memory in which the subject is asked to retrieve information without the assistance of cues. (**Cues** are reminders or stimuli associated with a particular memory.) For example, an individual might be presented with a long list of words, and then at some specified time interval, the individual would be asked to repeat the words without the help of any cues. Usually, in the time interval between the presentation of information and retrieval, the researcher gives the subject an unrelated task, known as a **distractor task**. For instance, the subject might be asked to count backwards from 100 by 3's. The distractor task is designed to prevent the subject from rehearsing information before being asked to retrieve it. In general, recall is the most demanding test for measuring memory.

Recognition

Recognition is a task used to measure memory in which subjects are given cues and are asked whether particular information matches the information given initially. For example, a multiple-choice question is a recognition task, since the correct answer is provided and need only be recognized as the one correct answer. By contrast, an essay question is an example of a recall task. Recognition is a less demanding task than recall because of the presence of cues. Of course, the cues provided must accurately reflect the material to be remembered. Unfair multiple-choice questions, for example, can hinder the retrieval of information. In general, though, recognition tasks are a more subtle measure of memory, since they can give evidence of material that is only moderately well learned.

Relearning

Relearning is a task used to measure memory in which the subject is asked to relearn previously learned material. The increase in learning speed is an indication of how much of the original learning was retained. In general, relearning is an even more subtle measure of memory than either recognition or recall. For example, try to recall the first poem you memorized in grade four. You are probably unable to perform this little recall test. Now suppose that you are asked to choose correctly from a selection of the correct poem and several others that you never memorized. You might well be unable to perform this recognition test. However, if you were asked to memorize all the poems in the group, you would very likely memorize the grade-four poem more quickly than the others. Relearning is easier than learning new information.

Which task should be used in memory experiments: recall, recognition, or relearning? The answer depends on the hypothesis being tested and the type of memory being investigated.

TYPES OF MEMORY

The information processing model

In cognitive psychology, many investigators employ an **information processing model** (also known as a **compartments model**). According to this model, the human mind works in a logical series of separate steps, the way a simple computer does. When applied to memory, the information processing model focuses on the three fundamental mechanisms that we discussed earlier — namely, acquisition, storage, and retrieval. This model has proved to be very fruitful. Nevertheless, we should emphasize that our understanding of memory is far from complete. The computer analogy may turn out to be too limited. Research has already been conducted that examines the influence on memory of expectations, emotion, motivation, and other "higher" processes that are difficult to conceptualize in computer terms. Later in this chapter, we will consider an alternative model known as the levels of processing model. For now, we will continue to explore the information processing model.

According to the information processing model of memory, humans have three types of memory: sensory, short-term, and long-term. Sensory memory is our fleeting reception of information from the world. Short-term memory lasts longer but still has a limited and

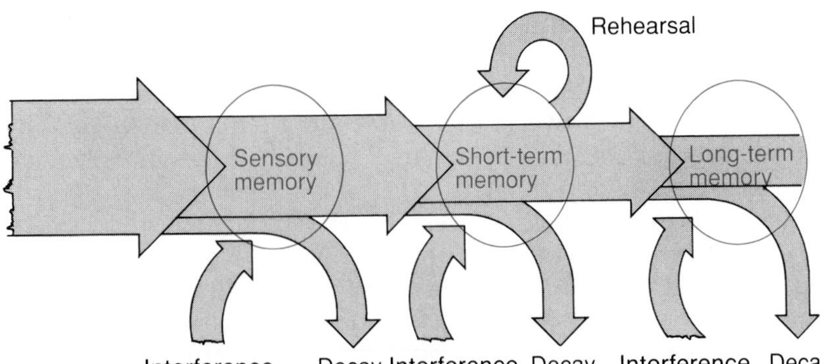

SOURCE: Adapted with permission from Allyn and Bacon, 1987.

FIGURE 7-1 The information processing model of memory

temporary capacity. Long-term memory permits more permanent storage of our experiences. A general schematic illustration of the information processing model of memory is given in Figure 7-1. Let us now examine the model in more detail.

Sensory memory

Before we can retain and retrieve information, we must first receive it. **Sensory memory** (also called **sensory register**) is the first and most temporary type of memory. It holds for very brief periods of time almost all the sensory information that we are exposed to. If we do not process the information further, we will lose it in under a second or two.

To date, research on sensory memory has concentrated on visual and auditory stimuli. In the visual system, it is as though the sensory memory has obtained a flash photograph of visual information, which it does not interpret in any significant way. If you were driving while conversing with a friend, and your friend suddenly asked, "What colour was the car you just passed?", you could probably answer. However, if your friend waited a few seconds to ask that question, you probably could not answer it. Information stored in the visual sensory register is sometimes called an **icon** (an exact replica), and the sensory memory for visual information is known as **iconic memory**. Without further processing, iconic memory usually lasts less than ½ second.

In the auditory system, it is as though the sensory memory briefly retains an echo of auditory information, which it does not interpret in any significant way. You have probably had the experience of being lost in your own thoughts while another person is talking to you. When that person complains, "You aren't listening to a thing I'm saying," you know perfectly well you haven't been. But you can say, "Yes I have! You just said (here you retrieve the last few words the other person said from sensory memory and repeat them)." "Okay," your friend says, "but it sure didn't seem that you were listening." This auditory record is very vivid and complete for about a quarter of a second and then available in diminished strength for about four seconds (Cowan, 1987). Information in the auditory sensory register is sometimes called an **echo**, and the sensory memory for auditory information is known as **echoic memory**.

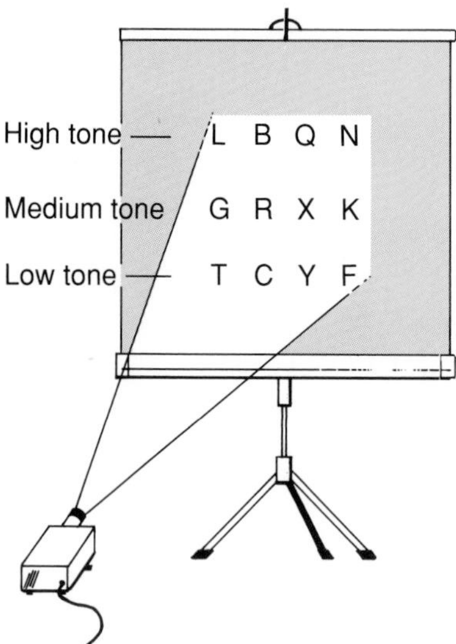

FIGURE 7-2 An example of the matrix of letters used in Sperling's experiment examining the visual capacity of sensory memory
SOURCE: Sperling (1960).

What evidence do we have for the existence of icons and echoes? In 1960, George Sperling conducted a revealing series of studies to examine the visual capacity of sensory memory. Subjects were very briefly shown three rows of letters, each four letters long. Then the subjects were asked to report as many letters as they could remember. Average performance on this task was only about three and one-half letters. This finding might suggest that the sensory register does not take a complete, accurate "photograph" of the image. But this conclusion is not necessarily true, as Sperling cleverly showed by modifying his experiment. Subjects were briefly shown the same sorts of letters as before, but now the subjects were instructed that they would only have to report one row, depending upon the tone that they heard. A high-pitched tone meant that they would be asked to repeat the top row, a medium-pitched tone meant the middle row, and a low-pitched tone meant the bottom row (see Figure 7-2). Sperling ordered the events so that the subjects had to rely on their sensory memories. The picture of the letters was presented for one-twentieth of a second, and the tone was played a fraction of a second later. Under these circumstances, subjects could almost always report all four letters correctly from whatever row they were asked for. It was as though a picture of the whole array of letters was held in the sensory register, but for only a very brief period of time. Presumably the subjects in the first experiment had scored so poorly because by the time they were reporting on the fourth or fifth letter, the icon had disappeared from their sensory memory.

Short-term memory

We have probably all had the experience of looking up a number in the telephone book but then forgetting it before we got to the phone. How can we explain this? When we looked up the number in the telephone directory, the information was stored in our sensory memory. However, the time between finding the phone number and actually dialing the number was greater than the time limit of sensory memory. Therefore, we "forgot" the number.

To retain information that initially enters the sensory register, we have to process it or rehearse it in some way. This allows us to transfer the information to short-term memory. When looking up a telephone number, we can process the information visually by consciously forming a mental picture of the number. More commonly, we process the information auditorily by repeating the number over and over again to ourselves. This process of repetition, known as **rehearsal**, enables us to keep the information active.

Short-term memory is the second kind of memory. Information is processed from sensory memory and then stored here, probably electrically. Short-term memory can hold information for up to about 30 seconds. As we mentioned above, the information must be processed in some way to enter short-term memory. We use the technical word **encode** to refer to the processing of information from the environment into forms that can be stored in short-term or long-term memory. We use the technical word **retrieval** to refer to the accessing of information stored in memory (i.e., "remembering").

How much information can we store in our short-term memory? Research has shown that the capacity of short-term memory, known as **immediate memory span**, is approximately seven (plus or minus two) discrete pieces of information. In the late 1800s Ebbinghaus (1913) conducted important research on the limits of short-term memory. But it was largely the work of George Miller (1956) that established seven as the "magic number" to describe our immediate memory span. This number may vary somewhat, although it is generally thought that at any given time our short-term memory capacity is between five and nine pieces of information (seven plus or minus two).

How do we operate with such a limited short-term memory? As you are reading this sentence, how do you remember the first words by the time you have reached the last ones? The answer would seem to be that we can extend the capacity of short-term memory by grouping distinct pieces of information together to make larger "chunks" of information. This process is known as **chunking**. For example, Canadian telephone numbers are seven digits (the magic number seven). Very often we "chunk" this string of digits to form three pieces of information. We can consider the exchange (the first three numbers) as the first unit, the next pair of digits as the second unit, and the final pair of digits as the third unit. Now we have only three pieces of information rolling around in short-term memory. As we shall see later in the chapter, chunking is also a useful technique for storing information in more permanent (i.e., long-term) memory.

Short-term memory is extremely vulnerable to information loss. After we dial the number, do we remember it? Information loss can take place in one of two ways. First, through a process known as **decay**, information seems to "evaporate" with the passage of time. (We have already encountered this phenomenon with sensory memory.) Second, through a process known as **displacement**, information stored in short-term memory is constantly being pushed out ("displaced") by new information. We noted above that the capacity of short-term memory is quite limited. For example, if we immediately look up a second telephone number and happen to exceed our seven-bit capacity, the earlier information is effectively pushed out of short-term memory and lost. It is very difficult to distinguish between decay and displacement in memory research. Generally, a continuous stream of thoughts and images is flowing through our consciousness.

In the late 1950s, Lloyd and Margaret Peterson (1959) developed a way to study short-term memory, which continues to serve as an important paradigm, or model design, for research in this area. They asked their subjects to try to remember a three-consonant sequence, such as "XFL." They then asked for recall after varying time spans, during which the subject engaged in a distractor task which prevented rehearsal. As the interval increased before recall, accuracy was found to decrease. The results indicated that information loss usually took place during the first 18 seconds. Moreover, some information was often lost after just a few seconds. Many other researchers have made use of this paradigm of (1) the presentation of information, (2) a distractor task, and (3) recall or recognition. Their studies show that short-term memory can hold information for up to 30 seconds, but it can lose information within a few seconds (Ellis & Hunt, 1989).

How do we remember a telephone number for longer than 30 seconds? Evidently we are able to process further the information in short-term memory and store it in a more lasting way.

Long-term memory

The third and longest lasting type of memory is known as **long-term memory**. It stores information through chemical changes in the brain. Long-term memory is relatively permanent and limited only by the storage capacity of the brain. This kind of memory holds a wide range of information, including our address and telephone number, our childhood memories, the knowledge we have acquired in the past, and, if we're lucky, information necessary for passing the final exam.

Long-term memories are sometimes forgotten, but the mechanisms behind this are not clearly understood. It is likely that our inability to remember such information arises from a failure in retrieval rather than from the disappearance of the memories. Long-term memory can be thought of as a warehouse full of filing cabinets. In these filing cabinets are file folders, and within these folders are sheets of papers containing information. Very often, our failure to retrieve a bit of information on one page, in one file folder, in one of these filing cabinets, stems from an ineffective strategy for searching for and accessing the information. It might seem that it would be an easier task if all of our memories could be stored alphabetically. However, our memories are very complex and varied, containing facts, experiences, ideas, and skills. It is quite amazing that we can remember anything at all, particularly considering that we sometimes file information without any apparent conscious effort.

FIGURE 7-3 The information processing model of memory
This is a more detailed diagram than the one shown in Figure 7-1. Visual and auditory memory storage processes are shown separately, but they do interact with each other.

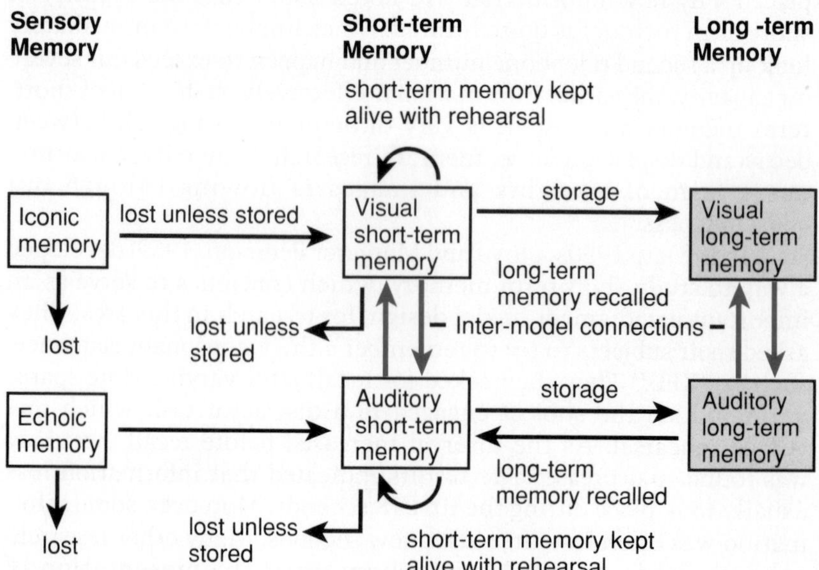

SOURCE: Adapted with permission from Allyn and Bacon, 1989.

In general, however, we consciously rehearse information in our short-term memory in order to store it in our long-term memory. (Later in this chapter we will examine in detail how information can be processed for long-term storage.) The relationships between the three types of memory — sensory, short-term, and long-term — are shown in Figure 7-3. This diagram depicts the information processing model of memory, with subdivisions into the visual and auditory branches.

Ebbinghaus (1913), whom we have already encountered in our study of short-term memory, conducted important experiments on long-term memory in the late 1800s. Ebbinghaus served as his own subject in these studies. In order to prevent practice effects and any reliance on old associations, he developed the nonsense syllable. A **nonsense syllable** is a three-letter "word" consisting of consonant-vowel-consonant that has no meaning. Examples would be "ZAC," "RIL," and "GAH." He devised 2300 of these to use in his research. He would then randomly select a number of nonsense syllables and try to memorize them as an ordered list. He carefully tabulated and assessed his efforts.

Figure 7-4 illustrates some of Ebbinghaus's findings. It shows one of his forgetting curves, indicating the amount of information lost over time. It is not surprising that Ebbinghaus found that specific memories diminish over time. But more importantly, he discovered that this memory loss does not occur at a steady rate. His most rapid forgetting came in the first hours and days after initial learning. This finding by Ebbinghaus seems very discouraging because if it is accurate, it means that we forget the majority of what we learn within a day. Postman (1975), however, has pointed out that more recent research shows that forgetting curves are usually less steep. This is not a reflection on Ebbinghaus's intelligence. He was learning virtually meaningless material, which is terribly difficult to remember because we can't incorporate it into our existing memory organization.

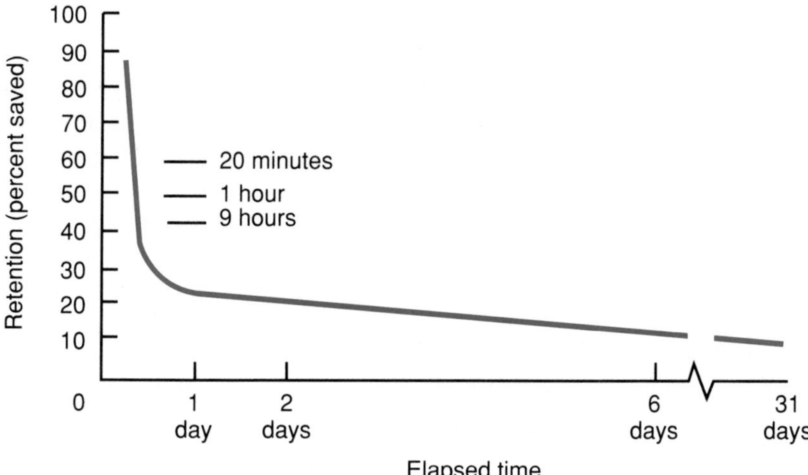

SOURCE: Ebbinghaus (1913).

FIGURE 7-4 A forgetting curve of Ebbinghaus
This curve illustrates the loss of information over time.

FIGURE 7-5 A graph showing the primacy and recency effects
Recall of information depends in part upon its position in the list presented.

Number of times word is recalled (in percent)
100
90
80
70
60
50
40
30
20
10
0
Primacy effect
Recency effect
Long-term memory
Short-term memory
1 2 3 4 5 6 7 8 9 10 11 12 13 14 15
Position in series

SOURCE: Adapted with permission from Allyn and Bacon, 1987.

Many studies have since been conducted in which subjects are asked to memorize and recall lists of words or nonsense syllables. (In general, the list of information to be remembered in a memory study is called the **target list**.) One reasonably consistent finding has been that the recall of a particular item depends in part upon its position in the list. Figure 7-5 represents a curve from one of these studies. According to the graph, information from the beginning of a list is more likely to be recalled than information from the middle of the list. This phenomenon is referred to as the **primacy effect**. The graph also indicates that information from the end of a list is more likely to be recalled than information from the middle of a list. This phenomenon is known as the **recency effect**. Note that according to Figure 7-5, the recency effect is slightly more powerful than the primacy effect. It is no wonder that effective speeches present major points at the beginning and at the end.

In preparing to execute his jump, Milt Ottey is probably concentrating on procedural memory.
SOURCE: Claus Anderson Photo Ltd.

How do we explain these phenomena? The primacy effect occurs probably because we have the most time to rehearse and process the first pieces of information. Therefore, we can store them best in long-term memory. By contrast, the recency effect occurs probably because we can store the last pieces of information best in short-term memory. We are assuming here that the time interval between the presentation of the information and recall does not exceed about 30 seconds (our immediate memory span). Information from the middle of a list does not enjoy either advantage. Too much time might elapse for retention in short-term memory, and there might not be enough time for secure storage in long-term memory.

Divisions of long-term memory

The mechanisms of our long-term memory may well depend on the nature of the information stored there. Some theorists divide long-term memory into two types: declarative memory and procedural memory (Anderson, 1985). **Declarative memory** is memory for "what"—namely, facts, rules, and ideas. It contains information that can be expressed verbally in a clear fashion. **Procedural memory** is memory for "how"—namely, learned responses to external stimuli. It contains skills that are extremely difficult to express verbally. Perhaps you remember how you learned to ride a bicycle as a young child. Your parents probably started by trying to explain the process to you in simple words. But soon after they were likely running along behind you balancing your bike. Instead of trying to explain the skill anymore, they probably advised you to relax and just do it. After numerous attempts — and perhaps a few spills — you eventually learned "how to do it." You probably still retain this "how-to-do-it" knowledge in your procedural memory.

The study of amnesia and certain types of brain damage (from physical injury or disease) provides dramatic evidence that declarative memory and procedural memory are in fact different kinds of memory. Some victims have forgotten their brother's name and what month it is, but they are still able to ride a bike and do their old job (Squire, 1987). In other words, they have lost declarative memory but not procedural memory.

In his research at the University of Toronto, Endel Tulving has suggested that declarative memory can be further subdivided into two categories. He calls them episodic memory and semantic memory (Tulving, 1972; 1985; and 1986). Once again this division of long-term memory is based on the type of information stored there. **Episodic memory** is memory for particular events ("episodes") that an individual personally experiences. Episodic memory might include what you had for breakfast this morning, or what happened in your last class. Episodic memory is contextual—that is, it is tied to specific places and times. When you recall an item from episodic memory, you can usually picture it as it actually occurred. By contrast, **semantic memory** is memory for items of knowledge that depends on the meaning of words and ideas ("semantics"). Your semantic memory will probably soon include the facts, ideas, and theories presented in this chapter. Unlike episodic memory, semantic memory is not contextual—that is, it is not necessarily linked to a specific time or place.

Some researchers reject this division of declarative memory into episodic memory and semantic memory. They concede that we do store different types of information in long-term memory. But they argue that it does not necessarily follow that we have separate memory systems for procedural memory, episodic memory, and

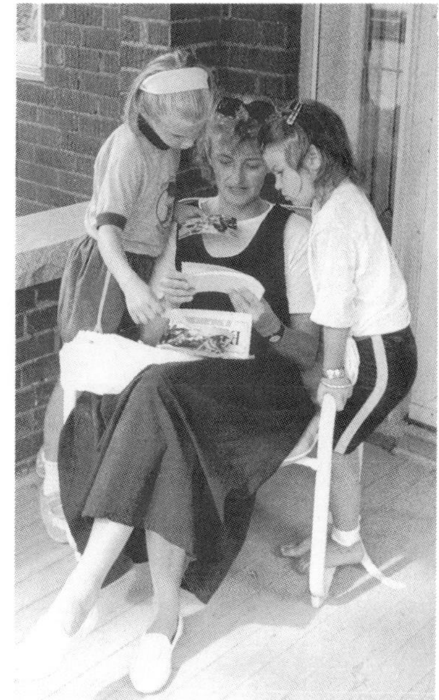

Episodic memory provides a kind of replay of an event.
SOURCE: Dick Hemingway.

Semantic memory provides abstract information which is not necessarily linked to one's personal experience.
SOURCE: *Jeopardy!* Steve Crise Photography. Photo courtesy of Merv Griffin Enterprises.

semantic memory (Humphreys, Bain, & Pike, 1989; Ratcliffe & McKoon, 1986). Other researchers agree with Tulving and have provided strong evidence for the existence of three separate kinds of memory (Mitchell, 1989). The issue is not yet settled. We do not fully understand the organization of long-term memory. Once we resolve the controversy about the divisions of long-term memory, we will be able to devise more effective models for teaching and learning.

Encoding and Storing into Long-term Memory: Getting and Keeping the Information In

A great deal of what we experience is never encoded and stored in memory. Most of what passes through sensory memory is never processed further—the colour of the cars we pass on the road, each throat-clearing sound we hear, the buzz of the fluorescent lights above our heads, and billions of other stimuli that bombard our senses. Even information that makes it into short-term memory is often displaced by new information before it can be stored in long-term memory. Let us now consider how and why certain information is selected and stored for remembering in long-term memory.

Automatic versus effortful processing

Encoding or processing information for storage in memory requires varying degrees of effort. Certain types of information seem to be much easier to encode than others. Hasher and Zacks (1979) draw a distinction between automatic processing and effortful processing. **Automatic processing** refers to the encoding of information for memory storage apparently without deliberate effort. Hasher and Zacks have shown that we often encode information about time, space, and frequency into episodic memory without having to try. For example, if you have ever been in a car accident or a near miss, you probably remember vividly the position of the cars and their movement. You did not have to work at articulating these events; they were encoded automatically. Where did you sit the last time you went to a movie? About what time of day was it when you last talked to your best friend? These are questions about time and space which you probably could answer, even though you made no effort to store the information. A question about frequency would be, About how many people sat near you yesterday at lunch? Hasher and Zacks argue that the brain probably evolved to store data about time, space, and frequency because this type of information is especially important for survival.

By contrast, we usually have to make some sort of effort to encode other types of information, including items of knowledge that depend on the meaning of words and ideas (i.e., semantic memory). For example, we have to try in order to store the idea of "the information processing model." The term **effortful processing** refers to the encoding of information for memory storage by deliberately rehearsing or transforming the information in some way. Let us now turn to some of the methods we employ for effortful processing.

Organization: Chunking and hierarchies

If our memories were simply randomly stored in the brain, life would be impossibly tedious as we would have to take time to remember our name or yesterday's date. Try saying the days of the week as fast as you can. Now try saying them in alphabetical order. This simple exercise illustrates that we have an organized and well practised way of remembering the days of the week. What is the fifth letter after L in the alphabet? Almost all of us have to say the letters from L to P mentally to answer this question because we have organized the alphabet in a particular order.

Chunking

We have already encountered the process known as chunking in our discussion of short-term memory. We also package distinct pieces of information into larger chunks for storage in long-term memory. For example, early in life we learn to group individual words into meaningful phrases. We also soon learn to group words and ideas into various types of categories (e.g., the "animal," "vegetable," and "mineral" categories of the game Twenty Questions). In fact, chunking plays an important role in the organization of most semantic memory.

Chunking enables us to organize new information into more familiar patterns. For instance, suppose that you are working for the government as an undercover agent. You are told to memorize the following code and destroy all written record of it:

CH2UN4KI6NG8PR1OC3ES5S

As 22 unrelated characters, this sequence might well strain your ability to encode it into long-term memory. However, with your training in memory, you look for larger groups and try to impose simple patterns. Soon you discover that you can treat the code as two interlocking series:

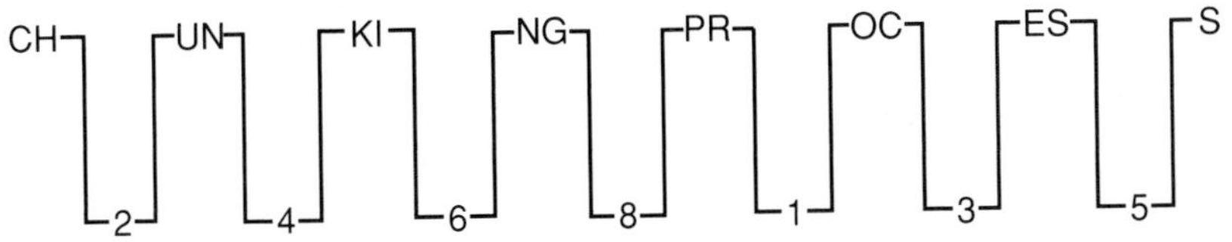

CH UN KI NG PR OC ES S

2 4 6 8 1 3 5

Then it is very easy to recall. You need only commit to memory the words "chunking process" and the rule that each pair of letters is followed by a number (even numbers in order for the first word and odd numbers in order for the second word).

Hierarchies

In the previous subsection, we mentioned that we often group words and ideas into various types of categories for memory storage. How are these categories related to one another? Some research suggests that they may be arranged in hierarchies. A **hierarchy** is an organizational framework in which more general categories branch out into narrower categories at each level. It is often represented by a so-called *tree diagram*. An example of a hierarchical organization is shown in Figure 7-6. It shows that "dog" is a subcategory of "mammal" which is a subcategory of "vertebrate" which is a subcategory of "animal." Each category has its own characteristics, but it also shares those characteristics of all the categories directly above it. Thus, for example, a dog barks (it is a dog), but it also has fur (it is a mammal), has a backbone (it is a vertebrate) and reproduces (it is an animal). Some sort of hierarchical organization seems to operate in the encoding (and retrieval) of semantic memory. For instance, one study has shown that words arranged in meaningful hierarchies are recalled more accurately than the same words presented in random order (Bower, Clark, Winzenz, and Lesgold, 1969).

The hierarchy model makes use of the idea of **associative networks in memory**. According to this idea, memories are linked to other memories through association. The more links that exist between a particular memory and others in the network, the better it is remembered. A point of meaning in an associative network is called a **node**. For example, in Figure 7-6 the concept of "dog" is a node.

The straightforward hierarchy model is useful, but it seems to be an oversimplification of how our memories actually work. Not all categories at the same level carry equal weight. For instance, in Figure 7-6, "dog" and "whale" are both subcategories of "mammal." However, people would take longer to answer the question "Is a whale a mammal?" than "Is a dog a mammal?" Evidently in our memory we have a concept of what a typical mammal is. A dog has more of this "mammalness" than does a whale. Therefore, "dog" is easier to classify (and hence, to encode and retrieve in the context of "mammal"). Another way to explain this is to say that "dog" has more associative links to the general concept of "mammal" than "whale" has.

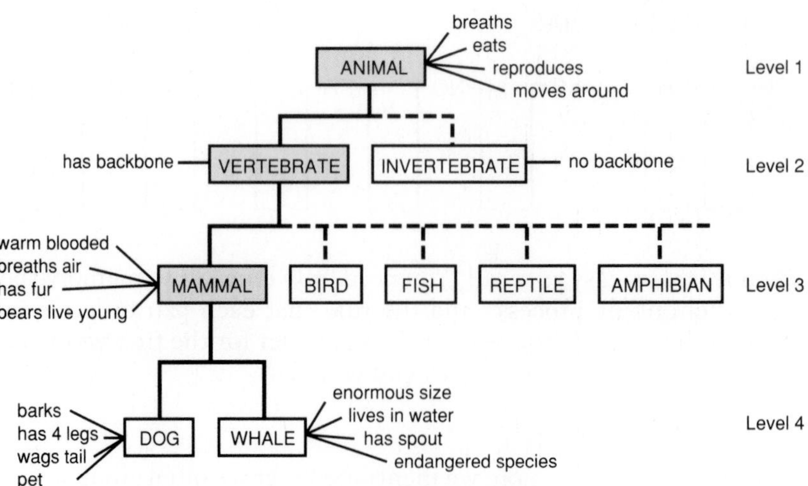

FIGURE 7-6 An example of hierarchical organization of concepts

According to the hierarchy model, when we encounter new information, we try to place it in the hierarchy nearest the nodes it is most related to. By forming connections with as many related nodes as makes sense, we encode the new information into the organization of memory. There is a practical side to this discussion. If we simply rehearse new information by rote, we will recall it less well than if we weave it in with what we already know. We will return to this point in the next section. The study of associative networks is one of the most promising and exciting in the area of memory.

Rehearsal and elaboration

In our discussion of short-term memory, we have already referred to *rehearsal*. When we look up a new telephone number in the phone book, we often repeat it mechanically over and over again to ourselves on the way to the phone so that we don't forget it. This process works well enough to keep the information active in our short-term memory. But how effective is rote repetition for transferring information from short-term memory to long-term memory? The answer is that rote repetition is not as effective as many people seem to think. Although the findings of experiments vary, it may well be that simple rehearsal leads to very little long-term storage (Rundus, 1977).

Research has conclusively shown that elaboration is much more effective than rehearsal for storing information in long-term memory (Craik & Tulving, 1975). **Elaboration** is a process of encoding in which the subject actively relates the given information to other items and experiences in meaningful ways. Methods of elaboration include reorganization, chunking, thinking of examples, and personalizing the information. Thus, to remember the word "trapeze" you might personalize it by thinking of a time you went to the circus. To remember the concept of memory "node," you might think of examples other than "mammalness" to illustrate it, such as how some chairs are more "chairlike" than others. You might also associate the concept of "node" with tree diagrams and think of other examples of hierarchies, such as the classification of minerals.

To remember this scene, you might focus on its unique features. This will help you to distinguish it from other similar scenes.
SOURCE: Dick Hemingway.

Elaboration is most useful for enhancing semantic memory and episodic memory. One experiment has demonstrated that elaboration can be effectively applied to the information presented in a textbook (Anderson, 1985). Two groups of subjects were given a chapter to read, and later they were asked test questions about it. The first group was also given a set of questions about the material before they started to read. These questions were different from the test questions. The second group—the control group—was not given any advance questions. According to the results of the experiment, the first group scored significantly higher on the test questions than the second group. Presumably, the advance questions encouraged the first group to elaborate the information more thoroughly and thus encode it more securely.

There are two main reasons why elaboration improves encoding. First, it increases the amount or depth of processing of the information. According to the model of associative networks (discussed in the preceding section), elaboration would be a means of actively forming connections with other memory nodes. Second, elaboration increases the "distinctiveness" of the information (Hunt & Mitchell, 1982; Ellis & Hunt, 1989). By focusing on the unique properties of the new information, we make it specific and distinguish it more clearly from other memories and information. Therefore, it is easier to retrieve later.

Parallel processing

Many of the older models of memory imply that memory is a one-track (serial) process, working in a step-by-step fashion. More recently, however, Rumelhart and McClelland (1986) have developed a **parallel distributed processing model** of memory. According to this model, many systems in the human brain process information at the same time. In other words, the systems operate in parallel, not serially. In Chapter 9, we will discuss evidence that the brain has independent "modules," all processing information simultaneously. This is an example of parallel processing.

Models of human memory have important applications in the area of **artificial intelligence**, the field in which computers are designed to simulate human thought processes. As researchers try to make computers "really think," they are drawing on the parallel distributed processing model. Traditionally, computers can perform only one little step at a time. Because they do the steps so fast, a lot seems to happen instantaneously. However, this is an illusion. By contrast, newer computers do have several processing units operating in parallel. The units work simultaneously to solve a given problem.

Imagery

We do not always rely solely on verbal meaning to store information in our long-term memory. Sometimes, we seem to encode information in a form that corresponds to each of our five senses. For instance, many people are able to bring to mind the faces of their parents (sight), remember a tune or recognize a friend's voice on the telephone (sound), identify the smell of burning rubber (smell), recall the taste of a grapefruit (taste), and recognize the feel of suede (touch).

For most of us, sight is the most important of our five senses for long-term memory. Allan Paivio of The University of Western Ontario (1986) argues that we normally store some memories verbally and other memories as mental images. It follows, then, that we do not always need words to think and remember. In some cases, images may well result in superior memory because they can be more detailed and distinctive than verbal memories. We do not yet fully understand how we encode visually as opposed to verbally. Perhaps the processes underlying imaged and verbal memories are the same (Kosslyn, 1986).

Imagery can be particularly helpful for procedural memory. In recent years, for example, sports psychologists have placed more and more emphasis on imagery as a means of improving the level of an athlete's performance. In some instances, competitors are advised to spend less time physically practising and more time visualizing a successful performance. This technique seems to work for recreational athletes as well as professionals.

One relatively rare ability in the field of visual memory is known as **eidetic imagery**, which is the ability to store detailed images with almost photographic accuracy. In fact it is popularly referred to as "photographic memory." Some people with eidetic imagery are able to reproduce verbatim long passages from material they have read only once. Haber (1979) found that only about 4% of the school-age children he tested had eidetic imagery. He let children view a complex picture on an easel for about 30 seconds. When the picture was removed, most children could describe its general features but not all of its smaller elements. These children's eyes normally wandered around as they tried to remember details. By contrast, the children with eidetic imagery were able to describe the picture in vivid detail. When they were asked about a particular part of the picture, they would usually stare at the easel where the image had been.

The levels of processing model

So far we have been looking at the *information processing model* (or *compartments model*) of memory. As we discussed earlier, the compartments model divides memory into three different kinds: sensory, short-term, and long-term. However, some theorists (Craik and Lockhart, 1972; Craik and Tulving, 1975) have proposed a different model, known as the **levels of processing model**. According to this model, memory is *not* divided into three distinct types. Instead, this model says there are an *infinite* number of "levels" of memory, as on a continuum. The more deeply we process information, the better we remember it.

The main difference between the compartments model and the levels model is shown in Figure 7-7. Do not be misled by the depiction of the levels model. The listing of three levels of processing (shallow, deep, and elaborative) is quite arbitrary. We could show any number of levels for this model. The important point to understand is that

FIGURE 7-7 A comparison of the information processing model of memory (three compartments) and the levels of processing model of memory (one continuum)

SOURCE: Adapted with permission from Allyn and Bacon, 1987.

COMPARTMENTS MODEL

- Sensory memory
- Short-term memory
- Long-term memory

LEVELS MODEL

Shallow processing
Deep processing
Elaborative processing

here memory is considered to consist of one continuum of increasing depth of processing.

The levels model was formulated as a result of some of the research into encoding. We have already talked about important processing methods, such as chunking, hierarchical organization, rehearsal, elaboration, and imagery.

In their experiments to support the levels model, Craik and Tulving (1975) asked subjects different questions about lists of words in order to encourage different types of processing. The subjects were not told ahead of time that they would be asked to recall the words. One group of subjects was asked to notice whether each word was written in capital letters. This group scored low when later tested for recall. Presumably these subjects used a relatively shallow level of processing. A second group of subjects was asked whether each word rhymed with another given word. This group evidently used a deeper level of processing, for they scored higher when later tested for recall. Finally, a third group of subjects was asked whether each word would make sense if used in a given sentence. This group scored highest of all. Presumably these subjects used the deepest level of processing. In general, we might conclude that deeper processing requires more semantic elaboration. It results in better memory even when it takes less time than shallower levels of processing.

It is controversial whether the levels of processing model is an adequate replacement for the compartments model of memory (Nelson, 1977). On the one hand, short-term memory does seem to operate differently from long-term memory. On the other hand, "deeper" processing certainly seems to facilitate memory. Eventually, the levels of processing model and the information processing model will probably be integrated into a more satisfactory model of memory.

RETRIEVAL AND FORGETTING FROM LONG-TERM MEMORY: GETTING THE INFORMATION OUT

We have encoded and stored a lot of information that we may never be able to use because we cannot retrieve it. Psychologists are interested in both how we access information stored in memory (i.e., retrieval) and why we forget.

Retrieval

As we discussed earlier, we can usually access information in short-term memory fairly easily. However, information is stored in short-term memory for only a very brief time. By contrast, tapping memories in long-term memory is more complicated. It usually requires an effort of some kind, at least with complex and less familiar memories.

Some memories seem to come to us automatically, but this is usually simply because we have rehearsed or retrieved them so often. The memory of your own name is an obvious example, even though it might seem odd. Many people would say, "But I don't have to remember my own name, I just know it." Clearly, though, "knowing" your own name requires retrieval of a memory that is so practised and familiar that the process seems effortless and automatic. Thus, we can see that one factor in retrieving memories is familiarity.

Cues

Another important variable in the search process of retrieving memories is the availability of retrieval *cues*. As we have explained earlier, cues are reminders or stimuli associated with a particular memory. A large part of memory seems to be organized into meaningful hierarchies of associated concepts and events. Therefore, one piece of information can act as a cue to help retrieve another piece of information. Suppose you wanted to remember what happened at the end of class last Wednesday. It would help to check the course outline and remember what the lecture was about, whom you were sitting with, where you were in the room, and so on. As you go through this list of cues, it is likely that you will suddenly be able to remember what happened.

We can use cues to jog our own memories. We have all probably had the frustrating experience of having to say, "Give me a minute. I *know* that I know that, but I just can't get it out right now." And we *do* know the information. The problem is one of retrieval, not of knowledge. The term **tip-of-the-tongue-phenomenon (TOT)** is used to refer to the inability at a particular moment to retrieve a piece of information that one is certain one knows. Yarmey (1973) studied the TOT by showing pictures of famous people to subjects and then asking the subjects to name them. Many subjects experienced TOT feelings. They found that they could eventually retrieve the memory by thinking of the famous person's profession, going over hunches about the person's initials, and thinking of the last time that they had heard about or seen pictures of the famous person.

All the external factors present when encoding takes place are known collectively as the **context**. These factors can later act as cues for retrieval. In other words, context improves memory. Therefore we will do better on tests if we take them in the room where we learned the material. We will even do better if the professor is in the room than if an assistant administers the test.

Our own internal state or condition at the time of learning can also provide cues for later retrieval. The effects of the internal factors present in the learner during encoding and retrieval are known collectively as **state-dependent learning**. Thus, the overall context of learning includes external cues and internal cues. If we are hungry when we study, we will later be able to retrieve the information more easily when we are hungry. If we are happy when we meet a new person, his or her name will be easier to remember when we are happy (Bower, 1981). Some studies suggest that state-dependent learning is stronger for memory about internal events (such as imagining, thinking, and reasoning) than it is for memory about external events. A shift in mood is more likely to reduce memory for one's own thoughts than for events actually happening at the time (Eich & Metcalfe, 1989).

We will remember better if we learn in a context similar to the one in which we will have to recall our knowledge.
SOURCE: Dick Hemingway

There are many striking stories of intoxicated people hiding large sums of money and then not being able to find the money when they sober up. They simply cannot remember. We might be tempted to attribute this to an alcohol-induced failure to notice what they were doing. But in most instances we would be wrong. Most people *can* remember the location of the money the next time they are drunk —back in the same state in which they encoded the memory. In a fascinating demonstration of state-dependent learning, Ehrlichman and Halpern (1988) asked college women to recall events and experiences. The researchers divided the subjects into three groups. During the questioning, the first group was exposed to a pleasant odour, the second group to an unpleasant odour, and the third group (the control group) to no special odour at all. All the women were then asked how happy the events were that they recalled during the experiment. The subjects who were exposed to the pleasant odour recalled happier events than the subjects who were exposed to the unpleasant odour. This study indicates that one's general emotional state (or mood) can act as a cue for the retrieval of memories with similar emotional associations. This phenomenon is sometimes called **mood-congruent recall**. Mood-congruent recall is one example of state-dependent learning. The "state" of the learner is his or her mood. For example, when people are depressed, they tend to remember more unhappy events than when they are not (Teasdale & Fogarty, 1979).

State-dependent learning has been clearly demonstrated in a number of well-known studies. However, many other recall experiments do not exhibit any effects of state-dependent learning (Blaney, 1986). What should we conclude from these results? Evidently one's emotional state acts as a strong cue for retrieval only in certain situations. More generally, we might argue that the failure to use cues is just one possible explanation of forgetting. Let us now turn to some of the other causes of forgetting.

Decay

As discussed earlier, *decay* is the loss of information caused by the passage of time. Some researchers have described this phenomenon in terms of a fading memory trace, where the trace itself is some form of physiological representation of an event in memory. Most of the research that supports decay as a cause of forgetting concerns sensory and short-term memory. We have already referred to the study by Peterson and Peterson (1959) which shows that short-term memory usually suffers information loss after just 18 seconds. However, other studies suggest that decay is only a minor cause of forgetting from long-term memory. Unfortunately, it is difficult to isolate decay in research studies because the passage of time is inevitably accompanied by some cognitive activity. On the one hand, as time passes we do subjectively find that our recollections become blurred, confused, or lost. On the other hand, the cause may well be that new cognitive activity has "interfered" with the old memories. Earlier we mentioned that displacement seems to be an important cause of forgetting from short-term memory. Now let us consider interference as a likely cause of forgetting from long-term memory.

Interference

Interference is the tendency for an item to be forgotten because of competition from other information in memory. The interfering information may have been learned before or after the item in question. One explanation that has been suggested for interference is that it is likely to occur when more than one item is associated with a particular cue.

In many laboratory studies investigating interference, subjects are asked to learn more than one list of words. The subjects are then tested for recall of only one list (the so-called target list). The researchers use the other lists to provide interference. The results are then compared to control trials or control groups, where subjects have to learn only one list. The studies indicate that two types of interference can occur. First, a list learned before the target list can hinder recall of the target list. This interference on the recall of information by other information learned earlier is called **proactive interference**. Second, a list learned after the target list can also hinder recall of the target list. This interference on the recall of information by other information learned later is called **retroactive interference**. Briggs (1957) studied retroactive interference by having subjects memorize a list of adjective pairs. Then different groups of subjects learned a second list 2, 4, 10, or 20 times. The more times the second list was learned, the more interference there was with remembering the first list.

Both types of interference seem to be common. Nevertheless, research suggests that proactive interference is a more powerful cause of forgetting than retroactive interference.

Motivated forgetting

"Motivated forgetting" sounds like a contradiction in terms. Why should we be motivated to forget? The answer lies in the theories of Sigmund Freud (to be examined in more detail in Chapters 9 and 10), in particular his concept of repression. According to Freud, **repression** is a defence mechanism by which we unintentionally eliminate painful and threatening thoughts from our consciousness and memory. Freud went on to argue that even when we succeed in repressing thoughts, they still exert an influence on our behaviour. Freud's ideas about repression are controversial. Many practising psychotherapists argue that their experience clearly indicates that repressed thoughts do influence people. However, experimental psychologists have shown that most of the psychoanalytical research on repression has been flawed. Furthermore, experimental psychologists reject clinical experience as valid support for Freud's complicated theory of repression. Nevertheless, some researchers have recently presented evidence to support a new model of learning theory and brain functions that incorporates the concept of motivated forgetting (Galin, 1974; Glucksberg & King, 1974; and Martin, Hawryluk, Berish, & Dushenko, 1984). We will examine this evidence in Chapter 9.

Implicit memory

When we speak of remembering, we usually assume that a person either remembers or does not remember. In other words, we assume that a sharp line exists between remembering and forgetting. But this assumption is not justified. There are many indications that we can have partial memories. Go watch professors wandering around the parking lot with their partial memories of where they parked their car this morning (we'll discuss partial memories more in Chapter 9). Or think of the tip-of-the-tongue phenomenon that we described earlier.

In addition, we seem to have a memory for information that we cannot consciously recall but that does have a demonstrable effect on our behaviour. This kind of memory is called **implicit memory** (Schacter, 1987; Schacter & Graf, 1989). Eich (1984) devised a dichotic listening study to demonstrate the existence of implicit memory. In general, **dichotic listening** is a procedure in which a subject is given two different messages simultaneously, one in each ear (see Figure 7-8). In Eich's study, subjects were instructed to repeat verbatim a prose passage being read into their right ear and to ignore whatever "distracting" information was being read into their left ear. For the experimental group, the distracting information included word combinations such as "taxi fare." For the control group, whenever the information given to the left ear included the sound "fair," the word was not biased by context to mean "fare." In a later spelling test, experimental subjects were more likely to spell the word as "fare," whereas control subjects tended to use the more common spelling "fair." The subjects could not consciously remember any of the words presented to their left ear. Nevertheless, those words clearly affected their later performance. Thus, in some unconscious way, subjects did "remember" those words. This experiment vividly illustrates what we mean by implicit memory.

FIGURE 7-8 Dichotic listening In Eich's dichotic listening study, subjects ignored the left-ear input and could not recall it later, but their performance was affected by it.

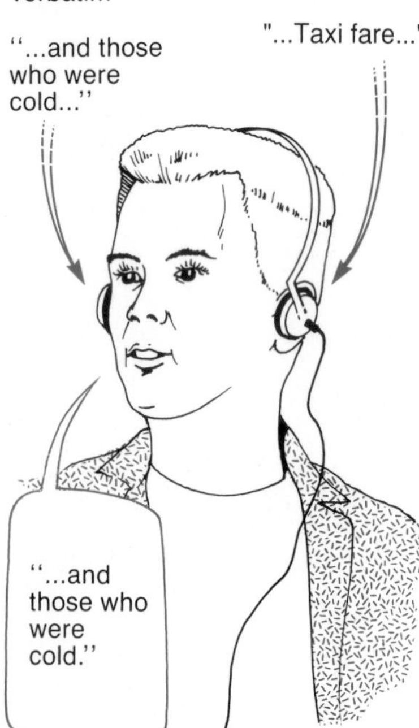

Amnesia

Amnesia is pathological (i.e., abnormal) forgetting that results from disease, physical injury, or emotional trauma. It is characterized by a failure in normal encoding or retrieval or both, especially with regard to episodic memory. There are different types of amnesia, depending on the nature of the disease, injury, or trauma.

Amnesia can affect short-term memory, long-term memory, or the interaction between them. The process by which information is transferred from short-term memory (reverberating neural circuits) to long-term memory (permanent chemical changes) is known as **consolidation**. Research suggests that consolidation takes about 30 minutes. Thus it is possible that an injury to the brain can disrupt the consolidation process and prevent the transfer of information to long-term storage.

Retrograde amnesia is amnesia that occurs after a head trauma in which the patient loses memory of some period before the trauma. Often retrograde amnesia affects the period just prior to the trauma. The classic line of the person who has been knocked out is "Where am I? How did I get here? The last thing I remember is . . . ." A friend of ours was once driving a car and was hit by a train as he crossed the tracks. In relating the incident to us later, our friend said that he could remember starting his car and driving toward the tracks but nothing after that. He was worried that before the accident he had somehow "blacked out" or suffered some kind of loss of control. We assured him that the theory of consolidation provided a more likely explanation of what had happened. Evidently, starting his car and going toward the tracks were information that he had securely stored in long-term memory. However, the next events were probably only in short-term memory at the time of the crash. His head injury would have disrupted the electrical activity in his brain and prevented the chemical changes necessary for long-term storage. Thus, his memory of those last few events before the crash was lost forever.

Another type of amnesia affects the ability to create new long-term memories. **Anterograde amnesia** (also called **post-traumatic amnesia**) is amnesia that occurs after a head trauma in which the patient is unable to remember information or experiences originating after the injury. Usually, the long-term memory for information prior to the trauma is unaffected. Individuals suffering from anterograde amnesia can often recall details preceding their injury such as their childhood experiences, old friends and family, and the knowledge they acquired in school. But after their injury, they are unable to remember someone they have met hours earlier.

Later in this chapter we will explore the physiology of memory. There we will again discuss various types of memory impairment caused by trauma and disease.

THE CONSTRUCTION AND RECONSTRUCTION OF MEMORIES

Memory is not a passive process that just happens to us. In order to store information in our memories, we actively filter, organize, and elaborate it. However, one consequence of our active participation is that we sometimes create distorted memories. When we discussed perception in Chapter 4, it was humbling to discover that "seeing is not necessarily believing." Through our perceptual processes, we construct a somewhat inaccurate version of reality. Further distortions occur with memory. When we retrieve memories, we often actually recall only part of what happened in the past and then reconstruct other parts of the particular memory. Because we don't do this consciously, we might believe strongly that what we remember is what we actually experienced. The reconstructive nature of memory was studied over 50 years ago by Bartlett (1932). He presented individuals with stories from other cultures that were unlike traditional Western fiction in structure and focus. He later asked the individuals to recount the stories. He found that the individuals often recalled the stories incorrectly by adding material that wasn't in the original,

SOURCE: *Bizarro* by Dan Piraro. Reprinted by permission of Chronicle Features, San Francisco, CA.

leaving out large parts, and revising other sections. In effect the given stories were altered to resemble the type of stories the individuals were used to. In one given story, for example, an Indian warrior joins a war party which later turns out to consist of ghosts. As subjects in Bartlett's experiment retold the story, all references to ghosts eventually dropped out. Subjects not only eliminated the unfamiliar mystical element of the original, they also added motives for some of the characters in the story in order to reflect Western values such as duty to family. Many subjects also tacked on a moral at the end, following the pattern of Western fables.

More recent research has provided additional evidence that we tend to reconstruct our memories (Loftus, 1980; Neisser, 1982). One fruitful area of investigation has been the study of eyewitness accounts. We will look at such studies in the Special Topic of this chapter.

Schemas

A **schema** is an abstract representation of a typical object, procedure, or event that we build from our knowledge and experiences of the world around us. Schemas are blueprints of what we expect particular things and situations to be like when we encounter them. We each have our own schemas for classrooms, textbooks, professors, lectures, writing exams, and all sorts of other objects and events. We use schemas to filter, process, and interpret information. Thus when we encounter a new situation, we don't have to go through the incredibly complex processing of every detail. For example, when we enter a classroom, we use the blueprint of a "classroomness" schema to form a memory of this particular classroom. We usually pay close attention only to what stands out.

Schemas save us a lot of time and effort. However, they also distort our memories. If you are later asked to describe the classroom you were just in, some of the details will come from the memory

Although schemas can sometimes save us a lot of time and effort, they can also mislead us into *seeing* what we think we should see. A traditional wedding photo might not be quite as normal as it first appears to be.
SOURCE: Courtesy the Sindrey family.

you constructed from the actual classroom, but other details may come from your schema. Therefore, some of the details that you "remember" may actually be incorrect. You may have had the disconcerting experience of reporting something that you remembered quite clearly, but then finding that others insisted that it never happened that way at all. Evidently, the subjects in Bartlett's experiments had strong schemas for what stories should be like. They honestly remembered the stories as fitting their own "blueprints."

A schema for an event is called a **script** (Schank & Abelson, 1977). We have powerful expectations for the course that most particular events will follow. For example, when taking an exam, we may be accustomed to a procedure in which the professor passes out soft-leaded pencils. This detail will then form part of our script for exam-taking. Suppose at one particular exam, a student passes out the pencils instead. It is possible that later we will quite clearly "remember" the professor passing out the pencils. What we remember is the reconstructed memory based partly on a script.

THE BIOLOGY OF MEMORY

Trying to locate memory

We don't know exactly where in the brain memories are stored and processed. It may well be that nearly all of our brain participates in some fashion in the function of memory. It is unlikely, for example, that specific memories are localized in one place. Memory seems to be stored diffusely. In other words, the memory of a particular event, concept, or skill probably involves many sites in the brain (Woody, 1986). This redundancy, if true, has great survival value. If memories are stored in several places, they will be difficult to destroy through injury.

Nevertheless, researchers have discovered that certain brain structures figure prominently in the functioning of memory. In particular, the temporal lobes and the hippocampus seem to play important roles (see Figure 7-9). This does *not* mean that memory traces are actually laid down in these anatomical areas. It simply means that the temporal lobes and the hippocampus participate in the storage or retrieval of memory.

FIGURE 7-9 The temporal lobes and the hippocampus seem to play important roles in the functioning of memory

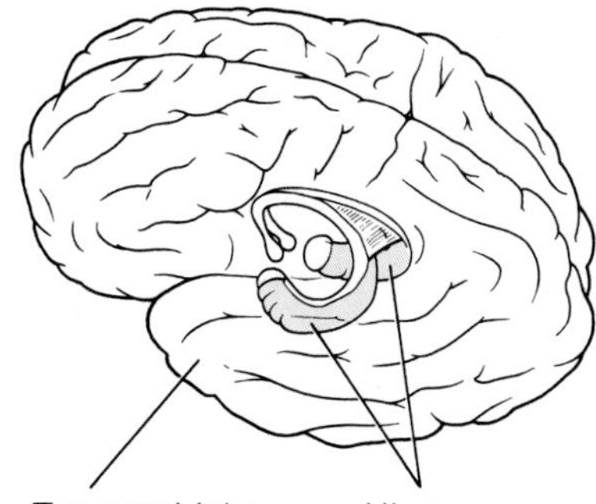

The **temporal lobe** is the lower, side portion of each hemisphere of the cerebral cortex. As we discussed in Chapter 2, the temporal lobes are primarily responsible for hearing. But other evidence suggests that the temporal lobes are also among the most important anatomical structures for the functioning of memory. For example, damage to these regions often produces significant impairment in memory. Furthermore, the famous Montreal neurosurgeon Wilder Penfield has demonstrated that electrical stimulation of certain areas of the temporal lobe can result in vivid recollections of past experiences (Penfield & Perot, 1963).

The **hippocampus**, a structure of the limbic system, is also crucial for the functioning of memory. When the hippocampus is affected by disease or injury, various types of memory disturbance result. For example, encephalitis (i.e., inflammation of the brain) often disrupts the normal activities of the hippocampus. Victims of encephalitis usually lose some memories. The hippocampus is also adversely affected by **Korsakoff's syndrome**, a brain disorder associated with vitamin deficiency caused by alcoholism. Not only do victims of Korsakoff's syndrome suffer memory losses, they also **confabulate**, or unwittingly fill in the blank spaces in their memory by creating false memories. Yet another type of memory impairment related to the hippocampus is provided by the patient H.M., whom we mentioned near the beginning of this chapter. To treat H.M.'s epilepsy, surgeons removed part of his hippocampus. The results were documented and studied by Scoville (1957) and by Brenda Milner of the Montreal Neurological Institute (1966). H.M. was able to remember events that occurred before the surgery. But he lost the ability to transfer new information and experiences from short-term memory to long-term memory. H.M. could retain information only as long as he was able to rehearse it. Once he was distracted, the information was lost. Subjectively, every day was literally a new one for H.M. Even after several years, it seemed to H.M. that his surgery had occurred just yesterday.

Trying to understand the physiology of memory

Although we know that particular brain structures are important in the functioning of memory, we still do not fully understand the physiology of how memory works. Traditionally, scientists looked for specific physical changes within the brain that might be responsible for actual memory storage. The assumption was that each memory would result in some form of physical change in the brain and serve as a permanent record of our experience. More recent efforts, however, have suggested that we modify this assumption.

A major physiological theory of memory was proposed by the Canadian psychologist Donald Hebb in 1949. Hebb suggested that when groups of neurons are stimulated, they form patterns of activity. If this same pattern of neural activity tends to be restimulated, a regular and reverberating neural circuit is established. This **cell assembly** then serves as the basis of short-term memory. With continued activity, permanent structural changes appear that result in long-term memory. Thus, according to this theory, consolidation is the process by which temporary reverberating circuits change to more permanent structures.

Research and clinical observations appear consistent with Hebb's theory. For example, electroconvulsive therapy, which causes a disruption of the brain's electrical activity, also produces memory impairment. Similarly, a physical blow to the brain that causes a disruption of neural activity also leads to memory loss. As we noted earlier, an individual who has suffered a severe head injury in an accident is often unable to recall the events of the accident and the period immediately preceding it.

Today, we use the term **engram** to refer to the trace within the nervous system by which a memory is stored. In short-term memory, the engram seems to be an active electrophysiological process. In long-term memory, the engram seems to be a relatively permanent chemical change.

Our current understanding of the chemical changes involved in long-term memory is based on discoveries in biochemistry and genetics. Our brains are "prewired" to develop into human brains (instead of ape brains or fish brains) because of deoxyribonucleic acid (DNA). This inherited "memory" is common to all of us of the human species. But how do we account for the different memories of individuals? One theory is that a large messenger molecule called ribonucleic acid (RNA) may be the biochemical mediator of more personal memories. Research to support this theory was originally conducted by Hyden and his colleagues (Hyden & Lange, 1972). They exposed a group of rats to various learning tasks and later investigated the chemical composition of these animals' brains. They predicted that the brains of the trained rats would differ from those of untrained rats. In fact, they did find greater amounts of RNA in the brains of the trained animals. They concluded that an organism's brain chemistry is very subtly changed by its experiences. Later theorists have suggested that the more vigorously a neuron fires, the more RNA is produced.

Integrating neuroscience and cognitive psychology

There are many ways to look at memory. Cognitive psychologists ask how memory works at the level of information-processing. They study such phenomena as sensory, short-term, and long-term memory; declarative and procedural memory; and patterns of interference. Neuropsychologists ask how memory works at the level of physiological functioning. They study such phenomena as injury, disease, brain structures, biochemistry, and neural activity. Sometimes, cognitive psychologists and neuropsychologists argue over whose approach is the more fruitful. However, both approaches are necessary and they should complement each other. We are now coming to the stage where the theories of cognitive psychology are dovetailing with the findings of neurological research on memory. For example, Squire (1987) argues that the brain is organized into separate and independent neural systems, and Hirst (1989, p. 124) points out that "a wide range of evidence suggests that each of these neural systems has its own memory capacity, both short-term and long-term." Another illustration of this dovetailing has emerged in the study of amnesia (Baddeley, 1982). Researchers have found that certain kinds of amnesia damage declarative memory but not procedural memory. In one study, subjects with anterograde amnesia were able to learn and remember the skill (i.e., the procedure) of reading words inverted in a mirror reflection just as well as non-amnesic subjects. The non-amnesic subjects also remembered the actual words used in the experiments better than they remembered other words. However, this was not the case for the amnesic subjects. Evidently, they had no declarative memory for the specific words.

The victims of Alzheimer's disease include not only the patients themselves but also their families and friends.
SOURCE: "Sonia" (S-19186), National Film Board of Canada

Memory in old age

Generally, the older we get, the more forgetful we appear to be. Memory problems in the aged can be caused by poor diet, impaired blood circulation to the brain, the overuse of prescription drugs, or disease (Smith, 1979). Senility, for example, is a disease that is not the same as the normal aging process. **Senility** (or senile dementia) is a pathological state. The term refers to the progressive degeneration of brain tissue in people over the age of 65. Senility is characterized by the deterioration of memory, particularly the ability to acquire and store new information. Older memories, such as those of childhood, appear to be relatively unaffected.

In its symptoms, Alzheimer's disease closely resembles senility. **Alzheimer's disease** is a chronic brain disorder marked by the progressive degeneration of neurons. Victims gradually lose their memory capabilities and other cognitive functions. The tragic consequences of Alzheimer's disease have become well known in recent years. It is the leading cause of mental deterioration among the elderly. Some say Alzheimer's disease may become the most prevalent neurological disorder in history (Bloom, Lazerson, & Hofstadter, 1985). Its cause is unknown. In their search for a cure, researchers are looking at a number of possible causes: viruses, chemical deficiencies in some areas of the brain, and elevated levels of some toxins, particularly aluminum, in the system of victims. There may even be different types of the disease, some of which may have a hereditary component (St. George-Hyslop, Tanzi, Polinsky et al., 1987). The victims of Alzheimer's disease include not only the patients themselves but also their family and friends. Even though patients may retain full physical ability, they suffer increasing helplessness and confusion, often swinging from irrational anger to childlike emotionality. The treatment of Alzheimer's disease is frustrating. According to May and Rapoport (1989, p. 184): "The devastation that is Alzheimer's disease is at once so immutable and frighteningly commonplace; understandably, this has led to the avid search for a cure, even though its root cause is unknown. . . . Because the pathogenesis of Alzheimer's disease is unknown, all therapeutic approaches are necessarily highly speculative."

Drugs and memory

As we pointed out earlier in this chapter, it takes some time for our short-term memories to consolidate into long-term memories. Anything that disrupts brain functioning during this time will influence memory storage and thus memory retrieval. Therefore, any drug that interferes with normal brain activity will influence memory. Such drugs can include alcohol and medications that depress the central nervous system. Marijuana seems to affect short-term memory and thus interferes with later recall of information learned while "high." In one study, a direct relationship was established between the strength of dose and the degree of interference with memory (Darley, Tinklenberg, Roth, Hollister, and Atkinson, 1973). Weil and Zinberg (1969) report that marijuana users often start a sentence and then lose the meaning before the sentence is finished. On the other hand, some drugs appear to improve memory. Drugs related to the hormone vasopressin seem to increase the learner's motivation and ability to recall information. Epinephrine (adrenaline) also seems to improve memory, especially when it is administered immediately after learning takes place (Gold and Delaney, 1981).

STRATEGIES FOR IMPROVING MEMORY

With all the material that we have discussed in this chapter, what have we learned that will enhance our memories?

Improving encoding

Because we are bombarded with enormous amounts of information in our day-to-day activities, it is not surprising that we forget some of it. To remember material over a long period, we first have to store it in short-term memory and then transfer it to long-term memory. Information that is trivial or meaningless is usually held or stored for only very brief periods of time. In general, we transfer only important or meaningful information from short-term to long-term memory. Even then, many of the details which were held in short-term memory may be lost in the translation. If we do not transfer information to long-term memory, it will not be there for us to retrieve later.

Sometimes we try to store too much information in short-term memory. We will then lose details that are not at all trivial. This can happen when we try to cram for examinations. We may overload our memories and prevent information from being transferred to long-term storage. Even if we possess powerful memories, we will forget information if we do not encode it properly. Poor attention, concentration, and comprehension at the encoding stage will inevitably lead to a failure to remember.

Sometimes, though we may have stored information in long-term memory, we may be unable to recall it. This is a problem of retrieval. Given the tremendous amount of information we hold in memory storage, it is surprising that we are able to remember the amount of information that we do. We should realize, however, that retrieval failure is often caused by poor encoding. Therefore, at the encoding stage we should do our best to use effective cues and forge strong associations with other material in our memories.

Minimizing interference

Earlier in this chapter we spoke of interference. According to this theory, both proactive and retroactive interference can lead to forgetting. It makes sense, then, that minimizing interference should result in better remembering.

One strategy that has proven useful in enhancing memory is called overlearning. **Overlearning** is the process of repeating and reviewing material after it has already been learned. Perhaps overlearning minimizes interference. Or perhaps overlearning facilitates the chemical changes needed for long-term memory. Whatever the reason, overlearning does enhance recall (Nelson, 1977).

Another strategy that seems to reduce interference is to increase the meaningfulness of the information. For example, words are more easily recalled than nonsense syllables. Whatever we can do to enhance the meaningfulness of information is important. Thus, we will be able to remember dates and events in history better if we try to grasp an overview of the chronological framework and seek to understand the significance of each event.

In keeping with the theory of retroactive interference, research has shown that we can enhance recall by minimizing activity in the period between learning and retrieval. An old study (Jenkins & Dallenbach, 1924) indicated that students performed better on examinations if they slept after studying rather than engaging in their more normal activities. Other studies have shown that retroactive interference is greatest when the interfering information is very similar to the information which is initially learned. Less interference would occur, for example, if your studying included two very different subjects rather than two that were similar. Strand (1970) showed a more subtle way to minimize interference. He demonstrated that we can improve recall by studying different subjects in different rooms, thereby associating each subject with a different set of cues.

Finally, taking short breaks between periods of studying appears to enhance recall. Thus we should avoid massed practice, where we might spend six straight hours studying for a test. We will remember more if we use spaced practice, spending the same six hours in three two-hour blocks separated by breaks (Wickelgren, 1981).

In short, if we have a lot of studying to do, we should space study sessions, try to review dissimilar subjects together, overlearn the material, add to its meaningfulness, and get a good night's sleep before the exam.

SCUBA is an acronym for Self-Contained Underwater Breathing Apparatus.
SOURCE: Aqua Images

Mnemonic devices

Mnemonics are techniques or systems that aid memory. Although they may take many forms, all mnemonics make use of certain encoding methods that provide cues for retrieval. A simple type of mnemonic device is a set of verses which provide a rhythmic series of cues for later retrieval. "Thirty days has September . . . " is an example that helps us remember the number of days in each month. Acronyms and acrostics are other verbal formulas that can be used as mnemonic devices. An **acronym** is a new "word" that is formed by the first letters of a series of words. Examples include NATO (North Atlantic Treaty Organization), WHO (World Health Organization), and LSAT (Law School Admission Test). An **acrostic** is a poem (or sentence) in which the first letter of each line (or word) spells out a word, phrase, or other information. For instance, "Every Good Boy Does Fine" permits those of us with little musical training to remember that the names of the musical notes written on the lines of the treble staff are E, G, B, D, and F.

More elaborate mnemonics, described by Higbee (1977), make use of the power of imagery and our ability to encode visually. Such mnemonic devices include the link system, the loci system, and the peg system. Each of these systems relies on our drawing an association between an image and a particular word, fact, or detail that we wish to remember.

The link system

In the **link system**, one forms a mental picture or image of the first item to be remembered. Then one forms an image of the second item that is physically attached ("linked") to the first. For example, if the first two items are "chair" and "cat," we might first visualize a chair and then picture a cat sitting on it (see Figure 7-10). The link system can be applied to a set of items that must be remembered in order, since a series of images are built up, each relying on the previous one.

The loci system

One shortcoming of the link system is that forgetting one item can lead to problems in recalling the remaining items. The loci system can help to overcome this shortcoming. It was developed by Greek orators of antiquity, who found it a very effective aid in remembering long speeches (Yates, 1978). The **loci system** is a mnemonic system in which one first chooses a familiar set of places ("loci"), usually in a building. Then one forms an image of ("imagines") each thing to be remembered. Finally, one stores each image in one of the selected places. For example, you might choose a set of locations in your apartment or house. You could remember the series of locations by walking around the rooms in your imagination. Therefore, even if you forgot the item associated with one location, you could easily move on to the next location. An example of using the loci system is shown in Figure 7-11. Experimental support for the effectiveness of this mnemonic system is very convincing. A study conducted by

FIGURE 7-10 Using the link system
One could visualize this image to remember the following ordered list: chair, cat, man, horse, and boat.

FIGURE 7-11 Using the loci system
One could remember a grocery list (coffee, potatoes, detergent, chicken, and milk) by imagining the listed objects as placed in specific and unusual locations.

Bower (1973) indicated that individuals who were taught to use this system were able to recall 72% of five 20-word lists, whereas others not using this system were able to recall only 28%.

The peg system

As we mentioned earlier, one disadvantage of the link system is that forgetting one item can lead to problems in recalling the remaining items. The peg system is another device that can help to overcome this shortcoming. Like the loci system, the peg system is suited for sequential or numerical recall. The **peg system** is a memory aid in which one learns an ordered set of mental "pegs," forms an image of each item to be remembered, and visually associates each image to one of the pegs. These pegs usually consist of number-word pairs (e.g., one-bun, two-shoe, three-tree, four-door, and so on) or letter-word pairs (e.g., A-apple, B-ball, C-cup, D-duck, and so on). Note that peg systems often make use of rhyme or spelling so that they may be easily learned. After one masters a set of pegs, one forms an image of each item to be remembered. Then one visually associates each image to one of the pegs. For example, suppose you wanted to remember the names of 20 celebrities in a particular order. You could start with an alphabetized set of pegs (e.g., A-apple, B-ball, C-cup, and so on). Then you could form an image of the first person eating an apple, the second person playing basketball, the third drinking coffee, and so on (see Figure 7-12).

The "pegs" in the peg system act in the same way as the "places" in the loci system. They function as cues for the ordered retrieval of information. The peg system does have some disadvantages, however. It is cumbersome to use for long lists of material, and it requires that different associations be formed for every peg.

SQ4R

SQ4R is an acronym for a very effective study strategy: Survey, Question, Read, Reflect, Recite, and Review. This strategy is extremely useful in learning and recalling the details of large amounts of factual information such as that found in a textbook. Many students simply open the book to the first chapter and start plowing through the words. Then two pages later they find that only about six words have stuck. An important principle in the SQ4R method is to prepare properly before you start detailed reading.

To "Survey" means gaining an overview of the information to be learned and subsequently recalled. With this textbook, for example, you should consider the outline of major headings given at the beginning of each chapter. By familiarizing yourself with the scope of the chapter and the information to be covered, you will find each paragraph easier to understand. You will be able to place the details into the larger picture.

The "Question" stage of SQ4R means formulating questions about the material surveyed. For example, after looking at the major headings of this chapter, you should ask yourself what might be contained in each section. It would be useful to write down a set of questions relating to each topical area for later review.

To "Read" may seem straightforward. Obviously, the reading should be thorough and complete. However, during this stage, you should also think of the questions that you formulated about the material. In your reading, you should try to acquire the basic facts as well as a clear understanding of each topic. Making notes would help here.

To "Reflect" on what you have read means thinking about its meaning. You should also try to relate the new material to other information and elaborate it in various ways.

To "Recite" means repeating in your own words the information that you have just read. You will find it helpful both to recite it aloud and to write it down. You may switch back and forth between reading and recitation, with the pace determined by the complexity of the material. Complex material might require recitation after phrases; more straightforward information might be recited after reading a paragraph. A common experience for teachers is that they understand the material vastly better after they have had to explain it to someone else. If you have studied with a friend, you may have had the same experience. Even if you thought you understood certain information quite well, you probably understood it much better if you had to articulate it to your friend. Articulating information to yourself can work just as well.

To "Review" means periodically going back over the material. You should review the questions you formulated as well as the notes you made during the reading, reflecting, and reciting stages. Review can also include rereading the summary at the end of the chapter or skimming through the entire chapter again.

It might seem that all these steps are cumbersome. Nevertheless, you will end up remembering more if you follow the SQ4R strategy than if you spend the same amount of time simply reading and rereading the book.

Some of the ideas that we have discussed in this chapter help to explain why SQ4R is such an effective study strategy. The Survey gets us to organize the material in our own minds. By dividing the material into "chunks," we are able to deal with what would otherwise be an overwhelming amount of information. Forming Questions continues this process and encourages us to begin elaborating the material. (Recall the textbook experiment described by Anderson,

FIGURE 7-12 Using the peg system
A. You are given a list of names to memorize in sequential order.
B. Establish a set of mental "pegs," such as a = apple, b = ball, c = cup, d = duck, e = egg, and so on.
C. Finally, associate each person on the list with the appropriate mental "peg."

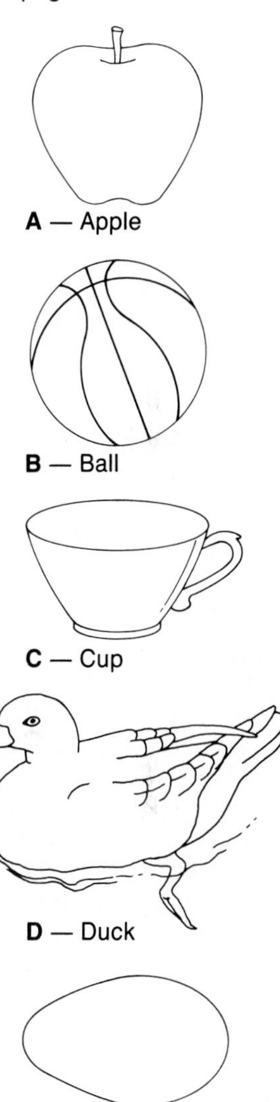

1985, that we discussed earlier.) By making notes, we provide ourselves with cues for later recall. By actively Reading, Reflecting, and Reciting, we elaborate the material more thoroughly and thus make it easier to retrieve later. Finally, by Reviewing the material, we make use of overlearning, which enhances recall.

We should realize from this chapter that memory is most effective when it is an active process. It is not sufficient simply to think we can absorb information passively. We should actively strive to organize, associate, rehearse, elaborate, and use cues in order to make new information meaningful.

SPECIAL TOPIC Eyewitnesses—Is Seeing Believing?

One of our traditional assumptions about memory is that permanent, unalterable traces of information of past experience exist in our brains. However, this assumption is being questioned by research on eyewitness testimony in civil and criminal legal cases (e.g., Loftus, 1979; Hall and Loftus, 1984; Wells and Loftus, 1984; and Yarmey, 1984). Canadian researchers are also participating in the debate. At least six Canadian universities have research programs that are investigating the phenomenon of eyewitness reports (Wells and Turtle, 1987).

In one American study (Loftus, Miller, & Burns, 1978), subjects were shown a series of slides depicting a car accident in which a Datsun came up to either a stop sign or a yield sign. Later the subjects were asked questions about what they had "witnessed." Some questions were deliberately misleading. For example, subjects who had seen a stop sign might be asked, "Did another car pass the Datsun while it was stopped at the yield sign?" In later questioning, subjects who had not been asked misleading questions correctly identified the type of sign they had seen over 90% of the time. The shocking thing is that subjects who had been asked misleading questions were *wrong* over 80% of the time. Evidently, the question had planted new, erroneous information that the subjects later incorporated when they *constructed a new memory*.

The implications of this research for the legal system are disturbing. We depend on eyewitness testimony in criminal trials. Buckhout (1974) staged a mugging scene which was shown on American television. Immediately after the scene was broadcast, viewers saw a lineup of suspects and phoned in to identify the mugger. Of 2000 viewers who phoned in, less than 10% chose the right suspect! Although the mugger

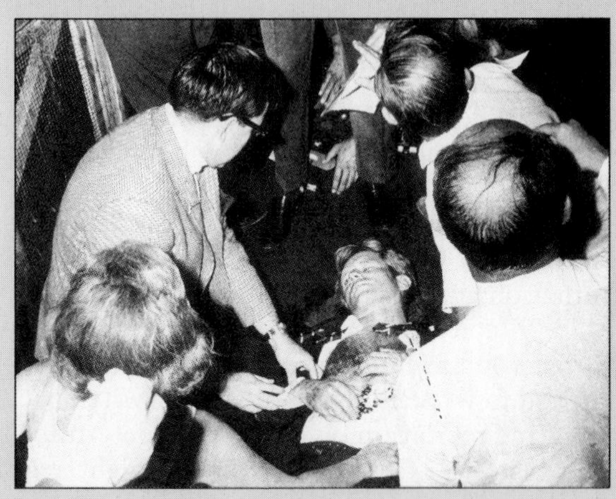

How well could you describe this scene after viewing it for several minutes? Would you construct distorted memories if a clever questioner planted suggestions in your mind?
SOURCE: The assassination of Robert Kennedy. UPI/ Bettmann Newsphotos.

was Caucasian, about a third of the viewers picked out a suspect who was Black or Hispanic. Evidently those viewers held schemas about crimes and particular minority groups that led them to construct distorted memories of the staged event.

Moreover, it may well be that some criminal lawyers are adept at "creating memories" in suspects and witnesses (Dershowitz, 1986). If a stop sign can be changed into a yield sign in memory so easily, clever "suggestions" of what happened can soon become reality for a witness. The newly reconstructed memory would then seem to be true to the witness. He or she would not be consciously lying.

Before we decide that all eyewitness testimony is unreliable, however, we need a great deal more evidence. Most of the studies that challenge the accuracy of eyewitnesses have been experiments and not research on actual eyewitnesses to real crimes. Such field research is very difficult to do. Nevertheless, two researchers from the University of British Columbia organized a study around an actual crime (Yuille and Cutshall, 1986). They studied 13 witnesses to a shooting in which one person was killed and another wounded in broad daylight. The witnesses' descriptions of events at the time of the shooting and several months later were remarkably accurate and showed little change over time. The researchers also reported that the witnesses were not significantly misled by leading questions. Therefore, the researchers concluded that eyewitnesses can be trusted. This one study does not, of course, settle the issue of the accuracy of eyewitness reports. But it does underline the necessity for more field research on real situations. On the one hand, memory has been shown to be constructive and subject to significant distortions. On the other hand, the significant responsibility of witnessing a crime may help individuals resist these distortions.

In the legal system itself, lawyers often challenge the reliability of eyewitness testimony in general and the credibility of particular witnesses. However, an early study by Loftus (1974) suggests that it is difficult to discredit the testimony of an eyewitness. Loftus created a hypothetical case and had her subjects act as jurors. The subjects were strongly influenced by an eyewitness, even when it was disclosed that the witness had poor eyesight and was not wearing glasses. In one scenario, only 9 of 50 subjects voted a defendant guilty on the basis of physical or circumstantial evidence alone. However, an eyewitness identification by a bystander changed the result to 36 of 50 voting for a guilty verdict. Even when the testimony of the eyewitness was shown to be suspect, 34 of 50 subjects voted for a guilty verdict. Loftus coined the term "discrediting failure hypothesis" to refer to the difficulty of discrediting the testimony of an eyewitness. Yet since 1974, other experimenters have not been able to replicate Loftus's results consistently. The general opinion today seems to be that "eyewitness testimony is readily disbelieved when there is reason to do so, at least in [experiments]" (Elliot, Farrington, & Manheimer, 1988).

Seven eyewitnesses identified the man on the right, Father Bernard Pagano, as an armed robber. The actual robber was Ronald Clouser, the man on the left.

SOURCE: UPI/Bettmann Newsphotos

Chapter Summary

1. Memory can be thought of either as a place where information is stored or as a process by which information is retrieved. In both cases, the concept of memory implies three stages of remembering behaviour: acquisition, storage, and retrieval. To research memory scientifically, one needs to use tasks that provide objective measurements. The most common tasks are recall, recognition, and relearning. In general, recall is the hardest task, and relearning is the easiest. Relearning provides the most subtle measure of memory.

2. Most investigators of memory use an information processing model of memory. This model has greatly increased our understanding of memory. However, it does not adequately account for the influence of "higher" processes (such as expectations, emotion, and motivation) on memory. According to the information processing model, humans have three major types of

memory: sensory memory, short-term memory, and long-term memory.

3. Sensory memory is usually retained for no more than a second or two. Visual information is stored as an exact replica called an icon. Auditory information is stored as an exact record called an echo. Information decays very rapidly unless it is processed and stored in short-term memory.

4. Short-term memory can be retained for up to 30 seconds. Our immediate memory span is about 7 discrete pieces of information. We can increase the capacity of short-term memory by grouping pieces of information together to form larger chunks. Information can be lost from short-term memory in a matter of seconds through decay and especially through displacement. For experiments on short-term memory, an important paradigm consists of the presentation of information, a distractor task, and recall or recognition.

5. The transfer of information from short-term memory to long-term memory generally requires rehearsal. Long-term memory is relatively permanent. The failure to remember something once stored in long-term memory usually arises from a failure in retrieval rather than from the disappearance of the memory. Forgetting curves indicate that information loss occurs most rapidly soon after storage. Other studies reveal that the recall of information depends in part upon its position in the sequence presented. We are more likely to remember information from the beginning of a list (the primacy effect) and the end of a list (the recency effect) than information from the middle of a list.

6. Long-term memory can contain a wide variety of information, including facts, ideas, experiences, and skills. Some theorists have divided long-term memory into memory for "what" (declarative memory) and memory for "how" (procedural memory). Other researchers have subdivided declarative memory into memory for experienced events (episodic memory) and memory for ideas (semantic memory). It has not yet been determined whether different memory systems exist for these divisions of long-term memory.

7. Memories must be encoded or translated into a form that the brain can store. We often seem to need no more than automatic processing to encode information about time, space, and frequency into episodic memory. By contrast, we usually have to employ effortful processing to encode information into semantic memory.

8. Memories appear to be organized in different ways in the brain. We can use chunking to reorganize new information into more familiar patterns for storage in long-term memory. Hierarchies seem to play a leading role in the organization of semantic memory. The hierarchy model (with its tree diagrams) relies on the hypothesis of associative networks (and nodes). The more associative links we forge between a given concept and other memories, the better we will remember it.

9. Rehearsal, or rote repetition, is certainly not the best way to encode information in long-term memory. Elaboration is much more effective, especially for semantic memory. By creating associations between the new information and existing memory, we increase both the amount of processing and the distinctiveness of the new information.

10. Some theorists support a non-serial model of memory called the parallel distributed processing model. According to this model, the brain performs several operations simultaneously. The parallel distributed processing model has been used to design new computers in the field of artificial intelligence.

11. Sight is generally the most important of our five senses for long-term memory. In some instances, visual memories are superior to verbal memories because imagery is more detailed and distinctive than words. Imagery can be particularly helpful for procedural memory. Some athletes have found that visualizing successful performances is an effective way to improve their performance.

12. In contrast to the information processing model (and its three types of memory), the levels of processing model views memory as one continuum of increasing depth. Craik and Tulving have supported the levels model by demonstrating that deeper or more elaborative types of processing result in better recall. The information processing model and levels of processing model each has advantages. Perhaps they will eventually be integrated into a more complete model of memory.

13. Memories that are accessed often from long-term memory are easier to remember. Familiarity facilitates retrieval. Cues also play an important role in the retrieval of information. When we experience the tip-of-the-tongue phenomenon, we can use cues to try to jog our memories. The surrounding environment during encoding — the so-called context — can provide cues. We can retrieve information more easily if we are in the same place where we originally learned it. According to state-dependent learning, our own internal state during encoding can also act as a cue. We can retrieve information more easily if we are in the same mood in which we originally learned it.

14. Decay, or the passage of time, seems to be at most a minor cause of forgetting from long-term memory. According to the theory of interference, an item is more commonly forgotten because of other information learned before (proactive interference) or after (retroactive interference) the item in question. According to Freud, we engage in motivated forgetting when we unintentionally try to eliminate painful and threatening thoughts from our consciousness and memory. This notion of repression is very controversial.

15. Some dichotic listening experiments reveal that we have a memory for information that we cannot consciously recall but that does have a demonstrable effect on our behaviour. The concept

of implicit memory implies that there is no sharp dividing line between remembering and forgetting.

16. Pathological forgetting known as amnesia assumes two main forms. Patients suffering from retrograde amnesia are unable to remember some period prior to the trauma. Their memory loss is probably caused by a disruption in the consolidation process during the trauma. Patients suffering from anterograde amnesia are unable to create long-term memories of material originating after the trauma.
17. Memory is an active process. When we retrieve a memory, we often reconstruct part of it. Schemas allow us to filter, process, and interpret an enormous amount of information. But by relying on schemas, we are liable to distort memory inadvertently.
18. Memory is probably stored diffusely in the brain. The most important anatomical parts of the brain for the functioning of memory seem to be the temporal lobes and the hippocampus.
19. For short-term memory, storage may result from an electrophysiological process. According to Hebb, short-term memories are produced when patterns of neurons are restimulated so that temporary reverberating neural circuits are established. For long-term memory, storage may result from a relatively permanent chemical change. Recent research suggests that ribonucleic acid (RNA) may help to carry personal memories in humans. Today the findings of neurological research are beginning to confirm some of the theories of memory of cognitive psychology.
20. Senility and Alzheimer's disease are the leading causes of memory disorder in the elderly. Both diseases are characterized by progressive degeneration of brain tissue. There are no known causes or cures for these diseases.
21. Depressants interfere with memory storage and retrieval by disrupting the consolidation process.
22. To enhance our memories, we should strive to minimize interference. Therefore, we should overlearn material, increase its meaningfulness, reduce competing information and activities, and space our study sessions. To aid our memories, we can also employ mnemonic devices such as the link system, the loci system, and the peg system. To learn large amounts of factual information, we should apply the study strategy known as SQ4R: Survey, Question, Read, Reflect, Recite, and Review.

KEY TERMS

Acronym A new "word" that is formed by the first letters of a series of words. It can serve as a mnemonic device.

Acrostic A poem (or sentence) in which the first letter of each line (or word) spells out a word, phrase, or other information. It can serve as a mnemonic device.

Alzheimer's disease A chronic brain disorder marked by the progressive degeneration of neurons.

Amnesia Pathological forgetting that results from disease, physical injury, or emotional trauma.

Anterograde amnesia Amnesia that occurs after a head trauma in which the patient is unable to remember information or experiences originating after the injury. It is also called *post-traumatic amnesia.*

Artificial intelligence The field in which computers are designed to simulate human thought processes.

Associative networks in memory Memories are linked to other memories through associations. The more links that exist between a particular memory and others in the network, the better it is remembered.

Automatic processing The encoding of information for memory storage apparently without deliberate effort.

Cell assembly Hebb's notion of patterns of neurons that are restimulated by repeated experiences.

Chunking Grouping distinct pieces of information together to make larger "chunks" of information.

Compartments model Another term for an *information processing model.*

Confabulate To unwittingly fill in the blank spaces in memory by creating false memories.

Consolidation The process by which information is transferred from short-term memory (reverberating neural circuits) to long-term memory (permanent chemical changes).

Context All the external factors present when encoding takes place. These factors can later act as cues for retrieval.

Cues Reminders or stimuli associated with a particular memory.

Decay The loss of information, particularly in sensory and short-term memory, caused by the passage of time.

Declarative memory Memory for "what" — namely, facts, rules, and ideas. It contains information that can be expressed verbally in a clear fashion.

Dichotic listening A procedure in which a subject is given two different messages simultaneously, one in each ear.

Displacement The loss of information stored in short-term memory caused by the flow of new information into short-term memory.

Distractor task In memory research, an unrelated task given to the subject in the interval between the presentation of information and retrieval. It is designed to prevent the subject from rehearsing the information before being asked to retrieve it.

Echo Auditory information stored in sensory memory.

Echoic memory Branch of sensory memory that briefly stores pieces of auditory information as echoes.

Effortful processing The encoding of information for memory storage by deliberately rehearsing or transforming the information in some way.

Eidetic imagery The relatively rare ability to store detailed images with almost photographic accuracy.

Elaboration A process of encoding in which the subject actively relates the given information to other items and experiences in meaningful ways.

Encode The processing of information from the environment into forms that can be stored in short-term or long-term memory.

Engram The trace within the nervous system by which a memory is stored. In short-term memory, the engram seems to be an active electrophysiological process. In long-term memory, it seems to be a relatively permanent chemical change.

Episodic memory A subtype of declarative memory. It is memory for particular events ("episodes") that an individual personally experiences.

Hierarchy An organizational framework in which more general categories branch out into narrower categories at each level.

Hippocampus A structure of the limbic system. It is crucial for the functioning of memory.

Icon Visual information stored as an exact replica in sensory memory.

Iconic memory Branch of sensory memory that briefly stores pieces of visual information as icons.

Immediate memory span The capacity of short-term memory. It can hold seven pieces of information, plus or minus two.

Implicit memory A memory for information that we cannot consciously recall but that does have a demonstrable effect on our behaviour.

Information processing model A model of cognitive psychology in which the human mind is seen to work in a logical series of separate steps, the way a simple computer does. According to this model, there are three types of memory: sensory, short-term, and long-term.

Interference The tendency for an item to be forgotten because of competition from other information in memory.

Korsakoff's syndrome Brain disorder associated with vitamin deficiency caused by alcoholism. It is marked by memory losses and confabulation.

Levels of processing model A model of memory according to which there are an infinite number of levels of memory, as on a continuum. The more deeply we process information, the better we remember it.

Link system A memory aid in which one forms images of the objects to be remembered and then links the images together in the order given.

Loci system A memory aid in which one selects a set of places, forms an image of each thing to be remembered, and stores each image in one of the selected places.

Long-term memory The third and longest lasting type of memory. It stores information relatively permanently, probably through chemical changes in the brain.

Memory The persistence of experience and learning over time.

Mnemonics Techniques or systems that aid memory. Mnemonics use certain encoding methods that provide cues for retrieval.

Mood-congruent recall The tendency to retrieve memories that are similar in emotional tone (mood) to one's current emotional state.

Node A point of meaning in a network of associations in memory.

Nonsense syllable A meaningless three-letter "word" consisting of consonant-vowel-consonant. It is often used in memory research.

Overlearning The process of repeating and reviewing material after it has already been learned.

Parallel distributed processing model A model of memory according to which many systems in the human brain process information at the same time; that is, the systems operate in parallel, not serially.

Peg system A memory aid in which one learns an ordered set of mental "pegs," forms an image of each item to be remembered, and visually associates each image to one of the pegs.

Post-traumatic amnesia Another name for *anterograde amnesia*.

Primacy effect The phenomenon in which information from the beginning of a list is more likely to be recalled than information from the middle of a list.

Proactive interference The interference on the recall of information by other information learned earlier.

Procedural memory Memory for "how" — namely, learned responses to external stimuli. It contains skills that are extremely difficult to explain verbally.

Recall A task used to measure memory in which subjects are asked to retrieve information without the assistance of cues.

Recency effect The phenomenon in which information from the end of a list is more likely to be recalled than information from the middle of a list.

Recognition A task used to measure memory in which subjects are given cues and are asked whether particular information matches the information given initially.

Rehearsal The process of repeating information in order to keep it active in short-term memory.

Relearning A task used to measure memory in which the subject is asked to relearn previously learned material.

Repression A defence mechanism by which we unintentionally eliminate painful and threatening thoughts from consciousness and memory.

Retrieval The accessing of information stored in memory (i.e., "remembering").

Retroactive interference The interference on the recall of information by other information learned later.

Retrograde amnesia Amnesia that occurs after a head trauma in which the patient loses memory of some period before the trauma.

Schema An abstract representation of a typical object, procedure, or event that we build from our knowledge and experiences of the world around us.

Script A schema for an event.

Semantic memory A subtype of declarative memory. It is memory for items of knowledge that depend on the meaning of words and ideas ("semantics").

Senility A pathological state. It refers to the progressive degeneration of brain tissue in people over the age of 65.

Sensory memory The first and most temporary type of memory. It holds for very brief periods of time almost all the sensory information that we are exposed to.

Sensory register Another term for *sensory memory*.

Short-term memory The second type of memory. Information is processed from sensory memory and then stored here, probably electrically. It can hold information for up to about 30 seconds. See also *immediate memory span*.

SQ4R An acronym for a study strategy: Survey, Question, Read, Reflect, Recite, and Review.

State-dependent learning The effects of the internal factors present in the learner during encoding and retrieval. The presence of the same factors can act as a cue.

Target list In memory research, the list of information that is to be remembered.

Temporal lobe The lower, side portion of each hemisphere of the cerebral cortex.

Tip-of-the-tongue phenomenon (TOT) The inability at a particular moment to retrieve a piece of information that one is certain one knows.

Suggested Readings

Ellis, H. C., & Hunt, R. R. (1989). *Fundamentals of human memory and cognition*. 4th ed. Dubuque, Iowa: Wm. C. Brown Publishers. This is a fairly advanced and well-written textbook that will take you further into the field of memory and the nature of thinking.

Loftus, E. (1980). *Memory: Surprising new insights into how we remember and how we forget*. Reading, MA: Addison Wesley. The author is a leading researcher on memory. We have discussed some of her work on eyewitness testimony in this chapter. This book is written for the lay reader and provides many suggestions, based on solid research, for improving memory.

Luria, A. R. (1968). *The mind of a mnemonist*. New York: Basic Books. An interesting book by one of the world's leading brain researchers. Luria investigates the amazing feats of recall by a Russian reporter who had an extraordinary memory.

Neisser, U. (1982). *Memory observed: Remembering in natural contexts*. San Francisco: Freeman. Rather than emphasizing laboratory experiments, this book focuses on studies of memory carried out in everyday situations.

CHAPTER 8

A
BC
DEF
GHIJ
KLMNO
PQRSTU
VWXYZ12
34567890

Thinking and Language

WHAT IS A thought? Where is a thought when it is not being thought? Most people have trouble with the first question and reject the second question as silly, even though they can't quite say why. These questions raise some troubling, fundamental issues about what it means to be human, to be conscious, to be aware. Are thoughts *things* that we possess in a place called our mind? Or are thoughts *processes* that occur in our brain? It seems more fruitful to view thoughts as processes. If a thought is a process, then it doesn't exist anywhere when it is not being "thought." It simply isn't happening right now, even though the brain is still structured so that the thought might happen again in the future. We should emphasize, however, that not everything that goes on in the brain qualifies as thinking. Most of us have said something like, "I did that without thinking," even though we performed some complicated act that clearly required extensive brain activity.

In this chapter, we will explore some fundamental questions about thinking and language. This material will enable us to investigate some of the complexities of thinking and consciousness in the following chapter.

Thinking and language are unique areas in psychology. We have to use our limited capacity to think about what thinking is and our limited language to explain what language is. Nonetheless, these topics, along with memory, are among the main concerns of cognitive psychology. As we pointed out in Chapter 1, **cognitive psychology** is the theory that cognitions (thinking, learning, remembering, and other mental processes) are the most important causes of behaviour. We also use the term cognitive psychology to refer to that branch of psychology which studies the "higher" mental processes, including attention, concentration, memory, reasoning abilities, planning, organizing, decision-making, problem-solving, and communication. Cognitive psychology investigates the processes that go on between the time a stimulus affects an organism and the time that organism responds. Thinking and problem-solving play major roles here.

WHAT IS THINKING?

It is difficult to define thinking precisely. Let us tentatively define **thinking** as the internal manipulation of symbols in order to process information. Symbols would include words, images, and special notations such as mathematical and musical symbols. Symbols can be combined into rules, concepts, and principles. Later in this chapter and in Chapter 9 we will see some difficulties with this definition because of the limits it places on what thinking is. For example, we all sometimes perform actions "without thinking," even though the act involves some kind of information processing. For now, though, let us limit thinking to information processing that manipulates symbols.

Our personal identity is largely determined by how we think. This is reflected in how we behave, how we solve problems, and how we make decisions and judgments. Indeed, thinking may form the cornerstone of our species, homo sapiens (literally, the knowing man). Are humans unique in having the capacity to reason, plan, problem-solve, remember the past, anticipate the future, form concepts, and use abstractions? Some other animals possess some of these abilities. One question we will grapple with is whether the difference between animals and humans is quantitative rather than qualitative. Is human thinking more complex than animal thinking but otherwise exactly the same (a quantitative difference)? Or do we have some particular ability that animals lack (a qualitative difference)? Another question we will address is whether computers can be designed to simulate all aspects of human thinking. Are we merely very complex machines?

Researching thinking

The study of internal and private processes is difficult. Nevertheless, research methods have been developed that help us understand what goes on inside the "black box." Let us examine four such methods.

Introspection

In the later 1800s, the structuralists began to apply scientific principles to their study of brain mechanisms. They devised a research method known as **introspection** in which trained observers examine their own mental processes and report their mental experiences in detail. The structuralists tried to develop consistent methods for describing feelings, images, sensations, and thoughts.

Introspection has at least two serious weaknesses, however. First, there is no way to resolve a discrepancy between the reports given by two different individuals on the same sort of inner experience. Second, introspection addresses only conscious experience, neglecting preconscious or unconscious activities. We will see in the next chapter that unconscious influences are important in our understanding of human behaviour.

A psychologist may make behavioural observations of a child under different circumstances and then make inferences about the child's thought processes.
SOURCE: Dick Hemingway.

Behavioural observation

Another method for investigating cognitive processes is known as **behavioural observation.** Here, we directly observe how people solve problems or deal with given situations under controlled conditions. From the changes in observed behaviour, we can make inferences about the thinking or reasoning processes involved. Behavioural observation is particularly suitable for research on the thinking and problem-solving of young children. For example, we can take babies of differing ages and expose them to different objects which are then hidden from view. When we uncover the objects at specified time intervals, we can observe movements and facial reactions of the babies to these objects and to others that they have not seen before. Differences might shed light on the cognitive processes of recognition.

An offshoot of behavioural observation is the study of errors made in problem-solving. The researcher generally assumes that our errors are not random. The usual assumption is that errors reflect a systematic, though faulty, problem-solving strategy.

Reaction-time studies

Another way to research cognitive processes is to use **reaction-time studies**. By measuring the time an individual takes to react to a given stimulus, situation, or problem, we can make inferences about the amount and complexity of mental processing that takes place. Here we assume that the more mental processing a task requires, the longer the subject will take to respond. This approach is usually used with relatively simple tasks, but some tasks may involve higher mental processing. For example, an individual may be presented with word pairs and asked to determine whether the words belong to the same category. In these sorts of studies, faster performance is often observed when word pairs are presented visually one after the other, rather than at the same time. From such results we might conclude that serial processing is more efficient than simultaneous processing.

Physiological studies

We can also investigate cognitive processes by measuring particular physiological responses of subjects as they deal with given stimuli, situations, or problems. Recording a subject's eye movements to visual stimulation, for example, gives us an indication of how individuals scan and solve visual problems (Janisse, 1973). The recording of minute muscle movements around the mouth and throat can give us an indication of whether an individual is "subvocalizing" in solving a particular problem.

Research has also been conducted by looking at electrical brain waves recorded on an electroencephalogram (EEG), which traces the electrical activity of the brain. EEG activity can help determine which parts of the brain are active in solving a particular problem and which types of problems result in greater brain activity. More sophisticated radiological and scanning techniques permit us to see which parts of the brain are most metabolically active during particular types of problem-solving activities. Such information gives us a better understanding of thinking and of the structure and organization of the brain.

HOW DO WE THINK?

Thinking is an incredibly complex process. In spite of its complexity, we usually do it with relatively little effort.

Images, words, and concepts are the major components of our thinking. When we think about vacations, for example, we may have images of snow or sand or water. An **image** is a brain process that gives a sensory representation of an object or event. We rely on our memories to visualize images. Interestingly, some of us visualize in black and white, whereas others visualize in colour. When we think about vacations, we may also think in terms of words. "Airplane," "customs," and "packing" identify specific objects and events which we might associate with vacations. A **word** is a verbal symbol, consisting of a combination of letters, that represents an object, event, idea, or concept. When we think about vacations, we might think of the concept of "freedom." A **concept** is a mental category of objects, events, or ideas based on common characteristics. Of course, we use words to describe concepts, but each concept consists of more than one element. For example, the concept of "freedom" might include the notions of getting away from work, sleeping in, choosing one's activities, and fulfilling one's own goals.

Images

We usually think of images as visual pictures, but they can involve other sensory modalities as well. Most of us would have no difficulty in forming an image of a carnival merry-go-round with brightly coloured horses on a revolving platform. We may also be able to form an auditory image of a rock group and its music. Perhaps, with some effort, we can conjure up the smell of hot buttered popcorn. You may have noticed that different senses are not recalled with equal intensity (Lindsay and Norman, 1977). People usually experience visual, spatial, and motion images most strongly. Images of sound, taste, touch, and smell are less frequent and generally less intense.

Our images are seldom complete. (See Figure 8-1.) An image of a merry-go-round might omit the covering over the platform and the background surroundings such as discarded candy wrappers and the colour of the sky. Images also vary in their vividness or intensity. We might be able to visualize quite clearly what that special person was wearing on our first date, but we might have only a vague recollection of where we may have first heard a familiar song.

It is difficult to determine precisely what role images play in our thinking. We must rely upon an individual's self-report about the images, and these reports are highly subjective. However, there do appear to be consistent differences between individuals in their preferred type of imagery. For example, Roe (1951) found that physical scientists were more apt to think in visual images whereas social scientists preferred auditory ones.

FIGURE 8-1 It is possible to think with images, some of which may be only partial

Imagery and creative thought

Much of our thinking is done with words, symbols, and concepts. It is possible, however, to think with images, which sometimes enable us to overcome the limitations of language. For example, the discoverer of the chemical structure of benzine, F.A. Kekulé, often worked with images of dancing atoms hooking themselves into chains of molecules (Schachter, 1976). While he was dreaming, he visualized an image in which a snake-like chain of molecules grabbed its own tail, forming a ring. This led to Kekulé's discovery that benzine has a ring structure at the molecular level. In particular, he hypothesized

FIGURE 8-2 The ring structure of the benzine molecule
Kekulé was led to this structure by dreaming of a snake-like chain swallowing its own tail.

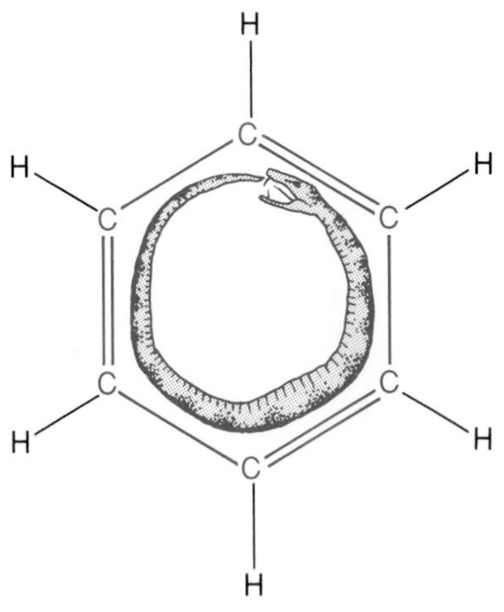

that the six carbon atoms of benzine form a ring, with a hydrogen atom attached to each carbon atom. See Figure 8-2. Similarly, Albert Einstein apparently made considerable use of visual images in his scientific thought. He often formulated ideas visually and then translated them into mathematical formulae. In fact, he sometimes said he knew a concept or idea long before he could put it into words (Shepard, 1978).

In the realm of aural imagery, we might mention that many composers create pieces of music without recourse to physical sound. They rely on their capacity to imagine the sounds in their minds. Several famous examples are well documented. Ludwig van Beethoven was almost completely deaf when he composed his late works, including his *Ninth Symphony* of 1824 (Cooper, 1985). In the 20th century, the Russian composer Sergei Prokofiev chose to compose a symphony without working out his ideas at the piano. The result of this mental exercise was his *Classical Symphony* of 1917 (Austin, 1966).

Words

Words are not the only type of symbolic representation we have, but they are usually the most useful in oral and written communication. Other types of signs are sometimes better able to communicate meaning, either in visual or auditory form. Drawings, gestures, facial grimaces, and non-verbal sounds often get across complex and unmistakable messages. Mathematical symbols and musical notes are examples of written languages that communicate information effectively without the use of words.

We use words as stand-ins for images and concepts. Different words can evoke different images. As we think, we often manipulate words rather than the concepts they represent. Words can be combined and rearranged to form various images. For example, "mother's father" and "father's mother" result in different images. Even though words can serve as a shorthand for broad concepts, they are useful only to the extent that people assign the same meaning to particular words. Words can lead to misunderstanding, particularly when they represent complex concepts. There would be considerable disagreement among a group of people about the meaning of the word "conservative" or the word "love."

Concepts

Some concepts represent categories of objects (such as toys or furniture), events or behaviours (such as studying or gesturing), or living organisms (such as dogs or whales). Other concepts represent abstract ideas (such as love or hate) or relationships (such as "longer than" or "better than").

A concept is a means of classifying information. In order to make sense out of the world, we form categories of objects, events, and ideas. "Dogs are animals" is a concept, as is "Hard work is good." We all have a concept of "boyishness" and a concept of "girlishness."

Concepts help us think more efficiently because we can know much about an element that fits one of these categories. Because related characteristics tend to occur together, we don't have to find out everything about each new situation, person, or object. These categories are mental representations of *kinds* of objects, events, and ideas. In our discussion of memory in Chapter 7, we have already mentioned an important type of concept known as *schemas*. You will recall that schemas are blueprints of what we expect particular objects and situations to be like when we encounter them.

Without concepts, our world would be perpetually novel. We could not benefit from past experience. We would have no way of drawing any comparison between a lighted match burning our fingertips and a hot soup spoon on our lips, for example. But we have a concept that could be called "dangerous because of heat." This is a category that includes matches that are burning down and soup that is very hot, although it does not include unlit matches and warm soup. The concept of "dangerous because of heat" is an example of a category that helps us organize the world and make predictions about the consequences of different behaviours.

Concepts can be based on various criteria. Some concepts rest on physical properties such as colour, size, or shape. Other concepts rest on abstract properties such as beauty, evil, or truth. In order to form a concept, we need to establish the criteria or features common to all objects or situations which fall within that class. We also need to determine which features or properties exclude membership. For example, see Figure 8-3.

In formulating our "dangerous because of heat" concept, we undoubtedly developed rules and criteria for including or excluding a new situation in the concept. "Flame near skin" is a criterion for inclusion, as is "other people scream when they do this." "Glows red" is an ambiguous criterion that requires further data, but "dull green" is a criterion for exclusion from the concept. In deciding whether a new instance is included or excluded from a particular

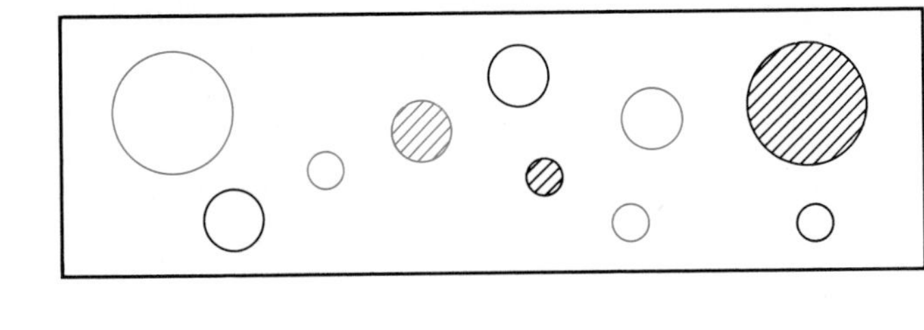

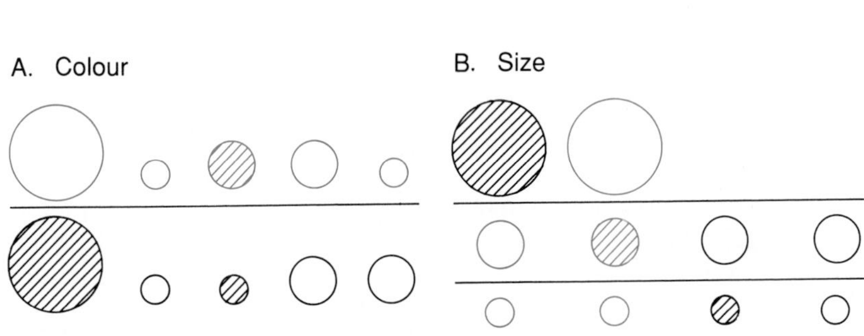

FIGURE 8-3 The defining properties of concepts
Different concepts rest on different properties. Suppose we want to organize the objects in the top compartment into two categories. If the organizing concept is based on colour, we will sort the objects as in A. However, we might choose an organizing concept that is more complex. If we adopt as the rule for categorization "a group of objects, no two of which are the same size," then we will sort the objects as in B.

concept, our definitions or boundaries can be either very precise or based on general tendencies. Less precisely defined concepts have "fuzzy" boundaries.

Fuzzy boundaries

Concepts in science tend to be precisely defined. If an animal is not a vertebrate and does not nurse its young, it is not a mammal. In everyday thinking, however, concepts tend to be more vague. For example, the whale fits the scientific concept of "mammal." However, it is hard not to think of a whale as a fish because it appears to share characteristics more common to our concept of "fish." In practice, we frequently make use of so-called fuzzy concepts (Zadeh, 1965; Rosch, 1978). A **fuzzy concept** is a concept whose criteria for inclusion or exclusion are based on tendencies rather than on precise rules. The boundaries of such concepts are not clearly drawn. For example, board games, card games, sports, and many recreational activities might be considered under the concept of "games" even though they share few common properties. We would be hard pressed to give a precise definition of the criteria underlying our notion of "game." As we noted in our discussion of memory in Chapter 7, "dog" has more associative links to the general concept of "mammal" than "whale" has. By the same token, people are much faster in deciding that a robin fits the category "bird" than they are in deciding whether to include an ostrich as a bird (Kintsch, 1974). The robin is more representative of the category "bird", at least in our culture. Likely, in the thinking of people in the tropics, a parrot is more "birdlike" than a robin. But cultural differences are beside the point here. Many concepts (such as "birdness" or "mammalness") are fuzzy ones based on tendencies.

Hierarchical concepts

Concepts are often arranged into hierarchies. A **hierarchy** is an organizational framework in which more general categories branch out into narrower categories at each level. The more general categories are often relatively abstract, and the narrower categories are often more concrete. It can be represented by a tree diagram, as we illustrated in the preceding chapter (see Figure 7-6). For example, the category of mammal has many subcategories, including dog, horse, and man. At the same time, "mammal" is itself a subunit of larger categories such as vertebrates, animals, and living organisms.

The formation of concepts

When we form a concept, we must decide on what basis an object or event is to be included or excluded. To do this, we use the processes of *generalization* and *discrimination*. (We have already encountered these technical terms in our discussion of conditioning in Chapter 5. There they have somewhat different meanings.) In concept formation, **generalization** is the process of expanding a concept by finding new examples that fit it. A child who has a loving and friendly dog will probably generalize good feelings to dogs in general and initially form a positive concept of dogs as friendly. Positive feelings will generalize to all dogs if generalization alone is operating. However, discrimination, the opposite of generalization, usually operates as well. In concept formation, **discrimination** is the process of narrowing a concept by finding new examples that do *not* fit it. Rules for exclusion are developed. After being hurt by snarling dogs, the child will likely refine the concept "dogs are friendly" to "non-snarling dogs are friendly." We are oversimplifying the process of concept formation in order to illustrate the underlying principles. Our concepts are numerous and complex. They are continually changing as we test new objects and situations to see whether they fit into our categories. We do determine rules (perhaps not always logical ones) for deciding which features are to be included in our concepts and which are to be ignored.

The primary strategy for forming concepts is known as hypothesis testing. In concept formation, **hypothesis testing** is the process of guessing what properties define a given concept and then testing new instances that have these properties to see whether they belong to the concept. The initial guess is a tentative hypothesis often based on relatively few examples. After testing new instances, we may retain, refine, or reject our initial guess.

Through hypothesis testing, we look for rules that will indicate whether a new item should be included in a particular concept. Some rules for inclusion or exclusion are easier to discover than others. The most difficult type is the **conditional rule**. (In logic, the term "conditional" refers to *if . . . then* statements.) This rule states that if the new instance meets one criterion or condition, then it must meet another particular criterion to be included in the given concept. An example of a conditional rule is, "If it is round, then it must be blue to belong to the concept." The second most difficult rule is the **disjunctive rule**. (In logic, the term "disjunctive" refers to *either . . . or* statements.) This rule states that if the new instance meets either one criterion or another criterion but not both criteria, then it is included in the given concept. An example of a disjunctive rule is, "If it is round or blue but not both, then it belongs to the concept."

The easiest rule to identify is the **conjunctive rule**. (In logic, the term "conjunctive" refers to statements in the form *A and B*.) This rule states that if a new instance meets two criteria at the same time, then it is included in the given concept. An example of a conjunctive rule is, "If it is round and blue, then it belongs to the category."

Researchers have conducted many experiments to investigate hypothesis testing. Let us work through a simple example.

From a child's point of view, one of the most important concepts to learn is that of "toy." The child might be handling a wooden block which an adult identifies as a toy. The child's working hypothesis might start out as "toys are cubic wooden objects I enjoy manipulating" (a conjunctive rule). This hypothesis could be tested by picking up a small wooden clock. When adults loudly pronounce, "Put that down. It's not a toy you know," the child must modify the hypothesis being tested to "wooden objects I enjoy manipulating but not if they have round dials" (a disjunctive rule). The child has learned an exclusionary rule. The concept of "toy" will be expanded by the inclusion

FIGURE 8-4 Hypothesis testing In forming a concept for "toy," the child examines many different objects and forms hypotheses about which fit the concept. He or she may test the hypothesis that "all objects that are fun to pick up and manipulate are toys" by picking up the family cat. Feedback (usually from adults, though in this case probably from the cat) confirms or disconfirms the hypothesis. The child then adds criteria for inclusion or exclusion from the concept. The child might add the criterion "not living" to the list of criteria for inclusion of an object in the concept "toy."

of new objects when a rag doll is identified as a toy. Through repeated testing and modifying of hypotheses about the concept, the child learns "if I enjoy manipulating an object and that activity is sanctioned by adults then the object is a toy" (an if-then rule that includes a conjunctive rule). Even a concept that seems as simple as "toy" is really quite complex. Is a stick a toy? It is under certain circumstances. Imagine the child's confusion when an adult refers to a sports car as "my new toy." The car qualifies as a toy because of characteristics that include impractical fun. The rules defining these characteristics are subtle and complicated. See Figure 8-4.

In concept formation experiments, most individuals form a guess or hypothesis and then modify this hypothesis based upon feedback they get from testing it. The way subjects use this feedback is very revealing. People tend to try to confirm their current beliefs. Generally, subjects have more trouble using disconfirming evidence. They tend to adopt a greater number of strategies which they expect to confirm the hypothesis they come up with first. This poor use of disconfirming evidence is particularly significant because it also seems to occur with concept formation in everyday life. For example, in testing our hypotheses about people or situations, we tend to look harder for confirming evidence than nonconfirming evidence. This tendency is called **confirmation bias**. For an example, see Figure 8-5. Moreover, we sometimes ignore altogether any evidence which is not consistent with our hypothesis. In its extreme, this rejection of disconfirming evidence results in prejudice.

Figure 8-5 illustrates the confirmation bias in an experiment devised by Johnson-Laird and Wason (1977). Subjects were to test the hypothesis "if a card has a vowel on one side, then it will have an odd number on the other side." Nearly everyone turned over the first card to see if the vowel was paired with an odd number. It was. The most efficient second move would be to turn over the card with the 8 showing, since this move might disconfirm the hypothesis and settle the issue. Even many pieces of confirming evidence cannot establish the hypothesis as true because there still might exist one piece of disconfirming evidence. This one disconfirmation would prove the hypothesis wrong. However, most subjects' second move was to turn over the card with a 7, seeking another piece of confirming evidence. In fact, this move was useless. If the back of the 7 contained a vowel, we would have another confirmation of the hypothesis but no proof that it always holds. If the back of the 7 contained a consonant, we would have learned nothing because the hypothesis does not require that *all* odd numbers be paired with vowels.

Subjects in this experiment used an inefficient strategy because they looked for confirmatory evidence. Researchers are not sure how to explain this bias, but it seems plausible that we learn a strong need to confirm our belief systems about reality. We are threatened by disconfirmations of existing beliefs, even when that leads to a distorted view of the world. We probably also are comforted by orderly relationships. If a hypothesis is true, the world seems safer because it is better understood.

FIGURE 8-5 Illustrating the confirmation bias
Johnson-Laird and Wason (1977) demonstrated the confirmation bias in an experiment. The subject's job was to examine cards similar to those in this figure in order to test the hypothesis "if a card has a vowel on one side, then it will have an odd number on the other side." Most subjects turned over more cards than necessary because they tended to choose cards that would confirm the hypothesis rather than those that would disconfirm it. What strategy would you use? See the text for an explanation of the best moves.
SOURCE: Johnson-Laird & Wason (1977).

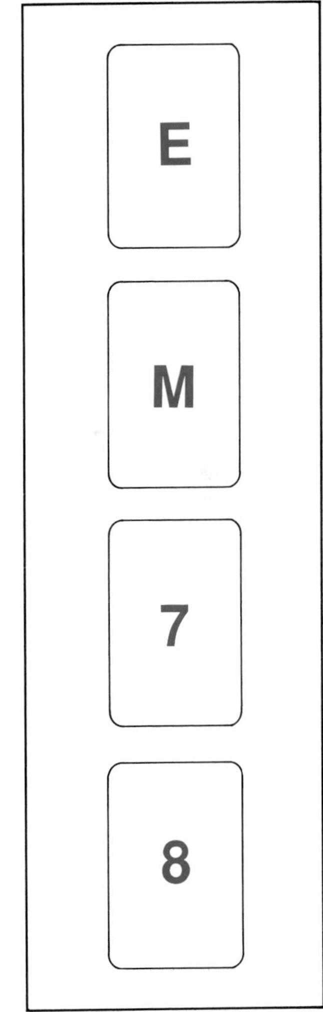

How Do We Solve Problems?

So far, we have been describing general principles. Now we will apply those principles to practical problem-solving.

What is a problem?

A **problem** is a situation or event that is currently not desirable. Change is required for a desirable outcome. Some problems seem to be easier to solve than others, but their apparent simplicity may be partly based upon how familiar we are with the situation. How to make it to first class in the morning is less of a problem now than it was on the first day of school. What to do when you finish your program of studies, however, is a larger, more complex problem. It contains many sub-problems and has life-changing consequences.

In general, we can distinguish three components that make up the process of problem-solving. We begin with the **initial state**, which is the less desired, current situation that one wishes to change. These initial conditions are the "givens," the circumstances we start with. The desired result of the problem-solving is called the **goal state**. This is the outcome we are seeking. Intervening between the two states are the means by which we manipulate the givens in order to reach the goal. These actions that we take to achieve the desired result are

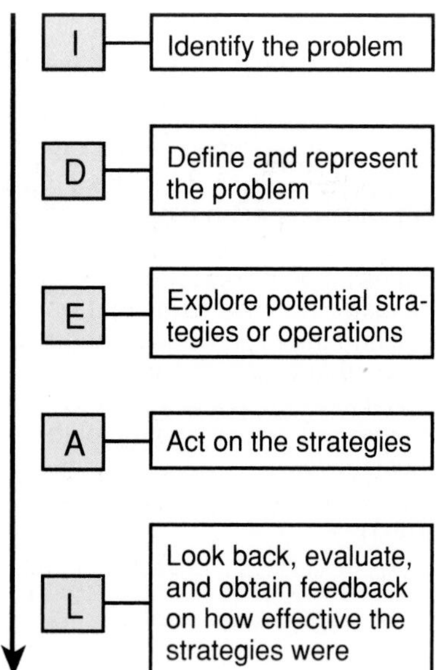

FIGURE 8-6 The IDEAL problem-solver

called **operations** (Newell and Simon, 1972). Thus we can define **problem-solving** as the process of changing from a less desired state (the initial state) to a more desired state (the goal state) by performing actions (operations).

To solve problems, we can make use of available information, past experience, and learned methods. There are many different operations that we might use to try to solve a particular problem. Part of the process of problem-solving is to choose the most effective set of operations.

Steps in problem-solving

A useful analysis of the steps used in problem-solving was presented by Bransford and Stein (1984). They also proposed an acronym as aid in remembering the steps. Their acronym is the **IDEAL problem-solver**: I = identify the problem; D = define and represent the problem; E = explore potential strategies or operations; A = act on the strategies; and L = look back, evaluate, and obtain feedback on how effective your strategies were. See Figure 8-6.

Identify and define (and represent) the problem

Some problems have a well-defined initial state, set of operations, and goal. An algebra problem is one example. Others, however, are less well defined and require clear articulation before we can formulate effective operations. In some cases, there may not even be a single "correct" solution to the problem. Writing a symphony, designing a home, or choosing a career are examples. As problem solvers, our first major task is to define what the problem is. We need to list what givens are present, what the ideal outcome or result would be, and what various strategies are available to try to achieve the goal.

The initial representation of a problem can strongly influence our search for a solution. Many childhood riddles depend on misleading the listener by the way they represent a problem. For example, if a plane crashes exactly on the border between two countries, where will the survivors be buried? You probably remember from grade school that the *survivors* won't be buried anywhere because they're not dead. The representation of the problem focused the listener on the crash and legal issues irrelevant to the stated problem. A dresser drawer contains a mixture of single black and grey socks in the proportion of 5:2. If it were totally dark, how many socks would a person have to remove to be sure to get a matched pair? You probably know that the simple answer is 3, but most people struggle with mathematical formulas and complex logic because of the initial mathematical representation of the problem. See Figure 8-7.

When defining and representing a problem it is wise to formulate several very different versions of the problem. For example, you might define the problem visually, logically, and then mathematically.

Explore strategies and act on them

Once a problem has been defined, it is time to develop strategies for solving it. Some problems are best solved by applying a systematic set of steps. A clearly stated series of rules and procedures that leads to the solution of a particular problem is called an **algorithm**. Computers require algorithms to solve problems because computer programs must be written in a clear, step-by-step way. Algorithms are dependable and useful in limited circumstances. Often, though, they are clumsy and inefficient. Suppose the given problem is to find how many smaller words can be made from the letters in the word "interdependent." One algorithm we could use would be to form all possible combinations of two or more letters and compare each combination with a list of English words. The possible combinations, numbering in the hundreds of thousands, would be hopelessly tedious to construct without a powerful computer. A more efficient strategy would be to look for combinations of letters common in English. Here we would be using a rule-of-thumb strategy known as a **heuristic**. Less structured than an algorithm, a heuristic often — but not always — leads to a solution. Wickelgren (1979) has identified four heuristics with which we might reduce the number of possible operations in an effort to reach our goal.

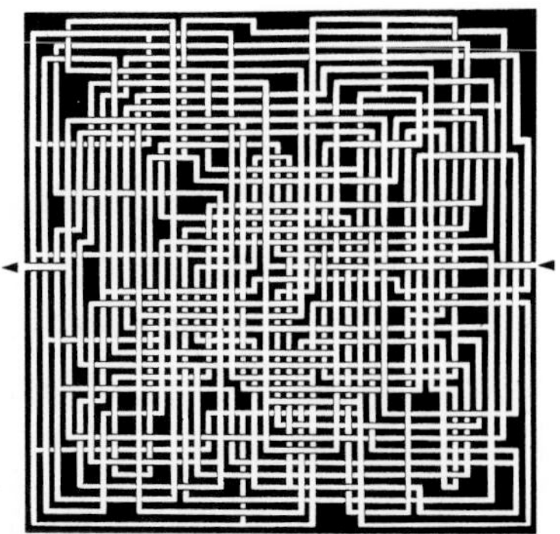

We use the second heuristic to solve puzzle mazes. We evaluate one series of actions and then either proceed or move back depending on whether or not that series will help us reach our goal.
SOURCE: M.J. Costello. Reprinted, by permission of the publisher, from Les Wood, *Mazes and Mandalas*. Copyright © by Prentice-Hall, Inc., Englewood Cliffs, NJ.

First, we might recognize that several operations belong to the same method class. In problem-solving, a **method class** is a group of operations that are so similar that if one operation in the class fails, then we know that the other operations in the class will fail as well. Consider, for example, the problem of reaching a socket in the ceiling to change a light bulb. We might stack a number of objects and stand on top of them in an attempt to reach the socket. Suppose we try this and we are still not close enough to change the light bulb. We would then know that rearranging the stacked objects is not going to provide the solution. There is no point in persisting with this particular method class. To solve the problem, we should try another set of operations.

The second heuristic we might use to reduce the number of operations would be to try out a few steps of a possible solution to see whether it seems to be leading to success. We would go through a *sequential series of actions*, evaluating our progress at each stage. After evaluating each action or group of actions, we try to decide whether our current course is likely to result in our attaining the goal state. We often employ this heuristic when we attempt to solve a puzzle maze. We may proceed up an alley, make

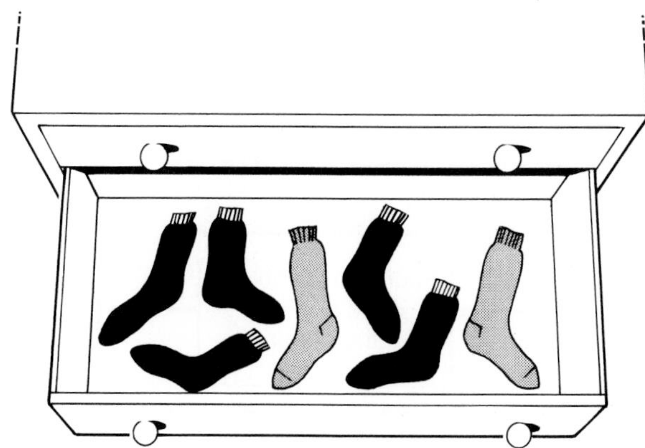

FIGURE 8-7 The initial representation of a problem
The drawer contains black and grey socks in the proportion of 5:2. In total darkness, how many socks would a person have to remove to be sure of getting a matched pair? The first time most people try to solve this well-known problem, they think in mathematical terms because the problem is represented in mathematical terms. A simple visual representation indicates that the answer is 3 socks.

Many large tasks are overwhelming unless they are broken down into subgoals.
SOURCE: Dick Hemingway.

a turn, and then evaluate our progress toward the goal. If it seems that we are making headway, we continue. If not, we reject this series of actions and choose another route.

The third method we might use is to **work backward from the goal**. As its name suggests, this heuristic consists of beginning at the goal state and working back to the initial state in an attempt to solve a given problem. This method is most fruitful when the information relating to the goal state is clearer than the information available at the initial state. For example, to plan a program of study in order to get into medical school, we might first determine which courses are required for admission. We could then work backwards and select all the prerequisite courses for these required courses.

The fourth method we might use is **setting subgoals**. This heuristic consists of breaking down the goal of a problem into smaller, more manageable objectives. For example, consider the complex problem of obtaining a university degree. It can seem overwhelming unless it is broken up into small, achievable subgoals. Thus, we could first tackle the objective of completing the first-year requirements. Even this objective could be usefully broken up into smaller subgoals, such as passing the psychology course or preparing for the next test. The final examination of this course may depend upon knowing thoroughly the information in this entire text, but mastery and subgoal attainment can begin with each chapter, section, or subsection.

Another term for the heuristic of setting subgoals is **means-ends analysis**. The word "ends" refers to the process of defining the goal, and the word "means" refers to the ways we might achieve that goal. In means-ends analysis we break down a large problem into smaller subproblems and then tackle each subproblem. Figure 8-8 illustrates how we can apply means-ends analysis to the problem of writing a good term paper.

Even the task of writing the first draft of something quite short can sometimes be daunting. Many of us have struggled with writer's block at one time or another. It is not a pleasant experience to stare at a blank page and wonder how we are ever going to accomplish our task. One solution that often works is to

FIGURE 8-8 An example of solving a problem through means-end analysis

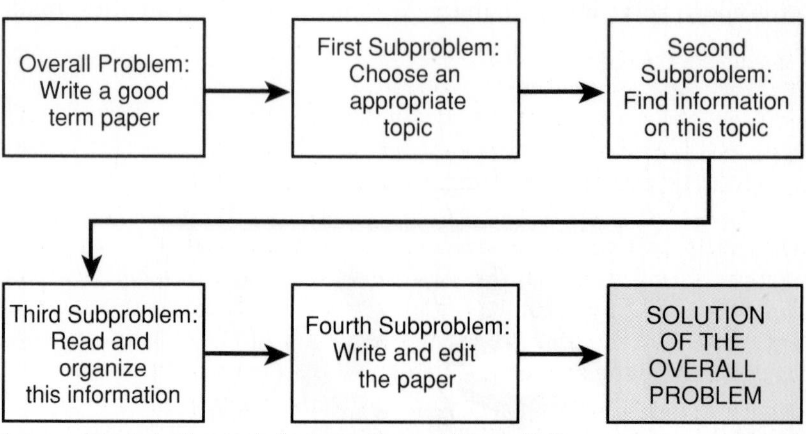

SOURCE: Adapted with permission from Allyn and Bacon, 1989.

decide to write only those few sentences that are clearest in our minds, regardless of where those sentences will fall in the final piece. Once that is done, we usually find it easier to tackle "just one more little section" and then "just one more" and so on until we have a complete first draft.

Look back, evaluate, and obtain feedback

Especially when the larger goal is broken into subunits, we should strive to evaluate our progress and get feedback on our performance. The essence of effective problem-solving is the ability to assess and modify one's approach if necessary. Problem-solving is a fluid process. Often, our knowledge about the initial state and goal state is incomplete. As we acquire this knowledge, we may be forced to re-evaluate our problem-solving strategies regarding the main goal. Feedback and evaluation are critical to the operations in problem-solving. Without evaluation of our performance, we have no way of determining whether we are making reasonable progress. In addition, the utility or attractiveness of our overall goals may change, as might the probability or likelihood that these ultimate goals can be reached. Without continuous feedback, we can easily miss the changes necessary to attain new goals.

A person might have defined a goal as seeking a particular career and established a strategy of action to reach that goal. Periodically, the person should evaluate and redefine the problem and the goals, rather than blindly following the established strategy. Perhaps the person consistently earns higher grades in courses unrelated to the original career goal. Job opportunities may have changed. These and many other kinds of new information need to be considered in the "look back."

Factors that affect problem-solving

It is not always easy to use the feedback we get on our problem-solving. There are many factors that interfere with the process. There are also general strategies we can adopt for improving problem-solving.

Emotional interference

Problem-solving is affected by our emotional state. If we are anxious, angry, or depressed, either from problem-solving efforts or other influences in our lives, our ability to solve problems suffers. A moderate level of anxiety or other arousal can facilitate problem-solving, but a high level interferes with it. Some emotions can make it difficult to carry out plans and they can hinder our thinking of other alternatives. In general, we should strive to reduce anxiety because it constricts thinking. This is especially true when flexible, creative thinking is required. For example, Glucksberg (1962) gave subjects a box of matches, two candles, and some thumbtacks. The problem was to mount the two candles on the wall. Can you think of a way to solve this problem? The solution requires thinking of the available objects in unusual ways. We will discuss the solution to this problem later in this chapter. For now, the relevant point is that subjects who were told they might win a $20 reward for the solution did more poorly than subjects who were offered no reward. The pressure of the possibility of winning money apparently constricted thinking.

Attention span

Human memory and cognition are not unlimited. For most chess positions, for example, even chess masters cannot hold in memory all of the possible combinations of moves. Moreover, as a game unfolds, the good chess player refocuses attention and energy on particular subgoals. For problem-solving in general, we use the term **attention span** to refer to the limits of human memory and cognition. To help overcome some of these limits, we can make use of external aids such as written records. For instance, we might take notes as reminders, recording each step of the problem-solving process, in order to focus clearly on the goal state. We might also employ computers to tackle problems that involve numerous calculations and parameters.

Sets

You will recall that in Chapter 4 we examined the concept of a **set**, a well-learned predisposition about how to perform a specific task or how to perceive a particular situation. We have already demonstrated how some sets are expectations that can distort perception. Similarly, some sets can distort thinking and problem-solving. Our expectations of how to solve problems are often based on strategies that have served us well in the past. On the one hand, a set may help to enhance our problem-solving efforts. A set can be considered to be a type of hint because it suggests a set of operations that might be appropriate to a given problem. On the other hand, a set may hamper our search for new, creative solutions. A strong expectation about how to solve a given type of problem may "blind" us to alternative operations which may be called for. A rigid set of thinking of objects in terms of their normal function is called **functional fixedness** (Dunker, 1945). Functional fixedness hinders us from thinking of novel uses of objects and hence new approaches to problems.

Figure 8-9 illustrates how functional fixedness can interfere with solving the Maier string problem (adapted from Maier, 1931). A person is standing between two strings which are hanging from the ceiling. The goal is to tie the strings together. If the person holds one of the strings, the other is just out of reach. On the table is a pair of scissors. If this problem is presented as "the famous scissors problem," few people will see the solution. They will usually try to think of solutions that involve cutting. However, if the problem is described as the famous "pendulum problem," the solution is easy to see. We have a powerful set about scissors. We automatically expect them to be used for cutting. This set often saves us a lot of time and effort because it is usually appropriate. In this case, however, it can lead to functional fixedness. We may be prevented from seeing alternative uses of the scissors because our expectations are so strong.

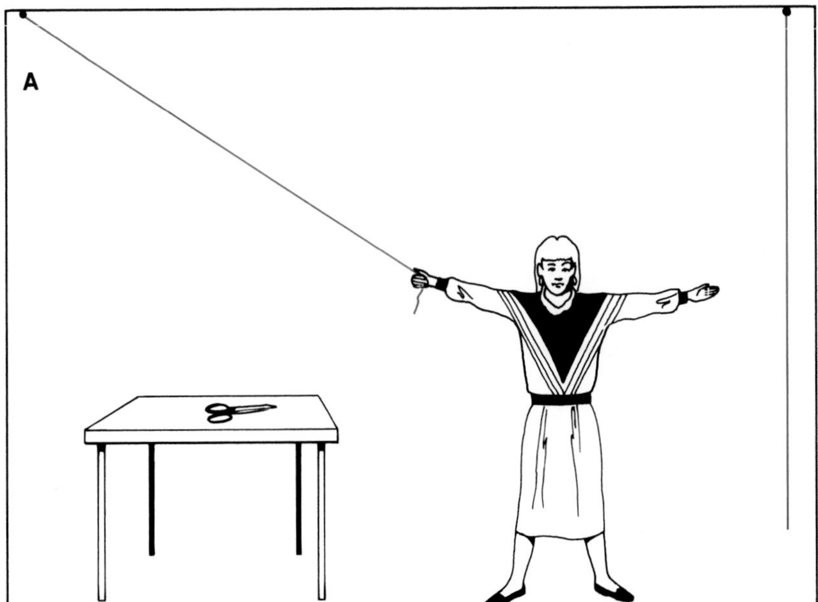

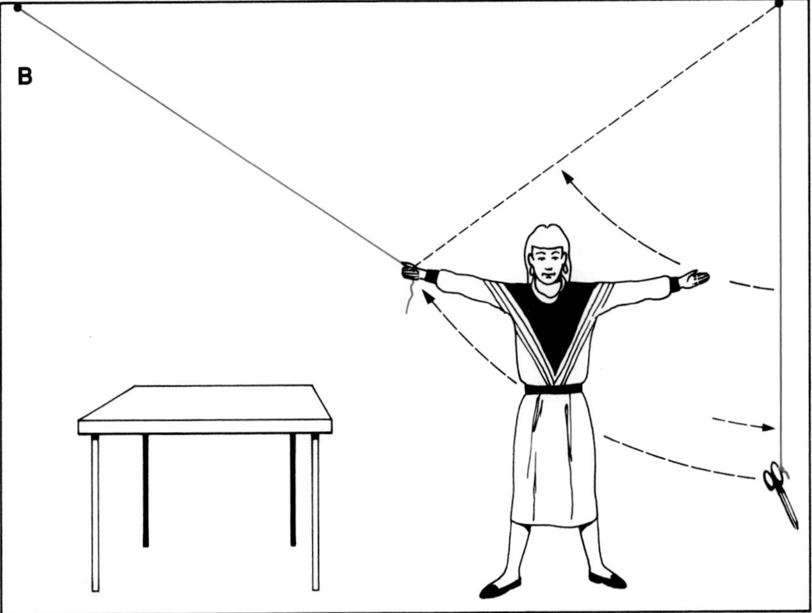

FIGURE 8-9 Functional fixedness and the Maier string problem How can this woman tie both ends of the string together, using only the scissors provided? Functional fixedness makes most people think of the scissors only in terms of cutting. Using them as a weight on a pendulum is the solution.

Self-deception

If a goal is especially attractive, we often disregard any negative aspects and overestimate the likelihood of a positive outcome. This self-deceptive denial may encourage us to misjudge the probability of finding a solution. Many aspiring entrepreneurs are so motivated by their dreams of success that they fail to evaluate accurately the market for their product. This principle also lies behind the saying that "love is blind." New lovers often overlook realistic problems and shortcomings in their partners because the goal is so attractive.

We may oversimplify complex situations by not considering all the alternatives or relevant facts. Both undue optimism (positive preconceptions) and undue pessimism (negative preconceptions) can blind us to certain facts. We may then make poor decisions because of our distortions. Many sources of error are nonrational and should have no place in problem-solving efforts. Unfortunately, humans cannot operate like Mr. Spock (of *Star Trek*) and the Vulcans. If we recognize the nonrational parts of ourselves, we may be able to reduce the effects of distortions on our problem-solving.

Problem-solving by computers

In Chapter 7 (Memory), we briefly examined **artificial intelligence**, the field in which computers are designed to simulate human thought processes. Today, much research is being done to construct programs that will enable computers to solve problems the way that humans do. One of the most challenging and controversial questions in the field is, "Will computers ever really think?" The answer will tell us much about ourselves as humans. But it may not be an answer that we want to discover. Do emotions, for example, differentiate our mental processing from that of mere machines? Or are humans merely very complex machines? A frequent plot in science fiction stories features a computer getting smarter and smarter until, say, it is ready to play for the world chess championship. At the last minute the computer quits because it is too upset to continue. Is some "nonrationality" an essential part of "real thinking"? We are far from being able to answer any of these questions definitively. Nevertheless, researchers in artificial intelligence are developing programs that more and more closely resemble human thinking.

The general strategy of artificial intelligence is to try to develop a model of human problem-solving by making its steps as explicit as possible. Then these steps are imitated through computer programs (in the form of algorithms), and the resulting solutions are compared with the results of human problem-solving (Schank and Hunter, 1985).

The field of artificial intelligence requires a knowledge of both machines and the complex psychology of human cognition. It is

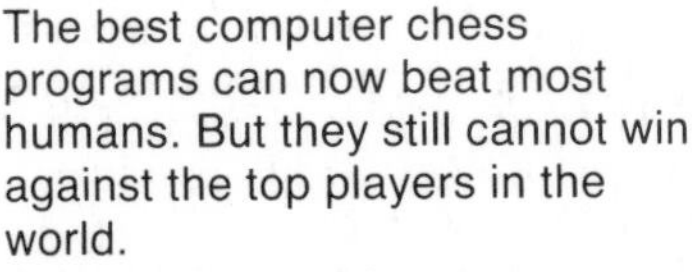
The best computer chess programs can now beat most humans. But they still cannot win against the top players in the world.
SOURCE: Dick Hemingway.

necessary to understand well the processes of human learning before we can design computers that can imitate them. Human learning and thinking contain many nuances. For instance, human attention is attracted by features in the environment that have *high salience* (i.e., that stand out as having more meaning). But as Martin (1989) points out, this salience is very dependent upon the *context* in which the features appear. For instance, the meaning of a small clicking noise is determined in large part by the particular setting and one's past experience. The noise might be highly salient if we hear it while driving a new car, but it might be meaningless if we hear it while walking. We have already discussed the importance of context in sensation, perception, and memory. In human thinking and learning, **context** refers to the setting of a statement, which includes the surrounding statements, preceding and following events, and previous knowledge. All these elements contribute to the interpretation of the meaning of a particular statement. "Intelligent" computer programs will have to take into account the notion of context.

One of the most interesting and socially important jobs in artificial intelligence is the development of expert systems. An **expert system** is a computer program that uses a series of decision rules derived from the thinking processes of human experts. Expert systems have been devised to diagnose human illness, identify automobile malfunctions, recognize images in photographs, and make decisions about where to drill for oil. At present, these programs are useful enough to help with human decision-making, but they are not refined to the point where they can serve as the exclusive decision maker.

To develop an expert system, the programmer first studies human experts in the process of making decisions. Newell and Simon (1972) argued that much human decision-making can be reduced to a series of conditional decision-making rules. Each so-called **if-then rule** is a logical rule in the form of an if . . . then statement. Such rules seem to operate informally in the execution of much skilled behaviour. The expert person acts and then chooses the next action according to the outcome of the last one. "If there is no fever, then look at disease list A, rather than B" is an example of an if-then rule in the field of medical diagnosis. This might lead to another if-then rule, such as "If a skin rash is present, ask the patient about recent food intake." To most of us, our problem-solving seems as though we "just did it," but in fact often we are rapidly going through a series of if-then decisions.

The program developer interviews several human experts with proven success records and observes them in decision-making. The experts sometimes "think out loud" during this observation process. Thousands of rules can be devised to guide the computer's "thinking." It is amazing how many steps must be programmed to do simple tasks, such as making a tower out of three blocks. But some expert programs work quite well. The medical diagnosis program, MYCIN, was tested against human experts for the ability to diagnose meningitis. The test ended in a tie for accuracy. Both human experts and computers were right about 69% of the time (Mason, 1985).

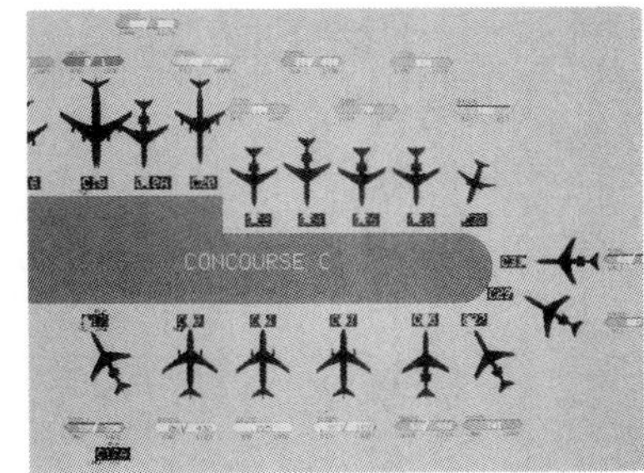

Texas Instruments' knowledge engineers worked closely with United Airlines to develop a gate control system that has dramatically reduced flight delays.
SOURCE: Courtesy Texas Instruments, Inc.

Nevertheless, much controversy surrounds the question of whether all human abilities can eventually be reduced to if-then rules and thus be performed by a computer. Many human skills involve an artistry that seems too complex for words. However, the goal of the developers of expert systems is to show that even these complicated processes can be reduced to a series of if-then decisions carried out very rapidly. Success in this field poses a real challenge to our deep-rooted notion that humans are uniquely creative. There is an anecdote about one human expert who was studied for months so that a programmer could develop an expert system. When the computer started making good decisions, the expert quit his profession in discouragement because what had felt so creative to him could now be reduced to if-then rules.

In the course of mastering a skill, most people usually experience what Gagné (1984) calls automatization. The term **automatization** refers to the process by which a complex activity is done so frequently that it comes to seem automatic. Many well-practised activities eventually become effortless. In the beginning, the novice probably has to struggle with awkward use of if-then rules, but with experience the activity becomes automatic. This process happens in many human activities, including artistic ones such as playing the piano. The beginner is constantly thinking about where the fingers go, if-then decisions about "if I want to produce a middle C, then my finger must strike there." By contrast, the expert piano player "just does it" and is free to focus on higher goals such as phrasing, dynamics, and large-scale structure.

CREATIVITY

We all have some notion about what creativity is. We can point to literary, musical, architectural, and scientific examples. Kekulé's discovery of the ring structure of the benzine molecule, described early in this chapter, is a striking example of a creative solution. We have already emphasized the important role that imagery can play in creative thought. Providing a precise definition of creativity, however, is difficult.

Johnson (1972) has listed five properties that he argues are necessary for a solution to be creative. The first is *appropriateness* to the situation. The complexity of the solution should fit the complexity of the problem. Other aspects of appropriateness include acceptability, practicality, and realism. A second property is *usefulness*. The problem-solving effort must be of some use or benefit to the situation. This does not necessarily mean immediate or direct practical utility. The benefit can be meeting some emotional or intellectual need. A third property of creativity is *ingenuity*, as opposed to systematic, mechanical, or repetitive problem-solving efforts. A fourth property is *breadth*. Creative works generally cover a wider range of application than noncreative solutions to problems. The final property is uncommonness or *novelty*. Breaking away from a strong set such as functional fixedness is a form of novelty. Arthur

Koestler (1970) argues that creativity involves the perceiving of two or more ideas that were previously not connected with each other. Surprising new combinations appear with qualities that the old ideas by themselves did not have. This is the essence of novelty.

Thus, we can define **creativity** as the process of problem-solving that has the properties of appropriateness, usefulness, ingenuity, breadth, and novelty. This definition implies an element of subjectivity in evaluating creativity. It also suggests that there are degrees of creativity. The following is a relatively modest example of a creative solution.

Previously we alluded to an experiment in which subjects had to mount two candles on the wall using only a box of matches, thumbtacks, and the two candles (Glucksberg, 1962). The solution required creative thinking because it is so common to think of the matchbox only in terms of the functions of matches (see Figure 8-10). After the matches have been emptied from the box, part of the box can simply be tacked to the wall and used as a support for the candles. This solution is *novel* because it is new and unexpected. It is *appropriate* because it is practical, acceptable, and realistic. It is *useful* because it serves a needed function. It is *ingenious* because it is clever and uses skill. It is *broad* because the solution could be applied in many different settings.

FIGURE 8-10 A creative solution Subjects in Glucksberg's (1962) experiment were given the materials in Panel A and told to mount the candles on the wall. The solution, shown in Panel B, requires a creative use of the matchbox.

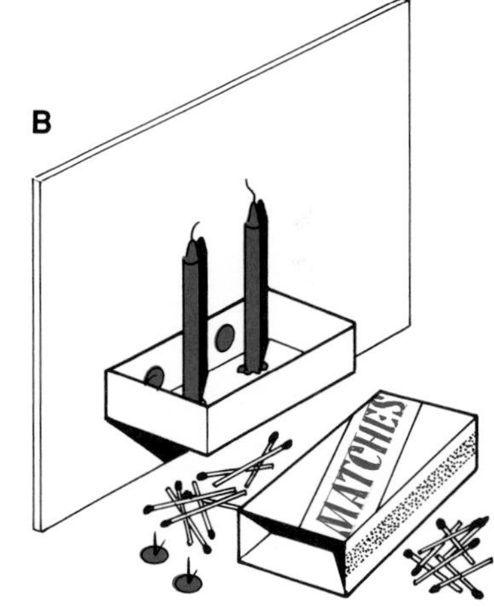

Psychological research into creativity has focused on two major goals. The first is to develop measures to assess creativity. The second is to clarify the relationships between creativity and other areas, such as intelligence.

In assessing the cognitive characteristics of creativity, Guilford (1967) contends that we are capable of two types of thinking: *divergent thinking* and *convergent thinking*. **Divergent thinking** is thinking that is directed to generating many different potential solutions to a given problem. It is a characteristic of creativity. Thinking of as many uses as possible for a brick is an example of divergent thinking or creative thinking. **Convergent thinking**, on the other hand, is thinking that is directed to generating one solution to a problem. It is a characteristic of logical problem-solving, which we have discussed earlier in this chapter. Examples of convergent thinking include solving a mathematical equation and performing well on an intelligence test. In short, creative persons tend to be divergent in their thinking, without losing sight of the appropriateness of their solution.

Researchers have tried to determine the relation between creativity and intelligence. The results of such studies tend to be mixed. Some indicate a positive relation, whereas others find no relation (e.g., Dellas and Gaier, 1970; Barron and Harrington, 1981). The lack of a conclusive relation between creativity and intelligence is not surprising, in view of our previous description of divergent and convergent thinking. Intelligence tests are designed to measure convergent thinking. They require much different thinking skills than do tests of creativity. In general, research studies show a greater relation between creativity and an individual's interests, attitudes, and motivation, than between creativity and other cognitive abilities.

Written music is a form of artificial language.
SOURCE: Jacques de Chambonnières, *Les pièces de clavessin* (Paris, 1670). "Sarabande," vol. 1, p. 29.

WHAT IS LANGUAGE?

Language is the most common means by which we communicate. In fact, throughout history all human societies have used language as a means of communication. Some researchers have argued that language represents one of the highest achievements of human cognition.

Language, like thought, relies on symbols. We can distinguish two broad categories of language. **Natural language** is a form of spoken, written, or gestured communication based on verbal symbols. English as well as sign language belong to this category. By contrast, **artificial language** is a form of written communication based on a notation that is not verbal. Musical scores and mathematical treatises are forms of artificial language.

Until recently, the study of language was exclusively the domain of linguistics. **Linguistics** is the field of study that investigates the production of speech, the structure of language, and the use of words and sentences. But psychologists have shown an increasing interest in language, both as a behaviour and as a window on human cognition. A relatively recent merger of psychology and linguistics has produced the discipline of psycholinguistics. **Psycholinguistics** is the field of study that investigates how language is acquired, perceived, and comprehended. Before we discuss language acquisition, it will be helpful to consider the structure of language.

The structure of language

We can analyse the structure of language at several different levels. Below and at the level of individual words, we can distinguish the subunits of language known as *phonemes*, *graphemes*, and *morphemes*. At higher levels, we can analyse phrases and sentences in terms of *syntax*, *grammar*, and *semantics*. The various levels of analysis are shown in Figure 8-11.

FIGURE 8-11 The analysis of language at different levels

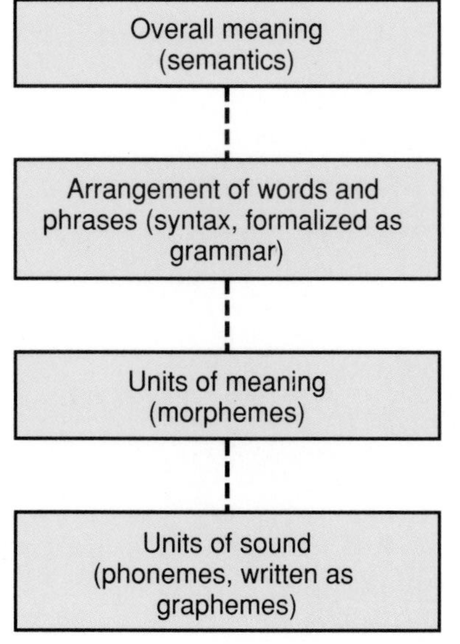

A **phoneme** is the smallest unit of sound in a language. For example, in English, the word *chat* consists of three phonemes: the sounds of the letters "ch," "a," and "t." Because a phoneme is a sound, it is sometimes hard to express clearly in writing. The phoneme represented by "t," for example, is not the sound *tee* but rather a sound close to *tuh*. Different languages have different phonemes. To facilitate research, linguists have developed the *International Phonetic Alphabet*, a collection of symbols that can represent the phonemes of various languages. The English language is composed of 45 different phonemes. In English, there are more phonemes than letters in the alphabet for two reasons. First, some letters have more than one phonemic sound (e.g., the "a" in *chat* and the "a" in *case* represent two different phonemes). Second, some combinations of letters can comprise a single phonemic unit (e.g., the "ch" combination in *chat*).

A **grapheme** is a letter or combination of letters representing a phoneme. Graphemes are features of written expression that cannot be analysed into smaller meaningful units. In short, graphemes are visual representations of the basic units of language, and phonemes are their auditory equivalent. For instance, the grapheme "ch" represents in writing the first phoneme in the word *chat*.

The level above phonemes and graphemes in the structure of language consists of morphemes. A **morpheme** is the smallest unit of meaning in a language. We can distinguish two general types. A **free morpheme** is a morpheme that can stand alone as a word. In English, the word *go* (which consists of two phonemic units) is an example of a free morpheme. By contrast, a **bound morpheme** is a morpheme that must be combined with one or more other morphemes to form a word. Even though they are not words by themselves, bound morphemes have specific positions and, like free morphemes, specific meanings. In English, the prefix "un-," meaning *not*, is a bound morpheme. So is the suffix "-s" indicating the plural. Bound morphemes are also used to produce *inflections* of words, such as the different tenses of verbs. In a given language, we can combine morphemes into larger units that communicate greater meaning. In all, English has about 50 000 morphemes, from which we can form the hundreds of thousands of words that comprise the language.

Syntax is the arrangement of words into acceptable phrases and sentences. We know that in English "John loves young Mary" means the same as "Young Mary is loved by John." We also know "John loves Mary young" means something different. The new syntax changes the meaning. Some arrangements destroy meaning. Thus, "Loves Mary John young" is not an acceptable combination in English. As children, our first use of syntax usually consists of combinations of word pairs, such as "doggie come" or "milk gone." These phrases are not very eloquent, but they do get the message across.

As we grow older, we learn to master the grammar of English. When we study a foreign language, we also strive to learn its grammar. In general, **grammar** is the formal codification of rules for word inflection, word formation, and syntax. Each language has its own rules for declining nouns, conjugating verbs, creating compound words, forming clauses, relating subjects and objects with verbs, and punctuating sentences.

Semantics is the study of meaning in language. In semantics, we analyse the meaning and organization of morphemes, words, phrases, and sentences. On occasion, people say that an argument boils down to a "semantic problem." By this, they mean that two individuals seem to be using the same words with different meanings. Suppose two people go out together for an evening. If one of them says, "I'd like to go home *soon*," and the other person eventually agrees to leave one hour later, we might assume that they disagree about the meaning of the word *soon*. Semantics also depends heavily on the relationships between words. Correct syntax does not by itself guarantee an acceptable expression of meaning. For example, the following sentence is correct syntactically but not semantically: "My car persuaded me not to go on the trip." Literally speaking, this is not correct semantically, because cars cannot persuade. Nevertheless, in certain contexts, words can be used to form metaphors. If you know that my car is in terrible condition, you would be able to infer that what I mean by my statement is "Because of the poor mechanical condition of my car, I decided not to go on the trip."

SOURCE: *Cathy* by Cathy Guisewite. Copyright 1990 Universal Press Syndicate. Reprinted with permission.

THE RELATIONSHIP BETWEEN LANGUAGE AND THOUGHT

Does the way we think determine our language? Or does our language dictate how we think? The precise relationship between thinking and language is a controversial issue. Nevertheless, the consensus appears to be that thinking and language interact to influence each other. On the one hand, our mental apparatus and the way we think seem to govern the development of human languages in general. On the other hand, the confines and limitations of any particular language seem to influence our thought and reasoning ability. For instance, particular concepts may not even occur to us because of the limitations of the English language. An interactive model for thought and language has not always been popular. There have been strong advocates for both extreme positions.

The American linguist Benjamin Whorf (1956) emphasized the influence of language on thought. He proposed the hypothesis, known as **linguistic determinism**, that the structure of a particular language determines how the users of that language think. Whorf argued that cultural differences in language lead to different perceptions of the environment and thus to different mechanisms of thought. Thus, members of different cultures organize and view the world differently. He cited the many different words for *snow* used by Inuit people and the multiplicity if names for *camel* in the Arabic culture. For instance, the Inuit have separate words for "snow that is falling," "snow already on the ground," and "snow packed hard like ice." Labels for different types of snow may have been developed because of the importance of snow to the Inuit way of life. This feature of their language may actually lead the Inuit to see the world differently than other people.

We might also support Whorf's hypothesis by arguing that an unlabelled object (or one that is not distinguished from other similar objects) cannot form part of long-term memory. Therefore, it will not be incorporated in the network of associations that play such an important role in our thinking. Memories of the same event or scene can be different for people with different languages.

In response to Whorf's hypothesis, some linguists and psycholinguists have adopted an opposing position. They maintain that people in different cultural circumstances learn to think differently about their environment and later develop language to express those differences. In other words, thinking develops first and then it structures language, rather than the other way around.

Two main arguments have been offered to support the primacy of thought over language. First, many languages share the same syntactical structure: subject, verb, and object, in that order. Presumably this syntax reflects an important characteristic of human thought. But this particular syntactical structure is far from universal. (For example, in German, the verb is placed at the end of the sentence.) To overcome this objection, we might make use of the analytical ideas developed by the American psycholinguist Noam Chomsky (1975). Chomsky differentiates between the surface structure and deep structure of any given sentence. **Surface structure** is the arrangement of phonemes, morphemes, words, and phrases in a sentence as it is actually written or spoken. **Deep structure** is the underlying meaning of a sentence. In a given language, sentences with different surface structures can express the same deep structure. For example, the following three English sentences have the same underlying meaning:

(1) Claudette put the package in the house.

(2) The package was put in the house by Claudette.

(3) The house contains the package that was put there by Claudette.

Chomsky further argues that even though various languages may have different surface structures, the deep structure of virtually all human languages is the same. He concludes that this uniformity in languages indicates similar ways of thinking in different cultural environments. Chomsky asserts that we are biologically predisposed to think in certain ways regardless of the culture we grow up in.

The second main argument that supports the primacy of thought over language rests on the observation that some people are able to think quite well without language. For instance, as we mentioned in Chapter 2, studies of aphasic patients reveal that individuals who have lost language abilities because of brain impairment are still able to reason and solve problems. Moreover, those deaf children who have virtually no spoken, written, or signing language ability still perform as well as other children on many thinking and problem-solving tests (Furth, 1971).

Today, the most accepted views of the relationship between language and thought lie between the two extreme positions. The interactive model stresses the importance of the interdependence of language and thought. The structure of thought determines language, and at the same time the structure of language imposes some limits on thought.

The Inuit have various words for *snow* in their language, probably because snow is so present in their environment.
SOURCE: Douglas Walker, Economic Development and Tourism.

Language Acquisition

Innate or learned?

We somehow change the guttural utterances, squeaks, and other random babblings that we make when infants into meaningful language as we grow older. Gradually we develop the ability to string together phonemes, morphemes, and words to communicate our thoughts. Psycholinguists try to discover the extent to which language ability is built-in and the extent to which it is a learned skill.

In earlier chapters, we have already encountered debates about the relative importance of biology (nature) and environment (nurture) in the fields of perception and learning. The nature-nurture controversy also arises in the area of language acquisition. From the

Noam Chomsky is a leading psycholinguist.
SOURCE: John Cook, MIT Department of Linguistics.

research done to date, it seems that language is strongly influenced *both* by innate brain structures and by learning.

The role of biology

The ability of infants to utter phonemic and morphemic units spontaneously, despite the complexity of language, suggests that we possess an innate capacity for language acquisition and expression. Moreover, a physiological comparison of our left and right cerebral hemispheres seems to point to our innate capacity for language. In most individuals, the hemisphere responsible for speech and language is the left one. And it is the left hemisphere that contains larger structures in certain areas.

Noam Chomsky (1975) is one of the leading proponents of the view that we have an innate capacity for language. On the basis of his analysis of language, Chomsky concludes that some kind of "wiring" in the human brain enables us to acquire and produce language. In the preceding section, we discussed Chomsky's differentiation between *surface structure* and *deep structure*. In the course of his research, Chomsky helped to develop a **transformational grammar** — a grammar (i.e., a formal system of rules) designed to analyse language and clarify its deep structure. Chomsky has emphasized the similarities between different languages. He has argued that most of the differences between various languages concern surface structure only. According to Chomsky, all human languages share common properties of deep structure (called *universals*).

Lenneberg (1967) is another researcher who stresses the innateness of language acquisition. He maintains that we possess a *biological determinant* of language behaviour. Both Lenneberg and Chomsky claim that we are born with the capacity for language and that we have an innate readiness to produce it. They conclude that language is not wholly learned and that some portions are innate.

Lenneberg also argues that we have a critical period for language acquisition. This **critical period** is the specific time period during which language can be learned relatively easily, starting at about 12 to 18 months of age and ending at about 13 years of age. It is called "critical" because at younger or older ages, it is extremely difficult for humans to master *general* language skills. Before about 12 to 18 months, we do not have the necessary neurological apparatus. However, once we reach that age, our nervous systems have matured sufficiently to permit us to acquire and use language. Then, the process of language acquisition parallels that of brain development until about age 13. Throughout this period, our "prewiring" interacts with our environment for our acquisition and development of language. Our neurological sophistication enables us to become more adept at learning and using syntactical and grammatical rules. After the age of about 13, our innate capacity seems to decline. Some rare instances have been documented of children in their young teens who had never been exposed to any language at all. With subsequent teaching, such children can acquire some language skills, but they seem unable to attain a high level of proficiency (Fromkin et al., 1974).

Lenneberg and Chomsky propose a model far to one end of the nature-nurture continuum. Nevertheless, even they would not completely discount the importance of environment and experience in language acquisition.

The role of environment

Infants raised in a verbally enriched environment tend to develop language skills relatively early. They also tend to be more verbal than average in later life. Such observations suggest that environment affects our acquisition of language.

Learning theorists stress the importance of environment for language acquisition. These theorists adopt an approach based either on *operant conditioning* or on *modelling*.

As we explained in Chapter 5, **operant conditioning** is the process of learning in which the organism emits a response, and the consequences either strengthen or weaken that response. A typical operant-conditioning theory of language acquisition is presented by A. W. Staats and C. K. Staats (1963). They contend that parents provide reinforcement for language by becoming excited, poking, touching, smiling, and other parental gyrations in response to the infant's vocalizations. Parental reactions increase further when these vocalizations mean something. As a result, meaningful responses are *shaped* by social reinforcement. Eventually, language usage itself becomes reinforcing as communication and interaction increases. A study by Rheingold, Gewirtz, and Ross (1955) demonstrated that infant vocalizations could be increased or decreased depending upon whether reinforcement was provided or withheld.

However, the operant-conditioning theory of language contains some serious weaknesses. First, parents normally pay very little attention to grammar and grammatical structure. Thus, grammar develops with advancing age, apparently in the absence of direct reinforcement. Secondly, we can acquire a greater vocabulary without being directly reinforced for doing so. Third, and perhaps most importantly, we somehow learn to form new grammatical relations to express thoughts and ideas in ways that we have never expressed before. As they are new, they could not have been specifically reinforced earlier.

Another group of learning theorists advocate a modelling theory of language acquisition. You may recall from Chapter 5 that **modelling** is the act of imitating or matching one's behaviour to that of another person who acts as a model. According to the modelling theory of language, infants acquire language by imitating adult speech. Indeed, the repetitive imitation that often occurs with children's speech is quite noticeable. Presumably, by imitating the speech of an adult, a child copies not only the basic structures of language, but also the interrelationships of syntax and grammar. Obviously, children do imitate a certain amount of their parents' speech. Rural Newfoundland children seldom speak exactly like their British Columbian counterparts. And "eh?" is not in common use south of the border.

Nevertheless, the modelling theory does not provide a completely satisfactory explanation of language acquisition. Despite

Children raised in a verbally enriched environment tend to develop language skills relatively early.
SOURCE: Dick Hemingway.

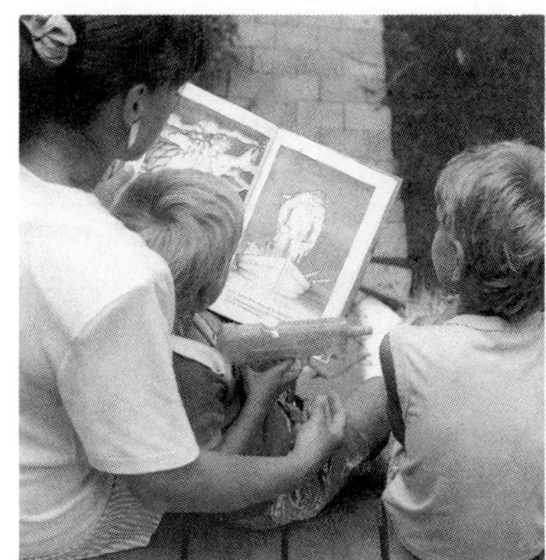

attempts at imitation, young children often produce grammatically incorrect sentences. Many parents have said "we have no more cookies" and winced at the child's enthusiastic agreement that "we got no more cookies." Furthermore, some psycholinguists claim that language is much too rich in combinations to be learned solely by imitation. Children could not possibly hear the millions of sentences that they eventually learn to express and comprehend (Miller, 1965).

From our consideration of the role of biology and the role of environment in the acquisition of language, we can draw the following conclusion. Humans do have a number of innate neurological structures that predispose them to learn language very easily and in very similar ways, even in different cultures. This predisposition, however, would not develop into language without specific learning experiences.

FIGURE 8-12 **Knowledge needed to produce meaningful speech**
SOURCE: Adapted with permission from Allyn and Bacon, 1989.

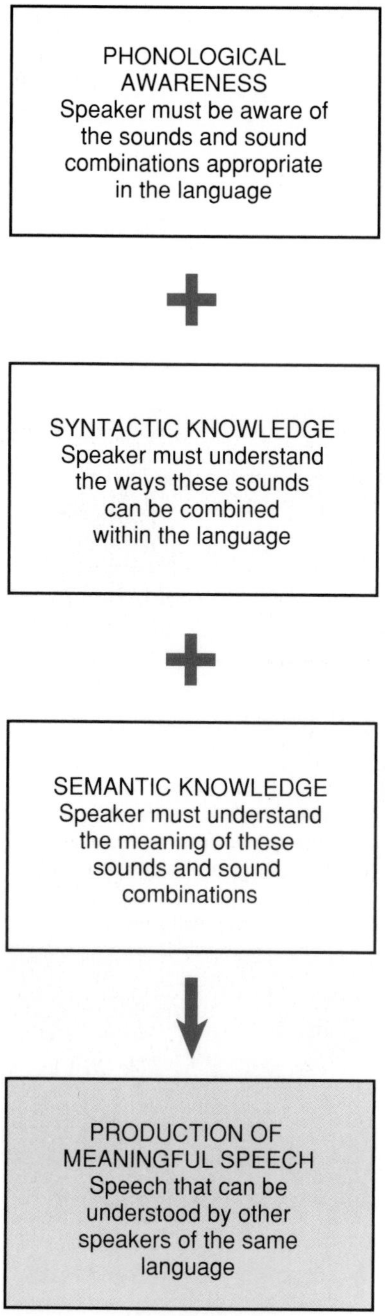

PHONOLOGICAL AWARENESS
Speaker must be aware of the sounds and sound combinations appropriate in the language

SYNTACTIC KNOWLEDGE
Speaker must understand the ways these sounds can be combined within the language

SEMANTIC KNOWLEDGE
Speaker must understand the meaning of these sounds and sound combinations

PRODUCTION OF MEANINGFUL SPEECH
Speech that can be understood by other speakers of the same language

Stages of language development

In order to produce meaningful speech, children must acquire three types of knowledge. (See Figure 8-12.) They must become aware of phonemes, morphemes, and words. They must gain syntactic knowledge to understand how these sounds can be combined and arranged in a form that is grammatically acceptable. And they must acquire semantic knowledge to understand the meaning of these sounds.

Most children follow a similar pattern of development in their acquisition of language. Researchers have identified four stages in this development during the early years of life. The exact ages at which infants progress from stage to stage varies somewhat, depending upon the individual. In the following descriptions, the ages that we cite are simply the typical ones.

The first stage of language development, which usually begins during the second or third month of life, is called the **cooing stage**. It is characterized by vowel-like vocalizations. At this stage, infants are more capable of discriminating and recognizing sounds than they are of producing them. At about age 5 months, infants begin making more babbling and rambling utterances. They seem to be trying to imitate the sounds of language that they hear.

The second main stage of development, known as the **one-word stage**, generally appears at about age 12 months. As its name suggests, the one-word stage is characterized by the use of single words, usually simple nouns and verbs such as "dada" and "go." The child starts to associate words with specific objects in the environment, first as a way of naming them and then as a means of request. For example, "toy" is first used to identify a particular play object, and subsequently to indicate the child's request for that object. This stage marks the beginnings of *true speech*, in which words and word combinations are used.

The third main stage of development, known as the **two-word stage**, usually begins at about age 20 months. As its name implies, the two-word stage is characterized by the use of pairs of words. "There milk" and "Mama shoe" are typical examples. In many cases, the listener must know the context in order to understand the communication. For instance, "Mama shoe" may mean "That is Mama's shoe" or "Mama is wearing the shoe." During this stage, the child often seems to be using word pairs to categorize objects, rather than to communicate requests.

The fourth main stage of development, which usually begins at about age 30 months, is called the **telegraphic-speech stage**. It is characterized by short phrases and sentences whose meaning is clear but which usually lack auxiliary verbs, articles, prepositions, and proper word inflections. "Milk all gone" would mean "All the milk is gone." Similarly, "It time Sonia sleep" would mean "It is time for Sonia to go to sleep." Nevertheless, by this stage the child has come to recognize the importance of word order (syntax). The child is now able to communicate thoughts relatively effectively.

By the age of 5 or 6 years, children have learned to produce complete sentences that are grammatically correct. Throughout their early years, children acquire new vocabulary at astounding rates. At the age of 2, the average child's vocabulary consists of approximately 50 words. By the age of 3, the vocabulary has increased to about 1 000 words (Lenneberg, 1969). And by the age of 5, the typical child has acquired a vocabulary of about 5 000 to 10 000 words.

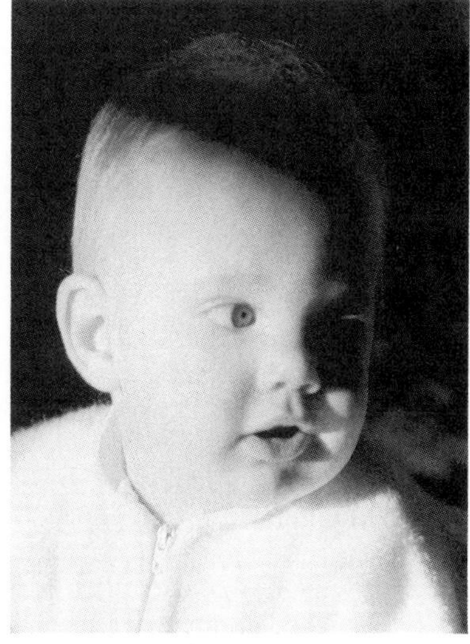

The first stage of language development is known as the cooing stage.
SOURCE: Dick Hemingway.

SPECIAL TOPIC Nonhuman Language

Many dog owners can tell when their pet wants a dog biscuit and when it wants to go outside. Does this mean that their dog is using language? Or do dogs use another type of communication system? To clarify these questions we should emphasize that in addition to communicating information to others, human language permits us to combine words in unique ways to represent novel ideas or abstractions. We may think we know what our pets are thinking and feeling. But are they actually able to use some form of language to plan, abstract, and develop new concepts? Considerable controversy surrounds the question of whether any nonhuman animals can use true language. Some of that controversy has even included uncivil accusations between researchers. Perhaps this issue arouses such intense feelings because we humans want to hang onto something that is unique to us. The underlying philosophical issue is whether we differ from animals *qualitatively* (we have something unique that they don't have) or only *quantitatively* (we do the same things as animals, only better and at a higher level).

Psychologists have been interested in determining the language capabilities of nonhuman primates for many years. Early attempts to train apes to use spoken language met with failure (e.g., Hayes, 1951; Kellogg and Kellogg, 1933), but this was primarily because apes lack an adequately developed vocal apparatus. It still wasn't

Washoe, a chimpanzee trained to use sign language, here gives the sign for "drink."
SOURCE: Paul Fusco/Magnum Photos.

known if the animals could acquire and use language as we know it. More recently, some researchers have tried to teach apes (chiefly chimpanzees and gorillas) to use sign language or plastic symbols representing words to communicate in a language-like fashion (e.g., Rumbaugh, Gill, and von Glaserfeld, 1963; Fouts and Rigby, 1977).

The Gardners adopted a chimpanzee, Washoe, when she was ten months old (Gardner & Gardner, 1972). They treated her as much like a human child as possible when they were with her and always spoke in American Sign Language (ASL) when in her presence. They wanted to recreate the environment in which human children learn language. Within four years, Washoe had learned about 160 signs. Moreover, she often seemed to use the signs in novel ways (Gardner & Gardner, 1972). The first time she saw a mask, she called it an "eye hat." She put together novel combinations of words such as "you drink" and even sequences of dialogue such as, "me drink orange juice." When informed that the juice was gone, she would ask to have the refrigerator opened. When told it was empty, she signed "drive to store." She and other chimpanzees have even used sign language to lie to their caretakers, thereby showing clear intent of symbolic use of the words.

One of the most moving and significant aspects of Washoe's life was her relationship with her adopted son, Loulis. Washoe had a baby that died, and she was almost inconsolable. When her caretaker entered her compound, she would rush over asking for her baby. When she was told that, no, there was no baby, she slouched grieving in the corner. She enthusiastically adopted the infant Loulis. Remarkably, she taught him over 50 signs, with some help from other chimpanzees who could sign. This intergenerational transfer is sometimes cited as evidence that Washoe was using true language.

Patterson has run a similar study with a gorilla named Koko. Koko has been well publicized for her adoption of kittens, whom she treats with the utmost gentleness. For our purposes, though, it is more important to note that Patterson has taught Koko more than 600 signs. Koko sometimes signs to herself when alone (Patterson & Linden, 1981). In a somewhat different study, the Premacks provided a group of chimpanzees with plastic symbols to use as words. Premack (1976) maintains that through reinforcement, the animals learned to use their "language" to communicate with each other, to solve problems, and to share in rewards. Another group of researchers, led by Rumbaugh, taught a chimpanzee named Lana to use a keyboard linked to a computer to "talk." Lana often made up new words, such as "finger bracelet" for a ring the first time she saw one (Rumbaugh, 1977).

How should we assess these studies? There is little doubt that other primates can learn to use words that carry meanings in much the same way as humans do. But there is a lot of doubt that nonhuman primates can combine those words into the sentence structures that are a feature of language. The conclusions one draws from the studies described above depends on how one defines language.

One apparent difference between human language and chimpanzee "language" is that human language is *productive*. By this we mean we can produce new structures, words, and meanings by new combinations of morphemes and words. With just 45 phonemes we can produce 50 000 morphemes that can be combined into hundreds of thousands of English words. Moreover, you could even make up hundreds of new words right now if you wanted to because you understand how to combine English morphemes. These words could be your attempt to communicate a feeling or concept for which existing words are inadequate. There is no conclusive evidence that other primates can produce words this way, although "finger bracelet" and "eye mask" can probably be called productive combinations of old words. That is a simpler task than creating a new word such as "gritchel." A second difference is that human language consists of *levels*, whereas chimpanzee language does not. There is a clear difference between specific sounds, which do not have semantic meaning, and morphemes, which do. Chimpanzees seem to give equal meaning to both. Some researchers argue that nonhuman primates simply use words to name things, rather than to develop complex semantic meaning. A third difference is that human language is strongly based on the *ordering* of words (i.e., syntax). "Gina hit Marc" means something much different than "Marc hit Gina." But it is not certain that nonhuman primates recognize syntactical rules.

One of the strongest criticisms of chimpanzee language has come from Herbert Terrace (1979, 1980, and 1985). He was quite enthusiastic about teaching language to a chimpanzee, whom he named Nim Chimpsky (after the famous psycholinguist Noam Chomsky). At the end of his study, however, Terrace concluded that much of what passes for evidence of language among lower primates is no more than object-naming and simple operant behaviour. He argued that the animals learned to work for rewards by generating certain signs, just as they might push a lever. He also argued that other investigators were unconsciously cuing their animals and mistaking imitative behaviour for true language.

In turn, some researchers have objected that Terrace's criticisms are not valid. They point out that Nim Chimpsky was kept in a cage and brought out for language lessons, which were often given by many different trainers. They argue that even a human baby would have trouble learning language under such conditions. The Gardners have also reacted strongly against Terrace's conclusions (Gardner & Gardner, 1986). As evidence that chimpanzees use true language, the Gardners point to the second-generation development of language (as learned by Loulis) and to the use of inflection in chimpanzee vocalizations.

Other researchers (Savage-Rumbaugh et al., 1983; Sanders, 1985) concede that chimpanzee language may exist. However, they maintain that it would have to be fundamentally different in purpose than human language. Human children, unlike chimpanzees, spontaneously name things and seek to assign meaning to words.

Do nonhuman animals have language? That depends on how we define *language*. They certainly can communicate in complex ways. Clearly, humans can do this better. But we still don't know whether our language ability is qualitatively different or only quantitatively different from other animals.

SPECIAL TOPIC The Psychology of Bilingualism

Barry McLaughlin points out that "Canada represents a modern industrialized society in which the issue of linguistic diversity has enormous social and educational consequences" (McLaughlin, 1985, p.60). He might have added *psychological* consequences as well. Canada's linguistic history is unique in the world in many ways, and there is a growing body of research aimed at understanding the impact that bilingualism has on Canadians.

Canada may be described as a linguistic "mosaic," as opposed to a "melting pot" as typified by the United States (see Figure 8-13). Canada's history has created distinct French and English cultures. Furthermore, many immigrant groups have worked to retain their cultural and linguistic identity. They have tried to avoid assimilation into the main culture. Native peoples also have their own languages. Four of their languages are widely used among Native Canadians: Algonquin, Athabascan, Iroquoian, and the language of the Inuit. According to the 1986 census, about 62% of Canadians have English as their mother tongue, and only about 8% of these speakers are bilingual. By contrast, about 25% of Canadians have French as their mother tongue, and about 33% of these speakers are bilingual (Alcock, Carment, & Sadava, 1991).

What factors affect the learning of a second language? The first is age, but not in the way most people think. The late Montreal neurosurgeon Wilder Penfield argued that the young child

FIGURE 8-13 Percentage distribution by mother tongue of the population by provinces and territories, 1986

Mother Tongue	Nfld.	P.E.I.	N.S.	N.B.	Que.	Ont.	Man.	Sask.	Alta.	B.C.	Yukon	N.W.T.
	%	%	%	%	%	%	%	%	%	%	%	%
English	98.9	94.8	94.6	65.9	9.2	79.6	75.7	84.2	84.1	83.7	90.0	55.5
French	0.4	4.1	3.6	33.0	84.5	4.9	4.6	2.1	2.1	1.4	2.5	2.6
Other	0.7	1.0	1.8	1.2	6.3	15.5	19.7	13.7	13.8	14.9	7.5	41.9

SOURCE: 1986 Census of Canada. From *The Nation* (Statistics Canada: Minister of Supply and Services, 1987), Catalogue 93-102.

could learn language more easily because the young brain was more "plastic." However, it appears that the child's advantage applies only to acquiring the accent of the language. Given the same amount of training and opportunity to use the new language, adults tend to learn a second language faster than children (Harley, 1986).

The second factor that affects the learning of a second language is intellectual ability. Ability is less important if one learns a second language in elementary school, rather than waiting until adolescence (Fiorucci and Preston, 1986). Among Ontario children who started learning French in grade 6 or earlier, intellectual ability was not correlated with their later French language competence in grade 12. The children were of about equal linguistic ability. Among children who started during adolescence, however, the brighter children were superior in grade 12. In general, intellectual ability is an important factor in learning a second language later in life.

The third and perhaps most crucial factor in determining success in learning a second language is attitude (Gardner and Lambert, 1972). Attitudes are important because they determine the level of a person's motivation. It takes a lot of motivation to make the effort needed to learn a language. People who tackle a second language simply to get a better job don't do as well as those who are more motivated to "live" in the language in their social relationships (Gardner, 1984). Another aspect of attitude seems to be how the individual regards the other linguistic community (Clément, Gardner, and Smythe, 1977). Francophone high school students learned English better if they had positive feelings about Anglophones.

Bilingualism seems to exert a detectable impact on cognition. When first learning a new language, a person usually thinks in the mother tongue and then mentally translates the words into the new language before speaking. Advanced progress occurs when the person starts to think (and even dream) in the new language. Subtle differences exist between languages, and these differences affect how one thinks. There are words for particular emotions in French that have no precise counterparts in English or German. If you don't speak French, you can't talk about that emotional state with a friend. Probably, you don't even think or feel exactly that way. Furthermore, knowing two languages can even enhance our use of metaphors in thinking. Marie Bountrogianni (1986) studied 45 bilingual Greek-English Canadian children and 45 unilingual English-speaking Canadian children. She found that the bilingual children were better able to infer the moral of proverbs presented in English. From these findings she concluded that bilingual children may be better able to detect metaphorical meanings in English sentence structure.

Language has such sweeping effects on how we think and act that we can confidently assert that being bilingual will affect the personality and interactions of an individual with others. Indeed, language is probably the single most powerful factor in maintaining one's cultural identity (Edwards, 1989). Only relatively recently have researchers begun to study the social and psychological effects of bilingualism. Although much more evidence needs to be gathered, we can make a few observations to illustrate the effects of language on behaviour.

One of Canada's national goals is to improve the attitudes that members of different linguistic communities hold toward each other. In Chapter 16 (Social Influence) we will see how some kinds of contact between different racial groups can help lessen prejudice. There is reason to believe that learning a second language will improve feelings toward members of the other linguistic community. At least early in some French immersion programs, students showed more positive attitudes toward Francophones than students in English schools showed (Genesee, 1984). It is discouraging to learn that these positive attitudes faded later in high school, but the findings offer some hope for improved relations in the future.

Another effect of bilingualism has been observed in English-French speaking families in which the father is the only parent who transmits one of the languages. In unilingual families, the mother usually speaks to the children more repetitiously and simply than the father does. The father can then build on the linguistic foun-

Language is probably the single most powerful factor in maintaining one's cultural identity.
SOURCE: Dick Hemingway.

dation established by the mother. By contrast, in the English-French families, both the mother and the father tend to speak in a similar style, using much repetition and simple language. Presumably, in such families, the father is responding sensitively to the child's efforts in acquiring the second language (Goodz et al., 1986).

The consequences of learning a second language also depend on the relative size and social prominence of the two linguistic communities. For example, Dion, Dion, and Pak (1989) found that linguistic competence affected the social and psychological adjustment of 184 bilingual members of Toronto's Chinese community. Those who were more confident in English (the majority language) had higher self-esteem, but they were less involved in the Chinese community. Those who were more confident in Chinese (the minority language) were more active in the Chinese community, but they reported lower self-esteem, less internal control, and less happiness. Thinking, emotion, and our very personalities are affected by our language.

Attitudes toward Canada's policy of official bilingualism vary according to the threat a community feels to its own cultural identity and socio-economic status. Residents of Cornwall, Ontario, for example, are more negative toward bilingualism than residents of Kingston, Ontario, where French is perceived as less of a threat to the English culture (Berry and Bourcier, 1989). The psychology of bilingualism is very much a political concern in Canada. There is a desperate need for more research to explore this subject.

Chapter Summary

1. Thinking and language are two of the main concerns of cognitive psychology. Thinking might be the most important characteristic of our species as a whole and of each of us as individuals. During the past one hundred years, researchers have developed four methods to investigate our thinking processes: introspection, behavioural observation, reaction-time studies, and physiological studies.

2. The major components of our thinking are images, words, and concepts. The most frequent and intense images are visual, spatial, and motion images. However, we can also experience images of sound, taste, touch, and smell. Because images enable us to overcome the limitations of language, they often play an important role in creative thinking.

3. Words are our most widely used symbols for oral and written communication. They represent images and concepts. For effective communication, it is essential that people agree on the meanings of the words they use.

4. Concepts enable us to classify information and organize our complex world. Concepts are often arranged in hierarchies. Different concepts may be based on different criteria. In practice, we employ many fuzzy concepts.

5. To form and refine concepts, we apply the processes of generalization and discrimination. Our primary, overall strategy for forming concepts is hypothesis testing. We seek to discover rules for inclusion or exclusion, which may take the form of conditional rules, disjunctive rules, or conjunctive rules. Unfortunately, many people hold a confirmation bias and make poor use of disconfirming evidence.

6. To solve problems, we can focus on three components: the initial state, the goal state, and effective operations. The IDEAL problem-solver is a useful acronym for the steps used in problem-solving. The way we identify, define, and represent a given problem can strongly influence our search for a solution. The strategies we might explore for solving a problem can include various algorithms and heuristics. Once we start acting on our strategies, we should strive to be flexible by looking back over our efforts, evaluating them, and obtaining feedback.
7. Various factors can affect problem-solving. Our emotional state may interfere with our efforts. Our attention span imposes some limits on our abilities, but we can partially overcome these limits by employing external aids. A set might facilitate the solving of some problems. However, a rigid set, such as functional fixedness, hampers our search for creative solutions. Sometimes, we engage in self-deception, which leads to poor decisions.
8. Research in artificial intelligence raises many questions about human thought processes. Some psychologists have emphasized the importance of context in cognition. Other psychologists have studied the process of automatization. Programmers have developed some expert systems based on if-then rules.
9. Creativity is characterized by appropriateness, usefulness, ingenuity, breadth, and novelty. Creativity seems to require divergent thinking. By contrast, logical problem-solving relies on convergent thinking. Research studies suggest that creativity and intelligence are not strongly related.
10. Language, our most common means of communication, relies on symbols. We make use of natural language as well as artificial language. The disciplines of linguistics and psycholinguistics investigate various aspects of language, including its production, structure, acquisition, and perception.
11. The structure of language can be broken down into phonemes, graphemes, morphemes, and words. At higher levels, language can be analysed in terms of syntax, grammar, and semantics.
12. The relationship between language and thought is perhaps best represented by an interactive model. On the one hand, according to Worf's hypothesis of linguistic determinism, the structure of a particular language may determine how its users think. On the other hand, according to Chomsky's linguistic analysis, all languages reveal a uniformity of deep structure and therefore similar ways of thinking regardless of culture.
13. The nature-nurture controversy is prominent in the area of language acquisition. Some psycholinguists maintain that we are born with an innate capacity for language. Chomsky supports this position by using a transformational grammar to show certain universals of language. Linneberg argues that we must be prewired for language because we have a critical period for its acquisition. By contrast, some learning theorists maintain that we acquire language through operant conditioning or modelling.

However, reinforcement and imitation do not adequately account for all aspects of acquisition. We can try to resolve the nature-nurture resolution here by concluding that we do have innate neurological structures that enable us to acquire language, but that this predisposition will not develop without specific learning experiences.

14. To produce meaningful speech, children must gain phonological awareness, syntactic knowledge, and semantic knowledge. Most young children pass through the following stages of language development: the cooing stage, the one-word stage, the two-word stage, and the telegraphic speech style.

Key Terms

Algorithm A clearly stated series of rules and procedures that leads to the solution of a particular problem.

Artificial intelligence The field in which computers are designed to simulate human thought processes.

Artificial language A form of written communication based on a notation that is not verbal.

Attention span In problem-solving, the limits of human memory and cognition.

Automatization The process by which a complex activity is done so frequently that it comes to seem automatic.

Behavioural observation A method of investigating cognitive processes in which we directly observe how people solve problems or deal with given situations under controlled conditions.

Bound morpheme A morpheme that must be combined with one or more other morphemes to form a word.

Cognitive psychology The theory that cognitions (thinking, learning, remembering, and other mental processes) are the most important causes of behaviour.

Concept A mental category of objects, events, or ideas based on common characteristics.

Conditional rule In concept formation, a rule that if the new instance meets one particular criterion, then it must meet another particular criterion to be included in the given concept. See also *if-then rule*.

Confirmation bias In testing hypotheses, the tendency to look harder for confirming evidence than disconfirming evidence.

Conjunctive rule In concept formation, a rule that if a new instance meets two criteria at the same time, then it is included in the given concept.

Context In human thinking and learning, the setting of a statement, which includes the surrounding statements, preceding and following events, and previous knowledge.

Convergent thinking Thinking that is directed to generating one solution to a given problem.

Cooing stage The first stage of language development, which usually begins during the second or third month of life. It is characterized by vowel-like vocalizations.

Creativity Process of problem-solving that has the properties of appropriateness, usefulness, ingenuity, breadth, and novelty. It is characterized by divergent thinking.

Critical period In language acquisition, the specific time period during which language can be learned relatively easily, starting at about 12 to 18 months of age and ending at about 13 years of age.

Deep structure The underlying meaning of a sentence.

Discrimination In concept formation, the process of narrowing a concept by finding new examples that do not fit it.

Disjunctive rule In concept formation, a rule that if the new instance meets either one criterion or another criterion but not both criteria, then it is included in the given concept.

Divergent thinking Thinking that is directed to generating many different potential solutions to a given problem.

Expert system A computer program that uses a series of decision rules derived from the thinking processes of human experts.

Free morpheme A morpheme that can stand alone as a word.

Functional fixedness A rigid set of thinking of objects in terms of their normal function. It hinders us from thinking of novel uses of objects and hence new approaches to problems.

Fuzzy concept A concept whose criteria for inclusion or exclusion are based on tendencies rather than on precise rules.

Generalization In concept formation, the process of expanding a concept by finding new examples that fit it.

Goal state In problem-solving, the desired result of the problem-solving.

Grammar The formal codification of the rules for word inflection, word formation, and syntax.

Grapheme A letter or combination of letters representing a phoneme.

Heuristic A rule-of-thumb strategy for problem-solving.

Hierarchy An organizational framework in which more general categories branch out into narrower categories at each level.

Hypothesis testing In concept formation, the process of guessing what properties define a given concept and then testing new instances that have these properties to see whether they belong to the concept.

IDEAL problem-solver An acronym for the steps in problem-solving: Identify, Define, Explore, Act, and Look back.

If-then rule A logical rule of deductive reasoning in the form of an if . . . then statement.

Image A brain process that gives a sensory representation of an object or event.

Initial state In problem-solving, the less desired current situation that one wishes to change.

Introspection A research method devised by structuralists in which trained observers examine their own mental processes and report their private mental experiences in detail.

Language See *artificial language; natural language.*

Linguistic determinism The hypothesis, proposed by Whorf, that the structure of a particular language determines how the users of that language think.

Linguistics The field of study that investigates the production of speech, the structure of language, and the use of words and sentences.

Means-ends analysis Another term for the heuristic of *setting subgoals.* The process of breaking a large problem down into smaller subproblems and then solving each subproblem.

Method class In problem-solving, a group of operations that are so similar that if one operation in the class fails, then we know that the other operations in the class will fail as well.

Modelling The act of imitating or matching one's behaviour to that of another person who acts as a model.

Morpheme The smallest unit of meaning in a language. See also *bound morpheme; free morpheme.*

Natural language A form of spoken, written, or gestured communication based on verbal symbols.

One-word stage The second stage of language development, which usually begins at about age 12 months. It is characterized by the use of single words, usually simple nouns and verbs.

Operant conditioning The process of learning in which the organism emits a response, and the consequences either strengthen or weaken that response.

Operations In problem-solving, the actions one takes to achieve the desired result.

Phoneme The smallest unit of sound in a language.

Problem A situation or event that is currently not desirable.

Problem-solving The process of changing from a less desired state (the initial state) to a more desired state (the goal state) by performing actions (operations). See also *IDEAL problem-solver.*

Psycholinguistics The field of study that investigates how language is acquired, perceived, and comprehended.

Reaction-time studies A method of investigating cognitive processes in which the speed with which the subject responds to a given stimulus, situation, or problem is taken as a measure of the amount and complexity of cognitive processing used.

Semantics The study of the meaning in language.

Set A well-learned predisposition about how to perform a specific task or how to perceive a particular situation.

Setting subgoals A heuristic that consists of breaking down the goal of a problem into smaller, more manageable objectives.

Surface structure The arrangement of phonemes, morphemes, words, and phrases in a sentence as it is actually written or spoken.

Syntax The arrangement of words into acceptable phrases and sentences.

Telegraphic-speech stage The fourth stage of language development which usually begins at about age 30 months. It is characterized by short phrases and sentences whose meaning is clear but which lack auxiliary verbs, articles, prepositions, and proper word inflections.

Thinking The internal manipulation of symbols in order to process information.

Transformational grammar A grammar (i.e., a formal system of rules) designed to analyse language and clarify its deep structure.

Two-word stage The third stage of language development, which usually begins at about age 20 months. It is characterized by the use of pairs of words.

Word A verbal symbol, consisting of a combination of letters, that represents an object, event, idea, or concept.

Work backward from the goal A heuristic that consists of beginning at the goal state and working back to the initial state in an attempt to solve a given problem.

Suggested Readings

Best, J. B. (1986). *Cognitive psychology.* St. Paul, MN: West. A good text on the topic of cognition.

Carroll, D. W. (1985). *Psychology of language.* Monterey, CA: Brooks/Cole. A good textbook on language.

Gardner, H. (1985). *The mind's new science.* New York: Basic Books, Inc. This widely respected book is perhaps the best source to use to extend your knowledge of thinking and language. It provides an excellent overview.

Koestler, A. (1970). *The act of creation.* London: Pan Books Ltd. This is a scholarly treatment of the psychology of creativity. It brilliantly explores art, humour, science, and other topics that are based on the unexpected combinations of creative thinking. The first half is designed for the educated layperson, and the second half is more formal and scholarly.

Linden, E. (1986). *Silent partners: The legacy of the ape language experiments.* New York: Times Books. Although this book is not specifically about the acquisition of language, it offers a provocative and disturbing look at the lives of the ape subjects in some of the language-training programs. Some of these animals no longer fit into their natural, animal society. Their fate in human society is dependent on research funding, which has a tendency to disappear. The treatment of some of these animals has not been good.

Pinker, S. (1984). *Language learnability and language development.* Cambridge, MA: Harvard University Press. A relatively advanced treatment of language which includes a discussion of Chomsky's theories.

Tartter, V. C. (1986). *Language processes.* New York: Holt, Rinehart & Winston. A useful testbook on language.

CHAPTER 9

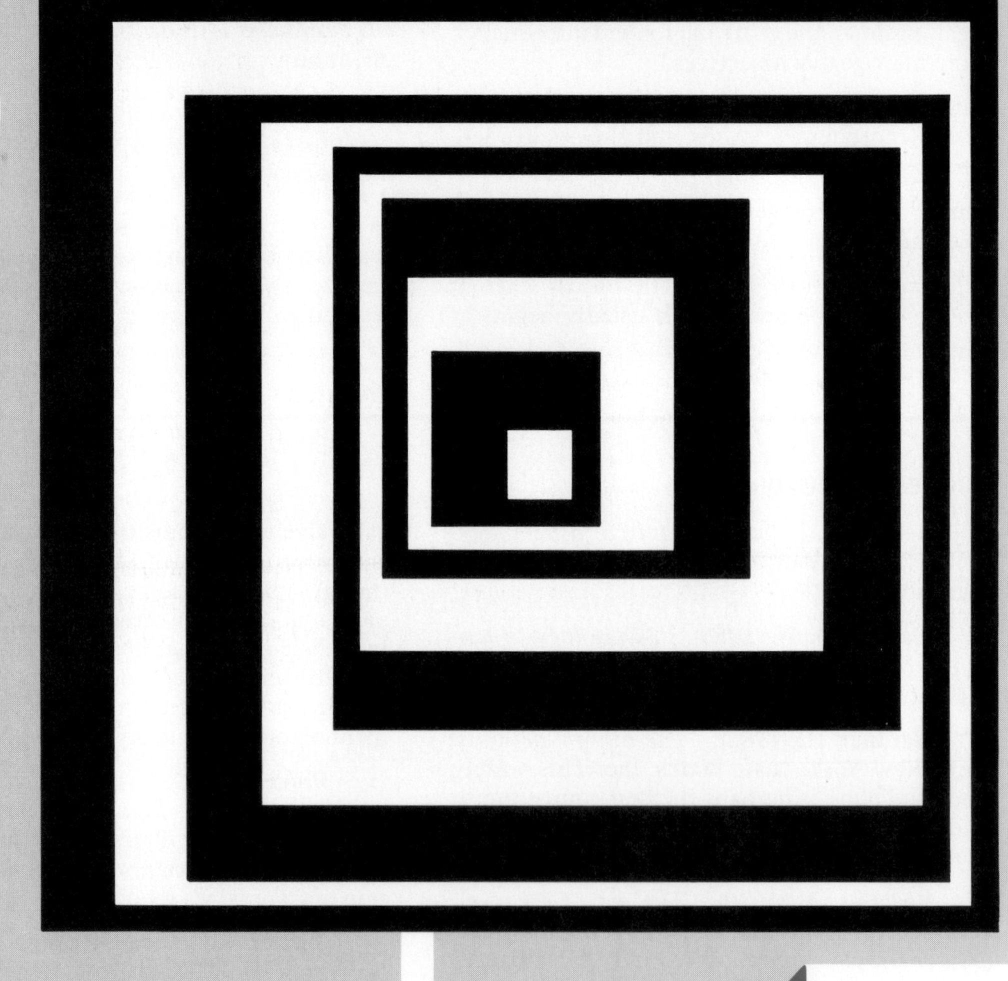

The Psychology of Consciousness

WE OFTEN CONFIDENTLY offer explanations for why we do what we do. Sometimes, though, our explanations, even about our own motives, turn out to be wrong. On occasion, we might say, "That wasn't like me to do that. I just wasn't myself. I wasn't conscious of what I was doing." But obviously, we were our "self" and we were "conscious." Nevertheless, we use such expressions when we do something that we have not consciously controlled as much as we would have wished. Many people have experiences in which the world seems a bit unreal. Every day we enter an *altered state of consciousness* in which the rules of reality are temporarily suspended: we sleep and dream. Some people seek new states of consciousness through meditation or drugs. A vastly complex sphere of experience lies outside ordinary awareness, and we will try to understand some of it in this chapter.

Endel Tulving, of the University of Toronto, has said, "Of all the mysteries of nature, none is greater than that of human consciousness. Intimately familiar to all of us, our capacity to contemplate the universe and to apprehend the infinity of space and time, and our knowledge that we can do so, have continued to resist analysis" (Tulving, 1985, p. 1). Everybody "knows" what consciousness is, but almost nobody can readily formulate a satisfactory definition. One problem is that the term *consciousness* has a great many meanings. For example, Natsoulas (1978) discusses six. Armstrong discusses three kinds of consciousness. However, he observes that "consciousness is a dizzying phenomenon. It is not even clear that those who use the word always refer to the same thing" (Armstrong, 1979, p. 234). Papalia and Olds propose that "while there is no universally agreed-upon definition of consciousness, we can adopt as a working definition *our awareness of ourselves and of the world around us*" (Papalia and Olds, 1988, p. 119) Myers suggests that we think of consciousness as *selective attention to ongoing perceptions, thoughts, and feelings* (Myers, 1989, p. 193). But these working definitions are far from satisfactory. For example, what is "awareness"? Is consciousness nothing more than simply awareness? Does consciousness of one's own self imply nothing more than selective attention to mental processes? Are animals conscious by these definitions? Our questions reveal some of the obstacles to defining consciousness in an adequate manner.

Consciousness enables us to contemplate the universe and the infinity of space and time.
SOURCE: Courtesy U.S. Naval Observatory.

The study of consciousness is one of the most controversial areas in psychology. In fact, some introductory psychology textbooks do not even include a chapter on consciousness. In our chapter, we will be looking at several issues over which psychologists are currently arguing. Some say that ideas such as consciousness are mystical and unscientific. Others say it makes no sense to exclude from psychology something so obviously important in human behaviour. We agree that it is a subject well worth discussing.

The scientific method operates through the formulation of theories and the testing of derived hypotheses. To explain an unusual phenomenon, a theoretical explanation may be proposed that is later found to be invalid. But this does not mean that we should then dismiss the phenomenon itself. We should try to keep an open mind. The phenomenon may actually be occurring, even though we lack a satisfactory explanation for it. Unfortunately, in the history of science, there has been a tendency to reject certain phenomena when the theories for them have been discredited. Later in this chapter, we will encounter this tendency in our historical survey of hypnotism—a phenomenon that was first explained in terms of magnetic forces.

The importance of consciousness has flourished and declined at various times throughout the history of psychology. Many of the trends we have already discussed about schools of thought have been reflected in the attitudes toward consciousness. In the early days of the discipline, in 1887, Ladd defined psychology itself as "the description and explanation of states of consciousness as such" (cited in Hilgard, 1980, p. 2). The *structuralists* agreed that consciousness should be the main focus of psychology. Therefore, one of their main methods of investigation was **introspection**, in which trained observers examine their own mental processes and report their private mental experiences in detail. By contrast, the *behaviourists* adopted a stance that was rooted in the biological sciences. In 1913, Watson clearly formulated the behaviourist position. He argued that psychology should exclude the concept of consciousness and instead study only observable behaviour:

> Psychology as the behaviourist views it is a purely objective experimental branch of natural science. Its theoretical goal is the prediction and control of behavior. Introspection forms no essential part of its methods, nor is the scientific value of its data dependent upon the readiness with which they lend themselves to interpretation in terms of consciousness (Watson, 1913, p. 158).

This view virtually dominated psychology until four decades ago. It still is a powerful influence, perhaps the most powerful influence, among psychologists in universities. For instance, some experimental psychologists reject the ideas of Freud because they are based on *unconscious* influences. In the 1950s, however, the so-called *cognitive revolution* began, and more attention was devoted to ideas about mental processes such as consciousness, awareness, thinking, feeling, altered states of experience, repression, and unconscious influences on behaviour. Researchers have been trying to subject these areas to scientific studies by focusing on brain function. Now that these topics are more fashionable in psychology, Larry Jacoby has said, "The sexual revolution made it permissible, and sometimes even obligatory, to discuss sex in public. The cognitive revolution seems to have done the same for discussion of the unconscious" (Jacoby, 1987, p. 357).

Consciousness includes awareness and an awareness of being aware.
SOURCE: Dick Hemingway.

THE CONCEPT OF CONSCIOUSNESS

We have pointed out that psychologists do not agree on a complete definition of *consciousness*. Nevertheless, most theorists would agree that *awareness* is a major part of consciousness. As we mentioned, Papalia and Olds (1988) made awareness the basis of their working definition. In this chapter, we too will use the term **consciousness** to mean roughly the same thing as *awareness*, although some definitions of consciousness would include other qualities such as "awareness of one's own being aware."

Here, we do not want to fall into the trap of substituting one unclear concept (awareness) for another (consciousness). Therefore, let us define awareness with care. **Awareness** is the degree to which a person can repeatedly express his or her own brain processes in symbolic ways. There are three important aspects of this definition of awareness. First, *only some of what goes on in the brain qualifies as awareness*. A great deal of brain functioning occurs without awareness. This obviously includes such automatic processes as brain control of hormonal secretions, but it also includes more complex brain functioning. For example, when first driving a new car, a person often tries to put the key in the ignition where it was in the old car "without being aware of what I was doing"—or "without thinking." Hebb has pointed out that he found it possible to read out loud for some time (perhaps to a child) and then to realize that he had "no notion at all of what the heroine had been up to" (Hebb, 1972, p. 31). Complex brain behaviour can occur "without thinking." We would like to understand how the brain can do things "outside awareness."

It is difficult to imagine, however, that reading out loud does not involve some of what we call awareness. This points to a second critical aspect of our definition. Awareness is a matter of *degree*. We should view awareness as a continuum. Strictly speaking, we would not be speaking precisely if we described someone as being *either* aware *or* unaware. A person can be partially aware. Presumably, Hebb was partially aware of more than one thing at a time as he read out loud while thinking about something else.

Finally, our definition refers to expressing something *in symbolic ways*. Evidence of awareness is a person's ability to express the relevant thought. If a person was suffering from anxiety but could not express any understanding of the causes, we would say he or she was *not aware* of the source of the anxiety. By the same token, if the person said, "I feel anxious and it seems to have something to do with my parents; but that's all I know," then we would conclude that he or she was *partially aware* of the causes. Symbolic expression usually takes the form of words. However, awareness can also be expressed symbolically through gestures, drawing pictures, or other non-verbal modes.

Some researchers have tried to determine the role of "normal" awareness. Psychologists also recognize the existence of other types of awareness. We use the term **altered state of consciousness** to denote a state of awareness of brain processes that an individual subjectively finds different from those of normal, waking experience.

Altered states of consciousness can occur under a variety of conditions, such as during sleep, meditation, and hypnosis. They can also be induced by certain drugs.

Let us now investigate how consciousness works. We will start by examining research that concerns brain functions.

Consciousness and the Brain

Brain hemispheres and awareness

Some researchers have studied the effects of having the brain hemispheres surgically separated by cutting the *corpus callosum*. Their findings have many implications for our understanding of consciousness. We will see that many important brain functions operate outside of awareness and yet they still help shape our conscious beliefs.

From Figure 9-1, you may recall our discussion in Chapter 2 of the lateralization of brain functioning. The left hemisphere is usually superior to the right at processing linear tasks, such as logic and language. In most people the left hemisphere controls speech. The left hemisphere always processes the right visual field and controls the right hand. By contrast, the right hemisphere is usually superior at processing spatial data and material that requires perceiving whole patterns. For example, it is usually superior at the recognition of faces. The right hemisphere also seems more involved in the recognition of emotion, especially strong emotion. The right hemisphere always processes the left visual field and controls the left hand.

To control the spread of epileptic seizures from one hemisphere to the other, a number of patients have undergone surgery in which the corpus callosum is severed. When the image of an object is flashed to their left visual field, these patients can choose by touch with the left hand that object from a group of items hidden behind a screen. (See Figure 9-2.) But when asked what the item is, the patients cannot identify it verbally at all (Sperry, 1984). The right hemisphere (processing the left visual field and controlling the left hand) is aware and can identify the item with manual gestures, but the left hemisphere (controlling speech) is not aware of what the item is. When asked how they could pick out the designated item every time, the patients replied that they had no idea and were just making lucky guesses.

It seems odd to say that the right hemisphere was aware of something but the left wasn't. Was the *person* aware? There are some fascinating anecdotes about split-brain patients. Trevarthen relates the following episode: "One of the patients obtained a dishwashing job in a hospital, and one day found that his left hand was throwing the dishes on the floor—not dropping, throwing. He was so ashamed that he ran away" (Armstrong, 1979, p. 245). Apparently, "one part" of a person can feel and behave in a manner that is totally opposite to the way "another part" feels and behaves. In an even more dramatic example, a man with a split brain was attacking his wife with one hand while struggling to stop the attack with his other hand.

FIGURE 9-1 Some features of the lateralization of brain functioning

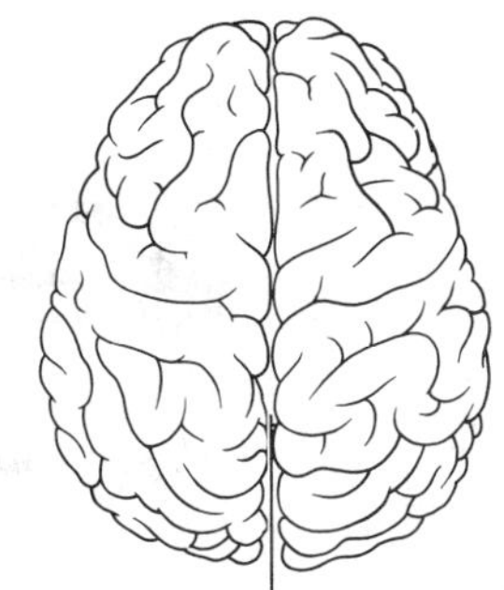

Corpus callosum

Left hemisphere	Right hemisphere
logic	spatial perception
language	recognition of faces
speech	recognition of emotion
right visual field	left visual field
right hand	left hand

FIGURE 9-2 Apparatus used in the study of split-brain patients A picture of an apple is flashed on the screen to the left visual field, which goes to the right hemisphere. The patient is able to identify the apple by touch with the left hand but is unable to say what it is, because neither the picture nor the information from his left hand can reach his left hemisphere.

SOURCE: Adapted with permission from Sperry (1984).

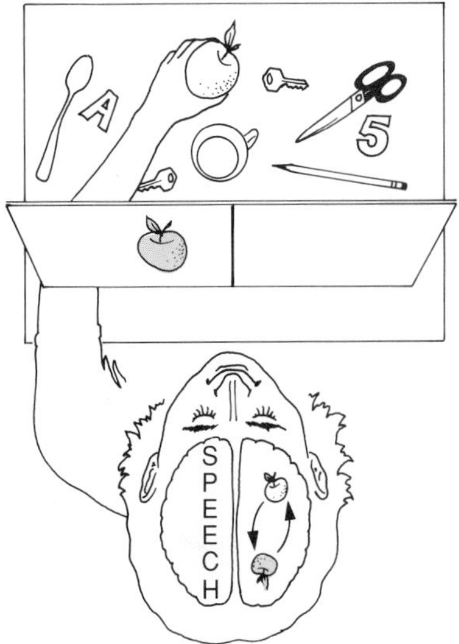

Gazzaniga (1967) reported that a split-brain patient of Sperry's was being shown neutral figures in the left and right visual fields. The figures were flashed so quickly that the patient was not able to centre her eyes on them. Thus, some stimuli went only to one hemisphere and some only to the other. Without warning, a picture of a nude woman was flashed in the left visual field (processed by the right hemisphere). The patient flushed and acted uncomfortable and confused but insisted that she had seen only a flash of light. All she could think to say about the experience was, "Oh, Dr. Sperry, you have some machine!" She was bothered by something occurring in her right hemisphere, but she was "not aware" of what it was in the sense that she couldn't describe it in words. (Remember that speech and language are controlled by the left hemisphere.) At the same time, however, her right hemisphere was "aware," and she probably could have used gestures or drawn a picture with her left hand to show she knew the picture was of a nude.

Gazzaniga's social brain theory

How can we make sense out of internal conflicts, contradictory beliefs, and responses to unconscious influences? Gazzaniga (1985) has proposed the theory, known as the **social brain theory**, that the brain is a sort of "society" made up of many different modules that can act independently of each other. Each module has different talents and functions. Only some modules belong to what we call consciousness or awareness. The so-called *non-verbal modules* do not belong to awareness, but they do process information and experience many kinds of emotion. According to this theory, flashes of insight may reflect long, complex mental processes that were initially done in non-verbal modules. When the results are somehow transferred to "conscious" modules, we experience "sudden" understanding.

Michael Gazzaniga.
SOURCE: Michael Gazzaniga, Ph.D.

Our conscious beliefs are often inaccurate. Gazzaniga asserts that they represent our simple attempts to make sense out of what is happening in modules of our brain that lie outside of our awareness. Gazzaniga supports this hypothesis with the findings of some of his split-brain studies. In one study, a split-brain patient was shown a picture of a chicken claw to the right visual field (the left hemisphere) and a snowy scene to the left visual field (the right hemisphere). (See Figure 9-3.) The patient was then asked to pick out cards relating to what he had seen. He chose a chicken with his right hand (left hemisphere) and a shovel with his left hand (right hemisphere). When asked to explain his choices, the patient said, "Oh, that's easy. The chicken claw goes with the chicken, and you need a shovel to clean out the chicken shed" (Gazzaniga, 1985, p. 72). The verbal explanation came from his left hemisphere, which had no knowledge of the snowy scene. Nevertheless, it instantly came up with a plausible explanation—a conscious belief—of why his left hand had chosen the shovel.

Gazzaniga argues that this same sort of "explanatory" process also occurs in human beings whose brain hemispheres are not severed. It seems to be part of the normal human condition. We often do things that are inconsistent with our conscious knowledge. Then

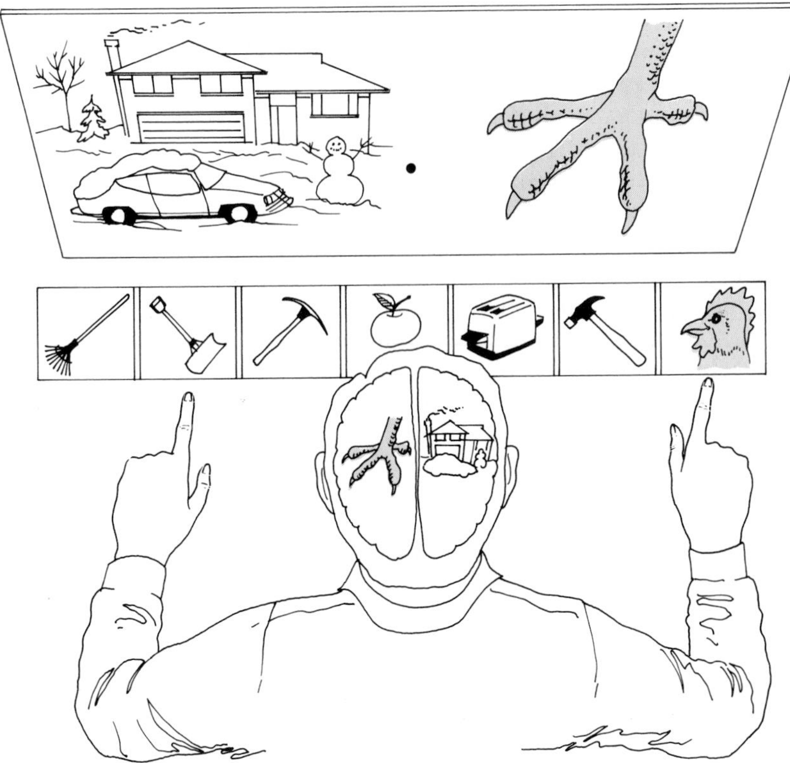

FIGURE 9-3 The design of a split-brain study
A split-brain patient views a snowy scene flashed quickly to the left visual field and a chicken claw flashed quickly to the right visual field. The small pictures on cards are continuously in full view. The patient picks out the chicken with his right hand (left hemisphere) and the shovel with his left hand (right hemishere). His talking (left) hemisphere is unaware of the snowy scene, and it verbally "explains" that the shovel is for cleaning out the chicken shed.

SOURCE: Adapted with permission from Gazzaniga (1985).

we work to "make sense" out of what we have done, often by ignoring that knowledge and changing our beliefs (Turner, 1988). Nisbett and Wilson (1977) set up a display of nylon hosiery in a store and asked people which stockings they thought were of superior quality. In fact, the stockings were identical. There is a general tendency for people to prefer an object at the right-hand end of a line of objects, everything else being equal. Shoppers quite consistently chose stockings to the right. They quite confidently "explained" their choices as being based on qualities such as weave and texture.

We will see that Gazzaniga's *social brain theory* fits in with the findings in some other areas of study on human consciousness. More recently, another prominent brain scientist has published a theory similar to Gazzaniga's. According to Ornstein's **multimind theory**, the brain is a collection of talents and policies and modules that are loosely integrated by a mental operating system (Ornstein, 1987). He also uses this concept to account for unconscious influences and the irrational beliefs that we all have.

UNCONSCIOUS INFLUENCES

One of the most controversial and pragmatically important issues in abnormal behaviour is the role played by awareness in the control of behaviour. We often behave in irrational ways that we cannot explain. Sometimes we have fears that seem to have no cause. We tend to forget threatening memories, even though they are well learned and important to remember. We distort memories in ways that make them more comfortable for us. How can we understand such *unconscious influences* (i.e., influences that lie outside our awareness)?

There are marked differences among psychologists in their acceptance of unconscious influences. Nearly all theories developed in clinical settings have emphasized the importance of unconscious influences on behaviour. By contrast, some (but not all) theories developed in experimental settings have rejected outright the possibility of unconscious influences. Many cognitive psychologists have argued that awareness is a *precondition* for the pervasive influence of cognitions on behaviour. Three decades ago, proponents of behaviour modification adamantly dismissed "clinical" concepts such as subliminal perception and repression. For example, Eysenck categorically stated, "Learning theory does not postulate any such 'unconscious' causes, but regards neurotic symptoms as simply learned habits" (Eysenck & Rachman, 1965, p. 10). Similarly, Wolpe argued, "It does not appear that the repression as such plays any part in the maintenance of neurosis" (Wolpe, 1958, p. 94). The existence of unconscious influences has been dismissed in some circles because the validity of Freud's original ideas seems highly questionable. However, this negative reaction ignores the possibility that Freud might have accurately observed processes such as repression but offered incorrect explanations for them.

More recently, the study of unconscious influences in terms of brain functioning has led to theories and research that meet the rigorous standards of the modern scientific approach. Shevrin and Dickman (1980) marshal a wide range of evidence to support the view that unconscious processes are a necessary assumption of all psychological theory. Kenneth Bowers observes that "the entire concept of unconscious influences on thought, behaviour, and feeling is enjoying a renaissance" (Bowers, 1987, p. 93).

Emotion and cognition

You may recall from Chapter 6 that three main theories of emotion emphasize the importance of awareness and cognition. Nevertheless, some researchers have questioned whether cognition is a necessary prerequisite for emotion. Zajonc (1980) has summarized evidence that *emotional reactions* and *cognitive processes* can and do operate independently of each other. He concludes that "preferences need no inferences," meaning that we can have emotional preferences (i.e., likes and dislikes) without having any conscious understanding of the reasons for those preferences. Wilson (1979) performed a *dichotic listening* experiment whose results support this view. He presented subjects with a complex task called *shadowing*. The subjects had to repeat every word said through earphones into their right ears, while he played different patterns of musical notes in their left ears. The subjects were selectively attending to the words read into the right ear and ignoring the musical patterns in the left ear. Subsequently, subjects were not able to discriminate the tone patterns they had heard from new tone patterns. (Other subjects, who had been instructed to attend to the tone patterns, discriminated them with 100% accuracy.) But when they were asked which patterns they preferred, subjects tended to choose the patterns that they had been exposed to. Even without being *aware* of what musical note patterns they had heard, the subjects developed a preference for the familiar patterns. Wilson argued that his findings illustrated the **simple exposure effect**, that is, the tendency of people to prefer familiar stimuli. Wilson concluded that the simple exposure effect does not require awareness to operate.

Zajonc and Lazarus have disputed which comes first, affect or cognition ("On the primacy of affect," Zajonc, 1984; "On the primacy of cognition," Lazarus, 1984). A resolution of this issue would clarify how we change emotions. If cognitions cause emotions, as Ellis (1985) maintains, then we could change an individual's emotions by changing that person's thinking. However, Zajonc argues that emotions can occur independently of cognitions.

Part of the debate between Zajonc and Lazarus boils down to a difference of opinion over the meaning of the word "cognition" (Kleinginna & Kleinginna, 1985). Zajonc uses the term to mean thinking and reasoning, whereas Lazarus uses the term to refer to any discrimination the body makes, even if the person is not aware of it. Thus, Zajonc's use of the term is closer to our rough definition of cognition as "awareness." Zajonc does present convincing evidence that emotions can occur independently of reason.

On balance, the position that seems most consistent with experimental findings is that emotion and cognition (defined as thought of which the person has some awareness) are separate systems in humans. They can operate independently, but they often do influence each other.

How can cognition influence emotion? Earlier in this book (in Chapter 5), we encountered a revealing process in our discussion of conditioned emotional responses (CER) such as fear. We noted that the only way to weaken a fear was through extinction. It is necessary to experience the fear to change it. All the reasoning (cognition) in the world cannot weaken the conditioned response. What cognition *can* do is suppress the fear temporarily by interfering with it. Thus, cognition can influence emotion, but to change emotion probably requires a combination of cognition and emotional experience.

How can emotion influence cognition? In our discussion of Gazzaniga's social brain theory, we have already seen that people sometimes form cognitive beliefs — even false ones — to "explain" their preferences and emotional reactions. Emotion may also influence cognition through *repression*, a concept that we will explore below. Everything else being equal, we are likely to forget or distort memories that are emotionally threatening.

Learning without awareness?

Clearly, we learn more when we are aware of what we are learning. One controversial question, however, is whether one *must* be aware of a particular contingency in order to learn it. Is it possible to learn

The fear of heights cannot be eradicated by reason alone. The best way to extinguish such a fear is to experience the emotion again under controlled circumstances.
SOURCE: Dick Hemingway.

a relationship between a behaviour and its reinforcement without being aware of that relationship? Is it possible to be classically conditioned without being aware of the relationship between the CS and the US? Even though some argue to the contrary (Dawson, 1970), there is evidence that both operant and classical conditioning can take place without the person being able to articulate anything about the learning contingency.

We will first look at two ingenious demonstrations of *operant conditioning* without awareness. Carter (1973) had subjects press a key in different patterns and rhythms. They were told they would earn points whenever they pressed the key according to particular patterns which they had to figure out. These points would be indicated by a flashing light and on an electronic counter they could see. In fact, Carter was watching through a one-way mirror and awarded points when the subject blinked his or her right eye. Blinking increased dramatically until the experimenter stopped awarding points for it. The blinking then extinguished, even though subjects continued to press the key rapidly, trying to find the "right pattern." The subjects could explain nothing about their change in blinking behaviour. They often would not believe Carter, when he explained the whole experiment to them, until he let some of them observe other subjects in the procedure.

Hefferline and Keenan (1963) reported a similarly convincing demonstration. They fastened many electrodes to the skin of each subject, but only one electrode was of critical interest. It was positioned to measure tiny contractions of the muscle at the base of the thumb, contractions which the subjects could not feel. A subject sat in front of an electronic counter and was told that he or she could earn a nickel for each increase of the counter, but nothing was said about how to make the counter increase. When the critical muscle contracted within a certain range, neither too little nor too much, the counter increased. When nickels were being awarded, the number of muscle contractions of the specified level increased. When the experimenters stopped giving nickels, the response extinguished. None of the subjects could explain how the nickels were earned, and they all expressed considerable irritation when the nickels stopped coming. In fact, one subject got so frustrated during extinction that he ripped off the electrodes and stormed out of the experiment room.

Some other experiments have demonstrated *classical conditioning* without awareness. In one experiment (Martin, Stambrook, Tataryn, & Beihl, 1984), subjects wore stereo earphones. In the right ear, they heard a new word every two seconds, and their task was to say a synonym for each word. This task was designed to keep the left hemisphere very busy with verbal processing. They were told that they would hear in their left ear "distractor noises" to see how well they could ignore them. In fact, the left-ear noises were different patterns of musical tones. One tone pattern was always followed by a half-second blast of very loud noise. The experimenters predicted that particular pattern would become a conditioned stimulus and arouse a conditioned electrodermal response (electrical activity in the sweat glands) called an SPR or skin potential response. Later in the experiment, on four blocks of trials the critical tone pattern was played with no loud noise following it. Figure 9-4 illustrates that, among subjects in the experimental group, there was a conditioned response to the critical tone. (Subjects in the control group had received identical exposure to the tones and loud noises, except that the tones and loud noises were presented at random times.) The difference between the experimental and control groups disappeared over time. The experimenters speculated that the conditioned response might have been extinguishing. (See Figure 9-4.) The important finding for our discussion is that a classically conditioned response was established without subject awareness. Several approaches were used to assess whether the subjects were aware of the contingency being used. They were questioned orally, and then the entire contingency was explained to them. Different tone patterns were then played in both ears of the subjects to see whether they could pick out the critical tone pattern.

The results of this dichotic listening experiment support the idea that awareness is a continuum. One subject immediately described the contingency and picked out the critical tone pattern. He seemed completely aware. Four said they had no idea what was going on, but when they heard the patterns played, they could pick out the one being used as a CS. Two of these subjects said that as soon as they heard it they "knew," but the other two subjects insisted they were just guessing when the experimenter told them they had consistently picked the right one. These subjects seemed partially aware to different degrees. Eleven subjects could articulate nothing about the contingency and could not pick out the CS tone pattern with better than chance accuracy. They were the subjects who were used as evidence that classical conditioning occurred without awareness.

FIGURE 9-4 Classical conditioning without awareness
In a dichotic listening experiment, subjects concentrated on a complicated verbal task presented to the right ear. In the left ear they heard tone patterns and loud noises. Experimental group subjects always had one pattern paired with the loud noise. On later trials with only the tone pattern (now a CS) and no loud noise, their skin potential response (SPR) demonstrated a conditioned response, even though they were not aware that the conditioning had taken place. Over time this CS weakened and was extinguished.
SOURCE: Martin et al. (1984).

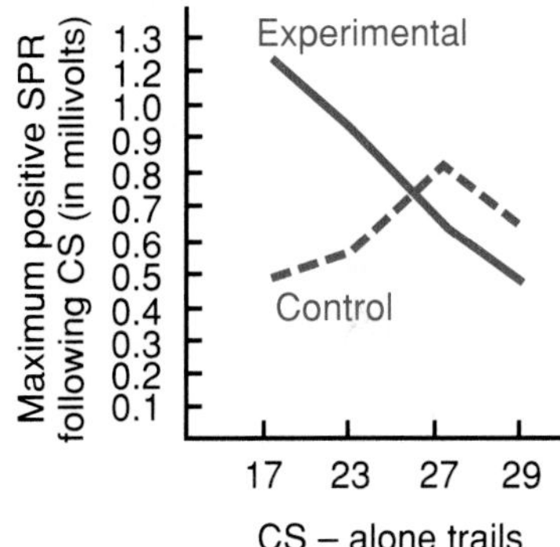

Self-deception

According to Sackeim and Gur (1978), **self-deception** is a process that occurs when an individual holds two contradictory beliefs at the same time and yet denies to the self or fails to notice one of these beliefs. Notice how well the idea of holding "two contradictory beliefs at the same time" fits Gazzaniga's social brain theory.

In a cleverly designed series of experiments, Sackeim and Gur supported their hypothesis that self-deception occurs "outside of awareness" (Sackeim & Gur, 1978, 1979; Gur & Sackeim, 1979). They based their study on considerable preliminary evidence that *self-confrontation* (hearing one's own voice) produces strong autonomic arousal. In the experiments by Sackeim and Gur, subjects heard very brief samples on tape (less than a second) of either their own voice or the voice of another person of the same sex and similar age. Self-deception occurred when subjects incorrectly identified their own voice as that of someone else. In such instances, a contradiction was revealed. At a conscious level, the subjects believed (incorrectly) that the voice belonged to another person. However, their autonomic responses reached the same levels of arousal normally related to hearing one's own voice. Thus, at some level outside awareness, the subjects "knew" it was their own voice.

People sometimes deceive themselves through a process of **denial**, a refusal to acknowledge the truth of a painful or threatening fact. Goleman (1986) has pointed out that denial is sometimes hurtful and sometimes actually helpful. On the one hand, for example, surgery patients who were unrealistically optimistic before surgery recovered more quickly. On the other hand, if a person denies the dangerousness of symptoms of a serious disease, the consequences can be fatal.

The evidence on repression

Repression may be defined as the unintentional forgetting of otherwise well-learned aversive memories. Freud claimed that repression is the main way that people defend themselves from anxiety. Freud argued that even though we tend to forget threatening or painful memories, they can still affect us without our awareness. Of course, not all aversive memories are forgotten, but there is a tendency for this to occur. Freud spoke of repression in words such as "pushing threatening memories into the unconscious mind." Brain scientists argue that such language doesn't make sense. The unconscious mind is not a *place*. The modern scientific approach is to view thinking as brain functioning. But do these objections necessarily mean that repression itself does not exist? Some researchers have shown that repression can make sense in terms of learning theory and brain function (Dollard and Miller, 1950). Thoughts that are followed by discomfort are likely to be inhibited, just like any other punished response. In addition, threatening thoughts might be avoided by displacing them with competing thoughts. These competing thoughts will be strongly reinforced because they help avoid the painful thought (Skinner, 1972; Chandra, 1976).

Thus, repression can be explained within different psychological theories. But what is the evidence that repression actually occurs? Some psychologists argue that forgetting aversive memories is not an unconscious process but rather a repeated, conscious process of suppression. **Suppression** is the intentional forgetting of aversive memories through conscious effort. The purposeful avoidance of thinking about a painful memory may become a habit that leads to suppression of that memory. Holmes (1974) favours this explanation and claims that there is no good evidence that repression even occurs. He quite correctly points out many shortcomings in the research on repression. It is difficult to do well-controlled research in which we have to show that something happened unconsciously. Holmes limits his criticisms to studies that tested a narrow definition of repression. He evaluated only research based on Freud's theory that "ego-threatening thoughts" are repressed.

However, other psychologists argue that repression applies to all aversive thoughts — painful as well as threatening. Using this broader definition, researchers have found scientific evidence for repression. For example, let us consider the elegant series of experiments conducted by Glucksberg and King (1967). Their procedure was a bit complicated, but it is worth understanding as an example of how scientific research can be done on cognitive processes.

Glucksberg and King began by choosing word pairs through a special procedure. They wanted pairs of words that are related to each other in subtle ways. For instance, the word "stem" is related to the word "smell," even though the connection is not immediately obvious to most people. Both "stem" and "smell" are strongly associated with the word "flower." Similarly, "command" and "disorder" are indirectly related because of the linking associate word "order." Glucksberg and King's entire set of words is shown in Figure 9-5. Words in the First word list are associated with words in the Second word list because of their common link to the Inferred linking associate word.

Glucksberg and King told their subjects nothing about the Second word list or the Inferred linking associates. First, they had their subjects learn to associate each Nonsense syllable with the corresponding word in the First word list. For example, through rehearsal, the subjects learned that "cef" was a cue to say "stem." Then, the experimenters asked the subjects to recite slowly each word from the Second word list. By means of very mild shocks, the experimenters punished the subjects for saying three of those words. No shocks were given when the subjects uttered the other seven words from the Second word list. In keeping with their hypothesis that repression can occur, Glucksberg and King predicted that by punishing the saying (and thus thinking) of the word "smell," they were also subtly punishing the thinking of the word "stem," although the subject would be unaware that this had happened. In fact, the results of their experiments confirmed their hypothesis. In the final phase of the study, the subjects were tested for their memory of the words from the First word list when they were cued by the Nonsense syllables. Subjects had more trouble remembering words associated with words from the Second word list for which they had been punished (Glucksberg and King, 1967; Glucksberg and Ornstein, 1969).

If we accept that repression does occur, we are still faced with the problem of explaining how it works. Some researchers suggest that repression arises when right-hemisphere processes are somehow inhibited from reaching the left hemisphere. For example, a person might be bothered by something occurring in the right hemisphere but might not be able to explain the trouble in words because the

Nonsense syllable	First word list	Inferred linking associate	Second word list
cef	stem	(flower)	smell
dax	memory	(mind)	brain
yov	soldier	(army)	navy
vux	trouble	(bad)	good
wub	wish	(want)	need
gex	justice	(peace)	war
jid	thief	(steal)	take
zil	ocean	(water)	drink
laj	command	(order)	disorder
myv	fruit	(apple)	tree

SOURCE: Adapted with permission from Glucksberg and King (1967).

FIGURE 9-5 Words used in Glucksberg and King's repression study
Words in the First word list are semantically linked in a subtle way to words in the Second word list. Corresponding words in each list are both primary associates of an Inferred linking associate. After subjects were punished for saying the word "smell," they found it harder to remember the word "stem" when cued by the Nonsense syllable "cef."

verbal left hemisphere does not get the information. This explanation may help to account for the common experience of anxiety. It suggests that on occasion we, with an intact corpus callosum, might be like the woman with the split brain discussed earlier. The nude picture that her right hemisphere saw embarrassed her, but she couldn't talk about the cause of her embarrassment. Fingarette (1969), Ornstein (1977), and Sackeim and Gur (1978) all stress the possibility that a hemisphere difference plays a leading role in the process of self-deception. The review by Galin (1974) of left and right cerebral specialization sparked a number of laboratory studies on cognition (e.g., Martin et al., 1984; Martin, Verman, & Miles, 1984). The results support the theory that repression operates through an inhibition of information flow from the right to left hemispheres.

Information processing without awareness?

Figure 9-6 Perception of emotion without reportable awareness
Stambrook and Martin (1983) presented a face in one visual half-field and a face-shaped figure in the other. When presentation time was so short that subjects could not correctly report the location of the face better than chance, they still could "guess" the emotion expressed by the face at better than chance levels.
Source: Adapted with permission from Ley and Bryden (1979).

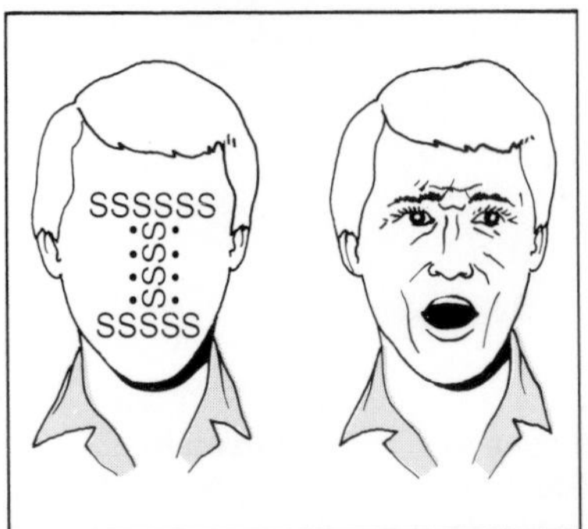

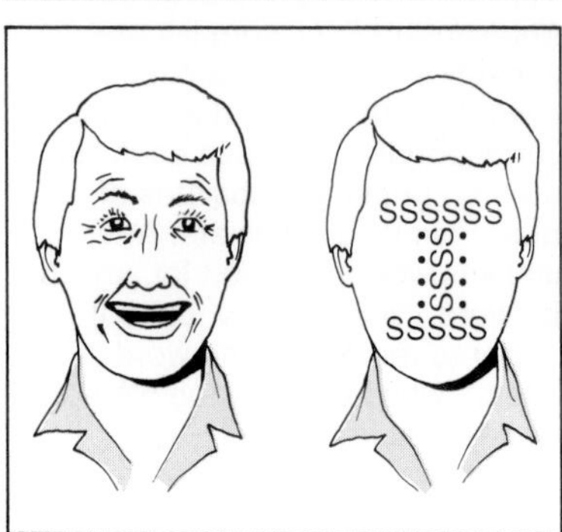

Another controversial question in the area of unconscious influences is whether complex information processing is possible without awareness. As we noted in the Special Topic of Chapter 3, many of the early claims for subliminal perception have been rightfully dismissed on methodological grounds (Eriksen & Pierce, 1968). However, as two reviewers (Dixon, 1971, 1981; Erdelyi, 1974) point out, we would not be justified in extending this dismissal to the field as a whole. In fact, some recent research (e.g., Martin, Hawryluk, & Guse, 1974; Marcel, 1978, 1983) supports the hypothesis that subliminal perception does exist. In one study, Stambrook and Martin (1983) used a tachistoscope to flash a picture of a face in one visual half-field and a face-shaped figure in the other. (See Figure 9-6.) Even when presentation speed was so fast that subjects could not correctly report the location of the face better than chance, they still could "guess" the emotion expressed by the face at better than chance levels. These findings indicate that complex information processing can occur in the absence of reportable awareness.

You may recall from Chapter 4 that **selective attention** is a state of focused processing of one set of stimuli among many competing stimuli. We do seem to be limited in the number of stimuli that we can consciously attend to at any given moment. But it does not necessarily follow that we are unable to process other information at the same time. In fact, studies on selective attention offer evidence to support a high level of "preconscious" analysis of information. Posner and Boles conclude that "conscious awareness is itself rather late in the sequence of mental processing" (Posner & Boles, 1971, p. 407).

A revealing type of experimental procedure makes use of binocular rivalry. In such experiments, each eye sees a distinct stimulus, but the subject is asked to concentrate entirely on only one of them. The results indicate that even though the subject can report correctly on only one of the stimuli, both stimuli affect the person. The effect of a stimulus presented to one eye of a subject who is reporting on a different stimulus presented to the other eye is called **binocular rivalry effect**. The findings that "the suppressed stimulus in rivalry is being fully analyzed and evaluated" have been reviewed by Walker (1978).

Research on preconscious or unconscious information processing is difficult to design because one must demonstrate the subject's lack of awareness (Derryberry, 1988). Some psychologists have criticized the validity of many of the experiments. For example, Holender (1986) concludes that only a handful of studies show meaningful semantic processing without conscious identification. Nevertheless, as Marcel (1986) points out, if such a subtle phenomenon is not found by several experiments but is demonstrated by a few studies, those few stand as supporting the phenomenon.

We have been exploring conscious and unconscious functioning as it occurs in normal, waking experience. Now, let us turn to a consideration of altered states of consciousness, beginning with the daily altered state of sleep.

Sleep and Dreams

We often think of the one-third of our lives spent sleeping as a time when we are unconscious. However, it is probably more accurate to think of it as a different state of awareness, our most common *altered state of consciousness*. We could whisper in your ear when you are sleeping, "Raise your hand if you are asleep." If you raise your hand, are you conscious? Are you aware? According to our definition of awareness, you are, to some extent, because you performed a symbolic gesture, even though you will not remember it when we wake you in a few minutes. Parents may sleep through all kinds of noise but wake instantly when their own baby cries out. Another demonstration of some sort of awareness during sleep is the Bowery El effect, which we discussed in terms of perceptual adaptation in Chapter 4. In New York, elevated trains used to run past some apartments every night at the same time. After the route was torn down, many people would wake up at the time the trains used to pass by. Evidently, while asleep they perceived something different in the surrounding stimuli. During some portions of sleep, we are also mentally engaged in our internal dreams. The intriguing phenomena of sleep and dreams have been the subjects of many studies in recent years.

Functions of sleep

What causes us to sleep? Pappenheimer has isolated a chemical substance (called "Factor S") from the cerebrospinal fluid of animals and from the urine of sleepy humans (Pappenheimer, 1976; Krueger, Pappenheimer, & Karnovsky, 1982). When this substance is injected into well-rested animals, it induces sleep. Possibly, it influences the **reticular activating system (RAS)**, a neural structure in the brain stem that helps control arousal, attention, and sleep. Beyond this, we don't know much about what makes us sleep. We might speculate that for us and for other visually oriented animals, sleep probably evolved as a way to conserve energy and to avoid night-prowling predators who would have an advantage over us in the dark (Webb, 1983).

Some people complain that there simply isn't enough time to do all the things they want to do and that it seems a shame to waste so much time sleeping. Some researchers (Friedman et al., 1977; Mullaney et al., 1977) have suggested that it is possible to *shape* oneself into getting along with less sleep without loss of function. Their subjects followed a procedure of gradually cutting back sleeping time, a half hour at a time, by going to bed later but waking at the same time as usual. Over six months, they reduced sleeping time to about five hours a night. They performed well at work and in tests of their functioning, even though they felt quite tired and felt less efficient. Interestingly, even a year after the experiment was over, the subjects were sleeping less than when they had started. About a third of them slept six hours a night. We will soon see, however, that sleep provides us with necessary physical and psychological rejuvenation.

Stages of sleep

Each night we sleep, we go through a cycle of five stages of brain activity, known as Stage 1 sleep, Stage 2 sleep, Stage 3 sleep, Stage 4 sleep, and REM sleep. Each stage has a distinctive pattern of electrical activity, as measured by the electroencephalogram (EEG). These stages are illustrated in Figure 9-7. **Alpha waves** (or **alpha rhythms**) are brain waves of 8-12 cycles per second (Hz) as measured on an EEG. They are characteristic of the brain activity of a person who is awake and extremely relaxed. As an individual dozes off, he or she enters *Stage 1 sleep*, in which the EEG pattern shows less amplitude, few alpha waves, and considerable irregularity. During this stage, the person is still easy to waken. *Stage 2 sleep* is marked by **spindles**, bursts of EEG activity slightly faster than alpha waves. During Stage 2 sleep, the fluctuation of wave amplitude (voltage) becomes more pronounced, as shown in Figure 9-7. In *Stage 3 sleep*, delta waves appear. **Delta waves** are brain waves of large amplitude and 1 to 2 cycles per second as measured on an EEG. During Stage 3 sleep, the amplitude of the brain waves becomes even more variable, sometimes giving a weak signal and sometimes a strong one. During *Stage 4 sleep*, the deepest stage, the slow delta waves predominate and the EEG tracing becomes more regular. In both Stage 3 and 4, the person will be difficult to wake up. Nevertheless, we know that much information is still being processed, because the person will waken to stimulation with personal meaning, such as a baby's cry.

The progress from Stage 1 sleep to Stage 4 sleep is marked by waves of increasing amplitude (voltage) and decreasing frequency (rate). After spending some time in Stage 4, the sleeper returns to Stage 3 and Stage 2. Then, instead of reentering Stage 1, the sleeper enters *REM (rapid eye movement) sleep*. The entire cycle of sleep stages — from Stage 1 or REM to Stage 4 and back to REM — lasts about 90 minutes. A normal night of sleep consists of four or five complete cycles. As shown in Figure 9-8, REM sleep tends to get longer in the later cycles.

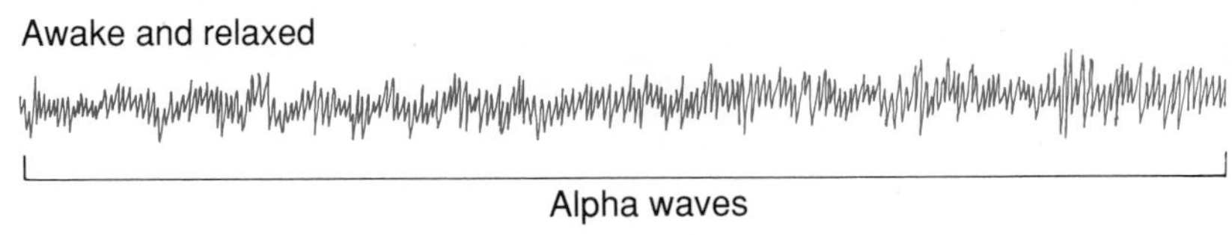

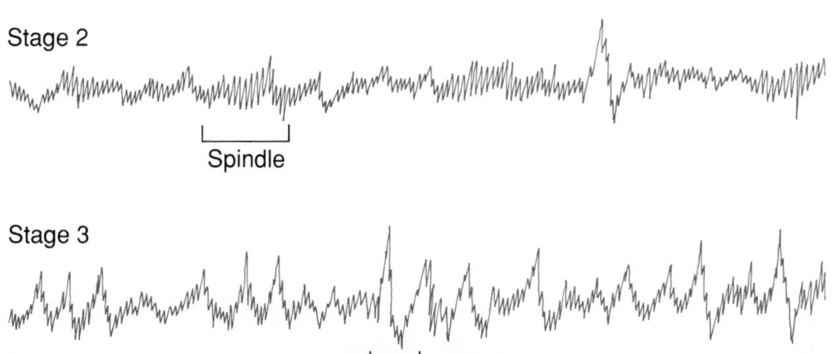

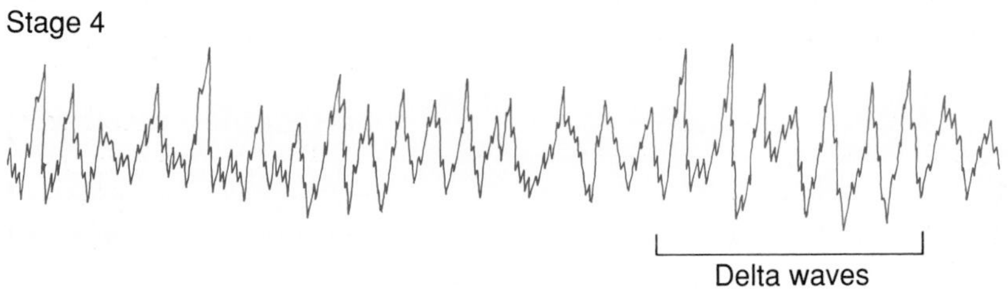

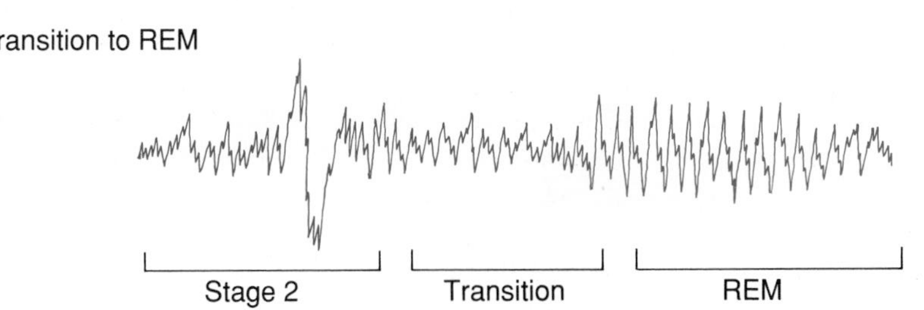

FIGURE 9-7 EEG patterns of brain activity during a relaxed state and during the different stages of sleep
The horizontal dimension in these tracings represents time, measured in seconds. The vertical dimension (amplitude) represents electrical activity, measured in microvolts.

SOURCE: Adapted with permission from Dement (1974).

FIGURE 9-8 The cyclic pattern of sleep during a normal night
We usually go through four or five cycles of sleep during the night. Each cycle lasts about 90 minutes. Observe that the periods of REM sleep tend to increase in the later cycles.

SOURCE: Adapted from Cartwright (1978).

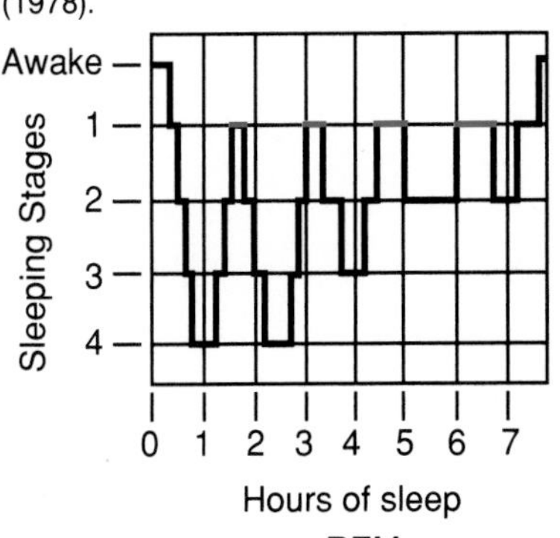

REM sleep

REM sleep is the stage of sleep marked by rapid eye movements (REM's) during which most dreaming seems to occur. If you observe a sleeping person during REM, you can actually see the eyes moving around under the eyelids. REM sleep is a very distinctive phase. Therefore, we use the term **NREM sleep** (non-rapid eye movement sleep) to refer to all the stages of sleep other than REM sleep—namely, Stage 1, Stage 2, Stage 3, and Stage 4 sleep.

REM sleep is sometimes called **paradoxical sleep** because it is a time of extensive mental activity, even though much of the musculature of the sleeper is virtually paralysed. The brain activity resembles that of an awake person, but motor functioning is shut down almost completely. This state may have evolved to prevent the sleeper from carrying out the intense and often irrational behaviour being dreamed about. Part of the apparent paradox that often surprises the layperson is that sleepwalking occurs during NREM sleep, rather than during REM when dreaming is more common.

When wakened during REM sleep, a person will almost always report a dream. When wakened during NREM sleep, a person will often report no dreaming. About 30% of the time, subjects do report dreaming during NREM sleep, but the dreams are usually unemotional and dull. In contrast, the dreams of REM sleep tend to be emotionally charged, vivid, and often bizarre. Since we normally go through the sleep cycle four or five times a night, it seems likely that everyone dreams several times every night. Some people say, "I never dream," but the reason for their assertion is probably that they habitually wake up in the morning during NREM sleep. If they change their usual schedules, they may find that they start remembering dreams.

As we go through the cycles of sleep stages, REM sleep increases throughout the night. (See again Figure 9-8.) During REM sleep, some physiological arousal does occur, even though the motor muscles are inactive. Heart rate increases, and breathing becomes more rapid. Even when there is no sexual content in dreams, the vagina is likely to receive an increased blood flow and the penis usually becomes erect.

REM sleep seems to serve an essential function. It performs a kind of psychological restoration. We probably use NREM sleep to replenish ourselves physically and REM sleep for some sort of mental operations (which we will discuss below in the section on dreams). On the one hand, increased physical activity during the day leads to more Stage 4 NREM sleep. On the other hand, times of emotional stress are often accompanied by increased REM sleep (Hartmann, 1984).

Researchers have discovered the so-called **REM rebound effect**, the tendency for the amount of REM sleep to increase following periods of REM deprivation. Dement (1960) suggests that the REM rebound effect represents an attempt to compensate for lost "dreaming time." Dement deprived his subjects of sleep by waking them either after a certain amount of REM sleep or after a corresponding amount of NREM sleep. He found that the rebound effect occurred only when REM sleep had been cut short. One bitter irony of using prescription sleeping pills is that they greatly reduce REM sleep relative to NREM sleep. Thus, the longer one uses them, the more disturbed a person's sleep will be on subsequent nights because of the REM rebound effect. Alcohol can have the same influence. In humans and in many animals, REM sleep is so necessary that it is very difficult to suppress it for long. The deprived subject will become irritable and have difficulty concentrating. Even if there is a normal amount of total sleep, the drive to enter REM sleep will become very strong.

The meaning of dreams

Psychologists disagree on the function and meaning of dreams. Some see dreams as filled with purpose and personal significance. Others see them as random and meaningless. Research studies to date do not conclusively support one particular theory.

Even though we all dream, some people are more likely to remember dreams than others. This is partly a function of sleep schedule, as we said above, and partly dependent on what we do immediately upon waking. If there is a distraction-free period during which we can *rehearse* our dreams, then we are more likely to consolidate them into our long-term memory (Koulack & Goodenough, 1976).

Two of the most influential psychotherapists in the history of psychology are Freud and Jung. Each considered the dreams of their patients in order to diagnose emotional disorders and formulate treatments. Both Freud and Jung concluded that dreams are an extremely important part of mental life and carry enormous psychological meaning. However, Freud and Jung disagreed on the general function and meaning of dreams.

Sigmund Freud (1900) called dreams "the royal road to the unconscious." Freud interpreted them as expressions of unconscious wishes that the dreamer finds unacceptable because of their sexual or aggressive nature. Therefore, Freud maintained not only that dreams are symbolic expressions but that they emerge in disguised forms. He called the actual words, images, and plots that the dreamer remembers the **manifest content of dreams**. By contrast, Freud used the term **latent content of dreams** to refer to the hidden meanings or wish fulfilments symbolized in dreams. Freud argued that the manifest content of dreams conceals from the dreamer's consciousness the latent content of sexual or aggressive wish fulfilments. As we

According to Freud and to Jung our dreams have much to teach us about our inner lives.
SOURCE: "The Nightmare" by Henry Fuseli, 1781. Courtesy the Detroit Institute of Arts. Gift of Mr. and Mrs. Bert L. Smokler and Mr. and Mrs. Lawrence A. Fleischman.

shall see in Chapter 10, Freudian theory stresses sexuality and aggression as underlying influences in almost all aspects of human functioning.

Carl Jung (*Collected Works*, 1953-1979) viewed the meaning of dreams much differently. He argued that although dreams are symbolic expressions, they are *not* concealments. Therefore, Jung did not interpret dreams as collections of general symbols whose meanings are obscure to the individual. Instead, he tried to work through each dream to clarify its specific meaning for the dreamer. Jung believed that aspects of our personalities that we ignore or disregard will often emerge in dreams. Therefore, he considered dreams to be potential learning experiences that have unique meaning for each individual.

Jung's view has been pursued and developed by some contemporary theorists. Hall (1966) describes each dream as "a letter to oneself." Cartwright (1978) considers dreaming to be a kind of problem-solving process in which real, current problems can be rehearsed and worked through, both to address recent events and to prepare for future activities. A few well-known scientists and artists have actually reported discovering answers to their creative problems in their sleep. As we mentioned in Chapter 8, Kekulé's dream of a snake led to his theory that benzine has a ring structure at the molecular level.

Two other theories of dreams have been proposed in recent times. One view is that dreams function as mental housecleaning. According to Crick and Mitchison (1983) and Evans (1984), the dreaming brain is "running old programs" like a computer that is cleaning up its daily accumulation of data that are no longer needed. This process helps to eliminate many random and useless associations. Furthermore, dreaming can help us come to terms with cognitive material and emotional experiences that might otherwise trouble us during our waking hours. According to this theory, we usually forget our dreams because their very function is to eliminate or resolve needless, redundant, or bizarre information that has accumulated during the course of the day. Occasionally, we do remember dreams because we have woken up during them. Recurring dreams probably deal with subjects that arouse considerable anxiety and therefore they are likely to waken the dreamer. If the purpose of dreams is to get rid of troublesome thoughts, then we are probably better off not remembering our dreams. At the same time, this theory does not exclude the possibility that dreams may carry important personal meaning, perhaps even in disguised form.

A second modern theory of dreams is radically different. According to Hobson and McCarley (1977), dreams are random phenomena that carry no meaning at all. They argue that dreams are simply the result of the physiological works of the brain. During REM sleep, the forebrain becomes unusually active and generates rapid and random bursts of stimulation in many parts of the brain. This theory provides an explanation for the often irrational nature of dreams. The brain has to contend with a great deal of fragmented information from all this random stimulation. Therefore, the brain tries to make sense out of it all by "constructing" dreams.

Sleep disorders

Insomnia can be a minor, occasional discomfort to some people and a major, constant disruption to others.
SOURCE: Dick Hemingway.

Sleep is such an essential part of our lives that problems with it can cause severe disruptions affecting all aspects of living. Considerable research is being done on the causes and potential treatments for these disorders.

Insomnia, the inability to fall asleep or to stay asleep throughout the night, is probably the most common sleep disorder in our culture. It has many different causes, ranging from physiological problems to anxiety or even the anticipation of a happy event. For instance, one common sign of depression is waking up too early in the morning and being unable to get back to sleep.

All humans have a daily physiological rhythm that seems to be regulated internally by some sort of biological clock. Insomnia can be brought on by a disruption of the **circadian rhythm**, a rhythm of bodily functions whose cycle lasts about 24 hours. We have a 24-hour cycle of alertness that usually is low at night and high during the day. Thompson & Harsha (1984) have speculated that the afternoon drowsiness slump that many people experience is a part of the circadian rhythm that we inherited from ancestors who needed to rest during the heat of the day. If our circadian rhythm is thrown off schedule by something such as jet lag, we may have trouble sleeping for several days. Our internal clock cannot immediately adjust to a new time-zone.

A very serious cause of insomnia is **sleep apnea**, a sleep disorder marked by the inability to breathe continuously during sleep. When people with sleep apnea fall into deep sleep, they literally stop breathing. Soon the intense discomfort of carbon dioxide build-up wakens them, and they desperately gasp for air to restore their oxygen shortage . Some victims may wake up hundreds of times during the night, but they are not aware of it the next morning. Much to their puzzlement, they are sleepy throughout the following day. Other victims are painfully aware of the problem and fear going to sleep. Sleep apnea can affect people of all ages, but it is more common among infants and the elderly. Some researchers suspect that sleep apnea may be one of the main causes of **sudden infant death syndrome (SIDS)**, otherwise known as *crib death*. Perhaps the signals the infants receive from oxygen debt are blocked by an underdeveloped respiratory centre, and as a result they don't wake up when they stop breathing. Sleep apnea may also lead to heart problems in adults.

The frustrating paradox of insomnia is that we can lie there, desperate to go to sleep. But the harder we try, the less likely we are to sleep. What should we do? It sometimes helps to remember that losing a night's sleep is not a big problem. We can make up for it later. Regular sleep habits are important because they can stabilize our circadian rhythm. To avoid setting up a vicious circle of sleepless nights and dozing in class, we should continue to get up in the morning at our regular time and we should avoid napping during the day. Regular exercise helps, but we should avoid doing it just before bedtime because our system will still be too aroused for us to fall asleep. As many people know, caffeine is a stimulant, and therefore drinking coffee can keep one awake. Unfortunately, some people use alcohol and many more people use sleeping pills to help them fall asleep. However, sleeping pills and alcohol are more of a cause than a cure of insomnia because, as we discussed earlier in this chapter, they disrupt the sleep cycle by reducing the amount of REM sleep. By contrast, some foods, such as milk and tuna, help to facilitate sleep, apparently because they are high in the amino acid tryptophan, which helps produce the neurotransmitter serotonin, needed for sleep.

Many people have trouble falling asleep. A few people can't help falling asleep. **Narcolepsy** is a sleeping disorder in which a person suddenly falls asleep at odd times during the day, usually at times of excitement or anxious arousal. Narcolepsy seems to stem from a deficiency of the neurotransmitter dopamine (Mefford et al., 1983). This brain disorder probably has a genetic component both in humans and in animals. When a narcoleptic person is aroused, it is as though there is a sudden intrusion of REM sleep in the awake brain. Treatment with amphetamines can provide partial relief of the symptoms.

HYPNOSIS

Hypnosis has long been considered a strange and sometimes mystical state of consciousness. For many years it was not a respectable subject of study within psychology. For several decades now, however, psychological research has shed light on what hypnosis is and is not. There are also many clinical uses of hypnosis, particularly in the control of pain, even though there is controversy about how hypnosis works. We can define **hypnosis** as a process of social influence in which the subject is in a much heightened state of suggestibility. The process by which a hypnotic state is caused in a subject is known as the **induction process**. By means of the induction process, the hypnotist aims to lead the subject to accept suggestions and orders. Induction usually involves deep relaxation and highly focused attention. Sometimes there is an obvious trance state, in which the person seems to be in a combination of sleep and wakefulness, but that is not always the case. The person might even finish the experience never having "gone to sleep" in any way. The individual might staunchly deny having been hypnotised, even though dramatic effects occurred during the session. For example, hypnosis anaesthesia might have been induced so that the person laughed while being jabbed with a needle.

We have all seen pictures of the swinging pendulum and piercing eyes of the stage hypnotist, but no mysterious props are necessary for hypnotic suggestion. The basic principle of the induction process is that susceptibility to suggestion is increased with each step. A classic method, for example, is to hold a small object just in front of and slightly above the eyes, with instructions to concentrate on a spot on the object. The eyes are then slightly converged and turned upward, which is very fatiguing. The hypnotist times the suggestion that the eyes will begin to feel tired to occur just as they become fatigued. This increases the validity the subject gives to the hypnotist's suggestions. Suggestions then become gradually more complex and as each one "comes true," the power of the next one increases.

Other methods can be more obvious or more subtle, but their purpose is the same. All induction techniques are designed to increase the power and credibility of the hypnotist. For example, Milton Erikson was famous for his subtle methods of induction. One of his approaches was the *confusion technique*, in which he would say very confusing things that sounded potentially meaningful to the subject, who struggled to make sense of it all. When Erikson next said something sensible, the subject was so desperate for structure the comment or suggestion had enormous impact.

Subjects with hypnotic talent can learn **self-hypnosis** and put themselves into a hypnotic trance. This usually requires prior training with hypnosis induced by another person.

Hypnotic phenomena

Individuals under hypnosis exhibit a number of fascinating behaviours. Very often, the hypnotist suggests that the person forget what happened during hypnosis. This forgetting of events or other material as suggested by the hypnotist is called **post-hypnotic amnesia**. Experiments have shown that highly hypnotizable subjects forget nearly all of what happened but are able to recall all events as soon as the hypnotist suggests a return of memory. Clearly, this is not a true forgetting but rather a temporary blockage of the memory (Kihlstrom, 1985).

Hypnosis has also been used to enhance the accuracy of memory, an effect that police agencies are often interested in using with witnesses. Hypnosis does seem to reduce anxiety and thus can lead to improvements in memory. However, a serious problem arises because the subject is highly motivated to follow the hypnotist's suggestions. Even if the hypnotist has only a subtle expectation, the subject often senses that expectation and creates "memories" to fulfil those expectations. This can happen even when the hypnotist tries to hide his or her expectations. Courts will therefore almost never accept testimony taken under hypnosis. The manufactured "memories" are mixed in with what seem to be actual improvements in memory. There is no way to distinguish the creations from the real memories. Perry and Laurence (1983b) summarize the history of the use of hypnosis to enhance the memory of legal witnesses. In 1981, an Alberta judge set a legal precedent in Canada by permitting evidence from a hypnotized witness to be heard by a jury. Perry and Laurence caution that Canadian courts would do well to benefit from the experience of the United States legal system by treating such evidence sceptically.

The process of hypnotic induction can take many forms. Its purpose is to increase the subject's suggestibility.
SOURCE: David Martin.

Some psychotherapists use hypnosis to help clients retrieve and relive emotionally charged memories. Hypnosis is sometimes applied to treat symptoms (such as smoking and overeating) directly, but hypnosis is not noticeably more effective than other methods. Most *hypnotherapists* focus on the more complex process of enhancing the client's memory for past events and then helping the person face past emotions of which they may have been unaware.

One purpose of post-hypnotic amnesia is to facilitate a **post-hypnotic suggestion**, a particular suggestion that the subject is asked to carry out after the hypnotic session. An example might be the suggestion given during the trance that whenever the hypnotist says the word "over," the subject should stand up. Some time after the hypnosis session, the hypnotist includes "over" in the conversation and the person stands up, giving some plausible reason for doing so. "I felt a need to stretch," for instance. Remember Gazzaniga's patients who "made sense" out of their behaviour after the fact? In our example the hypnotist could start saying "over" quite often and create a difficult and embarrassing situation in which the subject was standing up so frequently he or she couldn't explain it.

Hypnosis can also induce hallucinations. A **positive hallucination** is one in which the hypnotic subject sees or hears something that is not actually there. With the suggestion that "Fred" has just joined the group, for example, the subject will include Fred (who doesn't exist) in counting the number of people in the room. A **negative hallucination** is one in which the hypnotic subject fails to see or hear something that is actually there. If told that Susan has left the room when she actually hasn't, the subject will act as though Susan doesn't exist and will insist that she is not present. Such distortions can also occur as post-hypnotic suggestions.

The clinical use of hypnosis centres around **analgesia** (the reduction and control of specific pain) and **anaesthesia** (the temporary elimination of pain). In many experiments, pain is induced by holding a hand in a bucket of ice water. Hypnosis seems able to reduce such moderate levels of pain, although strong social suggestion and methods of distraction can also do so. More dramatic are instances of surgery performed only with hypnoanaesthesia.

Age regression is the hypnotic process in which the subject is "taken back in age" and acts as though he or she were actually that age. This effect of hypnosis is quite controversial. Under suggestion that they are getting younger and younger, subjects will revert to baby talk, drawing childishly, and acting as though they were actually younger. However, sometimes they act in ways that children of the target age seldom act. They seem to be acting the way they *think* they acted then. This effect may therefore be another case of unconsciously giving the hypnotist what is expected.

Hypnotic susceptibility

It is very difficult to hypnotize a person who does not want to be hypnotized. It has also been well established that subjects will not do what they consider morally unacceptable while under hypnosis. It is possible to tell a subject to "throw that bottle of acid in the experimenter's face" and have the person comply, but it is likely that the "acid" is assumed to be exactly what it is, a harmless liquid.

When circumstances are more persuasively harmful, the subject normally simply comes out of the trance. On the other hand, we will see in Chapter 16 that social psychologists have been able to induce people to act in some very antisocial ways by using authoritarian suggestions without hypnosis. It seems likely that hypnosis, cleverly applied, could induce similar actions.

Some people are more hypnotizable than others. Hypnotizability is a consistent personal quality that Bowers and Davidson (1986, p. 468) describe as "nearly as stable a psychological characteristic as intelligence." When doing research on hypnosis, it is critical to take this variable into account. If we were trying to understand musical genius and did our research on a cross-section of introductory psychology students, we might well conclude that averages in our data prove that there is no such thing as musical genius. We have obviously not chosen the best sample. There are also hypnotic "virtuosos" and it is their experiences that will teach us the most about hypnosis (Graham, 1986). We are all on a continuum of hypnotizability, and there are several tests to determine how susceptible a person is.

Various characteristics have been proposed as correlated with hypnotic susceptibility: gullibility, weakmindedness, strongmindedness, and intelligence. But research has shown that these particular ones are *not* correlated with hypnotizability. Having a good imagination, rich and vivid in its imagery, seems to be the only consistent correlate of hypnotic talent (Hilgard, 1975). For an effect to be convincingly the result of hypnosis, it is necessary to show that the person was relatively high in hypnotic susceptibility (Bowers,1984).

Is hypnosis a *special state*?

Hypnosis is one of the most controversial topics in psychology. Throughout history, there have been battles over its nature, and those in the field seem to fall into two camps: the "credulous supporters" and the "sceptics" (Sutcliffe, 1961; St. Jean, 1986). In general, the sceptical view has more often proven correct, as hypnosis has become more and more "demystified." Hypnosis was first called *mesmerism*, after Franz Anton Mesmer who, in the late eighteenth century, believed that many physical symptoms were the result of disturbances of a magnetic fluid in the body. He flamboyantly treated patients' disorders by touching them with rods that he said transmitted *animal magnetism.* With his purple robes and grand manner, he seemed to help a lot of people with symptoms. However, he was eventually discredited by an investigative panel led by Benjamin Franklin.

In its current form, the sceptic-supporter debate is far from settled. The question is whether hypnosis is some kind of *special state.* Is it qualitatively different from ordinary consciousness or is it simply a heightened state of suggestibility of the sort that social-psychological influence can create without any hypnotic trance. An article written by a sceptic (Spanos, 1986) was published along with

22 responses from researchers on both sides of the argument. This would be a good source for further reading on this debate. We will summarize a few of the many issues involved.

Role enactment theory

Role enactment theory is a sceptical theory of hypnosis as simply a process of social-psychological influence and not a special state of consciousness. According to this "non-special state" theory, behaviour under hypnosis is an involuntary playing out of a social role as a response to obvious and subtle social demands (Barber, 1969, 1979; Coe & Sarbin, 1977; Spanos, 1986). Spanos, for example, reports many studies in which hypnotic phenomena such as amnesia and analgesia can be induced by creating strong expectations and motivation. These effects cannot be distinguished from the reactions of hypnotized subjects. The implicit argument is that if the same effect can be demonstrated both ways, hypnosis is no different from social-psychological influence. However, Rosenthal has pointed out that establishing the effectiveness of such social influence is not enough to eliminate hypnosis as a *special state* that achieves the same effects. "No procedure (A) for producing behavior can prove that some alternative procedure (B) is ineffective in producing that behavior; it can only show that procedure B is not necessary to produce the behavior. Drugs are not shown to be ineffective simply because their effects can also be obtained by placebo" (Rosenthal, 1986, p. 479-480).

Dissociation theory

Dissociation theory is the theory that hypnosis is a special state of consciousness in which some mental functions are sharply separate from others. This *special-state* view of hypnosis is consistent with our previous discussion of the brain as functioning with many different modules—namely, the social brain theory. According to this view, people are capable of separate streams of thought simultaneously. In hypnosis, these streams of thought are separated more dramatically than in a normal situation, such as absent-mindedly reading to a child or arguing existential philosophy while driving through city traffic. The *dissociation* of these separate functions is exaggerated by hypnosis. Hilgard (1977) has presented evidence for a *hidden observer* during hypnosis among highly hypnotizable subjects. This so-called hidden observer functions as another part of consciousness or another module. Hilgard devised experiments in which subjects could report different experiences at the same time. For example, subjects might be exposed to the pain of immersing a hand in ice water. Hypnotic analgesia was then induced, and the subjects reported significant reductions in pain. They were asked if "some other part" of them knew what the experience was like physically. This "other part" was to use "automatic writing" or pressing numbered keys with a hand "out of awareness" to report the intensity of the pain experienced. Often this hidden observer could report an accurate understanding of the entire process that the conscious reporter knew nothing of (Hilgard & Hilgard, 1983). Figure 9-9 shows that with increasing time in ice water, subjects given hypnotic analgesia reported almost no pain with overt verbal reports. However, the hidden observer reported increasing pain, even though this pain never reached the levels reported by subjects who were not hypnotized. Under hypnosis, people have also engaged in automatic writing on one topic while they were reading aloud completely different material or naming colours on a chart (Knox, Crutchfield, & Hilgard, 1975). It is difficult for most of us to imagine doing this normally, but it would probably be possible to learn, just as we learned to read aloud and think of something else at the same time. According to this theory, hypnosis simply exaggerates the dissociation among processes in the brain.

To answer the criticism that these acts are simply *role enactment*, experimenters have compared (a) highly hypnotizable subjects under hypnosis with (b) subjects not very susceptible to hypnosis who were told to simulate hypnosis. The two groups behaved similarly, but their subjective descriptions of their experiences differed significantly (Hilgard et al., 1978; Zamansky & Bartis, 1985). In another approach to comparing simulators and nonsimulators, researchers used hidden cameras to observe subjects. When they thought they were being observed, subjects simulating hypnosis were significantly more responsive to suggestions. However, the subjects who had been hypnotized were equally affected by suggestions regardless of whether they thought they were being observed. Such findings suggest that hypnosis differs from simple role enactment (Kirsch et al., 1989).

Probably the most persuasive argument that hypnosis is different from simply meeting social expectations is its use in relieving extreme pain. Pain can be influenced in clinical settings by relaxation, diversion of attention, and social expectations, but this is qualitatively different from the pain relief resulting from hypnotic analgesia and anaesthesia (Perry & Laurence, 1983a; Turk & Rudy, 1986). Hilgard (1977) tells of five women who delivered babies by Caesarean section using only hypnoanaesthesia. We personally know a woman who had an appendectomy under self-hypnosis, after being trained by a hypnotist. Graham reports his work with a 13-year-old boy with extensive severe burns on his left leg.

> According to the nurses, he cried, writhed, and had to be held down whenever the burn was redressed by the surgeon. After one hypnosis session he was able to have his burn debrided and redressed while remaining calm. After three sessions he laughed as the surgeon debrided the most seriously burned area. To argue that this change in experience was nothing more than a desire to be seen as a good hypnosis role player is sheer sophistry (Graham, 1986, p. 473).

The evidence suggests that hypnosis is not a mystical process. It works by the same processes that normally operate in us. However, it greatly exaggerates those processes, especially in those individuals who are highly hypnotizable. Role enactment theory and dissociative theory each have some truth in them. They are constantly being refined in an attempt to integrate them (Perry & Laurence, 1986).

FIGURE 9-9 Overt and covert pain as reduced by hypnotic suggestion

The highest curve shows the normal waking pain when the hand is immersed in ice water. The lowest curve shows the overt, consciously reported pain when hypnotic analgesia is used. The middle curve is the level of pain reported by the person's "hidden observer," of whose reports the person is not consciously aware.

SOURCE: Adapted with permission from Hilgard and Hilgard (1975).

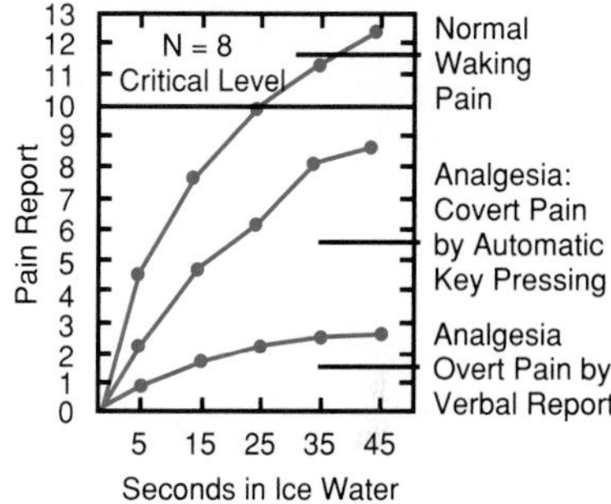

SOURCE: *Calvin and Hobbes* by Bill Watterson. Copyright 1989 Universal Press Syndicate. Reprinted with permission.

MEDITATION AND THE RELAXATION RESPONSE

Another way to achieve an altered state of consciousness or awareness is through *meditation*. At one level meditation seems easy. Dworetzky, for example, calls it a

> very simple technique that can be practiced by anyone. If you sit back, close your eyes, breathe deeply, and if you wish, concentrate on a particular sound or word for about 15 minutes, a number of changes will probably occur. Your heart rate will slow, your blood pressure will lower, and the amount of oxygen you consume will decrease. Body temperature at the extremities will rise. Muscles will relax. That's all there is to meditation (Dworetzky, 1985, p. 164-165).

However, as with hypnosis, there are "sceptics" and "supporters." Sceptics view meditation as simply a form of relaxation. Supporters view it as a complex process producing a special state of consciousness. Dworetzky represents the sceptical end of the continuum. Most who meditate and study meditation would find his description hopelessly simplistic, a kind of relaxation technique that is only one aspect of meditation. Meditation centres around the astonishingly difficult task of "not thinking." There are many different methods of meditation. Some make use of a **mantra**, a particular phrase, word, or sound which the meditator mentally repeats over and over again. The goal of meditation is to induce a state of consciousness that is not dominated by the structure and drive of ordinary rational thinking. The meditator strives to attain a *one pointedness* in concentration. If outside thoughts slip in, they are not to be fought but rather to be observed and released. With much practice, often extending for years, a meditator can be in a state that is difficult to describe but combines alertness, profound relaxation, detachment from the world and self-awareness. One reason meditation is a controversial area of psychology is that, as with hypnosis, both the experience and the historical background of meditation have "mystical" overtones with which psychologists tend to be uncomfortable.

Let us define **meditation** as a process for inducing a special state of consciousness characterized by the diminishing of everyday forms of thinking. There are many kinds of meditative practice. Most fall into two large categories: concentrative meditation and opening up meditation. Concentrative meditation is the more familiar. **Concentrative meditation** is the meditative practice marked by concentrating on one's own breathing, a mantra, object, or symbol repeated over and over, without the intrusion of structured thinking. One commercialized and widely promoted approach to concentrative meditation is called **transcendental meditation (TM)**. Lessons are offered in which a teacher interviews the novice, introduces certain semi-mystical rituals, and assigns the individual a personal mantra that is to be kept secret. The mantra is normally a sound such as "ohm" or "aim." The student receives guidance in concentrative meditation and is usually asked to practise twice a day.

Opening up meditation is the meditative practice marked by a total engagement of the present moment throughout daily life. For example, in response to the question "What is your meditative practice?" a Zen master might say, "My meditative practice is talking to you." Whatever is done is performed with full *mindfulness* of the moment, something very few of us ever achieve.

Eastern meditation has a long, respected history. Today people from many different cultures realize that, through the power of meditation, they can achieve an altered state of consciousness.
SOURCE: The Bettmann Archive.

Research findings on meditation and relaxation

Psychologists know relatively little about meditation, primarily because it is very difficult to study scientifically such complex states as *one pointedness* and *mindfulness*. So we study what we can: relaxation and its physiological correlates.

The main physiological correlates of relaxation are a decrease in heart rate, blood pressure, breathing rate, oxygen consumption, and muscle tension plus an increase in alpha waves. Are the physiological correlates of meditation identical? This question has provoked much controversy. Early researchers concluded that meditation creates a physiological state different from that created by resting and simple relaxation. Recently, Herbert Benson, an American medical researcher, has argued that meditation indeed brings about a special state of profound relaxation (Benson, 1975; Benson, Arns, & Hoffman, 1981; Benson & Friedman, 1985). In fact, Benson uses the term **relaxation response** to refer to the physiological patterns observed during meditation. This is a special state that is more than that which arises from simply closing one's eyes and relaxing. At the same time, Benson maintains that the mystical aspects of transcendental meditation are unnecessary. Benson claims that a person can achieve the same sort of special meditative state by sitting comfortably, closing one's eyes, relaxing one's muscles, focusing on breathing, and concentrating on the word "one."

Heated debate about the comparison between meditation and relaxation has been sparked by Holmes (1984, 1985a, 1985b) through his review of the research literature. As a "sceptic," Holmes concludes that not only is meditation no different from other relaxation methods, it is no different from simply resting with one's eyes closed—at least in terms of physiological relaxation. A number of supporters of meditation responded that Holmes was biased in his review, misrepresented some of the evidence, and left out important considerations (Suler, 1985; Shapiro, 1985; Benson & Friedman, 1985). One of the most interesting responses was made by Dillbeck and Orme-Johnson (1987) who analyzed research studying TM specifically (rather than combined studies of various types of meditation). They used a statistical method called *meta-analysis* in which the results from several studies can be combined to find overall effects. They reported that, contrary to Holmes' conclusion, there were physiological differences in some measures of physiological arousal. In particular, they reported that TM was often accompanied by an increase in alertness, as indicated by EEG readings and improved reflex responses. They argued that this supported the view of meditation as a state of "restful alertness."

Transpersonal psychology

Psychologists from many schools of thought are interested in meditation. However, the greatest interest is probably shown by humanistic psychologists and those specializing in transpersonal psychology. Transpersonal psychology is described by its followers as the "fourth force" in psychology. (We will see in Chapter 10 that psychoanalysis, learning theory, and humanism are the other three forces.) It has its own journal and society (Tart, 1975). We can briefly define **transpersonal psychology** as that branch which focuses on the esoteric and mystical aspects of human functioning. It argues against the exclusive use of rational methods of inquiry. In other words, it emphasizes the limitations of the traditional scientific *paradigm* or world view. One argument is that modern physics, especially the mysterious predictions of quantum theory, is showing us that contemporary psychology is based on a limited view of reality, that of Newtonian physics. One of transpersonal psychology's most articulate writers is Ken Wilbur (1983). He argues that there are many ways of "seeing" and the scientific "eye" is only one limited way to knowledge. This view is not acceptable to many other psychologists, as was made obvious when supporters tried to establish a transpersonal psychology division of the American Psychological Association. They were turned down on the general ground that transpersonal psychology isn't psychology at all. It is more like religion. This debate was especially interesting because it pointed out the problems in trying to define what psychology is and what it is not.

Albert Ellis has probably been the psychologist most dramatically critical of transpersonal psychology. He has used phrases such as "dangers of transpersonal psychology." He also asserts that "psychologists who hold transpersonal . . . ideas not necessarily but very often promulgate almost exactly the kind of absolutistic ideology that is devoutly held by the religious and political sectarians who may some day atomically annihilate the whole human race" (Ellis, 1989, p. 336). This is very strong language and has drawn vigorous rebuttal from Wilbur (1989a) and Walsh (1989), both of whom expressed their alarm that the article by Ellis "seemed severely, even dangerously, flawed" (Walsh, 1989, p. 338). If you are interested in this debate, you should also consult May (1989), Rowan (1989), and Wilbur (1989b).

Perspectives change over time. Only the future will tell whether transpersonal psychology becomes accepted as part of the profession. Regardless, transpersonal psychology may yet make a significant contribution to the discipline as a whole, as Hilgard suggests by the following remarks:

> Sometimes extreme groups lead those who are nearer the center to show that they have not been oblivious to the problems that the extreme groups focus upon. Then the new "movement" may have made its contribution through enriching the topics that psychologists study, even though most psychologists do not become disciples, and even if the new movement disappears in any recognizable form (Hilgard, 1980, p. 14).

SPECIAL TOPIC

The Chemistry of Consciousness

We know the brain functions by means of chemicals called neurotransmitters that cause neuron synapses to be crossed. Whenever we change the chemical environment of the brain, experience changes, sometimes dramatically. In our culture, we call some chemical substances *drugs* because they alter thinking and emotion, but our definition of "drugs" is usually not rational. To many people, nicotine, alcohol, and caffeine are "not really drugs," whereas LSD, heroin, and marijuana are. But, strictly speaking, **drugs** are any chemical substances other than food that change bodily or mental functioning. Drugs that affect the central nervous system are referred to as **psychoactive substances**. They can change perception, thinking, and emotion — they induce altered states of consciousness.

Some basic terminology

People talk a lot about these chemical substances, and terms are often used inaccurately, so we need to define some terms. When a person develops **tolerance** for a drug, a larger and larger dose is needed to cause the same effect. **Withdrawal symptoms** are the aversive physical discomforts that occur when a person stops taking a physically addictive drug. Withdrawal symptoms generally develop when the body has started to depend on an external source of a particular chemical and has therefore stopped producing some of its own substances internally. **Physical dependence** (or **addiction**) is the bodily changes resulting from the use of an addictive drug so that stopping the drug causes a painful period of readjustment.

The most common way to decide if a drug is physically addictive is to judge whether it results in tolerance and withdrawal symptoms. This definition of addiction, however, is often difficult to apply, because it is difficult to distinguish *psychological dependence* from *physical dependence*. **Psychological dependence** is a powerful need for a drug that is often difficult to distinguish from physical dependence. This dependence is probably based primarily on the drug's ability to reduce anxiety and pain. At one time, the tranquilizer diazepam (Valium) was thought not to be physically addictive. It was known that people became terribly dependent on it, but this was attributed to psychological dependence. Subsequent evidence convinced people that Valium is also physically addictive, and many patients have to be hospitalized in order to get free of a long-standing use of Valium.

There are several important lessons to be learned from the history of Valium. First, psychological dependence can be extremely powerful. It can look so much like physical addiction that professionals can't see the difference. Thus, it is misleading to refer to a drug as causing "only psychological dependence," as though psychological dependence isn't much. Second, it is dangerous to be casual about whether a substance is addictive or not. A more tragic example is that for years cocaine use was promoted with the "common knowledge" that it was not addictive, but this no longer seems true. It is now commonly believed that cocaine is addictive in all its forms but particularly in its concentrated, crystallized form called *crack*. Withdrawal is extremely painful.

Psychoactive substances are drugs which affect the central nervous system. They can change perception, thinking, and emotion. They can be classified into three major groupings. There are also some drugs that seem to be in classes by themselves.

Stimulants

Stimulants are a class of psychoactive substances that arouse, sensitize, and energize the sympathetic nervous system. In moderate doses, they make the person feel alert and awake, but high doses often cause anxiety and irritability. In general, when the sympathetic nervous system is aroused, the person feels a temporary energetic high. This high is usually followed by a "crash" or letdown that can include depression, fatigue, and anxiety. One way out of the letdown is to use the stimulant again and keep the cycle going. However, this must be continued to prevent an eventual crash.

Cocaine is one of the most powerful natural stimulant drugs available. It is derived from the bark of the coca tree. It has been in use since the late 1800s. It was part of the original formula of Coca-Cola. Freud used it at various times in his life, although he later struggled with a dependency on it. Native peoples in South America have chewed the raw coca bark for thousands of years. It has become a widely used drug because of its

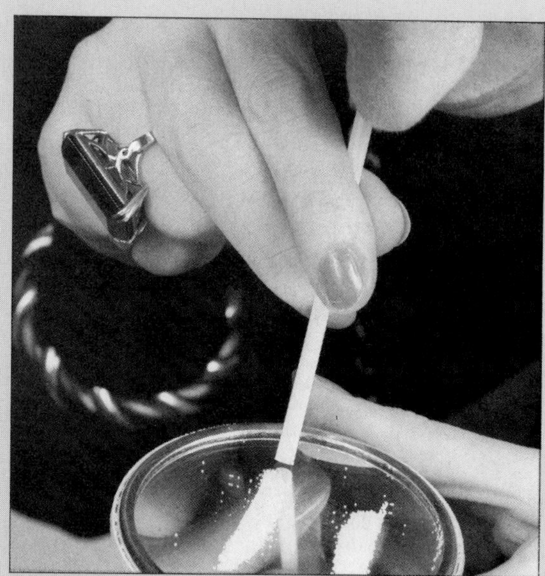

Cocaine is a powerful stimulant that produces its effect by interfering with the sympathetic nervous system.
SOURCE: Canada Wide/Barry Gray.

powerful stimulant powers. It is usually taken by "snorting" (sniffing into the nose) the powdered form, but it can also be injected or smoked.

Cocaine delivers a rush of euphoric pleasure. Within the nervous system, cocaine blocks the natural destruction of the neurotransmitter norepinephrine. As the norepinephrine continues to build up, the synapses affected become more and more active. Large doses can lead to **cocaine intoxication**, which can include very unpleasant hallucinations, paranoia, confusion, anxiety, and death. The post-cocaine letdown may bring headache and dizziness, but it is sometimes followed by a long sleep after which the effects are gone.

Cocaine use is one of our culture's most worrisome substance-abuse problems (Spitz & Rosecan, 1987). **Crack** is an extremely addictive, concentrated, and crystallized form of cocaine.

> The cocaine epidemic continues unabated despite massive federal government efforts. The spread seems to be particularly fuelled by the appearance of 'crack,' a highly potent form of the euphoriant. While its use by the middle-aged, middle- and upper-income groups who originally embraced it and touted its supposed 'virtues' has leveled off, it has now been passed on to a younger, poorer, and largely urban population (Lewis & Dworkin, 1989, p. 400-401).

Amphetamines are a group of stimulant drugs that work by increasing the neurotransmitter norepinephrine. They are commonly referred to as "speed." They include Benzedrine, Dexedrine (dextroamphetamine), and Methedrine (methamphetamine). They have an effect similar to cocaine, but they accomplish the purpose by increasing norepinephrine, rather than by blocking its destruction. Among other effects, amphetamines reduce appetite. They were used for many years as diet drugs. This use is no longer considered medically acceptable, since there is an almost universal "crash" and a boomerang effect in which the patient quickly regains any weight lost and more. Tolerance also builds quickly. Many patients required constantly increasing doses to prevent deep depression and exhaustion, until doses became life threatening and impossible to continue.

Caffeine is one of the most widely used stimulants in our culture. It is an element in coffee and is usually not even thought of as a drug. Caffeine has been used as a stimulant throughout history, and it is addictive for many people. Formerly heavy coffee drinkers often experience painful headaches and deep fatigue for a week or more after they stop. In some ways, **nicotine** addiction is our culture's most severe health problem, but it is so much a part of our culture that only recently has it become thought of as a drug problem. It is apparently as addictive as heroin, at least among heavy smokers. Nicotine addiction certainly causes more death than any other drug problem.

Depressants

Depressants are a major class of drugs that work by suppressing the central nervous system. Nerve activity is suppressed and slowed down. Paradoxically, depressants sometimes seem to arouse and stimulate the person. This is because certain neural centres usually function to inhibit behaviour. If these centres are suppressed, there is less to inhibit the person and behaviour becomes more animated and wild.

Alcohol is the most common of the depressant drugs. It is the clearest example of a depressant that often results in apparent stimulation. When inhibitory centres are suppressed, the person first feels more relaxed and easygoing and may feel free to do things that otherwise would have been inhibited. As alcohol ingestion increases, more and more centres are depressed, so speech can become slurred and thinking can

Most experts agree that alcohol is the most dangerous drug in our culture.
SOURCE: Canada Wide/Norm Bett.

be impaired. With excessive doses there can be brain damage, coma, and even death.

Alcohol is certainly addictive for some persons. It has been estimated that during some period of their lifetimes, about 10% of women and nearly a third of men will have an alcohol addiction severe enough to be called **alcoholism**. Withdrawal often involves nausea, vomiting, extreme fatigue, and shaking. It can include **alcohol withdrawal delirium**, the tremors, anxiety, depression, confusion, and possible hallucinations that accompany the cessation of alcohol consumption in an addicted drinker.

Most experts agree that alcohol is the most dangerous drug in our culture. This is ironic because it is legal, available, and an important part of many of our cultural practices. About 70% of males killed in car accidents were legally intoxicated at the time (Ray, 1983) and about half of violent crimes are alcohol-related.

Another class of depressants includes the many derivatives of the opium poppy, the **opioids**. In its oldest form, *opium*, the product of poppy seeds, was smoked. In the early 1800s **morphine** was derived from opium and was welcomed by the medical community because it seemed to be an effective painkiller that was not addictive. Morphine is still widely used medically, but we now know that there are no forms of opioids that are not addictive. These addictive derivatives include *heroin* and *codeine*. There are some synthetic drugs, such as **methadone**, that seem to operate in similar ways and are classified with the opioids.

As it suppresses the central nervous system, an opioid such as **heroin** produces a euphoric high that is very attractive to the user. There is little pain or anxiety, and the outside world — including sex — holds little interest. When the high passes, however, severe withdrawal symptoms are nearly inevitable. Heroin is very addictive. In order to keep the high going, the user must continually seek another "fix." Supporting a heroin habit often costs hundreds of dollars a day because tolerance builds so much the addict needs large amounts of the drug. The danger to society is that addicts often have to resort to prostitution and crime to obtain heroin. The dangers to the user include the addiction itself, fatal overdoses, the effects of impurities used to "cut" or dilute the drug, and the high rate of AIDS among intravenous drug users. AIDS is commonly spread through shared needles, and addicts seldom think of such dangers. It is often said that if you think you're going to die immediately without a "fix," the fear of AIDS has little impact.

Drugs that produce a calming effect at low doses are called **sedatives**. At higher doses, these drugs can induce sleep and are called **hypnotics**. There are two general classes of these drugs: barbiturates and minor tranquilizers.

Barbiturates depress central nervous system centres in much the same way as alcohol does. They were once used as tranquilizers and as sleeping pills. The discovery of better tranquilizers and of the dangers of barbiturates has meant that sleep-induction is now the main use for barbiturates. They are quite addictive, and

Because tolerance to heroin builds so quickly, it is a highly addictive substance.
SOURCE: Canada Wide.

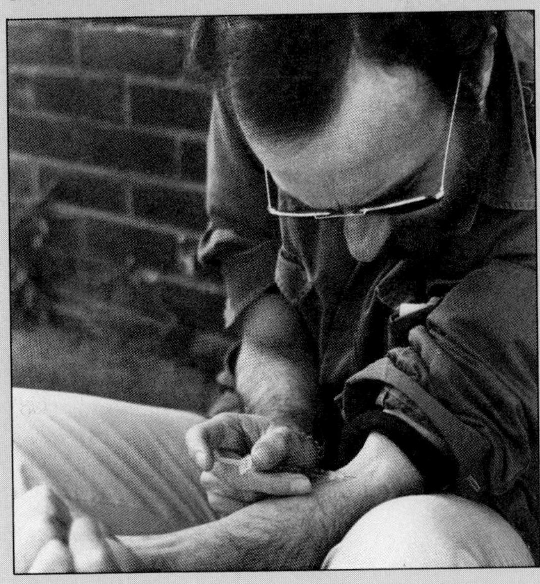

they can slow neural centres down so drastically that death can result from suppression of the respiratory centres. The user is often so groggy and unable to think clearly that an accidental overdose is relatively easy to take.

The **minor tranquilizers**, such as Valium and Librium, reduce anxiety without making the person so drowsy, are less addictive than barbiturates, and don't suppress respiratory centres.

Hallucinogens

The term **hallucinogens** was coined for drugs that result in radical alterations of perception—even to the point of causing hallucinations. **LSD (lysergic acid diethylamide)** is probably the best known of these drugs. It causes an intensification and distortion of experience. Tiny doses can cause hallucinations, quickly changing geometric designs that appear and disappear, sharply vivid "visions" that seem filled with cosmic meaning, sights that can be "heard," and sounds that can be "seen." LSD and other hallucinogens are sometimes called **psychotomimetic drugs**, because this experiencing resembles experiences reported by persons with the severe mental disorder called "psychosis" (see Chapter 14). At one time it was hoped that LSD would mimic psychosis so closely we could use the drug to learn things about schizophrenia and other psychotic problems. Now we know that the two operate differently in the brain.

LSD is a synthetic drug invented by Albert Hoffman in 1938. In April 1943, he accidentally ate a tiny speck of it (with his lunch, the story goes) and for two hours took the first LSD trip. **Mescaline** is another psychotomimetic drug which is derived from the peyote cactus plant. Whether synthetic or natural, hallucinogens all work the same way in the brain. They disrupt the synaptic connections that are sensitive to the neurotransmitter serotonin.

Marijuana and "designer drugs"

Marijuana is a psychoactive substance derived from the hemp plant. Its active chemical ingredient THC (delta-9-tetrahydrocannabinol) is so unlike the chemicals of other psychoactive drugs that marijuana is difficult to classify. We still don't know how marijuana works in the brain. It is also difficult to classify this drug because its effects are a mixture of depressive, excitatory, and hallucinatory. It gives an experience of euphoria that is quite long lasting, and the user often has distorted experiencing that can feel like new insights. However, these "insights" usually are expressed as disjointed verbalizations and thinking. Exaggerated claims about the benefits and dangers of marijuana make it difficult to sort out what is true. It now seems that the drug is not as harmful as was once thought. However, it probably does impair mental functioning in the short term and may have some subtle damaging effects on intellectual performance in the long term. There is also some risk to the reproductive system and respiratory system. In general, marijuana use has been decreasing in recent years (Johnson, Bachman, and O'Malley, 1987).

Designer drugs include a wide range of synthetic, hallucinogenic drugs that are frequently modified to keep them off the illegal drugs lists. There is an underground industry for these chemically modified drugs (Beck and Morgan, 1986), some of which have become fairly widely used. These drugs are also difficult to classify because they have effects that are combinations of hallucinogens, depressants, and stimulants. **Phencyclidine (PCP)** is a designer drug sometimes called "angel dust." It was developed as a painkiller but quickly turned into a street drug when its extreme effects on mood swings was recognized. **Methylene dioxy-metaamphetamine (MDMA)** has an amphetamine-like impact and is referred to by street names such as "Ecstasy" and "Adam." MDMA illustrates the confused state of affairs with designer drugs. Some people make claims of enormous benefits from personal insights with the drug (Leverant, 1986), while others warn of severe dangers such as impaired immune system functioning and depletion of serotonin in the brain. The fact is that we know very little about any of the "designer drugs" (Seymour, Wesson, and Smith, 1986).

1. The study of consciousness is one of the most controversial areas in psychology. Behaviourists argued that psychology should exclude the concept of consciousness and instead focus on observable behaviour. However, with the cognitive revolution, the study of consciousness has increased in recent years.

2. *Consciousness* is a rich term with many meanings. The main property of consciousness is *awareness*, the degree to which a person can repeatedly express his or her own brain processes in symbolic ways. From this definition, it follows that (1) only some of what occurs in the brain qualifies as awareness; (2) awareness is a continuum; and (3) awareness is measured by the ability to express something symbolically through words, gestures, images, or other non-verbal modes.

3. Studies of split-brain patients help to shed light on the concept of consciousness. For example, a split-brain patient can hold an object out of sight in the left hand and be able to describe it with left-hand gestures but not be able to describe it with words. The right hemisphere is "aware" of the object, but the left hemisphere is not.

4. According to Gazzaniga's social brain theory, only some modules of the brain belong to consciousness. The non-verbal modules lie outside of awareness, but they too process information and experience emotion. Gazzaniga argues that our conscious beliefs (which are often false) arise from the attempt by the conscious modules to make sense of what is happening in the non-verbal modules.

5. The role played by awareness in the control of behaviour has been the subject of much debate. Many learning theorists reject Freudian theory, including the very existence of unconscious influences. Nevertheless, recent experimental studies have led to an increasing acceptance of unconscious influences in terms of brain functioning.

6. Awareness does not seem to be a necessary condition for emotion, learning, or information processing. The evidence to date suggests that emotion and cognition are separate systems that can operate independently even though in practice they often influence each other. Other experiments indicate that operant conditioning and classical conditioning can occur outside of awareness. Binocular rivalry experiments demonstrate complex information processing in the absence of reportable awareness.

7. By definition, the controversial phenomena of self-deception, denial, and repression operate outside the individual's awareness. Repression can be understood as the inhibition of the flow of certain information from the right to left hemispheres.

8. Sleep is an altered state of consciousness in which we exhibit some sort of awareness. Sleep provides us with necessary physical and psychological rejuvenation.

9. There are five stages of sleep, each of which is marked by a different pattern of brain activity as measured by the EEG. The progress from Stage 1 sleep to Stage 4 sleep is marked by a gradual shift to delta waves. Each night, we usually go through the cycle of sleep four or five times. Rapid eye movement, dreaming, and the virtual paralysis of motor functioning characterize the stage

of sleep known as REM sleep or paradoxical sleep. REM sleep seems to perform a psychologically restorative function. Increased emotional stress leads to more REM sleep, and deprivation of REM sleep leads to the REM rebound effect.

10. Various theories have been proposed to explain the meaning of dreams. Freud argued that the manifest content of dreams conceals from the dreamer's consciousness the latent content of sexual or aggressive wish fulfilments. Jung agreed that dreams contain important symbolic meaning for the individual, but Jung did not view dreams as concealments. More recently, some theorists have suggested that dreaming is a process of mental housecleaning, helping us to eliminate or resolve the useless, redundant, or unusual information that has accumulated during the day. Another group of theorists argue that dreams have no meaning because they are simply the result of random brain-firing.

11. Insomnia is the most common sleeping disorder in our culture. It can arise from various causes, such as a disruption of the circadian rhythm, sleep apnea, anxiety, or depression. Despite widespread practice, taking sleeping pills or alcohol simply makes the problem worse because these substances hinder REM sleep. The sleeping disorder known as narcolepsy probably has a genetic component. Narcolepsy may be caused by a deficiency of the neurotransmitter dopamine.

12. Hypnosis can be considered a heightened state of suggestibility. Induction techniques vary widely, but they are all designed to increase the power and credibility of the hypnotist. People with hypnotic talents can learn self-hypnosis.

13. Hypnosis can provide a wide range of phenomena. Experiments suggest that through post-hypnotic amnesia, memories are not really forgotten but rather temporarily blocked. Hypnosis can help a person remember events, primarily by decreasing anxiety. However, a hypnotized person often invents memories to fulfil what are perceived as the hypnotist's expectations. Post-hypnotic suggestion can lead the person to perform specific actions after the hypnotic session is over. Hypnosis can produce positive and negative hallucinations. Analgesia and anaesthesia have both been demonstrated under hypnosis. Age regression is possible under hypnosis, but the results are not reliable, as the person is partly trying to fulfil the hypnotist's expectations.

14. Individuals vary considerably in their susceptibility to hypnotism. The only characteristic that has been conclusively correlated with hypnotic susceptibility is possessing a good imagination.

15. Hypnotism is a controversial topic. Throughout history the sceptics have often been proven correct. According to role enactment theory, hypnotism is not a special state but is simply a social-psychological phenomenon — a response to demands made by

the hypnotist. The opposing special-state view, known as dissociation theory, says that hypnosis is related to the social brain theory. It suggests that hypnosis exaggerates the dissociation of brain modules from each other, permitting dissociations in experience. One of the strongest arguments that hypnosis is a special state is its dramatic use in decreasing pain.

16. Meditation is another controversial phenomenon. Sceptics view meditation as simply a form of relaxation, whereas supporters view meditation as a complex process of not-thinking. Several different forms of meditation are designed to induce a state of consciousness undominated by the drive and structure of ordinary thinking. Sceptics argue that there is no physiological evidence that differentiates meditation from simple relaxation. Supporters have reported evidence that meditation is a special state that can best be described by the phrase "restful alertness."

17. Transpersonal psychology is emerging as a relatively small "fourth force" in psychology. It emphasizes the mystical and esoteric aspects of human functioning, while stressing the limitations of scientific understanding.

Key Terms

Addiction Another term for *physical dependence.*

Age regression The hypnotic process in which the subject is "taken back in age" and acts as though he or she were actually that age.

Alcohol The most common of the depressant drugs.

Alcoholism Severe addiction to alcohol.

Alcohol withdrawal delerium A process that can accompany the cessation of alcohol consumption in an addicted drinker. It can include tremors, anxiety, depression, confusion, and possibly hallucinations.

Alpha rhythms Another name for *alpha waves.*

Alpha waves Brain waves of 8-12 cycles per second (Hz) as measured on an EEG. They are characteristic of an extremely relaxed state.

Altered state of consciousness A state of awareness of brain processes that an individual subjectively finds different from those of normal, waking experience.

Amphetamines A group of stimulant drugs that work by increasing the neurotransmitter norepinephrine; commonly referred to as "speed."

Anaesthesia The temporary elimination of pain.

Analgesia The reduction and control of specific pain.

Awareness The degree to which a person can repeatedly express his or her own brain processes in symbolic ways.

Barbiturates Sedatives that depress central nervous system centres.

Binocular rivalry effect The effect of a stimulus presented to one eye of a subject who is reporting on a different stimulus presented to the other eye.

Caffeine One of the most commonly used stimulant drugs in our culture. It is present in coffee.

Circadian rhythm A rhythm of bodily functions whose cycle lasts about 24 hours.

Cocaine One of the most powerful natural stimulant drugs available; derived from the bark of the coca tree.

Cocaine intoxication Extreme reaction to large doses of cocaine. It can include paranoia, anxiety, confusion, hallucinations, and death.

Concentrative meditation The meditative practice marked by concentrating on one's own breathing, a mantra, an object, or symbol repeatedly, without the intrusion of structured thinking.

Consciousness Roughly the same as *awareness.*

Crack An extremely addictive form of cocaine; it is concentrated and crystallized.

Delta waves Brain waves of large amplitude and 1 to 2 cycles per second as measured on an EEG. They appear during Stage 3 sleep and predominate during Stage 4 sleep.

Denial A refusal to acknowledge the truth of a painful or threatening fact.

Depressants A major class of drugs that work by suppressing the nervous system.

Designer drugs A wide range of synthetic, hallucinogenic drugs that are frequently modified to keep them from being listed as illegal drugs.

Dissociation theory A theory that hypnosis is a special state of consciousness in which some mental functions are sharply separate from others.

Drugs Any chemical substances other than food that change bodily or mental functioning.

Hallucinogens Drugs which cause marked alterations in perception, including what are experienced as hallucinations.

Heroin An opioid that suppresses the central nervous system and produces a state of euphoric high; very addictive.

Hypnosis A process of social influence in which the subject is in a much heightened state of suggestibility.

Hypnotics A term for sedatives when used at high doses, since at these higher dosages they can induce sleep.

Induction process The process by which a hypnotic state is caused in a subject.

Insomnia The inability to fall asleep or to stay asleep throughout the night.

Introspection A research method used by structuralists in which trained observers examine their own mental processes and report their private mental experiences in detail.

Latent content of dreams Freud's term for the hidden meanings or wish fulfilments symbolized in dreams.

LSD (lysergic acid diethylamide) The most widely known hallucinogen.

Manifest content of dreams Freud's term for the actual words, images, and plots that the dreamer remembers.

Mantra A particular phrase, word, or sound which a meditator mentally repeats over and over again.

Marijuana (THC) A psychoactive substance derived from the hemp plant.

Meditation A process for inducing a special state of consciousness characterized by the diminishing of everyday forms of thinking.

Mescaline A natural psychotomimetic drug derived from the peyote cactus plant.

Methadone A synthetic drug that operates much like the opioids and is usually classified with them.

Methyline dioxy-metaamphetamine (MDMA) A designer drug with an amphetamine-like impact. It is referred to by street names such as "Ecstasy" and "Adam."

Minor tranquilizers Sedatives, such as Valium and Librium, which reduce anxiety without making the person as drowsy as barbiturates.

Morphine An opioid that is widely used medically as a pain killer; very addictive.

Multimind theory Ornstein's theory that the brain is a collection of talents, policies, and modules that are loosely integrated by a mental operating system.

Narcolepsy A sleep disorder in which a person suddenly falls asleep at odd times of the day.

Negative hallucinations A hallucination in which the hypnotic subject fails to see or hear something that is actually there.

Nicotine A commonly used stimulant.

NREM sleep Non-rapid eye movement sleep. All the stages of sleep other than REM sleep—namely, Stage 1, Stage 2, Stage 3, and Stage 4 sleep.

Opening up meditation Meditative practice marked by a total engagement of the present moment throughout daily life.

Opioids A group of addictive depressant drugs derived from the opium poppy plant. They include opium, morphine, and heroin.

Paradoxical sleep Another name for *REM sleep*.

Phencyclidine (PCP) A designer drug sometimes called "angel dust."

Physical dependence (also called *addiction*) Bodily changes resulting from the use of an addictive drug so that stopping the drug causes a painful period of readjustment.

Positive hallucination A hypnotic hallucination in which the subject sees or hears something that is not actually there.

Post-hypnotic amnesia The forgetting of events that occurred during a hypnotic session or of other material, as suggested by the hypnotist.

Post-hypnotic suggestion A suggestion that the hypnotic subject is asked to carry out after the hypnotic session.

Psychoactive substances Drugs which affect the central nervous system. They can change perception, thinking, and emotion.

Psychological dependence Powerful need for a drug that is often difficult to distinguish from physical dependence. This dependence is probably based primarily on the drug's ability to reduce anxiety and pain.

Psychotomimetic drugs Drugs whose effects seem to stimulate experiences similar to the psychoses.

Relaxation response The physiological patterns observed during meditation.

REM rebound effect The tendency for the amount of REM sleep to increase following periods of REM deprivation.

REM sleep The stage of sleep marked by rapid eye movements (REM's) during which most dreaming seems to occur. It is also known as paradoxical sleep because it is a period of extensive mental activity, even though much of the musculature of the sleeper is virtually paralyzed.

Repression The unintentional forgetting of otherwise well-learned aversive memories.

Reticular activating system (RAS) A neural structure in the brain stem that helps control arousal, attention, and sleep.

Role enactment theory A sceptical theory of hypnosis as simply a process of social-psychological influence and not a special state of consciousness.

Sedatives A group of drugs that provide a calming effect at relatively low doses.

Selective attention A state of focused processing of one set of stimuli among many competing stimuli.

Self-deception A process that occurs when an individual holds two contradictory beliefs at the same time and yet denies to the self or fails to notice one of these beliefs.

Self-hypnosis Hypnotic trance induced on oneself.

Simple exposure effect The tendency of people to prefer familiar stimuli.

Sleep apnea A sleep disorder marked by the inability to breathe continuously during sleep.

Social brain theory Gazzaniga's theory that the brain is a sort of society made up of many different modules that can act independently of each other.

Spindles Bursts of EEG activity slightly faster than alpha waves. They are characteristic of Stage 2 sleep.

Stimulants A class of psychoactive substances that result primarily in sympathetic nervous system arousal.

Sudden infant death syndrome (SIDS) Unexplained deaths that may be related to sleep apnea in which the infant's undeveloped respiratory system does not respond normally to the stopping of breathing.

Suppression The intentional forgetting of aversive memories through conscious effort.

Tolerance The phenomenon in which an increasingly larger dose of a drug is needed to achieve the same effect.

Transcendental meditation (TM) A commercialized and widely promoted approach to concentrative meditation.

Transpersonal psychology A small but growing "fourth force" in psychology that focuses on the esoteric and mystical aspects of human functioning and that argues against the exclusive use of rational methods of inquiry.

Withdrawal symptoms The aversive physical discomforts that occur when a person stops taking a physically addictive drug.

SUGGESTED READINGS

Bowers, K. S. (1983). *Hypnosis for the seriously curious.* New York: Norton. A well-written overview by a prominent Canadian researcher of various studies on hypnosis and their applications.

Bowers, K. S. (1987). Revisioning the unconscious. *Canadian Psychology*, 28, 93-104. An excellent summary of recent research into the role of unconscious influences on thought, behaviour, and feeling. This issue of the journal also contains responses to Bowers by several other researchers.

Dement, W. C. (1974). *Some must watch while some must sleep: Exploring the world of sleep.* New York: Norton. Written for the educated layperson, this book gives details of research methods and findings of sleep research. It emphasizes the functions of REM sleep and dreaming. Although a bit dated, it is a good summary of the field.

Gazzaniga, M. S. (1985). *The social brain.* New York: Basic Books. A fascinating theory we discuss in this chapter. This well-written book by one of the pioneers in brain laterality research explores the implications of the social brain for such topics as the inevitability of religious beliefs, unconscious influences, and how the evolution of our brains dooms us to interesting but conflictual lives.

Holender, D. (1986). Semantic activation without conscious identification in dichotic listening, parafoveal vision, and visual masking: a survey and appraisal. *The Behavioural and Brain Sciences*, 9, 1-66. A lively debate on information processing without awareness. Holender's critical review of studies is followed by 25 responses by prominent researchers.

Wallace, B., & Fisher, L. E. (1987). *Consciousness and behavior*, 2nd ed. Boston: Allyn & Bacon. A good, comprehensive source for information on psychology's growing interest in states of consciousness. A combination of research-oriented and applied material is provided.

Zilbergeld, B., Edelstien, M. G., & Araoz, D. L. (Eds.) (1986). *Hypnosis: Questions and answers.* New York: Norton. A clinically oriented book that gives thorough answers to many common questions about hypnosis. Methods of induction and clinical applications are covered.

PART IV

DEVELOPMENT AND PERSONALITY

CHAPTER 10

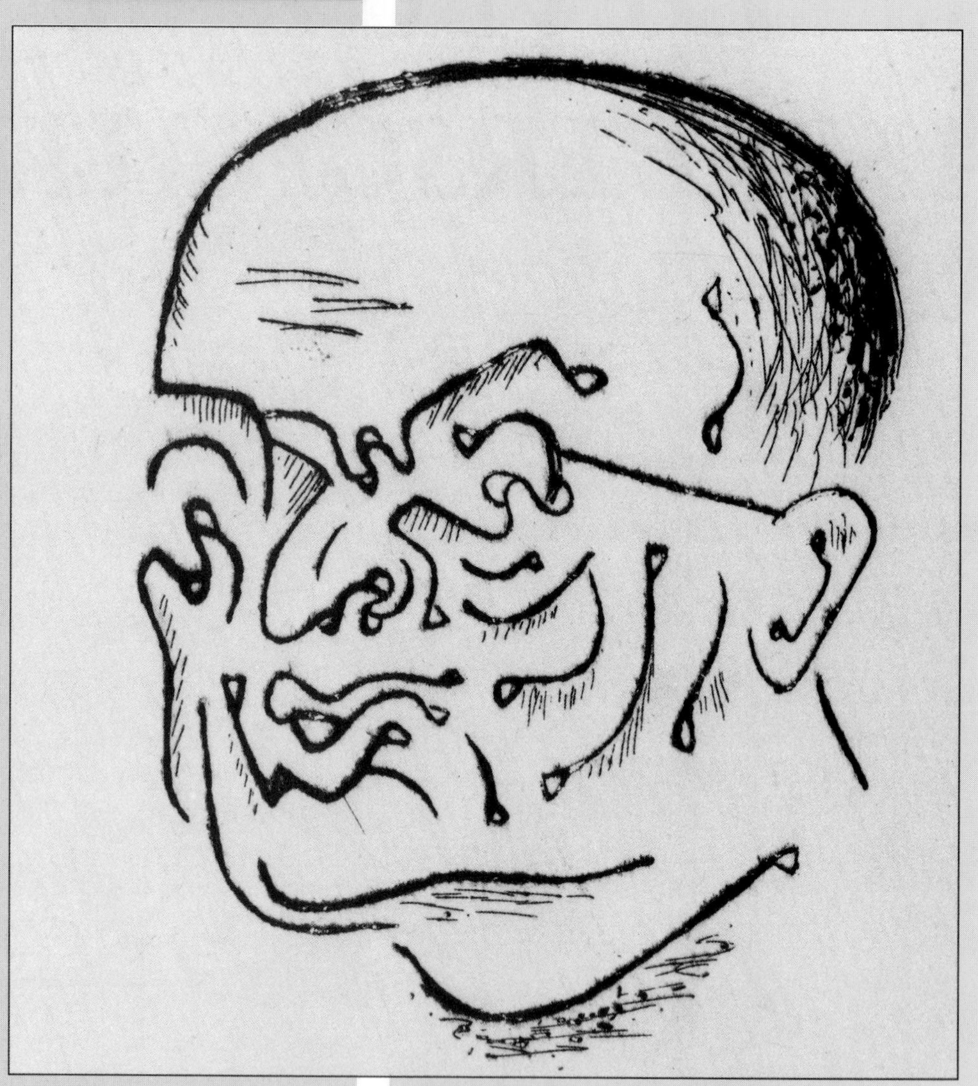

SOURCE: Sorel Etrog, Detail from Untitled [*Head of a Man*] (1969).

Theories of Personality

ALTHOUGH NEARLY all of us feel that we know what it means, the word "personality" is surprisingly difficult to define. Our language implies that personality is some kind of entity or *thing* that we possess and that has something to do with social interaction. We say, "He has a personality," and even, "She has a lot of personality." Apparently, this thing we have comes in different quantities. The first statement might apply to anyone, since presumably we all have a personality. The second statement implies that a particular person is attractive and socially effective. Our language is misleading, however. If personality is an entity, where is it? If you say, "I have a personality," is the "I" somehow different from the personality that it possesses? If an operation on your brain changed you from an aggressive person to a timid person, we might say that you have a new personality, but wouldn't you still be the same person? These questions point up the difficulty in defining personality, but the word must mean *something* since it is used so much in psychology. Some writers are so impressed by the lack of agreement on a definition that they claim, "There may be as many different meanings of the term 'personality' as there are theorists who have tried to define it" (Mischel, 1986, p. 4). But personality does refer to persons, and we can attempt a reasonably general definition of the word. **Personality** is a collective term which encompasses all of an individual's overt (observable) and covert (internal) behaviours (thoughts and feelings). These behaviours are perceived by the individual or others as having a unity, that is, of being consistent and characteristic.

WHY SO MANY PERSONALITY THEORIES?

When our knowledge is very incomplete, as it is in the study of human behaviour and personality, it is likely that several different theories will conflict with each other. However, it is precisely when our knowledge is incomplete that a good theory is especially needed and especially useful.

People sometimes say, "That's fine in theory, but it's not really true." This is a misuse of the word "theory." The main purpose of a theory is to organize our knowledge in a way that points us toward our best approximation of what is true. A theory that fulfils this purpose can be considered to be useful. There are four main criteria for judging whether a theory is useful.

First, a good theory must *integrate knowledge*. It must incorporate all relevant well-established present knowledge. Otherwise, it is a failure. In the personality area, however, there will be great disagreement over what is "well-established" present knowledge.

Second, a good theory must have *internal consistency*. The various parts of the theory must be logically consistent with each other. Many people have their own personal theory of the nature of human personality, but they apply different principles in different circumstances. To explain group behaviour they might refer to a "social instinct" and to explain individual differences they might refer to an "innate need for individuality" without reconciling how both principles can be inborn.

Third, a good theory should enable us to *make predictions*. For the purposes of science, it is important that present knowledge be organized in ways that suggest *new* ideas or that allow us to predict other possible truths. These predictions guide future research.

Fourth, a good theory should be capable of *guiding practice*. Especially in the study of human behaviour, we are interested in gaining knowledge that can improve life and relieve suffering. Every personality theorist defines at least (implicitly) what "the good life" is and how individuals who have behavioural problems can be helped.

Those who work in a young science dealing with a complex subject will have many conflicting views. This is certainly true of the psychology of personality. Philosophy, medicine, literature, and psychology have all influenced our understanding of personality. As a result we are faced with a bewildering diversity of personality theories. Most of these theories grew out of the thinking of one or two individuals who have attracted disciples. Until recently the different theories have been based not on scientific findings but on "armchair" speculation and on poorly defined concepts. The attempt to shore up such shaky foundations has led to hostility and disagreement among personality psychologists. Such doctrinaire attitudes have had some advantages. Because followers of a particular approach have adamantly committed themselves to their positions, they have sometimes worked hard to develop their chosen theory. However, inflexible commitment has also hampered communication, and communication is especially important in an area in which knowledge is young and tools of measurement are crude and unreliable.

Although there are a great many theories of personality, they can be roughly divided into five groups, each with an identifiable perspective on human nature. Keep in mind, though, that there is overlap between these theories. Later in this chapter we will talk about how important it is to be *eclectic*—that is, to draw from many different theories. Since no single personality theory is entirely correct, we have to be open to integrating a number of such theories. In the following paragraph, we will give a brief general overview of the five groups of personality theories. Then, for the rest of this chapter, we will investigate these theories in greater detail.

(1) First, there are several *psychodynamic theories*. The best known of these is *psychoanalysis*, the approach developed by Freud and elaborated by many of his followers. **Psychoanalysis** is both an instinct theory of personality and an approach to psychotherapy. **Instinct theory** proposes that human motivation is fundamentally biological and controlled by innate drives. (2) **Trait theories** are primarily concerned with describing and categorizing human characteristics, rather than explaining their underlying dynamics. (3) **Learning theories** state that virtually all behaviour is the result of prior learning. Humans are born with biological limits and needs,

Some of those who have influenced our ideas about personality.

The philosopher Bertrand Russell (1872–1941).
SOURCE: The Bettmann Archive.

The novelist Virginia Woolf (1882–1941).
SOURCE: Bettmann/Hulton.

The early medical theorist and practitioner Hippocrates (460–377 B.C.).
SOURCE: Art Resource.

but nearly all of what we call personality is learned. It is the result of experience. (4) In general, **humanistic theories** are less concerned with scientific aspects of the study of personality and more interested in individual experience and personal growth. Humanism, often referred to as the "third force" (psychoanalysis and learning theory are generally taken as the main two), takes a more optimistic view of human nature and personal freedom of choice. (5) Finally, **cognitive theories** stress the importance of thoughts, feelings, and impulses in the control of behaviour and the development of personality. Adherents of cognitive *learning* theories direct their criticisms against the more behaviouristic learning theorists for ignoring these internal processes (Mahoney, 1977). **Cognitive learning theories** take the position that the most important behaviours are internal (thoughts, feelings, and impulses) and follow the same laws as other behaviours.

Each theory of personality has important implications for the treatment of human emotional and behavioural problems. In this chapter, we will describe the different theories of personality. In Chapter 15 we will discuss the ways in which those theories lead to different approaches to the practice of psychotherapy.

PSYCHOANALYTIC THEORIES

One of the most powerful influences on the whole field of psychology in the first half of this century was Sigmund Freud's presentation of psychoanalysis (Freud, 1900 and 1935). Until the 1940s, psychoanalysis stood nearly alone as *the* psychotherapeutic treatment technique and theory of personality. Currently, psychoanalysis has less influence than some other personality theories, particularly in university settings. However, medical schools still stress Freud's thinking quite strongly.

The term "psychoanalysis" is used broadly to include a theory of personality development, a theory of neurosis, and an approach to psychotherapy. Many people think that "psychoanalysis" and "psychotherapy" are synonymous, but they are not. Psychoanalysis is one kind of psychotherapy. Therapists who subscribe to Freud's theories and/or therapeutic techniques describe themselves as "psychoanalysts" or as "analytically-oriented" therapists.

Even before the development of humanistic and learning theories, some of Freud's followers deviated from his ideas to establish their own approaches. Some of these "deviations" were clearly derived from Freud, but some of them represented dramatic disagreements on basic principles. Freud himself often deviated from his earlier ideas. Many of his later theoretical writings contradict his earlier writings, and he made no apparent attempt to reconcile some of these contradictions. Freud saw his thinking as an emerging, changing theoretical structure and often modified his position on the basis of new evidence. These shifts in position make it somewhat difficult to present a clearly organized view of the history of psychoanalysis, so this section will deal primarily with Freud's later contributions to the field.

Sigmund Freud was born in 1856, was, throughout his school days, a good student, and became a physician in 1881 after having made some original contributions in neurological research. He was influenced by the studies of Charcot (1825-1893) and Breuer (1842-1925) in the areas of hypnosis and hysteria. Partly because of their influence, he began to develop his ideas about the "talking cure" and about the importance of sexuality in human motivation. At the time—during the Victorian era—his ideas were rejected and often looked upon as repugnant and dangerous. In the early 1900s, however, his writings began to attract favourable attention. From 1909, when Freud gave a series of lectures in the United States, until his death in 1939, he enjoyed immense influence and was enormously productive. It is probably illustrative of Freud's character that he refused narcotics to kill the pain of his fatal cancer so that his mind would remain clear.

Josef Breuer (1842–1925).
SOURCE: Archiv für Kunst und Geschichte.

Structure of personality

Freud conceived of mental phenomena in a topographic way, as though the mind were a place. The three major regions or characters of the mind are the *id*, the *ego*, and the *superego* (see Figure 10-1). The **id** is that part of the personality driven by primitive biological strivings that are aimed entirely toward the attainment of pleasure. It operates on the **pleasure principle** which directs the individual to strive for immediate gratification. The id's motto is "if it feels good, do it." Id strivings are illogical and without relation to reality and are the original source of all *psychic energy* (which we will discuss below). These strivings toward gratification are also unconscious.

The **ego** is concerned with relationships to reality and develops through contact with the environment. In Freudian theory, the term "ego" does not include the commonly-used meaning of "conceit." The ego works on the basis of the **reality principle** which directs the individual to deal adaptively with the environment. That is, effective functioning in the environment guides the ego. The ego is poorly developed and weak in the infant. As the ego develops, it takes on

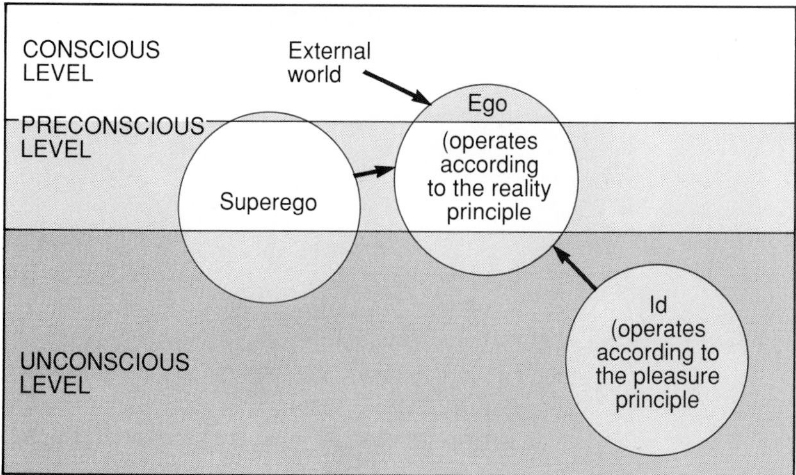

SOURCE: Reprinted with permission from Allyn and Bacon, 1989.

FIGURE 10-1 Freud's view of personality structure: id, ego, and superego
Freud believed that personality consists of three major components: id, ego, and superego. The id is largely unconscious and operates in terms of the pleasure principle, the desire for immediate, total gratification. The ego is partly conscious and operates in terms of the reality principle. It takes account of the external world and directs behaviour so as to maximize pleasure and minimize pain. Finally, the superego, too, is located only partly in the realm of consciousness. It is concerned with morality and permits gratification of id impulses only when it is morally correct to do so.

characteristics that are partly conscious and partly unconscious. It is responsible for our behaving "wisely" in the world and for repression. **Repression** is a defense mechanism which causes thoughts, impulses, and feelings that are unacceptable and/or cause anxiety to be forgotten (i.e., to be pushed into the unconscious). The job of the ego is to assist the id in gaining gratification, except where such gratification would be harmful in any way. The ego tries to control the harmful, primitive, and unrealistic strivings of the id.

The third "mind structure" in psychoanalytic theory is the **superego**. It is made up partly of moral standards adopted in childhood and partly of inherited unconscious moral ideas. It is roughly synonymous with the popular idea of "conscience." (The idea of inherited ideas is Jung's notion, which Freud mentioned in his later writings but did not stress.) The superego stems primarily from unconscious sources and is engaged in a battle with the amoral id. It too must be controlled by the ego.

Levels of consciousness

The id, ego, and superego exist at three levels: the *conscious*, the *preconscious*, and the *unconscious* (see Figure 10-2). In Freudian theory, the **conscious mind** is that part of the mind that is currently in awareness or can easily be brought to awareness. The **preconscious mind** is that part of the mind that consists of material (thoughts, memories, and feelings) that is not currently in awareness but that can be brought to awareness with effort. The preconscious is usually thought of as memory. Some painful ideas in the preconscious level are difficult to retrieve because of the censorship exercised by the ego (which strives to reduce anxiety and deal effectively with reality). The **unconscious mind** is that part of the mind that consists of material (thoughts, memories, and feelings) that is outside awareness and usually cannot be brought to awareness. It is Freud's study of the

Among those attending the Clark University Twentieth Anniversary Celebration Psychology Conference in September 1909, were Sigmund Freud (seated left) and Carl Jung (seated right). SOURCE: Clark University Archives.

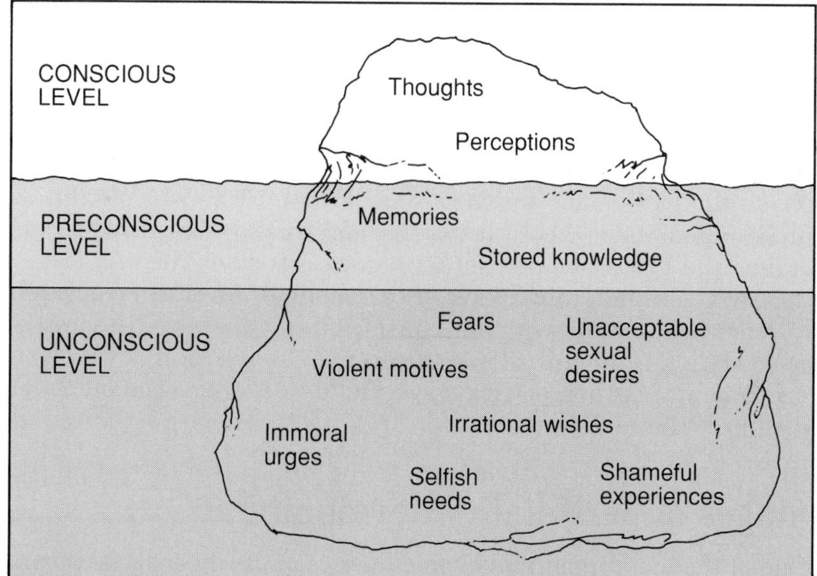

SOURCE: Reprinted with permission from Allyn and Bacon, 1989.

FIGURE 10-2 Freud's view of the human mind: the mental iceberg Freud believed that the human mind operates at three distinct levels: conscious, preconscious, and unconscious. The conscious mind includes our current thoughts. Beneath the conscious realm is the much larger preconscious which contains memories which are not part of current thoughts but can be brought to mind. Finally, beneath the preconscious, and forming the bulk of the human mind, is the unconscious—thoughts, desires, and impulses of which we remain largely unaware.

unconscious mind that is one of his most widely-known contributions to personality theory (although the idea of the unconscious had several earlier proponents). Freud conceived of thoughts, memories, and feelings as *excitations* that can be pushed, if they are painful or unacceptable, from the conscious level to the unconscious level by the ego. Once deeply-buried in the unconscious, these mental experiences become irrational. They also continue to be active. Unconscious fear, drives, desires, needs, and memories can enable the unconscious to exert irrational and sometimes crippling influences on behaviour.

Psychic energy and dynamics

It is crucial to understand that Freud's theory is a **dynamic theory**, that is, a theory based on the distribution of psychic energy. Freud saw mental activity as a form of **psychic energy**, which is different from physical energy. He labelled the basic, instinctual energy of mental life **libido** and considered it to flow from the life instinct, or *Eros*. Libido is the most important form of psychic energy. According to Freud, each individual possesses only a limited amount of libido. Because the amount of libido is limited, some mental functions must be sacrificed in favour of others. The distribution of available libido to different mental functions is an idea basic to psychoanalysis. For example, people who are terribly conflicted about expressing aggression might expend so much of their available psychic energy in such conflicts that they might not be able to function in other areas of their mental or emotional life. Creative abilities that might have developed would wither for lack of psychic energy.

Freud also proposed (though he did not develop the idea in detail) that we have a death instinct called **Thanatos**. It operates in opposition to Eros, motivating self-destructive behaviour when turned inwards or cruelty and aggression when turned outward. The conflict between Eros and Thanatos exemplifies Freud's emphasis throughout his writings on conflicting forces within the personality. Other examples of such conflict exist between the ego and the id, and the pleasure principle and the reality principle.

By calling the life instinct "Eros," Freud was stressing the essentially sexual nature of human motivation. In his view, virtually all physically pleasurable sensations are sexual. He considered this as fundamental to his theory. It was this idea that so scandalized people around the 1900s (and probably still does, actually). The very idea—that even children might have sexual feelings! Most of Freud's followers who later split with him considered sexuality to be less important than Freud did. This difference of opinion was often instrumental in their parting ways. Freud was quite adamant about the importance of sexuality.

Stages of personality development

One of the most important characteristics of psychoanalytic theory is its approach to the developmental stages through which a person passes. According to Freud, although these stages occur at different ages in different individuals, their sequence is always the same. Freud argued that these stages are determined by instinctual forces and thus are inevitable. At different stages in early life, libido functions primarily in different areas of the body (see Figure 10-3).

In Freudian theory, the stage of life occupying approximately the first two years is commonly known as the **oral-erotic stage**. Satisfactions and psychic energy are centered around the mouth and feeding. During the second stage, the **anal-erotic stage**, which occurs in approximately years three and four, libido is concentrated in the organs of elimination. In the following two years, which Freud called the **phallic stage**, libido centres around the genital organs. ("Phallus" means "penis.") At about the time of the phallic stage, the most important emotional conflict in the individual is the Oedipus complex (sometimes called the Electra complex in girls). According to Freud's theory of the **Oedipus complex**, the child in the phallic stage unconsciously desires the opposite-sex parent sexually and wishes to be rid of the same-sex parent (sometimes called the **Electra complex** in girls). The complex is named after a Greek myth in which Oedipus slays his father and marries his mother without being aware of his relationship to either. This Oedipal desire in the five-to-seven-year-old boy is expressed primarily by the boy's need for physical contact, by his wanting to be "mommy's little man," and by other disguised forms. The father is seen as a rival for the mother's affection. The boy, however, also fears retaliation by the father. This fear takes the primary form of **castration anxiety**, a fear that the father will take away the boy's penis. In normal development the intense conflict created is ultimately resolved by the boy's identification with the father, so that the father's manliness can be incorporated as the boy's own. This process is summarized by the phrase "identification with the aggressor." The boy acquires the father's power by identifying with him.

Freud's phrase "anatomy is destiny" reflects what he saw as inevitable sexual determinism. His theory is clearly male-dominated and centred around the importance of the penis. This emphasis has been strongly criticised by many who see his theory as indefensibly sexist. According to Freud, a similar problem accompanies the five-to-seven-year-old girl's development. Her Oedipus complex (or Electra complex, after another Greek myth) comes from a different source and is more slowly resolved. Freud decided that a girl of this age suffers **penis envy**, rather than castration anxiety, when she feels that she is deficient because she does not have a penis. She blames her mother (who is similarly "deficient"), and the resulting hostility causes her to turn to her father for gratification and love. Ultimately this "hopeless romance" is *sublimated* (displaced toward other objects). The mother is not very available to the girl as a person with whom to identify (because she is "deficient" too) so the girl takes much longer to resolve her Oedipal problem than the boy. Freud said this problem was not fully resolved until a girl bore children, which in Freud's view made her complete.

Karen Horney (1926) was one of the most articulate critics of the sexism inherent in Freud's theory. Her writing was especially important because she was trained as a psychoanalyst. She argued that Freud incorrectly equated the concept of "human" with the concept of "man." She also said that whatever envy women feel toward men is related to differences in social status and power, rather than to an instinctive desire to have a penis. In fact, many men envy women for such attributes as the ability to bear children—the ultimate creative act. This is sometimes half-seriously referred to as "womb envy." In general, Horney brought an emphasis on social and cultural influences to psychoanalytic theory.

(One wonders if Freud ever listened to the conversation of little girls. On one side of the question, there is the little girl who saw a boy urinating behind a bush at a picnic and said, "What a handy thing to take to a picnic!" On the other side of the argument, a five-year-old girl saw her first naked boy when her mother gave her a bath with a visiting neighbour boy. She played it very smoothly and said nothing until later that night when her mother was putting her to bed. Her only comment was, "Isn't it a blessing he didn't get it on his face?")

During the years from seven until puberty, the child is, according to Freud, in the **latency period** during which time sexual needs become relatively dormant. At the onset of puberty the child enters the **genital period** and is faced with the task of directing libidinal energy to an object-choice outside himself or herself and other than the parents. In other words, he or she is faced with the task of developing a love relationship as part of adulthood.

Figure: 10-3 Freud's psychosexual stages of development
According to Freud, all human beings pass through a series of discrete psychosexual stages of development. Freud believed that normal personality development can be derailed at any of these stages by either too much or too little gratification.
Source: Reprinted with permission from Allyn and Bacon, 1989.

GENITAL STAGE
Sexual desire is blended with affection; the capacity for adult love results

Puberty

LATENCY PERIOD
Sexuality decreases to low levels; Same-sex friendships are strong

Six Years Old

PHALLIC STAGE
Pleasure focused on genitals. Oedipal conflict arises and must be resolved

Four Years Old

ANAL STAGE
Pleasure focused on elimination. Toilet training; concerns with cleanliness, control over bodily fuctions

One Year Old

ORAL STAGE
Pleasure focused on mouth. Concern with receiving food, biting, chewing

Birth

Theory of neurosis

Freud's theory of neurosis attempts to explain how the mind copes with *neurotic anxiety* (as opposed to real anxiety, which he defined as fear of identifiable external threats).

Neurotic anxiety

Freud considered **real anxiety** to be a realistic fear with an identifiable cause, roughly equivalent to the common use of the word "fear." **Neurotic anxiety** is more complicated. It is an irrational fear of one's own unconscious thoughts, memories, and impulses, including id impulses. These impulses are unacceptable to the ego and frighten the person. As these impulses begin to emerge, the ego attempts to prevent them from entering consciousness. It represses them back into the unconscious. Material thus repressed still retains its psychic energy, however. Some of this energy is transformed into neurotic anxiety, a sign that there are unconscious conflicts.

The ego can become incapable of controlling anxiety-arousing material and less capable of dealing with reality. The psychic energy consumed in the process of repression and the energy retained by the repressed material in the unconscious are drained from the total amount of libido. This leaves the ego with less psychic energy to deal with the environment and with internal threats. Hence, according to Freudian theory, people with neurotic problems often function poorly in their everyday lives because their egos don't have sufficient psychic energy available for dealing with reality.

Fixation and neurotic symptoms

The picture is further complicated if, at some stage in development, a particular psychosexual problem is inadequately solved. **Fixation** is the tendency for a certain amount of psychic energy to remain attached to and tied up in the unresolved problems of an earlier developmental stage. Any unacceptable impulses of the fixated stage (incestuous desires, for example) consume psychic energy. Because the fixated amount of libido is not available for dealing with reality, one's ability to adjust to the demands of the environment is weakened.

When subjected to sufficient stress from either external or internal threats, the individual sometimes experiences regression. **Regression** is the return to an earlier stage of adjustment and behaviour as a response to stress. The individual returns to the stage at which he or she is most strongly fixated — that is, the stage that is invested with the most psychic energy.

An individual fixated at the phallic and Oedipal stages, for example, might develop conversion hysteria under stress. **Conversion hysteria** is the expression of psychological conflicts and the transformation of psychic energy into physical symptoms, such as the "heart attack" your uncle has every time your cousin gets engaged. Conversion symptoms are disguised expressions of sexual impulses that represent a compromise between the id forces seeking expression and the controlling censorship of the ego. They modify the original id impulses into forms that are acceptable to the ego. There are many other forms these "neurotic symptoms" can take, but they are all disguised expressions of internal conflicts.

Defence mechanisms

In 1938, Freud described a number of defence mechanisms that individuals use to protect themselves from anxiety. A **defence mecha-**

nism is an unconscious, self-deceptive mental process or manoeuvre that enables the individual to avoid anxiety but that also introduces distortions into the person's mental life.

Each of the following examples illustrates that a defence mechanism somehow protects a person from anxiety about himself or herself.

The fundamental defence mechanism is *repression*. Threatening memories and impulses are more likely than other memories and impulses to be denied access to consciousness. Freud said they are pushed into the unconscious. Defence mechanisms are a form of self-deception, since the individual is unaware of the true nature of the repressed mental processes. This self-deception can take many forms. **Projection** is the unconscious tendency to attribute to others one's own unacceptable impulses. The dishonest person who can't accept his own dishonesty and therefore believes that everybody else is a liar is suffering from projection. This belief protects him from the anxiety of his own impulses. **Reaction formation**, another defence mechanism, is an unconscious tendency to adopt ideas and behaviour that are the opposite of one's own unacceptable impulses. It is sometimes said that the most fervent reformer is often the most strongly tempted. The fanatic anti-homosexual campaigner might well be unconsciously proving to himself that he has no feelings of physical affection for the same sex. **Displacement** is the unconscious tendency to express unacceptable emotions and impulses in a disguised form that is more acceptable to the ego and less threatening to the individual. (You may be angry with your professor because of his rudeness, but it is safer to kick the dog.) Freud often spoke of sublimation. **Sublimation** is the redirection or displacement of psychic energy away from unacceptable impulses and toward more socially-acceptable or beneficial goals. Displacement refers to specific emotions being directed at substitute targets. Sublimation refers to a longer term, broader process or rechanneling psychic energy from an unacceptable outlet (usually sexual or aggressive) to a more acceptable outlet. (You may be angry with your professor because of his rudeness and it may be safer to kick the dog, but it may be more socially acceptable to go out and run five kilometres, or it may be more socially beneficial to study hard, become a university professor yourself, and always treat your own students with courtesy.)

Post-Freudian and neo-Freudian theories

Freud attracted many followers, but some of them became dissatisfied with many aspects of his theory. In the early part of this century, some of these colleagues broke with Freud to establish their own schools of thought, even though most of them acknowledged his enormous influence. We will briefly discuss two examples.

Carl Jung

Carl Jung was a Swiss psychiatrist and was a close friend and ally of Freud's from 1907 until 1913, when they parted ways with a great deal of bitterness. Jung developed a very complex theory that had many spiritual overtones (Jung, 1953-1979). Although he continued

Mythic "little folk" (elves, dybyks, leprechauns) appear in the folklore of many nationalities.

to use the term "libido," he downplayed the role of sexuality in motivation. This may have been the point that most infuriated Freud.

It is impossible to capture even a small part of Jung's theory quickly. However we will discuss several of his most important concepts. In Jungian theory, the **personal unconscious** is that part of the mind that is made up mainly of personal memories and impulses that have been repressed. It is roughly equivalent to Freud's concept of the individual unconscious. Jung, however, also believed that we are all born with a collective unconscious. This **collective unconscious** includes inherited ideas or, more accurately, the potentiality for these ideas, and it is sometimes called the racial unconscious. Since it has a quality derived from one's own relatives, different races or cultures might have differences in the collective unconscious. In the collective unconscious are **archetypes**, generalized potentialities for ideas. The general tendency toward religiosity is one such archetype. Two of the most important archetypes are the **anima** which is one's basic female nature, and the **animus** which is one's basic male nature. Each person has both a male and a female nature and is fundamentally a combination of these. We do ourselves a disservice to deny the reality of either of these parts of ourselves.

Jung emphasized the importance of mythology as an expression of our archetypes. Within the collective unconscious are many common patterns, so it is no surprise that the myths and legends of different peoples reflect similar fears, symbols, hopes and creatures.

Jung's influence has seemed to increase and decrease at different times in our culture. Because of the spiritual and religious implications of much of his thinking, he is often popular among people interested in those areas of human life. For example, he often spoke of the soul and said that many events are related by more than simple coincidence. Through "synchronicity," what appear to be coincidences often result from the spiritual interrelatedness of peoples' lives.

Ego psychology

Ego psychology is probably the most important of the current modifications of psychoanalysis. **Ego psychology** stresses positive ego functioning and the importance of interpersonal relations. Both of these principles are departures from Freudian theory. Freud placed more emphasis on instinctive drives than on ego functioning, and he was more concerned with the internal dynamics of each person's functioning (an *intra*-psychic approach) than with the dynamics between people. Ego psychologists (or "neo-analysts," as they are sometimes called) stress *inter*- personal functioning and dealing with the environment. Practitioners believe that emphasizing ego functioning gives the individual a more active role in living his or her own life.

Critical evaluation

Freudian psychoanalysis has, in one way or another, influenced nearly all psychotherapists and many of its ideas have become integral parts of our culture. For example, it is hard for us to imagine that

In the eighteenth and nineteenth centuries, many people saw children as miniature adults.
SOURCE: "The Graham Children" by Hogarth; reproduced by courtesy of the Trustees, the National Gallery, London.

at the beginning of this century most people saw children as nothing more than miniature adults and did not appreciate the extent to which childhood experiences mould adult personality. The commonly-held view that human behaviour follows at least partially predictable laws grew out of Freud's theory. The importance of sexuality in personality development was at first adamantly rejected but is now widely accepted. The idea of a "talking cure" was popularized by Freud and has influenced almost all forms of psychotherapy. Finally, most therapists recognize the importance of unconscious influences on behaviour. These are all important contributions, and some of them are supported by empirical evidence (Masling, 1986). As Bachop (1989) notes, however, psychoanalytic theory is so complex (and often vague) that it is difficult to do scientific research on it. After nearly a hundred years, current research "is still a beginning of this process, and much hard work remains to be done" (Bachop, 1989, p. 467).

Until the 1940s psychoanalysis was probably the strongest force in psychology, at least in the practice of psychotherapy. It is still very influential in particular settings (such as many medical schools) and, for various reasons, in particular areas (such as the eastern United States). In general, however, the influence of psychoanalysis is diminishing. Much of this loss of influence has resulted from rejection of some of its basic theoretical concepts. Although Freud may have accurately observed some important human characteristics, many psychologists believe that he explained them in indefensible terms. Few theorists today accept such Freudian notions as *psychic energy* and a *topographical mind* (as though the mind were a place with various parts). He is also criticised for developing a theory of the nature of *all* humans on the basis of his contact with relatively few well-to-do European therapy patients.

This rejection of certain theoretical concepts has sometimes resulted in the rejection of all of Freud's ideas, especially by some learning theorists. One adamant learning theorist we know consistently refers to "Sigmund Freud" as "Sigmund Fraud," reflecting the often hostile feelings between adherents of learning theory and Freudian theory. However, as we mentioned in Chapter 9, some of Freud's ideas have been reformulated into other theories, including learning theory, and have found research support. This is especially true of his ideas about repression and unconscious influences on behaviour.

TRAIT THEORIES

Some theorists have attempted to describe and categorize personality by developing interconnected lists of human traits. (As we have already mentioned, such theorists are not concerned with the underlying dynamics of personality.) It is those theorists who are interested in human *traits* and those who are interested in human beings as *types*. It is important to distinguish between traits and types. **Typologies** (or **type theories**) classify people into a small number of categories or types. When we use the words "extrovert" and "introvert" as labels for individuals who have certain characteristics, we are typing people.

William Sheldon's attempts to relate body types and personality is another example of a typology (1954). He said that there are three body types, and each is related to a different kind of personality. The **endomorphic** person has a plump, soft body and tends to be easygoing, gregarious, and food-loving (see Figure 10-4). The **mesomorphic**

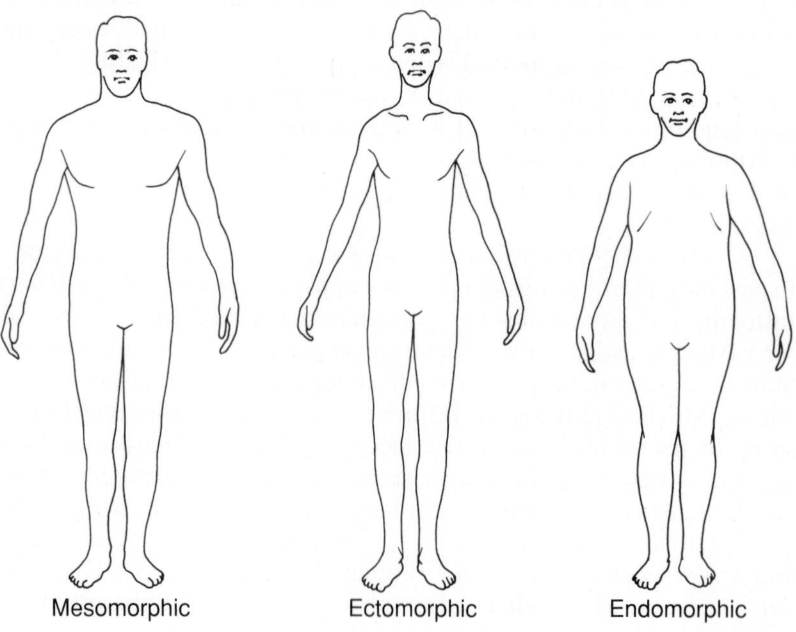

FIGURE 10-4 Sheldon's three body types
William Sheldon attempted to relate each of these body types to a particular personality type.

person is muscular, lean, athletic, and tends to be assertive, brave, and energetic. Finally, the **ectomorphic** person is tall, thin, and fragile, and tends to be fearful and introverted. Sheldon published very high correlations between these body types and certain personality characteristics. However, his research was somewhat flawed because he and his co-workers made the personality ratings without being "blind" to each subject's body type. They knew what findings they expected, and it appears that their judgments were strongly influenced by their expectations. Other researchers have not been able to satisfactorily replicate Sheldon's findings.

On the other hand, **traits** are organized tendencies within people which influence them to act in certain ways. Traits are sometimes thought of as inner characteristics that guide behaviour. We might say that a person "shows a lot of extroversion." We would then be using the term "extroversion" to describe a characteristic of that person rather than to label him or her as a particular type.

We believe that a trait can most usefully be thought of as a tendency to act in a particular way, rather than as a *thing* that a person has. Otherwise, it is easy to get trapped in circular reasoning with trait labels. How do we know that a person has a "lot of extroversion?"—because she acts so outgoing. Why does she act so outgoing?—because she has a "lot of extroversion." A trait label should be just a *description* of behaviour, but in this circular argument we have inappropriately tried to use it as an *explanation* of behaviour.

Gordon Allport (1897–1967).
SOURCE: Harvard University/Office of News and Publications.

The search for basic traits

Gordon Allport was one of the first and one of the most influential trait theorists. He thought of traits as general and enduring predispositions to respond in particular ways (Allport, 1937). He believed that a person's "personality structure" consists of that individual's pattern of dispositions to act in certain ways. This structure is made up of *cardinal* traits, *central* traits, and *secondary dispositions*. **Cardinal traits** are extremely generalized tendencies to act in certain ways. These are pervasive traits that affect nearly everything that a person does. For example, a person might be power-oriented to the extent that whatever he or she does is somehow influenced by this tendency. Traits that are quite general in their influence but which don't affect all areas of a person's life are called **central traits**. **Secondary dispositions** are traits that are highly specific attitudes that apply to specific situations (see Figure 10-5).

Allport coined the term **proprium** to describe the self as perceived by the individual. It is the "me" as known by the person. Allport emphasized the *individual differences* between people. In his research, he made an intensive study of individual lives, and he was much less concerned with groups of individuals. This emphasis is an important aspect of most trait theories. While many other personality theorists look for ways of grouping people according to their common characteristics, trait theorists tend to stress the uniqueness of the individual.

FIGURE 10-5 Allport's trait theory of personality

EMPHASIS
The importance of individual lives and of proprium (the unifying core of the personality)
TYPES OF TRAITS
Cardinal traits generalized tendencies, pervasive traits
Central traits traits that are fairly general
Secondary Dispositions highly specific attitudes

Raymond Cattell.
SOURCE: Courtesy Raymond Cattell.

FIGURE 10-6 Cattell's trait theory of personality

EMPHASIS
The importance of the correlations or statistical relationships among traits (factor analysis)
TYPES OF TRAITS
Source traits basic elements of personality – sixteen traits
Surface traits traits that are influenced by the situation of the moment

Factor analysis and trait lists

The statistical method called factor analysis has been used by many trait theorists to try to "boil down" human behaviours and characteristics to meaningful trait labels. A researcher using this method might give a list of a thousand adjectives to a large number of subjects and ask them to mark the adjectives that accurately describe themselves. Factor analysis would then cluster or group together those adjectives that tend to be chosen together. Thus, we might find that people who choose the adjective "enthusiastic" also have some tendency to describe themselves as "careless." If there is a cluster (or factor) of many similar adjectives that seem to "hang together," the researcher might argue that she had found a trait typical of humans. She might label the trait something like "carefreeness," depending, of course, on what adjectives were included in the factor.

Raymond Cattell (1950, 1965) was one of the pioneers of the factor-analysis approach to personality. He identified a number of **source traits**. These are pervasive characteristics that affect nearly all of a person's life. They are similar to Allport's cardinal traits. Some examples of source traits are "dominance versus submissiveness" and "ego-strength versus emotionality and neuroticism." (See Figure 10-6.) The more superficial surface traits are based on these source traits. **Surface traits** are influenced more by the situation of the moment. They do not result from a single source and they tend to be less stable over time. Surface traits include "honesty versus dishonesty" and "disciplined thought versus foolishness." For example, we might know a person who is both polite and honest in our presence and we might think of these correlated qualities as representing a source trait. However, the honesty could be based on one source trait and the politeness on another. If we asked the person to lie about our stealing something, either the honesty or the politeness would probably change dramatically.

By using factor analysis, Cattell was able to reduce his list of 170 traits to 16 independent factors because most of the characteristics on his list were correlated. Cattell believed that each of the 16 source traits was unique. In other words, each trait represented a pure factor in factor analysis. No other factor correlated strongly with each unique trait. For example, a person might be high on "superego strength" and thus be conscientious and responsible. This trait, however, would not predict that person's score on the other traits, such as "excitability-insecurity." The source traits provide a complete description of the person, since other characteristics—surface traits —are derived from the 16 basic traits.

An influential modern trait theorist is Hans Eysenck (1961, 1973, Eysenck and Rachman, 1965). He has identified what he thinks are two basic trait dimensions that have explanatory and predictive usefulness. Eysenck's **two-trait theory** argues that all human behaviour can be reduced to two fundamental, independent traits: emotional stability versus neuroticism and introversion versus extroversion. These traits have a strong genetic component. (See Figure 10-7.) This means, for example, that it is possible for a person to be high on emotional stability and be introverted while another person might be high on emotional stability and extroverted. It is not, however, possible for a person to be high on emotional stability and high on neuroticism. Although there can be fluctuations in trait strength, Eysenck has argued that these general trait dimensions apply to all humans. He even argues that they have some biological foundation and therefore much power as a way of describing personalities

FIGURE 10-7 Eysenck's trait theory of personality

EMPHASIS
The basic dimensions and broad categories that underlie the multiplicity of traits. A genetic, biological component to these dimensions
TYPES OF TRAITS
Neuroticism-emotional stability trait dimension
Introversion-extroversion trait dimension

Hans Eysenck.
SOURCE: Courtesy W.H. Allen.

Five-factor model of personality

The trait theory that has the most support at present is Tupes and Christal's (1961). Their **five-factor model of personality** is a recent formulation of trait theory that adds three further dimensions to Eysenck's two to describe personality along five dimensions. Since they did their research, a number of researchers have replicated their findings. Digman went so far as to say Tupes and Christal's findings are "consistent enough to approach the status of a law." He went on to say, "If a large number of rating scales is used and if the scope of the scales is very broad, the domain of personality descriptors is almost completely accounted for by five robust factors" (Digman, 1986, p. 117). McCrae and Costa (1986, 1987, 1989) report that these five factors emerge from subjects' descriptions of themselves and from others' descriptions of the subjects.

The five-factor dimensions are as follows:

(1) *Neuroticism versus emotional stability* A person can be rated on a dimension marked, at the neurotic end, by worry, insecurity, temperamentalness, self-consciousness, and negative affect. Emotional stability is marked by calmness, self-confidence, even-temperedness, and positive affect.

(2) *Extroversion or surgency versus introversion* Extroverted individuals tend to be friendly, outgoing, talkative, affectionate, sociable, and to like others, even though others don't necessarily like them. Introversion is marked by withdrawal, shyness, lack of expression of affection, and fear of others.

(3) *Openness to experience versus constriction of experiencing* Openness to experience is marked by imagination, daring, originality, and a wide range of interests. This factor is sometimes called "culture" or "intellect," but it is far broader than the concept of "intelligence." Constriction of experiencing includes a narrowing of activities to the dull and unimaginative. It implies an impoverishment of the expression of originality.

(4) *Consideration versus hostile noncompliance* Another phrase that describes this trait-dimension is "agreeableness versus antagonism." The antagonistic person tends to be in opposition to others and has trouble forming interpersonal bonds. The agreeable person is very relationship-oriented and can be overly dependent.

(5) *Conscientiousness versus undirectedness* The conscientious person has a strong will to achieve, to plan, and to persevere. Lack of direction is related to laziness.

The five-factor model says that a complete description of an individual personality can be constructed by knowing where the person falls on each of these five dimensions (Miller, 1988). The evidence for the usefulness of the model is extensive, but it does have its critics. Waller and Ben-Porath (1987) argue that supporters of the five-factor model are exaggerating when they say that the field of personality has reached consensus on these factors. Many other well-established descriptions of personality are not included in this model, and much of the research has used tests specifically designed to find the five factors. They feel that the model is useful and promising, but "... the field of ... personality should refrain from prematurely jumping onto a 'big five' bandwagon" (Waller & Ben-Porath, 1987, p. 888).

Critical evaluation

Trait theorists are deeply involved in the controversial issue of "persons versus situations." In essence, the argument is between those who believe that behaviour is most influenced (and best predicted) by the inner characteristics of individuals (trait theory) and those who believe that behaviour is most influenced by the outcomes of particular responses to particular situations (learning theory). Currently, this is one of the most important controversies in the personality field (Pervin, 1985). It is interesting to note that people tend to make "trait attributions" about the behaviour of others and "situation attributions" about their own behaviour (Jones & Nisbett, 1971; Nisbett & Ross, 1980). The guy next door smells bad because he's "slobbish." We smell bad because we're too busy to wash and are trying to conserve water.

SOURCE: *Bizarro* by Dan Piraro. Reprinted by permission of Chronicle Features, San Francisco, CA.

Trait theorists have been criticized as saying that individuals will act in particular ways because of the influence of their traits, regardless of the demands of the situation (Mischel, 1968; Mischel & Peake, 1982). On the other hand, learning theorists have been criticised as saying that the situation controls behaviour and traits are inconsistent over situations (or even that there are no traits). These are exaggerated presentations of the two positions. The real issue is not over whether it is traits *or* situations that influence behaviour, but rather over the relative contribution of each. The debate has been as lively as debates tend to get in psychological journals (Mischel & Peake, 1983; Epstein, 1983). However, most of the major trait theorists have taken the position that the debate is a little silly because both the attackers and the defenders seem to be referring to an extreme view of trait theory (Eysenck, 1982). Trait theorists don't say that *only* traits influence behaviour. Allport (1961) clearly included the influence of situations in his theory, and Cattell (1983) included situational influences in several aspects of his work. However, it seems clear that this debate has led to a useful softening of both extreme positions. Most personality psychologists pay more attention to situational influences than they used to, but they also recognize the importance of stable characteristics of the individual (Kenrick & Funder, 1988).

In our introduction to this discussion, we mentioned another problem with trait theories. They tend to be descriptive rather than explanatory, and it is easy to fall into the error of using traits as explanations. Further, as Pervin (1985) points out, trait theories tend to focus on the "surface" of human functioning—the overt or manifest level. This focus tends to ignore such things as unconscious dynamics. Finally, trait theories tend to be quite static. They describe what *is* right now but say little about how things got that way. The dynamic processes by which a person develops and changes are not part of trait theories.

LEARNING THEORIES

Different versions of learning (or behavioural) theory are probably the most powerful influences in personality theory in North American universities today. (The influence of psychoanalysis and humanism tends to centre more in clinical settings.) Learning theory tends to stress the scientific method and has extrapolated research and treatment methods from experiments with animals.

Essentially, the learning theorist says that the individual is born with a few biological motives and the capacity to learn. What we call personality is the sum total of a person's behaviours, including internal behaviours such as thinking and feeling. Personality is the result of an individual's experiences, as these experiences interact with his or her genetic make-up. In its extreme form, learning theory refers to the person as a **tabula rasa** or blank slate that is written on entirely by learning experiences. In this view, the infant is born without defined characteristics, and experience and environment determine the person's character. Nowadays, most learning theorists say that this is an oversimplified view and that genetic inheritance does influence development, to the extent that it *interacts* with experience.

We can contrast learning theory with psychoanalysis and humanism. Learning theory sees human nature as essentially mouldable, not driven by instincts (as in psychoanalysis) nor by a growth motive (as we will see in humanism). On the optimism-pessimism continuum, it seems to be somewhere between psychoanalysis and humanism. Humans are neither good nor bad. They are simply as their environment forms them.

Bobby and Brett Hull at the 1990 NHL Awards dinner. Genetic inheritance and learning experiences influence development.
SOURCE: Bruce Bennet Studio.

The process of acquiring personality

Learning theorists have had little to say about the *content* of human personality and a great deal to say about the *process* of how personality is acquired. A psychoanalyst, for example, might talk about a specific problem, such as the Oedipal problem, but a learning theorist would say that a person could have thousands of different specific problems. It all depends on his or her learning experiences. According to learning theory the processes by which personality develops are essentially those we discussed in Chapter 5, Principles of Learning.

It is necessary to understand that chapter to understand the learning view of personality. We will briefly review those principles, emphasizing those aspects which are particularly relevant for personality development.

As we discussed in Chapter 5, **classical conditioning** is the process of learning in which a neutral stimulus is paired with some unconditioned stimulus. If this is done repeatedly, eventually the neutral stimulus will become a conditioned stimulus. The response will now be a conditioned response. For example, repeatedly presenting a red light just before poking a person with a long pin could establish the colour red as a cue or conditioned stimulus for fear. This is a very simple example, of course, but it illustrates the fundamental learning principle that *any emotional responses* are *conditioned emotional responses (CER's)*.

Operant conditioning is the process of learning in which the organism emits a response and then the consequences which follow either strengthen or weaken that response. In operant conditioning the process of reinforcement is sometimes complex and subtle. However, what the learning theorist says, in essence, is that people do what they are somehow reinforced for doing. If a person has an Oedipal problem, it is because he or she has been reinforced and conditioned in particular ways to have that problem.

Once conditioned responses have become a part of the personality, they can be changed in one of two ways: extinction or counterconditioning.

To extinguish a classically-conditioned response, the individual must (1) be exposed to the conditioned stimulus (for example, in our red light/long pin experiment, the red light would be the CS); (2) perform the conditioned response (feel fear at the onset of the red light); and (3) not be exposed to the unconditioned stimulus (experience no pin prick and no pain following the onset of the red light).

An operant behaviour is weakened if the behaviour is performed and is not followed by reinforcement. *Counterconditioning* seeks to weaken the power of a particular response or behaviour by pairing the original stimulus with another that will bring about a competing response or behaviour. (For example, in our red light/long pin experiment, the red light that evokes fear would be paired with something pleasurable, with perhaps our favourite food.)

Because learning theorists recognize that there is a great deal that simply cannot be learned through direct reinforcement and conditioning, they place great stress on *generalized imitation* and *observational learning*. **Generalized imitation** is a broad class of imitative behaviours that is established at least in part through frequent and unpredictable reinforcement for imitating others. **Observational** (or **vicarious**) learning is the process of learning by watching others' behaviours. This type of learning underlies much human learning, including much of what we call personality.

Unlike psychoanalytic theories, learning theory proposes no particular stages or specific patterns of *personality development*. Learning theorists would say that our title for Chapter 12, Development through the Life Span, represents their general view of personality development. The development of one's personality and the patterns of that development depend on one's reinforcement, conditioning, and observational-learning history. There are no specific stages of development within learning theory.

Theory of neurosis

It should come as no surprise to hear that learning theorists think that human emotional problems (they prefer the term "behaviour problems") develop because of destructive conditioning experiences and faulty reinforcement histories.

They consider irrational fear and other debilitating emotions to be the result of classical conditioning. It is all too easy to oversimplify this general position, and much recent writing stresses instead its great complexity. However, in the earlier days of the development of behavioural treatments, writers such as Eysenck and Rachman (1965) essentially presented neurotic problems as a case of "surplus conditioned responses." They said, "Learning theory does not postulate any such 'unconscious' causes but regards neurotic symptoms as simply learned habits; there is no neurosis underlying the symptom but merely the symptom itself. Get rid of the symptom (skeletal and autonomic) and you have eliminated the neurosis" (Eysenck & Rachman, 1965, p. 10).

In its simple form, then, this idea suggests that a person who fears school has had a painful experience at school. More complex formulations, however, are possible within learning theory. For example, a child who seems to simply fear school might really fear that his or her mother will leave. The behaviour of fearing school (remember that emotions are seen as covert behaviours) could be reinforced by the enormous anxiety-relief of staying home where an eye can be kept on mother. Most learning theorists today would argue for the more complex formulation, or at least argue that it is a possibility.

Another emphasis of learning theorists is that one's own thoughts can become fear cues through conditioning. If these thoughts and feelings are highly motivated, the person can both need to feel and think them but also be terribly frightened by them. This is one possible learning theory explanation for the experience of anxiety based on internal conflicts (Dollard & Miller, 1959; Martin, 1983).

Learning theorists generally see severely self-defeating behaviours (what are usually called "neurotic symptoms") as behaviours that are reinforced by the immediate reduction of anxiety. These become powerfully reinforced, long-lasting behaviours, even though they lead to later negative consequences for the individual.

In addition to such anxiety-based problems, learning theorists would look for other kinds of reinforcers to explain maladaptive behaviour. For example, a child who is continually getting into trouble may be reinforced by getting attention for such behaviour. Attention of whatever kind may be a reinforcer. A learning theorist would say that *whatever* behaviours a person performs are being reinforced somehow. If the behaviour appears maladaptive, the reinforcers may be hidden and subtle, but they are there.

Cognitive learning theory

Pervin (1985) says that, "Psychology has gone cognitive generally, and personality is no exception" (p. 93). Learning theorists have moved away from talking only about reinforcers and conditioned stimuli in our external environments and moved toward speaking about internal processes. Thoughts and feelings can also be reinforcers and conditioned stimuli.

Since cognitive learning theory is largely a modification of learning theory, it is difficult to know whether to call it a separate approach. If we understand thinking and feeling as behaviour that goes on inside the skin, we can embrace Mahoney's proposal that "we adopt a broad conceptualization of 'learning principles' and entertain the possibility that these principles are directly relevant to the modification of cognition . . ." (Mahoney, 1977, p. 11).

The cognitive-learning approach to person variables

Mischel (1986), a well-known cognitive-learning theorist, is one of the most vocal critics of trait-theory explanations of behaviour. He has described *person variables* from a cognitive learning view, to try to explain individual differences in how people function. In essence, **person variables** are learned tendencies to think in particular ways. They are generalized strategies of thinking rather than thoughts about particular things. They are not even necessarily ways that the individual consciously chooses to think. They can be semi-automatic modes of operating cognitively. (See Figure 10-8.) We will describe a few of these person variables.

Expectancies are strongly learned beliefs about the relationships between certain behaviours and the outcomes or consequences of those behaviours. A trivial example might be our belief that kicking other people is often followed by unfortunate consequences. This is a prediction that we make about the nature of the world. There are times when we are in a hurry and kicking people out of the way would save time, but we don't even consider the option consciously

FIGURE 10-8 Mischel's cognitive-learning person variables

Summary of Cognitive Social Learning Person Variables

1. COMPETENCIES: ability to constuct (generate) particular cognitions and behaviours. Related to measures of IQ, social and cognitive (mental) maturity and competence, ego development, social-intellectual achievements and skills. Refers to what the person knows and *can* do.
2. ENCODING STRATEGIES AND PERSONAL CONSTRUCTS: units for categorizing events, people, and the self.
3. EXPECTANCIES: behaviour-outcome and stimulus-outcome relations in particular situations; self-efficacy or confidence that one can perform the necessary behaviour.
4. SUBJECTIVE VALUES: motivating and arousing stimuli, incentives, and aversions.
5. SELF-REGULATORY SYSTEMS AND PLANS: rules and self-reactions for performance and for the organization of complex behaviour sequences.

SOURCE: Reprinted with permission from Mischel (1986).

because of our strongly held expectancy. We also have expectancies about the relationships between stimuli in the environment and particular outcomes. When we see another person scowl, we semi-automatically make a number of predictions about what will happen next. We have thousands of these predictive beliefs, and knowing a person's expectancies can help predict that person's behaviour.

Self-regulation refers to beliefs, rules, and plans that we learn to apply to our own behaviour. The cognitive learning theorist would say that originally the contingencies that influence the individual are learned from external influences such as reinforcement and classical conditioning. However, the person learns to differentiate him or herself from the rest of the environment and develops a powerful set of rules and procedures that operate internally as cognitions. We eventually can reinforce ourselves with praise, for example. We make demands on ourselves. We can withhold or give particular rewards to ourselves. Each of these is a learned cognitive person variable.

One other example of a person variable might be the individual assigning of *subjective values*. Each of us attaches worth to different things. One person might place enormous value on honesty and refuse to lie to protect a friend. Another person's value could be that loyalty matters so much that lying would be justified for the friend's sake. These values are learned, cognitive, person variables, according to cognitive learning theory.

Walter Mischel.
SOURCE: Courtesy Walter Mischel.

Critical evaluation

One indication that learning theory is indeed a powerful influence in North America today is the popularity of behaviour modification as an approach to treatment of emotional and behavioural disorders (see Chapter 15). Another is the extensive research literature that is dominated by learning-oriented workers.

The one learning principle that has probably had more influence than any other on the study of personality is that reinforcement has great importance in the establishing of certain behaviours. To say that people do what they are reinforced for doing sounds, on one hand, so obvious that it seems simple-minded. But on the other hand, it is actually a powerful bit of knowledge whose full implications few see. A clear understanding of reinforcement is leading, we think and hope, to more positive ways of dealing with people and a movement away from punitive relationships and organizations.

The principles of conditioning contribute enormously to our understanding of emotions and of how to change emotions. To get rid of a fear, we must feel that fear in small steps. That has sweeping implications for how we do therapy.

The problem is that some learning theorists have tended to apply their theoretical principles in oversimplified ways. Messer and Winokur (1980) have argued that behaviour therapists are naive about the complexity of human problems. They draw a parallel between the typical North American's belief in behavioural therapies with his or her faith in technical solutions. Most important for our discussion, Messer and Winokur point to the behaviour theorists' tendency to focus on factors external to the person, rather than on internal factors such as cognitions and emotions. These are fair criticisms of *some* learning theorists, but the current trend in the field is clearly toward more complexity — the complexity of including thoughts and feelings as behaviour.

HUMANISTIC THEORIES

Humanistic personality theory states that humans are self-actualizing throughout their lifetime.
SOURCE: Dick Hemingway.

Humanistic theories, the "third force" in psychology, have had a considerable influence, especially on psychologists interested in the clinical practice of psychology. Humanistic theories present a more optimistic and less deterministic view of human nature than either Freudian or learning theories.

Self-actualization

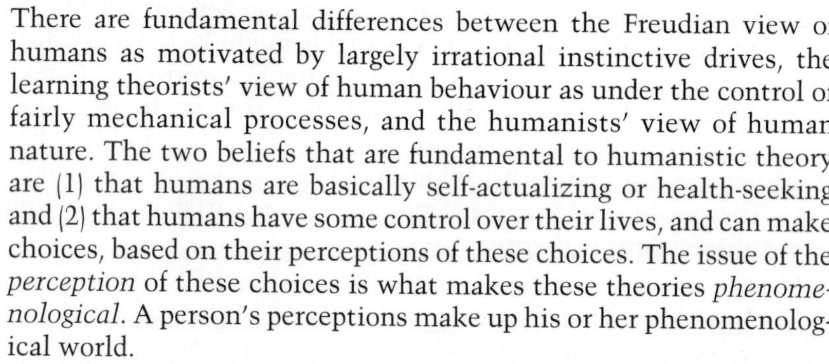

There are fundamental differences between the Freudian view of humans as motivated by largely irrational instinctive drives, the learning theorists' view of human behaviour as under the control of fairly mechanical processes, and the humanists' view of human nature. The two beliefs that are fundamental to humanistic theory are (1) that humans are basically self-actualizing or health-seeking and (2) that humans have some control over their lives, and can make choices, based on their perceptions of these choices. The issue of the *perception* of these choices is what makes these theories *phenomenological*. A person's perceptions make up his or her phenomenological world.

Just as there are many variations of psychoanalytic theory there are also many different and quite distinct kinds of humanistic theories, the advocates of which sometimes disagree among themselves.

Much of our discussion in this section will focus on the formulations of Carl Rogers, the humanistic psychologist who developed his theory the most completely.

Very few researchers or theorists in psychology have been concerned with describing the emotionally healthy person. We seem more comfortable and confident describing disorder. However, the humanists have been exceptions to this generalization according to Abraham Maslow (1968, 1971). Maslow was a leading humanist who stressed the importance of self actualization. One reason for this interest in the healthy personality is that the humanists believe people are inherently self-actualizing. Unless the individual's development is interfered with, he or she will grow in emotionally healthy directions. Rogers (1959, 1980a, 1980b) has developed this point of view most systematically. He argues that a tendency toward self-actualization is innate — born into the person.

> It has been my experience that persons have a basically positive direction. In my deepest contacts with individuals in therapy, even those whose troubles are most disturbing, whose behaviour has been most antisocial, whose feelings seem most abnormal, I find this to be true (Rogers, 1961, p. 26).
>
> It is evident not only in the general tendency of clients to move in the direction of growth when the factors in the situation

> are clear; but is most dramatically shown in very serious cases where the individual is on the brink of psychosis or suicide. Here the therapist is very keenly aware that the only force upon which he can basically rely is on the organic tendency toward ongoing growth and enhancement (Rogers, 1951, p. 489).

The basic humanistic position can be summarized as, "The person chooses the best course of action or thought (because of self-actualization), as he or she perceives the alternatives available." The first part of this statement indicates that we are not puppet-like victims of the past. Rather, our behaviour is determined by our choices about the future. It is clear that humanists come very close to talking about free-will, as opposed to the deterministic view of the psychoanalysts and the learning theorists. The second half of our opening statement reveals the meaning of phenomenology. Whatever objective reality may be, what matters in understanding another person is reality *as perceived* by that person.

Phenomenologically, the sun rises and sets as it moves around the earth, and the room spins when one is dizzy. We have other information to convince us otherwise in both cases, but we perceive the sun rising and the room spinning. Such phenomenological perceptions guide our behaviour.

Person-centred theory

Carl Rogers first developed his humanistic theory as an approach to psychotherapy, which we will discuss further in Chapter 15. Then he elaborated a general theory of personality that expanded on his ideas about therapy (1959). Figure 10-9 shows how Rogers saw his theory of therapy as the foundation for a general theory of personality, of the emotionally healthy person, of interpersonal relationships, and of many human activities. He called his approach *person-centred* psychology to emphasize his belief that the individual person is responsible for his or her life and is the best source of information about that life. His theory is rooted in the ideas of self-actualization and phenomenology. He wanted to take the focus away from outside experts and place it in the individual.

In order to explain how self-actualization works, Rogers postulated an organismic valuing process. The **organismic valuing process** is the expression of the self-actualizing motive. This is an internal process that is attracted to growth-producing experiences. Through this process individuals evaluate all of their experiences as congruent with or incongruent with the self-actualizing tendency. Based on this evaluation, the individual either approaches or avoids particular experiences. It is important to understand that this is the basis of the person's *true experiencing* because it is motivated by the basic motive.

In addition to this inborn characteristic, the person develops a number of others: *a self, a need for positive regard, a need for positive self-regard,* and *conditions of worth.*

The person develops a concept of self, as separate from the environment. This *self* is a complex and well-organized "perceptual

Pablo Picasso, here at 76, is evidence that age need not interfere with the self-actualizing process.
SOURCE: The Bettmann Archive.

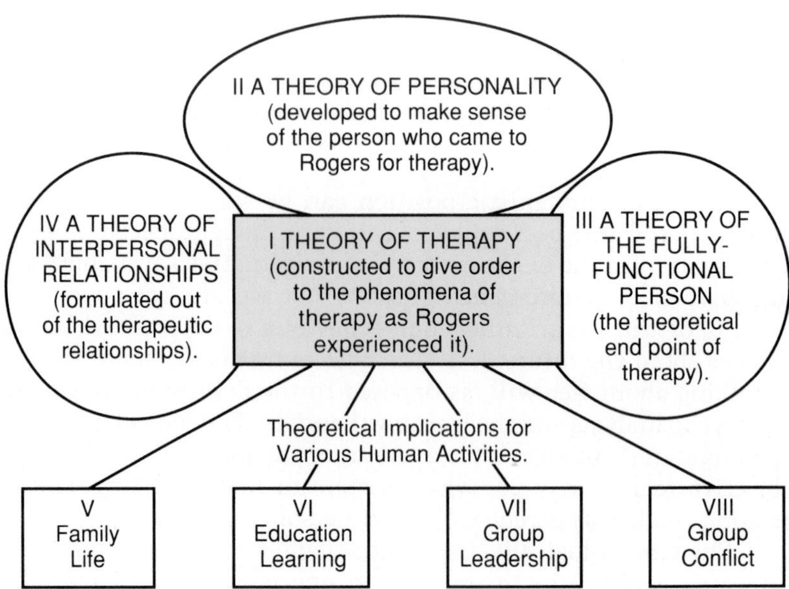

FIGURE 10-9 Rogers' theory of therapy as the foundation for understanding human behaviour Carl Rogers (1959), first developed (I) his theory of therapy. Then, using his theory of therapy as a base, he went on to develop (II) a theory of personality, (III) a theory of the fully-functional person, and (IV) a theory of interpersonal relationships. Finally, he set out the implications that his theory of therapy (I) has for a cluster of human activities: (V) family life, (VI) education and learning, (VII) group leadership, and (VIII) group conflict.

SOURCE: Adapted with permission from Rogers (1959).

object." It is an individual's picture of himself or herself. Because of the nature of early life, everyone develops a powerful need to be loved, *a need for positive regard*. Once this need develops it can become even more powerful than the organismic valuing process because, to the young child, even a momentary loss of love can feel like a loss of *all* love. So in that moment, the need for love would be overwhelmingly threatened. Next, the person develops a need to love himself or herself, *a need for positive self-regard*.

Theory of neurosis

Within their generally optimistic view, humanists explain maladaptive behaviour as resulting from inaccurate perceptions. These perceptions are largely based on interpersonal experiences. Remember that the person chooses the best alternatives *as he or she perceives them*. However, perceptions can be distorted by many factors. In Rogers' theory, for example, the person develops a need to be loved and to love himself or herself. If the child is punished by love withdrawal and made to feel guilty or worthless, he or she can learn that love is conditional. Certain feelings and actions make a person unlovable or unworthy. For example, if children experience a withdrawal of love when they are angry, they could learn that they are not lovable when they feel anger. A person could internalize this as a *condition of worth*, a standard he or she had to meet in order to be worthwhile. Conditions of worth are the foundation of emotional problems. A condition of worth is a limitation on unconditional self-acceptance. If the person doesn't meet certain conditions, he or she feels not acceptable or worthwhile. In our example, a condition of worth might be "I am worthy only if I don't feel anger." Sometimes, however, it is emotionally healthy to feel anger. Problems arise when the self-actualizing tendency motivates an individual to act a particular way, but the person has learned that he or she is not worthy when feeling that way. An inescapable conflict is set up. The individual *must* feel self-love but at the same time is motivated to experience the particular thought or feeling that threatens the experience of self-love. The conflict is resolved by distorting the threatening experience. However, this can lead to trouble because now the person has inaccurate perceptions. For example, in order to continue to feel self-acceptance, the person might falsely believe, "I never feel anger." This false belief will inevitably lead to distortions and inappropriate choices in interpersonal relations. These inaccurate perceptions lead to unwise choices and self-defeating behaviour.

Critical evaluation

In the popular press, humanistic theory had a large surge of influence in the 60s and 70s. This popularity was particularly associated with the encounter group movement, but that seems to have faded. Encounter groups were similar to group therapy sessions but were designed for personal growth rather than treatment of emotional problems. Today many practising clinicians would describe themselves as humanistic, although few medical settings or university training programs would describe themselves this way.

Probably the strongest influence and most lasting effect of Rogers' humanistic approaches have been felt in the practice of counselling and psychotherapy. It is interesting to note that, although Rogers is very influential, relatively few therapists being trained today seem to use the label "person centred" to describe their philosophy. In 1982, Smith surveyed 422 clinical and counselling psychologists. Carl Rogers was clearly ranked as the therapist who was "most influential today," but only 9% of the respondents described themselves as "person centred."

Humanistic theory has suffered from two basic problems that have made it unacceptable to many. First, it is difficult to defend the idea of self-actualization as innate. The humanists have tended to say that their belief in it grows out of their own experiences, but most other theorists do not accept this as evidence. Critics point to many examples of violent and fundamentally self-destructive behaviours as counter examples to the principle of self-actualization. They also argue that examples are not evidence. The second problem concerns what is perceived to be a logical flaw in the phenomenological theory. The phenomenologist says that the person's perceptions determine behaviour, so the person's behaviour is not determined by the past but by the future. The critic can ask, "But what determines perceptions?" The phenomenologist must either answer that past experiences determine perceptions (which is what a learning or cognitive theorist would say) or that we are born with these perceptions, a position that is difficult to defend. In this criticism, phenomenology boils down to a learning theory that simply hasn't taken the last step in logic. That is, it hasn't explained *why* we perceive or misperceive our alternatives the way we do.

Although they may have problems accepting humanistic theory, even Rogers' critics have had to acknowledge that considerable research supports the effectiveness of his approach to therapy. For example, he argued that successful therapy is based on empathy, acceptance and genuineness. There is research evidence that therapy is more effective when the client perceives these qualities in the therapist. We will examine this evidence more in Chapter 15, on psychotherapy.

COGNITIVE THEORIES

Cognitive theory draws from many different theories, so it is difficult to know exactly whom it includes. Cognitive theorists all emphasize the importance of cognition in understanding human behaviour. As we discussed in the section of this chapter on "Learning Theories," some of these psychologists are called *cognitive-learning theorists*. They say that cognition is important and is behaviour just like any other behaviour. It just happens to occur inside the skin. Others, however, would best be called simply *cognitive theorists*. They say that cognition is more than just behaviour. It is a different kind of functioning. Thoughts, feelings, and impulses are important in the development of personality and in the control of behaviour. These theories have developed largely as a protest over the learning theorists' tendency to talk primarily about external behaviour and to ignore the importance of thinking and feeling in understanding humans.

In some ways, the cognitive viewpoint resembles the phenomenological perspective. From both of these perspectives, we act according to our self-concept, according to the way we perceive ourselves and the way we perceive the world in relation to ourselves. In response to a learning theorist, a cognitive theorist would be likely to say that stimuli and reinforcement are important but we must not lose sight of the fact that thinking also influences behaviour. They would even say that thinking is what ultimately controls behaviour. Thus, if we want to change behaviour, we should first change the person's thinking. Cognitive theorists seem to place great emphasis on conscious thought and have little to say about unconscious influences on behaviour (Seligman & Johnston, 1973).

FIGURE 10-10 A-B-C sequence of Ellis' rational-emotive theory Rational-emotive theory proposes an A-B-C sequence to explain negative emotions. A, an Activating event seems to cause C, a negative emotional Consequence. However, Ellis says that B, the individual's Belief system, intervenes between A and C, and it is the belief that actually causes the negative emotion.

WHAT SEEMS TO HAPPEN

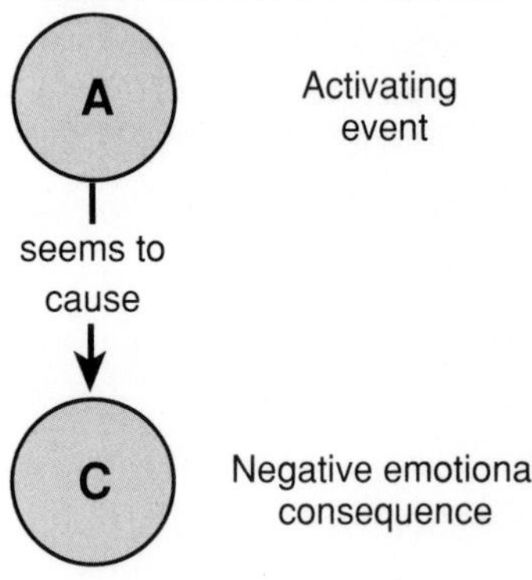

WHAT ACTUALLY HAPPENS

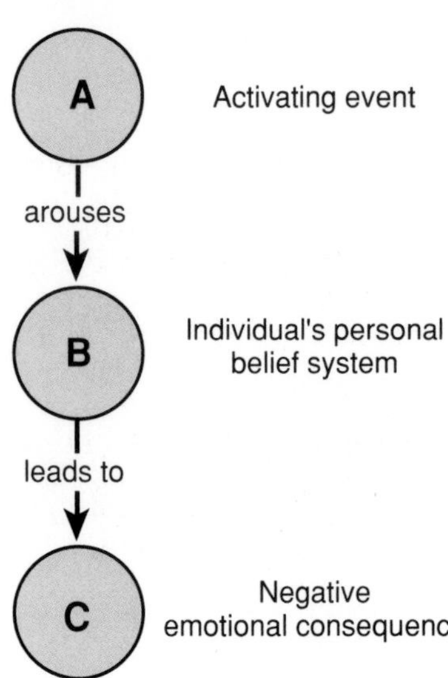

Rational-emotive theory

The cognitive focus is predominant in Albert Ellis' rational-emotive theory of therapy and personality (1962 and 1977). **Rational-emotive theory** states that our personal belief system (our assumptions and thoughts) guide our self-concept and our emotional reactions. Therefore, irrational, self-defeating emotional reactions and behaviours can be eliminated by changing erroneous assumptions and thoughts. Rational emotive theory proposes an A-B-C sequence to explain negative emotions. First A occurs. This is an activating event that seems to cause C, a negative emotional Consequence. However, Ellis says that A is not really the cause of C. B, the individual's Belief system intervenes between A and C, and it is the belief that actually causes the negative emotion (Ellis, 1973). (See Figure 10-10.)

Ellis argues that individuals with emotional problems strongly hold some irrational beliefs. These beliefs may be fairly common but in most cases they are not so severe that they debilitate the person. For example, the belief that "an adult human must be loved or approved by everyone" could have a crippling effect on a person who tried to live according to such an incorrect principle. Similarly, the belief that "when things are not the way you want them to be it is a catastrophe" could easily cause a person enormous and needless suffering. Ellis' goal in therapy is essentially to convince the person who holds such beliefs that they are irrational and thereby to free the person from the negative emotions they cause.

Although the effectiveness of Ellis' application of cognitive principles has been questioned (Wilson & O'Leary, 1980), his basic emphasis has had an important influence on the practice of cognitive behaviour modification, which we will discuss further in Chapter 15.

Albert Ellis.
SOURCE: Courtesy Dr. Albert Ellis.

BEING ECLECTIC

It must seem confusing to realize just how diverse and contradictory many of the theories of personality are. Each presents a different basic model of human nature, so they can't all be correct. We would emphasize this last statement very strongly, even saying that *none* of these theories can be entirely correct. It is rather amusing to hear someone say, "Well, psychologists say that. . . (here the speaker presents his or her *own* pet theory)." We have to ask, "*Which* psychologists?" If no single theory is entirely correct, it is up to each of us to be tentative but knowledgeable, sifting through the various theories for what seems valid in each of them. In doing this, we are trying to be *eclectic*, to draw from and integrate parts of each theory. The key word here is "integrate." "By the seat of your pants," or "off the top of your head" sometimes passes for eclecticism, but a truly eclectic position must be internally consistent. It should not contain contradictory ideas. As you develop your own understanding of human nature, draw from each theory of personality what seems useful to you and try to integrate your thinking.

SPECIAL TOPIC

Current Issues in Personality

The field of personality is a dynamic and exciting one in which several fascinating issues are being pursued. Courses in personality and chapters in introductory psychology books, however, often focus on past theories, just as we have done in this chapter. Singer and Kolligian (1987) have lamented, "One continues to wonder why personality is still so widely taught as a 'procession through the graveyard' in the pungent phrase of a prominent personality researcher" (p. 535). We think that a walk through the graveyard of old theories is probably necessary to give the student a perspective on the many radically different views of human nature among personality theorists. It is not sufficient, however, to merely give an accurate picture of the history of the field of personality. We want also briefly to mention some current issues and controversies in personality theory. In most cases these are issues discussed in other chapters of this book. Personality is such a broad field and is so interconnected with all aspects of human psychology that the subject often appears in other areas as well.

The affect versus cognition controversy

In Chapter 9, The Psychology of Consciousness, we described the argument between those who think that cognition is primary over and in control of emotion (affect) and those who think that emotion is primary. There are psychologists who argue for a view that combines these two positions. This integrated view is based on a belief that affect and cognition are separate systems in humans. They influence each other in reciprocal ways. Thus, it is misleading to argue that one is entirely primary over the other. This integrated view has many implications for our view of human nature and for the way we treat human problems therapeutically. If reason rules, we should try to change people's false beliefs to change their emotions. If affect dominates, then we should develop treatments based on emotional experiencing and downplay reason. If there is a fairly equal interaction between cognition and emotion, both should be integrated in treatment. Each of these three positions has strong advocates, and clearly somebody must be wrong. (Probably everybody is wrong to some extent.) It matters very much which approach is most accurate, so we must do meaningful research. (Also see the more detailed discussion of this controversy in Chapter 9.)

Consciousness and the private personality

The issue of conscious and unconscious influences on behaviour is very controversial. (See Chapter 9 for more details on this topic too.) After several decades in disrepute, our conscious beliefs about ourselves and about others have returned as a central concern of psychology. For many years, no self-respecting psychologist would talk about introspection, much less use it as a source of data. Now it is returning as one useful approach to research, even though it has serious limitations (Singer and Kolligian, 1987). Similarly, words such as "unconscious" and "subliminal" were scarcely heard among respectable researchers for many years, but that has been changed by research evidence.

Persons versus situations

We discussed this issue earlier in this chapter when we talked about trait theories. In a nutshell, the argument is over whether persons have traits that govern their behaviour across different situations or whether the demands of the situation more accurately predict what an individual will do.

In recent years, both extreme positions have been softened. Several decades ago, psychologists strongly emphasized that persons have traits that determine their behaviour. Today, most personality psychologists pay more attention to situational influences. On the other hand, most of the psychologists who argued that the situation determines behaviour, now acknowledge that some behaviours are quite stable over time (Kenrick & Funder, 1988).

Idiographic versus nomothetic approaches

Most recent research in personality has been **nomothetic research**. This is a research strategy in which the researcher seeks to understand human nature by studying groups of people to ascertain general laws or findings about human behaviour. It usually involves brief contact with a large number of subjects who perform under well-controlled and limited circumstances. On the other hand, there has been recent emphasis on idiographic approaches, in which there is intense focus on fewer individuals. **Ideographic research** is a research strategy in which the researcher seeks to understand human nature by studying a few people in great depth to ascertain what is unique about each individual. This type of research is designed to look for complex patterns in behaviour and for what people actually do in their lives (Lamiell, 1981, 1982; Lamiell, Foss, Larsen & Hempel, 1983; Rorer & Widiger, 1983; Silverstein, 1988). Actually, this is not a new approach but rather a return to an older approach that now is being integrated into other research methods. Arguments can be made for and against both approaches to research. Nomothetic research permits greater experimental control, but idiographic research can find the human complexity that nomothetic researchers miss. Idiographic data cannot be subjected to sophisticated statistical analysis, but then statistical analysis can mask or distort findings. The debate continues, but we strongly suspect that there is a valid place for both strategies in the study of personality. Strict adherence to one or the other would be needlessly limiting.

1. Psychologists of different schools of personality theory seldom agree on a definition of the term "personality." The one we use is that personality can be thought of as all of a person's observable and internal behaviours (actions, thoughts, feelings) that are perceived by self and others as part of a unitary whole.

2. A good theory of personality must meet the criteria of any good theory. It should integrate knowledge, have internal consistency, enable us to make predictions, and guide practice. A theory is an attempt to organize current knowledge in a way that points us toward a more clear understanding in the future. It is probably because psychology is still a young science and humans are so complex that we don't yet have one theory of personality. The five main types of personality theory are: psychoanalysis, trait theories, learning theories, humanistic theories, and cognitive theories.

3. Psychoanalysis originated with the ideas of Sigmund Freud. According to Freud, the three major regions or structures of the mind are the id (which operates according to the pleasure principle), the ego (which operates according to the reality principle), and the superego (which is roughly synonymous with the popular notion of "conscience"). The id, ego, and superego exist at three levels: the conscious, the preconscious, and the unconscious.

4. Freud's theory is essentially a dynamic theory. He proposes that each person has a limited amount of psychic energy, which he called libido. Libido flows from Eros, the life instinct, and is sexual in nature. Thanatos operates in opposition to Eros and is the cause of destructive, aggressive behaviours.

5. In psychoanalytic theory, the growing child goes through several stages of personality development: (1) the oral-erotic stage, during approximately the first two years, when sexual satisfactions are centred around the mouth; (2) the anal-erotic stage, during approximately the third and fourth years, when libido functioning is concentrated on the organs of elimination; (3) the phallic stage, during the following two years, when pleasure and gratification centre around the sex organs; (4) the latency period, during the years until puberty, when sexual needs become relatively dormant; and (5) the genital period, at puberty and beyond, when sexual energy is directed to an object-choice outside himself or herself and other than the parents. One of the central problems of development, the Oedipus conflict, occurs during the phallic stage. The successful resolution of this conflict is an important part of normal development.

6. Real anxiety is a rational reaction to a genuine threat. Neurotic anxiety is an irrational fear aroused by id impulses that are unacceptable to the ego. Such unacceptable impulses, when they are repressed into the unconscious mind, fixate psychic energy in the unconscious. This libido is then unavailable to the ego for dealing with reality. Freud coined the term defence mechanism

to describe such self-deceptive manoeuvres as conversion hysteria, repression, projection, reaction formation, displacement, and sublimation.

7. The major criticisms of Freudian psychoanalytic theory are that the notion of psychic energy and Freud's construction of the topography of the mind are extremely difficult to defend in the light of modern psychological knowledge. Although some research has been influenced by psychoanalysis and although most therapists recognize some debt to Freud's thinking, psychoanalysis in general seems to be on the wane.
8. Trait theories of personality attempt to describe human nature by describing our basic traits. Traits are, in this view, inner characteristics that guide behaviour. However, critics of trait theory argue that traits are simply descriptions rather than explanations of why people are as they are.
9. From Allport's perspective, individual differences between people are more important than group characteristics. He theorized that cardinal traits, central traits, and secondary dispositions are the internal characteristics that influence behaviour.
10. Through the use of factor analysis, some researchers believe they have found correlations between large numbers of specific human characteristics. From these correlations, they have distilled a few general traits. Cattell's deductions, using this method, are that there are two distinct types of traits: source traits and surface traits. Eysenck has identified two distinct trait dimensions: emotional stability versus neuroticism and introversion versus extroversion.
11. Currently, the most popular and most reliable trait theory is Tupes and Christal's five-factor model which adds three further dimensions to Eysenck's original two dimensions: openness to experience versus constriction of experiencing, consideration versus hostile noncompliance, and conscientiousness versus undirectedness.
12. Some trait theorists have been embroiled in the recent "persons versus situations" controversy: whether internal characteristics or external situations cause people to act as they do. The most productive attitude seems to be that *both* character traits and situations influence behaviour.
13. Learning (behavioural) theories are the most influential theories in psychology departments of North American universities. Even in the study of personality, learning theorists stress the scientific method and often extrapolate principles from experiments with animals. In their view, personality is seen as the result of the sum total of a person's learning experiences. Learning theory emphasizes the principles by which personality develops rather than any particular content of personality. In fact, some learning theorists would argue that there is no particular content to human nature. The specific issues of a person's life

depend on the experiences that person has in a particular environment. Emotions are basically conditioned responses. The principle of reinforcement explains why people do as they do or think as they think.

14. Learning theory suggests that human emotional problems develop as a result of destructive conditioning experiences and faulty reinforcement histories. Fear and other painful emotions result from classical conditioning. One's thoughts can become fear cues through conditioning. Internal conflict can result when a person a) is motivated to think the particular thoughts and b) fears those thoughts.

15. Cognitive learning theory emphasizes the importance of thinking, feeling, and other internal processes. As a countertheory to trait theories, Mischel has described generalized strategies of thinking called person variables, which include expectancies, self-regulation, and values.

16. If the principles of learning theory (as adapted to personality theory) are to have value, they must not be oversimplified and they must take into account internal as well as external behaviours. Today, behaviour modification (an outgrowth from learning theory) is very popular in North America. Both reinforcement and conditioning have become important topics in the study of personality and of human emotion.

17. Humanistic psychology encompasses a broad variety of different theories. The central ingredient of these approaches is self-actualization which is a more optimistic view of our ability to make choices—we are more the master of our own fate—than that of either psychoanalysis or learning theory. Humanistic theories are often referred to as phenomenological theories. In general, the phenomenological position is that what the individual perceives as reality is reality for that person. On the basis of a cognitive appraisal of the alternatives available, the individual chooses the most life-enhancing course of action as he or she perceives the alternatives.

18. One of the most influential humanistic psychologists has been Carl Rogers, whose person-centred theory of personality is based on the belief that the human organism has an innate tendency toward self-actualization. The person, through life experiences, develops a self, a need for positive regard, a need for positive self-regard, and conditions of worth. Ideally the person comes to have an unconditional sense of personal worth, but this often does not happen. Maladaptive behaviour results from misperception of the alternatives possible to the individual.

19. Many practising clinicians today describe themselves as humanistic though not specifically as adherents of Rogers' person-centred theory. Some critics of Rogers' theory cite examples of destructive behaviour as a challenge to his principle of self-actualization. Others question the logic of his belief that our perceptions are directed by the future rather than by the past.

20. While *cognitive learning* theorists suggest that thinking is just internal behaviour, *cognitive* theorists believe that thinking is a different kind of functioning from behaviour. Cognitive theorists stress the importance of thinking and feeling as causes of human behaviour. Ellis' rational-emotive theory suggests that, since behaviour is caused not by events so much as by the responding individual's personal belief system, a change in behaviour must be based on a change in that system.

21. Because of the diverse and sometimes contradictory nature of the many personality theories that exist today, it is necessary to be eclectic. We need to draw from these theories what we consider to be of value and then to integrate these ideas into our own understanding of human nature.

KEY TERMS

Affect vs. cognition controversy The controversial issue whether reason controls emotion, emotion controls reason or the two interact reciprocally.

Anal-erotic stage In Freudian theory, the second stage of development, in which libido is concentrated in the organs of elimination.

Anima One of Jung's fundamental archetypes. It is the person's basic female nature, possessed by both men and women.

Animus One of Jung's fundamental archetypes. It is the person's basic male nature, possessed by both men and women.

Archetypes Jung's notion of generalized potentialities for ideas that exist in the collective unconscious. The general tendency toward religiosity is one such archetype.

Cardinal traits In Allport's theory, extremely generalized tendencies to act in particular ways. Pervasive traits that affect nearly everything that a person does.

Castration anxiety In Freudian theory, the boy's fundamental unconscious fear in the Oedipus complex — that his rival, the father, will retaliate by cutting off the boy's penis.

Central traits In Allport's theory, traits that are quite general in their influence but which don't affect all areas of a person's life.

Classical conditioning The process of learning in which a neutral stimulus is paired with some unconditioned stimulus. If this is done repeatedly, eventually the neutral stimulus will become a conditioned stimulus and the response will now be a conditioned response.

Cognitive learning theory Cognitive theories that take the position that the most important behaviours are internal (thoughts, feelings, and impulses) and follow the same laws as other behaviours.

Cognitive theory Theories that stress the importance of thoughts, feelings and impulses in the control of behaviour and development of personality.

Collective unconscious In Jungian theory, this is a part of the mind that we share with others. It includes inherited ideas or, more accurately, the potentiality for these ideas, and it is sometimes called the racial unconscious.

Conditions of worth In Rogers' theory, circumstances under which the person does not feel worthy; self-acceptance is conditional.

Conscious mind In Freudian theory, that part of the mind that consists of material that is currently in awareness or can easily be brought to awareness.

Conversion hysteria The expression of psychological conflicts in physical symptoms (see Chapter 14).

Defence mechanism An unconscious, self-deceptive mental process that enables the individual to avoid anxiety but that also introduces distortions into the person's mental life.

Displacement A defence mechanism. The unconscious tendency to express unacceptable emotions and impulses in a disguised, more acceptable form or toward a less threatening target.

Dynamic theory In psychoanalysis, a theory based on the distribution of psychic energy.

Eclectic theory Position that draws from many different theories to extract the best elements of each in an internally consistent way.

Ectomorphic person In Sheldon's theory, an individual who is tall, thin, and fragile, and tends to be fearful and introverted.

Ego In Freudian theory, the part of the personality that deals with reality and develops through contact with the environment.

Ego psychology A post-Freudian, psychoanalytic theory which stresses positive ego functioning and the importance of interpersonal relations.

Electra complex In Freudian theory, a term sometimes used for the girl's version of the Oedipus complex.

Endomorphic person In Sheldon's theory, an individual who has a plump, soft body and tends to be easygoing, gregarious, and food-loving.

Eros In Freudian theory, the life instinct from which most mental energy flows; it is basically sexual in nature.

Expectancies A person variable in cognitive learning theory; strongly learned beliefs about the relationships between behaviours and the consequences of those behaviours.

Eysenck's independent traits Eysenck argues that emotional stability versus neuroticism and introversion versus extroversion are the two fundamental traits.

Five-factor model of personality A recent formulation of trait theory that adds three further dimensions to Eysenck's two to describe personality along five dimensions.

Fixation In Freudian theory, the tendency for a certain amount of psychic energy to remain attached to and tied up in the unresolved problems of an earlier developmental stage.

Generalized imitation A broad class of imitative behaviours that is established at least in part through frequent and unpredictable reinforcement for imitating others.

Genital period In Freudian theory, the fifth developmental stage, in which libidinal energy is directed to an object-choice outside himself or herself and other than the parents.

Humanistic theories Personality theories which are, in general, less concerned with scientific aspects of the study of personality and more interested in individual experience and personal growth.

Id In Freudian theory, the part of the personality driven by primitive biological strivings that are directed entirely toward the attainment of pleasure. These strivings are illogical, without relation to reality, unconscious, and the original source of all psychic energy.

Idiographic research A research strategy in which one attempts to understand human nature by studying fewer people in great depth to seek what is unique about the person.

Instinct theory The position that human motivation is fundamentally biological and controlled by innate drives.

Latency period In Freudian theory, the fourth developmental stage, in which sexual interest is relatively dormant.

Learning theories Theories which state that virtually all behaviour is the result of prior learning. Humans are born with biological limits and needs, but nearly all that we call personality is learned.

Libido In Freudian theory, the basic, instinctual energy of mental life. It is derived from the life instinct, Eros.

Mesomorphic person In Sheldon's theory, an individual who is muscular, lean, athletic, and tends to be assertive, brave, and energetic.

Need for positive regard In Rogers' theory, the acceptance from others that all humans crave.

Neurotic anxiety In Freudian theory, irrational fear of one's own unconscious thoughts, memories, and impulses, including id impulses.

Nomothetic research A research strategy in which the researcher seeks to understand human nature by studying groups of people to ascertain general laws or findings.

Observational learning (also called *vicarious learning*) The process of learning by watching others' behaviours. It underlies a great deal of human learning, including, according to learning theorists, much of what we call personality.

Oedipus complex In Freudian theory, the central psychological conflict in the phallic stage. The child unconsciously desires the opposite-sex parent sexually and wishes to be rid of the same-sex parent.

Operant conditioning The process of learning in which the organism emits a response and then the consequences which follow either strengthen or weaken that response.

Oral-erotic stage In Freudian theory, the first stage of development, in which psychic energy is centred around the mouth and feeding.

Organismic valuing process In Rogers' humanistic theory, the expression of the self-actualizing motive. This is an internal process that is attracted to growth-producing experiences.

Penis envy In Freudian theory, the girl's fundamental unconscious fear in the Oedipus or Electra complex — that she is deficient because she lacks a penis.

Person-centred psychology Carl Rogers' humanistic theory based on self-actualization and phenomenology. He called it "person-centred" to emphasize his belief that the individual person is responsible for his or her life and is the best source of information about that life.

Person variables Learned tendencies to think in particular ways, generalized strategies of thinking.

Personal unconscious In Jungian theory, that part of the mind that is made up mainly of personal memories and impulses that have been repressed. It is roughly equivalent to Freud's concept of the individual unconscious.

Personality A collective term which encompasses all of an individual's overt (observable) and covert (internal) behaviours (thoughts and feelings). These behaviours are perceived by the individual or others as having a unity, that is, of being consistent and characteristic.

Phallic stage In Freudian theory, the third stage of development, in which psychic energy is centered around the genital organs.

Pleasure principle The principle on which the id acts and which directs the individual to strive for immediate gratification.

Preconscious mind In Freudian theory that part of the mind that consists of material (ideas, memories, and feelings) that can be brought to awareness with effort but is not currently in awareness.

Projection The unconscious tendency to attribute to others one's own unacceptable impulses. A defence mechanism.

Proprium In Allport's theory, the self as perceived by the individual.

Psychic energy In psychoanalysis, the energy that drives mental functioning.

Psychoanalysis A term used to describe both the instinct theory of personality and the approach to psychotherapy proposed by Sigmund Freud.

Rational-emotive theory Ellis' cognitive theory which states that our personal belief system (our assumptions and thoughts) guide our self-concept and our emotional reactions.

Reaction formation The unconscious tendency to adopt ideas and behaviours that are diametrically opposed to one's own unacceptable impulses. A defence mechanism.

Real anxiety In Freudian theory, realistic fear with an identifiable cause, roughly equivalent to the common use of the word "fear."

Reality principle The principle on which the ego acts and directs the individual to deal adaptively with the environment.

Regression The return to an earlier stage of adjustment and behaviour as a response to stress.

Repression A defence mechanism which causes thoughts, impulses, and feelings that are unacceptable and/or cause anxiety to be forgotten (i.e., to be pushed into the unconscious).

Secondary dispositions In Allport's theory, traits that are highly specific attitudes that apply to specific situations.

Self-actualization In humanism, the fundamental human motive — to seek emotional growth.

Self-regulation A person variable in cognitive learning theory; beliefs, rules, and plans that we learn to apply to our own behaviour.

Source traits In Cattell's theory, a pervasive characteristic that affects nearly all of the person's life. They are similar to Allport's cardinal traits.

Sublimation In Freudian theory, the redirection of psychic energy from an outlet where it is blocked to some other form of expression.

Superego In Freudian theory, the part of the personality which is made up partly of moral standards adopted in childhood and partly of inherited unconscious moral ideas. It is roughly synonymous with the popular idea of "conscience."

Surface trait In Cattell's theory, a characteristic that is influenced by the situation of the moment, does not result from a single source, and tends to be less stable than a source trait.

Tabula rasa (literally "empty slate") The position that the infant is born without defined characteristics, and that experience and environment determines the person's nature.

Thanatos In Freudian theory, the death instinct which operates in opposition to Eros, motivating self-destructive behaviour when turned inward, or cruelty and aggression when turned outward.

Theory A set of ideas and propositions designed to organize our knowledge in a way that points us toward our best approximation of what is true.

Traits Organized tendencies within people which influences them to act in certain ways. Traits are sometimes thought of as inner characteristics that guide behaviour.

Trait theories Theories which are primarily concerned with describing and categorizing human characteristics, rather than explaining their underlying dynamics.

True experiencing In Rogers' theory, the feelings, wishes and actions that are motivated by the self-actualizing tendency.

Two-trait theory Eysenck's personality theory which argues that all human behaviour can be reduced to two fundamental traits: emotional stability versus neuroticism and introversion versus extroversion.

Typologies Attempts to classify people into a small number of categories or types.

Unconscious mind In Freudian theory, that part of the mind that consists of material that is outside of awareness and cannot be brought to awareness.

Vicarious learning See *observational learning.*

Suggested Readings

Hall, C.S., & Lindsey, G. (1986). *Introduction to theories of personality.* New York: Wiley. This is one of the many good university textbooks on personality theories. This might be the best bet to find general summaries of the theories discussed in this chapter.

Throughout this chapter, we have referred to specific writings of each major theorist. Those references are in the bibliography at the end of this book. However, the following might be of particular interest:

Freud, S. (1900/1965). *The interpretation of dreams.* New York: Avon/Discus. Any person interested in personality theory should read some of Freud's own writings. This book is a good one to start with. This book outlines how he saw the significance of dreams early in his career. Freud called dreams the royal road to the unconscious.

Masson, J.M. (1985). *The assault on truth.* New York: Penguin. This author had access to a wide range of correspondence and documents related to Freud. He came to the controversial conclusion that Freud and others, partly to preserve elements of Freud's theory, suppressed evidence that some of his patients may have been sexually abused. This book has been widely condemned and praised, depending on the perspective of the commentator.

Rogers, C.R. (1980). *A way of being.* Boston: Houghton Mifflin. This is a collection of papers and essays that Rogers wrote over a period of time. They include some very personal insights into his life and some important theoretical and applied works. They read well.

CHAPTER 11

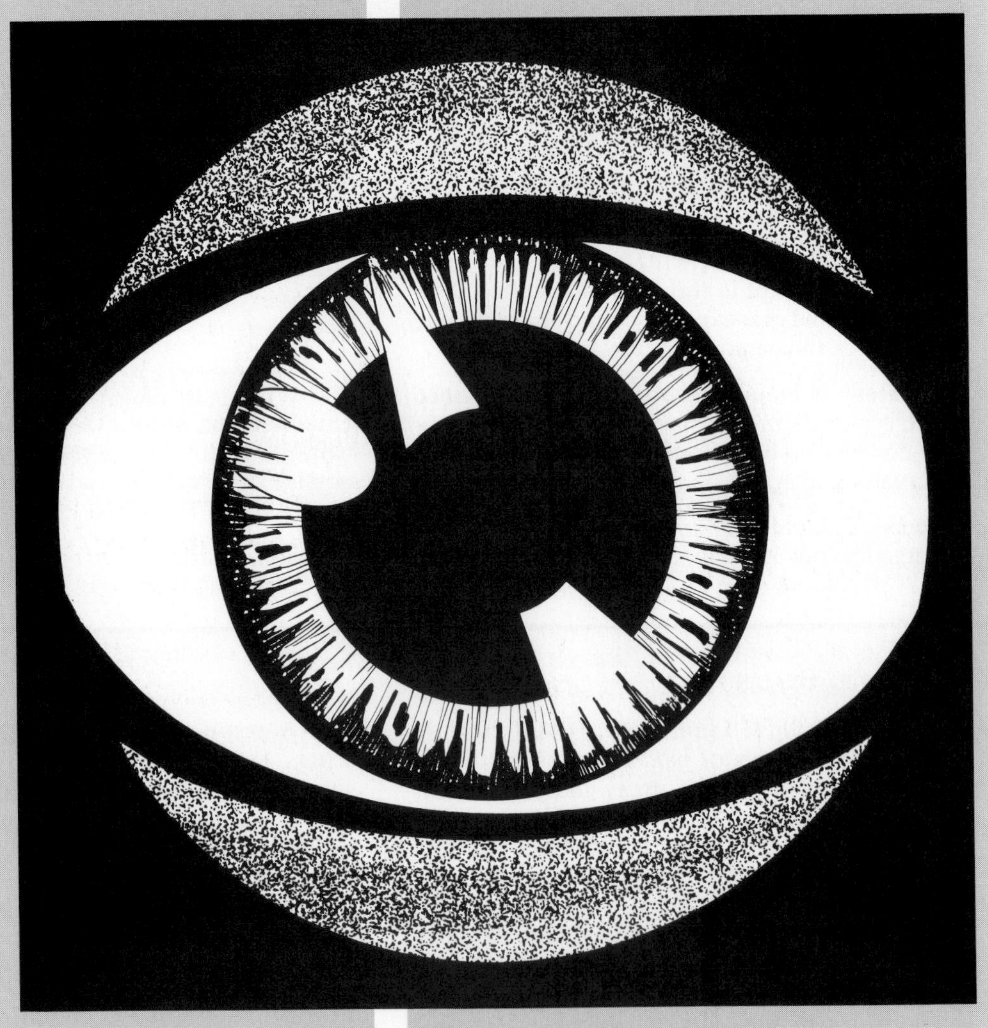

Measuring Human Behaviour

IT IS ALMOST certain that your life has been affected in important ways by psychological assessment. Assessment is the process through which psychologists make judgments about human functioning by quantifying various kinds of performance. You have probably taken intelligence tests, achievement tests, vocational tests, and perhaps personality tests. Most of us have been interviewed by a teacher or counsellor or club sponsor, with the purpose of measuring us in some way so a decision could be made. But what if you were incorrectly measured in some way? Instead of reading this book, you might be working at a job in an area ill-suited to you.

Many of us even know a single number that we carry around as "My IQ." That number is probably based on about one hour's worth of answered questions, either with paper and pencil or by way of oral responses. As H. Gardner says, "the score on an intelligence test does predict one's ability to handle school subjects, though it foretells little of success in later life" (Gardner, 1983, p. 3). He goes on to say, "There must be more to intelligence than short answers to short questions — answers that predict academic success; and yet, in the absence of a better way of thinking about intelligence, and of better ways to assess an individual's capabilities, this scenario is destined to be repeated universally for the foreseeable future" (Gardner, 1983, p. 4).

We are also interested in assessing personality, vocational interests, and brain function. Decisions have to be made about how to treat a particular disorder, who is best suited to be the new executive secretary, whether this child is doing badly in school because of low ability or emotional problems, and even whether she should be taken out of her home for her own benefit. Someone has to make these difficult decisions, and psychologists have developed techniques for gathering information to help make them. It is a frightening reality that incorrect information can significantly damage a life. On the other hand, having no information can also do damage. Our instruments are imperfect, but they are the best we have at the moment. Psychological assessment is here to stay and we need to understand it.

We are all constantly conducting informal psychological assessments. Assessment is simply quantifying—in this case, putting into numbers — our judgments of others. Even a statement such as "He seems anxious" is a measurement statement. It means "Relative to other people, his behaviours (or at least the ones that I can observe) seem more strongly to indicate a particular feeling that I label anxiety." In this statement we are using an internal norm or standard based on our idea of the level of "anxious behaviour" that we consider typical. We will see that formal **norms** are developed by testing large groups of people in order to establish what scores are typical of the population. Our internal norms are developed from our personal experience. We develop an idea of what "typical anxiety" is, for example. We are making a judgment about a particular individual's behaviour compared with those norms. We could arbitrarily assign numbers to these judgments, but that would only be for the purpose of making them more manageable. We could, for example, use a 3-point scale in which the judgment that the individual is suffering more anxiety than the typical person is assigned the number 1. The typical amount of anxiety could be called 2 and less than typical 3. The use of numbers in this instance would not suddenly turn our judgment into measurement. It would simply be a different way of making a statement about personality.

OBSERVABLES

We have stated that psychology is concerned with the description of behaviour. The first stage in this description process begins with assessment. **Assessment** is the process by which psychologists make judgments about human functioning by quantifying various kinds of performance.

The specific purpose of an assessment guides the type of assessment used. For example, if we were interested in assessing a friend's interests in sports, we probably wouldn't begin by asking questions about political parties. The assessment process is guided by the *assessment question*. The direction and presentation of this question depends on the specific information sought after in the assessment process.

A more realistic example, and one which psychologists frequently encounter, might be a "personality assessment." Physicians and other health workers often refer patients to psychologists for formal assessments. Typically, they send a referral letter describing the patient's circumstances and asking referral questions. To assess an entire "personality" is a huge task. The assessment question needs to be more specific. More useful assessment questions might be "Do this person's thought patterns suggest severe emotional disturbance? If so, what psychiatric diagnosis best describes that disturbance?" or "What are this person's intellectual strengths?" These questions provide a focus for the assessment. A further refinement of the first question might be "Does Mr. X. have a paranoid disorder?" This refines the focus of the assessment further, and the individual making the referral is more likely to receive a more specific answer. Generally in assessment, the more specific the referral question, the more specific the answer.

As psychologists, we are interested in *observing behaviour*, which is essentially the foundation in the assessment process. Whether the behaviours we are observing are the words that are spoken to us by the person we are assessing, documentation regarding his or her past history, or performance and scores on psychological tests, they are observables.

The second phase of the assessment process usually involves integrating these data and drawing inferences or conclusions from them to answer the assessment questions. These inferences are often made by comparing individuals to *norms* and other *standardized* data from psychological tests which we'll discuss later in this chapter. The point is that psychological assessment methods are based on observables of many types. They are not "psychic x-rays" with which the psychologist can directly probe the mysteries of the mind. Even those assessment techniques that do attempt to explore the person's underlying personality are based upon observables.

Kinds of error

The purpose of assessment is to answer questions as accurately as possible. However, inevitably there will be errors in assessment. Error in assessment falls into one of two categories. The first type of error is **false positive**, which is saying that something is the case when it is not. These are often referred to as Type 1 errors. The second type is **false negative**, which is saying that something is not the case when it is. These are commonly called Type 2 errors. The consequences of each type of error are different with different assessment questions. For example, in assessing suicidal potential, the consequences of a Type 1 error (false positive) are less dangerous than a Type 2 error (false negative). If we say there is no danger of suicide when there is, the results can be tragic. We would rather take precautions to prevent a suicide even if it turns out that they were unnecessary, than not take precautions and wish we had.

Before we discuss specific assessment procedures and psychological tests, a word about theory is necessary. In Chapter 10 we said that some theories of personality stress traits and underlying drives within the person. Other theories are more interested in observable behaviour and the influence of a given situation on behaviour. These differences are reflected in the kinds of tests psychologists use. Some tests look for underlying traits and dispositions. Others look more at behaviour.

TYPES OF ASSESSMENT

There are three major perspectives or approaches to assessing human characteristics. These perspectives overlap and most psychologists emphasize one or the other of them depending on the circumstances.

Psychometric assessment

Most people think of psychological tests when they think of assessment. **Psychometric assessment** emphasizes formal tests, usually with numerical scoring procedures ("metric" refers to the use of measures). These tests use standardized procedures for gathering data from subjects. Most of this chapter will be devoted to various kinds of psychometric tests, so we will simply mention this emphasis here and return to it later.

Behavioural assessment

The second major perspective is behavioural assessment. Behaviourism or learning theory contends that legitimate observation focuses on behaviour, without resorting to a search for underlying motivations, dynamics, or inferences. Both psychological tests and behavioural observations are designed to gather information with which to answer questions or make predictions about a person. Psychological tests use a standardized set of questions to accomplish this. **Behavioural assessment** uses methods that focus on observing behaviour rather than on the internal causes of that behaviour. Such assessments often use naturalistic observation. For example, assume that the assessment question relates to whether or not a person is "shy." A psychologist using the psychometric approach might administer a test of "shyness" to the individual. A behavioural psychologist, on the other hand, might observe the person directly in his or her environment.

The behavioural approach includes much more than simply watching the individual. Behaviours associated with "shyness" must first be operationally defined. To **operationalize** is to describe in terms that are observable and testable. This might mean that certain behaviours might be designated as socially-avoidant. Such behaviours might include leaving social situations, having speaking difficulties in the presence of others, or making little eye contact.

Our assessment would be most accurate if we could observe the individual on a 24-hour basis, perhaps for the rest of his or her life. This is obviously not practical. In fact, the purpose of doing a psychological assessment is to draw conclusions from a **sample** of behaviour. This sample is a small set of behaviours which should be representative of the entire **domain**, or the range of all behaviours which might be expected to occur in that situation. This point is similar to our discussion of research in Chapter 1, in which we randomly selected a sample to be representative of a population.

Clinical assessment

Both psychological testing and behavioural assessment may take place in the course of the broader **clinical assessment** process. This approach to assessment generally begins with a referral question. Then, the clinician collects many kinds of data that will help answer the referral question. Information might come from interviewing the person, making observations in natural settings such as a family discussion, interviewing relatives, and administering psychological tests. Finally, all of these sources of information are integrated for the purpose of describing the subject and making recommendations for action. This process uses a wide range of measures to answer questions with implications for the treatment of psychological disorders.

Psychological Tests

Psychological tests are standardized behavioural observations which are usually expressed as test scores. These scores are then used to make inferences about the individual who has been tested. These inferences can include predicting future behaviour, classifying the person relative to other people, and providing some understanding of the person's behaviour. In order to make these inferences valid, we must compare an individual to some kind of reference group. For example, we can use psychological tests to determine whether people are likely to have suffered brain damage, what vocational interests they have, or whether they are likely to succeed at a particular job or educational level. Implicit in all these judgments is the phrase "relative to other people." In order to compare one person's results with another's, we need to know that the test conditions are the same for both. That is, we need to know that the test is *standardized*.

Standardization

A **standardization sample** is a large sample of subjects from the population of interest who take a test to establish typical scores or norms. For example, it is common for university students who wish to enter law school in a Canadian university to write a set of examinations called LSATs. The law school is interested in predicting who will graduate. When these tests were initially developed, they were given to undergraduate university students and *standardized* on this population. The researchers kept track of individuals who took their test and later determined the average test score of individuals completing law school. They computed a similar average for students who did not graduate. They may also have submitted these scores to further statistical analysis and determined the best "cut-off score" to determine whether an individual would succeed in law school. University administrators could then look at an applicant's scores, compare them to these data, and have some idea about whether an applicant was likely to complete this particular course of studies.

It is important that the students of the standardization sample be similar to the students who will take the test in the future. Imagine if this test had been standardized only on students who had attended an expensive boarding school designed for university-preparation. The test would not be appropriate for use with a cross-section of university students. The standardization group must be drawn randomly from the population that the test is meant to assess. This concept is identical to that used when designing an experiment (see Chapter 1). The sample must be carefully drawn from the specific population being studied.

Standardized tests are used to make many decisions about individuals.
SOURCE: Courtesy of the University of Toronto.

In the development of psychological testing, we can ensure a quite accurate correspondence between the standardization group and the population from which it is drawn. For example, we might want to ensure that our sample contains the correct proportion of males versus females, individuals of higher versus lower socioeconomic status, and those with a rural versus an urban education.

Using standard procedures

Psychological tests are *standardized* behavioural observations, so they must be administered as they were during test development. For example, if our admissions test did not have time limits set in the original standardization, but some students tested later only had

Summary of Rules for Administering The WAIS-R Tests

1. Information	• Start with Item 5. • Give credit for Items 1-4 if both Items 5 and 6 are passed. If either Item 5 or Item 6 is failed, administer Items 1-4. • Discontinue after 5 consecutive failures.
2. Picture Completion	• Start with Item 1. • Give help if either Item 1 or Item 2 is failed. • Allow 20 seconds for each item. • Discontinue after 5 consecutive failures.
3. Digit Span	• Start with Item 1 of Digits Forward. • Give both trials of each item. • Discontinue after both trials of any item are failed. • Repeat for Digits Backward.
4. Picture Arrangement	• Start with Item 1. Present second trial if first is failed. • Time each item individually. • Discontinue after 4 consecutive failures.
5. Vocabulary	• Start with Item 4. • Give credit for Items 1-3 if some credit is earned on each of items 4-8. If any of items 4-8 are failed, administer Items 1-3. • Discontinue after 5 consecutive failures.

SOURCE: Reprinted with permission from The Psychological Corporation.

FIGURE 11-1 Summary of rules for administering the WAIS-R tests

a certain amount of time to complete the test, the results would not be comparable. Standardization of administration goes much beyond this fairly obvious example, however. Tests usually have detailed manuals to specify exactly how the test is to be administered (see Figure 11-1). Standard procedures should also be used to score tests. For many tests, the scoring procedures are standardized to the point that computers can do the scoring. We will see that some tests require subjective judgments by the scorer, but it is important to minimize the chance for the scorer's personal biases to influence the scoring process.

Norms

In order to make comparisons between people taking a test, we need *norms.* As we said earlier in our discussion, norms are scores or values obtained in the testing of the original standardization group. They establish a standard for comparison. For example, in our admissions test the average score of individuals who later completed law school might have been 72%, while those who did not graduate might have obtained an average of 48%. These norms can be specified in other ways. Statistical analyses may have determined that the best hit rate of this instrument follows from using a "cut-off score" of 64%. The **hit rate** is the frequency with which the test accurately predicts performance. This means that we can most accurately predict who will or will not complete law school by using 64% as a cut-off score or dividing line. We predict those above the cut-off score will complete the course of studies and those below will not.

Reliability

A test would not be much good if its results were erratic. **Reliability** is the consistency with which a measure yields readings on the quality it purports to measure (Anastasi, 1982).

In Chapter 1 we learned that a correlation coefficient was the degree of correspondence between two variables. This is how reliability is measured. For example, a set of scores obtained at one time might be correlated with another set of scores obtained by the same individuals at another time. This correlation coefficient is called a **reliability coefficient**. It is a statistic that indicates the degree of consistency of a measure. In our example, it is a measure of the test's results. A reliability coefficient of 1.0 would mean that each individual had scored exactly the same on the second testing as on the first. This degree of correspondence is rare in psychological testing, and a reliability coefficient of .80 or greater is usually considered acceptable. There are several subtypes of reliability.

Test-retest reliability

Our example above was one of test-retest reliability. **Test-retest reliability** is a measure of the degree of consistency between the results of a test given to the same individuals at two different times. This type of reliability would be appropriate only for those tests on which we would not expect any significant change in the subject to occur between the two testings. If we were assessing mood, which tends to fluctuate, test-retest reliability would not be an appropriate way to measure the reliability of the test.

When we say that test scores are consistent over a period of time, we do not mean they are identical. In our admissions test example, test-retest reliability could be high when individuals were re-administered the test after one year of law school. The acquisition of knowledge is presumed to be progressive and cumulative, rather than random, and thus if the test is reliable individuals scoring high on the first test will also tend to score high on the second test. Of course, individuals might vary in their ability to remember questions from the first testing, thus we would be assessing not only knowledge, but also "memory for test items." To avoid this problem, alternative forms of tests are often constructed.

Alternate-form reliability

Alternate-form reliability is a measure of the degree to which different versions of a test correlate with each other. When it is possible that re-administration of a test might occur, another test or tests are often developed to be as equivalent as possible to the first test. They are developed, standardized, administered, and scored in the same fashion as the original test and cover the same content area. If the tests are equivalent, there should be a reasonable consistency between an individual's performance on the original test and on the alternate form. This would result in a *high* alternate-form reliability.

We said that the alternate form should cover the same information as the original form. In a university admissions test, this would likely refer to knowledge that we would normally acquire over our previous school years. Sampling all of this knowledge, or *content sampling*, is an important concept which applies to alternate-form reliability. Both test forms must adequately sample the content area under study. How often have you taken an exam and felt that you had "lucked out" by having studied those areas which were heavily emphasized during the examination? This might be an example of poor content sampling. All of the information that should have been covered by the examination was not proportionately represented in the choice of test items.

Split-half reliability

Split-half reliability is a measure of the degree to which one half of a test correlates with the other half. In this case, two scores are obtained for an individual from one testing. The test-items are divided into two groups and the results of these two half-tests are compared with each other. If a test is internally consistent, the two groups of items should correlate highly with each other. One way that the grouping of these two subtests can be generated is the *odd/even method*. One group of test items is made up of odd-numbered items and one from even-numbered. If the content area is adequately covered, we would not expect an individual to obtain significantly different scores on the odd- and even-numbered test items. In general, the split-half reliability of a test tells us whether it has internal consistency.

Some ways of dividing up the test items would not be appropriate. For example, if we divided the test items into the first half and the second half, we might have other factors interfere with our results. Some individuals might do more poorly on the first few items because of anxiety and not being "warmed-up" to the test. Conversely, some individuals might do poorly in the second half because of fatigue or boredom. These factors would introduce error into our measurements and provide artificially low split-half reliability estimates.

Inter-scorer and inter-rater reliability test

Test reliability can also be assessed by comparing the judgments of two or more individuals scoring the same test data. **Inter-scorer reliability** is a measure of the degree to which two or more people agree when they score the same test. This type of reliability is important when some degree of judgment is required on the part of the scorer. For example, it is not an issue with multiple choice or true-false tests, but essay tests require scorer judgment. High inter-scorer reliability usually occurs when answers are clearly right or wrong, or when the scoring instructions accompanying the test provide very precise guidelines.

Scorer reliability can also be determined with behavioural observations. This is often referred to as *inter-rater reliability*, which is a measure of the degree to which two or more observers agree when they rate the same behaviour or quality. Inter-rater reliability is usually high if the behaviours being observed are clearly and concretely *operationalized*. Operationalization of a behaviour includes breaking the behaviour down into clearly specified observable units. For example, a wink might be defined as the complete closure of a single eye for a minimum of .5 seconds to a maximum of 3.0 seconds if the other eyelid remains at least 30 mm from the bottom lid without interruption during the process. We are more likely to get agreement between two observers following this operationalized definition than to ask them merely whether a person has winked or not.

In order for a test to be a good test, it must be reliable. This is a necessary condition for successful psychological testing, but high reliability does not guarantee that a test is adequate. We can have tests that are very reliable and yet they can be useless. The usefulness of a test depends upon its *validity*.

Validity

Validity is a measure of the degree to which a test actually ascertains what it purports to ascertain. A test with high *validity* measures what it is supposed to measure. We determine validity coefficients to see if a test measures what its name implies. A **validity coefficient** is a statistic that indicates the strength of relationship between a particular measure and some other variable being used to establish that measure's validity. If our admissions test did not correlate with educational success, it would not be valid. It might, however, relate very well to an individual's vocabulary level, so it would be a valid indicator of word knowledge. It is important to ask not only, "Is this test valid?" but also "What is it valid for?"

As is the case with reliability, there are a number of subtypes of validity. The relative importance of these types of validity depends on what a particular test is intended to measure.

Content validity

Content validity is a measure of the degree to which a test contains a fair balance of items from each area of the body of knowledge it is designed to test. If a test does this, it is said to have good content validity. The test must not only adequately sample a content area but also contain test items in the correct proportion. For example, if our admissions test was designed to sample the content area of previously acquired knowledge, it should sample all areas in a balanced fashion. A test of general achievement should not be made up of 99% mathematical questions.

Face validity

Content validity should not be confused with face validity. **Face validity** is a measure of the degree to which a test has the appearance of assessing what it is supposed to assess. This is a superficial kind of validity, since it only refers to what a test appears to measure, not what it actually measures. Even though a test may have face validity, it could be lacking in other, more essential types of validity. For example, a test asking questions about stars and space vehicles might look as though it could be used for astronaut selection. However, it may have absolutely no validity in assessing the attributes necessary to make a good astronaut.

Face validity does have an important function, however. Tests which appear irrelevant to a particular purpose may be resisted or approached with less motivation by individuals taking the test. For example, some tests of anxiety include questions such as "Do you often have diarrhea?" or "Does your neck spot with red often?" These questions are related to anxiety level. However, many people would consider them irrelevant to their emotional feelings and would resist a test of anxiety that consisted of such questions. The test would seem foolish.

Criterion validity

Criterion validity is a measure of the effectiveness of a test in predicting an individual's behaviour or performance in specified situations. To measure this, test performance is compared against a *criterion*. A criterion is a direct and independent measure of whatever the test is intended to predict. In our admissions test example, the criterion might be completion of a law degree. Criterion validity is especially important in situations where selection and classification of individuals for training or hiring is important. Since we are trying to predict a future outcome, this kind of validity is often referred to as *predictive validity*. Unfortunately, with this type of validation there usually is a long time interval between the initial test administration and the criterion measure. Even in our law school admissions test example, the researchers who standardized the instrument would have had to wait a minimum of three to four years before they had sufficient data to be usable.

Concurrent validity

Concurrent validity also relates to prediction. It is a measure of the degree to which a test correlates with other tests designed to assess the same quality. In this case, the test is used to predict performance on other tests that are available at the time the test is being standardized. These could include scores on other tests, ratings by a supervisor, or current grade point averages. For example, a test of mechanical aptitude could be administered to successful machinists or mechanics to determine the relationship between test scores and present (concurrent) performance.

Tests are used to predict some very complex behavioural outcomes. For example, what constitutes a "successful" mechanic? Is this assessment to be based upon productivity, earnings, employer ratings, or some set of mechanics' examinations? Further, the abilities assessed by a test of mechanical aptitude may be only some of the reasons that an individual is "successful." These other contributors to success, which might include motivation, opportunity, and

FIGURE 11-2 A table of intercorrelations among four tests of anxiety
This table is taken from the manual for the State-Trait Anxiety Scale (STAI) by Spielberger (1983). As evidence of construct validity, Spielberger showed that his test was strongly related to two other tests of the same construct: the Taylor Manifest Anxiety Scale (TMAS) and the IPAT Manifest Anxiety Scale (IPAT). It was less strongly related to the Zuckerman Affect Adjective Checklist (AACL).

Correlations between the State-Trait Anxiety Scale[1] and Other Measures of Trait Anxiety

Anxiety Scale	College Females (N = 126)			College Males (N = 80)			NP Patients (N = 66)	
	STAI	IPAT	TMAS	STAI	IPAT	TMAS	STAI	IPAT
IPAT	.75			.76			.77[2]	
TMAS	.80	.85		.79	.73		.83	.84
AACL	.52	.57	.53	.58	.51	.41		

[1]Based on Form X.
[2]N = 112 for the correlation between the STAI and the IPAT.
SOURCE: Adapted with permission from Spielberger (1983).

personality attributes, would interfere with and weaken the predictive and concurrent validity of a test. Jobs also change with time, and what might be defined as "successful" at the time of test standardization may not define "successful" several years later.

Construct validity

Construct validity is a measure of the degree to which a test is consistent with the theoretical notions (constructs) to which it is supposed to be related. It is a more complex kind of validity than the others we have discussed. A construct can best be thought of as a concept, a complex idea, rather than as a thing. Constructs can never be directly measured. They are inferred structures or processes. Examples of constructs include "intelligence," "anxiety," "motivation," and "shyness." Constructs are assumed to underlie and influence behaviours that can be observed or measured. If we are interested in developing a test which can assess "anxiety," we must operationalize the construct "anxiety" by specifying those behaviours that we believe reflect anxiety. These may include increased heart rate and respiration, subjective descriptions of fearfulness or apprehension, and so on. Construct validation usually involves the gradual accumulation of data from a variety of sources.

Construct validity may be determined by correlating a test with other tests that seem to measure the same construct. For example, if we were devising a new intelligence test, one way that we could verify that intelligence is in fact what we are measuring might be to determine the correlation between our test results and those of other tests of intelligence. Figure 11-2 shows a table of intercorrelations among four tests of anxiety.

We have now reviewed some of the essential aspects of good psychological tests. A good test must have been standardized on an appropriate population. It must have appropriate norms and it must be both reliable and valid.

ASSESSING INTELLIGENCE

We all have some notion of what intelligence is. In the past, words such as "immoral," "good," "evil," "insane," and "virtuous" were all confused with the notion of intelligence. Today we no longer believe that such words describe intelligence. However, we still use words that imply a judgment, words such as "smart," "dumb," "capable," and "incompetent." The fact is that no one has come up with a satisfactory definition of "intelligence." Some psychologists are sceptical about the use of this construct and sarcastically define "intelligence" as "a person's performance on an intelligence test." Others define it as an indicator of "adaptive abilities."

For the moment, we will define **intelligence** as the ability to learn and adapt existing knowledge to new situations. We will discuss the controversies around the definition of the term "intelligence" in a later section. However, in order to appreciate the controversies, we first need some background.

Alfred Binet.
SOURCE: Archives of the History of American Psychology.

The history of intelligence testing

Throughout history, people have been making comparisons amongst one another. They have ranked and categorized individuals in everything from sports to oratory. Usually, these comparisons have been subjective and non-systematic. Even before societies became as complex as they are now, it was obvious that some people did better at certain tasks than at others. Divisions of labour occurred, and educational systems developed. But there was no good way to establish what vocation or educational level was appropriate for any particular individual. This problem was evident in France in the late 19th century. The Minister of Public Education faced the challenge of developing an educational program for those individuals who did not appear capable of learning in the existing school system. In 1904 he commissioned Alfred Binet to develop such a program.

Binet and his colleague Theodore Simon felt that the first step was to develop some way to identify those individuals who would benefit from this program. Their original test was designed to identify retarded individuals who would benefit most from a modified program. This test evolved into the first published "intelligence test," the Binet-Simon Scale (Binet and Simon, 1905). This instrument was the first to demonstrate that intellectual skills were quantifiable and measureable.

Theodore Simon.
SOURCE: Georges Bareau.

Simon and Binet standardized their test by administering various types of problems to children at different age levels to determine the capacity of a "normal" child at each age level. Then, depending upon the number of questions answered correctly, an individual child could be assigned a *mental age*. **Mental age** is the measurement of a child's intellectual abilities according to the chronological age of children in the standardization group who obtained the same score. If a child's mental age was below his or her *chronological age* (actual age in years), educators could reduce expectations for that child. Simon and Binet found that children below the average of their chronological peer group tended to fall farther and farther behind their age mates as they grew older. For example, a six-year-old child with a mental age of four might, at age nine, have achieved a mental age of six. They also found that the ratio of the differences tended to remain about the same. This observation led to the use of a ratio where an individual's mental age (MA) was divided by the chronological age

Lewis M. Terman (1877–1956).
SOURCE: Courtesy of Stanford University Archives.

(CA), yielding an *intelligence quotient*. An **intelligence quotient** (or IQ) is a measure of a person's intellectual ability relative to a standard population. The average is set at 100. Binet-Simon's formula for IQ was (MA/CA) × 100. This yielded an average IQ of 100 for the standardization group. The mathematical precision with which an individual's IQ could be determined led the public to believe that intelligence was something that was "real" and could be accurately and precisely measured. This belief persists to the present and has contributed to the considerable controversy surrounding intelligence testing.

This intelligence test came to North America and was revised by Lewis Terman of Stanford University, to become the Stanford-Binet Intelligence Test (Terman, 1916). Revisions of this test are still in use in clinical practice.

During the First World War, the immediate classification of military recruits was necessary to ensure that individuals of different capabilities were used to their appropriate potential. The U.S. Army Alpha and Beta Tests (Yerkes, 1921) led to group intelligence testing and to the greater popularity and influence of intelligence tests. Subsequent to this, many tests of abilities appeared, and the *psychometric*, or test based, assessment of mental abilities accelerated.

The next major step in intelligence test development occurred in 1944 with David Wechsler's development of the Wechsler-Bellevue Intelligence Scale (Wechsler, 1944). Before we discuss the development of Wechsler's scales, a brief statistical diversion is necessary.

Normalized abilities

Many quantifiable attributes in the population are distributed in a *normal distribution* (for a further discussion of statistics, see Appendix A). A **normal distribution** is a symmetrical bell-shaped curve that is formed by plotting a large number of individual performances in a frequency distribution. That is, if we obtain measurements from a

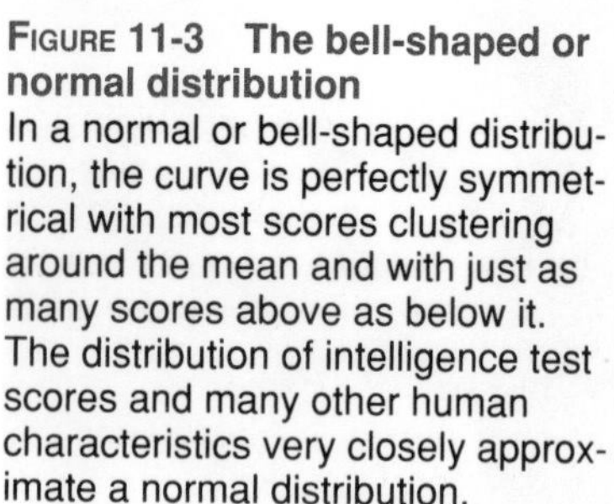

FIGURE 11-3 The bell-shaped or normal distribution
In a normal or bell-shaped distribution, the curve is perfectly symmetrical with most scores clustering around the mean and with just as many scores above as below it. The distribution of intelligence test scores and many other human characteristics very closely approximate a normal distribution.

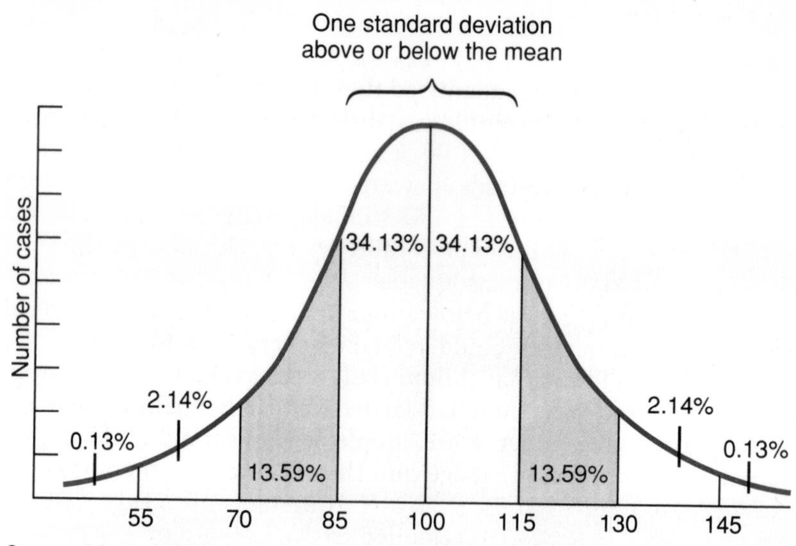

SOURCE: Adapted with permission from Allyn and Bacon, 1989.

large sample of people, we can obtain not only a mean but we can also draw a graph of the spread of individual scores around this mean. The **mean** is the numerical average of a group of numbers. In a *frequency distribution*, scores on most human attributes (including IQ) tend to cluster around the mean, with fewer and fewer scores occurring as we move away from the mean in either direction (see Figure 11-3). A **frequency distribution** is a graph in which the number of instances of a particular score are plotted along a line. The graph will be highest where the highest frequency of scores falls. Statistical analyses have determined what proportion of the scores will fall within specified values on a normal curve. For example, Figure 11-3 shows that half the scores fall above the mean and half below. About 68% of scores fall within one standard deviation of the mean on either side of the standard normal curve. The **standard deviation** is a statistical measure of how much variability there is among the scores in a distribution.

David Wechsler.
SOURCE: Archives of the History of American Psychology.

Wechsler's scales

The Stanford scales based the IQ score on a comparison between a person's mental age and chronological age. In tests developed by David Wechsler, however, an IQ score was computed by comparing the person with others of the same age. Wechsler gathered norms by testing standardization groups of different ages. For each age group, he assigned a score of 100 to the average performance. Then each standard deviation above or below the mean represented 15 IQ points. Figure 11-3 illustrates that 34.13% of those above the mean fall within one standard deviation from the mean. Thus, a child with an IQ of 115 scored better than 84% of the children in the standardization group. Other IQ scores are spread proportionately across the normal distribution. In fact, both methods of figuring IQ produce about the same results, but Wechsler's makes more sense statistically.

Critics of the Standford-Binet test claimed that it was heavily dependent upon previous education and verbal ability. Because of

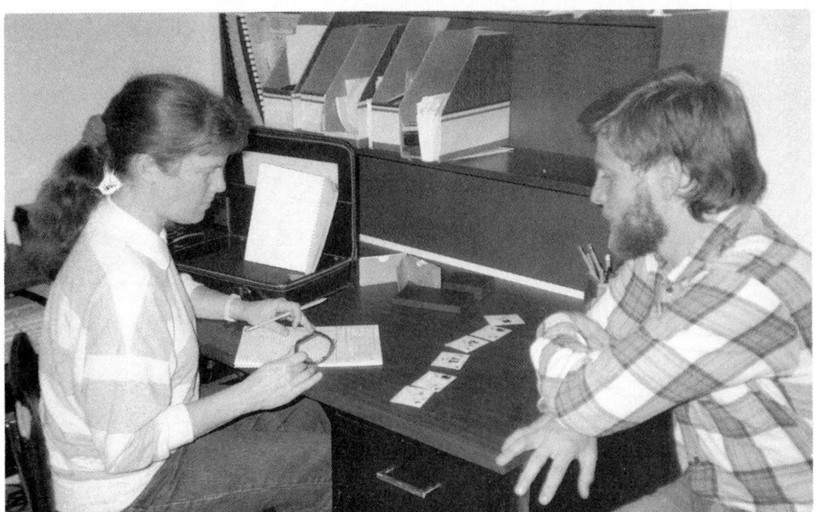

The Wechsler intelligence tests are administered individually to one subject at a time. They include subtests that tap both verbal and non-verbal (performance) abilities. This tester is timing the subject as he arranges cartoon panels into a sequence that makes a story.
SOURCE: Courtesy David Martin.

this emphasis, critics said, it put some cultural groups at a disadvantage. In response to this, Wechsler developed his scale to assess both verbal and nonverbal abilities as independently as possible. His test yields scores for verbal IQ, for performance (non-verbal) IQ, and for a combined full-scale IQ.

The Wechsler test has been revised several times through the years. There are now three commonly used tests for assessment of intellectual abilities: the Wechsler Pre-School and Primary Scale for Infants (Wechsler, 1967), the Wechsler Intelligence Scale for Children—Revised (WISC-R) (Wechsler, 1974), and the Wechsler Adult Intelligence Scale—Revised (WAIS-R) (Wechsler, 1981). These scales are the most widely used devices for assessing intellectual abilities today. See Figure 11-4 for a hypothetical profile sheet from WAIS-R.

FIGURE 11-4 A hypothetical profile sheet from a Wechsler Adult Intelligence Scale
This 27-year-old nurse earned an IQ score of 115. Her ability on non-verbal tests (performance IQ) was better than on verbal tests.

WAIS-R RECORD FORM

WECHSLER ADULT INTELLIGENCE SCALE—REVISED

NAME ____________

ADDRESS ____________

SEX F AGE 27 RACE ______ MARITAL STATUS ______

OCCUPATION Nurse EDUCATION R.N.

PLACE OF TESTING ____________ TESTED BY ____________

TABLE OF SCALED SCORE EQUIVALENTS*

Scaled Score	RAW SCORE											Scaled Score
	VERBAL TESTS						PERFORMANCE TESTS					
	Information	Digit Span	Vocabulary	Arithmetic	Comprehension	Similarities	Picture Completion	Picture Arrangement	Block Design	Object Assembly	Digit Symbol	
19	—	28	70	—	32	—	—	—	51	—	93	**19**
18	29	27	69	—	31	28	—	—	—	41	91-92	**18**
17	—	26	68	19	—	—	20	20	50	—	89-90	**17**
16	28	25	66-67	—	30	27	—	—	49	40	84-88	**16**
15	27	24	65	18	29	26	—	19	47-48	39	79-83	**15**
14	26	22-23	63-64	17	27-28	25	19	—	44-46	38	75-78	**14**
13	25	20-21	60-62	16	26	24	—	18	42-43	37	70-74	**13**
12	23-24	18-19	55-59	15	25	23	18	17	38-41	35-36	66-69	**12**
11	22	17	52-54	13-14	23-24	22	17	15-16	35-37	34	62-65	**11**
10	19-21	15-16	47-51	12	21-22	20-21	16	14	31-34	32-33	57-61	**10**
9	17-18	14	43-46	11	19-20	18-19	15	13	27-30	30-31	53-56	**9**
8	15-16	12-13	37-42	10	17-18	16-17	14	11-12	23-26	28-29	48-52	**8**
7	13-14	11	29-36	8-9	14-16	14-15	13	8-10	20-22	24-27	44-47	**7**
6	9-12	9-10	20-28	6-7	11-13	11-13	11-12	5-7	14-19	21-23	37-43	**6**
5	6-8	8	14-19	5	8-10	7-10	8-10	3-4	8-13	16-20	30-36	**5**
4	5	7	11-13	4	6-7	5-6	5-7	2	3-7	13-15	23-29	**4**
3	4	6	9-10	3	4-5	2-4	3-4	—	2	9-12	16-22	**3**
2	3	3-5	6-8	1-2	2-3	1	2	1	1	6-8	8-15	**2**
1	0-2	0-2	0-5	0	0-1	0	0-1	0	0	0-5	0-7	**1**

*Clinicians who wish to draw a profile may do so by locating the subject's raw scores on the table above and drawing a line to connect them. See Chapter 4 in the Manual for a discussion of the significance of differences between scores on the tests.

	Year	Month	Day
Date Tested	90	06	15
Date of Birth	63	05	14
Age	27	1	1

SUMMARY

	Raw Score	Scaled Score
VERBAL TESTS		
Information	22	11
Digit Span	14	9
Vocabulary	60	13
Arithmetic	15	12
Comprehension	24	11
Similarities	23	12
Verbal Score		68
PERFORMANCE TESTS		
Picture Completion	19	14
Picture Arrangement	17	12
Block Design	43	13
Object Assembly	37	15
Digit Symbol	75	14
Performance Score		66

	Sum of Scaled Scores	IQ
VERBAL	68	105
PERFORMANCE	66	124
FULL SCALE	134	115

THE PSYCHOLOGICAL CORPORATION
HARCOURT BRACE JOVANOVICH, PUBLISHERS

9-991829

SOURCE: Reprinted with permission from The Psychological Corporation (Harcourt Brace Jovanovich Publishers, 1981).

Cultural differences

Cultural bias is a problem with all tests of intelligence, and the Wechsler scales are no exception. This is a particular problem for Canadian psychologists. The development of the Wechsler tests was based upon a United States standardization sample, with a disproportionate number of middle-class caucasians. The tests contain many items (particularly in verbal areas) relating to U.S. knowledge. This bias in standardization penalizes lower socio-economic groups, minority racial groups, and test subjects from other countries (including Canada, where the tests are widely used). Canadian investigators have done considerable research in an effort to modify some content areas of the Wechsler scales for Canadian use with adults (Fellers, McInnis, Cappelli, Cragg, and Vaillancourt, 1987; Pugh and Boer, 1987; Violato, 1986) and with children (Cyr and Atkinson, 1987; Marx, 1984; Vernon, 1977; Beal, Prifitera, & Daniel, 1989). They have also suggested cautions for using these instruments with a Canadian population (Quintin, 1985). Standardization studies have also been done with Canadian minority groups such as the Native Indian and Inuit (Seyfort, Spreen and Lahmer, 1980; Wilgosh, Mulcahy and Watters, 1986) who are clearly disadvantaged when using these scales. One question asked of children (in the original Wechsler version) is, "Who discovered America?" If the child answers, "The Indians," no credit is given. A follow up question asks, "Yes, but who was the first European to discover America?" Questions such as these reflect both a cultural bias and a subtle racism. Afterall, how can one *discover* a country where people already live?

Intelligence testing has developed rapidly and is used in many settings. Such tests are used to stream individuals into specific training or educational settings, to provide the basis for social and educational planning, to determine competence in legal proceedings, and to guide people in a large number of other life-changing decisions. And yet, in spite of the wide-spread use of such tests, we still really don't know what intelligence is.

What is intelligence?

Although many people see intelligence and intelligence quotients as something real and tangible, intelligence is only a construct, a theoretical notion. In addition, there is little agreement on the definition of the construct.

Working definitions of intelligence often include some reference to abilities, either learned or innate. They often include the ability to learn and acquire knowledge, the rate of learning, and the ability to use this knowledge in different or novel situations. Traditional assessments of intelligence have relied heavily on verbal abilities, but most psychologists today include both verbal abilities and problem-solving skills in their definition of intelligence. Sternberg, Conway, Ketron, and Berstein (1981) asked both professionals and laypersons to judge which of 250 behaviours were typical of an intelligent person. Figures 11-5 and 11-6 give typical behaviours chosen as intelligent and show the results of this study. There was high

SOURCE: *Calvin and Hobbes* by Bill Watterson. Copyright 1988 Universal Press Syndicate. Reprinted with permission. All rights reserved.

Factor I. Practical problem-solving ability	Factor loading	Factor II. Verbal ability	Factor loading	Factor III. Social competence	Factor loading
Reasons logically and well.	.77	Speaks clearly and articulately.	.83	Accepts others for what they are.	.88
Identifies connections among ideas.	.77	Is verbally fluent.	.82	Admits mistakes.	.74
Sees all aspects of a problem.	.76	Converses well.	.76	Displays interest in the world at large.	.72
Keeps an open mind.	.73	Is knowledgeable about a particular field of knowledge.	.74	Is on time for appointments.	.71
Responds thoughtfully to others' ideas.	.70	Studies hard.	.70	Has social conscience.	.70
Sizes up situations well.	.69	Reads with high comprehension.	.70	Thinks before speaking and doing.	.70
Gets to the heart of problems.	.69	Reads widely.	.69	Displays curiosity.	.68
Interprets information accurately.	.66	Deals effectively with people.	.68	Does not make snap judgments.	.68
Makes good decisions.	.65	Writes without difficulty.	.65	Makes fair judgments.	.66
Goes to original sources for basic information.	.64	Sets aside time for reading.	.64	Assesses well the relevance of information to a problem at hand.	.66
Poses problems in an optimal way.	.62	Displays a good vocabulary.	.61	Is sensitive to other people's needs and desires.	.65
Is a good source of ideas.	.62	Accepts social norms.	.61	Is frank and honest with self and others.	.64
Perceives implied assumptions and conclusions.	.62	Tries new things.	.60	Displays interest in the immediate environment.	.64
Listens to all sides of an argument.	.61				
Deals with problems resourcefully.	.61				

SOURCE: Adapted with permission from Sternberg et al. (1981).

FIGURE 11-5 Factors underlying people's conceptions of intelligence: laypersons rating characteristics in ideal person

agreement that intelligence was defined by verbal abilities and problem-solving abilities such as "makes good decisions . . . is able to apply knowledge to problems at hand . . . reasons well." Factor analysis extracted three factors from laypersons' conception of intelligence and three slightly different ones from experts' descriptions. The experts were all psychologists with doctoral degrees doing research on intelligence in major university and research centres in the United States. The laypersons were nonstudents recruited through newspaper ads.

Subtle cultural biases in the defining of intelligence

Sternberg's results probably seem intuitively obvious. However, it is difficult for any of us to see that we have a culturally biased view of intelligence. Most of us probably would not include in our definition of intelligence abilities such as "accurately senses mood in others . . . is able to reproduce musical scores from listening to music . . . drives for basket with full knowledge of nine other players' position . . . senses position of sea canoe accurately." Each of these abilities requires the complex integration of extraordinarily complex brain functions with spatial movement. Why aren't they part of "intelligence"? We will return to these questions after we trace the history of attempts to define intelligence.

Factor I. Verbal intelligence	Factor loading	Factor II. Problem-solving ability	Factor loading	Factor III. Practical intelligence	Factor loading
Displays a good vocabulary.	.74	Able to apply knowledge to problems at hand	.74	Sizes up situations well.	.84
Reads with high comprehension	.74	Makes good decisions	.73	Determines how to achieve goals.	.83
Displays curiosity.	.68	Poses problems in an optimal way.	.73	Displays awareness to world around him or her.	.69
Is intellectually curious.	.66	Displays common sense.	.66	Displays interest in the world at large.	.63
Sees all aspects of a problem.	.66	Displays objectivity.	.66		
Learns rapidly.	.65	Solves problems well.	.66		
Appreciates knowledge for its own sake.	.65	Plans ahead.	.64		
Is verbally fluent	.65	Has good intuitions.	.62		
Listens to all sides of an argument before deciding.	.64	Gets to the heart of problems.	.62		
Displays alertness.	.64	Appreciates truth.	.61		
Thinks deeply.	.64	Considers the end result of actions.	.61		
Shows creativity.	.64	Approaches problems thoughtfully.	.60		
Converses easily on a variety of subjects.	.64				
Reads widely.	.63				
Likes to read.	.62				
Identifies connections among ideas.	.60				

SOURCE: Reprinted with permission from Sternberg et al. (1981).

FIGURE 11-6 Factors underlying people's conceptions of intelligence: experts rating characteristics in ideal person

Early attempts to define intelligence

One of the most important controversies over the definition of intelligence is over whether there is a general intelligence factor. There are those who think there is. On the other hand, there are those who believe that intelligence is made up of many separate abilities that often do not correlate with each other.

At the same time that Binet in France was addressing pragmatic concerns regarding school placement, Spearman (1904) in England was attempting to understand and define intelligence. His studies led him to the conclusion that intelligence was a single or unitary factor. He referred to this as a **G-factor** or general intelligence factor. According to Spearman, this G-factor has secondary or **S-components**. The secondary components are specific abilities that are subordinate to the general intelligence factor. Investigators in the United States took a very different view. Researchers such as Thorndike and his colleagues (Thorndike, Lay, and Dean, 1909) determined that abilities tended to fall in clusters. They argued that these clusters did not correlate highly with each other. Thus, intelligence is composed of many different clusters, not one over-all ability. These findings were extended by Thurstone and Thurstone (1941) who developed measures of **primary mental abilities**. These are the several different mental abilities that make up intelligence and that do not correlate well with each other.

There is evidence for both the general-factor view and the primary mental abilities view. However, the debate is complicated by some complex statistical problems. Some statistical procedures are more likely to find one overall ability and other procedures are more likely to find separate clusters of abilities. In common usage, people tend to speak of intelligence as though it were accurately represented by one score. Thus, in common usage, the general-factor seems more popular. However, this view of intelligence has been strongly attacked in recent years by writers such as Howard Gardner and Robert Sternberg.

Gardner's seven frames of mind

Howard Gardner has challenged traditional notions of intelligence in a book called *Frames of Mind* (1983/85). He argues that intelligence is not "a general capacity or potential which every human being possesses to a greater or lesser extent" (Gardner, 1985, p. ix). Rather, there are seven areas of ability that all must be considered in defining intelligence. These are relatively autonomous from each other, so there is no one overall intelligence but rather "multiple intelligences."

Gardner argues that our definition of intelligence is limited and culture-bound. According to his theory, each of the following activities reflects a different kind of intelligence.

Ophra Harnoy, cellist.
SOURCE: Courtesy Ophra Harnoy/Photographer Gordon Clarke.

Debbie Brill, high-jumper.
SOURCE: Claus Andersen.

Albert Einstein, scientist.
SOURCE: UPI/Bettmann.

Gardner does not claim that he has given the final definition of human intelligence. However, he does argue that there are multiple intelligences and he provides a description of seven that make sense to him. Two of his intelligences, *linguistic intelligence* and *logical-mathematical intelligence*, are the abilities that have traditionally been used to define intelligence. Gardner also says that there is a *musical intelligence* that is relatively independent of the other intelligences and that emerges early in life. In describing *spatial intelligence*, Gardner quotes the former world chess champion, Jose Raul Capablanca, saying, "To play chess requires no intelligence at all" (Gardner, 1985, p. 170). While this may sound absurd, Capablanca's point was that neither verbal nor mathematical skills are very important in chess. The chess master works in a visual way, "seeing" thousands of potential board positions in very quick succession. *Bodily-kinesthetic intelligence* is, according to Gardner, an ability that most people in our culture have trouble considering to be part of intelligence. Bodily-kinesthetic intelligence is the control of one's bodily movements and the ability to handle objects skilfully. Wayne Gretzky is clearly a genius in this area. He knows (senses? intuits?) where his teammates and opponents are and where they will be in the next half-second. Then his own body suddenly and effortlessly moves in a new direction. He has had no time to "analyse" or "think" about what he is doing. Is this a form of intelligence? Why not? asks Gardner. It is cultural blindness to call such complex brain/body activity non-intelligent. Finally, Gardner describes two "personal intelligences," the *understanding of oneself* and the *understanding of others*. This last intelligence forms the basis of social relationships. We might admire the enlightened individual who can accurately "read" other people and get along well with them. But most of us would not classify this as intelligence unless the person also has a large vocabulary and high SAT scores.

Gardner's ideas are a severe challenge to many approaches to the testing of intelligence. He questions "the assumption that intelligence, however defined, can be measured by standardized verbal instruments, such as short-answer, paper-and-pencil tests" (Gardner, 1985, p. ix).

Sternberg's triarchic theory of intelligence

Like Gardner, Robert Sternberg (1985, 1986, 1987) thinks that traditional intelligence tests tap only part of human intelligence. He has developed a theory that proposes three kinds of intelligence. He recognizes that many people who aren't good at reading, writing, and arithmetic are very good at activities such as creative thinking and getting along with others. For Sternberg, *componential intelligence* is close to the customary definition of intelligence. This type of intelligence enables an individual to process information, solve problems, and acquire and store information. *Experiential intelligence* enables the individual to be creative, insightful, and able to learn to perform many tasks automatically. This frees up energy and attention to solve other problems. Sternberg's theory is probably best known for his emphasis on *contextual intelligence* or "practical intelligence." (See Figure 11-7.) It is no secret that some people who

FIGURE 11-7 Sternberg's triarchic theory of intelligence According to Sternberg's triarchic theory, there are three distinct types of intelligence: componential, experiential, and contextual.
SOURCE: Adapted with permission from Allyn and Bacon, 1989.

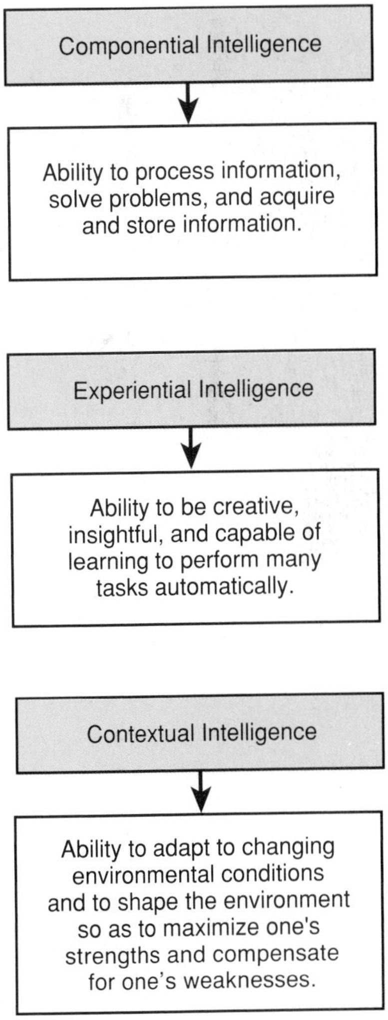

Componential Intelligence
↓
Ability to process information, solve problems, and acquire and store information.

Experiential Intelligence
↓
Ability to be creative, insightful, and capable of learning to perform many tasks automatically.

Contextual Intelligence
↓
Ability to adapt to changing environmental conditions and to shape the environment so as to maximize one's strengths and compensate for one's weaknesses.

FIGURE 11-8 Sternberg says that the ability to "read" other people is a form of practical intelligence

These pictures are designed to test that ability. The two pictures on the left are supervisor-supervisee pairs. The two pictures on the right depict two couples, only one of which is a real couple. The subject's task is to use non-verbal cues to decide which are the supervisors and which is the real couple. (In the top left photo, the supervisor is on the left; in the bottom left photo, the supervisor is on the right. The couple in the top right photo is the real couple.)

SOURCE: Reprinted from Sternberg (1985).

score very well on IQ tests constantly make social blunders. "How can he be so smart and not know how much that hurt her?" The practical knowledge one picks up from life, as opposed to "book learning," is called *tacit knowledge*. We gain tacit knowledge almost without conscious effort, and Sternberg argues that this tacit knowledge is probably more important to success in life than formal academic knowledge. He has designed some clever tests of contextual knowledge, and you can test yourself (just for fun, not a serious testing) by looking at Figure 11-8.

PERSONALITY TESTS

Psychologists have difficulty with the definition and measurement of intelligence, and the same situation exists with personality. As we said in Chapter 10, some personality theorists focus on *traits* that are consistent across situations. Others think that personality is much more a function of the demands of the given *situation*. The methods that individual psychologists use to assess personality reflect their definition of what personality is. In general, the situational-theorists use behavioural assessment. Trait theorists are more likely to use tests of personality to describe the individual's lasting characteristics or traits.

In general, psychological tests fall into two groups: *objective tests* and *projective tests*. **Objective tests** are psychological tests with highly structured answering formats for which standardized scoring procedures are used. The word "objective" has a nice rigorous ring to it. However, all it means when applied to tests is that the questions and answers are well-structured. That is, they can be answered in ways that can easily and consistently be scored by anyone. Multiple choice and true-false questions are common examples. An objective personality test might include true-false items such as "I frequently have an urge to sneeze during lectures." **Projective tests** are psychological tests in which an ambiguous stimulus is presented, and the subject produces responses, presumably based on projections from within. Vague pictures or inkblots, for example, might be presented. The subject then says what they seem to be. Presumably the person *projects* his or her own underlying personality dynamics to give the vague stimuli structure and meaning.

Objective tests

Objective *personality* tests rely on the answers that a person gives to questions in describing him or herself, and they emphasize structured scoring and interpretation. As with intelligence tests, standardization data and norms are used. However, the interpretations based on these tests are more complex and more dependent on the skill of the clinician than is the case with intelligence tests. Since the test data are based on a person's self-description, these tests are often called **self-report inventories**.

Self-report inventories vary in their type and format of questions. They may include answering true-false questions, choosing between two or more alternative responses, or rating a particular item on a numbered rating scale. They depend on the person's honesty and ability to critically self-analyze, so they are vulnerable to faking. To counteract this, many tests include **validity scales** which are designed to detect invalid responding and various kinds of faking. Some validity scales correct for "faking good" by asking questions that almost everyone would have to answer in the unflattering direction. If a person answers true to a series of statements such as "I never laugh at off-colour jokes," or "I have never told a lie," we will consider the possibility that the person is trying to make a good impression. Few people can honestly say they *never* do these things. Other scales try to detect answering biases such as "faking bad" and answering randomly. For example, some subjects might fear leaving the safety of a hospital or wish to appear emotionally damaged to obtain a legal settlement. Under such circumstances, they sometimes try to "fake bad," that is, to appear as more disturbed than they actually are.

Anyone can make up a test, as is obvious from "personality" tests in popular magazines and ads for tests such as the famous psychologist's personality test for helping customers choose the right carpet. We are not making this up. A carpet company published the test in its ads. However, legitimate objective personality tests are developed through *the analytical approach*, *empirical criterion keying*, or *factor analysis*.

Analytical approach

The **analytical approach** is the least sophisticated method of test development, in which the test developer simply makes up questions judged to test the quality to be measured. This approach depends heavily on face validity. The process starts with the question, "what do I want to measure?" The test developer then constructs a set of questions that he or she assumes taps the quality to be measured. A group of experts may be asked their opinion on items to be used. Development of such tests is based on how the developer theorizes about the quality being tested.

The original self-report personality inventory was the Woodsworth Personal Data Sheet. It was developed for use as a psychiatric screening device for persons entering the armed forces in World War I (Woodsworth, 1920). This was a paper-and-pencil test that was designed to be a standardized clinical interview. It asked about neurotic symptoms and simply added up the number of symptoms the person endorsed as true of himself or herself. It attempted to sample a certain content area, that of psychiatric symptoms, so it was developed through the analytical approach. More recent examples of such tests present a list of potential problems and ask the subject to check the ones that apply to him or her. The usefulness of this method depends entirely on the appropriateness of the items selected by the originator of the test.

These tests are sometimes designed to reflect the concepts in a particular personality theory. One example that is currently popular is the **Myers-Briggs Type Indicator (MBTI)**, which is based on the work of Carl Jung. This is a pencil-and-paper measure of people's preferences with regard to perception and judgment. It categorizes people into 1 of 16 types, based on scores on the four dimensions: EI—extroversion versus introversion; SN—sensing versus intuitive; TF—thinking versus feeling; and JP—judgment versus perception. The subject chooses between pairs of statements that reflect his or her preference and ends up with a numerical score for each of the eight poles. The person's type is then indicated by a four-letter code based on which end of each scale is preferred. There are sixteen possible types with this test, so a person with a pattern of ESTJ (Extroversion, Sensing, Thinking, Judgment) would be highly outgoing and rationally oriented toward life, for example (see Figure 11-9).

This test has a great deal of popular appeal, because people find it personally meaningful. It seems to have high face validity. For this reason it is sometimes used in counselling, education, and public workshops (Carlson, 1989). Many psychologists, however, criticize the MBTI for its lack of established validity and say that it requires a great deal more work before it can be trusted (Healy, 1989). One sign of its popularity is that a French-language version has been developed and standardized in Canada (Casas, 1989).

	Sensing Types		Intuitive Types	
Introverts	**ISTJ** Serious, quiet, earn success by concentration and thoroughness. Practical, orderly, matter-of-fact, logical, realistic, and dependable. See to it that everything is well organized. Take responsibility. Make up their own minds as to what should be accomplished and work toward it steadily, regardless of protests or distractions.	**ISFJ** Quiet, friendly, responsible, and conscientious. Work devotedly to meet their obligations. Lend stability to any project or group. Thorough, painstaking, accurate. Their interests are usually not technical. Can be patient with necessary details. Loyal, considerate, perceptive, concerned with how other people feel.	**INFJ** Succeed by perseverance, originality, and desire to do whatever is needed or wanted. Put their best efforts into their work. Quietly forceful, conscientious, concerned for others. Respected for their firm principles. Likely to be honored and followed for their clear convictions as to how best to serve the common good.	**INTJ** Usually have original minds and great drive for their own ideas and purposes. In fields that appeal to them, they have a fine power to organize a job and carry it through with or without help. Skeptical, critical, independent, determined, sometimes stubborn. Must learn to yield less important points in order to win the most important.
Introverts	**ISTP** Cool onlookers—quiet, reserved, observing and analyzing life with detached curiosity and unexpected flashes of original humor. Usually interested in cause and effect, how and why mechanical things work, and in organizing facts using logical principles.	**ISFP** Retiring, quietly friendly, sensitive, kind, modest about their abilities. Shun disagreements, do not force their opinions or values on others. Usually do not care to lead but are often loyal followers. Often relaxed about getting things done, because they enjoy the present moment and do not want to spoil it by undue haste or exertion.	**INFP** Full of enthusiasms and loyalties, but seldom talk of these until they know you well. Care about learning, ideas, language, and independent projects of their own. Tend to undertake too much, then somehow get it done. Friendly, but often too absorbed in what they are doing to be sociable. Little concerned with possessions or physical surroundings.	**INTP** Quiet and reserved. Especially enjoy theoretical or scientific pursuits. Like solving problems with logic and analysis. Usually interested mainly in ideas, with little liking for parties or small talk. Tend to have sharply defined interests. Need careers where some strong interest can be used and useful.
Extraverts	**ESTP** Good at on-the-spot problem solving. Do not worry, enjoy whatever comes along. Tend to like mechanical things and sports, with friends on the side. Adaptable, tolerant, generally conservative in values. Dislike long explanations. Are best with real things that can be worked, handled, taken apart, or put together.	**ESFP** Outgoing, easygoing, accepting, friendly, enjoy everything and make things more fun for others by their enjoyment. Like sports and making things happen. Know what's going on and join in eagerly. Find remembering facts easier than mastering theories. Are best in situations that need sound common sense and practical ability with people as well as with things.	**ENFP** Warmly enthusiastic, high-spirited, ingenious, imaginative. Able to do almost anything that interests them. Quick with a solution for any difficulty and ready to help anyone with a problem. Often rely on their ability to improvise instead of preparing in advance. Can usually find compelling reasons for whatever they want.	**ENTP** Quick, ingenious, good at many things. Stimulating company, alert and outspoken. May argue for fun on either side of a question. Resourceful in solving new and challenging problems, but may neglect routine assignments. Apt to turn to one new interest after another. Skillful in finding logical reasons for what they want.
Extraverts	**ESTJ** Practical, realistic, matter-of-fact, with a natural head for business or mechanics. Not interested in subjects they see no use for, but can apply themselves when necessary. Like to organize and run activities. May make good administrators, especially if they remember to consider others' feelings and points of view.	**ESFJ** Warm-hearted, talkative, popular, conscientious, born cooperators, active committee members. Need harmony and may be good at creating it. Always doing something nice for someone. Work best with encouragement and praise. Main interest is in things that directly and visibly affect people's lives.	**ENFJ** Responsive and responsible. Generally feel real concern for what others think or want, and try to handle things with due regard for the other person's feelings. Can present a proposal or lead a group discussion with ease and tact. Sociable, popular, sympathetic. Responsive to praise and criticism.	**ENTJ** Hearty, frank, decisive, leaders in activities. Usually good in anything that requires reasoning and intelligent talk, such as public speaking. Are usually well informed and enjoy adding to their fund of knowledge. May sometimes appear more positive and confident than their experience in an area warrants.

SOURCE: Reprinted with permission from Myers (1984).

FIGURE 11-9 Myers-Briggs Type Indicator: The characteristics frequently associated with each type

Empirical criterion keying

The most widely used objective personality tests were developed through **empirical criterion keying**. This is a test development procedure in which large numbers of items are chosen on the basis of whether they discriminate clearly defined groups from each other in preliminary testing. One problem with this approach is that one must have an accurate way to define the two groups to be tested. For example, if we want a test of depression, we could test a group of depressed subjects and a group of non-depressed subjects. But how do we determine who is in which group in the first place? We probably would use very extensive diagnostic procedures including self-report, expert opinion, and behavioural observations. Even then, the validity of the test we are developing is dependent on the validity with which we set up our original test groups.

In empirical criterion keying, it is interesting that the test developers don't really care what the test items say, as long as they work. If we want a test to identify reckless drivers, we could try hundreds of questions on groups of good and bad drivers. If good drivers tend to answer "true" to "I think the universe is essentially random" and bad drivers tend to answer "false," we will use the item and not care about why the item discriminates the two groups.

In the development of personality tests, however, the comparison is usually made between individuals within specific psychiatric categories versus "normals." The best known example of this approach is the **Minnesota Multiphasic Personality Inventory (MMPI)**. The MMPI is the most widely used objective personality test. Its items were empirically derived to discriminate psychiatric patients from non-patients. It contains a number of subscales to print actual test items. It was developed in the early 1940s by Hathaway and McKinley (1943). These investigators collected over 1000 true-false, self-descriptive statements and administered them to a group of individuals considered normal (mostly hospital visitors) and to patients. The patients had been diagnosed as having specific psychiatric problems, based on the psychiatric diagnostic categories in use at that time. Statistical analyses determined which items were answered in a particular way by individuals in the different diagnostic categories, in contrast to the normal control group.

Scales were derived for ten different diagnostic categories (see Figure 11-10). The developers also developed four validity scales to check on the accuracy of the subjects' responses. These validity

FIGURE 11-10 Table describing MMPI clinical scales and sample items

1. Hs (Hypochonriasis). Thirty-three items to identify patients with unusual concern over bodily symptoms. ("I notice the speed of my heart several times a day." Answered true.)
2. D (Depression). Sixty items that differentiate patients with overwhelming hopelessness, sad affect, and lethargy. ("I approach life with enthusiasm." Answered false.)
3. Hy (Conversion hysteria). Conversion hysteria refers to physical symptoms with no physical cause. Sixty items contribute to this scale. ("Under stress, my hands often go numb." Answered true.)
4. Pd (Psychopathic deviate). Fifty items from patients who show little feeling for others, emotional shallowness, untrustworthiness, damaging actions toward others, and inability to learn from experience. Such patients respond primarily to immediate gratification and are now referred to as "anti-social personalities." ("I am often in trouble with others who are mad at me." Answered true.)
5. Mf (Masculinity-feminity). Sixty items that differentiated men and women in the original test sample. ("I enjoy watching sports." True for masculinity and false for femininity.)
6. Pa (Paranoia). Forty items that identified patients who were abnormally suspicious or had delusions of grandeur. ("People frequently watch me in public places." Answered true.)
7. Pt (Psychasthenia). Forty-eight items that identify those who tend to be fearful, indecisive and obsessive. ("I seldom worry about a job once I finish it." Answered false.)
8. Sc (Schizophrenia). Seventy-eight items that describe patients with bizarre thought patterns, social withdrawal, hallucinations and delusions. ("I sometimes smell things that others cannot." Answered true.)
9. Ma (Hypomania) Forty-six items that tend to be chosen by patients who are extremely excitable, act in highly energized ways, and think in fleetingly unpredictable ways. ("I often just can't sit still." Answered true.)
10. Si (Social introversion). Seventy items from shy, insecure persons. ("I have no trouble meeting new people." Answered false.)

SOURCE: Reprinted with permission from The Psychological Association.

scales were designed to detect faking bad (malingering) and faking good. They seem to work quite well (Gillis, Rogers, & Dickens, 1989).

There have been over 90 foreign language translations of the MMPI (Butcher, 1984), and research studies using this instrument accumulate at the rate of several hundred per year. A review by Butcher and Keller (1984) found that 84% of research articles published on objective personality assessment between 1972 and 1977 used this 40-year-old instrument.

Factor analytic development

Factor analysis is a statistical procedure that correlates many variables with each other and groups variables into clusters (factors) that occur together. A large number of self-descriptive questions are administered to many people. Factor analysis then finds groups of items which tend to be answered in the same way. Subjects who choose "I like flower arranging" might also tend to select "Good art can't be described in words" and "Human experience goes beyond the limits of science." Because they tend to be chosen together, these items would load on the same factor. The same subjects might tend to reject items such as "If it's not logical, it's not worth doing." These rejected items would also be included in the factor but would have a negative loading on it. This means that a failure to choose the item would raise one's overall score on the factor. It might be that an item such as "I like vegetables" did not correlate, positively or negatively, with the other items at all. This item would not be included in the factor. The test developer looks at all the items that cluster into a factor and tries to give the factor a meaningful name such as "experience-oriented versus intellectualizing" (for the example we have been discussing).

Factor analysis has been used in the development of several personality tests. The best known is the Sixteen Personality Factor Questionnaire (16PF) (Cattell, Eber, and Tatsuoka, 1970). This inventory yields 16 scores on personality dimensions, such as reserved versus outgoing, humble versus assertive, shy versus adventuresome, and trusting versus suspicious. In Chapter 10, we discussed Cattell, a leading trait theorist. The 16PF grew out of his efforts to develop a list of human traits. This test is often used to assess nonclinical populations. It is sometimes used in clinical settings but much less often than the MMPI (Butcher and Keller, 1984).

Projective techniques

The rationale for projective techniques is based primarily on psychoanalytic theories of personality, which we discussed in Chapter 10. These theories stress the importance of internal dynamics, conflicts, and motivations in determining our behaviour and our personalities. In responding to an ambiguous stimulus, the individual is thought to reveal personal characteristics. Internal dynamics, motivations and conflicts are presumably *projected* onto the ambiguous stimuli. Have you ever noticed how different individuals see different things in clouds? It is this kind of experience on which projective techniques were developed. In order to enhance an individual's projection in

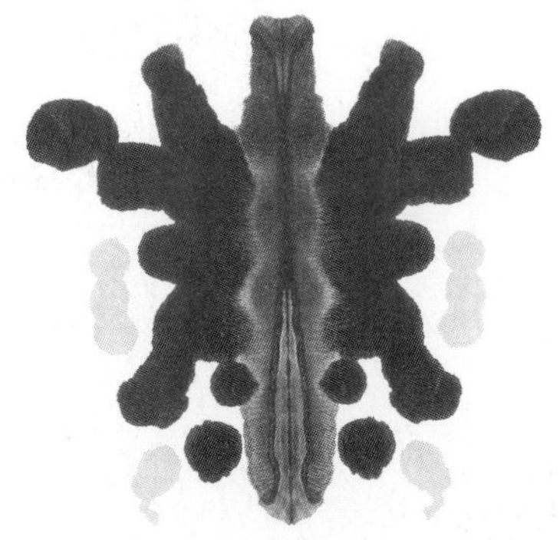

FIGURE 11-11 An inkblot resembling those used in the Rorschach test

these tests, instructions tend to be brief and vague. The way an individual interprets the test material or structures the situation is thought to reflect fundamental aspects of psychological functioning. Because there are no right or wrong responses, projective techniques are also thought to be less susceptible to conscious distortion than are objective tests.

Perhaps the best known projective technique is that developed by Hermann Rorschach (1921). The **Rorschach test** is a projective test in which a subject is presented with a series of ambiguous inkblots and asked to say what they look like. It is the most widely-known "ink blot test." In the original development of the technique, Hermann Rorschach experimented with a large number of ink blots (see Figure 11-11) which were administered to different psychiatric groups. He made careful clinical observations to determine the response characteristics that differentiated the various psychiatric syndromes under study.

Many scoring systems were subsequently developed. These systems considered different aspects of the subject's responses, such as: Which parts of the blot were used? Was colour or shading important in the response? How unusual was the response? Administering and scoring the Rorschach is heavily dependent upon the skill, training, and experience of the examiner.

The **Thematic Apperception Test (TAT)** is a projective test in which a subject is presented with a series of ambiguous pictures and is asked to tell a story about each picture. Test materials consist of 19 cards containing vague pictures (see Figure 11-12). The person is asked to indicate what led up to the event shown in the picture, describe what is happening at the moment, what the characters are feeling and thinking, and what the anticipated outcome might be. Normative data generated by research provide a general framework for interpreting individual responses. However, most clinicians rely heavily on their own "subjective norms" built up through their training and experience with the test. The TAT, like most projective techniques, is heavily reliant upon the skills of the clinician.

There are several advantages and disadvantages of projective techniques. Such tests appear intrinsically interesting, and they can be a good "ice-breaker" in the testing situation. They are less susceptible to "faking" than are self-report inventories, although they are not immune. On the other hand, they depend heavily on the skill and experience of the clinician. There is a general lack of norms for such tests, and it is difficult to assess their reliability and validity.

FIGURE 11-12 Card 12F from the Thematic Apperception Test

The examinee is asked to make up a story about this picture. As with the Rorschach, it is assumed that the individual's response reflects his or her own feelings, needs, and thoughts.

NEUROPSYCHOLOGICAL ASSESSMENT

Neuropsychology is concerned with brain-behaviour relationships. **Neuropsychological assessment** is assessment based on testing procedures designed to clarify the relationship of brain function, brain damage, and brain disease to intellectual and behavioural functioning. Neuropsychological assessment probably began many centuries ago when individuals noticed that people who had suffered damage to the brain also displayed behavioural changes. The investigation of these behavioural changes accelerated with the study of soldiers suffering bullet wounds to the brain during the First and Second World Wars.

This clinical investigation of individuals suffering brain injury was soon augmented with psychological testing. In many cases tests developed for other purposes were used in these early assessments. The first systematic psychometric investigations of brain damage began with Ward Halstead in the 1930s. He used an empirical validation approach. He administered a number of tests to individuals with brain impairment and to individuals without brain impairment, in an effort to determine which tests reliably differentiated these two groups (Halstead, 1947). The result was the development of a battery of ten tests. One of Dr. Halstead's students, Ralph Reitan, extended and elaborated this test battery, deleting some subtests and adding others. This resulted in the **Halstead-Reitan Neuropsychological Test Battery**, probably the most widely researched and used battery in North America for the assessment and description of brain damage and its effects on behavioural and intellectual functioning.

Since the 1960s, the use of neuropsychological assessment has grown rapidly. This has resulted in new research and in the development of new tests and test batteries (Stambrook, Hawryluk and Martin, 1987).

A neuropsychological assessment can be used to plan a rehabilitation strategy for a brain-damaged individual. It can help in making decisions about the best type of placement or accommodation for such a person. It can also play a part in legal decisions such as determining an individual's competence in managing his or her affairs.

A natural outgrowth of the process of neuropsychological assessment is the emerging field of *cognitive remediation*. **Cognitive remediation** is any treatment program designed to retrain people affected by brain damage or brain disease in the use of their intellectual abilities. Neuropsychologists use information related to brain functions and the behavioural data from assessments to design treatment programs for recovery from such brain damage. Since neuropsychological tests are based on the condition of the brain, a neuropsychologist must have a good background in neuroanatomy and neurophysiology, as well as the training in behaviour and assessment provided in most programs of psychology.

There are special problems in test construction that are unique to the field of neuropsychology. For example, individuals who undergo neuropsychological assessment may have severe physical disabilities, cognitive impairment, or a combination of the two. Thus, they may be extremely difficult to assess with the usual psychological instruments. We said earlier that psychological tests must be administered in a standardized way. With individuals suffering brain impairment, this is not always possible. The clinician must be aware of whatever deviations from standardization apply in a particular instance, in order to interpret the results properly. Sometimes, individuals have physical impairments preventing the use of their hands, or severe language impairments called *aphasia*, which prevent

Recovering stroke patients can be retrained to use their intellectual abilities through cognitive remediation.
SOURCE: Courtesy of the Riverdale Hospital, Toronto.

verbal communication. An individual may be blind, have a very short attention span, be uncooperative, or suffer from wide fluctuations in mood. Sometimes the clinician must deviate from standard procedures in an effort to come up with an accurate assessment.

VOCATIONAL ASSESSMENT

Psychological tests are also used to help people with vocational planning. **Vocational assessment** is the use of tests and other measures to evaluate an individual's interests, abilities, and personality characteristics. Such assessments may be used to help individuals make vocational decisions or to help companies to make personnel decisions. On the individual side, we are all faced with the prospect of choosing a career, a decision which may influence the rest of our lives. It is a complex decision which will influence future plans in many aspects of our lives, including our education. From industry's point of view, there may be considerable expense in hiring and training individuals. Vocational testing is used to facilitate good hiring and advancement decisions.

Individual vocational assessment

"What do you want to do when you grow up?" This question is often asked of us from the time of our preschool years. It is a question with which we wrestle for a good portion of our lives. Even when we are settled in an occupation or career, we may wish to change directions in the future. Vocational assessment is directed toward assisting us with these decisions.

Many factors enter into occupational choices. Some are personal and not measured by psychological tests. For example, we may be influenced by our parents' occupations, the expected income we can tolerate, and job availability. But there are some factors, such as abilities and interests, that can be assessed by testing.

Ability testing

It is important that we have a realistic appraisal of our assets as we make our occupational decisions. Intelligence is only one of these factors. We may also have more specific aptitudes or abilities in certain areas. For example, we might have good manual dexterity but lack mechanical aptitude. Over the years, many specific tests have been developed to assess these abilities. Among the more widely used instruments that serve this purpose are the General Achievement Test Battery and the Differential Aptitude Tests. The **General Achievement Test Battery (GATB)** is a group of ability tests that measure the amount a person has learned in various areas of knowledge. It is more a test of material learned than of intellectual ability. The **Differential Aptitude Tests (DAT)** are a group of tests that measure a person's ability to learn in various areas such as verbal reasoning, numerical ability, and mechanical ability. These can be used to guide our decisions by either giving us a picture of our relative strengths and weaknesses or by comparing us with specific occupations which demand a certain minimal level of ability in a particular area.

Interest testing

Satisfaction in an occupation is only partly based on being able to do the work. Personal *interests* are also important. Tests have been developed to compare a person's interests with the interests of individuals who are successful and satisfied in specific occupations. A popular example of this type of test is the **Strong-Campbell Interest Inventory (SCII)**. In developing such tests, items relating to school subjects, occupations, and activities were administered to individuals in various occupations and occupational groups. By the method of empirical validation, items were chosen which discriminate successful members of different occupations from each other. As with all uses of empirical validation, face validity of the items is not considered important. For example, if in the original standardization sample most bankers answered "yes" to "I like to handle money," the item was included in the test. If a subject also answered yes to this question, that person would get a point on the "banker's scale," for fairly obvious reasons. On the other hand, if there were a question such as "I like to arrange flowers," which was also answered "yes" by most bankers, it would also be included in the "banker's scale."

Institutions and vocational assessment

Organizational psychologists often develop and use tests to select applicants for a job or to fit individuals into specific areas within an organization. This process may go beyond testing and may also involve detailed behavioural job analysis. Behavioural analysis is often used to identify problems in job performance or the design of a job. This analysis can help specify modifications needed to increase productivity, worker efficiency, or worker satisfaction.

FORENSIC ASSESSMENT

Another expanding role of psychological assessment is in the area of forensic assessment. **Forensic assessment** is psychological assessment procedures that are used within the legal and court systems. These assessments are made of individuals who have been charged with a legal offence. Forensic assessment attempts to provide further understanding of the individual, specifically with regard to motivations underlying the act.

Forensic psychologists frequently use traditional intelligence or personality measures, but their focus is somewhat different from that of the usual applications of these tests. For example, intelligence and personality assessment may be used to determine whether an individual was able to appreciate the consequences of his or her act. This information may influence the judgment or sentencing. Assessments can also be used to determine fitness to stand trial or competence to advise legal counsel. Neuropsychological assessment may be used to determine whether any particular act was the result of some disorder in brain functioning. Or it might be used to determine whether an individual is likely to benefit from rehabilitation or some form of treatment. It is often important to determine whether an individual is considered dangerous or not, or whether he or she is likely to commit a similar offense in the future. Forensic assessments can also be used to design rehabilitation programs for offenders and to judge their suitability for parole.

SPECIAL TOPIC **Nature Versus Nurture**

It is difficult to determine how much of our intelligence is determined by physiology and genes and how much by our educational and cultural experiences. The controversy over this question is heated, partly because the debate is often based on social or political concerns, rather than scientific evidence. In the 19th century, intelligence was often seen as a reflection of "moral fibre." Specific abilities, however, were generally thought of as being biologically-based. Only in the era of the Great Depression did environmental, cultural, and learning influences become more accepted as factors in the development of abilities.

Most psychologists would agree that both genetic inheritance and learning experiences are important in the development of intelligence. They interact with each other. Genetic inheritance may set the limits of our intellectual potential. But whether or not we reach this potential is dependent upon our opportunity to do so, a factor determined largely by our *environment*. Within the limits of our genetic inheritance, intelligence can be increased by a more favourable or enriched environment (e.g. Eysenck and Kamin, 1981; Gottesman, 1963).

Race and intelligence

Particularly in the United States, considerable furore has been caused by arguments that some races are less intelligent than others, based upon lower performance on intelligence tests (e.g. Jensen, 1969, 1973, 1985). Recently, this has also become a Canadian issue, with publicity given to the writing of J. Philippe Rushton (1989a, 1989b), of the University of Western Ontario. Jensen and Rushton both argue that intelligence is largely inherited. Thus, the observation that whites generally tend to score better than blacks on traditional IQ tests could be attributed to racial differences in intelligence. Jensen says that **associative learning** encompasses rote memory, attention, simple reasoning skills, and short-term memory. He asserts that the races are approximately equal in this kind of intelligence. However, he says that caucasians are better than other racial groups at **cognitive learning**, which includes abstract thinking, verbal problem solving, concept formation, and symbolic thought.

Jensen's arguments are based on two assumptions. He presents data showing 1) IQ is primarily genetic and 2) whites do better on measures of intelligence. Critics have vigorously attacked both assumptions.

Jensen and his supporters estimated the proportion of intelligence determined by genetics at 80% (Loehlin & Nichols, 1976). However, a literature-review done by Henderson (1982) estimated it at about 50%. Most psychologists would accept the second figure as the more accurate one. Jensen's data relied heavily on the work of Sir Cyril Burt (1966, 1972), but Burt's data have been discredited in one of the most dramatic cases of scientific fraud on record. Burt not only manufactured data, he created some fictitious co-authors for his articles. Jensen presents other evidence that indicates that among white children, heredity powerfully influences IQ. For example, identical twins reared apart still have IQ scores more similar to each other than do fraternal twins reared together. Although we need to understand how this can be true, Jensen's critics can still say that genetics only accounts for about half of the development of intelligence.

An exaggerated example might clarify the point. If we took 100 caucasian children and reared them all in identical enriched environments with equal training, then any differences among them in running speed would be largely the result of genetic differences. We could rear another 100 caucasian children in identical small cages with only subsistence needs met. Any differences in running speed among these children could also be primarily attributed to genetic differences. For both groups, the environment was held constant for all members of the group, so any differences would be due largely to genetic differences. Thus, we could present strong evidence for the heritability of running speed. But it would be absurd to conclude that since nearly all of the first group could run faster than all of the second group, the second group was genetically inferior in running speed. Jensen's evidence for the heritability of intelligence is almost all taken from within homogeneous groups such as middle-class white children. Thus he can argue that intelligence is highly heritable because he is comparing children from one fairly homogenous environment. But, as with running speed, intelligence is based on a genetic potential which may or may not be reached, depending on the environment. It is not appropriate to compare children from different environments on intelligence and say that the differences are the result of genetics.

To date, the best understanding we can gain from the evidence is that while a particular cultural group may score lower on intellectual tests, this is not because of any genetic or biological inferiority. As we've said before, the interactive model suggests that our genes determine our "upper limits." Whether we reach this potential largely depends on our environmental and educational opportunities.

White children do typically perform better on IQ tests than black children. However, critics point out that the tests are biased toward whites, and that they only measure a small portion of what can reasonably be included in intelligence. Virtually all traditional IQ tests have been standardized on samples that included disproportionately few disadvantaged subjects. In Figure 11-13, you can test your own IQ on the Dove Counterbalance Intelligence Test, which Adrian Dove designed to be culturally unfair to middle-class whites (1968).

Finally, it is worth commenting on Rushton's ideas, which go far beyond racial differences in intelligence. He says that persons of Oriental descent are superior in intelligence and social organization and are low in aggressiveness and sexual behaviour. Caucasians are at medium levels in these characteristics, and blacks are low on intelligence and social organization and high on aggressiveness and sexual behaviour (Rushton, 1989a, 1989b). Rushton argues that these differences are the result of genetic differences. His ideas have aroused passionate argument. They obviously have enormous political and social implications. His arguments are complicated and extensive. We can't cover them all, but it is important to note that the vast majority of social scientists reject them. We have covered some of the arguments against his reasoning in this discussion, but a debate between Rushton and Lynn (1989a, 1989b) can give a more complete picture. Lynn makes several points. Rushton cites relevant literature in a selective and biased way. He misrepresents both theory and data from other writers. He applies many inappropriate findings from lower animals to humans. And finally, the race differences predicted by his hypothesis can be explained by environmental causes.

FIGURE 11-13 The Dove Counterbalance Intelligence Test

Adrian Dove wanted to make the point that most intelligence tests favour middle-class caucasians, so he constructed this test. Find out what your IQ is by taking this test. Unless you are black and grew up in a particular setting, you might be depressed by your results.

Almost everyone is curious about how they would score on an intelligence test. If you would like to get a rough estimate of your IQ, take the following self-administered test.

Dove Counterbalance Intelligence Test

Time limit: 5 minutes
Circle the correct answer.

1. T-bone Walker got famous for playing what?
   a. trombone *b.* piano *c.* T-flute
   d. guitar *e.* "hambone"

2. A "gas head" is a person who has a
   a. fast-moving car *b.* stable of "lace"
   c. "process"
   d. habit of stealing cars
   e. long jail record for arson

3. If you throw the dice and 7 is showing on the top, what is facing down?
   a. 7 *b.* snake eyes *c.* boxcars
   d. little joes *e.* 11
4. Cheap chitlings (not the kind you purchase at a frozen-food counter) will taste rubbery unless they are cooked long enough. How soon can you quit cooking them to eat and enjoy them?
   a. 45 minutes *b.* 2 hours
   c. 24 hours
   d. 1 week (on a low flame)
   e. 1 hour
5. Bird or Yardbird was the jacket jazz lovers from coast to coast hung on
   a. Lester Young *b.* Peggy Lee
   c. Benny Goodman *d.* Charlie Parker
   e. Birdman of Alcatraz
6. A "handkerchief head" is
   a. a cool cat *b.* a porter
   c. an Uncle Tom
   d. a hoddi *e.* a preacher
7. Jet is
   a. An East Oakland motorcycle club
   b. one of the gangs in West Side Story
   c. a news and gossip magazine
   d. a way of life for the very rich
8. "Bo Diddly" is a
   a. game for children
   b. down-home cheap wine
   c. down-home singer *d.* new dance
   e. Moejoe call
9. Which word is most out of place here?
   a. splib *b.* blood *c.* gray
   d. spook *e.* black
10. If a pimp is uptight with a woman who gets state aid, what does he mean when he talks about "Mother's Day"?
    a. second Sunday in May
    b. third Sunday in June
    c. first of every month
    d. none of these
    e. first and fifteenth of every month
11. How much does a "short dog" cost?
    a. 15¢ *b.* $2 *c.* 35¢
    d. 5¢ *e.* 86¢ plus tax
12. Many people say that "Juneteenth" (June 19) should be made a legal holiday because this was the day when
    a. the slaves were freed in the United States
    b. the slaves were freed in Texas
    c. the slaves were freed in Jamaica
    d. the slaves were freed in California
    e. Martin Luther King was born
    f. Booker T. Washington died
13. If a man is called a "blood," then he is a
    a. fighter *b.* Mexican-American
    c. Negro *d.* hungry hemophile
    e. red man or Indian
14. What are the Dixie Hummingbirds?
    a. a part of the KKK
    b. a swamp disease
    c. a modern gospel group
    d. a Mississippi Negro paramilitary strike force
    e. deacons
15. The opposite of square is
    a. round *b.* up *c.* down
    d. hip *e.* lame

Answers: **1.** *d* **2.** *c* **3.** *a* **4.** *c* **5.** *d* **6.** *c* **7.** *c* **8.** *c* **9.** *c* **10.** *c* **11.** *c* **12.** *b* **13.** *c* **14.** *c* **15.** *d*

If you scored 14 on this exam, your IQ is approximately 100, indicating average intelligence. If you scored 11 or less, you are mentally retarded. With luck and the help of a special educational program, we may be able to teach you a few simple skills!

SOURCE: Dove (1968). Reprinted with permission from *Newsweek* (July 1968), pp. 51-52.

1. Psychological tests are methods psychologists use to put judgments of others in measurable, sometimes numerical form. The first stage in the process of describing behaviour is assessment, the collecting of data for the purpose of understanding an individual. The assessment process begins with the need to observe behaviour and is guided by the assessment question. In psychological assessment, the more specific the question asked, the more specific the answer can be. Errors in assessment can be of two types: false positive and false negative.

2. Assessment techniques which use formal tests are called psychometric approaches. Behavioural assessment uses naturalistic

observation. Clinical assessment is a general process that uses many different assessment methods, including psychometric tests and behavioural observation.

3. Psychological tests are standardized behavioural observations. These observations are used to make inferences or statements about an individual and to predict some future behaviour or event. This is done by comparing the observations made on the individual to some kind of reference group. It is critical, before making such comparisons, to find out about the population on which the test was standardized. A person's test results cannot be valid if the person is not a member of that population. The scores obtained from the standardization sample during the development of the test are called the norms of the test.

4. One of the most important characteristics of a test is its reliability, the stability or repeatability with which it measures people. An unreliable test will yield markedly different scores under different circumstances and is useless. There are several kinds of reliability: test-retest, alternate-form, split-half, inter-scorer, and inter-rater reliability.

5. A second critical characteristic of a good test is its validity, the ability of a test to measure what it claims to measure. A good test will have several kinds of validity: content, criterion, concurrent, and construct validity. Face validity is not essential.

6. Intelligence can be broadly defined as the ability to learn and to adapt existing knowledge to new situations. Since the beginning of this century, several tests of intelligence have been developed, and most use an Intelligence Quotient (IQ) as a comparative measure of intelligence. An IQ of 100 is established as the norm for the average person in the population on whom the test was developed.

7. Intelligence tests have been criticized as being culturally biased. Even the definition of "intelligence" is determined differently in different cultures and social classes. Some theorists argue that there is a G (general) intelligence factor, while others suggest that intelligence is made up of several independent factors. One such theory proposes seven kinds of intelligence or primary mental abilities. IQ tests only measure one definition of intelligence. It is sometimes said sarcastically that intelligence is whatever intelligence tests measure.

8. Personality tests fall into two categories (1) projective tests, which use ambiguous stimuli to which subjects respond in a free-form manner and (2) objective tests, which require a structured way of answering.

9. Objective personality tests are self-report inventories which are dependent on structured scoring and interpretation. They have been developed through analytical approaches (the MBTI, for example), through empirical criterion keying (the MMPI), and through factor analysis (the 16PF).

10. Projective tests assume that the ambiguous stimulus (such as an inkblot or vague picture) will lead the subject to structure his or her response according to internal needs, motives, and perceptions. It is argued that this kind of responding is less vulnerable to conscious distortions.
11. Neuropsychological assessment measures brain-behaviour relationships. This is a rapidly growing area in psychology, and several test batteries have been developed to assess the nature and severity of various kinds of neuropsychological disorders.
12. Psychological testing is also used in vocational assessment where it can assist an individual in making a vocational choice or an employer in making a personnel decision. Tests assess an individual's abilities and/or interests.
13. Forensic assessment is used by the legal system to determine the motivation and responsibility of an alleged offender.

KEY TERMS

Alternate-form reliability A measure of the degree to which different versions of the same test correlate with each other.

Analytical approach The least sophisticated method of test development, in which the test developer simply makes up items judged to test the quality to be measured. It depends heavily on face validity.

Assessment The process by which psychologists make judgments about human functioning by quantifying various kinds of performance.

Associative learning Learning that encompasses rote memory, attention, simple reasoning skills, and short-term memory.

Behavioural assessment Assessment based on methods that focus on observing behaviour, rather than determining internal traits.

Binet-Simon Scale The first published intelligence test, designed in France to identify retarded children.

Chronological age One's physical age as measured by the calendar.

Clinical assessment The process of using a wide range of measures to answer questions with implications for treatment of psychological disorders. The process starts with a referral question, continues with the gathering of data, and finishes with recommendations for action.

Cognitive learning Learning that encompasses abstract thinking, verbal problem solving, concept formation, and symbolic thought.

Cognitive remediation Any treatment program designed to retrain people affected by brain damage or brain disease in the use of their intellectual abilities.

Concurrent validity A measure of the degree to which a test correlates with other tests designed to assess the same quality.

Construct validity A measure of the degree to which a test is consistent with the theoretical notions (constructs) to which it is supposed to be related.

Content validity A measure of the degree to which a test contains a fair balance of items from each area of the body of knowledge it is designed to test.

Criterion validity (also called *predictive validity*) A measure of the effectiveness of a test in predicting an individual's behaviour or performance in specified situations.

Differential Aptitude Tests (DAT) A group of tests that measure a person's ability to learn in various areas, such as verbal reasoning, numerical ability, and mechanical ability.

Domain (of behaviour) The entire set of behaviours from which a sample of behaviours is drawn in behavioural assessment.

Empirical criterion keying Test development procedure in which items are chosen on the basis of whether they discriminate clearly defined groups from each other in preliminary testing.

Face validity A measure of the degree to which a test has the appearance of assessing what it is supposed to assess.

Factor analysis Statistical technique that correlates many variables with each other and groups variables into clusters (factors) that occur together.

False negative errors (also called *Type 2 errors*) In assessment, the error of saying something is not the case when it is.

False positive errors (also called *Type 1 errors*) In assessment, the error of saying something is the case when it isn't.

Forensic assessment Psychological assessment procedures that are used within the legal and court systems.

Frequency distribution A graph in which the number of instances of a particular score are plotted along a line. The graph will be highest where the highest frequency of scores falls.

G-factor General intelligence factor.

Gardner's seven frames of mind The position that there are seven different "intelligences": linguistic, logical-mathematical, musical, spatial, bodily-kinesthetic, understanding oneself; understanding others.

General Achievement Test Battery (GATB) A group of ability tests that measure the amount a person has learned in various areas of knowledge. It is more a test of material learned than of intellectual ability.

Halstead-Reitan Neuropsychological Battery Probably the most widely researched and used battery of tests in North America for the assessment and description of brain damage and its effects on behavioural and intellectual functioning.

Hit rate A measure of the frequency with which a measure accurately predicts performance.

Intelligence The ability to learn and adapt existing knowledge to new situations.

Intelligence quotient (IQ) A measure of a person's intellectual ability relative to a standard population. Average is set at 100.

Inter-rater reliability Measure of the degree to which two or more observers agree when they rate the same behaviour or quality.

Inter-scorer reliability Measure of the degree to which two or more people agree when they score the same test.

Mean The numerical average of a group of numbers.

Mental age Binet-Simon's measurement of a child's intellectual abilities according to the chronological age of children in the standardization group who obtained the same score.

Minnesota Multiphasic Personality Inventory (MMPI) The most widely used objective test of personality; consists of true-false questions the subject answers about him or herself.

Myers-Briggs Type Indicator (MBTI) A personality test based on Jung's theory of personality. It categorizes people into 1 of 16 types, based on scores on the four dimensions: extroversion versus introversion, sensing versus intuitive, thinking versus feeling, and judgment versus perception.

Naturalistic observation A behavioural assessment method in which the subject's behaviour is recorded in the person's usual environment.

Neuropsychological assessment Assessment based on testing procedures designed to clarify the relationship of brain function, brain damage, and brain disease to intellectual and behavioural functioning.

Normal distribution The symmetrical bell-shaped curve that is formed by plotting a large number of individual performances in a frequency distribution.

Norms Test scores established as typical by administering a test to a large sample of subjects from the population of interest.

Objective tests Personality tests with highly structured answering formats for which standardized scoring procedures are used.

Odd/even method One kind of split-half reliability, in which one half is made up of even-numbered items and the other half of odd-numbered items.

Operationalize To describe in terms that are observable and testable.

Population (also called *domain*) A complete set of individuals, items, or data about which knowledge is sought.

Predictive validity Another term for *criterion validity.*

Primary mental abilities Thurstone and Thurstone's development of Thorndike's notion that intelligence is made up of several different mental abilities that do not correlate well with each other.

Projective tests Tests in which an ambiguous stimulus is presented and the subject produces responses, presumably based on projections from within.

Psychological tests Standardized behavioural observations which are usually expressed as test scores.

Psychometric assessment Assessment based on techniques which use formal tests, usually with numerical scoring procedures ("metric" refers to the use of measures).

Reliability The consistency with which a measure yields readings on the quality it purports to measure.

Reliability coefficient A statistic that indicates the degree of consistency of a measure.

Rorschach Test A projective test in which a subject is presented a series of ambiguous inkblots and asked to say what they look like.

S-components The secondary components of Spearman's theory, specific abilities which are subordinate to a general level of intelligence.

Sample (of behaviour) A small number of behaviours that are observed in assessment, on the assumption that they are representative of all the potential behaviours of interest.

Self-report inventories Tests in which the subject answers questions and makes judgments about him or herself.

Split-half reliability The degree to which one half of a test correlates with the other half.

Standard deviation A statistical measure of how much variability there is among the scores in a distribution.

Standardization sample A large sample of subjects from the population of interest who take a test to establish typical scores or norms.

Sternberg's triarchic theory of intelligence The position that intelligence can be grouped into three general kinds: componential intelligence, experiential intelligence, and contextual intelligence.

Strong-Campbell Interest Inventory A popular vocational interest test; matches the subject's personal interests with those of successful people in various occupations.

Test-retest reliability A measure of the degree of consistency between the results of a test given to the same individuals at two different times.

Thematic Apperception Test (TAT) A projective test in which a subject is presented a series of ambiguous pictures and asked to tell a story about each picture.

Type 1 error Another name for false positive errors.

Type 2 error Another name for false negative errors.

Validity A measure of the degree to which a test actually ascertains what it purports to ascertain.

Validity coefficient A statistic that indicates the strength of relationship between a particular measure and some other variable being used to establish that measure's validity.

Validity scales In self-report tests, questions included to detect invalid responding, such as "faking good" or "faking bad."

Vocational assessment The use of tests and other measures to evaluate an individual's interests, abilities, and personality characteristics. Such assessments may be used to help individuals make vocational decisions or to help companies make personnel decisions.

Wechsler Adult Intelligence Scale — Revised (WAIS-R) One of the most commonly used intelligence tests; consists of subtests arranged in verbal and performance (nonverbal) scales.

Suggested Readings

Some of the most interesting and provocative books you might want to read have already been referred to in this chapter—especially those concerning the nature of intelligence.

Anastasi, A. (1988). *Psychological testing*. New York: Macmillan. One of the best-known texts on psychological testing, this book gives a good overview of both the construction and uses of tests.

Gardner, H. (1983/85). *Frames of mind*. New York: Basic Books. This book is one of the most important modern interpretations of intelligence. Gardner reviews older conceptions of intelligence and develops his theory of multiple intelligences. Although written for professionals, the book is readable and interesting for the educated layperson.

Lanyon, R.I., & Goodstein, L.D. (1982). *Personality assessment*, 2nd ed. New York: Wiley Interscience. This text focuses on the measurement of personality, while Anastasi's book is more concerned with assessing cognitive abilities. Both are university textbooks.

Scarr, S. (1981). *Race, social class, and individual differences in IQ*. Hillsdale, NJ: Lawrence Erlbaum Associates. This is a good review of both the theoretical issues surrounding the race and intelligence issue and the research done up to the end of the 70s.

Sternberg, R.J. (1985). *Beyond IQ*. New York: Cambridge University Press.

Sternberg, R.J. (1986). *Intelligence applied*. San Diego: Harcourt, Brace, Jovanovich. Like Gardner, Sternberg is making the point that our definition of intelligence should be broadened. He reviews several conceptions of intelligence and describes his three-part or "triarchic" theory of intelligence. This book is written for the professional reader.

CHAPTER 12

SOURCE: Jamasie, *Inside the Igloo* (1966).

Development Through the Lifespan

THE ONE THING that's certain in life is change. Developmental psychology studies the processes and stages of that change as a person develops from one cell into a complete human being who lives a life and eventually dies. At each age or developmental stage there are special lessons to be learned and tasks to be mastered if the individual is to live an effective life. We hope that this chapter on development will raise a number of thought-provoking questions. Most of us have probably wondered what we would have been like if we had grown up as part of the family across the street or even in a different country. Would we have the same beliefs, attitudes, and feelings? Would we still be the same person? Are we the same person we were 14 years ago? Had we been born into a different family under different circumstances we might not have had the same beliefs or attitudes that we have today. To that extent we might have been a different person. Are we the same person we were 14 years ago? Well, yes and no. Even though every cell in our body has been replaced twice in the last 14 years, we are still the same individual. But we are also different. We have changed and developed through these 14 years, partly because of the process of maturation and partly because of the particular life experiences (good and bad) that we have had.

Sometimes it seems that (both as an individual and as a society) the life issues we are dealing with today are the issues people are supposed to be dealing with. But these weren't the staggering issues of our life a decade and a half ago. For example, 14 years ago, we weren't, as a society, as concerned about the environment as we are today. On an individual level, perhaps 14 years ago some of us were going through the experience of adjusting to kindergarten, while others were experiencing the joy and turmoil of the birth of a child. A few years from now, other issues will be more central in our lives. Understanding the principles of development can help put issues such as these in perspective.

This chapter is loosely divided into three sections. First, we will look at some general concepts about development. Then, several theories about the stages of development will be described. Finally, we will trace the major life changes from birth to death.

Before we look at development itself, we need to examine several general issues that will give us an overview of what follows.

Until fairly recently, it was generally understood that a developmental psychologist was actually a child psychologist. The field paid little attention to growth beyond adolescence. But it is now clear that development is a lifelong process, with significant changes in physical, cognitive, and social development at every stage.

Throughout this chapter we will be interested in the relative importance of what we inherit physically and what we learn — the "nature versus nurture" issue again. We want to understand how much of any particular individual characteristic — personality, height, eye colour, fearfulness—is inherited biologically (nature) and how much is shaped by life-experiences and the environment (nurture). This is one of the most fundamental questions in developmental psychology and one of the most controversial. Some psychologists say that inheritance dominates by controlling the person's **maturation** (the rate and manner of development of an individual's physical potential). Others argue that environment dominates. A person is essentially a *tabula rasa* (blank slate) at birth and what he or she becomes is largely the result of learning. We will see that both of these positions are extreme and that it is necessary to integrate them.

A puppy turns into a dog through a continuous process.
SOURCE: Courtesy Catherine O'Neill.

Up until the early 1900s, it was widely believed that children were essentially small adults. This position argues that development is *continuous*. **Continuous development theories** are theories which state that development is on a continuum of gradual change and is not marked by discrete stages. That is, whatever changes occur are simply changes in complexity rather than in *quality*. In general, this perspective is stressed by those who emphasize learning principles and see development as a gradual process of shaping personality and other behaviour. These theorists focus on the *process* of how a person develops. For example, they would be most interested in *how* a person learns, rather than in the specific *content* of that learning.

Throughout this century an alternative view has been advocated, the view that behaviour develops in distinct stages, with dramatic qualitative differences between these stages. A kitten turns into a cat through a continuous process; a caterpillar turns into a butterfly through a stage process. Stage theorists focus on the *content* of the person's development.

Stage theories argue that each person passes through the same stages in the same sequence. The timing of each stage might be different for different individuals, but the order of stages is the same. Each stage presents the person with a task that needs to be mastered or a problem that needs to be resolved for successful growth into later stages. We will be looking at several stage theories in the next section.

Stage Theories of Development

Initially, we will briefly describe some of the most influential stage theories. We will be returning to many of these concepts later in the chapter.

Freud and Erikson on stages of psychosocial development

Freud's theory has been one of the most influential stage theories of this century. You will recall that Freud's argument was that every person (driven by instinctual forces) passes through the same stages of personality development. In Chapter 10 we saw that in Freud's view there are five distinct developmental stages, each with its own issues and tasks:

(1) *Oral Stage* (*from birth to 1½ years*) The focus is on feeding issues.

(2) *Anal Stage* (*from 1½ to 3 years*) Toilet functioning is central.

(3) *Phallic Stage* (*from 3 to 6 years*) Sexual development has important implications for the individual and for family relations.

(4) *Latency Stage* (*from 6 years to puberty*) Sexual interest is dormant and environmental skills are developed.

(5) *Genital Stage* (*puberty*) The focus is on moving toward sexual and emotional attachments outside the family.

Freud argued that the conflicts of each stage must be successfully resolved before moving on to the next stage or else an individual could become fixated at an early stage. **Fixation**, in Freudian theory, is the tendency for a certain amount of psychic energy to remain attached to and tied up in the unresolved problems of an earlier developmental stage. For example, a child who has not passed successfully through the phallic stage will probably not resolve his or her Oedipus complex and will still feel hostility toward the parent of the same sex. While later theorists saw some merit in Freud's notion of developmental stages, many of them could not agree with his stress on specific sexual issues and behaviours.

Figure 12-1 illustrates that Erikson's stages are similar to Freud's, both in ages and in general themes. However, Erikson describes a person's emotional tasks both in terms of relationships with others and with his or her own feelings. Erikson also extended the developmental stages into adulthood. It is important to remember that, for Erikson, each of these stages must be successfully resolved to lay the groundwork for the next stage. His stages and the approximate ages involved are as follows:

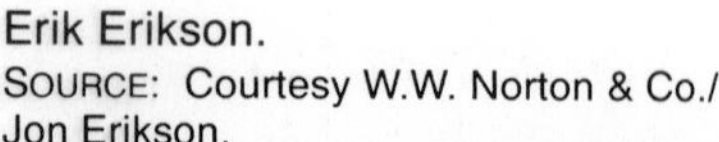
Erik Erikson.
SOURCE: Courtesy W.W. Norton & Co./ Jon Erikson.

(1) *Basic trust versus basic mistrust* (*from birth to 1½ years*) During this time, the infant is learning a basic attitude that will colour his or her life—a sense of whether or not the world is a dependable, trustworthy place. This sense of trust comes from having comfortable, predictable, and dependable love and care. It can only be called an attitude (rather than a belief) because the child is not equipped to store the memory of its experiences in verbal and conceptual terms. A failure to develop an attitude of trust will result in a sense of insecurity and anxiety.

(2) *Autonomy versus shame and self-doubt* (*from 1½ to 3 years*) During this time, the child develops a sense of control over self and environment. The gaining of this control often centres on the task of learning toilet control. The advent of walking (which also happens during this time) leads to the

remarkable discovery that "I have power to make things happen." A failure to gain this sense of autonomy leads to feelings of helplessness and inadequacy to control life's events.

(3) *Initiative versus guilt* (*from 3 to 6 years*) At this stage, it is not enough simply to have autonomous control. The child goes beyond that stage to create and initiate events. Failure to move in this direction will lead to feelings of low self-worth.

(4) *Competence versus inferiority* (*from 6 years to puberty*) In this stage, the child enters the world of intellectual and social achievement, and develops a sense of skill. Not doing so leads to low self-confidence and feelings of failure.

(5) *Identity versus role confusion* (*adolescence*) The adolescent needs a clear sense of him or herself as a unique individual, separate from parents, with a well-defined identity. Without this, the person will have a fragmented, changing self-view.

(6) *Intimacy versus isolation* (*early adult*) The major psychosocial task of this stage is to form intimate bonds with and commit oneself to another person. Failure to do this leads to a sense of loneliness and separation. A destructive denial of the need for intimacy may follow such failure.

(7) *Generativity versus stagnation* (*middle adult*) During these years, the individual focuses on being a productive member of society, creating family, creating achievements, and looking toward the future. Otherwise, the person will be self indulgent and not have a perspective on the future.

(8) *Ego-integrity versus despair* (*later adult*) In later years of adulthood and in old age, facing the end of life, the person develops a sense of having lived a meaningful full life that gives him or her a deep satisfaction. The essence of this sense of integrity seems to be self-acceptance. The meaningfulness of life includes a good feeling about oneself and a sense of fellowship with men and women of all ages. The person develops wisdom, which Erikson defines as a combination of knowledge and mature judgment. Otherwise, the person feels disappointment, regret, and futility. Despair is marked by a sense of not having lived well and not having time to change things. There is a hopelessness about the quality of one's life. The inevitability of death is difficult to accept.

Figure 12-1 Freud and Erikson's stage theories of development According to Freud, as children proceed from one stage of life to the next they adjust their view of the world. If a child has not successfully passed through a stage, fixation occurs. According to Erikson, a person must master each developmental stage successfully in order to deal fully with subsequent stages.

SOURCE: Adapted with permission from Allyn and Bacon, 1989.

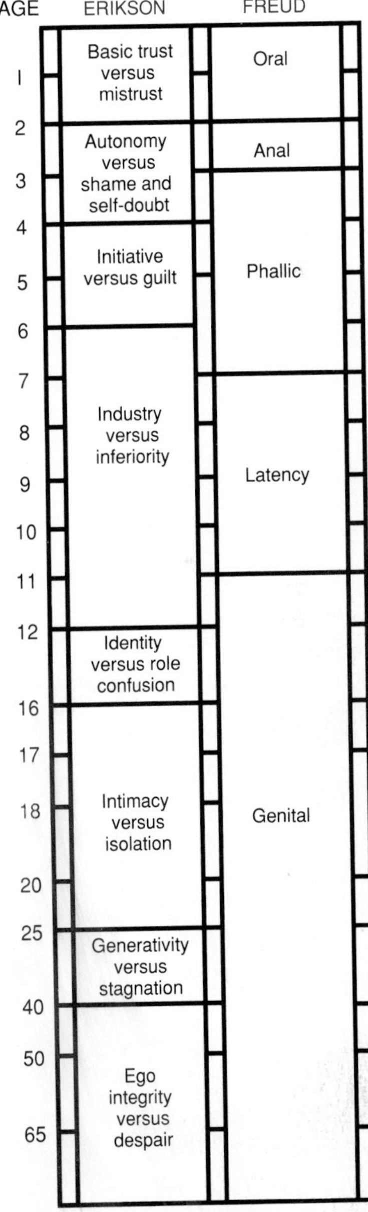

Evaluating Erikson

Many people are attracted to Erikson's stage theory because it "feels right" in describing life tasks. However, it is a difficult theory to test empirically. Concepts such as "ego integrity" are difficult to define in a way that can be studied.

A more telling criticism has been that Erikson's stages are limiting and sex-biased. Such criticism says that his stages emphasize instrumental tasks to the detriment of nurturing and relationship tasks. In the past, such instrumental tasks were thought of as typically male and the nurturing tasks were thought of as typically female. Even though Erikson does stress the importance of intimacy in young adulthood, in general his theory places far more emphasis on independence and competence. (We will evaluate these *traditional gender roles* in Chapter 18.) Gilligan (1982) has been critical of the narrowness of this formulation. She says, "Although the initial crisis in infancy of 'trust versus mistrust' anchors development in the experience of relationship, the task then clearly becomes one of individuation." She argues that Erikson stresses individual achievement, competence, and industry as the central tasks for human development and neglects nurturance and relationship tasks. His key terms are "autonomy, initiative," and "industry" for the developing child.

> Next comes adolescence, the celebration of the autonomous, initiating, industrious self through the forging of an identity. . . . But about whom is Erikson talking?
>
> Once again it turns out to be the male child. For the female, Erikson (1968) says, the sequence is a bit different. She holds her identity in abeyance as she prepares to attract the man by whose name she will be known, by whose status she will be defined, the man who will rescue her from emptiness and loneliness by filling 'the inner space'. . . .
>
> Yet despite Erikson's observation of sex differences, his chart of life-cycle stages remains unchanged: identity continues to precede intimacy as male experience continues to define his life-cycle conception (Gilligan, 1982, p. 12).

Piaget on stages of cognitive development

In studying cognitive development, we want to understand how a person learns to think, remember, solve problems, predict future events, and develop expectations and hopes. In this field, close attention has been paid to cognitive development in childhood, when change is the most rapid. The person who has contributed the most to our understanding of the development of children's cognitive processes is the Swiss psychologist, Jean Piaget (1930, 1952, 1967, 1972). His remarkable formulations were derived partly from his intensive study of his own children's thinking processes. While most researchers design controlled experiments to study one or two specific phenomena in groups of subjects, Piaget studied a few children in great depth. His approach was to give them a cognitive problem to solve and observe how they seemed to solve it. He then would modify the task slightly to tease out subtle differences in problem-solving approaches. Piaget's theories were based primarily on this intensive study of a few children (including his own children). Later in his life he also studied larger groups of children at his Centre of Genetic Epistemology in Geneva.

Jean Piaget.
SOURCE: UPI/Bettmann Newsphotos.

Assimilation, accommodation and schemas

Piaget said that the child was engaged in two interwoven processes as he or she approached new learning. **Assimilation**, the first of these cognitive processes, enables the child to take in new information and fit it in with existing conceptions. **Accommodation**, the second of the cognitive processes, enables the child to change or accommodate current conceptions when new information contradicts them. (See Figure 12-2.) For instance, when a child first sees porpoises swimming in a large tank of water, he or she interprets this information within existing mental frameworks and labels them "fish." This is an example of assimilation. Later, the child learns that porpoises breathe air and like to be petted. As a result, he or she forms a new concept for air-breathing but water-loving animals. This is an example of accommodation.

At many places in this book we encounter the concept of schemas. Piaget was one of the earliest theorists to discuss the importance of schemas in thinking. A **schema** is an organized, complex expectation we hold about the nature of reality. Schemas help us deal with the world efficiently. A schema is like a stereotype, a blueprint, or a generalized picture of how we learn to expect the world to be. Schemas start as simple expectations, such as a "sucking activity" schema in a very young child and become very complex in later years. For example, we all have powerful schemas for what is "masculine" and "feminine," or what is "religious."

Assimilation, accommodation, and schemas operate at all ages, but different ages are marked by very different modes of thinking. Often it is hard to imagine what it is like to think as a child. Whether we mean to or not, we frequently interact with a child as though he or she were a miniature adult who's just a little less bright than most adults we know. One of Piaget's most important contributions is his insight that we need to look differently when we look through a child's eyes. Children hear that babies start from seeds and grow in women's tummies. Then they are afraid to eat sunflower seeds. Or they stand staring at the ocean looking for the "undertoad" the adults keep warning them about. Or they think that death is "just sleeping" and so they are terrified to go to bed. Try to understand the child's world through each of the cognitive stages Piaget proposes. Keep in mind that the age ranges given are only approximate. Piaget would say that everybody goes through the stages in the same order but at different rates.

Sensorimotor stage (birth to 2 years)

The young child interacts with the world through direct contact, rather than through more symbolic or abstract ways. What exists for the child is what can be seen, touched, sucked, and stomped on. The child's two main tasks are to develop adaptive responses and to develop object permanence. **Adaptive responses** are behaviours that manipulate the environment. Initially, the child knows only simple relationships such as that turning the head is often related to finding food. During the second year of life, he or she learns to manipulate the environment more and more and can develop fairly complex goal-oriented adaptive responses. Near the end of the second year, the child is starting to represent objects symbolically and is able to extend adaptive responses beyond situations that must be seen and touched. Throughout this period, there is a growing understanding of object permanence. **Object permanence** is the concept that objects

FIGURE 12-2 Assimilation and accommodation in cognitive development
Assimilation refers to the tendency to fit new information into existing frameworks. Accommodation is the tendency to alter existing concepts or mental frameworks in response to new information.
SOURCE: Reprinted with permission from Allyn and Bacon, 1989.

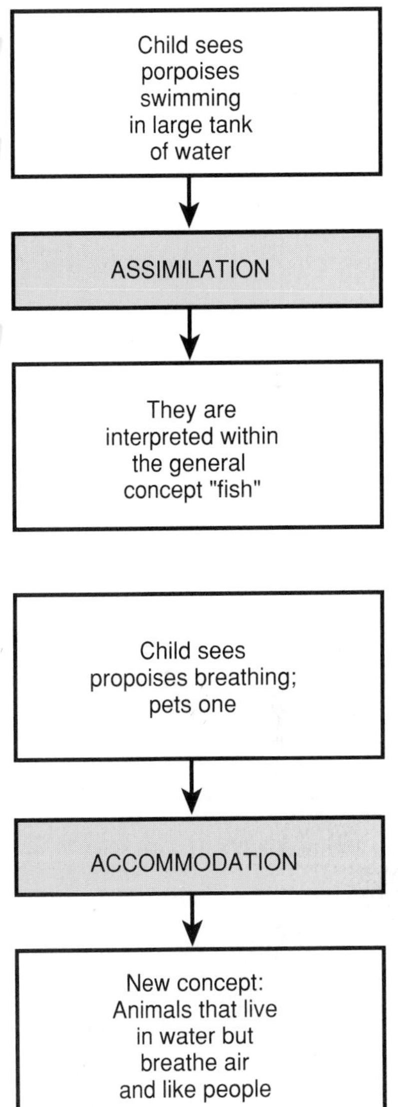

exist even if they are hidden from view. At about eight months, if we put a doll under a blanket the child will look for it at least for a few seconds. Within a few months, the child will go searching even if restrained for a few seconds after the doll is hidden. At about the same time and largely because of the development of object permanence, the baby shows **stranger anxiety** (which is distress the infant shows at strange faces). "Making strange" often appears quite suddenly, much to the distress of aunts, uncles, and grandparents. The baby seems to have developed schemas for the faces that are permanent to him or her, and their loss is upsetting.

Preoperational stage (2 to 7 years)

Object permanence helps the child learn to think symbolically or representationally. Objects can be represented by words and other symbols. This symbolic thinking is still *pre*-operational, however, because it is centred around how things appear, rather than around rules of thinking. Early in this period the child is learning that some people are girls and some are boys and that it is important to remember which of these one is. Interestingly, boys are taught this more strongly, but that discussion is for another chapter (Chapter 18). One boy we know was shown pictures of various persons, including himself. He was very clear that he was a boy. However, when the interviewer put a picture of a dress over his picture and asked, "If I put a dress on you would you be a boy or a girl?" the boy was clearly upset. He said, "I'd be a girl, but I'm not a girl. I'm a boy." He knew that objects are permanent but not that some qualities of objects are permanent (sex, race, eye colour), and some qualities are impermanent (mood, size, hair length, dress), an important rule of cognition.

The child is also ego-centric at this age. **Ego-centric** refers to the child's perspective that he or she is at the centre of the universe perceptually. This does not mean that the child is self-centred. He or she does not know that others see objects differently because they are in different positions. The child is at the centre of reality. Piaget (Piaget & Inhelder, 1967) showed children a three dimensional model of a mountain scene and asked what a teddy bear on the other side would see. Only near the end of the preoperational stage could children "look through another's eyes" and speculate on what the teddy bear might see. Using simple and more familiar stimuli, however, other researchers have found children able to do this kind of task at younger ages (Borke, 1975). In many cases, it appears that Piaget underestimated the mental abilities of younger children.

An important mental operation the child has difficulty with at this stage is **conservation**. This is the ability to take into account more than one dimension of an object. If we give a child two identical balls of clay, he or she will know that they are the same amount. However, if we roll one ball out into a "snake," the non-conserving child will now say that the long thin piece has more clay, even though it is the same piece as before. Similarly, we can take two identical glasses of liquid. The child will know they are the same amount, until we pour one into a tall thin glass, which will now be "more" to the child. (See Figure 12-3.)

Concrete operations stage (7 to 11 years)

Once one has learned rules of thinking, logic is possible. The person can perform mental operations by mentally manipulating relationships, reversing relationships previously thought, and forming new connections. This logical thinking, however, tends to be concrete. It deals with real objects and relationships rather than with hypothetical and abstract relationships. Concrete operations permit the child to comprehend concepts such as mathematical transformations. Now the child can recognize that objects that have been transformed in some way, such as by undergoing a change in shape or placement, remain the same objects and represent the same amount of weight or volume. Conservation becomes possible for the child because he or she can perform the necessary operations mentally. The child begins to discover rules and understand the reasons for them. In a typical conservation task, a child is shown two beakers: one short, squat and half-full of water, the other tall, thin, and empty. The experimenter pours the water from the short beaker into the tall beaker and asks the child which beaker had more water. A child who does not understand the principles of conservation will claim that the taller beaker has more. A child who is able to *conserve* volume will recognize that the same water was in both beakers and therefore the amount of water in both beakers is equal.

FIGURE 12-3 The concept of conservation

During the concrete operations stage children discover rules and understand the reasons for them. The hallmark of this stage is conservation: the ability to recognize that objects that have been transformed in some way, such as by undergoing a change in shape or placement, remain the same objects and represent the same amount of weight and/or volume.

SOURCE: Reprinted with permission from Allyn and Bacon, 1989.

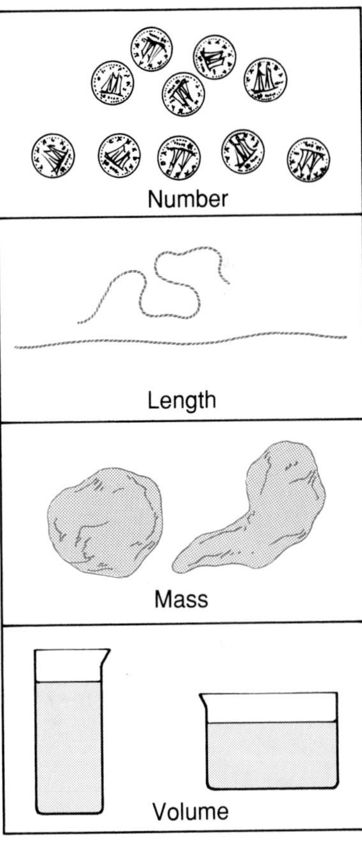

Formal operations stage (11 and older)

Finally, the adolescent and adult are able to think abstractly as opposed to the concrete way children reason about specific observations. Adolescents and adults can develop complex rules that govern even philosophical debate. For example, young children explain that a nail sinks because it is heavy and a block of wood floats because it is light. They become confused when shown that the block of wood is heavier than the nail. Older children extract the principle that both weight and size must be considered in relation to each other to determine whether an object will float.

Evaluating Piaget

Piaget is still the most influential thinker on the nature of children's cognition, even though his basic work was done many years ago. However, there are some criticisms of his work. One criticism is that he ignores the great variation among children, even though he may have described the average child quite well. Piaget described the stages of development as occurring within fairly narrow age ranges, but some children are able to understand conservation much younger than 7, for example, and some adults have trouble with the concept. Some researchers (Selman, 1980; Botvin & Murray, 1975) have found that many children can perform mental tasks at younger ages than Piaget said, especially when the problems are designed to use situations and objects familiar to the child (Borke, 1975). Smolucha and Smolucha (1986) have also suggested that there might be a "fifth Piagetian stage," in which logical thinking and highly imaginative mental processes are integrated in artistic creativity.

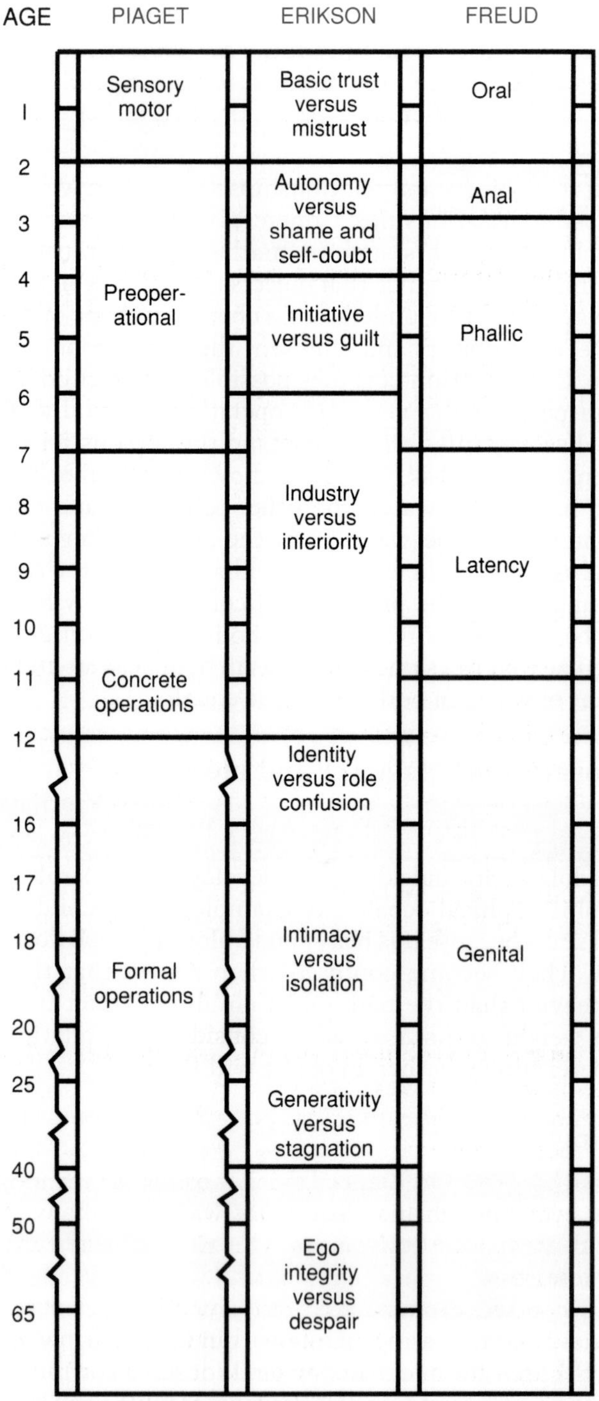

FIGURE 12-4 Stage theories of development: Freud, Erikson, and Piaget

AGE: 1, 2, 3, 4, 5, 6, 7, 8, 9, 10, 11, 12, 16, 17, 18, 20, 25, 40, 50, 65

PIAGET	ERIKSON	FREUD
Sensory motor	Basic trust versus mistrust	Oral
Preoperational	Autonomy versus shame and self-doubt	Anal
	Initiative versus guilt	Phallic
Concrete operations	Industry versus inferiority	Latency
Formal operations	Identity versus role confusion	Genital
	Intimacy versus isolation	
	Generativity versus stagnation	
	Ego integrity versus despair	

The fundamental issue that still divides Piaget from many learning theorists is whether, as Piaget believes, there are great leaps in ability (stage theory), or whether there is simply an accumulation of more and more knowledge (continuous development). Piaget believed that mental growth occurs in large qualitative changes, as opposed to steady quantitative changes in complexity. Piaget argued that the child at one stage simply could not think in ways typical of higher stages, no matter how much training the child was given. Each stage marked a different *kind* of thinking, rather than simply a different *amount* of ability. He said that changes from one stage to another depend on the child maturing and these changes happen fairly quickly. This issue (whether advancement in learning occurs in discrete stages or in continuous development) is unresolved.

Freud and Erikson developed stage theories for psychosocial development. Piaget's stage theory deals with cognitive development. The theories are similar in that they argue that development progresses in sudden, qualitative changes or stages. According to stage theorists, these stages always occur in the same order, although the ages at which they begin varies from person to person. Figure 12-4 compares the stage theories of Freud, Erikson, and Piaget.

Kohlberg on stages of moral development

Finally, we will look at the theory that a person's moral reasoning develops in stages, as proposed by Lawrence Kohlberg (1964, 1973, 1981). He originally suggested moral development occurs in six stages and has more recently added a seventh stage that appears very rarely among humans (see Figure 12-5). As with other stage theories, an individual goes through these stages always in the same order. However, Kohlberg's stages are not linked to particular ages. Nor are they inevitable in an individual's life. In fact, several writers, including Kohlberg, argue that most people in our society rise no further than Stage 3 or 4, the level of conventional morality. This theory has three levels of moral development, and each level has stages within it.

FIGURE 12-5 Kohlberg's theory of moral development

SOURCE: Adapted with permission from Allyn and Bacon, 1989.

Level I–Preconventional

Stage 1	avoid punishment
Stage 2	gain rewards

Level II–Conventional

Stage 3	meeting expectations of important people
Stage 4	fulfilling duties, upholding laws

Level III–Postconventional

Stage 5	importance of social contracts and individual rights and relativity of rules
Stage 6	self-selection of overriding ethical principles
Stage 7	universal or cosmic orientation

First, largely in childhood, we find **preconventional morality**. Morality is based on avoiding punishment and gaining rewards. It centres around immediate gratification rather than social principles. In Stage 1, moral decisions are based on avoiding discomfort and not getting caught — on obedience and punishment. In Stage 2, the "right" thing to do is whatever brings the most rewards and pleasure. The person's morals are hedonistic (to get pleasure) and instrumental (based on rewards).

The second level is **conventional morality**. Morality is based on being good and following rules. Moral guidance now comes from within rather than from outside the individual. The first stage of this level (Stage 3) is centred around getting acceptance and avoiding disapproval—the "good child" orientation. The second stage of this level (Stage 4) is the one that most adults seem to reach and not to go beyond — the "law and order" orientation. Much emphasis is placed on obedience to authority and to following rules.

The third highest level is called **postconventional morality**. Principles, rather than rules, guide moral thinking. This is the level

Lawrence Kohlberg.
SOURCE: Harvard University/Office of News & Public Affairs.

at which the individual begins to take the intentions and opinions of others into account. In Stage 5, the principles of making social contracts and of the importance of individual rights might be invoked to put aside some rules as unjust or immoral. It is this kind of morality that underlies the welfare of the society in general. In Stage 6, the person is guided by overriding ethical principles about the nature of justice. Kohlberg has added a seventh stage to this level, but it is rare among humans. Stage 7 could be called a universal or cosmic orientation, in which the person follows universal principles that rise above even social norms.

Evaluating Kohlberg

There is considerable evidence that Kohlberg's theory can be quite useful. It has given us a good framework for conceptualizing morality. He set the stage for understanding children's moral reasoning and laid the groundwork for a great deal of research on morality. However, Kohlberg's work has also been criticized in some specific ways. For example, it is hard to apply his theory reliably (Rosen, 1980). It has been shown that subjects' moral judgments can be quite variable in different situations, a variability which Kohlberg's scoring system smooths over (Krebs, et al., 1989).

Recent work at Simon Fraser University and the University of British Columbia has revealed important differences between how people score on Kohlberg's tests of morality and what they do in real-life situations. Kohlberg's testing procedure asks what a person should do in hypothetical situations. When researchers asked subjects what they would actually do, people tended to report that they would act at an even higher level than demanded by their moral obligation. However, they tended to say that others would act at a lower level. The researchers called this a *self-righteous attributional bias* (Denton, Krebs, & Carpendale, 1989). When faced with real-life situations, subjects actually tended to make lower-level moral judgements than they did to Kohlberg's hypothetical situations (Carpendale & Bush, 1989; Schroeder, 1989; Vermeulen & Denton, 1989).

A major problem with Kohlberg's system, as with Erikson's, seems to be a built-in sex bias. (This is a problem with many psychological theories, by the way. There has been an unfortunate tendency for psychologists—mostly male—to define what is typically male as the same as what is typically human.) With the two levels of "conventional morality," for example, the "lower" level is seen as more typical of women's orientation toward interpersonal factors such as approval. The "higher" one is seen as more typical of the traditional male emphasis on rules and authority. Both are conventional and not based on principles, but who is to say which one is higher? Even more difficult, men's socialization has emphasized (at least in the past) independence while women's has tended to stress interdependence. According to these stereotypes, men might consider it "higher" morality to stick to abstract principles even when it hurt individuals' well-being. Women might consider it "higher" to think of compassion and fairness (Loevinger & Knoll, 1983; Gilligan, 1982).

THE BEGINNINGS

We have discussed how a person develops in different ways—cognitively, psychosocially, and morally. Now we will look at each age period to cover some general issues that have not come up in the specific theories of development. We will have the most to add about the earliest ages.

Almost no modern psychologist thinks that a baby is a true *tabula rasa*, or "blank slate." Even the most behaviourally-oriented psychologists say that genetic inheritance places limits on how a person might develop. At the other end of the spectrum, some theorists say that a great deal of what we are interested in psychologically is inherited. The story of development starts long before birth.

Conception and genetics

Characteristics from our biological mother and father are passed on to us via our genes. Each cell in the body contains between 30 000 and 100 000 genes. **Genes** are the inherited genetic information for specific physical characteristics. They are carried in chains on chromosomes. **Chromosomes** are chains of genes. Humans have 46 chromosomes arranged in pairs (23 from each parent).

In each pair, one chromosome was inherited from the father and one from the mother. Thus, every cell in the body has these 23 pairs of chromosomes except for the **germ cells** or reproductive cells,

FIGURE 12-6 Each parent contributes half of a child's genetic material

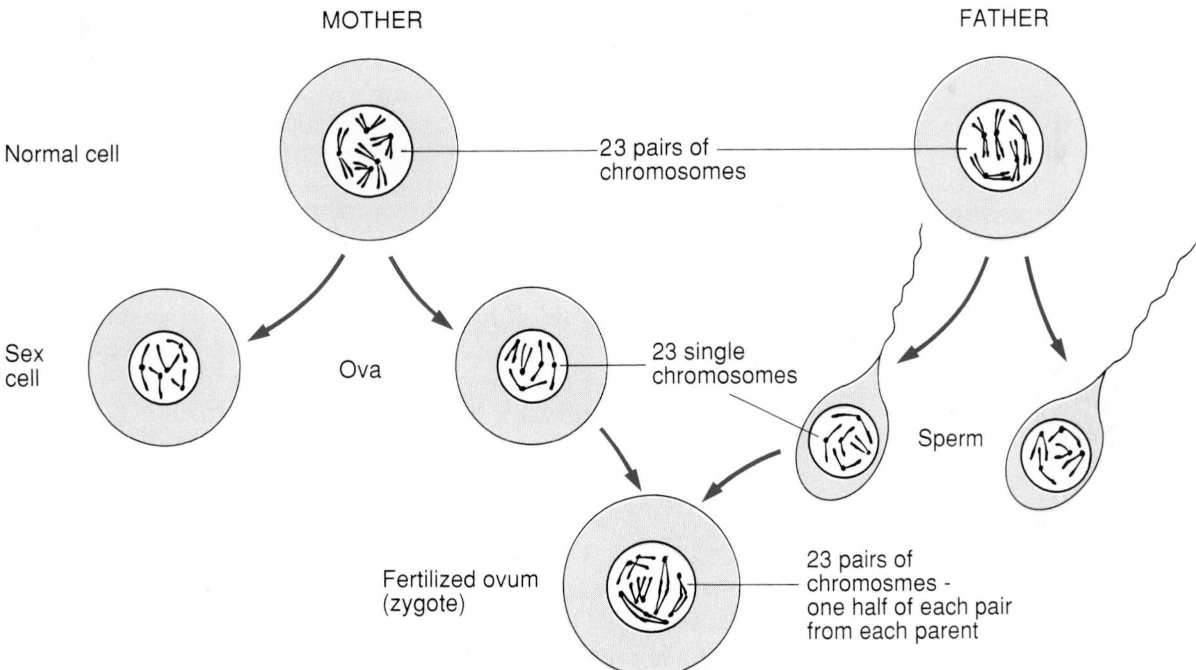

SOURCE: Adapted with permission from Allyn and Bacon, 1989.

the ova and the spermatozoa. During the cell division that produces these cells, each chromosome pair splits so that each ovum or sperm cell has only 23 single chromosomes. When a sperm cell from a man joins with the ovum from a woman, fertilization occurs. In the fertilized ovum (now called a zygote), the 23 single chromosomes from the mother are paired with those from the father. Thus each parent contributes half of their child's genetic material. (See Figure 12-6.) The number of genetically different offspring that a single couple could produce is astronomical. Each parent can produce over eight million genetically different sperm or ova. Together, a single couple has the *genetic* potential to produce over *70 trillion* unique offspring.

Dominant and recessive characteristics

While it is simplest to think of physical characteristics as being transmitted by having one gene for eye colour and another for, say, pain threshold, in most cases this is too simple. Most inherited characteristics are **polygenic**, that is, they are the result of the complex interactions of many different genes. Eye colour, however, is largely controlled by one gene pair, so we can use its simplicity to explain dominance and recessiveness in genes. Remember that in each chromosome pair, one chromosome is from the mother and one from the father. The pair of chromosomes link together so that the eye colour gene from the mother is linked to the eye colour gene from the father. Each gene is linked with its counterpart. Some genes are dominant. **Dominant genes** are genes for characteristics that will be expressed in the person, whether the gene it is paired with is the same or different. Thus, if one parent has contributed a dark-eye gene, the child will have dark eyes, regardless of the colour contributed by the other parent, because dark eye colour is dominant over light. Only if both parents have contributed a light-colour gene will the child have light-coloured eyes. In this case, two *recessive genes* will have been paired up. **Recessive genes** are genes for characteristics that will be expressed in the person only if paired with another recessive gene for the same attribute. With the pairing of two recessive genes, the light colour will not be suppressed by a more dominant gene. Normally, then, two blue-eyed parents will always have blue-eyed children, because we know that the parents can have only blue-colour genes. The eye colour of the offspring of brown-eyed parents is less predictable. A brown-eyed parent might have two brown-eye genes or might have one brown-eye gene and one blue-eye gene. In both cases the parent will have brown eyes because brown is dominant. In the second case, however, half of the parent's egg or sperm cells will contain a blue-eye gene and half will contain a brown-eye gene. Thus two brown-eyed parents could have a child with two blue-eye genes and thus with blue eyes.

Sex-linked characteristics

One of the chromosome pairs is the sex chromosome pair. It is the only pair of chromosomes that differs in males and females. This chromosome pair determines the child's sex and carries sex-linked characteristics. In the female, the sex chromosome pair looks like other pairs. It is called an XX chromosome, as opposed to the male's, which is called an XY chromosome. (See Figure 12-7.) In the male, the Y chromosome is not homologous with (doesn't look like) the X chromosome. In fact, the Y chromosome carries very little genetic information. Thus, in the male's sex chromosome pair, the genetic information on the X chromosome is far more likely to be expressed. This fact is the basis for understanding sex-linked characteristics. During cell division, the mother's sex chromosome pair divides so that every ovum contains a complete X chromosome. In the father, cell division leaves half of the newly formed sperm with an X chromosome and half with a Y chromosome. If the new baby results from one of the first half it will get two X chromosomes and become a girl. If one of the other sperm cells gets to the egg first, the new human will have a Y chromosome from the father combined with the X chromosome from the mother and become a boy.

The important issue for our discussion is that many characteristics are carried on the X chromosome and therefore are inherited along sex-linked lines. The genetic inheritance of colourblindness is an example of a sex-linked characteristic. It is common in males and uncommon in females. It is a *recessive* characteristic, so it won't be expressed if it is paired with the opposite dominant gene. In the female, even if she inherits a gene for colour-blindness from one parent, it is extremely unlikely that she will also get one from the other parent. She won't be colour-blind, but she will be carrying a gene for colour-blindness. However, if the male inherits this gene from his mother, because it is on the X chromosome, the Y chromosome from his father won't contribute any opposing gene, and he will be colour-blind. Thus, if the mother's father is colour-blind, there is a chance that the mother's sons will be also.

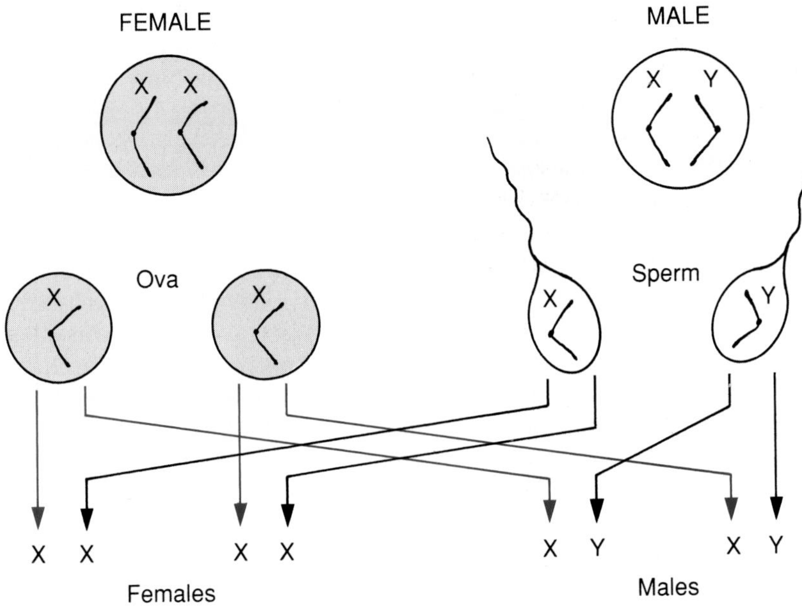

SOURCE: Reprinted with permission from Allyn and Bacon, 1989.

FIGURE 12-7 The genetic determination of sex
Females have two X chromosomes (XX). Thus, all the ova that a woman produces will contain an X chromosome. Males, meanwhile, have an X and a Y chromosome (XY). When a man's sex chromosomes divide, half the sperm contain an X chromosome and the other half a Y chromosome. A Y-bearing sperm produces an XY fertilized ovum, and therefore a male child. An X-bearing sperm produces an XX fertilized ovum, and therefore a female.

Nature versus nurture

We now return to a very basic issue that we have already discussed. People often ask questions such as, "Is intelligence the result of inheritance or environment?" or "Is temperament inherited?" The most sensible answer seems to be that the effects of inheritance and environment cannot be disentangled from each other. We seem to inherit **genetic boundaries** which are physical limits that set an upper and lower limit on an individual's growth and development. What happens within those boundaries is a function of environmental influences. Some genetic boundaries are very wide and some are very narrow. A quality such as a "lovingness" might well be influenced somewhat by inherited temperament but be strongly influenced by experience, while eye colour might have narrow boundaries. To change eye colour through environmental influence would take massive intervention such as injecting pigment-inhibiting chemicals. But it could be done.

Inheritance and environment interact

The important principle is that nature and nurture *interact*. The clearest example might have to do with temperament. At birth, babies differ dramatically in how emotionally responsive they seem to be. If we took two babies with different thresholds for reacting to pain and followed them from birth to adulthood, we would probably discover that the one who felt the most pain grew up to be more fearful. But we could not conclude that "fearfulness" was inherited. What was inherited was a *genetic predisposition* to feel pain more easily. **Genetic predisposition** is an inherited weakness or strength that makes it more likely for one person to develop a particular characteristic (for example, a disease or personality trait) than another. It would have been possible to raise the babies differently, so that the one who felt pain the most easily was given a safe, loving environment and the other one a pain-filled frightening environment. As adults, their patterns of fear would be reversed. Now what can we say was inherited? Genetic inheritance certainly is important. However, at least with humans, it is unlikely that psychological characteristics are inherited. Physical predispositions are inherited and interact with experience.

One of the most dramatic illustrations of this was reported by Skeels (1966). He had observed that some babies labelled as "retarded" seemed to make remarkable improvements when some caretaker took special interest in them. He tried to test this idea more systematically. He found 13 very young children in an orphanage. The group had an average IQ of about 65, which is very low. He moved them all to a home for adult mentally retarded persons as "house guests." Each child was "emotionally adopted" by one of the retarded women who developed an important relationship with the child, with the support of the staff. Thus each child was now getting intense personal love and care from one of the retarded women. Within three years, the group's average IQ was within the normal range. Within five years, 11 of the children had been adopted. Among a comparable group of children who had not been given this new environment, IQ scores dropped dramatically. Many years later, Skeels located all of these children, except one in the comparison group who had died. All of the "house guests" were self-supporting and their average educational level was grade eleven. In contrast, nearly half the comparison group were still institutionalized and they had completed grade four, on average. Eleven of the group that had received special care had married, and their children had IQ scores within the average range. Is "retardation" nature or nurture? Not all kinds of mental retardation would have been affected as much as this, but we must recognize the importance of both inheritance and experience and how they interact.

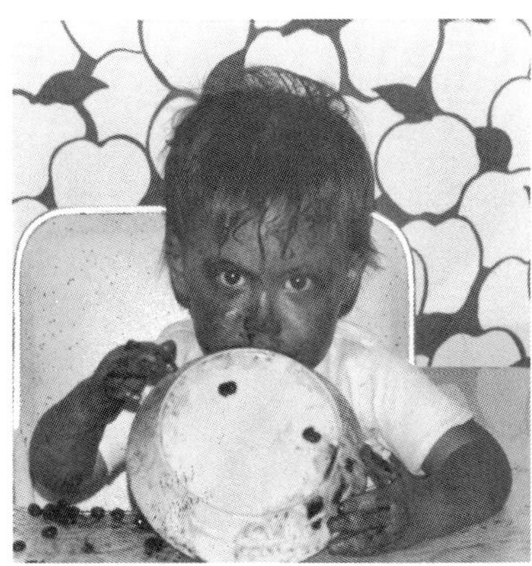

From earliest childhood, one's temperament influences the way one reacts to environmental stimuli.

SOURCE: "Child, Part 2," National Film Board of Canada.

Temperament

Temperament is a collective term that refers to an inborn, general mode of responding to environmental stimulation. Even at birth, there are measurable differences among individuals. About 40% of newborns tend to be "easy children," who show positive mood, regular bodily functions, low or moderately intense reactions, and a tendency to adapt to, rather than withdraw from, new situations (Thomas, Chess, & Birch, 1970; Thomas & Chess, 1977, 1981). At the other end of the continuum are about 10% who are "difficult children." They react harshly to stimuli, withdraw from new situations, have irregular bodily functions, and show considerable negative mood. Other babies seem "slow to warm up" (about 15%). About a third of these babies are difficult to categorize. Researchers have found that babies could be reliably classified by the age of 2 or 3 months. The "difficult babies" tended to have more behaviour problems, at least during the first 10 years of life. Identical twins are more similar in temperament than fraternal twins (Buss & Plomin, 1975; Goldsmith, 1983), and babies of Asian descent are more placid when restrained than are Caucasian or black babies (Freedman, 1979).

This all makes a convincing case that people are "born different," as long as we keep in mind that what has been inherited are physical characteristics such as reactivity to stimuli. A "difficult personality" is not inherited. A "difficult baby" can readily grow up to be a caring, gentle person, just as an "easy baby" can grow up to be mean and lonely.

Twin studies

Researchers have found some cases of spectacular similarity between identical twins who were reared in separate homes. In general, personality tests given to identical and fraternal twins find greater similarities among the identical pairs. However, this could be the result of genetic influences or it could be because identical twins are more likely to be treated in similar ways (Floderus-Myrhed, Pedersen, & Rasmuson, 1980; Loehlin & Nichols, 1976). A more powerful investigative method is to study large groups of identical and fraternal twin pairs, some of whom have been reared together and some reared apart. One such study of over 700 pairs of twins found that genetic factors significantly influenced four personality variables: neuroticism, extroversion, impulsivity, and the avoidance of monotony (Pedersen et al., 1988).

The Jim twins.
SOURCE: Bettmann Archive.

Some researchers have taken advantage of the reunions of adult twins who had been separated from infancy and reported similarities that were so striking that they received widespread publicity (Bouchard, 1984; Holden, 1980a, 1980b). They reported similarities in general personality similar to what other studies had found, and they found individual cases such as the "Jim twins." James Springer and James Lewis were identical twins separated at birth. Not only do they have the same first name, they both had married and divorced women named Linda and then married women named Betty. They chain smoked the same brand of cigarette. Both had dogs named Toy and sons named James Alan and James Allen. Both had basement workshops, had built white benches around trees in their yards, liked stock car racing, drove Chevrolets, chewed their fingernails excessively and had similar medical histories. Actually, we are even leaving out some of the similarities. Dramatic stuff. Critics, however, argue that if we intensively studied a large number of pairs of non-twins who were similar in age, sex and race, we would eventually find a pair where similar coincidences would apply. In fact, Myers (1989) cites an Associated Press report of two women who were not genetically related. Both were born March 13, 1941, and named Patricia Ann Campbell. They both had fathers named Robert, had two children the same ages, worked as bookkeepers, studied cosmetology, painted as a hobby, and married military men at about the same time. On balance, the data from the study of twins strongly suggests that genetics influence personality development, perhaps more than psychologists used to admit, but we need to view the data cautiously.

Prenatal development

The period of development prior to birth is divided into three stages. For two weeks after conception, the *zygote* is travelling down the fallopian tube toward the uterus, where it will become implanted in the uterine wall. During this journey, cell division is progressing rapidly. This is called the **period of the ovum**. From the third to eighth weeks is the **period of the embryo**. Cells begin to emerge with specialized functions. At about three weeks, the embryo has a recognizable shape and the beginning of vital organs. By the end of the fourth week, a primitive heart is beating, there is a spine with vertebrae, and a nervous system has started to develop. By the end of the embryo stage, the developing baby is about one inch long and has recognizable facial features. The third stage is the **period of the fetus**. It extends from week eight to birth, at week 38. During this period human features become more differentiated and movement can be detected by the third or fourth month, turning into kicks by about the seventh month.

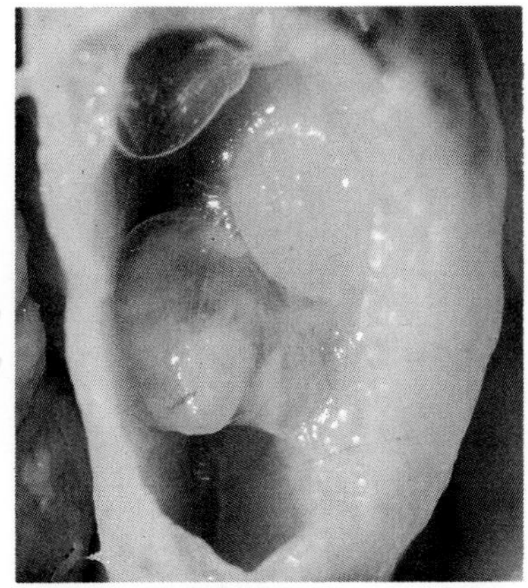

Intrauterine pregnancy of six weeks gestation.
SOURCE: Courtesy of Kernodle Clinic.

The most important environmental influence on prenatal development is the various substances passed from the mother's placenta, through the umbilical cord to the fetus. The fetus is subject to dramatic changes if harmful substances are imposed on it. This is especially true from the third to eighth weeks after conception. Nourishment and oxygen are provided in concentrated form, but so are any other chemicals in the mother's bloodstream. Cigarettes and alcohol are the two most damaging sources of such chemicals because of their common use. Women who smoke are more likely to have underweight babies, sometimes dangerously underweight (Joffe, 1969; U.S. Department of Health and Human Services, 1983). Even relatively light drinking by a pregnant woman can have dramatic effects on the infant. (See Figure 12-8.) *Fetal alcohol syndrome*

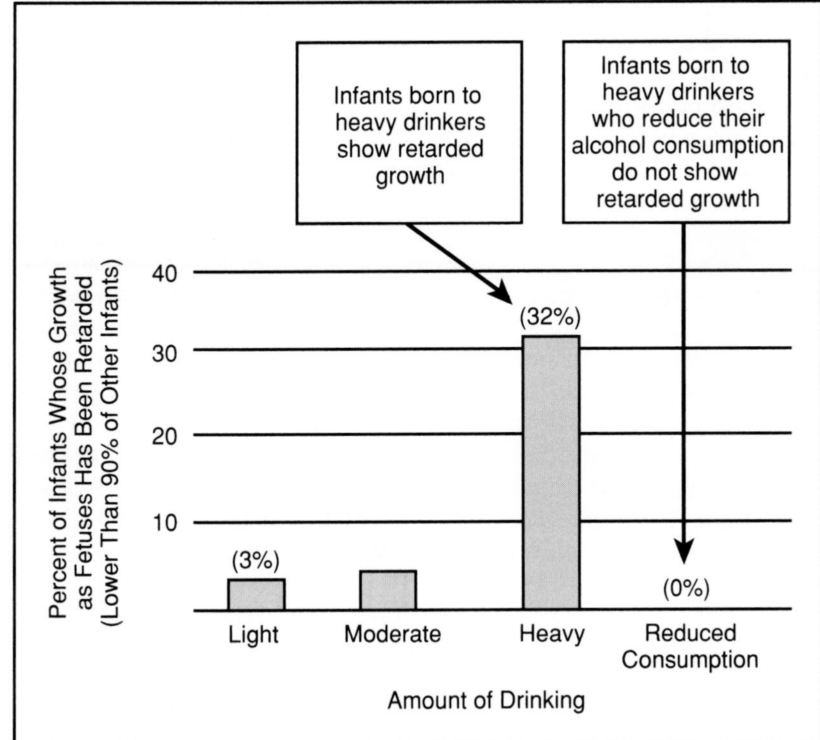

SOURCE: Reprinted with permission from Allyn and Bacon, 1989.

FIGURE 12-8 Effects on the fetus of prenatal alcohol use by mother
According to a study conducted by Rosett and Weiner in 1985, women who are heavy drinkers (consume more than 4 ounces of alcohol per day) have babies whose growth is retarded relative to the babies of women who are light or moderate drinkers (one ounce of alcohol or less per day). However, if mothers who are heavy drinkers reduce their consumption of alcohol, the damaging effects on the fetus are reduced.

can result in premature birth; retardation; and deformities of the heart, face and fingers.

Learning can also take place during the last month or so of the prenatal period (Munn, 1965). Fetuses can be conditioned to kick at certain sounds, for example. This should be no surprise, however, since an infant born prematurely at, say, seven months certainly can learn.

THE CHILD AT BIRTH

One of our single colleagues once remarked to a class how it distressed him to see perfectly rational people become completely illogical when they had a baby, which was obviously little more than a "blob of protoplasm." Until fairly recently, his view was shared by most people, who thought of infants as senseless reactors to the environment. "They don't notice anything the first six months anyway, so it doesn't much matter what you do with them then." With new ways of studying infants' abilities, we are discovering they are quite capable, alert, and very affected by their experiences from the beginning.

The infant brain

At birth, the infant has already developed nearly all the nerve cells it will ever have, but these nerve cells are not finished growing. The myelin sheath that covers neurons is not fully developed at birth, and the connections among neurons—the neural networks that enable us to perform complex acts—are not well formed. Parts of the brain are genetically "committed" to what they will do (as we said in Chapter 2). However, the cortex, where most of what we call thinking occurs, is fairly unstructured (Penfield, 1969).

We now know that *experience structures the cortex.* Evidence from animal studies has shown that animals raised in stimulating environments have more complex networks of neural connections—more axons, dendrites, and synaptic connections—than similar animals raised in dull environments (Rosenzweig, 1984; Rosenzweig, Bennett, & Diamond, 1972). In addition, well-used, specific areas of the brain develop while unused areas tend to degenerate (Greenough & Green, 1981). Humans have immature, still-growing brains at birth. It seems that both physical maturation and experience are essential for the brain's continued growth. Perhaps we should all buy our babies good mobiles. Better yet, we should make it one they can influence (see Figure 12-9).

There is evidence that the most stimulating environment, which is most effective in promoting cognitive development, is one in which the infant's behaviour has tangible effects. Three sets of babies were used to test this hypothesis (Watson & Ramey, 1972). The babies whose head movements caused a specially constructed mobile to rotate learned to move their heads, and they continued to do so when tested two weeks and six weeks later. They had learned the contingency between head-turning and mobile movement. When the babies in the second group were later given the opportunity to make the mobile move by turning their head, they readily learned to do so. However, the babies for whom the mobile had moved randomly on its own did not learn to control it. It was as if they had learned that nothing they could do affected the movements of the mobile. These results may have implications for infant-rearing practices: many babies reared in unresponsive, unstimulating environments stop trying to affect anything in their environments and become passive and apathetic.

FIGURE 12-9 The importance of early control of the environment An environment in which the infant's behaviour has tangible effects seems to promote cognitive development best.

SOURCE: Adapted with permission from Allyn and Bacon, 1989.

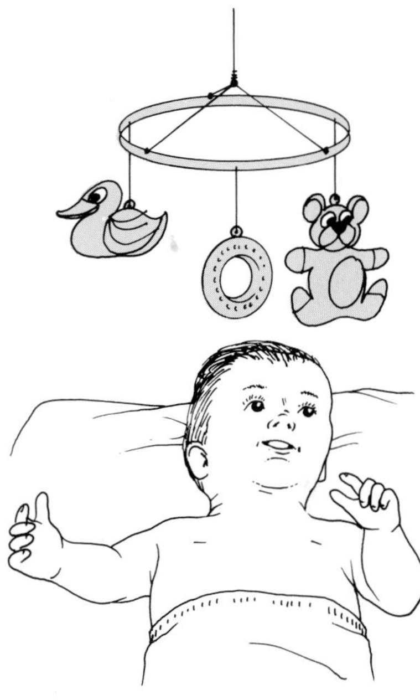

First condition	Later condition
Group A Head turning causes mobile to move. *Babies learn to move head.*	Group A Head turning causes mobile to move. *Babies continue to move head.*
Group B Mobile remains stationary.	Group B Head turning causes mobile to move. *Babies learn to move head.*
Group C Mobile intermittently moves on its own.	Group C Head turning causes mobile to move. *Babies do not learn to move head.*

Perceptual development

In the late 1900s, the famous psychologist William James theorized that, to the baby, the world was just "blooming, buzzing confusion." As we improve our research methods, however, we discover more and more that the baby is built to perform and to perceive in ways that make sense of its world and to draw certain kinds of responses from that world. For instance, the baby seems partly "preprogrammed" for social interaction. He or she kicks and moves more when it hears a female human voice than when it hears a bell (Freedman, 1971). Condon and Sander (1974) even found that infants' movements were synchronized with changes in inflection and content in adults' speech. Shortly after birth, infants can distinguish levels of light and track moving objects with their eyes. Even more interesting, they show a preference for stimuli that look like human faces or human eyes when they have a choice of different patterns. This even holds true when they have a choice between a picture of a face and a similarly shaped picture in which the facial features are incorrectly arranged (Fantz, 1961).

Within the first few days of life, many infants can discriminate their mother's smell, face, and voice. We know this from experiments in which the infant is permitted to choose between stimuli by looking one direction or another, by turning its head, or by sucking on a "soother" wired to start a recording of mother's voice or another woman's voice. The baby sucks harder to hear mother's voice (Mills & Melhuish, 1974). Many women claim that their babies recognized their voices immediately after birth. This seems possible, since the fetus can learn and it has been exposed to the sounds and patterns of its mother's speech for months. Remarkably, some babies even tend to imitate others' facial expressions in the first two weeks (Field et al., 1982; Meltzoff & Moore, 1977).

One of the most important effects of these "relationship oriented" perceptual abilities is the response they get from people around the baby. Babies who are stimulated and loved do better. Adults who see a two-week-old baby imitating them do tend to get excited. They then will spend hours making faces at the baby, which is very good for the baby. "Blob of protoplasm" indeed! We're offended, since we have personally known some absolutely brilliant infants and would be glad to show you pictures.

Motor development

At birth, the infant is also equipped with some built-in behaviours that help it survive. These reflexes appear with no prior learning. **Reflexes** are simple, innate response patterns to specific stimuli. Reflexes include quickly withdrawing an arm or leg from pain, rapid head movements when an object is covering the baby's face, and a sucking or "rooting" reflex. When its cheek is touched, the infant will start sucking movements and enthusiastically moving its mouth around. If he or she encounters a nipple, the baby nurses. If not, the baby will often cry, and this usually leads to the delivery of food.

The infant quickly starts to go beyond these reflexes as it learns new motor behaviours. Of course, each child develops at a different rate, but Figure 12-10 outlines the general ages at which different motor abilities emerge. Normal motor development follows a distinct pattern, although individual children progress at different rates. Development of motor skills requires two ingredients: maturation of the child's nervous system and lots of practice. Motor development is not merely a matter of using different neuromuscular systems once they develop. Physical development of the nervous system depends, to a large extent, on the baby's own movements while interacting with the environment. By the end of its first year of life, a baby can get from place to place very efficiently by crawling. However, it soon begins to struggle with standing upright and taking a few steps. If the baby tries to get somewhere fast, it drops to all fours and crawls. But if it is exploring in a more leisurely fashion, it tries to walk, even though the process is slow, tedious, and punctuated by frequent falls. For the infant mastery of the skill of walking seems to serve as its own reward.

For many of these abilities, such as walking, physical maturation seems to govern the onset of the activity. Before a certain level of muscular and neurological development, all the training in the world won't teach the baby to walk. After that point, almost nothing will prevent him or her from walking. In fact, even babies who have been strapped to a cradleboard for the first year seem to walk at about the same age as those with achievement-driven parents who have had the child in a "walker" for months (Dennis, 1940; Ridenour, 1982).

Cognitive development

We have said that Piaget called infancy the sensorimotor period of cognitive development. Piaget actually outlined six stages of cognitive development during infancy, but we focused on the infant's two main tasks, learning adaptive responses and object permanence. Learning of adaptive responses can be shown to occur within a few hours of birth, if the task is designed cleverly enough to tap the infant's abilities. Siqueland and Lipsitt (1966), for example, arranged for newborns to receive a sweet taste if they turned their heads one direction at a tone and the other direction at a buzzer. The babies learned this quickly. Then they had to learn to switch the direction by turning to the reverse pattern and did so in an average of just ten trials.

FIGURE 12-10 Milestones in a child's motor development

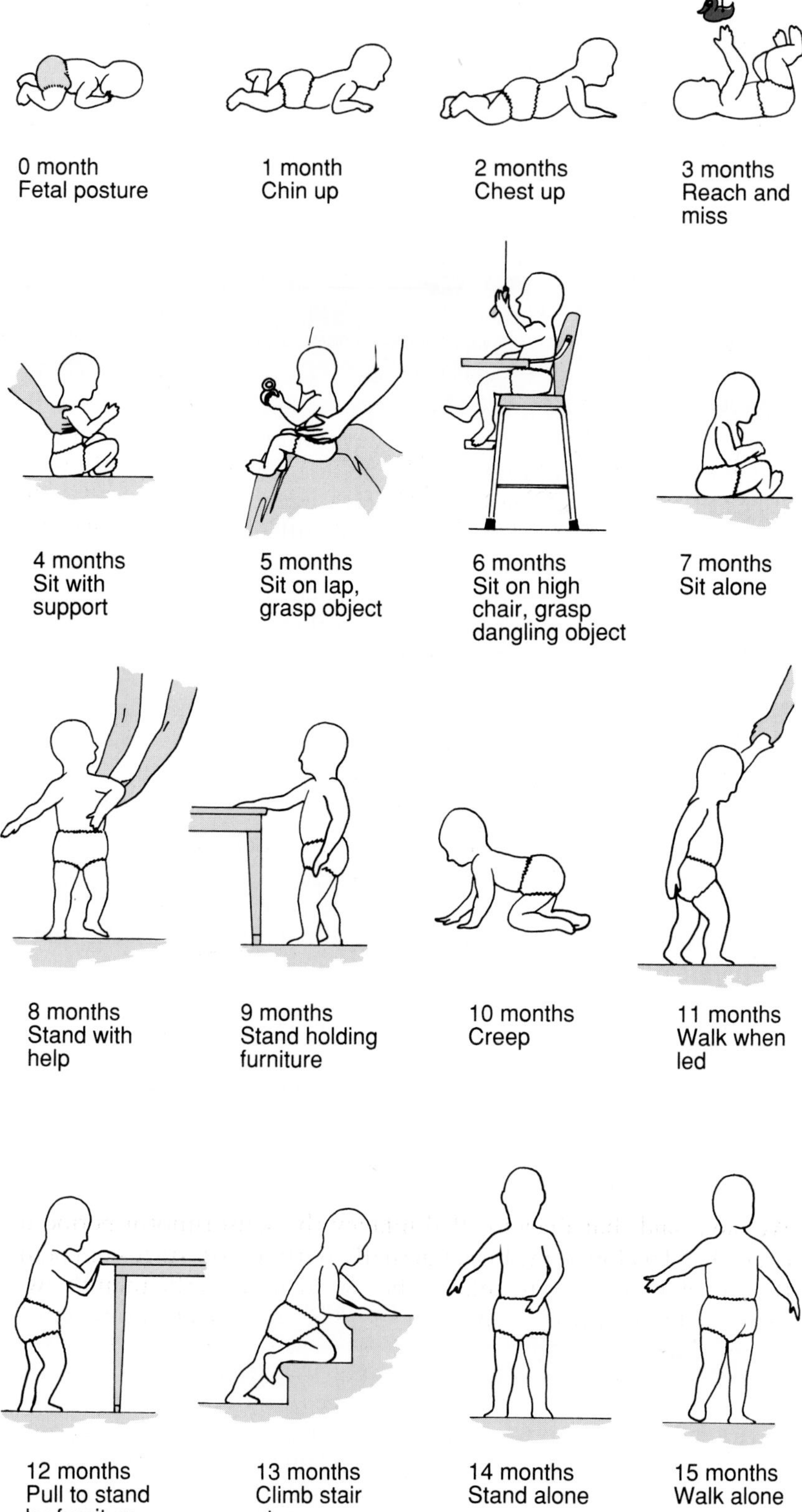

SOURCE: Reprinted with permission from Allyn and Bacon, 1989.

It is difficult to know how much an infant is capable of remembering. Learning object permanence usually begins near the end of the first year. We adults seem unable to remember our infancy. Freud called this failure to remember "infantile amnesia." There probably are several reasons for this. For one thing, the brain is not yet fully developed physically, and, for another, the infant has no symbolic system (such as language) to organize information. It is interesting that animals that are born with physically mature brains, such as guinea pigs, are able to establish memories that persist from birth. Animals with immature brains at birth, such as rats, cannot (Campbell & Coulter, 1976). This suggests that the human brain's immaturity is a major factor in infantile amnesia.

Even though the early months of development don't produce retrievable memories, the stimulation and learning of this period seem to have a lasting impact on later development. We have already discussed the increased physical development of the brain that results from early stimulation. Beyond this, the first two years seem to be critical in laying a groundwork for language development. Children who are deaf from birth have more difficulty learning language than children who became deaf at age two, for example (Lenneberg, 1967). More generally, children who spend the first two years in a dull environment seem never to reach their full potential, even if they are given intensive training later in life (Kagan, 1976).

Social development

We have already shown how the infant is a social being in terms of perception and early learning. Erikson argued that the major psychosocial task of the first year or two is to acquire a sense of basic trust. This trust or lack of trust is largely a result of the nature of the baby's human relationships.

Children who are more secure in their relationship to the parent are more free to explore and be independent.
SOURCE: Dick Hemingway.

Attachment and bonding

By about six months, most infants show strong signs of attachment to their primary caretakers. Up until about 18 months of age, there is no more devastating loss than the loss of a mother (or of a father if he is the primary caretaker). The baby will become very distressed, sometimes when the parent simply leaves the room. It has been said that in World War II bombings of London, infants who were taken to rural areas for safety suffered more emotional upset than those who had stayed with their mothers in the bombing.

If a strong attachment has formed, the child has a "home base" from which to explore the world more confidently. Mary Ainsworth (1979; Ainsworth et al., 1978) described an important difference between infants who were "securely attached" and those who were "insecurely attached." Securely-attached infants were able to explore their environments calmly and independently when their mother was present. They cried and showed distress when she left but then went to her for contact when she returned. Once they had established contact, these babies resumed their exploring. The insecurely-attached babies were more "clingy" when mother was present and less likely to play independently. They showed great distress when she left but seemed angry and aloof from her when she returned. There were clear differences in the parenting styles of the mothers. These differences reveal important clues about what infants need from their parents. The mothers of the securely-attached infants seemed alert and tuned-in to what their babies needed and were doing. The mothers were quick to respond to those needs. The mothers of insecurely-attached infants were more unpredictable. Sometimes they responded to the child and sometimes they did not, depending more on the mother's needs.

In the past, the connection between children and their mothers has been the primary focus of research, but recent work is starting to emphasize the importance of connection with fathers as well. Given the opportunity (or if they take the opportunity), fathers can be as nurturing as mothers, although they often meet different needs than the mother does. A close connection between fathers and their children has significant and lasting benefits for the child (Greenglass, 1982; Lamb, 1986).

An interesting parallel to the relationship between unresponsive parenting and infant insecurity can be found in the classic studies Harry Harlow reported with monkeys (Harlow, 1958; Harlow & Harlow, 1962 and 1969). He noticed that baby monkeys reared alone for reasons of disease control became intensely attached to cheesecloth blankets put in their cages. He theorized that contact comfort might be strongly linked to attachment. **Contact comfort** is the powerfully motivating affect of an infant's having a soft object to cling to. His results suggested that touch is even more important than food as a cause of attachment. He provided baby monkeys with two "surrogate mothers" such as those in Figure 12-11. One of them was made of wire but provided food. The other provided a soft body but no food. Later when the monkey was frightened it consistently ran to the cloth mother and clung. When it wanted to explore some new object it would repeatedly return to the cloth mother to "touch base." Even though the cloth mother was preferred to the wire one, neither surrogate could be called the ideal responsive parent. The infant monkeys showed dramatic effects of this when faced with almost any change in their environments. They were terrified and unable to do much but cower and cover their faces.

Even more dramatic was the monkeys' later inability to relate to other monkeys and to mate normally. If they were artificially impregnated, they were terrible mothers themselves. Sometimes they would act caring but often were abusive and erratic toward their infants, not unlike some human parents. The behaviour of the infant offspring of these monkeys was painfully pathetic to watch. They would cling desperately to their abusive mothers, in spite of being unpredictably flung across the cage, having their faces rubbed into the floor of the cage, and being hit. Attachment was more important than the physical pain.

FIGURE 12-11 Monkeys raised in isolation have a great need for contact comfort
Harlow's monkeys showed that the "contact comfort" of a soft surrogate mother was more powerfully attractive than the wire mother that provided food.
SOURCE: University of Wisconsin Primate Laboratory.

Parenting styles

There have been many swings in fashion in what is the most effective way to be a parent. It seems common for people to believe that there are only two choices: permissive parenting and authoritarian parenting. We now have evidence, though, that these are not the only choices. In addition, what is best for a child is different at different ages.

In the first two years, the critical ingredients seem to be social and physical stimulation; a closely *interactive* relationship with adults; and much loving, sensitive, predictable contact. In a sense, the evidence suggests that "permissive parenting" is what is best for an infant. In a later section we will return to the issue of parenting styles for older children. We will discuss how damaging permissive parenting can be for an older child and what the alternatives are. The answer to the parenting styles question is very complex (Clarke-Stewart, 1973).

Effects of disruptions

A dramatic way to show the importance of attachment is to study the effects on children who do not have much of it. We already saw one striking example in Skeels' study. Not only were the "retarded children" who got loving care vastly improved, the comparison group that stayed institutionalized suffered dramatic deterioration. In a classic study of infants in foundling homes in Canada and the United States (Spitz & Wolf, 1946), good food and adequate medical care were provided but the babies received little holding and stimulation because of lack of staff. More than a third of the children died, mostly in the second half of the first year. Even among the survivors there were high levels of physical retardation and emotional disorders. Some of this damage can be overcome by later good treatment, but Kagan & Klein (1973) report that damaging effects can linger at least throughout childhood and probably beyond.

If an infant loses its parents, there are often strong disruptions and even despair (Mineka & Suomi, 1978). If the child quickly enters a new, stable, loving environment, he or she usually seems to recover from the shock. The child will probably not be measurably different from other children by about age ten (Yarrow et al., 1973).

CHILDHOOD

From the end of infancy until adolescence is a period of fairly steady physical, mental, and social growth. We have already said a fair amount about this age, so this section will be quite general.

Physical development

The first two years of life include a dramatic growth spurt. Childhood, however, is a time of gradual and steady growth, both of the body and the brain. There certainly are individual differences in body size, but these differences usually don't become pronounced until adolescence.

Childhood is a time of gradual and steady growth, both of the body and of the brain.
SOURCE: Dick Hemingway.

Cognitive development

Piaget said the child's tasks include developing a sense of *conservation* and overcoming the limits of an *egocentric* cognitive stance. Near the end of this period, the child starts *concrete operations*. Piaget probably underestimated the ability of children to think at early ages, but his concepts remain useful in helping adults understand children by "seeing through their eyes."

Language development

Probably the most important cognitive task of this age is one we seldom think of, the acquisition of language. It is astonishing what a complex set of rules and vocabulary a three-year-old has already learned. It is common for an adult to struggle trying to learn a second language and then, when visiting Quebec or a French immersion school, to be amazed at how brilliant the little children are in speaking two languages. When Penfield referred to the "uncommitted cortex," he was talking mostly about how the young brain is open to learning language. In most cases, those who become bilingual later in life have great difficulty losing the accent of their first language. This simply means they have trouble learning a new one. The bilingual child is more likely to have two different accents, appropriate to two different linguistic communities.

As we noted in Chapter 8, the *nature versus nurture* issue is especially interesting when discussing language. The strict learning view (Skinner, 1957) is that language is similar to any other skill and comes about due to reinforcement. Obviously, training and reinforcement are important in language learning. Each child is capable of making all the sounds of every human language, but, over time, many of these sounds drop out through extinction while others are reinforced and survive. For example, in some oriental languages, the sound spectrum is divided differently than in western languages. Many who learn an oriental language first have trouble distinguishing the sound of "l" from "r." A person who learned German first may have trouble with "v" and "w." If you learned English first, it may seem odd to you that people really can't hear the difference between "v" and "w." However, there are sounds in other languages that most English-speakers simply can no longer hear because of their learning history. A person whose native language is Hindi, for example, might find it strange that you can't hear the difference between "gh" and "gh." See? We can't even write about this example because of the limitations of English. We have a Hindi-speaking friend who finds it amusing that we really can't hear the difference.

As important as learning is, though, there is strong evidence that brain maturation plays an important role in language learning. When the brain is ready, language seems to develop, even though parents give little direct language training. There is a fairly specific language area in the brain, usually in the left hemisphere. If this area is removed or damaged late in childhood, it is extremely difficult to develop language. If this damage occurs early in childhood (usually before the age of three) the "uncommitted" brain does develop language in the opposite hemisphere, but it is impaired language. The brain seems partly "prewired" for language. Chomsky (1968, 1975) argues strongly that the basic structure of human languages is so similar that it must have some inherited characteristics. More details of language acquisition can be found in Chapter 8, on Thinking and Language.

Children learn how to function in relationships by relating to siblings, friends, and other family members.
SOURCE: Courtesy of Yvonne Wilson Spitz.

SOURCE: Courtesy of Catherine and Brian O'Neill.

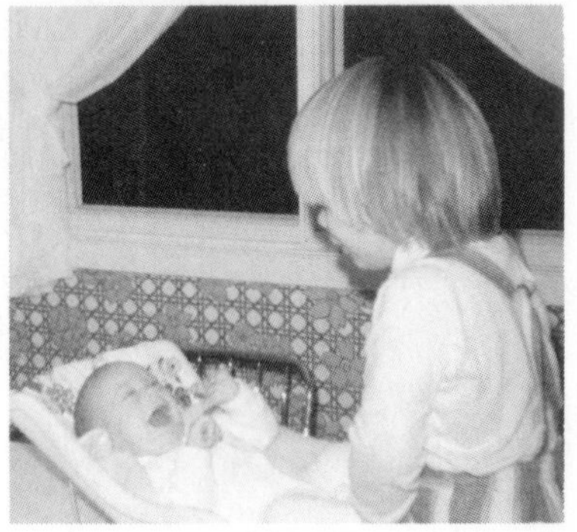

Psychosocial development

This is the time of Erikson's stages of autonomy versus self-doubt, of initiative versus guilt, and competence versus inferiority. These psychosocial skills prepare the child to function in a social world with a sense of personal worth. Remember, though, that Erikson has been criticized for overlooking the importance of developing relationship skills through this period. Children are learning how to function in relationships by relating to parents, friends and siblings. The quality of these relationships will affect the quality of their later relationships. Erikson seems to have ignored the absolutely essential part of development that is usually associated with the feminine role. We will have more to say about the real risks in this incomplete picture in Chapter 18, on Gender Roles.

Parenting styles

One of the most common misunderstandings people have of psychology is the belief that psychologists promote permissive parenting. Gordon (1976) has called this "you win-I lose" parenting. Beyond about age two, it can have damaging effects on a child (Clarke-Stewart, 1973). A theme that appears several places in this book is that most people seem to think that there are only two choices in dealing with other people, being either *permissive* or *authoritarian*. We often hear and read that "the trouble with kids today is not enough discipline. Parents are too permissive." What this usually means is that we must return to an "I win-you lose" style in which the parent has the power and uses it to control the child. In parenting, as in other relationships, there is a third alternative. There is evidence that this third approach results in children with good self-esteem and emotional health, as well as better relationships with their parents. **Authoritative parenting styles** have been called "firm and loving," and "no-lose parenting." The parent combines firm and consistent limit-setting that teaches rules and honours the parents' needs *and* warmth, dependable acceptance, communication, and a participatory process so the child also has a say in how events are run. We will see in later chapters that this combination of strength and sensitivity is essential in many kinds of relationships. It seems to require at least two basic skills: effective listening and non-destructive confrontation.

The children of permissive parents tend to be immature and demanding. The children of authoritarian parents tend to be "disaffiliated," resentful, and have difficulty forming close relationships. The children of "firm and loving" parents tend to have high self-esteem, high self-reliance, and good relationships with others (Baumrind, 1973; Coopersmith, 1967).

SOURCE: *Calvin and Hobbes* by Bill Watterson. Copyright 1989 Universal Press Syndicate. Reprinted with permission. All rights reserved.

ADOLESCENCE

It is interesting that some cultures do not have a period similar to our adolescence. Children quickly take on adult responsibilities when they are physically able to. For us, though, the teenage years are a time of essential learning and preparation for adulthood.

Physical development

The second growth spurt starts with *puberty*, at about 11 in girls and about 13 in boys, on the average. Along with marked changes in height, the adolescent develops *primary* and *secondary sex characteristics*. **Primary sex characteristics** include adult forms of genitalia and reproductive structures. This includes **menarche** (the onset of menstruation for girls) and the appearance of erections and ejaculations, through night dreams, for boys. **Secondary sex characteristics** include the changes in body shape and body hair that differentiate male and female. The changes in this period are so dramatic that they have tremendous impact on the tumult that many adolescents go through.

The age of onset of puberty is related to adjustment in this period, especially for boys. An early start for puberty tends to give a boy an advantage in adjustment and social acceptance (Jones, 1957). For girls, however, the picture is mixed. Being too tall too soon can be inhibiting, but later in adolescence these girls who have an early start seem to have some advantage in confidence (Brooks-Gunn, 1986).

Cognitive development

In Piaget's system, the adolescent is moving into the highest stage of thinking and is now able to perform *formal operations*. He or she can think abstractly and symbolically and develop systems of

Physical development in adolescence is accompanied by the increased importance of peer contacts.
SOURCE: Dick Hemingway.

thought. It is debatable whether or not preadolescents are capable of formal operations, but it is clear that this becomes a central part of adolescent thinking and discussion. Topics such as the meaning of life, the nature of love, and world peace become important issues to adolescents at this time.

Psychosocial development

The most difficult issues in adolescence seem to centre around human relationships and around finding an *identity*. Erikson said that there are four parts to the task of finding an identity: accepting one's own sexuality, being a person on one's own and not just somebody's son or daughter, becoming committed to some beliefs, and finding a direction toward a social or vocational role.

Erikson probably underestimated the importance of forming *peer* relationships and sexual and romantic involvements. These relationships help prepare the adolescent for the task of finding intimacy in early adulthood. Peers become extremely important as a source of information, acceptance, and activities. This is inevitably accompanied by a necessary separation from parents (Connolly & Ondrack, 1989; Johnson & Connolly, 1989). It is sometimes said that the teenager's greatest need is not to need his or her parents, and the parents' greatest need is still to be needed. This is a difficult dilemma that often leads to hostility and rejection, as the adolescent separates. Some of this hostility is probably a reaction to authoritarian parenting, to parents who have based their relationship with their children on power. Parents lose their power in this period and don't have a constructive foundation for a new relationship. But this is only part of the story. The teenager really needs to get free psychologically. Even with a good parent-teenager relationship, there is often pain in this process.

A father and daughter supper can be especially important during adolescence which is inevitably a time of increased independence. The growing separation of parent and child requires sensitivity on both sides.
SOURCE: David Martin.

ADULTHOOD

For many years, psychology neglected adulthood as a stage of life and of development. However, there are many developmental tasks unique to adult years. Understanding can help prepare for them.

Physical development

There is a general decline in physical abilities that starts in early adulthood. Unlike the more rapid decline of old age, changes for the adult are less obvious and very much a function of lifestyle factors such as eating, exercise, smoking, and drinking. The decline is much more gradual than is commonly believed when individuals remain active and engage in regular exercise (see Figure 12-12). There is truth in the ads comparing the 60-year-old Swede and the 30-year-old Canadian, in terms of "physiological age." Since our culture so values youth and beauty, the inevitable physical decline can be a source of

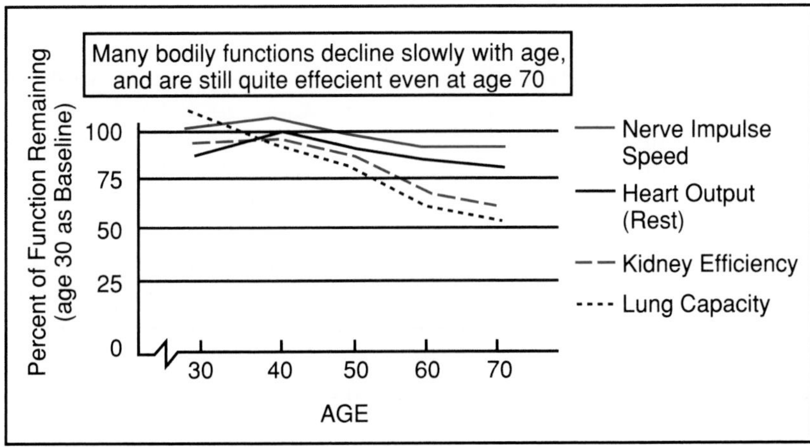

SOURCE: Adapted with permission from Allyn and Bacon, 1989.

FIGURE 12-12 Aging and physical decline
Physical decline with aging is actually more gradual and smaller than most people believe. When individuals remain active, and especially when they engage in regular exercise, they can be strong and vigorous for many years.

lowered self-esteem for many and a source of raised income for sellers of hair growers and wrinkle eliminators.

The most obvious physical change for women comes with **menopause** (or **climacteric**), the cessation of the menstrual cycle and the ability to conceive. This usually happens at around 50 years of age, give or take a few years (Lennon, 1982). It is traditional to associate menopause with anxiety, distress, and physical symptoms such as "hot flashes." The evidence is, however, that, while some women are troubled by menopause, the majority welcome the freedom that it brings. Neugarten (1968) found that most women under 45 said it was not true that after menopause "women generally feel better than they have for years." However, two thirds of women past menopause said this was true. If menopause is markedly early or late, the woman is more likely to have emotional distress about it. Many of the problems reported around menopause seem to be cultural. They are not a direct result of menopause but of social attitudes toward it and toward aging (Ballinger, 1981).

Men do not have as clear-cut a physical change late in adulthood. However, they do have a general decrease in physical aspects of sexuality (Beard, 1975), and they do have some cycles in the production of hormones (Kimmel, 1974). Testosterone production seems to fluctuate in cycles and some studies of men's mood level have found subtle but regular cycles. As with women, though, whatever physical changes occur seem secondary in their impact to the psychological and social influences. If one fears age, one suffers more.

Cognitive development

There seems to be a gradual reduction in *fluid intelligence* throughout adulthood. **Fluid intelligence** refers to the speed of mental processing and the creative arrangement of new concepts. However, this change is scarcely noticeable except with specially designed tasks because of a steady growth in **crystallized intelligence**. This is the growth of knowledge and the ability to use that knowledge in practical ways, in "wisdom," and in professional and productive knowledge and ability.

Psychosocial development

Erikson's two major tasks for adulthood are to establish *intimacy* rather than *isolation* and *generativity* rather than *stagnation*. The adult is to establish family and to contribute productively to society. It is interesting how similar this is to Freud's answer to, "What can the normal person do that the neurotic cannot?" He said that the normal person can love and work.

The fact is that we don't have much solid evidence about the developmental stages of adulthood. We have many popularized concepts such as "empty nest syndrome" and "midlife crisis." However, many such ideas are based largely on reporters' looking for "trends." The few research studies that have been done are not very consistent with each other.

As she did with menopause, Neugarten has gathered data that challenge common ideas about the "empty nest syndrome" that occurs when children leave home. Contrary to the idea that women who have committed themselves to motherhood now mourn the loss of their reason for being, "Most women are glad to see their children grow up, leave home, marry and have their careers" (Neugarten, 1974, p. 38).

For men, Levinson (1978) gathered extensive data that led him to conclude that between 40 and 50 nearly all men do go through a crisis that involves extensive redefinition of the self and the structure of life. Two other studies (Gould, 1978; Vaillant, 1977) also came to the conclusion that the early forties are a time of change and upset for men. Gould described it as painful and tumultuous, while Vaillant thought men's problems were relatively mild. All three of these studies have been criticized for being biased toward highly-educated and intelligent men, so it is difficult to generalize from them to the general population of men.

The more important lesson to note in all this is that we don't know much about midlife stages of development. What we do know will probably change within a few years. The major issues of the middle part of life are far more a function of social changes than of maturation and physical changes.

THE LATER YEARS

Erikson's last developmental stage, the search for *ego integrity*, is essentially a search for meaning and satisfaction. In the years past 60 or 70 this means finding self-acceptance and meaning in the present, evaluating the quality one's life has had, and facing the reality of death. These issues are all faced in the context of declining abilities.

Physical development

As we have seen, a gradual physical decline starts early in adulthood. This decline accelerates at different ages for different abilities. Generally around 60 or 70, there is a noticeable drop off in hearing, sight, smell, muscle strength, adaptation to light levels, and most other physical functions. At 75, Art Linkletter commented that sex was less like the Fourth of July and more like Thanksgiving.

There is also an unfortunate relationship between physical illness and emotional deterioration. Many older people say that the most important factor for them is to keep their health. Loss of health often leads to depression and anxiety, which can contribute to a worsening of the physical illnesses. Thus a vicious circle is established. However, there is great variability among individuals over 65. This variability results largely from differences in illness and from some lifestyle factors. Those who take regular exercise, don't smoke, and pursue healthy eating habits seem to be able to remain active into their eighties and beyond (Woodruff, 1977). There also is evidence to support the "use it or lose it" philosophy with sexuality (Masters and Johnson, 1966; Pfeiffer, 1977), mental functioning (Kra, 1986), and physical functioning (Perlmutter and Hall, 1985). Masters and Johnson reported that people can remain sexually active well into old age. This is especially true for those who had engaged in sex regularly in earlier years. The physical ability to have sex seems partially a function of regular use. Kra (1986) has summarized evidence that also dispels common beliefs about the loss of memory and mental functioning. Older persons who maintained or resumed a lively interest in learning remained more able to think and remember. It is especially interesting that apparent memory and thinking loss can be reversed by renewed mental activity. Finally, Perlmutter and Hall (1985) stress the importance of continued physical activity as the most effective way to slow down the decline of physical functioning. Regular moderate exercise and stretching can have remarkable effects on the physical quality of life for older people.

People who, like Jackrabbit Johannsen, engage in regular exercise can remain healthy into their eighties and nineties.
SOURCE: "Jackrabbit," National Film Board of Canada.

Cognitive development

One of the cruel stereotypes of the aging in our culture is that they are unable to think clearly or to remember recent events. There certainly are disorders of aging that involve loss of cognitive functioning. However, when we look at those elderly who are in the majority and living in the community, we find a much more complicated picture.

Decline or stability?

Whether or not we see a sharp decline in cognitive ability with aging depends in part on how we collect our data. In **cross-sectional studies**, different data is collected on individuals of groups of different ages at one point in time. These studies tend to find that younger people are more intelligent than older people. However, **longitudinal studies** test the same subjects over the course of many years. These data generally show little decline in intelligence with age. (See Figure 12-13.) How can we understand this discrepancy? With cross-sectional studies, there are many possible *alternative explanations* for the differences between older and younger subjects. For example, it is possible that younger subjects have grown up in a time when there

FIGURE 12-13 Changes in intellectual ability with age: longitudinal and cross-sectional data
These graphs show that intellectual abilities do not decline dramatically with age when the same subjects are studied over time (longitudinal data). Cross-sectional data give the incorrect impression that there are such dramatic declines.
SOURCE: Adapted with permission from Schale and Strother (1968).

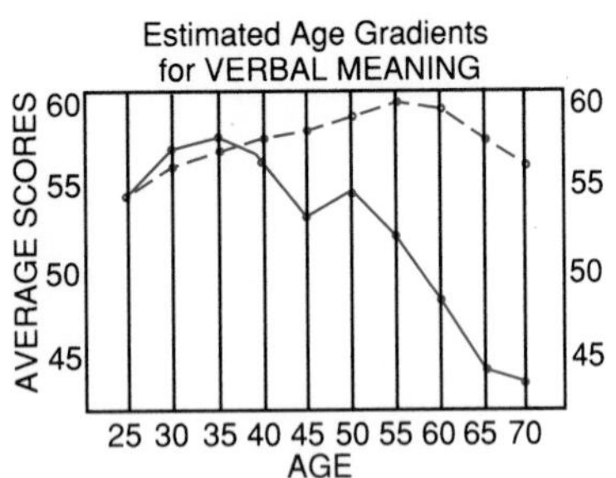

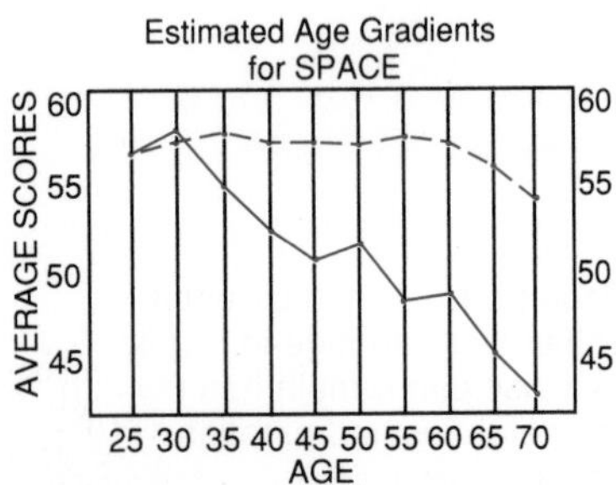

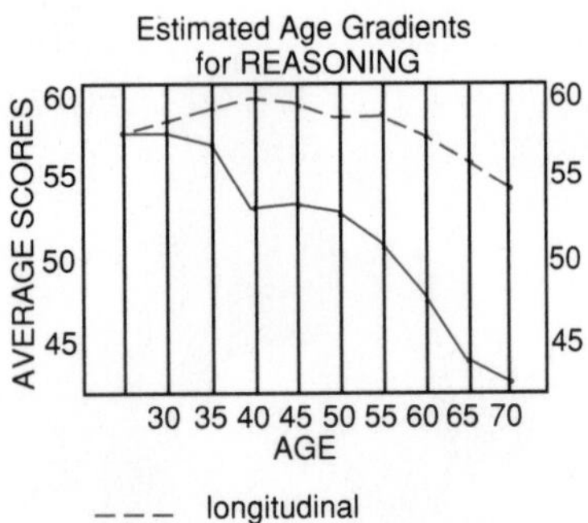

are more educational opportunities. Another factor is that intellectual ability declines rapidly near the end of life. Thus, each individual loses little cognitive ability until near the end. However, if we test a large number of older people, the average score will be lower because of those subjects whose ability has declined. This lower average score masks the fact that many subjects retained their ability. Finally, we have to ask what kind of intelligence we are measuring at different ages.

What kind of intelligence?

One of the biggest problems with any discussion of intelligence is captured in the slightly cynical definition that intelligence is "whatever intelligence tests measure" (see Chapter 11). We often arbitrarily define one ability (such as speed at adding numbers) as intelligence. Another ability, such as sensitivity to nonverbal cues from others is often excluded from the definition of intelligence. Why? As we said in Chapter 11, the decision is often a question of who has the power to make up the tests. With the elderly, it is important to recognize that many of their abilities are ignored by testing.

Some common tests, however, do find that older persons do better than younger ones, particularly tests that tap stored knowledge such as vocabulary and general information. As we noted, this is referred to as *crystallized intelligence*. On the other hand, *fluid intelligence* requires speed of associations and abstract problem solving. This kind of intelligence seems to decline with age.

An interesting difference in memory among older subjects was reported by McIntyre and Craik (1987). They tested college students and retired people living in the community in Manitoba and Ontario and found that older people could remember facts they had just learned quite well. However, they were less likely to remember the source of those facts. McIntyre and Craik drew a parallel between this and the **source amnesia** sometimes seen with certain kinds of brain damage. The significance for the thinking of older people is that there may be a loss of *episodic memory*, relative to loss of *semantic memory*. **Episodic memory** is a subtype of declarative memory. It is memory for particular events ("episodes") that an individual personally experiences. **Semantic memory** is also a subtype of declarative memory. It is memory for items of knowledge that depend on the meaning of words and ideas ("semantics"). (See Chapter 7 on memory.)

Psychosocial development

As with cognitive functioning, we often have negative stereotypes about older people being unhappy with life and "crotchety." This seems to result largely from our selective perceptions based on a minority of the elderly.

Satisfaction and meaning

Surveys of satisfaction with marriage and with life in general tend to find older people happier than adults in early or middle stages. This information often surprises people. The finding may reflect older people's being more peaceful or "mellow." The older person may have come to terms with life, compared with a more driven quality in other stages of adulthood (Herzog, Rogers, & Woodworth, 1982). Of course, this satisfaction differs greatly depending on the person's life circumstances, particularly whether one has good health. Other factors that contribute to satisfaction are being married; having sufficient money; having a religious commitment; and the presence of friends, siblings, and other social supports (Depner, Ingersoll-Dayton, 1988).

Edwin Shneidman (1989) has studied people in their seventies. He says that this decade can be "the Indian Summer of life." The seventies can be seen pessimistically as a time of loneliness, illness, rejection by children and society, sudden termination of meaningful work, and great losses. But they also

> . . . can be (and often are) a very special time of fulfilment, independence, increased opportunities for selfhood, and freedom and release. Consider that when one is a septuagenarian, one's parents are gone, children are grown, mandatory work is done; health is not too bad, and responsibilities are relatively light, with time, at long last, for focus on the self (Shneidman, 1989, p. 684).

CLOSE-UP How to Tell What a Baby Hears

Learning to use sounds in language depends on the infant's ability to discriminate one sound from another. Even infants as young as one month old have been studied using an apparatus on which the infant sucks a rubber nipple (Terhub, 1976). A recording device first measures the speed with which the infant sucks and second plays an auditory stimulus after each suck. When infants hear a new sound, they tend to suck more rapidly. As the novelty of the new sound wears off, sucking slows down. When another sound is played, sucking increases. This permits experimenters to tell whether the infant can discriminate one sound from another. The graph in Figure 12-14 shows that the infant sucks at a rapid rate in order to hear the sound "zah." After several minutes, sucking slows down until a new sound, "rah," is introduced and the rate increases. Thus we can infer that the infant could discriminate these two sounds. Evidence from such studies tells us that young infants can make very fine discriminations between sounds.

FIGURE 12-14 Data from Trehub's study of sound discriminations in infants

SOURCE: Adapted with permission from Trehub (1976).

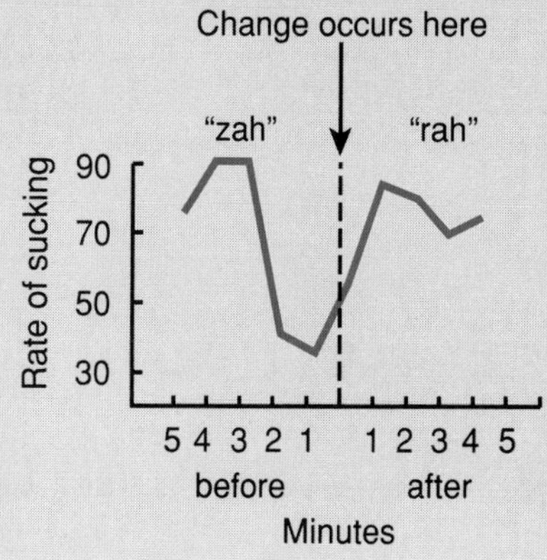

SPECIAL TOPIC Facing Death

"There's not enough time," is perhaps the most common thought of a person facing death at any age. Younger people often avoid even thinking about death. However, as one gets older it becomes more difficult to deny the reality and finality of death. Companions die with increasing regularity, shrinking the person's social world and being a constant reminder of his or her own mortality. The person must both mourn the loss of others and come to terms with the certainty of his or her own death.

Elisabeth Kubler-Ross (1969) has worked with dying people for many years and has developed a widely quoted description of the process of dying. On the basis of her experience, she argued that most people go through the same five stages of dying in roughly the same order. First, there is *denial*, a conviction that this just can't possibly be true. The denial can be so powerful that health workers often report that patients who have been told they are dying will later insist that they had never been told. Second is a stage of *anger*, at God, at the doctors, at family members, or just generalized rage: "Why me?" The third stage is *bargaining*, usually with God. The person often asks for a second chance and promises changes in return. There can also be desperate bargaining with health care workers for miracles and family members for special help. Fourth is *depression* at the impending loss of all of life's good things and missed opportunities. This is often accompanied by a sense of hopelessness. Fifth, and finally, the dying person comes to an *acceptance* of the inevitability of death. Even more, there is a sense that it is all right, that it is time to go now. This acceptance can bring a sense of deep peace.

Elisabeth Kubler-Ross.
SOURCE: UPI/Bettmann.

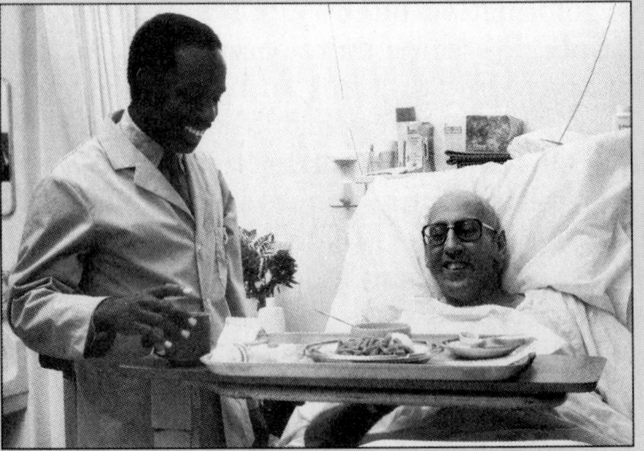

Over the past decade there has been an increasing emphasis on the importance of palliative care.
SOURCE: "Time for Caring," National Film Board.

Kubler-Ross' stages are widely known and widely used in dealing with those who are dying. We think they have had some helpful uses, but they have also carried risks. A professional man we know suffered the death of his wife from cancer. Afterward he said he wanted to write a book called *How Not to be Helpful* to give to some of the people he and his late wife had dealt with. "What *really* made me angry," he said, "was all those people telling her that she should be angry now." Many people trying to be helpful grab onto theories such as Kubler-Ross' and attempt to fit everybody into them. Kubler-Ross presented her observations as a stage theory, but there is evidence that many dying people don't go through all these stages. Furthermore, some go through them in a different order (Kastenbaum & Costa, 1977; Shneidman, 1976). We can hurt people by trying to be helpful unless we humbly respect the other person's experiences and the limits of our own knowledge.

The death of a loved one can be devastating and can happen to anyone. It is more likely to happen to women. About three quarters of all women can expect to suffer the death of a spouse, one of the most traumatic events adults ever go through. For anyone who goes through the death of a loved one there seems to be a process of *mourning* that is essential but is often prevented by our culture (Schulz, 1978). We are often expected to "be strong" and "put the past behind" us and go on living. This is to deny a natural and necessary working through of the loss. At first, the mourning person seems to be in a state of shock and disbelief. One of the most common experiences is an overwhelming feeling of unreality. It all actually feels as though it *couldn't* have happened. After some period, usually a few weeks, the numbness fades into overwhelming sadness. This sadness can be expressed in insomnia, physical symptoms, frequent crying, and loss of appetite. Then, continuing for about a year, the person frequently thinks about death, searching to give it meaning, and reliving it. Commonly in the second year there is a renewing of other relationships and interests and a sense of having developed new strengths by having come through the tragedy. The successful resolution of this process depends on being able to express the feelings involved.

As with Kubler-Ross' stages, though, there is a danger in describing the stages of mourning. We have often talked with people who feel hurt and isolated that friends and professionals say they should be over their grief by the end of the first year. The friends and professionals misunderstand what is expected to happen at the end of the first year. Certainly there is a renewing of life and interests, but this does not mean an end to sadness and the sense of the loss of one who was loved so much. A little knowledge can be dangerous, especially when trying to understand another unique human being. We will discuss grieving in more detail in a Special Topic in Chapter 13, on stress.

We all go through the experience of mourning in our own way and in our own time.
SOURCE: Dick Hemingway.

Chapter Summary

1. The individual continues to develop in cognitive, physical, and social areas throughout life. The question of whether inheritance or learning plays the more important role in how the person develops is called the nature vs. nurture debate. Another important issue in developmental psychology is whether development occurs in discrete stages or is more continuous, with growth resulting from gradual change.

2. Stage theories argue that the person goes through discrete developmental stages in a particular order. Although there may be some differences in the ages at which the stages occur for each individual, the order itself is fixed. Changes between stages are rather clear and sudden. Freud's stages (discussed in Chapter 10) have been translated into more social and interpersonal terms by Erik Erikson.

3. Piaget proposed a stage theory of cognitive development, in which the child's conception of the world develops in large leaps forward with each stage. Piaget's stages are sensorimotor, preoperational, concrete operations, and formal operations.

4. Kohlberg proposed a stage theory for the development of moral reasoning. He defined increasingly more mature levels of morality. He proposed three levels of development, with two stages in each level. In the preconventional level are Stages 1 (morality is based on not getting caught) and 2 (morality is based on maximizing rewards). In the conventional level are Stages 3 (getting

acceptance and avoiding disapproval) and 4 (obedience to authority and following rules). Kohlberg thinks most adults don't get beyond these stages. The postconventional level is marked by Stage 5 (principles rather than rules guide moral decisions) and Stage 6 (overriding ethical principles of justice prevail). Recently he added a seventh and very rare stage in which the person follows universal principles that rise above even social norms.

5. Freud, Erikson, and Kohlberg have all been criticized for proposing male-biased theories of behaviours appropriate to different stages of life.

6. Our genetic inheritance comes from the chromosomes of our biological mother and father. Humans have 46 chromosomes (23 pairs) in every cell except for germ cells, which have 23 single chromosomes. A germ cell from each parent unites with one from the other parent to form the new 23 chromosome pairs of the baby. Most characteristics transmitted genetically result from complex interactions of different genes. One chromosome pair determines the baby's sex. Some characteristics also carried on this chromosome pair can thus be sex-linked.

7. The nature/nurture question seems best answered by saying that inheritance and experience interact. Nature sets genetic boundaries to development, and the environment determines what happens within those boundaries. Psychological characteristics don't seem to be inherited as such. Some inherited physical characteristics make it more likely that an individual will learn certain psychological characteristics.

8. Prenatal development is divided into three stages. The first two weeks is the period of the ovum. From two weeks to eight weeks is the stage of the embryo. The stage of the fetus is the final stage.

9. At birth, the nervous system is completely formed. The infant is alert, predisposed to social experience, and capable of considerable cognitive activity. The infant has some preprogrammed responses called reflexes, such as an automatic tendency to suck. Infants can make discriminations and learn within a few hours of birth. Cognitive development in this period is critical for later language development, even though individuals can't remember this period.

10. By about six months a strong attachment develops for the mother and continues to be strong until about 18 months. Infants who develop a secure attachment are more able to explore the environment independently. Insecurely-attached infants show more distress and clinging behaviour. This phenomenon has many implications for later adjustment.

11. Childhood is a time of gradual growth of body and brain. The most important task of this period is acquiring language. The young brain is quite malleable, in the sense that it is dramatically moulded by experience.

12. Both permissive and authoritarian parenting styles have destructive consequences for children. A combination of firm, consistent limits and warmth, communication, and a participatory process seems most effective as a parenting style.

13. Adolescence is marked by the growth spurt in which dramatic changes in body shape and size are accompanied by development of primary and secondary sex characteristics. Finding an identity seems to be the adolescent's most important psychological task.

14. Beginning in early adulthood, there is a general decline in physical abilities, but these are strongly affected by the person's lifestyle. For women, climacteric (menopause) is the most obvious physical change. Many women report feeling considerable freedom associated with this change. For men, there is not such a clear-cut change point. Although there is a gradual reduction in the speed of cognitive processing, there is a compensating increase in knowledge and the ability to apply it. This is called crystallized intelligence. Much of the evidence about psychological development in adulthood is contradictory. The prevalence of the "midlife crisis" and the "empty nest syndrome" is not really known.

15. In later life, physical decline accelerates, and health becomes a primary concern. Again, lifestyle is a critical factor in the speed and severity of decline. Cognitive abilities in the elderly may remain fairly high until near the end of life, at which time there is a rapid decline. Our assumption of widespread unhappiness among the elderly may be inaccurate, depending on how measures are taken.

Key Terms

Accommodation In Piaget's theory, the cognitive process of changing or accommodating current conceptions when new information contradicts them.

Adaptive responses Behaviours that manipulate the environment. This is one of the child's two major cognitive tasks in Piaget's theory.

Assimilation In Piaget's theory, the cognitive process of fitting new information into existing conceptions.

Authoritarian parenting styles Ineffective style in which coercive power is used to control the child.

Authoritative parenting styles A more effective parenting style often characterized as "firm and loving." It is marked by participatory problem solving, clear limits, and considerable warmth.

Bonding The process of forming emotional attachment between infant and caretaker.

Chromosomes Chains of genes that carry genetic coding. Humans have 46 chromosomes arranged in pairs (23 from each parent).

Climacteric Another term for *menopause*.

Conservation In Piaget's theory, the child's ability to take into account more than one dimension of an object.

Contact comfort The powerfully motivating effect of an infant's having a soft object to cling to.

Continuous development theories Theories which state that development is on a continuum of gradual change and is not marked by discrete stages.

Conventional morality Kohlberg's second level of moral development. Morality is based on being good and following rules.

Cross-sectional studies Research method in which data is collected on individuals or groups of different ages at one point in time.

Crystallized intelligence Mental operations that depend on stored knowledge, "wisdom," and productive knowledge and abilities.

Development The patterns of change and growth that mark the passage of years.

Dominant genes Genes for characteristics that will be expressed in the person, whether the gene it is paired with is the same or different.

Ego-centric In Piaget's theory, the child's perspective that he or she is the centre of the universe perceptually.

Empty nest syndrome The notion that parents, especially women, suffer a traumatic loss when the children grow and leave home.

Episodic memory A subtype of declarative knowledge. It is memory for particular events that an individual personally experiences.

Fetal alcohol syndrome The severe damage often done to the embryo or fetus when the mother ingests alcohol.

Fixation In Freudian theory, the tendency for a certain amount of psychic energy to remain attached to and tied up in the unresolved problems of an earlier developmental stage.

Fluid intelligence Mental operations that depend on the speed of mental processing and the creative arrangement of new concepts.

Genes The inherited genetic information for specific physical characteristics. They are carried in chains on chromosomes.

Genetic boundaries The physical limits that set an upper and a lower limit on an individual's development by inherited characteristics.

Genetic predisposition Inherited weakness or strength that makes it more likely for one person to develop a particular characteristic (for example, a disease or personality trait) than another.

Germ cells The ovum and sperm cell that each parent contributes to a new offspring.

Infantile amnesia The forgetting of experiences from the first years of life.

Longitudinal studies Research method which tests the same subjects over the course of many years.

Maturation The rate and manner of development of an individual's physical potential.

Menarche The onset of menstruation.

Menopause (also called *climacteric*) The woman's cessation of the menstrual cycle and the ability to bear children.

Midlife crisis A period of turmoil, especially for middle aged men, in which the meaning of life and the structure of the man's life comes into question.

Nature vs. nurture The debate over the relative influence on development of genetic inheritance (nature) and environmental influences (nurture).

Object permanence The concept that objects exist even if hidden from view. The gaining of this concept is one of the child's two major cognitive tasks in Piaget's theory.

Period of the embryo The time from two to eight weeks in pregnancy.

Period of the fetus The time from nine weeks to birth in pregnancy.

Period of the ovum The time of the first two weeks of pregnancy.

Permissive parenting styles Ineffective style in which limits are not set, the parent's needs are not met, and the child learns to have excessive expectations of others.

Polygenic characteristics Inherited characteristics that result from the complex interactions of many different genes.

Postconventional morality Kohlberg's third level of moral development. Morality is based on principles.

Preconventional morality Kohlberg's first level of moral development. Morality is based on not getting caught and on obtaining rewards.

Primary sex characteristics Adult forms of genitalia and reproductive structures that develop in puberty.

Psychosocial development theories Theories such as Freud's and Erikson's in which the emphasis is on developmental tasks centred around interpersonal and social issues.

Puberty The period of dramatic change and growth initiated by hormonal changes in the teen years.

Recessive genes Genes for characteristics that will be expressed in the person only if paired with another recessive gene for the same attribute.

Reflexes Simple, innate response patterns to specific stimuli.

Schema An organized, complex expectation we hold about the nature of reality.

Secondary sex characteristics Adult forms of development that develop in puberty, including the changes in body shape and body hair that further differentiate male and female.

Semantic memory A subtype of declarative knowledge. Memory for items of knowledge that depend on the meaning of words and ideas ("semantics").

Sex-linked characteristics Inherited characteristics that are carried on the sex chromosomes.

Source amnesia The ability to remember particular facts but not to be able to remember where those facts were learned.

Stage theories Theories of development that propose that the child changes in fairly sudden large steps that occur in a fixed order.

Stages of dealing with death Kubler-Ross' theory that dying persons go through stages marked by denial, anger, bargaining, depression, and acceptance.

Stranger anxiety Distress the infant shows at strange faces; sometimes called "making strange."

Temperament A collective term that refers to an inborn, general mode of responding to environmental stimulation.

Zygote The fertilized egg during the first two weeks of pregnancy.

Suggested Readings

Berger, K. (1986). *The developing child,* 2nd ed. New York: Worth. This is a well-written textbook that summarizes current research and theory on development up through adolescence. It is one of the best choices for a more detailed overview of the field.

Bringuier, J. (1980). *Conversations with Jean Piaget*. Chicago: University of Chicago Press. Piaget's writings are difficult to read in their original form. This series of interviews with Piaget helps to clarify his theories and to give a more personal view of this leading theorist in developmental psychology.

Flavell, J. H. (1985). *Cognitive development,* 2nd ed. Englewood Cliffs, NJ: Prentice-Hall. If you want to focus on cognitive and intellectual development from early childhood up through adolescence, this is one of the most respected texts.

Gilligan, C. (1982). *In a different voice: Psychological theory and women's development*. Cambridge, MA: Harvard University Press. We have cited this book in this chapter for its challenges to many popular theories of development as being male-biased. Gilligan draws from psychological writing and research and from literature to develop her case. Both men and women can gain much from this book.

Gordon, T. (1976). *Parent effectiveness training in action*. New York: Wyden. This is a practical book on how to communicate with children so that both parents and children get their needs met. The principles are similar to those being taught in many parenting courses such as Systematic Training in Effective Parenting (S.T.E.P.).

Silverstone, B., & Hyman, H.K. (1981). *You and your aging parent: The modern family's guide to emotional, physical, and financial problems*, 2nd ed. New York: Pantheon. Another practical book that speaks to the younger person about how to care for an aging parent responsibly but without overinvolvement. It applies considerable modern knowledge about aging.

Wass, H., Berardo, F. M., & Neimeyer, R. A. (eds.). (1988). *Dying: Facing the facts*, 2nd ed. Washington, DC: Hemisphere/Harper & Row. This book draws together the writing of several different researchers. It is a bit advanced and probably most useful as a graduate level text. However, it also includes a series of exercises on one's own personal awareness of death and suggestions for finding resources on the topic of death.

PART V

DISORDER AND THERAPY

CHAPTER 13

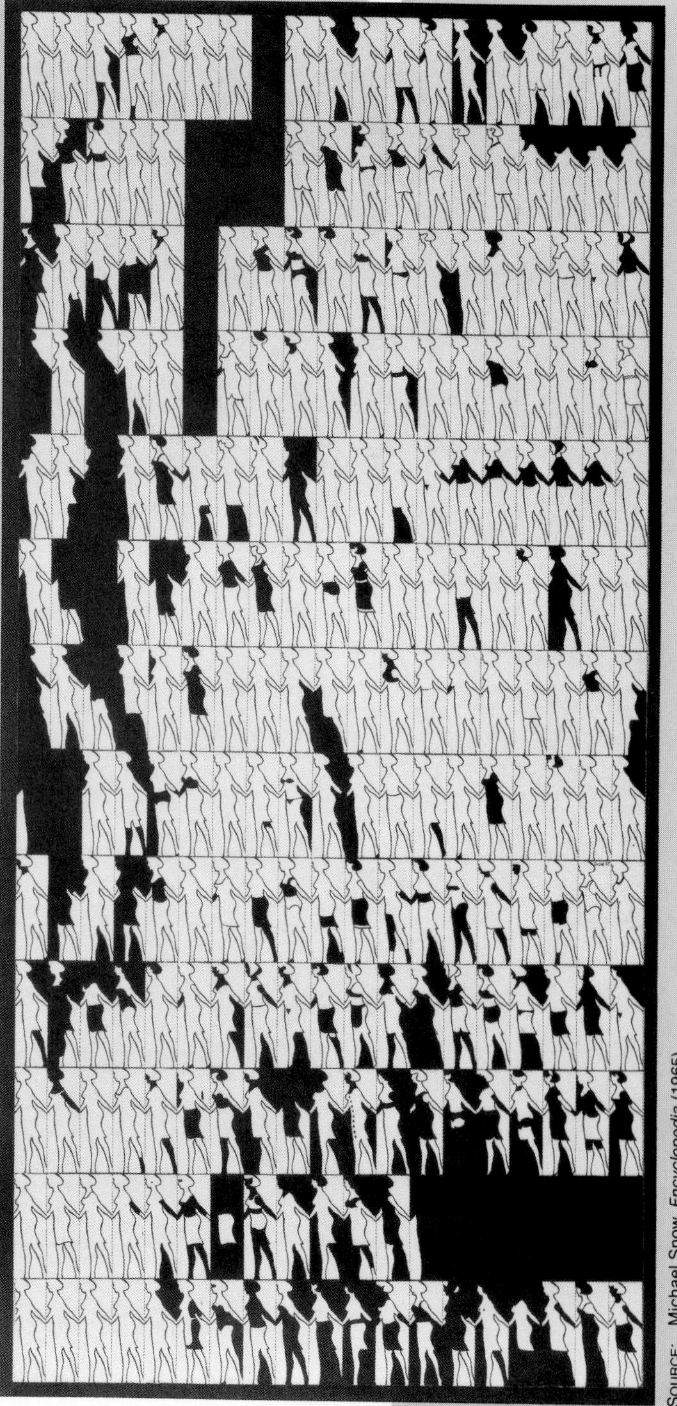

SOURCE: Michael Snow, *Encyclopedia* (1965).

Stress

NO MATTER WHAT we do—at school, at home, in relationships, on the job, or for that matter, on vacation — our lives are full of stresses. They challenge us and sometimes overwhelm us. Stress can change our bodies, our thoughts, our emotions, and our behaviours. There is evidence that stress can contribute to nearly all forms of illness, psychological pain, and deterioration in the quality of life. This is the negative side of stress. There is also a positive side to stress. Research has given us insights into how people are able to cope with and manage stress. This kind of knowledge can help in designing treatments for those who do suffer from stress reactions. It can also help all of us in dealing with the stressors in our lives. A life without stress is not possible. If we can come to understand the way we respond to stress, we can better prepare ourselves and others to cope.

WHAT IS STRESS?

Natural disasters such as the 1989 San Francisco earthquake are obvious sources of stress.
SOURCE: Canapress Photo Service.

What is stressful for one person may not be stressful for someone else. One individual may look forward to a public speaking engagement, while another may feel intense anxiety and lose self-confidence. Any definition of stress must take into account that it is a relative concept.

In its most general sense, **stress** can be defined as the pattern of an organism's responses to demands for change or threatening circumstances. Stress results when an organism's physical and psychological equilibrium is disturbed. Another view emphasizes that stress results when an organism's adaptive resources are taxed or exceeded by environmental or internal demands. It is useful to distinguish between **stress**, which is the pattern of responses made to demands, and **stressors**, which are the external sources of demands for change. In other words, stressors are the stimuli that arouse stress reactions. Stressors could include a car accident, the injury sustained, the close brush with death, the hassles with insurance companies, and the resulting lack of transportation. The stress would be the internal feelings of anxiety, fear, frustration, and anger at what happened.

An analogy to stress is trying to balance on one leg and being pushed a little off balance. In this physical analogy, the person's sense of balance or equilibrium has been disturbed. The individual is forced to take action or risk falling to the ground. The same is true for stress. An event disrupts the person's psychological equilibrium. As the person deals with the stress, change occurs on a number of levels: physiological, behavioural, cognitive, and emotional. Whether the person falls to the ground or meets the challenge of stress is determined by many factors, as we will see throughout this chapter.

Many forms of stress exist. We would all readily agree that disasters, medical emergencies, arguments with our parents, accidents, and missing the bus are stressful events. They lead to negative emotional states such as anxiety, fear, and anger. But what of events that are positive? How should we consider leaving home, graduating, entering a new program of studies, starting a new job, getting married, or having a child? Selye (1974) argued that *all* forms of change in life are stressful. All lead to adjustments in lifestyle, even those that lead to positive changes. He distinguished between **distress**, which is a negative reaction to stressors and **eustress**, which is a positive reaction to stressors. All adjustment is stressful. Whether a particular event leads to distress or eustress depends upon the meaning that the person gives the event. The meaning assigned to news of a pregnancy, for example, will determine whether the prospective mother is happy or distressed.

Research on stress has accelerated markedly in the past 10 to 15 years. This research focuses on the influences of stress, how stress leads to physical disease, and what moderates the effects of stress. It also examines the forces that are conducive to health, coping, and adaptation to stressful lifestyles. As a result, two new specialty areas have emerged (Stone, Cohen, and Adler, 1979). **Behavioural medicine** is the field of study that applies psychological knowledge to the treatment of physical disease. And **health psychology** is the field of study that applies psychological knowledge to all aspects of maintaining wellness and treating illness. We will explore health psychology in detail in Chapter 19.

Even the positive change of graduating from high school can create stress.
SOURCE: Courtesy Karen O'Neill.

STUDYING AND MEASURING STRESS

We all have some intuitive understanding of what stress is, but scientific exploration of stress demands that the concept of stress be *operationalized*. In Chapter 2 we discussed how the *sympathetic nervous system* is aroused in times of danger. Thus, one measure of stress is the degree of arousal of the sympathetic nervous system. We can study stress by means of a **laboratory analogue study**. Such a research method is designed to stimulate real-life scenarios in the laboratory so that the subject's reactions can be studied under well-controlled conditions. We can also investigate stress as it actually occurs in the natural environment by conducting a **field study**. We might also design a **survey study** and use questionnaires or interviews to ask groups of subjects about the kinds of events they find stressful in their lives.

Laboratory measurement

Laboratory analogue research measures the effects of stress in terms of physiological changes, emotional changes, cognitive changes, and behavioural changes. If the focus of a particular study is on physiological changes, for example, measurements may be taken of heart rate, blood pressure, respiration rate, and perspiration in response to stimuli that are thought to be stressful. This research can be carried out with humans as well as infrahuman species, such as rats, dogs and monkeys. We will discuss examples of such research later in this chapter.

Stress in the environment

For the study of human stress, it is unethical (even if it were feasible) to study the effects of severe forms of stress in a laboratory. Severe stress is measured in the natural environment. Psychologists have learned a great deal by assessing the effects of extreme stress and by providing mental health treatment following catastrophes such as earthquakes, tornados, and floods. Following the eruption and ashfall of Mount St. Helens in 1980, Adams and Adams (1984) reviewed community records of such stress indicators as illness rates both before and after the disaster. They observed that stress illnesses such as high blood pressure were aggravated and increased almost 200%. The number of cases of mental illness had also increased. They also found an increase in alcohol-related problems, violence, and family stress that lasted at least three to four months following the disaster. Similar research has been carried out on the effects of terrorism, plane crashes, and war. The Vietnam war experience was especially stressful. It resulted in unusually damaging long-term effects for those involved in the fighting. Research such as this is needed in developing appropriate disaster relief, emergency services, and long-term counselling for people who deal with extreme stressors.

Life-change units

One major approach in stress research is to survey people to determine their sources of stress. Holmes and Rahe (1967) were the first to attempt this type of research. In the next section, we will discuss the impact of changes in life events. In this section, we will talk about the development of scales to measure these changes. Holmes and Rahe developed a test called the **Social Readjustment Rating Scale**, in which people were asked to rate how much adjustment would be needed for each of 43 different life events. Marriage was used as the comparison point and was arbitrarily assigned a value of 50 *life-change units*. Each of the other life events was assigned a value relative to this 50, depending on how much readjustment, adaptation and change was required. The results of the original survey study are shown in Figure 13-1.

Holmes and Rahe did not ask people to assess whether an event is positive or negative, just the amount of change required to deal with it. The researchers then suggested that one could use this scale to calculate the amount of stress (or change) that a person has been exposed to over a certain period of time by adding up the number of life-change units. Holmes and Rahe believed that there is a strong relationship between amount of stress and later development of psychological problems or physical illness. A life-change unit score of 300 or more over a 12-month period was thought to indicate major

FIGURE 13-1 The Social Readjustment Rating Scale
All events are measured in terms of life-change units to indicate the amount of change and adaptation they require. Marriage is arbitrarily assigned a value of 50 life-change units.

Rank	Life Event	Life-change units
1	Death of spouse	100
2	Divorce	73
3	Marital separation	65
4	Jail term	63
5	Death of close family member	63
6	Personal injury or illness	53
7	Marriage	50
8	Fired at work	47
9	Marital reconciliation	45
10	Retirement	45
11	Change in health of family member	44
12	Pregnancy	40
13	Sex difficulties	39
14	Gain of new family member	39
15	Business readjustment	39
16	Change in financial state	38
17	Death of close friend	37
18	Change to different line of work	36
19	Change in number of arguments with spouse	35
20	Taking out a mortgage or loan for a major purchase	31
21	Foreclosure of mortgage or loan	30
22	Change in responsibilities at work	29
23	Son or daughter leaving home	29
24	Trouble with in-laws	29
25	Outstanding personal achievement	28
26	Wife begins or stops work	26
27	Begin or end school	26
28	Change in living conditions	25
29	Revision of personal habits	24
30	Trouble with boss	23
31	Change in work hours or conditions	20
32	Change in residence	20
33	Change in schools	20
34	Change in recreation	19
35	Change in church activities	19
36	Change in social activities	18
37	Taking out a mortgage or loan for a lesser purchase	17
38	Change in sleeping habits	16
39	Change in number of family get-togethers	15
40	Change in eating habits	15
41	Vacation	13
42	Christmas	12
43	Minor violations of the law	11

SOURCE: Reprinted with permission from Holmes & Rahe (1967).

life stress. It resulted in an 80% chance of later illness. A score between 200 and 299 indicated a moderate degree of stress, with a 50% chance of subsequent illness.

The Social Readjustment Rating Scale has been criticized for two main reasons. First, it does not sample all possible major stresses that a person may face. It underrepresents events that are stressful to the poor, women, and students. Second, in some instances, the impact of a particular major event may be substantially different from the value of life-change units given by the scale. For some individuals, for example, divorce may not be one of the most stressful events that the person will deal with. The death of a close friend may require a much greater adjustment than that indicated by the scale. Abortion would be another example of a life event that might bring about widely varying reactions and needs for adjustment. For some, abortion may arouse little stress. For others, it may be a devastating experience that could dramatically alter self-esteem, coping, and self-image.

The **Life Experiences Survey** (Sarason, Johnson, and Siegel, 1978) is a 60-item scale that attempts to deal with these criticisms. On this scale, people rate each event in terms of the amount of change required and the quality of its impact on their life (i.e., positive or negative). Thus, an experience such as abortion can be rated in terms of its desirability as well as its impact. The Life Experiences Survey also contains ten items specifically for students, and it leaves room for each respondent to list three unique personal experiences. This scale is more flexible and possibly more accurate than the Social Readjustment Rating Scale. See Figure 13-2.

Other ways of measuring sources of stress have been developed as well. One intriguing approach which focuses on daily experiences rather than major life events was designed by Kanner, Coyle, Schraeger, and Lazarus (1981). They developed a scale measuring daily *hassles* and daily *uplifts*. Hassles are everyday negative experiences and

FIGURE 13-2 The Life Experiences Survey: Instructions to respondents and the first twelve items

Instructions to Respondents

Listed below are a number of events which sometimes bring about change in the lives of those who experience them and which necessitate social readjustment. Please check those events which you have experienced in the recent past and indicate the time period during which you have experienced each event. Be sure that all check marks are directly across from the items they correspond to.

Also, for each item checked below, please indicate the extent to which you viewed the event as having either a positive or negative impact on your life at the time the event occurred. That is, indicate the type and extent of impact that the event had. A rating of −3 would indicate an extremely negative impact. A rating o 0 suggests no impact either positive or negative. A rating of +3 would indicate an extremely positive impact.

	0 to 6 mo	7 mo to 1 yr	extremely negative	moderately negative	somewhat negative	no impact	slightly positive	moderately positive	extremely positive
1. Marriage			−3	−2	−1	0	+1	+2	+3
2. Detention in jail or comparable institution			−3	−2	−1	0	+1	+2	+3
3. Death of spouse			−3	−2	−1	0	+1	+2	+3
4. Major change in sleeping habits (much more or much less sleep)			−3	−2	−1	0	+1	+2	+3
5. Death of close family member:									
a. mother			−3	−2	−1	0	+1	+2	+3
b. father			−3	−2	−1	0	+1	+2	+3
c. brother			−3	−2	−1	0	+1	+2	+3
d. sister			−3	−2	−1	0	+1	+2	+3
e. grandmother			−3	−2	−1	0	+1	+2	+3
f. grandfather			−3	−2	−1	0	+1	+2	+3
g. other (specify)			−3	−2	−1	0	+1	+2	+3
6. Major change in eating habits (much more or much less food intake)			−3	−2	−1	0	+1	+2	+3
7. Foreclosure on mortgage or loan			−3	−2	−1	0	+1	+2	+3
8. Death of close friend			−3	−2	−1	0	+1	+2	+3
9. Outstanding personal achievement			−3	−2	−1	0	+1	+2	+3
10. Minor law violations (traffic tickets, disturbing the peace, etc.)			−3	−2	−1	0	+1	+2	+3
11. *Male*: Wife/girlfriend's pregnancy			−3	−2	−1	0	+1	+2	+3
12. *Female*: pregnancy			−3	−2	−1	0	+1	+2	+3

SOURCE: Reprinted with permission from Sarason, Johnson, and Siegel (1978).

concerns that produce stress. Uplifts are everyday positive events that nevertheless lead to change and adjustment. Figure 13-3 lists some examples of hassles and uplifts.

There is considerable controversy at present about all these tests measuring sources of stress. Some researchers (Dohrenwend and Shrout, 1985) believe that the scales confuse stressors with indicators of psychological distress. Is an event such as a change in health, for example, a stressor, the result of stress, or both? There is no easy answer to this question. Stress is a result of an interaction of events and the interpretation of them. Thus, it is quite possible for an event such as an illness to be both the result of stress and a major stressor at the same time.

Stressors

Stressors can range from minor inconveniences and frustrations, such as losing a coin in a drink machine, to intense, overwhelming and destructive circumstances such as internment in a concentration camp. Stressors also differ on many other dimensions. They may be short-lived (**acute**) or long-lasting (**chronic**). They can be interpersonal and social, or entirely within the individual. A stress reaction may be the result of one stressor or a combination of many stressors. The stressor may be events others are also experiencing or uniquely one's own. A stressor may be part of normal development, such as marriage, entering college or university, or starting a new job. We all face different challenges as we grow up and grow old. The reaction of an individual to the death of a parent will differ quite substantially, depending upon whether the individual is an infant, a toddler, an adolescent, a young adult, or a middle-aged person. The event will be painful at any age, but the stress and meaning will be different (Stambrook & Parker, 1987).

Life events versus hassles

Life events are the major kinds of changes we all face. They include marriage, divorce, receiving a promotion, having a child, and death of a spouse. Such events represent the inescapable challenges and stressors that necessitate considerable readjustment (Holmes and Rahe, 1967). Holmes and Rahe's *life-change units* discussed above attempt to quantify life events for research. The life events listed in Figure 13-1 all require adjustment and therefore can be stressors.

There is a large body of research that shows a correlation between a high rate of changes in life and susceptibility to physical illness, psychological distress, and accidents. Six months before a group of sailors went to sea, Rahe (1968) examined changes in their lives that led to readjustment. The results showed that the high-risk portion of this group (i.e., those with a high rate of life changes) had 90% more illness while at sea than the lower-risk groups.

Research indicates that the risk to health increases with the accumulation of stressors. The cumulative impact of many life

FIGURE 13-3 Some typical hassles and uplifts

SOURCE: Reprinted with permission from Kanner et al. (1981).

Hassles
Misplacing or losing things
Troublesome neighbors
Concerns about owing money
Too many responsibilities
Planning meals
Having to wait
Being lonely
Too many things to do
Too many meetings
Gossip
The weather
Difficulties with friends
Silly practical mistakes
Difficulties with getting pregnant
Auto maintenance
Filling out forms
Unchallenging work
Concern about the meaning of life
Declining physical abilities
Problems with your lover

Uplifts
Getting enough sleep
The weather
Not working (on vacation, laid-off, etc.)
Staying or getting into good physical shape
Quitting or cutting down on smoking
Sex
Spending time with family
Shopping
Making a friend
Looking forward to retirement
Being complimented
Going someplace that's different
Giving love
Being "one" with the world
Flirting
Fixing/repairing something (besides at your job)
Having good ideas at work
Getting a present
Having fun
Socializing (parties, being with friends, etc.)
Good news on local or world level

Minor hassles can contribute to ill health.
SOURCE: Dick Hemingway.

changes occurring in close successions is known as the **pile-up effect**. Adjustment to one major life event is made more difficult by other major life changes occurring one after the other. The person might lose a job, go bankrupt, become seriously ill, have a mortgage foreclosed, and become separated. Each of these personal disasters may have contributed to the next. The person's reaction to one problem may also have helped to cause the next. Such a "piled up" string of stressors is very likely to cause emotional and physical problems.

In contrast to this focus on personal disasters, some psychologists believe that it is more common for the *hassles* of daily life to be associated with stress and eventual ill-health (Lazarus, 1981a). In fact, DeLongis, Coyne, Dakof, Folkman, and Lazarus (1982) found that ill-health was more correlated with the stress of minor hassles than with major life events. The reason seems to be that the minor stresses and hassles add up faster. They produce a lifestyle or pattern of behaviour that may, in time, be more likely to cause psychological distress and illness.

Dimensions of stressors

The impact of any stressor will depend primarily on its type, intensity, duration, and how predictable and controllable it is. We have already discussed the types of stressors in terms of life events versus hassles. We have also examined some attempts to measure the intensity of stressors by means of various scales.

When we consider the duration, it is important to know how long a stressor is present. Is it acute (short-lived) or chronic (long-lasting)? It is equally important to know how frequently it occurs and how long the intervals are between occurrences. An interval that allows an individual to recoup and rest may make the stress easier to deal with than if there were no such respite. It is not uncommon to hear people say that when dealing with stressors, they have no breathing room or time to recharge before being dealt another blow.

The predictability and controllability of stressors has been the subject of intense study. One of the initial investigations looking at the effects of being able to control stressful events was carried out by Joseph Brady in 1958. This classic study investigated *executive monkeys* and the development of gastrointestinal ulcers.

Gastric ulcers are lesions of the stomach lining that are caused by excess secretions of acid. They often result from stress. Ulcers can lead to physical debility and even death.

In Brady's experiment, one group of monkeys were exposed to painful electric shock which they could learn to avoid by pressing a button. Brady called this group **executive monkeys** because they could exercise control over the shocks. The other group of monkeys were exposed to exactly the same number, intensity, and duration of shocks, but these passive monkeys were not able to avoid them. They helplessly received uncontrollable shock. This experiment was thought to be an analogue of the real-life experiences that human executives face. Just like humans, the executive monkeys had to be on guard, vigilant, and ready to make responses that had major effects on their well-being. The results of this experiment were striking. All of the executive monkeys developed severe stomach ulcers, whereas the helpless monkeys did not. The experiment seemed to indicate that always being on guard and ready to act results in a heightened state of physical arousal that eventually leads to a breakdown of functions. (See Figure 13-4.)

However, these results are not as clear cut as they first seemed. Other researchers found flaws in Brady's work. They noted that Brady did not randomly assign the monkeys to receive either controllable shock or noncontrollable shock. The executive monkeys were chosen because of their ability to learn the avoidance response faster than the other monkeys. As Seligman (1975) points out, the executive monkeys may have learned to avoid the shock faster *and* may have developed more severe ulcers because they were more emotional by nature. Thus, they would have been more vulnerable to the effects of shock, regardless of their ability to control it.

A comparison with the findings of other experiments in this field underlines the importance of using adequate *controls*, such as random assignments to groups. For example, Weiss (1977) conducted his own series of studies to investigate the issues of controllability and predictability. In one experiment, Weiss randomly assigned rats to an executive group or a passive group, but he was unable to duplicate Brady's results. In another experiment, Weiss randomly assigned rats to different experimental conditions in which some could predict the onset of shock and others could not. All animals received the same number and intensity of shocks. Weiss also used a third group of rats who were placed in the same apparatus but who received no shock and no signals. They functioned as the control group. His research has clarified the relationship between stress and predictability and controllability. If a stressor is not controllable, it is less stressful when it is predictable. Rats who received unpredictable shocks had significantly more gastrointestinal ulcers than animals receiving the same number of shocks preceded by a reliable warning signal such as a buzzer. Many people know from experience that it is often preferable to know when a stressor is going to occur, especially if there is a way to prepare for it. There is another advantage to being able to predict when a stressor will occur. A reliable warning indirectly provides a safety signal. We know that for the interval between a shock and a signal, there will be no shock or stressor. This provides a rest period. For Weiss's rats, not having some predictor of when the shock was going to occur led to chronic fear and anticipation of the painful stimulus. They had to be constantly vigilant. On the other hand, the rats who did receive the warning learned that the absence of the warning was a sign of safety so they could relax.

Seligman's (1975) research on *learned helplessness* demonstrates dramatically the widespread effects of a lack of control over stressors. **Learned helplessness** is a generalized tendency to give up in the face of stress. It results from frequent experience with uncontrollable stressors. Seligman's basic experiment used three groups of dogs. The first group was placed in an apparatus where they received electric shocks to the foot, but they were able to learn to escape the shocks by pushing a panel with their noses. The second group received exactly the same number of shocks, but they could not

FIGURE 13-4 An executive monkey
In Brady's experiment, the executive monkeys (who could control the shocks) all developed ulcers. By contrast, the passive monkey did not develop ulcers.
SOURCE: Based on Brady (1958).

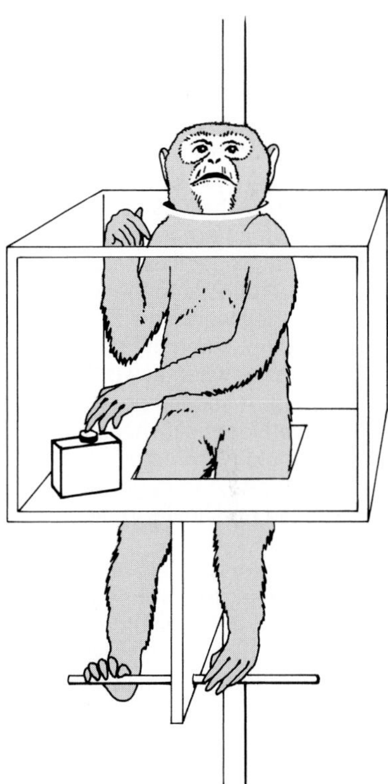

escape the shocks. The third group was placed in the apparatus but received no shocks. They functioned as the control group to account for the effects of being restrained in the laboratory.

After this first phase of the experiment, all subjects were taken to a second apparatus where they again received electric shocks. However, now it was possible for all of them to learn to escape shock by jumping over a shoulder-high barrier. Since they were given signals to predict the shock, they could learn to avoid the painful stimulus. The results were striking. The group who originally had received the uncontrollable shock apparently had learned that nothing they could do would be effective in controlling the shock. This learned helplessness made them act passive and helpless in the new situation where they could, in fact, control the shock. These dogs tended to cower in the corner and whimper. Both of the other groups were able to learn the escape response very quickly in the second situation. (See Figure 13-5.)

This general finding has been noted in many species, including humans. Learned helplessness has been shown to lead to motivational, cognitive, and behavioural deficits that are similar to depression. The stress of having no control over events has been shown to cause stomach ulcers. Some research has even shown that it can lead to decreases in the immune system's ability to fight infections (Turkkan, Brady, and Harris, 1982).

To complicate the picture, it may not be the ability to control a stressor that is most important. Our perception or belief that we can control events or stressors may be the crucial point. In an experiment conducted by Geer, Davison, and Gatchel (1970), subjects who thought they had control over an aversive electric shock were less stressed than subjects who thought they had no control over the shock. All subjects in this experiment received the same number of shocks, but one group was falsely told that if they responded fast enough, they would be able to terminate the shock. Thus they believed that they had some control over it. The other group were simply told that the shock would occur. Results such as this suggest that it is important to understand a person's thoughts, perceptions, and attributions about stressful events in understanding an individual's reactions to stressors. It is conceivable that a person might actually have some control over particular stressors but not perceive

FIGURE 13-5 Seligman's apparatus for inducing learned helplessness in dogs

A) In the first phase of the experiment, three groups of dogs were placed in a harness apparatus. The first group, illustrated here, received shocks to the foot, which they were able to learn to avoid by pushing the panel with their noses when a warning light dimmed. A second group received identical shocks, but they could not predict them or avoid them. A third group received no shocks in the apparatus.

B) In the second phase of the experiment, the groups of dogs were placed in a shuttle box. A shoulder-high barrier divided the floor into two sections. The left section contained rods that could be electrified. The right side could not be electrified at all. The group of dogs who had previously received inescapable shock tended to cower when the floor on the left was electrified (B1). By contrast, the other two groups quickly learned to avoid the shocks by jumping over the barrier (B2).

SOURCE: Based on Seligman (1975).

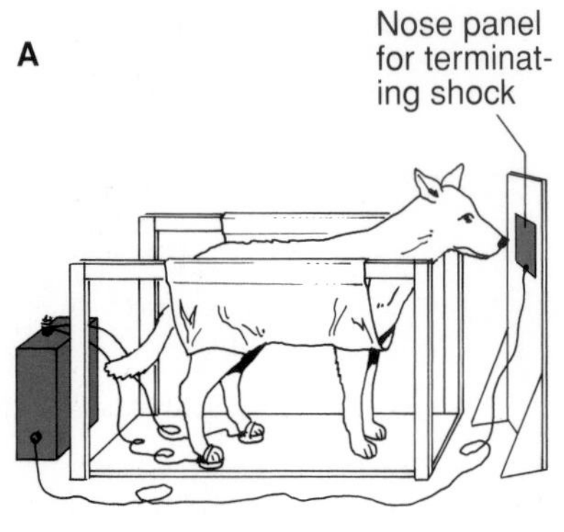

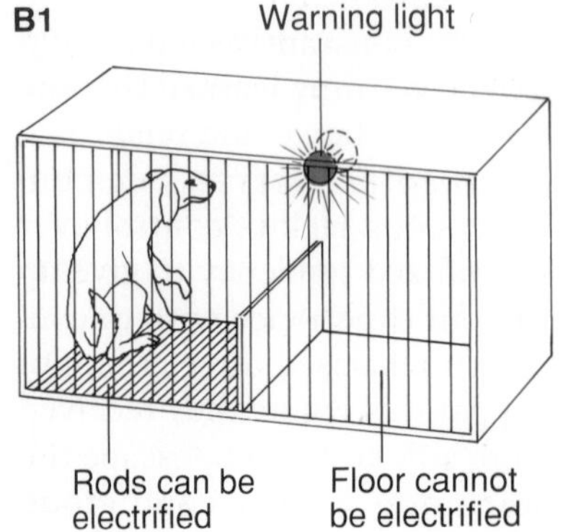

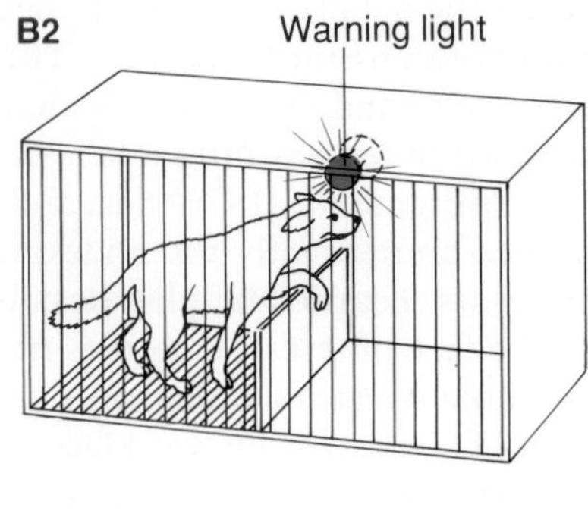

this control. Ironically, this person would experience more stress than individuals who falsely believed they had some control when they did not.

This appreciation of cognitive factors has led to a reformulation of the learned helplessness theory. In order to understand learned helplessness, we must include factors such as expectations, attributions, and interpretations of events. A person's ability to deal with major stressors in life depends partly on previous experience with stress. The person who is accustomed to having control develops a generalized tendency to believe that stress is controllable. This reduces future stress, especially when that control is attributed to internal factors such as hard work or skill. In contrast, if previous experiences with control of stressors is attributed to external factors such as luck or ease of the challenge, the person will benefit less from that experience. The person who has a sense of control and believes that success is the result of ability and effort will cope more effectively with stress.

SOURCE: *Calvin and Hobbes* by Bill Watterson. Copyright 1989 Universal Press Syndicate. Reprinted with permission. All rights reserved.

Frustration and conflict

Frustration is the stressful reaction to being blocked from attaining an expected and desired goal. Confidently applying for a new job and not getting it may result in intense frustration, for example. Frustration may come from being delayed in achieving goals, not having adequate resources to be able to reach the goals, having the goals taken away, or failing to achieve the goal.

Some research indicates that when frustration is intense enough, aggression commonly results. The so-called **frustration-aggression hypothesis** is the hypothesis that once frustration reaches a threshold level it will arouse the organism to attack. (In Chapter 17, we will discuss this hypothesis in more detail.) In some instances, frustration leads to displays of direct aggression. In other instances, frustration leads to aggression displaced from the original target onto a less threatening, more vulnerable target—in other words, a *scapegoat*. There is evidence of correlations between economic hardship and social scapegoating such as increased racism and violent actions towards minority groups. As well, some data suggests that as the rate of unemployment (a form of frustration) increases, so does the rate of child abuse (Steinberg, Catalano, and Dooley, 1981). This may be one reason for the vandalism, gang fights, and high crime rates in poverty-stricken core areas of cities where stressors such as crowding, poor housing, lack of medical services, lack of employment, and drug abuse are pervasive.

Psychological conflicts also lead to stress. A **conflict** is a source of frustration that results from having two or more incompatible motives or goals at the same time. Because the goals are incompatible, one of them cannot be performed. Thus, conflict is a form of frustration because the person is blocked from at least one of the desired goals (Miller, 1944).

We can distinguish four major types of conflict. First, an **approach-approach conflict** is the conflict of wanting two goals, one of which must be sacrificed if the other is to be obtained. We often

FIGURE 13-6 Approach-Approach conflict
A person experiencing this conflict is torn between two desirable but mutually exclusive goals.

experience this conflict when we must choose between two alternatives that are equally attractive. (See Figure 13-6.) If you strongly want to be a high-ranking executive who travels a great deal and if you equally strongly want to have time to devote to a family, you will have to make some painful choices. Choosing one almost inevitably means giving up the other. You will be frustrated by losing one of your goals.

Second, an **approach-avoidance conflict** is the conflict of having a single goal that is both desired and feared at the same time. In other words, the goal both attracts and repels the person. Someone in this kind of conflict sometimes vacillates for long periods before taking some definitive action. (See Figure 13-7.) An example we mentioned in Chapter 5 involved a person who was conditioned to jump up to avoid a shock whenever a red light came on and to crouch down to receive a reward whenever a yellow light came on. The jumping was a fear-induced avoidance response, and the crouching was an approach response toward a desired goal. Because of generalization, the unexpected presentation of an orange light will arouse both fear and desire at the same moment because both yellow and red are similar to orange. The person will probably freeze in place, quivering in conflict. The person both fears and desires the colour orange. It is our nature to be able to feel contradictory emotions toward one object or situation. A highly paid job in a city hundreds of miles away from family and friends could create an approach-avoidance conflict. Many people desperately want an intimate relationship and desperately fear intimacy. Our lives are filled with examples of approach-avoidance conflicts.

The stress is compounded in the third type of conflict, known as **double** or **multiple approach-avoidance conflict**. In this conflict, there are two or more goals, each of which is desired and feared at the same time. Such conflicts are typical of the complications of real life. A person might want to graduate from university to obtain qualifications but also not want to because of the uncertainty of facing new social groups. Furthermore, if she doesn't graduate, parents will be hurt and the person will feel guilty, but she will also feel some satisfaction in hurting the parents, whom she both loves and resents.

FIGURE 13-7 Approach-Avoidance conflict
A person experiencing this conflict both desires and fears a particular goal.

Fourth, an **avoidance-avoidance conflict** is the conflict between two undesirable goals, one of which must be attained if the other is to be avoided. In the vernacular, it would be described as a no-win situation. (See Figure 13-8.) A person may dislike sex, but at the same time fear losing his or her spouse by refusing sexual relations. A student could be late turning in a paper and fear facing the professor with the late submission. The person will also fear waiting longer, however, because the consequences become worse as time passes. Avoidance-avoidance conflict forces a choice between evils. If the evils are equally strong, the stress of being unable to act will become severe.

All of these conflicts lead to stress and result in psychological manoeuvres designed to counteract the effects of the stress. Let us now examine various reactions to stress and then move on to various methods of coping with stress.

FIGURE 13-8 Avoidance-Avoidance conflict
A person experiencing this conflict has to choose between two undesirable goals.

REACTIONS TO STRESS

Stress affects us in multiple ways: physically, emotionally, cognitively, and socially. The first step in understanding reactions to stress is to look at some of the processes that are involved in our initial assessment of an event as stressful. What makes different individuals react differently to stressful situations?

Cognitive appraisal

According to Lazarus (1981a, 1981b), stress results from a "transaction" or relationship between an individual and the environment. This transaction, Lazarus postulated, is our assessment or evaluation of a stressor, our interpretation of what the stressor means to us personally. The process of interpreting the meaning of a stressor is known as **cognitive appraisal**. Any event (such as a pregnancy or receiving a grade of B+) can have different meanings for different people. For one it can be a source of joy, for another a source of stress. The appraisal process is one factor that accounts for our varying reactions to similar stressors.

Lazarus differentiated between two forms of cognitive appraisal: the initial or *primary appraisal* and the later *secondary appraisal*.

Primary appraisal: assessing the threat

Primary appraisal is the initial cognitive appraisal made in response to a possible stressor in order to determine whether that stressor is

The stress reaction on seeing an accident depends in part on the individual's primary appraisal.
SOURCE: Canada Wide/Warren Bekker.

relevant and threatening to the individual. For example, if we encounter a bad accident on the highway, a primary appraisal might conclude that although the accident is tragic, it is not personally relevant and not threatening. This appraisal would differ markedly if we see that the car is a close friend's. Then the primary appraisal would conclude that indeed the event is personally relevant and threatening. In both situations, the environmental stimuli are essentially the same: a car wreck at the side of the road. However, our reaction differs dramatically depending upon the primary appraisal.

An investigation of the importance of cognitive appraisal in stress reactions was conducted by Lazarus, Speisman, Mordkoff, and Davison (1962). They showed three groups of subjects a very explicit film of a genital operation carried out as part of an Australian Aboriginal rites-of-passage ritual. The film shown for all three groups was identical, but the groups heard different sound tracks. The "trauma" group saw the film with a sound track that focused on the pain and suffering involved in the procedure. The "intellectual" group heard a sound track that was clinical, cold, and devoid of emotion in its discussion of the ritual. The "denial" group was exposed to a sound track that minimized the pain and suffering. Physiological indicators of stress reactions taken during the showings were highest among the subjects in the trauma group. Evidently, the different sound tracks induced different primary cognitive appraisals by the three groups of the same movie, and therefore very different levels of stress resulted. This study is a powerful demonstration of the effects that primary cognitive appraisal has on reaction to stress.

Secondary appraisal: evaluating resources

Secondary appraisal is the later cognitive appraisal made in response to a stressor in order to evaluate the resources that are available to deal with that stressor. Should the stressor be confronted, avoided, or worked through? Should more information be collected or should the person simply try to relax and accept the situation? The resources to be evaluated are both internal (psychological and personality resources) and external (family, friends, and other support groups). The kind of resources available will depend on personality development, learning history, previous experience with coping, controllability of the stressor, and the attributions one has given for previous successes or failures.

In the helping professions, one of the helper's tasks is to assess the resources and capabilities of clients or patients in dealing with stressors. For example, in rehabilitation settings, therapists often deal with young adults who have suffered permanent and disabling diseases and traumas. Therapists must try to assess the patient's and family's ability to cope, adjust, and adapt to life under altered circumstances. Patients try to evaluate and assess these factors on their own as well. They attempt to come to terms with their situation and mobilize themselves to cope with the altered circumstances. This may mean re-arranging the household, scheduling work in different ways, making financial sacrifices, and changing expectations. The ease with which this is done will depend on the resources of the patient and family as they live with the disability.

Physiological mechanisms

Stress is a biological event that activates our central nervous system and many other organ systems in our body. This helps us prepare for action. It also can lead to the development of many so-called *stress diseases* and disorders.

Flight or fight reaction

As we saw in Chapter 2, the *autonomic nervous system (ANS)* is a division of the peripheral nervous system outside of the brain and spinal column. (Figures 2-7 and 2-8 will refresh your memory.) The ANS helps to maintain the stability of our internal systems. It also provides an important survival mechanism. When the organism is threatened, the *sympathetic nervous system* becomes aroused. This leads to diffuse bodily changes, including increases in heart rate, respiration, and blood pressure; dilation of pupils; dilation of air passages in the lungs; decreased digestion; increased sweating; and increased secretion of adrenaline. All of these responses prepare the organism to attack or to run. Cannon (1929) introduced the term **flight or fight reaction** to refer to this set of responses.

This reaction has survival value if there really is a need to run or fight. However, for humans living in a technological age, this extreme type of reaction is rarely necessary. The autonomic nervous system is not efficient for us when it becomes aroused just before a major speech, in an examination, or in confrontations with important people in our lives. We become highly mobilized and physiologically aroused when we want to remain calm, collected, and relaxed in dealing with psychological and interpersonal stressors. When the sympathetic nervous system is chronically activated, the organ systems that are stimulated are sometimes aroused to the point of dysfunction. We will discuss several such psychophysiological disorders in Chapter 14 (Abnormal Psychology).

ANS/pituitary interaction

Stress affects us both cognitively and physiologically. One important physiological reaction involves the secretion of hormones by the endocrine system. The autonomic nervous system stimulates this secretion of hormones. The following details of our physiological reactions to stress will build on our discussion of the biology of behaviour in Chapter 2.

The autonomic nervous system is regulated by the *hypothalamus*, which receives input from the cortex and from the reticular activating system. Thus, the hypothalamus is a key area in determining the body's response to stress. Stimulation of the hypothalamus causes activation of the autonomic nervous system. The sympathetic nervous system then activates many body systems. In particular, the sympathetic nervous system stimulates the interior of the adrenal glands, known as the **adrenal medulla**, to release **epinephrine** (commonly called *adrenaline*) that in turn leads to bodily activation. The hypothalamus also activates the attached **pituitary gland**, which is the "master gland" of the body. The pituitary gland secretes a hormone known as **adrenocorticotropic hormone (ATCH)** into the blood stream. This hormone then stimulates the outside of the adrenal glands, the **adrenal cortex**, to release a class of hormones known as **corticoids**, which are stress hormones. This chain of responses is summarized in Figure 13-9. Stress hormones affect the body's metabolism. With prolonged stress, in combination with the activation of the sympathetic nervous system, excessive levels of hormones can lead to bodily system breakdown. This can be seen in

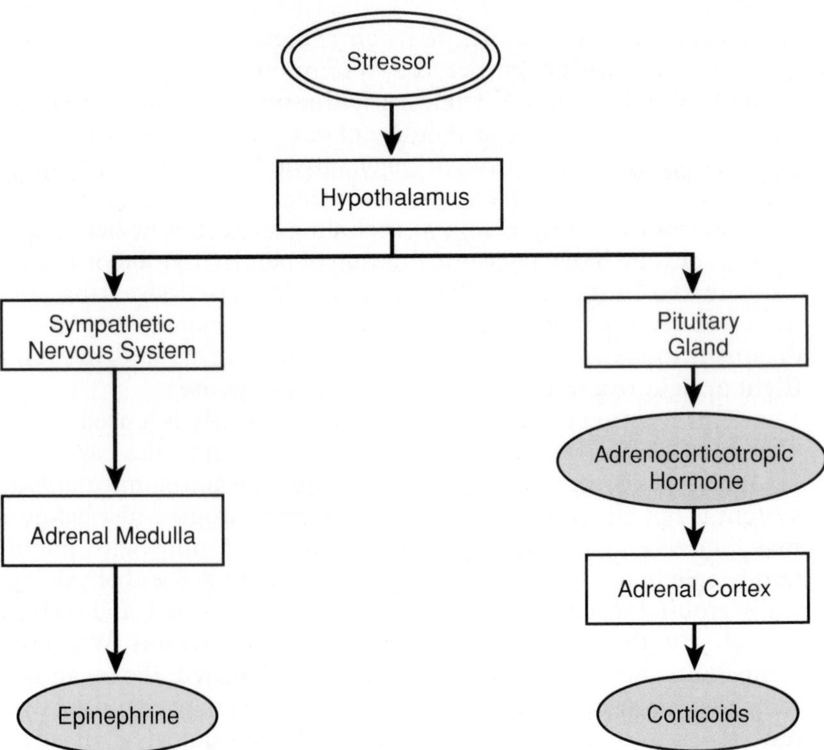

FIGURE 13-9 The secretion of hormones in response to stress

gastrointestinal ulcers, dysfunction of the adrenal glands, and even decreased immunity because of the decreased production of white blood cells and antibodies (Selye, 1982).

Common physical symptoms of stress include increased heart rate, upset stomach, diarrhea, difficulty catching one's breath, headaches, difficulty sleeping, increased frequency of urination, heart palpitations, skin problems, and increased susceptibility to colds and other illnesses. Sometimes these physical effects of stress are relatively mild and can serve as warnings that we are under too much stress. However, they can also become severe enough to lead to major medical problems if the warnings are not heeded.

General adaptation syndrome

There is a relatively consistent pattern of responses to any form of stress. Hans Selye, the late Canadian physiologist from McGill University postulated that "stress is the nonspecific result of any demand on the body" (Selye, 1982, p. 7). Selye called this nonspecific response the **General Adaptation Syndrome (GAS)** (Selye, 1956). In contrast to Cannon's *flight or fight reaction*, the General Adaptation Syndrome goes beyond the organism's initial reaction to threat. It describes the long-term pattern of response to a stressor in terms of three stages: alarm, resistance, and exhaustion. See Figure 13-10.

The *alarm phase* involves an initial response to any stressor, whether it is physical (such as the introduction of a virus) or psychological (such as coping with the loss of a loved one). There is an initial shock that results in a decrease in coping. Then the alarm phase continues with a mobilization of resources and an increase in physical and emotional arousal. One reason Selye believed that this syndrome is a rather general pattern in response to all stressors was that people tend to suffer the same kinds of generalized symptoms regardless of the specific illness or stressor. These reactions include decreased energy, headache, and some increase in temperature. These are the nonspecific effects of many forms of illness and occur as resources are being mobilized.

The *resistance phase* begins when bodily defences start to work and psychological defences are mobilized if there is a psychological stressor. During this phase of the syndrome, tolerance for the initial stressor increases as resistance builds. At the same time there is a decreased tolerance for other stressors. When we are fighting off a cold, our resistance may be lower for other infections. On the psychological front, we may become more irritable about unrelated issues when we are stressed by a specific situation.

Most stressors are dealt with completely either in the alarm phase or in the resistance phase. However, if the stressor is prolonged, resources become depleted and the *exhaustion* phase follows. Physiologically, this is the stage where the stress hormones become depleted and the organs which have been chronically aroused begin to break down. If the stressor does not stop, death may occur. On a psychological level, there can be emotional exhaustion with inappropriate and exaggerated defences, such as uncontrolled weeping, blatantly unrealistic denial of obvious facts, or uselessly repetitive

FIGURE 13-10 The General Adaptation Syndrome (GAS) According to Selye, the body reacts to a stressor in three stages: alarm phase, resistance phase, and exhaustion phase. Immediately after the stressor begins, there is a drop in resistance followed by a mobilization of defences. Then the body maintains a steady, high level of resistance. If the stressor lasts too long, the body's resources become depleted, and exhaustion or even death will follow.

SOURCE: Adapted from Seyle (1956).

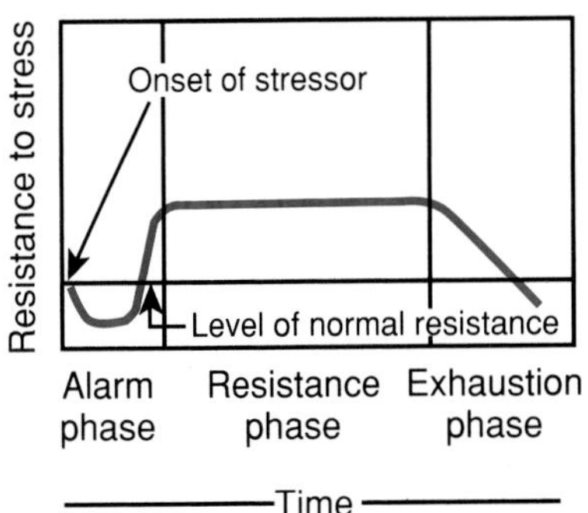

behaviours. There may also be substantial psychological *decompensation* or breakdown where the individual may lose contact with reality.

Stress diseases

Unremitting activation of the sympathetic nervous system and secretion of the corticoid hormones from the adrenal glands can lead to a number of stress-related diseases. These can include hypertension (high-blood pressure), ulcers, cardiovascular and cerebrovascular disorders, skin problems, asthma, rheumatoid arthritis, ulcerative colitis, and various forms of headache. Stress has even been linked with cancer development. In addition, stress sometimes leads to disease indirectly, because many people who are overwhelmed with stress neglect their health, increase their smoking, increase their drinking, maintain a poor diet, do not get sufficient sleep, and fail to seek medical assistance in the early stages of potentially serious illnesses. In fact, in Chapter 19 (Psychology and Health), we will argue that virtually all diseases are affected by psychological factors.

The development of a physical disorder that is stress-related is not a simple all-or-none proposition. As is indicated by Vulcano, Barnes, and Breen (1983), stress-related physical disorders are only one possible outcome resulting from stress. The development of such disorders also depends on many other factors. These factors include the types of stress as well as personality factors such as depression, anxiety, and cognitive problem-solving skill. Social factors such as the kinds of supports available and the person's ability to use the social support system can also be factors. Vulcano, Barnes, and Breen surveyed over 500 Canadian police officers, whose occupation is considered a highly stressful one. They found that the incidence of psychophysiological disorders was higher than that reported for the general population. Particularly striking was the increased prevalence of symptoms such as nervous stomach, diarrhea, indigestion, stomach ulcers, and colitis. The results further suggested that psychophysiological symptoms and conditions were more frequent in officers who were lonely and did not have the social supports available that others did.

Stress related diseases are not "all in the head." They involve actual damage to body-tissue. There are other kinds of disorders where psychological turmoil leads to physical symptoms without physical causes or tissue damage. We will discuss these disorders more in Chapter 14 (Abnormal Psychology). Our purpose in this chapter is to discuss the basic principles of stress. In later chapters we will apply these principles to specific disorders (Chapter 14) and consider their implications for the maintenance of health (Chapter 19).

Psychological reactions to stress

Stress has both physical and psychological impact. Emotional and cognitive functioning can be affected in many ways by stress. On a behavioural level for example, increased stress can lead to motoric restlessness, jumpiness, and tremors. As stress increases, whole-body shaking can occur. The person can even become immobilized and freeze in the face of extreme stress.

An optimal level of stress

Moderate stress can enhance performance. Extreme stress usually leads to disruption in functioning. We have all had trouble concentrating when we are anxious or under pressure. Initially, however, an increase in anxiety may be adaptive. For example, we will probably be more motivated and conscientious in studying if we feel some anxiety before an exam. However, there is an optimal level of stress. If the optimal level is exceeded, performance can decline rapidly. If we become too anxious during an exam, we may freeze, our mind may go blank, and we may not be able to recall well-learned information. As shown in Figure 13-11, the **Yerkes-Dodson inverted-U function** describes the relationship between level of arousal and performance (Yerkes & Dodson, 1908).

Complex behaviour requiring high levels of mental effort and cognitive activity tend to break down earlier under stressful conditions than do well-learned activities that demand less mental work. A highly anxious individual may be able to drive quite safely and competently (a well-learned activity) to school to take an oral exam but may not perform well in the more novel task of answering academic questions orally.

FIGURE 13-11 Yerkes-Dodson inverted-U function

Moderate levels of arousal or stress can enhance performance. Too much arousal may debilitate performance, whereas too little arousal may fail to produce sufficient motivation.

SOURCE: Based on Yerkes & Dodson (1908).

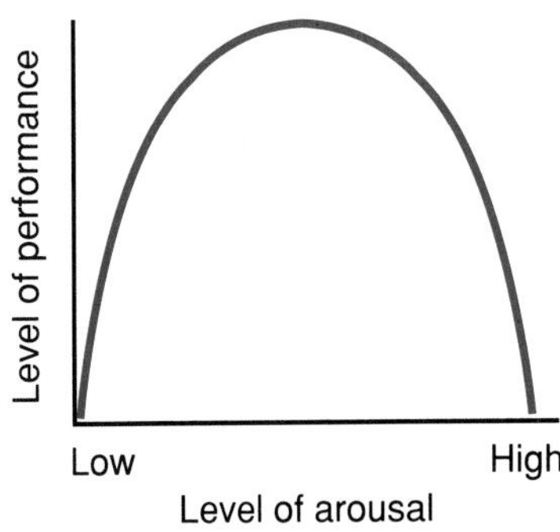

Defence mechanisms

As we discussed in Chapter 10, *defence mechanisms* help to protect the individual from anxiety and distress. However, they do this by distorting reality. Defence mechanisms such as *denial, repression*, and *reaction formation* take mental energy and often cause psychological blind spots. This can be costly. If there is evidence at work that our performance is deteriorating, we may be blind to it and not be able to make the necessary corrections to upgrade our performance. We may be very surprised if fired and feel that the firing is arbitrary, unfair, and discriminatory. Others might correctly believe that we received much warning, prior notice, and opportunities for improvement.

Adjustment disorders

Adjustment disorders are extreme behaviour disruptions that result from identifiable stressors. Such disorders can take the form of a disruption in social relationships or work functioning. The behavioural symptoms often go well beyond the normal or expected reaction to a particular stressor. Everyone reacts strongly to certain stressors in life, such as illness, relationship breakdown, and major financial losses. The reactions would not be diagnosed as adjustment disorders unless they exceed the "typical" response to such stressors. Expected reactions to the stress of beginning school for a 6-year old may be initial anxiety, a disruption in psychological stability, and a transient fear of separation. However, an adjustment disorder may be present if the child's behaviour changes dramatically and he or she is not able to meet the developmental challenge of beginning school. The child could become depressed, withdrawn, or anxious, leading to very noticeable impairment in functioning.

Stressors leading to an adjustment disorder may be single or multiple. They may also be unique or recurrent. They can involve interpersonal relationships (deteriorating communication patterns, physical and psychological abuse, separation and divorce), or physical health (terminal illness, chronic illness, general effects of aging). They can affect an individual or large social groups (natural disasters and catastrophes, such as high-rise hotel fires, earthquakes, and plane crashes). Stressors that lead to adjustment disorders may also be associated with unemployment, persecution, and relocation.

The disorder is defined by the reaction to the stressor. It usually develops within three months of the stressor's occurrence and involves extended and relatively continuous behavioural disruption (American Psychiatric Association, 1987). What forms do adjustment disorders take? They may appear as depression, tearfulness, and hopelessness. Anxiety and nervousness may predominate, or the disorder may appear as a mixture of anxiety and depression. Individuals may show radical changes in behaviour such as poor performance at school or work, social withdrawal, vandalism, truancy, or promiscuity. All of these forms of the adjustment disorder represent unsuccessful attempts to cope with stress. Although adjustment disorders are intensely stressful for the sufferer and disconcerting for those around him or her, there are other reactions to stress that are even more severe. In Chapter 14 (Abnormal Psychology), we will discuss the range of abnormal behaviour and see some reactions to stress that are more disabling than adjustment disorders.

Post-traumatic stress disorder can be a consequence of a sudden and traumatic loss such as that suffered by this young woman. She has just lost her home and members of her family in a tornado.
SOURCE: UPI/Bettmann.

Post-traumatic stress disorder (PTSD)

Some stressors are exceedingly traumatic: the death of one's family in an explosion, a soldier's experience of killing a blood-soaked enemy who dies in his arms, the unexpected loss of a business for which a person had worked for years, natural disasters, and even severe car accidents. Such catastrophic stressors often lead to a stress disorder called **post-traumatic stress disorder (PTSD)**. PTSD is characterized by flashbacks, emotional numbness, recurrent dreams, lack of interest in others, and emotional constriction. The person may be hypervigilant and have exaggerated startle responses and sleep disturbance. There can also be cognitive symptoms such as memory problems, lack of attention, and difficulties in problem-solving (American Psychiatric Association, 1987). This order can also lead to re-experiencing the initial trauma and a worsening of symptoms in situations that remind the person of the original traumatic event.

Post-traumatic stress disorder is a relatively new diagnostic label that was largely developed after the Vietnam war. The symptoms of PTSD have been noted for centuries, but now they have received an official designation as a diagnosable mental disorder. Post-traumatic stress disorder may occur immediately after the trauma or within the following months. When the symptoms last less than six months, the disorder is diagnosed as *acute*. When the symptoms begin within six months of the trauma and last longer than six months, the disorder is considered *chronic*. Of particular interest is the fact that post-traumatic stress disorder may be delayed. Symptoms can begin six or more months after the initial trauma.

The severe mental pain and anguish associated with post-traumatic stress disorder may lead to alcohol and drug abuse, marital breakdown, unemployment, increased hostility, suspiciousness, and suicide. The stress of war, particularly the Vietnam war, has been described by Blank (1982). Soldiers are exposed to poor living conditions, disease, the risk of physical injury, capture, torture, the sights and sounds of war, death, dismemberment, and disfigurement. In Vietnam, they also had to deal with stressors unique to that war. The objectives of the war were not clear. Guerilla warfare carries special threats of terrorist attack, tropical diseases, and poisonous snakes and other dangerous animals. When the soldiers came home, the stress was compounded by a lack of social support. In previous wars, homecoming aided the soldiers' ability to deal with, and get over, the war experience. Unfortunately for Vietnam veterans, given the political tension and ambivalence the war created in the United States, veterans were sometimes confronted by feelings of disgust, anger, and ridicule. They usually did not go through the kind of talking-down that is needed in dealing with this kind of experience. Only since the late 1970s have special programs been initiated to deal with the aftermath of the extreme stress suffered by veterans of the Vietnam war. Canadians who volunteered to fight in Vietnam have had even less support because no official agencies were formed to deal with the problem.

Post-traumatic stress disorder develops in the wake of a disaster or catastrophic event. During the crisis of a disaster, a different pattern emerges. How have people reacted during disasters such as earthquakes, train crashes, tornadoes, and airplane crashes? Researchers have uncovered a basic pattern of behaviour or syndrome associated with disasters. The first phase of the reaction consists of shock and a general disbelief about what has occurred. In extreme cases, people may become disoriented, stuporous, and later may not recall what had initially occurred. The next phase is one of heightened suggestibility. People are quite passive and willing to do what they are told. They will follow directions and be concerned about others, but they will not be efficient or able to use all their cognitive or physical resources to initiate their own behaviour. The third stage is a recovery stage in which the impact of what has happened begins to sink in. This phase is marked by a tense, apprehensive, and anxious mental state. In this stage, people feel and intensely need to talk and relive the event.

As time passes, it is possible that recovery may be complicated by grief over loss of acquaintances, friends, and family. Survivors often feel guilt remembering that they were not able to act more efficiently or were paralysed with fear watching somebody else die and were not able to do anything about it. Most survivors of the Nazi concentration camps later suffered in this way. They felt guilt because they survived and others did not. This *survival guilt* can lead to philosophical questioning and may be a major stumbling block in getting over the catastrophe. A post-traumatic stress disorder could develop, including flashbacks and intense mental anguish.

Stress is also experienced by those who are involved in rescue operations, medical evacuation, and, in fact, by the community at large. Imagine both the stress involved in being in a hotel during a major fire that led to multiple deaths and the stress involved in the

Disasters produce tremendous stress in the rescuers as well as the victims.
SOURCE: Canada Wide/Jim Garnett.

rescue operation. The rescuers had to remove charred bodies, see and hear tremendous human suffering, and deal with fast-paced and chaotic events. Disasters arouse great heroism, but they can also lead to increases in illness, alcohol abuse, family stress, violence, aggression, and other related adjustment problems (Adams and Adams, 1984).

Professional burnout

Professionals who work in settings marked by intense emotions and demands can also develop stress-related disorders. A nurse working in a critical care area sees anguish, suffering, and death every day. A worker in a crisis centre constantly deals with individuals in the midst of major life challenges, suicidal despair, and marital breakdown. Psychotherapists hear hours of human misery, depression, and intense anxiety.

Professionals who work in such emotionally charged environments may fall victim to **professional burnout**. The stress of dealing with intense emotional arousal on a day-to-day basis may lead to physical exhaustion and emotional exhaustion (such as despair and depression). Another symptom of professional burnout is a cynical, depersonalized, and almost uncaring attitude toward patients or clients. Along with this depersonalization, there can be a lack of enjoyment of work, a feeling that the person is just putting in time. Sometimes there is a greatly reduced sense of personal accomplishment and pleasure in work that before was stimulating and challenging. This kind of burnout can lead to absenteeism, physical illness, and eventually to psychological breakdown.

The risk factors for the development of professional burnout are relatively easy to define. Those who are at high risk usually work in settings where there are long hours with heavy demands and little feedback or positive appreciation for the work being done. In health care and social-service settings, a heavy caseload in an emotionally charged atmosphere is frequently a risk factor. Workers usually feel that they have little control and that they always have to "give out."

Preventative factors that protect against burnout include manageable caseloads and flexibility in schedules. Flexibility permits balancing of intensely emotionally charged work with other kinds of activity such as paperwork, research, teaching, or administration. A strong administrative support system is essential. There should be frequent reinforcement and feedback about performance, as well as permission to take care of oneself in dealing with the stress of the workplace. In some settings, staff have their own support groups that allow them to express their feelings, receive support from others, and jointly to tackle the problems of managing the stressful situation. Unless professional burnout is dealt with and prevented, there will be rapid job turnover, worker dissatisfaction, less efficient service, and a failure to serve adequately the needs of the clientele.

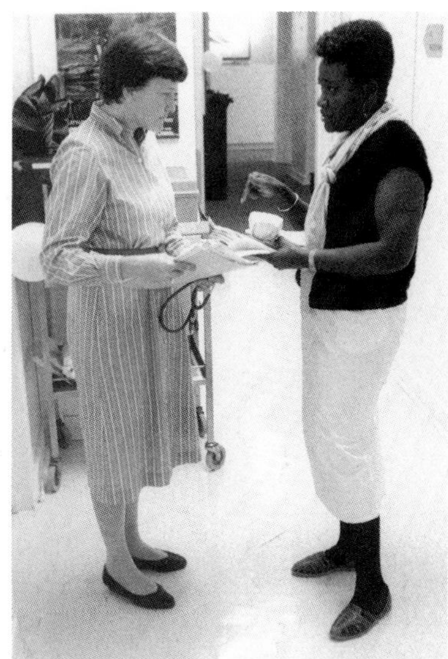

Professional burnout can lead to despair and cynicism.
SOURCE: Dick Hemingway.

COPING WITH STRESS

What can be done about stress? Psychologists have defined two primary methods that people use to cope with stress (Moos & Billing, 1982). One approach focuses on cognitions, especially problem-solving. Here, the person employs active coping methods to confront the problem directly. The other approach focuses on emotions, primarily anxiety. Here, the person copes with stress by doing "internal work."

Problem-focused methods

As we discussed earlier, the initial steps in reacting to any stressor are primary and secondary appraisal. Methods to deal with stress may involve a re-appraisal, re-definition, or re-analysis of the stressor. With respect to the primary appraisal, we should ask, "Has the stressor been seen accurately in all of its dimensions and does it really apply to us?" For instance, we may have misinterpreted our instructor's bad mood. It may not have resulted from his perception of our work but from his marital difficulties. With regard to the secondary appraisal, we may be able to prevent or decrease our stress level by re-evaluating our own set of resources. We might seek out more information, ask the advice of others, watch how similar people deal with the same stress, or attempt to restructure our thoughts about our relationship to the stressor. This restructuring may consist of attempting to see the stressor in a more favourable light, deciding that it could have been worse than it is, judging that we are better off than others, or concluding that some good may come out of dealing with the stressor.

Taylor (1983) has described the forms of cognitive restructuring and reappraisal that occur among those who deal with tragedies or threatening events. Taylor intensively interviewed 78 women who were diagnosed as having breast cancer. She also interviewed many of their family members. She found that the cognitive adaptation to the stress of cancer could be analyzed in terms of three major adjustments. First, the patients attempted to find an explanation for why the cancer occurred. The women examined the meaning of the cancer in terms of larger issues such as the meaning of life. They often reappraised life and valued it to a greater degree. Second, the patients attempted to gain some sense of mastery or control over the threatening event. They learned about the nature of cancer, its causes, and specific ways to prevent it from recurring. They changed their diet, readjusted their lifestyle to decrease stress, and learned to believe that through their own actions they could maintain good health. The third cognitive change was a restoration of self-esteem. The diagnosis of cancer in a healthy person is a tremendously stressful event that erodes the sense of invulnerability and well-being and the sense of self. Taylor discovered that self-esteem returned when patients began to see some value and good in their illness, believing that it had changed them for the better. Patients also felt themselves better off than others who had worse cancers.

Therefore, Taylor argued that successful adjustment to the stress and threat of cancer worked through the ability of the patients to sustain and develop illusions of control about their illness. These illusions had the effect of buffering them from the true magnitude of their situation. In other words, psychological defences may be beneficial if used sparingly. As Taylor states, "Not only did patients see themselves as genuinely well-adjusted at the time of the interview, and as better adjusted than they were during the cancer bout, they also saw themselves as better adjusted than before they had any signs of cancer!" (Taylor, 1983, p. 1165).

Moos and Tsu (1977) have listed the types of cognitive coping strategies that people use in their adjustment to serious physical illness. These methods include (1) denying or minimizing the seriousness of the illness, (2) seeking additional information about the illness, (3) asking for reassurance and emotional support, (4) learning about the medical complications related to the illness and various treatments, (5) establishing appropriate goals for themselves, (6) mentally rehearsing various outcomes, and (7) attempting to find some meaning or reason for what is occurring.

Sometimes people need to learn new skills to cope with stress. For example, this could be the case with people who are widowed after lengthy marriages in which traditional roles had been maintained. This may be especially true for widowers who are unaccustomed to household management, cooking, budgeting, and laundry. It could also apply to widows who may find themselves needing to learn about pension management, financial planning, and dealing with sex-role prejudices at the local service station.

Emotion-focused methods

Emotion-focused methods of dealing with stress entail lessening anxiety and finding more internal peace and acceptance. In using these methods, the person is not dealing directly with the environment. However, internal changes often make it possible to deal with external problems more effectively.

Changing emotions

Moos and Billing (1982) outline three methods of changing one's emotions: emotional discharge, acceptance, and affective regulation.

Emotional discharge is the release of emotion through actual expression, such as yelling when faced with a real frustration, or crying when faced with a loss. **Acceptance** occurs in situations where there is no control over a particular stressor. The person adapts to a particular outcome and lets it occur without struggle. **Affective regulation** involves controlling the emotional arousal that occurs through the activation of the sympathetic nervous system. This can be accomplished in many ways, depending on the situation. It may be best to hold the feelings in and not react immediately. Alternatively, it may be best to confront and deal with the feelings, particularly when they involve painful, anxiety-arousing and depressing emotion.

Exercise

Exercise is a physical method of dealing with stress. Physical activation is lessened through an intense and vigorous work-out. Exercise often provides a considerable amount of stress reduction, as well as positive effects that lead to increased physical health.

Drugs

The taking of various kinds of drugs is also an emotion-focused method. Drugs can decrease emotional tension and the physiological activation that occurs with stress. Many forms of tranquilizers are available that artificially decrease sympathetic nervous system functioning, help with sleep disorders, and make one feel more relaxed. Benzodiazepines, such as Valium, barbiturate sleeping pills, alcohol, and many forms of nonprescription drugs (e.g., marijuana and hashish) are used extensively in our drug-taking society. Unfortunately, there is evidence that the use and abuse of these drugs can lead to new problems. In the short-term, a tranquillizing medication may be useful in helping an individual to cope better with stresses in life. However, the long-term use of these medications can lead to addiction, health problems, and a failure to cope with life's stresses adaptively.

Relaxation methods

Psychological techniques, such as learning to relax, can be very effective in decreasing the bodily arousal of intense stress. **Progressive relaxation** (Jacobson, 1970) is one method to decrease muscle tension, blood pressure, heart rate, and sympathetic nervous system activity. Progressive relaxation can be learned quite easily by willing subjects. It involves learning to relax multiple muscle groups. *Meditation* is another method that can lower bodily arousal. As we noted in Chapter 9, it is unclear whether meditation can reduce bodily arousal more than simple relaxation or resting (Holmes, 1984; Suler, 1985; and Shapiro, 1985). For an effective relaxation exercise, see the first Close-up at the end of this chapter.

Biofeedback

As we discussed in Chapter 2, **biofeedback** is a treatment procedure in which a person who is provided with ongoing information about his or her autonomic functions can learn to modify those functions.

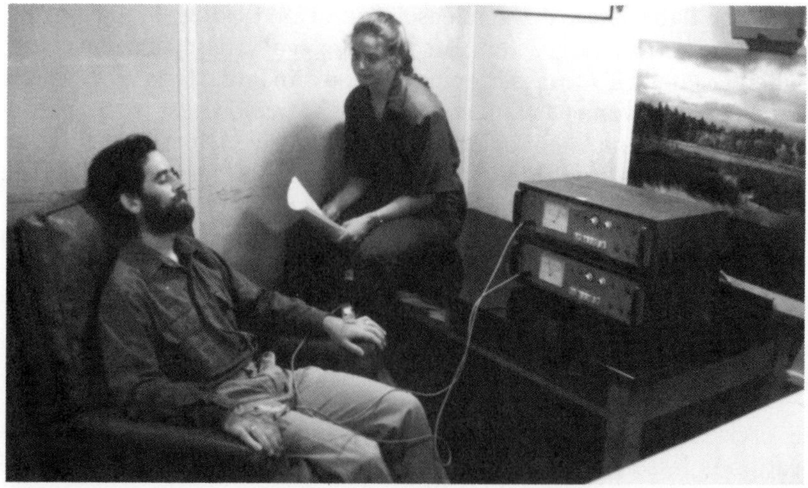

Biofeedback can often give a person control over bodily functions that are normally considered "automatic." This client is learning to relax by monitoring activity in his sweat glands.
SOURCE: Courtesy David Martin.

Biofeedback utilizes sensitive equipment to detect, amplify, and signal measurements of physiological responses, such as blood pressure, heart rate, skin temperature, brain waves, and muscular tension (Blanchard and Epstein, 1978). Biofeedback can be used to reduce physiological stress reactions. Using feedback about their bodily functions, people are able to learn to control their physiological activity to some extent. Thus, in one particular biofeedback application, the goal may be to control heart rate in stressful situations. To do this, an individual is given information, either visually or auditorily, about heart rate. The person uses this information to decrease the heart rate by employing mental mechanisms, such as particular kinds of images, to induce different kinds of bodily sensations and relaxation. As we said in Chapter 2, it is controversial whether biofeedback is any more effective than relaxation, exercise, stress-management techniques, lifestyle changes, and counselling in helping people control stress (White and Tursky, 1982).

Social support

A comprehensive prescription for the prevention of stress would be hard to write. It would include an individual recognizing and accepting limits of skill, endurance, and energy, having appropriate expectations and goals, having the ability to organize oneself, and the ability to slow down and carefully assess both stressors and challenges. It would take into account the availability of both internal resources and resources that exist in the natural social support system. A healthy lifestyle, a healthy diet, adequate vacations, and plentiful exercise are important contributors to good health and reduction of stress.

As important as all these ingredients are, the importance of social support is probably most critical. Studies have been uniform in showing that decreased social contact, loneliness, and isolation are related to poor outcomes in stressful situations (Mitchell, Billings, and Moos, 1982). In times of stress and turmoil, we frequently look to the people around us to assist us in coping. They give us reassurance, caring, joint problem-solving, love, and goodwill. We also look to others for more instrumental assistance such as making sure we are well fed, have clean clothes, and have a roof over our heads. We seek out others at times when we are stressed (Schachter, 1959). Research has indicated that social support does reduce psychological fall-out at times of stress. It contributes to greater recovery in people who are ill. It is also effective in helping terminally-ill patients deal with the stressors that they are facing (Taylor, et al., 1986).

The benefits of talking about trauma

James Pennebaker and his co-workers have reported some dramatic evidence about the impact of disclosing and confronting traumatic events from one's life. Pennebaker and O'Heeron (1984) studied people whose spouses died in accidents or through suicide. The more these spouses discussed the deaths with friends and the less they brooded and ruminated, the fewer health problems they reported. In other research, subjects spoke into a microphone about the most traumatic experiences of their entire lives. Control-group subjects talked just as much but simply discussed their plans for the remainder of the day. Those who talked about emotionally significant topics showed signs of lower stress afterward. For example, they showed "large drops in systolic blood pressure . . . after talking about profound topics" (Pennebaker & Susman, 1988, p. 331).

Even more convincing, Pennebaker, Kiecolt-Glaser, and Glaser (1988a) randomly assigned university students to groups in which they either wrote about "the most traumatic and upsetting experiences of your entire life" or about superficial topics such as daily activities and social events attended recently. There were four separate 20-minute writing sessions on four different days. Prior to doing the writing, each subject had blood drawn and measures of autonomic system arousal taken. Blood samples taken after the writing permitted the experimenters to assess changes in the immune system. It was found that subjects who had disclosed traumatic events were more likely to have improved functioning of the immune system relative to the control subjects. In addition, university health-service records revealed that these students made fewer visits to the doctor in the months after the study than did the control subjects. Pennebaker and Beall (1986) reported a similar reduction in health service use after self-disclosure sessions.

These are dramatic findings with sweeping implications for health care and psychotherapy. Some writers caution against drawing unwarranted conclusions from the findings (Neale, Cox, Valdimarsdottir, and Stone, 1988). For example, we can't know that the reduction in visits to the health service was a direct result of changes in immune functioning. But even these critics "find the disclosure treatment quite exciting and look forward to new work in this area" (Neale et al., 1988, p. 637). Pennebaker has responded to these critics both by acknowledging the need for more research and by arguing that the data are strong enough to be "cautiously optimistic" (Pennebaker, Kiecolt-Glaser, and Glaser, 1988b, p. 639.)

Confronting one's traumatic memories by disclosing them to a person one trusts can lead to less inhibition and brooding. It may also have a beneficial impact on physical health.
SOURCE: Courtesy David Martin.

CLOSE-UP Relaxing in Your "Safe Spot"

When giving workshops on relaxation, we have found one of the most effective exercises to be deep breathing in a vividly imagined "safe spot." We use this exercise ourselves to relax before giving a workshop. Participants report it is almost immediately helpful. You may find it useful too.

First, think of a specific time and place when you strongly felt the way you want to feel now. Think of a good memory. Then think of the specific word that describes the feeling you had. Make it the unique word for your experience. It might be a general word such as "relaxed," "peaceful," or "calm." Or it might be something that comes from your own personal needs, such as "safe," "alone," "loved." We even knew a teenage boy who chose "angry." That sounds paradoxical, but he felt most calm that way. Choose what is best for you.

Get in a comfortable position with eyes closed or open, whichever feels better. Imagine the scene of your specific incident as vividly as you can. Use all of your senses. What sounds were there? Imagine them. Was the air moving? What did it smell like? Could you feel it on your skin? Could you feel grass or the fabric of a chair or movement? How were you being touched? What did you see? Make your imagined scene as vivid and as alive as possible.

As you hold this image, experience the feeling that you liked. Breathe deeply, pulling the air all the way into your belly. As you breathe in, slowly say to yourself, "I am." Hold the breath for a few seconds and slowly exhale, silently saying the word you chose to describe your feeling. As the air leaves your body, imagine that tension is draining out with it. Focus on your body. Where is the most tension? Focus on draining that tension out with your breath. Do this for as many times as you wish. Most people find that four or five deep breaths are the minimum to achieve the benefits of relaxation.

The beauty of this exercise is that you can do it anywhere, anytime, and no one will know what you are doing. We know people who do it to control anger. Sometimes they are even looking at the person with whom they are angry and secretly calming themselves. Others can sometimes diminish the effects of an asthma attack or relieve pain caused by chronically tense shoulders. At first it takes some effort and practice, but the relaxation is usually so immediate that it is quite rewarding to learn this exercise. With practice, you can use this relaxation tool almost automatically.

CLOSE-UP The Stress of Survival from Cancer

Medical discoveries have resulted in the ability to detect cancer in early stages. New treatments have changed the popular view of this disease from one that was inevitably fatal to one that can often be curable. In fact, the five-year survival rate for all forms of cancer is greater than 50%. But what does survival after cancer lead to? Koocher and O'Malley (1981) have written about the psychological adjustment that occurs in children who survive cancer. They have documented what they call the **Damocles Syndrome**. Patients feel the constant threat of recurrence of the disease, as though the sword of Damocles were suspended above their heads and could fall at any time. This syndrome can leave survivors of cancer anxious, depressed, and in constant fear as they attempt to put their lives back into gear. They are under the chronic stress of knowing that the very treatments that cure cancer are toxic, create tissue destruction and may even lead to an increased risk of a secondary cancer later in life (Li, Cassady, and Jaffe, 1975). Cella and Tross (1986) have compared 60 survivors of Hodgkin's Disease (a cancer of the lymph nodes and spleen) with a sample of physically healthy men. The cancer patients in this study had been free of symptoms for an average of two years prior to the study. Their results showed that there were no major psychological difficulties after the stress of the cancer. However, there were some subtle psychological effects that had markedly changed the patients. Some of these may be positive changes. Often the patients' brush with their own mortality led to an increased appreciation of life compared with those who did not deal with the stress of cancer. On the negative side, there were some psychological costs. The stress led to subtle distress and decreases in motivation for interpersonal intimacy. In addition, the patients showed lowered work capacity as well as bodily distress reflected in decreases in physical stamina, less sleep, and appetite disturbance. Thus the good news regarding cure from cancer should be tempered with the knowledge that lasting psychosocial changes may result.

SPECIAL TOPIC Grief

Grief is a stress reaction that almost all of us will have to deal with in life. In Chapter 12, we briefly discussed some issues of facing one's own death. In this section, we will discuss grieving the death of another. **Grief** refers to the painful psychological state that follows an important loss, particularly the loss of a loved one. In fact, this loss is one of the most stressful that people must deal with. But we may also experience grief following other losses, such as a loss of innocence, virginity, youth, health, or a loss of opportunities. There are also the kinds of losses people deal with in debilitating illnesses and disorders, such as the loss of independence and functioning for a young person rendered *quadriaretic* (paralysed from the neck down) by a recent spinal cord injury. Such an injury is a tremendously stressful event that involves serious feelings of grief.

Many factors will influence the way a loss is dealt with and the consequent grief syndrome. In loss through death, factors such as the suddenness of death, relationship with the lost one, residual guilt or ill-feeling, ambivalent feelings, family supports, prior level of psychological adjustment, and understanding of death are all important.

Grief in children

The understanding of death is particularly important for children. Their reaction to death will depend quite substantially on how they understand it. Children's ability to conceptualize death depends on their level of cognitive functioning and what they have been taught about death. Parents' and other significant people's reactions to the death and how they communicate these to the child also play an important role (Stambrook & Parker, 1987). A child under the age of 6 or 7 is still in the preoperational stage of cognitive development. Thinking is based on how things appear, and the child uses few rules of thinking (as we discussed in Chapter 12). The child may easily misinterpret what death is and become confused and disturbed about the loss of a parent, for example. Telling a child that a parent is in heaven and that heaven is up in the sky may create intense fear the next time the child goes to the airport for a flight or watches the remaining parent depart on a plane. Clear, consistent, and concrete information should be given to prevent such misunderstandings. When information is embedded in a religious context, there must be sufficient information given to prevent misinterpretation. A parent who listens carefully to both what the child says and does not say will be in a good position to help a child deal with the stress of losing a loved one. Children can adapt well following loss when they are allowed to grieve and express their feelings in age-appropriate ways. It is normal for children to show their reactions and healthy for them to see the pain and distress of surrounding adults.

The grieving child has specific fears that must be dealt with sensitively.
SOURCE: "The Umpire," National Film Board.

Instead, if adults attempt to hide all their pain, the child is still able to perceive the distortions in communication patterns, the tension, and the changed circumstances. This can be a breeding ground for misconceptions about what has happened, particularly about their own role in the loss. Koocher (1986) states that children will attempt to deal with three questions related to the death of a loved one: (1) Did it happen because of something I did (or failed to do)? (2) Will it happen to me (or someone else I care about)? and (3) Who will take care of me if and when it does happen?

Grief in adults

As we noted in Chapter 12, when adults face the loss of a loved one, the normal grief reaction begins with the death and can continue for months or even years. Initially there is shock, then disbelief and a psychological numbness. This stage gives way to very intense and deep feelings of loss, yearning, regret, and the tears and weeping associated with depression. There may be quite paralysing anxiety at these times too, with symptoms such as shortness of breath, dizziness, and panic. Sleep is disrupted and appetite may be disturbed as well. The second major phase in normal grief or bereavement may begin three or four weeks after the loss. It can include dwelling on the circumstances surrounding the death. Could something have been done sooner? Could the doctor have been called earlier? What if I hadn't asked him to go out for the paper? What if I had done things differently? There is also a search for the meaning of the death (why did this have to happen?) and times when the bereaved searches for the deceased. This searching may entail thinking the loved one is present in a room, thinking one hears the lost person, or anticipating seeing the person in a particular place. It is very hard to break old habits, and these actions are based on well established behaviour patterns that are built on the previous interaction between the bereaved and the deceased.

The bereaved person may return to work after two or three weeks following the death of a loved one. Acute symptoms of loss tend to lessen in the first few months after the death. However, it often isn't until one year has elapsed that recovery from such a loss begins. Sometimes there is a conscious decision that life must be carried on again. The final recovery phase of bereavement involves reintegrating oneself back into social life, integrating the loss, and being willing to move on psychologically (Schulz, 1978). It is important to remember that the symptoms of grief may last significantly longer than this first year. The grieving person often feels "abnormal" when others say that grief "should" last just one year because that's what the book says. Grief can last for years. It is important not to interpret these "stages" of mourning rigidly. Each individual's experiences are different.

Mourning a suicide

Death by suicide presents unique adjustment challenges to those who survive. The guilt associated with having someone close commit suicide is staggering. It can lead to many psychological problems for years to come.

Some psychologists speculate that suicides can run in families not because the act of suicide can be inherited but because of the psychological legacy that is left behind. Anniversary dates of suicides (or any death) are particularly stressful for survivors. When a suicide has occurred in a family, the natural inhibitions for this kind of behaviour may be lowered because the act may be seen as a legitimate solution to life problems.

There are special forms of treatment available for family and friends of those who die by suicide. There are also mental health treatments available to deal with the stress that many other forms of death bring. These include support groups available for cancer victims and survivors and for parents who have lost children through sudden infant death syndrome. Organizations such as Compassionate Friends also assist in dealing with various kinds of loss through death.

Chapter Summary

1. Stress is a relative concept. Stress results when an organism's physical and psychological equilibrium is disturbed. All change leads to stress, but not all stress is harmful. Negative reactions to stressors are called distress. Positive reactions are called eustress.

2. Psychological research into stress has expanded dramatically over the past two decades. It has given rise to two subfields in psychology: behavioural medicine and health psychology.

3. Although we all have personal experience with stress, scientific study requires that we operationalize the concept of stress. To investigate the phenomenon, researchers use laboratory analogue studies, field studies, and survey studies.

4. One of the important tools in the assessment of stress is the use of rating scales such as the Social Readjustment Rating Scale and the Life Experiences Survey. In general, the higher the rate of life changes, the higher the rate of subsequent physical illness.

5. Stressors can differ in type (life events versus hassles), intensity, and duration (acute versus chronic). The impact of a stressor also depends on its predictability and controllability. Brady's studies of executive monkeys seemed to indicate that some controllability over stressors leads to ulcers. However, Brady's work has been discredited because he did not randomly assign monkeys to groups. Follow-up studies by Weiss have shown that controllability and predictability of stressors are desirable and beneficial.

6. Seligman's research on learned helplessness showed that animals exposed to inescapable shock suffered more stress and learned not to respond in effective ways, even in later situations where the shock was avoidable. The ability to control stressors is important. But the perception or belief that we can control stressors may be even more important.

7. Frustration is a common source of stress. According to the frustration-aggression hypothesis, an organism will attack once frustration builds up to a certain level. This hypothesis has important social consequences for understanding scapegoating and urban violence.

8. Conflict arises when there are two or more incompatible motives or goals. There are four main types of conflict: approach-approach conflict, approach-avoidance conflict, double or multiple approach avoidance conflict, and avoidance-avoidance conflict.

9. The same stressors can have markedly different effects on different people. Each individual makes his or her own primary appraisal and secondary appraisal of a given situation.

10. Perceptions of stressors activate the sympathetic branch of the autonomic nervous system, which produces the fight or flight reaction. Hormones are released by several endocrine glands, particularly the adrenal glands. The chronic overactivity of these systems can lead to stress diseases and tissue damage.

11. Selye has called the long-term pattern of response to stressors the General Adaptation Syndrome. It consists of three stages: the alarm phase, the resistance stage, and the exhaustion stage.

12. Moderate stress can enhance performance. According to the Yerkes-Dodson Inverted-U Function, too much arousal can debilitate performance, and too little arousal may fail to produce sufficient motivation.

13. Stress disrupts cognitive functioning such as memory, problem-solving, and concentration. We sometimes use defence mechanisms to lessen the impact of stress, but this leads to distortions in thinking.

14. Adjustment disorders are extreme disruptions in functioning that result from identifiable stressors. Post-traumatic stress disorder (PTSD) often results from catastrophic events. During a catastrophe, people usually respond first with disbelief, then with heightened suggestibility, and then with intense anxiety.

15. People working in helping professions who experience intense emotions and demands may fall victim to professional burnout. The person may become physically and emotionally drained and may develop a cynical attitude toward clients.

16. To cope with stress, we can use two main strategies. Problem-focused methods include cognitive reappraisal, cognitive restructuring, and the learning of new skills. Emotion-focused methods include the changing of emotions, exercise, drugs, relaxation, biofeedback, and social support. Some research suggests that talking about trauma reduces stress diseases.

Key Terms

Acceptance Adapting to a stressful outcome and letting it occur without struggle.

Acute Short-lived.

Adjustment disorders Extreme behaviour disruptions that result from identifiable stressors.

Adrenal cortex The outer part of the adrenal gland which secretes stress hormones called corticoids.

Adrenal medulla The inner portion of the adrenal gland which secretes epinephrine and norepinephrine.

Adrenaline See *epinephrine*.

Adrenocorticotrophic hormone (ACTH) Hormone secreted by the pituitary gland as part of stress response. It stimulates the adrenal cortex.

Affective regulation Controlling the emotional arousal that occurs through the activation of the sympathetic nervous system.

Approach-approach conflict The conflict of wanting two goals, one of which must be sacrificed if the other is to be attained.

Approach-avoidance conflict The conflict of having a single goal that is both desired and feared at the same time.

Avoidance-avoidance conflict The conflict of two undesirable goals, one of which must be attained if the other is to be avoided.

Behavioural medicine The field of study that applies psychological knowledge to the treatment of physical disease.

Biofeedback Treatment procedure in which a person who is provided with ongoing information about his or her autonomic functions can learn to modify those functions.

Burnout See *professional burnout*.

Chronic Long-lasting.

Cognitive appraisal The process of interpreting the meaning of a stressor.

Conflict A source of frustration that results from having two or more incompatible motives or goals at the same time.

Corticoids Stress hormones secreted by the adrenal cortex.

Damocles Syndrome The fear felt by patients who have recovered from cancer that the disease will recur.

Distress Negative reaction to stressors.

Double or multiple approach-avoidance conflict Having two or more goals, each of which is desired and feared at the same time.

Emotional discharge The release of emotion through actual expression.

Epinephrine Hormone secreted by the adrenal medulla to arouse emergency responses. It is commonly called adrenaline.

Eustress A positive reaction to stressors.

Executive monkeys In Brady's classic studies, those monkeys who could exercise control over the shocks. They developed ulcers, whereas the passive monkeys did not.

Field study Research method in which behaviour is studied in the natural environment.

Fight or flight reaction Cannon's term for the response to threat made by the autonomic system. The ANS produces a quick arousal that prepares the organism for either fleeing or resisting.

Frustration The stressful reaction to being blocked from attaining an expected and desired goal.

Frustration-aggression hypothesis The hypothesis that once frustration reaches a threshold level, it will arouse the organism to attack.

Gastric ulcers Lesions of the stomach lining that are caused by excess secretions of acid. They often result from stress.

General Adaptation Syndrome (GAS) Selye's description of the long-term pattern of response to stress. It consists of three stages: alarm, resistance, and exhaustion.

Grief The painful psychological state that follows an important loss.

Health psychology The field of study that applies psychological knowledge to all aspects of maintaining wellness and treating illness.

Laboratory analogue study Research method designed to simulate real-life scenarios in the laboratory so that the subjects' reactions can be studied under well-controlled conditions.

Learned helplessness A generalized tendency to give up under stress. It results from frequent experience with uncontrollable stressors.

Life Experiences Survey A test compiled by Sarason, Johnson, and Siegel in their survey study of stress. Each event is rated in terms of the amount of change required and the quality of its impact (i.e., positive or negative).

Multiple approach-avoidance conflict See *double or multiple approach-avoidance conflict.*

Pile-up effect The cumulative impact of many life changes occurring in close succession.

Pituitary gland The "master gland" of the endocrine system. In stress, it secretes adrenocorticotrophic hormone (ACTH), which stimulates the adrenal gland.

Post-traumatic stress disorder (PTSD) A stress disorder resulting from a catastrophic stressor. It is characterized by flashbacks, emotional numbness, recurrent dreams, lack of interest in others, and emotional constriction.

Primary appraisal The initial cognitive appraisal made in response to a possible stressor in order to determine whether that stressor is relevant and threatening to the individual.

Professional burnout A condition in which professionals can be overwhelmed by demands on their personal resources and develop exhaustion, despair, and a cynical attitude toward clients.

Progressive relaxation A method of decreasing the activity of the sympathetic nervous system through the relaxation of multiple muscle groups.

Secondary appraisal The later cognitive appraisal made in response to a stressor in order to evaluate the resources that are available to deal with that stressor.

Social Readjustment Rating Scale A scale compiled by Holmes and Rahe in their survey study of stress. All events are measured only in terms of life-change units.

Stress The pattern of an organism's responses to demands for change or threatening circumstances.

Stressor The external source of demands for change. The stimuli that arouse stress reactions.

Survey study Research method in which groups of subjects are asked for information through questionnaires or interviews.

Yerkes-Dodson Inverted-U Function The relationship between level of arousal and performance as described by Yerkes and Dodson. Too much arousal debilitates performance; too little does not motivate performance.

Suggested Readings

Eliot, R.S., & Breo, D.L. (1984). *Is it worth dying for?* New York: Bantam. Just the title of this book is a gripping reminder. We once gave a workshop and cited this title. Some months later a woman told us that our comment had such an effect that she switched jobs, even though she took a pay cut. Written by a physician whose stressful lifestyle led to a heart attack ("when the elephant sat on my chest"), the book is full of useful advice on understanding and managing stress.

Hanson, P.G. (1986). *The joy of stress.* Kansas City: Andrews, McMeel, & Parker. This is a practical, well-written book for the layperson. It shows how stress is not necessarily bad and can even be good for the person when handled properly. A cassette tape is available with effective stress-reducing methods and exercises.

Lazarus, R.S., & Folkman, S. (1984). *Stress, appraisal, and coping.* New York: Springer. This is a scholarly resource that summarizes the literature well. It expands on our discussion of how one's interpretation or appraisal of stress is significant in how we react to stress.

Schulz, R. (1978). *The psychology of death, dying, and bereavement.* Reading, MA: Addison-Wesley. This older book is still a classic about the grieving process.

White, L., & Tursky, B. (eds.) (1982). *Clinical biofeedback: efficacy and mechanisms.* New York: Guilford Press. This collection of essays is a good introduction to the use of biofeedback. It presents research findings, clinical applications, and theoretical explanations of how biofeedback works.

CHAPTER 14

SOURCE: Caven Atkins, Detail from *Mountain Vision* (1932).

Abnormal Psychology

AT SOME TIME in our lives, we all experience emotional problems of some kind. We are often confused about how to make sense of the kind of human behaviour that seems destructive to the individual and those who are close to him or her. In this chapter, we will be discussing problems that all of us face, although these problems are usually not extreme enough to be called "abnormal." In fact, one of the most important lessons to be learned in this chapter is that we all have emotional problems. Even though most of these are problems in living rather than illnesses, the principles by which everyday behaviour develops are the same as the principles that underlie problems serious enough to be called "mental disorders."

We hope and believe that you will learn much that will interest you and increase your understanding. However, it is especially important in this chapter to remember that this is not a self-help book that will give you answers to your problems. It would be wrong to expect answers to complex problems in a brief discussion that is intended only to introduce the basic principles of abnormal behaviour. Treat this as academic material that may have some application to your life. It will not make you into an expert. Please don't go home and say, "Mother, I finally found out what's wrong with you." We also hope you don't fall prey to the "medical student's disease." As medical students learn the symptoms of each new disease, it is quite customary for them to "contract" that disease, seeing in themselves all the signs that surely mean imminent death. Don't be surprised, then, if you see yourself somewhere in this chapter. Indeed, it is likely that you will see yourself, because most of the problems we will discuss occur in everyone to some extent. For many "mental disorders" there is little qualitative difference between "normal" and "abnormal." The difference may be in degree of severity. For some disorders, abnormal behaviour does involve biochemical dysfunction, so it will be important to distinguish between disorders that are primarily psychological and those that include physical factors.

To some extent, we all suffer from problems in living, from painful emotions, and from self-defeating behaviours.
SOURCE: Canada Wide.

DEFINING "ABNORMAL"

The word "abnormal" has many meanings. Literally, it simply means "different from what is common." Thus, in one sense, a very intelligent person is abnormal. However, "abnormal" usually carries a negative connotation. When used to describe human problems it often implies sickness. In the past it even implied an evil. Most "abnormal behaviour" is not the result of illness at all but rather stems from the problems in living that each of us suffers. We hope that, after you study this chapter, you will never again refer to someone as "a neurotic" or "a schizophrenic," as though he or she were different from the rest of us in some qualitative way. Generally speaking, normal and abnormal are on a continuum. To some extent, we all suffer from problems in living, from painful emotions, and from self-defeating behaviours. If these problems become severe enough they may be labelled "abnormal," but they are not different *in kind* from other problems. They are different in complexity and in severity.

We are emphasizing this issue because our experience has been that many people still think primarily in terms of "mental illness," a way of thinking that hampers understanding of human behaviour problems. It *is* true that physical and genetic factors seem to be factors in some kinds of emotional problems, and we will discuss these factors at the appropriate places. But the important fact to keep in mind is that people *have* schizophrenic problems—not that they *are* schizophrenics. (There is real danger in labelling people.)

The *psychological perspective* suggests that many behavioural disorders are better understood in terms of our basic human processes (such as learning and cognition) rather than as "mental illness." This perspective has important implications for helping people deal with such disorders. It suggests that our efforts should concentrate not so much on curing mental illness as on altering maladaptive ways of thinking, perceiving, and behaving (see Figure 14-1).

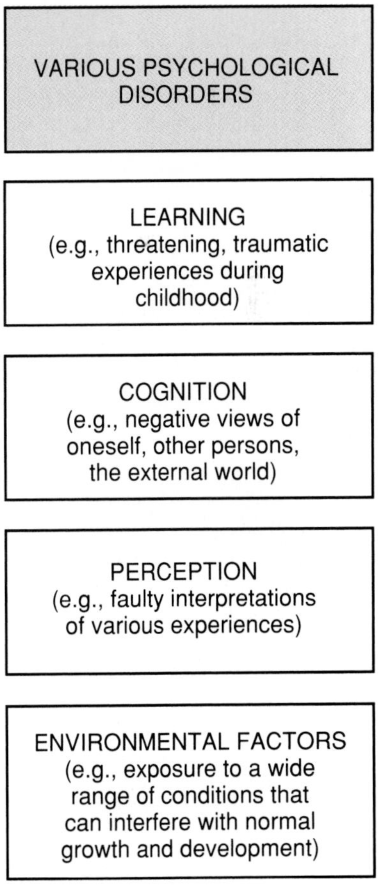

The most authoritative definition of "mental disorder" is found in the American Psychiatric Association's *Diagnostic and Statistical Manual IIIR* (DSM-IIIR), (1987). We will make frequent reference to DSM-IIIR, since it is the most widely used system for classifying abnormal behaviour. As its title implies, it has been through three major versions (the "R" stands for "revised").

The definition of "mental disorders" from DSM-IIIR includes several elements. A mental disorder is a *syndrome* or pattern of behaviours, thoughts, and feelings that are associated with (1) *present distress* (a painful symptom) or (2) *disability* (impairment in one or more important areas of functioning) or (3) a *significantly increased risk* of death, pain, disability, or an important loss of freedom. To qualify as a mental disorder, the behaviours, thoughts, and feelings must be more than an "expectable" response to a traumatic event such as the death of a loved one (American Psychiatric Association, 1987, p. xxii).

FIGURE 14-1 The psychological perspective on behavioural disorders

SOURCE: Adapted with permission from Allyn and Bacon, 1989.

VARIOUS PSYCHOLOGICAL DISORDERS

LEARNING
(e.g., threatening, traumatic experiences during childhood)

COGNITION
(e.g., negative views of oneself, other persons, the external world)

PERCEPTION
(e.g., faulty interpretations of various experiences)

ENVIRONMENTAL FACTORS
(e.g., exposure to a wide range of conditions that can interfere with normal growth and development)

The diathesis-stress perspective

We have mentioned both psychological and physical factors in understanding abnormal behaviour. Different theorists argue for the primacy of one kind of cause over the other. We think that the most useful way to think about the causes of abnormal behaviour is to take a diathesis-stress perspective (Davison & Neale, 1990). The **diathesis-stress perspective** says that mental disorders are the result of an interaction between an inherited predisposition (diathesis) to a particular disorder and the stressors (environmental events and stimuli that precipitate that disorder). For example, a person might have a genetic predisposition toward schizophrenia. That person might develop the disorder under stress that would not cause it in another person. However, under the right life conditions, the first person might never develop schizophrenia. On the other hand, the second might become schizophrenic if exposed to sufficient stress of the right sort. This general idea probably applies to virtually all disorders to different degrees. If two children were born with different pain thresholds and had exactly the same experiences, the one with the lower threshold (a predisposition or diathesis) would experience more pain and therefore probably have more fears. This person would not have inherited "fearfulness," just the lower pain threshold. We could only understand the difference between the two as the result of both diathesis and stress.

DIAGNOSING PSYCHOPATHOLOGY

We have mixed feelings about this section. It is devoted to the process of classifying kinds of emotional problems and to the process of diagnosing individual persons. We have, however, put considerable emphasis on the dangers of labelling people. These dangers are further compounded by the fact that the reliability and validity of diagnoses of abnormal behaviour are dependent on relatively few research studies. It is bad enough to label a person in a limited category, even when there is some accuracy to the label. It is worse when those labels are sometimes inaccurate. It distresses practising psychologists to talk to people who say, "Well, the doctor said I was an obsessive-compulsive (or whatever), so I guess that's what I am." The truth is that few people fit any category perfectly.

If diagnosis is so unreliable, then why bother with it at all? There are both good and not so good reasons for developing a diagnostic system. The mental health professions have tried to imitate other branches of medicine. Systems of medical diagnosis in some other areas are fairly reliable and valid. They are useful in guiding treatment of different disorders. Psychiatric diagnoses can be made reliably within gross categories such as "psychosis," "anxiety-based disorders," and "personality disorders." Such categories do have implications for treatment.

Even though it has weaknesses, DSM-IIIR is superior to previous diagnostic systems in many respects. It can be argued that we are constantly improving diagnosis, so someday our diagnoses will be more useful. This is one of the most important justifications for having a diagnostic system. It seems a valid argument, as long as we acknowledge the limitations of current approaches. We will discuss these limitations further later in the chapter. Figure 14-2 gives a brief overview of the major categories of mental disorders as defined in DMS-IIIR (APA, 1987).

In Chapter 11 we described the various tools and methods psychologists use to assess people. In this chapter, we will discuss the categories and descriptions arrived at after using those tools.

Defining disorders

It may be helpful to have a brief, simplified overview of the major kinds of disorders. **Psychosis** is a severe disorder which is marked by a loss of contact with reality. These are the disorders that most people

FIGURE 14-2 Table of major DSM-IIIR diagnostic categories

Category	Examples
Disorders usually first evident in childhood or adolescence	Mental retardation, Tourette's syndrome, hyperactivity, anorexia nervosa
Organic mental syndromes and disorders	Alzheimer's disease (senile dementia) and other disorders that result from brain malfunction.
Psychoactive substance-use disorders	Abuse of or dependence on such drugs as alcohol, barbiturates, amphetamines, PCP, LSD
Schizophrenia	Disorganized, catatonic, paranoid, undifferentiated, and residual schizophrenia, all of which involve thought disturbances or hallucinations or both
Delusional (paranoid) disorders	Differing degrees of paranoia, which involves the delusion that one is being persecuted
Psychotic disorders not elsewhere classified	Brief reactive psychosis (psychotic symptoms in response to a trauma). Other psychosis that fits no other category.
Mood disorders	Disorders of mood such as depression and mania
Anxiety disorders	Phobias, panic disorders, obsessive-compulsive disorder, post-traumatic stress disorder
Somatoform disorders	Hypochondriasis, conversion disorder, psychogenic pain disorder. The person exhibits physical symptoms for which no physiological basis can be found
Dissociative disorders	Multiple personality, amnesia, fugue, all of which involve a sudden, temporary alteration in consciousness, identity, or motor behavior
Sexual disorders	Masochism, sadism, inhibited orgasm, premature ejaculation, gender identity disorders
Sleep disorders	Sleep problems of more than one month duration.
Factitious disorders	Physical or psychological symptoms that are under the control of the individual. Symptoms are intentionally produced.
Impulse control disorders not elsewhere classified	Kleptomania (compulsive stealing), pyromania (fire setting), pathological gambling
Adjustment disorders	Impaired functioning in response to some stressful life event (divorce, illness, natural disaster) or a developmental stage (leaving the parental home, becoming a parent), which may include a depressed or anxious mood or inhibition with work
Psychological factors affecting physical condition	Tension headaches, asthma, ulcerative colitis, acne
Personality disorders	Paranoid, narcissistic, antisocial, passive-aggressive, schizoid, borderline
Conditions not attributable to a mental disorder that are a focus of attention or treatment	Malingering, problems in school or on the job, marital problems, parent-child problems

SOURCE: Adapted with permission from the American Psychiatric Association (1987).

think of as "insanity." The most common psychosis is schizophrenia. **Anxiety-based problems** are serious problems in living without the marked loss of contact with reality. The individual might suffer intense anxiety and behave oddly, but he or she knows that the behaviour is unusual and understands its implications. This kind of problem used to be called "neurosis." Even though that term is no longer officially sanctioned it is often used in informal discussions. Personality disorders are more difficult to define. A **personality disorder** is a long-lasting maladaptive pattern of behaviour, that appears to be part of the person's basic character, rather than a temporary disorder. For example, a person who is chronically very suspicious might be said to have a paranoid personality disorder. One very important personality disorder is "antisocial personality," which used to be called "psychopathic personality." The anti-social personality is characterized by chronic dishonesty and disregard for others. Such a person responds primarily to immediate gratification, regardless of the long-term consequences.

DMS-IIIR

The third edition of the diagnostic system of the American Psychiatric Association was designed to improve on previous editions by describing disorders in more operational ways. Its definitions of disorders focus on observable, definable criteria. It also provides a more useful description of a person by requiring judgements along five different dimensions or "axes." This procedure gives a fairly complete picture of the patient. (See Figure 14-3.) Axis I is most similar

FIGURE 14-3 The five axes of DSM-IIIR
Each patient is diagnosed on all of the five axes.

AXIS I. CLINICAL SYNDROMES.
This axis includes one of the disorders listed in Figure 14-2. Usually, a subcategory of the disorder is named. For example, if an Anxiety disorder is diagnosed, this judgement might also narrow down to social phobia, obsessive-compulsive disorder, or panic disorder.

AXIS II. DEVELOPMENTAL DISORDERS OR PERSONALITY DISORDERS.
This axis is either reserved for a disorder of development such as mental retardation or autism *or* it is used to identify any personality disorder present. Personality disorders might include antisocial personality, dependent personality, or one of the other personality disorders we will discuss later in this chapter.

AXIS III. PHYSICAL DISORDERS AND CONDITIONS.
Medical problems other than psychiatric ones often have an important impact on adjustment, so any such problems present are listed here.

AXIS IV. SEVERITY OF PSYCHOSOCIAL STRESSORS.
Our understanding of a disorder will be different depending on the severity of stressors in a person's life. DSM-IIIR includes a 7-point rating scale for describing such stressors. Ratings go from "none" through "catastrophic" (death of child, natural disaster, captivity as a hostage).

AXIS V. GLOBAL ASSESSMENT OF FUNCTIONING.
Finally, a scale is provided for judging overall ability to function. Examples are given for assigning a score from 1 (persistent danger of hurting self or others, for example) through 90 (absent or minimal symptoms such as mild anxiety before an exam.)

SOURCE: American Psychiatric Association (1987).

to a traditional diagnosis of a disease. It includes all of the categories of disturbance except personality disorders. Axis II calls for a decision about whether there is a personality or developmental disorder present. Axis III includes the presence and severity of any physical disorders. Axis IV is a rating of how severe the psychosocial stressors are in the patient's life. For example, a mild stressor might be a monthly deadline for an assignment at work and a severe one a natural disaster. Axis V asks for a rating of the patient's highest level of adaptive functioning during the previous year.

Having a multiaxial system provides a more accurate view of an individual person. We might see two patients with similar levels of depression, for example, but our understanding of them would be much different if we knew that one of them was under severe pressure financially and had cancer.

The usefulness of diagnosis and classification

There are many advantages and uses for diagnosis and classification. (1) We need to make predictions about persons who might be a threat to themselves or to others. (2) Professionals need to communicate with each other about persons under care. (3) A treatment that is appropriate for one kind of disorder might be inappropriate or even destructive for another. As we refine our classification system, we often even discover that disorders that appear to be similar turn out to be quite different. (4) Different problems have different kinds of causes. In order to advance knowledge of these causes, we need to discriminate one disorder from another.

Given all these valid reasons for a diagnostic system, we still need to recognize that a diagnostic system carries with it some serious problems, especially when it is as imperfect as our current systems are.

Reliability problems

As we said in Chapter 11, **reliability** refers to the consistency with which a measure yields readings on the quality it purports to measure. In diagnosis, we would be especially interested in how well different diagnosticians agree on their independently done assessments of individuals. Reliability is essential because without it, we cannot trust the validity of our measurement system. **Validity** is a measure of the degree to which a test actually ascertains what it purports to ascertain. If any particular test gives different diagnoses under different circumstances, we have no way of knowing which is correct. The reliability of diagnosis of abnormal behaviour has been only moderately good in the past. "Only moderately good" is not acceptable if the effects of making a diagnosis mean people get labelled for life or are hospitalized or suffer other life-changing consequences. In one famous study using earlier versions of DSM, independent diagnosticians agreed on the presence of schizophrenia only 53% of the time (Beck et al., 1962). This study involved carefully planned procedures and took many steps to ensure accuracy of diagnosis.

DSM-IIIR was designed to increase reliability by giving clearer descriptions of criteria that are more strongly tied to observable behaviour. In fact, this design has resulted in somewhat better reliabilities for DSM-IIIR users (Robins & Helzer, 1986), but only for most of the major categories. Finely detailed diagnoses still result in low agreement among raters, even under the best conditions. Field trials published with DSM-IIIR give some illustrative reliability figures that include about 80% agreement on diagnosing schizophrenia, 63% on anxiety disorders, over 90% on psychosexual disorders, and only 56% agreement diagnosing personality disorders. Later in this chapter we will see that each of these categories has several subcategories. For example, there are several kinds of "anxiety disorder." If agreement on the general class "anxiety disorder" is about 63%, agreement on the many subcategories will be even lower. In a summary of the literature on these problems, Garfield (1986) added a personal observation that most practising clinicians would recognize as true.

> Anyone who has worked in a large clinical setting has probably noticed that there is no unanimity among the staff in diagnostic conferences. I have participated in staff conferences in which the final decision (on a patient's diagnosis) was conclusively settled by an eight to seven vote of the staff members present (Garfield, 1986, p. 101).

We must be very cautious about how we use diagnostic labels.

Troubling issues

Even if we could depend on diagnoses to be reliable and valid, there are still some problems we need to recognize in any classification system. In classifying a person, we inevitably lose information that is unique to the individual. When we say "He's a schizophrenic," we group the person with a large number of other individuals with similar behaviour. It is easy then to focus on the similarities of all the people in that group because that saves us some complex thinking. Categorization serves that worthwhile purpose. We also, however, will be more likely to overlook the many ways each individual is *different* from the rest in the group. We might even build our categories around trivial similarities among the individual members of the group. A rigid classification system might prevent us from investigating what we call schizophrenia. Rather than asking if it is really a group of several different disorders with very different causes we might be inclined to stay with our established classification.

Having classification names makes it easier to isolate a "patient" with a nameable disease as different in *kind* from the rest of us. We have already mentioned the important idea that there is a continuum between "normal" and "disturbed." We are all vulnerable to emotional problems, and there is no dividing line where one suddenly is in the "disturbed" category. Using categories too rigidly makes this harder to remember.

Classification can also stigmatize the person who is so categorized, both in the person's own eyes and in the eyes of others. There is a real risk of a self-fulfilling prophecy if a person strongly believes that he or she *is* an hysteric, for example. Others who "know what the person is" might also reinforce behaviour that confirms this "knowledge" and might ostracize the person, which would lead to further problems.

Problems with actual clinical practice

Finally, we want to describe a very upsetting study reported by Temerlin (1970). So far our discussions of reliability and the usefulness of diagnosis have assumed the careful application of recommended diagnostic procedures. In actual practice, it often seems that diagnosis is not done so carefully.

Temerlin tape-recorded an interview with an actor who played the role of a person with good mental health. In this role, the actor portrayed a man who had a meaningful job in which he was happy and productive, good relationships with friends and in his community, a good marriage with a good sexual relationship, self-acceptance without being arrogant, and no "symptoms" that could have marked any kind of diagnosable disturbance. Temerlin created the actor's script based on many descriptions of mental health. According to the script, the man had read a book about therapy and stopped by a clinic to discuss it with a professional person out of interest in the book. Temerlin played the tape for groups of professionals and asked them to diagnose the man in one of four categories: mentally healthy, neurosis, character disorder, or psychotic. Temerlin emphatically asked the professionals to base their judgements only on evidence actually presented in the interview and all agreed to do this.

When the tape was introduced as an employment interview or with no context given, none of the professionals rated the man as psychotic. However, it is disconcerting that about a third classified him neurotic or as having a personality disorder. The most worrisome finding came when Temerlin provided a "prestige suggestion." Just before the tape was played for some of the professionals, a respected person said, "I know the man being interviewed today. He's a very interesting man because he looks neurotic but actually is quite psychotic." Under these conditions, 60% of the psychiatrists and 30% of the clinical psychologists called the man "psychotic"! Only 12% of the psychologists chose "mentally healthy", and the rest said the man was neurotic or had a personality disorder. Temerlin had confederates posing as professionals in the group, and they asked people how they had made their decisions. Many of the professionals offered elaborate "evidence" they had gotten from the tape. One said, "I thought he was psychotic from the moment he said he was a mathematician, since mathematicians are highly abstract and depersonalized people who live in a world of their own" (Temerlin, 1970, p. 115). Clearly the prestige suggestion strongly biased the diagnoses, which were later rationalized to fulfil the professionals' expectations. Similar results have been reported by other researchers (Langer & Abelson, 1974). The clear risks inherent in classifying and diagnosing individuals should make us all cautious in our own judgments and in accepting the judgments of experts.

Critics of diagnosis

The majority of psychologists and psychiatrists seem to support the use of DSM-IIIR as a diagnostic tool. However, a number of behavioural and humanistic psychologists have criticized it severely. Eysenck (1986), for example, is a leading behaviourist who has attacked DSM-IIIR strongly for being based more on political issues than on scientific evidence.

> DSM-IIIR, like its predecessors, is the outcome of large-scale committee work, designed not so much to ascertain facts and to arrive at the truth, but rather to reconcile different power groups and pacify semipolitical Tammany Hall-type organizations whose influences are incommensurate with their scientific status. . . . It is clearly necessary to throw out the whole approach, hook, line, and sinker before anything better can take its place. DSM-IV, if ever such a misshapen fetus should experience a live birth, can only make confusion worse confounded and make the psychiatric approach to classification even less scientific than it is at the moment (Eysenck, 1986, pp. 74, 96).

Angelo Boy (1989) has criticized psychodiagnosis from a person-centred perspective. He argues that the act of diagnosis interferes with psychotherapy by inappropriately establishing the client as an inferior and dependent recipient of the clinicians' expertise. He also argues that the diagnostic process is fatally flawed by several weaknesses. (1) Diagnosis is notoriously unreliable. (2) The clinician's personal biases distort the process. (3) DSM-IIIR is largely a political document that protects the interests of medical practitioners. (See also Garfield, 1986; Shlien, 1989; Seeman, 1989).

Probably the strongest critic of diagnosis is the psychiatrist Thomas Szasz (1984). He even questions the notion of mental illness or mental disorders as being problems that individuals have. (His 1960 article was called "The Myth of Mental Illness" to underline his attack on traditional psychiatry.) Rather, he argues that cultures define certain behaviours as "sick" when in fact it is the culture that is sick. He argues that mental health practitioners have acquired too much power and authority in our society, and that much of this power is political, rather than scientific or medical.

Anxiety-based Disorders

This section was difficult to name. Some years ago, we could have called it "neurotic disorders." The term "neurosis", however, is falling into disuse, largely because it has acquired many surplus meanings. It seems to imply that neurotic problems are illnesses somehow related to the nerves rather than problems in living. We may at times use the terms "neurosis" or "neurotic," but we use them only as a kind of shorthand way to mean "learned patterns of maladaptive behaviour based on anxiety."

An overview of "neurotic" problems

A general description of problems severe enough to be called "neurotic" would include all or some of the following three characteristics: (1) painful emotions such as anxiety, depression or guilt; (2) self-defeating behaviours that are usually called "neurotic symptoms"; and (3) impaired problem-solving. It seems clear that each of these characteristics is true of all of us to some extent. We have at times felt anxious or apprehensive without knowing what the cause was. At times we have done things that were not in our own best long-term interest. We have sometimes failed to think clearly because of anxiety. Whether or not our behaviour would be called neurotic depends on the severity of our problems. There is no magic line to cross between normal and abnormal. These are problems in living that we all have.

Understanding anxiety

There are many theories of anxiety. Usually, anxiety is differentiated from fear by the degree to which the victim can identify the cause of the aversive feelings. **Anxiety** is the sense of dread, apprehension, panic, and other fear-related emotions when the cause of the emotion is not clear. However, since we can be aware of what is bothering us to different *degrees*, this definition of anxiety is often difficult to apply. What if I am pretty sure I know what I am afraid of? What if I am absolutely sure I know what is cuing my fear and it turns out I am wrong? The fact that we can be affected to any degree of awareness confuses this issue.

What should not confuse us is that the experience of anxiety can be terribly frightening and consuming. We might be afraid of stimuli in the environment and we might also fear our own powerful but only vaguely understood thoughts, memories, and desires. Anxiety can be so painful that a person would do almost anything to avoid it.

Self-defeating behaviour ("symptoms")

The victim of anxiety will even do things that are very self-defeating in order to avoid the anxiety. From the psychoanalytic viewpoint such behaviour might be explained as the ego creating some behaviour that is a substitute for an unacceptable id impulse. From the learning theory perspective, the behaviour might be understood as being immediately reinforced by anxiety-reduction. Anxiety-reduction is an extremely powerful reinforcer, so a person might perform quite bizarre behaviours to get it. Remember too that this whole process can occur with little awareness on the individual's part.

These self-defeating behaviours are often called "neurotic symptoms." However, this term implies that somehow they are like medical symptoms, in which a particular illness usually results in particular symptoms such as a red rash or dizziness. Psychoanalytic theory does suggest that underlying psychic conflicts are manifested in overt symptoms. However, *anxiety-avoiding behaviours that are self-defeating* can be understood as just that, rather than as symptoms. This is made especially clear when we realize that all of us perform self-defeating acts frequently. How severe does this behaviour have to be before it qualifies as "neurotic"? This is an entirely arbitrary social judgement that changes over time and over cultures. If your lecturer for this course chain-smokes while lecturing, that would be considered a little unusual. Twenty years ago it would hardly have aroused notice. If he or she walks around spitting into the corner while lecturing, you have probably already told people about your weird (neurotic?) professor. If current trends continue, twenty years from now, smoking in public will be considered in the same light as spitting is now because of the health threat to others. Will it be neurotic then? Who knows? What is and is not a "neurotic symptom" is an arbitrary social judgement based on the amount of damage a particular behaviour does to the individual and to others.

Impaired problem solving

Finally, we need to talk about what Dollard & Miller (1950) have called "neurotic stupidity," which is not a polite term but which captures this phenomenon well. Anxiety and the avoidance of anxiety often lead people to think unwisely, and to solve problems foolishly. We often marvel at how a person can't see something when "it's as plain as the nose on his face." It seemed to be so obvious to everybody that she was trying to get rid of him, why couldn't he see it? There are at least two reasons for distortions. First, *anxiety constricts behaviour*, including the behaviour of thinking. When anxious, the person simply doesn't take in as much information as at other times and doesn't think freely. Second, *repression* makes it difficult to remember threatening memories and to think threatening thoughts. Thoughts of which we are unaware can still affect us but not be available for thinking and planning wisely.

Some famous "neurotic symptoms"

We have stressed that the words "neurotic" and "symptom" are somewhat misleading when discussing anxiety-based problems. What gets defined as a neurotic symptom is *any* behaviour sufficiently problematic to the person's life that the behaviour is considered to be socially deviant and unacceptable to others and/or to the person with the problem. This means that any behaviour *can be* a symptom if carried to excess, including studying, playing hockey, and going to parties. However, some patterns of behaviour are more commonly associated with anxiety-based disorders than others and have been identified as "symptom syndromes." These different patterns are not different illnesses. We know we have said this often, but we also know that it is commonly believed in our culture that disorders such as phobias are illnesses. We have even read articles in newspapers and magazines that call different phobias different illnesses. It will help to understand anxiety-based problems in general to have a deeper understanding of some specific kinds of neurotic disorders.

Our discussion of stress in Chapter 13 is relevant here. For example, post-traumatic stress disorder could have fit just as easily

Any behaviour can be a "neurotic symptom" if it is carried to excess. SOURCE: Courtesy of the University of Toronto.

in this chapter, but we presented it in the chapter on stress. Professional burnout and grief are other examples of what could be considered anxiety-based problems that also appear in Chapter 13.

Fear of heights can mask deeper, more frightening fears.
SOURCE: Metropolitan Toronto Convention and Visitors Association.

Phobias

A phobia can be defined as a very extreme fear of a specific stimulus. The fear is out of proportion to the actual threat represented by that stimulus. We will discuss some specific phobias, but remember that a person could be phobic to just about anything. There are instances of individuals so phobic to the number seven, for example, that they couldn't walk down the street for fear of passing a house with a seven in its address. In the past, psychologists coined names for different phobias by combining root words with "phobia." We are familiar with "claustrophobia" and "agoraphobia." "Homilophobia" is a morbid fear of sermons, "parthenophobia" is a morbid dread of virgins, and "ergasiophobia" is a fear of writing. The list could go on and on, but that would not be helpful. Being able to apply a fancy name to a fear does not tell us anything about that fear.

Phobias are more common than most other diagnostic categories. Researchers estimate that from 6 to 8% of the population suffer from phobias (Myers et al., 1984). Many of these, however are phobias that do not debilitate the person. About 2% of the population seem to have debilitating phobias.

There are two general theories about the causes of phobias. Both theories are probably partly correct. They may explain two quite different kinds of problems that look similar. It is possible that some irrational fears are directly conditioned fears. A **directly conditioned fear** is a fear that results from direct classical conditioning. A person might be trapped in a mine collapse and then fear long dark hallways. We could see this as a case of traumatic conditioning. More subtly, the person might have had a series of smaller conditioning experiences which had a cumulative effect of establishing a strong fear. This is the simpler kind of phobia. Other phobias can have more complicated patterns of development. For example, a phobia may serve to help the person avoid some more horrifying fear or internal conflict. It may be the "lesser of two evils." A person might have a powerful unconscious urge to commit suicide by jumping from a high place. This problem might be totally unacceptable and impossible to deal with. If the person developed a "phobia for heights," however, he or she would have an "acceptable" problem that was strongly reinforced by the avoidance of any situation where the more serious conflict would arise.

Agoraphobia is a fear of crowds and public places.
SOURCE: Courtesy of the Canadian National Exhibition, Toronto, Canada.

The phobia most commonly seen and treated in clinical settings is **agoraphobia**, which literally means "fear of the gathering place or marketplace." This set of fears centres around an inability to leave home or other safe refuge and go into public places. Often it includes a fear of not being able to escape or find help if overwhelming fear strikes in public, of looking "crazy" to others, of fainting or vomiting in public, of actually "going crazy" if panic strikes, and of generally losing control. The problem often develops after one or several panic attacks occur. Then the person comes to "fear the fear," which he or

"Reuben! The Johnsons are here! You come up this instant . . . or I'll get the hose!

SOURCE: *The Far Side* by Gary Larson. Reprinted by permission of Chronicle Features, San Francisco, CA.

she feels might strike at any time. This fear can persist months or even years after the last panic. Most individuals with agoraphobia are women, and the problem usually starts in late adolescence or early adulthood. A sad irony about this problem is that, even though it is the most commonly seen problem in clinics, it is doubtless more common than anyone knows. There are thousands of people who are too fearful to leave home to seek help, and they are never counted.

Somewhat less common is **social phobia**, an irrational fear associated with the presence of other people. This phobia can extend from extreme stage fright to a fear of eating in public, writing one's name in the view of others, and using public washrooms. Social phobias commonly begin in adolescence and are only slightly more common among women than among men.

Simple phobias are severe fears of specific things such as small animals, chairs, or insects. A person who suffers from such a fear does not find it a "simple" problem, however. These fears can include specific animals, heights, injections, blood, thunder, germs, running water, and virtually any other object. Again, what defines such fears as "phobic" is arbitrary and depends on the degree to which the person is incapacitated.

The anxiety states

Three kinds of problems are categorized as "anxiety states": *panic disorders, generalized anxiety,* and *obsessive-compulsive disorder*. The first two involve much *felt* anxiety and the third is an example of a "symptom" that develops to avoid severe anxiety.

Panic disorders

A **panic disorder** is marked by attacks of intense anxiety and panic that are unpredictable and overwhelming. A panic attack is an experience that is almost too horrible to capture in words. The person is suddenly and unexpectedly swept by terror and feelings of impending doom. The heart starts pounding, breathing increases rapidly, and there might be sweating, dizziness, and shaking — all the result of intense autonomic nervous system arousal. There may be a fear of dying immediately or of going crazy. This fear is increased by frequent experiences of **depersonalization and derealization**, in which the person feels separated from himself or herself, outside the body, and in a state of unreality. DSM-IIIR specifies that to qualify as panic disorder there must be at least three panic attacks in a three week period. By this definition, slightly less than 1% of the population has panic disorder. However, the incidence of panic attacks is much higher than this would indicate. In fact, they are relatively common. One study (Norton et al., 1985) found that 30% of college students had had a panic attack in the previous year. A large majority of individuals with other diagnosed anxiety disorders have some panic attacks but not enough to meet the criterion for panic disorder. In a study of Manitoba undergraduates, among those who read the DSM-IIIR description of panic attacks, over half reported having had such an attack. If a brief clinical example of a panic attack was included with the description, this figure dropped to about one-third. Apparently the description of an attack led the students to limit their definition to exclude less severe situational anxiety attacks (Sandler et al., 1989).

Little is known conclusively about panic disorder, but some individuals may be more susceptible physiologically than others (Torgerson, 1983). One clue to psychological factors is the finding that persons with panic disorder tend to brood about having illnesses (Hibbert, 1984).

Generalized anxiety

Panic attacks come and go, **generalized anxiety** is a chronic sense of apprehension and fear when no cause is apparent. It is evidenced by chronic worry, apprehension, tension, and somatic arousal. It is often called "free-floating anxiety" to describe its vague, indefinable, haunting presence. The experience can be like having an evil and dangerous being always just behind your head where you can never quite see it. The person often sweats frequently and can have diarrhea, racing heart, frequent urination, and many other signs of fear. These signs result from high levels of autonomic nervous system arousal. The person worries nearly constantly, often cannot make simple decisions, and is overly sensitive. It is almost always fruitless to look for specific cues for anxiety, the experience is so diffuse and all-pervading.

The psychoanalytic explanation of free-floating anxiety is that the ego is in conflict with unacceptable id impulses. The unconscious id impulses are usually non-rational sexual and aggressive urges pushing to find expression. The ego is threatened by these impulses and fights to keep them unconscious, but they often emerge in partial and disguised forms that can arouse severe anxiety. The behavioural view is quite different. The person is thought to fear external cues that are frequently present. Wolpe, for example, described a patient who had developed a fear of shadowy objects, and since shadows are nearly everywhere the individual was always afraid (Wolpe, 1958).

There is a cognitive-behavioural view, however, that resembles the psychoanalytic view but uses cognitive behavioural principles. In this theory, one's own thoughts, feelings and desires are seen as internal behaviours that can become fear cues. For example, if a person were frequently punished while thinking about sex, the *act* of thinking about sex would become an aversive conditioned stimulus. Such thoughts would arouse fear. If the person had many thoughts and desires that were both well motivated *and* aversive because they had been punished, he or she would be continuously frightened by these thoughts and desires. Much of this could happen without awareness of the source of the fear (Martin, 1983).

Obsessive-compulsive disorder

Obsessive-compulsive disorder is an anxiety-based disorder marked by specific thoughts the person cannot stop thinking (obsessions) and behaviours the person cannot stop performing (compulsions). The afflicted person cannot stop performing the compulsive behaviours

FIGURE 14-4 Obsessive-compulsive disorders
Individuals who develop an obsessive-compulsive disorder tend to have elevated levels of arousal and to overreact to emotion-producing stimuli. As a result, they experience anxiety in a response to recurrent (obsessional) thoughts and are unable to terminate them. These thoughts tend to persist and may lead such persons to adopt compulsive rituals which help to reduce their anxiety.
SOURCE: Reprinted with permission from Allyn and Bacon, 1989.

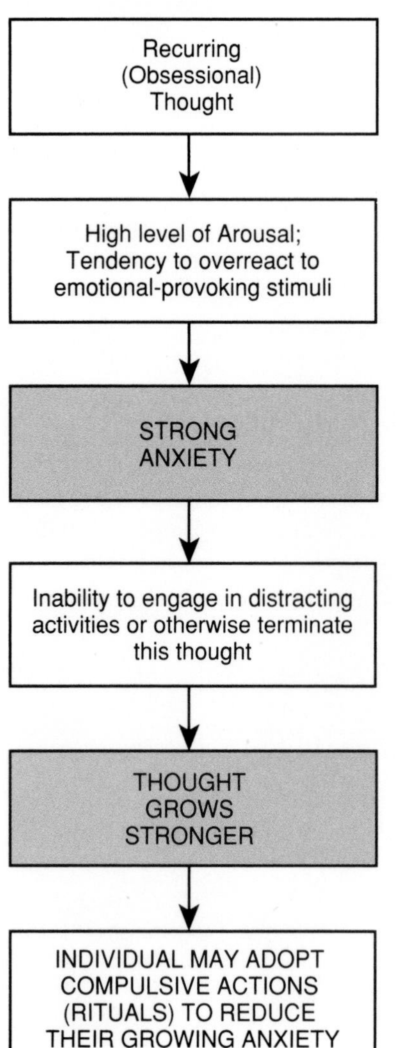

without suffering enormous fear, anxiety, and apprehension. They can take the form of "rituals" (tapping the side of the sink *exactly* 18 times) or repetitive behaviours (Lady Macbeth's continuous hand-washing after the murder of Duncan). These two characteristics often appear together, hence the name "obsessive-compulsive." (See Figure 14-4.) They can consume a person's life. We knew a young boy who took hours getting home from school because he *had* to pick up every piece of trash he saw. Then all night long he worried about bits he might have overlooked. If he tried not to pick up the trash, he suffered intense fear and dread. Many obsessive-compulsive problems are much more debilitating than this one.

This boy was unusually young for a sufferer of this disorder. It most commonly begins in young adulthood and is often preceded by some kind of stressful event (Kringlen, 1970). Obsessive-compulsive disorders are recognized by the person as irrational and usually as "not really a part of me." The etiology of obsessive-compulsive problems is not clearly understood, but the thoughts and behaviours seem to perform some kind of protection against anxiety. It is possible that being consumed by the obsessive thoughts and compulsive behaviours, as awful as they are, is another case of the "lesser of two evils." They may help the person avoid some other more frightening conflict.

SOMATOFORM DISORDERS

Somatoform disorders are disorders with symptoms that take physical form but that have no discernible physical causes. The two most common are *conversion disorder* and *somatization disorder*. A **conversion disorder** is one in which the nerves and muscles malfunction with no physical cause. Specific problems are sometimes called hysterical symptoms. For example, the person could be partially paralyzed, insensitive to feeling, or even blind. In **somatization disorder**, the person may have conversion symptoms but also reports very frequent physical complaints: bodily pains, headaches, fatigue, allergies, and cardiac symptoms such as heart palpitations.

Conversion (hysterical) disorder

Conversion disorder is the most common of the somatoform disorders. These physical impairments can include various degrees of muscular paralysis and loss of sensation. They often take forms that would be impossible if they had a true neurological basis. For example, in "glove anaesthesia", the hand can feel nothing from the wrist down, but there is no way this could result from neurological damage (see Figure 14-5).

Other conversion symptoms can include "hysterical blindness" (in which the person can develop tunnel vision or even entirely lose his or her vision), loss of voice, and even false pregnancy (with swelling of the abdomen, cessation of menstrual periods, and morning sickness).

The two terms we use for these problems, hysteria and conversion disorders, have interesting origins. Even though their original meaning is no longer considered valid, we still use the older terms. Originally, "conversion" referred to Freud's theory that psychic energy was being converted into a physical symptom. The term "hysteria" is even older. Hippocrates explained that certain disorders in women were caused by arbitrary or wilful wanderings of the womb (uterus) round and about the body! "Hysteria" is derived from the Greek word for uterus.

FIGURE 14-5 Glove anaesthesia A person who could feel nothing in the area of the hand (that is, the area that would be covered by a glove) would probably be suffering from a conversion disorder. It would be most unlikely that the lack of feeling in the hand could have a neurological basis.

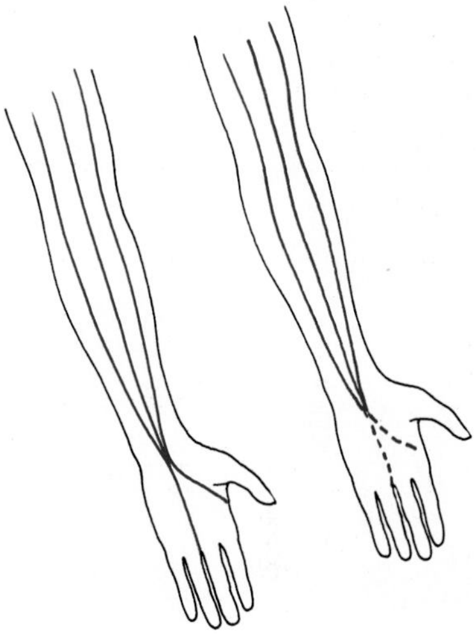

DISSOCIATIVE DISORDERS

Dissociative disorders are a class of disorders in which the normal continuity and integration of experience is lost. Such disorders include, according to DSM-IIIR, *psychogenic amnesia, psychogenic fugue, and multiple personality*. DSM-IIIR defines a dissociative disorder as "a disturbance or alteration in the normally integrative functions of identity, memory or consciousness" (American Psychiatric Association, 1987, p. 269). Normally, a person perceives himself or herself as one unified personality. The disruption of this unity involves severe gaps of memory and the "dissociation" of portions of life that are (in most people) normally associated.

Types of dissociative conditions

Psychogenic amnesia is the loss of specific portions of memory as the result of psychological stress or trauma. Amnesia can also occur as the result of organic injury, but cases of psychogenic amnesia do not include such injury. Perhaps the loss of a loved one, the trauma of being raped, or some similar shock might lead to the forgetting of specific information but not to the loss of the ability to speak, read, think, and perform other previously learned skills. This can last anywhere from hours to years. Psychogenic amnesia usually goes away just as suddenly as it came and it is unlikely to recur. As with the other dissociative disorders, psychogenic amnesia attracts a great deal of attention. Probably because of this publicity (soap opera writers would be helpless without psychogenic amnesia) people think it is more common than it actually is.

Psychogenic fugue is a pervasive amnesia in which personal identity is lost and a new identity may be assumed. The individual may assume a new identity with no memory of the old one. There have been milder cases of psychogenic fugue. In wartime soldiers have been known to perform actions such as driving a motorcycle from Berlin to Paris over the course of a week or two. They functioned effectively enough on the journey except for having lost personal identity. Later the soldiers woke up in Paris with absolutely no memory of the trip. In more extreme cases, some individuals have adopted entire new identities and maintained them over long periods of time. Recovery from such fugues is usually complete, and the recovered person loses memory of the period of the fugue.

Three of the personalities of the young woman, Sybil (as portrayed by Sally Field), who suffered from multiple personality disorder.
SOURCE: "Sybil," Photofest.

Multiple personality is the dissociative disorder that has attracted the most attention—attention far out of proportion to its frequency. Books and movies such as *The Three Faces of Eve* and *Sybil* portray patients who suffer from this disorder. **Multiple personality** is a dissociative disorder in which the person has two or more distinct identities or separate "ego states." Most of us perceive one relatively unified "self" no matter how much our behaviour may vary in different circumstances. Sometimes we say, "I just wasn't myself when I did that," but we don't mean it literally. In multiple personality disorder, at least one "ego state" exists without knowledge of at least one other, and these different states exist over some time for the person. Multiple personality is *not* the same as schizophrenia, as we will discuss later in this chapter.

Theories of dissociative disorders

The massive memory loss and later sudden recovery that occur in dissociative disorders strongly suggest that repression is a factor in these disorders. Dissociative disorders are typically related to early traumatic experiences. The person must be protected from horribly threatening memories or impulses. Simple repression is not sufficient, so large parts of the personality are hidden from awareness. Learning theorists tend to emphasize dissociative behaviour as avoidance behaviour, designed to escape some kind of punishment. This analysis, however, does not deal with the almost bizarrely "unconscious" nature of the process. As we saw in Chapter 9, it is possible to understand repression within a learning perspective. It seems likely that some combination of the psychoanalytic approach and learning approach will emerge as the most complete explanation for dissociative disorders.

Psychophysiological Disorders

When we discussed conversion disorders, we pointed out that they were not accompanied by actual physical causes or changes. They are not the same thing as "psychosomatic" problems, although the two terms are frequently confused in the popular press. "Psychosomatic" problems are, however, more accurately called "psychophysiological disorders." **Psychophysiological disorders** are caused by chronic overactivation of the autonomic nervous system. They are often accompanied by actual organ damage. Particularly the sympathetic nervous system is aroused in times of stress (see Chapters 13 and 19), and stress can affect virtually all illnesses. It is thus misleading to speak of psychological effects on illness and on health as "just in the person's head." This phrase seems to imply that the problem is therefore under the individual's conscious control and all that's required to be well is a little will power.

Stress and illness

The evidence seems to be growing that stress has a damaging effect on the body's immune system and therefore may affect a wide range of illnesses. Sklar and Anisman (1979) demonstrated that stress increased the speed of growth of cancers in mice. Although the evidence is not conclusive, various kinds of chronic stress have been related to cancer in humans, as we will see in Chapter 19 on Psychology and Health. If stress suppresses the immune system, we would expect it to be related to increases in infectious diseases. This does seem to be the case for a wide variety of disorders, such as respiratory infections, mononucleosis, tuberculosis, and herpes simplex (Jemmott and Locke, 1984).

It is important to note that not all individuals are equally affected by stress. The same stressors can lead to physical illness in one person but not in another. This is why tests that measure life stress are only moderately effective at predicting illness. Research has been done to identify the personal characteristics of individuals resistant to illness under stress — individuals with "hardiness." Kobasa and her coworkers (Kobasa, 1979; Kobasa, Maddi, & Kahn, 1982) say, "Persons high in hardiness easily commit themselves to what they are doing (rather than feeling alienated), generally believe that they can at least partially control events (rather than feeling powerless), and regard change to be a normal challenge or impetus to development (rather than a threat)" (Kobasa & Puccetti, 1983, p. 840). They have demonstrated that "hardy" individuals have fewer physical illnesses.

Theories of psychophysiological disorders

We will focus on a few illnesses that seem particularly linked to stress of various kinds. These disorders have been identified as psychophysiological disorders because they are the most closely linked to psychological factors. This close link seems to result from the role

Some occupations, such as that of stock exchange trader, are more stressful than others.
SOURCE: Courtesy of the Toronto Stock Exchange.

of chronic activation of the autonomic nervous system in such problems as ulcers and essential hypertension (the two disorders we will discuss). Other problems, such as heart attack, asthma, skin eruptions, colitis, headache, lower-back pain, and hyperventilation are also often classified as psychophysiological disorders, but we will not deal with them in this chapter.

There are a number of puzzling questions to be answered about psychophysiological disorders. First, why do some people develop them, while others, under similar stress, do not? Second, why does stress sometimes produce a physical disorder rather than a psychological one? Why does one person under stress develop one disorder while another person develops a different one? There are a number of theories that attempt to answer these questions, but no one theory seems entirely satisfactory.

Physiological theories

The **somatic-weakness theory** is a physiological theory that says that specific psychophysiological disorders are due to genetic inheritance. Under stress, the genetically most vulnerable organ system is likely to be affected. The **specific-reaction theory** states that, probably for genetic reasons, different individuals react to stress with different autonomic responses. One person, for example, might have increased heart rate, while another might have increased respiration rate. Lacey (1967) has demonstrated that there is considerable variety among individual patterns of autonomic responsiveness. One other physiological theory is that *evolution* has prepared us for short-term emergencies (remember the GAS syndrome in Chapter 13). However, we humans also have the mental capacity to prolong emergencies by anticipating stress and carrying resentment for years. We can make the stress chronic, leading to the damage of long-term arousal.

Psychological theories

Psychoanalytic theories of psychophysiological disorders have stressed the symbolic meaning of suppressed psychic conflicts to explain particular disorders (Alexander, 1950). They say that ulcers, for example, are related to frustrated feelings of dependency and longing for parental love. The stomach constantly prepares itself for the food that represents love, and the unnecessary digestive acids cause ulcers. High blood pressure (essential hypertension) reflects suppressed anger, and asthma might be a kind of suppressed crying for love. **Behavioural theories of psychophysiological disorders** stress how classical and operant conditioning can affect psychophysiological problems. Usually, conditioning worsens an already existing physiological disorder. Some asthmatics, for example, develop breathing problems when shown pictures of horses, if horses are an important allergen for them. The mere sight of horses could well have become a conditioned stimulus, as could barns, helping explain how such a problem could "spread" through classical conditioning. As with other kinds of "neurotic symptoms," having a problem such as an ulcer could be reinforced by anxiety reduction. The person might escape an intolerable situation by being sick, for example.

Multiple factor theory is the position that no single theory of psychophysiological disorders is adequate. Such disorders probably result from a combination of genetic predispositions, emotional conflicts, and conditioning. There is some evidence to support each of the theories we have discussed but no one theory seems complete by itself. We need to include both physical and psychological explanations to develop a complete diathesis-stress understanding of psychophysiological disorders. The person with ulcers probably does have a genetic predisposition to them. The ulcers probably are related to stress, but perhaps stress that is no greater than that of another person who doesn't get ulcers.

Some specific disorders

We have chosen to discuss two psychophysiological disorders in more detail in order to illustrate the principles involved and the kinds of evidence available.

Ulcers

Ulcers are inflamed crater-like lesions in the lining of the stomach and duodenum. Ulcers eat into the lining because excess amounts of normal digestive juices (hydrochloric acid and pepsin) are secreted and because the layer of mucous that normally protects the lining has been weakened. If the mucous layer is weakened and there is too much acid, the lining of the stomach and duodenum is actually digested itself. (See Figure 14-6.) This process results from stress: chronic overactivity of the autonomic nervous system can simultaneously increase the secretion of digestive juices and reduce the bloodflow to the mucosa.

Many sources of stress have been related to ulcers in humans and in animals. One of the earliest studies was done by Selye (1936). He immobilized rats by wrapping them in towels. The immobilized rats developed more ulcers than control rats which had not been restrained in this way. Animals in approach-avoidance conflicts often develop ulcers. They might be in a cage where they have to cross an electrified grid to reach food. They have to cross the grid or starve, but the grid causes pain. The inescapable conflict leads to chronic arousal (Sawrey, Conger, & Turrell, 1956). Air-traffic controllers have twice as many ulcers as pilots, probably because of the constant vigilance required of the controllers (Cobb & Rose, 1973).

There is strong evidence of a physiological predisposition component in the acquiring of ulcers. It is possible to breed strains of animals that are especially vulnerable to ulcers. Humans have been shown to be especially likely to develop ulcers under stress if they tend to secrete high levels of pepsinogen, which is converted into pepsin for digestion. In a very persuasive study, researchers (Weiner et al., 1957) identified new soldiers who were high and low in pepsinogen secretion. None of the soldiers had any sign of ulcers. Sixteen weeks later, after basic training, none of the low pepsinogen group had ulcers, but 14% of the high pepsinogen group did.

FIGURE 14-6 Ulcerated stomach lining
Ulcers result from chronic overactivation of the autonomic nervous system that causes excess hydrochloric acid and pepsin to eat away the stomach lining.

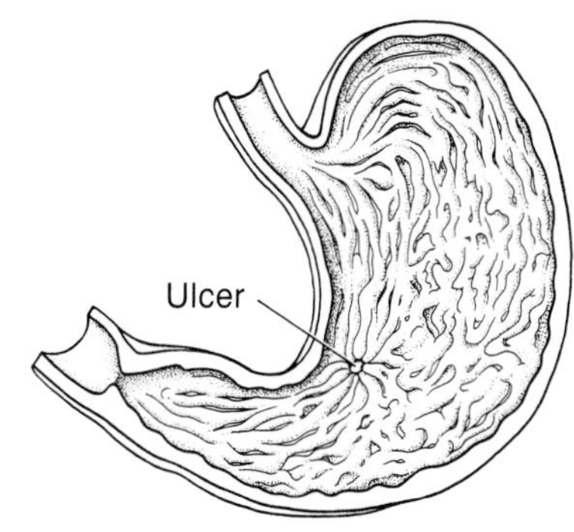

Stressful situations and professions can have a damaging effect on the body's immune system. Air-traffic controllers have twice as many ulcers as pilots.
SOURCE: Courtesy Transport Canada.

Essential hypertension

Essential hypertension is high blood pressure that has no apparent organic cause. This cardiovascular problem is called the "silent killer." It has been estimated that as many as one-third of North Americans have essential hypertension. However, because it produces no apparent symptoms, many of these people are unaware of the problem. Hypertension does its insidious damage by weakening the walls of blood vessels. After it starts, the average life expectancy of the victim is about twenty years (Lyght, 1966). Several autonomic reactions contribute to hypertension. Primarily because of the sympathetic nervous system arousal of stress, blood vessels constrict and the heart pumps more blood. This is similar to turning the water on full blast and squeezing the hose. Under such circumstances, the hose is far more likely to burst. In an emergency, this reaction gets more needed oxygen and nutrients to the muscles. However, if the "emergency" is an emotion such as smouldering resentment for your boss, the muscles can't use the help for fight or flight and the pressure stays high for a long time. Kasl & Cobb (1970) found that anticipating the loss of one's job raised blood pressure and that those who were unemployed the longest had the longest periods of hypertension.

As with ulcers, there is evidence that hypertension is associated with some kind of physical predisposition. Some individuals seem to be "cardiovascular responders" who are more likely to develop essential hypertension under stress (Rose, Jenkins, & Hurst, 1978).

MOOD DISORDERS

Mood disorders are long lasting disturbances of emotion or affect that pervade the person's whole life. They are evidenced by either intense depression or intense elation, referred to as mania.

Describing the experience

Depression has been called the common cold of psychopathology because so many people experience it. This certainly understates the potential severity of the experience of depression, however. In its extreme form, depression can be totally debilitating, and a manic episode can lead to life-destroying foolishness in the name of exuberant self-expression. Try to project from your own experience of feeling depressed to understand what extreme forms might feel like.

In **depression** the overriding feeling is one of deep sadness usually marked by hopelessness, guilt, and self-blame. The person is lethargic and apathetic, often unable to get up in the morning because there seems no point in doing so. The experience is often accompanied by disturbances of appetite with concomitant weight loss or gain. Sleep disturbances can include insomnia and the inability to fall asleep after waking in the night or very early in the morning. Some sufferers may have a desire to sleep a great deal of the time. Zest and meaning in life disappear—forever, it seems to the sufferer.

The individual frequently feels horribly worthless and deserving of blame and guilt. Death is frequently thought of and suicide sometimes results.

At nearly the opposite end of the continuum, **mania** is marked by extreme feelings of elation, frenetic activity, and irrational animation. We remember one of our professors describing mania as being "too happy." That seemed an odd emotion to label as a disorder. The problem is that in a state of mania the person is constantly on the move, sometimes staying awake for days at a time, perhaps writing letters to everyone in parliament, planning to open a chain of stores, borrowing huge sums of money to start the business, and deciding to walk 200 miles to the next town. The person feels enormously talented and worthwhile and often speaks very rapidly. When the mania passes, there can be consequences such as huge debts and no way to account for the money.

Bipolar and unipolar depression

There are rare instances of mania appearing in a person who did not also swing into depression, but nearly always it appears as one extreme in **bipolar depression**. This is also called **manic-depressive disorder**. The person cycles between severe bouts of depression and episodes of mania. This disorder often follows a cycle in which the person goes through a period of normal adjustment between the extreme "poles" of disturbance.

Unipolar depression is depression without manic periods. The person has cycles of depression and of feeling normal. There seems to be evidence that bipolar and unipolar depression are distinctive disorders with notable differences between them. Bipolar depression may include some kind of genetic predisposition and tends to appear at an earlier age (median age in the early thirties) than does unipolar depression (median age in the early forties) (Depue & Monroe, 1978). Unipolar depression also seems to include a more agitated, anxious quality than does the depression of the bipolar disorder.

There is a marked tendency for mood disorders to be "self-limiting." It has been reported that about 80% of depressed patients recovered after five years, while a similar group of patients with schizophrenia had only a 14% recovery rate. These depressed patients did not receive medications or electroshock therapy, so this seemed an indication of a "natural" rate of recovery (Morrison et al., 1973).

Theories of depression

Freud proposed a complex **psychoanalytic theory of depression** that is best characterized by the phrase "depression is aggression turned inward." Freud saw this self-aggression as the complex outcome of the loss of a significant other person, for which the person blamed him- or herself symbolically. The aggression turned inward is partly a self-punishment and partly a form of anger toward the one being mourned. Later developments in psychoanalytic theory introduced the idea of "symbolic loss," since it was apparent that many depressed persons had not suffered an actual loss.

Currently the most influential theories of depression and its treatment seem to be cognitive theories, especially that of Aaron Beck (1967). **Cognitive theories of depression** take the position that depression is caused by distorted beliefs based on inaccurately negative self-evaluation.

Some typical cognitive errors Beck might try to change in therapy for depression would include **overgeneralization**. The person incorrectly interprets one incident as applying to many situations. In **selective abstraction**, the person takes one negative element out of many possible parts of a situation. The student who has a B+ average selectively remembers and dwells on the one C+ received on one paper last term. In **arbitrary inference**, the person draws a discouraging conclusion on the basis of little or no evidence. None of my friends have called for days, and I'm absolutely sure it's because they have finally seen me for what I really am.

The learning theories of depression take the position that depression results from the loss of reinforcements that used to be available to the person and from the learning of a helpless attributional style. Through loss of a loved one, loss of some other significant source of meaning, or even through loss of ability to get others to provide reinforcement, the individual is frustrated and discouraged. These feelings are expressed as depression.

A more complex theory is a combination of cognitive and learning elements that is based on the concept of **learned helplessness** that we mentioned in Chapter 13. This is sometimes called the *control perspective* on depression. It focuses on the person's experiences which lead to a sense of lack of control over life. (See Figure 14-7.) Seligman (1974) suggested that evidence from experiments with animals provides a strong analogy to human depression. In experiments, some dogs received shocks which were inescapable. Others received the same number and intensity of shocks, but could perform activities to control the shocks. The first group eventually simply cowered and whimpered. Even in later situations, where escape and control were possible, these animals showed "learned helplessness." They never even tried.

Some theorists believe that humans develop a *depressive attributional style* in the face of experiences of helplessness. They attribute unpleasant events to their own faults of character, faults that are fundamental to themselves and that are long-lasting. This "internal and long-lasting" attribution is especially devastating and disheartening because the flaws are experienced as "who I *am* is bad" and this cannot be changed. The hopelessness of depression is likely to follow. There is some evidence to support this formulation (Peterson & Seligman, 1984; Metalsky et al., 1982; Robins, 1988). It has been suggested that the higher incidence of depression in women may be linked to elements of traditional feminine sex roles, in which the woman is taught that she has little control. Abramson, Metalsky, and Alloy (1989) have reformulated this theory of depression and propose that there is a subtype of depression called *hopelessness depression*. They suggest that hopelessness is a cause of this kind of depression and not just a symptom of it.

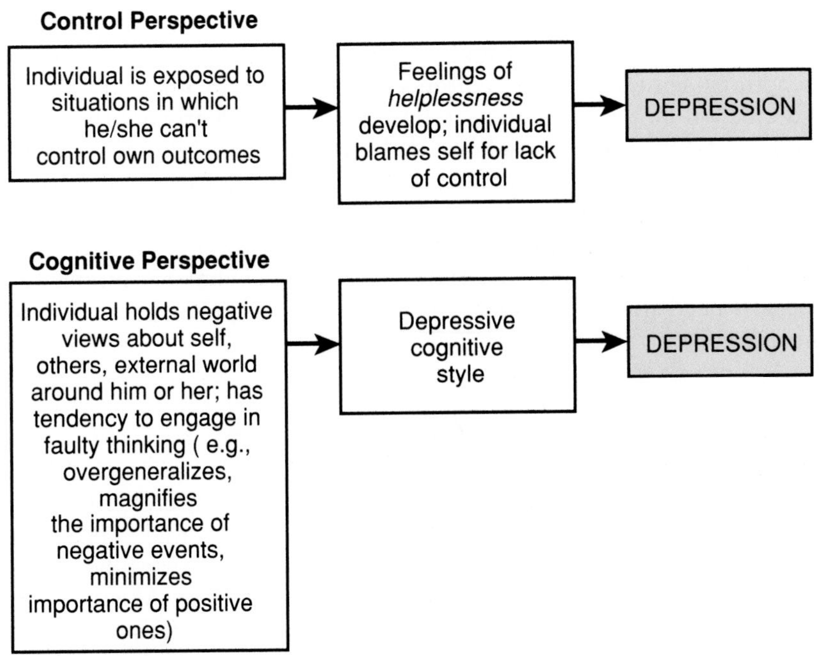

SOURCE: Adapted with permission from Allyn and Bacon, 1989.

FIGURE 14-7 Depression: Control and cognitive perspectives According to the control perspective, exposure to situations in which individuals cannot control their own outcomes leads to feelings of helplessness which generalize to a wide range of situations. Such feelings, in turn, contribute to depression. The cognitive perspective suggests that depression results from negative views about oneself, others, and the external world, plus certain faulty types of thinking.

Depression seems to result from a combination of psychological and physiological factors. **Physiological theories of depression** state that depression has a genetic component and is the result of disorders of neurotransmitters. There are major theories of depression that focus on reduced levels of two particular neurotransmitters — norepinephrine and serotonin. We have already discussed neurotransmitters. They are the chemicals that control the functioning of the nervous system by controlling the crossing of the synapses between neurons. It would make sense that reduced levels of neurotransmitters could have a debilitating effect on normal functioning. There is some evidence that depression can involve either or both of these chemicals. This has led to the use of **antidepressant medications** as a common element of treatment programs for both unipolar and bipolar depression.

Suicide

Not all people who commit suicide do so while depressed, but depression is a factor in the majority of attempted and successful suicides. Suicide is the tenth most common cause of death among adults, but it is second only to accidents among young people. Tragically, the suicide rate among young people is increasing. For every "successful" suicide, there are about eight attempted suicides. These attempted suicides are more common among women by about a three-to-one ratio. However, more men actually kill themselves, partly because they use more deadly methods such as guns. It used to be that about three times as many men as women killed themselves, but that ratio is shrinking toward two-to-one. In general suicide rates are highest during periods of economic depression and lowest in times of war.

There are a number of common false beliefs about suicide that are worth mentioning because they sometimes lead to unfortunate reactions. For example, it is often said that a person who talks about suicide will not commit the act, but this is quite clearly not the case. From 70–80% of those who kill themselves send out warnings, through direct threats and indirect cries for help. It also seems untrue that suicidal people really want to die. Most of them are very ambivalent about it. If the attempt is thwarted somehow, they are grateful later to have lived. People of all social classes commit suicide. A person need not be "insane" or even deeply depressed to commit suicide.

PSYCHOSEXUAL DISORDERS

In this context, "disorders" refers to kinds of sexual problems that are usually thought of as deviant or severely abnormal. The term "sexual dysfunctions" refers to the kinds of problems that huge numbers of people have in enjoying a rewarding sex life. Masters and Johnson (1970) have estimated that half the marriages in North America are sexually dysfunctional. They mean there is enough difficulty over sex to interfere with the quality of the relationship. Problems this widespread would, of course, not be called "disorders", in the sense of abnormal and disturbed behaviour.

A number of thought-provoking issues are raised by the information in this section. For example, psychologists are still puzzled over why some individuals feel they are really one sex trapped in the body of the other sex. We have very few hints from research about the causes of this problem, so it makes us wonder how such a powerful feeling could be just the result of training. On the other hand, one's gender role is largely the result of learning, so how could such a feeling be inborn? We are only somewhat less confused by the paraphilias. **Paraphilias** are disorders in which uncommon or bizarre objects become the focus of sexual attraction. Some students may have difficulty with what we have to say about homosexuality. We will see that homosexuality is no longer considered to be a "disorder" unless it causes the individual severe distress to be homosexual. In these cases it is called **ego dystonic homosexuality**. This simply means that the person rejects his or her own homosexuality. Otherwise, most psychologists argue that homosexuality is simply a way of life.

Gender identity/transsexualism

Transsexual persons feel that their "true sex" is the opposite of their biological sex. This is more common among men. The person persistently wishes to be rid of the genitalia, and this wish lasts for many years. A minimum of two years is the criterion to define this as transsexualism. The transsexual person is not delusional about which sex he or she is, as a schizophrenic person might be. The desire to change sexes is a heartfelt wish which is frequently granted through surgery and hormone-replacement therapy.

It is not at all clear what causes transsexualism. Biological explanations are not well supported by evidence. Some studies find, for example, elevated levels of male sex hormones among female transsexuals, but other studies do not (Meyer-Bahlburg, 1979). Surgical treatment through sex-change operations involves removal of the genitalia and construction of an artificial vagina from some of the penile tissue for men. The person who becomes a woman this way is capable of sexual intercourse as a woman but obviously not of becoming pregnant. The woman who wants to become a man surgically has a much harder time of it. Surgical construction of a sexually-workable penis is very difficult. On the other hand, this change does not require extensive electrolysis to remove an unwanted beard. One study of 40 transsexual men randomly chose 20 of them to receive a sex change operation quickly, while the others had to wait the usual period of two years after meeting the criteria to qualify for the operation. After two years, the men who had been operated on had improved their sexual and psychosocial functioning, but the other men had not changed (Mate-Kole & Robin, 1989).

Until 1973, *homosexuality* was listed in DSM-II as a "sexual deviation." After considerable debate, the American Psychiatric Association voted to eliminate this designation on the ground that homosexuality was simply one form in which sexual preference is expressed. This recognized that studies generally show groups of homosexuals to be about as well-adjusted in all other ways as heterosexuals. It was difficult to defend the idea that homosexuality was a kind of disorder. It *is* considered a disorder however to have *ego-dystonic homosexuality*. Ego-dystonic means that the person cannot accept his or her own homosexuality and is caused great distress by it. In this case the distress is the problem.

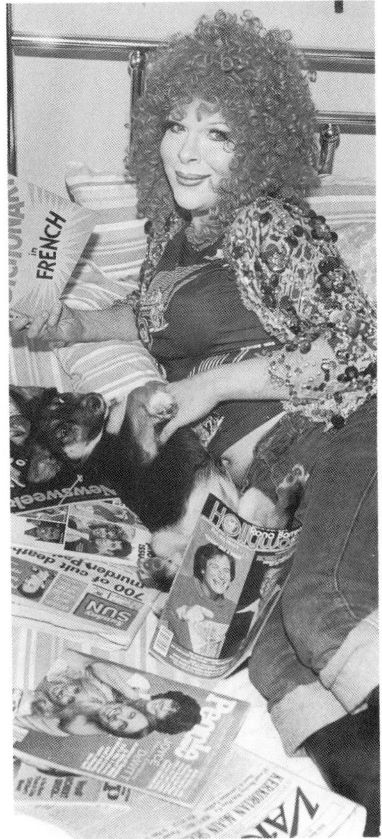

Transvestism is sometimes part of a well-developed subculture.
SOURCE: Canada Wide/Jonathon Gross.

Paraphilia

With the *paraphilias*, something unusual (para) is loved (philia). DSM-IIIR says that "unusual or bizarre imagery or acts are necessary for sexual excitement" (American Psychiatric Association, p. 266). We will describe a few examples of paraphilias.

If this disorder involves preference for use of nonliving objects for sexual arousal, it is called a **fetish**. The person with a fetish is nearly always male. He can be sexually stimulated by—even absolutely require—an object such as shoes, fur, or underpants. Anything can be a fetish object, but most of them have some connection to female sexuality. Some fetishes are so powerful that the person will change jobs to ensure contact with the objects, attack others if necessary to get them, and generally pay a very high price to obtain the fetish object. This is different from another paraphilia, **transvestism**, in which the person is sexually aroused by wearing clothing traditional to the opposite sex. It is the cross-dressing that is exciting, rather than just fondling a particular object (a fetish). Note that transvestism is not the same disorder as transsexualism. Transvestism does not involve a wish to change sex.

One of the most troublesome paraphilias is **pedophilia**. The person (usually a man) has a compelling sexual attraction to children.

Pedophilia often occurs in a person with rigid religious and moralistic beliefs and feelings. It is very difficult for the person to change. Pedophilia seldom involves physical violence against the child victim, but child sexual molestation is greeted with far more revulsion and anger than are other sexual offences. Especially in the subculture of prisons, pedophiles are treated as the lowest form of life imaginable, even though their behaviour seems so pathetically and compulsively uncontrollable.

SCHIZOPHRENIA

We now will deal with the most common psychotic disorders. To most people, these are the disorders they think of as "insanity" or "real craziness," although neither of these terms is used by professionals. "Insanity" is a legal term that is not used in the mental health professions. This helps to explain why mental health professionals often cannot agree on the issue of "sanity" in court. The essential difference between psychotic problems and "neurotic" problems is that psychosis is evidenced by a marked loss of contact with reality.

We want to expand on one common misconception about schizophrenia. It is not "split personality," although this is a favourite belief of newspaper writers. We discussed multiple personalities earlier in this chapter as one kind of dissociative disorder. The confusion seems to have arisen because the word "schizophrenia" is from the same root as "schism" or split. "Schizophrenia" was meant to convey "split" in the sense of "fragmented." The person's thinking and talking are disorganized, illogical, bizarre, and split off from reality. In contrast, the person with multiple personality speaks logically but has two or more separate self-concepts.

In this section we will see that there is evidence that schizophrenia involves some physical factors. It will be important to understand how the diathesis-stress paradigm applies to schizophrenia. If you understand this, you should be able to answer the question "Is schizophrenia inherited?"

Defining schizophrenia

Schizophrenia is a puzzling disorder that may include several different kinds of disorders with similar external symptoms. Field trials of DSM-IIIR diagnoses of schizophrenia yielded fairly good reliability results. Inter-rater agreements was about 80%. For a number of years, this category was used with increasing frequency in North America. From the 1930s to the 1950s, the percentage of hospitalized patients diagnosed as schizophrenic remained at about 20% in Europe but went from 20% to 80% in some North American hospitals (Kuriansky, Deming, & Gurland, 1974). The definition of schizophrenia was clearly expanding to the point where it was losing much of its meaning. DSM-IIIR, however, has again narrowed the definition of schizophrenia. For our purposes we will define **schizophrenia** as the most common of the psychoses. It is marked by fragmentation of thinking, perceptual distortions, and odd motor behaviours.

There are several kinds of disturbances that make up schizophrenia, but no one characteristic is *essential* to a diagnosis being made. We will not describe the several sub-categories of schizophrenia but rather give an overview of the major kinds of disturbance that lead to the general diagnosis of schizophrenia.

Thought disorders

One of the most striking symptoms of schizophrenia is grossly illogical, fragmented thinking that can sound quite startling. It is sometimes possible to follow a kind of logic in the person's thinking, but it is as though the train of reason were somehow "short circuiting." We once gave an intelligence test to a young girl in whom schizophrenia had not been suspected previously. To test her comprehension we asked, "What is the thing to do if you cut your finger?" She quickly replied, "Cut it off" and saw nothing odd about her answer. This clue led to further testing that revealed many similar disturbances of thought. Such loose illogical associations are sometimes called **cognitive slippage** (Meehl, 1962). This phrase captures the flavour of this kind of talk. Cameron (1947) gives another illustration of cognitive slippage. An interviewer asked a patient, "Why are you in the hospital?" The patient answered, "I'm a cut donator, donated by double sacrifice. I get two days for every one. That's known as double sacrifice; in other words, standard cut donator. You know, we considered it. He couldn't have anything for the cut, or for these patients" (Cameron, 1947, p. 466). The DSM-IIIR manual gives this example: "Parents are the people who raise you. Parents can be anything—material, vegetable, or mineral—that has taught you something. A person can look at a rock and learn something from it, so a rock is a parent" (American Psychiatric Association, 1987, p. 399).

Disturbances in the *content* of thinking are illustrated by **delusions**, which are grossly false beliefs. The person might believe that he has to walk around looking only at the ground because his gaze carries poisonous rays that could harm those he looks at. These delusions can also be *persecutory*. Each new room must be checked for radio devices that control one's behaviour, or one must constantly watch everyone on the bus to see which one is the agent assigned to one's case. **Delusions of reference** lead the person to believe that whatever happens is somehow related to him or her. People laughing on the other side of the room, for example, would be assumed to be laughing at the person with the delusion.

Perception and attention disorders

Almost everyone occasionally has a sense of the world seeming "unreal" and distorted, but this experience can be very extreme with schizophrenia. It can seem as though the world is a dream or that people literally are mechanical devices moving awkwardly through space. **Hallucinations** are dramatic instances of perception disorders. They are gross distortions of perception in which non-existent

A person suffering from catatonic immobility may remain in one (sometimes quite awkward) position for long periods of time.

objects, sounds, or smells are perceived as existing (positive hallucinations) or real things are perceived as not existing (negative hallucinations). With visual hallucinations, the person sees objects and people that don't exist. In auditory hallucinations one can hear such sounds as instructions, audible thoughts, verbal arguments, and scoldings, all "really there" for the person. Olfactory hallucinations involve smells that don't exist. Tactile hallucinations can include overwhelmingly vivid sensations of stimuli such as bugs crawling on the skin. With schizophrenia, the most common kind of hallucinations are auditory.

Motor, mood, and social disturbances

The person with schizophrenia sometimes engages in bizarre behaviour that can include wild grimacing, and strange and repetitive gestures in which he or she seems to be interacting with some invisible other being. These behaviours can include odd postures that are held motionlessly for long periods of time. This extreme immobility is referred to as **catatonic immobility** or **waxy flexibility**. It is a condition in which the patient maintains one physical position for long periods of time and can be moved to a new position as though made of flexible wax.

Schizophrenia is often accompanied by mood (affective) disturbances. Such disturbances can take the form of either flattened or inappropriate affect. **Flattened affect** is a dull, unvarying emotion. **Inappropriate affect** is emotional behaviour that is unrelated to any apparent cause. For example, inappropriate giddy laughter or sudden sobbing. The person may start giggling when told that a friend has died or perhaps act terrified in response to "good morning."

Finally, *social withdrawal*, an aloofness and lack of connection with others is typical of schizophrenia. The person withdraws from others, both physically and psychologically, perhaps turning the head away when spoken to or hiding in corners.

Etiology of schizophrenia

Trying to understand the causes of schizophrenia requires a clear understanding of the diathesis-stress concept. It does seem that both environmental stressors and an inherited predisposition are prerequisites for the onset of schizophrenia. We have learned a great deal about these factors in the last few decades, but there are still many unanswered questions. We have to be cautious in our analyses.

Psychological factors

Two psychological factors have received research attention as possible causes of schizophrenia: *social class* and *family relationships*.

There is a disproportionate frequency of schizophrenia among the lowest social class. One explanation, the **sociogenic hypothesis of schizophrenia**, is that the degrading and stressful life of homelessness, joblessness, and lower-class living contributes to schizophrenia. On the other hand, the **social-drift hypothesis** says that persons with schizophrenia are unable to function well in jobs and social relationships, so they are likely to "drift" into the lowest social class possible. Both theories seem to have some truth to them. For example, schizophrenic patients are more likely to have a father from a low social class, even when the father was not schizophrenic. This supports the sociogenic theory. At the same time, however, schizophrenic patients often tend to have a lower social class job than their fathers, pointing toward the social-drift idea (Turner & Wagonfeld, 1967; Goldberg & Morrison, 1963).

Studies of patterns of communication within the family have yielded unclear results. Fromm-Reichmann (1948) coined the term **schizophrenogenic mother**, to describe a cold, over-protective, and rigid pattern of mothering that is supposed to cause schizophrenia. Bateson's famous term **double bind parenting**, described a close-bound connection between schizophrenia and a parent who gives impossibly contradictory messages (Bateson et al., 1956). In one example, a son with schizophrenia put his arm around his mother, who noticeably stiffened up. When he withdrew his arm, she asked, "Don't you love me anymore?" When he blushed, she said he shouldn't get embarrassed so easily and be so afraid of his feelings. He was trapped. Both of these theories seem intuitively plausible, and many practising clinicians have seen examples supporting them. However, controlled studies have not been able to establish that these two specific patterns are especially prevalent in the families of those with schizophrenia.

It has been shown, however, that there is more conflict between the parents of those with schizophrenia than between other parents. If a schizophrenic patient is discharged from hospital to a home where there is much intense emotion expressed (either as hostility or as overinvolvement) he or she is more likely to return to hospital than patients who are discharged to homes with less intense emotional expression (Fontana, 1966; Brown et al., 1966; Vaughn & Leff, 1976). Certainly family stress does make a difference in schizophrenia, but it seems unlikely that there is a particular pattern that causes it.

The genetic data

There are several clues from *twin studies* that a predisposition to schizophrenia is inherited. These studies report *concordance rates* among twins. **Concordance rate** is the measure of how often a disorder appears in different members of specific groups. Twin studies investigate the percentage of cases in which, if one twin has schizophrenia, the other one does also. Among fraternal twins, the concordance rate tends to run about 10–20%. This is only slightly higher than the concordance rate for siblings who are not twins. However, among identical twins concordance rates tend to run about 30–60%. (There is great variability among studies, so we are giving ranges.) This strongly suggests some genetic component. However, it is important to note that we cannot say that schizophrenia is inherited. Otherwise the concordance rate for identical twins would be close to 100%. There also is a tendency for children borne by women with schizophrenia and then adopted into families without the disorder to have a disproportionately high incidence of schizophrenia.

Schizophrenic behaviour can include fragmented thinking, frightening delusions, and social withdrawal.

Brain functioning

In recent years, considerable progress has been made in identifying brain malfunctions related to schizophrenia. One prominent hypothesis is that there is *excess dopamine activity* in the brains of schizophrenics. **Dopamine** is a neurotransmitter essential to brain functioning. It is possible that too much of it or an oversensitivity to it could be a factor in schizophrenia. The evidence for this hypothesis is extensive, but we must be cautious in interpreting it. It appears that excess dopamine activity is a factor in at least some kinds of schizophrenia, but we don't know if this is a cause of schizophrenia or if it develops as a result of schizophrenia.

A number of *neurological abnormalities* have also been found to be associated with schizophrenia, so brain structure abnormalities may be important. The study of neurological structures is one of the most important frontiers in our understanding of schizophrenia. Postmortem analyses of the brains of schizophrenia patients frequently reveal abnormalities of brain structure, although different studies report different specific problems. Recent studies using CAT scans and PET scans have also found deterioration of brain tissue, especially in the frontal lobes (Buchsbaum et al., 1984).

Paranoid disorder and paranoid schizophrenia

Paranoid thinking is marked by extreme suspiciousness and feelings of being persecuted. We will see in the next section that the diagnosis **paranoid personality disorder** describes a person who is chronically suspicious and, even though the problem pervades his or her life, he or she is not sufficiently out of contact with reality to be called psychotic. **Paranoid disorder** is a relatively rare psychosis in which the person does not display the erratic logic of schizophrenia but has a well-developed system of paranoid beliefs (extreme sense of being persecuted, suspiciousness, and mistrust). A person suffering from a paranoid disorder has an **encapsulated delusion**. This is an elaborate and well-developed delusional system which does not show the "cognitive slippage" of thought disorder or include hallucinations or bizarre delusions. The person sounds quite rational and is able to function in society but has a persistent false belief that usually includes feelings of persecution and jealousy, or notions of grandiosity (a grossly inflated belief in one's own importance or place in life). Often if we accept one or a few basic premises as being true (perhaps that there *is* a world-wide conspiracy to poison the person), much of what he or she says makes logical sense. **Paranoid schizophrenia**, on the other hand, is more common and is a combination of paranoid delusions and the fragmented, illogical thinking we discussed in the last section.

PERSONALITY DISORDERS

The second axis of a DSM-IIIR diagnosis deals with personality disorders. A diagnosis of personality disorder "should be made only when the characteristic features are typical of the individual's long-term functioning and are not limited to discrete periods of illness" (American Psychiatric Association, 1987, p. 305). The key phrase here is "long-term functioning." Axis I asks for a decision about a currently active disorder. The personality disorder of Axis II describes a way-of-being that is part of a person's general character. In fact personality disorders are sometimes called "character disorders." Even if a person is assigned a diagnostic label on Axis I, there may or may not be a personality disorder label that applies on Axis II. Usually just over half the formal diagnoses made with DSM-IIIR include the naming of a personality disorder. Personality disorders are considered quite difficult to treat. They often seem so deeply ingrained in character that changes come very slowly.

The diagnosis of personality disorders is notoriously unreliable. Prior to DSM-IIIR, agreement among diagnosticians on personality disorders was almost nonexistent. DSM-IIIR has improved the definition of personality disorders somewhat, but even in field trials of DSM-IIIR, the reliability of the decision whether *any* personality disorder was present was lower than for any other major diagnostic category. Judgments about specific disorders are, of course, even less reliable. The personality disorders are sometimes referred to informally as "wastebasket diagnoses," sometimes used if no other diagnosis fits. This difficulty arises largely because the personality disorders are exaggerated forms of common ways of functioning. It is difficult to get raters to agree on just where "disorder" begins.

Some specific personality disorders

Given these cautions, we can best explain what a personality disorder is by describing a few of them. As you read these descriptions, you probably will recognize someone you know. Remember that these are simply common patterns that would be called personality disorders only in their extreme forms.

Paranoid personality disorder

Paranoid personalities are chronically suspicious, secretive and blaming of others. They seem always tensely vigilant, on the lookout for how someone is going to do them harm. Argumentative and aloof, they are sensitive and quick to take offence.

Borderline personality disorder

This category has been the most widely used "wastebasket" term, but it has been somewhat more clearly defined in recent years. Extreme, sudden, and unpredictable change marks **borderline personality disorder**, especially in the three areas of self-concept, relationships, and mood. In relationships, psychoanalytic language would say these individuals have "weak ego boundaries." This means that they enter into a series of intense attachments that develop quickly and dissolve just as quickly, often in a torrent of stormy accusations that catch the other person off guard. Then the attachment can return in a way that seems as though they were psychologically merged with the other person. They may use suicide threats manipulatively one day and seem to care for nothing the next. Under stress, they can appear psychotic but the episode often passes and the person returns to a pattern of erratic attachments. Millon says that this disorder is "faddish . . . (and) overdiagnosed, having become a wastebasket for many patients who demonstrate that protean constellation of multiple symptoms that characterize the syndrome" (Millon, 1988, p. 902).

It is clear that such a person would be difficult to relate to. Prognosis for treatment is quite discouraging, unless the person also has a mood disorder (Pope et al., 1983). The mood disorder component of the person's problems often responds well to medication, improving the person's overall functioning.

Schizoid personality disorder

Schizoid personality disorder is a chronic, long-lasting way of relating to the world by withdrawal and thinking that is unusual but not severe enough to be diagnosed as a schizophrenic psychosis. This category includes individuals who generally maintain a good contact with reality but would be described by others as "odd." Usually this means the person is withdrawn and unable to make emotional contact with others, a kind of "loner" who has trouble sensing another person's thoughts or feelings. Hermits and extremely eccentric individuals might be examples of this disorder.

Schizotypal personality disorder

Schizotypal personality disorder is more severe than schizoid personality disorder. Schizotypal personality includes serious difficulty with forming relationships and making emotional contact with other people. It is more serious, though, since it also includes behaviours and thinking patterns that resemble those of schizophrenia but are not severe enough to be called psychotic. This is often a difficult discrimination to make, and so reliability of diagnosis is difficult to establish. Schizotypal personality disorder can include superstitious ideas or magical thinking that resemble delusions. **Magical thinking** is a tendency to attribute events to highly implausible causes. The person may often feel unreal, outside his or her body, and "sense the presence" of something that is not there (Lenzenweger & Loranger, 1989).

Passive-aggressive personality disorder

Our previous examples were of "character structures" that resembled psychotic problems. Other personality disorders are more "neurosis-like." One example is the **passive-aggressive personality disorder**. The passive-aggressive person inconveniences and even hurts others through indirect methods that are thought to be disguised aggression. The person is often late in ways that are extremely annoying and damaging to others. The person can apologize profusely for being late and never have to express aggression openly. By "forgetting" important events and being "ineffectual" the person maintains a self-image of non-aggressiveness but controls others in a hostile way.

Compulsive personality disorder

Compulsive personality disorder is a long-standing way of acting that is marked by excessive orderliness, cleanliness, and/or precision. More commonly a problem with men than women, compulsive personalities tend to be rigidly perfectionistic. Everything must be in place, on schedule, serious, and done "the right way." They work hard and manage their time determinedly, but they also have trouble making decisions and staying on their self-imposed schedules, because nothing is ever good enough.

Antisocial personality disorder

We are going to give special attention to one of the personality disorders. As with the other syndromes, terminology is changing and DSM-IIIR refers to "antisocial personality" instead of the more commonly known terms, "psychopathy" and "sociopathy." It includes antisocial personality in the personality disorders, along with the other more "neurosis-like" personality disorders. This is a bit misleading. It is useful to understand antisocial personality as having different causes than the other personality disorders. This is an oversimplification, but there is some truth in saying that neurotic problems result from too much anxiety, and psychopathic disorders from too little anxiety.

Antisocial personality disorder is a long-standing way of acting that is marked by lack of feeling for others, harmful behaviour towards others, lack of remorse or guilt, and a focus on immediate gratification. The primary characteristic of the antisocial personality is a tendency to respond to impulsive momentary pleasure with little feeling of guilt or remorse over negative consequences to self or others. We're repeating ourselves, but such problems are on a continuum with normal problems, so it would be inappropriate to call a person "a psychopath" or "a sociopath."

Let us also caution that only some antisocial behaviour results from "true psychopathy." Some people perform antisocial behaviours because those behaviours are somehow anxiety-reducing. Remember our previous discussion of "symptom" development. Any behaviour can be a symptom if it leads to anxiety reduction. Thus, stealing might somehow reduce anxiety because it brought social acceptance or relieved guilt by getting the person caught. Secondly, some people perform antisocial behaviours because that is what they are reinforced for in their cultural setting. It is the "normal" way to act under the circumstances.

The classic descriptions of sociopathy were developed by Cleckley (1976) and McCord and McCord (1964). The major elements of their descriptions are:

(1) *Inability to delay gratification.* Criminal acts are poorly planned and often lead to arrest because the person ignores realistic risks and seeks immediate pleasure. Relationships tend to be short, and the person may hold many jobs, leaving whenever frustrated or bored for the moment.

(2) *Lack of feelings of empathy for others or remorse.* One quality that enables most of us to live in a social setting is that we feel some guilt over hurting others. The lack of such remorse among some persons with antisocial personality can be stunning to the rest of us. One we know of said, "I shot him and all I felt was the recoil of the rifle."

(3) *Inability to learn from experience.* This is related to the impulsivity of item (1). Even after being punished, the person often commits similar acts, repeatedly receiving the punishment.

(4) *Lack of emotional connections with others.* Even if intimate relationships are formed, they are usually soon broken abruptly and aggressively. A family member is just as likely to be exploited and harmed as anyone else.

(5) *Stimulus seeking.* These individuals seem to need high levels of stimulation, even to the extent that they take great chances and seem to revel in the danger, which is preferable to the boredom of normal life.

(6) *Superficial charm and intelligence.* They are not actually more intelligent than the rest of the population, but they have learned how to appear charming and intelligent for purposes of manipulating others. This charm, mixed with a nearly total lack of loyalty or conscience, makes forming a relationship with such a person extremely dangerous.

Family factors have been the focus of a great deal of research with antisocial personality. Early studies reported a relationship

Those who suffer from antisocial personality disorder may appear to be quite charming, but their charm is used to mask the aggression evidenced by their manipulation and exploitation of others. In general, such people evidence a lack of remorse for genuine harm caused by their actions and a lack of emotional commitment to the other people in their world.

between antisocial personality and lack of affection, parental inconsistency, and severe rejection. However, these studies were all *retrospective*. That is, they studied individuals already identified as antisocial personalities and then studied their memories of childhood. This is difficult data to interpret. Virtually all the factors identified have also been associated with other behaviour disorders, and most children subjected to such parenting do not develop sociopathic behaviour.

It seems likely that *genetic* and *neurological factors* may be involved (Mednick, Gabrielli, & Hutchings, 1984). There do seem to be an unusually high number of EEG abnormalities among groups of these individuals, although these abnormalities certainly do not appear in all. Some of the most interesting evidence is from laboratory experiments in which subjects diagnosed as antisocial personality conditioned more slowly than others and learned to avoid punishment more slowly. When they were given injections of adrenaline, however, these subjects learned avoidance behaviour at a "normal" rate, presumably because the drug had raised their general level of anxiety (Schachter & Latane, 1964; Chesno & Kilmann, 1975).

SPECIAL TOPIC Historical Perspective

It is important to learn from the past, from the history of diagnosis and treatment of the emotionally disturbed. While we can look back at what seems to be cruel and useless victimization of helpless people, we wonder how textbooks in the next century will portray our treatment and judgments of people with emotional problems.

Until fairly recently (up to the early or mid-nineteenth century), events that could not be explained were often attributed to supernatural causes. Human behaviour that was bizarre was thought to be the work of demons. **Demonology** is the study of the ancient belief that mental disorders are caused by possession by demons. Autonomous evil beings were thought to enter a person and control his or her mind and body. The "treatment" for these disorders might include rituals to drive out the demon or even torture, maiming, and killing the possessed person. In about 300 B.C., Hippocrates (the founder of modern medicine) proposed a **somatogenic hypothesis**. He said there were physical causes for mental disorders. ("Soma" means "body" and "genic" refers to causes.) His system of medical explanations is not consistent with modern knowledge, but he did lay the groundwork for a more humane and scientific view of behaviour disorders. However, in about 300 A.D. the dark ages

Early beliefs about abnormal behaviour resulted in cruel "treatments" to drive out demons.
SOURCE: The Bettmann Archive.

began for science and medicine. Demonology once again became the common theory of abnormality, especially as it related to the devil. The mentally disturbed either were thrown out on their own or, at best, they had rituals performed on them and were given magic potions to drink (only after the full moon had passed). Belief in the power of the devil increased rapidly in the dark ages. The Roman Church countered this demonic power by starting the Inquisition in the mid 1200s. For the next few centuries, papal inquisitors were empowered to torture victims until they confessed and to execute, usually by burning, those "convicted" of consorting with the devil. Some witches were even found to have had sex with the devil. Protestant authorities also conducted witch hunts. Over the centuries from the mid 1200s to the mid 1600s, hundreds of thousands of people of all ages were tortured and killed. A large portion of these were certainly mentally deranged. In fact, the manual of instruction (the *Malleus Maleficarum* or *Witches' Hammer*) provided by the Roman Catholic Church specified that a sudden loss of reason was a sign of possession by a demon, which should be driven out by burning.

Later, during the fifteenth and sixteenth centuries, *asylums* were provided for a variety of society's misfits. Asylums were ugly warehouses for the emotionally disturbed. "Treatment" was either ignored or consisted of inhumane procedures such as drawing up to six quarts of a patient's blood over a period of a few months (Farina, 1976). Philippe Pinel (1745–1826) brought in important reforms during the French Revolution by promoting **moral treatment** for the mentally ill. He released patients from shackles and chains and tried to bring them some comfort. However, it wasn't until the end of the 1800s that *somatogenic* and *psychogenic* approaches became popular. This change probably resulted from many causes. The rise of the scientific method led to physical explanations and physical treatments, as did Darwin's influence. Near the end of the nineteenth century, physicians were more open to "talking cures" and hypnosis. There was an acceptance of psychological explanations to replace demonology. It is now believed that "mental illness" is a complex result of physical and psychological causes and that those who are afflicted need to be treated humanely.

Philip Pinel, a French physician (1745–1826) introduced humane treatment of the mentally ill. This painting by Charles Miller depicts him demanding the removal of chains from the insane at the Bicentre Hospital in Paris. SOURCE: The Bettmann Archive.

CHAPTER SUMMARY

1. Everyone has emotional problems. These are usually problems in living rather than illnesses. "Normal" and "abnormal" behaviour are on a continuum and develop through the same processes. The DSM-IIIR (the most popular diagnostic system extant today)

defines a mental disorder as a syndrome or pattern of behaviours that occurs in a person, associated with present distress, or disability or significantly increased risk of suffering. The syndrome is not a mental disorder if the symptoms result from a typical reaction to an event such as the death of a loved one.

2. The diathesis-stress model of mental disorders says that such disorders are caused by both physical and psychological factors. A predisposition to a particular disorder might be inherited but any disorder a person develops is the result of an interaction between the predisposition and life stress.

3. According to the DSM-IIIR, the major types of mental disorders include (1) psychosis, disorders characterized by marked loss of contact with reality; (2) anxiety-based disorders (formerly called "neurotic disorders"), serious problems in living without a loss of contact with reality; and (3) personality disorders, long-lasting patterns of behaviour in which maladaptive behaviour seems to be a part of the person's character. DSM-IIIR focuses on observable, definable criteria to make a diagnosis. It requires judgements along five different dimensions or axes to give a complete picture of the patient.

4. The diagnostic process of psychopathology carries some risks to patients, such as the harmful effects of being labelled and categorized. These risks are compounded by problems with the reliability and validity of psychiatric diagnoses. Detailed diagnoses in clinical practice are notoriously unreliable. However, major categories of mental disorder can now be diagnosed fairly reliably, and reliability is improving. Thus, we can expect the usefulness of diagnosis to increase in the future.

5. Anxiety-based disorders used to be called "neuroses," but this term is misleading and is falling into disuse. These problems are characterized by (1) painful emotions, (2) self-defeating behaviours (sometimes called "neurotic symptoms"), and (3) impaired problem-solving. Anxiety can be so powerful and painful that the person will do virtually anything to reduce it. Many self-defeating behaviours can be seen as attempts to reduce anxiety, despite the harmful effects they have on the person. Anxiety constricts behaviour, including thinking, and can cause the afflicted person to think unclearly and solve problems inadequately.

6. Examples of "neurotic symptoms" include phobias (extreme fears out of proportion to the actual threat) such as agoraphobia and social phobia and compulsive cleanliness and ritualistic behaviours. Any behaviour can become a symptom if carried to the extreme that it is severely self-defeating to the person.

7. Panic disorders, generalized anxiety, and obsessive-compulsive disorders are all anxiety states. Panic attack is characterized by feelings of doom, a fear of dying, feelings of depersonalization, increased heart rate, shaking and sweating. Generalized anxiety is sometimes called free-floating anxiety, to capture its flavour of chronic worry and tension. Obsessive-compulsive behaviours

are marked by thoughts the person cannot stop thinking and behaviours the person cannot stop performing.

8. Somatoform disorders are physical symptoms that have no physical cause. The most common is conversion disorder (sometimes called hysterical disorder) in which symptoms develop with no actual physical damage or change.

9. Dissociative disorders are evidenced by a severe loss of the normal integration and continuity of experience. Psychogenic amnesia causes loss of large portions of memory. Psychogenic fugue is more extensive loss of identity, in which the person develops a new identity. Multiple personalities also can develop. It seems that a combination of psychoanalytic and learning theory is most likely to lead to an understanding of these disorders.

10. Psychophysiological disorders result from chronic overactivation of the autonomic nervous system. These disorders often lead to actual damage to organ systems. We are now discovering that virtually all illnesses are affected by psychological factors. Examples of specific psychophysiological disorders include ulcers (which result from excessive acid secretion in the stomach) and high blood pressure (which can result from stress). Specific-reaction, psychoanalytic, behavioural, and multiple-factor theories have all been used to explain the phenomena of psychophysiological disorders.

11. Mood disorders are disorders of affect or emotion. Depression is the most common and has been called the common cold of psychopathology. Severe depression is very debilitating and is characterized by feelings of worthlessness, guilt, and self-blame. Bipolar depression (manic-depressive disorder) is marked by fluctuations between severe depression and manic periods of extreme elation and irrational animation. Some depression seems to include a genetic predisposition, especially bipolar depression. Suicide is often related to depression. Psychoanalytic, cognitive, learning and physiological theories have been used to explain mood disorders.

12. Psychosexual problems include sexual dysfunctions (the problems that many people have in enjoying a rewarding sex life) and psychosexual disorders (which are more severely deviant problems). Persons who feel strongly that they are the opposite sex of their genetic sex are called transsexual. When unusual or bizarre imagery or objects are required for sexual excitement, a paraphilia is diagnosed. Wearing cross-sex clothes is called transvestism. Sexual attraction to young children is called pedophilia. Homosexuality is not considered a sexual deviation. If one is troubled by one's own homosexuality, this distress is called egodystonic homosexuality.

13. Schizophrenia is the most common psychosis and is characterized by a marked loss of contact with reality. It is a puzzling disorder which may include several different kinds of disorders

with similar symptoms. Thought disorder is a major part of schizophrenia; the person makes loose, illogical associations and may hold grossly false beliefs called delusions. There may also be distortions of perceptions called hallucinations, in which the person seems to perceive non-existent things. Motor disturbances that accompany schizophrenia can include catatonia, in which the person moves very little. Disturbances in emotion or affect are also apparent. Schizophrenia may be characterized by flattened or inappropriate affect. The diathesis-stress model seems to fit schizophrenia well. There is evidence for a genetic predisposition that may interact with stress to produce schizophrenia. Because of this, medications are often useful in treating the disorder.

14. Paranoid thinking includes feelings of being persecuted and extreme suspiciousness. When this thinking accompanies the disordered thought patterns of schizophrenia, it is called paranoid schizophrenia. Paranoid disorder is the term used to describe severely paranoid thinking in an otherwise realistically thinking person.

15. Personality disorders are maladaptive patterns of behaviour that last over long periods of time. It is as though the behaviour is an ingrained part of the person's character.

16. Personality disorders are difficult to diagnose reliably and are notoriously difficult to treat. Examples include paranoid personality disorder and borderline personality disorder. This latter is marked by extreme, sudden, and unpredictable change, especially in relationships. Schizoid and schizotypal personality disorders are marked by withdrawal from emotional contact with others. Those who suffer from passive-aggressive disorders harm others through disguised aggression. Those who suffer from compulsive personality disorders are usually rigid perfectionists. Antisocial personality disorder is marked by a lack of feeling and of responsibility for others, and by a focus on immediate gratification.

Key Terms

Agoraphobia Fear of crowds and public places. The phobia most commonly seen in clinical practice.

Antidepressant medications Drugs used to treat unipolar and bipolar depression.

Antisocial personality disorder A long-standing way of acting that is marked by lack of feeling for others, harmful behaviour toward others, lack of remorse or guilt, and a focus on immediate gratification. This was formerly called "psychopathy" and "sociopathy."

Anxiety The sense of dread, apprehension, panic and other fear-related emotions when the cause of the emotion is not clear.

Anxiety-based problems Severe problems in living that do not involve loss of contact with reality. These were formerly called "neurotic" problems.

Arbitrary inference A source of false beliefs in cognitive theory of depression. The person draws a discouraging conclusion on the basis of little or no evidence.

Behavioural theories of psychophysiological disorders Theories that classical and operant conditioning act to worsen an already existing physiological disorder.

Bipolar depression (Also called *manic-depressive disorder.*) Disorder in which the person cycles between periods of severe depression and mania.

Borderline personality disorder A long-standing character structure marked by extreme, sudden, and unpredictable changes of feeling, especially in the three areas of self-concept, relationships, and mood.

Catatonic immobility (also called *waxy flexibility*) One possible symptom of schizophrenia in which the patient maintains one physical position for long periods of time and can be moved to a new position as though made of flexible wax.

Cognitive slippage The thinking processes typical of schizophrenic disorders. Loose, illogical associations are the primary characteristic.

Cognitive theories of depression The position that depression is caused by distorted beliefs based on inaccurately negative self-evaluation.

Compulsive personality disorder A long-standing way of acting that is marked by excessive orderliness, cleanliness and/or precision.

Concordance rate The measure of how often a disorder appears in different members of specific groups.

Conversion disorder A somatoform disorder in which the nerves and muscles malfunction with no physical cause. Specific problems are sometimes called hysterical symptoms.

Delusions Grossly false beliefs that often are part of schizophrenic disorders.

Delusions of reference The grossly false belief that whatever happens is somehow related to the deluded individual.

Demonology The ancient belief that mental disorders are caused by possession by demons.

Depersonalization and derealization One of the experiences that sometimes accompanies a panic attack; the person feels separated from the self, outside the body, and in a state of unreality.

Depression Severe feelings of sadness, usually marked by hopelessness, guilt, and self-blame.

Diathesis-stress perspective The model that mental disorders are the result of an interaction between inherited predispositions (diathesis) to a particular disorder and stressors (environmental events and stimuli that precipitate that disorder).

Directly conditioned fear Fear that results from direct classical conditioning.

Dissociative disorders A class of disorders in which the normal continuity and integration of experience is lost. They include psychogenic amnesia, psychogenic fugue, and multiple personality.

Dopamine A neurotransmitter that is suspected of being involved in schizophrenia.

Double bind parenting hypothesis A psychological theory of the cause of schizophrenia in which there is a close-bound connection between schizophrenia and a parent who gives impossibly contradictory messages.

Ego dystonic homosexuality A disorder in which the person is distressed by his or her own homosexuality.

Encapsulated delusion The paranoid system of paranoid disorder. The person has an elaborate and well-developed delusional system which does not show the cognitive slippage of thought disorder or hallucinations or bizarre behaviours.

Essential hypertension High blood pressure that has no apparent organic cause.

Fetish Preference for the use of a nonhuman object for sexual arousal.

Flattened affect The dull, unvarying emotion that sometimes is part of schizophrenia.

Generalized anxiety The chronic sense of apprehension and fear when no cause is apparent. It is also called "free-floating anxiety."

Hallucinations Gross distortions of perception in which non-existent objects, sounds, or smells are perceived as existing (positive hallucinations) or real things are perceived as not existing (negative hallucinations).

Inappropriate affect Emotional behaviour that is unrelated to any apparent cause, for example, inappropriate giddy laughter or sudden sobbing.

Learned helplessness A tendency to give up in the face of challenge because of previous experiences with failure to control the environment.

Learning theories of depression The position that depression results from the loss of reinforcements that used to be available and from the learning of a helpless attributional style.

Magical thinking A tendency to attribute events to highly implausible causes.

Mania Extreme elation, frenetic activity, and irrational animation.

Manic-depressive disorder See *bipolar depression.*

Mood disorders Long-lasting disturbances of emotion or affect that pervade a person's whole life.

Moral treatment Philippe Pinel's reforms during the French Revolution in which he released mental patients from shackles and chains and tried to bring them some comfort.

Multiple factor theory The position that no single theory of psychophysiological disorders is adequate. Such disorders probably result from a combination of genetic predispositions, emotional conflicts, and conditioning.

Multiple personality A dissociative disorder in which the person has two or more distinct identities or separate "ego states."

Obsessive-compulsive disorder An anxiety-based disorder marked by specific thoughts the person cannot stop thinking (obsessions) and behaviours the person cannot stop performing (compulsions).

Overgeneralization One source of false beliefs in cognitive theory of depression. The person incorrectly interprets one incident as applying to many situations.

Panic disorder A disorder marked by attacks of intense anxiety and panic that are unpredictable and overwhelming.

Paranoid disorder A relatively rare psychosis in which the person does not display the erratic logic of schizophrenia but has a well-developed system of paranoid beliefs (extreme sense of being persecuted, suspiciousness and mistrust).

Paranoid personality disorder A long-standing way of thinking marked by suspiciousness and mistrust.

Paranoid schizophrenia A disorder marked by a combination of paranoid delusions and fragmented, illogical thinking.

Paraphilias Disorders in which uncommon or bizarre objects become the focus of sexual attraction.

Passive-aggressive personality disorder A long-standing way of acting in which the person inconveniences and hurts others through indirect methods that are thought to be disguised aggression.

Pedophilia Compelling sexual attraction to children.

Personality disorder A long-lasting pattern of maladaptive behaviour that appears to be part of the person's basic character, rather than a temporary disorder.

Phobias Severe, morbid fears of specific objects, far out of proportion to the actual threat posed by the objects.

Physiological theories of depression The position that depression has a genetic component and is the result of disorders of neurotransmitters.

Psychoanalytic theories of depression The position that depression results from unconscious conflict and from aggression turned inward toward the self.

Psychoanalytic theories of psychophysiological disorders Theories that psychophysiological disorders are the result of underlying psychic conflicts.

Psychogenic amnesia The loss of specific portions of memory because of psychological stress or trauma.

Psychogenic fugue Pervasive amnesia in which personal identity is lost and a new identity may be assumed.

Psychophysiological disorders Disorders caused by chronic overactivation of the autonomic nervous system. They are often accompanied by actual organ damage.

Psychosis A severe disorder that is marked by loss of contact with reality.

Reliability The consistency with which a measure yields readings on the quality it purports to measure.

Repression The unintentional forgetting of otherwise well-learned aversive memories.

Schizoid personality disorder A chronic, long-lasting way of relating to the world by withdrawal and thinking that is unusual but not severe enough to be diagnosed as a schizophrenic psychosis.

Schizophrenia The most common of the psychoses. It is marked by fragmentation of thinking, perceptual distortions, and odd motor behaviours.

Schizophrenogenic mother A mother whose cold, over-protective, and rigid pattern of mothering is supposed to cause schizophrenia.

Schizotypal personality disorder More severe than schizoid personality disorder but not severe enough to be called schizophrenia. The person has difficulty with forming relationships and making emotional contact with other people, is withdrawn, and demonstrates eccentric patterns of thinking such as magical thinking.

Selective abstraction A source of false beliefs in cognitive theory of depression. The person takes one negative element out of many possible parts of a situation.

Self-defeating behaviours Behaviours performed for immediate escape from anxiety, in spite of serious negative consequences; when severe, formerly called "neurotic symptoms."

Sexual dysfunction The kinds of sexual problems that often deprive otherwise normal individuals of sexual satisfaction.

Simple phobias Severe fears of specific objects, such as small animals, chairs, insects, or any specific thing.

Social-drift hypothesis The theory that the reason there is more schizophrenia in poorer areas of cities is that individuals with schizophrenia are likely to suffer decreases in social class.

Social phobia A severe generalized fear of the presence of other people.

Sociogenic hypothesis of schizophrenia The theory that the reason there is more schizophrenia in poorer areas of cities is that the degrading and stressful life of homelessness, joblessness, and lower-class living contribute to schizophrenia.

Somatic-weakness theory A physiological theory that says that specific psychophysiological disorders are due to genetic inheritance. Under stress, the genetically most vulnerable organ system is likely to be affected.

Somatization disorder A somatoform disorder in which the person may have conversion symptoms but also reports very frequent general physical complaints such as bodily pains, headaches, fatigue, allergies, and cardiac symptoms.

Somatoform disorders Disorders with symptoms that take physical form but that have no discernible physical causes. The two most common are conversion disorder and somatization disorder.

Somatogenic hypothesis Hippocrates' theory that mental disorders had a physical cause.

Specific-reaction theory A physiological theory that states that, probably for genetic reasons, different individuals react to stress with different autonomic responses.

Transsexual A person who is convinced that his or her "true sex" is the opposite of his or her biological sex.

Transvestism A behaviour in which a person is sexually aroused by wearing clothing traditional to the opposite sex.

Ulcers The inflammation of the stomach lining from excess acid; can sometimes be a psychophysiological disorder.

Unipolar depression Depression without manic periods; cycles between periods of depression and periods of feeling normal.

Validity The ability of a measure to measure what it claims to measure.

Waxy flexibility See *catatonic inflexibility*.

Suggested Readings

Cleckley, H. (1976). *The mask of sanity*, 5th ed. St. Louis: C. V. Mosby. This is considered the classic work on antisocial personality. Cleckley's description of the disorder is widely used, and he provides some interesting case material.

Davison, G. C., & Neale, J. M. (1990). *Abnormal psychology*, 5th ed. New York: John Wiley & Sons. One of many undergraduate textbooks on abnormal psychology, this is one of the best balanced and most readable. It would probably be the best bet for a general follow-up to this chapter.

Kaplan, B. (ed.) (1964). *The inner world of mental illness*. New York: Harper & Row. It is sometimes difficult to imagine what the experience of mental disorders is actually like. This book is a collection of first-person accounts by individuals who suffered and wrote about the experience.

Millon, T., & Klerman, D. L. (eds.) (1986). *Contemporary approaches to psychopathology*. New York: Guilford Press. This is a collection of chapters written by different authorities on the different disorders. There is considerable discussion of the general process of diagnosing and classifying mental disorders and suggestions for how the system might be improved.

Sheehan, S. (1982). *Is there no place on earth for me?* Boston: Houghton-Mifflin. This documents the life of a girl who developed schizophrenia and spent much of her life in mental hospitals. It is at times gripping and upsetting. It won the Pulitzer Prize.

CHAPTER 15

SOURCE: Claude Tousignant, Detail from *Sculpture* (1974).

Approaches to Therapy

ONE OF THE MOST important activities of psychologists is the relief of human suffering. There are many different forms of therapy available. Now that we have studied personality theories in Chapter 10 and the nature of psychological problems in Chapters 13 and 14, we are ready to look at several approaches to treatment. Before reading this chapter, it will be especially important to recall the material on personality theories in Chapter 10. Most approaches to therapy are closely linked to one or another of the theories of personality.

WHAT IS THERAPY?

At the end of this chapter we will briefly consider some medical approaches to the treatment of psychological problems, but our main focus will be on methods that use human interaction as the mode of treatment. Many of these approaches are based primarily on conversations that take place between a therapist and a patient (or client). One early term for Freud's brand of psychotherapy was "the talking cure." **Psychotherapy** is not some strange or frighteningly special process. In general, it is a specialized structured human relationship that operates between a socially sanctioned healer and a client who comes for help with emotional problems.

Our culture provides many structures for dealing with emotional problems, so it is sometimes difficult to define exactly what is and is not psychotherapy. Advice columnists, bartenders, ministers, and best friends may pull us through some tough problems, but what they do is not usually called psychotherapy. This term is reserved for a specialized relationship that generally meets the following three criteria (Frank, 1961). First, one person is sanctioned by the sufferer and the culture as a specially trained healer. Second, there is a sufferer who seeks help from the healer. Third, there is a structured series of contacts between these two parties for the purpose of healing. These contacts are primarily based on talking, acts, and rituals in which the sufferer and healer participate.

This definition covers a large variety of treatment modes, such as psychiatric treatment, psychiatric counselling, pastoral counselling, and behaviour therapy. The definition also makes it clear that "psychotherapy" refers to a specifically structured kind of help and not to more casual contacts, no matter how helpful they might be.

Who are therapists?

This section will be of special interest to those who would like to be a therapist or counsellor. There are many pathways into such a profession.

The professions

Psychiatrists are medical doctors who, after earning an M.D. degree, complete a three or four year residency for diagnosis and treatment of emotional disorders. This residency is usually done in a hospital setting. In North America, psychiatrists are the only group of psychotherapists who are legally permitted to prescribe medication as part of treatment. **Psychoanalysts** are one, relatively small, group of psychiatrists who have been especially trained in the psychoanalytic approach of Sigmund Freud (see the next section). Note that many people incorrectly refer to all psychotherapists as psychoanalysts. **Lay analysts** belong to an even smaller group of non-medical practitioners of psychoanalysis who have undergone psychoanalytic training (which takes many years). **Clinical psychologists** are practitioners who are trained in psychology departments in universities and nearly always have a Ph.D. degree or a Psy.D (doctor of psychology) degree. This training usually takes about five years after a B. A. (honours) plus one year of internship. Some clinical psychologists practise with an M. A. degree, but they usually must work under direct supervision or in an institutional setting. Most provinces and states require a Ph.D. or Psy.D. degree to be a registered or licensed psychologist. Generally speaking, the clinical psychologist is more likely to be trained in principles of human behaviour and research methods than the other professionals we have mentioned. **Social workers** are practitioners who are trained in a school of social work, usually with a MSW degree or a Ph.D degree. They often receive specific training in psychotherapy and work in settings where they help individuals, groups, and families. There are also training programs for **family therapists** who then specialize in seeing clients as members of family units.

Other roles

The truth is that in our culture, the methods of psychotherapy are used in a great many jobs that are not formally "psychotherapy jobs." Probation officers, group-home workers, family workers in homes for the elderly, and workers in many other settings clearly require formally structured contacts that fit our definition of therapy. It has been our experience that many workers are not well prepared for this work and often suffer uncertainty in doing their jobs. It is essential that such "paraprofessional counsellors" receive careful training (Kendall and Norton-Ford, 1982). Many of these people are excellent natural counsellors, but many of them have simply been thrown in and expected to swim without being shown how to do so.

PSYCHOANALYTIC APPROACHES

As we said in Chapter 10, **psychoanalysis** is one approach to psychotherapy and is based largely on the work of Sigmund Freud. It is based on an instinctual model of human behaviour and its main methods are free association, interpretation, and transference.

FIGURE 15-1 The goals of psychoanalysis

The main goal of psychoanalysis is to provide an individual with insight into repressed inner conflicts. This process of making the unconscious conscious frees up psychic energy. Once these insights are recognized, an emotional release occurs, and the person can attain "mental health."

SOURCE: Reprinted with permission from Allyn and Bacon, 1989.

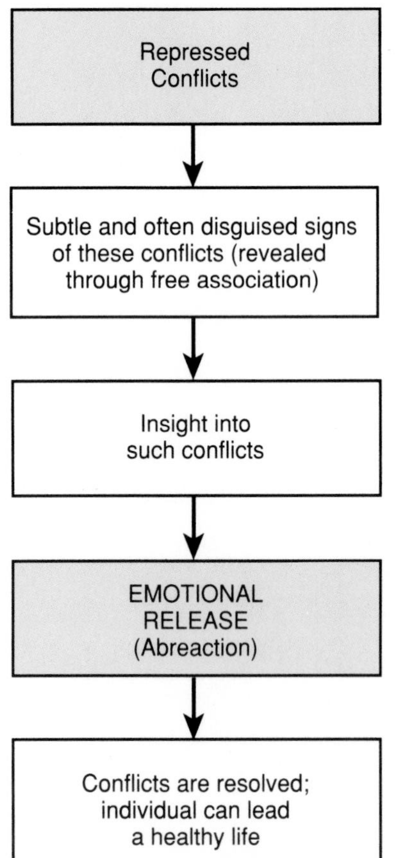

In theoretical terms, the goal of psychoanalytic treatment is to free up trapped psychic energy for use by the ego. To say it simplistically, "making the unconscious conscious" relieves repression and fixations, making more psychic energy available for everday living (see Figure 15-1). Because psychoanalytic approaches are based on "dynamic" theories (having to do with the distribution of psychic energy), they are often also referred to as "psychodynamic approaches" to therapy.

Most psychoanalytic writing (including Freud's) is concerned with theoretical constructions about the nature of personality and emotional disturbance. Little attention has been paid to specific therapeutic techniques. This state of affairs may exist, in part, because many psychoanalysts are convinced that techniques can best be taught through actual situations in which the apprentice analyst's work is supervised by an experienced analyst. Budding psychoanalysts also learn techniques when they go through the experience of being analyzed themselves. This analysis is considered part of the training process for a psychoanalyst. Further, individual analysis is a very complex procedure and it is difficult to lay down absolute rules or techniques that would work in all circumstances. It has also been said (perhaps with tongue in cheek) that the reason Freud didn't write more on techniques is because he didn't want his future patients to read his books and start second-guessing him in analysis.

However, there are some psychoanalytic techniques that we can describe and many of these came about through Freud's establishment of the "talking cure" (Freud, 1935). A number of these Freudian techniques are still widely used in the practice of therapy.

Free association

The central technique of psychoanalysis is "the rule of free association." In classical analysis the patient lies on a couch, with the analyst sitting out of sight behind him or her. The patient is instructed to practise **free association**, that is, to say whatever comes to mind without censoring or editing, and no matter how painful, apparently trivial, or illogical the material may be. He or she is simply to spill out all thoughts as they occur. This is very difficult to do, and when the person is unable to make associations or think of anything to say, the patient is said to be resisting. **Resistance** is the patient's unconscious avoidance of threatening material, an inability to think of anything because of emotional blocks. In the early stages of analysis during free association, the analyst may offer mild interpretations of the patient's resistances in an unthreatening way. The analyst uses the **manifest content** — that is, the verbalized content of the free associations or of dreams—to derive his or her own understanding of the latent content. **Latent content** is the hidden, often symbolic content of free associations and dreams that lies behind the words of the manifest content. Dream analysis serves as a starting point for the free-association procedure. Because the ego's censorship is weakened during sleep, threatening unconscious material often is able to appear in dreams. The analyst uses this material to help formulate ideas about the patient's personality dynamics. Freud strongly believed that dream content symbolically represented the nature of unconscious conflicts.

Much of the value of free association in psychoanalytic treatment is the *catharsis* it allows the patient. Freud conceived of the mind as a place where memories, thoughts, and emotions exist as "excitations." Talking results in the releasing of these mind-contents and thus results in relief. The strong emotional release that usually comes from the catharsis of talking about feeling-laden content is called **abreaction**.

Interpretation

Since much of psychoanalysis consists of free association, the patient does most of the talking, especially early in treatment. The therapist intervenes, however, when he or she thinks intervention will free bound-up psychic energy and make unconscious material conscious. The function of interpretation is to speed the process of uncovering unconscious material — material whose existence the analyst has inferred from what the patient has said. **Interpretation** is a psychoanalytic technique in which the therapist explains to the patient a deeper understanding of a particular personal issue than the patient has discovered. The analyst listens for gaps and inconsistencies in the patient's story, makes inferences about the meaning of the dreams the patient reports, observes the patient's behaviour in the therapy session and listens to what is said about behaviour outside the session, and is ever alert for indications of the patient's feelings toward the therapist. These data are sifted and organized by the analyst, within the framework of the psychoanalytic understanding of personality structure, to formulate the real nature of the patient's problems.

The analyst is careful not to impose very threatening interpretations clumsily. As Menninger describes it, the analyst "tells the patient what he has *almost* seen for himself" (Menninger, 1958, p. 134). This method of timing interpretations is often referred to as *interpreting at the preconscious level*. The analyst delicately goes beyond what the patient is conscious of by giving interpretations that are new but not so threatening that the patient will reject them. It is usually ineffective to interpret material that is deeply unconscious. Such material would probably be denied by the patient.

Transference and working through

One of the most important issues that the analyst interprets is *transference*. **Transference** is the patient's experience toward the therapist of emotional responses (positive and negative) which are unconsciously transferred from other relationships in his or her life. Transference is an essential part of the psychoanalytic cure, for it allows a patient to attach to the therapist any troublesome feelings carried over from other relationships. The patient might, for example, transfer to the therapist some unresolved Oedipal attachments or hatreds. The analyst becomes a current substitute for the parent and fills a progressively more important role in the patient's life. During a transference, the patient may think about the analyst frequently. He or she may even fall in love with or make life plans that centre around the analyst. The patient may also develop a passionate hatred for the analyst. Transference is based primarily on fantasy—a fantasy necessary for the patient's "working through" the unresolved complexes with the analyst. **Working through** is the process, both cognitive and emotional, of resolving old conflicts by re-experiencing them in the safety of therapy and transference relationship. Some of Freud's followers insist that only transference interpretations can lead to real changes in the ego (Strachey, 1934, as cited in Bernstein, 1965). Others say that true psychoanalysis requires a full-blown "transference neurosis," in which the patient is deeply involved with feelings about the analyst, although Freud apparently never stated this point of view (Marmor, 1968).

If an analyst develops an excessive attachment to or dislike of a particular patient, **countertransference** becomes a problem. The analyst might develop emotional responses (positive and negative) toward the patient because of the analyst's own unconscious conflicts and distortions. These irrational reactions may stand in the way of dealing with the patient's problems. The analyst may require consultation with a colleague to deal with this effectively.

Psychoanalytic psychotherapy

Very few therapists practise psychoanalysis the way Freud did. He saw his patients daily, had them lie on a couch, and the therapy sometimes lasted for years. Obviously, this kind of therapy would be very expensive and any one psychoanalyst could see only a few patients. Many therapists, however, consider themselves to be psychoanalytic and apply Freud's general theories and techniques in different settings. For example, it is common for a *psychoanalytically oriented psychotherapist* to meet with a patient for one or perhaps two hours a week, sitting face to face with the person. They may talk sitting on either side of a desk or simply in two comfortable chairs arranged facing each other.

These therapists likely will use free association, interpretation, and the transference relationship and will interpret the patient's problems within the framework of Freud's notions of fixations, Oedipal problems, stages of life, and so forth. They are also more likely to offer advice than classical psychoanalysts are. This more flexible approach is well represented by *The Chicago Group* of Alexander and French (1946; Alexander, 1956, 1963). Depending on the nature and severity of a problem, Alexander and French would see a patient on a highly individualized schedule. At first, the patient might come in every day and then taper off to once a week or even less frequently. If the therapist was concerned about excess dependency developing, he or she might even suggest less frequent contact or a break from therapy. These therapists were also likely to make directive suggestions about actions the patient might take. Freud said a patient should not make any major life decisions while in treatment, a rule, by the way, that could create problems for patients who were in treatment for several years. Alexander and French, however, often suggested such changes when the therapist and patient agreed on their wisdom.

One of the most important contributions of The Chicago Group was the emphasis of its adherents on *corrective emotional experiences*. Many people who misunderstand psychoanalysis think that it is largely an intellectual process in which progress comes about because the patient gains new *insights*. These insights are often thought of as sudden, new, more accurate understandings of the causes of the person's problems. However, it is clear to nearly all practising therapists that purely intellectual understanding of one's problems is often not accompanied by any meaningful change. Alexander and French stressed that there must also be emotional experiencing for change to take place. They used the transference relationship for the reliving—emotional as well as intellectual—of old conflicts. This time, going through some old unresolved problem with the therapist, they felt that the outcome could be constructive and could help undo the old damage. "Re-experiencing the old, unsettled conflict *but with a new ending* is the secret of every penetrating therapeutic result" (Alexander and French, 1946, p. 338).

Another group of psychodynamic therapists called *ego analysts* place greater emphasis on current functioning. An **ego analyst** is a therapist who subscribes to the fundamentals of psychoanalysis but who strongly emphasizes the patient's ego strengths and control of his or her life. They give the patient credit for considerable control through ego functioning and stress current functioning more than the exploration of the past. These therapists take a much more optimistic view of the potential for creativity and love and they reject Freud's male-dominated approach. Ego analysts draw much from Freud's view of unconscious influences and other psychoanalytic ideas but they practise therapy in ways that recognize that the patient "directs his own activity and deals constructively with his environment" (Ford and Urban, 1963, p. 181). Modern psychoanalytic therapy is more likely to stress such supportive approaches and to encourage emotional expression in therapy. Wallerstein (1989) reported results from a 30-year study of psychoanalytic therapy carried out at the Menninger Foundation. Traditional (or Freudian) psychoanalysis produced less positive outcomes than had been anticipated, but psychoanalytic psychotherapy achieved more than predicted. The supportive and expressive (emotional) aspects of psychoanalytic psychotherapy seemed to be the elements most related to patient progress.

HUMANISTIC APPROACHES

There are many approaches to the treatment of emotional problems that fall under the label of "humanistic therapy." **Humanistic therapy** is the term used for several approaches to therapy that are all based on a belief in the client's own tendencies toward growth and in the importance of the client's perspective on his or her problems. It is remarkable how different those approaches can be, in spite of their underlying emphasis on self-actualization and phenomenology. We will examine Carl Rogers' person-centred therapy and Fritz Perls'

Gestalt therapy. Both approaches are designed to help the client experience present feelings and thoughts more fully and accurately. This greater self-understanding helps the person live more wisely, well, and meaningfully. There is considerably more attention paid to the present than in psychoanalysis, in which past causes of behaviour play a more significant role. Of course, humanists do talk about the past, and psychoanalysts do talk about the present a great deal. The difference is in the emphasis.

Person-centred therapy

Carl Rogers' approach to therapy is often called "client-centred therapy," to indicate the respect paid to the client as the source of direction in therapy. More recently, Rogers applied the principles of his approach to many circumstances beyond therapy and came to prefer the term "person-centred." **Person-centred therapy** stresses the core conditions of accurate empathy, dependable acceptance, and therapist genuineness.

Since Rogers argues that the individual will normally develop in constructive directions unless the growth process is somehow distorted or interfered with, his treatment is designed to reverse the experiences that led to conditional self-acceptance and to the distortions in experience that result. He would say that the therapist *facilitates* the client's improvement, not that the therapist treats the client, in the sense of doing things *to* him or her. The client solves his or her own problems, within a special kind of emotional environment created by the therapist. The innate self-actualizing tendency ensures growth, if the conditions are right (Rogers 1951, 1957, and 1980; Raskin & Rogers, 1989).

Rogers' proposals are, obviously, quite different from the psychoanalyst's role as the expert guide and interpreter. Rogers' three conditions — accurate empathy, dependable acceptance, and genuineness—are often referred to as the "therapeutic triad" or even the "core conditions." Person-centred therapy has received some research support, as we shall see later in this chapter.

Basic attitudes

Notice that we have called the therapeutic triad "conditions" for therapy and not "techniques." Rogers was even happier with the term "basic attitudes" of the therapist. He believed that therapists who try to apply these three qualities simply as techniques miss the whole point of a real human encounter. Although the "core conditions" should be expressed in the therapist's behaviour, it is the attitude behind them that is essential.

Accurate empathy is the therapist's experience and expression of a deep understanding of what the client is experiencing and trying to communicate. The therapist, through words or gestures or even silence, somehow gives the client the feeling, "Oh, right! That's exactly what I meant, but I never thought that anyone would be able to understand it. Now I feel like talking more." The client makes discoveries and experiences feelings more deeply, as this empathic response makes it easier and easier to explore material that would otherwise be too threatening. Accurate empathy is often misunderstood to be a passive kind of repeating back what the client just said, but this is clearly a misunderstanding of what Rogers meant.

Another of Rogers' core conditions for therapy is **dependable acceptance**. The therapist values the client as a worthwhile person, regardless of what the client thinks, feels, or says. The more formal term that Rogers often uses is **unconditional positive regard**. Although this term is sometimes misunderstood too, his choice of words shows the function that the relationship serves. Remember that in his theory, the person's problems are largely the result of the experience being accepted only *conditionally*. Self-acceptance is only conditional. The therapist gives the client the experience, "Here is a person who *really* knows me as I am and still values me. Lots of people say they accept me, but they don't know some of the things I think and feel. This person proves he or she knows me (because of the accurate empathy) and accepts me, so I can accept myself."

Of course, the client doesn't think all this explicitly, but client-centred therapy is designed to move the person more toward unconditional self-acceptance. Then the person is free to experience all of his or her perceptions accurately. Because of the self-actualization tendency, the accurately experiencing person will then live healthily.

Earlier in his career, Rogers stressed empathy and positive regard. More recently he has said that none of this will be effective if the therapist is not genuine and honest in the relationship. **Therapist genuineness** implies that the therapist does not play a role but acts in ways that are consistent with how he or she feels. He has moved more toward being himself in the therapist-client relationship, sharing some of his own reactions and at all times trying to experience himself accurately, so he can relate as the person he is at the moment.

We will examine some research evidence relevant to person-centred therapy later. For now it is interesting to note that some researchers have concluded that Rogers' "core conditions" are also necessary for teachers and for the fullest development of thinking processes in educational settings (Aspy, Roebuck, and Benoit, 1987).

Gestalt therapy

Fritz Perls described his approach to therapy as an *encounter* between therapist and patient, and many of his approaches were evident in the encounter-group movement that was popular a few years ago and still has some adherents today. The Gestalt approach to the practice of psychotherapy is above all else present-oriented. Perls has a formula that reads "now = experience = awareness = reality." In his view, "the past is no more and the future not yet. Only the now exists" (Perls, 1970, p. 14).

Although Rogers might have claimed the same goals, the two therapists went about doing therapy quite differently. The Gestalt therapist may be questioning, may seem aggressive and challenging and may intentionally frustrate the client. But all the therapist's attitudes are aimed at helping the client discover and enhance awareness of present functioning. The Gestalt therapist promotes current

Fritz Perls.
SOURCE: Photo by Hugh Lyon Wilkerson.

experiencing through such techniques as forbidding the word "it" and other detached language and challenging the client when he or she attempts to play games. The therapist urges the client to focus on bodily sensations, on perceptions of the environment, on sensory awareness, and on feelings toward self and others. In other words, the Gestalt therapist could be said to actively prompt experiencing, while the client-centred therapist would try to facilitate experiencing.

Encounter groups

Humanism's great emphasis on awareness and personal growth was instrumental in the 1960s and 1970s in the great popularity of **encounter groups**. The word "encounter" was well chosen for these groups, because they centred around the participants interacting with each other in ways that led to intense contact and experiencing. Their aim was to help participants to experience themselves, their feelings, and their life more fully. This was often accomplished through body exercises, group dream work, and psychological "games" such as having the whole group try to communicate with each other non-verbally and without the use of hands. Many of these groups were based on the principles of gestalt therapy and were highly confrontative. Often, for example, one member would be put in the "hot seat" and each other member would tell this person what he or she didn't like about the person.

Although many participants reported positive changes as a result of encounter groups, there were also many reports of "bad trips" that led to severe problems for individuals. A critical turning point for the encounter group movement came with the publication of Yalom and Lieberman's (1971) finding that the encounter groups they studied had a "psychiatric casualty rate" of about 10%. In other words, a totally unacceptable number of participants had such severely destructive experiences that they required immediate therapeutic intervention after an encounter group experience.

Encounter group sessions can be either supportive or confrontative.
SOURCE: "Old Monkeys on Young Backs." UPI/Bettmann.

It is important to note that Yalom and Lieberman described seven kinds of group leaders. The one that was most likely to do damage was the "aggressive stimulator" who was described as "intrusive, confrontive, challenging, caring, . . . self-revealing, . . . charismatic, and as focusing on the individual" (Lambert, Bergin, and Collins, 1977, p. 471). Yalom and Lieberman's report was a significant factor in the sharp decline in popularity of encounter groups. It is interesting that one of the few continuing programs, the La Jolla program, is based on the approach of Carl Rogers and is not centred around a highly confrontative approach.

BEHAVIOURAL APPROACHES

In the early 1960's, the explicit application of behavioural principles to treatment became a popular approach, and behaviour therapy is now one of the most influential perspectives on treatment. According to Garry Martin, by 1981 "In various settings in Canada the behavioural approach has developed a firm foundation, is well respected, and is growing rapidly" (Martin, 1981, p. 20). That conclusion still seems valid. By now, the general term **behaviour modification** refers to a large number of techniques that are explicit applications of conditioning princples to human problems. We have discussed these principles in Chapter 5 and again in Chapter 10, where we saw how they applied to the process of personality development. The techniques derived from conditioning principles can be categorized into three major classes: 1) desensitization methods, 2) changing reinforcement contingencies, and 3) aversive conditioning.

Desensitization

Desensitization techniques are designed to change unpleasant emotions. The basic principles (as we discussed in Chapter 5) are extinction and counterconditioning. To get rid of a conditioned response, one must perform the response in the absence of an unpleasant experience (extinction) or in the presence of a pleasant stimulus (counterconditioning). We will look at two ways to apply these methods.

Systematic desensitization

Systematic desensitization is probably the best-known behavioural method for relieving undesired emotions (Wolpe, 1958; 1987), although there are a great many ways to apply the basic principles. **Systematic desensitization** uses counterconditioning by pairing deep relaxation with imagined scenes arranged along an anxiety hierarchy. In this approach the therapist goes through three steps. First, the therapist and patient work together to establish an **anxiety hierarchy** (an ordered list) of feared cue situations that range from the most fear-inducing situation the patient has to deal with down through progressively less fear-arousing cues or situations.

After the construction of agreed-upon anxiety hierarchies, the second step is to train the patient in *deep-muscle relaxation*. Third,

Joseph Wolpe was one of the first behaviour therapists. He popularized systematic desensitization.
SOURCE: Courtesy of Pepperdine University.

the therapist instructs the patient to imagine one of the less anxiety-arousing situations and at the same time to relax. Thus, the anxiety response is counterconditioned by the pairing of deep muscle relaxation with an imagined fearful situation. The therapist then systematically progresses up the anxiety hierarchy by moving to more intensely aversive situations and continuously pairing deep muscle relaxation with the imagined fear-arousing situation. (See Figure 15-2.)

For example, a man with sexual fears might be instructed to imagine himself on a date with a woman and use his relaxation skills. When he is comfortable with this scene, a more intense scene would be imagined, progressing to vivid scenes of sexual encounter. Presumably, the treatment will eventually generalize to real life.

Systematic desensitization is not only conducted using mental imagery. **In vivo desensitization** is a process of extinction and counterconditioning exercises carried out in the natural environment. The process is the same. That is, an individual moves gradually through a hierarchy of feared events or objects while applying relaxation skills. For example, a person with diabetes may experience terror at the prospect of giving himself an injection. While relaxed, the individual might progress through a series of steps ending with the actual experience of a self-administered injection. These steps might include looking at a syringe from a distance, touching a syringe, practising on an orange, observing another person performing an injection and finally giving himself the injection. The hierarchy must be individualized, depending on the particular circumstances and the individual's fears, and each step in the hierarchy must be done thoroughly before proceeding to the next.

Systematic desensitization is only one way the general principles can be applied. The basic procedure involves gradual exposure to the feared cues paired with positive experience. This, of course, assumes that one accurately knows what the feared cues are, and this is often a very complex matter in human emotional problems.

FIGURE 15-2 Systematic desensitization
In systematic desensitization an individual practices feeling relaxed while imagining scenes or events which initially produced anxiety. Because opposite emotional states tend to inhibit each other, it is expected that the stimuli will gradually lose their capacity to evoke anxiety.
SOURCE: Reprinted with permission from Allyn and Bacon, 1989.

Individual constructs hierarchy of anxiety-inducing scenes or events
↓
Individual learns to induce muscle relaxation
↓
Individual relaxes while imagining each scene or event; they become signals for positive feelings
↓
These scenes or events no longer induce anxiety

Extinction approaches

Graduated extinction is similar to systematic desensitization. The client is exposed to the feared cues in small steps along an anxiety hierarchy. The difference is that little attention is paid to providing a specific counterconditioning agent, such as relaxation. These exposure methods depend on the patient's experiences of fears in situations where there is no actual threat. Without the specific instructions from the therapist, the patient would run from such situations. This would result in strengthening avoidance of the feared situation and would prevent extinction from taking place. Remember from Chapter 5 that extinction requires that the person feel the fear. By facing the feared situation in graduated steps, the person should experience a reduction in fear.

A very different kind of extinction therapy argues that intense exposure to the feared cues is more effective than a graduated exposure. This therapy is sometimes called **flooding** and sometimes **implosive therapy**. This flooding can be done through vividly presented imaginary scenes (which are often very frightening) or *in vivo*. *It is essential that a flooding session not be ended* until the anxiety has diminished, or the person can be left more fearful than at the beginning.

Changing reinforcement contingencies

Reinforcement contingencies are the relationships between specific behaviours and the consequences that follow. We have discussed the power of positive reinforcement in Chapter 5, with the phrase "people do what they are reinforced for doing." Behaviour therapists argue that the application of this powerful principle is only limited by the imagination of the person doing the treatment.

A classic illustration of the application of reinforcement principles treatment was reported by Baer and Harris (1963). Analyses of the reinforcement contingencies provided to an individual child in a classroom revealed that disruptive behaviour was often followed by attention from the teacher. Although the teacher's intent was to weaken the behaviour, the increased attention served to strengthen it. Similarly, desired behaviour was often ignored or given minimal attention, which to the child may have been punishment, or at least nonreinforcement. Baer's procedure was to establish a baseline rating of a particular target behaviour and to instruct the teacher to ignore disruptive behaviour and to respond positively to desired behaviour as often as possible. Desired behaviours increased significantly. In a further stage, the teacher was instructed to return to the original mode of response to the child for a period — a step designed to establish that the change in the child's behaviour was indeed due to the change in responses from the teacher. Disruptive behaviour increased. Ultimately, the new reinforcement contingencies were reinstated.

Contingency contracting

Many behaviour therapists explain the principles of reinforcement to the client and then develop **contingency contracting**. This is a contractual arrangement in which the therapist and client work out a system for the client to be rewarded or punished for particular behaviours. For example, a person who wanted to stop pulling out his or her own hair might give the therapist a large sum of money for safekeeping. Each day that the client passed without any hair-pulling could see $10 go into a fund to buy some special reward with special meaning to the client — perhaps a new wardrobe or a new guitar. Each day that the "symptom" is acted out, however, would mean that $10 would be sent to the organization most disliked by the client. These contingencies would be agreed upon and monitored somehow.

Stuart (1971) proposed five elements that a contingency contract would normally include: (1) a statement of the client's and therapist's responsibilities, (2) rewards for complying with the contract, (3) a system for monitoring whether the client complies with the conditions, (4) extra reinforcers for unusually good performance, and (5) some kind of punishment for failures.

Token economies

The principles of reinforcement have often been applied to institutional settings, where therapists have considerable control over the contingencies in patients' lives. In the normal environment, reinforcement contingencies are often poorly structured. Money, for example, is supposed to be a system of tokens that reinforce desired behaviours. There are many drawbacks to these "natural" contingency systems, however. In most jobs, money is not really contingent on the quality of work, except in some very loose way. Often undesirable activity brings more money than other behaviours, for example. In a **token economy**, there are clearly specified target behaviours that are quickly reinforced with some kind of structured reinforcement token system such as poker chips or gold stars. A **target behaviour** is a specific behaviour that is to be changed by a behavioural treatment program. These quickly provided tokens then can ultimately be exchanged for **backup reinforcers**. These are the larger rewards available from using the tokens earned. Such rewards might include extra food, special privileges, and better living conditions.

FIGURE 15-3 Effects of a token economy on children's disruptive behaviour
Eight disruptive children were observed both during a baseline period and after a token system for reinforcing good behaviour was introduced. There was an abrupt drop in disruptive behaviour. Delay of reinforcement was gradually increased to four days with no increase in negative behaviours.
SOURCE: Adapted from O'Leary and Becker (1967).

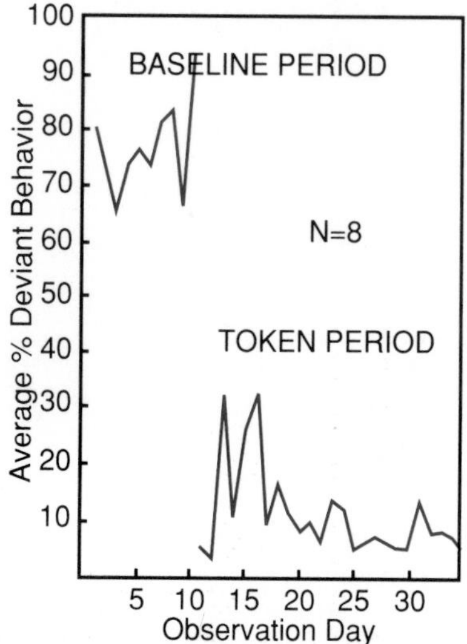

Token economies have been used successfully to increase self-care behaviours in a mental hospital (Ayllon and Azrin, 1965), to decrease disruptive behaviour in classrooms (O'Leary and Becker, 1967), and even to increase the rate of participation in community activities in the natural environment (Miller and Miller, 1970). Figure 15-3 illustrates the dramatic impact of a token economy on the disruptive behaviour of eight children in a classroom setting. General reinforcers (such as "Good for you") had not worked with these children. When teacher ratings of specific behaviours were linked to rewards such as trinkets and candy, behaviour improved (O'Leary and Becker, 1967).

Aversive counterconditioning

Aversive counterconditioning is the application of punishment methods to rid the client of undesired behaviours. The elimination of maladaptive behaviours through the use of painful stimuli, such as nauseating drugs, has been a treatment techniques for many years. It is most frequently used with alcoholism and deviant sexual behaviours. For example, *emetic* drugs cause violently painful nausea shortly after the person takes a drink of alcohol. This is designed to punish the drinking behaviour and to condition an aversive reaction to alcohol. Used alone, aversion procedures probably result in only a temporary suppression of target behaviours and can even result in the eventual increase of the maladaptive behaviour (Menaker, 1967; Rachman and Teasdale, 1969; Rimm and Cunningham, 1985). They do have some usefulness in suppressing an undesirable behaviour while establishing substitute behaviours with more positive approaches, such as the use of positive reinforcement of desirable behaviours.

FIGURE 15-4 The treatment of shyness with graduated exposure (extinction) and social skills training
Cappe and Alden showed that social skills training (behavioural treatment) combined with graduated exposure (extinction) to social situations was effective in treating severe shyness. Graduated extinction alone was more effective than no treatment but less effective than the combination of treatments.

SOURCE: Adapted with permission from Cappe and Alden (1966).

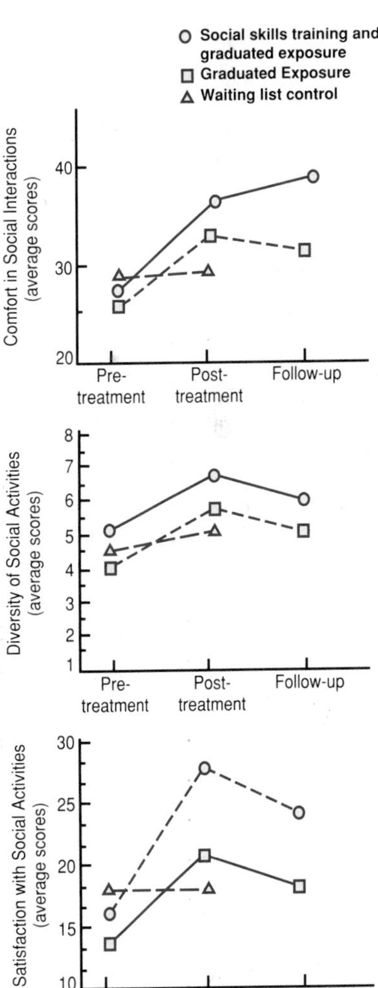

Complexities in application

The most common criticism of behaviour therapy is that it is simplistic, and the discussion of specific illustrative techniques may have strengthened this impression. It should be noted that we have only described the basic principles, and in practice, behaviour modifiers take into account many complexities of human problems. In the next section we will be discussing an important trend in this direction, the trend toward what has been called "cognitive learning theory." Behavioural principles can be applied both to explicit overt behaviours and to the complex covert behaviours of thinking and feeling.

Robin Cappe and Lynne Alden (1986) of the University of British Columbia have reported a well controlled study that nicely illustrates the application of behavioural treatment to severe shyness. Most of their subjects were so shy they would probably qualify as having social phobias. Most had never dated or hadn't dated for years, and less than 20% were married. Cappe and Alden randomly assigned the subjects to one of three treatments. One group received systematic desensitization. One received systematic desensitization plus a program of social skills training. And a control group was assigned to wait for treatment. Later the control group was to receive whichever of the treatments proved superior. Both treatment groups improved more than the control group on the number of social interactions they had and on their own ratings of social comfort and satisfaction with treatment. The group that had also received social skills training improved the most (See Figure 15-4.)

COGNITIVE APPROACHES

It is important to remember that cognitive approaches are primarily intended as a corrective to the strict behavioural ones that tend to focus on external behaviour. They try to bring some needed complexity to a generally learning-oriented approach. Some cognitive therapists say that cognitions are simply behaviours that occur inside the person and follow the same laws as overt behaviours. These would be the "cognitive learning theorists." Others, "cognitive theorists," say that cognitions differ from overt behaviours in important ways and are primary in controlling behaviour (Schwartz, 1982). In the practice of therapy, though, this distinction doesn't make much difference. All of these therapists stress the importance of cognition in the development of emotional problems and see the proper focus of therapy as changing cognitions. They argue that emotional problems are primarily the result of irrational or improper thinking. They work on changing both specific thoughts and more general strategies of thinking.

Cognitive behaviour modification

Cognitive behaviour modification has become one of the most popular new approaches to therapy. It has its theoretical roots in behavioural theory, but in many ways it resembles the more talking-oriented approach of traditional approaches to therapy.

Cognitive traps

Aaron Beck is a prominent cognitive therapist who has worked mostly with those who suffer from depression.
SOURCE: Courtesy of Aaron T. Beck, M.D.

Aaron Beck has developed a cognitive approach to the treatment of depression that has been widely adopted and has been supported by clinical studies (Beck, 1976; Rush et al, 1977; Kovacs et al, 1981). He has argued that people fall into **cognitive traps**, certain illogical ways of thinking that lead them to feel self-deprecating. **Arbitrary inference** is one example of a cognitive trap. In this situation a depressed person draws conclusions about him or herself on the basis of irrelevant or limited information. For example, making an error such as spilling soup on one's suit is exaggerated into evidence of general incompetence.

Magnification is another cognitive trap. A small problem—the new car has a light burn out—is exaggerated and "catastrophized." The owner is upset for days about the low quality of cars and about how he has been ripped off because he's so stupid. The other side of magnification is **minimization**, in which the person automatically discounts positive evidence. A glowing annual evaluation is dismissed because "those things aren't valid anyway" or "they don't really know how incompetent I am, and they're going to find out eventually."

Cognitive strategies

The cognitive therapist tries to help the client change these distorted beliefs by first understanding the "negative cognitive triad" — the sequence that goes from *cognition to emotion to behaviour*. The therapist argues that faulty cognitions lead to negative emotions and these emotions result in self-defeating behaviour. Then the client may be urged to monitor and record instances of this sequence in everyday life. The therapist may then help the client examine the evidence for and against the client's personal beliefs and help substitute more realistic cognitions. The therapist might also assign "homework" to help change false beliefs. A physically attractive client who thinks she is ugly, for example, might be assigned the task of standing in some public place and counting the number of women who seem to her to be above average in attractiveness. In one such instance, the client found that almost nobody was "above average" by her standards. The therapist used this to point out her unrealistic beliefs about attractiveness.

Clients as collaborators

Cognitive therapists often use a variety of techniques to help the client understand and change faulty ways of thinking. In general, cognitive therapists take the role of a "facilitative teacher." They are less directive toward the client than many interpretive analysts would be but are more likely to actively teach the lessons they want the client to learn than, say, a person-centred therapist would be. One of the most important principles of cognitive therapy is that the client should be seen and treated as a collaborator, rather than having the therapist play the role of expert advice giver.

Rational-emotive therapy

One of the best-known cognitive approaches is Albert Ellis's rational-emotive therapy (RET). Ellis's 1962 book, *Reason and Emotion in Psychotherapy*, was clearly the pioneer work in this area and came years before cognitive behaviour therapy became popular. In **rational-emotive therapy** Ellis takes the "reason controls emotion" position more strongly than nearly any other writer. He outlines the ABC's of RET as the basic principle of his approach. "(W)hen a highly charged emotional Consequence (C) follows a significant Activating Event (A), A may seem to but actually does not cause C. Instead emotional Consequences are largely created by B—the individual's Belief System" (Ellis, 1973, p. 167). His approach to therapy, then, is centred on changing the person's belief system. Ellis often quotes Shakespeare's Hamlet: "There is nothing either good or bad but thinking makes it so."

In order to change the client's thinking, Ellis uses very direct and directive methods (Ellis and Bernard, 1985). He likes the word "disputation" to describe his frontal attack on the client's irrational beliefs. He often argues and persuades and assigns specific homework assignments. For example, Ellis might assign a client the task of introducing himself to several strangers. In a subsequent session, Ellis and the client would then discuss the impact of carrying out this homework. Another client might be told to keep a record of instances of anxiety feelings and another might be told to initiate an argument with a friend if Ellis thought that would teach a useful lesson.

Some research and theory issues

Cognitive therapy has received some research support for its effectiveness, although, as we will see, no particular "school" of therapy has been demonstrated to be superior to others. One review of research (Shapiro and Shapiro, 1982) reported considerable support for cognitive approaches and especially argued that they were superior to systematic desensitization. However, a later article (Berman,

Miller, and Massman, 1985) reviewed a larger number of studies and argued that there was no demonstrated difference in effectiveness between the two approaches. These authors said that most of the studies reviewed by Shapiro and Shapiro had been "conducted by investigators with an allegiance to cognitive therapy" (Berman, Miller, and Massman, 1985, p. 451). Cognitive behavioural approaches are quite popular and seem to be increasing in influence (Borgen, 1984; Hollon and Najavits, 1988).

The theoretical issue that needs to be answered about cognitive therapy is related to a discussion that has come up several times in this book. There is real controversy over the notion that cognitions control emotions (see Chapter 9, for example). Critics can point to "false beliefs" such as "arbitrary inferences" or "minimization" and ask *why* the person holds that false belief in the face of evidence to the contrary. Many would say that the belief is distorted by painful emotion, rather than the emotion being caused by the false belief. Most practising therapists, for example, have often had the experience of hearing a client say, "I am absolutely sure that you are correct, and my belief is false, but I still feel worthless (or whatever the feeling might be)." Recently, cognitive therapists have included more and more notions that sound like unconscious influences in their theories. For example, many of these therapists talk about "automatic thoughts," many of which the person is not aware of. This makes it hard to define exactly what a "belief" is.

OTHER FORMATS

Traditionally, most psychotherapy has been conducted between an individual therapist and individual client. There are good reasons, however, for doing therapy in other formats.

Group therapy

In **group therapy** it is most typical that one therapist (sometimes two) meets with six to ten clients for about an hour and a half once a week. Of course there are many variations on this pattern. Group therapy is sometimes thought of as a cheap substitute for individual therapy, but cost is a minor variable in justifying group therapy. Individual and group therapy each has its own advantages under different circumstances. Just as there are many approaches to individual therapy, the methods used in any particular group will depend on the style of the therapist.

Yalom (1985) has described several factors that make group therapy especially useful for some clients. These "curative factors" are not available in the same way in individual therapy. For example, *universality* refers to the experience of being with other people who also are troubled and struggling in similar ways. This can make a client feel less alone and different. *Development of socializing techniques* can result from the interactions within the group. The group provides a safe setting in which to learn and practise social skills with a number of other persons.

SOURCE: *Bizarro* by Dan Piraro. Reprinted by permission of Chronicle Features, San Francisco, CA.

Group therapy can provide unique benefits, especially in dealing with social problems.
SOURCE: Ken Karp.

The group therapy client often benefits from *imitative learning* in a way that is unlikely if the person is only interacting with a therapist. The client has a chance to watch others talking and interacting and to see the therapist (we hope) provide a constructive model of how to communicate with others.

Family and couple therapy

Family and couple therapy is a format for therapy in which both members of a couple or all members of a family are seen at the same time by one or two therapists. This is one of the fastest growing specialties in psychotherapy. The therapist (or sometimes a team of co-therapists) sees several or all members of a family unit at the same time. The critical difference between family therapy and individual therapy — or even group therapy — is that the family is a *system*. Many family therapists argue that if a client is a member of a family system, it is often fruitless to treat the individual without also treating and changing the system. The word "system" stresses that every change in one part inevitably leads to changes in other parts. The family is an interrelated whole.

The relationship is the client

Family therapists stress that they are treating the whole family, so that no one person becomes *the identified patient*. Often part of a family system includes one person serving as the "disturbed one," and other family members come to therapy "in order to help" the identified patient. The therapist treats the whole system as the patient or client. Often the family needs for the identified patient to stay "sick" to fill some essential role. In some cases, for example, the intense focus on the problems of a child help the parents avoid the reality of their own crumbling relationshp. If the child is no longer a problem, the parents may fight bitterly and, at some level, everybody knows this and works to keep the child "disturbed" for the sake of harmony.

Family therapy is a complex process in which all members of the family participate.

Treatment methods

Family therapists have developed many different techniques. In general, family therapy involves considerable intervention by the therapist in the interactions of the family members. When the family is communicating destructively, for example, the therapist might assertively stop the process and model alternative ways of communicating or perhaps suggest that people move about the room to rearrange patterns of interaction or have one person speak as though he or she were another person in the family. The general goals of these methods is to increase family members' understanding of what is happening in their system and to help them learn more constructive ways of communicating. They then must find new ways for the family to function without the identified patient fulfilling his or her "sick role."

Community psychology

Some psychologists believe that traditional methods of intervention to help people with problems are inefficient. They think that more meaningful and effective change can be brought about by making changes in the social environment, by changing the community. The basic principle of community psychology is that human behaviour develops out of the interactions between people and the many characteristics of their environment. **Community psychology** is an approach to intervention in human problems that focuses on changing the social environment, prevention of emotional problems, and crisis intervention. Community psychologists deal with the physical environment as well as the social, political and economic environment (Nietzel & Bernstein, 1987).

Basic principles

Community psychologists have an *ecological perspective* on therapy. They are much less likely to look just at an individual with problems because human problems are the result of interactions among the person, the social structure, the political structure, and economic conditions. Rather than focusing on change for the individual person, the community psychologist works more toward *social-system change*. Much of this change is aimed at *prevention* of human problems. Rather than waiting until people are troubled, the community psychologist tries to anticipate situations that will contribute to the development of problems and change those situations. The community psychologist might, for example, start up parenting training courses for disadvantaged families. One example is the Cambridge Prevention Project in a high-risk neighbourhood of Cambridge, Ontario. The project provided such services as a toy lending library, a parent education group, and fitness classes. An evaluation of the program showed that program participants had significant reductions in emotional distress and greater knowledge of community resources (Pancer, 1989). Community psychologists also do *crisis intervention*. By being available in the community when crises occur, the professional can often have a very significant impact at a time of great change and thus bring about positive change instead of waiting for the crisis to lead to emotional problems. Finally, the community

Community psychologists can sometimes intervene to prevent a confrontation or can help a community heal itself once the crisis has passed.
SOURCE: Canada Wide/Bill Sandford.

psychologist tries to promote a *psychological sense of community.* The goal is to strengthen the resources and ability of a community to handle its own problems and make constructive changes — to empower the community (Rappaport, 1981).

Current status

In the 1970s and 1980s community psychology flourished and seemed to be developing as a very distinct branch of psychology. There have been problems, however, with defining the exact nature of this branch of psychology, and many of the principles and approaches of community psychology have been absorbed into other areas of psychology. "As prevention is absorbed into other subfields of psychology, community psychology is threatened with a loss of distinctiveness" (Nietzel & Bernstein, 1987, p. 229). Park Davidson, an eminent Canadian psychologist who died in a car accident in 1981, said that "community psychology has a long tradition but a very short history in Canada" (Davidson, 1981, p. 319). He meant that the traditions of health care in Canada have long been consistent with a community approach to human problems, but the formal development of community psychology programs has not advanced quickly, lagging about 5 to 10 years behind similar developments in the United States.

SOMATIC APPROACHES

Most intervention methods called "psychotherapy" use techniques that can be called "psychological." These techniques can include some kind of verbal exchange between therapist and patient, role playing, prescribing particular behaviours, and emotional release. Throughout the history of the treatment of behavioural disorders, however, **somatic therapies** have also been used. They use direct manipulations of the body. In the late nineteenth and early twentieth centuries, patients were dunked into hot or cold water, nearly to point of drowning; wrapped in cold, wet sheets; hung by the arms and twirled, often to the point of unconsciousness. In the 1930s, patients were put into convulsions and comas with insulin injections that sometimes killed them.

There is a great attraction to finding somatic treatments for psychopathology, and practitioners have had some success in treating some disorders chemically and surgically.

Chemotherapy

Not until the 1950s was there real progress in finding drug treatments for behavioural disorders. Since that time, two classifications of disorder have shown quite positive response to particular chemical treatments.

Antipsychotic drugs

There is a large class of drugs called the **neuroleptics** (including phenothiazines and haloperidol) which have a specific effect in relieving many of the syptoms of schizophrenia (see Chapter 14). These symptoms include severe withdrawal, thought disorder, and hallucinations. It is believed that these drugs work by making receptors in the brain less sensitive to the neurotransmitter **dopamine** which is believed to be a factor in schizophrenia.

There has been some controversy about whether these drugs work by simply sedating the patient, but evidence strongly suggests that they work quite specifically by relieving symptoms of schizophrenia. Other drugs, such as barbiturates, do only sedate the patient and don't help specifically with schizophrenic symptoms. Phenothiazine drugs often do have side effects, such as inducing symptoms that mimic Parkinsons's disease, and other drugs must be used to control these side effects. For individual patients, however, the tradeoff in relief from schizophrenic symptoms is often worth it.

Antidepressants

Drugs that increase the amount of the neurotransmitters **norepinephrine** and **serotonin** seem to relieve many of the symptoms of severe depression for some individuals. The mechanisms by which they work are not well understood, and often what works for one person will not work for another. Interestingly, these "antidepressants" seem to have little effect on persons who are not depressed to begin with (Cole and Davis, 1975), and this seems to suggest some kind of biochemical involvement in at least some forms of depression.

The two major types of antidepressants are monoamine oxidase (MAO) inhibitors and tricyclics. The tricyclics tend to be used more, partly because they have fewer side effects.

Lithium carbonate

As we said in Chapter 14, bipolar depression (manic-depressive disorder) seems to have some biochemical component and probably some hereditary component. **Lithium carbonate** has been found to have a beneficial effect on many victims of manic-depressive disorder, although it is potentially quite toxic and must be monitored with regular blood tests. The evidence suggests that lithium is considerably more helpful with the manic phase of bipolar depression than with the depressive phase. This may be because it reduces the availability of the neurotransmitter norepinephrine. This would be opposite to the effect of the antidepressant drugs. Of course this does not help explain why it would help, as it sometimes seems to, with the depressive phase of bi-polar depression (Fieve, 1975; Berger, 1978).

Minor tranquilizers

The antipsychotic drugs discussed earlier are often referred to as "major tranquilizers," and a large group of other chemicals, not all from the same "drug family," are called "minor tranquilizers." These include diazapam (Valium), chlordiaxepoxide (Librium), and meprobamate (Miltown, Equanil). These drugs are used mostly for the control of anxiety in individuals who do not have psychotic symptoms. They are the most prescribed drugs in North America.

One significant difference between this group of drugs and the previous groups is that the minor tranquilizers exert an effect on nearly everyone, rather than having a specific effect on a specific disorder and little effect on persons who don't have that disorder. This suggests that the anxiety problems for which minor tranquilizers are used are less likely the result of specific biochemical deficiencies. These drugs can be physically addictive, if a person takes large doses for long periods, and they are often not treated with sufficient caution.

Psychosurgery

Psychosurgery refers to any surgical procedure that is designed to correct behavioural and emotional problems. Surgical resection of the brain is one approach psychiatrists have tried in treating various disorders, but, with one major exception, this is not done much in modern treatment. The best known psychosurgery procedure is **prefrontal lobotomy**. Surgeons cut the connections, in whole or in part, between the prefrontal lobes of the brain and the thalamus. According to the neurological theories of the time when this procedure was first used, the prefrontal lobes controlled emotion, and the thalamus was the location of thinking. Thus, the operation was to relieve the thinking process of the disruptions of emotion. The operation did result in considerable blunting of emotion and sometimes led to the control of disruptive behaviour—but at enormous cost. Other brain functions, such as the ability to maintain attention for periods of time and to plan for future consequences, were also impaired. The evidence that we have does not show the proposed benefits to offset the costs (Robbin, 1958; Maher, 1966). Few, if any, prefrontal lobotomies are being performed in North America now.

One surgical technique that is currently used is **localized resection of the cortex** for the control of *intractable* (not treatable by other means) epilepsy with focal onset. Some epilepsy can be localized as having seizures start in highly specific places in the brain. Once such seizures start, their effects spread to other parts of the brain, causing a generalized disruption of many functions. If more conservative treatments, such as anti-convulsant drugs, don't work, the area of origin of the seizures can be surgically separated from the rest of the brain. This surgical procedure sometimes results in loss of some functions, but if carefully planned, this loss can be more than compensated for by the increased effectiveness of the parts of the brain that were being disrupted by the epilepsy.

Electroconvulsive therapy

Insulin injections were once used to induce convulsions as a treatment for severe mental disorders. The theory was that patients with epilepsy seldom had schizophrenic problems, so the seizures had some kind of anti-psychotic effect. This theory was later found to be incorrect, and insulin shock therapy is not used now.

Another induced-convulsion treatment that is used fairly frequently in some places now, however, is **electroconvulsive shock**

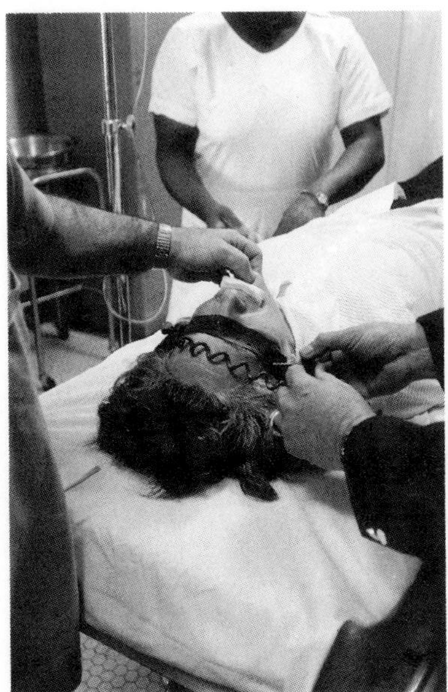

Electroconvulsive therapy may be used to relieve severe depression.
SOURCE: Paul Fusco.

treatment, or **ECT**. A moderate current is passed through the brain for about half a second. Two electrodes are placed on the head — sometimes on either side of the head so the current passes from one hemisphere to the other (bilateral ECT) and sometimes on the front and back of one side of the head so one hemisphere is primarily affected (unilateral ECT). This induces an immediate loss of consciousness and a convulsive state similar to an epileptic seizure. Patients are usually given anaesthetics and muscle relaxants prior to treatment to prevent violent movements that could result in broken bones.

ECT was originally used for schizophrenia, but well controlled evidence suggests that it is only effective with severe depression, particularly among patients who have not responded to drug treatments. There is evidence that ECT can relieve depression among many patients who do not respond to drug treatment, and it seems to work faster than drugs (Cole and Davis, 1975; Small et al., 1986).

No one knows how ECT works to relieve depression, and it has observable side effects such as memory impairment. It is likely that any current strong enough to induce a seizure is also strong enough to damage brain tissue, so physicians use ECT sparingly. It sometimes seems jusitified when there is a clear and present danger of suicide and when nothing else has worked (Kalinowsky, 1975). Unilateral ECT seems to have fewer deleterious effects on patients and is thus being used more at present. The use of ECT is very controversial, and there are strongly held views on both sides (Weiner, 1984; Pinel, 1984). Some former ECT patients have even formed groups to fight its use.

BEING ECLECTIC

The field of psychotherapy includes a staggering number of theoretical "schools," each with followers who sometimes resemble religious fanatics. Some of these believers are absolutely sure all other approaches are wrong. Sometimes this confidence of the therapist may be helpful, since it can contribute to the client's faith and hope in the process. It also, however, sometimes leads therapists to dismiss the ideas of others with scorn and misunderstanding.

The majority of therapists now refer to themselves as "eclectic," and Strupp and Bergin, as early as 1969, said "The barriers separating the major schools of psychotherapy are gradually being eroded, and the predominant direction of research is toward a nonschool approach" (Strupp and Bergin, 1969, p. 24). Goldfried said, "Psychoanalytic, behavioural, and humanistically oriented clinicians are starting to raise serious questions about the limits of their respective approaches and are becoming more open to contributions from other paradigms" (Goldfried, 1980, p. 991). Parloff, London, and Wolfe (1986) argued that there is a strong trend toward the "integration" of different approaches, and Lazarus (1987) is trying to develop a systematic approach to being eclectic. In a science as young as psychotherapy, it is unlikely that any one approach is entirely correct. It seems important that therapists remain open to learning from all approaches. It is important to be eclectic.

SPECIAL TOPIC

Evaluating Psychotherapy

Herink's book, *The Psychotherapy Handbook* (1980), describes 255 different approaches to therapy. While it includes the ones we've discussed, it also lists "Horticultural Therapy," "Placebo Therapy," and "Soap Opera Therapy." Some therapists have a distressing tendency to propose a "new" approach to therapy and name it after themselves (such as the infamous "tickling therapy" of a few years ago, whose originator called it "Z Therapy," since his last name started with Z). We need reliable evidence to help us distinguish the effective from the noneffective therapies. Virtually any therapy approach can be "supported" through anecdotes about clients who were helped. There is a Yiddish proverb that says, "For example is no proof." It is not sufficient to show cases where therapy works. One must provide evidence. Research on psychotherapy is very difficult to do well, but over the last four or five decades enough evidence has accumulated to enable us to draw several conclusions.

Challenges to therapy

Until the 1950s there was a great deal of therapy being done but almost no research on its effectiveness. The impetus to change this came mostly from a severe attack on psychotherapy by Hans Eysenck (1952), who concluded from his survey of the literature that there was no evidence that psychotherapy (he was looking primarily at psychoanalytic psychotherapy at the time) had any more beneficial effect than the simple passage of time. His reading of the evidence was that about 60% of therapy patients improved, but at least that large a percentage of people with neurotic problems also improved over the course of two years, *without* formal treatment. Since then, Eysenck's analyses of the data have been severely criticized, and his conclusions have been contradicted by new evidence. However, at that time there was considerable truth to his statement that sufficient evidence had not been collected to support the effectiveness of psychotherapy.

Conclusions from research

Even though psychotherapy research is extremely difficult to do well, the work that has been done can make us fairly confident of a number of useful conclusions. We will state these conclusions and refer to more detailed references that support them.

1. Overall, having psychotherapy is better than having no treatment, but no one "school" of therapy has deen demonstrated to be superior to any other "school." Notice that this refers simply to grouping therapists according to the school of therapy with which they identify themselves (Meltzoff and Kornreich, 1971; Smith and Glass, 1977; Frank, 1979; Landman and Dawes, 1982; Miller and Berman, 1983; Casey and Berman, 1985; Kazdin, 1986; Thompson, Gallagher, and Breckenridge, 1987).
2. Desensitization and operant reinforcement procedures are effective with clearly definable problems, at least for short-term change (Bergin and Suinn, 1975; Smith and Glass, 1977; Gomes-Schwartz, Hadley, and Strupp, 1978; Casey and Berman, 1985). In a review of research on therapy with children and adolescents, Weisz, Weiss, Alicke, and Klotz (1987) concluded that therapy was generally better than no treatment and that behavioural approaches were superior to other approaches across the range of problems. Remember though that most reviews find different approaches about equally effective.
3. There is a strong relationship between successful therapy and the *client's perception* of the therapist as empathic, accepting, and genuine (Gurman, 1977). Earlier we mentioned that there is research evidence supporting the effectiveness of the "core conditions"

described by Carl Rogers. This conclusion seems to apply to therapists from different schools of thought. For example, some studies have shown that behaviour therapy tends to be more successful when the client perceives high levels of the core conditions in the therapist. From a psychoanalytic perspective, Waterhouse and Strupp (1984) reviewed evidence on the therapist-client relationshp and concluded that if the client felt accepted, understood, and liked by the therapist by the third session, therapy tended to be successful. This is a remarkable conclusion that supports the belief in the importance of the client's perception of the "core conditions" of therapy. Another study by Luborsky, McLellan, Woody, O'Brien, and Auerbach (1985) had similar results. They found that the quality of the relationship early in treatment correlated strongly with later success of therapy.

4. There is a moderate relationship between successful therapy and the therapist's level of "core conditions," *as rated by outside observers*. Most of these studies have used rating scales used by raters who listen to tape recordings of therapy, and there are serious shortcomings of this as a way to study therapy (Gurman, 1977). Lambert, DeJulio and Stein (1978) would argue that this relationship is "only modest," but it is widely agreed that even this rather crude method of measuring therapist behaviour shows that the "core conditions" are important.

5. Some therapists do serious damage to clients. This disturbing finding has been called the *deterioration effect* by Bergin (1963, 1980) who first noted it. He says "the empircal case for therapist-induced deterioration is compelling" (Bergin, 1980, p. 93). Luborsky, McLellan, Woody, O'Brien, and Auerbach (1985) found in their study that "profound differences were discovered in the therapists' success with the patients in their caseloads" (Luborsky et al., 1985, p. 602). It is clear that not all therapists are created equal.

   It is not yet completely clear how to identify the few therapists who are destructive, but the evidence we do have is consistent with Yalom and Lieberman's description of the "aggressive stimulator" in encounter groups mentioned earlier: "intrusive, confrontive, challenging, caring, . . . self-revealing, . . . charismatic, authoritarian" (Lambert, Bergin, and Collins, 1977, p. 471). We repeat this description to make the point strongly that if you are ever in a therapy or counselling relationship in which you feel damage is being done, be careful to take good care of yourself. The evidence is that the client is usually right, although you should discuss your concerns with the therapist.

Chapter Summary

1. Psychotherapy is a structured human relationship which operates within certain limits to relieve human suffering. The relationship consists of (1) a socially-sanctioned healer, (2) a client who seeks help from the healer, and (3) a series of structured contacts for the purpose of healing.

2. Several professions practise psychotherapy, including psychiatrists, psychoanalysts, clinical psychologists, and social workers.

3. Psychoanalytic psychotherapy is based on the theories and methods of Sigmund Freud. The general goal of psychoanalysis is to release psychic energy for use by the ego by "making the unconscious conscious." One central technique of psychoanalysis is free association. The analyst uses interpretation to help uncover the hidden or latent meaning in what the patient says during free association. Dreams are frequently used as a source of material

for interpretation. Transference is a central part of psychoanalysis. In the safety of the therapeutic relationship, it is possible to work through old relationships in a more healthy way. The process of psychoanalysis is both an intellectual one and an emotional working through.

4. Many modern therapists have been influenced by Freud but do not do formal psychoanalysis. They are called psychoanalytically oriented psychotherapists. Some of them subscribe to ego analysis, which places more emphasis on the patient's ego strengths.
5. The humanistic approach to psychotherapy is characterized by an emphasis on helping the client experience current feelings and thoughts more fully and accurately. Carl Rogers' person-centred therapy is designed to facilitate client improvement within a special kind of emotional environment created by the therapist. This environment is created through three core conditions or therapist attitudes: (1) accurate empathy, (2) therapist genuineness, and (3) dependable acceptance or unconditional positive regard.
6. Another humanistic approach, Gestalt therapy, is described by Fritz Perls as an encounter between therapist and client. To focus on the present moment, the therapist uses fairly confrontative methods, such as frustration and manipulation of the client. Much of the encounter group movement grew out of gestalt therapy.
7. Behaviour modification refers to a large number of techniques used by therapists who directly apply learning principles to human problems. Behavioural techniques used to change unpleasant emotions are called desensitization techniques. Behaviour therapists use extinction and counterconditioning. Principles of reinforcement are often used to establish desired behaviours through such methods as contingency contracting. A third set of techniques are called aversive counterconditioning.
8. Cognitive approaches to therapy stress the importance of thoughts in causing human problems. Irrational thought patterns, sometimes called cognitive traps, are changed through instruction, exercises, discussion, and other techniques. It is believed that changes in beliefs will lead to changes in behaviour and emotions. The most extreme cognitive therapy is rational emotive therapy, proposed by Ellis. He believes that reason controls emotion, and uses more disputation and strong persuasion to change beliefs than do other cognitive therapists.
9. Some therapy is conducted with more than one client at a time. In group therapy, usually six to ten clients meet with one or two therapists. Group therapy has some advantages and disadvantages compared with individual therapy. Each client receives less attention and trust is harder to build. However, group therapy also provides an opportunity to be helpful to others, a sense of not being alone with one's problems, and other benefits. Group therapy is also less expensive than individual therapy. Couple

therapy and family therapy are also popular formats for therapy, especially with problems involving the interactions among the members of a family unit. The family is seen as a system in which change in one part inevitably leads to change in another part. Community psychologists work with larger social goups. They tend to have an ecological perspective and work more towards social-system change.

10. Somatic approaches to treatment use physical methods such as drugs, surgery, and electroconvulsive therapy (ECT). Tranquilizers, antipsychotic and antidepressant drugs, and lithium carbonate are widely used, especially with psychotic disorders. Currently, surgery can help control otherwise intractable epilepsy, and ECT is used for severe depression.

Key Terms

Abreaction Strong emotional release that usually comes from the catharsis of talking about feeling-laden content.

Accurate empathy One of Rogers' core conditions for therapy; the therapist experiences and expresses a deep understanding of what the client is experiencing and trying to communicate.

Anxiety hierarchy A list of anxiety-arousing situations that are arranged in order of increasingly strong impact on the client.

Arbitrary inference A cognitive trap in which a depressed person draws conclusions about him or herself on the basis of irrelevant or limited information.

Aversive counterconditioning The application of punishment methods to rid the client of undesired behaviours.

Backup reinforcers In a token economy, the larger rewards available from using tokens earned.

Behaviour modification The explicit application of the principles of learning to the relief of human problems.

Clinical psychologist A practitioner who has a Ph.D. or Psy.D. degree and who has served a psychological internship.

Cognitive traps In cognitive approaches to therapy, illogical ways of thinking that lead clients to feel self-deprecating.

Community psychology An approach to intervention in human problems that focuses on changing the social environment, prevention of emotional problems, and crisis intervention.

Contingency contracting A behaviour therapy technique in which the therapist and client agree on a system in which particular client behaviours are rewarded or punished in particular ways.

Countertransference In psychoanalysis, the irrational feelings (positive and negative) that the analyst might develop toward the patient because of the analyst's own unconscious conflicts and distortions.

Couple and family therapy A format for therapy in which both members of a couple or all members of a family are seen at the same time by one or two therapists.

Dependable acceptance One of Rogers' core conditions for therapy; the therapist's valuing of the client as a worthwhile person, regardless of what the client thinks, feels, or says.

Dopamine A neurotransmitter that is believed to be a factor in schizophrenia.

Ego analyst Therapist who subscribes to the fundamentals of psychoanalysis but who strongly emphasizes the patient's ego strengths and control of his or her life.

Electroconvulsive shock treatment (ECT) Somatic treatment in which short, intense electrical current is passed through the brain. It is usually used for severe depression.

Encounter groups Group experiences designed as therapy or for growth-enhancement. They are often but not always based on confrontative methods.

Family therapist A therapist who specializes in dealing with clients as members of family units.

Flooding (also called *implosive therapy*) Extinction technique in which the client is exposed to the feared cues more suddenly and strongly than in graduated extinction.

Free association Psychoanalytic technique in which the patient is instructed to say everything that comes to mind without censoring or editing.

Gestalt therapy Perls' approach to therapy in which faulty perceptions are blocked so that healthier ones can form.

Graduated extinction Extinction technique in which the client is exposed to the feared cues in small steps along an anxiety hierarchy.

Group therapy A format for therapy in which several clients (usually 6-10) are seen together by one or two therapists.

Humanistic therapy A term for several approaches to therapy that all are based on a belief in the client's own tendencies toward growth and in the importance of the client's perspective on his or her problems.

Implosive therapy See *flooding*.

In vivo desensitization Extinction and counterconditioning exercises carried out in the natural environment.

Interpretation Therapeutic technique in which the therapist explains to the patient a deeper understanding of a particular personal issue than the patient has discovered.

Latent content In psychoanalysis, the hidden, often symbolic content of free associations and dreams that lies behind the words of the manifest content.

Lay analyst A non-medical practitioner of psychoanalysis who has undergone psychoanalytic training (which takes many years).

Lithium carbonate Medication often used with bipolar affective disorder (manic-depression).

Localized resection of the cortex A general term for the surgical procedure of cutting highly specific lesions in the brain. In psychosurgery, it is usually used to control intractable epilepsy with focal onset.

Magnification A cognitive trap in which a small problem is exaggerated and "catastrophized."

Manifest content In psychoanalysis, the verbalized content of free association or of dreams.

Minimization A cognitive trap in which the person automatically discounts positive events.

Neuroleptics A large class of drugs (including phenothiazines and haloperiodol) which have a specific effect in relieving many of the symptoms of schizophrenia.

Norepinephrine A neurotransmitter that seems to be a factor in depression.

Person-centred therapy Carl Rogers' humanistic approach to therapy which stresses the core conditions of accurate empathy, dependable acceptance, and therapist genuineness.

Prefrontal lobotomy Psychosurgical procedure in which the frontal lobes of the brain are separated from the brain. This procedure was used in the past to control extreme emotionality.

Psychiatrist A medical doctor who has completed a three or four year psychiatric residency for diagnosis and treatment of emotional disorders.

Psychoanalysis Sigmund Freud's approach to both personality theory and psychotherapy. It is based on an instinctual model of human behaviour. Its main methods are free association, interpretation, and transference.

Psychoanalyst A psychiatrist who has received special training in the psychoanalytic methods of Sigmund Freud.

Psychosurgery Surgical procedures designed to correct behavioural and emotional problems.

Psychotherapy A specialized, structured human relationship betwteen a socially sanctioned healer and a client who comes for help with emotional problems.

Rational-emotive therapy Ellis's cognitive approach to therapy, in which reason is seen to control emotion. The client's belief structure is changed through persuasion and disputation.

Reinforcement contingencies The relationship between specific behaviours and the consequences that follow.

Resistance In psychoanalysis, the patient's unconscious avoidance of threatening material, an inability to think of anything (such as in free association) because of emotional blocks.

Serotonin A neurotransmitter that seems to be a factor in depression.

Social worker A practitioner trained in a school of social work, usually has an MSW degree, although he or she may also have a Ph.D. Some but not all social workers are trained in psychotherapy.

Somatic therapies Therapy approaches that focus on physical interventions such as drugs, surgery, and electroconvulsive shock.

Systematic desensitization Behavioural method for relieving undesired emotions; uses counterconditioning by pairing deep relaxation with imagined scenes arranged along an anxiety hierarchy.

Target behaviour The specific behaviour that is to be changed by a behavioural treatment program.

Therapist genuineness One of Rogers' core conditions for therapy; the therapist does not play a role but acts in ways that are consistent with how he or she feels.

Token economy A behaviour therapy technique in which institutional settings use a structured reinforcement token system based on earning tokens for specific target behaviours.

Transference In psychoanalysis, the patient's experience towards the therapist of emotional responses (positive and negative) which are unconsciously transferred from other relationships in his or her life.

Unconditional positive regard Rogers' more formal term for dependable acceptance in therapy.

Working through In psychoanalysis, the process, both cognitive and emotional, of resolving old conflicts by re-experiencing them in the safety of therapy and the transference relationship.

Suggested Readings

Corsini, R. J., & Wedding, D. (eds.) (1989). *Current psychotherapies*, 4th ed. Itaska, IL: F. A. Peacock Publishers. This recent edition is an excellent source of overviews of different therapy approaches written by experts in each of the schools of therapy.

Garfield, S. L., & Bergin, A. E. (eds.) (1986). *Handbook of psychotherapy and behavior change*, 3rd. ed. New York: Wiley. This is one of the classic standards in the therapy area. It is a collection of chapters by different authors on both research and practice in psychotherapy.

Martin, G. L., & Pear, J. J. (1988). *Behavior modification: What it is and how to do it*, 3rd ed. Englewood Cliffs, NJ: Prentice-Hall. The title of this book says it all. A practical, informative textbook, this recent overview will provide a good next step if behaviour modification interests you.

Menninger, K., & Holzman, P. S. (1973). *Theory of psychoanalytic technique*, 2nd ed. New York: Basic Books. Much psychoanalytic writing is abstract and theorteical, but this one is more clearly oriented toward methods of practice.

Rogers, C. R. (1970). *On becoming a person: A therapist's view of psychotherapy*. Boston: Houghton Mifflin. This may be Rogers' most widely read book. Its style is personal and often touches the reader as personally relevant.

Yalom, I. D. (1975). *The theory and practice of group psychotherapy*, 2nd ed. New York: Basic Books. This is probably the best known overview of group psychotherapy. It is an excellent guide to different approaches and to practical advice about doing group therapy.

Zilbergeld, B. (1983). *The shrinking of America: Myths of psychological change*. Boston: Little, Brown. Written by an active therapist, this provocative book argues that many therapists have oversold the need for and impact of therapy. The author says that therapy can have beneficial effects, particularly in helping people with self-acceptance, but he also cautions against giving up one's own uniqueness and power to "gurus."

PART VI

SOCIAL BEHAVIOUR

CHAPTER 16

SOURCE: Jamasie, Detail from *Summer Games* (1973).

Social Influence

THE POWER OF SOCIAL CONTEXT

In previous chapters we have explored primarily the behaviour of individuals. Now we want to investigate the powerful effects of the social environment. Consider for a moment how much of what we do is determined by our perception of what others think, what is expected, and what we think will happen if we do otherwise. Sets of social rules and rituals are involved in many of our everyday activities. We readily accept these rules, even though we seldom think of them.

Our behaviour on an elevator is a good example of the influence of the social context in deciding what is appropriate. On an elevator, we think nothing of being squeezed tightly into a very small enclosure, in bodily contact with people of both sexes who are strangers. The vast majority of people will avoid eye contact, face straight ahead, and be very cautious in their movements. There is rarely much talking in the elevator, and even people who get on the elevator in the midst of a conversation will reduce their volume or stop talking altogether. Such behaviour on elevators is a function of the particular social environment and context, as we would quickly discover if we tried to violate any of the unspoken or unwritten rules. Try striking up a conversation with a stranger in a crowded elevator. Try looking someone straight in the eye and holding their gaze. While waiting for the elevator to arrive, try to stand as close as you would in the elevator. But don't blame us if you're arrested.

We can define **social context** as all facets of any situation in which people interact with other people. This includes the particular individuals involved; their behaviours; the pattern of interactions that occur; the generally accepted rules and etiquette of the situation; each person's own perception of the context; and the cognitions that each person has about what is expected, what is desired, and what may happen later. The social context is the social environment which defines our roles and strongly influences our behaviour. We are often surprised by the power of a social context.

Social psychology is the discipline that studies individual behaviour within the social context. Unlike other areas of psychology, social psychology focuses on **situational factors** — that is, on those influences in the current environment that affect behaviour, as distinct from individual internal tendencies to act in certain ways. Social psychology straddles the intrapsychic, person-focused theme of psychology on the one hand and broader disciplines such as anthropology and sociology on the other hand. In social psychology, the emphasis is still on an individual's behaviour, but it is now viewed from a situational perspective. By contrast, sociology and anthropology investigate global social and cultural factors, such as the family, the judicial system, and the health-care system.

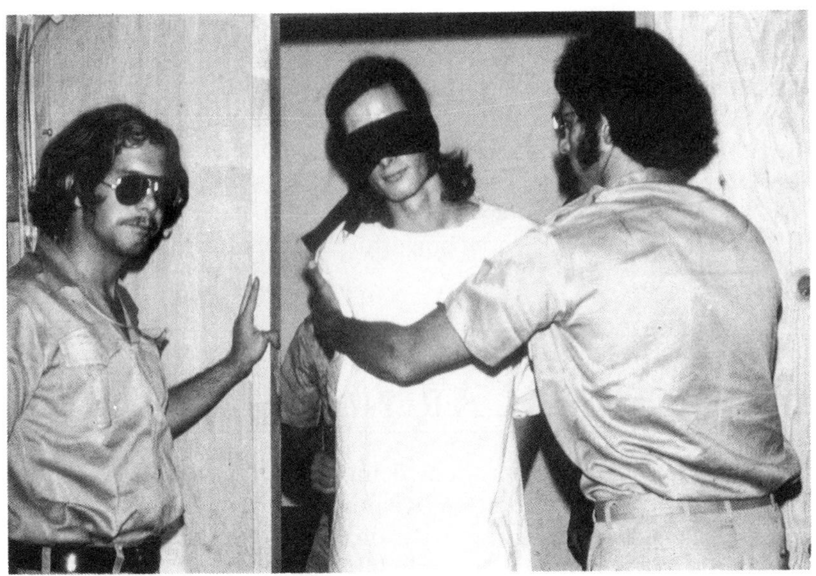

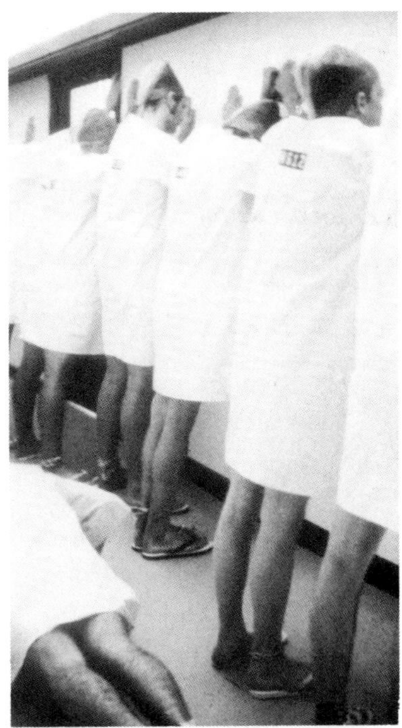

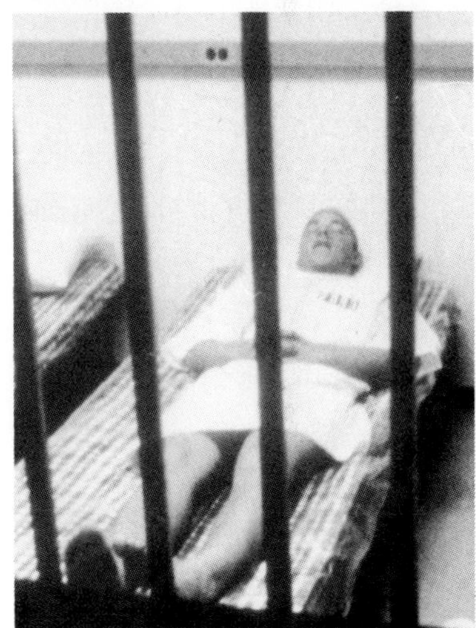

These photos were taken during the Stanford prison experiment conducted by Philip Zimbardo. The experiment was cut short because the participants became too involved in their roles as guards and prisoners.
SOURCE: Philip G. Zimbardo.

The Stanford prison experiment

One Sunday morning, a young male college student is arrested, charged with a crime, searched, handcuffed, fingerprinted, stripped, put into a uniform, and jailed. In prison he encounters guards who are authoritarian, harsh, and punitive. Our prisoner finds that he is frequently punished by a loss of privileges and made to perform dehumanizing and undignified menial tasks, such as scrubbing the floors and cleaning the toilets with his bare hands. Very quickly this college student begins to act and feel like a prisoner, while the guards seem determined to come up with new tasks to make the prisoner feel useless, helpless, and undeserving. This was an ingenious social psychological experiment designed by Philip Zimbardo. Known as the Stanford prison experiment, it was carried out at Stanford University in the mid-1970s (Zimbardo, 1975).

The guards were not real guards; nor was the prisoner a real prisoner. All the people who took part in this experiment responded to ads placed in newspapers asking for volunteers to participate in a psychological study of prison life. All the participants were normal, healthy, middle-class college students. They were selected because they were law-abiding, mentally normal, and physically healthy. The volunteers were randomly divided into guards and prisoners by the toss of a coin. They were not given any instructions about how to behave as guards or prisoners.

However, soon after the experiment began, it was obvious that powerful social psychological forces were operating. The people chosen to be guards soon assumed the attitudes and behaviours of guards. The "prisoners" quickly became demoralized victims. The remarkable fact to remember is that there were no differences between guards and prisoners prior to the study.

This experiment was scheduled to last for two weeks but was abandoned after six days because of its dramatic impact on the participants. "Prisoners" were suffering severe distress, and some were so upset they were unable to continue in the experiment. "Guards" who initially were passive became sadistic and authoritarian. This striking experiment demonstrates the power of the social context to cause behavioural changes. The participants in this experiment quickly began to play out new roles that took on a life of their own. Can you project yourself into this study? Do you believe that the role would have so strongly influenced your behaviour? It is sometimes hard to appreciate how powerful the social context can be.

THE INDIVIDUAL IN THE SOCIAL ARENA

The Stanford prison experiment demonstrates the powerful influences of *situational factors* on behaviour. We should also consider what the person brings to the situation to understand the interaction between social situations and individual dispositions. There is usually a difference between what actually exists in a social situation and what the person perceives. Your social reality depends on your own **phenomenological perspective**, that is, your subjective perception of reality. We all interpret situations differently and may see social reality from slightly different perspectives. As we explained in Chapter 4 on Perception, we often see what we want to see or expect to see. This has important consequences for social psychology.

Self-fulfilling prophecies —getting what you expect

The act of seeing the social arena somewhat differently than others will influence our own behaviour. Moreover, we often influence the behaviour of others to conform to what we expect them to do. Sometimes, this is not even to our advantage. The tendency to subtly reinforce in others behaviour we expect is known as a **self-fulfilling prophecy**. You might expect a policeman to be rough, aggressive, unfriendly, and unsympathetic, and hence treat him in a manner that may lead him to act in just these ways. Your first impression may have been made even before you meet the individual, based on the stereotype formed from your social schema for police officers.

I once took over an introductory class half way through the year. I did not realize that nearly the whole class had been in an experiment in which they watched a film of me giving a lecture that was intended to be as bad as possible. (The experiment was concerned with the effects of different teaching styles.) At first, the course was a terrible experience for all concerned. The students were thinking "Oh, no. It's *him*." They expected, and therefore saw, a cold, humourless lecturer to whom they didn't respond well. As the lecturer, I was puzzled and frustrated to have run into the most unresponsive class ever. It was tempting to give up and stop trying as hard as possible to teach well. We were in a vicious circle of self-fulfilling prophecies. As soon as the cause was discovered, about a month after I took over, we discussed what had happened. We were then able to develop a good teacher-student rapport.

In the example just described, more than just the feelings of the teacher and students was at stake. In a study by Jamieson, Lydon, Stewart, and Zanna (1987), the researchers created high expectations in selected students about a new high-school teacher's ability and motivation. The students who expected the teacher to be good engaged in more appropriate verbal behaviour, and they actually scored significantly higher on the teacher's tests than did students who had not been given the initial expectations. Through subtle changes in interactions, we tend to get from others what we *expect* to get.

A self-fulfilling prophecy was also demonstrated in an experiment in which male subjects were led to believe they were going to be involved in telephone conversations with either an attractive woman or a plain-looking woman (Snyder, Tanke, & Berscheid, 1977). The expectation of attractiveness was manipulated by having the subjects look at pictures of the woman with whom they were supposedly going to speak. The men's expectations actually shaped the conversations. Those who thought they were talking with an attractive woman were more animated, warm, and friendly than men who thought they were talking with a plain-looking woman. We can regard this as an example of how the perception of social reality held by the male subjects was manipulated, and how this created behaviour in them that in turn influenced the telephone behaviour of the women with whom they were speaking.

Social reality is in the eye of the beholder. Rubin, Provenzano, and Luria (1974) found that when parents described characteristics of newborn infants, boys were described as being stronger, bigger, more robust, and more coordinated than girls, even though there were no real sex differences in health, weight, or length. Parents had expectations for their children that were based on gender stereotypes. These expectations caused them to see what they expected, regardless of what was actually present. There are many circumstances in which we subtly misperceive others and then influence them to fit our perceptions.

Social schemas

Earlier in this book we have emphasized the importance of schemas in perception, memory, and problem-solving. You will recall that a **schema** is an abstract representation of a typical object, procedure, or event that we build from our knowledge and experiences of the world around us. A schema is a complex, long-lasting expectation. One class of schema, known as a **social schema**, concerns other individuals or groups of individuals. Our social schemas help determine the impressions we form of others and the theories we develop to explain why people behave in the way they do.

A social schema functions as a kind of cognitive blueprint or organized map that we use to perceive others relatively efficiently. If we had to find out everything about every new person we met, we

We each have our own social schema of what constitutes good looks in a male.

SOURCE: "The Secret of My Success." Copyright © 1987 by Universal City Studios, Inc. Photofest.

would not have time to establish many relationships. So we have developed, for example, a "good-looking male" schema. We could write out a general description of what good-looking males are like, even though we know that every person is different. On the one hand, this social schema probably serves us well because it saves us time figuring out each new good-looking male. On the other hand, the schema will inevitably cause us to misjudge any individual good-looking male in some way.

Social schemas are powerful influences on our thinking. We have a strong tendency to perceive information about a particular person in an integrated, unified way and to reject information that is not consistent with our schemas (Brown, 1986).

ATTITUDE DEVELOPMENT AND CHANGE

Hundreds of millions of dollars are spent annually by individuals, companies, and institutions to change our behaviour in particular ways. Advertisers want us to buy more of their product, politicians want us to vote for them, and Revenue Canada encourages us to submit our income tax accurately and on time. We are told of the dangers of drugs, AIDS, and not wearing seat belts, in order to induce us to change. Attitudes are at the core of this tremendous outlay of money and are a central focus of research for many social psychologists.

What is an attitude?

An **attitude** can be usefully defined as a combination of beliefs, values, and emotions that leads to a predisposition to act in a particular way. Attitudes, particularly ones that are very broad, function as social schemas that determine what we see, what we remember, how we collect information, and how we assess information. Attitudes include

1) beliefs about the order of things—what is right, what is true, and what is just
2) feelings about whether something is positively or negatively valued
3) the resultant predisposition to act in certain ways and to justify those actions.

The effects of attitude on behaviour

What is your attitude toward abortion, capital punishment, bilingualism, the nuclear arms race, the Soviet Union, equal opportunity, energy conservation, premarital sex, and the legalization of marijuana? A person who asked about your attitudes would probably be most interested in predicting what you will do as a result of your attitudes. People often makes statements such as "He acts that way because of his attitude." It seems intuitively obvious that there would be a strong relationship between attitudes and behaviour. However, research has not borne this out conclusively (Wicker, 1971). Many factors affect the attitude-behaviour relationship (Jamieson & Zanna, 1989). For example, when there are strong *situational demands*, those demands predict behaviour better than attitudes. In fact, we will see that we often look at our own behaviour in order to form our attitudes.

Early research by LaPiere (1934) provides an insight into the lack of correspondence between attitudes and behaviour. LaPiere travelled throughout the United States with an Oriental couple. He was quite surprised that this couple had no difficulty receiving service in over 200 hotels and restaurants, considering the prejudice that existed at that time. Following their trip, LaPiere sent a letter to each of the establishments assessing their attitudes regarding service to non-whites. Out of 128 replies, 92% stated they would not serve Orientals, despite the fact that they had previously done so. This illustrates the low correlation between attitudes and behaviour. It suggests that situational factors can overcome prejudicial attitudes. It may be relatively easy to say one would not serve Orientals in the abstract, but when actually confronted with the Oriental couple, it is not as easy to deny them service.

We should point out, however, that some circumstances actually strengthen the relationship between attitudes and behaviour. If an attitude is linked to important personal consequences or if it is based on personal experiences, we tend to act consistently with the attitude. Moreover, attitudes that we have thought through or that we remember easily are quite likely to influence behaviour. For example, two people might both say they have very positive attitudes toward a particular political party. However, if one person's attitude is based on family tradition and the other's is based on personal experience with individual candidates, then the second person is more likely to vote in accordance with those attitudes.

A need for structure empowers attitudes

David Jamieson and Mark Zanna (1989) show how a need for structure can also lead a person to act more in accordance with previously held attitudes. A **need for structure** is a strong need for clarity and an intolerance of ambiguity that can inhibit the process of seeking new knowledge. A person may tend to become rigid and may not want to be confused with new facts. Here, the person is more likely to look inward toward attitudes for guidance in how to act.

In one experiment, Jamieson and Zanna divided subjects into (i) "high self-monitors," who tended to adapt their behaviour to situational cues and (ii) "low self-monitors," who tended not to monitor the environment but to use personal principles to guide their behaviour. Each subject was given a description of a complex court case concerning a female biologist who had sought a job at the University of Toronto but had lost out to a slightly less qualified male applicant. The subject was instructed to be an "involved but impartial decision maker." The experimenters had previously collected information

Leon Festinger.
SOURCE: Karen Zebulon.

about each subject's attitudes toward affirmative action in hiring and were interested in how much those attitudes would bias decisions in the court case.

When the subjects were given lots of time to make their decision, both high and low self-monitors rendered judgements independent of their attitudes. They went with the evidence. The interesting finding is that when a need for structure was induced by giving subjects only three minutes to make their judgements, the low self-monitors were strongly influenced by their attitudes, but other subjects were not. Similar results were found for other topics, such as making a decision in a capital murder case.

The effects of behaviour on attitude

Cognitive dissonance

Attitudes may or may not affect behaviour. Can behaviour affect attitudes? What happens when a person's behaviour is very inconsistent with the attitude he or she holds? In certain situations a person may feel compelled to perform a behaviour for what later turns out to be insufficient justification. An experiment by Festinger and Carlsmith (1959) investigated this possibility. Subjects participated in a dull, monotonous, and routine experimental task. They then were asked by the experimenter to misrepresent the task to new subjects by saying that it was really quite exciting and interesting. One half of the subjects were paid one dollar to do this, and the other half were paid twenty dollars. The critical measure in this study was the ratings the subjects gave for their liking of the experiment. The subjects who received one dollar for lying rated the monotonous task as significantly more intersting than did those who had been paid twenty dollars. Festinger (1957) argued that those who were paid twenty dollars could easily justify the inconsistency between what they said and what the task was actually like because they had been well-paid to lie. By contrast, those who were paid only one dollar did not have sufficient financial justification. They were in what Festinger termed a state of **cognitive dissonance**—a state of conflict that occurs when attitudes and behaviours are inconsistent with each other. Because being in conflict is aversive, there is pressure for dissonance reduction. Festinger believed that the subjects who were paid one dollar reduced dissonance by changing their attitude about the experiment, stating honestly that they thought it was more fun than they had believed initially. See Figure 16-1.

FIGURE 16-1 Experimental evidence for cognitive dissonance The subjects rated their enjoyment of the task on a scale from -5.0 to +5.0. The theory of cognitive dissonance would explain why the subjects who were given the lesser incentive of $1 changed their attitudes towards the task.
SOURCE: Based on Festinger and Carlsmith (1959).

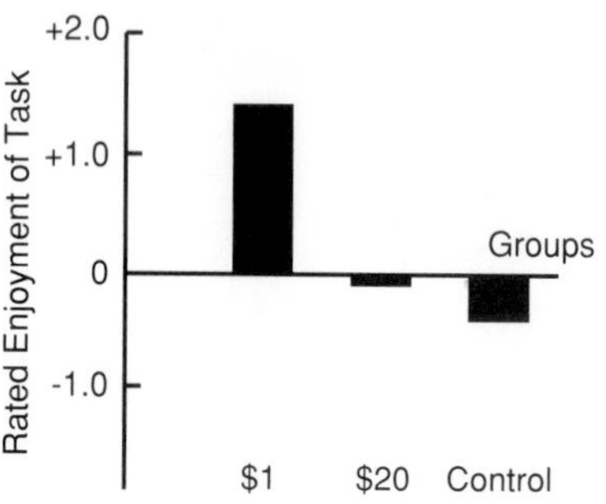

The concept of cognitive dissonance leads to an intriguing prediction. In situations where individuals are offered rewards for engaging in attitude-discrepant behaviour, the dissonance produced, and therefore the amount of attitude change that follows, will be maximum when such rewards are just barely sufficient to induce the inconsistent actions. If the rewards are any smaller, attitude-discrepant behaviour is unlikely to occur. If the rewards are any larger, the increased justification provided by large payoffs will serve to lessen the total amount of dissonance. See Figure 16-2.

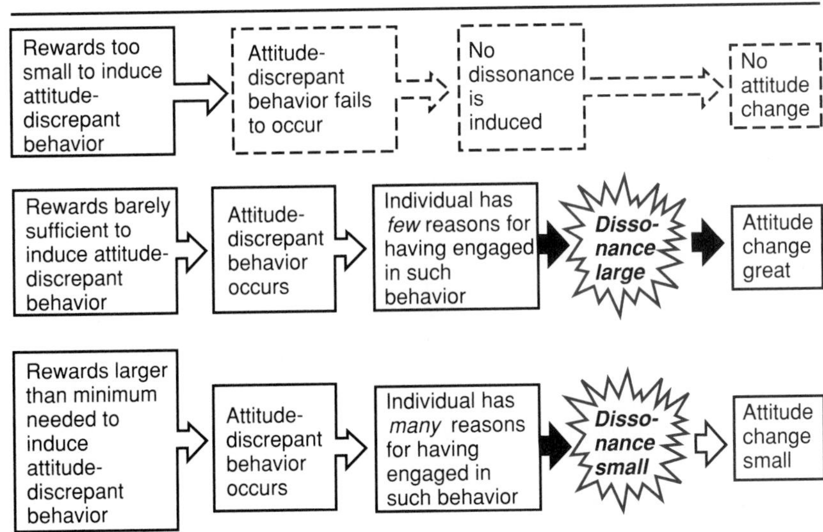

FIGURE 16-2 Cognitive dissonance and rewards: Why less sometimes leads to more

SOURCE: Reprinted with permission from Allyn and Bacon, 1989.

However, recent evidence suggests that the "less leads to more effect" occurs only under certain conditions. First, as might be expected, such effects occur only in situations where individuals believe that they had a choice of whether to perform the attitude-discrepant behaviour. Second, small rewards lead to greater amounts of attitude change only when individuals feel that they were *personally responsible* both for the chosen course of action and any negative effects produced. And finally, the effect does not occur when individuals view the payment they receive as a bribe, rather than as well-deserved pay.

In other words, dissonance occurs most frequently when people feel that they are given a free choice and then publicly commit themselves to a course of action for which there is little external reward or justification. Under such circumstances, people feel personal responsibility for their actions. In order to reduce the dissonance, they make their behaviour explainable by changing their attitudes.

Consider the situation outlined in Figure 16-3. Here, a person holds two incompatible attitudes. If the person feels that he or she originally chose both attitudes freely, then cosiderable dissonance will result. However, if someone else had openly forced the person to comply with Attitude I ("Affirmative action is good and should be implemented"), then the person would experience less dissonance.

In general, there are three main ways to try to reduce or eliminate dissonance. First, we could attempt to add consonant elements to the situation—thoughts consistent with one or the other of those producing dissonance. Second, we could seek to minimize the importance of some of the cognitive elements involved. Third, we could actually alter one or both of the cognitive elements producing the dissonance. In overcoming dissonance, we seem to opt for the path of least resistance to change.

Fazio, Zanna, and Cooper (1977) concluded that cognitive dissonance occurs most readily in situations where the behaviour carried out is quite discrepant from the attitude held. Most of us have

FIGURE 16-3 Pressures for attitude change arising from cognitive dissonance

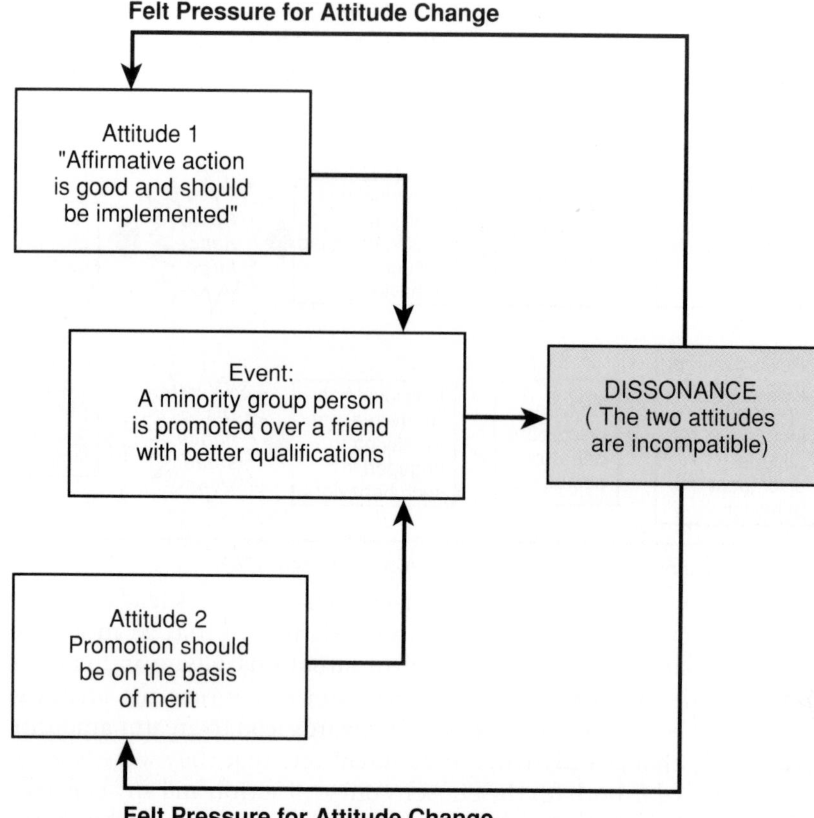

SOURCE: Reprinted with permission from Allyn and Bacon, 1989.

been cajoled or pressured into doing something we didn't want to do and then said that we really did enjoy it despite ourselves. Is this cognitive dissonance at work, or did we really enjoy the activity?

The self-perception hypothesis

Daryl Bem (1972) has suggested an alternative explanation for the cognitive dissonance effect. Festinger asserted that we change our attitude to fit our behaviour in order to relieve the discomfort of conflict. But Bem argues that inner conflict is not necessary to explain the dissonance effect. We often simply look at our own behaviour and conclude from what we see that we must hold a particular attitude or feeling. The extreme case is the person who says, "I won't know what I think until I hear what I have to say." Often a person does something for reasons that are not entirely conscious. If asked about how you feel about a particular acquaintance, you might remember walking somewhat out of your way to talk with him and then conclude from this behaviour that, "I must like him fairly well." According to Bem's so-called **self-perception hypothesis**, we form our attitudes simply by observing and perceiving our own behaviour.

One of the clearest lines of evidence for Bem's hypothesis is the observation that if people are paid excessively for performing behaviours they *like* to do, their attitude toward that activity often becomes more *negative* (Deci & Ryan, 1980; Ross & Fletcher, 1985).

Children in one experiment were given a chance to play with coloured markers. One group of the children were given external rewards (**extrinsic reinforcement**) for producing pictures, whereas the other group of children simply played with the markers. A week later, the children who had been paid had lost interest in using the markers again, while the others had not (Lepper, Greene, & Nisbett, 1973). Bem would argue that the extrinsic reinforcement led to the self-perception that "I am receiving rewards for making pictures, so that must be why I am doing it." The other children observed themselves drawing for no external reason and therefore concluded, "I must be doing this because it is fun."

This effect of extrinsic reinforcement has important implications for how we influence others. To the extent that rewards are seen as controlling our behaviour, our attitudes are likely to change in a negative direction. If everything you do for this course is closely tied to getting a high grade, you might discount the material as being uninteresting. If you were induced to study one chapter hard even though it would not be on the test, you might find the material much more engaging.

PERSUASION AND ATTITUDE CHANGE

Attitudes are formed through socialization. They are taught through child rearing, formal education, and contact with others. They are heavily influenced by (1) **social norms** (i.e., the rules and standards for behaviour established and held by groups for their members) and by (2) **reinforcement contingencies** (i.e., the relationship between specific behaviours and the consequences that follow). We are rewarded for saying certain things and behaving in certain ways. There are many sources that have the potential to change attitudes, including parents, friends, radio, newspapers, and television. **Persuasion** is the process by which people induce others to change their attitudes. Attitude change is a continuous process, as individuals are constantly trying to influence each other. With so much at stake and so many people involved in being persuaders, it is important to know what contributes to effective persuasion.

The source

The same message delivered by different speakers will have vastly different impacts. A speaker with high *credibility* will be more persuasive, especially when the attitude being changed concerns facts and opinions, rather than personal preferences.

Credibility depends on a number of different factors. If the persuader appears to have a lot of knowledge about the topic of the message, then he or she will be credited with a high level of *expertise*. Aronson, Turner, and Carlsmith (1963) have demonstrated the importance of expertise in persuasion. In one experiment, they first asked

FIGURE 16-4 The amount of attitude change produced by persuaders

A) A persuader credited with a high level of expertise will cause a change that increases with the initial discrepancy between the subject's and the persuader's expressed attitude. Thus, when the initial discrepancy is large, the persuader will produce the greatest amount of attitude change.

B) A persuader credited with little expertise is still able to cause some change in the attitudes of the subjects. However, when the initial discrepancy is large, the persuader's influence declines significantly.

Based on Aronson, Turner, and Carlsmith (1963). Adapted with permission from Allyn and Bacon, 1989.

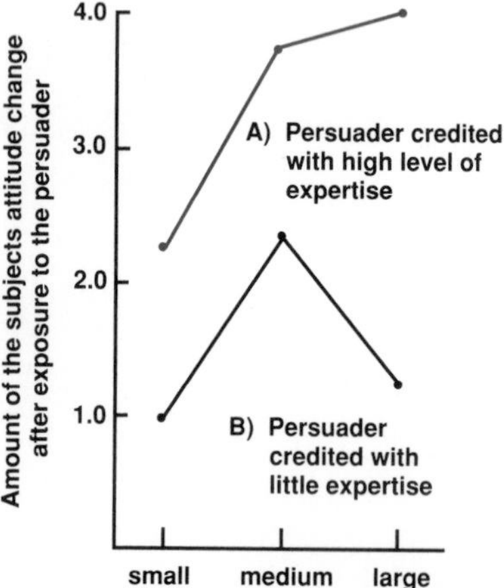

college students to evaluate two anonymous passages of poetry. Then, they showed the students an evaluation of these passages. One group of students was told that the evaluation was written by the famous poet T.S. Eliot (i.e., a source they would credit with a high level of expertise). The other group of students was told that the evaluation was written by a student at a small college (i.e., a source they would credit with little expert status). The experimenters also manipulated the size of the discrepancy between the initial attitude of the student and that of the outside evaluation. In both groups, the students read an evaluation that was very similar to their own (small discrepancy), somewhat different (medium discrepancy), or very different (large discrepancy). Later, the subjects were asked to evaluate the passages of poetry again, and the experimenters measured the amount of shift in their opinions. The results are shown in Figure 16-4. The messages supposedly written by the communicator with a high level of expertise were much more effective in altering the students' opinions than were those supposedly written by another student of little expertise. The difference in the results was greatest when the initial discrepancy was large. Here, the subjects resisted the "other student's" influence especially strongly.

A speaker can increase his or her credibility by communicating a *lack of ulterior motive.* One technique for doing this is to appear to be objective by presenting both sides of an issue. Another technique is to argue unexpectedly against one's own self-interest — or, more accurately, to *seem* to do so. A lawyer who is arguing against a new law might say, "As a lawyer, I agree the more laws the better; I get more business. Even so, I have to be against this law." The implication is that this law is so bad, the lawyer is willing to sacrifice important self-interest to oppose it. In fact, one law more or less won't make any difference to this speaker's income. Nevertheless, the speaker's credibility might be increased using this approach.

A speaker's credibility depends on a number of different factors.
SOURCE: Photo by Bill McCarthy. Courtesy of the Office of the Prime Minister.

Much advertising rests on the portrayal of attractive, successful people rather than on the presentation of rational argument.
SOURCE: Metropolitan Toronto Convention & Visitors Association.

A speaker can also increase credibility by making frequent eye contact with the listener and by talking at a slightly faster than average rate. Skilled speakers also use their props effectively to produce the impression of sincerity. They might reach for the glass of water on the podium and act as if they are quite thirsty. But when the glass is half way to their lips, a compellingly important thought occurs and can't wait. They seem to forget the much needed drink and set down the glass. The implication is that they are about to raise a very important point.

When the attitudes to be changed have more to do with personal preferences than facts, people are more influenced by the *attractiveness* of the source of a message and by the source's *similarity* to themselves. This is what lies behind "life-style" advertising. There is no way to persuade rational people to smoke or drink by using reason. However, a powerful influence can be made by the portrayal of attractive, successful people who are similar to us and to how we wish to be.

The message

The most effective form for a persuasive message depends on who is speaking and who the audience is. If the audience already agrees with the message or is unlikely to hear opposing arguments, it is more effective to present only one side of the case. If the audience is sophisticated, however, it is better to present both sides to show that the speaker has considered counter-arguments. This is especially important if the audience is likely to hear the other side soon. In this case, it is advantageous to speak first, as long as we anticipate the next speaker's main arguments and present them as "one side of the issue." We lead the audience to anticipate the main points *and* to have the refuting points in mind. This makes the second speaker's job more difficult. If the other side is not to be presented until much later or if a decision is called for right after the second presentation, the advantage shifts from the first speaker to the second speaker.

"Six boxes of cookies for you, and no arguments."

SOURCE: *Herman* by Jim Unger. Copyright 1980 Universal Press Syndicate.

If the speaker is very credible, taking an extreme and one-sided stance sometimes works well. However, in general it is more effective to stay closer to what the audience already believes and to moderate what is said.

Fear can be an effective tool in a persuasive communication. But at times the use of fear can backfire and cause a hardening of attitudes opposite to what one intends. This surprises many people. Paradoxically, because fear is so powerful, persuaders often incorporate it in their messages without sufficient thought. The key is that fear works only when it is accompanied by concrete ways for the audience to deal with and reduce the fear. Showing an addicted smoker's black lung tissue and films of lung cancer patients dying painfully is likely to lead to a fierce avoidance, not of smoking but of the person presenting the communication. This avoidance probably will include denial, repression, and a *polarization* of attitudes about "do-gooder crusaders who are always exaggerating anyway." The fear is overwhelming and the chances for useful change seem remote. It would be much more effective to offer achievable goals and a means of reaching them, perhaps along with some fear-inducing information (Beck, 1979; Leventhal, Singer, & Jones, 1965).

Another important aspect of the message is its **framing**, or the way in which it is worded. The persuasiveness of two messages carrying the same information in different framings can be significantly different. In one experiment (Levin, Schnittjer, & Thee, 1988), the first group of subjects were told that "65% of the students had cheated during their college career," and the second group of subjects were told that "35% of the students had never cheated." Both sentences mean exactly the same thing. However, the first group of subjects later rated the incidence of cheating higher than did the second group. Similarly, subjects who were told that a new medical treatment had a "50% success rate" thought the treatment was more effective and they were more likely to recommend it to others than subjects who were told that the treatment had a "50% failure rate."

The power of the framing effect was studied by Meyerowitz and Chaiken (1987), who wanted to persuade university women to do breast self-examinations. Their subjects read a three-page pamphlet on self-examination, but there were two versions of the pamphlet. The first version was framed to stress the potential gains of doing self-examinations, whereas the second version was framed to stress the potential losses of not doing them. The first version included the following paragraph:

> By doing breast self-examinations now, you can learn what your normal healthy breasts feel like so that you will be better prepared to notice any small, abnormal changes that might occur as you get older. Research shows that women who do breast self-examination have an increased chance of finding a tumour in the early, more treatable stage of the disease (Meyerowitz & Chaiken, 1987, p. 504).

In the second version the corresponding paragraph read as follows:

> By not doing breast self-examination you will not learn what your normal, healthy breasts feel like so that you will be ill-prepared to notice any small, abnormal changes that might occur

> as you get older. Research shows that women who do not do breast self-examination have a decreased chance of finding a tumour in the early, more treatable stage of the disease (Meyerowitz & Chaiken, 1987, p. 504).

Four months later, the women who had read the second, loss-oriented message were almost twice as likely to be doing breast self-examinations as the other group. In fact, the first group was no more likely to be doing the self-examinations than was a control group who had read neither pamphlet. Perhaps, the second version was so effective because it was a fear-arousing communication in which a concrete, achievable solution was offered. However, there was no demonstrated difference in the expression of fear by the subjects in these groups. From this study, we cannot logically conclude that "negative" framing is always more effective. Nevertheless, we can see that the way a message is worded has a significant impact on its persuasiveness.

The channel

In general, face-to-face communication is more persuasive than mass-media messages and mailed messages (Eldersveld & Dodge, 1954). However, because face-to-face contacts are expensive and impractical for large-scale campaigns, the mass media are used more often. Huge sums are spent on advertising—$50 to $60 billion each year in North America—and much research is conducted to determine what type of advertising works best.

The average high-school graduate will have spent more time watching television than in school (Adler, Lesser, Meringoff, Robertson, & Ward, 1980). Given all this exposure, we might expect television advertising to exert a large impact. However, it is surprising how little firm evidence we have about the effectiveness of advertising. We commonly hear anecdotes about the effectiveness of a particular ad campaign, but there is only a weak relationship between the amount spent advertising particular products and the market share that those products gain (Assmus, Farley, & Lehmann, 1984). Children are somewhat more affected by television ads, but that seems partly to be because they do not discount the credibility of the advertiser's self-interested message (Gaines & Esserman, 1981).

The written word seems more effective in communicating complex information. Most people say that they get their information from television more than newspapers. But some studies show that people remember the printed material better (Lichty, 1982; McGuire, 1985).

The audience

Many speakers and teachers seem to think that their job is simply to present certain information accurately. The effective speaker, however, has a constant, almost empathic, sense of what is going on inside the minds of the audience. What matters most is the process of change in the audience, whether one is teaching, persuading, or entertaining. The good teacher or persuader *leads* the audience to come to certain conclusions and to make particular discoveries. If facts and principles are presented to lay a firm foundation, then a rhetorical question can have a powerful effect. The speaker may never even state the conclusion, as long as the audience is silently answering the critical question for themselves.

Audiences differ in how easily they can be influenced. A persuasive communicator quickly learns that he or she is wasting time with listeners who are already committed, either for or against the speaker. On the whole, young audiences are less likely to hold strong opinions. Therefore, they can more easily be influenced by persuasion.

The history of research into possible gender differences about who is more easily influenced reveals the need to design studies with care. Older research often concluded that women were more vulnerable than men to persuasion (McGuire, 1969). However, Eagly and Carli (1981) reviewed more recent work and concluded that there is only a slight tendency for this gender difference to occur. Furthermore, they claimed that earlier studies were marred by at least two biasing factors. First, only research conducted by male experimenters found women to be influenced more. Second, most of these studies concerned attitudes about "male oriented" topics. Because males would be more informed about these topics, they should be less easily influenced to change. In fact, Karabenick (1983) found that men were easier to influence about "female oriented" topics.

GROUP DYNAMICS

In social psychology, the term *group* refers to more than just a collection of individuals. A **group** is three or more people who (1) interact in a structured and regular way, (2) share some common goals, and (3) have a sense of belonging to the group (Hare, 1976; Shaw, 1976). The need to belong is powerful. Everyone is a member of at least several groups, some formal and others informal. One's membership in informal, unofficial groups is often a very important part of one's identity. In nearly every high school, there is an "in group" and peripheral "out groups"—and everybody knows who belongs to each group.

Membership in informal groups is often an important part of one's identity.

SOURCE: Courtesy of the University of Toronto.

The power of roles

A *role* is a set of behaviours that a group deems socially appropriate under particular circumstances. We all have many roles, and their power should not be dismissed lightly. In Chapter 18 we will discuss how much our sex role affects our thinking and behaviour. On the basis of gender, we are assigned a set of behaviours that we will have difficulty breaking out of. In the Stanford prison experiment, the guard role and the prisoner role had a disturbingly strong influence, much to the surprise of the experimenter and the subjects. All of our life we are reinforced for living within roles and punished for violating the boundaries of our roles. We are not concerned here with the

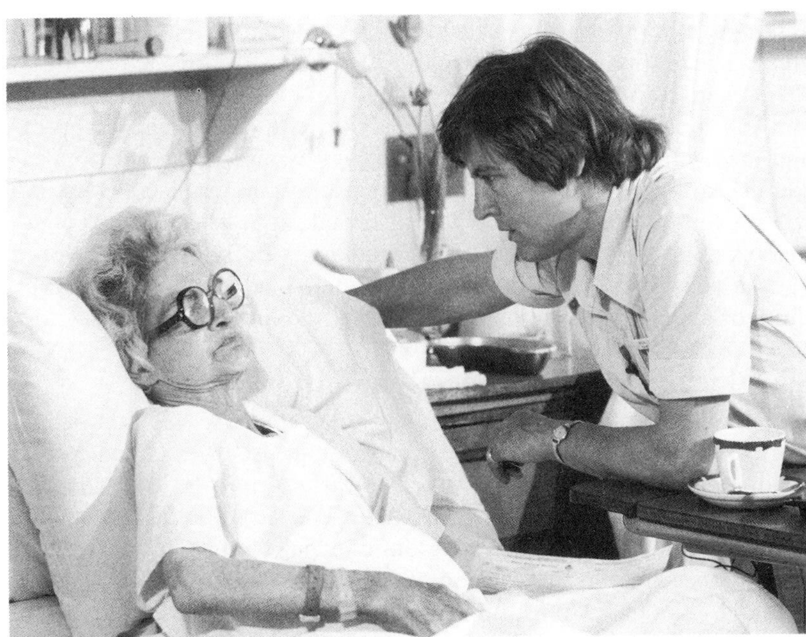

Adopting the role of patient is not always entirely in the individual's best interests.

SOURCE: "Last Days of Living," National Film Board of Canada.

characteristics of particular roles. The "good student" role clearly differs from the "rebellious authority-kicker" role. The point we wish to emphasize is that we learn a generalized tendency to live within roles, within prescribed sets of behaviours.

Roles can be helpful or harmful. If we had to figure out in every group we entered which gestures were appropriate for males and which were appropriate for females, we would be a wreck. Once we learn a role, we don't have to think much about what to do as a student when that's called for, and what to do as a best friend when that's called for. We can switch quickly from one to the other because we know the correct behaviour set. This is very efficient. The negative aspect of roles arises when socially appropriate behaviour is not in our best interests. In hospitals there is a *patient role* in which the patient is expected to quietly and passively accept treatments and procedures. As a result, physical and mental health may suffer. However, violating this role by asking questions carries the risk of being labelled as a troublemaker. People who in other circumstances would be quite assertive about what was being done to them often become unquestioning lambs when such a role is clearly defined.

Group influences on performance and decision making

Social loafing

Being in a group sometimes leads people to ease up on their own efforts, sometimes to try harder and do better, and sometimes to try so hard that they do worse.

When responsibility for a group effort can be spread around, there is a tendency for social loafing to occur. **Social loafing** is the phenomenon of diminished performance resulting from the diffusion of responsibility in a group. Because no one person's effort stands out as the main contributor to the effort, no one can be identified as not giving the best possible performance. Latané, Williams, and Harkins (1979) gathered male students in the middle of a football stadium and had them make as much noise as they could—yelling, clapping, and stamping their feet in whatever way would make the loudest sound. An individual person made markedly more noise alone than when even one other person was also making noise. A group of six made a noise only about a third as loud as six individual men would have made. Even when isolated, the men made less noise if they thought another person was also yelling in another isolated setting.

Social facilitation and social inhibition

Social loafing notwithstanding, it has long been observed that people work harder to perform when in the presence of others. Under such conditions, the performance of some tasks improves, but the performance of other tasks declines. Robert Zajonc (1965) has suggested a useful explanation of this apparent contradiction. The presence of others raises overall motivation or drive-level for humans and many animals. (Zajonc even found this effect with cockroaches.) This rise in general drive-level strongly motivates our **dominant responses**, the best-learned responses among a group of competing possible responses. Thus, when we are in the presence of others, our performance of dominant responses usually improves. This enhancement of performance is known as **social facilitation**. It often concerns simple tasks, as they are commonly overlearned.

By contrast, if we want to do something complex or unfamiliar in the presence of others, the rise in drive-level will usually detract from our performance. Or to put it another way, the arousal of our dominant responses will usually interfere with our execution of the desired response. The phenomenon of diminished performance of non-domninant responses when in the presence of others is known as **social inhibition**. See Figure 16-5.

Therefore, for a particular task, we would expect a skilled person to improve and a beginner to deteriorate in the presence of an audience. This was borne out in an experiment concerning good and poor pool players. When four observers moved in to watch the players closely, the accuracy of the good players increased about 10 percent whereas the accuracy of the poor players decreased about 10 percent (Michaels et al., 1982). The practical applications of these results are very useful. If we are being tested for information we know very well, it is helpful to have an audience because it will raise our arousal level. If our skills or knowledge are new and uncertain, we should try to perform alone and keep a low arousal level.

Group problem solving and decision making

Under "good" circumstances, two heads really are better than one for decision making and problem solving (Gordon, 1977). We will discuss an approach to this process in Chapter 20 on Organizational Psychology. The problem is that "good" circumstances include tolerance, openness of communication, creativity, and explicit protection against the enormous power of a group setting to pressure members to conform to the group norm.

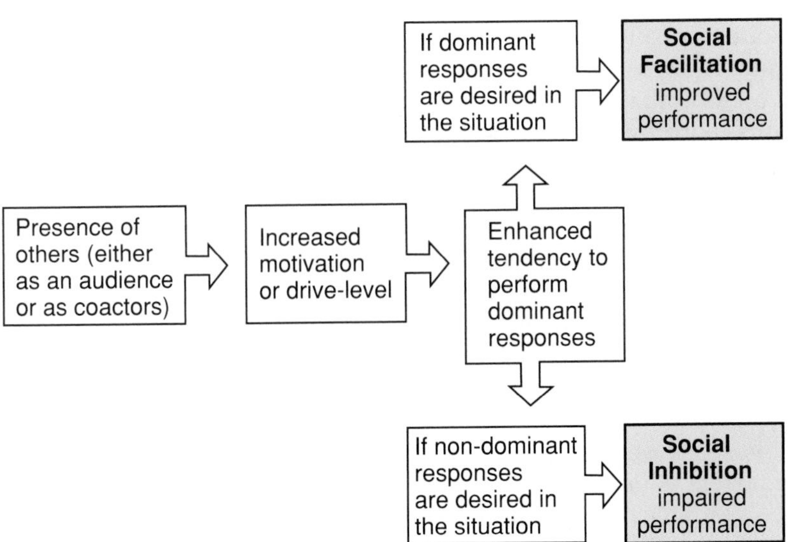

SOURCE: Adapted with permission from Allyn and Bacon, 1989.

FIGURE 16-5 The effects of the presence of others on performance
On the one hand, the presence of others will improve the performance of well-learned responses *(social facilitation)*. On the other hand, the presence of others will impair the performance of responses that have yet to be mastered *(social inhibition)*.

One possible dangerous consequence of group problem solving is **groupthink**, the tendency for group members to go along with what they perceive to be the group opinion. A risky or inappropriate solution may be proposed which gathers momentum despite a lack of enthusiastic support. Each member interprets the silence of others as support for the idea. No one wants to look foolish by bringing up objections. Each member starts to feel a kind of group invulnerability. As a result, some very stupid decisions can be made. One of the most commonly cited examples of groupthink was the decision by the U.S. to back the invasion of Cuba's Bay of Pigs in 1961. After the invasion failed miserably, it seemed obvious to everyone that it was a foolish act. President Kennedy himself wondered, "How could we have been so stupid?"

Irving Janis (1983) analyzed the Bay of Pigs process and other similar policy decisions and fiascoes. He has pointed out that groupthink is especially likely to occur in a group with a dynamic, highly respected leader. Janis has also identified three characteristics that can help us anticipate groupthink. The first characteristic is **cohesiveness**, the strong feeling of belonging to a tightly knit group. The

Group decision making can easily be distorted. The effective leader must be aware of the dangers of groupthink.
SOURCE: Courtesy of the Office of the Prime Minister.

excitement and camaraderie of being part of an intelligent, powerful group is intoxicating. It is hard for members to question the wisdom of a group that they value so highly. Each person suppresses objections, both by failing to bring them up to confront others and by minimizing them internally as unimportant and probably silly. This suppression of objections leads to the second characteristic—an **illusion of unanimity**, in which group members incorrectly interpret each other's silence as agreement with the group opinion. No one else is objecting, which must mean they all agree; so how could this course of action be wrong? In fact, many members might have objections but are also staying silent under the illusion that they are the only ones. Cohesiveness and the illusion of unanimity can arouse such intense feelings that an **illusion of invulnerability** develops. This sense of strength that comes from group membership leads members to underestimate realistic risks.

To prevent groupthink, Janis (1983) suggests that a group leader should specifically encourage the expression of doubts. Perhaps one member could take the role of devil's advocate and actively challenge ideas "just as an exercise." Bringing in outsiders to address the group and breaking the group into small subgroups also help to prevent distortion in the decision-making process. Groups can be painfully blind and distort facts to fit the shared view of reality. It is wise to build formal protections into the group's structure.

Conformity

We are all members of various groups, and each group exerts its own influence on us. As we mentioned earlier in this chapter, the rules and standards for behaviour established and held by groups for their members are known as *social norms*. Even though these norms are seldom formally stated, they powerfully affect what we do and even what we think. One norm that nearly every group holds is that one is required to behave in ways that are similar to other group members. Behaviour that coincides with the behaviour of others because of group expectations is called **conformity**. By its very nature, a group encourages conformity.

Solomon E. Asch.
SOURCE: Courtesy Solomon E. Asch.

One of the classic experiments in psychology was Solomon Asch's (1951) demonstration of the power of conformity. Seven subjects sat around three sides of a table. The experimenter displayed two large stimulus cards with lines. One card had a standard or criterion line, and the other card had three different comparison lines, one of which matched the criterion line in length. See Figure 16-6. The cards were presented as a size discrimination task, and each subject was simply asked to say which comparison line matched the criterion line. This task was so easy that when control subjects were tested in isolation, they were accurate more than 99 percent of the time. However, in the experimental scenario, six of the subjects were confederates working for the researcher, and the actual subject was seated second from the last around the table. For the first two trials, there was unanimous agreement on the correct answer as Asch went around the table asking for responses. On the third trial, however, the first five "subjects" all chose the same, obviously incorrect, line.

Subject number six was understandably puzzled. The critical data for the experiment concerned this so-called *conformity trial*. Would the subject go along with the crowd or would he choose the line he knew was correct? Subsequent trials were also held where there was unanimous agreement on the correct line, but every now and then a conformity trial was inserted.

The 50 subjects in this experiment might well have been expected to resist the pressure to conform, because they didn't know any of the other "subjects" and therefore had no group ties to them. Moreover, the confederates were presented to the subject as his peers. Therefore, he wouldn't have expected them to have any superior knowledge. Still, about three-quarters of the subjects did conform on at least some of the conformity trials. About one-third of all responses to the conformity trials were conforming responses.

A number of factors have been found to increase conformity. One critical factor in Asch's experiment was the unanimity of the group. If just one other member failed to go along with the false responses, the conformity rate dropped to about five percent (Asch, 1956). Even a small unanimous group exerts more power than a fairly large one with one or two nonconformers in it. In general, the ambiguity of the correct way to respond also increases conformity, as we tend to look to others for cues on the right thing to do. The more ambiguous the situation is, the more likely people are to conform to others. The intensity of the contact with others is another factor that enhances conformity. Being in close contact with the other subjects increased conformity in Asch's study. When subjects were in private booths and responded with button pushes, conformity decreased (Deutsch & Gerard, 1955). When the person was told that it would be necessary to interact with group members at a later time, conformity increased (Aronson & Osherow, 1980). In addition, being of lower status increases conformity, as does having low self-esteem.

We can distinguish between external conformity and internal conformity. **External conformity** is a change of outward behaviour to conform to that of the group without changing one's thoughts and attitudes. **Internal conformity** is a change of attitudes and ideas to conform to those of the group. In practice, we often change our thoughts and feelings to go along with others we value. In Asch's experiments, though, interviews with subjects suggested that they

Figure 16-6 The stimulus cards for Asch's conformity experiment The card on the left contains the standard or criterion line. The card on the right contains the three comparison lines. Clearly, comparison line 2 matches the standard line. Here the lines are drawn to scale. In the experiment, the cards were separated by about 100 cm and presented a few metres away from the subjects.

Source: Based on Asch (1956).

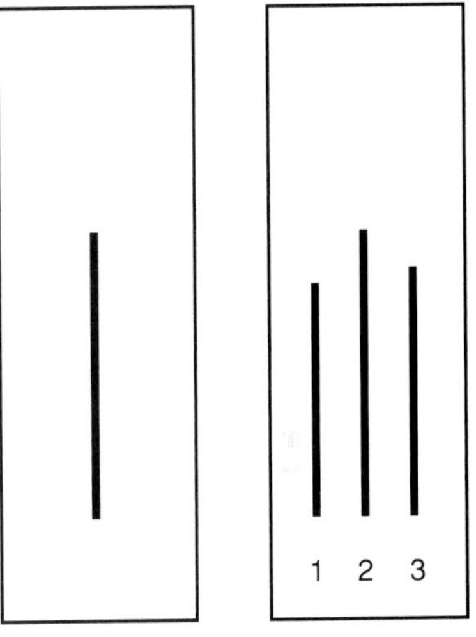

In Asch's conformity experiment, all of the "subjects" are secret confederates of the researcher except subject number 6 (the sixth from the left in the first photo). In the second photo, he leans forward anxiously to study the cards after hearing incorrect answers from the others.

Source: William Vandivert.

strongly believed that the group was wrong on the critical trials but they didn't want to be considered "misfits" or "fools." We could describe their behaviour as external conformity. They behaved outwardly to conform to group pressure without actually changing their own thoughts. We can conclude that the punishments for nonconformity are quite serious, and it is the fear of these consequences that induces people to conform. A number of experiments have shown that the person who looks odd by current group standards is more likely to be excluded, ostracized, and deprived of whatever rewards the group controls.

When we conform internally as well, we *internalize* the attitudes and ideas held by others. They become our own attitudes and ideas. This often happens because of our *identification* with others. We want to be similar to those we admire and by whom we want to be accepted. This kind of conformity has much more lasting effects on us. We will act consistently with the belief system (now our own) even when the group members are absent and even if we fail to recognize the source of those ideas.

We should point out that conformity is not entirely negative. Some conformity is absolutely necessary in order for people to live with others. Destructive features arise only when the degree of conformity is extremely large or extremely small. The person who always conforms would relinquish his or her own judgement and could be led to do things that are destructive to self and others. Individuals who never conform would be so antagonistic they would be impossible to live with.

RESPONDING TO THE REQUESTS AND DEMANDS OF OTHERS

Inducing compliance

We once saw one of our students selling windsurfers at a local sports show. He was very excited about the training he had taken in sales techniques and how they fit in with what he had learned in psychology. We responded, "Yes, some of the things in psychology can be used manipulatively." His boss took offence at this and claimed, "We don't manipulate people. We just help them know what they want"—which, by coincidence, always turns out to be a windsurfer. **Compliance** is behaviour that accedes to an explicit request from another person or a group. Selling is a clear case in which one person is trying to get another to *comply* with a certain course of action. We also try to have others comply in less obvious situations. Research has identified several strategies for increasing the likelihood of compliance. Let us examine three of them.

The **foot-in-the-door technique** starts with a small request that is almost certain to be granted. Once the person has gone along with that small favour, he or she is far more likely to agree to a much more costly demand. Freedman and Fraser (1966) phoned homemakers and asked if they would answer an eight-question survey about soap use. Several days later they called these women and another group of women who had not been surveyed to ask permission for a group of six men to visit the home and inventory all her household products. Women who had agreed to be interviewed previously were twice as likely to comply with this excessive intrusion. The researchers argued that the first act of compliance may have established a self-image as a cooperative person in this circumstance, an image that was difficult to violate.

A reverse strategy is the **door-in-the-face technique**. First, we make an outrageous request and probably get the door slammed in our face. But the other person is softened up for the much more reasonable request which we then make. The other person may feel obligated to "compromise" after turning us down once. One group of researchers (Cialdini et al., 1975) asked a control group of subjects to take needy children on a two-hour tour of the zoo. About 33% of the people agreed. The researchers first asked the experimental group to commit themselves to be volunteer counsellor to delinquents for two years, and all of them refused. Later, however, when this group was asked to help with the zoo trip, over 50% of them agreed.

If you have bought a car recently, you may have been the victim of the **low-ball technique**. The salesperson gets the customer committed to buying a particular car at a low price. The customer seems to cross a line of some kind when this psychological commitment is made. He or she undoubtedly wants this car now. The customer engages in an internal process of rationalization and self-persuasion about why this car is just the right one. Then the person who is trying to obtain compliance changes the terms to make them more stringent. In the sales setting, the usual method is to get the customer to sign some kind of agreement to purchase and then say, "I'll see if I can get the sales manager to go along with this." Crestfallen, the salesperson returns to say that the manager won't go along with it because they'd be losing money on the deal. In most cases, the customer will still buy the car, at a price that would have been unacceptable just a few minutes previously.

Obedience

Obedience is behaviour that accedes to a direct command from another person, particularly a person in authority. Obedience can be considered to be an extreme instance of compliance. Like conformity, obedience can lead to positive or negative consequences. In this section, we will focus on the dangers of obedience.

History is filled with instances where barbaric acts have been carried out by people who were "simply following orders." Obedience often results in extreme deeds by those who obey. We tend to judge these inhumane actions as abnormal and as actions that we ourselves would never perform. However, there is disturbing evidence that normal people can be induced to do terrible things by "the proper authorities" without very much pressure being brought to bear. Hannah Arendt (1963), in her book about the Nazi war criminal Adolph Eichmann, concluded that evil is usually quite banal—that is, ordinary and plain. Some of the Nazi leaders were almost certainly psychopathic, but the majority of atrocities were committed by very average people.

Adolph Eichmann (1906–1962), the notorious Nazi war criminal, admitted to the many atrocities he committed. He offered the excuse that he was only following orders.
SOURCE: The Bettmann Archive.

Stanley Milgram (1933–1984).
SOURCE: Alexandra Milgram. Photo by Eric Kroll, 1982.

The classic research that brought home the dangers of obedience was done by Stanley Milgram (1963, 1968). Milgram wondered just how far ordinary people would go when ordered by an authority figure to inflict harm on others. He advertised for community members who were not students to participate in an experiment on learning to be held at Yale University. Each subject was paid $4.00 for an hour's participation. The subject was introduced to a "fellow subject" who was actually Milgram's confederate. The confederate was a middle-aged accountant who had been trained to act as the "learner" in the experiment. The two drew lots to see who would be the "teacher" and who would be the "learner," but the draw was fixed so that the actual subject was always the "teacher." An "experimenter" wearing a lab coat explained that the purpose of the study was to investigate the effects of punishment on learning. The "teacher" first saw the "learner" being strapped into a chair and electrodes attached to his wrists. The teacher was then placed in an adjacent room. He could not see the learner, but he could communicate with him over an intercom and he could hear him through the wall. The teacher read a list of word pairs to the learner, who was to memorize which word went with which stimulus word. The learner gave his answers by pressing the appropriate lever on the table in front of him. If the learner made an error, the teacher was to administer an electric shock to him by means of a convincing-looking "shock machine." The switches on the panel of this machine were labelled from a benign "Slight" through to "Danger: Severe shock" and the ominous "XXX" (450 volts). Before the experiment started, the subject (i.e., the "teacher") was given a sample shock of 45 volts, so he could experience what the upper end of "Slight" was like—a definite jolt. This sample strengthened the authenticity of the procedure for the subject, who didn't know that the "shock machine" was a fake. The 45-volt shock came from a separate battery. Although the machine and its panel appeared to be very elaborate, they generated nothing but "electrical noises."

With each error, the teacher was to increase the voltage level by one step of 15 volts. The "learner" committed errors fairly frequently, and so the shock level rose quickly. When it reached 75 volts the "learner" started to moan. When the shock level rose further, he yelled and swore, begging to be released from the experiment, saying he had a heart condition and couldn't stand anymore. At 300 volts, he started pounding on the wall in addition to screaming he wanted out. At this point, he stopped responding to questions. The experimenter told the subject to consider no response as an incorrect answer. At 315 volts, the learner pounded on the wall again and then made no more sounds for the remainder of the experiment.

Most of us think it is quite amazing that any of the "teachers" would even get to the 300-volt level in the face of the "learner's" begging and screaming. Certainly we ourselves wouldn't. Before you read the results, imagine how high you think you would have gone before refusing to continue, in spite of pressure from the experimenter. The experimenter was wearing a lab coat and stood near the "teacher" urging him to continue all the way up to the maximum shock. He used a firm, insistent voice giving commands such as,

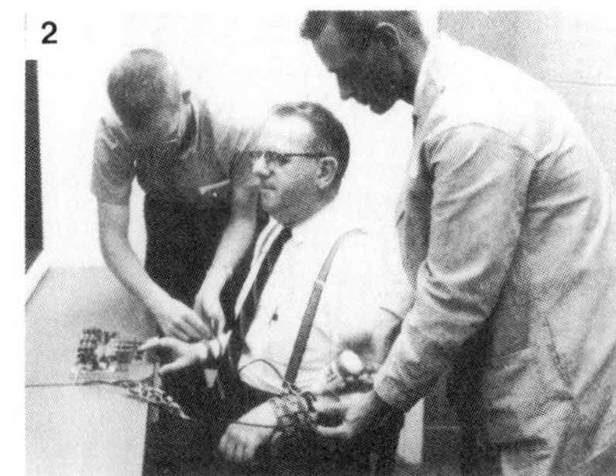
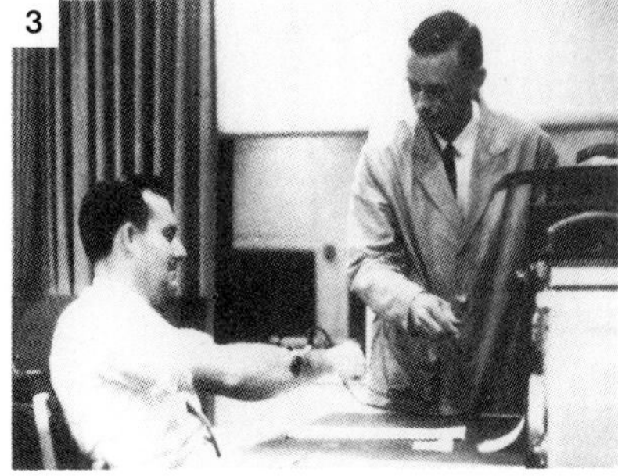

In Milgram's obedience experiment, the subjects were tricked into believing that if they pressed switches on an elaborate-looking panel, they would be administering electrical shocks. The illusion was strengthened by giving the subjects a sample, mild shock, but this came from a separate battery. The "learner," actually a confederate of Milgram's, was strapped into a chair and had electrodes strapped to his wrists. Some subjects refused to continue the experiment at some point.

1. Shock generator used in the experiments. Fifteen of the thirty switches have already been depressed.

2. Learner is strapped into chair and electrodes are attached to his wrists. Electrode paste is applied by the experimenter. Learner provides answers by depressing switches that light up numbers on an answer box.

3. Subject receives sample shock from the generator.

4. Subject breaks off experiment. On right, event recorder wired into generator automatically records switches used by the subject.

SOURCE: From the film "Obedience," distributed by the New York University Film Library. Copyright 1965 by Stanley Milgram.

"Please go on . . . The experiment requires that you continue . . . You have no choice. You must go on." The teachers showed signs of intense distress during the experiment. They trembled, perspired heavily, dug their nails into their hands, made obvious moaning and sighing sounds, and asked if they could please stop. They uttered statements such as, "He can't stand it! He's hollering, he's going to die! What if something happens to him?" One of the most powerful ways to keep the subject going higher was for the experimenter to say that he himself would take responsibility for whatever happened. Subjects would accept this and continue raising the shock level.

Milgram asked a group of psychiatrists to read a description of the procedure and to predict how high people would go. Their consensus was that most people would not go beyond 150 volts, and only extreme sadists or psychopaths would go to the full 450 volts. He also surveyed many people to estimate how high they felt they would go. Nobody said they would go higher than the 300-volt level. Less than 25% predicted that they would even go higher than 160 volts. We cite these findings so you can compare your view of yourself with them.

In the actual experiment, *everyone* went at least to the 300-volt level (see Figure 16-7). Even more disconcertingly, 65% of the subjects delivered the highest shock-level ("XXX") of 450 volts. In addition, all of those who refused to comply with the command to go to 450 volts simply walked out without checking on the condition of the "learner."

Milgram (1965) also conducted a second experiment to show the influence of peer behaviour on obedience. He introduced two confederates who were to act as "subjects" in full view of the actual subject. One confederate refused to go on after the 150-volt level and walked out. The second confederate refused to continue after the

FIGURE 16-7 The results of Milgram's obedience experiment
After each incorrect response by the "learner" (a confederate), the experimenter ordered the "teacher" (the subject) to administer a larger shock. At the 300-volt level, the learner pounded on the wall and then stopped responding to the questions. At the 315-volt level, the learner pounded on the wall again. The experimenter told the subject to consider no answer as an incorrect response. When the subject hesitated to deliver a shock, the experimenter urged him to go on, finally with the statement, "You have no choice. You *must* go on." Sixty-five percent of the subjects gave the learner what they believed to be a 450-volt shock.

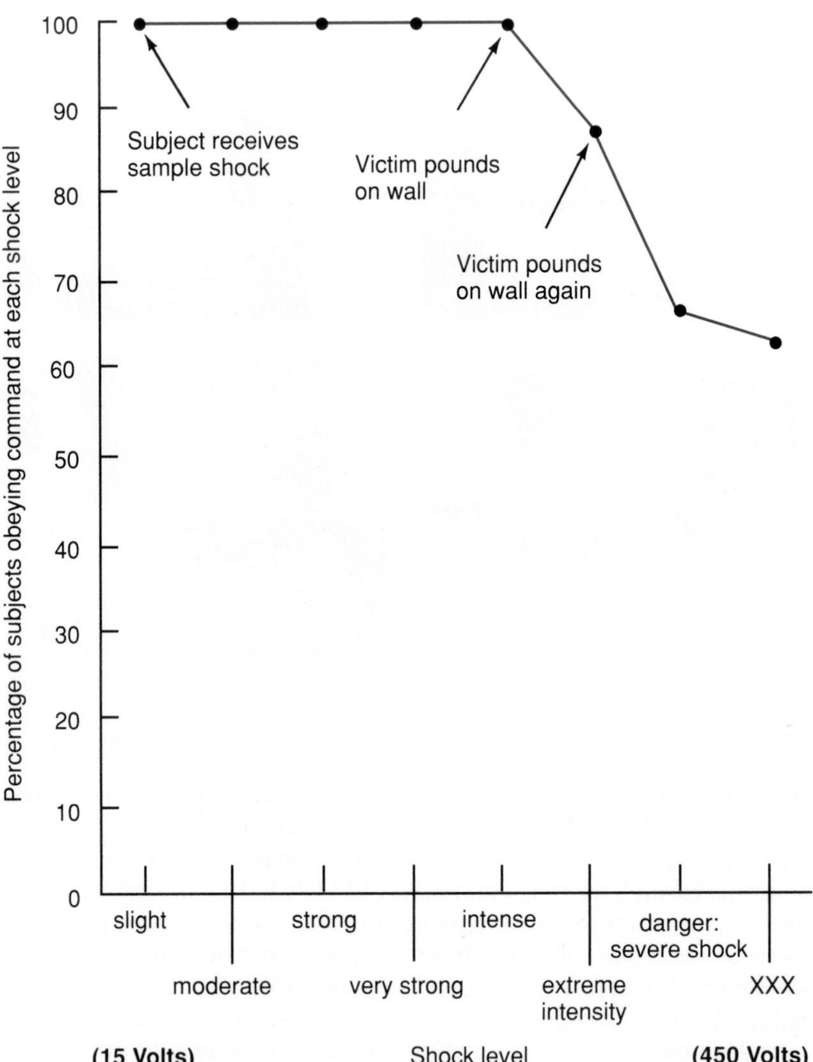

SOURCE: From Milgram (1963). Reprinted with permission from Allyn and Bacon, 1989.

210-volt level and also walked out. In both instances, the experimenter himself took over and kept increasing the shock level. In this experiment, more subjects refused to comply and stopped sooner than in Milgram's original experiment. (See Figure 16-8.) Evidently, when we are in the company of others who refuse to obey orders to hurt someone else, we ourselves are more likely to refuse to continue causing harm.

Nevertheless, both studies indicate that under certain circumstances we can be surprisingly cruel. Milgram's original experiment reveals that in the company of ruthless people, we tend to be ruthless ourselves. We might wish that Milgram's finding was a fluke, but it has been replicated many times in many different countries. About two thirds of the subjects reliably go all the way to "XXX." His subjects learned something very disturbing about themselves. Actually, we should all learn a disturbing lesson, unless we try to deny it by arguing that somehow we're different than all the people in these experiments.

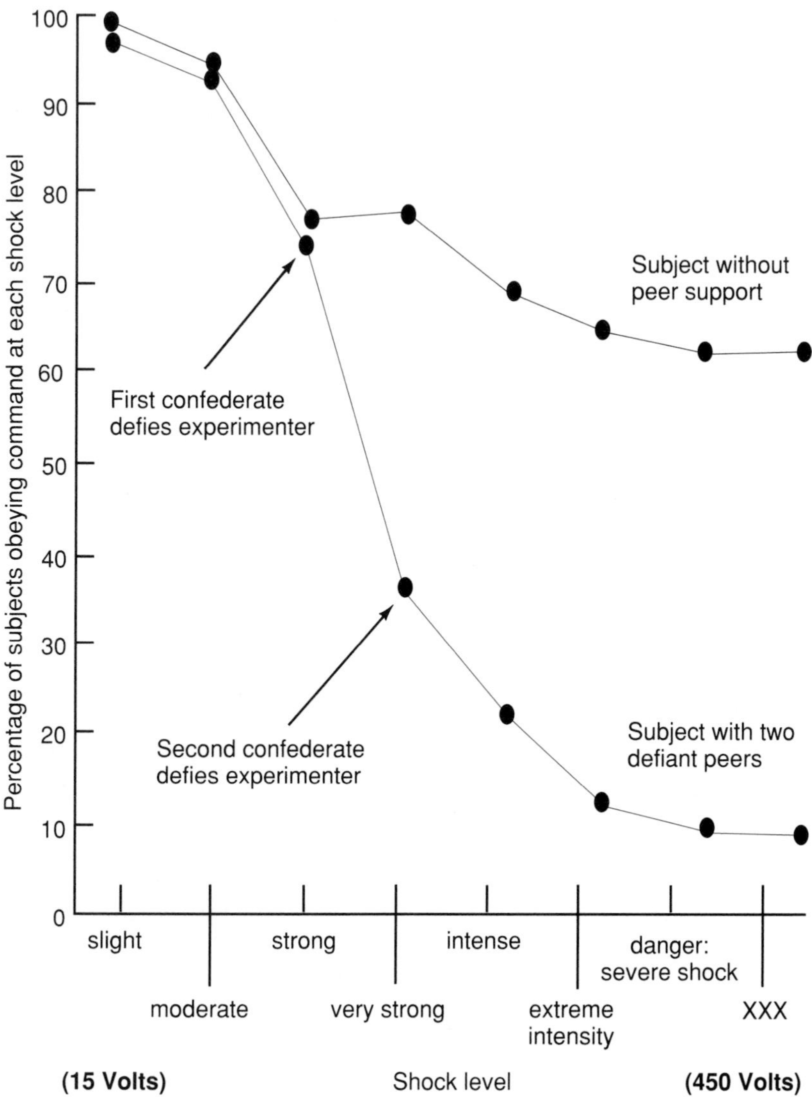

SOURCE: From Milgram (1965). Reprinted with permission from Allyn and Bacon, 1989.

FIGURE 16-8 The results of Milgram's second experiment comparing behaviour with defiant "peers" and behaviour without them
In Milgram's second experiment, one confederate "subject" refused to continue beyond 150 volts and the second confederate "subject" refused to continue beyond 210 volts. The actual subjects tested (in the presence of these confederates) who eventually refused to continue (see the coloured curve in the graph) stopped sooner than those subjects tested without peer support (see the black curve in the graph). Moreover, with peer support, only 10 percent of the subjects eventually administered the full 450-volt shock.

One might try to explain away Milgram's findings by claiming that his experimental scenario was artificial and might not apply to normal life. However, there is evidence for dangerous obedience reactions in other settings too. Consider the study conducted by Hofling et al. (1966). Nurses were misled into obeying a doctor's orders to administer a drug in a way that would have been dangerous had the experimenter not stopped the procedure in time. Each nurse received a phone call while on regular hospital duty. A doctor whom she did not know but whose name she recognized from a listing of hospital staff said, "This is Dr. Smith from Psychiatry calling. I was asked to see Mr. Jones this morning, and I'm going to have to see him again tonight. I'd like him to have had some medication by the time I get to the ward. Will you please check your medicine cabinet and see if you have some Astroten? That's Astroten." In fact, "Astroten" is a fictitious drug that had been planted in the medicine cabinet but which was not on the hospital's stock list of approved medications. The drug was labelled "ASTROTEN — 5 mg capsules. Usual dose: 5 mg. Maximum daily dose: 10 mg." After the nurse found the drug, the doctor said, "Now will you please give Mr. Jones a dose of 20 milligrams of Astroten. I'll be up within ten minutes. I'll sign the order then, but I'd like the drug to have started taking effect." This procedure was carefully designed to lead the nurse into greater and greater commitment to act. Just as with Milgram's subjects, the person was induced to perform early easy steps, and this made it harder to resist the pressure to continue. None resisted the initial instructions, even though they didn't know the doctor and in spite of that fact that it was against regulations to take such an order over the phone. About 95% of the nurses actually started to administer the medicine, even though the dosage ordered was clearly excessive. This study revealed that results similar to those found by Milgram do occur outside the laboratory.

Milgram's research has been criticized for being unethical. Opponents claim that the experiments were misleading and stressful to the subjects. By contrast, supporters of Milgram argue that the benefits of his research have been enormous and were worth the cost of the deception he used. Awareness of the dangers of blind compliance and obedience is the first step toward the preservation of individual freedom.

We can identify five factors that contribute to obedience. First, persons of high status induce obedience. Even though the "experimenter" in Milgram's studies was actually powerless to punish subjects for disobeying, he evidently was seen to possess a high degree of status and authority. (Recall that he was dressed in a lab coat.) Second, when the authority figure "takes responsibility" for the consequences, subjects are more likely to obey. Third, a gradual escalation of demands increases obedience, probably because the person finds it difficult to draw the line clearly at some point and disobey. Fourth, once a person obeys early, moderate demands, he or she is more likely to obey later, greater demands. Apparently, people feel somewhat trapped into obeying because of their own previous behaviour. Fifth, the absence of dissenting peers increases obedience, as demonstrated by Milgram's second experiment. These five factors are described in Figure 16-9.

FIGURE 16-9 The tendency to obey: Five contributing factors

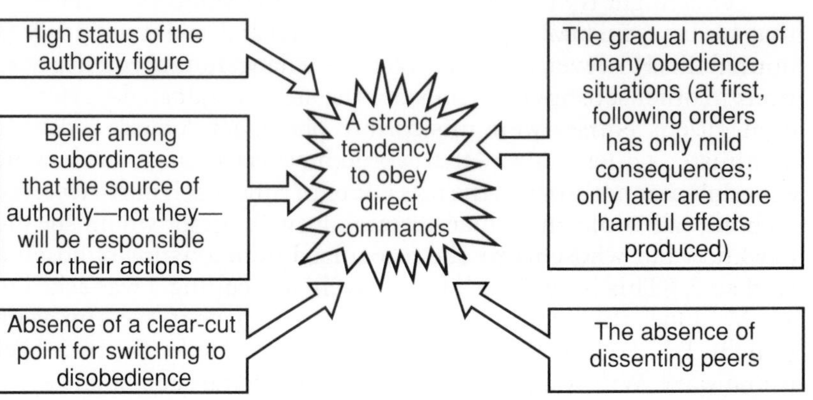

SOURCE: Adapted with permission from Allyn and Bacon, 1989.

PREJUDICE AND AUTHORITARIAN PERSONALITIES

Prejudice, stereotyping, and scapegoating

The knowledge that ordinary people can fairly easily be manipulated into performing acts they know to be wrong requires us to think through how people relate to each other as members of different groups. Our prejudices can lead us to think of some people as appropriate targets for violence, both physical and psychological. The word *prejudice* literally means "pre-judging" others. Humans base much of their reaction to others on well-organized patterns of expectations, rather than on the actual characteristics of the individual. It can be argued that this saves time and effort, because it is not possible to assess every individual one meets. However, there are enormous dangers in prejudice. It inevitably distorts reality.

Prejudice, literally the "pre-judging" of others, is strongly resistant to change.
SOURCE: Graffiti directed against Bill 101. The Gazette, January 12, 1989. Photo by Michael Dugas.

We can define **prejudice** as having three characteristics. First, it normally involves negative opinions and hostile feelings toward members of a group of people. Second, these opinions and feelings are based on inaccurate or incomplete information. Third, prejudices are extremely difficult to change, even in the face of overwhelming evidence against them. Prejudices often lead to the mistreatment of members of other groups with justifications such as, "Well, we know that people like that are (insert your favourite prejudice) anyway." Usually prejudice is negative, but of course it is possible to have unrealistically positive expectations for members of a particular group. Even this is damaging because it sets up false expectations. In either event, the individual person is not assessed accurately, and consequently, effective interaction with that person is highly unlikely.

A **stereotype** is a collection of expectations and beliefs about a certain group. A stereotype is a very powerful schema. We have often discussed *schemas* as being like a "blueprint" or expected pattern that describes our reality. It is an organized picture of what we expect to perceive. It can be so powerful that it helps determine what we do perceive, even when that involves distorting actual events and situations.

We tend to maintain our stereotypes even when they are contradicted by reality. There are several reasons for this. Probably most importantly, it is threatening to find that our belief systems are wrong. This is true even if that "belief system" involves fairly minor expectations. Suppose we have a subordinate whom we think of as lazy and irresponsible, and one day that person starts acting conscientiously and helpfully. We will have a strangely mixed reaction, probably without full awareness of what is happening. On the one hand, we will welcome this behaviour that we have always said we wanted from the person. On the other hand, we will also be threatened, because our "belief system" is being challenged. There is much evidence that under these circumstances we will subtly reinforce laziness and punish conscientiousness in order to fulfil our expectations. This is another instance in which we are likely to create a *self-fulfilling prophecy*. We want our "predictions" about the nature of reality to be true, even when they predict events we don't consciously want (Rosenthal & Rubin, 1978). If our expectations are as elaborate as a stereotype, it is even more important to us that they not be violated.

Thus, one way we protect our stereotypes is by influencing others to fit them. There are three other methods by which we try to maintain our prejudices and stereotypes. First, we apply **selective attention**, the tendency in social relations to direct our attention more toward information and events that are consistent with our existing expectations and beliefs. When a member of a minority group acts in a way we expect, it confirms our expectations and we pay attention closely—"Isn't that just like those people?" On the other hand, when the person acts inconsistently with our stereotype, there is a tendency to pay attention to other input, to selectively block out this new information. Second, we apply **selective memory**, the tendency in social relations to remember information and events that are consistent with our existing expectations and beliefs. When we perceive information that is inconsistent with our stereotypes, we are less likely to remember it. In Chapter 7, we pointed out that human memory is often inaccurately revised. We "construct" the details of our memories to fit our schemas and our other perceptions, and to avoid feelings of threat. Thus, not only is our memory selective to maintain stereotypes, it can also be distorted.

A fourth way we maintain our stereotypes and prejudices is by means of an **attributional bias**, dismissing unexpected behaviour from a member of a stereotyped group by attributing it to some unusual or impermanent cause. When we make judgements about why a person performs a particular act, we are making attributions about causes. How does the prejudiced person handle undeniable evidence against prejudice. To what cause does he or she attribute the other person's behaviour? Often a "Yeah, but . . . " attribution is used. Milton (1972) studied male police officers who had been assigned a female partner. Most of the men had to admit that the partner had done a good job, contrary to their general expectations. The evidence was overwhelming. But the evidence could be acknowledged and then explained away with a causal attribution such as, "Sure, she was good, but that's because she works so hard." The evidence is accounted for, but the stereotype that women aren't as good as men at police work can be maintained. We will discuss attributional biases further in Chapter 17.

Attributional bias enables people to retain their stereotypes in the face of disconfirming evidence.
SOURCE: Courtesy of Metropolitan Toronto Police.

The most serious danger of prejudice is that it helps rationalize **scapegoating**, the unjust treatment of minority groups. When an individual or group is frustrated, a scapegoat is often singled out for aggression. If our stereotypes let us think of some people as "less than we are" in some way, the ground is laid for racial violence and aggression.

Frustration is not the only cause of scapegoating. One theory suggests that competition can lead to scapegoating, especially when resources are scarce. In the 1800s, for example, Chinese immigrants were welcomed to the United States to help build the railroads in

Scapegoating, whether from frustration, competition, or cultural norms, has led to barbaric acts of horror.

SOURCE: Slave labourers in the Buchenwald concentration camp liberated by the Allies in 1945. Nobel Prize winner and novelist Elie Wiesel is the man whose face can be seen on the far right of the centre bunk. UPI/ Bettmann.

the West. Books and newspaper articles of the time described the strong family life of these people and praised their honesty and industriousness. After the U.S. Civil War, however, many Caucasians moved west and needed jobs. With amazing speed, the popular writings focused on how dishonest and inferior the Chinese were. Why didn't people direct their animosity against the individuals who were competing for the job, whether Chinese or Caucasian? We often don't do this because it is easier to label a group that is "them" and "we" are against them.

The role of competition in scapegoating was illustrated in a well-known experiment with twelve-year old boys attending a camp (Sherif & Sherif, 1953). As is often done with children's groups, two competing subgroups were formed, the Bulldogs and the Red Devils. As the competition was increased in the games, members of the two groups developed strong hostility toward each other. Later the researchers were able to reduce this hostility but only by giving the boys tasks in which they had to cooperate with each other to achieve the desired goals. This study should make us pause to think when we pit one group against another in order to achieve some short-term goal such as increased performance that might be stimulated by the competition. We will also pay a price in intergroup hostility. Richard Lalonde (1989) followed a hockey team through a series of eight games and found that they always portrayed the other team as being dirtier than their own team, regardless of the outcome of the games.

We have seen that frustration and competition can cause and increase prejudice. A third contributing factor is *cultural norms*. The musical *South Pacific* contains the lyrics "You've got to be taught to hate and fear. You've got to be taught from year to year, to hate all the people your relatives hate." It is no surprise that children do tend to have the same racial prejudices as their parents and are exposed to fewer opportunities to learn anything else about minorities (Ashmore & DelBoca, 1976; Stephan & Rosenfield, 1978).

Authoritarian personalities

The tendency to stereotype and to scapegoat victims is frightening, especially because under certain conditions ordinary people can be led by "the proper authorities" to commit violent acts against others. Are certain types of personalities more likely to obey authoritarian orders without questioning them? Shortly after World War II, Adorno et al. (1950) claimed that such an **authoritarian personality** did exist. These researchers further argued that an individual's personality was more important than the surrounding conditions in determining whether that person would obey authority.

Recent study has provided additional insights into the authoritarian person. In 1986, Bob Altemeyer was awarded the Prize for Behavioural Science Research from the American Association for the Advancement of Science for his research in this field, which he conducted in Canada and the United States (Altemeyer, 1988a and 1988b). He introduced the term **right-wing authoritarianism (RWA)** to refer to a set of attitudes marked by hostility which are in compliance with a society's traditions and established authorities, whether that society is communist, capitalist, or fascist. By reviewing previous research and developing a test (called the RWA Scale), Altemeyer defined three characteristics of the authoritarian personality. First, the person is relatively submissive to established authority and usually accepts its pronouncements unquestioningly. Second, the person tends to be very conventional and to value what is "proper." Third, the person will become relatively aggressive when it seems sanctioned by established authority figures.

In order to encourage more accurate self-descriptions, Altemeyer's RWA Scale is presented as a public opinion poll. It asks the degree to which the person agrees with statements such as the following:

1) "It is always better to trust the judgement of the proper authorities in government and religion."
2) "It is important to protect fully the rights of radicals and deviants."

The questions are worded in a way that an authoritarian person would strongly agree with half of them (such as (1) above) and strongly disagree with the other half (such as (2) above). People with high RWA scores tend to make harsher statements about ethnic, racial, and religious minorities. They also tend to be more tolerant of abuses of power by politicians. And they tend to impose harsher sentences in hypothetical court cases.

Altemeyer surveyed about 600 Canadian university students and many of their parents, with some startling results. He was interested in how people who scored high on the RWA Scale would differ from others in response to this hypothetical situation:

> "Suppose the Canadian government, sometime in the future, passed a law outlawing the Communist Party in Canada. Government officials then stated that the law would be effective only if it were vigorously enforced at the local level, and appealed to every Canadian to aid in the fight against Communism."
>
> This was followed by six statements, and the subjects were asked to indicate on a scale of −4 to +4 how well each statement applied to them.
>
> Would they tell their friends it was a good law? Identify any Communists they happened to know? Help the police hunt them down? Participate in an attack on the Communist headquarters if it were organized by "the proper authorities"? Endorse the use of "physical force" to make captured Communists reveal the identities of others? Support the execution of Communist leaders? (Altemeyer, 1988a, p. 33).

A solid majority of subjects said they would be unlikely to carry out these acts. But the interesting finding for our purposes was that high-RWA subjects were only *slightly* unlikely to support the "new law" actively. Altemeyer argues that these people are near the boundary between disagreeing and agreeing. A carefully planned persuasion campaign would likely sway many of them, certainly more than enough to form many "posses" or perhaps even an "elite corps" of enforcers.

Even more revealing, high-RWA subjects were more likely to support the persecution and killing of members of groups that are traditionally considered "right wing," such as the Ku Klux Klan, *if they were outlawed by the proper authorities.* In general, high-RWA persons are more likely to support the Progressive Conservative Party of Canada. However, in response to a hypothetical law in which that party was outlawed, a high-RWA person is more likely than others to "accept the 'necessity' of destroying the party . . . It is not just an authoritarian's hostility that sets him apart. It is his submissiveness —his readiness to substitute an authority's judgment, however depraved, for his own" (Altemeyer, 1988a, p. 35).

Two factors seem especially important in leading to the combination of submissiveness and aggression found with RWA. First, there is an *instigator factor* or motive that arouses the aggression. Second, there is a *disinhibitor factor* that enables the person to engage in violence. Even if very angry, most people are inhibited in some way from acting violently. Therefore, for RWA, both arousal and lack of inhibition are necessary. Research suggests that with RWA the most important instigator is *fear*, particularly the fear of the world as a dangerous place. If the person also has strong feelings of *self-righteousness*, he or she can feel justifed (disinhibited) in acting, by any means, against the dangerous forces in the world.

SPECIAL TOPIC Blind Obedience—Can It Happen Here?

The people surveyed by Milgram were sure they wouldn't follow orders to do something as destructive as committed by the subjects in his obedience experiment. Many people would like to believe that Milgram's findings were the result of sampling error. However, as we mentioned earlier, Milgram's results have been replicated many times with male and female subjects in different countries. In fact, Altemeyer (1981) reported several similar findings with both students and non-students in Canada. The experiments took the following two-part form. In the first part, subjects thought they were punishing another subject for making errors. Unlike Milgram's "teachers," these subjects were permitted to set the level of shock they thought was appropriate by choosing one of five "shock-level" switches. Also on the table in front of the subject was a small metal box with a large red pushbutton and wires running to and from the box. The button was labelled, "Danger. Very severe shock. Do not push this button unless you are instructed to do so." During the first part of the experiment no reference was made to this box after it was pointed out initially. One finding was that authoritarian subjects set higher levels of shock than others during the initial phase of the experiment. The results of the second part of the experiment were much more disconcerting. At the end of the "teaching" procedure, the experimenter said, "That concludes the experiment. It's obvious the learner hasn't been trying as hard as he should. Push the red button on your right to administer an extra strong shock as punishment for not trying." If the subject resisted, the experimenter quietly but firmly urged compliance for fifteen seconds. Within those fifteen seconds, *more than 85% of the subjects obeyed orders*, whether they were high or low RWA, whatever their religious convictions, and however their parents had raised them.

Altemeyer also administered a survey to 38 Canadian Armed Forces recruits who had just finished basic training. The questionnaire was given by an officer that the recruits did not know. Their answers were anonymous. The men were asked how they would respond in several hypothetical cases. One case read as follows:

> Suppose you are stationed near Ottawa. One day the Prime Minister declares that Canada is in a state of emergency. He orders strict censorship of all newspapers, radio and TV stations, suspends the civil liberties of Canadian citizens, and declares Parliament closed until further notice. As there are no laws giving the Prime Minister such powers, he has to rely upon the military to back him up. The military leaders agree to do so, and your unit is ordered to Parliament Hill to keep the House of Commons from meeting. Would you obey this order and move out to take up such positions? (Altemeyer, 1981, p. 274).

Here is another scenario growing out of the preceding one:

> Suppose a Member of the House of Commons attempted to cross your lines and enter the building. Your commander ordered you to place him under arrest and take him to a military prison. Would you do so? (Altemeyer, 1981, p. 275).

It is sobering to learn that 76% of the recruits said they would follow orders to shut down the House of Commons, and 92% said they would put the Member of Parliament under arrest. When members of the U.S. military fired on and killed student demonstrators at Kent State University in 1970 during protests against the Vietnam war, there was shock, outrage and disbelief. Altemeyer set up a similar situation and asked the Canadian recruits to consider the following scenario:

> Suppose a demonstration was organized to protest the closing of Parliament and a crowd of persons carrying signs and chanting slogans began to march toward your lines. The officer commanding your detachment orders them to stop or they will be fired upon, but they continue to march toward you. The officer orders you to open fire at the crowd. Would you shoot at the demonstrators? (Altemeyer, 1981, p. 275).

Sixty-three percent of the recruits said they would open fire. The findings in this whole section are frightening and humbling. Almost all of us underestimate the degree to which we would follow orders to hurt others, to discriminate, to scapegoat, and to undermine the foundations of freedom. We need to be vigilant.

SPECIAL TOPIC Reducing Intergroup Hostility and Prejudice

We hope that learning the material in this chapter will decrease your own tendency to stereotype others. To be realistic, however, it is likely that this knowledge will have only a modest impact. To change prejudice dramatically seems to require interpersonal contact with members of other groups. Stuart Cook (1979) reviewed the research and concluded that five aspects of interpersonal contact help reduce prejudice.

The most powerful factor is the one the Sherifs used to reduce hostility between the Bulldogs and Red Devils. Members of different groups need to be involved in tasks that require *cooperation* to achieve goals. They need to be interdependent rather than in competition with each other. In one important study (Aronson & Osherow, 1980), elementary school children were placed in newly racially integrated classes. Study groups were set up so that to do well on exams, members had to cooperate and support each other. Each member of a group contributed a part of various assignments. The children quickly stopped the racial slurs and "out group" attacks that had been occurring. The second factor identified by Cook was that the members of different groups should encounter each other on an *equal status*. Contact alone is not enough. In fact, extended contact between, say, Caucasians of high status and Natives of low status will tend to maintain and even increase prejudice. Third, Cook concluded that *individual contact* is essential, rather than simply being in the same larger group together. There should be opportunities to get to know the other person as a unique person. The fourth factor identified by Cook was that *social norms* should be established and promoted that encourage positive attitudes toward the other group. Finally, Cook concluded it is important that the stereotyped group frequently *exhibit behaviours that violate the stereotype.* This is most likely to happen when members of each group have similar interests.

CHAPTER SUMMARY

1. Social context and situational factors strongly influence our behaviour, as was dramatically demonstrated by the Stanford prison experiment. The study of social context and its effect on individual behaviour is the subject matter of social psychology.
2. A person's phenomenological perspective partly determines social behaviour. In self-fulfilling prophecies, our expectations of what others will do may actually encourage them to act in precisely that way. Our social schemas are complex long-lasting expectations that can save us time. However, social schemas can also cause us to misjudge particular individuals or groups of individuals. We tend to reject information that is inconsistent with our internal schemas.
3. An attitude can be thought of as a combination of beliefs, values and emotions that leads to a predisposition to act in a certain way. Research has revealed a surprisingly low correspondence between expressed attitudes and actual behaviours, except for attitudes in which we have a very strong personal investment. A need for structure tends to lead low self-monitors to act more in accordance with their attitudes.
4. According to the theory of cognitive dissonance, a conflict between attitudes and behaviour may lead to a change in attitude. Rewards that are barely sufficient to induce inconsistent actions will cause the maximum amount of attitude change. The self-perception hypothesis offers an alternative explanation to

the theory of cognitive dissonance. Studies of extrinsic reinforcement support the hypothesis that we form our attitudes by observing and perceiving our own behaviour.

5. Attitudes are formed through a socialization process. They are heavily influenced by social norms and reinforcement contingencies. Attitude change is a continuous process as individuals constantly try to influence each other. Effective persuasion depends upon (i) the source of the communication (especially its credibility), (ii) the form of the communication (including its framing), (iii) the channel through which the communication is conveyed, and (iv) the audience or target of the communication.
6. We all belong to several groups and learn various roles throughout our lives. Roles are efficient, but they may not always be in our best interests.
7. Group dynamics can lead to social loafing, social facilitation, or social inhibition. If our skills or knowledge are new or uncertain, we should try to perform alone and keep a low arousal level. Cohesiveness, an illusion of unanimity, and an illusion of invulnerability characterize the phenomenon known as groupthink.
8. Social norms, though rarely stated formally, encourage conformity. Asch performed a classic experiment in which subjects clearly violated their own perceptions in order not to deviate from the group norm. Conformity is increased through the unanimity of the group, the ambiguity of the situation, the intensity of the contact with others, being of lower status, and possessing low self-esteem. There seem to be two kinds of conformity. With external conformity, we avoid looking odd to other group members. With internal conformity, we identify with group members and internalize their attitudes and ideas. Conformity is not entirely bad. It is often necessary in order to live with others.
9. In many situations we try to have others comply with our requests. Effective strategies for inducing compliance include the foot-in-the-door technique, the door-in-the-face technique, and the low-ball technique.
10. Obedience to authority can be thought of as an extreme instance of compliance. Milgram's classic studies reveal that normal people can be induced to commit cruel deeds by an authority figure. Milgram's findings have been replicated by other studies. Five factors contribute to obedience: (i) an authority figure of high status, (ii) an authority figure who takes responsibility for whatever happens, (iii) a gradual escalation of demands, (iv) obeying earlier mild demands, and (v) the absence of dissenting peers.
11. Prejudice, literally the "pre-judging" of others, inevitably distorts reality. Stereotypes are very powerful schemas. We tend to maintain our stereotypes through self-fulfilling prophecies, selective attention, selective memory, and attributional biases. Prejudice and stereotyping often to lead to the mistreatment of others through scapegoating. Scapegoating may be increased through frustration, competition, and cultural norms.

12. People with an authoritarian personality are especially prone to obey. Altemeyer has devised the RWA scale to investigate the characteristics of such a personality. Right-wing authoritarianism is frequently promoted by fear (an instigator factor) and by self-righteousness (a disinhibitor factor).

Key Terms

Attitude A combination of beliefs, values, and emotions that leads to a predisposition to act in a particular way.

Attributional bias Dismissing unexpected behaviour from a member of a stereotyped group by attributing it to some unusual or impermanent cause.

Authoritarian personality A personality characterized by the following attitudes and behaviours: (i) submissiveness to established authority, (ii) tendency to be very conventional and value "proper" things, and (iii) aggressiveness when this seems to be sanctioned by authority figures.

Cognitive dissonance A state of conflict that occurs when attitudes and behaviours are inconsistent with each other.

Cohesiveness The strong feeling of belonging to a tightly knit group.

Compliance Behaviour that accedes to an explicit request from another person or a group.

Conformity Behaviour that coincides with the behaviour of others because of group expectations. See also *External conformity* and *Internal conformity*.

Dominant responses The best-learned responses among a group of competing possible responses.

Door-in-the-face technique A compliance-inducing technique in which one first makes an outrageous request which is denied, and then one makes a much more reasonable request.

External conformity A change of outward behaviour to conform to that of the group without changing one's thoughts and attitudes.

Extrinsic reinforcement External rewards given for behaviour.

Foot-in-the-door technique A compliance-inducing technique in which one first makes a small request and obtains compliance, and then one makes a much larger request.

Framing The way in which a message is worded.

Group Three or more people who (1) interact in a structured or regular way, (2) share common goals, and (3) have a sense of belonging to the group.

Groupthink The tendency for problem-solving to be hampered by group members going along with what they perceive to be the group opinion.

Illusion of invulnerability The sense of strength that comes from group membership, which leads members to underestimate realistic risks.

Illusion of unanimity A characteristic of groupthink in which group members incorrectly interpret each other's silence as agreement with the perceived group opinion.

Internal conformity A change of attitudes and ideas to conform to those of the group.

Low-ball technique A compliance-inducing technique in which one first obtains compliance under certain terms, and then one changes the terms to make them more stringent.

Need for structure A strong need for clarity and an intolerance of ambiguity that can inhibit the process of seeking new knowledge.

Obedience Behaviour that accedes to a direct command from another person, particularly a person in authority.

Persuasion The process by which people induce others to change their attitudes.

Phenomenological perspective The individual's subjective perception of reality.

Prejudice Literally, the act of pre-judging others. It is usually characterized by negative opinions and hostile feelings, which are based on inaccurate or incomplete information, and which are strongly resistant to change.

Reinforcement contingencies The relationship between specific behaviours and the consequences that follow.

Right-wing authoritarianism (RWA) A set of attitudes marked by hostility which are in compliance with a society's traditions and established authorities, whether that society is communist, capitalist, or fascist.

Role A set of behaviours that a group deems socially appropriate under particular circumstances.

Scapegoating The unjust treatment of minority groups.

Schema An abstract representation of a typical object, procedure, or event that we build from our knowledge and experiences of the world around us.

Selective attention In social relations, the tendency to direct attention more toward information and events that are consistent with our existing expectations and beliefs.

Selective memory In social relations, the tendency to remember information and events that are consistent with our existing expectations and beliefs.

Self-fulfilling prophecy The tendency to subtly reinforce in others behaviour we expect.

Self-perception hypothesis In cognitive dissonance, the theory that we form our attitudes simply by observing and perceiving our own behaviour.

Situational factors Influences in the current environment that affect behaviour, as distinct from individual internal tendencies to act in certain ways.

Social context All facets of any situation in which people interact.

Social facilitation The phenomenon of improved performance of dominant responses when in the presence of others.

Social inhibition The phenomenon of diminished performance of non-dominant responses when in the presence of others.

Social loafing The phenomenon of diminished performance resulting from the diffusion of responsibility in a group.

Social norms Rules and standards for behaviour established and held by groups for their members.

Social psychology The discipline that studies individual behaviour within the social context.

Social schema A schema specifically about other individuals or groups of individuals.

Stereotype A collection of expectations and beliefs about a certain group.

Suggested Readings

Alcock, J. E., Carment, D. W., & Sadava, S. W. (1990). *A textbook of social psychology*, 2nd ed. Scarborough, Ontario: Prentice-Hall Canada Inc. This excellent textbook is probably the best bet as a next step in the study of social psychology. It contains considerable Canadian content and covers important issues that seldom appear in textbooks, such as bilingualism and the impact of Canadian law on behaviour.

Altemeyer, B. (1988) *Enemies of freedom: Understanding right-wing authoritarianism*. San Francisco: Josey-Bass. A provocative book that is especially interesting to Canadian readers because much of the research was done in Canada.

Aronson, E. (1984). *The social animal*, 4th ed. San Francisco: W. H. Freeman. One of the classic textbooks on social psychology. It treats the topics of this chapter in more depth but it still gives a good overview.

Brown, R. (1986). *Social psychology,* 2nd ed. New York: Free Press. Another widely used textbook for more advanced social psychology courses.

Cialdini, R. B. (1984). *Influence: How and why people agree to do things.* New York: Morrow. (In paperback as *Influence: science and practice.* Glenview, IL: Scott, Foresman.) A practical book that attempts to apply the knowledge gained from social psychological research to actual instances of persuasion.

Milgram, S. (1974). *Obedience to authority.* New York: Harper & Row. The classic and complete description of Milgram's work. He also discusses the social implications of his findings and the ethical problems of doing research such as his on obedience.

CHAPTER 17

SOURCE: Photo by Kathy Bellesiles.

Person to Person

SOURCE: *Single Slices* by Peter Kohlsaat. Copyright 1987 Los Angeles Times Syndicate. Reprinted with permission.

WE HAVE SEEN how powerful social influences are. In many ways the most distinctive features of being human come from our relations with others. Now let's look at the most personal kinds of social relations, our face-to-face interactions with others. These range from first impressions and fleeting encounters to the compelling grip of love. As a friend of ours said, "It's awful. There is nothing more difficult than making a relationship work. But you can't just quit, because there is nothing more important." The complexities and mysteries of relationships are beyond our complete understanding. However, psychology does provide some useful information about the person-to-person aspect of life. We will start with some basic processes and move on to relationships that affect our lives more directly.

PERSON PERCEPTION

An important area in social psychology is that of **social perception** or **person perception**, the processes by which individuals form impressions of others. Two basic questions arise here. How do we form impressions of others? And how do we learn about the motives and reasons for the actions of others?

Person perception is a special case of other forms of perception that we have dealt with in this book. The same sensory and perceptual processes operate. All perception involves our interpretation of the concrete data from our environment. Just as visual perceptions can be distorted, so can social perceptions. We only know the concrete sensory data through our inferences, theories, and speculations. These are what form our impressions of others and our attributions for their behaviour. Thus, our impressions and atrributions can be distorted and may need correction.

When we perceive other people, we have a strong tendency to form *social schemas* (as discussed in the previous chapter). We develop an overall, integrated picture that we use to categorize each individual.

First impressions

First impressions are very important. To form our first impressions of people, we tend to focus on their looks, what they wear, the circumstances we see them in, the first interaction we have with them, how we are introduced to them, and other superficial cues. For example, attractiveness is a very important but superficial cue. Researchers have found that people who are rated highly on attractiveness are also seen as smarter, more social, stronger, and more sensuous than unattractive people (Dion, Berscheid, & Walster, 1972). A person who wears glasses may be perceived as more intellectual than a person who does not. Even first names may affect what people first think of another person and expect of him or her. Such superficial initial information is one of the clearest examples of a **social schema**, a schema specifically about other individuals or groups of individuals. Our social schemas are complex, long-lasting expectations that we use as cognitive "blueprints" to organize our thoughts about other people. We all have powerful cognitive schemas that are **stereotypes**, collections of expectations and beliefs about groups in society (Anderson & Klatzky, 1987). Think of a nurse, a football player, a homosexual, a police officer, a doctor, and you will be able to focus on your own image or stereotype of members of these groups. These stereotypes are over-generalizations that may in some circumstances be true. However, they are inevitably inaccurate for many people who are members of the particular groups. You are using schemas from your personal repertoire of schemas. When schemas are accurate, they are helpful as mental shorthand devices. But when they are inaccurate, they are potentially dangerous and may lead to and foster prejudicial attitudes.

Impression formation is the process by which we form a picture or series of judgments about other people. Research has demonstrated that first impressions play a large role in impression formation (Luchins, 1957). The phenomenon that one's first impressions of others carry a powerful influence that is difficult to change has been labelled the **primacy effect**. The first information we have about someone biases later impressions. One reason is that we are usually quite attentive when we first meet somebody. Thus, this first impression may form the kernel around which a schema for a person is developed. These schemas are difficult to change because they develop so automatically. Frequently, the expectations that are developed support a pre-existing stereotype. These expectations in turn lead to behaviour that is self-fulfilling. As we learned in Chapter 16, we often act in ways that influence others to behave as we expect, thus "confirming" our first impressions through self-fulfilling prophesies.

The primacy effect is especially powerful for negative first impressions (Rothbart & Park, 1986). For example, a long-lasting undesirable impression can be made by telling one lie, whereas a good impression usually requires many instances of truthfulness and can more easily be destroyed. A good image is hard to earn and easy to lose. A bad one is easy to get and hard to shake.

Impression formation

Not only do we have first impressions that are difficult to change, we also have social schemas about how certain personality traits and dynamics go together. In particular, we have **prototypes**, our specific schemas for types of persons (Mayer & Bower, 1986). And we have **implicit personality theories**, our beliefs about what personality characteristics occur together in people (Schneider, 1973). In other words, we have expectations of what qualities go with other qualities. For example, we might believe that if a person is friendly, he or she will also be generous, good-natured, honest, and fair. We might also believe that somebody who is rotund will be gregarious, happy, and boisterous. These implicit theories help us to process information about social perception, as well as remember it and have it accessible for retrieval when required. They are necessary because it takes too much time and mental work to "individuate" each person (Hamilton & Trollier, 1986). Our implicit theories provide the memory structures and organization to help us make sense out of a complex, fast-moving world. However, there is some cost involved because our theories can lead to inaccuracies.

An experiment by Snyder and Uranowicz (1978) demonstrates the negative consequences of our implicit personality theories. Students read a lengthy story about a woman named Betty Kay. Following their reading, one group of subjects was told that the woman was heterosexual, another group was told that she was homosexual, and a third group was told nothing about her sexual orientation. Later, subjects were asked to report on the story they had read. The results showed that the information remembered was primarily consistent with what they were told about the woman's sexual orientation. In other words, what they remembered was schema-consistent. Errors of memory were also consistent with the prototype they formed. Thus, those who were led to believe the woman was homosexual "remembered" information that was consistent with their homosexual schema but that was not necessarily in the story at all. Other experiments have shown that we remember more about people if we can use schemas to assist and organize the information than if we are given a set of traits and descriptions to remember. It is easy to remember certain information about a person who has been identified as a bank manager, because all we need to do is pull out our bank-manager prototype when it comes time for recall. We do this at the cost of actually "manufacturing" some of our memories (Asch & Zukier, 1984). McFarland and Ross (1987) had subjects rate their dating partners on personal traits such as honesty, dependability, and sociability. The subjects made the same ratings two months later and then tried to remember their first set of ratings. Not surprisingly, those who rated their partners more negatively also inaccurately remembered the first ratings as being more negative that they actually were. Those who were more positive about their partners also remembered the initial ratings incorrectly, but they erred in the positive direction. The point is that the subjects distorted their memories and reconstructed them in a way that was more consistent with present feelings. We explained in Chapter 7 that such selective memory is a common phenomenon. It certainly distorts our perceptions of others.

In general, we can distinguish four stages in the process of impression formation. First, we engage in **initial encoding**, during which information about another person is transformed into an internal representation and becomes part of our cognitive system. Second, we compare this new information with our current social schemas through **elaborative encoding**. That is, we elaborate or expand on our initial impression. Third, we combine our new information and previous social schemas into a consistent whole through **integration**.

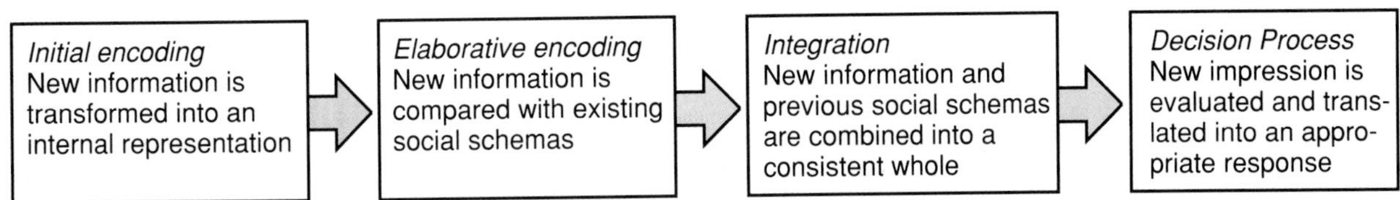

SOURCE: Adapted with permission from Allyn and Bacon, 1989.

FIGURE 17-1 The process of impression formation

Finally, in the fourth stage, we evaluate our new impression, and through a **decision process** we translate it into an appropriate response (e.g., a rating, a smile, or some overt action). See Figure 17-1.

Attributions of causality

After we have formed an impression of persons, we begin to evaluate their motives or reasons for their actions. Why did they compliment us? What do they want from us? What are their motives? The essential question here is "Why?" We want to come to some understanding of the meaning and causes of their behaviour. The study of causes, or attributions of causality, has been a well-researched area of social psychology (Heider, 1958). **Attributions of causality** may be defined as the process by which we attempt to infer the traits, motives, and intentions of other people from our observations of their overt behaviour. Here we are developing explanations for what caused a person to behave in a particular way.

In any interaction, all we actually see are behaviours. We can only infer or speculate about the causes of the behaviour. We see a young, frazzled parent in a supermarket, with a child having a tantrum in a shopping cart. The parent becomes agitated and then hits the child on the hand for upsetting a display of produce. That's the behaviour. What is the cause? What reasons might we speculate regarding the parent's actions, or the child's actions for that matter? Do we make attributions about the parent's authoritarian personality or about the child being manipulative (dispositional attributions)? Or do we speculate about long line-ups and over-tiredness (situational attributions)? On one hand, we could try to look inside the actors of this drama and search for causes in their personality or *disposition*, or we could look for causes in the particular environment or *situation*. In general, we can distinguish between (1) **dispositional determinants**, causes within a person for that person's behaviour, and (2) **situational determinants**, causes in the environment for a person's behaviour.

The process of assigning or attributing causes for behaviour pervades our own interactions. Although we never really know the causes of others' actions, we act as if we do.

Rules for making attributions

In assigning causes to actions, we make use of a number of rules that guide us in our decision-making. We speculate about causes by viewing effects. In our example of the child in the supermarket, the child's behaviour is the effect. We might speculate that the adult's poor parenting skills is the cause. An important rule is the **co-variation rule**, based upon our beliefs that particular events tend to occur together, or co-vary. Kelley (1967, 1973) has outlined three important components that assist in judging co-variation: distinctiveness, consensus, and consistency. *Distinctiveness* is the extent to which the effect occurs only in the presence of the speculated cause. In our supermarket example, distinctiveness would be high if the child's tantrum occurred only with that particular parent and not with the other parent or other adults. *Consistency* is the extent to which the particular effect occurs when the presumed cause is present. In our example, consistency would be high if the misbehaviour occurred every time this parent was present. *Consensus* is the extent to which the presumed cause will have the same effect on other people. In our example, if other people demonstrate poor parenting skills, then the same effect should result: their children will misbehave in supermarkets.

According to Kelley, we use the components of co-variance to decide between internal and external causes. When we observe the combination of low distinctiveness, high consistency, and low consensus, then we tend to attribute the cause to dispositional determinants. When we observe the combination of high distinctiveness, high consistency, and high consensus, then we tend to attribute the cause to situational determinants. See Figure 17-2.

FIGURE 17-2 Use of co-variance components in attributions of causality, according to Kelley

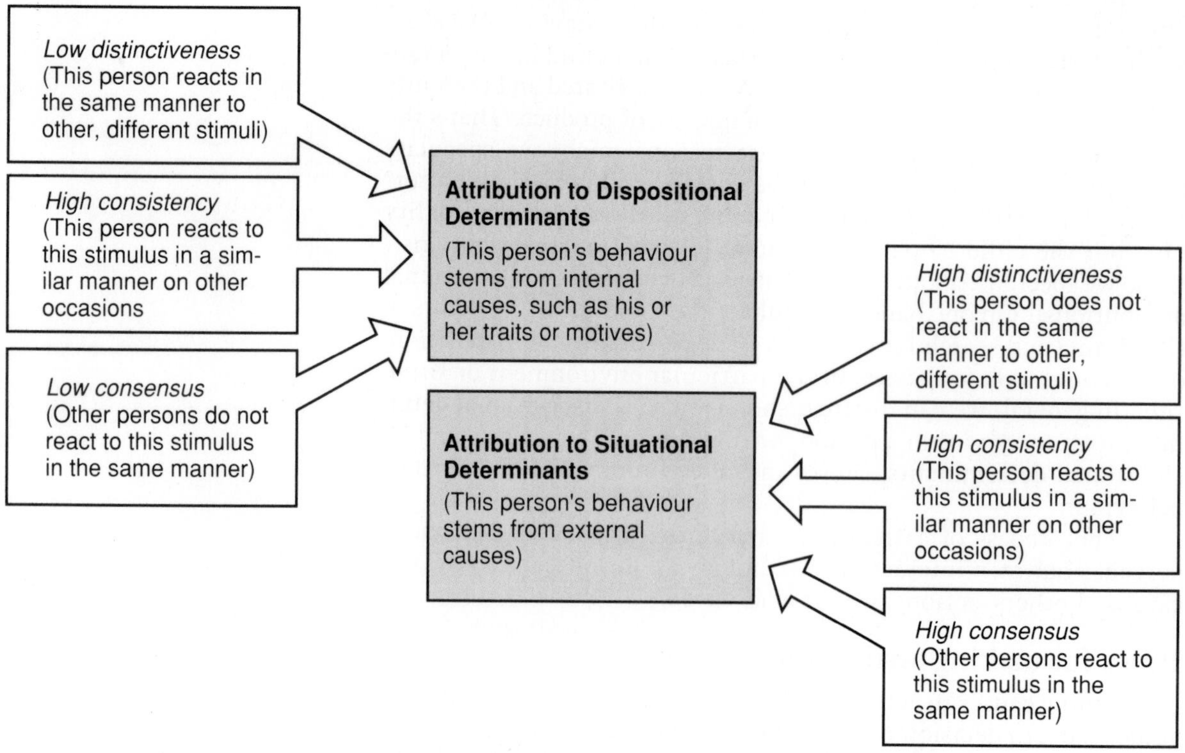

SOURCE: Adapted with permission from Allyn and Bacon, 1989.

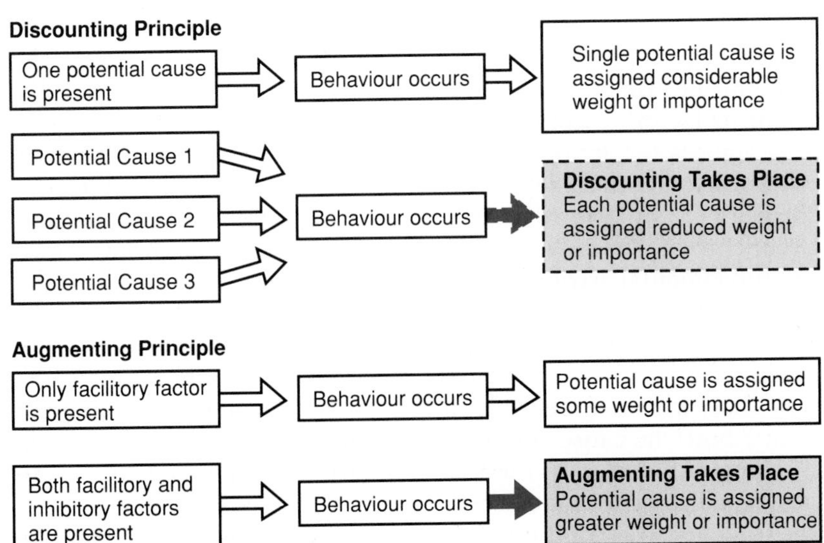

SOURCE: Adapted with permission from Allyn and Bacon, 1989.

FIGURE 17-3 Discounting and augmenting: Two basic principles of causal attribution

Often we must try to understand the causes of someone's behaviour on the basis of only a single incident. In such cases, Kelley (1967, 1973) suggests that we employ two strategies. According to the **discounting principle**, we tend to reduce the importance of any potential cause of another person's behaviour to the extent that other plausible causes are also present. Suppose a friend of ours is grouchy one day. If we know that he stayed up all night studying, then we will assign considerable weight to his lack of sleep as the cause of his grouchy behaviour. But if, in addition, we also know that he recently broke up with his girlfriend and that he is often moody, we will assign each potential cause considerably less weight. The second strategy is called the **augmenting principle**. When both a facilitory factor and an inhibitory factor are present, we tend to assign greater importance to a potential cause. Suppose a friend of ours says she is hungry and then crosses a dangerous street to get some food. We will tend to place great emphasis on hunger as the cause of her behaviour because she performed it despite the danger (an inhibitory factor). See Figure 17-3.

Although these principles are helpful, our ability to make accurate attributions about the causes of others' behaviour is far from high. But that doesn't stop us from making attributions all the time. Despite the fact that we really do not know what causes behaviour, we seldom suspend judgment and rarely conclude that we don't know why another person is acting in a particular way.

Attribution errors and biases

Jones and Harris (1967) asked subjects to listen to speeches presenting arguments for and against racial segregation. Subjects were told that the speakers were given no personal choice about the side that they were to take in the debate. The subjects nevertheless attributed the speaker's position to be his or her own. Overlooking the explicit situational determinant, they made a dispositional or internal attribution. The subjects in this experiment failed to make use of the discounting principle in attributing causation, even though the "discounting factor" was made clear.

Causes for actions are commonly attributed to dispositional determinants rather than to situational determinants. The tendency to overlook situational factors and to make internal attributions occurs frequently and is a powerful phenomenon. It has been termed the **fundamental attribution error** (Ross, 1977).

We respond to circumstances—others are just that way. The fundamental attributional error has been found to be most powerful when we are attributing causes to the behaviour of others. It is much less likely when we are explaining our own behaviour. The tendency to attribute the causes of one's own behaviour to situational determinants rather than to internal dispositions is known as the **actor-observer bias** (Jones and Nisbett, 1971). For example, it is not unusual for students to attribute their own poor performance on exams to such factors as lack of effort, difficulty of the test, or not enough preparation time (situational determinants). However, they attribute similar poor performances of their colleagues on the same exams to internal or dispositional causes, such as lack of skill, lack of knowledge, or lack of intelligence.

The actor-observer bias is partly a function of perceptual salience (what is prominent or sticks out). To ourselves, the actors, the environment is salient when we look for the causes of our own behaviour. But when we observe the behaviour of another, that person is the most salient stimulus we perceive. This resembles the perceptual principle of figure versus ground. Here, the other person is the salient figure and the situation is the less important background. Taylor and Fiske (1975) have shown that salience is a factor that determines a perceptual figure and ground for causal attributions. In their experiment, subjects observed two individuals in conversation. Despite the fact that the speakers were equally involved in conversation, subjects differed dramatically in terms of whom they attributed the conversational control to. The differential attribution was a function of which of the two speakers the subject was closer to and could see most readily. The speaker who was most visible was most salient. This may have relevance for getting due credit for work done. In teamwork efforts, the member who is most salient (for example, by virtue of presenting the work) may get more credit than is justified.

There are other forms of biases that distort the attributional process. Because we all use different, personally idiosyncratic social schemas when we observe interactions, we have different memory structures with which to organize our experience. This can lead to **egocentric** (or **self-serving**) **recall**, which is inaccurate memory that serves the interests of the person doing the remembering. Couples know this phenomenon all too well when each person remembers a particular argument quite differently (Ross & Sicoly, 1979).

Among troubled couples, spouses tend to attribute the other person's negative behaviour to causes that are both dispositional (internal) and stable (long-lasting). For example, she broke the lamp "because she is filled with hate." Positive actions are attributed to causes that are both situational (external) and temporary (short-lived). For example, he was pleasant "because his team won last night." Happily married couples tend to do just the opposite (Bradbury & Fincham, 1988; Hanson, 1989).

Another bias in attributing causation is the **just world bias**, the belief that people get what they deserve (Lerner, Miller, & Holmes, 1976). If the world is just—if wrongdoing is punished and good deeds are rewarded—then we feel in control of our own destiny. This bias helps to explain our tendency to attribute disasters and catastrophes to some action of the victim. Frequently we hear people say "It's not going to happen to me," but many of the tragedies that do strike people are random, senseless, and could happen to anyone. When they do happen to others, we distance ourselves from the event, proclaiming that we are more careful; we wouldn't be out there at that time; we are quicker, better drivers; or we wouldn't be in that bad neighbourhood, for example. This is an unfortunate bias because it often leads to blaming victims for their misfortunes.

ALTRUISM: PEOPLE HELPING PEOPLE

Making personal sacrifices for the welfare of others is a common human act that seldom receives attention. It isn't as interesting as tragedy and cruelty, but in many ways, altruism is the cement that holds society together. We can define **altruism** as behaviour in which time, energy, or money is given to others without obvious reward to the giver. Altruistic behaviour is an important topic in psychology. We won't try to cover the complex issues of why parents sometimes even sacrifice their lives for their children or why a person might devote a lifetime to easing the pain of the dying. We suspect that there is much here beyond our current understanding. We will focus on the social psychology of individual acts of helping, particularly on **bystander intervention** — the actions of individuals when they encounter others who are in emergency situations.

John M. Darley.
SOURCE: John M. Darley.

Probably no other area of psychology grew so clearly out of one historical incident. In the early hours of the morning of March 13, 1964, Kitty Genovese was walking to her apartment in Queens, New York. A man attacked her with a knife, and she screamed repeatedly for help. Thirty-eight people heard her screams, many turned on their lights, and in one apartment they turned off the lights so they could see better. But no one came to her help. No one even phoned the police until after the attacker had stabbed the screaming woman, run away, returned to stab her some more, and sexually molested her. This all took more than a half hour, during which Kitty continued to call for help until she died. There was a horrified outcry in the popular press, and the notion of *bystander apathy* became a part of our language. Many people concluded that part of the modern human condition is a numb, uncaring, indifferent disregard for others, especially in big cities such as New York.

Partially in response to this incident, Darley and Latané began a long and revealing series of studies that showed that many factors determine whether bystanders will give help or not. It wasn't just numbness or indifference that led Kitty Genovese's neighbours not to act. In fact, many of the neighbours later expressed distress and confusion, saying things such as, "I just don't know" when asked why they hadn't at least phoned the police. They seemed almost to watch with paralyzed fascination. Latané and Darley (1976) described them as "unable to act but unwilling to turn away."

There have since been many demonstrations of bystander apathy. Therefore, much as we might like, we can't write off the Genovese case as an isolated incident. For example, Takooshian and Bodinger (1982) had students commit over 200 "burglaries" from a locked car on a busy New York street. To prevent legal trouble, each "thief" carried proof of ownership of the car being broken into. However, to bystanders it looked like a crime when the person "cased" a row of cars, forced the door on one with a piece of wire, removed a large valuable object, locked the door, and hurried away. Only six people ever questioned what was happening, and three of these were police officers. In similar experiments held in a number of other cities in Canada and the U.S., bystanders intervened more often, but still only about 10% of the time.

This series of photos was taken during the "robberies" staged in Takooshian and Bodinger's experiments. Most bystanders simply ignored or quietly watched the "burglars."
SOURCE: Courtesy Harold Takooshian.

Factors that inhibit people from helping

Many factors influence the decision of whether to give help.
SOURCE: Dick Hemingway.

If we can understand the factors that inhibit or facilitate helping behaviour, we have a chance of increasing altruism. In fact, we have reason to hope that reading this chapter will increase the likelihood that you will give help. In one study, undergraduates were divided into three groups who either heard a lecture on altruism research, saw a film about it, or received no information on the topic. Two weeks later, each subject was walking with another person (a confederate in the experiment) when they came upon a man lying in a hallway. The confederate acted indifferent to the situation. Only 25% of those who had not heard the lecture or seen the film offered help, but almost 50% of the others did (Beaman et al., 1978).

The prospect of risks

It is seldom real indifference that causes a bystander not to offer help. The inhibiting factor of which the bystander is probably most aware is the genuine risk involved in helping. There could be physical danger involved. Intervening might result in entanglement in legal proceedings. If the situation has been misinterpreted, the helper might look foolish or even arouse attack and resentment from the "victim." Moreover, few people have the skills or confidence to handle the unpredictable events that might happen in emergencies. All of these factors could be operating at different times. However, evidence indicates that there are also more subtle conditions that affect helping behaviour, conditions of which the potential helper is usually unaware. One of Kitty Genovese's neighbours could have placed an anonymous phone call to the police and not been exposed to any of these risks. When they later tried to explain why they had not, saying, "I don't know why; I just don't know," they were revealing a lack of awareness of the causes of their own behaviour. What might some of those causes have been?

Interpreting the need for help

Two events must happen before we define a situation as an *emergency* that calls for action (Darley & Latané, 1968). First, we have to notice the event. One powerful social norm is that we respect the privacy of others. We don't stare at people. In many circumstances, we turn our attention inward, stare straight ahead, and tune out the events around us. This is more likely to occur in a crowd, which gives us a clue to one of the most common causes of bystander nonintervention. In general, *the presence of other people diminishes helping behaviour*. This has been called the **bystander effect**.

Second, even after we notice an unusual event, we have to interpret it accurately as an emergency. The presence of others often interferes with this. If we see smoke coming out of a vent in the wall, we likely will go for help or take some other action. But what if we were one of three people in the room, and the others glanced at the smoke and went on chatting or reading with apparent indifference? We would be more likely to interpret the smoke as harmless. Not wanting to look foolish, we would also chat and read. The other people might also be interpreting our overt indifference as evidence of there being no problem here. We will have developed **group ignorance** or **pluralistic ignorance**. This is exactly what happened in one experiment (Latané & Darley, 1968). Subjects alone in the room reported the smoke 75% of the time, but fewer than 13% of those in small groups did so. The experimenters ended the procedure after six minutes, but by this time the room was full of smoke. The subjects in small groups rationalized to themselves that it must be smog or steam or something else "safe."

Because interpreting whether a situation is an emergency is a major determinant of helping, it is no surprise that bystander intervention is less likely in ambiguous situations. "Those screams could just be kids playing. Who wants to look like a fool?" Twenty-five witnesses passively watched a rape in which the woman screamed for help. Later one said, "We thought . . . it might be her boyfriend" (Shotland & Goodstein, 1984).

Diffusion of responsibility

Social norms and group ignorance are not the only ways that the presence of others inhibits helping behaviour. Some situations are undeniably interpreted as emergencies, and yet if others are present, an individual is less likely to act. The responsibility is spread around so each person can think that someone else will step in or that someone probably already had acted. This phenomenon is called **diffusion of responsibility**.

Darley and Latané (1968) demonstrated this tendency by means of another experiment. Subjects were told that they would be part of a discussion of personal problems students were experiencing. Each person in the discussion would take turns talking for two minutes into a microphone. Supposedly the privacy of an individual booth would encourage subjects to make more personal disclosures. The only microphone that would be turned on at any one time was that of the person speaking, and the experimenter would not be listening to the discussion. In fact, all the speakers were tape recordings except for the one who was the actual subject. At his first turn, one of the "other subjects" disclosed that he had seizures. During his second turn, this "subject" made noises as though he was having a seizure and begged the others to help him. The situation was set up so that the subject knew that there was an "emergency" and knew that the experimenter could not be aware of it. There was no way to know how "other subjects" were reacting. The actual subject only knew how many "other subjects" there were. If the subject thought this was a two-person experiment, and he or she was the only person who knew about the problem, 85% reported the emergency. If the subject thought there were three subjects in the group, about 60% took action. If the subject thought the group had six members, only 30% tried to help. Diffusion of responsibility enables each member of a group to justify not acting.

The bystander's emotional state

Research has established that a person who is in a good mood is more likely to help others. Alice Isen (Isen, 1970; Isen & Levin, 1972) demonstrated this in several ways. In one experiment, she dropped a bag of groceries near a pay phone in a parking lot. If a potential helper had just found an unexpected coin in the phone, he or she was more likely to help pick up the groceries. In other experiments, people who thought they had just performed well on a task gave more money to a collection and were more likely to help a person carrying an armload of books than were those who thought they had done poorly.

On the other hand, people under stress are less likely to give help. Milgram (1970) suggested that city people are less helpful than small-town people for several reasons. One important reason is the stress of the constant bombardment of stimulation in big cities. In order to survive, the person must shut out much of what happens. This makes it less likely that an emergency will even be perceived. Even within one city, there is a relationship between the level of stimulation and level of helping (Korte, Ypma, & Toppen, 1975).

Why people help

Despite the potential power of inhibitory factors, they are not always present and they do not always determine how a bystander will act. People do help others under certain circumstances. Piliavin, Rodin, and Piliavin (1969) set up a situation that was unambiguous and where responsibility was clear. The results were that people did give help — on the New York subway, no less. (When we contrast this study with the ones we discussed above, it is even clearer that "apathy" is not the main reason that bystanders often fail to help.) Two female experimenters sat in the subway car to record results while two male researchers stood in the car to play out the experimental scenario. One of the men staggered, fell to the floor, and lay staring at the ceiling until he received help from a bystander. If no one else helped him, the second experimenter eventually helped the fallen man to his feet. Sometimes the "victim" appeared drunk, whereas at other times he carried a cane. In some instances the "victim" was white, and in others he was black.

The experiment was designed to minimize the situational factors that inhibit helping behaviour. It was obviously an emergency. Because no one was helping the man, it was difficult for the bystanders to prolong any diffusion of responsibility. The majority of the time, a bystander tried to help the man. The race of the helper and helpee made little difference. When the "victim" had a cane, he received help quickly well over 90% of the time. Even when he seemed and smelled drunk, somebody tried to help about 50% of the time. Under the right circumstances, people do help. Let us now consider some of the theories that try to explain why people help others.

Belief in a just world

In our discussion of attributions of causality, we saw that the just world bias can lead people to blame victims for the misfortune that befalls them. If life is just and people get what they deserve, then victims must have done something to deserve their misfortunes.

There is a positive side to holding this type of belief, however. It can motivate people to try to restore fairness when they see injustice, including the injustice of suffering from a lack of help. **Belief in a just world** is a motive for altruism in which the helping person believes that such behaviour will be rewarded in some way. Zuckerman (1975) found that students who believed strongly in a just world were more likely to volunteer to read to blind persons than were other students *if* it was shortly before a final exam. But they were not more likely to volunteer if the exam was months away. Apparently the students believed at some level that doing good would be rewarded in the near future, by better performance on an upcoming exam.

Social exchange theory

They may not have been aware of it, but the students in Zuckerman's experiment were making a deal with the world. They were implicitly exchanging the help for others for benefit to themselves. According to the **social exchange theory**, people act altruistically because the social world operates like a market of equal exchanges between people. In other words, altruistic behaviour is implicitly some kind of exchange of benefits. This idea is an outgrowth of the theory that people do what they are *reinforced* for doing. Thus, altruistic behaviour occurs because it is somehow reinforced. The process is complex, but one example would involve the **norm of reciprocity**, the social norm that people should exchange social benefits fairly equally (Brown, 1986). You get back what you give to others. Reciprocity is a principle of social interaction that we are taught from a very early age. "If you do that for me, then I'll do this for you." If a person consistently receives benefits (e.g., acceptance, praise, or later rewards) for being helpful to others, then being helpful becomes a very strongly learned behaviour. It eventually becomes a *secondary reinforcer* itself. It feels good and satisfying to be helpful, even when there is no obvious reward.

In a sense, then, altruism is ultimately selfish. It may be true that the most gratifying life is a love-centred life. But it is important to see that *selfish* does not always mean **egoistic**, or self-serving and self-focused for the immediate benefit of the self (Batson et al., 1986). We can discriminate between (1) egoistic helping behaviour, which is designed to curry favour or gain immediate benefits and (2) true altruism, which is designed to benefit the *other* person without any clear "payback." True altruism is more likely to occur between people with an established relationship, but it can also happen between complete strangers (Batson, 1987).

Hans Selye (1976) coined the term **altruistic egoism** to describe the theory that altruistic behaviour ultimately serves the individual's own interests in very important ways. It keeps the person connected to others in mutually supportive ways. And being connected in relationships is strongly correlated with longer life and better health. In fact, some evidence indicates that men who do volunteer work live longer than average and that men engaged in hostile competitiveness live shorter than average (Growald and Luks, 1988).

Is helpfulness a trait?

Much of our discussion to this point in the chapter suggests that whether individuals help or don't help depends largely on the nature of the situation—on its degree of ambiguity and on the presence or absence of others. Nevertheless, many people commonly consider certain individuals to be "helpful people" (self-sacrificing) and others to be "unhelpful people" (markedly selfish). Is helpfulness a trait? Studies have tried to find personality differences between those who help and those who don't. However, even tests and questionnaires designed to tap social traits such as "humanitarian concern" and "responsibility" have not identified those likely to help in a real crisis situation (Huston et al., 1981). The evidence to date suggests that helpfulness is primarily a response to situational demands.

Albert Schweitzer (1875–1965) devoted much of his life to helping others in Africa. Was he innately self-sacrificing?
SOURCE: The Bettmann Archive.

Is there a biological basis for helping?

Sociobiologists are theorists who stress the inborn biological roots of human and animal behaviour. They argue that there must be some inherited tendency that supports helping behaviour (Wilson, 1978). Humans and animals often act in ways that may hurt the individual but are beneficial to the species as a whole. This would have considerable survival value for the species. In terms of evolution, a genetic tendency toward altruism would tend to survive and be passed on, as long as it supported helping behaviour that contributed to the survival of close genetic relatives of the "martyr." Some honeybees defend the nest by sacrificing their lives. Animals expose themselves to predators by giving warning cries that protect the herd or flock. It is not clear how such behaviour could be inherited, but it is compelling to note how easy it is for animals and humans to learn to sacrifice themselves.

When helping can hurt

Sometimes our attempts to help others leave both them and us worse off, in spite of our good intentions. We encounter this frequently in mental hospitals. The term **hospitalism** has been used to describe the increasing helplessness of being unable to function outside a hospital following a period of being cared for by others. But this sort of helplessness is not confined to hospitals. Relationships can be harmful if one member is consistently the helper and one the helpee, no matter how "good" the helper thinks he or she is being.

Being helpful is usually positive and is an essential part of relationships, but it is important to recognize the subtle messages that excessive helping communicates (Brickman et al., 1982). First, we imply that the other person lacks competence. Every time we rush to do something that another person could do, we deprive that person of a chance to learn some control of the environment. One example that might seem trivial is that of men holding doors open for women "to show respect." How does that show respect? It suggests that women need to be taken care of. The sensible arrangement would be for the person closest to the door or most able to open it to do so.

Second, if the helper does too much, the other person may learn to attribute success to others. This can be discouraging and self-defeating. In psychotherapy, good therapists don't fix things for the client. Instead, they treasure the moments when the client says, "I did this myself." Helpers often subtly encourage dependency by doing too much and then feel critical of the other person for not being stronger.

As we said in Chapter 13 (Stress), excessive helping leads to *professional burnout* when the helper reaches the limits of his or her resources. Many people become social workers, psychologists, psychiatrists, or probation counsellors out of a desire to help others. This is a laudable motive, but it carries with it the danger of trying to hold back the tide singlehandedly. The helper often does not balance personal needs with the demands created by the needs of others. The helper who can't say "no" to "just one more person" is headed for trouble. As soon as that person is added to the caseload, we can find a hundred more whose need is at least as compelling. Unless helpers are prepared for this reality, they quickly become discouraged and often withdraw emotionally from their clients (Edelwich and Brodsky, 1980; Cherniss, 1986).

In personal relationships, this same kind of emotional distancing can result from resentment—perhaps partially unconscious—in which the "helpful partner" tries to give and give and may even resist attempts by the other person to reciprocate. Eventually, though, the imbalance becomes the basis for anger at the "unfairness" of the relationship.

Is aggression an instinctual drive or is it a response that one learns through social reinforcement? SOURCE: Canada Wide/Tim McKenna.

Aggression: People Hurting People

Aggression and violence dominate much of society's thinking and pervade our entertainment media. Aggression and violence seem to be on the increase in personal relationships, in street crime, in international terrorism, and in certain global conflicts. It is vital that we understand aggression and ways to reduce it if we hope to survive. Unfortunately, there are two competing theories of aggression that completely contradict each other. We need to figure out which is the more accurate explanation of aggression. The conclusions we would draw about ways to reduce violence are very different depending on which theory we use. In fact, if we follow the advice of one, the other predicts that we will increase violence rather than decrease it.

According to the **catharsis theory of aggression**, aggression is an instinctual drive. It builds up inside the person and needs periodic release to prevent its reaching the point of explosion. By contrast, according to the **social learning theory of aggression**, aggression is behaviour that results from one's learning history and develops through social reinforcement. If we accept this theory, then we will conclude that being aggressive does not act to reduce aggression by releasing it. Aggression will lead to more aggression.

Before we go into these opposing views, let us try to define aggression. As is so often the case, a concept that seems fairly easy to define is not. One old standard definition is that **aggression** is behaviour intended to deliver harm to another organism. We can trace this back to the definition of aggression given by Dollard et al. (1939): "a response having for its goal the injury of a living organism." We would all agree that aggression delivers harm. But it is quite another matter to agree on the *intentions* of the individual. Intentions and awareness are on a continuum. Is it aggression the third time you accidentally shut the kitchen drawer on your brother's thumb? You apologize—we suspect you "sort of" meant to do it, but you're not sure about that.

Another problem arises concerning behaviour aimed at damaging nonliving objects. Is it aggression if a man stubs his toe on a chair and starts swearing and kicking the chair? It certainly looks aggressive, but the target is not a living organism. We might argue that it was an instance of "displaced aggression" actually aimed at himself or someone who made him mad earlier, but again we would be speculating.

Many acts are difficult to classify as aggression as opposed to nonaggression. Berkowitz (1989) suggests it is useful to distinguish between **hostile aggression**, which is designed to inflict injury, and **instrumental aggression**, which is designed to achieve some reward such as money or social approval.

Is aggression an instinctual drive?

Freud as well as some animal behaviour theorists (Lorenz, 1966; Ardrey, 1966; Morris, 1967) have argued that animals and humans possess an instinctual drive toward aggression. This drive is similar to a reservoir behind a dam. The drive builds up with time. If it is not given periodic release, eventually the dam will burst, leading to destruction. Thus, some of the drive should be "drawn off" harmlessly. This process of releasing aggression is called *catharsis*. People sometimes say, "That was a real catharsis" after a screaming match or a long cry or smashing tennis balls against a wall. Afterward, there is a sense of relief. **Catharsis** thus refers to the release of any emotion, not just aggression. In our everyday language, we sometimes refer to the release of emotional tension as a type of purging. "I feel better for telling him off. I got it out of my system." "Watching violent shows gives kids a harmless outlet for their natural aggression." As we stated earlier, the theory that aggression is an instinctual drive that builds up and needs periodic release is known as the catharsis theory of aggression. In a way, this theory is similar to Freud's notion of psychic energy being diverted or *sublimated* from one function to another.

Genetics and aggression

Many psychologists reject the notion that aggression is instinctive in humans. However, they do acknowledge that there are important biological influences on aggression. Among animals it is possible to breed selectively for aggression. Lagerspetz (1979) bred mice selectively for 25 generations by interbreeding the most aggressive animals from each generation with each other and the least aggressive mice with each other. The mice bred for aggression almost always attacked each other when placed together, whereas the nonaggressive mice would not attack under virtually any circumstance. Thus, genetic endowment certainly contributes to levels of aggression.

Some anthropologists have suggested that humans are biologically "wired" so that aggression is easy to trigger or inhibit under certain conditions. It does seem clear that humans learn aggression easily, partly for genetic reasons. However, this is quite different than saying that aggression is instinctive.

Hormones and aggression

The male sex hormone testosterone is related to aggressive behaviour in animals. It probably underlies one of the few human sex differences with some biological foundation (Moyer, 1983). Male animals who are castrated and therefore have lowered levels of testosterone become less aggressive. If they are then given injections of testosterone, their previous levels of aggression return.

The nervous system and aggression

Aggressive behaviours in most animals follow a fairly rigid, stereotyped form. Because the same response patterns are observed in animals raised in isolation, it seems likely that these behaviours are organized or programmed in the brain.

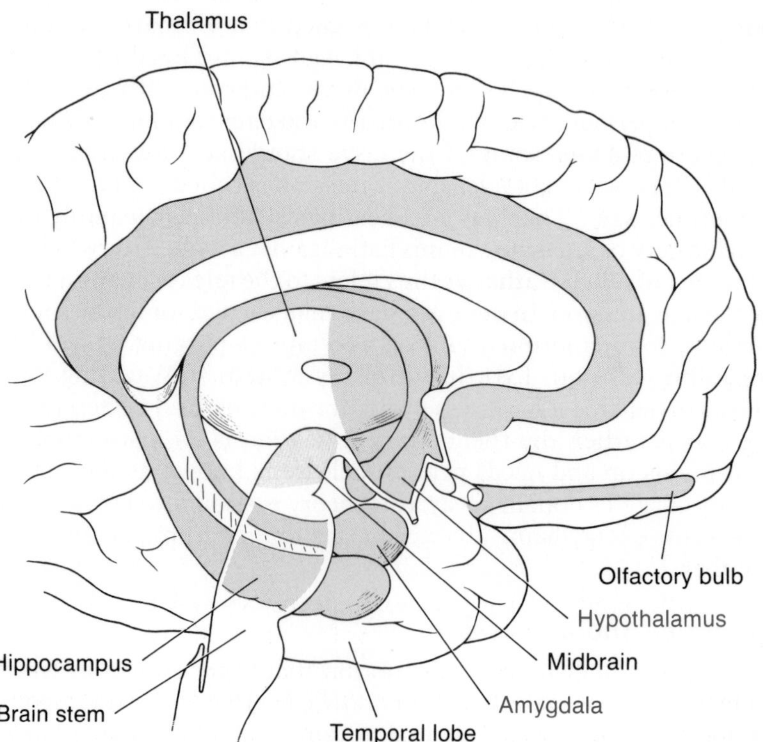

FIGURE 17-4 The hypothalamus and the amygdala: Two neural centres that influence aggression

As we discussed in detail in Chapter 2, two neural centres seem to be capable of dramatically arousing aggression or inhibiting it. First, the **hypothalamus**, located above the brain stem and below the thalamus, influences aggressive behaviour. Second, the **amygdala**, an almond-shaped structure of the limbic system located deep in the temporal lobe, also influences aggressive behaviour, though its precise role is uncertain. (See Figure 17-4.) In some cases, removing parts of the amygdala from animal brains has resulted in nearly constant attack behaviour. Then, further removing other parts can leave the same animal placid and unaggressive. Humans have had electrodes implanted in the limbic system for purposes of medical diagnosis. In some instances when these electrodes were stimulated, the person immediately became angry and aggressive, even though the electrical stimulus could not be felt (Moyer, 1983). Some investigators believe that the malfunctions of the amygdala account for some cases of irrational violence in humans.

The frustration-aggression hypothesis

Azrin (1967) presented evidence that in animals pain leads to aggression. He argued that because *pain-elicited aggression* appears without prior learning, it must be biologically built into animals, from pigeons to monkeys. He also demonstrated *extinction-elicited aggression*, which is actually the same phenomenon. However, in this case, the "pain" was the pain of having a previously given reinforcer withheld. For example, the animal was frustrated by not finding food where it was expected. The animal then turned to attack whatever was available as a target, preferably another animal.

This phenomenon was described years ago as the **frustration-aggression hypothesis** (Dollard et al., 1939). According to this hypothesis, frustration (i.e., being blocked from an expected goal) leads to aggression. In its strongest form, this hypothesis states that frustration *always* leads to aggression and does so for *innate* reasons. However, more recent evidence has shown that the way a person responds to frustration is mostly a function of his or her previous learning experiences. Aggression often is reinforced by the control it gives over others, especially when one has just been frustrated in some way, such as having someone grab a favourite toy. If some other behaviour, such as whining or acting helpless, is reinforced when the child is frustrated, then that will be the likely response to future frustration. There also seem to be instances of aggression that are not preceded by frustration. For example, Kaufman (1970) has demonstrated that the aggression of college students is largely a function of learned social attitudes and expectations.

Is aggression a learned behaviour?

In opposition to the catharsis theory, the social learning theory of aggression states that aggression is a learned behaviour that is socially reinforced. Although there are a few built-in reflexes that contribute to learning aggression easily, aggression develops because it has been reinforced. Thus, according to this theory, aggression is not inevitable in humans.

The built-in reflexes make it very likely that humans will learn aggression, however. In response to pain, there seems to be an unlearned tendency to move intensely. This kicking and thrashing often gets rid of the source of the pain. Thus, it is reinforced. There also is an unlearned reaction to frustration. This reaction is aversive internal arousal that is a kind of a pain. The intense activity of aggression probably blocks much of this pain because it "closes the gates" on pain, as we learned in our discussion of gate-control theory in Chapter 4. Thus, the aggressive acts will be reinforced by the reduction in pain. Consequently, it is also likely that aggression will be learned as a response to frustration. Thus, the social learning theorist would say that aggression is not innate, but it is almost inevitable that humans will learn it.

Vicarious aggression

Experiencing aggression by watching it is known as **vicarious aggression**. A socially significant implication of the social learning view concerns the effect of the mass media on violent behaviour. According to the catharsis theory, viewing aggression on television provides a structured, safe outlet. It provides a necessary release. However, according to the more convincing social learning theory, viewing aggression on television generally causes the viewer to be more violent for three reasons. First, it teaches aggression by example. In other words, new aggressive responses may be acquired through observational learning. Second, it provides cues to stimulate aggression. Third, it lowers inhibitions against aggression by getting people used to it — by making it commonplace and acceptable. Viewers may become desensitized to violence and their inhibitions against engaging in violence may be weakened.

Berkowitz (1979; 1983) conducted a series of studies that examined the effects of watching either an exciting footrace or a bloody fight scene from the movie *Champion*, in which Kirk Douglas plays

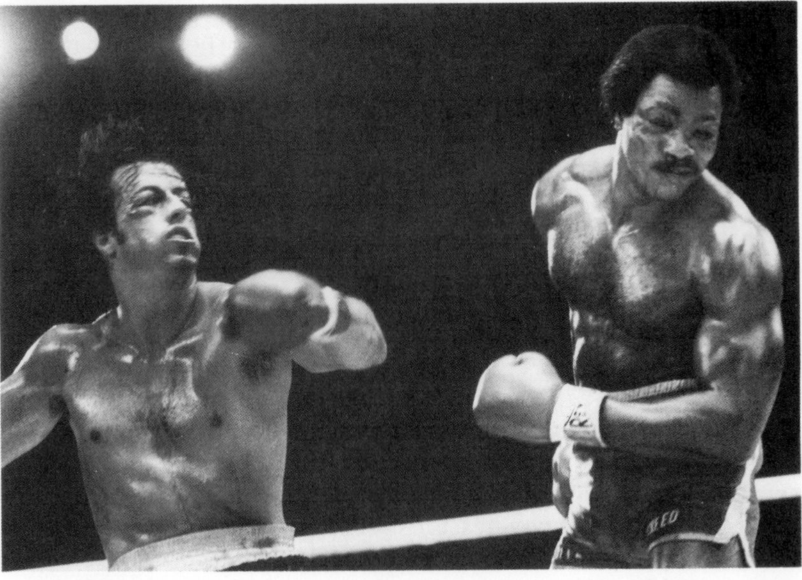

According to the social learning theory of aggression, vicarious aggression stimulates violence.
SOURCE: "Rocky II." Copyright © 1979 by United Artists Corporation. Photofest.

a boxer who receives a bad beating. In the second phase of the experiment, after watching the film, subjects were asked to deliver an electrical shock to another "subject," who in fact was a confederate of the experimenter and never actually received any shocks. The measure of interest was the intensity of shock the subjects chose to deliver to the other person. The general finding was that subjects who had watched the bloody fight scene set higher shock levels. Even more significantly, subjects who had been told that the beating was justified gave significantly stronger shocks than subjects who just watched the movie. There is a powerful lesson in this. Watching *justified aggression* is especially likely to arouse the viewer's own violence. We can define **justified aggression** as viewed aggression that tends to arouse strong aggression in the viewer because it seems morally right.

In Berkowitz's experiment, another group of subjects who watched the bloody fight scene were told that Douglas died as a result of the beating. These subjects set lower levels of shock than those subjects who simply watched the film. Thus, it is possible for viewed violence to be so excessive that it has a horrifying effect that in turn inhibits the viewer's own aggression. However, the problem and danger in our society is that most public aggression—movies, television, executions—is "justified" because the "good people" use it to win. Therefore, showing horrifying aggression will have a two-fold effect. At first, the viewers may experience some inhibition. But eventually viewers will extinguish the horror. What used to be unthinkable will become quite ordinary and therefore arouse viewer aggression.

For several decades, researchers have been trying to answer the question whether watching violence on television in the natural environment increases violence in viewers. Not all studies have found a positive relationship (Milavsky et al., 1982). However, the weight of the evidence is that vicarious aggression does contribute to violence in the viewer. In 1982, the National Institute of Mental Health in the United States adopted the strong position that children imitate the behaviour they see on television. The Institute argued that because of the media, children internalize the value that violence and aggression are socially acceptable behaviour. In his longitudinal study of eight-year-olds, Eron (1980; 1982) found that eleven years later, the best predictor of the males' violent behaviour from their previous testing was the violence of the television they liked to watch.

A revealing series of experiments

We will now describe a series of studies that provide a nice illustration of how science develops an idea. These experiments help explain why people commonly feel that the catharsis theory of aggression is correct. We often feel that we do "get it out of our system" by fighting back when frustrated and angry.

Two initial studies seemed to support this view with male subjects (Hokanson & Shelter, 1961; Hokanson & Burgess, 1962). The subjects received aversive stimulation from another person and had a rise in blood pressure when they were aggressed against. If the subject made an aggressive counterresponse, his blood pressure returned to normal fairly quickly. If he was prevented from responding or did not counterattack, his blood pressure returned to its previous level more slowly. These results seemed to support the catharsis view that the aggression was discharged by striking back. But the issue quickly became complicated. If the other person was of high status, blood pressure returned to normal slowly whether the subject counterattacked or not. Aggressing against some person other than the original attacker did not lower blood pressure. Even more interestingly, female subjects showed a different pattern (Hokanson & Edelman, 1966). Females who were friendly in response to aggression from another female recovered just as fast as those who struck back.

It didn't seem plausible that the catharsis theory might apply to males but not to females. Therefore, some researchers proposed a social learning explanation. It seems likely that males learn to meet aggression with counteraggression. In fact, they are often traditionally punished for friendly responses under such circumstances. Females, however, are generally punished for being "too aggressive" and are often reinforced for friendly responses. Hokanson, Willers, & Karapsak (1968) supported this explanation by giving male subjects some experience of receiving reward for friendly counterresponses and receiving punishment for striking back. Females received the opposite training. When these subjects underwent the experiments, the rate of recovery of their blood pressure was quite different from that of the "untrained" subjects. We can conclude that it does "feel good to get it out of your system" for some people, whereas just the opposite holds true for others. It all depends on the person's learning history.

Interpersonal Attraction

For most people, the highest highs and the lowest lows come from their close personal relationships. No one can build us up more than a friend or lover who knows us intimately *and* finds us attractive and worthwhile. No one can tear us down so painfully and destructively as that same person. Relationships usually follow a course of increasingly close contact, starting with simple social exchange and progressing through acquaintanceship, friendship, intimacy, and being lovers. Most relationships stop somewhere along this progression. What determines how far each of our encounters will lead? To whom are we attracted?

What attracts us to others?

Proximity

When people are asked how they choose their friends, few say they pick people who live close by. However, research has shown that physical proximity is the best single predictor of whether two people will become friends. This has been demonstrated in university dormitories, neighbourhoods, police academies, and even in the addresses of people who apply for marriage licences.

Ellen Berscheid.
SOURCE: Courtesy Ellen Berscheid.

Physical attractiveness

A second factor that people seldom mention in what attracts them to others is physical appearance (Tesser & Brodie, 1971). However, there is strong evidence that people are kidding themselves or at least trying to kid others about what they look for in a new acquaintance (Berscheid, 1985). Walster and her co-workers (1966) gave a dance billed as a "computer dance" in which partners were supposedly matched to each other. In fact, couples were randomly paired together. Halfway through the dance, participants filled out anonymous questionnaires about their partners. Earlier, the experimenters had conducted several personality, intelligence, and social-skills tests on the participants, and they had collected independent ratings of each person's physical attractiveness. The only factor that accurately predicted whether a person liked his or her partner was physical attractiveness.

Even nursery school children can be reliably ranked for attractiveness by adults. When children then rate each other for personality traits, the less attractive child is seen as more aggressive and less independent (Berscheid & Walster, 1972). Women were given a written description of an incident in which a child misbehaved. The child's picture was attached to the report. In fact, the reports were always identical and only the pictures were changed, sometimes showing an attractive child and sometimes a plain one. If the misbehaviour had been fairly serious, the less attractive child was described as chronically antisocial, but the attractive one was judged not likely to repeat the offence.

However, the implications of physical attractiveness are not always so simple. Women in their forties and fifties were ranked for their beauty in their college-yearbook pictures from 25 years previously. In interviews, it was found that physical beauty in college was related to *less* satisfactory adjustment later in life. The choice of a marriage partner also seems less influenced by physical attractiveness than does the initial forming of relationships (Stroebe et al., 1971). At the level of a "computer dance," physical attractiveness is a strong determinant of liking. However, for the long term, for actual dating and for marriage, observation suggests that the **matching principle** seems to operate. According to this principle, people tend to seek out and choose marriage partners of about equal physical attractiveness to themselves (Folkes, 1982; McKillip & Reidel, 1983).

Similarity

Which is true: "opposites attract" or "birds of a feather flock together"? Research suggests that the matching principle also extends to our choice of partners in terms of interests, personality, values, social class, and race (Byrne, Clore, & Smeaton, 1986). In one study, students who had just transferred to the University of Michigan were given free rent in exchange for filling out questionnaires about their relationships in the dormitory. Early in the term, physical

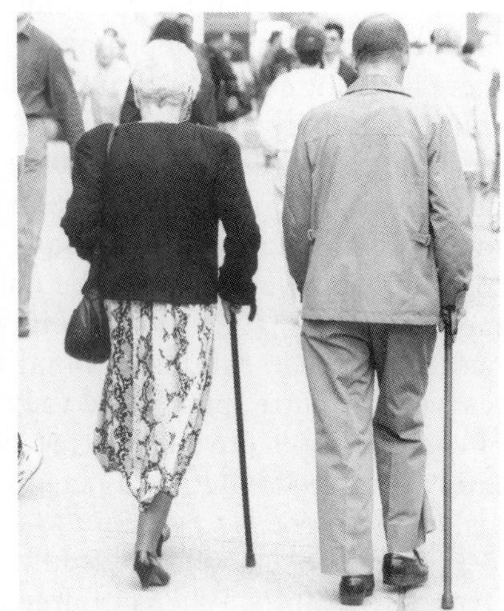

According to the matching principle, people tend to seek out partners of about equal physical attractiveness to themselves.
SOURCE: Photos by Dick Hemingway.

proximity was the best predictor of friendship. However, later in the term, similarity of interests was the best predictor (Newcombe, 1961). In another study, Hill, Rubin, and Peplau (1976) followed dating couples over the course of a year. They found that couples who were more similar in background and interests were more likely to be together still at the end of the study. More recently, Rosenbaum (1986) has added a new interpretation to the observation that similar people remain together. He has accumulated evidence for the **repulsion hypothesis**, which says that people choose partners who are similar to themselves because dissimilarity fosters dislike.

Some research suggests that different kinds of similarity are attractive to different kinds of people. In general, we can distinguish between two types of people based on the importance they place on the impression they make on others. **Low self-monitors** pay great attention to their internal feelings and attitudes to guide their own behaviour. By contrast, **high self-monitors** pay great attention to cues from other people in the environment to guide their own behaviour. In one study (Jamieson, Lydon, & Zanna, 1987), students were first assessed in terms of their self-monitoring. The researchers then found that the students who were low self-monitors were most attracted to people who held similar *attitudes* to those they held themselves. By contrast, the students who were high self-monitors were found to be attracted to people whose *preferred activities* were similar to their own.

The theory that opposites attract is based on the **needs-complementarity hypothesis**. This refers to a more subtle kind of similarity-dissimilarity dimension than the attitudes and activities that psychologists usually study. According to this hypothesis, well-matched couples complement each other's weaknesses. In other words, each partner fills in a weakness in the other person's character or meets an important need. Thus, a very dominant person might seek a submissive partner. Most people can think of some couple they know that fits this kind of pattern. Nevertheless, even here there is a fundamental similarity. For such a complementary relationship to work, both partners have to value this kind of uneven balance as "the way relationships should be." In general, research indicates that similarity is a better predictor of good adjustment in marriage than is complementarity (Meyer & Pepper, 1977).

Familiarity

We can find an old saying to support just about anything. Consider the old adage that "familiarity breeds contempt." Research has shown that this is quite wrong. In fact, it has been shown that in general, "familiarity breeds liking" (or as one person said, "familiarity breeds," but that's a different issue).

According to the **mere exposure effect** proposed by Zajonc (1968), familiarity with a stimulus (be it a word, object, or person) promotes positive feelings toward it. In other words, a subject's liking of a stimulus is a function of how many times he or she has been exposed to it. This effect has been found among both animals and humans. Rats developed a discriminated taste for the music of Mozart, but only if they had been exposed more to it than to other music. Human subjects were shown pictures of faces several times and then asked to rate the persons in the pictures for how much the subject would like the person. The faces that had been seen most frequently by a particular subject were seen as most likable. Another study used pictures of female subjects as well as the mirror image of each picture. The women themselves thought the mirror images were more attractive, but their friends and lovers preferred the normal versions. We often are unpleasantly surprised at how we look in photographs, partly because we virtually always see ourselves in a mirror image. Familiarity leads us to prefer it. In friendships and other social interactions, increased familiarity creates an impression of increased similarity between people (Moreland & Zajonc, 1982). So if you can hang around without being a pest, both familiarity and proximity should work to your benefit.

Robert J. Sternberg.
SOURCE: Courtesy Robert J. Sternberg, Yale University.

Three elements of love

It is difficult enough to discuss the general elements of what attracts people to each other. It is overwhelming to try to describe the experience of love. The word *love* has so many meanings that definitions seem impossible to agree on.

Nevertheless, some recent research provides a useful structure within which to think about love. A helpful description of love has grown out of the work of Robert Sternberg and his co-workers (Sternberg, 1986; Sternberg & Barnes, 1985; Sternberg & Grajeck, 1984). According to their **triangular theory of love**, a love relationship is

FIGURE 17-5 Various kinds of love according to Sternberg's triangular theory
SOURCE: Based on Sternberg (1986).

(a) CONSUMMATE LOVE

(b) FATUOUS LOVE

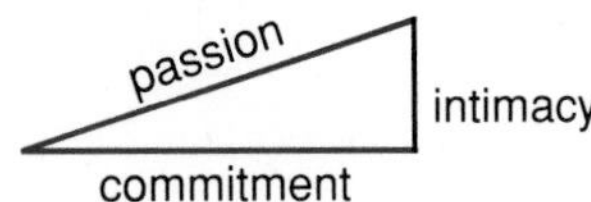

(c) LIKING

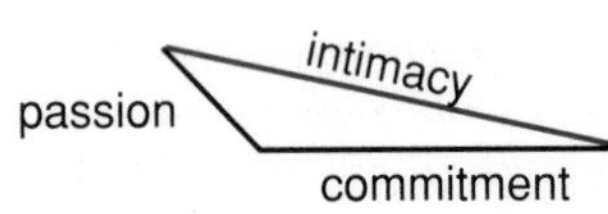

(d) COMPANIONATE LOVE

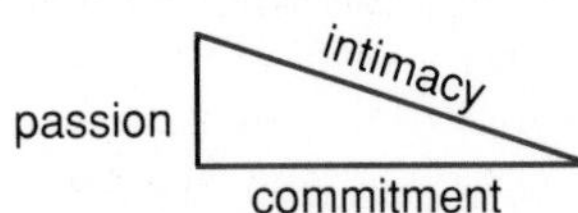

(e) INFATUATION

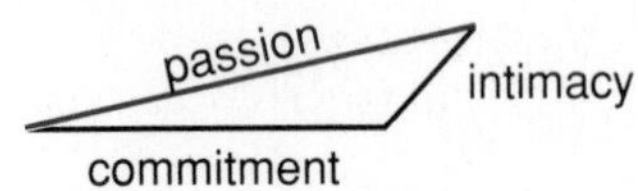

(f) EMPTY LOVE

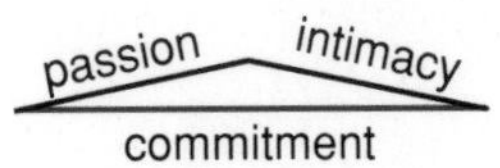

(g) ROMANTIC LOVE

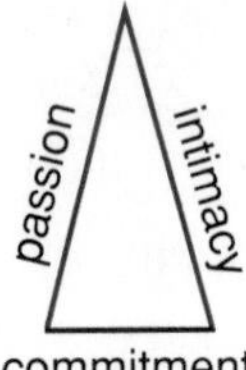

composed of three important elements: intimacy, passion, and commitment. *Intimacy* is the emotional sharing part of love, in which the couple communicate openly, share feelings, feel closeness, and give support. *Passion*, the second essential element, is the desire for sexual sharing. It makes partners want to be intensely joined in all ways, and it is often the initial motivation to enter a relationship. The third essential element is *commitment*, the shared knowledge that the relationship is dependable. This often involves a more cognitive decision than do passion and intimacy.

We can develop a visual image of seven different kinds of relationships by means of triangles whose sides represent each of the elements discussed above (see Figure 17-5). First, three long and equal sides will yield the largest triangle. It represents **consummate love**, the most fulfilling and healthiest love. Second, if passion and stated commitment are strong, but there is little intimacy, then we would have a wide, short triangle — what Sternberg calls **fatuous love**. It develops quickly and often doesn't work well, because there is little sharing. It is exemplified by a young man we knew who strongly believed statements such as, "Of course I love her. I'm still here, aren't I?" He was expressing commitment by staying, but he had trouble expressing the intimacy of directly saying he loved his partner. He also said, "As long as the sex is good, the rest will follow," reflecting the importance of passion. As Sternberg would predict of such relationships, this one didn't last long. Third, we can picture **liking** as a combination of much intimacy plus some commitment but with little or no passion. Fourth, if we increase the commitment, we arrive at **companionate love**, which would characterize a long-term friendship. This relationship also describes some marriages in which passion has faded. Fifth, **infatuation** is heavy on the passion, but there is seldom much intimacy or commitment. Sixth, what Sternberg calls **empty love** has high commitment but little intimacy and little passion. It is most typical of "stale marriages." The partners would never leave each other because of their strong sense of commitment. But they don't share and experience feelings together, and their passion has faded away. Many arranged marriages are like this from the beginning and may or may not develop into more complete love. Finally, the **romantic love** that so often passes for complete love in our popular music and culture is a combination of passion and intimacy without much commitment. This is usually what happens when people first fall in love.

The triangular model of love can be useful for understanding what each person in a relationship wants from it. The most powerful predictor of the success of a relationship is how closely it fits what the people in the relationship want, not whether it fits some "ideal relationship." If both people want companionate love and mutually understand this, they are probably much better off than a couple in which the man wants commitment and passion, while the woman wants commitment and intimacy. Mismatched combinations do not bode well for long-term success.

Sternberg strongly emphasizes that the balanced relationship of consummate love is both difficult to achieve and difficult to maintain. It is what most people seem to be seeking, but what few find.

CLOSE-UP Aggression and Anabolic Steroids

Canadian sport has been deeply affected by recent scandals over the use of anabolic steroids. Many athletes take these drugs in order to increase muscular strength, in spite of several dangerous side effects. It is less commonly known that one behavioural side effect in many steroid users is an increase in aggressive feelings and behaviours. Steroids were first used to make German soldiers more aggressive during World War II (Haupt & Rovere, 1984). Both Russian and U.S. athletes started using them during the 1950s.

Aggression is partly the result of hormonal and other chemical influences. Research has shown mood changes among steroid users. Arnold LeUnes and Jack Nation (1989) report that it is generally accepted that steroids often result in increased rage and aggression. For example, Dean Steinkuhler of the NFL Houston Oilers admitted that he had used steroids during his college days and early in his professional career. Steinkuhler said that the drugs "made me real moody, violent, I wanted to kill somebody" (LeUnes & Nation, 1989, p. 303).

SPECIAL TOPIC How to Be a Good Listener

Human relationships require many skills. We have to be able to confront others, to negotiate, to reassure, and to comfort. In this section, we would like to discuss the one interpersonal ability that is probably most important in helping others: being a good listener.

We often hear that communication is fundamental to relationships and that one must work at communication to be effective. The trouble is that few of us know *how* to work at it. Let us be very specific and concrete about some things we can do to improve our listening skills.

It may be trite to say that listening is a foundation of communication. But in spite of how often this has been said, the fact is that few people really listen. In the typical conversation, we are planning our next brilliant response, which the other person will find absolutely fascinating if he or she would just shut up long enough to listen to us. We tend to hear the first few words from the other person, *assume* that we know what he or she is going to say, and then start planning our next speech.

Often people don't explicitly say what they mean, or they may be using words differently than we would. They may not find just the words that capture what they mean. A quick assumption often dooms us to misunderstanding, and this results in poor communication. Our goal as a good listener should be to have the other person feel that we understood what he or she *meant* to say. If we do this effectively, he or she will then have the internal reaction, "Oh, right. That's exactly what I meant. You were really listening."

Many people assume that they are good listeners when they are not. An exercise we have done with people is to ask each person to answer honestly whether there is someone in their own life who really listens consistently and makes them feel understood. Many find this a depressing exercise. Research by Carkhuff and Berenson (1977) suggests that very few people do listen well. And yet effective listening is essential in a healthy, fulfilling relationship. The listening skills we will be describing are powerful. We hope that you will find them useful.

Most of us are more comfortable relating to others by giving advice and asking questions, particularly when the other person has come to us with a problem. We usually try to solve the problem for the other person, but this is seldom the best way to help. Imagine the following scenario and honestly consider what your most likely response would be. Your best friend says to you, "I just feel so useless lately. Nothing I do matters or makes any difference. I feel worthless. I'm just not any good." If you are like most people, you would probably answer with something encouraging such as "Look at all the people who like you. Your studies are going well. Your job prospects are good. Cheer up. Count your blessings." In many situations these are nice words to hear. We like to hear good things from our friends.

But let's turn the roles around. Try to remember as vividly as possible how you felt the last time you were depressed. Imagine that you felt very low and said to a good friend, "I feel so useless lately. Nothing I do seems to be any good, and what's the point anyway?" What would your internal reaction be if your friend said, "Come on, cheer up. There's lots of good things in your life. It doesn't make sense for you to feel so low." Your friend might be saying things that are factually true, but many of us would feel the frustration of not being understood. We might feel, "You don't know how I feel. You don't know how strong it is. All that's easy for you to say." Reassurance and advice have their place in relationships. However, if they result in the other person's feeling misunderstood, then they are useless.

In a sense, your friend would be trying to talk you out of your feeling. He or she is implying, "It's not all right to feel that way, so stop. There is not sufficient reason for you to feel these things, so apply your willpower and feel better. Anyway, I don't like hearing these negative things from you."

If you could reason your way out of the feelings, then you would. Your friend has left you feeling isolated and alone with your feelings. The foundation of communication is letting the other person know that we have heard what he or she is trying to say.

To describe good listening skills, let us start with a formal definition of **active listening** (or **empathic listening**). *It is the communicated understanding of the other person's intended message, including implied feelings.* It is not enough simply to understand. We must also somehow *prove* that we understand by communicating it. It is not enough to hear the words the person used. We must hear what the person *meant*—what the intended message was.

This skill seems so easy to most people that it is often misunderstood. Many people see it as sort of a weak permissiveness in which you nod your head and repeat back what the other person just said. This kind of parroting of the other person's words could hardly be further from what good listening really is. This is a misunderstanding that appears in a painfully large number of books, especially in the helping skills area.

Listen for what is meant

We need to practice listening for the implicit message. Many people erroneously take this to mean they should make fancy interpretations of the other person's "hidden meaning." But that is something very different from empathic listening. Although we want to go beyond the superficial level of what the other person says, we still want to stay within the bounds of what he or she meant to say.

Suppose one of your friends plops down in front of you and says, "They need more student advisors around here." You might respond to the surface meaning with, "They really have quite a few. Have you used the appointment sign-up system?" You could parrot back the words, "You think they need more student advisors." (Actually this might help some, although it looks silly on paper.) You could launch into an interpretation such as, "That's because you're too dependent on others. That attitude won't help you." None of these responses even acknowledges what the other person was implying.

To try to help, we should give an actively empathic response. "Sounds like you need help with something." "I guess things feel pretty confusing around here." "What's gone wrong?" Assuming you understand the feelings implied, you could say something like, "You sound pretty ticked off." Each of these responses (we like the first one best) acknowledges what the other person implied. It's fairly clear that the other person's words and manner all implied that he or she is overwhelmed by some minor disaster. Hearing this implicit message is not some mystical skill at deciphering hidden meanings. It is simply listening for what's being implied.

Thus a useful way to practice the skill is to take some time to focus on what the other person is saying and ask yourself to name the implicit message. Tomorrow at lunch practice by listening to others' conversations and silently paraphrasing statements you hear to capture the implicit message. Try not to be too obvious about this, though, or you might look strange talking to yourself.

In a sense, we should try to hear and see through the other person's ears and eyes. Another interesting exercise that might help improve this ability is to simulate the conditions under which other people live. A person who works with the blind, for example, might spend a day blindfolded.

Finding the words

Let's assume for the moment that you are good at hearing the implicit message. Now your task is finding some way to communicate to the other person that you have understood. We find that most people stumble for words when they first try to do this. It feels awkward to respond in such an unaccustomed way. It feels more natural to give advice and offer opinions. What feels "natural," though, is what you are used to doing. Once you have been practicing good listening skills for a while, it will gradually come to feel more comfortable.

People have such trouble with this that we are going to give you some "formula responses" to get you started, even though we are a bit reluctant to do so. Once you have heard the implicit message, you can say, "It sounds like you feel ____________ (because of ____________)." This lead-in phrase can be very helpful because it communicates that you are trying to understand the other person. It also gives your response a tentativeness that says, "I am not laying this on you, and if I'm wrong, just tell me. My goal is to be sure I understand." There are dozens of ways to communicate this "skillful tentativeness." Here are a few more such lead-in phrases. Read each one to get an idea of what purpose it serves in communicating your emphatic intentions:

— If I hear you correctly, you mean. . . .
— I think what you mean is. . . .
— So there's a feeling of. . . .
— I'm not sure this is what you mean, but. . . .
— I guess you feel. . . .

Be sure not to cling to this kind of formula too much. The point is not to follow a formula at all. *The point is to make the other person feel understood.* And it hardly matters how you do that. Think in terms of what would give the other person the feeling of, "Yeah! That's exactly what I meant."

Here is a final thought on finding the right words. Because there are always many parts of the other person's statement, your words usually respond only to some of the parts. The most important part of what people are trying to say is often the most neglected. It is the *feeling* part. Emotional reactions are nearly always the part of the message that are not stated explicitly. That's why so many of the useful lead-in phrases include the word "feel." Remember that you should not force feelings into your response in order to fit some formula. However, if the person has implied some kind of reaction (which is usually the case), try to include that in your understanding response.

You must practice

We can read about communication skills for years and pass tests about being a good listener. But the only way to learn these skills is to practice them. A person must actually do some listening and go through the awkwardness of trying a new way of responding.

When it's appropriate

Most of our social interactions don't involve intimacy or problems and conflicts. Intense active listening is *not* appropriate for most of our interactions. *Empathy*, however, can be given at all different levels. As we check out at the grocery store and the clerk gives a deep sigh, an empathic response might be, "Long day, eh?" This is a small incident, but it still represents empathic understanding. We responded at the level that the other person intended for us to hear. We wouldn't say, "If I hear you correctly, you feel overburdened by an oppressive employer." (We're being silly, but you get the point.) Sometimes the other person simply is asking for information, and the appropriate response is to prove we understood by answering the question. Suppose someone says, "How does this new computer work?" We wouldn't answer, "You seem to be saying you're confused." Tell the person how the computer works.

Active listening is *most* appropriate when we are helping another person solve his or her own problems or talk through some troublesome feelings. Empathic understanding at lower levels is probably appropriate in most other encounters, if only to get feedback from the other person that we are hearing accurately.

Empathy is not sympathy

Probably the most common misunderstanding of empathy is that it is the same as agreeing with or sympathizing with another person. However, we can be empathic with a person we hate or with a person we totally disagree with. We can communicate an understanding of his or her intended message—and that is all that empathy is. There are many other constructive qualities that usually accompany empathy. We usually express concern for the other person, for example. But caring and sympathy, although they have a place, should not be confused with empathy. Actually, sympathy often implies some pity. By contrast, empathy implies, "I am with you, and I trust your strength to deal with what you are talking about. Your feelings are not my feelings, but I will be with you as you talk about them."

1. Person perception, or social perception, influence interpersonal attraction, aggression, helping behaviour, and other kinds of dyadic (two-person) interactions. We have a strong tendency to use social schemas when we perceive people. As with other kinds of perception, we can distort reality through inference.

2. Our first impressions of others exert a powerful effect. We tend to use superficial information which feeds into our social schemas to form our impressions. Often we use this information to fit a person into a special kind of social schema, a stereotype. We also make use of prototypes and implicit personality theories. These ideas help us make judgments quickly but they also distort person perception. In general, we form impressions of others by means of initial encoding, elaborative encoding, integration, and a decision process.

3. We are constantly making attributions of causality to explain the behaviour of others. Sometimes we point to dispositional determinants; at other times we point to situational determinants. We often rely on the co-variation rule by focusing on distinctiveness, consistency, and consensus. We also make use of the discounting principle and the augmenting principle.

4. Unfortunately, we are prone to certain biases in our attributions of causality. We tend to commit the fundamental attribution error when explaining the behaviour of others. We tend to be influenced by the actor-observer bias when explaining our own behaviour. Other distortions of attribution include egocentric recall and the just world bias.

5. Psychologists have investigated altruism by studying bystander intervention. Research has shown that apathy does not adequately explain the lack of help offered by bystanders in instances such as the Genovese case. The presence of others can lead to group ignorance, the diffusion of responsibility, and the bystander effect. People can also be inhibited from helping by the prospect of risks, by the ambiguity of the situation, and by being in a poor emotional state.

6. People will help others because of a belief in a just world or an acceptance of the social exchange theory. Altruism may be selfish, but not egoistic. To date, research has failed to demonstrate that helpfulness is a function of personality. Moreover, it is not clear to what extent helpfulness is inborn.

7. Despite the good which altruism usually leads to, excessive helping can hurt either the helpee or the helper. Patients in a hospital who become reliant on the help of hospital staff are an example of how altruism can encourage dependency. Two factors seem to

contribute to this effect. The helper can communicate a lack of confidence in the helpee's competence. Second, the helpee may attribute success to others. The helper is also vulnerable to burnout.

8. The traditional definition of aggression is problematic because it involves the inference of intention. More recently, some researchers have attempted to identify hostile aggression, instrumental aggression, vicarious aggression, and justified aggression.

9. There are two opposing theories of aggression: the catharsis theory and the social learning theory. Each leads to opposite conclusions about appropriate ways to reduce violence and about the effects of viewing violence on television. The workings of the hormone testosterone and the functioning of the hypothalamus and amygdala indicate a biological foundation for aggression. However, the evidence to date seems to demonstrate that aggression is a learned response. Social learning theorists would argue that aggression is not an instinctive drive, but that because of our biological wiring it is almost inevitable that humans will learn it. Vicarious aggression seems to cause the viewer to be more violent because it teaches aggression by example, it provides stimulating cues, and it lowers inhibitions.

10. Research on interpersonal attraction suggests that the single best predictor of whether two people will become friends is physical proximity. People seldom mention physical attractiveness as a factor in attraction, but studies show that this is an important element. The matching principle seems to operate when people choose partners for dating and marriage. Similarity in terms of other factors is also important in partner choice. Low self-monitors seem most attracted to people who hold similar attitudes to those they hold themselves. High self-monitors seem most attracted to people who prefer the same sorts of activities as they do. The mere exposure effect also plays an important role in interpersonal attraction.

11. Sternberg suggests that there are three elements to a love relationship: intimacy (emotional sharing), passion (sexual sharing), and commitment (shared knowledge that the relationship is dependable). Consummate love consists of high, balanced levels of all three elements. It is the ideal relationship which most people seek. The triangular theory of love also describes various other types of relationships, including fatuous love, liking, companionate love, infatuation, empty love, and romantic love. The best predictor of success in a relationship is probably not the type of love involved but the extent to which both partners want the same kind of love.

Key Terms

Active listening The communicated understanding of the other person's intended message, including implied feelings.

Actor-observer bias The tendency to attribute the causes of one's own behaviour to situational determinants rather than to internal dispositions.

Aggression Behaviour intended to deliver harm to another living organism. See also *hostile aggression*, *instrumental aggression*, *justified aggression*, and *vicarious aggression*.

Altruism Behaviour in which time, energy, or money is given to others without obvious reward to the giver.

Altruistic egoism The theory that altruistic behaviour ultimately serves the individual's own interests in important ways.

Amygdala An almond-shaped structure of the limbic system located deep in the temporal lobe. It strongly influences aggressive behaviour.

Attributions of causality The process by which we attempt to infer the traits, motives, and intentions of other people from our observations of their overt behaviour.

Augmenting principle In causal attribution, the tendency to assign greater importance to a potential cause when both a facilitory factor and an inhibitory factor are present.

Belief in a just world A motive for altruism in which the helping person believes that such behaviour will be rewarded in some way.

Bystander effect The tendency for an individual bystander not to give help when other bystanders are present.

Bystander intervention The actions of individuals when they encounter others who are in emergency situations.

Catharsis The release of any emotion.

Catharsis theory of aggression The theory that aggression is an instinctual drive that builds up and needs periodic release.

Companionate love Love in which commitment and intimacy are high but passion is low.

Consummate love The most fulfilling and healthiest love, in which there is a high and balanced level of all three elements—passion, intimacy, and commitment.

Co-variation rule A rule for making attributions of causality, based on an individual's beliefs that particular events tend to occur together.

Decision process The fourth stage of impression formation, during which the new impression is evaluated and translated into an appropriate response.

Diffusion of responsibility The tendency for individuals in a group to assume less responsibility for giving help in an emergency than if he or she were facing it alone.

Discounting principle In causal attribution, the tendency to reduce the importance of any potential cause of a person's behaviour to the extent that other plausible causes are also present.

Dispositional determinants Causes within the person for that person's behaviour.

Egocentric recall Inaccurate memory that serves the interests of the person doing the remembering.

Egoistic Self-serving and self-focused for the immediate benefit of the self.

Elaborative encoding The second stage of impression formation, during which new information is compared with existing social schemas.

Empathic listening Another term for active listening.

Empty love Love in which commitment is high but passion and intimacy are low.

Fatuous love Love in which passion and commitment are high but intimacy is low.

Frustration-aggression hypothesis The hypothesis that frustration (i.e., being blocked from an expected goal) leads to aggression. In its strongest form, this hypothesis states that frustration always leads to aggression and does so for innate reasons.

Fundamental attribution error The tendency to attribute the causes of others' behaviour to dispositional determinants and to ignore the influence of situational determinants.

Group ignorance The tendency of individuals in the presence of others to interpret a situation as less dangerous than if he or she were facing it alone.

High self-monitors People who pay great attention to other people in the environment to guide their own behaviour.

Hospitalism The increasing helplessness of being unable to function outside a hospital following a period of being cared for by others.

Hostile aggression Aggression designed to inflict injury.

Hypothalamus A neural centre located above the brain stem and below the thalamus. It appears to play a role in arousing or inhibiting aggression.

Implicit personality theory An individual's beliefs about what personality characteristics occur together in people.

Impression formation The process by which we form a picture or series of judgments about other people.

Infatuation Love in which passion is high but intimacy and commitment are low.

Initial encoding The first stage of impression formation, during which information about another person is transformed into an internal representation.

Instrumental aggression Aggression designed to achieve some reward such as money or social approval.

Integration The third stage of impression formation, during which new information and previous social schemas are combined into a consistent whole.

Just world bias A bias in causal attribution resting on the belief that people get what they deserve.

Justified aggression Viewed aggression that tends to arouse strong aggression in the viewer because it seems morally right.

Liking A relationship characterized by much intimacy plus some commitment but with little or no passion.

Low self-monitors People who pay great attention to their internal feelings and attitudes to guide their own behaviour.

Matching principle The principle that people tend to seek out and choose marriage partners of about equal physical attractiveness to themselves.

Mere exposure effect The phenomenon that familiarity with a stimulus (be it a word, object, or person) promotes positive feelings toward it.

Need-complementarity hypothesis The hypothesis that well-matched couples complement each other's weaknesses.

Norm of reciprocity The social norm that people should exchange social benefits fairly equally.

Person perception The processes by which individuals form impressions of others. Also known as *social perception*.

Pluralistic ignorance Another term for *group ignorance*.

Primacy effect In social psychology, the phenomenon that one's first impressions of others carries a powerful influence that is difficult to change.

Prototype In person perception, a specific schema for a type of person.

Repulsion hypothesis The hypothesis that people choose partners who are similar to themselves because dissimilarity fosters dislike.

Romantic love Love in which passion and intimacy are high but commitment is low.

Self-serving recall Another term for *egocentric recall*.

Situational determinants Causes in the environment for a person's behaviour.

Social exchange theory The theory that people act altruistically because the social world operates like a market of equal exchanges between people.

Social learning theory of aggression The theory that aggression is a learned behaviour that develops because it is reinforced socially.

Social perception The processes by which individuals form impressions of others. Also known as *person perception*.

Social schema A schema specifically about other individuals or groups of individuals.

Sociobiologists Theorists who stress the inborn biological roots of human and animal behaviour.

Stereotype A collection of expectations and beliefs about a certain group in society. An instance of a powerful cognitive schema.

Triangular theory of love The theory that a love relationship is composed of three important elements: intimacy, passion, and commitment.

Vicarious aggression Experiencing aggression by watching it.

Suggested Readings

Aronson, E. (1984). *The social animal.* 4th ed. New York: Freeman. As we mention in the preceding chapter, this book is one of the most useful and interesting overviews of social psychology. It has much to say about impression formation, altruism, aggression, and interpersonal attraction.

Brehm, S. S. (1985). *Intimate relationships.* New York: Random House. Based on the psychological literature on love and other close relationships, this book gives much practical advice.

Johnson, D. W. (1986). *Reaching out: Interpersonal effectiveness and self-actualization.* 3rd ed. A practical and well-founded book on how to apply what we know about effective relationships. It includes many exercises that can be used as the basis of group discussion, as well as advice and exercises for the individual reader.

Welwood, J. (ed.) (1985). *Challenge of the heart.* Boston: Shambala. A fascinating collection of essays by various authors about love. It covers such topics as marriage as a path, erotic love (the puzzle and the promise), what men and women really want, sexuality (the meeting of two worlds), and larger visions of relationships. Some of the authors disagree with others completely. The editor's comments guide the reader in assessing the differences.

CHAPTER 18

Gender Roles and the Effective Person

SOURCE: *Cathy* by Cathy Guisewite. Copyright 1987 Universal Press Syndicate. Reprinted with permission. All rights reserved.

THESE ARE CONFUSING times in which to be a man or a woman. Some people are nostalgic for the days when "men were men, and women were women." As old-fashioned as this language sounds, we can appreciate how life was easier when the rules seemed clearer. But life was harder too. The main theme of this chapter is that our gender roles needlessly limit our lives in subtle but powerful ways. We hope that this chapter will provide some helpful insight into your own personal experiences and stimulate some interesting thoughts for the future.

THE POWER OF ROLES

A **role** can be defined as a set of behaviours that a group deems socially appropriate for a particular person in a particular situation. We all have many roles—a student role, a friend role, a son or daughter role, and so on. We can name a set of behaviours that are appropriate when we are "being a student" but that are not appropriate when we are "being a friend." Furthermore, we almost always acts in ways appropriate to our current role. We have learned our roles well, and they exert great influence on our behaviour, even when we are not aware of it.

Perhaps the most powerful and significant role is our *gender role*. We can stop being a student or friend sometimes, but our gender role is in effect always. Each of us has been rigorously taught our **gender role** — a pervasive, powerful set of behaviours that is prescribed as appropriate (and another set prescribed as inappropriate) based only on one's sex. Virtually none of these behaviours rests on inborn universal differences between the sexes. Moreover, the prescribed behaviours differ dramatically in different cultures. What we call "masculine" behaviour and "feminine" behaviour are essentially *learned differences in behaviour*. We will argue later in this chapter that the way gender roles are defined in our culture serves some positive functions, but it also deprives both men and women of much that makes a person "fully functioning." Our gender-role training needlessly limits our lives.

People often find it dramatic and a bit upsetting to learn that gender-role training is so powerful that they themselves *could* have been raised in the opposite gender role. There are instances in which a baby's sex has been misidentified because of ambiguous formation of the genitals. If these children are raised as either a male or female, then that is the gender they are *psychologically*, even though their *biological* sex may be later discovered to be opposite to their psychological sex. Money, Hampson, and Hampson (1957) report that in our culture, it is extremely difficult or even impossible to change such a psychological gender role after the age of about eighteen months to three years. We should note that it is much less difficult to correct such an error in cultures that do not teach these roles as adamantly as ours does.

Gender role is a characteristic of psychological maleness or femaleness (gender), not of biological maleness or femaleness (sex). A great deal of confusion over terminology exists in this field. We should note some terms that are not the same as gender role. (See Figure 18-1.) Gender role is not the same as one's **genetic sex**. One's genetic sex is determined biologically and can be identified by the structure of the sex chromosome pair. Females have the XX configuration and males the XY. Gender role is not the same as **anatomical sex**, which is determined by the presence of male or female genitals. Gender role is not the same as **sexual preference**, which refers to a person's choice of sexual partners in terms of anatomical sex (the same or different than themselves). Sexual preference is an independent concept from one's gender role. It is common, for example, for homosexual men to have strongly masculine gender roles (Bieber et al., 1962; Evans, 1969). Gender role is not the same as gender identity, although this term is used inconsistently within psychology. **Gender identity** usually refers to the degree to which a person identifies with and is comfortable with his or her biological sex. In rare cases, transsexual persons actually reject the fact of their biological sex, as we saw in Chapter 14. More commonly, people fall somewhere along a continuum of how comfortable they are with their bodies sexually. Another widely used term is *sex role*. Usually, this term means roughly the same as *gender role*. *Sex role* refers to nonbiological aspects of one's sex. It is the person's learned or psychological role. Deaux (1985) and others have recommended the use of the term *gender role* to clearly differentiate it from the term *sex*, which is biologically determined. We will follow that recommendation throughout this chapter.

Figure 18-1 Some terms related to maleness and femaleness

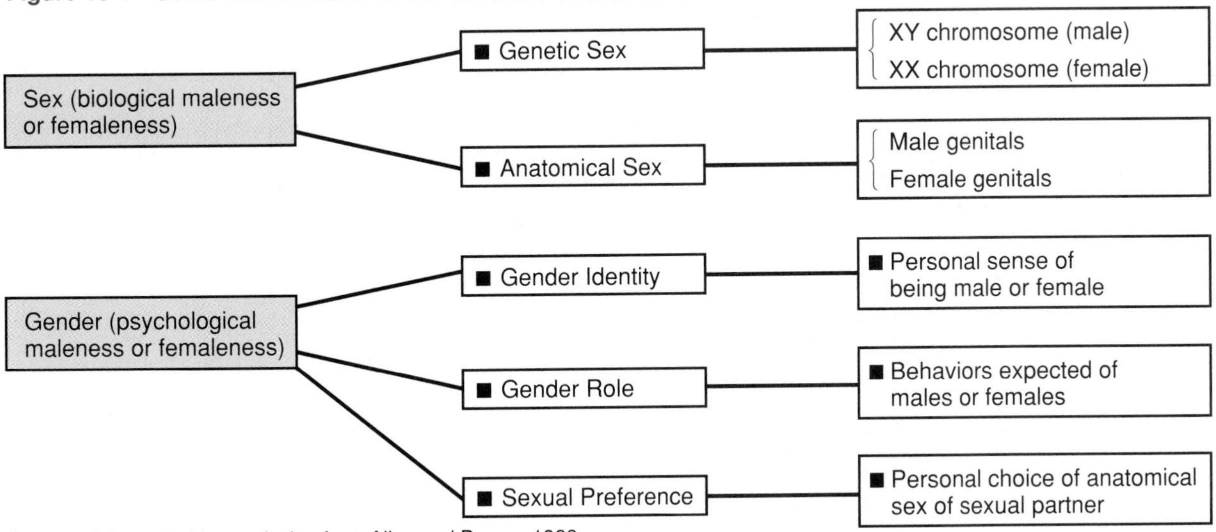

Sex (biological maleness or femaleness)
- ■ Genetic Sex — XY chromosome (male) / XX chromosome (female)
- ■ Anatomical Sex — Male genitals / Female genitals

Gender (psychological maleness or femaleness)
- ■ Gender Identity — ■ Personal sense of being male or female
- ■ Gender Role — ■ Behaviors expected of males or females
- ■ Sexual Preference — ■ Personal choice of anatomical sex of sexual partner

SOURCE: Adapted with permission from Allyn and Bacon, 1989.

Traditional gender roles

Nearly everyone can quite accurately describe the behaviours of our traditional gender roles. In general, the traditional *masculine role* is based on **instrumental behaviour**, actions aimed toward manipulating the environment and achieving goals. By contrast, the traditional *feminine role* is based on **relationship behaviour**, actions aimed toward facilitating human interaction. We could cite many specific beliefs that illustrate these two general statements. Men initiate relationship contacts more often. Women are more intuitive. Men should be responsible for things. Women are better with children. We could also cite some behaviours that are obviously trivial but that are very strongly enforced as gender-role appropriate. These are worth thinking about because they illustrate both how arbitrary and how powerful our gender roles are. Women may not smoke pipes. Men must not perform the gesture in which the forearm is pointed upward and the hand bends back at the wrist. Women may colour their lips; men must not. Why? There is no sensible answer to this question, but it is important to recognize that all of us are powerfully affected by our gender-role training.

The **feminine gender role**, the traditional female role, is characterized by passivity and relationship behaviour. The **masculine gender role**, the traditional male role, is characterized by activity and instrumental behaviour. The subtlety and power of gender-appropriate behaviour was demonstrated in a revealing study by Sande, Adams, and Freisen (1990). The researchers began with the knowledge that females tend to use a pattern of speech intonation that conveys powerlessness, uncertainty, and deference to others (Lakoff, 1975). Females use more "empty" adjectives such as *cute*, whereas males use more "power" adjectives such as *terrific*. Females are more likely to soften and modify statements and to end statements with a question such as "isn't it?" or with a rising intonation that implies a questioning stance. These are subtle but consistent differences with far-reaching consequences. Sande, Adams, and Freisen investigated whether this female style of speaking led women to be excluded from more powerful positions. Would adopting a more masculine speech style help a woman advance in the job market? Or would it hurt her chances by eliciting rejection for her violation of gender-role expectations? The researchers had Canadian university students listen to an audiotape that was presented as an interview with a job applicant. The students rated the job applicant on social traits, ability traits, competence, and dependability. They then assessed the applicant's suitability for two different jobs, one with higher status and pay than the other. Each subject heard one of four tapes: a male applicant speaking in the traditional male speech pattern; a male using the feminine speech pattern; a female using the masculine pattern; and a female using the feminine pattern.

Male subjects reacted strongly and negatively to the female applicant who used the more "powerful" pattern of intonations. Male subjects also reacted against the male job applicant who used a feminine style of speech, but they did not penalize him as harshly. By contrast, the female subjects did not downgrade either applicant for using gender-inappropriate speech patterns. This finding suggests that male students hold gender-role stereotypes more strongly and are more ready to enforce them in others than females are. We will also note later that, in general, gender-role training for boys starts earlier and is more strongly enforced than gender-role training for girls.

Both the male and female subjects in this experiment rated the two job applicants who used gender-appropriate speech patterns equal in social traits and ability traits. However, even though the qualifications of the two applicants were the same, both sexes consistently tended to award the higher paying job to the male.

One dimension or two?

One of the most insidious aspects of our gender-role training is that we are implicitly taught that the masculine and feminine gender roles are *opposites* (Constantinople, 1973). Even many psychological tests assign a score on the "M-F dimension." A person scores *either* in the masculine direction *or* in the feminine direction. The implication is that to become more masculine, one must become less feminine, and vice-versa. This one-dimensional view of gender roles subtly teaches us that one cannot be both instrumental, achieving, strong, and active *and* loving, sensitive, empathic, and open to emotion. If asked point-blank, "Is it *possible* for one person to be both strong and loving?," most people will answer, "Of course it is." Nevertheless, most of us act as though one cannot have the positive characteristics of both the masculine and feminine roles. They seem mutually exclusive of each other.

Bierman has surveyed a large body of research and concluded that "Much of social behavior can be represented by combinations of the two orthogonal dimensions of active expressiveness versus passive restrictiveness and of acceptance versus rejection" (Bierman, 1969, p. 339). Bierman suggested that we can use a graphic device, known as the **interpersonal behaviour circle**, to describe any social behaviour in terms of two independent dimensions: (1) active versus passive and (2) loving versus hostile. As you can see in Figure 18-2, the vertical axis represents the degree of activity, and the horizontal axis represents the degree of affection. We can place any social behaviour somewhere in the circle by plotting the appropriate points along the two axes. For example, a guarded friendly gesture might be somewhere in Quadrant III (lower right), since it is toward the right on the horizontal axis and below the middle on the vertical axis.

Each of the four quadrants represents a different set of behaviours. Quadrant III (lower right) represents the traditional feminine gender role—passive and loving. Quadrant I (upper left) represents the traditional masculine gender role—active and lacking in affection. If these were the only choices, then traditional gender roles would be opposites. However, according to the diagram we are dealing with two *independent* dimensions (which is what Bierman means by *orthogonal* dimensions). Thus, it is possible for a person to be in Quadrant IV (upper right) and act in both an active and loving manner. In fact, the most effective persons are probably those who

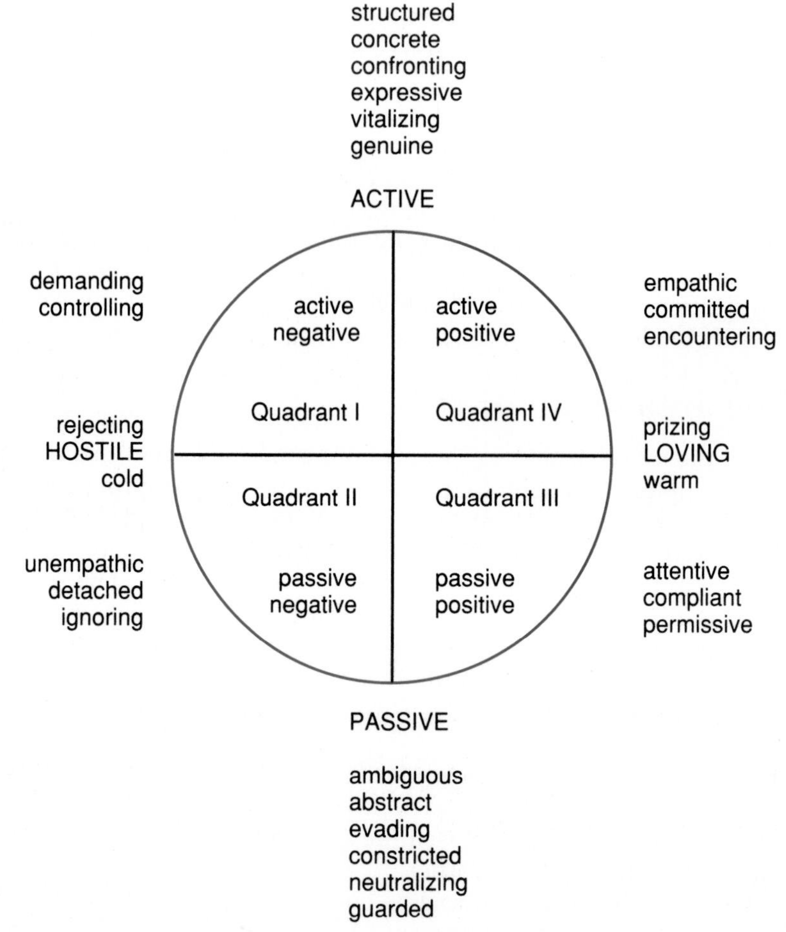

FIGURE 18-2 The interpersonal behaviour circle
According to Bierman, any social action can be considered in terms of two dimensions. The vertical axis of the circle shows the active-passive dimension. The horizontal axis of the circle shows the loving-hostile dimension. Quadrant III represents the traditional female gender role, and Quadrant I represents the traditional male gender role. The most effective behaviours are located in Quadrant IV.

SOURCE: Reprinted with permission from Bierman (1969).

operate with this combination of behaviours. Effective parents are "firm and loving." Effective managers are "instrumental and considerate" or "tough and fair." Effective therapists are "empathic and intensely engaged."

In recent years, the term *androgynous* has been used to describe a person, of either sex, whose behaviour falls in Quadrant IV (upper right) of the interpersonal behaviour circle. Such a person is both active and loving (tough and fair; firm and considerate, etc.). **Androgyny** can be defined as the combination, within an individual, of the positive qualities of both the traditional masculine and traditional feminine gender roles. The word androgyny comes from the two Greek root words "andro" (man) and "gyny" (woman). We will have more to say about androgyny after we examine some of the evidence about the current state of sex differences and gender roles.

Let us mention in passing that Quadrant II (lower left) represents the behaviour of a small minority of persons who are generally quite troubled. Most of them suffer from a *passive-aggressive personality disorder* (see Chapter 14).

PSYCHOLOGICAL SEX DIFFERENCES

In this section we will investigate sex differences (and sex similarities) in the areas of cognitive abilities and the personality characteristics of achievement motivation, aggression, and dependency. Many people become personally involved when discussing sex differences, and it is common to make statements that are easy to misunderstand. For example, in a few paragraphs, we will say, "After adolescence, boys develop a superiority in spatial abilities." All this statement means is that on *some* tests of spatial abilities, grouping the scores of all the boys together gives an *average* score that is higher than the *average* score of all the girls grouped together. In fact, this average difference tends to be quite consistent, although it is not a large difference. In other words, we have a small average difference that is *statistically significant*. As we discussed in Chapter 1, **statistically significant** refers to research findings whose likelihood (probability) of being "real" (that is, not due to chance) has been calculated to be at least 95%. Thus, according to our statement about spatial abilities, we can be at least 95% certain that if we could test all the children in our population, we would still get a small average difference favouring boys.

The danger with a phrase such as "boys are superior" is that it can be misinterpreted as a *polarized* statement. One might think that boys are at one end of the continuum and girls are at the other. But this would be wrong. See Figure 18-3. Suppose that on a test of, say, 80 points, the average score of the boys is 3 points higher than the average score of the girls (this would be a typical finding for spatial ability). Far from being polarized, the two groups overlap enormously (Matlin, 1987). And the differences between individuals varies considerably. It could easily be true that 47% of the girls were better at the test than the average boy. When we say "girls are better at . . . " or "boys have an advantage in . . . ," remember that we are using a kind of shorthand language.

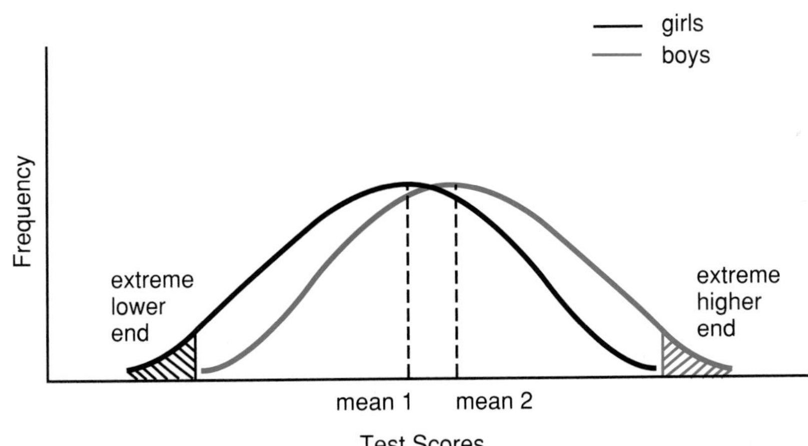

FIGURE 18-3 Hypothetical results with a small average difference that is statistically significant
These hypothetical distributions have different means. However, the enormous overlap between them indicates that we should treat each individual case uniquely and avoid making polarized generalizations. At the same time, the curves also illustrate that even though the average difference is small, the difference at the extreme ends is relatively large.

It is important not to think in polarized terms about general sex differences. However, we do need to recognize that "small differences in means [i.e., averages] translate into large differences in the proportions of males and females beyond some extreme cutoff point" (Eaton & Enns, 1986, p. 25). Thus, if we look at all males and females on some variable, such as spatial ability or general activity level, we might find a small but stable average sex difference. However, if we look only at the extreme ends of the continuum, the difference will be relatively large. For example, in one study, when only the 9% most active children were identified, boys outnumbered girls by 2 to 1 (Schachar, Rutter, & Smith, 1981). Figure 18-3 illustrates that at the extreme right of the distribution, boys are proportionately much more frequent than girls (and at the extreme left, girls are proportionately much more frequent than boys).

Cognitive abilities

A person's *cognitive abilities*—that is, the abilities to think, learn, remember, and solve problems—are all determined by an interaction between inborn skills and environmental influences. Each of us inherits a potential upper limit. Whether we actually reach that upper limit depends on our experiences. (In practice, many people probably function below their potential limit.) Because boys and girls are treated so differently from a very early age, it is very difficult to sort out whether any sex differences in cognitive ability are inborn. For example, males tend to do better at spatial tasks. However, it is very problematic to ascertain the reasons. How much should we attribute to inborn ability? And how much should we attribute to the fact that boys are usually given construction toys and encouraged to play catch more often than girls?

Who is more intelligent, boys or girls? As we pointed out in Chapter 11, the answer to this question will depend largely on our definition of *intelligence*. Tests can be constructed to measure and emphasize many different abilities. Thus, some research has resulted in the conclusion that females have higher general intelligence. This has usually been because the researchers used a test that stressed verbal ability, on which females are superior at certain ages. When more balanced tests are used, sex differences do not *appear*. Should we then conclude that sex differences do not *exist*? Certainly not. It would be invalid to draw such a conclusion because the "balanced" tests were *constructed* to eliminate sex differences. It is difficult to give an intelligent answer to the question of who is more intelligent in general. We can, however, make some statements about specific abilities.

Verbal ability

It is commonly believed that females are superior at verbal tasks throughout life. One extensive survey of the research literature, however, concluded that females are superior only in specific phases of development (Maccoby & Jacklin, 1974). Up to about 2 years of age, there seems to be very weak evidence, if any, that girls do activities such as babble and vocalize more than boys. From the age of 3 to about the age of 11 or 12, there seems to be no measurable difference between the verbal ability of boys and girls on reading and language tests. From then on, however, girls do show an advantage over boys both in uncomplicated skills, such as simple fluency, and in tasks that require considerable semantic processing, such as creative writing, reading comprehension, and verbal problem-solving. This female advantage seems to last past high school. The general statement that, as adults, females show some superiority at verbal tasks seems to be supported, but several recent reviews suggest that the difference is smaller than Maccoby and Jacklin concluded (Hyde, 1981; Benbow & Stanley, 1980).

Is this verbal superiority the result of inborn differences? The evidence is inconclusive. On one side of the argument, some researchers claim that females have verbal abilities represented in both brain hemispheres to a larger extent than males do. However, even this could be the result of either learning or inheritance. On the other side of the argument, some researchers maintain that girls are more reinforced for verbal performance in school, whereas boys are more reinforced for physical performance.

Spatial ability

After adolescence starts, boys develop a superiority in spatial ability. This ability includes skills such as visualizing objects in space, orienting oneself in space, doing "mental rotations" of images, and making designs with blocks. Recent evidence (Linn & Petersen, 1983) found that the male advantage is limited to these fairly simple spatial tasks, and that there were no apparent differences on complex spatial tasks that required analytic thinking. Both boys and girls continue to increase in spatial ability with age, but boys develop at a faster pace.

Traditionally, there is considerable pressure against girls' pursuing geometry and the physical sciences, including engineering. If we also take into account the clear differences in the kinds of play encouraged for boys and girls, it may well be that much of the observed sex difference in spatial ability is the result of training differences. Spatial abilities do increase with practice (Newcombe, Bandura, & Taylor, 1983; Halpern, 1986).

Nevertheless, the sex difference in spatial abilities is the one cognitive ability that seems most likely to have a biological basis. Spatial ability might be at least partly a genetically sex-linked characteristic. This would mean that it would be influenced by a recessive gene on the sex chromosome pair (see Chapter 12). According to one theory, the sex chromosome carries either a "good-spatial-ability" gene that is *recessive* or a "not-as-good-spatial-ability" gene that is *dominant*. The girls' sex chromosome pair is XX. It includes two X chromosomes, one from the mother and one from the father. Even if she inherits the "good-spatial-ability" gene from one parent, it will probably be suppressed by the dominant opposing gene. She would need to inherit the recessive gene from both parents to express the high spatial ability. The boy's sex chromosome pair, however, is XY, where the Y half is not actively expressed. Thus, he only needs to inherit one of the "good" genes for it to be expressed. Therefore, one can conclude from this theory that boys are more likely to express good spatial ability for genetic reasons. Can we verify this theory in any way? We know that the boy gets his X chromosome from his mother and the Y chromosome from his father. Thus, if the theory is true, there should be a higher correlation between spatial ability of mothers and sons than between fathers and sons. Several studies reported this finding (Bock & Kolakowski, 1973; Corah, 1965; Hartlage, 1970). However, the issue is still unsettled.

One review of research literature (Vandenberg & Kuse, 1979) cited some studies where this correlation was not found. Caplan, MacPherson, and Tobin (1985, 1986), in fact, said that there is no known basis in brain function to explain sex differences in spatial abilities. They have even argued that either "sex differences in spatial abilities do not exist" or at least the whole issue is ". . . by no means clear as yet" (Caplan, MacPherson, & Tobin, 1985, p. 797). They have dismissed the large amount of attention paid to this sex difference as a "magnified molehill and misplaced focus" (Caplan, MacPherson, & Tobin, 1986, p. 1016). Because virtually every topic in the field of sex difference is so controversial, it is not surprising to learn that Caplan and his co-researchers have received vigorous criticism. Hiscock (1986) agreed with Caplan that sex differences are *small* average differences and are in fact often inconsistent. He went on, though, to argue that the evidence is both extensive and consistent that there is a small advantage to males in spatial ability. Several other writers (Eliot, 1986; Burnett, 1986; Halpern, 1986) criticized Caplan and his co-researchers for not reviewing the research thoroughly enough. Halpern (1986) has probably best captured our current level of understanding on this topic. He states that there are small but fairly consistent differences between groups of males and females on most spatial tasks. There *may* be some biological component involved, although this probably has more to do with hormones and brain laterality than with the genetic theory. In any case, these differences are enormously influenced by the different training that males and females receive. "It seems likely that sex differences in spatial ability would be reduced, possibly even eliminated, if sex-role pressures and expectations became sex neutral" (Halpern, 1986, p. 1015).

Mathematical ability

A large part of mathematical ability depends upon spatial skills. Thus, as we might expect, males tend to do better than females on math-related tests. As with spatial abilities, this advantage doesn't seem to appear until junior high school or later. Again we are faced with the question of how much of this difference is cultural and how much is biological. If there is a biological difference in spatial ability, it would be reflected in mathematics, of course. However, there are so many cultural, personal, and reinforcement pressures on females to avoid math, that these factors seem to be the more important explanations of the observed differences (Shoemaker, 1977).

Girls are given very strong training to believe that mathematics is a male-appropriate skill and that females are deficient in it. This strong belief creates a powerful self-fulfilling prophecy. In fact, the term *math anxiety* is commonly applied to girls and women to describe a learned fear of anything to do with numbers (Tobias, 1976). Such a fear would make it very difficult to pursue studies in math. It is interesting to note that in some studies, math skills were tested in terms of "female-relevant" topics, such as cooking and sewing. In these tests, female subjects scored much higher than on tests where the identical problems were presented in terms of "masculine" topics such as guns and money (Milton, 1958).

Meredith Kimball

Boys tend to do better on standardized tests of math achievement. Benbow (1989) has interpreted these results as evidence that both environmental and biological factors cause this sex difference. Meredith Kimball (1989), of Simon Fraser University, has pointed out a further complication, however. Although boys tend to do better on standardized measures of math achievement, girls tend to earn better classroom grades in math. She offers three possible explanations for this. First, perhaps the boys' greater math experience gives them a special advantage on standardized tests. Second, perhaps boys have a more independent learning style in math, which facilitates performance on standardized tests, whereas girls use more rote learning, which works best in classroom settings. Third, perhaps girls do better in familiar situations such as their own classroom, whereas boys do better in novel situations such as a standardized test. There is some evidence to support each of these hypotheses, and only more research will tell which is the best explanation. In the meantime, we need to recognize that the male superiority in math depends partly on the setting.

We should add a cautionary note here. Sex differences in cognitive ability seem to be diminishing with relatively recent changes in the educational system and social values, as well as changes in the workplace and home. Rosenthal and Rubin (1982) have pointed out that in the areas of mathematical, spatial, and verbal ability, sex differences tended to shrink in tests from the 1960s to the early 1980s. This strongly suggests that whatever differences we find are at least very susceptible to change from environmental factors. The conclusions we draw today may very well be invalid in a few years.

Achievement motivation

The **need for achievement** is a socially acquired motive to produce and succeed. (See Chapter 6.) It is not enough to be able to achieve. One must also have the motivation to use that ability. It has been said that "the three A's of manhood are Achieve, Achieve, and Achieve" (Zilbergeld, 1978). This reflects the pressure placed on males in our society to produce tangible results. This standard is in many ways internalized by males as the essential way to define their own personal worth. It seems that achievement, in the sense of producing tangible products, is less central to a woman's life. This is both an advantage and a disadvantage for females. The productive person often receives many rewards but also often pays a price in life satisfaction.

The study of achievement motivation

In Chapter 6 on motivation we discussed how achievement motivation has been studied by means of TAT cards that tapped achievement imagery (McClelland et al., 1953). We should emphasize that almost all of this early research on achievement was done with male subjects. Now, with our greater sensitivity to gender-role issues, it seems as though the early researchers equated "achievement motivation in men" with the "general study of achievement motivation." In other words, they appeared to make male behaviour the standard for human behaviour.

It was found, for example, that if the researcher made a verbal reference to qualities such as intelligence and leadership, then the stories given by the male subjects to describe the cards included a higher need for achievement. Thus, with males, measures of achievement motivation correlated with achievement effort and academic performance. Among females, however, this correlation seldom occurred in the few cases where they were studied. The researchers tended to dismiss these different results in footnotes with words to the effect that the sex difference is an unresolved issue. But now, we can see that the resolution of the issue seems to centre around the definition of *achievement*. Men, on the one hand, tend to be more motivated to achieve in the production of things, and in competition. Women, on the other hand, seem to be just as motivated to achieve but in the areas of social skills and interpersonal relationships (Deaux, 1976b). "Yeah, but . . ." we sometimes hear (more from men than women), "that's not really achievement." Clearly, this is a problem of definition. Success in social and interpersonal areas certainly is central to success in life. Surely it should qualify as achievement.

Attributions of success and failure

There is an interesting difference in the way men and women tend to explain their own success or failure, when success is defined in terms of productivity as opposed to interpersonal relationships. In general, men attribute their performance more to internal causes, such as high or low ability. Women have some tendency to attribute performance to luck (Deaux, 1976a). This has important consequences for later behaviour. If a person attributes good performance to luck, then it is beyond her control to repeat the performance again. It is not a matter of trying hard next time. By the same token, if a person attributes poor performance to bad luck, then failure is not as devastating as it would be if it was attributed to a lack of personal skill. Maybe she will be luckier next time.

This general attitude seems to be contradicted by some evidence that women are more likely than men to respond to failure feedback by performing more poorly—in essence, giving up (Greenglass, 1982). Dweck and Bush (1976), however, noted that most of the evidence for this involved children receiving failure feedback from adults. They hypothesized that the *source* of the feedback is critical. In fact, they found that boys were more likely than girls to give up in the face of failure feedback from a male, especially a male peer. They were less affected by feedback from an adult, especially a woman. Girls were more likely to be adversely affected by failure feedback from a woman. Thus, we should conclude that this "helplessness in the face of failure feedback" is not a general characteristic of females.

Fear of success

In Chapter 6, we pointed out that individuals with a low need for achievement tend to have a strong fear of failure. During the 1970s, another idea that attracted great attention in the field of achievement was the hypothesis that women tend to have a strong **fear of success**. In other words, women tend to have a learned motive to feel threatened by their own successful performance. This hypothesis arose from research by Horner (1970). In one study, she asked men and women to write stories about the following sentence, which sometimes referred to a woman and sometimes to a man: "After first-term finals Anne (John) finds herself (himself) at the top of her (his) medical school class." Horner reported that 65% of college women wrote stories that indicated some fear of success. They included responses that denied the success or described it in a negative context, such as Anne was ugly or a "mistake had been made." Only 10% of the men wrote such stories. Horner related scores on her testing procedure to other achievement-avoiding behaviour and concluded that fear of success was a stable personality trait.

Subsequent research, however, has indicated that fear of success is probably not a very common personality trait. For example, if Anne is at the top of her *nursing* school class, then little fear of success emerges in the stories. Summaries of the research on fear of success (Tresemer, 1977; Hoffman, 1977a, 1982) generally find that the concept is difficult to measure. Whatever fear of success does exist is probably specific to situations and to the realistic consequences of success in specific settings. To illustrate the point, consider the stories we would have gotten if the study had used the sentence, "After first-term finals, John finds himself at the top of his Tammy Baker Make-Up School class." Subjects tend to write stories based on what are perceived as likely consequences. This is much different than basing them on stable personality traits. Thus, although fear of success was a popular topic for many years, interest in it is now diminishing (Deaux, 1985).

Aggression

There is considerable evidence that males are, on average, more aggressive than females, both in verbal and physical ways. This difference is found in a wide variety of cultures (Whiting and Edwards, 1973). In our culture, it appears as early as social play begins. In nursery school, boys more than girls exhibit disruptive behaviour, attention-seeking through misbehaviour, antisocial behaviour, and open physical aggression (Maccoby & Jacklin, 1974; Maccoby, 1980). It is also well established that males incorporate aggressiveness into their self-concepts and report themselves to be more aggressive and hostile than females, especially when frustrated (Bennett & Cohen, 1959).

In younger persons, this aggression is usually used to exert dominance and control over others. As they get older, males continue to try to dominate others more than women do, and men are more likely to approach leadership roles in authoritarian ways. This has some surprising and disturbing consequences that we will pursue later. For example, in Chapter 20 (Organizational Psychology), we will argue that both permissive and authoritarian leadership styles are less effective than a combination of assertiveness and helpfulness. We have also seen in Chapter 12 (Development) and Chapter 17 (Person to Person) that what works for young males may not work for adult males when dealing with others.

Biological influences

The sex difference in aggression may be one of the few behavioural differences that have some foundation in biological differences between males and females. Research with rats and monkeys has demonstrated that the levels of the male sex hormone androgen are related to levels of aggressive behaviour and dominance. If pregnant females are injected with androgen, their female offspring will show more threat behaviour and less withdrawal when dealing with other animals, as compared with normal females (Young, Goy, & Phoenix, 1964). In one study of humans, 17 girls had received doses of androgen prior to birth for medical reasons. Their later behaviour was described by their mothers as more "masculine," and this included engaging in more fighting than their sisters (Ehrhardt & Baker, 1973). These results should be interpreted cautiously, however. Their parents knew about the expected effects of the male sex hormone, and the girls received medical treatment for it throughout their childhood. These factors could easily have biased the parents' observations and may even have produced self-fulfilling prophecies.

Cultural pressures

There may well be an *average* difference in aggression between males and females. And we have seen that this difference may have a biological foundation. Nevertheless, it is clear that boys are trained for aggression far more than girls. The difference in training probably starts in the first few weeks of life. It includes buying aggressive toys for boys, strongly inhibiting aggression in girls, punishing boys for *not* being aggressive ("Don't be a sissy, son."), and surrounding children with models of male aggression. These cultural pressures almost certainly enhance—and even exaggerate—the human male's somewhat greater *potential* for aggression. It is easier for a boy to learn aggression, but it is also probable that we could take a group of babies and raise nearly all the girls to be more aggressive than nearly all the boys.

Dependency

The cultural stereotype in our society is that girls are more dependent than boys on others. However, the evidence for this in the early years of life is quite weak (Maccoby & Jacklin, 1974). Much depends on how one defines the word *dependency*. If dependency is defined as seeking help and social approval directly, then girls generally are seen as more dependent. Girls tend to stay closer to mother or teacher and to ask for help, for example (Greenglass, 1971; Golightly, Nelson, & Johnson, 1970). However, if dependency is defined as seeking attention and acceptance, then boys tend to appear more dependent, even in cross-cultural studies (Whiting and Edwards, 1973). In other words, males tend to express dependency less directly than females do. In general, the evidence on sex differences in dependency is not conclusive.

Sandra Bem.
SOURCE: Courtesy Sandra Bem, Cornell University.

ANDROGYNY

We mentioned earlier in this chapter that androgyny has become one of the most interesting and important issues in the psychology of gender roles. **Androgyny** is the combination, within an individual, of the positive qualities of both the traditional masculine and traditional feminine gender roles. An androgynous person would combine the characteristics of independence, strength, productivity, and self-reliance with those of sensitivity to others, openness to emotion, and the ability to love—just to mention a few of the desirable qualities of "masculinity" and "femininity." (See again Quadrant IV in Figure 18-2.) A great deal of research and writing about androgyny has been done, particularly by Bem (1974) as well as by Spence and her co-workers (Spence, Helmreich, & Stapp, 1974).

The advantages of flexibility

The most important argument that has been made for the desirability of androgyny is that a person with a rigid traditional gender role is needlessly limited. Life demands of us very different behaviours and abilities under different circumstances and at different times in our lives. At work, it is often necessary to compete vigorously, a traditional masculine characteristic. But then a few hours later, effective

A person with a rigid traditional gender role is needlessly limited.
SOURCE: A military policewoman learns to rappel during an exercise at CFB Gagetown, New Brunswick. Courtesy Canadian Forces Photos.

SOURCE: Kathleen Bellesiles.

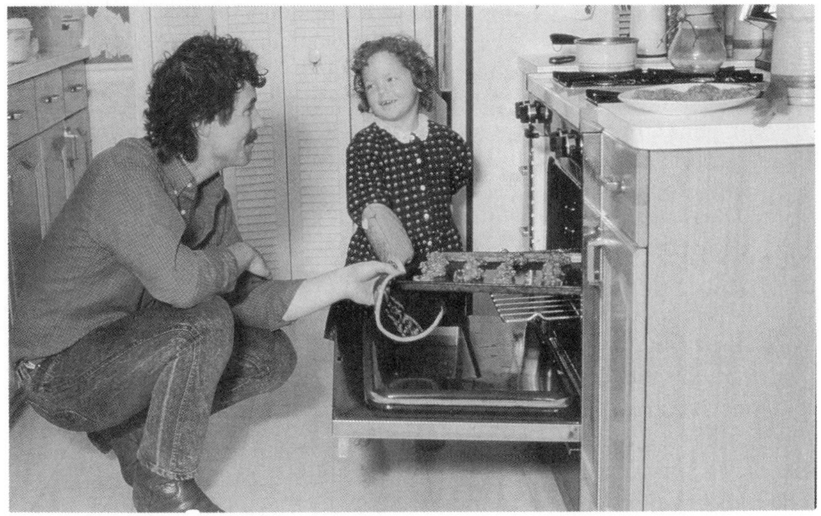

living requires empathic sensitivity with a close friend, spouse, or child. A person who is strongly bound to a traditional gender role will do well in only one of these circumstances. Similarly, what brings greatest rewards for a 20-year-old may be very different from what is most effective at 30 or 40. Bem has argued as follows:

> The highly sex-typed individual is motivated to keep his behaviour consistent with an internalized gender-role standard, suppressing any behaviour that might be considered undesirable or inappropriate for his sex. Thus, whereas a narrowly masculine self-concept might inhibit behaviours that are stereotyped as feminine, and a narrowly feminine self-concept might inhibit behaviours that are stereotyped as masculine, a mixed, or androgynous, self-concept might allow an individual to freely engage in both "masculine" and "feminine" behaviours (Bem, 1974, p. 155).

Before we continue our discussion of androgyny itself, we need to lay some background for a later argument. There is considerable evidence that individuals who are strongly sex-typed in the traditional feminine role tend to exhibit more anxiety than others, be somewhat less intelligent, and have lower self-esteem (Cosentino & Heilbrun, 1964; Sears, 1970; Webb, 1963). It is more difficult to generalize about the behaviour and characteristics of a person with a strongly sex-typed masculine role. A strongly held masculine role tends to correlate with somewhat lower intelligence and lower creativity (Maccoby, 1966). However, a classic study by Mussen (1961) reveals a fascinating pattern. Mussen tested adolescent boys and found that the boys with strongly masculine interests also had more self-confidence and more positive self-concepts than did boys with more feminine interests. Mussen then tested the same subjects when they were in their late thirties. The men who had been "masculine" as adolescents still tended to be masculine, being more self-sufficient, less social, and less introspective. The other men still tended to be more social (more "feminine") in orientation. Other qualities, however, had changed:

> During adolescence, highly masculine subjects possessed more self-confidence and greater feelings of adequacy than the other group, but as adults, they were relatively lacking in qualities of leadership, dominance, self-confidence, and self-acceptance. . . . In general there seems to have been a shift in the self-concepts of the two groups in adulthood, the originally highly masculine boys apparently feeling less positive about themselves after adolescence, and, correlatively, the less masculine groups changing in a favourable direction (Mussen, 1962, p. 440).

It seems likely that strongly masculine behaviour is well-reinforced for males in adolescence and young adulthood. The rewards this brings would contribute to self-esteem and confidence. From the perspective of our discussion of androgyny, however, we might argue that this is a dangerous and misleading trap for the young man. If he becomes committed to his sex-typed gender role, it will be difficult to change when life's demands change. Perhaps the meaning of life and affirmation of the individual come more from shared relationships later in life. It is not easy to shed a powerful gender role, and a strongly masculine role is correlated in adulthood with higher anxiety and lower self-acceptance (see also Harford, Willis, & Deabler, 1967).

Bem (Bem & Lenny, 1976; Bem, Martyna, & Watson, 1976) designed some interesting experiments to illustrate how androgyny can relate to greater flexibility and adaptability. In one experiment, subjects were paid for posing for photographs of themselves engaged in various simple, common tasks. Some of the tasks were sex-typed, and the subject was given a choice between pairs of photographs in which to pose. A subject, for example, could choose to pose oiling a squeaky hinge or ironing a handkerchief. In each case, posing for the "cross-sex behaviour" paid slightly more. For example, a male subject could earn a little more money posing ironing the handkerchief, and a female subject could earn a little more money posing oiling a squeaky hinge. It was most reasonable to choose the tasks that paid the most money. In the actual experiment, strongly sex-typed subjects tended to sacrifice the money, while androgynous ones chose the better-paying choice. The cost of "violating" their gender roles was so high that sex-typed individuals sacrificed the money, even with such innocuous activities as mixing baby formula and pounding in a nail.

A further finding makes an important and sad commentary on how powerfully one's gender role can be internalized. Sometimes subjects were required to choose between two "cross-sex" behaviours. In other words, they ended up having to pose for photographs "violating" their gender roles. After such an experience, strongly sex-typed subjects actually felt worse about themselves as persons.

In other experiments by Bem, subjects had to express their independent judgments, even when others disagreed with them. Masculine subjects did this well, and so did androgynous subjects. When a situation required effective listening skills, feminine subjects did well, and so did androgynous subjects. Bem's conclusion is that androgyny provides flexibility for different circumstances.

Criticism of androgyny

Since Bem's pioneering work, androgyny has become a popular topic in psychology. An enormous amount of research is being done on it, and it has been the basis of many books and articles. The idea has great relevance for life and for the current interest in changing gender roles. Taylor and Hall (1982) examined this research and offered a number of criticisms of the way androgyny is conceptualized and the way research findings have been interpreted. We will comment on some of their arguments.

Their central conclusion is that there is a general advantage to having a "masculine" orientation for both males and females. According to Taylor and Hall, there is no clear evidence that a "balanced" gender role is related to more effective functioning. "It is primarily masculinity, not androgyny, that yields positive outcomes for individuals in American society" (Taylor & Hall, 1982, p. 362).

We think that this conclusion deserves careful consideration and probably holds under many circumstances. However, there are some problems with taking Taylor and Hall's conclusion at face value. Much depends on how one defines "positive outcomes" and on who the subjects are in the research one is reviewing. Much of the research relating androgyny to measures of effective psychological functioning is based on paper-and-pencil tests that rely on the subject to report his or her own functioning. Part of the masculine role is to deny weakness, both to others and to oneself. In general, females are more willing to report personal weaknesses on questionnaires. Therefore, we should be careful about making broad generalizations from self-reported data (Hill & Sarason, 1966; Lekarczyk & Hill, 1969).

Our second and more important comment refers back to Mussen's findings discussed earlier. One serious problem with much research in psychology is that a greatly disproportionate amount of the data collected is gathered from undergraduate students. (They are clearly human and are easy to get at.) Because this is the case with most of the research reviewed by Taylor and Hall, it is probably not justified to generalize their findings to society as a whole. In fact, Mussen's findings would suggest that we should expect traditional masculine values to be most effective in the very age group being studied—late adolescence and young adulthood. However, just the reverse seems likely true among older subjects, which is exactly the point of stressing the relationship between androgyny and flexibility. We agree with Taylor and Hall that there is a great need for more research on androgyny, but we tend to see more value in the notion than they do.

GENDER ROLES AND THE EFFECTIVE PERSON

It is clear that gender-role training and sexist practices are very powerful in our culture. Is there any evidence of change in our society? What can we hope for the future? What are the personal implications of all this for us? What should we strive for?

There have been many attempts to describe what defines an "emotionally healthy person" or a "fully functioning person" (Rogers, 1961) or (the phrase we prefer) an "effective person." These descriptions share some common characteristics. Elsewhere, I have summarized them with four qualities that an effective person, male or female, would have (Martin, 1976). I have argued that the **effective person** is a person who possesses self-esteem, autonomy, emotional self-knowledge, and a capacity for intimacy. Two of these qualities are traditionally masculine in our culture, and two of them are traditionally feminine. If a person is a victim of strict gender-role training (and all of us are to some extent), then that person is being deprived of half of what makes life meaningful—half of what makes for an effective person. In the previous section we presented evidence that the great advantage of being androgynous is *flexibility*. Life makes very different demands at different times. Sometimes one must be tender and sensitive, at other times strong and independent. The effective person moves easily among these different ways of behaving.

Let's look at the four qualities of the effective person as they relate to gender roles. The first two—*self-esteem and autonomy*—are traditionally identified with the masculine gender role. We have found it easy to persuade women that their training has tended to deprive them of these valuable characteristics. The second two—*emotional self-knowledge* and a *capacity for intimacy*—are traditionally identified with the feminine gender role. Men tend to be deprived of these equally valuable characteristics. Although all four characteristics are essential to effective living, our gender roles try to limit us to two. We have found, however, that it is more difficult to persuade men that they are missing out on half of what makes life meaningful. We think this is because males are taught their gender roles more stringently (Maccoby & Jacklin, 1974; Block, 1978). Unfortunately, one of the powerful lessons men are taught is that emotion and intimacy are "women's things" and should be devalued. Maching (1986) reported that male and female university students had clearly different expectations for partners in a relationship. Moreover, the male subjects were considerably more resistant to changes in the traditional roles in marriage than were the female subjects. Rosaria Caporrimo concludes, "While it is clear that roles are changing, it is not clear that the pace is the same for women and men, and many stereotypes remain" (Caporrimo, 1989, p. 407).

Self-esteem

Nearly every description of the effective person stresses that he or she possesses **self-esteem**, a sense of personal worth. It is a kind of self-love that seems to consist mostly of a quiet feeling of being okay. This, of course, is quite different from conceit and braggadocio, which often seem to be a compensation for insecurity about oneself. In general, the evidence suggests that it is healthy to like oneself.

Some studies suggest that women who most strongly identify with the traditional feminine gender role are likely to have a lower self-esteem than other women. Furthermore, masculine characteristics tend to correlate with higher self-esteem (Basow, 1980). There is also evidence that males increase in self-esteem relative to females after elementary school (Loeb & Horst, 1978). Such findings, however, should be interpreted with care. Perhaps males tend to exaggerate their self-esteem as part of an inability to admit weaknesses.

Many other studies report weak or no differences in overall self-esteem. Deaux (1976b) suggested a helpful explanation for these puzzling results. She noted that most tests of self-esteem actually contain two general kinds of items. One kind tests **self-regard**, the way a person rates himself or herself in relation to others. The second kind tests **self-acceptance**, the degree to which a person likes himself or herself. It is possible to be high on one component and low on the other. Females tend to be somewhat lower on self-regard ("I'm not as good as other people") and higher on self-acceptance ("I am as good as I need to be for myself"). Males seem to be more likely to inflate their "quality" and at the same time to be dissatisfied with themselves, as though part of the male role is that one is never good enough. Stake (1979) found that women consistently evaluate themselves as lower on ability and performance. In fact, women tend to underestimate their own grades and other measures of success, whereas males tend to overestimate them.

In general, research suggests that females are taught to think less well of themselves and are therefore being denied one of the most important aspects of being an effective person. In addition, we suspect that the gender-role training received by males demands a kind of exaggerated, pseudo self-esteem ("It's hard to be humble when you're perfect in every way.") that almost certainly carries with it the intolerable burden of never being permitted to have weaknesses.

All of us are powerfully affected by our gender role training.
SOURCE: Nikki Abraham.

Autonomy

To deal with the world effectively, the person must possess **autonomy**, the ability to function independently and be productive. The concept of autonomy implies an independent confidence in one's own judgment and competence. Rogers describes the autonomous person as moving "away from meeting expectations, . . . away from pleasing others, . . . toward self-direction. . . . [The person] becomes responsible for himself" (Rogers, 1961, pp. 169–171). Two general characteristics of healthy autonomy emerge from Rogers' conception: an independence of self-judgment and a trust in oneself. The first seems related to self-esteem. The effective person seems more able than most people to make the judgment, "I am who I am and know that I have personal worth. I am my own judge." The second characteristic—trust in oneself—seems more related to confidence, competence, and control of oneself and one's environment.

The sense of competence and independent control probably starts to develop shortly after birth, often in ways that parents don't even think about. For example, male infants must perform more behaviours for the same rewards than female infants. At first glance, this seems to be a disadvantage for the little boys. In fact, however, they are starting to learn lessons such as persistence and control of the environment with their own behaviours. Parents seem likely to anticipate the needs of a girl baby and to be there meeting the infant's needs, often before she cries or reaches out or kicks. Her needs are being met, but they are not being met *contingent on her behaviour*. She is not learning that her behaviour has an impact (Block, 1976, 1978; Hoffman, 1977b). To a girl, adults seem more likely to say, "Here, honey, I'll show you how to do that." But to a boy, they seem more likely to say, "You can do that if you try." We often ask our undergraduate classes how often in a typical day they think this kind of subtle difference in treatment is given to boys and girls. Estimates have ranged from 5 to 20. Even if this subtle difference in "competence training" occurs only 5 times a day, that's over 1800 times a year—36 000 lessons by age 20!

One of our students was a nurse working with premature babies. She frequently observed that parents and visitors would look through the glass observation window at the tiny babies. If the baby was a boy, they would make comments such as, "Come on, you can do it! Look at him moving. You can tell he's trying!" If the baby was a girl, comments were more like, "The poor, sweet little thing. Oh, she's so tiny." Rubin, Provenzano, and Luria (1974) asked the parents of 30 newborn babies to describe their new boy or girl. Even though the babies did not differ on any objective measure, parents tended to describe girl babies as little, beautiful, pretty, and cute compared with boy babies. New fathers were most likely to make more extremely sex-typed judgments—all within 24 hours of the babies' birth. When we remember the power of self-fulfilling prophecies, in which people cause to happen what they expect to happen, we can see that early sex-typing and gender-role training will have powerful consequences.

Emotional self-knowledge

To know oneself requires both cognitive knowledge and emotional knowledge. All of us distort our memories and feelings and are subject to unconscious influences on our behaviour. However, the less one distorts, the more effectively one can live. The effective person possesses **emotional self-knowledge**, the ability to experience emotion and to accurately know one's own emotions.

We can't be wise about our lives if our information from our thoughts and feelings is inaccurate. From his classic study of *self-actualizing* individuals, Maslow concluded that "their ease of penetration to reality, their closer approach to an animal-like or child-like acceptance and spontaneity, implies a superior awareness of their own impulses, their own desires, opinions and subjective reactions in general" (Maslow, 1954, p. 210). Maslow goes on to note that self-actualized people have "a wonderful capacity to appreciate again and again, freshly and naively, the basic goods of life with awe, pleasure, wonder, and even ecstasy, however stale these experiences may be for other people" (Maslow, 1954, p. 214).

Can you picture Clint Eastwood as Dirty Harry talking about having an experience of "deep joy" or "appreciating with awe and wonder the basic goods of life"? The image seems funny somehow. Male gender-role training is strongly suppressive of virtually all strong emotion except anger and sexual desire. One of our students said he was permitted to feel two things—hostile and horny. To some extent, men are permitted jubilation *if* it is over an aggressive achievement such as scoring a goal. And men are permitted some sadness *if* it is over an event as serious as a death.

People often find the following thought experiment very revealing. Imagine that you are the parent of five-year-old twins, a boy and a girl. The girl comes home from kindergarten bubbling with happiness. She has had a wonderful day. She runs in the front door and skips to you in the kitchen, practically singing, "Guess what happened. Guess what happened." She's half holding onto you and half jumping up and down. What is your reaction to her? Now your other twin, the boy, comes home and does exactly the same thing—skips in the door practically singing, "Guess what happened. Guess what happened," and is now in front of you jumping up and down. Their behaviour is identical. Will you respond at all differently to the boy? Most people who picture this scene vividly feel mildly embarrassed by the boy's exuberance and say they would want to say something like "Calm down, son. You're being too silly. I'm glad you're happy, but calm down." The lesson being taught the boy is "be cool," meaning "don't feel things too strongly. That's silly." This is another one of those lessons that is taught in some subtle way several times a day and becomes incredibly powerful.

It is often said that men are prohibited from crying by their gender-role training, and therefore that training is dangerous and unnatural. Being able to cry in some circumstances is healthy. We would agree that this is true, but the problem is even deeper. Males are taught to suppress virtually all intense emotion, which means they must be distorting their own internal experiencing. Buck (1977) reported that boys as young as between 4 and 6 years old were already increasingly masking overt emotional reaction and inhibiting themselves in response to pictures of emotion-arousing scenes. Girls did not show this increasing inhibition with age. Among college students, there is some evidence that males may experience considerable emotion but inhibit its expression more than females (Cherulnik, 1979). It seems likely that there are no *inherent* reasons for males to feel less than females, but a lifetime of training to inhibit emotion has to have a significant impact.

Capacity for intimacy

It is worth repeating here that when Freud was asked what a normal person could do that a neurotic person could not he replied, "To love and work." This was the closest Freud came to describing the effective personality, but his comment is consistent with what we have been saying. It also points out that intimate relationships are central to life. The effective person should possess the **capacity for intimacy**, the ability to love and be loved. The contemporary sculptor Henry Moore has said, "My belief is that no matter what advances we make in technology and in the controlling of nature, and so on, the real basis of life is human relationships. It is through them that we are happy or unhappy and that we fulfill ourselves or we don't" (Grebstein, 1969, p. 125). We feel that we are in over our heads trying to comment on the nature of intimacy as it relates to gender roles in only a few paragraphs. It is clear, though, that gender-role training creates serious barriers to intimacy, especially for males.

Two essential interpersonal skills for making relationships work are active listening or empathy and the ability to confront another person constructively (see Chapters 17 and 20). Communication lies at the heart of successful relationships. Good communication requires sensitivity, trust, empathy, caring, self-disclosure, and nondestructive ways to confront another person. In general, men's verbal communications tend to be aimed at domination, whereas women's patterns involve more listening and empathy (Henley, 1977; Henley & Thorne, 1977; Haas, 1979). Men are more self-disclosing in the specific areas of work, interests, and opinions, but women reveal more personally intimate topics (Rosenfeld, Civikly,

& Herron, 1979). It is important to note that the limitation to reveal only nonpersonal information is found among sex-typed masculine men specifically and not among androgynous men (Lombardo & Levine, 1978).

As young as ages seven and eight boys have been shown to be significantly more uncomfortable than girls in situations that required intimate interaction (Foot, Chapman, & Smith, 1979). Other studies reveal that men tend to have fewer friendships than women. The friendships men do have tend to emphasize companionship rather than trust and confidentiality. There seems little question that in general, males are not well-prepared for intimacy.

It has been a part of our romantic myth to think that a traditionally masculine man and a traditionally feminine woman make a good match because their needs complement each other. If the effective person needs a balance of strength and connection with others, however, two androgynous partners should have a better chance at a satisfying relationship. And this is just what the evidence suggests (Spence, Deaux, & Helmreich, 1985).

CLOSE-UP

Bill Cosby Faces Manhood at 11

Bill Cosby tells of his first sexual encounter in a way that touches on the dilemma of a boy in our culture. He is expected to know everything about sex and certainly not to be so ignorant as to need ever to ask anything about it. How does the boy find out in the first place?

> So, man, Saturday comes, and I've been thinkin' all week about this p-u-s-s-y. You know, and I'm tryin' to ask people questions about how they get some p-u-s-s-y. And I don't want guys to know that I don't know nothin' about gettin' no p-u-s-s-y. But how do you find out how to do it without blowin' the fact that you don't know how to do it? So I come up to a guy, and I say, "Say, man, have you ever had any p-u-s-s-y?" And the guy says, "Yeah." And I say, "Well, man, what's your favorite way of gettin' it?" He says, "Well, you know, just the regular way." And I say, "Well, do you do it like I do it?" And the cat says, "How's that?" And I say, "Well, hey, I heard that there was different ways of doin' it, man." He says, "Well, there's a lotta ways of doin' it, you know, but I think that . . . you know, the *regular* way. . . ." I say, "*Yeah*, good ol' regular way . . . good ol' regular way of gettin' that p-u-s-s-y."
>
> So now, I'm walkin', and I'm trying to figure out how to do it. And when I get there, the most embarrassing thing is gonna be when I have to take my pants down. See, right away, then, I'm buck naked in front of this girl. Now, what happens then? Do you . . . do you just . . . I don't even know what to do. . . . I'm gonna just stand there and she's gonna say, "You don't know how to do it." And I'm gonna say, "Yes I do, but I *forgot*." I never thought of her showing me, because I'm a man and I don't want her to show me. I don't want *nobody* to show me, but I wish somebody would kinda slip me a note. . . . I stopped off at a magazine stand to look and see if there were any sexy magazines about it. I mean if I wasn't going to learn how to do it, I figured there might be some pictures in there of somebody *almost* getting ready to do it. But I don't find nothin'. [Bill Cosby, The regular way. *Playboy* (December, 1968) pp. 288–289. Reprinted with permission.]

Bill Cosby survived his encounter with the girl without having sex, but on the way home he brags about how good it was and tells a curious friend, "If you don't know how to do it, I ain't gonna tell you how to do it."

1. The most powerful and significant role we have is likely our gender role. It is well learned and nearly impossible to change after early childhood. Gender role refers specifically to psychological maleness or femaleness, not biological maleness or femaleness. Gender-appropriate behaviour is primarily learned, not innate. Gender role is not the same as genetic sex, anatomical sex, sexual preference, or gender identity.

2. Traditional gender roles divide behaviour into two classes. The masculine gender role is characterized by activity and instrumental behaviour, whereas the feminine gender role is characterized by passivity and relationship behaviour. Traditional roles imply that masculine and feminine are at opposite ends of one continuum. However, according to Bierman's interpersonal behaviour circle, any social behaviour can be described in terms of two independent dimensions: active/passive and loving/hostile. The traditional masculine role is active and hostile. The traditional feminine role is passive and loving. It is entirely possible to be both active and loving, combining the positive qualities of both roles in one person. In recent years, such a person has been described as androgynous.

3. Many studies that suggest the existence of psychological sex differences rest on results that are statistically significant but that exhibit only a small average difference between the two groups. Such findings can mean that the two groups overlap enormously and that the difference between individuals varies considerably. We should be careful not to turn such statements as "girls are better at . . ." into polarized generalizations.

4. Sex differences in intelligence depend largely on the definition of intelligence used. Females seem to be superior (on the average, of course) in verbal abilities at certain ages. Males seem to be superior in spatial abilities after adolescence. This difference may have some biological foundation. According to one theory, spatial ability is carried by a recessive gene on the sex chromosome pair. Males seem to be better at mathematical skills than females, but this difference seems largely caused by cultural factors. Sex differences in cognitive ability seem to be diminishing with changes in the educational system, workplace, and home, suggesting that environmental factors are very important.

5. Early studies of achievement motivation were unintentionally biased in that male behaviour was taken as the standard for human behaviour. Many researchers now reject the earlier conclusions that women characteristically give up more than men in the face of failure feedback and that women tend to have a strong fear of success. Studies reveal that men tend to be more motivated in the production of things and in competition, whereas women tend to be more motivated in social skills and in interpersonal relationships.

6. Males are probably more aggressive than females. This sex difference may well rest in part on hormonal differences. Nevertheless, boys are trained for aggression far more than girls.
7. The evidence for a sex difference in the area of dependency is inconclusive, despite our cultural stereotype. Girls seem to be more dependent in the sense of seeking help and social approval directly. Boys seem to be more dependent in the sense of seeking attention and acceptance indirectly.
8. The primary advantage of being androgynous is that the person is flexible and can adapt to a complex world better than a person who has a traditional gender role. Research evidence generally supports this. Critics of androgyny research suggest that masculine behaviour is more effective for both males and females in our society. However, this conclusion is based on studies that may well be biased in favour of masculine qualities for two reasons. First, most of the experiments have relied on self-reported data. Second, most of the studies have used undergraduate students as subjects.
9. The effective person seems to combine two general characteristics of the traditional masculine gender role (self-esteem and autonomy) and two characteristics of the traditional feminine gender role (emotional self-knowledge and the capacity for intimacy). Women seem more easily convinced than men of the need to modify gender roles. We can point to several possible reasons: the disadvantages of the traditional feminine role may be clearer; males are trained more stringently and rigidly in their gender roles than females; and our culture seems to devalue the positive feminine qualities such as emotionality and intimacy.

Key Terms

Anatomical sex Biological sex as determined by the presence of male or female genitals.

Androgyny The combination, within an individual, of the positive qualities of both the traditional masculine and the traditional feminine gender roles.

Autonomy The ability to function independently and be productive.

Capacity for intimacy The ability to love and be loved.

Effective person A person with four general characteristics: self-esteem, autonomy, emotional self-knowledge, and a capacity for intimacy.

Emotional self-knowledge The ability to experience emotion and to accurately know one's own emotions.

Fear of success The hypothesis that women tend to have a learned motive to feel threatened by their own successful performance.

Feminine gender role The traditional role assigned to women which is characterized by passivity and relationship behaviour.

Gender identity The degree to which a person identifies with and is comfortable with his or her biological sex.

Gender role A pervasive, powerful set of behaviours that is prescribed as appropriate (and another set prescribed as inappropriate) based only on one's sex. See also *feminine gender role* and *masculine gender role*.

Genetic sex Biological sex as determined by the structure of the sex chromosome pair.

Instrumental behaviour Actions aimed toward manipulating the environment and achieving goals. Such behaviour is typical of the traditional masculine role.

Interpersonal behaviour circle A graphic device to describe any social behaviour in terms of two independent dimensions: (1) active versus passive and (2) loving versus hostile.

Masculine gender role The traditional role assigned to men, which is characterized by activity and instrumental behaviour.

Need for achievement A socially acquired motive to produce and succeed.

Relationship behaviour Actions aimed toward facilitating human interaction. Such behaviour is typical of the traditional feminine role.

Role A set of behaviours that a group deems appropriate for a particular person in a particular situation.

Self-acceptance The degree to which a person likes himself or herself.

Self-esteem A sense of personal worth.

Self-regard The way a person rates himself or herself in relation to others.

Sexual preference One's choice of sexual partners in terms of anatomical sex.

Statistically significant Research findings whose likelihood (probability) of being "real" (that is, not due to chance) has been calculated to be at least 95%.

Suggested Readings

Gilligan, C. (1982). *In a different voice: Psychological theory and women's development*. Cambridge, MA: Harvard University Press. This book may well become a classic on gender. We referred to it in Chapter 12, on development through the lifespan, for its incisive criticisms of the inherent male bias in many psychological theories. Many readers, both male and female, have found much that is personally relevant in this book.

Greenglass, E. R. (1982). *A world of difference: Gender roles in perspective.* Toronto: John Wiley & Sons. An excellent textbook on gender roles. Written in Canada, it includes many interesting studies and statistics based on Canadian experience.

Tavris, C., & Offir, C. E. (1984). *The longest war.* 2nd ed. New York: Harcourt Brace Jovanovich. This is another very good text on gender roles. It makes for enjoyable reading.

PART VII

Using Psychology

CHAPTER 19

SOURCE: Frederick Horsman Varley, Detail from *Study for "Dhârâna"* (1932).

Psychology and Health

Personality, Stress, and Physical Illness
- Personality and disease
- General theories
- Stress and illness

Specificity Theories and Specific Diseases
- Coronary heart disease
- Cancer
- Diabetes

Psychology and Disease Prevention
- Psychological models of self-destructive behaviour
- Obesity
- Smoking
- Alcoholism
- AIDS
- Summing up

Psychology and Medical Intervention
- Crisis
- Typical reactions to crisis

Coping with Physical Illness
- Coping: Tasks
- Coping: Skills
- Determinants of success in coping
- The patient role: Gains and losses

Special Topic Adherence

PEOPLE USUALLY THINK of physical health in purely medical terms and of psychological health as a different matter. This way of thinking says that some illnesses may be partly "psychosomatic," but the majority are not. However, it is becoming clear that virtually *all* illnesses are affected by psychological factors. In fact, there is evidence (Turkington, 1987) that providing psychotherapy as a part of a health service results in lower overall health-care costs because patients require less medical care. The personal implications of this are compelling. Your own health will be significantly affected by your stress level, your unresolved conflicts, your emotional reactions, and your behaviour. According to the U. S. Center for Disease Control (1986), 54% of deaths in individuals under 65 can be attributed to lifestyle behaviours such as drinking, smoking, and driving habits.

Since the early 1970s, psychologists have been interested in the psychological aspects of illness and medical problems. The field of **health psychology** has developed rapidly and is now a maturing discipline of its own (Taylor, 1987). There are still questions about exactly what marks the boundaries of health psychology as a field (Turk, 1989), but in general it emphasizes the prevention of disease and psychological reactions to illness and injury. The rapid development of this field can be seen in the increasing number of books and publications in the area and in the growing number of psychologists employed in medical schools and hospitals in Canada (Arnett et al., 1987; Dunn, 1986; Lacroix, 1987) and in the United States (Thompson and Matarazzo, 1984). Interest in the psychological aspects of illness has also been shared by many physicians. They appreciate the importance of treating the patient, not just the illness.

Health psychology is concerned with the **etiology**, or cause, of disease; with the *course and treatment* of disease; and with the *maintenance* of health. The health psychologist is interested in (1) psychological factors predisposing us to illness and disease, (2) psychological factors which either retard or enhance recovery, and (3) research and treatment on modifying health-related habits and lifestyles.

In all of these areas, *stress* is an important variable, and we will be building on our discussion of the principles of stress in Chapter

13 and psychophysiological disorders in Chapter 14. We want to know how our knowledge of stress can be applied to the etiology, treatment, and prevention of specific illnesses.

Are specific personality styles directly related to the development of specific diseases?
SOURCE: Courtesy of Metropolitan Toronto Convention & Visitors Association.

PERSONALITY, STRESS, AND PHYSICAL ILLNESS

As discussed in Chapter 13, we all have an individual vulnerability to stress. Personality differences are one of the causes of these individual differences in susceptibility to stress.

Personality and disease

Personality characteristics may contribute to our vulnerability to disease in different ways. For example, research has investigated whether specific personality styles are directly related to the development of particular diseases. Is there an "arthritic" (or "ulcerative," or "asthmatic") personality? Another way in which our personalities may contribute is through the mechanism of stress. Are there certain kinds of personalities which result in inadequate coping strategies to life stressors or in lifestyles which tend to perpetuate stress? Do individuals with low self-esteem, for example, tend to be anxious or depressed more often? Do these negative emotions result in changes in physical functioning and the promotion of disease?

Research relating personality and disease falls into three broad categories. The first assumes that personality helps cause disease before symptoms occur. This usually implies that personality is somehow a factor in producing biochemical or pathological changes which result in the production of disease. The second approach emphasizes the role of psychological factors in the course and outcome of illness once symptoms are displayed. Research of this type generally considers illness as a stressor and assumes that the way we cope with stress can affect the course of our illness. This view assumes that physiological reactions to the stress of illness are affected by both biological factors and by psychosocial factors. **Biological factors** are those contributors to health and illness that are specifically physical in nature. **Psychosocial factors** are those contributors to health and illness that arise from psychological processes, relationships, and other environmental processes. These psychosocial factors include the extent to which we view illness as threatening or harmful and the degree to which we see ourselves as able to cope or take action to reduce the threat (Cohen and Lazarus, 1979; Krantz et al., 1981). The third category researches the results of being ill and receiving treatment. These circumstances can have a dramatic effect on changing one's personality. Receiving chemotherapy for cancer, losing a leg or arm, or being dependent on a kidney dialysis machine can have impact on such personality characteristics as independence, assertiveness, and mood (Fox, 1978; Haney, 1977).

General theories

In the next section, we will discuss how psychological factors contribute to some specific diseases. First, however, we need to look at general theories about the link between illness and psychology.

Nuclear conflict theory

One of the earliest formulations of the relationship between personality and illness was proposed by Franz Alexander and his colleagues (Alexander, 1950). He called it the **nuclear conflict theory**. This theory contends that unconscious conflicts and the emotions that they produce are associated with the onset of specific diseases. According to these researchers, the conflicts are involved both in predisposing an individual to a disorder and to the onset of specific symptoms. When specific psychological conflicts are "activated" by stressful situations, they generate emotions such as anger, depression, and anxiety. These emotions, in turn, result in autonomic and endocrine responses that precipitate the onset of the disease.

Alexander proposed that specific emotional conflicts underlie a variety of psychophysiological disorders, including asthma, hypertension, duodenal ulcers, migraine headaches, and rheumatoid arthritis. These conflicts do not always result in disease, however. Latent conflicts underlying these diseases could remain unactivated if there is no precipitating situation. Or an individual could resolve the conflicts through other means than the development of disease. Research on this theory is difficult to do, because the theory is based upon underlying conflicts which are difficult to measure. A few early investigations tended to support the nuclear conflict theory. For example, Weiner, Thaler, Reiser, and Mirsky (1957) were able to identify individuals who had what the researchers called "ulcer-prone conflict." These subjects did have excessive amounts of stomach secretions that predispose individuals to duodenal ulcers. However,it has been difficult to find specific diseases linked to specific unconscious conflicts.

There is evidence, however, to support the idea that there may be a "disease-prone personality." This personality pattern predisposes us to the development of diseases in general rather than to a particular disorder (Friedman and Booth-Kewley, 1987). We will be describing these predisposing characteristics thoughout this chapter.

Helplessness-hopelessness theory

One such theory is the **helplessness-hopelessness theory**. It suggests that ineffectual passiveness increases our susceptibility to illness of many types (Engel, 1968; Schmale, 1972). Among individuals who are biologically predisposed to a particular illness, feeling hopeless or helpless will increase the chances of getting that illness. This general state, called the **giving-up-given-up complex**, includes a psychological sense of powerlessness over the environment. Most investigators agree that this psychological state often accompanies disease. However, it must occur in an individual who has a biological predisposition to a disease in order to result in a disease process (Cohen, 1979; Weiner, 1977).

This general theory holds considerable promise, especially as researchers develop links between emotions such as grief and loss and changes in physiological functioning. The most important principle seems to be that reactions to stress often result in the suppression of the immune system. The working of the immune system is illustrated in Figure 19-1. This leaves the body vulnerable to a wide variety of diseases that can no longer be effectively resisted. Diseases affected by reduced immune functioning include cancer, heart disease, and most viruses and bacteria (Maier and Laudenslager, 1985; Jemmott and Locke, 1984; Kandil and Borysenko, 1987).

The field of **psychoimmunology** studies the link between immune system functioning and psychological factors. This field is growing rapidly as we understand better how important psychological factors are in immune system functioning. For example, the death of a close relative increases the likelihood of death in the next-of-kin, particularly as a result of coronary disease (Cottington et al., 1980; Parkes, Benjamin, and Fitzgerald, 1969). Up to 50% of those individuals who had recently lost a close relative and who died suddenly from coronary heart disease were reported to have had clinical

FIGURE 19-1 **The immune system**
The immune system is constantly fighting off disease. When it is weakened by stress or other causes, the person is more vulnerable to virtually all diseases.

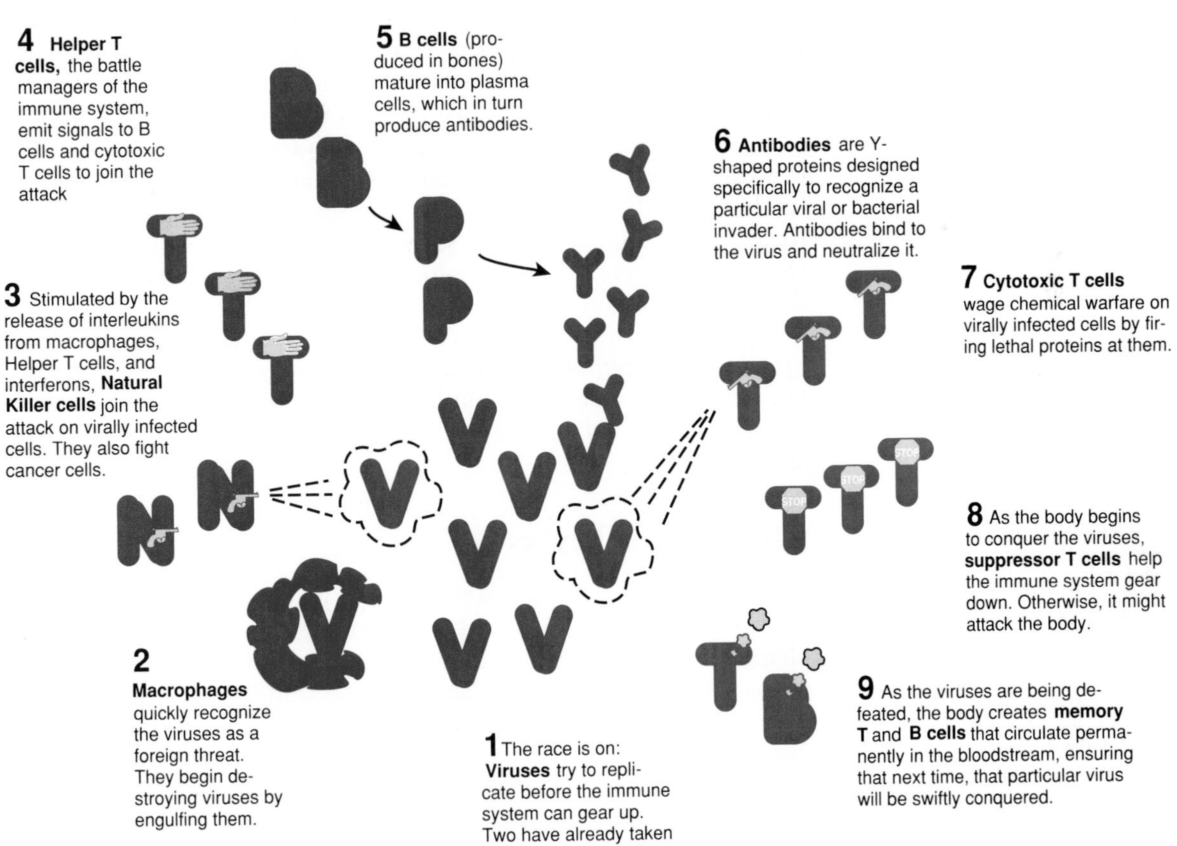

SOURCE: Reprinted with permission from *Nutrition Action Healthletter* (1988) by the Center for Science in the Public Interest.

symptoms of depression for some time prior to death. A sudden state of arousal (either positive or negative) seems to have precipitated the acute coronary event in many situations (Greene, Goldstein, and Moss, 1972). Irwin (1987) studied 45 women whose husbands either had recently died of lung cancer or were currently being treated for it. The women whose husbands had died were more depressed and had lower levels of the "natural killer cell" activity that is essential in immune system defence against virus-infected and tumour cells.

The helplessness of individuals does not come solely from bereavement. For example, lower immune functioning was found to be related to depression and despair, and higher functioning was related to effectiveness of coping in women who were about to undergo breast biopsy (Katz et al., 1970). Even the fluctuations of daily mood affect the immune system. Investigators measured levels of a particular antibody produced to resist "foreign invaders" in the blood. They found that levels were high when daily mood was high and low when mood was more negative (Stone et al., 1987).

Many of the studies linking helplessness/hopelessness to disease must be interpreted cautiously because they often don't include control groups and they usually depend on retrospective data. Asking sick patients how they used to feel gives us distorted information because being ill might make one remember previous feelings of helplessness more strongly.

A better source of evidence is *prospective research*. Prospective studies test large numbers of people who are not ill and then follow them to see which ones develop diseases. Kobasa, Maddi, and Kahn (1982) tested healthy executives and then followed the status of their health for two years. Those who stayed the most healthy were high on feelings of being in control of their lives and had positive attitudes toward change. They saw change as a challenge. Those who were likely to get ill saw change more as a setback over which they had little control. Maddi and Kobasa even reported some success in teaching the executives the psychological hardiness that seems to fight disease (Maddi and Kobasa, 1984; Fischman, 1987).

The bulk of the recent evidence suggests that the helplessness/hopelessness hypothesis is a useful theory. However, Dattore, Shontz, and Coyne (1980) and Gillum, Leon, Camp, and Becerra-Aldama (1980) did not find a link between illness and depression scores on the MMPI.

Stress and illness

In Chapter 13, we discussed the general principles of stress and saw how it can cause illness through physiological mechanisms. In this chapter we will briefly focus on individuals' different reactions to stress. **Stress** is a subjective aversive reaction to change. It depends upon our personalities and past experiences. As Lazarus (1966) points out, it is the subjective reaction that is crucial in the development of disease. A single event may be interpreted differently by different people, with some seeing it as stressful and others not. If a person has the resources to meet the challenge, has a positive evaluation of the situation, or does not perceive that danger exists, then less stress will occur. Individuals who are less likely to become ill tend to be those who reduce stress and conflict. They also avoid obsessive worry and brooding. In contrast, there is more illness among those who are hypersensitive about their life and environment (Cohen & Lazarus, 1979). There is also evidence to suggest that people with sufficient social supports live longer (Berkman, 1977) and have a lower incidence of illness (Cassel, 1976). When ill, they tend to develop less severe symptomatology (Luborsky, Todd, and Katcher, 1973).

The way a person copes with stress can reduce physiological arousal and the resulting biochemical changes associated with disease. Some research suggests that taking action, rather than remaining passive, can be effective in reducing stress and can influence the biochemical precursors to disease (Gal and Lazarus, 1975).

SOURCE: *Calvin and Hobbes* by Bill Watterson. Copyright 1989 Universal Press Syndicate. Reprinted with permission. All rights reserved.

Specificity Theories and Specific Diseases

In the previous section, we outlined the more general theories relating personality and stress to disease. We now move on to two examples of theories relating psychological factors to specific diseases.

Coronary heart disease

Considerable research has been done on psychological and social factors implicated in the causes of coronary heart disease. Despite this, there still is controversy over the relative importance of psychological and biological factors in producing this disease. The most consistent psychosocial predictors of coronary heart disease are the presence of disturbing emotions, such as anxiety and depression, and a syndrome of traits and behaviours called the Type A personality (Friedman and Rosenman, 1974; Jenkins, 1976). The behaviour of a **Type A personality** is described as "a particular complex of personality traits, including excessive competitive drive, aggressiveness, impatience, and a harrying sense of time urgency. Individuals displaying this pattern seem to be engaged in a chronic, ceaseless and often fruitless struggle—with themselves, with others, with circumstances, with time, sometimes with life itself. They also frequently exhibit a free-floating, but well-rationalized form of hostility, and almost always a deep-seated insecurity" (Friedman and Rosenman, 1974, p. 4). Individuals with a **Type B personality**, by contrast, exhibit a pattern of behaviours linked to lower incidence of heart disease. These behaviours are marked by calm resiliency, trustfulness, lack of time urgency, and faster recovery from stress (Jamieson and Lavoie, 1987).

Type A versus Type B behaviour is assessed by means of a structured interview (Rosenman et al., 1964) or through a questionnaire, the Jenkins Activity Survey (Jenkins, Rosenman, and Friedman, 1967). The interview seems to be a better predictor of heart disease than the questionnaire.

Type A behaviour has been consistently linked with the increased incidence and prevalence of heart disease. The death rate from heart disease is twice as high in Type A individuals than in Type B (Rosenman et al., 1970). This is true even when other risk factors, such as parental history of heart disease, smoking, high blood pressure, education, occupation, and high cholesterol level are considered. Work overload and chronic conflict may precede coronary heart disease, and aerobic fitness has a beneficial effect. However, none of these predict heart problems with as much accuracy as the Type A variables (Jenkins, 1976).

Biological mechanisms

The biological mechanisms of the Type A behaviour and their influence on heart disease are not completely understood. However, evidence suggests that disturbing life situations or conflict may lead to increases in cholesterol and other blood fats and may also be associated with increased blood pressure. Catecholamines such as epinephrine and norepinephrine may be implicated. Under stress, Type A's have more of the hormone norepinephrine in their blood than do Type B's (Simpson et al., 1974). This hormone can damage arteries and the heart and make blood platelets clump together more, promoting the blockage of arteries.

Cynical hostility and impatience kill

The elements of the Type A personality that seem most damaging are impatience and cynical hostility. **Cynical hostility** is marked by chronic mistrust of others and harsh, judgmental, and vengeful feelings. Barefoot, Dahlstrom, and Williams (1983) followed up medical students who had taken the MMPI 25 years earlier, when they were all healthy. Those who later developed coronary problems or had died from heart trouble were more likely to have been hostile. In the original testing they had a harsh view of others as deserving to be punished, as selfish and immoral, and as inconsiderate. Even more revealing is a study of borderline-hypertensive males. Some were classified as Type B and some as Type A, according to the structured interview that is usually used for this study. The men responded to aversive audiotaped stimuli such as a threat to their self-esteem and a frustrating auto-repair situation. They also were examined for the extent of physical damage their hearts had sustained over the years. As expected, the Type A men responded with more hostile cognitions and they showed more cardiac damage. In addition, some of the men classified as Type B responded to the audiotapes with hostility, and *they* also showed cardiac damage. "Type B's without cardiac damage reported significantly fewer hostile thoughts than all Type A's and those Type B's who did suffer cardiac damage" (Weinstein et al., 1987, p. 55).

Cathy Moser and Dennis Dyck (1989) frustrated Type A and Type B undergraduates from Manitoba by exposing them to a task in which they always failed. Nothing the subjects could do would bring success. Other subjects were not exposed to the uncontrollable failure experience or feedback. The subjects then recalled self-referent adjectives. Among Type A subjects, the failure experience increased their recall of hostile self-descriptive adjectives, but this did not occur among Type B subjects (see Figure 19-2). The researchers expected Type B subjects to recall more depressive self-descriptive adjectives after failing, but this did not occur. Moser and Dyck interpreted this finding as the arousal of Type A subjects' "hostile self-schemas."

FIGURE 19-2 Recall of self-descriptive adjectives after failure feedback

After receiving frustrating failure feedback on their performance, Type A subjects tended to recall more hostile adjectives as describing themselves. When subjects received no feedback, Type A and Type B subjects recalled equal numbers of positive, hostile, and depressed adjectives.

SOURCE: Reprinted with permission from Moser and Dyck (1989).

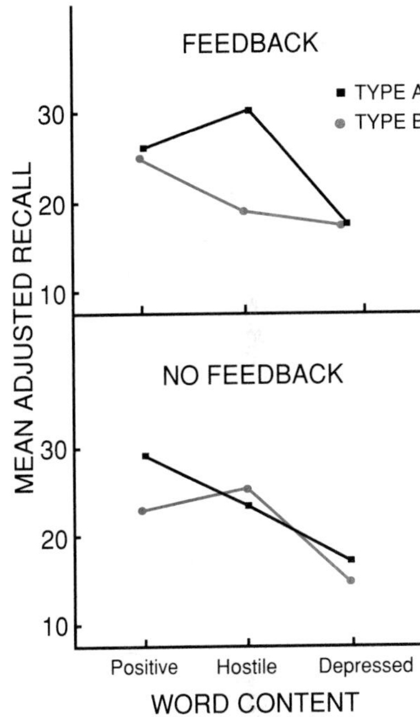

Treating Type A

One of the most promising treatments health psychology has to offer is changing Type A behaviour. Some programs use behavioural methods to change the intense drivenness of patients who have already had heart attacks. These programs can reduce the recurrence of heart attacks and the death rate. The Montreal Type A Intervention Project is an ambitious treatment program that has compared the effectiveness of ten weeks of different treatments (Roskies et al., 1986). Cognitive-behavioural stress management, weight training, and aerobic exercise were provided to different groups of healthy Type A men, all executives of two large Canadian corporations. Only the stress management treatment had any effect. It was able to change the men's behavioural reactivity so that they reacted less like the typical Type A pattern. This is an important accomplishment, but none of the treatments changed the men's physiological reactivity to stress. It is possible that a longer period of treatment would be necessary to accomplish this. An amusing but sadly revealing anecdote that therapists in these treatment programs sometimes report is that Type A patients may start competing with each other over who can become the most laid-back.

Cancer

Lizette Peterson (1986) has said it appears that "the psychological status of (cancer) patients is as relevant to outcome as their biological status" (Peterson, 1986, p. 591). This remarkable statement reflects the rapidly growing area of **biopsychosocial oncology**, the study of the relationship between the development and treatment of cancer and emotion, behaviour, physiology, and the social environment.

The relationship between psychological factors and cancer is less clear than with coronary disease. We are less able to use personality variables to predict who will get cancer. In the past, there has been evidence both for (Whitlock and Siskind, 1979) and against (Evans, Baldwin, and Gath, 1974) the idea that persons with psychopathology, particularly depression, are more likely to develop cancer. It is clear that cancer patients have a high incidence of depression, but that obviously is partly the result of having cancer. This question won't be resolved until some large prospective studies are conducted (Derogatis, 1986; Barofsky, 1981; Fox, 1978; Abse et al., 1974). Further, research relating different personality traits and different types of cancer has not, in the past, demonstrated a clear relationship (Schmale and Iker, 1971).

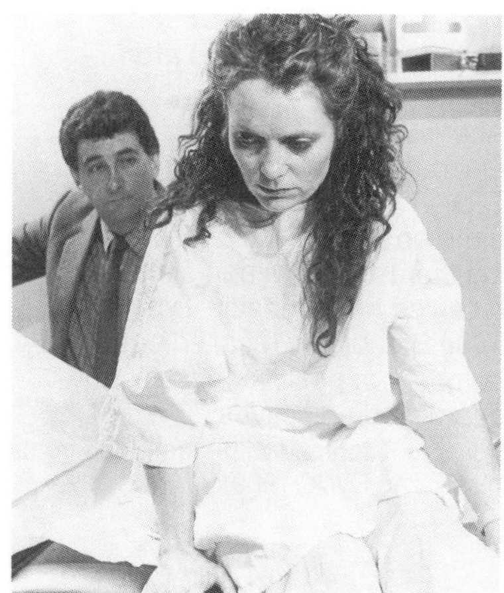

Compliant, unexpressive cancer patients seem to have a shorter survival time than those with a fighting spirit.
SOURCE: "Who Should Decide?" National Film Board of Canada.

More recently, however, Alastair Cunningham (1985), of the Ontario Cancer Institute, has drawn together three lines of evidence that strongly suggest a link between psychological factors and cancer. First, there is convincing evidence from animal studies that stress influences both the onset and rate of growth of some cancers. Second, some prospective human studies have been done linking repressed and depressive affect with cancer. Third, and more speculative, a number of clinical reports of the success of various kinds of psychological interventions at least deserve our attention. Although none of this evidence "is conclusive by itself, the convergence of views from three quite separate kinds of research is persuasive. . . ." (Cunningham, 1984, p. 24).

Personality and survival time

There is clearer evidence on how personality variables and coping styles are related to how long a cancer patient survives. Emotional expressiveness, rather than suppression, may be a factor in prolonging life once the diagnosis of cancer has been made (Cohen, 1979). As early as the 1950s, patients who died more quickly were described as "polite, cooperative, and unable to express negative affects, particularly hostility. Longer survivors were described as emotionally expressive, and in some cases, bizarre" (Derogatis, 1986, p. 635).

More recent evidence has confirmed this general finding. The fighting spirit of survivors is reflected in psychological test scores that are high on anxiety, hostility, and alienation. Normally, we would consider these characteristics undesirable, but they contribute to survival from cancer better than polite helpless-hopelessness (Edwards, DiClemente, and Samuels, 1985). This touched us personally when a friend with cancer said, "I'm not going 'softly into that dark night.' I'm going with rage." Interestingly, his cancer disappeared several years ago.

Gottschalk (1985) speaks of "hope and other deterrents to illness" (Gottschalk, 1985, p. 515). He recorded the speech of terminally ill cancer patients and analysed their patterns of language use. He scored the content of their speech for expressions that implied hope and found that "hope scores" correlated with survival time. A second conclusion Gottschalk reached was that the open expression of emotion helped to deter illness. Some medical in-patients had psychotherapy designed to bring out appropriate emotional reactions to being in the hospital. They recovered more quickly and needed less medication than other patients.

Biological mechanisms

As with heart disease, the physiological mechanisms in cancer are extremely complex. In general, they involve the immune system. A breakdown in our immune system can lead to the proliferation of cancer cells and their spreading or **metastasis** to other parts of the body. Any factor that compromises our immune system makes us vulnerable to a number of diseases, including cancer. Schwartz (1975) says that generally our immune system prevents us from developing cancer. Once this system is weakened, either through biological or psychological agents, cancer can develop more easily. The complexity of this system is not yet fully understood, and many biological factors play an important role (Amkraut and Soloman, 1977).

Diabetes

In Chapter 5, on motivation, we discussed the work of David McClelland. He gave TAT-like tests to subjects to test their need for achievement (nAch). In recent years, McClelland (1989) has been using the same method to study other social motives such as the need for power (n Power) and the need for affiliation in relationships (n Affiliation). He describes n Affiliation as a motive characterized by a need to be in close relationship with others, to be approved of and accepted. He has used this approach to study personality factors in juvenile-onset, insulin-dependent diabetes, usually referred to as type I diabetes. McClelland argues that previous research has not found a link between personality and diabetes because researchers have asked the patients directly about their need for affiliation. However, when he uses the more subtle projective measure he finds "an implicit motive syndrome" that differentiates diabetic subjects from control subjects.

> Compared with controls, the type I diabetics were more often characterized by at least a moderately high n Affiliation and a lack of assertiveness. Lack of assertiveness was here indicated by a lower n Power and/or a low inhibition score, signifying lack of assertiveness in controlling the self. We referred to this set of motivational characteristics as the Easygoing Affiliative Syndrome (or EAS) (McClelland, 1989, p. 675).

Easygoing affiliative syndrome (EAS) is marked by low assertiveness and high need for relationships. About 60% of the diabetic patients and only 30% of the controls showed this pattern.

Diabetics with EAS are at risk for having poor control of blood sugar levels for at least two reasons. First, arousing their need for affiliation leads them to eat more. Second, such arousal also causes higher levels of dopamine concentrations in their blood, which stimulates the release of sugar from the liver. For example, McClelland and his co-workers showed an affiliation-arousing romantic film to diabetic patients with EAS, other diabetic patients, and control subjects. After watching the film, the first group ate more than the other groups and had higher dopamine levels.

We cannot say that having EAS causes diabetes, of course. Quite likely, having diabetes makes it more probable that a person will develop a need for others. But the picture is complicated because, whatever the cause of the need for relationships, this personality factor can make the diabetes worse by affecting eating and blood sugar levels.

We have discussed psychological factors related to both general and more specific disease processes. We now turn to the ways that psychology can promote health.

Cigarette smoking and alcohol abuse are self-destructive behaviours.
SOURCE: Dick Hemingway.

Psychology and Disease Prevention

In this section, we will provide an overview of how psychology contributes to changing health-threatening behaviours. Changing some of these behaviours is a difficult task. Most people are aware that specific behaviours can contribute to disease and reduce life expectancy. We seem fairly adept at using denial, however, since these gruesome outcomes seem to apply more to other people than to ourselves.

Anything that decreases stress can have a beneficial impact on health. In fact, much of what goes on in psychotherapy is directed toward stress reduction or conflict resolution. Successful resolution of emotional problems leads to a happier person and likely a healthier one as well. There also are more specific self-destructive behaviours that have received considerable attention because of their direct relationship with illness. Specifically, a number of studies have indicated that high blood pressure; cigarette smoking; and a diet high in saturated fat, cholesterol, and sugar contribute to the risk of coronary heart disease. Obesity and lack of physical activity also contribute to coronary risk status and may result in a number of other physical conditions that interfere with quality of life and well-being. The relationship between diet, weight, and the increased incidence of diabetes is well established. Even stronger is the relationship between cigarette smoking and respiratory diseases such as lung cancer, emphysema, bronchitis, and diseases of the heart and blood vessels. Finally, alcohol abuse leads to a number of physical complications such as cirrhosis of the liver and kidney disorders as well as problems in emotional functioning and disruption in employment, marital and family relationships, and normal community functioning.

We will discuss general theories for why people behave self-destructively and then look at obesity, cigarette smoking, and alcohol abuse as specific examples of topics in health psychology.

Psychological models of self-destructive behaviour

Theories to explain self-destructive behaviours include (1) the rational model, (2) the psychodynamic model, and (3) the social learning model (Henderson, Hall, and Lipton, 1979).

Rational model

The **rational model of self-destructive behaviour** assumes that human behaviour is guided by objectivity and logical thought. The theory contends that given the appropriate information about health risks, we would modify our behaviour accordingly. Self-destructive behaviour, then, could be explained as the result of incomplete knowledge of the risks that accompany that behaviour. This lack of accurate knowledge could have many causes, such as misleading advertising, insufficient education, distortions from cognitive defences (Janis, 1975), or faulty perception caused by our own health or self-destructive behaviour (Becker, 1976).

Unfortunately, the practical results of applying the rational model to addictive behaviour is disappointing. Both large-scale information campaigns and smaller controlled studies indicate that information-only treatment is generally not an effective means of changing behaviour (Meyer and Henderson, 1974). We are more than logical, rational beings. We have evaluative and emotional reactions that affect our problem-solving skills.

Psychodynamic model

The **psychodynamic model of self-destructive behaviour** contends that within all of us there are unconscious conflicts among our instinctual, rational, and moralistic tendencies. The psychodynamic model views these unconscious conflicts as the root of self-destructive behaviour. The behaviour is merely a symptom of the underlying conflict. If the patient can understand the underlying conflicts and resolve them, the symptoms will disappear. The psychodynamic theorists say that simply treating the symptoms will result in symptom substitution. **Symptom substitution** is the emergence of a new problem after a specific symptom is removed without treating the underlying unconscious conflict. The person might stop smoking, for example, but the underlying conflict will result in some new problem.

To explain obesity psychodynamic theorists have proposed several unconscious conflicts. They include excessive oral dependency needs, rejection of pregnancy, and highly symbolic and metaphorical ideas such as "psychological cannibalism" — the person's eating is hypothesized to be linked to feelings of aggression and destruction toward others (Henderson, Hall, and Lipton, 1979). There is little or no research supporting the effectiveness of this model for changing specific self-destructive behaviours.

Social-learning model

Classical conditioning, instrumental conditioning, and modelling all are part of the social learning approach. The **social-learning model of self-destructive behaviour** proposes that we learn self-destructive behaviours, either through direct reinforcement, social reinforcement, or modelling. Reinforcers (particularly social reinforcers) tend to maintain this behaviour. Social-learning theorists would argue that individuals engaging in self-destructive behaviour do so because this behaviour has worked as an acceptable coping mechanism or is socially rewarding. As we said in Chapter 14, some self-destructive behaviour is probably reinforced by anxiety-reduction. To change behaviour, the social-learning approach would first identify what reinforces the behaviour. These reinforcers would be eliminated and other, more desirable, behaviours would be reinforced.

Many adults lose weight on their own through a combination of self-control, improved eating habits, and exercise.
SOURCE: Metropolitan Toronto Convention & Visitors Association.

Obesity

In general, professional treatment of weight control has produced disappointing results. Rational and psychodynamic approaches do least well in the treatment of obesity and the maintenance of weight loss. Behavioural approaches seem to produce the best results (Bellack, 1975; LeBow, 1984; Stunkard, 1972, 1977). Combining the rational approach and the behavioural approach is also sometimes successful (McReynolds et al., 1976).

Research results for treating obesity are quite inconsistent, but we can identify several specific interventions that appear to produce better outcome: (1) booster sessions, in which the dieter has periodic contact with the therapist during and after the treatment program (Hall, Bass, and Munroe, 1978); (2) development of environmental cues that reduce reminders of food and that associate eating with only one location (Weiss, 1977); (3) and methods to encourage independence and reduce therapist dependency (Hanson et al., 1976).

It is commonly believed that obesity is a nearly untreatable problem (Brownell, 1982). However, as we will see with the treatment of smoking, official statistics on the treatment of overweight may be misleadingly discouraging. It may be that many people successfully treat themselves for obesity, so only the difficult cases get into formal treatment programs. Schachter (1982) looked at a cross section of people who had an adult history of being overweight and found that the majority of them could be called "cured fat." They had successfully lost weight on their own through a combination of self-control, improved eating habits, and exercise. Only 15% of his sample had failed completely in their attempts. Even more encouraging, Orme and Minik (1987) found that even adults with diabetes were successful at self-treatment of obesity.

Smoking

The rational approach, simply providing information about the adverse effects of cigarette smoking, has been generally unsuccessful (Andrus, Hyde, and Fisher, 1964; Monk, Tayback, and Gordon, 1965). Adolescents in particular do not feel vulnerable to long-term health risks. They smoke because of peer pressure. Campaigns emphasizing the physical unattractiveness of smoking and interpersonal variables seem more effective than campaigns based on the rational approach (Evans, 1975).

Smoking has not been of great interest to psychodynamic theorists. Where research and theorizing has been done, underlying problems such as conflicts stemming from childhood, masochism, hostility toward parental figures, and symbolic masturbatory activity have been proposed (Henderson, Hall, and Lipton, 1979). The standard psychodynamic intervention is long-term psychotherapy, with poor outcome generally the case. It is interesting that Freud had a life-long nicotine addiction to cigars, which probably contributed to his fatal jaw cancer.

Social-learning theorists see smoking as a habit maintained by a variety of factors, including the physiological effects of nicotine, social reinforcement, and anxiety reduction. This formulation leads to specific treatment strategies, some of which appear more promising than others. Specific treatments have included aversive procedures in which smoking urges or smoking are paired with electrical shock. Another aversive technique is rapid smoking in which clients are instructed to smoke as many cigarettes as possible as quickly as possible until they reach the point of nausea. Sometimes rapid smoking is carried out in a small cubicle to increase its aversiveness. Self-control procedures are often used. They include confining smoking to a specific area (stimulus control) and gradually decreasing situations where smoking takes place, contractual agreements to quit smoking, and self-administered shock or punishment. When applied in a clinical setting, rapid smoking generally produces abstinence rates of 90% or greater at termination of treatment. However, the number drops to 60% after six months. Other behavioural studies have resulted in abstinence rates from 24 to 35% at follow-up from two to six years (Lichtenstein and Rodrigues, 1977).

Rapid smoking techniques are designed to be aversive, but they may also be dangerous for individuals with cardiac or pulmonary problems because of the rapid intake of carbon monoxide and nicotine. It is essential that a complete physical examination be undertaken before entering such a program.

It is important to remember that most of the discouraging statistics we read about treating smoking refer to professional treatment programs. Most smokers who quit do so on their own (Glasgow et al., 1985). There is a selection bias, so that smokers who get into formal treatment programs are by definition the more difficult cases who could not stop on their own. Among smokers who do try to quit on their own, quitting "cold turkey" is more effective than tapering off, and cognitive self-statements are quite different between those who quit and those who fail. Abstainers are more likely to use positively motivating self-statements such as, "think of the example I'll set by stopping smoking," while nonabstainers use self-punitive motivators such as, "think how weak I'll be if I give in and smoke."

Alcoholism

Providing information is not particularly effective in the treatment of alcoholism. This is not surprising considering that many have called alcoholism the "disease of denial." As with smoking, information relating to the personally unattractive aspects of alcohol consumption holds some promise. In Chapter 16 we said that lifestyle advertising is more effective in influencing personal preferences. It appeals to emotions rather than reason. It can be used to start people drinking and smoking. It probably is also necessary to discourage drinking and smoking. We are not entirely rational beings.

Psychodynamic formulations describe the alcoholic as an individual fixated at the oral stage of development. The person is overly dependent and has a history of poor relationships with parents. Again, intensive psychotherapy is the suggested cure. However, a problem that appears specific to alcoholics is the lack of motivation and commitment to enter into such an intensive program. In general, research indicates little evidence for the positive outcome of psychodynamic psychotherapy in alcohol treatment (Hill and Blane, 1967) or for the usefulness of group therapy (Baekeland, Lundwall, and Kissin, 1975).

Social-learning theory focuses on the role of alcohol in avoiding problems and in the induction of a positive, relaxed state. Modelling and social reinforcement are important factors in the development and maintenance of the problem. Alcoholism is sometimes treated with aversion therapies. A common method is to use drugs that induce intense nausea when the patient drinks alcohol. Aversive treatment of alcoholism is successful sometimes (Blake, 1967; Hsu, 1965), but only when it is combined with strong positive reinforcement for more adaptive behaviours (Bandura, 1969; Hunt and Azrin, 1973; Sobell and Sobell, 1972).

It is a very contentious issue whether the goal of treatment should be controlled drinking or abstinence. Some research indicates that some alcoholics can control drinking in a variety of situations and can go on to become social drinkers (Lloyd and Salzberg, 1975; Miller, 1977). This conflicts with the view of alcoholism proposed by many treatment facilities, including Alcoholics Anonymous. They see alcoholism as a progressive disease. This view says that treatment requires complete abstinence.

Sobell and Sobell (1976, 1978) reported that alcoholic patients given a combination of aversive therapy and positive alternatives to drinking did better if their goal was controlled drinking. Patients who tried for abstinence did not do as well. The Sobells' work, however, was strongly attacked (Pendery, Maltzman, and West, 1982) for incomplete reporting of controlled-drinking patients who did continue to drink excessively. This was part of a bitter dispute that involved lawsuits and investigations by the American Psychological Association. The stakes are very high, because for many alcoholics it is easy to use the rationalization that controlled drinking is all right when it may only be appropriate for a few.

AIDS

> Acquired Immunodeficiency Syndrome (AIDS) is perhaps the major public health threat of the twentieth century. The number of AIDS cases is increasing steadily and AIDS appears to be moving out of traditional 'high risk' groups, but undeterred, many Canadians continue to practice very high levels of unsafe sexual behaviour (Fisher, 1989, p. 420).

AIDS is caused by several different but related viruses that break down the immune system's ability to fight disease. Victims don't die of AIDS but of other diseases that the body is no longer able to suppress. It is very likely that AIDS will continue to be a fatal disease for many years, unless there is some unforeseen medical breakthrough. About 90% of the time, the virus is transmitted through the exchange of bodily fluids, primarily semen and blood, during homosexual or heterosexual contact, or when needles are shared by intravenous drug users (Castro et al., 1988).

The insidious characteristic of AIDS is that a person can carry the virus for years without showing any symptoms and thus unknowingly infect present and future sex partners. From the viewpoint of AIDS risk, it has been said that when you have sexual relations, you are also having sex with all the people your partner has had sex with in the last five years, plus all the people *they* had sex with in the previous five years.

AIDS presents several challenges to health psychologists. It is important to find ways to help victims cope with a painful, degenerative condition that often leads to social isolation. We also need to develop methods of prevention that clearly influence people's lifestyle decisions. There are lifestyle changes that will minimize one's chances of contracting AIDS, but many of these changes are not easy to make. The surest protection is abstinence from sex and from careless intravenous drug use. At least the first seems an unlikely solution to the problem. Being in a sexually monogamous relationship or reducing the number of sexual partners greatly reduces the risk, as does using a latex condom during all stages of genital contact. Among gay men, it is important to reduce the frequency of anal intercourse, because this often causes tearing and bleeding of the anus, making the mixing of blood and semen much more likely.

There are many reasons for the difficulty in getting people to make these changes in behaviour (Fisher, 1989). Sexual behaviours are complex behaviours that are seldom taught explicitly. Our sexual training includes powerful emotional barriers to learning freely about sex, especially about behaviours that would prevent AIDS. There is also a great deal of denial and misinformation related to AIDS. Hack and Devins (1989) administered questionnaires to 173 male students at the University of Calgary. They found that those men who thought they had high control over exposure to AIDS and low susceptibility to getting AIDS were actually at greatest risk for catching it. Another group of men who had little accurate knowledge of AIDS and perceived themselves as quite susceptible to contracting the disease were taking risk-reducing measures that reflected ignorance of how AIDS is spread. This is clearly an area of health psychology that requires a combination of information and changing of emotional reactions.

Summing up

At present, behavioural interventions seem to be the most effective in producing behaviour change for self-destructive behaviours. The rational approach may be used in combination with the behavioural approach for specific target groups and specific problems. We especially need research on understanding resistance to changing self-destructive behaviour and on the causes of relapse with obesity, smoking, and alcoholism (Brownell et al., 1986).

One of the most serious problems in changing self-destructive behaviour is that our society places little responsibility on the individual for remaining healthy and avoiding serious illness. So much illness is self-induced that we need to change the popular view that effective health care consists of going to health-care professionals to have problems fixed.

Psychology and Medical Intervention

In this section, we will review the relationship between psychology and the practice of medicine. We will look at the psychological impact of illness, particularly chronic illness; at specific difficulties with patient understanding and adherence; and finally at the impact of being a patient.

Crisis

Most of us have been or will be medical patients at one time or another. This can be a very traumatic time, depending on the particular circumstances of hospitalization or confinement. With significant illness, disease, or injury, the experience is often a form of crisis. We will discuss the crisis of physical illness, but much of the research and many of the principles apply to other crisis events as well.

Crisis theory is concerned with how people cope with or adapt to major life changes and transitions. It focuses on major adaptive tasks in life and the skills or strategies we employ to deal with these situations. For an individual who is affected by a serious illness or trauma, there is not only some degree of physiological imbalance but also a threat to psychological equilibrium. As Gruen puts it:

> [The patient] is faced with the sudden termination of his customary lifestyle, which has abruptly passed out of his control. He suffers pain, strange symptoms, and a frightening disruption of physiological processes that were once automatic or taken for granted. He is afraid of getting worse or even of death and dying. He must leave his immediate future up to the 'experts', most of whom he has never met before. He is concerned about the disruption in his family, friend, and work circles, and its consequences; and he worries about his capacity to re-enter these circles. He faces an uncertain future in which resumption of normal activities is questionable for him. He is concerned about whether he can make major changes to accommodate any physical residues of his illness. Finally, he questions the reasons why he became ill and what he can do to prevent a recurrence (Gruen, 1975, p. 223).

A crisis event produces stress which forces us into a state of psychological disequilibrium or imbalance. Since we are creatures of habit, when faced with a crisis we typically resort to previous problem-solving strategies. If the crisis is an unfamiliar one, or one with great impact, our coping mechanisms may fail to restore our psychological equilibrium. Not only do powerful unpleasant emotions result, but we also tend to regress or resort to more primitive problem-solving strategies that we used in our younger years.

In addition, we are less effective as problem solvers, and our coping strategies deteriorate when we experience high anxiety. In short, when we are in crisis we are undergoing an intense emotional experience which tends to leave us with fewer immediate resources with which to deal with the problem.

A distinction can be made between problem-solving efforts to deal with the threat itself (problem-solving function) and efforts to regulate the emotional distress (palliative function) (Cohen and Lazarus, 1979). Caring for a wound or seeking medical attention would be an example of a problem-solving function. Denying one is ill or taking tranquilizers to relax in the face of illness-induced anxiety might be examples of the palliative function.

At times, these functions may work against one another. Individuals sometimes avoid seeking medical help (avoid problem-solving) and resort to denying illness in the face of obvious physical signs.

The turmoil associated with the crisis of physical illness does more than cause emotional arousal, reduce our problem-solving abilities, and foster maladaptive behaviours. In such a state we are also in the confusing position of being more susceptible to external influence and guidance. At the same time, anxiety makes us less receptive or sensitive to our environment, so we may not hear or comprehend efforts to assist us.

Typical reactions to crisis

Anxiety tends to be the cornerstone of reactions to crisis. Some of our behaviour will be directed against this anxiety, in an effort to maintain psychological equilibrium. There are, however, other responses to crisis.

Denial is a failure to perceive an obvious situation or a failure to appreciate its significance. Denial is a defence mechanism used by most of us at one time or another to deal with anxiety or unpleasant events. Although denial is usually a maladaptive response to situations, researchers are beginning to appreciate the value of *some* denial—enough to prevent us from being overwhelmed by anxiety and thrown into a state of complete disorganization (Lazarus, 1974).

Denial is displayed in many ways. A woman with a lump on her breast who maintains "it's nothing," or "it'll go away," is displaying a form of denial. A patient who refuses to accept a diagnosis on the grounds that his physician was incompetent, the laboratory procedures must have been fouled up, or his results must have been confused with those of another patient, is likely displaying denial. A patient who refuses medication for an obvious ailment, claiming there is nothing wrong with him, is displaying denial. A "model patient" with obvious illness who displays no signs of distress or concern may be using denial.

Even though denial appears to be a common result of crisis, it is generally short-lived. The individual begins to more accurately perceive reality or appreciate the significance of the situation. If denial is persistent, it may signify a more serious form of psychological maladjustment.

Most of us become angry on occasion, usually in response to frustration. Anger can also be a response to loss. We can view loss as one kind of frustration, the frustration of losing something very important. With illness, our needs are frustrated in many ways, and the types of loss are many. In illness, our attempts to become well have been thwarted and this frustration may provoke an angry response. Most of us like to be in control of our lives, and with illness some of this control is relinquished.

Illness can bring many kinds of loss. This loss may relate to loss of control, loss of independence, loss of the former body image, loss of normal physiological functioning, or the loss of normal life circumstances and relationships.

Depression is usually associated with loss. There are many kinds of loss, and the way we deal with loss is influenced by many factors: our past experiences with loss, the importance or value of the loss object, and the environmental (cultural, psychosocial, economic, and family) supports we have available to us. While depression is a normal reaction to loss, severe or profound depression is not a typical reaction to physical illness and may require more active intervention.

Coping with Physical Illness

Coping: Tasks

Coping may be defined as "efforts, both action oriented and intrapsychic, to manage (that is master, tolerate, reduce, or minimize) environmental and internal demands, and conflicts among them, which tax or exceed a person's resources" (Lazarus and Launer, 1978).

In a way, coping may be seen as a defence, although the two words have different value connotations. Defence suggests striving to prevent some unwanted event, while coping implies a more active and adaptive problem-solving strategy.

Attempts to cope can occur prior to a stressful event, such as scheduled surgery. In this case they are referred to as **anticipatory coping**. Insufficient research attention has been paid to anticipatory coping, which appears to be one of the major mechanisms by which we deal with stressful events. We may go over in our minds possible future outcomes and strategies. In fact, one of the major ways cognitive behaviour therapists foster anticipatory coping is through mental rehearsal (Meichenbaum, 1977).

Cohen and Lazarus (1979) have identified four main modes of coping: *Information Seeking*, *Direct Action*, *Inhibiting Action*, and *Intrapsychic* (or cognitive) processes.

Information seeking

Information seeking is a coping method in which the patient increases control by gathering information that can be used against the illness. Information seeking is one of the most basic forms of coping in situations where knowledge is limited or conditions ambiguous. When faced with illness, some individuals seem insatiable in their quest for knowledge regarding their particular disease. Others actively avoid this information. The reasons for this marked difference between people is unknown.

Direct action

Direct action is a coping method in which the patient carries out specific behaviours aimed at reducing the impact of the illness. Direct actions include any active efforts to deal with the problem of the illness. Such actions might include seeking medical care, taking medication, or removing or eliminating situations or behaviours which accelerate the disease process.

Moos and Tsu (1977) see individuals as having to master certain adaptive tasks for which skills can be learned and developed. They divide adaptive tasks into two categories, including those which are illness related and those which are relevant to all types of life crisis. Figure 19-3 summarizes these coping tasks.

FIGURE 19-3 Coping tasks faced by the medical patient

SOURCE: Adapted with permission from Moos and Tsu (1977).

I. ILLNESS RELATED TASKS
  a. Dealing with pain and incapacitation.
  b. Dealing with the hospital environment and special treatment.
  c. Developing adequate relationships with professional staff.

II. GENERAL TASKS
  d. Preserving a reasonable emotional balance.
  e. Preserving a satisfactory self-image.
  f. Preserving relationships with family and friends.
  g. Preparing for an uncertain future.

These coping tasks may vary in individuals, based upon the type of crisis or stressors and the individual's habitual set of coping responses. The value of direct action was underlined by Holahan and Moos (1985), who said that stress resistance was most strongly related to an easy-going disposition and less use of avoidance coping. **Avoidance coping** is a coping method in which the patient keeps feelings bottled up and takes out negative feelings on others as a way to escape the realities of the illness.

Inhibiting action

Inhibiting action is a coping method in which the patient might choose not to act in a certain situation. The outcome of some actions may be ineffective or harmful to the problem-solving process or may lead to the development of further difficulties. For example, it may be tempting to rush frantically from doctor to doctor or to blindly medicate oneself. Restraint and calm can prevent self-harm.

Intrapsychic (cognitive) coping

Intrapsychic (cognitive) coping is a coping method in which the patient uses mental processes to handle stress. Such processes include denial, avoidance, and intellectualized detachment. Many of these processes we traditionally think of as defences. When a person is ill there may be relatively little that can be done actively to deal with the situation, and the individual is placed in a position of passivity and dependence. Under these circumstances, intrapsychic modes of coping appear the most important as the individual attempts to deal with the situation psychologically, using intellectual processes.

Coping: Skills

There are specific skills which can help deal with the crisis of illness.

Learning to ask for help

Most of us, at one time or another, have relied upon the emotional support of others to help us through crisis and stress. Sometimes this is readily available in our environment from family and friends, and at other times it is not. Benjamin Gottlieb (1987) has summarized a large body of research that shows how important social support is to the medical patient. As with other psychological factors, our social connections have a significant impact on the course of illness. A specific coping skill which can be learned is *the ability to request emotional support and reassurance* during the time of illness. Sometimes family and friends have difficulty in relating to an individual who has assumed the new role of patient. We can learn to request the support we need at the time others in our environment may find it difficult to offer.

In addition to these individualized supports, there are other ways that support can be found. There are many self-help groups for individuals with various diseases and disabilities, for example. These groups are composed of individuals with a similar disease or disability. They serve as a source of both information and mutual support. An individual with a serious illness often feels terribly alone and often reports that contact with individuals in a similar situation is a source of strength.

Learning the system

Another coping skill is *becoming accustomed to illness-related procedures*. One of the stressors we face with illness is a loss of control or competence in dealing with our environment. Willpower and previous problem-solving strategies are often ineffective against physical illness or disability. This loss of control need not be all-consuming, however. Our efforts to engage in our own treatment can both reduce demands on staff and — perhaps more importantly — demonstrate that some degree of control is possible. For example, self-catheterization in spinal cord injured patients or self-dialysis in patients with kidney disease can give the patient a meaningful sense of control.

Setting achievable goals

When attempting a new task or acquiring a new skill we need to receive feedback as to whether we are progressing or not. Essentially, we can *set concrete limited goals* with built-in feedback mechanisms. For example, an individual who has suffered a stroke may have as a goal the eventual return to walking unassisted. This process is facilitated by some forms of therapy but is usually disappointingly slow. Very little progress is seen on a day-to-day basis. Under these circumstances, one might wish to break the behaviour of walking into smaller units which are more easily or quickly mastered.

A search for purpose

Another skill which seems particularly helpful to the physically ill is that of *finding a meaning or purpose* to the events that have transpired. Meaning may be based on religious, interpersonal, or even random grounds. Any of these grounds serves to impose a meaningful perspective on events.

Determinants of success in coping

Determining who copes well with physical illness and who does not depends upon three general factors: personal characteristics, illness-related factors, and features of the environment.

Personal characteristics

Personal characteristics include age, intellectual abilities, cognitive and emotional development, and previous coping strategies and skills. Age is significant because coping strategies and their success might be fundamentally different for a child with heart disease compared with an elderly person, for example. Intelligence has an influence in that an individual of low intelligence may not be able to use information as effectively. Cognitive and emotional resources include the degree to which we perceive ourselves as having control over the environment and destiny, self-image, emotional stability, and so on. Previous coping strategies are also important, as is our previous success in using them. Philosophical and religious beliefs may exert an influence on our ability to relinquish control to a superior being, or to find meaning in current circumstances.

Illness-related factors

Important illness-related factors are the progressive or nonprogressive features of our disease, the extent of impairment or disability, the degree of rehabilitation required, and the extent of personal responsibility involved. The patient might feel a painful level of personal responsibility for injuries from a car accident caused by negligence, for example. Another important dimension of illness-related factors is the psychological significance (in contrast to the biological significance) of the disease. For example, the scarring produced by burns, while not life-threatening, may have considerable psychological impact. On the other hand, high blood pressure, which is life threatening, may not have such an impact.

Features of the environment

The environment has its impact as well. Different stresses are imposed by hospitalization than are found in outpatient treatment. The physical environment has an obvious impact with wheelchair accessibility for paralysed patients or the aids available to the blind. The environment also includes locally available resources for treatment or support for those with a particular illness. The interpersonal environment is also very important to the patient. Significant people in the patient's life can both hinder and help in adjustment and recovery. The environment even includes the culture's or society's view of a particular disease or disability.

The patient role: Gains and losses

Another way to look at the success of adjustment to physical illness is in terms of gains and losses associated with the **patient role**. As with other roles, the patient role consists of a set of behaviours that are socially defined as appropriate for a medical patient. Gains are the advantages that come from being a patient, and losses are the psychological liabilities associated with this role. If gains exceed losses, it is possible that the process will be a very difficult one that results in incomplete adjustment, slow recovery or rehabilitation, or development of a chronic patient role. On the other hand, if losses exceed gains, there is a stronger incentive for getting well. This can contribute to quicker recovery and more successful adjustment. Of course we are not suggesting that patients should be made uncomfortable to encourage them to get better faster. However, it is important to be aware of preventing the comforts of the patient role from encouraging illness behaviour.

Patients are placed in a position of dependency, so they experience the *removal of responsibility*. When we are sick, we are not expected to assume normal obligations or roles within society. This may be an important issue with individuals who see themselves as ill-equipped to deal with the outside world and its social, interpersonal, and financial responsibilities. Life for these individuals is often a struggle, characterized by conflict and anxiety, frustration and disappointment. Obligations may be so strong that the individual may be unable to escape these responsibilities or deal with them in a reasonable way. Suddenly, with hospitalization, these stressors are removed and "sick behaviour" is strongly reinforced by the anxiety reduction that comes from escaping the world.

The maintenance of sick behaviour by contingencies in the environment is not the same as *malingering*. In our discussion of awareness and learning we stressed that much of our behaviour has been shaped and reinforced without our being aware of all the contingencies involved. So it often is with the individual who is being reinforced for sick behaviour. Malingering, on the other hand, is a deliberate effort to emit sick behaviour where the rewards are clearly seen. This brings us to another potential advantage of the patient role, *financial gain*.

Although it is sometimes difficult to distinguish between malingering and illness behaviour that is maintained without the patient's conscious plan, malingering does occur. When it does, financial gain is often a factor. Financial gains can come from court settlements after injury or in the form of disability insurance after illness or injury.

Another potential advantage of being a patient is *social or interpersonal gain*. An example might be found in a disturbed marital relationship. Being sick might bring attention or changes in the dynamics of the relationship which otherwise would not occur. A spouse, for example, who receives very little attention from his or her workaholic partner, may find that once ill, he or she receives considerable attention and assistance. The weakness of illness is often a powerful tool for controlling others. In the individual case, it is often difficult to distinguish whether the sickness behaviour is maintained without the patient's awareness or whether malingering is occurring.

Another effect of the reinforcements that come with illness is *hospitalism*. This problem can include an excessive dependence on the hospital and its environment, the development of psychological reactions to proposed discharge from hospital, and attempts to prolong hospital stay. Some individuals become ill and improve but cling to hospitalization and a particular doctor or series of doctors. They may even become attached to the hospital or treatment unit as the major supportive structure in their lives.

The chronic patient

Related to gains and losses and to the syndrome of hospitalism is the problem of those individuals who appear chronically ill. We are not talking about the patient with a long-term physical disability or one with a progressive disease. Some patients have an absence of medical findings to account for subjective symptoms or report pain or incapacitation disproportionate to the physical findings. These are the patients who are seeing many physicians, who have been on innumerable kinds of medication, or who may have undergone several surgeries without apparent relief of their condition. While these individuals may be described as hypochondriacal, or display a conversion disorder (see Chapter 14), the underlying difficulties may be best understood on the basis of learning theory. This orientation is illustrated by Fordyce (1976) in his development of a behavioural model to understand these patients. He has also outlined a treatment strategy to assist these individuals to return to a more normal lifestyle.

Individuals who experience chronic pain can be taken as an example. At one time, these individuals have suffered from an illness or injury which results in pain, but they fail to recover. They continue to report pain and are incapacitated beyond the expected time of healing of the original illness or injury. Sometimes this happens because the pain behaviour has been reinforced.

This can happen in several ways. The first is through direct reinforcement of pain behaviour. Receiving attention for being sick can reinforce pain, for example. The second way is through anxiety reduction. Being in pain often helps the person avoid situations and responsibilities that arouse anxiety. A third possibility is that pain behaviour is maintained through punishment of "well" behaviour. This is less likely than the first two sources of reinforcement for pain. It is important to realize that such a patient is not malingering. The person actually feels pain and usually is not aware that it is the result of reinforcement. (See the Special Topic in Chapter 4, on the perception and management of pain.)

Figure 19-4 compares the disease model and the learning (behavioural) model perspectives on chronic pain. It illustrates how a learning model of chronic pain leads to a direct treatment of symptoms, rather than to a focus on underlying causes. Figure A illustrates the traditional disease model of treatment. The patient's symptoms

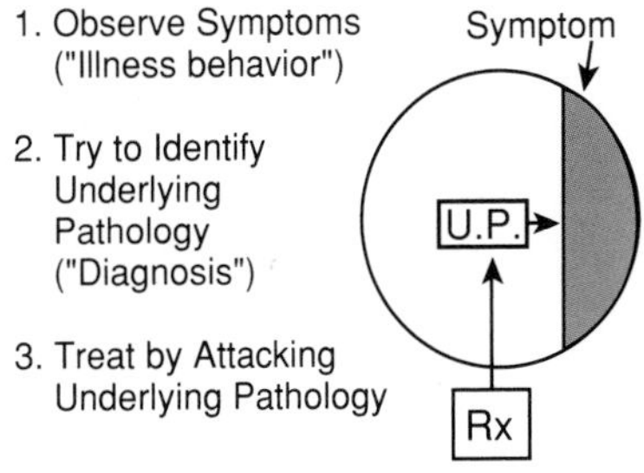

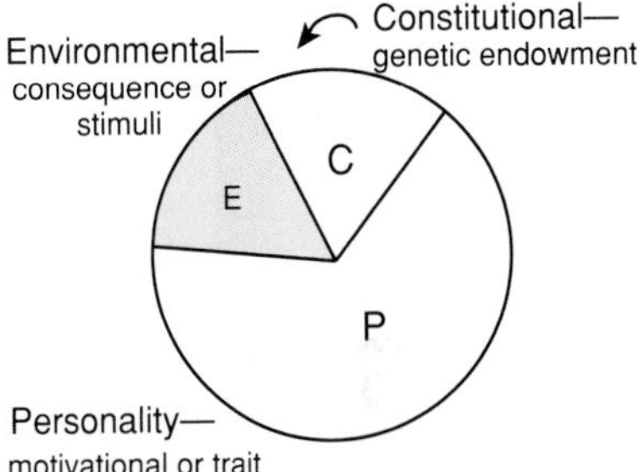

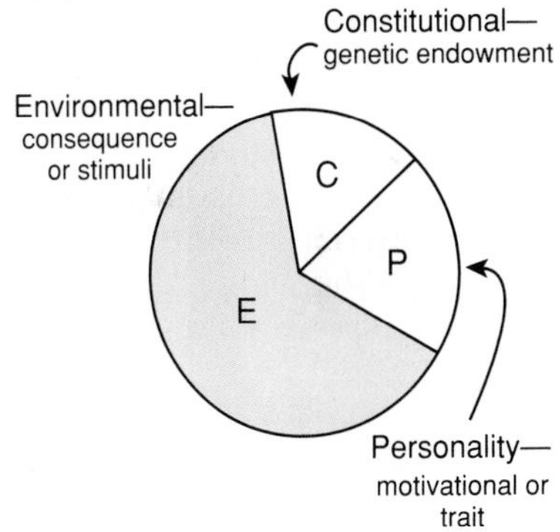

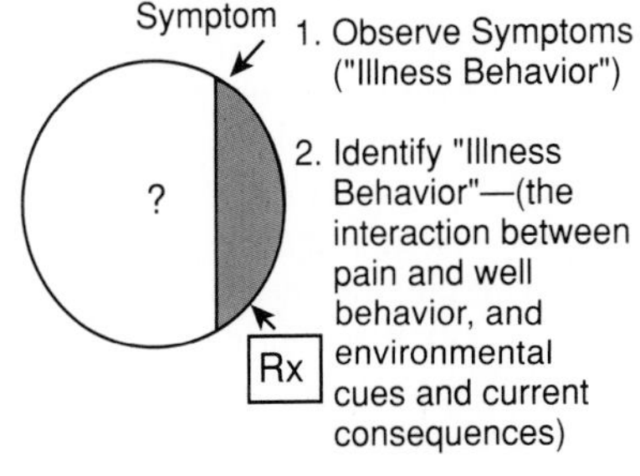

FIGURE 19-4 Comparing a disease model and a learning model for the treatment of chronic pain
Figure A illustrates the traditional disease model of treatment for chronic pain. Figure B shows the motivational model of factors influencing behaviour. Figure C shows the behavioural model of factors influencing behaviour. Figure D illustrates the learning model of treatment for chronic pain.
SOURCE: Adapted with permission from Fordyce (1976).

are largely ignored and treatment focuses on underlying causes. This approach to treating chronic pain would grow out of the motivational model of behaviour illustrated in Figure B (a traditional psychodynamic view). In Figure B, personality factors are seen as the most important underlying causes of problems such as chronic pain. Personality factors are given more weight than environmental or constitutional (genetic) factors. Thus, to relieve the chronic pain, one would treat the personality.

In contrast, Fordyce's learning (behavioural) model of behaviour is illustrated in Figure C. Environmental factors are given more weight than genetic or personality factors. This model leads to the treatment strategy illustrated in Figure D which is based on the learning model proposed by Fordyce. Symptoms are identified and treated directly through learning principles.

Fordyce's treatment model uses the principles of reinforcement to enhance "well" behaviour and to extinguish pain behaviour. He combines this behavioural treatment with other forms of treatment.

Special Topic **Adherence**

A major problem in the health-care system concerns individuals who lack an understanding of and do not participate in their treatment. This treatment may include changing self-destructive behaviours, taking medications, or following other forms of therapy (Richardson et al., 1987). Among patients with dangerously high blood pressure, only about half seek treatment when advised to do so. Of those who seek treatment, only about half follow the treatment advice given them (Leventhal, Zimmerman, & Gutmann, 1984).

There is some controversy in the health-care system as to which term, *compliance* or *adherence*, best describes a patient's following medical advice or treatment. It may seem that the choice of words is unimportant, but the terms reflect important differences in whether one views the doctor-patient relationship as a superior-subordinate one or as a collaborative effort. As the title of this section implies, we see it as more of a collaborative endeavour. The health-care professional and the patient work together toward a common goal, the restoration of a patient's health or maximization of potential in the face of disability.

Within health psychology, adherence to treatment programs is a major topic of concern and research. Unfortunately, a surprisingly small proportion of patients adhere strictly to any treatment program. Dunbar and Stunkard (1979) found that 20 to 50% of patients don't even arrive for scheduled appointments. With regard to treatment, 20 to 80% of patients make errors in taking their medication, and 25 to 65% stop taking medications before it is therapeutically desirable to do so. Among programs directed to changing lifestyle or self-destructive behaviour for health reasons, 20 to 80% of patients drop out of weight-management programs, and as many as 90 to 95% of participants in these programs fail to achieve a desirable weight. As indicated earlier, rates of permanent termination of smoking are equally poor, with a long-term abstinence of less than 25%. This is generally comparable to the success rate of studies on alcohol and heroin addiction (Best and Bloch, 1979).

Contrary to popular belief, many of these studies indicate that personality variables are not particularly associated with patient adherence. There is no systematic relationship between adherence and age, race, sex, marital status, educational level, intelligence, or motivation. The crucial variable seems to be the initial understanding of the instructions and subsequent memory for them. For example, a study by Ley (1976) found that immediately after the office visit with their physician, patients remembered only two thirds of the instructions they were given.

Several studies have looked at this problem (Dunbar, 1980) and suggest that information presented to the patient should be given in logical categories and tailored to the individual patient.

The health-care professional should take into account the individual's medical sophistication, intellectual level, and receptivity to the information. Information should be gradually presented over time to prevent overloading. It has also been suggested that the patient should repeat what he or she has heard and that instructions should be provided orally and in writing. Further, self-monitoring systems and record keeping for treatment are useful. It is often helpful to use frequent cues and reminders, either by notes or the assistance of other family members or by associating a particular treatment procedure with a common daily activity.

Much less research has been done on the role of the physician or care-giver in adherence. There is evidence to show, however, that patients are more adherent when the care-giver demonstrates warmth and empathy (Francis, Korsh, & Morris, 1969), and when care-givers are more approachable and receptive to the questions which the patient might have. Threatening the patient with the potential disasters which await nonadherence is not effective in promoting adherence to the treatment program.

One study asked physicians to rate themselves on their interpersonal skills, empathy, self-monitoring ability, and affective communication skill (DiMatteo, Hays, and Prince, 1986). The experimenters also obtained objective measures of how sensitive the physicians were to audio communications and how skillful they were at nonverbal communication. The physicians' views of themselves did not predict patient adherence, but this is not too surprising. Most health-care workers describe themselves as good communicators whether it's true or not. The objective measures gathered, however, provided interesting results. Doctors who were more sensitive to oral communication had fewer patients fail to show up for appointments. Those who were good at nonverbal communication had more satisfied patients and heavier workloads.

Finally, some research has investigated the nature of the treatment program itself. Complicated instructions, side effects (in the case of medication), length of treatment, and the degree to which an individual is asked to make major changes in lifestyle are all key variables. The more complex a treatment program, particularly when changes or modifications are required over time, the less likely the patient is to adhere to it. Simplifying instructions, providing cues, and gradually introducing the requirements of the program over time may be of benefit. It has not been demonstrated that the side effects of medications are related to adherence. A more crucial factor is how the patient's response to these side effects is dealt with. For example, adherence is more likely when complaints of side effects are dealt with in a supportive and concerned manner rather than being brusquely dismissed as unimportant. Interestingly, forewarning patients of side effects does not appear to affect adherence.

The issue of adherence is complex and does involve some ethical considerations. For example, what are our rights as patients and do these rights involve responsibilities for our own health care? From the health-care practitioner's point of view, how far can one go without violating an individual's rights to nonadherence if that is what is desired? Although we are dealing with behaviour in an area amenable to scientific investigation, values, morals, and judgments are also important considerations.

1. Nearly all diseases are affected by psychological factors. Providing psychotherapy as part of health service may reduce health-care costs. Health psychology focuses on the psychological aspects of health and illness. It emphasizes prevention as well as psychological reactions to illness and injury. Health psychology research focuses on (1) the etiology or causes of disease, (2) the course and treatment of disease, and (3) the maintenance of health.

2. Personality factors play a role in physical health in three major ways. (1) Personality helps cause disease before symptoms occur, suggesting that personality is a factor in the biochemical changes which result in disease. (2) Physiological reactions to the stress of illness are affected by both biological and psychosocial factors. (3) Illness can change personality.

3. Two general theories have been proposed to account for the link between personality and health. Nuclear conflict theory hypothesizes that specific unconscious conflicts and the emotions they produce are associated with specific diseases. The predictions of this theory are difficult to measure. Second, helplessness-hopelessness theory suggests that illness may develop in biologically predisposed people who respond to situations in a specific way called the giving up-given up complex. One of the most important principles in this model involves a link between stress and the immune system. This link is investigated in the field of psychoimmunology.

4. It is apparent that not all people respond the same way to stress. In a given situation, if a person feels that he or she has the resources to meet the threat, positively evaluates the situation, or does not perceive danger, the person is less likely to experience stress. Individuals who are less likely to become ill tend to avoid stress and conflict, don't brood over life goals, and aren't obsessively involved in life's activities. Those who have good social supports appear to live longer. They also have less incidence of illness, and when they are ill have fewer symptoms of illness.

5. Specificity theories link particular personality factors to particular diseases. The most consistent psychosocial predictor of coronary heart disease is a constellation of factors called the Type A personality. It appears that the biological link between the Type A personality and heart disease involves increases in cholesterol, blood lipid levels, and the hormone norepinephrine, which are caused by stress. The most damaging parts of the Type A personality appear to be impatience and cynical hostility.

6. Psychological processes have also been implicated in cancer, a topic investigated in the field of biopsychosocial oncology. Research seems to suggest a link between feelings of depression and development of cancer. Research somewhat more strongly shows a link between feelings and the length of survival of cancer patients. Emotional expressiveness and feelings of hope are related to longer survival. Again, the link between these feelings and the body appears to be the immune system, which affects the extent to which cancer spreads or metastasizes to other parts of the body.

7. Personality factors have also been found to be associated with the juvenile onset of (type I) diabetes. Specifically, McClelland believes that the need for affiliation is a major factor in diabetes.

8. The prevention of disease in health psychology involves reducing stress by dealing with conflict and promoting the expression of emotion. Other interventions include reducing self-destructive behaviours such as overeating, smoking, and drinking. Three models have been proposed to explain why people behave in ways that are not good for them. (1) The rational model assumes that human behaviour is primarily guided by logic and objectivity, so self-destructive behaviour arises from a lack of accurate information. The practical results from implementing this model

have been disappointing. (2) The psychodynamic model assumes that within all people are unconscious conflicts that lead to self-destructive behaviour. This model is difficult to implement and test and has not been widely useful. (3) The social-learning model proposes that self-destructive behaviours are learned and are maintained through reinforcement. Implementation includes reducing reinforcement for these behaviours and establishing new responses through learning principles.

9. The social-learning model appears to be the most effective in dealing with obesity. With smoking, most who quit do so on their own. Some formal treatments, such as rapid smoking treatment, have had some effect. Going "cold turkey" and using positively motivating self-statements appear to help with stopping smoking. With alcoholism, the rational and psychodynamic models appear to have little effect. Behavioural intervention strategies focus on modelling and social reinforcement in the treatment of alcoholism.

10. AIDS is perhaps the major health threat of the twentieth century. Health psychologists must find ways of helping victims cope with their incurable disease and of assisting in the change of lifestyle necessary to avoid AIDS.

11. Psychology and medical treatment are linked in health psychology. Illness has a great impact psychologically. Crisis theory explains how people deal with life changes and transitions, and illness can be a major life change. Illness often forces the person to find new coping strategies under highly emotional circumstances. In such a situation, any action that relieves anxiety is very reinforcing, whether it is adaptive or maladaptive. Efforts to deal with a crisis can be separated into two categories. Efforts which deal with the threat directly serve a problem-solving function. Efforts which regulate the emotional stress serve a supportive function.

12. The primary reaction to crisis seems to be anxiety. Other reactions include denial, anger and frustration, and depression.

13. To cope with physical illness one must manage environmental and internal demands and the conflicts among them. Anticipatory coping, information seeking, direct action, avoidance coping, and inhibiting action are all coping methods. Learning to ask for help, learning the system, setting limited concrete goals, and finding meaning in events are coping skills during the process of illness. The success of coping with illness is affected by personal characteristics, illness-related factors, and the environment.

14. The patient role offers gains for some people. Patients may experience the removal of the normal responsibilities of their lives, some financial gains, and social or interpersonal gains. Patients who are incapacitated beyond any medical reasons may be chronic patients. Such patients may have acquired these behaviours because past behaviours of similar kinds were reinforced.

Key Terms

Anticipatory coping Attempts to cope prior to a stressful event, such as scheduled surgery.

Avoidance coping In health psychology, a coping method in which the patient keeps feelings bottled up and takes out negative feelings on others as a way to escape the realities of the illness.

Biological factors In health psychology, those contributors to health and illness that are specifically physical in nature.

Biopsychosocial oncology The field that studies the links between the development and treatment of cancer and emotion, behaviour, physiology, and the social environment.

Coping In health psychology, the "efforts, both action oriented and intrapsychic, to manage (that is master, tolerate, reduce, or minimize) environmental and internal demands, and conflicts among them, which tax or exceed a person's resources" (Lazarus and Launer, 1978).

Crisis theory The area of study of how people cope with or adapt to major life changes and transitions.

Cynical hostility The most damaging element of Type A personality. It is marked by chronic mistrust of others and harsh, judgmental, and vengeful feelings.

Denial The failure to perceive or to appreciate the nature of obviously threatening circumstances.

Direct action In health psychology, a coping method in which the patient carries out specific behaviours aimed at reducing the impact of the illness.

Easygoing affiliative syndrome (EAS) A personality pattern associated with type I diabetes. It is marked by low assertiveness and high need for relationships.

Etiology The source or causes of something; in health psychology, the causes of an illness.

Giving-up-given-up complex A psychological sense of powerlessness over the environment. The emotional state that seems to contribute to vulnerability to disease. Part of helplessness-hopelessness theory.

Health psychology The discipline that studies psychological aspects of health and illness; emphasizes prevention, treatment, etiology, the course of illnesses, and reactions to illness.

Helplessness-hopelessness theory The idea that feelings of depression and giving up contribute to disease by suppressing the immune system.

Information seeking In health psychology, a coping method in which the patient increases control by gathering information that can be used against the illness.

Inhibiting action In health psychology, a coping method in which the patient might choose not to act in a certain situation.

Intrapsychic (cognitive) coping In health psychology, a coping method in which the patient uses mental processes to handle stress; denial, avoidance, and intellectualized detachment are examples.

Metastasis The process by which cancer spreads through the body.

Nuclear conflict theory The notion that specific unconscious conflicts and the emotions they produce lead to specific diseases.

Patient role A set of behaviours that are defined as appropriate to being a medical patient.

Psychodynamic model of self-destructive behaviour In health psychology, the theory that unconscious conflicts among our instinctual, rational, and moralistic tendencies are the root of all self-destructive behaviour.

Psychoimmunology The field that studies the link between psychological factors and the functioning of the immune system.

Psychosocial factors In health psychology, those contributors to health and illness that arise from psychological processes, relationships, and other environmental processes.

Rational model of self-destructive behaviour In health psychology, the theory that human functioning is fundamentally logical, so self-defeating behaviour is the result of inaccurate information.

Social-learning model of self-destructive behaviour In health psychology, the theory that health behaviours, including self-defeating behaviours, are learned either through direct reinforcement, social reinforcement, or modelling.

Stress The subjective aversive reaction to change. It depends on our personalities and our past experiences.

Symptom substitution The emergence of a new problem after a specific symptom is removed without treating the underlying unconscious conflict.

Type A personality A type of personality whose pattern of behaviours is linked to coronary heart disease. These behaviours are marked by competitiveness, aggressiveness, impatience, time urgency, insecurity, and — most importantly — cynical hostility.

Type B personality A type of personality whose pattern of behaviours is linked to lower incidence of heart disease. These behaviours are marked by calm resiliency, trustfulness, lack of time urgency, and faster recovery from stress.

Suggested Readings

Check the suggested readings in Chapter 13, Stress, if you are particularly interested in that aspect of health psychology.

Friedman, M., & Ulmer, D. (1984). *Treating Type A behavior—and your heart.* New York: Knopf. This is a popularized book with much useful advice about changing Type A behaviour. The research on Type A is developing rapidly, so a more recent book might put more stress on the cynical hostility factor, but this one is useful.

Levy, S. M. (1985). *Behavior and cancer.* San Francisco: Jossey-Bass. This is a scholarly but readable account of the psychological factors that are related to the development of cancer.

Taylor, S. E. (1985). *Introduction to health psychology.* New York: Random House. An introductory textbook to the area covered by this chapter and Chapter 13. This book is probably at the level you would want to pursue as a next step beyond our chapter.

The following two books are annotated bibliographies in the area of health psychology. If you want to write a paper or pursue some particular topic more fully, these are excellent sources. They are very complete, and each reference is accompanied by a summary of the article.

Hornig-Rohan, M., & Locke, S. E. (eds.) (1985). *Psychological and behavioral treatments for disorders of the heart and blood vessels: An annotated bibliography. Psychological and behavioral treatments for medical disorders, vol. 1.* New York: Institute for the Advancement of Health.

Locke, S. E. (ed.) (1986). *Psychological and behavioral treatments for disorders associated with the immune system: An annotated bibliography. Psychological and behavioral treatments for medical disorders, vol. 2.*

CHAPTER 20

SOURCE: Janet Kigusiuq, *Winter Camp Scene* (ca. 1974).

Organizational Psychology

Overview of Organizational Behaviour

One of the most useful applications of psychology is in the world of work. Some psychologists work directly for commercial organizations and call themselves "industrial psychologists" or "organizational psychologists." **Organizational psychology** (sometimes called "industrial psychology") applies psychological principles and findings to the world of work. Organizational psychologists use many of the principles discussed in this chapter. Of broader relevance, however, is the knowledge that psychology can offer for the person who wants to be a manager of other individuals' work. Effective leadership and management skills have received much attention in psychology. In this chapter, we will try to provide an understanding of both the nature of organizations and the skills and attitudes that contribute to being a better manager.

The effective manager must be both perceptive in analyzing situations *and* good at relating with people. This is not an easy combination of qualities to achieve. It requires an understanding of the content of the relevant theories as well as the way to apply those theories.

Katzell & Guzzo (1983) reviewed 207 experiments in which psychological approaches were used to increase productivity. In 87% of the studies there was improved productivity on at least one concrete measure. Psychology has a great deal to offer the organization.

Historical background

The goal of organizational psychology is the *scientific study of why people behave as they do in organizations*. Stated this way, we can see that organizational psychology became an issue as far back as the industrial revolution. Before that most workers were in small cottage industries. For thousands of years, individuals have tried to understand how to get others to work effectively, but this understanding has been largely intuitive and "seat of the pants." The science of organizational behaviour had its start in two major approaches: Scientific Management and the Human Relations movement. Much of contemporary organizational psychology is derived from these approaches.

Scientific management

In the early 1900s, Frederick W. Taylor conducted studies of the efficiency of various patterns of "time and motion" at a steel company. He was an industrial engineer looking for the most efficient way to perform various jobs. **Taylorism** or **scientific management** is often criticized — and misunderstood — as being a mechanical and

A steel mill of the early 1900s. In such a factory Frederick Taylor conducted his "time and motion" studies.
SOURCE: Hamilton Steel and Iron, 1906. Photo courtesy of Stelco Inc.

dehumanizing search for the "one best way" to do a particular job. However, Taylor was quite sensitive to matching a particular person to a particular way to do a job. "One best way" meant the best way for a particular individual to perform a job. His studies of efficiency often resulted in enormous increases in productivity, so he had considerable influence.

His logical and rational approach to motivating people to work was based on the theory that human behaviour is motivated primarily by economic rewards. Thus, one should (1) determine the most efficient way to perform a job, (2) prescribe this work method to the worker, and (3) pay for performance on a "piecework" basis. This efficiency-oriented philosophy still has considerable influence in organizations, which tend to be production oriented.

Taylor's efficiency-orientation probably grew as much out of his personality as out of any other causes. When he was young, he would carefully draw up lists of attractive and unattractive girls before going to a dance, so he could divide his time equally between them. He sometimes would scarcely participate in games because he was so concerned about the accurate measurement of the playing field.

The human relations movement

In the 1930s, a classic series of experiments forced managers to move away from mechanistic approaches to work behaviour and to consider mental and emotional factors that affect workers (Roethlisberger and Dickson, 1935). At the Hawthorne plant of the Western Electric Company, Elton Mayo and his co-workers tried to study the effects of various levels of lighting on work performance (Mayo, 1933). This fit nicely within the philosophy of scientific management. Mayo expected that as lighting increased, productivity would increase, up to some point, at which further increases would hamper productivity because of excessive brightness. This seemed a reasonable hypothesis, but he and his co-workers found very few relationships between illumination levels and productivity. It soon became

A steel mill of today.
SOURCE: Modern casting of hot steel, Lake Erie Works. Photo courtesy of Stelco Inc.

SOURCE: *Cathy* by Cathy Guisewite. Copyright 1990 Universal Press Syndicate. Reprinted with permission. All rights reserved.

obvious that other factors were having a significant impact—factors such as social relations, morale, freedom to choose work goals, and the like. This is commonly referred to as the Hawthorne Effect. The **Hawthorne Effect** refers to the influence that factors such as morale and social relations have on productivity. Specifically, it refers to the finding that in an experiment on levels of lighting, productivity went up no matter what changes were made. The attention of being studied brought about the change. In some cases, for example, productivity increased when it was predicted to decrease, apparently because some workers were responding to having been chosen to be in an experiment. The important conclusion was that efficiency is only a small part of work behaviour. Human relations count too.

The human relations movement has been criticized when it has stressed only the mental and emotional parts of work behaviour. It is sometimes sarcastically referred to as "cow sociology," because it seems to argue that the manager's job is to make workers contented and "contented cows give more milk."

The modern manager recognizes that *both* productivity and human considerations are essential to being effective, and that is the primary theme of this chapter. The effective manager can be described as "tough and fair" or "assertive and helpful" or "productive and considerate." These qualities are not easy to combine, but it does seem to be worth the effort. We will try to be as explicit as possible about how that can be done.

Motivation for Work

How can a person be induced to accomplish goals with enthusiasm and persistence? That is the basic question of work motivation. Actually, it is the basic question of any motivation. You might object if we said that you want to manipulate others, but surely you want to "influence" others' behaviour. You want your spouse or lover or child or friend to behave in certain ways and you try to facilitate that behaviour. As a manager, we would want our workers to perform and produce. To accomplish that we must motivate them. People will do what they are motivated to do. This is a paraphrase of the sentence from Chapter 5 on principles of learning, in which the learning theorist said, "People do what they are reinforced for doing." Learning theory is one approach to motivation which we will discuss.

Theories of motivation

Within organizational psychology, there are several important theories of motivation. As we noted in Chapter 10 in our discussion of theories of personality, many different theories in psychology contradict each other and are based on radically different views of human nature. This is also true of theories of motivation in the workplace.

Maslow's hierarchy

One of the best known theories of motivation is Abraham Maslow's "hierarchy of needs" (1943) which we have already discussed in Chapter 6 of this book. This theory says that each person's motivations are different at different times, so any application to individuals must be tailor-made. Maslow argues that human needs are arranged in a hierarchy, or ascending order of importance. Needs that are higher in the list have no motivating power unless lower needs have been satisfied (see Figure 20-1). Similarly, a need that has been satisfied no longer has motivating power.

Maslow's hierarchy includes:

1. *Physiological needs.* The most fundamental needs are for sleep, food, drink, avoidance of pain, and the like. If these needs are active, nothing else matters as a motivator until they are relatively satisfied. The desire for social prestige doesn't mean much in the streets of Calcutta.
2. *Safety needs.* When immediate physiological needs have been met, the person is most motivated to avoid external threats to safety and well-being.
3. *Social acceptance needs.* The need to belong and be accepted by others is next in the hierarchy.
4. *Esteem (status) needs.* Social position, prestige, self-worth, and self-importance become motivating, once the lower levels of needs are met.
5. *Self-actualization needs.* The search for meaningful work and living, fulfilling one's destiny in life, and reaching ultimate goals are all examples of powerful motivators, *if* the lower levels of needs have been met.

Maslow argued that what works as a motivator will vary greatly depending on the culture and on the individual person. The person or system providing the motivators will have to take the hierarchy into account.

Maslow's theory has wide acceptance as an explanation of behaviour. However, in its most literal form it has not been consistently supported by scientific studies of individual motivation in the workplace (Miner, 1980; Naylor & Ilgen, 1980; Wahba & Bridwell, 1976). Maslow himself (1965) cautioned that his theory came out of work with clients in therapy and may not be applicable to the study of work behaviour. It does seem that it is useful to classify needs in two broad categories: "deficiency" needs (physiological, safety, and social needs) and "growth" needs (esteem and self-actualization). The "hierarchy" of needs may not be strictly accurate, since there are many instances of humans in great danger or in situations of physiological deprivation who have acted in "actualizing" ways and performed noble actions. The manager, however, can probably find useful insights in Maslow's theory. Human motivation includes both kinds of needs and there is a tendency for the "growth" needs to be more important when the "deficiency" needs are met.

FIGURE 20-1 Maslow's hierarchy of needs

Organizational psychologists often refer to Maslow's theory that lower needs must be met before higher needs will be motivating. In addition, once a need is met, it no longer serves as an effective motivator of human behaviour.

SOURCE: Reprinted with permission from Allyn and Bacon, 1989.

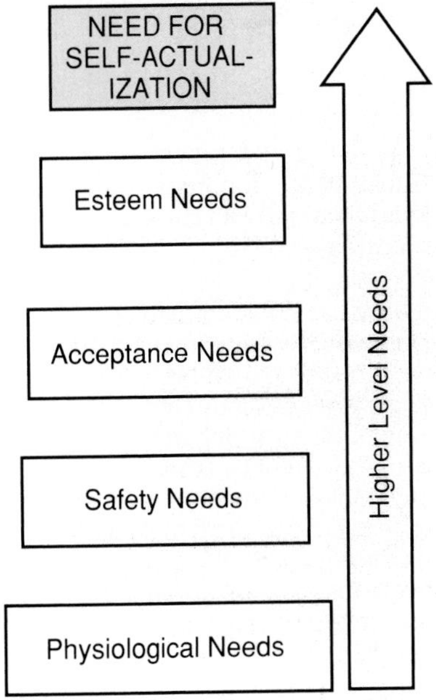

Hygienes and motivators

Herzberg and his co-workers (Herzberg, Mausner, & Snyderman, 1959; Herzberg, 1976) have proposed a two-factor theory of work motivation that has been frequently applied in organizations. It is common to think of motivational factors as on one dimension. This dimension or continuum has factors that give job satisfaction at one end and factors that cause job dissatisfaction at the other end. This would mean that removing a variable that causes dissatisfaction would automatically increase satisfaction and removing a "satisfier" would cause dissatisfaction. This seems intuitively obvious to most people, but Herzberg's argument is harder to grasp.

He said there were really two dimensions to be considered. Some factors, which he called **hygienes**, cause dissatisfaction if they are absent but do not function as motivators when they are present. In a sense, workers expect them as "givens" of the job. An obvious example might be cleanliness in company washrooms. This cleanliness can hardly be thought of as a motivator, but its absence will be dissatisfying and will affect work behaviour. These hygienes are represented by the dimension going from "no job dissatisfaction" to "job dissatisfaction." Other examples of hygienes in most work settings might include fringe benefits, working conditions, adequate supervision, and company policy. Usually none of these is particularly motivating to an individual worker, but their absence can lead to much dissatisfaction, as is often obvious in labour negotiations over such issues.

Herzberg's **motivators** are factors that have a direct effect on increasing productive behaviour in the worker. They are represented by the dimension going from "no job satisfaction" to "job satisfaction." Examples of motivators might include recognition, achievement, advancement, meaningfulness of particular work, and personal responsibility. (See Figure 20-2.)

Much of Herzberg's research supports his theory, although others have had difficulty repeating his work (Fein, 1974). We think that if one does not take the theory too literally, there is considerable instructive value in it. For example, Herzberg seemed to be quite strict about what was a motivator and what was a hygiene. However,

FIGURE 20-2 A comparison of Maslow's and Herzberg's theories

This diagram shows how Maslow's theory can be integrated with Herzberg's theory. In our culture, most needs low on Maslow's hierarchy are satisfied. Thus they no longer act as strong motives. This is exactly what Herzberg would say. Maslow's higher needs correspond to Herzberg's motivators. In a poorer culture, things that are hygienes for us might well be motivators because they are unmet needs.

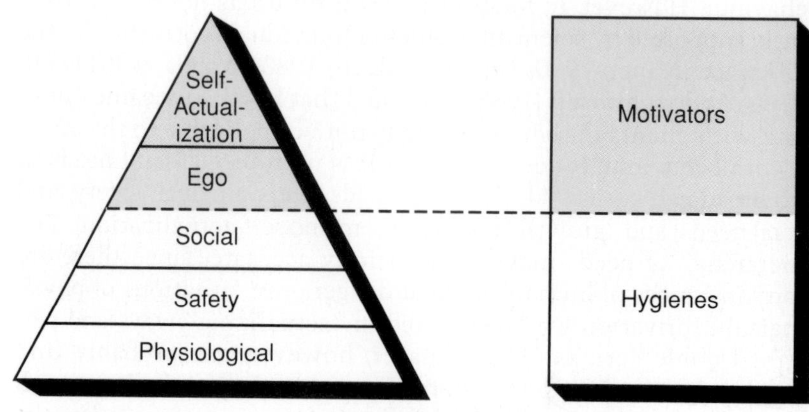

SOURCE: Reprinted with permission from Gray and Starke (1988).

there is evidence (House & Wigdor, 1967) that there is considerable individual variation in these factors. For example, factory workers may consider specific pay increases to be motivators while professionals might not. There is also evidence for general sex differences, in which female employees are more likely to consider interpersonal relations to be motivators, while male employees would be more likely to consider them hygienes. That is, they are not terribly relevant unless they go wrong.

Theory X and Theory Y

Within management circles, the best known theory of motivation is probably Douglas McGregor's *Theory X and Theory Y.* McGregor (1960) drew heavily from the humanistic theories of personality and from Maslow's work. He argued that traditional managers operate on a false set of assumptions about human nature.

Theory X is the usual view that humans are basically lazy and will get away with as much as they can unless they are forced to work. In general, people prefer to be controlled and directed, rather than to take personal responsibility. They are not motivated to achieve organizational goals and are basically driven only by physiological and safety needs. This seems a harsh representation of managers' views, but there are many examples of organizations and managers whose behaviour seems to be based on these assumptions. Such managers would argue that any other approach would be naive.

McGregor presented a different set of assumptions as **Theory Y** and said that these principles could guide the effective manager. (1) Employees find work natural and attractive if they are in an appropriate organizational setting characterized by trust and human values. People seem to be adverse to work because of oppressive organizational structures and past experience with adversarial work

According to McGregor, employees find work natural and attractive if they are in an appropriate organizational setting characterized by trust and human values.
SOURCE: Courtesy of IBM Corporation.

arrangements. In other words, there is a vicious circle in which workers resist authoritarian control and managers see this resistance in the light of Theory X. (2) Employees can be motivated by responsibility, independence, self-actualization, and other higher motives. (3) Employees are inherently motivated to seek responsibility, since it allows them to satisfy their own higher needs.

McGregor's theory does not lend itself well to empirical testing, since it is a generalized set of value statements and a generalized theory of human behaviour. There is an interesting parallel between Theory X and psychodynamic theory and Theory Y and humanistic theory, as discussed in Chapter 10. In their broadest forms, Theory X and psychodynamic theory say that human nature is fundamentally irrational and must be brought under control, while Theory Y and humanistic theory say that human nature is fundamentally positive and needs to be "released" to develop to its fullest potential.

Our own view is that each of these positions is an extreme and there are other alternatives that combine some qualities of each. Again, this is probably reflected best in the manager described as "tough and fair." The important lesson to be learned from Maslow, Herzberg, and Theory Y is that motivating humans is much more than a simple matter of providing basic rewards such as money. Realizing one's potential, doing meaningful work, having a sense of control over one's life, and relationships are also powerful motivators. This insight forms the historical foundation of modern management methods both in North America (Baxter & Bowers, 1985; Florida, 1985) and in Japan (Takanaka, 1985).

Organizational behaviour modification

At present, the most widely applied approach to motivation in the workplace is the specific use of behavioural principles to influence workers' behaviour. In a sense, this theory says that humans are neither good nor bad. How they behave depends on their learning histories. In its applications, this theory has elements both of control (using reinforcement to "shape behaviour") and more positive approaches (emphasizing the use of positive reinforcement over punitive approaches). We won't review all the principles of learning from Chapter 5 here, but a few illustrations and important principles are worth mentioning.

The power of reinforcement

The behaviour modifier would emphasize the *power of positive reinforcement*. To influence behaviour in the long run, we need to pay special attention to what is positively reinforcing in the worker's environment. The manager wants the worker to *want* to be productive and that will happen only with some system of reinforcement. The most effective way to influence behaviour in the long term is through much positive reinforcement combined with mild punishment of undesired behaviour.

Intrinsic and extrinsic reinforcement

It is most effective if this reinforcement can somehow be made *intrinsic* to the work to be done rather than extrinsic. This is not always possible of course, but it is probably more possible than most people realize. For example, we might try to reinforce a worker with extra time off for increased productivity or we could find some way to make the work more meaningful and important. The second approach would likely have the greatest long-term effects.

Partial reinforcement

The organizational psychologist needs to be aware of the *schedules of reinforcement* discussed in Chapter 5. Paying a worker once each week is reinforcement on a fixed-internal schedule, while piecework payments are an example of a fixed-ratio schedule. Each has different consequences for worker behaviour. *Partial reinforcement* schedules have been used in one factory to reduce absenteeism, especially on Mondays and Fridays (Gray & Starke, 1988). A weekly lottery was established so that all employees who had been at work all five days were entered in a draw for a portable TV. The draw was held on Friday afternoons. There was also a two-week lottery for those with perfect attendance, a seven-week lottery, etc., all with increasingly valuable prizes, up to the annual lottery for an all-expense trip to Hawaii. This scheme combined shaping small steps in behaviour with the unpredictable or partial reinforcement of lotteries. Absenteeism dropped from about 20% to less than 5%. The system was so effective that the company had to institute new rules to prevent people from coming to work when they were really sick. The company determined that the cost of the lotteries was about one-third of what they had been losing on absenteeism.

Using punishment

Finally, the issue of the use of punishment is critical in the organizational setting. **Punishment** is the delivery of discomfort for the purpose of weakening a particular behaviour. Much of traditional management style is based on punitive methods. Certainly the manager who holds to Theory X thinks that punitive methods are essential. Learning theory argues that there is a valid place for punishment, but that it is probably much overused. To repeat, the most effective way to influence behaviour in the long term is *to combine much positive reinforcement with mild punishment of the undesired behaviours*. A primarily punitive approach usually leads to quick compliance but long-term negative consequences such as resistance, sabotage, high turnover, and in some cases lower productivity (Likert, 1961).

Behavioural principles can be applied in many different ways. The principles are fairly simple, but their applications require creative thinking and can be extremely diverse. The examples we have used in this section are fairly direct applications of learning principles. Later, we will be talking about complex management styles that require good interpersonal skills and assertiveness. Even these more complex approaches still use the basic learning principle that long-term behaviour is best influenced by positive methods.

THE NATURE OF ORGANIZATIONS

It is not enough to understand the psychology of individual behaviour to be an effective manager. We must also understand the nature of organizations and the effect of different organizational structures on behaviour.

Organizational structure and behaviour

There are many different ways to structure an organization, and the chosen structure has an important impact on the behaviour of people in the organization.

Functional versus divisional structures

The most general way to look at organizations is to decide whether they are structured around different *functions* or different *divisions*.

The functional structure is illustrated by the organizational chart of Company A in Figure 20-3. This is the most commonly used structure in businesses. **Functional structure** is an organizational form in which a company is divided according to specific jobs to be done. Each division does only one job and does it for the whole organization. One subunit would take care of marketing, another subunit would take care of advertising, and another of finance. The advantages of a functional organization are (1) there is specialization of labour, so that the workers in one division do the same sort of work and become efficient at it; (2) workers tend to understand the whole structure better and see how their work relates to the work of others in the organization; and (3) there is little duplication of effort. However, the functional organization sometimes has trouble with workers not seeing the company in an overall perspective. They often become specialized to the point of feeling that they are not part of

FIGURE 20-3 Functional versus divisional organizational structures
The functional structure divides work according to different jobs to be done. The divisional structure divides work according to geography or product line so each division is more like an independent organization that has all important functions within it.

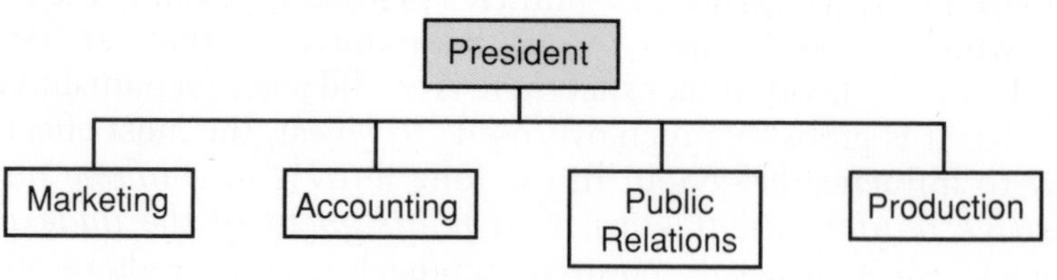

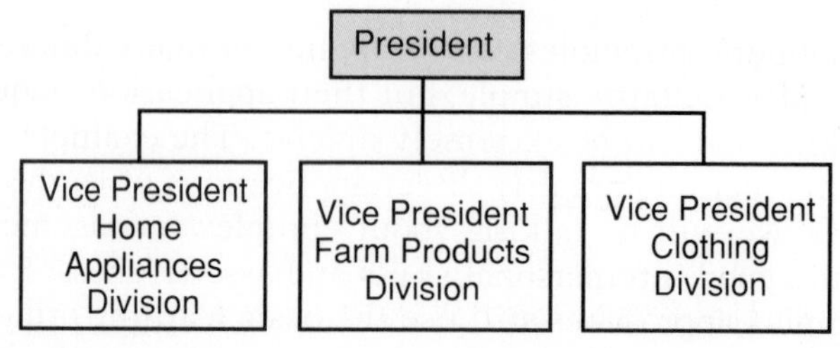

the whole system. It is also difficult to assign responsibility for productivity, since each unit does only part of the overall task, and working in one subunit in a functional organization does not groom potential management people well, since each worker has such a limited range of experience.

The divisional structure is illustrated by Company B. **Divisional structure** is an organizational form in which a company is divided into subunits at each geographical location, so that work is less specialized. Here all functions are carried out within each division. For example, in Company B, there is a Southern Division and an Eastern Division, and each is responsible for marketing, advertising, inventory, etc., within its division. Many of the disadvantages of the functional organization are overcome, since accountability is clear and potential managerial staff gain broader experience. However, in contrast to the functional system, there is often inefficient duplication of effort. An additional problem is that such companies often grow without clear planning, since it is possible simply to add divisions without integrating them into the overall structure.

Flat versus tall structures

Another way to view differences in organizational structure is to describe organizations by their "height." In the **flat structure**, there are few levels of hierarchy and many workers report to one supervisor. In the **tall structure**, there are more levels of reporting and supervision. See Figure 20-4. The rationale for a tall structure is that each boss has fewer subordinates and is therefore more able to give individualized attention. However, the evidence generally suggests that

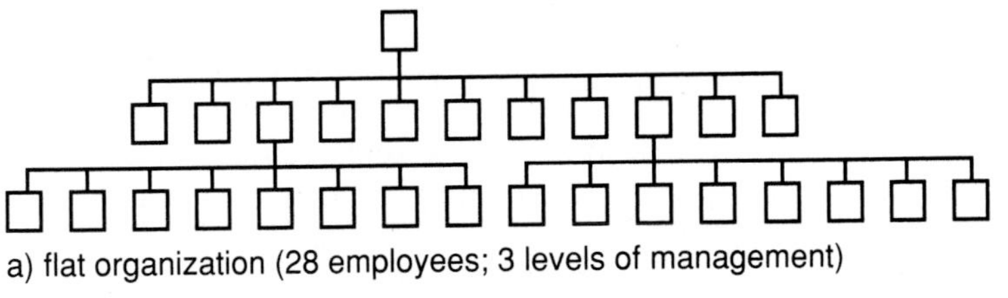

a) flat organization (28 employees; 3 levels of management)

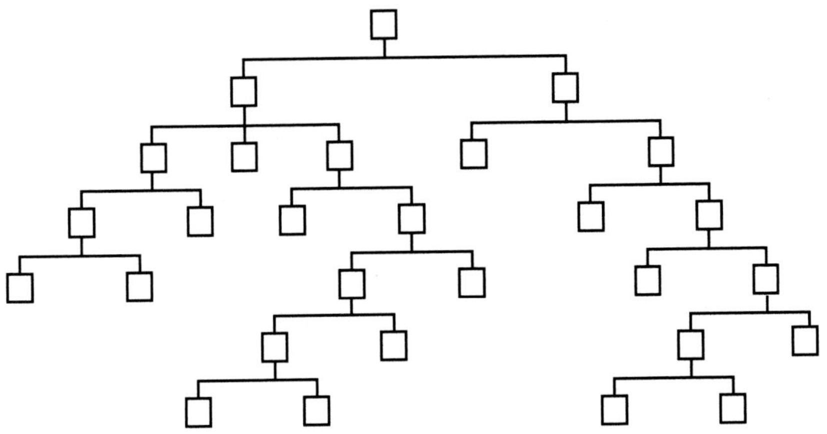

b) a tall organization (28 employees; 7 levels of management)

FIGURE 20-4 Flat versus tall organizational structures
In a flat organization, each supervisor will have many subordinates because there are few levels of hierarchy. This leads to more independence for each subordinate. The tall structure has more levels of authority, and each supervisor tends to have fewer subordinates.

workers prefer flat structures because they provide more autonomy for each worker. Worker satisfaction is greater in flat structures, and up to a point, productivity seems to increase along with this greater satisfaction. The "up to a point" qualification seems to result because a "too flat" structure will have so many workers reporting to one supervisor that there is insufficient supervision (Carpenter, 1971; Ivancevich & Donnelly, 1975).

Effects of bureaucracy

The term "bureaucracy" is often used in an insulting way to imply inefficiency and red tape. It is usually meant as an insult when a person says, "You're a real bureaucrat." However, there are both advantages and problems with bureaucratic structures in organizations. A **bureaucracy** is a highly structured organizational structure in which procedures are explicitly stated. Bureaucracies were first proposed as an ideal organizational structure to overcome a number of very difficult problems that existed with organizations in the early 1900s (Weber, 1947). Max Weber, a German sociologist and political scientist, saw many organizations, both private and public, operating in arbitrary and unfair ways that were determined more by power and influence than by principle. He wanted a system that would (1) provide equal and fair treatment for clientele, (2) be efficient in operation, and (3) provide rational decision making.

Weber argued that organizations should be highly specialized in job descriptions and that procedures and responsibilities should be highly structured and specifically described. Promotions were to be based on merit and technical qualifications. Authority was to be centralized, and complete written records were to be kept. In other words, the system was to be "rule bound" and personal factors were to be minimized. It is easy to see why such an organization can become awkward, frustrating to deal with, and impersonal, and we will discuss these disadvantages below. However, it is important not to lose sight of the fairness that such a system provides. In modern times, we sometimes take these advantages for granted and then complain about the rigidity of our bureaucracies.

It is also important to specify the disadvantages of bureaucratic structures. They have many implications for workers' behaviour. One of the most striking results of bureaucracy is the *rigidity of worker behaviour*. Every M*A*S*H fan is familiar with requisition form A765F/H, without which the desperately needed equipment cannot be unloaded from a truck. You may have your own favourite memory of a frustrating unwillingness to "bend the rules a little." The work norms of bureaucracies often do lead to excessively rule-governed behaviour. A *resistance to change* often develops, as well as *avoidance of responsibility*. Where there are no real decisions required, or even permitted, the individual can come to feel little involvement or caring for the consequences. Other problems can include a kind of *working to rule* in which workers simply perform the minimally required behaviour, and an *over-identification with subgoals*, in which the worker loses sight of the purpose of the organization in pursuing his or her own rule-bound goals. Baron & Bielby (1986) presented evidence that one sign of inefficiency is that large numbers of detailed job titles develop in bureaucracies, as compared with more flexible organizations. This proliferation of job titles leads to fragmentation, more status gradations, and gender distinctions.

It is commonly thought that public organizations are the most bureaucratic, but one study of 344 employees in six different organizations found more bureaucratic organization in industrial organizations (Allison, 1986). Some bureaucratic organization was seen as necessary, but it could easily become a threat to a company's survival.

The informal organization

So far we have discussed formal aspects of organizational structure, the kind of hierarchy that can be graphed in an organizational chart. These charts, however, almost never reflect what really happens in an organization. In many organizations, the boss's secretary is often introduced as "the person who really runs things around here." This is sometimes a condescending "pat on the head," but sometimes it is the truth. The formal organization can only specify some of the behaviours to be expected of workers. All the other events that occur are largely the result of the informal organization. The **informal organization** is the unofficial structure which is nearly inevitable in an organization. Patterns of influence and power develop within this social structure.

Ignore at your peril

The most important lesson to learn in this section is that there almost always is an informal organization that develops within the formal one, and this informal structure has very significant power. The danger of being a "book educated" manager instead of an "experience educated" one is that fancy rules, principles, and theories come to seem to be the truth. But unless we understand the power of the informal organization, we are going to make fools of ourselves. Real power often lies in the hands of a worker who is the informal leader and sets work norms. See Figure 20-5 for a somewhat humorous comparison between formal and informal structures. Sometimes the grapevine will undermine all of the organization's efforts to put out information. A manager running a problem-solving meeting might be totally confused by a resistance even to brainstorm suggestions because he or she is not aware that several workers made a decision over coffee the previous night. The manager must understand and work within the informal organization, rather than try to suppress it.

FIGURE 20-5 Formal versus informal organization of a company— a tongue-in-cheek perspective

FORMAL

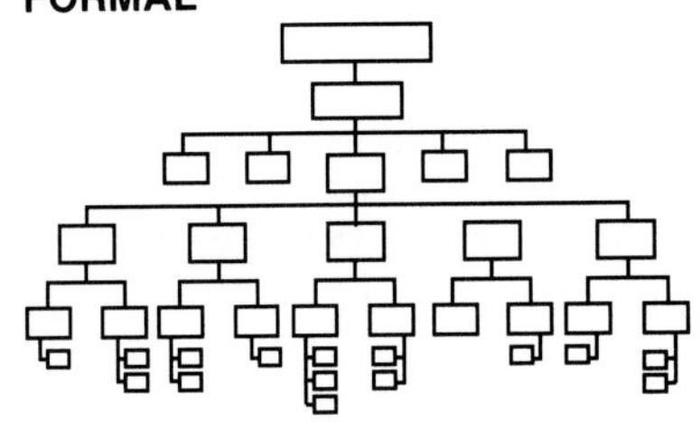

INFORMAL

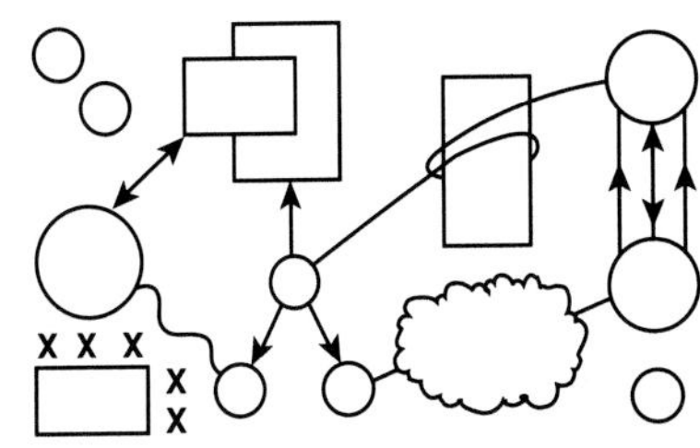

Functions of the informal organization

One purpose of the informal organization is *to satisfy worker needs* (and sometimes organizational needs) that are not met by the formal structure. In general, the organization only provides for the workers to the extent that organizational needs must be met. Employees subtly develop a system for getting their own needs met more thoroughly. A second purpose is to provide *stability and predictability in interpersonal relations*. Workers often gain *security* and a *sense of belonging* from forming subgroups that have no direct bearing on organizational goals. Finally, the informal organization *makes up for many deficiencies* in the formal structure. This becomes obvious when workers "work to rule" and activity slows down markedly. Even though they are doing everything formally demanded by the system's structure, the organization will nearly come to a halt. Much of what makes the organization work is the result of the informal procedures that develop within that organization.

Informal leaders

There is a great difference between power and authority. **Authority** is the formally stated right to influence others. **Power** is the ability to actually influence the behaviour of others. Many leaders have formal authority but little real influence over others. Most organizations develop informal leaders who have considerable real power to influence the behaviour of others. We can describe five sources of power, and it will be clear that only the first one is a function of the formal structure of the organization. (1) **Legitimate power** is roughly synonymous with formal authority. The subordinate accepts the norm that a person in a higher position has a "right" to have influence. (2) **Reward power** is much more complex. It is power that derives from a person's control of reinforcers, whether they be formal rewards such as money or informal rewards such as social acceptance. Commonly, formal leaders such as a manager have only very general control over specific rewards available to a worker. For example, salaries change infrequently and are usually only partially under the manager's control. However, other powerful rewards, such as social acceptance within the group, can be influenced by persons who may have no formal authority. (3) **Punishment power** is power that derives from a person's ability to deliver punishing consequences. These may include punishments such as social ostracism and subtle harassment. (4) **Referent power** is power that derives from others' identifying with a person and wanting to be like him or her.

We grant expert power to those who have superior knowledge in some particular area that has importance for us.
SOURCE: Courtesy Ontario Hydro.

A person who is admired and whom people would like to imitate has enormous influence over those people, whether or not he or she has formal authority. (5) **Expert power** is granted to the person who is seen as especially knowledgeable or skillful, again even if that person has no formal power.

The important lesson for the manager is to recognize the importance of informal power. The wise manager identifies those with power and influence and includes their influence in his or her management style.

LEADERSHIP STYLES

A great deal has been written about **leadership**. Anyone who aspires to advancement in the world of work has an investment in knowing what effective leadership is and how to achieve it. Jago (1982) has defined leadership as "the *process* of . . . noncoercive influence" and the *property* of "qualities or characteristics attributed to those who are perceived to successfully employ such influence" (Jago, 1982, p. 315). In other words, the successful leader both has a role (certain properties) and is effective at the process of influencing people. It is useful to think of three styles of leadership as an introduction to our discussion of how a manager can handle conflict.

The autocratic style

The autocratic leader believes that decision-making power must rest with the leader. The subordinate is expected to comply. The **autocratic style of leadership** is leadership based on the use of coercive power. This style may arise from the leader's belief in Theory X—that people are lazy or incompetent—or from a sincere belief that this is the most efficient way to operate. In fact, if the leader is competent, there can be savings in time and other efficiencies. Until recent years, this has probably been the most popular style of leadership. There are circumstances where it does seem to be the most effective style in terms of maximizing productivity. These circumstances require that the leader possess considerable coercive power, that workers be relatively unskilled and uninvested in their work, and that the work not involve the need for commitment over time. These circumstances do arise, but they are not what most managers will have to deal with (Hersey & Blanchard, 1982). Hamlin (1986) has also argued that effective supervisors sometimes need to use a directive style and sometimes a "participatory" style (which we will discuss extensively). He says that directive leadership is effective in situations such as emergencies and short-term production schedules.

There are also a number of disadvantages to the autocratic style. (1) Workers bear no responsibility for outcomes and often slavishly follow instructions, even when they know them to be wrong. (2) Workers know what to do but not why, leading to rigidity of behaviour and low morale. (3) Autocratic leaders tend to have high turnover among staff. (4) The work relationship usually becomes an adversarial one in which the worker may comply with orders in the short term but may resist and even sabotage the leader in the long term. There are hundreds of guerilla warfare methods to sabotage a boss, including answering the phone abruptly, phoning friends from work, and blowing your nose a lot while he or she is speaking to you.

The permissive style

It has been our experience that many people think there are only two ways to deal with others. If one is not autocratic, one must be permissive. We will argue that there is a powerful third alternative and that permissive leadership is destructive, ineffective, and terribly frustrating for the leader. This too is a power-oriented solution to problems. The **permissive style of leadership** is one in which the leader gives power to the subordinates by being unable to be assertive, set limits, and insist that his or her needs must be met. Almost everyone agrees that being permissive is not effective, so it is surprising how many managers are permissive. They ask people to do tasks and then quietly take no action when the worker fails to perform. Incompetent employees are permitted to continue with no consequences. Control and decision making are given over to subordinates, even when the decisions are bad for the organization and the leader.

There is one, fairly unusual, leadership situation that seems to call for permissive management. If one is the leader of a group of highly trained and very motivated professionals working on independent tasks for which they need very specialized skills, little intervention is called for. But in most other cases, permissive leadership is self-destructive.

This self-destructive leadership can have many sources. Some leaders are desperate to be liked by everyone and don't want to offend people. Some have been promoted from lower ranks and now must manage people who used to be their peers. Some are quite fearful of confrontation and conflict and may even be terrified by open expressions of anger. Finally, many leaders simply have never been taught effective ways to confront others and resolve conflicts. For this last category of leader, there is much useful information that psychology has to offer.

The participatory/democratic style

It is difficult to describe the "third alternative" that seems to mark the effective leader. Many people interpret a phrase such as "participatory/democratic" as implying permissiveness, but that is incorrect. The leader who uses the **participatory/democratic style of leadership** is the "tough and fair" person we have referred to often. He or she is concerned with both productivity and human needs, with both confrontation and helpfulness.

Although there still is controversy on the topic, the trend in both public and business organizations is toward more participatory leadership. The Canadian Manufacturing Association (1987) reports that, "Canadian companies are increasingly experimenting with innovative management styles, including: participatory management, management teams, quality circles and management by objectives" (Canadian Manufacturing Association, 1987, p. 18). We will be discussing these methods later in this chapter. Sashkin (1984) reviewed extensive research showing that "participative management is, when properly applied, effective in improving performance, productivity and job satisfaction" (Sashkin, 1984, p. 5). Figure 20-6 is taken from Sashkin (1984) and outlines the ways that participative management leads to increased job satisfaction, productivity, and performance. (See also Carson, 1985; and Van Katwyk, Cronshaw, & Williams, 1989). Others have argued that the evidence is not yet conclusive and factors in addition to participation are important motivators for workers (Locke, Schweiger, & Latham, 1986). This position seems reasonable but doesn't negate the powerful trend toward participatory management (Carson, 1987). Kolchin (1987) says that Japanese managers readily accept this approach but that there is resistance among North American managers, in spite of the evidence available. This resistance will return to complicate our understanding later in the chapter. Note the phrase in the quote from

FIGURE 20-6 A model of how participative management works
Sashkin (1984) argues that when workers participate in decision making, they experience greater autonomy and meaning in their work. This leads to increased challenge and satisfaction, as well as greater security and commitment to their work. Security and challenge lead to greater innovation. The final outcome is increased performance and productivity.

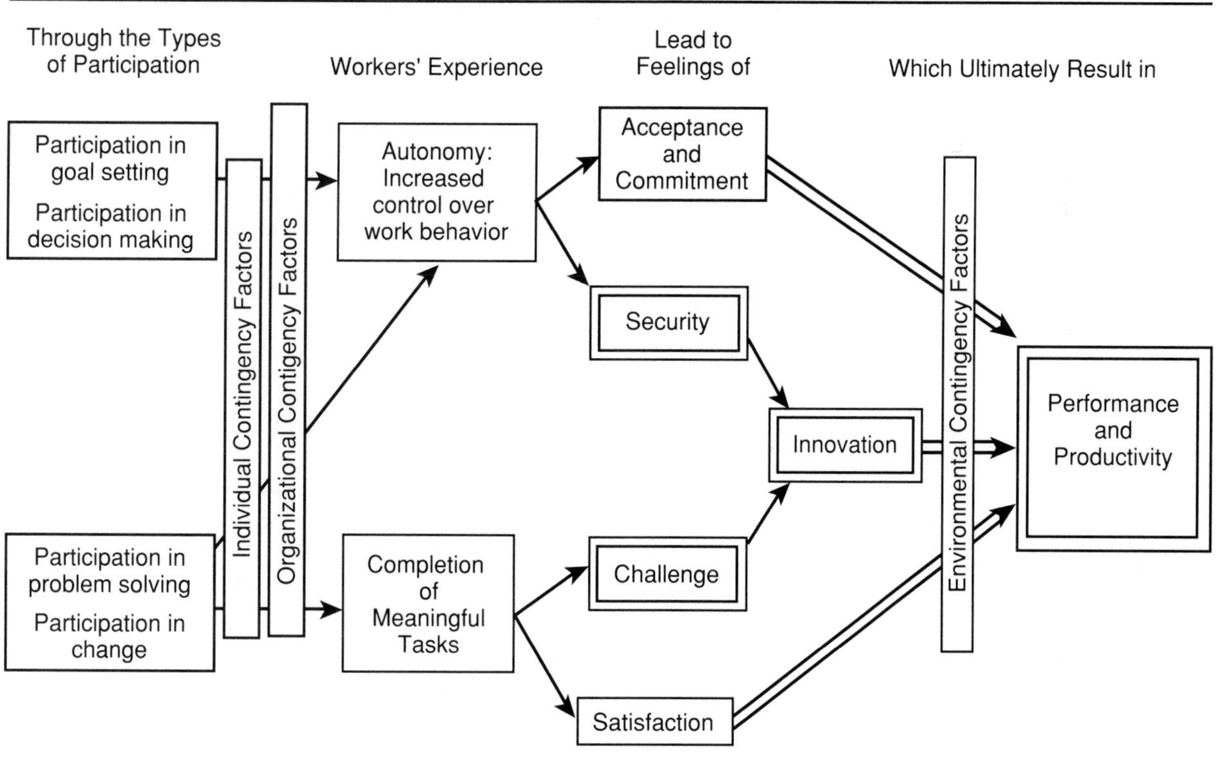

SOURCE: Reprinted with permission from Sashkin (1984) p. 12.

Sashkin earlier in this paragraph. Participatory methods work well "when properly applied," a critical distinction.

Before we can elaborate on the nature of the participatory/democratic style, however, we need to lay some background about the nature of conflict.

Conflict and Competition

Conflict arises when one person or group has reason to block the goals of another person or group. **Conflict** is the pursuit of incompatible goals in which the parties interfere with each other. The key here is that there are incompatible goals and there is active interference with another's behaviour. On the other hand, **competition** is the pursuit of incompatible goals (only one person can win a race) in which the parties do not actively interfere with each other. Competition is interesting and has many constructive and destructive effects, but our interest here is in how a good manager can deal with conflict — conflict between other workers as well as between the manager and others.

A new view of conflict

The traditional view of conflict in organizations was that it was destructive and to be avoided whenever possible. Historically, this view probably arose from the destructiveness on both sides in the formation of the labour movement and from some studies that focused on the destructive consequences of conflict. The usual response was to suppress conflict through direct orders and through isolating and specializing workers to prevent contacts that might lead to conflict. However, there were many costs to these measures, and a different view of conflict has arisen in recent years.

Conflict is inevitable

First, there has been the recognition that in any work setting (in any relationship actually) conflict is inevitable because resources are always limited. One person or group's best interest is at times going to diminish another's best interest. Management cannot successfully suppress conflict for very long. The informal organization will develop ways to deal with it if management does not. The issue then becomes not whether there will be conflict but rather the best way to deal with it. There are potentially constructive consequences of conflict that is handled well, and the effective manager needs conflict resolution skills.

Part of the new view of conflict is that there is an optimum level of conflict within an organization. Conflict can stimulate people to find new solutions to old problems. Too little conflict usually results in stagnation and loss of creative growth. Too much conflict leads to animosity and diversion of resources away from productivity and into fighting.

While conflict is inevitable, it can be resolved if all parties can take the time to sensitively listen to each other's grievances.
SOURCE: Metropolitan Toronto Convention & Visitors Association.

Managing conflict

Conflict is inevitable, and probably no other facet of the workplace holds as much potential for good or for harm. The effective manager needs to be skillful at managing conflict without being permissive or autocratic. Before we outline a method of constructive conflict resolution, we need to review some basic skills presented earlier in this book.

Review of basic communication skills

In Chapter 17, we discussed basic skills needed in an intimate relationship. Many writers (Gordon, 1977; Argyris, 1976; Halpin & Winer, 1957; Kahn & Katz, 1960; and Blake & Mouton, 1964) have argued that it is exactly these same skills that underlie effective management. We must be able to be sensitive and empathic and at the same time be able to confront others without doing damage. The effective manager is both "tough and fair" or "instrumental and considerate." There are two other sections of this book that have laid groundwork for this section: the Special Topic on active listening in Chapter 17 and the introductory part on the interpersonal behaviour circle in Chapter 18. For the sake of convenience, we will briefly review that material and add some new principles.

The evidence suggests that the most effective persons, in many different situations, are those that can combine the personal qualities of strength and activity along with sensitivity to the needs of others. Our training, especially our sex-role training, often teaches us that these qualities are incompatible with each other, that we must give up one to have the other. We often feel, for example, that to become more "feminine" means becoming less "masculine," and vice versa. But evidence (Bierman, 1969) suggests that these qualities are *independent* of each other, so it is possible to be high on both.

It has been argued (Larson, Hunt, & Osborn, 1976; Nystrom, 1978) that in the managerial setting the notion of a "high-high leader" (one who is high on both interpersonal skills and on production skills) is a "myth." This stems partly from the fact that very few managers *are* high on both. It is a difficult combination of qualities to have.

The interpersonal skill that is most related to being helpful and sensitive to the needs of others is active listening. **Active listening** is a communication skill in which the listener communicates an understanding of the speaker's intended message. In Chapter 17 we said that active listening sounds easy, is very difficult to do consistently, and has a remarkably powerful impact in relationships. At least four outcomes will result from good active listening. (1) People will want to talk and will be able to say things that would otherwise be difficult to say. (2) People will solve many of their own problems. (3) Feelings will change through the talking/listening process. (4) Communication will be more accurate because of getting and giving continuous feedback. Active listening is most effective in helping the speaker deal with a problem he or she "owns." It is an effective way to help others get their needs met.

But active listening is not enough. We must also get our own needs met. Conflict is inevitable, and we need to be able to confront the other person. Most confrontation seems to be **destructive confrontation** because it is based on attacks on the other person's character, rather than the *behaviour* the confronter finds unacceptable. A **non-destructive confrontation** consists of (1) naming the unacceptable behaviour, (2) naming your reaction to that behaviour, and (3) naming the tangible connection between the behaviour and your reaction.

Win-lose and win-win attitudes

All our lives we are trained in the **win-lose attitude**—at least we are so trained in our culture. We assume that for one person to win, someone else must lose. One of the most important trends in the psychology of organizations is the realization that in most settings this is a destructive attitude. Win-win methods are available. The traditional autocratic leader considers this naive, but there is evidence that it is possible to develop solutions to conflicts in which both parties end up with a solution they can live with. Acceptance of this possibility comes hard to many people. After a lifetime of playing Monopoly (or virtually any other game) it seems clear that only one person wins and the other must lose.

There is an interesting game in which four participants sit at the corners of a square with a spot in each corner. Each participant holds a string and all four strings are connected to an object in the middle of the square, as shown in Figure 20-7. Each time this object crosses the little circle in front of a player, that player earns a reward such as a point or some money. The most sensible strategy for this game is to cooperate and have the central object pass through each person's little circle in turn. Then everybody wins points quickly. Children playing this game, however, often act competitively and try to pull the central object to their own corners, tugging against the pull of their "competitors" whom they must "beat," even though

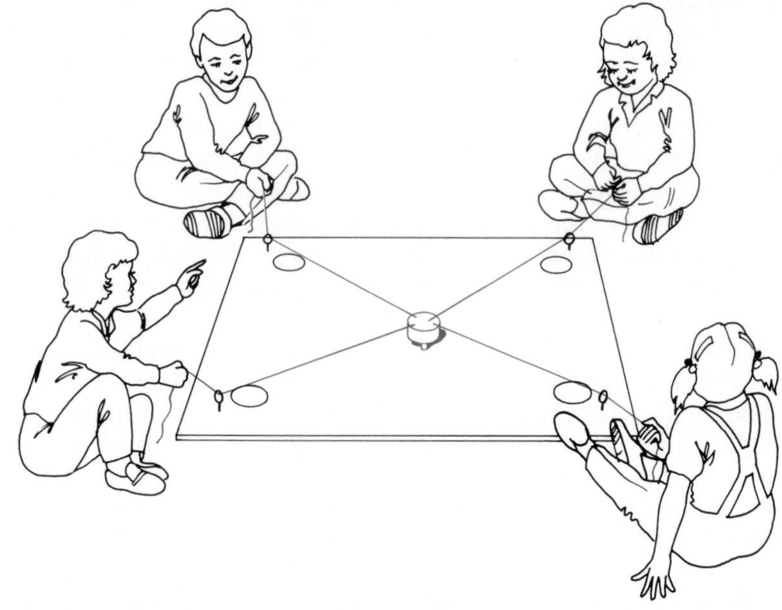

FIGURE 20-7 A game used to study competitiveness in children

Each child scores a point when the moving pointer passes through the circle in front of the child. The most efficient way to play is to cooperate by taking turns passing the pointer around. Highly competitive children struggle to monopolize the pointer and thus do poorly.

most of the effort expended is wasted in trying. It is revealing that North American children use this win-lose strategy more than Mexican children, and within North America, children from cities are more likely to adopt the competitive strategy than are rural children (Nelson & Kagan, 1972).

We once gave a workshop on communication skills to the faculty of a community college. We demonstrated the basic skills and then role played some win-win methods of conflict resolution (see the Special Topic in this chapter for the details of this approach). One role-played situation was a teacher with a student who was being disruptive in class, and we used the steps outlined in the Special Topic section. At the end of the role play, several teachers made comments such as, "That looks like it would work . . . Both people are satisfied with the solution." But one teacher was clearly angry. His face turned red and he said, "But that student thinks he won!" Several other faculty said, "But the teacher got what he wanted." The only response the angry teacher could think of was to repeat—several times—"But that student thinks he won!" In his mind, for the student to have won, the teacher had to have lost. Or at least it infuriated him that the student might think that. Win-lose was a part of that man.

We have tried to play some "non-competitive" board games and find most of them boring. What's the point if you're not trying to destroy somebody? We tell you this only to underscore the power of the cultural training we all have had in win-lose approaches.

We have repeatedly mentioned the "tough and fair" combination of qualities as effective in human relations of many kinds. Another pair of words with the same meaning is "assertive and helpful." The **win-win method of conflict resolution** is a problem-solving method in which both parties get their needs met. The method consists of (1) making an approach, (2) defining the problem, (3) generating and evaluating possible solutions, (4) choosing a solution, (5) implementing the solution, and (6) following up. The basic philosophy of win-win is neither permissive nor autocratic. It says (assertively), "I must get my needs met," *and* (helpfully), "I also recognize that you must get your needs met, and I will do what I can to see that that happens. Let's work on this together and find something we both can live with." This combination of characteristics is needed by the effective manager. It depends on the two basic skills of active listening and non-destructive confrontation. The Special Topic box for this chapter describes a process within which those two skills can help resolve conflicts in a way that can enable both parties to feel that they have won.

ORGANIZATIONAL DEVELOPMENT

The field of organizational development (usually referred to as OD) is large enough and important enough that some consultants and consulting companies do nothing but work with companies that want to improve and develop. **Organizational development (OD)** is the process of improving a company or other organization by making changes at the level of individual workers (micro) or in the structure of the organization (macro). Implementing OD implies that an organization is ready to make a long-range commitment to improve problem-solving and production methods and processes of renewal within the organization. It usually necessitates hiring outside help, although many of the approaches of OD could be implemented by an individual manager. The methods of OD can be roughly divided into **micro approaches**, which focus on changes at the level of the individual worker (through job enrichment, job changing, participatory goal setting, and individual counselling) and **macro approaches**, which concentrate on changes in the overall organization (through process consultation, often with an outside expert).

Micro approaches

Micro approaches are attempts to help the individual worker improve both task-oriented skills and interpersonal skills that will presumably lead to increased job satisfaction and greater productivity.

Participatory goal setting

We have used the word "participatory" often. It is one of the most important concepts in OD. Traditional approaches to goal setting and performance appraisal have meant that the boss sits down once a year with the employee, fills out an appraisal form that may contain a number of rating scales of the worker's performance, and reviews the worker's job description as determined by the boss or the organization.

One of the most significant influences in this area, however, was Peter Drucker's proposal of **management by objectives**, which is widely and frequently referred to as **MBO** (Drucker, 1954). This is a participatory method of goal setting and performance appraisal in which the manager and worker both contribute to the process. There have been over 4000 books, articles, films, and seminars on MBO (Kondrasuk et al., 1984). Drucker pointed out that employees usually felt little identification with the goals of large organizations, often because they had no involvement with establishing either the major

Participation in periodic planning conferences allows workers to share in the setting of goals. SOURCE: Metropolitan Toronto Convention & Visitors Association.

goals or individual goals that affected them. With MBO, there is a consultative process that differs from the traditional performance appraisal. The employee's input is a significant part of the procedure. Organizational goals are presented and held important, of course, but the employee participates in establishing the way she or he will contribute to those goals. This gives the employee a way to meet his or her own goals to a greater extent within the work context. In most work settings, MBO also includes subsequent feedback on how well proposed goals have been met.

MBO makes two major assumptions about why this process will contribute to both worker satisfaction and organizational goals. First, because the worker has participated in setting goals, motivation is increased by the much greater ego involvement. Second, participatory goal setting makes it more likely that workers will develop internal control over their work behaviour, making external control less necessary.

Thomas Gordon (1977) has proposed a similar process which he calls the *periodic planning conference*. Both Drucker and Gordon argue that any efforts put into such participatory goal setting will be more than rewarded by increased commitment and productivity. In actual practice, MBO has often been used successfully, but its purposes have also often been undermined by traditional managers. Some have used the *form* of MBO but subtly converted it into just another method to exert "control from the top." This is inevitably perceived as such by workers and can be resisted as just one more trick to get more work out of them. In fact, Leonard (1986) reported that in a study of Fortune 500 companies, MBO was found to be successful in only 25 to 30% of the cases. A study of unsuccessful cases showed that poor communication was the most common cause of failure. MBO will not work without good communication, explicit measuring of how results match with plans, and continuous feedback. Earlier in this chapter, we noted that Sashkin (1984) said that participatory methods work well "when properly applied." Any method is useless without commitment and effort. In fact, simply taking industries that claim to use MBO and comparing them to those that do not revealed no differences between the companies on corporate financial performance (Kondrasuk et al., 1984). This is not surprising, given the high percentage of unsuccessful implementations of MBO and the global measures used in this study.

Quality circles

Another popular method for implementing participatory management is to form **quality circles**, small groups of workers, usually with representatives of different levels in the organizational structure. They meet to express and discuss their ideas about their workplace. This approach has been used in Japan and led to the development of **Theory Z**, which is intended as an extension of the Theory Y we discussed earlier. Theory Z stresses worker participation in decision making, particularly in groups (Bachmann, 1984; Florida, 1985). Some see North American quality circles as evolving from participatory discussion groups into *Z teams*. These teams stress solidarity and loyalty within the corporation, rather than stressing competition, as is typical in North American organizations (Mroczkowski, 1984).

In showing how quality circles and Theory Z could be applied in a hospital setting, Rawson & Lasser (1983) stressed the principles of decision by consensus in small groups, the importance of organizational values, and the manager's ultimate responsibility for control. They showed how a hospital could effectively use Theory Z for goal-development, examination of patient care, and developing team skills, among other uses.

Job design and enrichment

Modern organizations are often criticized for being dehumanizing and forcing people into mind-numbing routines. In fact, many people see their work as unrewarding time to be put in so they can live the rest of their lives. One method of OD is to find ways to change individual jobs so that the worker finds more meaning in the work. The three general ways this is done are *job changing, job expansion,* and *job enrichment*. A worker can be rotated through a series of jobs, or new tasks can be added to a particular job. These two methods have both some utility and serious limitations. Being rotated through a series of boring jobs may be only slightly better than having one boring job. A job can be expanded just so much because of the limitations on how much one person can do.

Job enrichment, however, is significantly different because it is based on increasing the *level of responsibility* in a job. The worker is given more *decision-making discretion* in such factors as the pacing of work, the quality of work, and the methods to achieve particular goals. An important aspect of job enrichment is that workers must receive *feedback* on performance so that they know where their performance fits into organizational goals and performance. Finally, the real key to job enrichment seems to be that attention be paid to the *meaningfulness* of the job as perceived by the worker. This meaningfulness usually comes from whether the job is seen as having an impact on others and whether the worker is permitted to do the complete job. There is both accountability and satisfaction in saying, "I made that," rather than, "I fastened 4000 fenders on Volvos."

A macro approach

The other major approach to OD is to try to bring about changes in the organization at levels higher than individual workers.

Process consultation

Process consultation is the clearest example of how an outside consultant can be hired to diagnose situations and plan solutions to problems within the organization. In cartoons we often see the "efficiency expert" sneaking around the factory taking notes and then sitting down to tell the boss what changes to make. The process consultant works much differently than this. His or her effectiveness depends on joint consultation with management. Decisions and conclusions are left in the hands of the client organization, not the consultant. The consultant's major goal is to increase management's effectiveness at diagnosing and solving its own problems. The consultant brings a fresh perspective and an ability to see an organization in new ways and must be an expert at both *diagnosis* and *human relationships*.

Thus, the process consultant is a good illustration of what a person can do with a knowledge of organizational psychology.

SPECIAL TOPIC A Win-Win Method of Conflict Resolution

One practical application of basic communication skills is in resolving conflicts in a way in which both participants feel they have "won" a solution each can live with. It appears that participatory methods are especially effective where the leader has moderate levels of power and workers have moderate levels of sophistication and motivation. This describes most work settings.

The power of this method comes from the fact that it is *participatory*. People are far more committed to solutions which they have helped to formulate.

Making the approach. With relatively few words, it is possible to communicate all of the following: "I need for us to talk because there is a situation I cannot live with. I am insistent that there be a solution that is acceptable to me, but I am also committed to being as helpful as I can in finding one that is acceptable to you too. Let's engage in a mutual problem-solving process where neither of us starts out committed to a particular solution."

Of course one wouldn't use these exact words. It probably won't help to write them on your cuff. But all of these ideas can be expressed in just a few seconds with a comment such as, "John, do you have a few minutes? There's a problem that involves both of us that I really need to get some change on. I don't know what the best way is to handle it, but I'm sure we can find something we can both live with."

There probably is no completely non-threatening way to make this approach, but implying both an assertive stance and an openness to the other person's perspective is probably the least threatening and upsetting way to do it.

Defining the problem. Many people skip this step in the process, thinking that they already know what the problem is. Almost always there is some misunderstanding of what the main issues are. One or both of the people involved usually lack some information, especially from the other person's perspective. A process of trying to define the problem very often even reveals to the participants insights they didn't know about their own perceptions and feelings.

We start out by stating our position through non-destructive confrontation statements and using phrases such as "my perception is. . . . " Then we listen for the other person's perception and respond with active listening, followed by more of our perceptions and more active listening. Through this process a clearer picture emerges of what the problem is. We might tentatively conclude this step with a summary of our understanding of the main issues.

Generate and evaluate possible solutions. By "participatory brainstorming" we permit both ourself and the other person to "toss out" possible solutions without having to be committed to them. This gives us a chance to look at many possibilities and evaluate them.

Come to an agreement. As the brainstorming progresses, usually a consensus begins to emerge between us on what makes sense for both of us. In real life, there is no sharp line between one step of this process and another. We can merge into this next step by starting to summarize and articulate what seems to be the solution that is emerging. When both parties agree on one of these summaries, we can agree to try this particular solution.

Implement the solution. Now the discussion is over. It is up to each of the parties to dependably carry out the agreed upon solution.

Follow up. It is important to check up after some time has passed to see that both parties are satisfied that the solution they arrived at is workable and that both are living up to the agreement.

Questions about participatory methods

In workshops we have done with managers, several questions come up regularly and are worth commenting on here.

Does changing methods take a lot of time? One of the apparent attractions of authoritarian leadership methods is that they seem to work fast. We have argued that in most settings this apparent speed is an illusion because imposed solutions require tremendous amounts of time and energy for enforcement. They lead to subtle resistance and sabotage, and they are related to high turnover of staff. On the other hand, leaders and potential leaders often react to participatory methods with dismay at the time they look like they will take. Who has time to go through six steps of problem solving every time some conflict arises?

It probably is the case that participatory problem solving takes longer when it is first introduced into a system, especially if the system has been traditionally run in either an authoritarian or a permissive way. The permissive leader who starts using win-win problem solving is likely to meet resistance from workers who will perceive the shift from having their own way to a leader who is now being assertive. Permissive methods, however, certainly cannot be said to work quickly. They don't work at all. The leader rarely gets his or her needs met. The switch from authoritarian leadership to win-win methods is likely to be time-consuming at first because of problems with trust in the leader. The leader will need to be very explicit about the changes under way, making clear an intention to use more participatory methods and to be committed to them.

When a person first starts to use the steps of win-win conflict resolution, it is usually necessary to be quite conscious of going through the steps. When participatory methods are well established, however, conflict resolution tends to go very quickly and seldom takes the formal structure of "steps." The participants in the group implicitly know the process and have learned to trust the leader's commitment to it. They know the leader will be tough but will listen to reason and will try to accommodate the workers' needs. Once this is established it is usually only necessary to do a little problem definition, perhaps usually initiated by the leader, who might then say something like, "What's reasonable here?" This is the step of generating possible solutions. Everybody knows the rules. The worker knows this is not an adversarial battle and usually comes up with a solution both people can live with. The process is finished quickly and easily and is practically unnoticeable in the daily flow of interacting. Both leader and worker have a commitment to the solution. They both participated in finding it and agreeing to it, so compliance with the solution is vastly more likely than if the leader had unilaterally come up with exactly the same solution.

What if it doesn't work? One leadership workshop we conducted was attended by a man we think was a direct descendant of Atilla the Hun. After a role-playing demonstration of win-win problem solving, he said, "After about ten seconds of that, I would have fired both of you." He represented the traditional beliefs that participatory processes are naive and don't work. Only "Theory X" works, and people will respond only to power. We have presented evidence to the contrary, but many still hold this belief. But, of course, sometimes it doesn't work. Sometimes nothing will work. Some people are chronically hostile or have no intention of cooperating with anybody. Some even have emotional problems that make them unable to interact constructively with others. Win-win problem solving is not magic, but it *is* effective with the vast majority of people. It would be a mistake to focus on the exceptions and conclude that they represent what is typical. Leaders who consistently use win-win methods find that they are effective with nearly all workers. The sad fact seems to be that few leaders use these methods.

Think for a moment about the one specific person whom you would call the best boss or leader you have ever worked with. How typical is this person of leaders you have known? For most of you, this effective leader will stand out as one of very few effective leaders. Think of this person in terms of the combinations "tough but fair" and "assertive and helpful." In almost all cases, the description will fit. The conclusion to draw here is that the "tough but fair" leader is the most effective *and* that such leaders are rare.

Our point is that most leaders seldom use participatory methods or they try them half-heartedly and then conclude that they don't work. During a break at our workshop, Atilla the Hun was holding forth loudly to a group about how this approach just doesn't work. When he unexpectedly saw one of us standing at the edge of the group, he added, "Of course I've never tried it."

When the win-win conflict resolution process fails, you will know because of the follow-up step. If the solution has turned out to be the wrong one, then we return to step one and try again; that's fairly easy. A more difficult problem arises when the other person has not lived up to the agreed upon solution. Here again, the action to take is to return to step one, both to renegotiate the problem *and* to deal with the new factor of the violation of an agreement. The leader will directly confront the worker on this part of the issue. In our experience, it is sometimes necessary and useful to re-enter the conflict resolution process several times. In some cases, however, it has eventually been necessary to give up (two particular persons come to mind). "Give up" can have many different meanings, depending on the situation. It can mean ending the relationship, perhaps even through a firing. It can mean disciplinary action. It would be naive to think that such actions are never necessary, but it is important to keep in perspective that these are the extreme cases.

Will it be effective with my boss? Most people can see how to approach a subordinate or even a peer with this kind of confrontative and participatory process. However, many are concerned about using it with someone who has more power, especially if that person is authoritarian. Our usual first answer is that, yes, these same principles apply with someone above you in the system, but use them *very* nicely. The value of non-destructive confrontations is that they focus on specific behaviours and events. There is no blaming in them. Most bosses will respond well to such a specific discussion.

1. Organizational or industrial psychology is the subfield of psychology concerned with the world of work. The science of organizational behaviour had its beginnings in two major approaches: scientific management and human relations.
2. One of the earliest series of studies in scientific management was Taylorism, in which a logical and rational approach to work motivation assumed that behaviour is primarily motivated by economic rewards. Others, however, found that social relations, morale, and freedom to choose work goals — human relations variables—also affect productivity significantly.
3. One of the best-known theories of motivation is Maslow's hierarchy of needs. Inherent in this theory is the idea that only needs which have not been met are motivators. Maslow's hierarchy of needs, from lowest to highest, are physiological needs, safety needs, social needs, status needs, and self-actualizing needs.
4. Herzberg suggests that hygienes are factors whose absence produces dissatisfaction but which don't act as positive motivators. Factors that do increase productivity are called motivators.
5. McGregor's theories draw heavily on humanistic theories of behaviour and argue that many managers operate on a false set of assumptions about human nature. Theory X is the view that human beings are lazy and will get away with as much as they can if not forced to work. On the other hand, Theory Y suggests that human beings do not like working in oppressive situations. Rather, employees can be motivated by higher motives, and employees are inherently motivated to seek responsibility.
6. Currently, the most widely used set of principles used to motivate workers are behavioural principles. The manager reinforces

behaviours which promote productivity. Extrinsic reinforcement produces immediate but short-term effects. Intrinsic reinforcement has a longer-lasting effect. Partial reinforcement schedules are effective. Punishment usually leads to short-term compliance and long-term negative consequences.

7. The structure of the organization can also modify productivity. Functional structures divide work into subunits which perform all of a specific type of work for an entire company. This provides efficient division of labour, clear understanding of the job by each worker, and little duplication of effort. However, it can create over-specialization and isolation of workers, lack of commitment to the finished product, and lack of training workers for advancement. The divisional structure creates subunits for each geographic location of a company. This overcomes the disadvantages of the functional structure, but it results in duplication of effort and less efficient planning.
8. Another way to look at the organization of companies is to look at their "height." A flat structure has few levels of hierarchy and is preferred by workers because it allows greater autonomy. Tall structures are characterized by many levels of supervision, giving each boss fewer subordinates and more time for individual supervision. Up to a point, flat structures promote higher productivity.
9. Today the term "bureaucracy" has negative connotations. However, the bureaucratic structure was originally designed to provide equal and fair treatment for clientele, to be efficient, and to permit rational decisions. Bureaucratic structures tend to produce rigidity of worker behaviour and resistance to change, as well as avoidance of responsibility.
10. The informal structure of organizations is unofficial and not readily apparent. However, it still has significant influence on productivity. The real power of a group of workers often lies with an informal leader who sets group norms. An effective manager learns to work within the informal organization and not to try to suppress it.
11. The essence of leadership is to influence others' behaviour. There are several kinds of influence or power. The formally stated right to influence others is called authority, while the informal ability to influence others is called power.
12. There are several patterns of leadership style. The autocratic style uses coercive power to force compliance with the leader's decisions. This style works best when the leader possesses coercive power and workers are relatively unskilled and uninvested in their work. There are several disadvantages of this style in most organizational settings: workers bear little responsibility; there is high turnover and low morale; work becomes rigid; and resentment can lead to subtle sabotage. The permissive style is usually ineffective, in that the leader does not assert his or her needs or the needs of the organization. The permissive style is most effective with a group of highly trained and motivated

professionals working on independent tasks. Finally, the "tough and fair" leader uses the participatory/democratic style of leadership. Under most leadership circumstances, this style works best.

13. Competition occurs when two parties have incompatible goals but they do not interfere with each other. Conflict occurs when parties interfere with each other to accomplish incompatible goals. Historically, conflict was seen as something to be avoided.The modern view is that conflict is inevitable. It is believed that there is an optimal level of conflict in an organization. The issue is how to deal with conflict effectively. A good manager must combine active listening with an ability to confront others constructively to deal effectively with conflict. The manager must be both sensitive and assertive.

14. Organizational development of a company involves a long-term commitment to improve problem solving, production, and renewal methods. Changes which focus on individual workers are called micro approaches. Changes which focus on the overall organization are called macro approaches. Management by objectives (MBO) is one of the most significant approaches designed to influence individual workers. It uses participatory goal setting. Job changing and job enrichment are two micro approaches designed to help workers find more meaning in their work. An example of a macro approach is process consultation, in which an outside consultant works with management to diagnose situations and plan solutions.

Key Terms

Active listening Communication skill in which the listener communicates an understanding of the speaker's intended message.

Authority The formally stated right to influence others.

Autocratic style of leadership Leadership style based on the use of coercive power.

Bureaucracy A highly structured organizational structure in which procedures are explicitly stated.

Competition The pursuit of incompatible goals in which the parties do not actively interfere with each other.

Conflict The pursuit of incompatible goals in which the parties interfere with each other.

Destructive confrontation Confrontation marked by personal attacks on general character traits, rather than on behaviour.

Divisional structure An organizational form in which a company is divided into subunits at each geographical location, so that work is less specialized.

Expert power Power that is granted to a person who is seen as especially knowledgeable or skillful.

Flat structure An organizational hierarchy with few levels; each supervisor has a larger number of subordinates.

Functional structure An organizational form in which a company is divided according to specific jobs to be done. Each division does only one job and does it for the whole organization.

Hawthorne effect In general, the influence that factors such as morale and social relations have on productivity. Specifically the finding that in an experiment on levels of lighting, productivity went up no matter what changes were made. The attention of being studied brought about the change.

Hygienes Factors whose absence produces dissatisfaction but which don't act as positive motivators.

Informal organization The unofficial structure which is nearly inevitable in an organization. Patterns of influence and power develop within the social structure.

Job enrichment A micro method of organizational development in which jobs are redesigned to increase the worker's sense of personal responsibility and pride and the meaningfulness of the work.

Leadership The ability to influence others effectively.

Legitimate power Power that is granted by the formal organization. It is similar to authority.

Macro approaches to OD The process of improving a company or other organization by making changes at the level of organizational structure, through process consultation, often with an outside expert.

Management by objectives (MBO) A participatory method of goal setting and performance appraisal in which the manager and worker both contribute to the process.

Micro approaches to OD The process of improving a company or other organization by making changes at the level of individual workers, through methods such as job enrichment, job changing, participatory goal setting, and individual counselling.

Motivators Factors that have a direct effect on increasing productive behaviour.

Non-destructive confrontation A method of confrontation that consists of (1) naming the specific behaviour that is not acceptable; (2) naming your reaction to that behaviour; and (3) naming the tangible connection between the behaviour and your reaction.

Organizational development (OD) The process of improving a company or other organization by making changes at the level of individual workers (micro) or the structure of the organization (macro).

Organizational psychology The discipline that applies psychological principles and findings to the world of work; less often also called industrial psychology.

Participatory/democratic style of leadership A leadership style in which the manager is both "tough and fair" or "sensitive and assertive." This leader is concerned with both productivity and human needs, with both confrontation and helpfulness.

Permissive style of leadership A leadership style in which the leader gives power to the subordinates by being unable to be assertive, set limits, and insist that his or her needs must be met.

Power The ability to influence the behaviour of others.

Process consultation A macro approach to organizational development in which an outside consultant works with management to diagnose situations and plan solutions to problems in the structure of an organization.

Punishment The delivery of discomfort for the purpose of weakening a particular behaviour.

Punishment power Power that derives from a person's ability to deliver punishing consequences.

Quality circles A method for implementing participatory management in which small groups of workers are formed for discussion.

Referent power Power that derives from others' identifying with a person and wanting to be like him or her.

Reward power Power that derives from a person's control of reinforcers, whether they be formal rewards such as money or informal rewards such as social acceptance.

Scientific management The approach to organizational psychology that stresses logical and rational motivation factors, such as economic reward systems; sometimes called Taylorism.

Tall structure An organizational hierarchy with many levels. Each supervisor has fewer direct subordinates and those subordinates are more likely to have workers under them.

Taylorism An early name for the scientific management approach; named after an early theorist, Frederick W. Taylor.

Theory X The view that human beings are lazy and will get away with as much as they can if not forced to work.

Theory Y The view that human beings do not like working in oppressive situations, that employees can be motivated by higher motives, and that they are inherently motivated to seek responsibility.

Theory Z An extension of Theory Y. Theory Z stresses worker participation in decision making, particularly in groups.

Win-lose attitude The philosophy that for one person in a conflict to get his or her needs met, the other person must not.

Win-win method of conflict resolution Problem-solving method in which both parties get their needs met. The method consists of (1) making an approach, (2) defining the problem, (3) generating and evaluating possible solutions, (4) choosing a solution, (5) implementing the solution, and (6) following up.

Suggested Readings

Gray, J. L., & Starke, F. A. (1988). *Organizational behavior*, 4th ed. Columbus, OH: Charles E. Merrill. This textbook gives a good overview of organizational psychology. Written by Canadian authors, it includes some Canadian examples.

Gordon, T. (1977). *Leader effectiveness training*. New York: Wyden Books. This practical guide to being a participatory leader expands on the skills of active listening and effective ways to confront workers. Examples are drawn from the world of work.

APPENDIX

STATISTICS

BY ANNABEL EVANS COLDEWAY

STATISTICS: WHAT GOOD ARE THEY?

You're reading this section because you have to, right? Well, believe it or not, one of the most useful skills you will acquire in your university education might be a solid understanding of statistics. Read and think about the following hypothetical statements. They are similar to statements we have all seen reported in newspapers.

1. "The average yearly income of Canadians is $26,000," says the *US Daily Mail*.
2. "The average yearly income of Canadians is $32,000," says *Canada Today*.
3. "Don't take political science, young woman, if you hope to marry!", claims the *University Student Weekly*.
4. "Eight out of ten dentists agree that *Fluoro-supremo* reduces cavities."

I will refer to these statements again as we discuss basic statistical procedures.

Some students approach their statistics courses in a rather cavalier way. They seem to think that studying statistics is an *unnecessary* (though inevitable) evil in academic life. The fact of the matter is we all need and use statistics every day. There is nothing mysterious or underhanded about statistics. They are simply techniques which help us organize and interpret data.

DESCRIPTIVE STATISTICS: SUMMARIZING AND DESCRIBING DATA

We use **descriptive statistics** when we want to summarize an entire set of numbers that represent observations. These observations are measures of properties of things, events, people, and so on. People, things, and events have many properties which vary from person to person, thing to thing, and event to event. Height, for example, varies from person to person. Gas mileage varies from automobile to automobile. The size of the attending audience varies from rock concert to rock concert. A property which takes on different values—that is, which varies from one item to the next—is called a **variable**. Height of people, gas mileage of cars, attendance at rock concerts: these are all examples of variables. Other properties do not vary; for instance, your height, your car's gas mileage (hopefully), and the attendance at the Grateful Dead concert on October 25, 1968. A property which remains the same is called a **constant**.

Statistics are techniques which are used to summarize and interpret data, the varying properties of people, events, and things. Variables can be classified in terms of their role in research and in terms of the mathematical properties they possess.

Types of variables

One way to classify variables is in terms of the role they play in an experiment. The **independent variable** in an experiment is the variable manipulated by the researcher. The **dependent variable** is the outcome measure expected to be influenced by (depend on) the manipulation. In the memory-drug experiment described in Chapter 1, the independent variable was the administration or non-administration of the drug, and the dependent variable was the measure of memory performance. Statistical procedures help us determine if the manipulation of an independent variable in an experiment had a real or significant effect on the outcome measure (the dependent variable).

Variables can be classified in terms of their mathematical properties as well as the function they serve in experiments. Remember that a variable is a property of things, events, or people, that takes on different values. The *mathematical nature of those values* provides the basis for the mathematical classification.

A variable which is **continuous** has values which vary along an infinite continuum of possible values. Our weight is such a variable. Weight is a continuum whose values are only limited by the precision of the measuring instrument. In other words, weight could theoretically be measured to an infinite number of decimal places. My bathroom scale measures my weight to the nearest kilogram. It tells me that I weigh 54 kg. But in reality I might weigh 53.79 kg or 54.31 kg, although my scale would still insist that I weighed 54 kg. Theoretically, my weight could be measured to an infinite number of decimals. Therefore, weight is a continuous variable, in spite of the limitations of my K-Mart scale!

Other variables have only certain defined values. Number of children in families is such a variable. Even if the average number of children in a Canadian family is 2.3, no one has yet had 3/10 of a child. These variables categorize people, events, and things into different classes and are called **discrete** variables.

This differentiation is important statistically because certain procedures which are appropriate for continuous variables may not be suitable for discrete variables.

Organizing a distribution of numbers

Numbers, numbers, numbers! What do they mean? Let's imagine that the thirty-one numbers below are the scores received by your class on the first quiz in introductory psychology.

56 52 60
80 67 75 71 41
70 67 64
65 80 71 79 42
42
59 66 74 69
40 71 50 60
65 63 51
43
40 51

Do those numbers mean anything to you? Do you have any idea how well your class did? If your score was 79, do you have any idea how your score compares to everyone else?

Without a reasonable organizational scheme, numbers mean very little. It's very important that we agree on some way of organizing and presenting numbers in a consistent way. Statistics help us do this.

One of the most useful ways of organizing numbers is to construct a table called a **frequency distribution**. You have seen many frequency distributions, although you probably didn't know that's what they are called. A frequency distribution lists in tabular form all possible scores and the frequency with which each score occurred. This information is placed in columns from the highest possible score to the lowest. Figure A-1 shows a frequency distribution of the above numbers.

Certainly the scores are better organized now by this table, but you may still find it difficult to assess the performance of the class. In this type of frequency distribution, called a **simple frequency distribution**, most possible scores are listed, even some that never occurred. When we have many scores occurring or many scores that do not occur at all, we often choose to group the scores into intervals, rather than list all possible scores. Figure A-2 shows a **grouped frequency distribution** of the same scores.

Now do you have some idea of how the class did and how you did in comparison? You can certainly see that you did very well. Only three people scored as high or higher than you.

Organizing numbers using a frequency distribution makes it much easier to see trends in data. Another way of presenting numbers in an organized fashion is to construct a graph. Often, graphs are easier to understand than frequency distribution tables, they are certainly more eye-catching.

Several different types of graphs can be used to present numbers. Which graph is used depends on our purpose and also on the kind of data we have. Recall our discussion of continuous versus discrete variables. One graph that is typically used to display discrete variables is known as a **bar graph**. Imagine we have counted the number of dogs of different breeds competing in the obedience event of a dog show. We could present our tallies of 12 collies, 10 retrievers, 7 beagles, 11 poodles, and 3 Old English sheepdogs as shown in Figure A-3. The gaps between the bars indicate that the variable is discrete. They tell the reader that breed of dog is not a continuum but rather a categorical variable with only certain values. The height of each bar indicates the frequency (i.e., the number of dogs) for that category.

Continuous variables should not be presented in a bar graph. Several other graphs are suitable for these kinds of variables. One example, a **frequency polygon**, uses points rather than bars to indicate the frequency for each value of the variable. Let's present our psychology quiz data in a frequency polygon. We'll use the grouped frequency distribution we constructed earlier to do this. See Figure A-4. You may find it easier to see how the class did by examining this graph as opposed to looking at the frequency distribution tables. Many people can grasp data faster from a graph than from a table.

FIGURE A-1 An example of a simple frequency distribution

Score on test	Frequency (f)
80	2
79	1
78	0
77	0
76	0
75	1
74	1
73	0
72	0
71	3
70	1
69	1
68	0
67	2
66	1
65	2
64	1
63	1
62	0
61	0
60	2
59	1
58	0
57	0
56	1
55	0
54	0
53	0
52	1
51	2
50	1
49	0
48	0
47	0
46	0
45	0
44	0
43	1
42	2
41	1
40	2

FIGURE A-2 An example of a grouped frequency distribution

Score interval	Frequency (f)
76–80	3
71–75	5
66–70	5
61–65	4
56–60	4
51–55	3
46–50	1
41–45	4
36–40	2

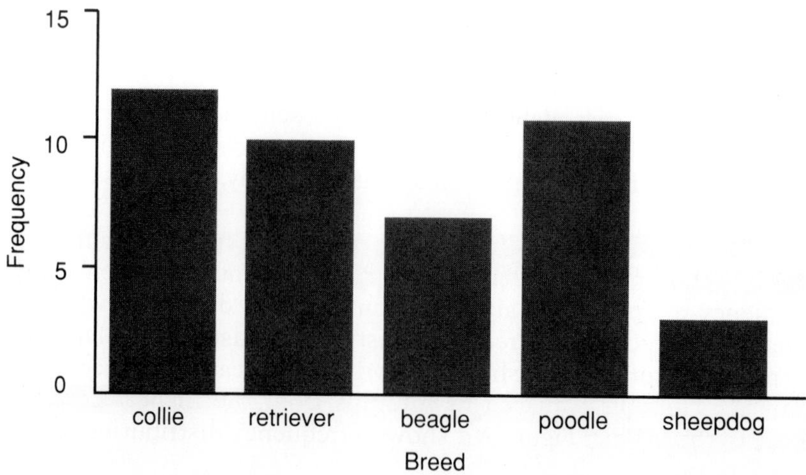

FIGURE A-3 An example of a bar graph

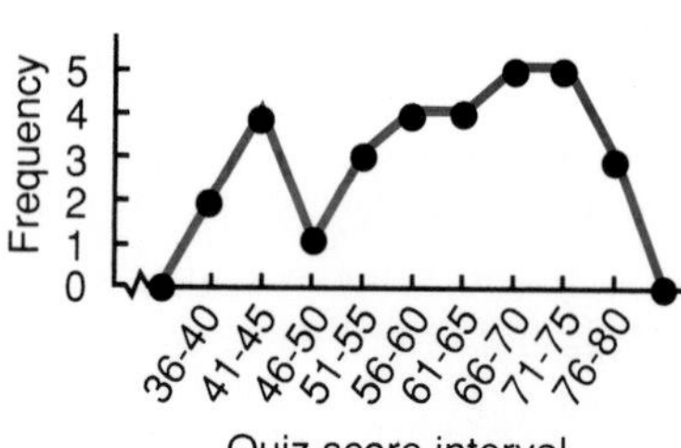

FIGURE A-4 An example of a frequency polygon

Organizing numbers into frequency distribution tables and presenting them graphically are important descriptive techniques. It is difficult to see any trends or meaning in an unorganized group of numbers. Consistent organizational and graphing techniques allow us to read any report and quickly see what is being presented. Adequate description of a distribution of numbers requires more than just organization, however. We need other descriptive measures to fully summarize a distribution.

Recall the first two newspaper statements mentioned earlier:

1. "The average yearly income of Canadians is $26,000," says the *US Daily Mail*.
2. "The average yearly income of Canadians is $32,000," says *Canada Today*.

Could two respected newspapers report such different averages and both be correct? Yes, they could.

Describing the average of a distribution of numbers

Average tells us where the centre of a distribution of numbers is. It is a very important statistic. You may be surprised to learn that there is not one but three averages which can be computed on the same set of numbers.

The "average" that you are probably most familiar with is called the **arithmetic mean** or simply, the **mean**. It is found by summing the scores in a distribution and dividing by the total number of scores. Statisticians usually call a set of scores the "X" distribution, and the total number of scores, "N". By convention, mathematicians use the Greek letter "Σ" to mean "the sum of." Thus, we can write the formula for the mean as follows:

$$\text{Mean} = \frac{\Sigma X}{N}$$

If you knew the class "average," you would have an even better understanding of how well you did. Let's calculate the mean for our hypothetical quiz. We need to add all the scores and divide by the number of people in the class.

$$\text{Mean of quiz scores} = \frac{\Sigma X}{N} = \frac{1884}{31} = 60.8$$

Now we have an even better idea of how the class performed on the quiz. You can see that a score of 79 was much higher than the class "average" of 60.8.

Another measure of average is based on the *number* of scores, rather than on their actual value. This average is called the **median**. The median is the middle value in a distribution of numbers. In other words, it divides the distribution in half. Let's find the median for our introductory psychology quiz. Here are the thirty-one scores in order from highest to lowest.

80, 80, 79, 75, 74, 71, 71, 71, 70, 69, 67, 67, 66, 65, 65, [64], 63, 60, 60, 59, 56, 52, 51, 51, 50, 43, 42, 42, 41, 40, 40

The median is the middle score: 64. There are 15 scores above it and 15 scores below it. If there is an even number of scores, then the median is the value halfway between the two central scores. Although the median is close to the mean, it is not exactly the same. The median is not as sensitive as the mean because it only reflects the number of scores above and below, not the actual value of the scores. The mean will always be pulled toward extreme scores. In the example above, the mean is slightly lower than the median because there are several quite low scores that pull the mean in their direction.

Consider, again, the two newspaper reports of the "average" income of Canadians.

1. "The average yearly income of Canadians is $26,000," says the *US Daily Mail*.
2. "The average yearly income of Canadians is $32,000," says *Canada Today*.

Perhaps one paper was referring to mean income while the other paper was reporting median income. Let's suppose this is the case. Can you surmise which would be which? It is not possible to have an income lower than zero, but it is possible to have an extremely high income. The mean would then be pulled up toward those high scores. Thus, it seems likely that the figure given by the *US Daily Mail* represents the median income, and the figure given by *Canada Today* represents the mean income.

The third type of "average" is called the **mode**. The mode is the number in a distribution which occurs more frequently than any other. It is the "typical" score, one obtained more often than any other. Can you see that the mode for our hypothetical psychology quiz is 71? More students scored 71 than any other single value. If your professor reported the class "average" in terms of the mode, your score of 79 would look somewhat mediocre. Mode is often only a crude measure of average.

Some statistical measure of average is very important in describing a distribution of numbers. It tells us where the "middle" of the distribution is or where the "average" score lies. In most cases, the mean is the most meaningful and useful measure of the "average". However, mean, median, and mode do not tell us how spread out the numbers are. The spread or *variability* of a distribution is another important characteristic to consider.

Describing the variability of a distribution of numbers

Remember that when we provide descriptive measures of a distribution of numbers, we are trying to tell others as much as possible about what the distribution is like. The mean, median, and mode provide information about the "average" score. Measures of **variability** provide information about the spread of the whole distribution. Were most of the scores bunched around the centre of the distribution or were there lots of extreme scores lying far from the centre?

Examine the two distributions in Figure A-5. The distribution in Graph A is more compact. Scores are more bunched around the middle with few extreme scores. By contrast, Graph B shows a more variable distribution with the scores spreading out to the extreme

Figure A-5 Distributions of different variability

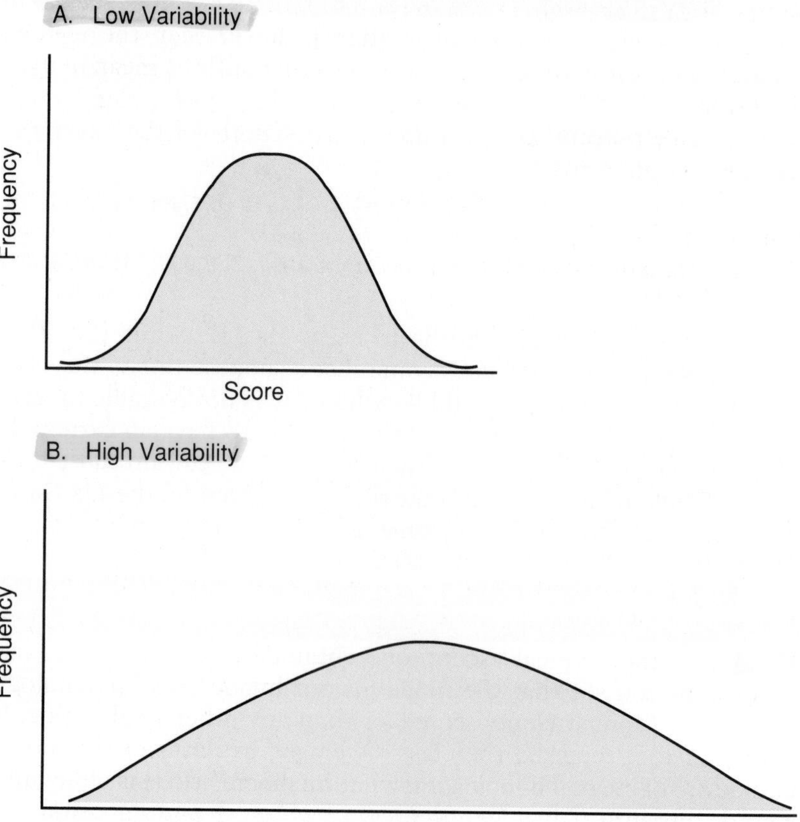

ends. These graphs illustrate that both the average *and* the variability of distributions are important.

Consider the following scenario. Josie wrote her final exams in psychology and in history. She received 72% in both tests and the class average (the mean) was 60% in both tests. Many of us might assume from this information that Josie did equally well in both tests. Aha! Not necessarily so. Josie must obtain one more piece of information before she can properly evaluate her performance. She needs to know the variability of the distribution. Let's imagine that the variability of scores on the history test was high. In other words, the class was spread out with very high scores and very low scores. Let's further suppose that the psychology scores were similar to one another and bunched together. The graphs in Figure A-6 depict the scenario we have just described.

FIGURE A-6 Two sets of test scores with the same mean but different variability

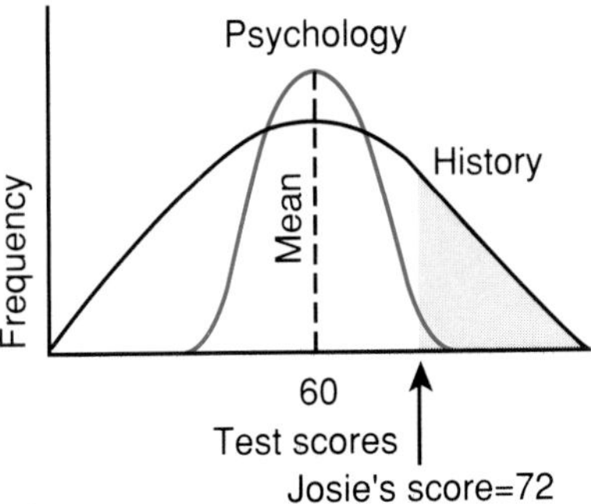

You can see that very few students writing the psychology test did better than Josie. On the history test, however, quite a few students did better than Josie. Josie's performance, relative to her classmates, was superior on the psychology quiz. So, knowing your score and the class average doesn't always provide enough information about relative standing. You must know something about the variability of the scores. It isn't necessary, however, to construct a graph to determine the variability of a distribution.

A quick but crude measure of variability is the **range**. The range simply tells us the span of the scores. It is found by subtracting the lowest from the highest score plus 1. In the hypothetical quiz described near the beginning of the Appendix, the highest score was 80 and the lowest score was 40. Therefore, the range of our quiz scores is 80 − 40 + 1 = 41. In other words, the scores ranged across 41 possible values. When the mode is used as the measure of average, the range is often used as the measure of variability.

A more sensitive measure of variability is the **standard deviation**. When the mean is provided as a measure of average, the standard deviation usually accompanies it. The standard deviation is a number which describes how far, on the average, the scores in a distribution are from the mean of the distribution. More specifically, it measures the average deviation (difference) between the scores and the mean.

The term *deviation* simply means the difference between a score and the mean of its distribution. If a distribution, with a mean of 60 has a standard deviation of 5, we know that, on the average, scores deviate or vary five points from the mean. The standard deviation is computed by summing the squared deviations of all the scores from the mean, dividing the sum by the total number of scores, and taking the square root of this ratio. Here is a formula for the standard deviation.

$$\text{Standard deviation} = \sqrt{\frac{\Sigma(X - \text{Mean})^2}{N}}$$

To calculate the standard deviation for any set of data, we first must compute the mean. Next, we subtract the mean from each score and square this difference. The standard deviation is then simple to obtain. Let's do an example.

Score (X)	Deviation (X − Mean)	Deviation squared $(X - Mean)^2$
23	10	100
22	9	81
17	4	16
14	1	1
12	−1	1
11	−2	4
9	−4	16
8	−5	25
8	−5	25
6	−7	49
$\Sigma X = 130$		$\Sigma(X - Mean)^2 = 2318$

$$\text{Mean} = \frac{\Sigma X}{N} = \frac{130}{10} = 13$$

$$\text{Standard deviation} = \sqrt{\frac{\Sigma(X - Mean)^2}{N}} = \sqrt{\frac{2318}{10}} = 5.64$$

For these data, then, the mean is 13 and the standard deviation is 5.64. This tells us that the scores, on the average, vary 5.64 points from 13.

The standard deviation is an extremely useful descriptive statistic. Not only does it provide a measure of variability but it can be used to tell us, at a glance, where the bulk of the scores in a distribution lie. In *any* distribution, at least 75% of the scores fall within 2 standard deviations of the mean of the distribution. With the distribution above then, we know that at least 75% of the scores fall between 7.36 (i.e., 13 − 5.64) and 18.64 (i.e., 13 + 5.64). You can see that this is correct since 8 of the 10 scores (i.e., 80%) do indeed fall between these two values.

If a distribution is fairly symmetrical (i.e., the right half looks much like the left half of the graph of the distribution), then at least 90% of the scores fall within 2 standard deviations of the mean. Consider a midterm quiz where the class mean was 55%. You received a score of 72%. If in addition to this information, you learn that the standard deviation of the quiz scores was 6 and the distribution was fairly symmetrical, you would then know that at least 90% of the class must be between 43% (2 standard deviations below the mean) and 67% (2 standard deviations above the mean). That leaves less than 5% of the class scoring above 67%. Your score of 72% is quite impressive!

The **normal curve**, mentioned in Chapter 11, is a very important distribution in statistics. Although the normal curve, is a theoretical distribution (i.e., theoretically rather than empirically constructed), many real-life variables distribute themselves more or less normally. Therefore, statisticians often use the normal curve as a model of how variables behave. Height, weight, and IQ are some of the many variables that approximate the normal curve in shape. The normal curve has been standardized in such a way that it has the following invariant properties: (1) the mean, mode, and median have the same value; (2) the distribution is perfectly symmetrical; and (3) the curve is shaped like a bell with few scores at the extreme ends. Because it is standardized, we know the precise percentage of scores between any two points under the curve.

Figure A-7 illustrates the normal curve as a frequency polygon. As you can see, 68.26% of the scores in a normal distribution lie between one standard deviation below and one standard deviation above the mean. More than 95% of the scores lie within two standard deviations of the mean. One reason why the normal curve is so important in statistics is that it can be used descriptively. Suppose you have taken a college entrance exam standardized to a normal distribution with a mean of 500 and a standard deviation of 85. Further suppose that you obtained a score of 755. Your score is 3 standard deviations above the mean! Because the scores on this exam are normally distributed you can see by examining Figure A-7 that you are in the top 0.13% of the population of people taking this test.

The normal curve is very important in *inferential statistics* as well, a topic we will discuss shortly. If a researcher knows that a variable he is studying is normally distributed, then he has certain expectations about the outcome of his particular study. Imagine that the principal of an innovative school believes that her program is superior to most others and that her students achieve higher levels of competence as a result. We, as interested researchers, might decide to examine her claim by giving her students a standardized test of academic achievement. We might choose a test that yields a normal distribution with a known mean and standard deviation. We would expect, if the principal's claim were false, that her students' scores would yield a mean not much different than the normative mean. If we found, on the other hand, that the scores were much higher than that, we might be compelled to agree with her claim. The normal curve, then, can serve as a model of expected results, thereby allowing the researcher to compare the actual outcomes of his or her study with those expected.

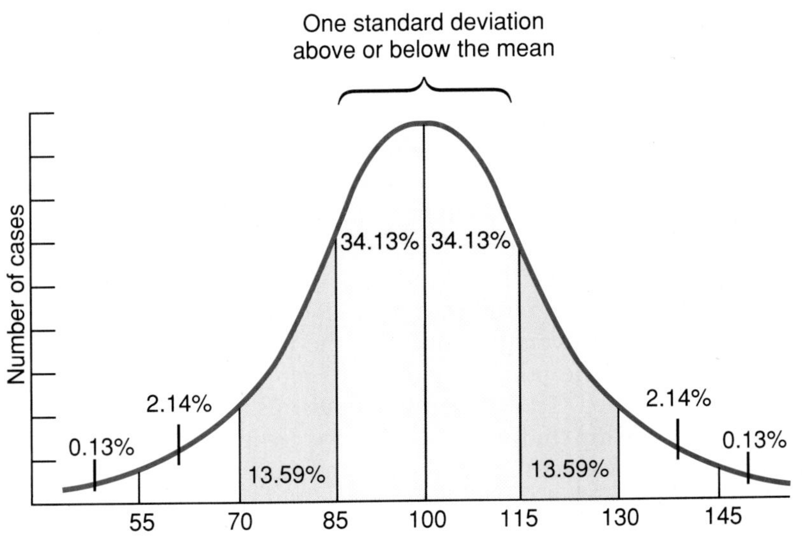

FIGURE A-7 The normal distribution

An adequate description of a distribution of numbers requires both a measure of average and a measure of variability. Taken together, these descriptive statistics tell us a great deal about a distribution of numbers. The average and variability also enable us to see trends that otherwise would be difficult, if not impossible, to observe.

DESCRIBING RELATIONSHIPS: CORRELATIONS

In the sections above, we have discussed the importance of describing the average and variability of a distribution of scores of a single variable, such as the scores on a quiz. We now know how to answer the following questions: What is the average performance? What is the spread of the scores around the average? Another important question we might ask is "What is the relationship between *two* variables?"

We have all heard about the relationship between smoking and lung disease. Smoking is a variable and lung disease is also a variable and they tend to vary together. In other words, people who smoke a lot tend to suffer from lung disease more often than people who do not smoke. Statisticians say that these two variables, smoking and lung disease, are **correlated**. Another correlation you are probably familiar with is the one between high-school graduating average and university performance. Students with higher averages in high school tend to do well in university, whereas students with poorer averages tend to do less well. How do we know this?

Let's imagine that we have obtained the high-school graduating averages of 20 students. Let's further imagine that these 20 students have just completed their first year at university and we have obtained their grade-point averages. We place these numbers in a frequency distribution to obtain the table shown in Figure A-8.

FIGURE A-8 An example of a bivariate frequency distribution

Student	High-school grade average	University grade-point average
1	55	3.8
2	57	3.2
3	57	4.5
4	57	4.2
5	60	4.0
6	61	6.2
7	61	5.0
8	65	4.6
9	68	5.7
10	69	7.2
11	69	6.3
12	69	6.0
13	72	5.3
14	72	6.9
15	73	5.9
16	74	6.7
17	76	7.1
18	78	7.6
19	84	7.8
20	86	6.5

A study of this **bivariate** (two variables) frequency distribution suggests that there might be a relationship. We can see that there is a trend for low high-school grades to be associated with low university grades. This is not always the case, however. Student 10 with 69% out of high school did well in university with a grade point of 7.2. Student 20 with the highest high-school average (86%) only got a grade-point average of 6.5 after first year university. So the correlation between high-school grades and university grades was not perfect, but there does seem to be a trend.

Graphing a bivariate frequency distribution is a good way to see if a relationship exists. This kind of graph is called a **scattergram**. Figure A-9 is a scattergram of the bivariate frequency distribution of high-school and university grades for the twenty students. In this scattergram a single point is plotted to represent the grades each individual received. The scattergram confirms that there does seem to be a relationship. Individuals with low grades out of high school tended to get low grades in university, and students with high grades in high school tended to get high grades in university as well. The points tend to rise from the lower left to the upper right portion of the graph. This relationship is called a **positive correlation** because low values of one variable are associated with low values of the second variable, and high values of the first variable are associated with high values of the second.

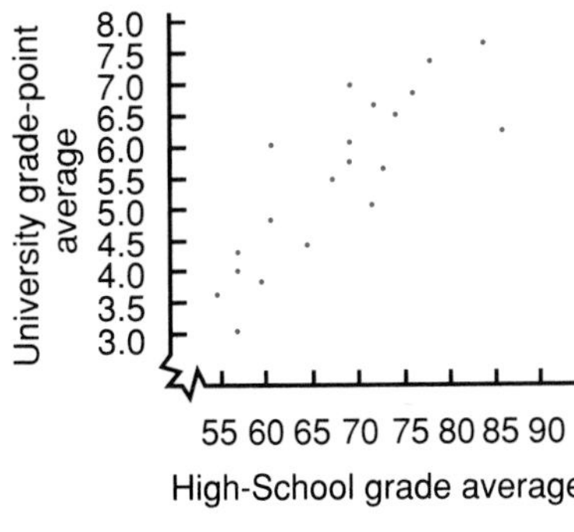

FIGURE A-9 A scattergram indicating a positive correlation

A **negative correlation** exists when *high* values of one variable are associated with *low* values of another and vice versa. Teeth flossing and the incidence of cavities are negatively correlated. In other words, people who floss more tend to get fewer cavities than people who floss less. A scattergram of this relationship might look like the graph in Figure A-10. You can see that the points tend to drop from the upper left to the lower right indicating that as flossing increases, the incidence of cavities decreases.

Constructing a scattergram is one way of determining whether two variables are correlated. A scattergram gives a visual picture of that relationship. The relationship can be quantified by computing a **coefficient of correlation**. There are several different statistical techniques to do this. Which is chosen depends on the nature of the variables. Some coefficients are appropriate when the variables are discrete, and others are appropriate when the variables are continuous.

Pearson's product-moment coefficient of correlation is often used when both variables are continuous. It is perhaps the most common coefficient, and most other coefficients are based on this one. The computation of Pearson's coefficient is complicated, but the concepts underlying it are really quite simple. Karl Pearson used a *least squares criterion* to fit a straight line to the points in a scattergram in order to quantify the linear relationship between two variables. In other words, a straight line (called the *regression line* or *line of best fit*) is laid down in such a way that the sum of the squared distances of the points from the line is as small as possible. Once the line is fit, the coefficient of correlation basically measures how variable the points are from that line. If the points all lie on the straight line of best fit, the correlation is said to be *perfect*. In other words, there is no variability of the points from the line; the two variables increase and decrease perfectly together. Knowing the value of one variable allows perfect prediction of the value of the second variable. If the points do not all line on the straight line, the correlation is less than perfect; predicting from one variable to the other will result in some amount of error. How close the points hug the line defines the strength of the relationship between the variables.

Another popular coefficient is the **Spearman rank-order correlation coefficient**. It is used when the values of both variables are ranks. For example, if we were interested in comparing CFL standings of the last two years, we might choose to use the Spearman correlation. We would compare the rankings of the teams last year with their rankings this year. The correlation coefficient would tell us if there is a relationship. Is the order of the teams from first to last similar this year to what it was last year? Rank order data are noncontinuous. They are discrete data on an ordinal scale of measurement.

Figure A-10 A scattergram indicating a negative correlation

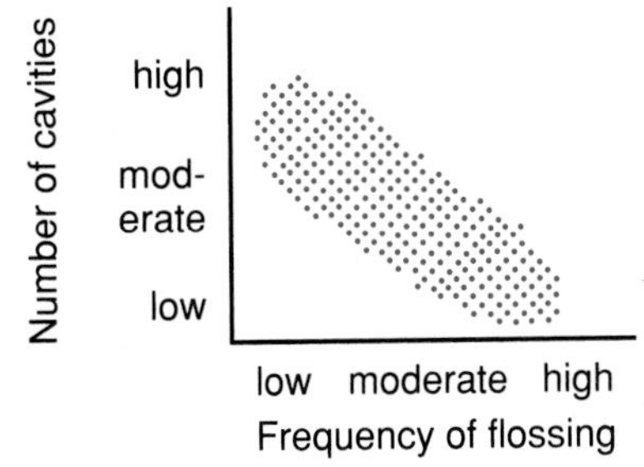

Regardless of which coefficient is used, the index of correlation ranges from -1 to $+1$. The number reflects the strength of the relationship, and the sign indicates whether the correlation is a negative or a positive one. The closer the coefficient is to ± 1, the stronger the correlation. For example, a coefficient of -0.86 reflects a very strong negative correlation, and a coefficient of $+0.86$ reflects an equally strong positive correlation.

A great deal of research involves correlational statistics. There are demonstrated correlations between many, many variables. "High fibre diet is negatively correlated with certain kinds of cancer." "Smoking is positively correlated with lung disease." "Alcohol consumption by pregnant women is negatively correlated with fetal weight gain." "Exposure to amplified music is positively correlated with hearing loss." You have probably read or heard many statements like these in newspaper articles, in magazines and on television. And you may have assumed these statements indicate the existence of a causal relationship. In other words, you might have thought that eating lots of fibre reduces the risk of cancer, smoking increases the risk of cancer, drinking during pregnancy decreases fetal weight gain, and listening to loud music causes hearing loss. In many cases the media themselves strongly imply a causal relationship. In fact, a causal relationship may well exist, but it is not *proven* by the existence of a correlation.

The demonstration of a correlation between two variables does not tell us about cause and effect. As you will recall from Chapter 1 of this book, **correlation does not infer causation**. This is an important truism that many psychology students will hear throughout their academic careers. A correlational relationship does not prove cause; it only shows that two variables are associated. Why they are associated is another matter entirely and can only be definitively resolved by an experimental procedure. Let's examine the statement "Exposure to amplified music is positively correlated with hearing loss." This statement says that people who listen to a lot of very loud music tend to have poorer hearing than people who do not. And that is all it says. It does not tell us whether the music caused the hearing loss, whether people with poor hearing prefer very loud music, or whether something else entirely is responsible for the relationship.

Let's look at one of the statements I presented at the beginning of this Appendix.

> "Don't take political science, young woman, if you hope to marry!", claims the *University Student Weekly*.

I used this particular statement because I remember several years ago coming across an article in a university news-sheet that caught my attention. Essentially, the article discussed how female political scientists tend not to marry whereas almost all home-economics coeds did marry. The article clearly implied that it was something about the discipline that was responsible for this relationship. In other words, women taking political science were somehow discouraged from engaging in romantic activities that might lead to marriage. I thought this was a perfect example of how people misinterpret the meaning of correlation. I don't claim to know for sure whether studying to be a political scientist causes a woman to avoid marriage. This could only be shown through an experimental procedure. But my guess is that it is not the discipline at all. I suspect that the kind of women who chose political science, particularly several years ago, were different than the kind of women who chose to study home-economics. They were different to begin with, *not* as a result of their studies. Women choosing political science as a career may not have been the "marrying kind" in those days, whereas women who intended to marry may well have selected home-economics in preparation for that event. I doubt that this correlation exists today.

PREDICTIVE STATISTICS: USING ESTABLISHED RELATIONSHIPS TO PREDICT FUTURE EVENTS

Being able to predict what will happen in the future can be very helpful in making decisions today. If two variables are strongly correlated, we can use values of the first variable to predict values of the second. This kind of statistical procedure, known as **predictive statistics**, is frequently seen in situations where we want to know if a person will benefit from a particular kind of training or educational experience, or if an individual will be effective in a particular kind of job or position. For example, if I have collected data over the years showing that students who attend more lectures tend to perform better on exams than students who rarely attend, I might use this correlation as a way of encouraging my students to attend my lectures. Of course, I might be wasting my time because we would not know that lecture attendance *per se* causes higher grades. It may well be that better students choose to attend more lectures and that my lectures have little to do with it! Nevertheless, knowledge about a variable known to be correlated with another is often used as a predictor of future performance. Let's examine a real-life correlation that was used to predict the performance of all of you taking this course: the one between high school grades and university performance that we discussed earlier.

Most, if not all, universities use high-school graduating average as an indicator of success in university. Most universities accept the correlation between these two variables as such a useful predictor that they use high-school average as a cut-off for admission to university. For the purpose of this discussion, let's assume that the cut-off for admission to first year at the "University of Greater Knowledge" (UGK) is 65%. Where did this cut-off come from? Well, presumably the "powers that be" at UGK have determined that students with high-school averages of less than 65% have a low probability of succeeding in university-level courses. They determined this by collecting data for many years where cut-offs were not used as admission criteria. In other words they have recorded the entry high-school grades of their students and the university grades of their students and found a positive correlation to exist. Suppose that Figure A-11 depicts this correlation.

FIGURE A-11 Hypothetical correlation between university performance and high-school average

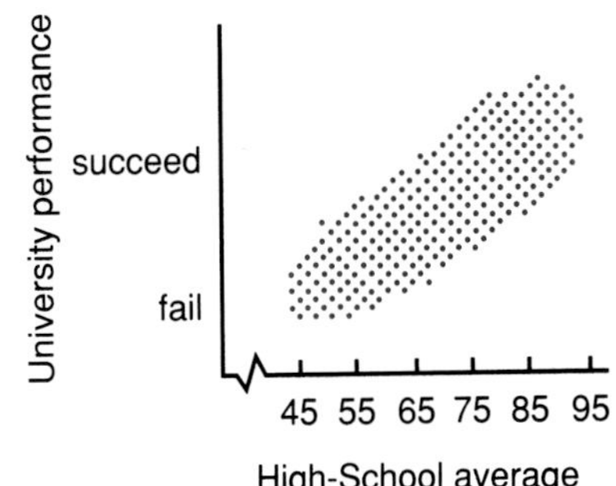

Figure A-12 Hypothetical situation for UGK

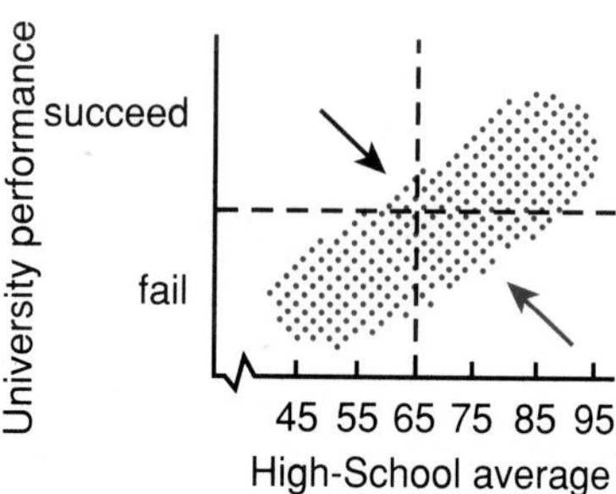

The existence of the positive correlation presented in Figure A-11 provides a basis for UGK to make decisions about who will be admitted to first year. You may be feeling somewhat indignant at this point, but consider the position of the university as well as that of the hopeful student. It is expensive to educate students. It is very expensive to admit students who later fail. On the other hand, it is tragic to reject a student who could have succeeded. It is a matter of balance. A wise university will select a cut-off such that the number of students admitted who later fail and the number of students rejected who would have succeeded are minimized.

Figure A-12 shows the hypothetical situation for UGK after it has introduced a cut-off of 65%. If we consider this scattergram to be a predictor of future performance, we can see that the cut-off would be successful at predicting performance for those students in the lower left and the upper right quadrants. The students in the lower left quadrant would not have been admitted to UGK, if the cut-off were used, and rightly so since they would not have succeeded. The students in the upper right quadrant would have been admitted, and again, rightly so, because they did succeed. The arrows point to the cases where the prediction would have been inaccurate. The black arrow points to the students who would have succeeded if only UGK had given them a chance. The coloured arrow points to those students who cost UGK money by failing to perform at the level predicted. The trick is to select a cut-off which will reduce the number of cases in both these categories.

Predictive procedures can be very useful in a variety of situations. Care must be taken, however, to ensure that the predictor variable in fact predicts performance. Did you know there is a positive correlation between amount of debt and number of years attending university? Yes, indeed, students who attend for more years have larger debts than those who attend for fewer years! Imagine the absurdity of using indebtedness as a cut-off for admission.

Descriptive statistics are needed whenever we wish to organize an entire set of observations, depict them in a graph, summarize their characteristics, and examine relationships, or make predictions, between one set and another. *Inferential statistics* come into play when the entire set of observations, the population, is not available to us to describe.

Inferential Statistics

I think that inference is the area where some people become suspicious of statistics. Inference is not mysterious. It's a probabilistic approach used when we cannot get our hands on the entire population we want to study.

If you are interested in the behaviour of the giant panda, it is likely that you will be able to study all the giant pandas in the cosmos. Psychologists, as you know, are interested in human behaviour: *all* humans. No psychologist, however, studies the behaviour of all humans. The population of interest to many psychologists, i.e., all humans, is not available for description. This is where **inferential statistics** comes into play.

Statistical inference is actually a two-step procedure. First, a subset of observations, called a **sample**, is selected for study from the population of interest. Second, the statistical properties of the sample are used to infer the statistical properties of the population from which the sample as taken.

Selecting a sample

How a sample is selected determines what proper inferences can be made. This point is one which I often think has been overlooked by many researchers. A researcher who is interested in all people must select a sample in such a way that the sample is likely to be *representative* of all people. If I want to determine whether women are smarter than men, it would not be fair if I selected a sample of women from the Faculty Club of a prestigious Canadian university and a sample of men from a run-down bar in Toronto's inner city. If I did so, it would be likely that I would have introduced a bias in favour of women, and any inferences I made to *all* women and *all* men would be faulty.

A typical procedure for selecting samples is called **random selection**, and samples so constructed are called **random samples**. The term random sample does not describe the nature of the sample; rather, it describes the nature of the selection procedure. As explained in Chapter 1, a random sample is selected in such a way that *every member of the population of interest has an equal probability of being included in the sample*. One way to ensure random selection is to number every member of the population, put all these numbers in a very large hat, and draw out enough numbers to make up the required sample. A better way is to use a **random number table** to select the members of the sample. A random number table is a table of digits, 0–9, generated such that each of the digits has an equal probability of appearing at any one point in the table. Figure A-13 presents a portion of a random number table generated by my MacIntosh computer (Microsoft Works). Suppose we had numbered each member of a population of 900 observations from 001 to 900. If we wanted to randomly select 25 observations to be included in our sample, we could use the random numbers table in Figure A-13 to do so. We might begin by throwing a dart at the table. Where the dart lands would be our starting point. Let's say that our dart (or finger stab with eyes shut) landed on the number 176. It really doesn't

773	389	669	100	435	098	046	693	507	780
381	507	**176**	673	718	654	794	227	980	831
338	660	754	143	961	667	142	261	410	126
430	671	746	802	626	417	903	975	202	615
132	540	258	542	711	969	110	537	314	944
961	209	489	065	049	988	529	699	114	824
461	713	050	313	872	955	029	564	073	236
661	127	726	177	126	743	555	853	150	270
059	494	240	378	870	954	377	953	477	382
718	161	369	084	668	423	248	476	204	226
803	455	727	046	780	401	741	475	790	665

FIGURE A-13 An example of a random number table

matter which direction we go, so let's go to the right. Since we have 900 possible participants in our sample, we must include each three digit number we can as a member of our sample until we have obtained 25 three digit numbers of 900 or less. We simply ignore numbers larger than the size of our population (such as 980). You can see from examining the table that our sample will consist of the observations numbered 176, 673, 718, 654, 794, 227, 831, 338, 660, 754, 143, 667, 142, 261, 410, 126, 430, 671, 746, 802, 626, 417, 202, 615, and 132.

Most researchers do not use a truly random sampling procedure, but all good researchers attempt to ensure that their samples are not biased in any systematic way. Nevertheless, it is important the sampling procedures be carefully scrutinized when inferences to populations are made.

Let's now consider the last hypothetical statement presented at the beginning of this Appendix:

> "Eight out of ten dentists agree that *Fluoro-supremo* reduces cavities."

This statement is one of my favourites because it is very close to a claim made by several toothpaste manufacturers and it exemplifies so many statistical no-nos. First, the relationship between the use of *Fluoro-supremo* and cavities, if there is one, is most likely correlational not causal. Second, the statement is incomplete since we don't know what the comparison group is. Do people who use *Fluoro-supremo* have fewer cavities than people who use *Fluoro-fantastico*, or is it that people who use *Fluoro-supremo* have fewer cavities than people who don't brush their teeth?! There is no way of knowing from the statement as it stands. Our concern now, however, is in the sampling procedures.

Eight out of ten dentists . . . hmm. What could this mean? Of course, the toothpaste company wants you to believe that 80% of *all* dentists agree. That is not what the statement says, however. Is it possible that the research director of the *Fluoro-supremo* toothpaste company interviewed dentist after dentist until she found eight who agreed and two who didn't or didn't have an opinion? One can only wonder!

I hope you are beginning to realize we cannot be misled by statistics *per se*, but we can be misled by the users of statistics. The accuracy and appropriateness of generalizations made about populations is limited by the representativeness of samples selected from those populations.

Inferring characteristics of populations

After the sample has been selected, the next step is to infer characteristics of the population from characteristics of the sample. Suppose that after we have randomly selected 100 dentists from the population of all dentists and asked them which toothpaste they recommend, we find that 80 of our dentists recommend *Fluoro-supremo* over other brands of toothpaste. Can we assume that 80% of the population of all dentists would say the same? This is a question that can only be answered by an inferential statistical procedure.

There are many techniques available to deal with this stage of the inferential process. Which procedure is chosen depends on the kinds of data involved and the researcher's interest. All of these techniques, however, have at least one thing in common. They all deal with **probabilities**. In our toothpaste example, whatever procedure is chosen should answer this question: "How likely is it that 80 out of 100 randomly chosen dentists would agree if the population proportion was *significantly* different from 80%?" The answer to this question determines whether or not an inference can be made with statistical reliability.

Perhaps a simpler way of stating this is to say that inferential statistics determine the probability that the characteristics of the population at large are reflected in the sample at hand. The characteristics of the population that the researcher is interested in determines whether he or she will use **parametric** or **non-parametric** procedures.

Parametric inference

A **parameter** is a single characteristic of a population. The mean of a population, for example, is a parameter. If our interest is in inferring mean performance of people on a new driving test, we would use a parametric approach. We might select a random sample and have each member take our new driving test. We would compute the mean performance for our sample and use this measure to infer the mean of the population. Let's say that our sample mean on the new driving test was much lower than we expected based on data from the old driving test. In fact, all of our drivers failed the new test! There are two possible explanations for this finding. Perhaps our new test is significantly more difficult to pass than the old one. On the other hand, perhaps by chance we got a sample of really poor drivers! If our sampling procedure was truly random, there would be no good reason why we would have a group of such "driving dead-heads." Therefore, the second explanation seems unlikely. We would probably feel quite confident that the first explanation is the correct one. We would infer that mean performance on the new driving test by the population at large is lower than on the old driving test.

Parametric inference then, uses sample measures to make inferences about those same measures in the population. We should realize that one random sample drawn from a population will not be identical to a second sample randomly drawn from that same population. Samples vary. Another sample of drivers may not do as poorly as the first sample. Perhaps, by chance alone, our first sample included particularly poor drivers. If this were the case, our inference to the population of all drivers would be in error. Good sampling procedures will reduce the likelihood of inferential error.

The term **statistical significance** is used to indicate that the likelihood of a chance, rare event being responsible for the outcome is very low. In the case of our driving test results, we would use an appropriate **test of significance** to support our claim that performance on the new driving test was significantly poorer than performance on the old test. This statement means that the statistical probability that our group of drivers would perform that poorly by chance alone is very low. We, therefore, make the inference that the new test is more difficult to pass than the old one. You may be wondering what "very low" means. To most statisticians, "very low" means less than about 5%. In other words, we will be confident in the veracity of our inferential conclusion if the probability that it is in error is less than about 5%. How do we know if a statistical inference is *true* or not? The answer is, we don't! No statistical inference, however conscientiously arrived at, is ever made with certainty. The only way to know *for sure* if the population of all drivers would do poorly on our new driving test is to test the entire population of drivers. Inferential statistics are used when for whatever reason we cannot test the entire population. We always take the risk that our sample outcome is a rare event that is not indicative of the population.

Statisticians are particularly concerned with two kinds of inferential errors: **Type I errors** and **Type II errors**. A Type I error occurs when the sample outcome leads the researcher to make a false inference about the population because the sample was *not* representative of the population from which it was drawn. For example, if for some bizarre reason, we had selected a sample of really incompetent drivers to use in our new driving test, we would be making a Type I error by concluding that the new driving test is more difficult than the old one. We would be wrong because it was not the test, necessarily, that produced such poor results but rather it was the lousy drivers in our sample. Again, a careful sampling procedure will reduce the likelihood of this kind of error. But it's important to recognize that no matter how careful a researcher is, there is always some probability of a Type I error. You may be wondering about the connection between the "very low" probability I referred to and this business of Type I error. A good statistical test of significance ensures that the probability of making a Type I error is low, usually less than about 5%.

Another kind of inferential error, a Type II error, is also of concern to researchers. Suppose for the moment that our new driving test really was more difficult to pass than the old one. In other words, if the entire population of drivers were to take our new test, they would not perform well at all. Suppose further that our sample of test drivers, in fact, did okay on the new driving test. This could happen, although it's not likely to, even if we used random selection procedures. We may have happened to get a sample of particularly good drivers! In such a case, our sample outcome would lead us to conclude that the new driving test was not more difficult than the old one. Our inference would be wrong and we would make a Type II error. A Type II error then occurs when we fail to detect a population characteristic because our sample, for whatever reason, does not represent that population characteristic. The various statistical tests of significance all try to reduce and balance the probability of a Type I and Type II error.

As you are probably beginning to realize, the design of good research is a difficult and demanding exercise. Research involving inferential statistics is a matter of probability: the probability of being correct in an inferential conclusion and the probability of being in error. A good researcher knows what these probabilities are and interprets his or her research outcomes accordingly.

Parametric inference deals with single characteristics of populations, such as means. In other words, every member of a sample is measured on some variable and the average of the sample is used to infer the average of the population. Measures of average are not the only parameters used in parametric inference, but they are the most common. Do you recall the example of the dentists used earlier? In that case, measures on some performance variable were not the data of interest. Rather, the dentists were simply categorized into those who like *Fluoro-supremo* and those who did not. These kinds of data require a different inferential approach.

Non-parametric inference

The Liberal party want to know how they are doing in the polls. The federal government wants to know how the public feels about abortion. A restaurant owner wants to know if his customers can tell the difference between butter and margarine. These are questions about frequencies or proportions rather than averages. They are suited to a non-parametric statistical analysis.

The Liberal party is interested in knowing what proportion of the population will vote for them. The federal government is interested in how many people feel abortion should be criminalized. The restaurant owner is interested in preference for butter over margarine. Since it would be costly, to say the least, to ask everyone in Canada how he or she feels on such issues, we need to select a sample and use those data to infer the attitude of the general public. As with parametric inference, the selection of the sample is of critical importance. If the sample is not representative of the population at large, then any inferences based on the sample data will fail to reflect the population.

Let's help out the restaurant owner. We'll randomly select 100 diners and have them declare their preference for one of two dishes: one cooked in butter and the same dish cooked in margarine. Suppose that 62 diners choose the butter dish over the margarine dish. Well, we know that if people can't tell the difference, we would expect about 50% of the sample to choose each alternative. Of course, we wouldn't expect *exactly* half of our sample to choose each dish because we know that sample outcomes vary by chance alone. The question is, if people in general can't tell the difference, how likely is it that 62% of our sample would choose the butter dish over the margarine dish? If it is extremely unlikely (perhaps less than about 5%) we might conclude that people can, in fact, tell the difference. If so, we will tell the restaurant owner to stock up on butter, not margarine.

Let's go ahead and answer the question plaguing the restaurant owner. A very common non-parametric technique suitable for our scenario is called a **chi-square test for goodness of fit**. This test simply compares the obtained frequencies in a study with those expected if a certain hypothesis is made. As we have already discussed, the restaurant owner would expect about half of his customers to choose the butter dish if they can't tell the difference between butter and margarine. The expected frequency of customers choosing the butter dish over the margarine dish, then, is 50%. A chi-square analysis of this study would compare the obtained frequencies of 62% (for the butter dish) and 38% (for the margarine dish) with the expected or predicted frequencies of 50% for each dish if customers had no preference. The statistic, chi-square, is a number obtained by squaring the difference between each expected frequency and obtained frequency, dividing this value by the expected frequency, and summing these ratios. For the present example the value of the chi-square statistic is calculated as follows:

$$\text{chi-square} = \frac{(62-50)^2}{50} + \frac{(38-50)^2}{50}$$
$$= 5.76$$

What does this number mean? Remember that our question asks whether it is likely to have 62% of our sample prefer the butter dish if people in general can't tell the difference. If the probability is very low then we can infer that people *can* tell the difference. Tables of chi-square values (called **critical values**) have been developed which help us answer this question. In this particular example the critical value is 3.84. Our obtained chi-square value of 5.76 is larger than this. Thus, the probability of getting our outcome if people in general can't tell the difference between butter and margarine is very low, less than about 5%. We should conclude that people *can* detect the difference and we would inform the restaurant owner accordingly.

Inferential statistics, then, include a host of techniques which allow us to make inferences about the characteristics of populations with a reasonable degree of confidence. We use these when the entire population is not available for description. Any inference we make can be wrong, but we reduce the probability of error by using good sampling procedures, good research techniques, and sensitive statistical tests.

If this discussion of statistics helps you understand better and question more carefully what you read and hear, I will have accomplished my purpose.

AEC, 1991

A

ABRAMSON, L.Y., MATALSKY, G.I., & ALLOY, L.B. (1989). Hopelessness depression: A theory-based subtype of depression. *Psychological Review, 96,* 358–372.

ABSE, D.W., WILKINS, M.M., VAN DE CASTLE, R.L., BUXTON, W.D., DEMARS, J., & BROWN, R.S., & KIRSCHNER, L.G. (1974). Personality and behavioral characteristics of lung cancer patients. *Journal of Psychosomatic Research, 18* (2), 101–113.

ADAIR, J.G. (1981). Canadian psychology as a profession and discipline: Developments, issues and trends in the seventies. *Canadian Psychology, 22,* 163–172.

ADAMS, P.R., & ADAMS, G.R. (1984). Mount Saint Helens's ashfall: Evidence for a disaster stress reaction. *American Psychologist, 39,* 252–260.

ADLER, R.P., LESSER, G.S., MERINGOFF, L.K., ROBERTSON, T.S., & WARD, S. (1980). *The effects of television advertising on children.* Lexington, MA: D.C. Heath.

ADORNO, J.W., FRENKEL-BRUNSWICK, E., LEVINSON, D.J., & SANFORD, R.N. (1950). *The authoritarian personality.* New York: Harper & Row.

AGRAS, W.S., SCHNEIDER, J.A., ARNOW, B., RAEBURN, S.D., & TELCH, C.F. (1989). Cognitive-behavioral and response-prevention treatments for bulimia nervosa. *Journal of Consulting and Clinical Psychology, 57,* 215–221.

AINSWORTH, M.D.S. (1979). Infant-mother attachment. *American Psychologist, 34,* 932–937.

__________, BLEHAR, M.C., WATERS, E., & WALL, S. (1978). *Patterns of attachment: A psychological study of the strange situation.* Hillsdale, NJ: Erlbaum.

AKIL, H. (1978). Endorphins, beta-LPH and ACTH: Biochemical, pharmacological, and anatomical studies. *Advances in Biochemical Psychopharmacology, 18,* 125–139.

ALBERT, D.J., & WALSH, M.L. (1984). Neural systems and the inhibitory modulation of agonistic behavior: A comparison of mammalian species. *Neuroscience and Biobehavioral Reviews, 8,* 5–24.

ALCOCK, J.E. (1981). *Parapsychology, science or magic?* New York: Pergamon.

__________, CARMENT, D.W., & SADAVA, S.W. (1991). *A textbook of social psychology,* 2nd ed. Scarborough: Prentice-Hall Canada Inc.

ALEXANDER, F. (1950). *Psychosomatic medicine.* New York: Norton.

ALEXANDER, F.M. (1956). *Psychoanalysis and psychotherapy.* New York: W.W. Norton & Co.

__________. (1963). *Fundamentals of psychoanalysis.* New York: W.W. Norton & Co.

__________, & FRENCH, T.M. (1946). *Psychoanalytic therapy.* New York: Ronald Press Co.

ALLISON, C.W. (1986). The industrial bureaucrat. *Journal of General Management, 11*(3), 47–56.

ALLPORT, G.W. (1937). *Personality: A psychological interpretation.* New York: Holt, Rinehart and Winston.

__________. (1961). *Pattern and growth in personality.* New York: Holt, Rinehart and Winston.

ALTEMEYER, B. (1981). *Right-wing authoritarianism.* Winnipeg: University of Manitoba Press.

__________. (1988a). Marching in step: A psychological explanation of state terror. *The Sciences, 28*(2), 30–38.

__________. (1988b). *Enemies of freedom: Understanding right-wing authoritarianism.* San Francisco: Josey-Bass.

AMERICAN PSYCHIATRIC ASSOCIATION. (1987). *Diagnostic and statistical manual of mental disorders.* 1st ed., 1952; 2nd ed., 1968; 3rd ed., 1980; 3rd ed., revised, 1987. Washington, D.C.: American Psychiatric Association.

AMERICAN PSYCHOLOGICAL ASSOCIATION. (1974). *Standards for educational and psychological tests.* Washington: American Psychological Association.

AMKRAUT, A.A., & SOLOMON, G.F. (1977). From the symbolic stimulus to the pathophysiologic response: Immune mechanisms. In Z.J. Lipowski, D.R. Lipsitt, & P.C. Whybrow (eds.), *Psychosomatic medicine: Current trends and clinical applications.* New York: Oxford University Press.

ANASTASI, A. (1982). *Psychological testing.* New York: The Macmillan Company.

ANDERSON, J.R. (1985). *Cognitive psychology.* New York: W.H. Freeman.

ANDERSON, S.M., & KLATZKY, R.L. (1987). Traits and social stereotypes: Levels of categorization in person perception. *Journal of Personality and Social Psychology, 53,* 235–246.

ANDRUS, L.H., HYDE, D.F., & FISCHER, E. (1964). Smoking by high school students: Failure of a campaign to persuade adolescents not to smoke. *California Medicine, 101,* 246–247.

ARDREY, R. (1966). *The territorial imperative.* New York: Dell.

ARENDT, H. (1963). *Eichmann in Jerusalem: A report on the banality of evil.* New York: Viking Press.

ARGYRIS, C. (1976). *Increasing leadership effectiveness.* New York: John Wiley & Sons.

ARMSTRONG, D.M. (1979). Three types of consciousness – commentary. In Wolstenholme, G., & O'Connor, M., (eds.), *Brain and mind.* Amsterdam: Excerpta Medica.

ARNETT, J.L., MARTIN, R.M., STREINER, D.L., & GOODMAN, J.T. (1987). Hospital psychology in Canada. *Canadian Psychology, 28,* 161–171.

ARONSON, E., & OSHEROW, N. (1980). Cooperation, prosocial behavior, and academic performance: Experiments in the desegregated classroom. In L. Bickman (ed.), *Applied social psychology annual,* vol. 1. Beverly Hills, CA: Sage Publications.

ARONSON, E., TURNER, J.A., & CARLSMITH, J.M. (1963). Communicator credibility and communication discrepancy as determinants of opinion change. *Journal of Abnormal and Social Psychology, 67,* 31–36.

ASCH, S.E. (1951). Effects of group pressure upon the modification and distortion of judgments. In H.S. Guetzkow (ed.), *Groups, leadership, and man: Research in human relations.* Pittsburgh: Carnegie Press.

________. (1956). Studies of independence and conformity: A minority of one against a unanimous majority. *Psychological Monographs, 70,* (9, Whole No. 416).

ASCH, S.E., & ZUKIER, H. (1984). Thinking about persons. *Journal of Personality and Social Psychology, 46,* 1230–1240.

ASHMORE, R.D., & DEL BOCA, F.K. (1976). Psychological approaches to understanding intergroup conflicts. In P.A. Katz (ed.), *Towards the elimination of racism.* Elmsford, NY: Pergamon Press.

ASLIN, R.N., & SMITH, L.B. (1988). Perceptual development. *Annual Review of Psychology, 39,* 435–473.

ASPY, D.N., ROEBUCK, F.N., & BENOIT, D. (1987). Person-centered education in the information age. *Person Centered Review, 2,* 87–98.

ASSMUS, G., FARLEY, J.U., & LEHMANN, D.R. (1984, February). How advertising affects sales: Meta-analysis of econometric results. *Journal of Marketing Research, 21,* 65–74.

ATKINSON, J.W., & LITWIN, G.H. (1960). Achievement motive and test anxiety conceived as motive to approach success and motive to avoid failure. *Journal of Abnormal and Social Psychology, 60(1),* 52–63.

AUSTIN, W. (1966). *Music in the 20th century from Debussy through Stravinsky.* New York: W.W. Norton & Company.

AX, A.F. (1953). The physiological differentiation between fear and anger in humans. *Psychosomatic Medicine, 15,* 433–442.

AYLLON, T., & AZRIN, N.H. (1965). The measurement and reinforcement of behavior of psychotics. *Journal of the Experimental Analysis of Behavior, 8,* 357–383.

AZRIN, N. (1967). Pain and aggression. *Psychology Today, 1(1),* 26–33.

B

BACHMANN, R. (1984). Panel 3—The applicability of the Japanese model to U.S. public sector organizations: Applications of theory Z to American public institutions. *Public Productivity Review, 8(2),* 128–135.

BACHOP, M.W. (1989). Current research on psychoanalytic ideas. *Contemporary Psychology, 34,* 466–467.

BADDELEY, A. (1982). Amnesia: A minimal model and an interpretation. In Cermak, L.S. (ed.), *Human memory and amnesia.* Hillsdale, NJ: Erlbaum.

BAEKELAND, F., LUNDWALL, L., & KISSIN, B. (1975). Methods for the treatment of chronic alcoholism: A critical appraisal. In Y. Isreal (ed.), *Research advances in alcohol and drug problems,* vol. 2. New York: Wiley.

BAER, D.M., & HARRIS, F.R. (1963). Control of nursery school children's behavior by programming social reinforcement from their teachers. *American Psychologist, 18,* 343.

BALL, K., & SEKULAR, R. (1982). A specific and enduring improvement in visual motion discrimination. *Science, 218,* 697–698.

BALLINGER, C.B. (1981). The menopause and its syndromes. In J.G. Howells (ed.), *Modern perspectives in the psychiatry of middle age.* New York: Brunner/Mazel.

BALOGH, R.D., & PORTER, R.H. (1986). Olfactory preferences resulting from mere exposure in human neonates. *Infant Behavior and Development, 9,* 395–401.

BANDURA, A. (1965). Vicarious processes: A case of no-trial learning. In L. Berkowitz (ed.), *Advances in experimental social psychology,* vol 2. New York: Academic Press.

________. (1969). *Principles of behavior modification.* New York: Holt, Rinehart and Winston.

________. (1977). *Social-learning theory.* Englewood Cliffs, NJ: Prentice-Hall.

BANDURA, A., & ROSENTHAL, T.L. (1966). Vicarious classical conditioning as a function of arousal level. *Journal of Personality and Social Psychology, 3,* 54–62.

BANKS, M.S., & SALAPETEK, P. (1984). Infant visual perception. In M.M. Haith & J.J. Campos (eds.), *Infancy and developmental psychobiology,* vol. 2 of P. Mussen (ed.), *Handbook of child psychology,* 4th ed. New York: Wiley.

BANNISTER, R. (1985). *Brain's clinical neurology,* 6th ed. New York: Oxford University Press.

BARBER, T.X. (1969). *Hypnosis: A scientific approach.* New York: Van Nostrand Reinhold.

________. (1979). Suggested ("hypnotic") behavior: The trance paradigm versus an alternative paradigm. In E. Fromm & R.E. Shor (eds.). *Hypnosis: Developments in research and new perspectives.* Chicago: Aldine-Atherton.

BARD, P. (1934). The interaction of cognitive and physiological determinants of emotional state. In L. Berkowitz (ed.), *Advances in experimental social psychology.* NY: Academic Press.

BAREFOOT, J.C., DAHLSTROM, G., & WILLIAMS, R.B. (1983). Hostility, CHD incidence, and total mortality: A 25-year follow-up study of 255 physicians. *Psychosomatic Medicine, 45(1),* 59–63.

BAROFSKY, I. (1981). Issues and approaches to the psychosocial assessment of the cancer patient. In C.K. Prokop & L.A. Bradley (eds.), *Medical psychology: Contributions to behavioral medicine.* New York: Academic Press.

BARON, J.N., & BIELBY, W.T. (1986). The proliferation of job titles in organizations. *Administrative Science Quarterly, 31,* 561–587.

BARRON, F., & HARRINGTON, D.M. (1981). Creativity, intelligence, and personality. *Annual Review of Psychology, 32,* 439–476.

BARTLETT, F.C. (1932). *Remembering.* Cambridge, England: Cambridge University Press.

BASOW, S.A. (1980). *Sex-role stereotypes: Traditions and alternatives.* Belmont, CA: Brooks Cole.

BATESON, G., JACKSON, D.D., HALEY, J., & WEAKLAND, J. (1956). Toward a theory of schizophrenia. *Behavioral Science, 1,* 251–264.

BATSON, C.D. (1987). Prosocial motivation: Is it ever truly altruistic? In L. Berkowitz (ed.), *Advances in experimental social psychology.* New York: Academic Press.

BATSON, C.D., BOLEN, M.H., CROSS, J.A., & JEURINGER-BENEFIEL, H.E. (1986). Where is the altruism in the altruistic personality? *Journal of Person ality and Social Psychology, 50,* 212–220.

BAUMRIND, D. (1973). The development of instrumental competence through socialization. In A. Pick (ed.), *Minnesota symposium in child development,* vol. 7. Minneapolis: University of Minnesota Press.

BAXTER, G.D., & BOWERS, J.K. (1985, August). Beyond self-actualization: The persuasion of pygmalion. *Training & Development Journal, 39,* 69–71.

BEAL, A.L., PRIFITERA, A., & DANIEL, M.H. (1989). WISC-III and DAS: Suitability for Canadian children. *Canadian Psychology, 30(2),* 470.

BEAMAN, A.L., BARNES, P.J., KLENTZ, B., & MCQUIRK, B. (1978). Increasing helping rates through information dissemination: Teaching pays. *Personality and Social Psychology Bulletin, 4,* 406–411.

Beard, R.J. (1975). The menopause. *British Journal of Hospital Medicine, 12,* 631–637.

Beck, A.T. (1967). *Depression: Clinical, experimental and theoretical aspects.* New York: Harper and Row.

_________. (1976). *Cognitive therapy and the emotional disorders.* New York: International Universities Press.

Beck, A.T., Ward, C.H., Mendelson, M., Mock, J.E., & Erbaugh, J.K. (1962). Reliability of psychiatric diagnosis: II. A study of consistency of clinical judgments and ratings. *American Journal of Psychiatry, 119,* 351–357.

Beck, J., & Morgan, P.A. (1986). Designer drug confusion: A focus on MDMA. *Journal of Drug Education, 16,* 287–302.

Beck, K.H. (1979). The effects of positive and negative arousal upon attitudes, belief acceptance, behavioral intention, and behavior. *Journal of Social Psychology, 107,* 239–251.

Becker, M.H. (1976). Sociobehavioral determinants of compliance. In D.L. Sackett & R.B. Haynes (eds.), *Compliance with therapeutic regimens.* Baltimore: Johns Hopkins University Press.

Bellack, A.S. (1975). Behavior therapy for weight reduction: An evaluative review. *Addictive Behaviors: An International Journal, 1(1),* 73–82.

Bem, D.J. (1972). Self-perception theory. In L. Berkowitz (ed.), *Advances in experimental social psychology,* vol. 6. New York: Academic Press.

Bem. S.L. (1974). The measurement of psychological androgyny. *Journal of Consulting and Clinical Psychology, 42,* 155–162.

Bem, S.L., & Lenney, E. (1976). Sex typing and the avoidance of cross-sex behavior. *Journal of Personality and Social Psychology, 33,* 48–54.

Bem, S.L., Martyna, W., & Watson, C. (1976). Sex typing and androgyny: Further explorations of the expressive domain. *Journal of Personality and Social Psychology, 34,* 1016–1023.

Benbow, C.P. (1989). Gender differences in mathematical talent: Why and what can be done. *Canadian Psychology, 30,* 385.

Benbow, S.L., & Stanley, J.C. (1980). Sex differences in mathematical ability: Fact or artifact? *Science, 210,* 1262–1264.

Bennett, E.L., Diamond, M.C., Kerch, D., & Rosenzweig, M.R. (1964). Chemical and anatomical plasticity of the brain. *Science, 146,* 610–619.

Bennett, E.M., & Cohen, L.R. (1959). Personality patterns and contrasts. *Genetic Psychology Monographs, 59,* 101–155.

Benson, H. (1975). *The relaxation response.* New York: Morrow.

Benson, H., Arns, P.A., & Hoffman, J.W. (1981). The relaxation response and hypnosis. *International Journal of Clinical and Experimental Hypnosis, 29,* 259–270.

Benson, H., & Friedman, R. (1985). A rebuttal to the conclusions of David S. Holmes's article: "Meditation and somatic arousal reduction." *American Psychologist, 40,* 725–728.

Berger, P.A. (1978). Medical treatment of mental illness. *Science, 200,* 974–981.

Bergin, A.E. (1963). The effects of psychotherapy: Negative effects revisited. *Journal of Counseling Psychology, 10,* 244–250.

_________. (1980, February). Negative effects revisited: A reply. *Professional Psychology, 11,* 93–100.

Bergin, A.E., & Suinn, R.M. (1975). Individual psychotherapy and behavior therapy. *Annual Review of Psychology, 26,* 509–556.

Berkman, L.F. (1977). Social networks, host resistance, and mortality: A follow-up study of Alameda County residents. Unpublished doctoral dissertation, University of California, Berkeley.

Berkowitz, L. (ed.). (1979). *Advances in experimental social psychology,* vol. 12. New York: Academic Press.

_________. (1983). Aversively stimulated aggression: Some parallels and differences in research with animals and humans. *American Psychologist, 38,* 1135–1144.

_________. (1989). Advanced aggression. *Contemporary Psychology, 33,* 962–964.

Berman, J.S., Miller, R.C., & Massman, P.J. (1985). Cognitive therapy versus systematic desensitization: Is one treatment superior? *Psychological Bulletin, 97,* 451–461.

Bernard, L.L. (1924). *Instinct.* NY: Holt, Rinehart and Winston.

Bernstein, A. (1965). The psychoanalytic technique. In B.B. Wolman (ed.), *Handbook of clinical psychology.* New York: McGraw-Hill.

Berry, J.W., & Bourcier, D. (1989). Attitudes towards official bilingualism in eastern Ontario. *Canadian Psychology, 30,* 437.

Berscheid, E. (1985). Interpersonal attraction. In G. Lindzey & E. Aronson (eds.), *The handbook of social psychology,* vol. 2, 3rd ed. New York: Random House.

Berscheid, E., & Walster, E. (1974). Physical attractiveness. In L. Berkowitz (ed.), *Advances in experimental social psychology.* New York: Academic Press.

Best, J.A., & Bloch, M. (1979). Compliance in the control of cigarette smoking. In R.B. Hayens, D.W. Taylor, & D.L. Sackett (eds.), *Compliance in health care.* Baltimore: Johns Hopkins University Press.

Bieber, I., Dain, H.J., Dince, P.R., Drellich, M.G., Grand, G.C., Gundlach, R.G., Kremer, M.W., Rifkin, A.H., Wilbur, C.B., & Bieber, T.B. (1962). *Homosexuality: A psychoanalytical study.* New York: Random House.

Bierman, R. (1969). Dimensions of interpersonal facilitation in psychotherapy and child development. *Psychological Bulletin, 71,* 338–352.

Binet, A., & Simon, T. (1905). Methodes nouvelles pour le diagnostic du niveau intellectuel des anormaux. *L'Année psychologique, 11,* 191–244.

Blake, B.G. (1967, May). A follow-up of alcoholics treated by behavior therapy. *Behavior Research and Therapy, 5,* 89–94.

Blake, R., & Hirsch, H.V.B. (1975). Deficits in binocular depth perception in cats after alternating monocular deprivation. *Science, 190,* 1114–1116.

Blaise, R., & Mouton, J. (1964). *The managerial grid.* Houston: Gulf.

Blakemore, C. *Mechanics of the mind.* New York: Cambridge University Press.

Blanchard, E.B., & Epstein, L.H. (1978). *A biofeedback primer.* Reading, Mass.: Addison-Wesley.

Blaney, P.H. (1986). Affect and memory: A review. *Psychological Bulletin, 99,* 229–246.

Blank, A.A. (1982). Stresses of war: The example of Vietnam. In L. Goldberger & S. Breznitz (eds.), *Handbook of stress.* New York: Free Press.

Block, A. (1980). An investigation of the response of the spouse to chronic pain behavior. *Pain, 9,* 243–252.

Block, J.H. (1976). Issues, problems, and pitfalls in assessing sex differences: A critical review of the psychology of sex differences. *Merrill-Palmer Quarterly, 22,* 283–308.

_________. (1978). Another look at sex differentiation in the socialization behaviours of mothers and fathers. In J.A. Sherman & F.L. Denmark (eds.), *The psychology of women: Future directions in research.* New York: Psychological Dimensions.

Bloom, F.E., Lazerson, A., & Hofstadter, L. (1985). *Brain, mind, and behavior.* New York: W.H. Freeman.

Bock, R.D., & Kolakowski, D. (1973, January). Further evidence of sex-linked major gene influence on human spatial visualizing ability. *American Journal of Human Genetics, 25,* 1–14.

Borgen, F.H. (1984). Counseling psychology, *Annual Review of Psychology, 35,* 579–604.

Borke, H. (1975). Piaget's mountains revisited: Changes in the egocentric landscape. *Developmental Psychology, 11*, 240–243.

Botvin, G.J., & Murray, F.B. (1975). The efficacy of peer modeling and social conflict in the acquisition of conservation. *Child Development, 46*, 796–799.

Bouchard, T.J., Jr. (1984). Twins reared together and apart: What they tell us about human diversity. In S.W. Fox (ed.), *Individuality and determinism*. New York: Plenum Press.

Bountrogianni, M. (1986). Metaphorical competence in bilingual children. *Canadian Psychology, 27*, 65.

Bower, G.H. (1973). Educational applications of mnemonic devices. In K.O. Doyle, Jr. (ed.), *Interaction: Readings in human psychology*. Boston: D.C. Heath.

———. (1981). Mood and memory. *American Psychologist, 36*, 129–148.

Bower, G.H., Clark, M., Winzenz, D., & Lesgold, A. (1969). Hierarchal retrieval schemes in recall of categorized word lists. *Journal of Verbal Learning and Verbal Behavior, 3*, 323–343.

Bowers, K.S. (1984). Hypnosis. In N.S. Endler & J. McV. Hunt (eds.). *Personality and behavioral disorders*, 2nd ed. New York: Wiley.

———. (1987). Revisioning the unconscious. *Canadian Psychology, 28*, 93–104.

Bowers, K.S., & Davidson, T.M. (1986). On the importance of individual differences in hypnotic ability. *The Behavioral and Brain Sciences, 9*, 468–469.

Boy, A.V. (1989). Psychodiagnosis: A person-centered perspective. *Person-Centered Review, 4*, 132–151.

Bradbury, T.N., & Fincham, F.D. (1988). Individual difference variables in close relationships: A contextual model of marriage as an integrative framework. *Journal of Personality and Social Psychology, 54*, 713–721.

Brady, J.S. (1958). Ulcers in "executive" monkeys. *Scientific American, 199(4)*, 95–100.

Bransford, J.D., & Stein, B.S. (1984). *The ideal problem solver*. New York: W.H. Freeman.

Breland, K., & Breland, M. (1961). The misbehavior of organisms. *American Psychologist, 16*, 681–684.

Brickman, P., Rabinowitz, V.C., Karuza, J., Coates, D., Cohn, E., & Kidder, L. (1982). Models of helping and coping. *American Psychologist, 37*, 368–384.

Briggs, G.E. (1957). Retroactive inhibition as a function of the degree of original and interpolated learnings. *Journal of Experimental Psychology, 53(1)*, 60–67.

Brody, E.B., & Brody, N. (1976). *Intelligence: Nature, determinants, and consequences*. New York: Academic Press.

Brooks-Gunn, J. (1986). Pubertal processes and girls' psychological adaptation. In R.M. Lerner & T.T. Foch (eds.), *Biological-psychosocial interactions in early adolescence: A life-span perspective*. Hillsdale, NJ: Erlbaum.

Brown, G.W., Bone, M., Dalison, B., & Wing, J.K. (1966). *Schizophrenia and social care*. London: Oxford University Press.

Brown, P.L., & Jenkins, H.M. (1968). Autoshaping of the pigeon's key peck. *Journal of the Experimental Analysis of Behavior, 11(1)*, 1–8.

Brown, R. (1986). *Social psychology*, 2nd ed. New York: Free Press.

Brownell, K.D. (1982). Understanding and treating obesity. *Journal of Consulting and Clinical Psychology, 50*, 820–840.

Brownell, K.D., Marlatt, G.A., Lichtenstein, E., & Wilson, T.G. (1986). Understanding and preventing relapse. *American Psychologist, 41(7)*, 765–782.

Bruner, J.S., & Goodman, C.C. (1947). Value and need as organizing factors in perception. *Journal of Abnormal and Social Psychology, 42*, 33–44.

Bruner, J., & Postman, L. (1949). On the perception of incongruity: A paradigm. *Journal of Personality, 18*, 206–223.

Buchsbaum, M.S., Kessler, R., King, A., Johnson, J., & Cappelletti, J. (1984). Simultaneous cerebral glucography with positron emission tomography and topographic electroencephalography. In G. Pfurtscheller, E.J. Jonkman, and F.H. Lopes da Dilva (eds.), *Brain ischemia: Quantitative EEG and imaging techniques*. Amsterdam: Elsevier.

Buck, R. (1977). Nonverbal communication of affect in preschool children. Relationships with personality and skin conductance. *Journal of Personality and Social Psychology, 35*, 225–236.

Buckhout, R. (1974, December). Eyewitness testimony, *Scientific American, 231(6)*, 23–31.

Burnett, S.A. (1986). Sex related differences in spatial ability: Are they trivial? *American Psychologist, 41*, 1012–1014.

Burt, C. (1966). The genetic determination of differences in intelligence: A study of monozygotic twins reared together and apart. *British Journal of Psychology, 57*, 137–153.

———. (1972). Inheritance of general intelligence. *American Psychologist, 27*, 175–190.

Buss, A.H., & Plomin, R.A. (1975). *A temperamental theory of personality development*. London: Wiley.

Butcher, J.N. (1984). Current developments in MMPI use: An international perspective. In J.N. Butcher & C.D. Spielberger (eds.), *Advances in personality assessment*, vol. 4. Hillsdale, NJ: Erlbaum.

Butcher, J.N., & Keller, L.S. (1984). Objective personality assessment. In G. Goldstein, & M. Hersen (eds.), *Handbook of psychological assessment*. New York: Pergamon.

Butcher, J.N., & Owen, P.L. (1978). Objective personality inventories: Recent research and some contemporary issues. In B. Wolman (ed.), *Handbook of clinical diagnosis of mental disorders*. New York: Plenum.

Butcher, R.A., & Harlow, H.F. (1954). Persistence of visual exploration in monkeys. *Journal of Comparative and Physiological Psychology, 47*, 258–263.

Butler, J.M., & Rice, L.N. (1963). Audience, self-actualization, and drive theory. In J.M. Wepman and R.W. Heine (eds.), *Concepts of personality*. Chicago: Aldine.

Butler, R.A. (1954, February). Curiosity in monkeys. *Scientific American, 190*, 70–75.

Byrne, D., Clore, G.L., & Smeaton, G. (1986). The attraction hypothesis: Do similar attitudes affect anything? *Journal of Personality and Social Psychology, 51*, 1167–1170.

C

Cameron, N. (1947). *The psychology of behavior disorders*. Boston: Houghton Mifflin.

Campbell, B.A., & Church, R.M. (eds.). (1969). *Punishment and aversive behavior*. New York: Appleton-Century-Crofts.

Campbell, D.T., & Coulter, X. (1976). The ontogenesis of learning and memory. In M.R. Rosenzweig & E.L. Bennet (eds.), *Neural mechanisms of learning and memory*. Cambridge, MA: MIT Press.

Canadian Manufacturing Association. (1987). *CMA—The Management Accounting Magazine, 61*, 18–24.

Canadian Psychological Association. (1986). *A Canadian code of ethics for psychologists*. CPA, Vincent Rd., Old Chelsea, Que., J0X 2N0.

Cannon, W.B. (1927). The James-Lange theory of emotions: A critical examination as an alternative theory. *American Journal of Psychology, 39(1)*, 106–124.

———. (1929). *Bodily changes in pain, hunger, fear and rage*. New York: Appleton.

Cannon, W.B., & Washburn, A.L. (1912). An exploration of hunger. *American Journal of Physiology, 29*, 441–454.

CAPLAN, P.J., MACPHERSON, G.M., & TOBIN, P. (1985). Do sex-related differences in spatial abilities exist? A multilevel critique with new data. *American Psychologist, 40,* 786–799.

________. (1986). The magnified molehill and the misplaced focus: Sex-related differences in spatial ability revisited. *American Psychologist, 41,* 1016–1018.

CAPORRIMO, R. (1989). Review of *Gender and Stress. Sex Roles, 19,* 406–408.

CAPPE, R.F., & ALDEN, L.E. (1986). A comparison of treatment strategies for clients functionally impaired by extreme shyness and social avoidance. *Journal of Consulting and Clinical Psychology, 54,* 796–801.

CARKHUFF, R.R., & BERENSON, B.G. (1977). *Beyond counseling and therapy,* 2nd ed. New York: Holt, Rinehart and Winston.

CARLSON, J.G. (1989). Affirmative: In support of researching the Myers-Briggs Type Indicator. *Journal of Counseling and Development, 67,* 484–486.

CARLSON, N.K., DRURY, C.G., & WEBBER, J.A. (1977). Discriminability of large weights. *Ergonomics, 20(1),* 87–90.

CARLSON, N.R. (1986). *Physiology of behavior.* Boston: Allyn and Bacon.

CARPENDALE, J.I., & BUSH, A.J. (1989). Real-life moral judgment. *Canadian Psychology, 30(2),* 354.

CARPENTER, H.H. (1971). Formal organizational structural factors and perceived job satisfaction of classroom teachers, *Administrative Science Quarterly, 16,* 460–465.

CARSON, S.A. (1985). Participatory management beefs up the bottom line. *Personnel, 62(7),* 45–48.

________. (1987). Good news for participation. *Management World, 16(1),* 26–28.

CARTER, E.N. (1973). The stimulus control of a response system in the absence of awareness. Unpublished doctoral dissertation, University of Massachusetts.

CARTWRIGHT, R.D. (1978). Sleep and dreams, Part II. *Annual Review of Psychology, 29,* 223–252.

CASAS, E.F. (1989). L'indicateur de types psychologiques—version Française du MBTI standardisée au Canada. *Canadian Psychology, 30(2),* 320.

CASEY, R.J., & BERMAN, J.S. (1985). The outcome of psychotherapy with children. *Psychological Bulletin, 98,* 388–400.

CASSEL, J. (1976). The contribution of the social environment to host resistance. *American Journal of Epidemiology, 104(2),* 107–123.

CASTILLO, M., & BUTTERWORTH, G. (1981). Neonatal localization of a sound in visual space. *Perception, 10,* 331–338.

CASTRO, K.G., LIFSON, A.R., WHITE, C.R., BUSH, T.J., CHAMBERLAND, M.E., LEKATSAS, A.M., & JAFFE, H.W. (1988). Investigation of AIDS patients with no previously identified risk factors. *Journal of the American Medical Association, 259,* 1338–1342.

CATTELL, R.B. (1950). *Personality: A systematic theoretical and factual study.* New York: McGraw-Hill.

________. (1965). *The scientific analysis of personality.* Baltimore: Penguin Books.

________. (1983). *Structured personality learning theory.* New York: Praeger.

CATTEL, B.B., EBER, H.W., & TATSUOKA, M.M. (1970). *Handbook for the Sixteen Personality Factor Questionnaire (16PF).* Champaign, IL: Institute for Personality and Ability Testing.

CELLA, D.F., & TROSS, S. (1986). Psychological adjustment to survival from Hodgkins disease. *Journal of Consulting and Clinical Psychology, 54,(5),* 616–622.

CHAMBONNIÈRES, JACQUES DE. (1967). *Les pieces de clavessin.* Facsimile of the 1670 Paris Edition. vol. 1. New York: Broude Brothers.

CHANDRA, S. (1976). Repression, dreaming and primary process thinking: Skinnerian formulations of some Freudian facts. *Behaviorism, 4,* 53–75.

CHERNISS, C. (1986). Different ways of thinking about burnout. In E. Seidman and J. Rappaport (eds.), *Redefining social problems.* New York: Plenum Press.

CHERRY, C. (1966). *On human communication: A review, a survey, and a criticism,* 2nd ed. Cambridge, MA: M.I.T. Press.

CHERULNIK, P.D. (1979). Sex differences in the expression of emotion in a structured social encounter. *Sex Roles, 5,* 413–424.

CHESNO, F.A., & KILMANN, P.R. (1975). Effects of stimulation intensity on sociopathic avoidance learning. *Journal of Abnormal Psychology, 84,* 144–151.

CHILD, I. (1985). Psychology and anomalous observations: The question of ESP in dreams. *American Psychologist, 40,* 1219–1230.

CHOMSKY, N. (1968). *Language and mind.* New York: Harcourt, Brace, & World.

________. (1975). *Reflections on language.* New York: Pantheon.

CIALDINI, R.B., VINCENT, J.E., LEWIS, S.K., CATALAN, J., WHEELER, D., & DARBY, L. (1975). Reciprocal concessions procedure for inducing compliance: The door-in-the-face technique. *Journal of Personality and Social Psychology, 31,* 206–215.

CLARKE-STEWART, K.A. (1973). Interactions between mothers and their young children: Characteristics and consequences. *Monograph of the Society of Research in Child Development, 38,* (6–7, serial no. 153.).

CLECKLY, J. (1976). *The mask of sanity,* 5th ed. St. Louis: Mosby.

CLÉMENT, R., GARDNER, R.C., & SMYTHE, P.C. (1977). Interethnic contact: Attitudinal consequences. *Canadian Journal of Behavioural Science, 9,* 205–215.

CLEMMER, E.J. (1986). Not so anomalous observations question ESP in dreams. *American Psychologist, 41(10),* 1173–1174.

COBB, S., & ROSE, R.M. (1973). Hypertension, peptic ulcer, and diabetes in air traffic controllers. *Journal of the American Medical Association, 224,* 489–493.

COE, W.C., & SARBIN, T.R. (1977). Hypnosis from the standpoint of a contextualist. *Annals of the New York Academy of Sciences, 296,* 2–13.

COHEN, F. (1979). Personality, stress, and the development of physical illness. In G.C. Stone, F. Cohen, & N.E. Adler (eds.), *Health psychology: A handbook.* San Francisco: Jossey-Bass.

COHEN, F., & LAZARUS, R.S. (1979). Coping with the stresses of illness. In G.C. Stone, F. Cohen, & N.E. Adler (eds.), *Health psychology: A handbook.* San Francisco: Jossey-Bass.

COLE, J.O., & DAVIS, J.M. (1975). Antidepressant drugs. In A.M. Freedman, H.I. Kaplan, & B.J. Saddock (eds.), *Comprehensive textbook of psychiatry II,* vol. 2. Baltimore: Williams & Wilkins.

COLLINS, A.M., & QUILLIAN, M.R. (1969). Retrieval time from semantic memory. *Journal of Verbal Learning and Verbal Behavior, 8,* 240–247.

CONDON, W.S., & SANDER, L. (1974). Neonate movement is synchronized with adult speech: Interactional participation and language acquisition. *Science, 183,* 99–101.

CONNOLLY, J.A., & ONDRACK, C. (1989). Peer networks, self-image and subjective wellbeing in adolescence. *Canadian Psychology, 30(2),* 272.

CONSTANTIOPLE, A. (1973). Masculinity-femininity: An exception to a famous dictum? *Psychological Bulletin, 80,* 389–407.

COOK, S. (1979). *Social science and school desegregation: Did we mislead the supreme court?* Boulder, CO: Institute of Behavioral Science, University of Colorado.

COOPER, M. (1985). *Beethovan: The last decade, 1817–1827.* London and New York: Oxford University Press.

COOPERSMITH, S. (1967). *The antecedents of self-esteem.* San Francisco: Freeman.

Corah, N.L. (1965). Differentiation in children and their parents. *Journal of Personality, 33*, 300–308.

Cosby, B. (1968, December). The regular way. *Playboy*, 288–289.

Cosentino, F., & Heilbrun, A.B. (1964). Anxiety correlates of sex-role identity in college students. *Psychological Reports, 14*, 729–730.

Cottington, E.M., Matthews, K.A., Talbott, E., & Kuller, L.H. (1980). Environmental events preceding sudden death in women. *Psychosomatic Medicine, 42*, 567–574.

Cowan, N. (1987). Auditory sensory storage in relation to the growth of sensation and acoustic information extraction. *Journal of Experimental Psychology, 13*, 204–215.

Craik, F.I.M., & Lockhart, R.S. (1972). Levels of processing: A framework for memory research. *Journal of Verbal Learning and Verbal Behavior, 11*, 671–684.

Craik, F.I.M., & Tulving, E. (1975). Depth of processing and the retention of words in episodic memory. *Journal of Experimental Psychology: General, 104*, 268–294.

Crick, F., & Mitchison, G. (1983). The function of dream sleep. *Nature, 304*, 111–114.

Cunningham, A.J. (1985). The influence of mind on cancer. *Canadian Psychology, 26*, 13–29.

Cyr, J.J., & Atkinson, L. (1987). Test item bias in the WISC-R. *Canadian Journal of Behavioural Science, 19(1)*, 101–107.

D

Darley, C.F., Tinklenberg, J.R., Roth, W.T., Hollister, L.E., & Atkinson, R.C. (1973). Influence of marijuana on storage and retrieval process in memory. *Memory and Cognition, 1*, 196–200.

Darley, J.M., & Latané, B. (1968). Bystander intervention in emergencies: Diffusion of responsibility. *Journal of Personality and Social Psychology, 8*, 377–383.

Darwin, C. (1873a). *On the origin of species by means of natural selection, on the preservation of favored races in the struggle for life.* London: John Murray.

________. (1873b). *The expression of the emotions in man and animals.* London: John Murray.

________. (1904). *The descent of man, and selection in relation to sex.* London: John Murray.

Dattore, P.J., Shontz, F.C., & Coyne, L. (1980). Premorbid personality differentiation of cancer and noncancer groups: A test of the hypothesis of cancer proneness. *Journal of Consulting and Clinical Psychology, 48*, 388–394.

Davidson, P.O. (1981). Some cultural, political and professional antecedents of community psychology in Canada. *Canadian Psychology, 22*, 315–320.

Davis, H.P., & Squire, L.R. (1984). Protein synthesis and memory: A review. *Psychological Bulletin, 96*, 518–559.

Davison, G.C., & Neale, J.M. (1990). *Abnormal Psychology*, 5th ed. New York: John Wiley & Sons.

Dawson, M.E. (1970). Cognition and conditioning: Effects of masking the CS-UCS contingency on human classical conditioning. *Journal of Experimental Psychology, 85*, 389–396.

Deaux, K. (1976a). A perspective on the attribution process. In J.H. Harvey, W.J. Ickes, & R.F. Kidd (eds.), *New directions in attribution research.* Hillsdale, NJ: Erlbaum.

________. (1976b). *The behavior of women and men.* Monterey, CA: Brooks Cole.

________. (1985). Sex and gender. *Annual Review of Psychology, 36*, 49–81.

Deci, E.L., & Ryan, R.M. (1980). The empirical exploration of intrinsic motivational processes. In L. Berkowitz (ed.), *Advances in experimental social psychology*, vol. 13. New York: Academic Press.

Deckner, C.W., Hill, J.T., & Bourne, J.R. (1972). Shaping of gastric motility in humans. *Proceedings of the 80th Annual Convention of the American Psychological Association.* Washington, D.C.

Delgado, J.M.R. (1969). *Physical control of the mind.* New York: Harper & Row.

Dellas, M., & Gaier, E.L. (1970). Identification of creativity: The individual. *Psychological Bulletin, 73(1)*, 55–73.

DeLongis, A., Coyne, J.C., Dakof, G., Folkman, S., & Lazarus, R.S. (1982). Relationship of daily hassles, uplifts, and major life events to health status. *Health Psychology, 1(2)*, 119–136.

Dement, W.C. (1960). The effect of dream deprivation. *Science, 131*, 1705–1707.

________. (1974). *Some must watch while some must sleep.* New York: Norton.

Dennis, W. (1940). Does culture appreciably affect patterns of infant behavior? *Journal of Social Psychology, 12*, 305–317.

Denton, K.L., Krebs, D.L., & Carpendale, J.I. (1989). The self-righteous bias in moral attribution. *Canadian Psychology, 30(4)*, 355.

Depner, C.E., & Ingersoll-Dayton, B. (1988). Supportive relationships in later life. *Psychology and Aging, 3*, 348–357.

Depue, R.A., & Monroe, S.M. (1978). Learned helplessness in the perspective of the depressive disorders: Conceptual and definitional issues. *Journal of Abnormal Psychology, 87*, 3–20.

Derogatis, L.R. (1986). Psychology in cancer medicine: A perspective and overview. *Journal of Consulting and Clinical Psychology, 54*, 632–638.

Derryberry, D. (1988). Experimental analysis of the unconscious? *Contemporary Psychology, 33*, 877–878.

Dershowitz, A.M. (1986). *Reversal of fortune inside the Von Bulow case.* New York: Random House.

Deutsch, J.A., Young, W.G., & Kalogeris, T.J. (1978). The stomach signals satiety. *Science, 201*, 165–167.

Deutsch, M., & Gerard, H.B. (1955). A study of normative and informational influences on social judgment. *Journal of Abnormal and Social Psychology, 51*, 629–636.

DeValois, R., & DeValois, K. (1975). Neural coding of color. In E.C. Carterette & M.P. Friedman (eds.), *Handbook of perception*, vol. 5. New York: Academic.

Digman, J.M. (1986). Further specification of the five robust factors of personality. *Journal of Personality and Social Psychology, 50*, 116–123.

Dillbeck, M.C., & Orme-Johnson, D.W. (1987). Physiological differences between transcendental meditation and rest. *American Psychologist, 42*, 879–881.

DiMatteo, M.R., Hays, R.D., & Prince, L.M. (1986). Relationship of physicians' nonverbal communication skill to patient satisfaction, appointment noncompliance, and physician workload. *Health Psychology, 5*, 581–594.

Dion, K.K., Berscheid, E., & Walster, E. (1972). What is beautiful is good. *Journal of Personality and Social Psychology, 24*, 285–290.

Dion, K.L., Dion, K.K., & Pak, A.W. (1989). Correlates of self-confidence in English vs. Chinese in members of Toronto's Chinese community. *Canadian Psychology, 30*, 438.

Dixon, N.F. (1971). *Subliminal perception: The nature of a controversy.* London: McGraw-Hill.

________. (1981). *Preconscious processing.* New York: Wiley.

Dohrenwend, B.P., & Shrout, P.E. (1985). "Hassles" in the conceptualization and measurement of life stress variables. *American Psychologist, 40*, 780–785.

Dollard, J., Doob, L.W., Miller, N.E., Mowrer, O.H., Sears, R.R., Ford, C.S., Hovland, C.I., & Sollenberger, R.I. (1939). *Frustration and aggression.* New Haven: Yale University Press.

DOLLARD, J., & MILLER, N.E. (1950). *Personality and psychotherapy: An analysis in terms of learning, thinking and culture.* New York: McGraw-Hill.

DOMJAN, M., & NASH, S. (1989). Conditioning of sexual and reproductive behavior: Extending the hegemony to the propagation of species. *Behavior and Brain Sciences, 12(1),* 138–139.

DOVE, A. (1968, July 15). Taking the chitling test. *Newsweek,* 51–52.

DRUCKER, P. (1954). *The practice of management.* New York: Harper & Row.

DRUCKMAN, D., & SWETS, J.A. (eds.). (1988). *Enhancing human performance: Issues, theories, and techniques.* Washington, DC: National Academy Press.

DUNBAR, J.M. (1980). Assessment of medication compliance: A review. In R.B. Haynes, M.E. Mattson, & T.O. Engebretson (eds.), *Patient compliance to prescribed antihypertensive medication regimens: A report to the National Heart, Lung and Blood Institute.* Bethesda, MD: National Heart, Lung and Blood Institute.

DUNBAR, J.M., & STUNKARD, A.J. (1979). Adherence to diet and drug regimen. In R. Levy, B. Rifkind, B. Dennis, & N. Ernst (eds.), *Nutrition, lipids and coronary heart disease.* New York: Raven Press.

DUNCAN, C.P. (1949). The retroactive effect of electroshock on learning. *Journal of Comparative and Physiological Psychology, 42,* 32–44.

DUNCAN, J. (1980). The locus of interference in the perception of simultaneous stimuli. *Psychological Review, 87,* 272–300.

DUNCKER, K. (1945). On problem solving. *Psychological Monographs, 58(5),* 1–114.

DUNN, R.J. (1986). General hospital psychology. *Canadian Psychology, 27(1),* 44–50.

DUTTON, D., & ARON, A. (1974). Some evidence for heightened sexual attraction under conditions of high anxiety. *Journal of Personality and Social Psychology, 30,* 510–517.

DWECK, C.S., & BUSH, E.S. (1976). Sex differences in learned helplessness: I. Differential debilitation with peer and adult evaluators. *Developmental Psychology, 12,* 147–156.

DWORETZKY, J.P. (1985). *Psychology,* 2nd ed. St. Paul, MN: West Publishing.

E

EAGLY, A.H., & CARLI, L. (1981). Sex differences in influenceability. *Psychological Bulletin, 85,* 86–116.

EATON, W.O., & ENNES, L.R. (1986). Sex differences in human motor activity level. *Psychological Bulletin, 100,* 19–28.

EBBINGHAUS, H. (1913). *Memory.* New York: Columbia University. (Originally published 1885, Liepzig: Altenberg).

EDELWICH, J., & BRODSKY, A. (1980). *Burnout: Stages of disillusionment in the helping professions.* New York: Human Services Press.

EDWARDS, J. (1989). The social psychology of language and identity. *Canadian Psychology, 30,* 438.

EDWARDS, J., DICLEMENTE, C., & SAMUELS, M.L. (1985). Psychological characteristics: A pretreatment survival marker of patients with testicular cancer. *Journal of Psychosocial Oncology, 3,* 79–94.

EHRHARDT, A.A., & BAKER, S.W. (1973). Hormonal aberrations and their implications for the understanding of normal sex differentiation. Paper presented at the meeting of the Society for Research in Child Development, Philadelphia.

EHRLICHMAN, H., & HALPERN, J.N. (1988). Affect and memory: Effects of pleasant and unpleasant odors on retrieval of happy and unhappy memories. *Journal of Personality and Social Psychology, 55,* 769–779.

EICH, E. (1984). Memory for unattended events: Remembering with and without awareness. *Memory and Cognition, 12(2),* 105–111.

EICH, E., & METCALFE, J. (1989). Mood dependent memory for internal versus external events. *Journal of Experimental Psychology: Learning, Memory, and Cognition, 15,* 443–455.

EKMAN, P. (1980). *The face of man: Expressions of universal emotions in a New Guinea village.* NY: Garland STPM Press.

________. (1984). Expression and the nature of emotion. In K.R. Schert & P. Ekman (eds.), *Approaches to emotion.* Hillsdale, NJ: Erlbaum.

EKMAN, P., SORENSON, E.R., & FRIESEN, W.V. (1969, April). Paracultural elements in facial displays in emotion. *Science, 164,* 86–88.

ELDERSVELD, S.J., & DODGE, R.W. (1954). Personal contact or mail propaganda? An experiment in voting turnout and attitude change. In D. Katz, D. Cartwright, S. Eldersveld, & A.M. Lee (eds.), *Public opinion and propaganda.* New York: Dryden Press.

ELIOT, J. (1986). Comment on Caplan, MacPherson, and Tobin. *American Psychologist, 41,* 1011.

ELLIOTT, R., FARRINGTON, B., & MANHEIMER, H. (1988). Eyewitnesses credible and discredible. *Journal of Applied Social Psychology, 18,* 1411–1422.

ELLIS, A. (1962). *Reason and emotion in psychotherapy.* New York: Lyle Stuart.

________. (1973). Rational-emotive therapy. In R. Corsini (ed.), *Current psychotherapies.* Itasca, IL: F.E. Peacock Publishers.

________. (1977). Rational-emotive therapy: Research data that support the clinical and personality hypothesis of RET and other modes of cognitive behavior therapy. *The Counseling Psychologist, 7(1),* 2–42.

________. (1985). Cognition and affect in emotional disturbance. *American Psychologist, 40,* 471.

________. (1989). Dangers of transpersonal psychology: A reply to Ken Wilbur. *Journal of Counseling and Development, 67,* 336–337.

ELLIS, A., & BERNARD, M.E. (eds.). (1985). *Clinical applications of rational-emotive therapy.* New York: Plenum.

ELLIS, H.C., & HUNT, R.R. (1989). *Fundamentals of human memory and cognition,* 4th ed. Dubuque, IA: Wm. C. Brown Publishers.

ENGEL, G.L. (1968). A life setting conductive to illness: The giving-up-given-up complex. *Bulletin of the Menninger Clinic, 32,* 355–365.

________. (1971). Sudden and rapid death during psychological stress: Folklore or folk wisdom? *Annals of Internal Medicine, 74,* 771–782.

EPSTEIN, S. (1983). The stability of confusion: A reply to Mischel & Peake. *Psychological Review, 90,* 179–184.

ERDELYI, M.H. (1974). A new look at the new look: Perceptual defense and vigilance. *Psycological Review, 81,* 1–25.

ERIKSEN, C., & PIERCE, J. (1968). Defense mechanisms. In E. Borgotta and W. Lambert (eds.), *Handbook of personality theory and research.* Chicago: Rand McNally.

ERIKSON, E.H. (1963). *Childhood and society.* New York: W.W. Norton.

________. (1968). *Identity: Youth and crisis.* New York: W.W. Norton.

ERON, L.D. (1980). Prescription for reduction of aggression. *American Psychologist, 35,* 244–252.

________. (1982). Parent-child interaction, television violence, and aggression in children. *American Psychologist, 37,* 197–211.

ESCHER, M.C. (1985). *Escher on Escher: Exploring the infinite.* New York: Harry N. Abrams, Inc.

EVANS, C. (1984). *Landscapes of the night: How and why we dream.* New York: Viking.

EVANS, F.J. (1985). Expectancy, therapeutic instructions, and the placebo response. In L. White, B. Tursky, & G.E. Schwartz (eds.), *Placebo: Theory, research and mechanisms.* New York: Guilford Press.

EVANS, N.J.R., BALDWIN, J.A., & GATH, D. (1974). The incidence of cancer among in-patients with affective disorders. *British Journal of Psychiatry, 124*, 518–525.

EVANS, R.B. (1969). Childhood parental relationships of homosexual men. *Journal of Consulting and Clinical Psychology, 33*(2), 129–135.

EVANS, R.I. (1975). Discussion facilitation statement for Session 'A': Lifestyle development and modification session. In S.M. Weiss (ed.), *Proceedings of the National Heart and Lung Institute Working Conference on Health Behavior.* DHEW Publication No. (NIH) 76–868. Washington, DC: U.S. Government Printing Office.

EYSENCK, H.J. (1952). The effects of psychotherapy: An evaluation. *Journal of Consulting Psychology, 16*, 319–327.

________. (1960). Learning theory and behaviour therapy. In H.J. Eysenck (ed.), *Behaviour therapy and the neuroses: Readings in modern methods of treatment derived from learning theory.* Oxford, England: Pergamon Press.

________. (1961). The effects of psychotherapy. In H.J. Eysenck (ed.), *Handbook of abnormal psychology: An experimental approach.* New York: Basic Books.

________. (1964). *Crime and personality.* Boston: Houghton Mifflin.

________. (1973). Personality and the law of effect. In D.E. Berlyne & K.B. Madsen (eds.), *Pleasure, reward, preference.* New York: Academic Press.

________. (1979). The conditioning model of neurosis. *The Behavioral and Brain Sciences, 2*, 155–166.

________. (1982). *Personality genetics and behavior.* New York: Praeger.

________. (1986). A critique of contemporary classification and diagnosis. In T. Millon and G.L. Klerman (eds.), *Contemporary directions in psychopathology.* New York: Guilford.

EYSENCK, H.J., & KAMIN, L. (1981). *The intelligence controversy: H.J. Eysenck vs. Leon Kamin.* New York: Wiley-Interscience.

EYSENCK, H.J., & RACHMAN, S. (1965). *The causes and cures of neurosis: An introduction to modern behavior therapy based on learning theory and the principles of conditioning.* San Diego: Knapp.

F

FAHRION, S.L., NORRIS, P., GREEN, A., & GREEN, E. (1986). The biobehavioral treatment of essential hypertension: A single group outcome study. *Biofeedback and Self-regulation, 11*, 257–278.

FANTZ, R.L. (1961, May). The origin of form perception. *Scientific American*, 66–72.

FARINA, A. (1976). *Abnormal psychology.* Englewood Cliffs, NJ: Prentice-Hall.

FAZIO, R., ZANNA, M.P., & COOPER, J. (1977). Dissonance and self-perception: An integrative view of each theory's proper domain of application. *Journal of Experimental Social Psychology, 13*, 464–479.

FEIN, M. (1974). Job enrichment: A reevaluation. *Sloan Management Review, 15*(2), 69–88.

FELLERS, G., MCINNIS, C., CAPELLI, M., & VAILLANCOURT, R. (1987). WAIS-R Information subtest bias for Canadian high school students. *Canadian Journal of Behavioural Science, 19*(1), 108–114.

FESTINGER, L. (1957). *A theory of cognitive dissonance.* Stanford: Stanford University Press.

FESTINGER, L., & CARLSMITH, J.M. (1959). Cognitive consequences of forced compliance. *Journal of Abnormal and Social Psychology, 58*, 203–210.

FIELD, T.M., WOODSON, R., GREENBERG, R., & COHEN, D. (1982). Discrim ination and imitation of facial expressions by neonates. *Science, 218*, 179–181.

FIEVE, R.R. (1975). Lithium (antimanic) therapy. In A.M. Freedman, H.I. Kaplan, & B.J. Saddock (eds.), *Comprehensive textbook of psychiatry II*, vol. 2. Baltimore: Williams & Wilkins.

FILSINGER, E.E., & FABES, R.A. (1985). Odor communication, pheromones, and human families. *Journal of Marriage and the Family, 47*, 349–359.

FINGARETTE, H. (1969). *Self-deception.* London: Routledge and Kegan Paul.

FIORUCCI, S., & PRESTON, J.M. (1986). Psycholinguistic abilities and early vs. later second-language acquisition. *Canadian Psychology, 27*, 204.

FISCHMAN, J. (1987). Getting tough. *Psychology Today, 21*(12), 26–28.

FISHER, W.A. (1989). AIDS prevention: A psychological analysis. *Canadian Psychology, 30*, 420.

FLEXNER, L. (1967). Dissection of memory in mice with antibiotics. *Proceedings of the American Philosophical Society, 111*, 343–346.

FLODERUS-MYRHED, B., PEDERSEN, N., & RASMUSON, I. (1980). Assessment of heritability for personality, based on a short-form of the Eysenck Personality Inventory: A study of 12,898 twin pairs. *Behavior Genetics, 10*, 153–162.

FLORIDA, I.H. (1985). America's gift to human resource management. *Office, 101*, 154.

FOLKES, V.S. (1982). Forming relationships and the matching hypothesis. *Personality and Social Psychological Bulletin, 8*, 631–636.

FONTANA, A. (1966). Familial etiology of schizophrenia: Is a scientific methodology possible? *Psychological Bulletin, 66*, 214–228.

FOOT, H.C., CHAPMAN, A.J., & SMITH, J.R. (1977). Friendship and social responsiveness in boys and girls. *Journal of Personality and Social Psychology, 35*, 401–411.

FORD, D.H., & URBAN, H.B. (1963). *Systems of psychotherapy: A comparative study.* New York: John Wiley.

FORDYCE, W.E. (1973). An operant conditioning method for managing chronic pain. *Postgraduate Medicine, 53*(6), 123–128.

________. (1976). *Behavioral methods for chronic pain and illness.* St. Louis: Mosby.

FORGUS, R., & SHULMAN, B. (1979). *Personality: A cognitive view.* Englewood Cliffs, NJ: Prentice-Hall.

FOUTS, R.S., & RIGBY, R.L. (1977). Man-chimpanzee communication. In T.A. Seboek (ed.), *How animals communicate.* Bloomington: University of Indiana Press.

FOX, B.H. (1978). Premorbid psychological factors as related to cancer incidence. *Journal of Behavioral Medicine, 1*(1), 45–133.

FRANCIS, V., KORSCH, B.M., & MORRIS, M.J. (1969). Gaps in doctor-patient communication: Patients' responses to medical advice. *New England Journal of Medicine, 280*, 535–540.

FRANK, J.D. (1961). *Persuasion and healing.* Baltimore: Johns Hopkins Press.

________. (1979). The present status of outcome studies. *Journal of Consulting and Clinical Psychology, 47*, 310–316.

FREDERICK, P., LI, F.P., CASSADY, J.P., & JAFFE, W. (1975). Risk of second tumors in survivors of childhood cancer. *Cancer 35(4)*, 1230–1235.

FREDERICKSEN, N. (1986). Toward a broader conception of human intelligence. *American Psychologist, 41(4)*, 445–452.

FREEDMAN, D.G. (1971). Behavioral assessment in infancy. In G.B.A. Stoelinga & J.J. Van Der Werff Ten Bosch (eds.), *Normal and abnormal development of brain and behavior.* Leiden: Leiden University Press.

________. (1979). *Human sociobiology: A holistic approach.* New York: Free Press.

FREEDMAN, J.L., & FRASER, S.C. (1966). Compliance without pressure: The foot-in-the-door technique. *Journal of Personality and Social Psychology, 4*, 195–202.

FREUD, S. (1900/1965). *The interpretation of dreams.* New York: Avon-Discus.

________. (1935). *A general introduction to psychoanalysis.* New York: Washington Square Press.

FRIEDMAN, G.D., URY, H.K., KLATSKY, A.L., & SIEGELAUB, A.M. (1974). A psychological questionnaire predictive of myocardial infarction: Results from the Kaiser-Permanente epidemiologic study of myocardial infarction. *Psychosomatic Medicine, 36,* 327–343.

FRIEDMAN, H.S., & BOOTH-KEWLEY, S. (1987). The "Disease-Prone Personality": A meta-analytic view of the construct. *American Psychologist, 42,* 539–555.

FRIEDMAN, J., GLOBUS, G., HUNTLEY, A., MULLANEY, D., NAITOH, P., & JOHNSON, L. (1977). Performance and mood during and after gradual sleep reduction. *Psychophysiology, 14,* 245–250.

FRIEDMAN, M., & ROSENMAN, R.S. (1974). *Type A behavior and your heart.* New York: Knopf.

FROMKIN, V., KRASHEN, S., CURTISS, S., RIGLER, D., & RIGLER, M. (1974). The development of language in Genie: A case of language acquisition beyond "the critical period." *Brain and Language, 1,* 81–107.

FROMM-REICHMANN, F. (1948). Notes on the development of treatment of schizophrenics by psychoanalytic psychotherapy. *Psychiatry, 11,* 263–273.

FUREDY, J.J. (1989). Variety of views on polygraph widely sampled but not well analyzed. *Contemporary Psychology, 34,* 459–460.

FURTH, H.G. (1971). Linguistic deficiency and thinking: Research with deaf subjects. *Psychological Bulletin, 75,* 52–58.

G

GAGNÉ, R.M. (1984). Learning outcomes and their effects: Useful categories of human performance. *American Psychologist, 39,* 377–385.

GAINES, L., & ESSERMAN, J.G. (1981). A quantitative study of young children's comprehension of television programs and commercials. In J.F. Esserman (ed.), *Television advertising and children: Issues, research and findings.* New York: Child Research Service.

GAL, R., & LAZARUS, R.S. (1975). The role of activity in anticipating and confronting stressful situations. *Journal of Human Stress, 1(4),* 4–20.

GALIN, D. (1974). Implications for psychiatry of left and right cerebral specialization. *Archives of General Psychiatry, 31,* 572–583.

GALL, F.J., & SPURZHEIM, G. (1810). Anatomie et physiologie du systeme nerveux. Paris: Schoell.

GALLISTEL, C.R. (1973). Self-stimulation: The neurophysiology of reward and motivation. In J.A. Deutsch (ed.), *The physiological basis of memory.* New York: Academic Press.

GARCIA, J., & KOELLING, R.A. (1966). Relation of cue to consequence in avoidance learning. *Psychonomic Science, 4,* 123–124.

GARDNER, B.T., & GARDNER, R.A. (1972). Two-way communication with infant chimpanzees. In A.M. Schier & F. Stollnitz (eds.), *Behavior of nonhuman primates,* vol. 4. New York: Academic Press.

________. (1986). Discovering the meaning of primate signals. *British Journal for the Philosophy of Science, 37,* 477–495.

GARDNER, H. (1983). *Frames of mind.* New York: Basic Books.

GARDNER, R.C. (1984). *Social aspects of second language learning.* London: Edward Arnold.

GARDNER, R.C., & LAMBERT, W.E. (1972). *Attitudes and motivation in second language acquisition.* Rowley, MA: Newbury House.

GARFIELD, S.L. (1986). Problems in diagnostic classification. In T. Millon and G.L. Klerman (eds.), *Contemporary directions in psychopathology.* New York: Guilford.

GARFINKEL, P.E., & GARNER, D.M. (1982). *Anorexia nervosa: A multidimensional perspective.* New York: Brunner/Mazel.

GAZZANIGA, M.S. (1967, August). The split brain in man. *Scientific American, 217,* 24–29.

________. (1985). *The social brain.* New York: Basic Books.

GAZZANIGA, M., & LEDOUX, J.E. (1978). *The integrated mind.* New York: Plenum.

GEER, J.H., DAVIDSON, G.D., & GATCHEL, R.I. (1970). Reduction in stress in humans through non veridical perceived control at aversive stimulation. *Journal of Personality and Social Psychology, 16,* 731–738.

GEER, J.H., & TURTLETAUB, A. (1967). Fear reduction following observation of a model. *Journal of Personality and Social Psychology, 6,* 327–331.

GENESEE, F. (1984). Beyond bilingualism: Social psychology studies of French immersion programs in Canada. *Canadian Journal of Be havioural Science, 16,* 338–352.

GEORGE, S.G., & JENNINGS, L.B. (1975). Effect of subliminal stimuli on consumer behavior: Negative evidence. *Perceptual and Motor Skills, 41,* 847–854.

GESCHEIDER, G.A. (1985). *Psychophysics: Method, theory and application.* Hillsdale, NJ: Erlbaum.

GESTELAND, R.C. (1986). Speculations on receptor cells as analyzers and filters. *Experientia, 42,* 287–291.

GEWIRTZ, J.L. (1971). The roles of overt responding and extrinsic reinforcement in "self" and "vicarious-reinforcement" phenomena and in "observational learning" and imitation. In R. Glasser (ed.), *The nature of reinforcement.* Columbus, OH: Charles E. Merrill Books.

GIBSON, E.J., & WALK, R.D. (1960, April). The "visual cliff." *Scientific American,* 64–71.

GIBSON, J.J. (1979). *The ecological approach to visual perception.* Boston, MA: Houghton Mifflin.

GILLIGAN, C. (1982). *In a different voice: Psychological theory and women's development.* Cambridge, MA: Harvard University Press.

GILLIS, J.R., ROGERS, R., & DICKENS, S.E. (1989). Detecting Malingering on the MMPI with an outpatient population. *Canadian Psychology, 30(2),* 292.

GILLUM, R., LEON, G.R., KAMP, J., & BECERRA-ALDAMA, J. (1980). Prediction of cardiovascular and other disease onset and mortality from 30-year longitudinal MMPI data. *Journal of Consulting and Clinical Psychology, 48,* 405–406.

GLASGOW, R.E., KLESGES, R.C., MIZES, J.S., & PECHACEK, T.F. (1985). Quitting smoking: Strategies used and variables associated with success in a stop-smoking contest. *Journal of Consulting and Clinical Psychology, 53,* 905–912.

GLASS, D.C., & SINGER, J.E. (1972). *Urban stress: Experiments on noise and social stressors.* New York: Academic Press.

GLEITMAN, H. (1987). *Psychology,* 2nd ed. New York: W.W. Norton.

GLUCKSBERG, S. (1962). The influence of strength of drive on functional fixedness and perceptual recognition. *Journal of Experimental Psychology, 63,* 36–41.

GLUCKSBERG, S., & KING, L.J. (1967). Motivated forgetting mediated by implicit verbal chaining: A laboratory analog of repression. *Science, 158,* 517–519.

GLUCKSBERG, S., & ORNSTEIN, P.A. (1969). Reply to Weiner and Higgins: Motivated forgetting is not attributable to a confounding original learning with retention. *Journal of Verbal Learning and Verbal Behavior, 8,* 681–685.

GOLD, P.E., & DELANEY, R.L. (1981). ACTH modulation of memory storage processing. In J.L. Martinez, Jr., R.A. Jensen, R.B. Messing, H. Ritger, and J.L. McGaugh (eds.), *Endogenous peptides and learning and memory processes.* New York: Academic Press.

GOLDBERG, E.M., & MORRISON, S.L. (1963). Schizophrenia and social class. *British Journal of Psychiatry, 109,* 785–802.

GOLDFRIED, M.R. (1980). Toward the delineation of therapeutic change principles. *American Psychologist, 35,* 991–999.

GOLDSMITH, H.H. (1983). Genetic influences on personality from infancy to adulthood. *Child Development, 54,* 331–355.

GOLEMAN, D. (1986). *Vital lies, simple truths: The psychology of self-deception.* New York: Simon & Schuster.

GOLIGHTLY, C., NELSON, D., & JOHNSON, J. (1970). Children's dependency scale. *Developmental Psychology, 3(1),* 114–118.

GOMES-SCHWARTZ, R., HADLEY, S.W., & STRUPP, H.H. (1978). Individual psychotherapy and behavior therapy. *Annual Review of Psychology, 29,* 435–471.

GOODZ, M.S., BILODEAU, L., & WHITE, K. (1986). Parent-to-child speech in bilingual families. *Canadian Psychology, 27,* 240.

GORDON, T. (1976). *Parent Effectiveness Training in Action.* New York: Wyden.

________. (1977). *Leader Effectiveness Training.* New York: Wyden Books.

GOTTESMAN, I.I. (1963). Genetic aspects of intelligent behavior. In N. Ellis (ed.), *Handbook of mental deficiency: Psychological theory and research.* New York: McGraw-Hill.

GOTTLIEB, B.H. (1987). Marshalling social support for medical patients and their families. *Canadian Psychology, 28,* 201–217.

GOTTSCHALK, L.A. (1985). Hope and other deterrents to illness. *American Journal of Psychotherapy, 39,* 515–524.

GOULD, R.L. (1978). *Transformations: Growth and change in adult life.* New York: Simon & Schuster.

GRAHAM, C.H., & HSIA, Y. (1958). Color defect and color theory. *Science, 127,* 675–682.

GRAHAM, K.R. (1986). Explaining "virtuoso" hypnotic performance: Social psychology or experiential skill? *The Behavioral and Brain Sciences, 9,* 473–474.

GRAY, J.L., & STARKE, F.A. (1984). *Organizational behavior.* Columbus, OH: Charles E. Merrill Publishing.

GREBSTEIN, L.C. (1969). *Toward self-understanding.* Glenview: Scott Foresman.

GREENE, W.A., GOLDSTEIN, S., & MOSS, A.J. (1972). Psychosocial aspects of sudden death. *Archives of Internal Medicine, 129,* 725–731.

GREENGLASS, E.R. (1971). A cross-cultural study of the child's communication with his mother. *Developmental Psychology, 5,* 494–499.

________. (1982). *A world of difference.* Toronto: John Wiley & Sons.

GREENOUGH, W.T., & GREEN, E.J. (1981). Experience and the changing brain. In J.L. McGaugh, J.G. March, & S.B. Kiesler (eds.), *Aging: Biology and behavior.* New York: Academic Press.

GREER, K. (1984). Physiology of motor control. In M.M. Smyth & A.M. Wing (eds.), *Psychology of human movement.* London: Academic Press.

GROWALD, E.R., & LUKS, A. (1988, March). Beyond self. *American Health,* 51–53.

GRUEN, W. (1975). Effects of brief psychotherapy during the hospitalization period on the recovery process in heart attacks. *Journal of Consulting and Clinical Psychology, 43,* 223–232.

GUILFORD, J.P. (1967). *The nature of human intelligence.* New-York: McGraw-Hill.

GUR, R.C., & SACKEIM, H.A. (1979). Self-deception: A concept in search of a phenomenon. *Journal of Personality and Social Psychology, 37,* 147–169.

GURMAN, A.S. (1977). The patient's perceptions of the therapeutic relationship. In A.S. Gurman & A.M. Razin (eds.), *Effective psychotherapy: A handbook of research.* Oxford, England: Pergamon Press.

H

HAAS, A. (1979). Male and female spoken language differences: Stereotypes and evidence. *Psychological Bulletin, 86,* 616–626.

HABER, R.N. (1969, April). Eidetic images. *Scientific American, 220,* 36–44.

HACK, T.F., & DEVINS, G.M. (1989). Coping with AIDS: Impact of AIDS on male university students. *Canadian Psychology, 30,* 225.

HALL, C. (1966). *The meaning of dreams.* New York: McGraw-Hill.

HALL, D.F., & LOFTUS, E.F. (1984). The fate of memory: Discoverable or doomed? In L.R. Squire, & N. Butters (eds.), *Neuropsychology of memory.* New York: Guilford Press.

HALL, S.M., BASS, A., & MONROE, J. (1978). Confirmed contact and monitoring as follow-up strategies: A long-term study of obesity treatment. *Addictive Behaviors, 3(2),* 139–147.

HALPERN, D.F. (1986). A different answer to the question, "Do sex-related differences in spatial abilities exist?" *American Psychologist, 41,* 1014–1015.

HALPIN, A.W., & WINER, B.J. (1957). A factorial study of the leader behavior descriptions. In R.M. Stogdill & A.E. Coons, (ed.), *Leader behavior: its description and measurement.* Columbus: Ohio State University, Bureau of Business Research.

HAMILTON, D.L., & TROLIER, T.K. (1986). Stereotypes and stereotyping: An overview of the cognitive approach. In J. Dovidio & S.L. Gaertner (eds.), *Prejudice, discrimination, and racism: Theory and research.* New York: Academic Press.

HAMLIN, R. (1986). Choosing between directive and participative management. *Supervisory Management, 31(1),* 14–17.

HANEY, C.A. (1977). Illness behavior and psychosocial correlates of cancer. *Social Science and Medicine, 11,* 223–228.

HANEY, W.V. (1979). *Communication and interpersonal relations.* Homewood, IL: Richard D. Irwin.

HANSON, K. (1989). Communicated attributions and conflict in close relationships. *Canadian Psychology, 30,* 287.

HANSON, R.W., BORDEN, B.L., HALL, S.M., & HALL, R.G. (1976). Use of programmed instruction in teaching self-management skills to overweight adults. *Behavior Therapy, 7,* 366–373.

HARE, A.P. (1976). *Handbook of small group research.* New York: Free Press.

HARFORD, T.C., WILLIS, C.H., & DEABLER, H.L. (1967). Personality correlates of masculinity-femininity. *Psychological Reports, 21,* 881–884.

HARLEY, B. (1986). *Age in second language acquisition.* San Diego, CA: College-Hill Press.

HARLOW, H. (1958). The nature of love. *American Psychologist, 13,* 673–685.

HARLOW, H., & HARLOW, M.K. (1962). The effect of rearing conditions on behavior. *Bulletin of the Menninger Clinic, 26,* 213–224.

________. (1969). Effects of various mother-infant relationships on rhesus monkey behaviors. In B.M. Foss (ed.), *Determinants of infant behavior,* vol. 4. London: Methuen.

HARLOW, H.F. (1971). *Learning to love.* San Francisco: Albion.

HARRIS, B. (1979). Whatever happened to Little Albert? *American Psychologist, 34,* 151–160.

HARTLAGE, L.C. (1970). Sex-linked inheritance of spatial ability. *Perceptual and Motor Skills, 31,* 610.

HARTMANN, E. (1984). *The nightmare.* New York: Basic Books.

HASHER, L., & ZACKS, R.T. (1979). Automatic and effortful processes in memory. *Journal of Experimental Psychology: General, 108,* 356–388.

HATHAWAY S.R., & MCKINLEY, J.C. (1943). *MMPI manual.* New York: Psychological Corporation.

HAUPT, H.A., & ROVERE, G.D. (1984). Anabolic steroids: A review of the literature. *The American Journal of Sports Medicine, 12,* 469–483.

HAYES, C. (1951). *The ape in our house.* New York: Harper.

HEALY, C.C. (1989). Negative: The MBTI: Not ready for routine use in counseling. *Journal of Counseling and Development, 67,* 487–488.

HEBB, D.O. (1949). *Organization of behavior.* New York: John Wiley & Sons.

________. (1972). *A textbook of psychology,* 3rd ed. Philadelphia: Saunders.

Hefferline, R.F., & Keenan, B. (1963). Amplitude induction gradient of a small-scale (covert) operant. *Journal of Experimental Analysis of Behavior, 6,* 307–315.

Heider, F. (1958). *The psychology of interpersonal relations.* New York: Wiley.

Held, R., & Hein, A. (1963). Movement produced stimulation in the development of visually guided behavior. *Journal of Comparative and Physiological Psychology, 56,* 872–876.

Henderson, J.B., Hall, S.M., & Lipton, H.L. (1979). Changing self-destructive behaviors. In G.C. Stone, F. Cohen, & N.E. Adler (eds.), *Health psychology: A handbook.* San Francisco: Jossey-Bass.

Henderson, N.D. (1982). Human behavior genetics. *Annual Review of Psychology, 33,* 403–440.

Henley, N.M. (1977). *Body politics: Power, sex and nonverbal communication.* Englewood Cliffs, NJ: Prentice-Hall.

Henley, N.M., & Thorne, B. (1977). Womanspeak and manspeak: Sex differences and sexism in communication, verbal and nonverbal. In A. Sargent (ed.), *Beyond sex roles.* St. Paul: West, 201–218.

Herbert, E.W., Gelfand, D.M., & Hartman, D.P. (1969). Imitation and self-esteem as determinants of self-critical behavior. *Child Development, 40,* 421–430.

Hering, E. (1920). Grundzuge der Lehr vs. Lichtsinn. Berlin: Springer-Verlag.

Herink, R. (1980). *The psychotherapy handbook.* New York: New American Library.

Herman, C.P., & Polivy, J. (1980). Restrained eating. In A. Stunkard (ed.), *Obesity.* Philadelphia: Saunders.

Hersey, P., & Blanchard, K. (1982). *Management of Organizational Behavior.* Englewood Cliffs, NJ: Prentice-Hall.

Herzberg, F. (1976). *The managerial choice: To be efficient and to be human.* Irwin.

Herzberg, F., Mausner, B. & Snyderman, B. (1959). *The motivation to work,* 2nd ed. John Wiley and Sons.

Herzog, A.R., Rogers, W.L., & Woodworth, J. (1982). *Subjective well-being among different age groups.* Ann Arbor: Institute for Social Research, University of Michigan.

Hibbert, G.A. (1984). Hyperventilation as a cause of panic attacks. *British Medical Journal, 288,* 263–264.

Higbee, K.L. (1977). *Your memory: How it works and how to improve it.* Englewood Cliffs, NJ: Prentice-Hall.

Hilgard, E.R. (1974, November). Hypnosis is no mirage. *Psychology Today.*

________. (1975). Hypnosis. *Annual Review of Psychology, 26,* 19–44.

________. (1977). *Divided consciousness: Multiple controls in human thought and action.* New York: Wiley-Interscience.

________. (1980). Consciousness in contemporary psychology. *Annual Review of Psychology, 31,* 1–26.

Hilgard, E.R., & Hilgard, J.R. (1975). *Hypnosis in the relief of pain* (Revised edition, 1983). Los Altos, CA: William Kaufmann, Inc.

Hilgard, E.R., MacDonald, H., Morgan, A.H., & Johnson, L.S. (1978). Covert pain in hypnotic analgesia: Its reality as tested by the real-simulator design. *Journal of Abnormal Psychology, 87,* 655–663.

Hill, C.T., Rubin, Z., & Peplau, L.A. (1976). Breakups before marriage: The end of 103 affairs. *Journal of Social Issues, 32(1),* 147–168.

Hill, K.T., & Sarason, S.B. (1969). The relation of test anxiety and defensiveness to test and school performance over the elementary school years. *Monographs of the Society for Research in Child Development, 31,* no. 104.

Hill, M.I., & Blane, H.T. (1967). Evaluation of psychotherapy with alcoholics: A critical review. *Quarterly Journal of Studies on Alcohol, 28(1),* 76–104.

Hill, O.W. (1986). Further implications of anomalous observations for scientific psychology. *American Psychologist, 41,* 1170–1172.

Hineline, P.N., & Rachlin, H. (1969). Escape and avoidance of shock by pigeons pecking a key. *Journal of the Experimental Analysis of Behavior, 12,* 533–538.

Hines, T. (1988). Negative reinforcement is *not* punishment. *Contemporary Psychology, 33,* 1009.

Hirsch, J., & Knittle, S.L. (1970). Cellularity of obese and nonobese human adipose tissue. *Federation of American Societies for Experimental Biology: Federation Proceedings, 29,* 1516–1521.

Hirst, W.C. (1989). Discovering how the brain remembers. *Contemporary Psychology, 34(2),* 123–125.

Hiscock, M. (1986). On sex differences in spatial abilities. *American Psychologist, 41,* 1011–1012.

Hoagland, H. (1960). Some endocrine stress responses in man. In J.M. Tanner (ed.), *Stress and psychiatric disorder.* Oxford: Blackwell Scientific Publications.

Hobson, J.A., & McCarley, R.W. (1977). The brain as a dream state generator: An activation synthesis hypothesis of the dream process. *American Journal of Psychiatry, 134,* 1335–1348.

Hochberg, J. (1968). In the mind's age. In R.N. Haber (ed.), *Contemporary theory and research in visual perception.* New York: Holt, Rinehart and Winston.

Hoebel, B.G., & Teitelbaum, P. (1966). Effects of force-feeding and starvation on food intake and body weight on a rat with ventromedial hypothalamic lesions. *Journal of Comparative and Physiological Psychology, 61(2),* 189–193.

Hoffman, L.W. (1977a). Fear of success in 1965 and 1974: A follow-up study. *Journal of Consulting and Clinical Psychology, 45,* 310–321.

________. (1977b). Changes in family roles, socialization, and sex differences. *American Psychologist, 32,* 644–657.

________. (1982). Methodological issues in follow-up and replication studies. *Journal of Social Issues, 38(1),* 53–64.

Hofling, C.K., Brotzman, E., Dalrymple, S., Grames, N., & Pierce, C.M. (1966). An experimental study in nurse-physician relationships. *Journal of Nervous and Mental Disease, 143,* 171–180.

Hohmann, G.W. (1962). Some effects of spinal cord lesions on experienced emotional feelings. *Psychophysiology, 3(1),* 143–156.

Hokanson, J.E., & Burgess, M. (1962). The effects of three types of aggression on vascular processes. *Journal of Abnormal and Social Psychology, 64,* 446–449.

Hokanson, J.E., & Edelman, R. (1966). Effects of three social responses on vascular processes. *Journal of Personality and Social Psychology, 3,* 442–447.

Hokanson, J.E., & Shelter, S. (1961). The effect of overt aggression on physiological arousal. *Journal of Abnormal and Social Psychology, 63,* 446–448.

Hokanson, J.E., Willers, K.R., & Karapsak, E. (1968). The modification of autonomic responses during aggressive interchange. *Journal of Personality, 36,* 386–404.

Holahan, C.J., & Moos, R.H. (1985). Life stress and health: Personality, coping, and family support in stress resistance. *Journal of Personality and Social Psychology, 49,* 739–747.

Holden, C. (1980a, March). Identical twins reared apart. *Science, 207,* 1323–1325.

________. (1980b, November). Twins reunited. *Science, 80,* 55–59.

Holender, D. (1986). Semantic activation without conscious identification in dichotic listening, parafoveal vision, and visual masking: A survey and appraisal. *The Behavioral and Brain Sciences, 9,* 1–66.

HOLLON, S.D., & NAJAVITS, L. (1988). Review of empirical studies on cognitive therapy. In A.J. Frances and R.E. Hales (eds.), *Review of psychiatry*, vol. 7. Washington, DC: American Psychiatric Press.

HOLMES, D.S. (1974). Investigations of repression: Differential recall of material experimentally or naturally associated with ego threat. *Psychological Bulletin, 81*, 632–653.

————. (1984). Meditation and somatic arousal reduction. A review of the experimental evidence. *American Psychologist, 39*, 1–10.

————. (1985a). To meditate or to simply rest, that is the question: A response to the comments of Shapiro. *American Psychologist, 40*, 722–725.

————. (1985b). To meditate or rest: The answer is rest. *American Psychologist, 40*, 728–731.

HOLMES, T.H., & RAHE, R.H. (1967). The social readjustment rating scale. *Journal of Psychosomatic Research, 11*(2), 213–218.

HORNER, M.S. (1970). Femininity and successful achievement: A basic inconsistency. In J.M. Bardwick, E. Douvan, M.S. Horner, & D. Gutmann (eds.), *Feminine personality and conflict.* Belmont, CA: Brooks Cole.

HORNEY, K. (1926). *Feminine Psychology.* New York: W.W. Norton.

HOUSE, R., & WIGDOR, L. (1967). Herzberg's dual-factor theory of job satisfaction and motivation, *Personnel Psychology, 20*, 369–389.

HSU, J.J. (1965). Electroconditioning therapy of alcoholics: A preliminary report. *Quarterly Journal of Studies on Alcohol, 26*, 449–459.

HUBEL, D.H. (1979, September). The brain. *Scientific American, 241*, 45–53.

————, & WIESEL, T.N. (1979, September). Brain mechanisms of vision. *Scientific American, 241*, 150–162.

HULL, C.L. (1943). *Principles of behavior: An introduction to behavior theory.* NY: Appleton-Century-Crofts.

HUMPHREYS, M.S., BAIN, J.D., & PIKE, R. (1989). Different ways to cue a coherent memory system: A theory for episodic, semantic, and procedural tasks. *Psychological Review, 96*, 208–233.

HUNT, G.M., & AZRIN, N.H. (1973, February). Community reinforcement approach to alcoholism. *Behavior Research and Therapy, 11*, 91–104.

HUNT, R.R., & MITCHELL, D.B. (1982). Independent effects of semantic and nonsemantic distinctiveness. *Journal of Experimental Psychology: Learning, Memory, and Cognition, 8*(1), 81–87.

HURVICH, L.M., & JAMESON, D. (1957). An opponent-process theory of color vision. *Psychological Review, 64*, 384–404.

HUSTON, T.L., RUGGIERO, M., CONNER, R., & GEIS, G. (1981). Bystander intervention into crime: A study based on naturally occurring episodes. *Social Psychology Quarterly, 44*, 14–23.

HUSTON-STEIN, A., & HIGGENS-TRENK, A. (1978). Development of females from childhood through adulthood: Career and feminine role orientations. In P. Baltes (ed.), *Lifespan development and behavior*, vol. 1. New York: Academic Press.

HYDE, J.S. (1981). How large are cognitive gender differences? A meta-analysis using w2 and d. *American Psychologist, 36*, 892–901.

HYDEN, H. (1961, December). Satellite cells in the nervous system. *Scientific American, 205*, 62–83.

————, & LANGE, P.W. (1972). Protein changes in different brain areas as a function of intermittent training. *Proceedings of the National Academy of Sciences, 69*, 1980–1984.

I

IRWIN, M., DANIELS, M., BLOOM, E.T., SMITH, T.L., & WEINER, H. (1987). Life events, depressive symptoms, and immune function. *The American Journal of Psychiatry, 144*, 437–441.

ISEN, A.M. (1970). Success, Failure, Attention and reactions to others: The warm glow of success. *Journal of Personality and Social Psychology, 15*, 294–301.

————, & LEVIN, P.F. (1972). Effect of feeling good on helping: Cookies and kindness. *Journal of Personality and Social Psychology, 21*, 384–388.

IVANCEVICH, J.M., & DONNELLY, J.H. (1975). Relations of organization structure to job satisfaction, anxiety-stress and performance, *Administrative Science Quarterly, 20*, 272–280.

IZARD, C. (1971). *The face of emotion.* NY: Appleton-Century-Crofts.

IZARD, C.E. (1982). *Measuring emotions in infants and children.* NY: Cambridge University Press.

J

JACOBSON, E. (1970). *Modern treatment of tense patients.* Springfield, IL: Charles C. Thomas.

JACOBY, L.L. (1987). Book reviews: The unconscious reconsidered. *Canadian Journal of Behavioural Science, 19*, 357–358.

JAGO, A.G. (1982). Leadership: Perspectives in theory and research, *Management Science, 28*(3), 315–336.

JAMIESON, D.W., LYDON, J.E., STEWART, G., & ZANNA, M.P. (1987). Pygmalion revisited: New evidence for student expectancy effects in the classroom. *Journal of Educational Psychology, 79*, 461–466.

JAMIESON, D.W., LYDON, J.E., & ZANNA, M.P. (1987). Attitude and activity preference similarity: Differential bases of interpersonal attraction for low and high self-monitors. *Journal of Personality and Social Psychology, 53*, 1052–1060.

JAMIESON, D.W., & ZANNA, M.P. (1989). Need for structure in attitude formation and expression. In A.R. Pratkanis, S.J. Breckler, & A.G. Greenwald (eds.), *Attitude structure and function.* Hillsdale, NJ: Erlbaum.

JAMIESON, J.L., & LAVOIE, N.F. (1987). Type A behavior, aerobic power, and cardiovascular recovery from a psychosocial stressor. *Health Psychology, 6*, 361–371.

JANIS, I.L. (1975). Effectiveness of social support for stressful decisions. In M. Deutsch, & H. Hornstein (eds.), *Applying social psychology: Implications for research, practice, and training.* Hillsdale, NJ: Erlbaum.

————. (1983). *Groupthink: Psychological studies of policy decisions and fiascoes,* 2nd ed. Boston: Houghton Mifflin.

JANISSE, M.P. (1973). Pupil size and affect. *Canadian Psychologist, 14*, 311–329.

JEANS, J. (1937). *Science and music.* Cambridge: Cambridge University Press.

JEMMOT, J.B., III, & LOCKE, S.E. (1984, October). Psychosocial factors, immunologic mediation, and human susceptibility to infectious diseases: How much do we know? *Psychological Bulletin, 95*, 78–108.

JENKINS, C.D. (1976). Recent evidence supporting psychologic and social risk factors for coronary disease. *New England Journal of Medicine, 294*, 987–994 and 1033–1038.

JENKINS, C.D., ROSEMAN, R.H., & FRIEDMAN, M. (1967). Development of an objective psychological test for the determination of coronary-prone behavior pattern in employed men. *Journal of Chronic Diseases, 20*, 371–379.

JENKINS, J.G., & DALLENBACH, K.M. (1924). Obliviance during sleep walking. *American Journal of Psychology, 35*, 605–612.

JENSEN, A.R. (1969). How much can we boost I.Q. and scholastic achievement? *Harvard Educational Review, 39*, 1–123.

————. (1973). *Educability and group differences.* New York: Harper & Row.

————. (1985). The nature of black-white differences on psychometric tests: Spearman's hypothesis. *Behavior and Brain Sciences, 8*, 193–263.

JOFFE, J.M. (1969). *Prenatal determinants of behavior.* Oxford: Pergamon Press.

JOHNSON, A.M., & CONNOLLY, J.A. (1989). Teenagers' perceptions of power in their relationships with peers and adults. *Canadian Psychology, 30*(2), 273.

JOHNSON, D.M. (1972). *Systematic introduction to the psychology of thinking.* New York: Harper & Row.

JOHNSON, L.D., BACHMAN, J.G., & O'MALLEY, P.M. (1987). *Student drug use in America.* Ann Arbor, MI: Institute of Social Research.

JOHNSON-LAIRD, P.N., & WASON, P.C. (1977). A theoretical analysis of insight in a reasoning task. In P.N. Johnson-Laird and P.C. Wason (eds.), *Thinking: Readings in cognitive science.* Cambridge: Cambridge University Press.

JONES, E.E., & HARRIS, V.A. (1967). The attribution of attitudes. *Journal of Experimental Social Psychology, 3*(1), 1–24.

JONES, E.E., & NISBETT, R.E. (1971). *The actor and observer: Perceptions of the causes of behavior.* New York: General Learning Press.

_________. (1971). The actor and the observer: Divergent perceptions of the causes of behavior. In E.E. Jones, et al. (eds.), *Attribution: Perceiving the causes of behavior.* Morristown, NJ: General Learning Press.

JONES, M.C. (1957). The later careers of boys who were early or late maturing. *Child Development, 28,* 113–128.

JULESZ, B. (1971). *Foundation of cyclopean perception.* Chicago: University of Chicago Press.

JUNG, C.G. (1953–1979). *Collected Works,* edited by H. Read, M. Fordham, and G. Adler, translated by R.F.C. Hull. Princeton: Princeton University Press.

K

KAGAN, J. (1976). Emergent themes in human development. *American Scientist, 64,* 186–196.

KAGAN, J., & KLEIN, R.E. (1973). Cross cultural perspectives on early development. *American Psychologist, 28,* 947–961.

KAHN, R., & KATZ, D. (1960). Leadership practices in relation to productivity and morale. In D. Cartwright & A. Zander (ed.), *Group Dynamics.* Evanston, IL: Row Petersen & Company.

KALAT, J.W. (1974). Taste salience depends on novelty, not concentration, in taste-aversion learning in the rat. *Journal of Comparative and Physiological Psychology, 86*(1), 47–50.

KALINOWSKI, L.B. (1975). The convulsive therapies. In A.M. Freedman, H.I. Kaplan, & B.J. Saddock (eds.), *Comprehensive textbook of psychiatry II,* vol. 2. Baltimore: Williams & Wilkins.

KANDEL, E.R., & SCHWARTZ, J.H. (1982). Molecular biology of learning: Modulation of transmitter release. *Science, 218,* 433–443.

KANDIL, O., & BORYSENKO, M. (1987). Decline of natural killer cell target binding and lytic activity in mice exposed to rotation stress. *Health Psychology, 6*(2), 89–99.

KANNER, A.D., COYNE, J.C., SCHAEFER, C., & LAZARUS, R.S. (1981). Comparison of two modes of stress measurement: Daily hassles and uplifts versus major life events. *Journal of Behavioral Medicine, 4*(1), 1–39.

KAPLAN, H.S. (1974). *The new sex therapy.* New York: Brunner/Mazel.

KARABENICK, S.A. (1983). Sex-relevance of content and influenceability: Sistrunk and McDavid revisited. *Personality and Social Psychology Bulletin, 9,* 243–252.

KASL, S.V., & COBB, S. (1970). Blood pressure changes in men undergoing job loss: A preliminary report. *Psychosomatic Medicine, 32*(1), 19–38.

KASS, J.H. (1987). The organization of the neocortex in mammals. *Annual Review of Psychology, 38,* 129–151.

KASTENBAUM, R., & COSTA, P.T. (1977). Psychological perspectives on death. *Annual Review of Psychology, 28,* 225–249.

KATKIN, E.S. (1985). Polygraph testing, psychological research, and public anxiety. *American Psychologist, 40,* 346–347.

KATZ, J.L., ACKMAN, P., ROTHWAX, Y., SACHAR, E.J., WEINER, H., HELLMAN, L., & GALLAGHER, T.F. (1970). Psychoendocrine aspects of cancer of the breast. *Psychosomatic Medicine, 32*(1), 1–18.

KATZ, J.L., WEINER, H., GALLAGHER, T.F., & HELLMAN, L. (1970). Stress, distress, and ego defences. *Archives of General Psychiatry, 23,* 131–142.

KATZELL, R.A., & GUZZO, R.A. (1983). Psychological approaches to productivity improvement. *American Psychologist, 38,* 468–472.

KAUFMAN, H. (1970). *Aggression and altruism.* New York: Holt, Rinehart and Winston.

KAZDIN, A.E. (1986). Comparative outcome studies of psychotherapy: Methodological issues and strategies. *Journal of Consulting and Clinical Psychology, 54,* 95–105.

KEITH-LUCAS, T., & GUTTMAN, N. (1975). Robust single-trial delayed backward conditioning. *Journal of Comparative and Physiological Psychology, 88,* 468–476.

KELLEY, H.H. (1967). Attribution theory in social psychology. In D. Levine (ed.), *Nebraska Symposium on Motivation,* vol. 15. Lincoln: University of Nebraska Press.

_________. (1973). The process of causal attribution. *American Psychologist, 28,* 107–128.

KELLOGG, W.N., & KELLOGG, L.A. (1933). *The ape and the child.* New York: McGraw-Hill.

KELLY, J.P. (1985). Cranial nerve nuclei, the reticular formation, and biogenic aminecontaining neurons. In E.R. Kandel & J.H. Schwartz (eds.), *Principles of neuroscience,* 2nd ed. New York: Elsevier.

KENDALL, P.C., & NORTON-FORD, J.D. (1982). *Clinical Psychology.* New York: Wiley.

KENRICK, D.T., & FUNDER, D.C. (1988). Profiting from controversy: Lessons from the person-situation debate. *American Psychologist, 43,* 23–34.

KIHLSTROM, J.F. (1985). Hypnosis. *Annual Review of Psychology, 36,* 385–418.

KIMBALL, M.M. (1989). A new perspective on women's math achievement. *Psychological Bulletin, 105,* 198–214.

KIMBLE, G.A. (1961). *Hilgard and Marquis' conditioning and learning,* 2nd ed. New York: Appleton-Century-Crofts.

KIMMEL, D.C. (1974). *Adulthood and aging.* New York: Wiley.

KIMURA, D. (1973, March). The asymmetry of the human brain. *Scientific American, 228,* 70–80.

KINSEY, A.C., MARTIN, C.E., & POMEROY, W.B. (1948). *Sexual behavior in the human male.* Philadelphia: Saunders.

_________. (1953). *Sexual behavior in the human female.* Philadelphia: Saunders.

KINTSCH, W. (1974). *The representation of meaning in memory.* Hillsdale, NJ: Lawrence Erlbaum.

KIRSCH, I., SILVA, C.E., CARONE, J.E., JOHNSTON, J.D., & SIMON, B. (1989). The surreptitious observation design: An experimental paradigm for distinguishing artifact from essence in hypnosis. *Journal of Abnormal Psychology, 98,* 132–136.

KLEINGINNA, P.R., JR., & KLEINGINNA, A.M. (1985). Cognition and affect: A reply to Lazarus and Zajonc. *American Psychologist, 40,* 470–471.

KNOX, V.J., CRUTCHFIELD, L., & HILGARD, E.R. (1975). The nature of task interference in hypnotic dissociation: An investigation of hypnotic behavior. *International Journal of Clinical and Experimental Hypnosis, 23,* 305–323.

KOBASA, S.C. (1979). Stressful life events, personality and health: An inquiry into hardiness. *Journal of Personality and Social Psychology, 37,* 1–11.

KOBASA, S.C., MADDI, S.R., & KAHN, S. (1982). Hardiness and health: A prospective study. *Journal of Personality and Social Psychology, 42,* 168–177.

KOBASA, S.C., & PUCCETTI, M.C. (1983). Personality and social resources in stress resistance. *Journal of Personality and Social Psychology, 45*, 839–850.

KOESTLER, A. (1970). *The act of creation.* London: Pan Books Ltd.

KOFFKA, K. (1935). *Principles of gestalt psychology.* New York: Harcourt Brace.

KOHLBERG, L. (1964). Development of moral character and moral ideology. In M.L. Hoffman & L.W. Hoffman (eds.), *Review of child development research*, vol. 1. New York: Russell Sage Foundation.

———. (1973). Continuities in childhood and adult moral development revisited. In P.B. Baltes & K.W. Schaie (eds.), *Lifespan developmental psychology: Personality and socialization.* New York: Academic Press.

———. (1981). *The philosophy of moral development: Essays on moral development*, vol. 1. San Francisco: Harper & Row.

KOHLER, W. (1947). *Gestalt psychology.* New York: Liveright.

KOLB, B., & WISHAW, I.Q. (1985). *Fundamentals of neuropsychology*, 2nd ed. San Francisco: W.H. Freeman.

KOLCHIN, M.G. (1987). Borrowing back from the Japanese. *SAM Advanced Management Journal, 52*(2), 26–36.

KONDRASUK, J.N., FLAGLER, K., MORROW, D., & THOMPSON, P. (1984). The effect of management by objectives on organization results. *Groups & Organization Studies, 9*, 531–539.

KOOCHER, G.P. (1986). Coping with death from cancer. *Journal of Consulting and Clinical Psychology, 54*(5), 623–631.

KOOCHER, G.P., & O'MALLEY, J.E. (1981). *The Damocles Syndrome: Psychological consequences of surviving childhood cancer.* New York: McGraw-Hill.

KORNETSKY, C. (1986). Effects of opiates and stimulants on brain stimulation: Implications for abuse. Paper presented at the convention of the American Psychological Association, Washington, D.C.

KORTE, C., YPMA, I., & TOPPEN, A. (1975). Helpfulness in Dutch society as a function of urbanization and environmental input level. *Journal of Personality and Social Psychology, 32*, 996–1003.

KOSSLYN, S.M. (1986). A computational analysis of mental image generation: Evidence from functional dissociations in split-brain patients. *Journal of Experimental Psychology: General, 114*, 311–341.

KOULACK, D., & GOODENOUGH, D.R. (1976). Dream recall and dream recall failure: An arousal-retrieval model. *Psychological Bulletin, 83*, 975–984.

KOVACS, M., RUSH, A.J., BECK, A.T., & HOLLON, S.D. (1981, January). Depressed outpatients treated with cognitive therapy or pharmacotherapy: A one year follow up. *Archives of General Psychiatry, 38*, 33–39.

KRA, S. (1986). *Aging myths: Reversible causes of mind and memory loss.* New York: McGraw-Hill.

KRANTZ, D.S., GLASS, D.C., CONTRADA, R., & MILLER, N.E. (1981). Behavior and health. In *Five year outlook of science and technology: 1981* (Source materials, vol. 2). Washington, D.C.: National Science Foundation.

KREBS, D.L., DENTON, K., VERMEULEN, S.C.A., CARPENDALE, J.I., & BUSH, A.J. (1989). The structural plasticity of moral judgment. *Canadian Psychology, 30*(2), 354.

KRINGLEN, E. (1970). Natural history of obsessional neurosis. *Seminars in Psychiatry, 2*, 403–419.

KRUEGER, J.M., PAPPENHEIMER, J.R., & KARNOVSKY, M.L. (1982). The composition of sleep-promoting factor isolated from humans. *The Journal of Biological Chemistry, 257*, 1664–1669.

KRUGER, L., & LIEBSKIND, J.C. (eds.). (1984). *Advances in pain research and therapy.* New York: Raven Press.

KUBLER-ROSS, E. (1969). *On death and dying.* New York: Macmillan.

KUPFERMAN, I. (1985). Hemispheric asymmetries and the cortical localization of higher cognitive and affective functions. In E.R. Kandel & J.H. Schwartz (eds.), *Principles of neural science.* New York: Elsevier.

KURIANSKY, J.B., DEMING, W.E., & GURLAND, B.J. (1974). On trends in the diagnosis of schizophrenia. *American Journal of Psychiatry, 131*, 402–407.

L

LACEY, J.I. (1967). Somatic response patterning and stress: Some revisions of activation theory. In M.H. Appley & R. Trumbull (eds.), *Psychological stress.* New York: Appleton-Century Crofts.

LACROIX, R. (1987). Stumbling blocks to the practice of health psychology: A Canadian perspective. *Canadian Psychology, 28*, 280–284.

LADD, G.T. (1887). *Elements of physiological psychology.* New York: Scribner's.

LAGERSPETZ, K. (1979). Modification of aggressiveness in mice. In S. Geahback & A. Faczek (eds.), *Aggression & behavior change: Biological & social processes.* New York: Praeger.

LAKOFF, R. (1975). *Language and women's place.* New York: Harper & Row.

LALONDE, R.N. (1989). Hockey from an intergroup perspective: The dynamics of group differentiation. *Canadian Psychology, 30*, 265.

LAMB, M.E. (1986). The father's role in a changing world. In M. Lamb (ed.), *The father's role: Applied perspectives.* New York: Wiley.

LAMBERT, M.J., BERGIN, A.E., & COLLINS, J.L. (1977). Therapist induced deterioration in psychotherapy. In A.S. Gurman & A.M. Razin (eds.), *Effective psychotherapy: A handbook of research.* Oxford, England: Pergamon Press.

LAMBERT, M.J., DEJULIO, S.S., & STEIN, D.M. (1978). Therapist interpersonal skills: Process, outcome methodological considerations, and recommendations for future research. *Psychological Bulletin, 85*, 467–489.

LAMIELL, J.T. (1981). Toward an idiothetic psychology of personality. *American Psychologist, 36*, 276–289.

———. (1982). The case for an idiothetic psychology of personality: A conceptual and empirical foundation. *Progress in Experimental Personality Research, 11*, 1–63.

LAMIELL, J.T., FOSS, N.A., LARSEN, R.J., & HEMPEL, A.M. (1983). Studies in intuitive personology from an idiothetic point of view: Implications for personality theory. *Journal of Personality, 51*, 438–467.

LANDMAN, J.T., & DAWES, R.M. (1982). Psychotherapy outcome. *American Psychologist, 37*, 504–516.

LANG, P.J. (1970, October). Autonomic control. *Psychology Today, 4*, 37–42.

LANGE, C. (1922). *The emotions.* Baltimore: Williams & Wilkins. (Originally published in 1885).

LANGER, E.J., & ABELSON, R.P. (1974). A patient by any other name—clinician group difference in labelling bias. *Journal of Consulting and Clinical Psychology, 42*(1), 4–9.

LANZETTA, J.T., CARTWRIGHT-SMITH, J., & KLECK, R.E. (1976). Effects of non-verbal dissimulation on emotional experience and autonomic arousal. *Journal of Personality and Social Psychology, 39*, 354–370.

LAPIERE, R. (1934). Attitudes versus actions. *Social Forces, 13*, 230–237.

LARSON, L., HUNT, J., & OSBORN, R. (1976). The great hi-hi leader behavior myth, *Academy of Management Journal, 19*, 628–641.

LATANÉ, B., & DARLEY, J.M. (1968). Group inhibition of bystander intervention in emergencies. *Journal of Personality and Social Psychology, 10*, 215–221.

———. (1976). *Help in a crisis: Bystander response to an emergency.* Morristown, NJ: General Learning Press.

LATANÉ, B., WILLIAMS, K., & HARKINS, S. (1979). Many hands make light the work: The causes and consequences of social loafing. *Journal of Personality and Social Psychology, 37*, 822–832.

LAZARUS, A.A. (1987). The need for technical eclecticism: Science, breadth, depth, and specificity. In J.K. Zeig (ed.), *The evolution of psychotherapy.* New York: Brunner/Mazel.

LAZARUS, R.S. (1966). *Psychological stress and the coping process.* New York: McGraw-Hill.

_________. (1974). Psychological stress and coping in adaptation and illness. *International Journal of Psychiatry in Medicine, 5,* 321–333.

_________. (1981a, July). Little hassles can be hazardous to your health. *Psychology Today, 15,* 58–62.

_________. (1981b). The stress and coping paradigm. In C. Eisdorfer, D. Cohen, A. Kleinman, & P. Maxin (eds.), *Theoretical Basis of Psychopathology.* New York: Spectrum.

_________. (1984). On the primacy of emotion. *American Psychologist, 39,* 124–129.

LAZARUS, R.S., & LAUNIER, R. (1978). Stress-related transactions between person and environment. In L.A. Pervin & M. Lewis (eds.), *Perspectives in interactional psychology.* New York: Plenum Press.

LAZARUS, R.S., SPEISMAN, J.C., MORDKOFF, A.M., & DAVISON, L. (1962). A laboratory study of psychological stress produced by a motion picture film. *Psychological Monographs, 6,* no. 34, 1–35. Washington, D.C.: APA.

LEBOW, M.D. (1981). *Weight Control: The behavioral strategies.* Chichester, NY: Wiley.

_________. (1984). *Child obesity: A new frontier of behavior therapy.* New York: Springer.

_________. (1988). *The thin plan.* Champaign, IL: Life Enhancement Publications.

LEFTON, L.A. (1985). *Psychology,* 3rd ed. Boston: Allyn and Bacon.

LEIBOWITZ, H.W. (1971). Sensory, learned, and cognitive mechanisms of size perception. *Annals of the New York Academy of Sciences, 188,* 47–62.

LEKARCZYK, D.T., & HILL, K.T. (1966). Self-esteem, test anxiety, stress, and verbal learning. *Developmental Psychology, 1*(2), 147–154.

LENNEBERG, E.H. (1967). *Biological foundations of language.* New York: John Wiley & Sons.

_________. (1969). On explaining language. *Science, 164,* 635–643.

LENNON, M.C. (1982). The psychological consequences of menopause: The importance of timing of a life stage event. *Journal of Health and Social Behavior, 23,* 353–366.

LENZENWEGER, M.F., & LORANGER, A.W. (1989). Psychosis proneness and clinical psychopathology: Examination of the correlates of schizotypy. *Journal of Abnormal Psychology, 98*(1), 3–8.

LEONARD, J.W. (1986, June). Why MBO fails so often. *Training & Development Journal, 40,* 38–40.

LEPPER, M.R., GREENE, D., & NISBETT, R.E. (1973). Undermining children's intrinsic interest with extrinisic reward: A test of the "overjustification" hypothesis. *Journal of Personality and Social Psychology, 28*(7), 129–137.

LERNER, M.J., MILLER, D.T., & HOLMES, J. (1976). Deserving and the emergence of forms of justice. In L. Berkowitz and E. Walster (eds.), *Advances in experimental social psychology.* New York: Academic Press.

LE UNES, A.D., & NELSON, J.R. (1989). *Sport Psychology.* Chicago: Nelson-Hall.

LEVENTHAL, H., SINGER, R., & JONES, S. (1965). The effects of fear and specificity of recommendation upon attitudes and behavior. *Journal of Personality and Social Psychology, 2,* 20–29.

LEVENTHAL, H., & TOMARKEN, A.J. (1986). Emotion: Today's problems. *Annual Review of Psychology, 37,* 565–610.

LEVENTHAL, H., ZIMMERMAN, R., & GUTMANN, M. (1984). Compliance: A self-regulation perspective. In D. Gentry (ed.), *Handbook of behavioral medicine.* New York: Guilford Press.

LEVERANT, R. (1986). MDMA reconsidered. *Journal of Psychoactive Drugs, 18,* 373–379.

LEVIN, I.P., SCHNITTJER, S.K., & THEE, S.L. (1988). Information framing effects in social and personal decisions. *Journal of Experimental Social Psychology, 24,* 520–529.

LEVINSON, D.J., with DARROW, C.N., KLEIN, E.B., LEVINSON, M.H., & MCKEE, B. (1978). *The seasons of a man's life.* New York: Knopf.

LEVY, G. (1985, May). Right brain, left brain: Fact and fiction. *Psychology Today, 19,* 38–44.

LEWIS, M.J., & DWORKIN, S.I. (1989). The cocaine epidemic. *Contemporary Psychology, 34,* 400–401.

LEY, P. (1976). Toward better doctor-patient communications. In A.E. Bennett (ed.), *Communication between doctors and patients.* New York: Oxford University Press.

LEY, R.G., & BRYDEN, M.P. (1979). Hemispheric differences in processing emotions and faces. *Brain and Language, 7,* 127–138.

LEZAK, M.D. (1983). *Neuropsychological assessment,* 2nd ed. NY: Oxford University Press.

LICHTENSTEIN, E., & DANAHER, B.G. (1976). Modification of smoking behavior: A critical analysis of theory, research, and practice. In M. Hersen, R.M. Eisler, & P.M. Miller (eds.), *Progress in behavior modification, vol. 3.* New York: Academic Press.

LICHTENSTEIN, E., & RODRIGUES, M.P. (1977). Long-term effects of rapid-smoking treatment for dependent cigarette smokers. *Addictive Behaviors, 2,* 109–112.

LICHTY, L.W. (1982). Video versus print. *Wilson Quarterly, 6,* 48–57.

LIKERT, R. (1961). *New Patterns of Management.* New York: McGraw-Hill.

LINDSAY, P.H., & NORMAN, D.A. (1977). *Human information processing,* 2nd ed. New York: Academic Press.

LINN, M.C., & PETERSEN, A.C. (1983). Emergence and characterization of gender differences in spatial ability: A meta-analysis. Unpublished manuscript, University of California, Berkeley.

LLOYD, R.W., & SALZBERG, H.C. (1975). Controlled social drinking. *Psychological Bulletin, 82,* 815–842.

LOCKE, E.A., SCHWEIGER, D.M., & LATHAM, G.B. (1986). Participation in decision making: When should it be used? *Organizational Dynamics, 14*(3), 65–80.

LOEB, R.C., & HORST, L. (1978). Sex differences in self and teacher's reports of self-esteem in preadolescents. *Sex Roles, 4,* 779–788.

LOEHLIN, J.C., & NICHOLS, R.C. (1976). *Heredity, environment, and personality.* Austin: University of Texas Press.

LOEVINGER, J., & KNOLL, E. (1983). Personality: Stages, traits, and the self. *Annual Review of Psychology, 34,* 195–222.

LOFTUS, E.F. (1974, December). Reconstructing memory: The incredible eyewitness. *Psychology Today,* 116–119.

_________. (1979). *Eyewitness testimony.* Cambridge, Mass.: Harvard University Press.

_________. (1980). *Memory.* Reading, MA: Addison-Wesley.

LOFTUS, E.F., MILLER, D.G., & BURNS, H.J. (1978). Semantic integration of verbal information into a visual memory. *Journal of Experimental Psychology: Human Learning and Memory, 4*(1) 19–31.

LOMBARDO, J.P., & LEVINE, L.J. (1978). Self disclosure: A function of sex or sex role? Paper presented at the Eastern Psychological Association convention, Washington, D.C.

LORENZ, K. (1966). *On aggression.* New York: Harcourt Brace Jovanovich.

LUBORSKY, L., MCLELLAN, A.T., WOODY, G.E., O'BRIEN, C.P., & AUERBACH, A. (1985). Therapist success and its determinants. *Archives of General Psychiatry, 42,* 602–611.

LUBORSKY, L., TODD, T.C., & KATCHER, A.H. (1973). A self-administered Social Assets Scale for predicting physical and psychological illness and health. *Journal of Psychosomatic Research, 17,*(2), 109–120.

LUBOW, R.E., RIFKIN, B., & ALEX, M. (1976). The context effect: The relationship between stimulus pre-exposure and environmental pre-exposure determines subsequent learning. *Journal of Experimental Psychology: Animal Behavior Processes, 2(1)*, 38–47.

LUCHINS, A. (1957). Primacy-recency in impression formation. In Hovland, C.I. (ed.), *The order of presentation in persuasion.* New Haven: Yale University Press.

LYGHT, C.E. (ed.). (1966). *The Merck manual of diagnosis and therapy,* 11th ed. Rahway, NJ: Merck Sharp and Dohme Research Laboratories.

LYKKEN, D.T. (1981). *A tremor in the blood: Uses and abuses of the lie detector.* NY: McGraw-Hill.

LYNN, M. (1989a). Race differences in sexual behavior: A critique of Rushton and Bogaert's evolutionary hypothesis. *Journal of Research in Personality, 23,* 1–6.

________. (1989b). Criticisms of an evolutionary hypothesis about race differences: A rebuttal to Rushton's reply. *Journal of Research in Personality, 23,* 21–34.

M

MACCOBY, E.E. (1966). Sex differences in intellectual functioning. In E.E. Maccoby (ed.), *The development of sex differences.* Stanford, CA: Stanford University Press, 25–55.

________. (1980). *Social development: Psychological growth and the parent-child relationship.* New York: Harcourt Brace Jovanovich.

MACCOBY, E.E., & Jacklin, C.N. (1974). *The psychology of sex differences.* Stanford, CA: Stanford University Press.

MACHING, A. (1986). *Talking career, thinking job: Gender differences in career and family expectations of Berkeley seniors.* Report. Center for Study Education and Advancement of Women. University of California at Berkeley.

MADDI, S.R., & KOBASA, S.C. (1984). *The hardy executive: Health under stress.* Homewood, IL: Dorsey Press.

MAHER, B.A. (1966). *Principles of psychopathology.* New York: McGraw-Hill.

MAHONEY, M.J. (1977). Reflections on the cognitive-learning trend in psychotherapy. *American Psychologist, 32,* 5–13.

MAIER, N.R.F. (1931). Reasoning in humans. *Journal of Comparative Psychology, 12,* 181–194.

MAIER, S., & LAUDENSLAGER, M. (1985, August). Stress and health: Exploring the links. *Psychology Today, 19,* 44–50.

MANDLER, G. (1985). *Cognitive psychology: An essay in cognitive science.* Hillsdale, NJ: Erlbaum.

MARCEL, A.J. (1978). Unconscious reading: Experiments on people who do not know that they are reading. *Visible Language, 12,* 392–404.

________. (1983). Conscious and unconscious perception: Experiments on visual masking and word recognition. *Cognitive Psychology, 15,* 197–237.

________. (1986). Consciousness and processing: Choosing and testing a null hypothesis. *The Behavioral and Brain Sciences, 9,* 40–41.

MARKS, D., & KAMMANN, R. (1979). *The psychology of the psychic.* Buffalo, NY: Prometheus Books.

MARKS, W.B., DOBELLE, W.H., & MACNICHOL, E.F. (1964). Visual pigments of single primate cones. *Science, 143,* 1181–1183.

MARMOR, J. (1968). *Modern psychoanalysis.* New York: Basic Books.

MARTIN, D.G. (1976). *Personality: Effective and ineffective.* Monterey, CA: Brooks Cole.

________. (1983). *Counseling and therapy skills.* Monterey, CA: Brooks Cole.

MARTIN, D.G., HAWRYLUK, G.A., BERISH, C., & DUSHENKO, T. (1984). Selective forgetting of aversive memories cued in the right hemisphere. *International Journal of Neuroscience, 23,* 169–176.

MARTIN, D.G., HAWRYLUK, G.A., & GUSE, L.L. (1974). Experimental study of unconscious influences: Ultrasound as a stimulus. *Journal of Abnormal Psychology, 83,* 589–608.

MARTIN, D.G., STAMBROOK, M., TATARYN, D.J., & BEIHL, H.O. (1984). Conditioning in the unattended left ear. *International Journal of Neuroscience, 23,* 95–102.

MARTIN, D.G., VERMAN, S.H., & MILES, J.M. (1984). Selective inhibition of vocal reaction time to aversive words in the left visual field. *International Journal of Neuroscience, 23,* 177–186.

MARTIN, G. (1981). Behaviour modification in Canada in the 1970's. *Canadian Psychology, 22,* 7–22.

MARTIN, J. (1989). Focusing attention for observational learning: the importance of context. (Georgia Institute of Technology.) Paper read at the International Joint Conference on Artificial Intelligence, Detroit, MI.

MARTIN, R.M., RITCHIE, P., & SABOURIN, M. (1988). The state of psychological practice in Canada: Current status and directions for the future. In P. Ritchie, T. Hogan, & T. Hogan (eds.), *Psychology in Canada: The state of the discipline, 1984.* Ottawa: Canadian Psychological Association.

MARX, R.W. (1984). Canadian content and the WISC-R Information subtest. *Canadian Journal of Behavioural Science, 16(1),* 30–35.

MASLING, J. (ed.). (1986). *Empirical studies of psychoanalytic theories,* vol. 2. Hillsdale, NJ: Analytic Press.

MASLOW, A.H. (1943). A theory of human motivation. *Psychological Review, 50,* 370–396.

________. (1954). *Motivation and personality.* New York: Harper & Row.

________. (1965). *Eupsychian Management.* Homewood, IL: Richard D. Irwin, 55–56.

________. (1968). *Toward a psychology of being,* 2nd ed. New York: Van Nostrand.

________. (1970). *Motivation and personality,* rev. ed. NY: Harper & Row.

________. (1971). *The farther reaches of human nature.* New York: Viking.

MASON, R.M. (1985). Artificial intelligence: Promise, myth, and reality. *Library Journal, 110,* 56–57.

MASTERS, W.H., & JOHNSON, V.E. (1966). *Human sexual response.* Boston: Little, Brown.

________. (1970). *Human sexual inadequacy.* Boston: Little, Brown.

MATARAZZO, J.D. (1972). *Wechsler's measurement and appraisal of adult intelligence,* 5th ed. Baltimore: Williams & Wilkins.

MATE-KOLE, C., & ROBIN, A. (1989). Gender reassignment surgery: A controlled study. *Canadian Psychology, 30(2),* 214.

MATLIN, M.M. (1987). *The psychology of women.* New York: Holt, Rinehart, & Winston.

________. (1988). *Sensation and perception,* 2nd ed. Boston: Allyn and Bacon.

MAY, C., & RAPOPORT, S.I. (1989). Treating Alzheimer's disease. *Contemporary Psychology, 34,* 184–185.

MAY, R. (1989). Answers to Ken Wilber and John Rowan. *Journal of Humanistic Psychology, 29,* 244–248.

MAYER, J.D., & BOWER, G.H. (1986). Learning and memory for personality prototypes. *Journal of Personality and Social Psychology, 51,* 473–492.

MAYO, E. (1933). *Human problems of an industrial civilization.* New York: Macmillan.

MCBURNEY, D.H., & COLLINGS, V.B. (1984). *Introduction to sensation/perception,* 2nd ed. Englewood Cliffs, NJ: Prentice-Hall.

MCCAULEY, C., PARMELEE, C.M., SPERBERG, R.D., & CARR, T.D. (1980). Early extraction of meaning from pictures and its relation to conscious identification. *Journal of Experimental Psychology: Human Perception and Performance, 6,* 265–276.

MCCLELLAND, D.C. (1965). Achievement and entrepreneurship: A longitudinal study. *Journal of Personality and Social Psychology, 1,* 389–392.

________. (1971). *Motivational trends in society.* Morristown, NJ: General Learning Press.

________. (1989). Motivational factors in health and disease. *American Psychologist, 44*, 675–683.

McClelland, D.C., Atkinson, J.W., Clark, R.A., & Lowell, R.L. (1953). *The achievement motive.* New York: Appleton-Century-Crofts.

McCord, W., & McCord, J. (1964). *The psychopath: An essay on the criminal mind.* New York: Van Nostrand Reinhold.

McCormick, D.A., & Thompson, R.F. (1984). Cerebellum: Essential involvement in the classically conditioned eyelid response. *Science, 223*, 296–299.

McCrae, R.R., & Costa, P.T. (1986). Clinical assessment can benefit from recent advances in personality psychology. *American Psychologist, 41*, 1001–1002.

________. (1987). Validation of the five-factor model of personality across instruments and observers. *Journal of Personality and Social Psychology, 52*, 81–90.

________. (1989). The structure of interpersonal traits: Wiggins's Circumplex and the five-factor model. *Journal of Personality and Social Psychology, 56*, 586–595.

McDougall, W. (1908). *An introduction to social psychology.* London: Methuen.

McFarland, C., & Ross, M. (1987). The relation between current impressions and memories of self and dating partners. *Psychological Bulletin, 13*, 228–238.

Mcginty, D.J., & Szymusiak, R. (1988). Neuronal unit activity patterns in behaving animals. *Annual Review of Psychology, 39*, 135–164.

McGregor, D. (1960). *The human side of enterprise.* New York: McGraw-Hill.

McGuire, W.J. (1969). The nature of attitudes and attitude change. In G. Lindzey & E. Aronson (eds.), *Handbook of social psychology*, vol. 3. Reading, MA: Addison-Wesley.

________. (1985). Attitudes and attitude change. In G. Lindzey & E. Aronson (eds.), *Handbook of social psychology*, vol. 2. New York: Random House.

McIntyre, J.S. & Craik, F.I.M. (1987). Age differences in memory of item and source information. *Canadian Journal of Psychology, 41*, 175–192.

McKillip, J., & Reidel, S.L. (1983). External validity of matching on physicial attractiveness for same and opposite sex couples. *Journal of Applied Social Psychology, 13*, 328–337.

McLaughlin, B. (1985). *Schoolage children*, vol. 2 of *Second language acquisition in childhood*, 2nd ed. Hillsdale, NJ: Lawrence Erlbaum Associates.

McReynolds, W.T., Lutz, R.N., Paulsen, B.K., & Kohrs, M.B. (1976). Weight loss resulting from two behavior modification procedures with nutritionists as therapists. *Behavior Therapy, 7*, 283–291.

Mead, M. (1939). *From the south seas: Studies of adolescence and sex in primitive societies.* NY: Morrow.

Mednick, S.A., Gabrielli, W.F., & Hutchings, B. (1984). Genetic influences in criminal convictions: Evidence from an adoption cohort. *Science, 224*, 891–894.

Meehl, P.E. (1962). Schizotaxia, schizotypy, schizophrenia. *American Psychologist, 17*, 827–838.

Mefford, I.N., Baker, T.L., Boehme, R., Foutz, A.S., Ciaranello, R.D., Barchas, J.D., & Dement, W.C. (1983). Narcolepsy: Biogenic amine deficits in an animal model, *Science, 220*, 629–632.

Meichenbaum, D. (1977). *Cognitive-behavior modification: An integrative approach.* New York: Plenum Press.

Meltzoff, A.N., & Moore, M.K. (1977). Imitation of facial and manual gestures by human neonates. *Science, 198*, 75–78.

Meltzoff, J., & Kornreich, M. (1971, July). It works. *Psychology Today, 5*, 57–61.

Melzack, R. (1973). *The puzzle of pain.* New York: Basic Books.

________. (1980). Psychology, and aspects of pain. In J.J. Bonicer (ed.), *Pain.* New York: Raven Press.

Melzack, R., & Dennis, S.G. (1978). Neurophysiological foundations of pain. In R.A. Sternbach (ed.), *The psychology of pain.* New York: Raven Press.

Melzack, R., & Wall, P.D. (1983). *The challenge of pain.* New York: Basic Books.

Menaker, T. (1967). Anxiety about drinking in alcoholics. *Journal of Abnormal and Social Psychology, 72*, 43–49.

Menninger, K. (1958). *Theory of psychoanalytic technique.* New York: Harper & Row.

Merikle, P.M., & Cheesman, J. (1986). Consciousness is a "subjective" state. *The Behavioral and Brain Sciences, 9*, 42–43.

Messer, S.B., & Winokur, M. (1980). Some limits to the integration of psychoanalytic and behavior therapy. *American Psychologist, 35*, 818–827.

Metalsky, G.I., Abramson, L.V., Seligman, M.E.P., Semmel, A., & Peterson, C. (1982). Attributional styles and life events in the classroom: Vulnerability and invulnerability to depressive mood reactions. *Journal of Personality and Social Psychology, 43*, 612–617.

Meyer, A.J., & Henderson, J.B. (1974). Multiple risk factor reduction in the prevention of cardiovascular disease. *Preventive Medicine, 3*, 225–236.

Meyer, J.P., & Pepper, S. (1977). Need compatibility and marital adjustment in young married couples. *Journal of Personality and Social Psychology, 35*, 331–342.

Meyer-Bahlburg, H. (1979). Sex hormones and female homosexuality: A critical examination. *Archives of Sexual Behavior, 8*(2), 101–119.

Meyerowitz, B.E., & Chaiken, S. (1987). The effect of message framing on breast self-examination attitudes, intentions, and behavior. *Journal of Personality and Social Psychology, 52*, 500–512.

Michaels, J.W., Blommel, J.M., Brocata, R.M., Linkous, R.A., & Rowe, J.S. (1982). Social facilitation and inhibition in a natural setting. *Replications in Social Psychology, 2*, 21–24.

Milavsky, J.R., Stipp, H.H., Kessler, R.C., & Rubens, W.S. (1982). *Television and aggression: A panel study.* New York: Academic.

Milgram, S. (1963). Behavioral study of obedience. *Journal of Abnormal and Social Psychology, 67*, 371–378.

________. (1965). Liberating effects of group pressure. *Journal of Personality and Social Psychology, 1*, 127–134.

________. (1968). Some conditions of obedience and disobedience to authority. *Human Relations, 18*(1), 57–76.

________. (1970). The experience of living in cities: A psychological analysis. *Science, 167*, 1461–1468.

Miller, A. (1988). Toward a typology of personality styles. *Canadian Psychology, 29*, 263–283.

Miller, G.A. (1956). The magic number seven, plus or minus two: Some limits on our capacity for processing information. *Psychological Review, 63*(2), 81–97.

________. (1965). Some preliminaries to psycholinguistics. *American Psychologist, 20*, 15–20.

Miller, L.K., & Miller, O. (1970). Reinforcing self help group activities of welfare recipients. *Journal of Applied Behavior Analysis, 3*(1), 57–64.

Miller, N.E. (1944). Experimental studies of conflict. In J. McV. Hunt (ed.), *Personality and the behavior disorders*, vol. 1. New York: Ronald.

________. (1948). Fear as an acquired drive. *Journal of Experimental Psychology, 38*(1), 89–101.

________. (1969). Learning of visceral and glandular responses. *Science, 163*, 434–445.

________. (1983). Behavioral medicine: Symbiosis between laboratory and clinic. *Annual Review of Psychology, 34*, 1–31.

———. (1985, February). Rx: Biofeedback. *Psychology Today, 19,* 54–59.

Miller, R.C., & Berman, J.S. (1983). The efficacy of cognitive behavior therapies: A quantitative review of the research evidence. *Psychological Bulletin, 94(1),* 39–53.

Miller, R.G., Ruben, R.T., Clark, B.R., Crawford, W.R., & Arthur, R.J. (1970). The stress of aircraft carrier landings: I. Corticosteroid responses in naval aviators. *Psychosomatic Medicine, 32,* 581–588.

Miller, W.R. (1977). Behavioral self-control: Training in the treatment of problem drinkers. In R.B. Stuart (ed.), *Behavioral self-management: Strategies, techniques, and outcomes.* New York: Brunner/Mazel.

Millon, T. (1988). Falling short of the border line. *Contemporary Psychology, 33,* 902–903.

Mills, M., & Melhuish, E. (1974). Recognition of mother's voice in early infancy. *Nature, 252,* 123–124.

Milner, B. (1966). Amnesia following operations on the temporal lobes. In C.W.M. Whitty & O. Zangwill (eds.), *Amnesia.* London: Butterworth.

Milner, P.M. (1966). *Physiological psychology.* New York: Holt, Rinehart & Winston.

Milton, G.A. (1958). Five studies of the relation between sex role identification and achievement in problem solving. Technical report no. 3. Department of Psychology, Yale University.

Milton, K. (1972). Women in policing. Washington, D.C.: Police Foundation.

Mineka, S., & Suomi, S.J. (1978). Social separation in monkeys. *Psychological Bulletin, 85,* 1376–1400.

Miner, J. (1980). *Theories of organizational behavior.* Hinsdale, IL: Dryden Press.

Mischel, W. (1968). *Personality and assessment.* New York: Wiley.

———. (1986). *Personality,* 4th ed. New York: Holt, Rinehart and Winston.

Mischel, W., & Peake, P.K. (1982). Beyond deja vu in the search for cross-situational consistency. *Psychological Review, 89,* 730–755.

Mischel, W. (1983). Some facets of consistency: Replies to Epstein, Funder, and Bem. *Psychological Review, 90,* 394–402.

Mitchel, J.S., & Keesey, R.E. (1974). The effects of lateral hypothalamic lesions and castration upon the body weight of male rats. *Behavioral Biology, 11(1),* 69–82.

Mitchell, D. (1981). Sensitive periods in visual development. In R. Aslin, J. Alberts, & M. Petersen (eds.), *The visual system,* vol. 2 of *Development of perception.* New York: Academic Press.

Mitchell, D.B. (1989). How many memory systems: Evidence from aging. *Journal of Experimental Psychology: Learning, Memory and Cognition, 15(1),* 31–49.

Mitchell, R.E., Billings, A.G., & Moos, R.H. (1982). Social support and well-being: Implications for prevention programs. *Journal of Primary Prevention, 3,* 77–98.

Money, J., Hampson, J.G., & Hampson, J.L. (1957). Imprinting and the establishment of gender role. *Archives of Neurology and Psychiatry, 77,* 333–336.

Monk, M., Tayback, M., & Gordon, J. (1965). Evaluation of an anti-smoking program among high school students. *American Journal of Public Health and the Nation's Health, 55,* 994–1004.

Moos, R.H., & Billings, A.G. (1982). Conceptualizing and measuring coping resources and processes. In L. Goldberger & S. Breznitz (eds.), *Handbook of Stress.* New York: Free Press.

Moos, R.H., & Tsu, V.D. (1977). The crisis of physical illness: An overview. In R.H. Moos (ed.), *Coping with physical illness.* New York: Plenum.

Moreland, R.L., & Zajonc, R.B. (1982). Exposure effects in person perception: Familiarity, similarity and attraction. *Journal of Experimental Social Psychology, 18,* 395–415.

Morrell, F. (1963). Information storage in nerve cells. In W.S. Fields & W. Abbott (eds.), *Information storage and neural control.* Springfield, IL: Charles C. Thomas.

Morris, D. (1967). *The naked ape.* New York: McGraw-Hill.

Morrison, J., Winokur, G., Crowe, R., & Clancy, J. (1973). The Iowa 500: The first follow up. *Archives of General Psychiatry, 29,* 678–682.

Moser, C.G., & Dyck, D.G. (1989). Type A behavior, uncontrollability, and the activation of hostile self-schema responding. *Journal of Research in Personality, 23,* 248–267.

Moskowitz, B.A. (1978, November). The acquisition of language. *Scientific American, 239 (11),* 92–108.

Moyer, K.E. (1983). The physiology of motivation: Aggression as a model. In C.J. Scheier & A.M. Rogers (eds.), *G. Stanley Hall Lecture Series,* vol. 3. Washington, D.C.: American Psychological Association.

Mroczkowski, T. (1984). Quality circles, fine—what next? *Quality Circle Digest, 4,* 44–47.

Mullaney, D.J., Johnson, L.C., Naitoh, P., Friedmann, J.K., & Globus, G.G. (1977). Sleep during and after gradual sleep reduction. *Psychophysiology, 14,* 237–244.

Munn, N.L. (1965). *The evolution and growth of human behavior.* Boston: Houghton Mifflin Company.

Murdock, B.B., Jr. (1962). The second position effect in free recall. *Journal of Experimental Psychology, 64,* 482–488.

Murphy, L.B. (1974). Coping, vulnerability, and resilience in childhood. In G.V. Coelho, D.A. Hamburg, & J.E. Adams (eds), *Coping and Adaptation.* New York: Basic Books.

Mussen, P.H. (1961). Some antecedents and consequents of masculine sex-typing in adolescent boys. *Psychological Monographs, 75,* no. 506.

———. (1962). Long-term consequents of masculinity of interests in adolescence. *Journal of Consulting Psychology, 26,* 435–440.

Myers, D.G. (1989). *Psychology,* 2nd ed. New York: Worth.

Myers, J.K., Weissman, M.M., Tischler, G.L., Holzer, C.E., Leaf, P.J., Orvaschel, H.A., Anthony, J.C., Boyd, J.H., Burke, J.D., Kramer, M., & Stoltzman, R. (1984). Six-month prevalence of psychiatric disorders in three communities: 1980–82. *Archives of General Psychiatry, 41,* 959–967.

N

National Institute of Mental Health. (1982). *Television and behavior: Ten years of scientific progress and implications for the eighties,* vol. 1. Washington, D.C.: U.S. Government Printing Office.

Natsoulas, T. (1978). Consciousness. *American Psychologist, 33,* 906–914.

Naylor, J., Pritchard, R., & Ilgen, D. (1980). *A theory of behavior in organization.* New York: Academic Press.

Neale, J.M., Cox, D.S., Valdimarsdottir, H., & Stone, A.A. (1988). The relations between immunity and health: Comment on Pennebaker, Kiecolt-Glaser, and Glaser. *Journal of Consulting and Clinical Psychology, 56,* 636–637.

Neill, W.T., & Westberry, R.L. (1987). Selective attention and the suppression of cognitive noise. *Journal of Experimental Psychology: Learning, Memory, and Cognition, 13,* 327–334.

Neisser, U. (1967). *Cognitive psychology.* New York: Appleton Century-Crofts.

———. (1982). *Memory observed.* New York: W.H. Freeman.

Nelson, L.L., & Kagan, S. (1972, September). Competition: the star-spangled scramble. *Psychology Today, 6,* 53–56, 90–91.

Nelson, T.O. (1977). Repetition and depth of processing. *Journal of Verbal Learning and Verbal Behavior, 16,* 151–172.

Neugarten, B. (1968). Adult personality: Toward a psychology of the life cycle. In B. Neugarten (ed.), *Middle age and aging.* Chicago: University of Chicago Press.

________. (1974). The roles we play. In American Medical Association, *Quality of life: The middle years.* Acton, MA: Publishing Sciences Group.

NEUGEBAUER, R., & SUSSER, M. (1979). Some epidemiological aspects of epilepsy. *Psychological Medicine, 9,* 207–215.

NEWCOMB, T. (1961). *The acquaintance process.* New York: Holt, Rinehart and Winston.

NEWCOMBE, N., BANDURA, M.M., & TAYLOR, D.C. (1983). Sex differences in spatial ability and spatial activities. *Sex Roles, 9,* 514–522.

NEWELL, A., & SIMON, H.A. (1972). *Human problem solving.* Englewood Cliffs, NJ: Prentice-Hall.

NIETZEL, M.T., & BERNSTEIN, D.A. (1987). *Introduction to clinical psychology,* 2nd ed. Englewood Cliffs, NJ: Prentice-Hall.

NISBETT, R., & WILSON, T. (1977). Telling more than we can know: Verbal reports on mental processes. *Psychological Review, 84,* 231–259.

NISBETT, R.E. (1972). Hunger, obesity and the ventromedial hypothalamus. *Psychological Review, 79,* 433–453.

NISBETT, R.E., & ROSS, L.D. (1980). *Human inference: Strategies and shortcomings of social judgment.* Century Psychology Series. Englewood Cliffs, NJ: Prentice-Hall.

NORTON, G.R., HARRISON, B., HAUCH, J., & RHODES, L. (1985). Characteristics of people with infrequent panic attacks. *Journal of Abnormal Psychology, 94,* 216–221.

NYSTROM, P. (1978). Managers and the hi-hi leader myth, *Academy of Management Journal, 21,* 325–331.

O

OLDS, J., & MILNER, P. (1954). Positive reinforcement produced by electrical stimulation of septal area and other regions of rat brain. *Journal of Comparative and Physiological Psychology, 47,* 419–427.

O'LEARY, K.D., & BECKER, W.C. (1967). Behavior modification of an adjustment class: A token reinforcement system. *Exceptional Children, 33,* 637–642.

ORME, C.M., & MINIK, Y.M. (1987). Recidivism and self-cure of obesity: A test of Schacter's hypothesis in diabetic patients. *Health Psychology, 6,* 467–475.

ORNSTEIN, R. (1977). *The psychology of consciousness,* 2nd ed. San Francisco: Freeman.

________. (1987). *Multimind.* Boston: Houghton Mifflin.

P

PAIVIO, A. (1986). *Mental representations: A dual coding approach.* New York: Oxford University Press.

PANCER, S.M. (1989). The Cambridge Prevention Project. *Canadian Psychology, 30,* 500.

PANKSEPP, J. (1986). The neurochemistry of behavior. *Annual Review of Psychology, 37,* 77–107.

PAPALIA, D.E., & OLDS, S.W. (1988). *Psychology,* 2nd ed. New York: McGraw-Hill.

PAPPENHEIMER, J.R. (1976, August). The sleep factor. *Scientific American, 235,* 24–29.

PARKES, C.M., BENJAMIN, B., & FITZGERALD, R.G. (1969). Broken heart: a statistical study of increased mortality among widowers. *British Medical Journal, 1,* 740–743.

PARLOFF, M.B., LONDON, P., & WOLFE, B. (1986). Individual psychotherapy and behavior change. *Annual Review of Psychology, 37,* 321–349.

PATTERSON, F.G., & LINDEN, E. (1981). *The education of Koko.* New York: Holt, Rinehart and Winston.

PATTERSON, G.R., RAY, R., & SHAW, D. (1968). Direct interventions in families of deviant children. Unpublished manuscript, University of Oregon.

PATTERSON, M.M. (1976). Mechanisms of classical conditioning and fixation in spinal mammals. In A.H. Riesen and R.F. Thompson (eds.), *Advances in psychobiology,* vol. 3. New York: Wiley-Interscience.

PAVLOV, I. (1927). *Conditioned reflexes.* (G.V. Anrep, translator). New York: Dover Publishing, Inc.

PEDERSEN, N.L., PLOMIN, R., MCCLEARN, G.E., & FRIBERG, L. (1988). Neuroticism, extraversion, and related traits in adult twins reared apart and reared together. *Journal of Personality and Social Psychology, 55,* 950–957.

PEDERSON, D.M., & WHEELER, J. (1983). The Muller-Lyer illusion among Navajos. *Journal of Social Psychology, 121,* 3–6.

PENDERY, M.L., MALTZMAN, I.M., & WEST, L.J. (1982). Controlled drinking by alcoholics? New findings and a reevaluation of a major affirmative study. *Science, 217,* 169–175.

PENFIELD, W. (1969). Consciousness, memory and man's conditional reflexes. In K.H. Pribram (ed.), *On the biology of learning.* New York: Harcourt Brace Jovanovich.

________. (1975). *The mystery of the mind.* Princeton: Princeton University Press.

PENFIELD, W., & PEROT, P. (1963). The brain's record of auditory and visual experience. *Brain, 86,* 595–697.

PENNEBAKER, J.W., & BEALL, S.K. (1986). Confronting a traumatic event: Toward an understanding of inhibition and disease. *Journal of Abnormal Psychology, 95,* 274–281.

PENNEBAKER, J.W., KIECOLT-GLASER, J.K., & GLASER, R. (1988a). Disclosure of traumas and immune function: Health implications for psychotherapy. *Journal of Consulting and Clinical Psychology, 56,* 239–245.

________. (1988b). Confronting traumatic experience and immunocompetence: A reply to Neale, Cox, Valdimarsdotir, and Stone. *Journal of Consulting and Clinical Psychology, 56,* 638–639.

PENNEBAKER, J.W., & O'HEERON, R.C. (1984). Confiding in others and illness rate among spouses of suicide and accidental-death victims. *Journal of Abnormal Psychology, 93,* 473–476.

PENNEBAKER, J.W., & SUSMAN, J.R. (1988). Disclosure of traumas and psychosomatic processes. *Social Science and Medicine, 26,* 327–332.

PERLMAN, D. (1975). Heart doctors clash over coronary risk factors. *San Francisco Chronicle,* January 22, p. 4.

PERLMUTTER, M., & HALL, E. (1985). *Adult development and aging.* New York: Wiley.

PERLS, F.S. (1970). Four lectures. In J. Fagan & I.L. Shepherd (eds.), *Gestalt therapy now.* Palo Alto: Science and Behavior Books, Inc.

PERRY, C., & LAURENCE, J-R. (1983a). Hypnosis, surgery, and mind-body interaction: An historical evaluation. *Canadian Journal of Behavioural Science, 15,* 351–372.

________. (1983b). The enhancement of memory by hypnosis in the legal investigative situation. *Canadian Psychology, 24,* 155–167.

________. (1986). Social and psychological influences on hypnotic behavior. *The Behavioral and Brain Sciences, 9,* 478–479.

PERVIN, L.A. (1985). Personality: current controversies, issues, and directions. *Annual Review of Psychology, 36,* 83–114.

PETERSON, C., & SELIGMAN, M.E.P. (1984). Causal explanations as a risk factor for depression: Theory and evidence. *Psychological Review, 91,* 347–374.

PETERSON, L. (1986). Introduction to the special series. *Journal of Consulting and Clinical Psychology, 54,* 591–592.

PETERSON, L.R., & PETERSON, M.J. (1959). Short-term retention of individual verbal items. *Journal of Experimental Psychology, 58*(3), 193–198.

PETRI, H.L. (1986). *Motivation: Theory and research.* Belmont, CA: Wadsworth.

PFEIFFER, E. (1977). Sexual behavior in old age. In E.W. Busse & E. Pfeiffer. (eds.), *Behavior and adaptation in late life;* 2nd ed. Boston: Little, Brown.

PIAGET, J. (1930). *The child's conception of physical causality.* London: Routledge & Kegan Paul.

________. (1952). *The origins of intelligence in children.* New York: International University Press.

________. (1972). Intellectual evolution from adolescence to adulthood. *Human Development, 15,* 1–12.

PIAGET, J., & INHELDER, B. (1967). *The child's conception of space.* New York: W.W. Norton.

PILIAVIN, J.M., RODIN, J., & PILIAVIN, J.A. (1969). Good Samaritanism: An underground phenomenon? *Journal of Personality and Social Psychology, 13,* 289–299.

PINCUS, J.D., & TUCKER, G. (1978). *Behavioral neurology,* 2nd ed. New York: Oxford University Press.

PINEL, J.P.J. (1984). After forty-five years ECT is still controversial. *The Behavioral and Brain Sciences, 7(1),* 30–31.

PITTENGER, D.J., & PAVLIK, W.B. (1989). Resistance to extinction in humans: Analysis of the generalized partial reinforcement effect. *Learning and Motivation, 20(1),* 60–72.

PLUTCHIK, R. (1980). *Emotion: A psychoevolutionary synthesis.* NY: Harper and Row.

POKORNY, J., & SMITH, V.C. (1986). Colorimetry and color discrimination. In K. R. Boff, L. Kaufman, & J.P. Thomas (eds.). *Handbook of perception and human performance (vol. 1).* New York: Wiley.

POMERANZ, B. (1984). Acupuncture and the endorphins. *Ethos, 10,* 385–393.

POPE, H.G., JONAS, J.M., HUDSON, J.I., COHEN, B.M., & GUNDERSON, J.G. (1983). The validity of DSM-III borderline personality disorder. *Archives of General Psychiatry, 40(1),* 23–30.

POSNER, M.L., & BOLES, S.J. (1971). Components of attention. *Psychological Review, 78,* 391–408.

POSTMAN, L. (1971). Human learning and memory. In G.A. Kimble & K. Schlesinger (eds.), *Topics in the history of psychology.* Hillsdale, NJ: Erlbaum.

________. (1975). Verbal learning and memory. *Annual Review of Psychology, 26,* 291–335.

PREMACK, D. (1965). Reinforcement theory. In D. Levine (ed.), *Nebraska Symposiumon Motivation.* Lincoln: University of Nebraska Press.

________. (1976). *Intelligence in ape and man.* Hillsdale, NJ: Erlbaum.

PRIBRAM, K.H. (1969, January). The neurophysiology of remembering. *Scientific American, 220,* 73–86.

PUGH, G.M., & BOER, D.P. (1987). Summing up: Ten Canadian substitute items for the WAIS-R Information subtest that work. *Canadian Psychology, 28(2a),* Abstract 488.

Q

QUINTIN, E.P. (1985). Note sur l'usage clinique du WPPSI. *Psychologie Canadienne, 26(3),* 214–218.

R

RACHMAN, S.T., & TEASDALE, J. (1969). Aversion therapy: An appraisal. In C.M. Franks (ed.), *Behavior therapy: Appraisal and status.* New York: McGraw-Hill.

RAHE, R.H. (1968). Life change measurement as a predictor of illness. *Proceeding of the Royal Society of Medicine, 61,* 1124–1126.

RANDI, J. (1980). *Flim-flam!* New York: Lippencott & Crowell.

________. (1983a, Summer). The Project Alpha experiment, Part 1: The first two years. *Skeptical Inquirer,* 24–33.

________. (1983b, Fall). The Project Alpha experiment, Part 2: Beyond the laboratory. *Skeptical Inquirer,* 36–45.

RAPPAPORT, J. (1981). In praise of paradox: A social policy of empowerment over prevention. *American Journal of Community Psychology, 9,* 1–25.

RASKIN, N.J., & ROGERS, C.R. (1989). Person-centered therapy. In R.J. Corsini and D. Wedding (eds.), *Current psychotherapies,* 4th ed. Itasca, IL: F.A. Peacock Publishers.

RATCLIFFE, R., & MCKOON, G. (1986). More on the distinction between episodic and semantic memories. *Journal of Experimental Psychology: Learning, Memory and Cognition, 12,* 312–313.

RAWSON, I.G., & LASSER, A.A. (1983). Theory Z: A useful tool for hospital management or another fad? *Hospital and Health Services Administration, 28(4),* 21–30.

RAY, O.S. (1983). *Drugs, society, and human behavior* (3rd ed.). St. Louis: Mosby.

REISENZEIN, R. (1983). The Schachter theory of emotion: Two decades later. *Psychological Bulletin, 94,* 239–264.

RHEINGOLD, H.L., GEWIRTZ, J.L., & ROSS, H.W. (1959). Social conditioning of vocalizations in the infant. *Journal of Comparative and Physiological Psychology, 52,* 68–73.

RHINE, J.B. (1977). History of experimental studies. In B.B. Wolman (ed.), *Handbook of parapsychology.* New York: Van Nostrand Reinhold.

RICHARDSON, J.L., MARKS, G., JOHNSON, C.A., GRAHAM, J.W., CHAN, K.K., SELSER, J.N., KISHBAUGH, C., BARRANDAY, Y., & LEVINE, A.M. (1987). Path model of multidimensional compliance with cancer therapy. *Health Psychology, 6(3),* 183–207.

RIDENOUR, M. (1982). Infant walkers: Developmental tool or inherent danger? *Perceptual and Motor Skills, 55,* 1201–1202.

RIMM, D.C., & CUNNINGHAM, H.M. (1985). Behaviour therapies. In S.J. Lynn & J.P. Garske (eds.), *Contemporary psychotherapies: Models and methods.* Columbus, OH: Charles E. Merrill.

ROBBIN, A.A. (1958). A controlled study of the effects of leucotomy. *Journal of Neurology, Neurosurgery and Psychiatry, 21,* 262–269.

ROBINS, L.N. (1988). Attributions and depression: Why is the literature so inconsistent? *Journal of Personality and Social Psychology, 54,* 880–889.

ROBINS, L.N., & HELZER, J.E. (1986). Diagnosis and clinical assessment: The current state of psychiatric diagnosis. In M.R. Rosenzweig & L.W. Porter (eds.), *Annual review of psychology: 1986.* Palo Alto, CA: Annual Reviews.

ROCK, I. (1983). The logic of perception. Cambridge, MA: MIT Press.

ROE, A.A. (1951). Study of imagery in research scientists. *Journal of Personality, 19,* 459–470.

ROETHLISBERGER, F., & DICKSON, W.J. (1935). *Management and the worker.* Cambridge: Harvard University Press.

ROGAWSKI, M.A. (1985). Norepinephrine. In M.A. Rogawski & J.L. Barker (eds.), *Neurotransmitter actions in the vertebrate nervous system.* New York: Plenum Press.

ROGERS, C.R. (1951). *Client-centered therapy.* Boston: Houghton Mifflin.

________. (1957). The necessary and sufficient conditions of therapeutic personality change. *Journal of Consulting Psychology, 21(2),* 95–103.

________. (1959). A theory of therapy, personality, and interpersonal relationships, as developed in the client-centered framework. In S. Koch (ed.), *Psychology: A study of a science,* vol. 3. New York: McGraw-Hill.

________. (1961). *On becoming a person.* Boston: Houghton Mifflin.

________. (1980a). *A way of being.* Boston: Houghton Mifflin.

________. (1980b). Client centered therapy. In H.I. Kaplan, B.J. Sadock, & A.M. Freedman (eds.), *Comprehensive textbook of psychiatry,* vol. 3. Baltimore: Williams & Wilkins.

RORER, L.G., & WIDIGER, T.A. (1983). Personality structure and assessment, *Annual Review of Psychology, 34,* 431–463.

ROSCH, E. (1978). Principles of categorization. In E. Rosch and B.B. Lloyd (eds.), *Cognition and categorization.* New York: Wiley.

ROSE, R.M., JENKINS, C.D., & HURST, M.W. (1978). *Air traffic controller health change study.* Report to the Federal Aviation Administration. Washington, D.C. United States Government Printing Office.

ROSEN, B.C., & DI'ANDRADE, R. (1959). The psychological origins of achievement motivation. *Sociometry, 22,* 185–218.

ROSEN, H. (1980). *The development of socio-moral knowledge.* New York: Columbia University Press.

ROSENBAUM, M.E. (1986). The repulsion hypothesis: On the non development of relationships. *Journal of Personality and Social Psychology, 51*, 1156–1166.

ROSENFELD, L.B., CIVIKLY, J.M., & HERRON, J.R. (1979). Anatomical sex and self-disclosure: Topic, situation, and relationship considerations. Paper presented at the International Communications Association convention, Philadelphia.

ROSENHAN, D.L. (1973). On being sane in insane places. *Science, 179*, 250–258.

ROSENMAN, R.H., FRIEDMAN, M., STRAUS, R., JENKINS, C.D., ZYZANSKI, S.J., & WURM, M. (1970). Coronary heart disease in the Western Collaborative Group Study. *Journal of Chronic Diseases, 23*, 173–190.

ROSENMAN, R.H., WURM, M., KOSITCHEK, R., HAHN, W., & WERTHESSEN, N.T. (1964). A predictive study of coronary heart disease: The Western Collaborative Group Study. *Journal of the American Medical Association, 189(1)*, 15–22.

ROSENTHAL, R. (1986). Nonsignificant relationships as scientific evidence. *The Behavioral and Brain Sciences, 9*, 479–481.

ROSENTHAL, R., & RUBIN, D.B. (1978). Interpersonal expectancy effects: The first 345 studies. *Behavioral and Brain Sciences, 1*, 377–386.

_________. (1982). Further meta-analytic procedures for assessing cognitive gender differences. *Journal of Educational Psychology, 74*, 708–712.

ROSENZWEIG, M.R. (1984). Experience, memory, and the brain. *American Psychologist, 39*, 365–376.

ROSENZWEIG, M.R., BENNETT, E.L., & DIAMOND, M.C. (1972, February). Brain changes in response to experience. *Scientific American, 226*, 22–29.

ROSETT, H.L., & WEINER, L. (1985). Alcohol and pregnancy: A clinical perspective. *Annual Review of Medicine, 36*, 73–80.

ROSKIES, E., SERAGANIAN, P., OSEASOHN, R., HANLEY, J.A., COLLU, R., MARTIN, N., & SMILGA, C. (1987). The Montreal Type A intervention project: Major findings. *Health Psychology, 5(1)*, 45–69.

ROSS, L. (1977). The intuitive psychologist and his shortcomings: Distortions in the attribution process. In L. Berkowitz (ed.), *Advances in Experimental Social Psychology*, vol. 10. New York: Academic Press.

ROSS, M., & FLETCHER, G.J.O. (1985). Attribution and social perception. In G. Lindsey and E. Aronson (eds.), *Handbook of social psychology*, 3rd ed. Reading, MA: Addison-Wesley.

ROSS, M., & SICOLY, F. (1979). Egocentric biases in availability and attribution. *Journal of Personality and Social Psychology, 37*, 322–336.

ROTHBART, M., & PARK, B. (1986). On the confirmability and disconfirm ability of trait concepts. *Journal of Personality and Social Psychology, 50*, 131–142.

ROWAN, J. (1989). Two humanistic psychologies or one? *Journal of Humanistic Psychology, 29*, 224–229.

RUBIN, J.Z., PROVENZANO, F.J., & LURIA, Z. (1974). The eye of the beholder: Parents' views on sex of newborns. *American Journal of Orthopsychiatry, 44*, 512–519.

RULE, B.G., & ADAIR, J.G. (1984). Contributions of psychology as a social science to Canadian society. *Canadian Psychology, 25*, 52–58.

RUMBAUGH, D.M. (ed.). (1977). *Language Learning by a chimpanzee: The Lana project.* New York: Academic Press.

RUMBAUGH, D.M., GILL, T.V., & VON GLASERFELD, E.C. (1963). Reading and sentence completion by a chimpanzee. *Science, 182*, 731–733.

RUMELHART, D.E., & MCCLELLAND, J.L. (1986). *Parallel distributed processing: Explorations in the micro-structure of cognition.* Cambridge, MA: MIT Press.

RUNDUS, D. (1977). Maintenance rehearsal and single-level processing. *Journal of Verbal Learning and Verbal Behaviour, 16*, 665–682.

RUSH, A.J., BECK, A.T., KOVACS, M., & HOLLON, S.D. (1977). Comparative efficacy of cognitive therapy and pharmacotherapy in the treatment of depressed outpatients. *Cognitive Therapy and Research, 1*, 17–38.

RUSHTON, J.P. (1989a). The evolution of racial differences: A response to M. Lynn. *Journal of Research in Personality, 23*, 7–20.

_________. (1989b). Race differences in sexuality and their correlates: Another look and physiological models. *Journal of Research in Personality, 23*, 35–54.

S

SACKEIM, H.A., & GUR, R.C. (1978). Self-deception, self-confrontation and consciousness. In G.E. Schwartz and D. Shapiro (eds.), *Consciousness and self-regulation, advances in research*, vol. 2. New York: Plenum Press.

_________. (1979). Self-deception, other-deception, and self-reported psychopathology. *Journal of Consulting and Clinical Psychology, 47*, 213–215.

ST. GEORGE-HYSLOP, P.H., TANZI, R.E., POLINSKY, R.J., HAINES, J.L., NEE, L., WATKINS, P.C., MYERS, R.H., FELDMAN, R.G., POLLEN, D., DRACHMAN, D., GROWDON, J., BRUNI, A., FONCIN, J., SALMON, D., FROMMETT, P., AMADUCCI, L., SORBI, S., PIACENTINI, S., STEWART, G.D., HOBBES, W.J., CONNEALLY, P.M., & GUSELLA, J.F. (1987). The genetic defect causing familial Alzheimer's disease maps on chromosome 21. *Science, 235*, 885–889.

ST. JEAN, R. (1986). Hypnosis: Artichoke or onion? *The Behavioral and Brain Sciences, 9*, 482.

SAMELSON, F. (1980). J.B. Watson's Little Albert, Cyril Burt's twins, and the need for a critical science. *American Psychologist, 35*, 619–625.

SANDE, G.N., & ADAMS, J.E., & FRIESEN, C. (1990). Consequences of gender-inappropriate speech. Unpublished manuscript, University of Manitoba.

SANDERS, R.J. (1985). Teaching apes to ape language: Explaining the imitative and nonimitative signing of a chimpanzee. *Journal of Comparative Psychology, 99*, 197–210.

SANDLER, L.S., WILSON, K.G., ASMUNDSON, G., LARSEN, D., & EDIGER, J. (1989). Panic attack among university students. *Canadian Psychology, 30(2)*, 446.

SANFORD, F.H., & WRIGHTSMAN, L.S. (1970). *Psychology: A scientific study of man*, 3rd ed. Monterey: Brooks/Cole Publishing Company.

SARASON, I.G., JOHNSON, J.H., & SIEGAL, J.M. (1978). Assessing the impact of life changes: Development of the Life Experiences Survey. *Journal of Consulting and Clinical Psychology, 46*, 932–946.

SASHKIN, M. (1984). Participative management is an ethical imperative. *Organizational Dynamics, 12(4)*, 4–22.

SAVAGE-RUMBAUGH, E.S., PATE, J.L., LAWSON, J., SMITH, S.T., & ROSENBAUM, S. (1983). Can a chimpanzee make a statement? *Journal of Experimental Psychology: General, 112*, 457–492.

SAWREY, W.L., CONGER, J.J., & TURRELL, E.S. (1956). An experimental investigation of the role of psychological factors in the production of gastric ulcers in rats. *Journal of Comparative and Physiological Psychology, 49*, 457–461.

SAXE, L., DOUGHERTY, D., & CROSS, T. (1985). The validity of polygraph testing. *American Psychologist, 40*, 355–366.

SCHACHAR, R., RUTTER, M., & SMITH, A. (1981). The characteristics of situational and pervasively hyperactive children: Implications for syndrome definition. *Journal of Child Psychology and Psychiatry, 22*, 375–392.

SCHACHTER, S. (1959). *The psychology of affiliation.* Stanford, CA: Stanford University Press.

———. (1964). The interaction of cognitive and physiological determinants of emotional state. In L. Berkowitz (ed.), *Advances in experimental social psychology.* NY: Academic Press.

———. (1971). *Emotion, obesity, and crime.* NY: Academic Press.

———. (1982). Recidivism and self-cure of smoking and obesity. *American Psychologist, 37,* 436–444.

SCHACHTER, S., GOLDMAN, R., & GORDON, A. (1968). The effect of fear, food deprivation, and obesity on eating. *Journal of Personality and Social Psychology, 10,* 91–97.

SCHACHTER, S., & LATANE, B. (1964). Crime, cognition, and the autonomic nervous system. In D. Levine (ed.), *Nebraska Symposium on Motivation,* vol. 12. Lincoln, NE: University of Nebraska Press.

SCHACTER, D.L. (1976). The hypnagogic state: A critical review of the literature. *Psychological Bulletin, 83,* 452–481.

———. (1987). Implicit memory: History and current status. *Journal of Experimental Psychology: Learning, Memory and Cognition, 13,* 501–518.

SCHACTER, D.L., & GRAF, P. (1989). Modality specificity of implicit memory for new associations. *Journal of Experimental Psychology: Learning, Memory, and Cognition, 15(1),* 3–12.

SCHACTER, D.L., & SINGER, J.E. (1962). Cognitive, social, and physiological determinants of emotional state. *Psychological Review, 69,* 379–399.

SCHALE, K.W., & STROTHER, C.R. (1968). A cross-sectional study of age changes in cognitive behavior. *Psychological Bulletin, 70,* 671–680.

SCHANK, R., & ABELSON, R. (1977). *Scripts, plans, goals, and understanding.* Hillsdale, NJ: Erlbaum.

SCHANK, R.C., & HUNTER, L. (1985). The quest to understand thinking. *Byte, 10(4),* 143–155.

SCHIFFMAN, H.R. (1976). Sensation and perception: An integrated approach. New York: Wiley.

SCHMALE, A.H. (1972). Giving up as a final common pathway to changes in health. *Advances in Psychosomatic Medicine, 8,* 20–40.

SCHMALE, A.H., & IKER, H.P. (1971). Hopelessness as a predictor of cervical cancer. *Social Science and Medicine, 5(2),* 95–100.

SCHNEIDER, D.J. (1973). Implicit personality theory: A review. *Psychological Bulletin, 79,* 294–309.

SCHNEIDMAN, E.S. (ed.). (1976). *Deaths of man.* New York: Quadrangle.

SCHROEDER, M. (1989). The relationship between moral reasoning and conduct. *Canadian Psychology, 30(2),* 461.

SCHULZ, R. (1978). *The psychology of death, dying, and bereavement.* Reading, MA: Addison-Wesley.

SCHWARTZ, B. (1984). *Psychology of learning and behavior,* 2nd ed. New York: W.W. Norton.

SCHWARTZ, R.M. (1982). Cognitive-behavior modification: A conceptual review. *Clinical Psychology Review, 2,* 267–293.

SCHWARTZ, R.S. (1975). Another look at immunologic surveillance. *New England Journal of Medicine, 293,* 181–184.

SCOVILLE, W.B., & MILNER, B. (1957). Loss of recent memory after bilateral hippocampal lesions, *Journal of Neurology, Neurosurgery, and Psychiatry, 20(1),* 11–21.

SEARS, R.R. (1970). Relation of early socialization experiences to self-concepts and gender role in middle childhood. *Child Development, 41,* 267–289.

SEEMAN, J. (1989). A reaction to "Psychodiagnosis: A person-centered perspective." *Person-Centered Review, 4,* 152–156.

SELFRIDGE, O.G. (1955). Pattern recognition and modern computers. *Proceedings of the Weskin Joint Computer Conference.* New York: Institute of Electrical and Electronics Engineer.

SELIGMAN, M.E.P. (1970). On the generality of the laws of learning. *Psychological Review, 77,* 406–418.

———. (1971). Phobias and preparedness. *Behavior Therapy, 2,* 307–320.

———. (1974). Depression and learned helplessness. In R.J. Friedman & M.M. Katz (eds.), *The psychology of depression: Contemporary theory and research.* Washington, D.C.: Winston-Wiley.

———. (1975). *Helplessness: On depression, development, and death.* San Francisco: Freeman.

SELIGMAN, M.E.P., & HAGER, J.L. (1972). *Biological boundaries of learning.* New York: Appleton Century-Crofts.

SELIGMAN, M.E.P., & JOHNSTON, J.C. (1973). A cognitive theory of avoidance learning. In F.J. Guigan and D.B. Lumsden (eds.), *Contemporary approaches to conditioning and learning.* Washington, D.C.: V.N. Winston and Sons.

SELMAN, R. (1980). *The growth of interpersonal understanding.* New York: Academic Press.

SELYE, H. (1936). A syndrome produced by diverse nocuous agents. *Nature, 138,* 32.

———. (1956). *The stress of life.* New York: McGraw-Hill.

———. (1974). *Stress without distress.* New York: New American Library.

———. (1976). *The stress of life,* 2nd ed. New York: McGraw-Hill.

———. (1982). History and present status of the stress concept. In L. Goldberger and S. Breznitz (eds.), *Handbook of stress: Theoretical and clinical aspects.* New York: Free Press.

SERAGANIAN, P. (1985). Behavioural aspects of coronary heart disease. *Canadian Psychology, 26(2),* 113–120.

SEYFORT, B., SPREEN, O., & LAHMER, V. (1980). A critical look at the WISC-R with Native Indian children. *Alberta Journal of Educational Research, 26(1),* 14–24.

SEYMOUR, R.B., WESSON, D.R., & SMITH, D.E. (1986). Editor's introduction. *Journal of Psychoactive Drugs, 18,* 287–289.

SHAPIRO, D.A., & SHAPIRO, D. (1982). Meta-analysis of comparative therapy outcome studies: A replication and refinement. *Psychological Bulletin, 92,* 581–604.

SHAPIRO, D.H., JR. (1985). Clinical use of meditation as a self-regulation strategy: Comments on Holmes's conclusions and implications. *American Psychologist, 40,* 719–722.

SHAW, M.E. (1976). *Group dynamics: The psychology of small group behavior,* 2nd ed. New York: McGraw-Hill.

SHEFFIELD, F.D. (1966). New evidence on the drive-reduction theory of reinforcement. In R.N. Haber (ed.) *Current research in motivation.* New York: Holt.

SHELDON, W.H. (with the collaboration of C.W. Dupertuis and E. McDermott). (1954). *Atlas of Men.* New York: Harper & Row.

SHEPARD, R.N. (1978). Externalization of mental images and the act of creation. In B.B. Randhawa and W.E. Coffman (eds.), *Visual learning, thinking, and communicating.* New York: Academic Press.

SHERIF, M., & SHERIF, C.W. (1953). *Groups in harmony and tension.* New York: Harper & Row.

SHETTLEWORTH, S.J. (1972). Constraints on learning. In D.S. Lehrman, R.A. Hinde, and E. Shaw (eds.), *Advances in the study of behavior,* vol. 4. New York: Academic Press.

SHEVRIN, H., & DICKMAN, S. (1980). The psychological unconscious: A necessary assumption for all psychological theory. *American Psychologist, 35,* 421–434.

SHLIEN, J.M. (1989). Boy's person centered perspective on psychodiagnosis. *Person-Centered Review, 4,* 157–162.

SHNEIDMAN, E. (1989). The indian summer of life: A preliminary study of septuagenerarians. *American Psychologist, 44,* 684–694.

SHNEIDMAN, E.S. (ed.). (1976). *Deaths of man.* New York: Quadrangle.

SHOEMAKER, J. (ed.). (1977). Women and mathematics: Research perspectives for change. *N.I.E. papers in education and work*, No. 8. Washington, D.C., Education and Work Group, The National Institute of Education, U.S. Department of Health, Education and Welfare.

SHOTLAND, R.L., & GOODSTEIN, L.I. (1984). The role of bystanders in crime control. *Journal of Social Issues, 40(1)*, 9–26.

SILVERSTEIN, A. (1988). An Aristotelian resolution of the idiographic versus nomothetic tension. *American Psychologist, 43*, 425–430.

SIMPSON, M.T., OLEWINE, D.A., JENKINS, F.H., RAMSEY, S.J., ZYZANSKI, S.J., THOMAS, G., & HAMES, C.G. (1974). Exercise-induced catecholomines and platelet aggregation in the coronary-prone behavior pattern. *Psychosomatic Medicine, 36*, 476–487.

SINGER, J.L., & KOLLIGIAN, J. (1987). Personality: Developments in the study of private experience. *Annual Review of Psychology, 38*, 533–574.

SINGER, W. (1986). Neuronal activity as a shaping factor in postnatal development of visual cortex. In W.T. Greenough and J.M. Jurasko (eds.), *Developmental neuropsychobiology*. New York: Academic Press.

SIQUELAND, E.R., & LIPSITT, L.P. (1966). Conditioned head turning in human newborns. *Journal of Experimental Child Psychology, 3*, 356–376.

SKEELS, H.M. (1966). Adult status of children with contrasting early life experiences. *Monographs of the Society for Research in Child Development, 31(3)*.

SKINNER, B.F. (1957). *Verbal behavior*. New York: Appleton-Century-Crofts.

_________. (1969). *Contingencies of reinforcement*. New York: Appleton-Century-Crofts.

_________. (1971). *Beyond freedom and dignity*. New York: Knopf.

_________. (1972). *Cumulative record*, 3rd ed. New York: Appleton-Century-Crofts.

SKLAR, L.A., & ANISMAN, H. (1979). Stress and coping factors influencing tumor growth. *Science, 205*, 513–515.

SMALL, I.F., MILSTEIN, B., MILLER, J.J., MALLOY, F.W., & SMALL, J.G. (1986). Electroconvulsive treatment—indication, benefits and limitations. *American Journal of Psychotherapy, 40*, 343–356.

SMITH, D. (1982). Trends in counseling and psychotherapy. *American Psychologist, 37*, 802–809.

SMITH, M.L., & GLASS, G.V. (1977). Meta-analysis of psychotherapy outcome studies. *American Psychologist, 32*, 752–760.

SMITH, S.M. (1979). Remembering in and out of context. *Journal of Experimental Psychology: Human Learning and Memory, 5*, 460–471.

SMOLUCHA, L., & SMOLUCHA, F. (1986). A fifth Piagetian stage: The collaboration between imagination and logical thought in artistic creativity, *Poetics, 15*, 475–491.

SNYDER, M., & URANOWITZ, S.W. (1978). Reconstructing the past: Some cognitive consequences of person perception. *Journal of Personality and Social Psychology, 36*, 941–950.

SNYDER, M.L., TANKE, E.D., & BERSCHEID, E. (1977). Social perception and interpersonal behavior: On the self-fulfilling nature of social stereotypes. *Journal of Personality and Social Psychology, 35*, 656–666.

SNYDER, S.H., & CHILDERS, S.R. (1979). Opiate receptors and opioid peptides. *Annual Review of Neuroscience, 2*, 35–64.

SNYDERMAN, M., & ROTHMAN, S. (1987). Survey of expert opinion on intelligence and aptitude testing. *American Psychologist, 42(2)*, 137–144.

SOBELL, M.B., & SOBELL, L.C. (1972). Alcoholics treated by individualized behavior therapy: One-year treatment outcome. *Behavior Research and Therapy, 11*, 599–618.

_________. (1976). Second-year treatment outcome of alcoholics treated by individualized behavior therapy: Results. *Behaviour Research and Therapy, 14*, 195–215.

_________. (1978). *Behavioral treatment of alcohol problems. Individualized therapy and controlled drinking*. New York: Plenum Press.

SOLOMON, R.C., & WYNNE, L.C. (1953). Traumatic avoidance learning: Acquisition in normal dogs. *Psychological Monographs, 67(4)*, 1–19.

SPANOS, N.P. (1986). Hypnotic behavior: A social-psychological interpretation of amnesia, analgesia, and "trance logic." *The Behavioral and Brain Sciences, 9*, 449–467.

SPEAR, P.D., PENROD, S.D., & BAKER, T.B. (1988). *Psychology: Perspectives on behavior*. New York: John Wiley & Sons.

SPEARMAN, C. (1904). "General intelligence" objectively determined and measured. *American Journal of Psychology, 15*, 201–293.

SPENCE, J.T., DEAUX, K., & HELMREICH, R.L. (1985). Sex roles in contemporary American society. In G. Lindsey and E. Aronson (eds.), *Handbook of social psychology*, 3rd ed. Reading, MA: Addison-Wesley.

SPENCE, J.T., HELMREICH, R., & STAPP, J. (1974). The personal attributes questionnaire: A measure of sex-role stereotypes and masculinity-femininity *JSAS Catalog of Selected Documents in Psychology, 4*, 43.

SPERLING, G. (1960). The information available in brief visual presentations. *Psychological Monographs, 15*, 201–293.

SPERRY, R. (1982). Some effects of disconnecting the cerebral hemispheres. *Science, 217*, 1223–1226.

SPERRY, R.W. (1964, January). The great cerebral commisure. *Scientific American, 210*, 42–52.

_________. (1968). Hemispheric disconnection and unity in conscious awareness. *American Psychologist, 23*, 723–733.

_________. (1984). Consciousness, personal identity, and the divided brain. *Neuropsychologia, 22*, 661–674.

SPETCH, M.L., WILKIE, D.M., & PINEL, J.P.J. (1981). Backward conditioning: A reevaluation of the empirical evidence. *Psychological Bulletin, 89*, 163–175.

SPIELBERGER, C.D. (1983). *Manual for the state-trait anxiety inventory*. Palo Alto, CA: Consulting Psychologists Press.

SPITZ, H.I., & ROSECAN, J.S. (1987). *Cocaine abuse: New directions in treatment and research*. New York: Brunner/Mazel.

SPITZ, R.A., & WOLF, K. (1946). Anaclitic depression. *Psychoanalytic Study of Children, 2*, 313–342.

SQUIRE, L.R. (1987). *Memory and brain*. New York: Oxford University Press.

STAATS, A.W., & STAATS, C.K. (1963). *Complex human behavior: A systematic extension of learning principles*. New York: Holt, Rinehart and Winston.

STAKE, J.E. (1979). The ability/performance dimension of self-esteem: Implications for women's achievement behavior. *Psychology of Women Quarterly, 3*, 365–377.

STAMBROOK, M., HAWRYLUK, G.A., & MARTIN, D.G. (1987). Lateralizing brain damage with the Luria-Nebraska Neuropsychological Battery: Effectiveness as compared with the Halstead-Reitan Neuropsychological Battery. *International Journal of Neuroscience, 35*, 73–88.

STAMBROOK, M., & MARTIN, D.G. (1983). Brain laterality and the subliminal perception of facial expression. *International Journal of Neuroscience, 18(1)*, 45–58.

STAMBROOK, M., & PARKER, K.C.H. (1987). The development of the concept of death in childhood. *Merrill Palmer Quarterly Journal of Developmental Psychology, 33*, 133–157.

STAPP, J., FULCHER, R., & WICHERSKI, M. (1984). The employment of 1981 and 1982 doctorate recipients in psychology. *American Psychologist, 39(12)*, 1408–1423.

STAPP, J., TUCKER, A.M., & VANDEBOS, G.R. (1985). Census of psychological personnel: 1983. *American Psychologist, 40(12)*, 1317–1351.

STEINBERG, L.D., CATALANO, R., & DOOLEY, P. (1981). Economic antecedents of child abuse and neglect. *Child Development, 52*, 975–985.

STEPHAN, W.G., & ROSENFIELD, D. (1978). Effects of desegregation on racial attitudes. *Journal of Personality and Social Psychology, 36*, 795–804.

STERNBERG, R.J. (1985). *Beyond IQ.* New York: Cambridge University Press.

________. (1986a). *Intelligence applied.* San Diego: Harcourt Brace Jovanovich.

________. (1986b). A triangular theory of love. *Psychological Review, 93(1)*, 119–135.

________. (1987). The future of intelligence testing. Paper presented at the meeting of the American Psychological Association, New York.

STERNBERG, R.J., & BARNES, M. (1985). Real and ideal others in romantic relationships: Is four a crowd? *Journal of Personality and Social Psychology, 49*, 1586–1608.

STERNBERG, R.J., CONWAY, B.E., KETRON, J.L., & BERNSTEIN, M. (1981). People's conceptions of intelligence. *Journal of Personality and Social Psychology, 41*, 37–55.

STERNBERG, R.J., & GRAJECK, S. (1984). The nature of love. *Journal of Personality and Social Psychology, 47*, 312–329.

STONE, A.A., COX, D.S., VALDIMARSDOTTIR, H., JANDORF, L., & NEALE, J.M. (1987). Evidence that secretory IgA antibody is associated with daily mood. *Journal of Personality and Social Psychology, 52*, 988–993.

STONE, G.C., COHEN, F., & ADLER, N.E. (1979). *Health psychology: A handbook.* San Francisco: Jossey-Bass.

STRAND, B.Z. (1970). Change of context and retroactive inhibition. *Journal of Verbal Learning and Verbal Behavior, 9*, 202–206.

STROEBE, W., INSKO, C.A., THOMPSON, V.D., & LAYTON, B.D. (1971). Effects of physical attractiveness, attitude similarity and sex on various aspects of interpersonal attraction. *Journal of Personality and Social Psychology, 18*, 79–91.

STRUPP, H.H., & BERGIN, A.E. (1969). Some empirical and conceptual bases for coordinated research in psychotherapy: A critical review of issues, trends and evidence. *International Journal of Psychiatry, 7(2)*, 18–90.

STUART, R.B. (1971). Behavioral contracting within the families of delinquents. *Journal of Behavior Therapy and Experimental Psychiatry, 2*, 1–11.

STUNKARD, A.J. (1972). New therapies for the eating disorders: Behavior modification of obesity and anorexia nervosa. *Archives of General Psychiatry, 26*, 391–398.

________. (1977). Behavioral treatment of obesity: Failure to maintain weight loss. In R.B. Stuart (ed.), *Behavioral self-management: Strategies, techniques, and outcome.* New York: Brunner/Mazel.

SUEDFELD, P. (1980). *Restricted environmental stimulation: Research and clinical applications.* NY: Wiley.

SULER, J.R. (1985). Meditation and somatic arousal: A comment on Holmes's review. *American Psychologist, 40*, 717.

SUTCLIFFE, J.P. (1961). "Credulous" and "skeptical" views of hypnotic phenomena: Experiments in esthesia, hallucination, and delusion. *Journal of Abnormal and Social Psychology, 62*, 189–200.

SWEET, R.C. (1969). RNA "memory pills" and memory: A review of clinical and experimental status. *Psychological Record, 19*, 629–644.

SZASZ, T. (1960). The myth of mental illness. *American Psychologist, 15*, 113–118.

________. (1984). *The therapeutic state: Psychiatry in the mirror of current events.* Buffalo, NY: Prometheus.

T

TAKANAKA, A. (1985). Some thoughts on Japanese management centering on personnel and labor management: The reality and the future. *International Studies of Management and Organization, 15(3–4)*, 17–69.

TAKOOSHIAN, H., & BODINGER, H. (1982). Bystander indifference to street crime. In L. Savitz & N. Johnston (eds.), *Contemporary criminology.* New York: Wiley.

TARKKAN, J.S., BRADY, J.V., & HARRIS, A.H. (1982). Animal studies of stressful interactions. In L. Goldberger & S. Breznitz (eds.), *Handbook of stress.* New York: Free Press.

TART, C.T. (ed.). (1975). *Transpersonal psychologies.* New York: Harper & Row.

TAYLOR, M.C., & HALL, J.A. (1982). Psychological androgyny: Theories, methods, and conclusions. *Psychological Bulletin, 92*, 347–366.

TAYLOR, S. (1983). Adjustment to threatening events: A theory of cognitive adaptation. *American Psychologist, 38*, 1161–1173.

TAYLOR, S.E. (1979). Hospital patient behavior: Reactance, helplessness, or control? *Journal of Social Issues, 35*, 156–184.

________. (1987). The progress and prospects of health psychology: Tasks of a maturing discipline. *Health Psychology, 6(1)*, 73–87.

TAYLOR, S.E., FALKE, R.L., SHOPTAW, S.J., LICHTMAN, R.R. (1986). Social support, support groups, and the cancer patient. *Journal of Consulting and Clinical Psychology, 54(5)*, 608–615.

TAYLOR, S.E., & FISKE, S.T. (1975). Point of view and perceptions of causality. *Journal of Personality and Social Psychology, 32*, 439–445.

TEASDALE, J.D., & FOGARTY, F.J. (1979). Differential effects of induced mood on retrieval of pleasant and unpleasant events from episodic memory. *Journal of Abnormal Psychology, 88*, 248–257.

TEITELBAUM, P. (1955). Sensory control of hypothalamic hyperphagia. *Journal of Comparative and Physiological Psychology, 48*, 156–163.

TEMERLIN, M.K. (1970). Diagnostic bias in community mental health. *CommunityMental Health Journal, 6(2)*, 110–117.

TERMAN, L.M. (1916). *The measurement of intelligence.* Boston: Houghton Mifflin.

TERRACE, H.S. (1979). How Nim Chimpsky changed my mind. *Psychology Today, 13*, 65–76.

________. (1980). *Nim.* New York: Alfred A. Knopf.

________. (1985). In the beginning was the "name." *American Psychologist, 40*, 1011–1028.

TESSER, A., & BRODIE, M. (1971). A note on the evaluation of a "computer date." *Psychonomic Science, 23(4)*, 300.

THELAN, M.G. (1969). Modeling of verbal reactions to failure. *Developmental Psychology, 1*, 297.

THOMAS, A., & CHESS, S. (1977). *Temperament and development.* New York: Brunner/Mazel.

________. (1981). The role of temperament in the contributions of individuals to their development. In R.M. Lerner & N.A. Bush-Rossnagel (eds.), *Individuals as producers of their own development: A life-span perspective.* New York: Academic Press.

THOMAS, A., CHESS, S., & BIRCH, H.G. (1970, August). The origin of personality. *Scientific American, 223*, 102–109.

THOMPSON, J.K., JARVIE, G.J., LAKEY, B.B., & CURETON, K.J. (1982). Exercise and obesity: Etiology, physiology, and intervention. *Psychological Bulletin, 91(1)*, 55–79.

THOMPSON, L.W., GALLAGHER, D., & BRECKENRIDGE, J.S. (1987). Comparative effectiveness of psychotherapies for depressed elders. *Journal of Consulting and Clinical Psychology, 55*, 385–390.

THOMPSON, M.J., & HARSHA, D.W. (1984, January). Our rhythms still follow the African sun. *Psychology Today*, 50–54.

THOMPSON, R.J., & MATARAZZO, J.D. (1984). Psychology in United States medical schools: 1983. *American Psychologist, 39*, 988–995.

THORNDIKE, E.L. (1911). *Animal intelligence.* New York: Macmillan.

THORNDIKE, E.L., LAY, W., & DEAN, P.R. (1909). The relation of accuracy in sensory discrimination to general intelligence. *American Journal of Psychology, 20*, 364–369.

THURSTONE, L.L., & THURSTONE, T.G. (1941). Factorial studies of intelligence. *Psychometric Monographs*, No. 2.

TOBIAS, S. (1976, September). Math anxiety: Why is a smart girl like you counting on your fingers? *Ms., 5*, 56–59 ff.

TOMPKINS, S. (1981). The quest for primary motives: Biography and autobiography of an idea. *Journal of Personality and Social Psychology, 41*, 306–329.

TORGERSON, S. (1983). Genetic factors in anxiety disorders. *Archives of General Psychiatry, 40*, 1085–1089.

TREHUB, S.E. (1976). The discrimination of foreign contrasts by infants and adults. *Child Development, 47*, 466–472.

TRESEMER, D.W. (1977). *Fear of success.* New York: Plenum.

TULVING, E. (1972). Episodic and semantic memory. In E. Tulving & W. Donaldson (eds.), *Organization of memory.* New York: Academic Press.

_________. (1985). Memory and consciousness. *Canadian Psychology, 26*, 1–12.

_________. (1986). What kind of hypothesis is the distinction between episodic and semantic memory? *Journal of Experimental Psychology: Learning, Memory, and Cognition*, 12, 307–311.

TUPES, E.C., & CHRISTAL, R.E. (1961). *Recurrent personality factors based on trait ratings.* (USAF ASD Technical Report No. 61–97). Lackland Air Force Base, TX: U.S. Air Force.

TURK, D.C. (1989). Promises to keep but miles to go. . . . *Contemporary Psychology, 34*, 453–454.

TURK, D.C., & RUDY, T.E. (1986). Hypnotic behavior dissected or . . . pulling the wings off butterflies. *The Behavioral and Brain Sciences, 9*(3), 485.

TURKINGTON, C. (1987). Help for the worried well. *Psychology Today, 21*(8), 44–48.

TURKKAN, J.S. (1989). Classical conditioning: The new hegemony. *Behavioral and Brain Sciences. 12*(1), 121–179.

TURKKAN, J.S., BRADY, J.V., & HARRIS, A.H. (1982). Animal studies of stressful interactions. In L. Goldberger & S. Breznitz (eds.), *Handbook of Stress*, New York: Free Press.

TURNBULL, C. (1962). *The forest people.* New York: Simon & Schuster.

TURNER, C.K. (1988). Don't blame memory for people's faulty reports on what influences their judgments. *Personality and Social Psychology Bulletin, 14*, 622–629.

TURNER, R.J., & WAGONFELS, M.O. (1967). Occupational mobility and schizophrenia. *American Sociological Review, 32*(1), 104–113.

U

UNITED STATES CENTER FOR DISEASE CONTROL. (1986, February 21). Supplement to *Research Institute Recommendations.*

UNITED STATES DEPARTMENT OF HEALTH AND HUMAN SERVICES. (1983). *Smoking and health bulletin.* Washington, D.C.: U.S. Government Printing Office.

V

VAILLANT, G.E. (1977). *Adaption to life.* Boston: Little, Brown.

VALENSTEIN, E.S. (1977). The brain and behavior control. In *Master lectures on behavior control.* Washington, D.C.: American Psychological Association.

VANDENBERG, S.G., & KUSE, A.R. (1979). Spatial ability: A critical review of the sex-linked major gene hypothesis. In M.A. Wittig and A.C. Peterson (eds.), *Sex related differences in cognitive functioning.* New York: Academic Press.

VAN KATWYK, P.T., CRONSHAW, S.F., & WILLIAMS, D. (1989). A quantitative review relating leader behaviour to individual work outcomes. *Canadian Psychology, 30*, 366.

VAUGHN, C.E., & LEFF, J.P. (1976). The influence of family and social factors on the course of psychiatric illness. A comparison of schizophrenic and depressed neurotic patients. *British Journal of Psychiatry, 129*, 125–137.

VERMEULEN, S.C.A., & DENTON, K. (1989). Moral judgment about interpersonal conflicts. *Canadian Psychology, 30*(2), 354.

VERNON, P.E. (1977). Final report on modifications of WISC-R for Canadian use. *Canadian Psychological Association Bulletin, 7*, 5–7.

VIOLATO, C. (1986). Canadian versions of the Information subtests of the Wechsler tests of intelligence. *Canadian Psychology, 27*(1), 69–74.

VOKEY, J.R., & READ, J.D. (1985). Subliminal messages: Between the devil and the media. *American Psychologist, 40*, 1231–1239.

VON EULER, U.S. (1933). *Shock and circulatory homeostasis.* New York: The Josiah Macy Jr. Foundation.

VULCANO, B.A., BARNES, G.E., & BREEN, L.J. (1983). The prevalence and predictors of psychosomatic symptoms and conditions among police officers. In A.J. Krakowski and C.P. Kimball (eds.), *Psychosomatic medicine.* New York: Plenum.

W

WAGNER, M.W., & MONNET, M. (1979). Attitudes of college professors toward extra-sensory perception. *Zetetic Scholar, 5*, 7–16.

WAHBA, M.A., & BRIDWELL, L.G. (1976). Maslow reconsidered: A review of research on the need hierarchy theory. *Organizational Behavior and Human Performance, 15*, 212–240.

WALKER, P. (1978). Binocular rivalry: Central or peripheral selective processes. *Psychological Bulletin, 85*, 376–389.

WALL, P.D. (1979). On the relation of injury to pain. *Pain, 6*, 253–264.

WALLER, N.G., & BEN-PORATH, Y.S. (1987). Is it time for clinical psychology to embrace the five-factor model of personality? *American Psychologist, 42*, 887–889.

WALLERSTEIN, R.S. (1989). The psychotherapy research project of the Menninger Foundation: An overview. *Journal of Consulting and Clinical Psychology, 57*(2), 195–205.

WALLIS, C. (1984, June 11). Unlocking pain's secrets. *Time*, 58–66.

WALSH, R. (1989). Psychological chauvinism and nuclear holocaust: A response to Albert Ellis and defense of non-rational emotive therapies. *Journal of Counseling and Development, 67*, 338–340.

WALSTER, E., ARONSON, E., ABRAHAMS, D., & ROTTMAN, L. (1966). Importance of physical attractiveness in dating behavior. *Journal of Personality and Social Psychology, 4*, 508–516.

WATERHOUSE, G.J., & STRUPP, H.H. (1984). The patient-therapist relationship: Research from a psychodynamic perspective. *Clinical Psychology Review, 4*, 77–92.

WATSON, J.B. (1913). Psychology as the behaviorist views it. *Psychological Review, 20*, 158–77.

WATSON, J.B. (1970). *Behaviorism*, rev. ed. New York: Norton.

_________, & RAYNER, R. (1920). Conditioned emotional reactions. *Journal of Experimental Psychology, 3*(1), 1–14.

WATSON, J.S., & RAMEY, C.T. (1972). Reactions to responsive contingent stimulation in early infancy. *Merrill-Palmer Quarterly, 18*, 219–227.

WEBB, A.P. (1963). Sex-role preferences and adjustment in early adolescents. *Child Development, 34*, 609–618.

WEBB, W.B. (1983). Theories in modern sleep research. In A. Mayes (ed.), *Sleep mechanisms and functions.* Wokingham, England: Van Nostrand Reinhold.

WEBER, M. (1947). *The theory of social and economic organization.* A.M. Henderson & T. Parsons, trans. & eds. Glencoe, IL: Free Press.

WECHSLER, D. (1944). *The measurement of adult intelligence.* Baltimore: Williams & Wilkins.

________. (1967). *Manual for the WPPSI.* New York: Psychological Corp.

________. (1974). *Manual for the WISC-R.* New York: Psychological Corp.

________. (1981). *Manual for the WAIS-R.* New York: Psychological Corp.

WEDDING, D. (1986). Neurological disorders. In D. Wedding, A.M. Horton Jr., & J. Webster (eds.), *The neuropsychology handbook.* New York: Springer Publishing.

WEIL, A., & ZINBERG, N.E. (1969). Acute effects of marijuana on speech. *Nature, 222*, 434–437.

WEINER, H. (1977). *Psychobiology and human disease.* New York: Elsevier.

WEINER, H., THALER, M., REISER, M.F., & MIRSKY, I.A. (1957). Etiology of duodenal ulcer: I. Relation of specific psychological characteristics to rate of gastric secretion (serum pepsinogen). *Psychosomatic Medicine, 19(1)*, 1–10.

WEINER, R.D. (1984). Does electroconvulsive therapy cause brain damage? *The Behavioral and Brain Sciences, 7(1)*, 1–53.

WEINSTEIN, K.A., DAVISON, G.C., DEQUATTRO, V., & ALLEN, J.W. (1987). Type A behavior and cognitions: Is hostility the bad actor? *Health Psychology, 6(1)*, 55.

WEISS, A.R. (1977). A behavioral approach to the treatment of adolescent obesity. *Behavior Therapy, 8*, 720–726.

WEISS, J.M. (1972, June). Psychological factors in stress and disease. *Scientific American, 276*, 104–113.

________. (1977). Psychological and behavioral influences on gastro-intestinal lesions in animal models. In J.D. Maser & M.E.P. Seligman (eds.), *Psychopathology: Experimental models.* San Francisco: Freeman.

WEISZ, J.R., WEISS, B., ALICKE, M.D., & KLOTZ, M.L. (1987). Effectiveness of psychotherapy with children and adolescents: A meta-analysis for clinicians. *Journal of Consulting and Clinical Psychology, 55*, 542–549.

WELLS, G.L., & LOFTUS, E.F. (1984). *Eyewitness testimony: Psychological perspectives.* Cambridge: Cambridge University Press.

WELLS, G.L., & TURTLE, J.W. (1987). Eyewitness testimony research: Current knowledge and emergent controversies. *Canadian Journal of Behavioural Science, 19(4)*, 363–388.

WERTHEIMER, M. (1923). Untersuchungen zur lehre von der gestalt, II. *Psychologische Forschung, 4*, 301–350.

WHITE, L., & TURSKY, B. (eds.). (1982). *Clinical biofeedback: Efficacy and mechanisms.* New York: Guilford Press.

WHITE, R.W. (1974). Strategies of adaptation: An attempt at systematic description. In G.V. Coelho, D.A. Hamburg, & J.E. Adams (eds.), *Coping and adaptation.* New York: Basic Books.

WHITING, J.W.M., & EDWARDS, C.P. (1973, December). A cross-cultural analysis of sex differences in the behavior of children aged three through 11. *The Journal of Social Psychology, 91*, 171–188.

WHITLOCK, F.A., & SISKIND, M. (1979). Depression and cancer: A follow-up study. *Psychological Medicine, 9*, 747–752.

WHORF, B.L. (1956). *Language, thought, and reality.* New York: MIT Press-Wiley.

WICKELGREN, W.A. (1979). *Cognitive psychology.* Englewood Cliffs, NJ: Prentice-Hall.

________. (1981). Human learning and memory. *Annual Review of Psychology, 32*, 21–52.

WICKER, A.W. (1971). An examination of the "other variables" explanation of attitude behavior inconsistency. *Journal of Personality and Social Psychology, 19(1)*, 18–30.

WICKRAM, I. (1989). Classical conditioning and the placebo effect. *Behavioral and Brain Sciences, 12(1)*, 160–161.

WILBUR, K. (1983). *Eye to eye.* Garden City, NY: Anchor Press.

________. (1989a). Let's nuke the transpersonalists: A response to Albert Ellis. *Journal of Counseling and Development, 67*, 332–335.

________. (1989b). Two humanistic psychologies? A response. *Journal of humanistic psychology, 29*, 230–243.

WILCOXIN, H.C., DRAGOIN, W.B., & KRAL, P.A. (1971). Illness-induced aversions in rat and quail: Relative salience of visual and gustatory cues. *Science, 171*, 826–828.

WILGOSH, L., MULCAHY, R., & WATTERS, B. (1986). Assessing intellectual performance of culturally different, Inuit children with the WISC-R. *Canadian Journal of Behavioural Science, 18(3)*, 270–277.

WILLIAMS, D.R., & WILLIAMS, H. (1969). Automaintenance in the pigeon: Sustained pecking despite contingent nonreinforcement. *Journal of the Experimental Analysis of Behavior, 12*, 511–520.

WILSON, E.O. (1978). *On human nature.* Cambridge, MA: Harvard University Press.

WILSON, G.T., & O'LEARY, K.D. (1980). *Principles of behavior therapy.* Englewood Cliffs, NJ: Prentice-Hall.

WILSON, W.R. (1979). Feeling more than we can know: Exposure effects without learning. *Journal of Personality and Social Psychology, 37*, 811–821.

WING, C.W., & WALLACH, M.A. (1971). *College admissions and the psychology of talent.* New York: Holt, Rinehart and Winston.

WINTERBOTTOM, M.R. (1958). The relation of need for achievement to learning experiences in independence and mastery. In J.W. Atkinson (ed.), *Motives in fantasy, action, and society.* NY: Van Nostrand.

WISPE, L.G., & DRAMBAREAN, N.C. (1953). Physiological need, word frequency, and visual duration threshold. *Journal of Experimental Psychology, 46(1)*, 25–31.

WOLPE, J. (1958). *Psychotherapy by reciprocal inhibition.* Stanford: Stanford University Press.

________. (1987). The promotion of scientific therapy: A long voyage. In J.K. Zeig (ed.), *The evolution of psychotherapy.* New York: Brunner/Mazel.

WOLPE, J., & RACHMAN, S. (1960). Psychoanalytic "evidence": A critique based on Freud's case of Little Hans. *Journal of Nervous and Mental Disease, 130(2)*, 135–148.

WOODRUFF, D. (1977). *Can you live to be one hundred?* New York: Chatham Square.

WOODSWORTH, R.S. (1920). *Personal data sheet.* Chicago: Stoelting.

WOODY, C.D. (1986). Understanding the cellular basis of memory. *Annual Review of Psychology, 37*, 433–493.

WOOLDRIDGE, D.E. (1968). *Mechanical man: The physical basis of intelligent life.* New York: McGraw-Hill.

Y

YALOM, I.D. (1985). *The theory and practice of group psychotherapy*, 3rd ed. New York: Basic Books.

YALOM, I.D., & LIEBERMAN, M.H. (1971). A study of encounter group casualities. *General Archives of Psychiatry, 25*, 16–30.

YARMEY, A.D. (1973). I recognize your face but I can't remember your name: Further evidence on the tip of the tongue phenomenon. *Memory and Cognition, 1*, 287–290.

________. (1984). Age as a factor in eyewitness memory. In G.L. Wells and E.F. Loftus (eds.), *Eyewitness testimony: Psychological perspectives.* Cambridge: Cambridge University Press.

YARROW, L.J., GOODWIN, M.S., MANHEIMER, H., & MILOWE, I.D. (1973). Infancy experience and cognitive and personality development at ten years. In L.J. Stone, H.T. Smith, & L.B. Murphy (eds.), *The competent infant.* New York: Basic Books.

YATES, F.A. (1978). *The art of memory.* Harmondsworth, England: Penguin Books Ltd.

YERKES, R.M. (ed.). (1921). Psychological examining in the United States Army. *Memoirs of the National Academy of Sciences,* 15.

YERKES, R.M., & DODSON, J.D. (1908). The relation of strength of stimulus to rapidity of habit-formation. *Journal of Comparative and Physiological Psychology, 18,* 459–489.

YOUNG, W.C., GOY, R.W., & PHOENIX, C.H. (1964). Hormones and sexual behavior. *Science, 143,* 212–218.

YUILLE, J.C., & CUTSHALL, J.L. (1986). A case study of eyewitness memory of a crime. *Journal of Applied Psychology, 71,* 291–301.

Z

ZADEH, L.A. (1965). Fuzzy sets. *Information Control, 8,* 338-353.

ZAJONC, R.B. (1965). Social facilitation. *Science, 149,* 269–274.

________. (1968). Attitudinal effects of mere exposure. *Journal of Personality and Social Psychology,* Monograph Supplement 9 (no. 2), 1–29.

________. (1980). Feeling and thinking: Preferences need no inferences. *American Psychologist, 35,* 151–175.

________. (1984). On the primacy of affect. *American Psychologist, 39,* 117–123.

ZAMANSKY, H.S., & BARTIS, S.P. (1985). The dissociation of an experience: The hidden observer observed. *Journal of Abnormal Psychology, 94,* 243–248.

ZBOROWSKI, M. (1969). *People in pain.* San Francisco: Jossey-Bass.

ZILBERGELD, B. (1978). *Male sexuality.* New York: Bantam Books.

ZIMBARDO, P.G. (1975). On transforming experimental research into advocacy for social change. In M. Deutsch & H. Hornstein (eds.), *Applying social psychology: Implications for research, practice and training.* Hillsdale, NJ: Erlbaum.

ZUCKERMAN, M. (1975). Belief in a just world and altruistic behavior. *Journal of Personality and Social Psychology, 31,* 972–976.

________. (1979). *Sensation seeking.* Hillsdale, NJ: Erlbaum.

ZUSNE, L., & JONES, W.H. (1982). *Anomalistic psychology: A study of extraordinary phenomena of behaviour and experience.* Hillsdale, NJ: Erlbaum.

Page numbers that refer to definitions of key terms are preceded by an asterisk. All key terms are also listed separately in the Key Term Index.

A

SUBJECT INDEX

Q

R

T

NAME INDEX

KEY TERMS INDEX

A

B

Q

R

Full Credits for Canadian Art from the AGO Found in Chapter Openings

CHAPTER 2

Sorel Etrog (b. 1933), Untitled lithograph on paper (n.d.); 40.6 × 31.8 cm. Art Gallery of Ontario, Toronto. Gift of Sam and Ayala Zacks, 1970. Reproduced with permission.

CHAPTER 3

William von Moll Berczy (1744-1813), *Study of a Right Hand* (n.d.); charcoal, heightened with white on laid paper bleute; 20.7 × 30.3 cm. Art Gallery of Ontario, Toronto. Gift of John Andre, Toronto, 1982. Reproduced with permission.

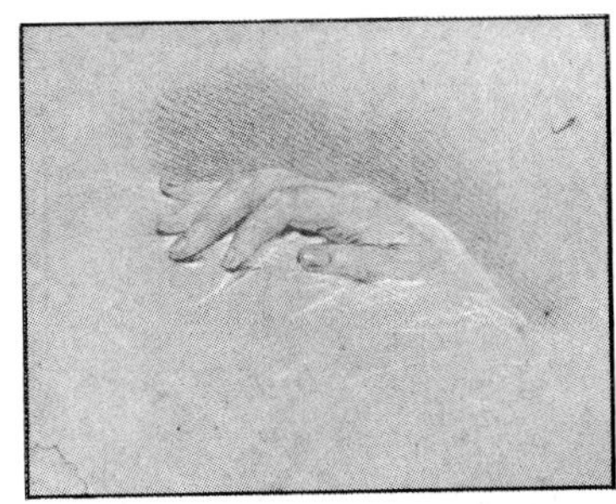

CHAPTER 5

Walter Trier (1890-1951), "Der Bücherbote," *Illustrierte Zeitschrift für Bücherfreunde* (n.d.); pen and ink and wash on paper; 25.6 × 18.1 cm (paper). Art Gallery of Ontario, Toronto. Gift of the Trier-Fodor Foundation, 1977. Reproduced with permission.

CHAPTER 6

Robert J. Flaherty (1884-1951), *Summer (August) Eskimo in Northeastern Hudson Bay* (ca. 1925); photogravure; 21.1 × 16.7 cm (image). Art Gallery of Ontario, Toronto. Gift of Sandra Ball and Marcia Reid, 1987. Reprinted with permission.

CHAPTER 7

G.A. Reid (1860-1947), *Sketch for "Adagio"* (n.d.); graphite on paper; 7.8 × 11.2 cm. Art Gallery of Ontario, Toronto. From the G.A. Reid Scrapbook, Edward P. Taylor Reference Library. Gift of Mrs. G.A. Reid, 1957. Reproduced with permission.

CHAPTER 10

Sorel Etrog (b. 1933), Untitled [*Head of a Man*] (1969); etching on paper; 14.3 × 10.8 cm (imp). Art Gallery of Ontario, Toronto. Gift of Ayala Zacks-Abramov, Jerusalem, Israel, 1984. Reproduced with permission.

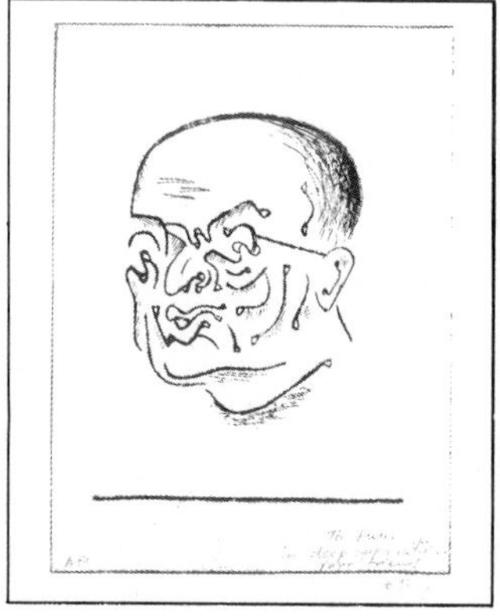

CHAPTER 12

Jamasie (1910-1985), *Inside the Igloo* (1966); engraving; 25.3 × 32.8 cm. Art Gallery of Ontario, Toronto. Gift of the Klamer Family, 1978. Reproduced with permission.

CHAPTER 13

Michael Snow (b. 1929), *Encyclopedia* (1965); ink on printed paper, acrylic resin varnish; 245.1 × 118.1 cm. Art Gallery of Ontario, Toronto. Purchased with assistance from Wintario, 1977. Reproduced with permission.

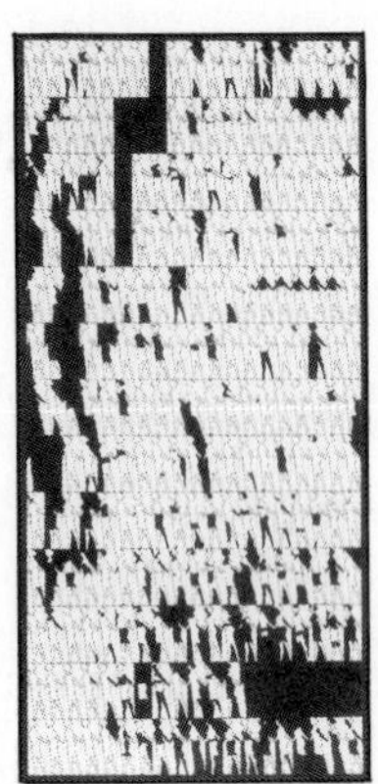

CHAPTER 14

Caven Atkins (b. 1907), *Mountain Vision* (1932); wood-block; 17.0 × 12.4 cm (imp.) Art Gallery of Ontario, Toronto. Gift from the Douglas M. Duncan Collection, through the Toronto Central Library, 1970. Reproduced with permission.

CHAPTER 15

Claude Tousignant (b. 1932), *Sculpture* (1974); screenprint on paper; 66.0 × 115.5 cm (sheet). Art Gallery of Ontario, Toronto. Gift of Judith Terry, 1988. Reproduced with permission.

CHAPTER 16

Jamasie (1910-1985), *Summer Games* (1973); stonecut; 61.1 × 85.8 cm. Art Gallery of Ontario, Toronto. Gift of the Klamer Family, 1978. Reproduced with permission.

CHAPTER 19

Frederick Horsman Varley (1881-1969), *Study from "Dhârâna"* (1932); graphite on board; 31.0 × 38.0 cm. Art Gallery of Ontario, Toronto. Purchased with assistance from the Government of Canada through the Cultural Property Export and Import Act, 1985. Reproduced with permission.

CHAPTER 20

Janet Kigusinq (b. 1926), *Winter Camp Scene* (ca. 1974); pencil and colour pencil; 50.8 × 66.2 cm. Art Gallery of Ontario, Toronto. Gift of the Klamer Family, 1978. Reproduced with permission.